UNIX® Secrets®, Second Edition

UNIX® Secrets®, Second Edition

James C. Armstrong, Jr.

IDG Books Worldwide, Inc.
An International Data Group Company

Foster City, CA ♦ Chicago, IL ♦ Indianapolis, IN ♦ New York, NY

UNIX® Secrets®, Second Edition

Published by

IDG Books Worldwide, Inc.

An International Data Group Company

919 E. Hillsdale Blvd., Suite 400

Foster City, CA 94404

www.idgbooks.com (IDG Books Worldwide Web site)

ISBN: 0-7645-3320-7

Printed in the United States of America

10 9 8 7 6 5 4 3 2 1

1B/SS/QX/ZZ/FC

Distributed in the United States by IDG Books Worldwide, Inc.

Distributed by CDG Books Canada Inc. for Canada; by Transworld Publishers Limited in the United Kingdom; by IDG Norge Books for Norway; by IDG Sweden Books for Sweden; by IDG Books Australia Publishing Corporation Pty. Ltd. for Australia and New Zealand; by TransQuest Publishers Pte Ltd. for Singapore, Malaysia, Thailand, Indonesia, and Hong Kong; by Gotop Information Inc. for Taiwan; by ICG Muse, Inc. for Japan; by Norma Comunicaciones S.A. for Colombia; by Intersoft for South Africa; by Eyrolles for France; by International Thomson Publishing for Germany, Austria and Switzerland; by Distribuidora Cuspide for Argentina; by Livraria Cultura for Brazil; by Ediciones ZETA S.C.R. Ltda. for Peru; by WS Computer Publishing Corporation, Inc., for the Philippines; by Contemporanea de Ediciones for Venezuela; by Express Computer Distributors for the Caribbean and West Indies; by Micronesia Media Distributor, Inc. for Micronesia; by Grupo Editorial Norma S.A. for Guatemala; by Chips Computadoras S.A. de C.V. for Mexico; by Editorial Norma de Panama S.A. for Panama; by American Bookshops for Finland. Authorized Sales Agent: Anthony Rudkin Associates for the Middle East and North Africa.

For general information on IDG Books Worldwide's books in the U.S., please call our Consumer Customer Service department at 800-762-2974. For reseller information, including discounts and premium sales, please call our Reseller Customer Service department at 800-434-3422.

For information on where to purchase IDG Books Worldwide's books outside the U.S., please contact our International Sales department at 317-596-5530 or fax 317-596-5692.

For consumer information on foreign language translations, please contact our Customer Service department at 800-434-3422, fax 317-596-5692, or e-mail rights@idgbooks.com.

For information on licensing foreign or domestic rights, please phone +1-650-655-3109.

For sales inquiries and special prices for bulk quantities, please contact our Sales department at 650-655-3200 or write to the address above.

For information on using IDG Books Worldwide's books in the classroom or for ordering examination copies, please contact our Educational Sales department at 800-434-2086 or fax 317-596-5499.

For press review copies, author interviews, or other publicity information, please contact our Public Relations department at 650-655-3000 or fax 650-655-3299.

For authorization to photocopy items for corporate, personal, or educational use, please contact Copyright Clearance Center, 222 Rosewood Drive, Danvers, MA 01923, or fax 978-750-4470.

Library of Congress Cataloging-in-Publication Data

Library of Congress Cataloging-in-Publication Data

Armstrong, James C., Jr.
    UNIX Secrets 2nd ed./
Armstrong, James C., Jr.
        p. cm.
    Includes index.
    ISBN 0-7645-3320-7 (alk. paper)
    1. UNIX (Computer file).
I. Zijleman, Erwin. II. Title
QA76.76.063A757   1999
005.4'32–DC21   99-30197
                                                 CIP

ABOUT IDG BOOKS WORLDWIDE

Welcome to the world of IDG Books Worldwide.

IDG Books Worldwide, Inc., is a subsidiary of International Data Group, the world's largest publisher of computer-related information and the leading global provider of information services on information technology. IDG was founded more than 30 years ago by Patrick J. McGovern and now employs more than 9,000 people worldwide. IDG publishes more than 290 computer publications in over 75 countries. More than 90 million people read one or more IDG publications each month.

Launched in 1990, IDG Books Worldwide is today the #1 publisher of best-selling computer books in the United States. We are proud to have received eight awards from the Computer Press Association in recognition of editorial excellence and three from Computer Currents' First Annual Readers' Choice Awards. Our best-selling ...For Dummies® series has more than 50 million copies in print with translations in 31 languages. IDG Books Worldwide, through a joint venture with IDG's Hi-Tech Beijing, became the first U.S. publisher to publish a computer book in the People's Republic of China. In record time, IDG Books Worldwide has become the first choice for millions of readers around the world who want to learn how to better manage their businesses.

Our mission is simple: Every one of our books is designed to bring extra value and skill-building instructions to the reader. Our books are written by experts who understand and care about our readers. The knowledge base of our editorial staff comes from years of experience in publishing, education, and journalism — experience we use to produce books to carry us into the new millennium. In short, we care about books, so we attract the best people. We devote special attention to details such as audience, interior design, use of icons, and illustrations. And because we use an efficient process of authoring, editing, and desktop publishing our books electronically, we can spend more time ensuring superior content and less time on the technicalities of making books.

You can count on our commitment to deliver high-quality books at competitive prices on topics you want to read about. At IDG Books Worldwide, we continue in the IDG tradition of delivering quality for more than 30 years. You'll find no better book on a subject than one from IDG Books Worldwide.

John Kilcullen
Chairman and CEO
IDG Books Worldwide, Inc.

Steven Berkowitz
President and Publisher
IDG Books Worldwide, Inc.

IDG is the world's leading IT media, research and exposition company. Founded in 1964, IDG had 1997 revenues of $2.05 billion and has more than 9,000 employees worldwide. IDG offers the widest range of media options that reach IT buyers in 75 countries representing 95% of worldwide IT spending. IDG's diverse product and services portfolio spans six key areas including print publishing, online publishing, expositions and conferences, market research, education and training, and global marketing services. More than 90 million people read one or more of IDG's 290 magazines and newspapers, including IDG's leading global brands — Computerworld, PC World, Network World, Macworld and the Channel World family of publications. IDG Books Worldwide is one of the fastest-growing computer book publishers in the world, with more than 700 titles in 36 languages. The "...For Dummies®" series alone has more than 50 million copies in print. IDG offers online users the largest network of technology-specific Web sites around the world through IDG.net (http://www.idg.net), which comprises more than 225 targeted Web sites in 55 countries worldwide. International Data Corporation (IDC) is the world's largest provider of information technology data, analysis and consulting, with research centers in over 41 countries and more than 400 research analysts worldwide. IDG World Expo is a leading producer of more than 168 globally branded conferences and expositions in 35 countries including E3 (Electronic Entertainment Expo), Macworld Expo, ComNet, Windows World Expo, ICE (Internet Commerce Expo), Agenda, DEMO, and Spotlight. IDG's training subsidiary, ExecuTrain, is the world's largest computer training company, with more than 230 locations worldwide and 785 training courses. IDG Marketing Services helps industry-leading IT companies build international brand recognition by developing global integrated marketing programs via IDG's print, online and exposition products worldwide. Further information about the company can be found at www.idg.com.   1/24/99

Credits

Acquisitions Editor
Laura Lewin

Development Editors
Matthew E. Lusher
Terrence P. O'Donnell

Technical Editor
William Rousseau

Copy Editors
Victoria Nuttall
Robert Campbell
Nicole LeClerc

Production
IDG Books Worldwide Production

Proofreading and Indexing
York Production Services

Cover Photo
© TSM/Mendola Ltd., 1999

About the Author

James C. Armstrong, Jr., is a 20-year UNIX veteran; his first exposure to UNIX was back in the mid-70s when his father showed him the system he used at Bell Labs. At Duke University, James sought out opportunities to learn UNIX as an undergraduate, as he felt it was the future of computing.

James graduated from Duke in 1982, and attended the University of St. Andrews for two more years of graduate work before deciding to return to industry. He has worked at Bell Labs, Tandem, and Netscape, and has been involved with several start-ups. He's currently at AOL after its acquisition of Netscape.

To Amy. Ea in cordibus illorum, qui eam amant, semper vivet.

Preface

You must be thinking, "Oh boy, another UNIX book. What makes this one so different from all the others?" It's true that a large number of books about UNIX are in the marketplace, and at first glance, you may think this is just another book. However, I feel there is a tremendous gap in the market, and I wrote this book to fill that gap.

Many good books are available for novice UNIX users: *UNIX For Dummies* by John Levine is one such book, and *Teach Yourself UNIX in a Week* by Dave Taylor is another good introductory book. For experts, books such as *UNIX Unleashed* provide encyclopedic detail on different aspects of UNIX. The gap in UNIX books exists for the knowledgeable UNIX user moving to become an expert. With this book, I attempt to address this transition. To do so, I wrote about how UNIX performs the underlying tasks. This approach provides you with not only the knowledge of commands but also an understanding of what really is happening in the system.

The second task of this book is to teach you how the tools can work in concert with one another. UNIX has many commands, and each attempts to perform a specific task with certain options. For complicated tasks, there may not be a single, specific tool. Instead, with a UNIX system, you need to combine these smaller tools in pipelines; these pipelines can perform complicated tasks quickly and efficiently.

What's in This Book

I have broken down *UNIX Secrets* into 12 parts, and each part discusses a feature set of UNIX in detail.

Each part of this book conforms to a format. The inner secrets of how UNIX really works in this field are described in depth in an introductory chapter. Then, the various commands and utilities available in that area are described in the next chapters. Lastly, each part is tied together with a chapter that discusses how to use the tools with other tools to increase the power of each individual tool.

Part I: Accounts

This part introduces the basics of account management, such as checking to see who is on the system and how to get onto the system.

Part II: Command Shells

Once you log in, your first interface is the command shell. This is a very powerful program, and this part enables you to get the most out of the command environment. Included is an introduction to shell programming and the creation of inline programs at the command prompt.

Part III: File System Navigation

Another area that offers many ways to improve your UNIX usage is hard disk management. Most UNIX users know that the ls command tells you what files you have, but how many users understand the usage of all 21 options? The details of this command, and others, are explained in this part.

Part IV: Editing

The process of creating documents is described here. A UNIX guru needs a good working knowledge of the ed text editor and regular expressions because many commands are built from these basic tools. The sed editor and awk are also detailed, and some hints on the common screen editors are also provided.

Part V: Processes

Although closely related to shell management, process management is a different area. This part describes the many tools available for examining and manipulating processes on UNIX.

Part VI: Networking and Communications

UNIX truly differentiates itself from other operating systems in its capability to interact easily with other systems. This part describes the uses of a local area network for sharing administrative information and file systems.

Part VII: UNIX and the Internet

The Internet, originally built on UNIX protocols, has become the single most important computing development in the past generation and promises to be the most socially transforming computer development in history. Knowing how to make best use of Internet technologies is an essential skill for any UNIX user, let alone an expert. This part covers the history of the Internet, the tools and protocols on which it's built, Web browsers, Web servers, HTML, and CGI programming.

Part VIII: The X Window System

The common interface for workstations is X Windows. With X, you have the capability to increase your productivity greatly. This part describes how you can create an X-based user environment, some basics of window managers, and a lengthy primer on some of the many varied X applications available.

Part IX: Software Development

UNIX is a software developer's system, perhaps more so than any other operating system you can choose. Many of the tools available are intended solely for use in the software development process. This part details many of those uses, and it provides a starting point for writing your own applications.

Part X: GNU Tools

One of the best resources for UNIX users is the Free Software Foundation. Its philosophy is that software should be available to all, and to that end it has written many applications for UNIX that are freely available via FTP.

Part XI: System Administration

Keeping a single-user UNIX system up and running is not difficult, but when you add multiple users, or an Internet connection, or if you want to recover from a crash, you should have some rudimentary system administration skills. This section, written by experts in system administration, gives details on the tasks involved in keeping a busy system running.

Part XII: UNIX Flavors and Directions

UNIX also provides some basic tools for managing calendars and the like. This part is really something of a catch-all section where the applications that don't readily fit into other categories are described. It also describes the many flavors of UNIX and the growing phenomenon of Linux, which promises to be the next great area of UNIX development.

Conventions Used in This Book

To get the most out of this book, you need to know something about its design. Almost every chapter contains boldfaced text, italicized text, bulleted lists, numbered lists, figures, listings, and tables of information. I think you'll agree that all these design features help you understand the material that is being presented.

Throughout the book, you are going to see icons. These mark different, important pieces of information and can help you get a better understanding of the system as a whole.

Note

A Note provides additional information not directly related to the body of the chapter.

Caution

A Caution is an additional piece of information that describes where you may make mistakes and provides tips on how to avoid those errors.

Secret

A Secret is an undocumented (or poorly documented) feature about a given single application or task.

Tip

A Tip is a helpful piece of advice on how to do something more efficiently or how to increase your powers with UNIX by using commands together.

In addition to these icons, some sidebars call out useful information. Some of these, headlined as a "Story," reflect my personal experience with the technology or application being discussed in the body text.

I've been a UNIX user since 1981. My first contact with UNIX was through my father. He worked at AT&T in Manhattan and occasionally needed to get output from the UNIX printers in Murray Hill. Once I got my driver's license, I'd get to use the car for the day if I'd take him to the train, and sometimes that meant going past Murray Hill.

As an undergraduate at Duke University, I changed my major from physics to computer science in 1980. One of my professors, William Smith, was a UNIX aficionado, so I arranged to work with him over the summer of 1981 on a statistical package for the Department of Cardiology at Duke Hospital. This was my first taste of UNIX as a user. In graduate school at the University of St. Andrews, I used UNIX for several projects, and when I left graduate school in 1984, I got a job with Bell Labs writing programs for managing telecommunication switches. I've been a UNIX user ever since, and am now working for AOL in Silicon Valley.

Still, I am the first to admit that I don't know everything about UNIX; I don't think any one person does. For that reason, I asked several people to help me with this book by writing chapters on their particular expertise. Dave Taylor wrote chapters on the Internet. Wes Morgan wrote about system administration. Matthew Merzbacher wrote a chapter on programming languages. Michael O'Neill wrote about archive and compression tools. John Wilson and Yves Lepage wrote about GNU, and Peter Salus wrote about crash recovery.

I hope you enjoy this book.

Acknowledgments

From the first edition:

No book is the work of one person, and this remains the case for *UNIX Secrets*. Special accolades should go to the folks at IDG Books Worldwide and, in particular, Ellen Camm, Erik Dafforn, and Jim Grey. These three people piloted the project and kept me on track. My supplemental authors, Cedric Higgins, Yves Lepage, Matthew Merzbacher, Wes Morgan, Michael O'Neill, Peter Salus, Dave Taylor, and John Wilson also deserve more credit than I can express in words.

There are, alas, victims, too, in the book writing process. My two companions Leela and Nyssa both suffered from neglect as I spent an inordinate amount of time at the keyboard. Other local friends have either suffered or celebrated my absence. I regret I was unable to offer Tai Jin assistance with his move, and I also want to mention Robert Diamond, who seemed to get a decent share of "I'm not available" messages from me. Rob — it's over, I'm free now!

I should mention my parents, since I forgot to mention them in my last book. Mother and Father, Mother and Father. There, that's twice; we're even now! Seriously, thanks for the support. Ditto my sister Lillian.

There are many other friends from mailing lists and other venues who have given me information and assistance. I doubt I'll remember them all, but John Carter, Steve Chapin, Orin Day, Scott Turner, and Jeff Burch all deserve a special mention. Bob Snader also made a special contribution to this book, without which it could never have been written.

Last, I should again mention Dave Taylor. If you have a friend who has been half the friend that Dave has been to me, you are truly a lucky person. I wish him and his wife, Linda Dunlap, many, many decades of happiness together.

For the second edition:

I'd also like to thank Laura Lewin and Matt Lusher for their assistance. Mike "Biff" Rosenberg also deserves credit for keeping me focused. Also, congratulations to Orin Day and Karen Grimes; they got married for my second edition . . . I wonder who's up for the third?

Contents at a Glance

Contents

Chapter 38: Development Tools **793**

Chapter 39: You Expect Me to Understand That? **825**

Part I

Accounts

Chapter 1

Understanding UNIX Accounts

In This Chapter

▶ Logging in

▶ Understanding files related to user accounts

▶ Understanding important UNIX accounts

Logging In

To begin a UNIX session, you must log in. The login process sets up your session's ID and permissions, without which you could not run even the most basic commands. When you log in, the system updates a file that keeps track of logged-in users to show that you have logged in.

When you log in, you use a *tty,* which is a special kind of file that enables a computer running UNIX to interact with remote physical devices. A system process called a *daemon* checks to see whether another process is running on your terminal. (A daemon is any process that continuously runs. For more information, see Part V.) If the daemon finds no processes there, it starts a process called *getty,* for "get tty," or get terminal type. getty presents a login prompt and reads your input. It expects you to enter your user ID, which is an alphanumeric string. When you do, getty executes the login process with your user ID as its argument.

getty accesses a file that defines characteristics on a line. This file is usually /etc/gettydefs, although it may have a different name on your system. Check the getty manual page for the name of this file on your machine. This file has several fields, each separated by a number sign (#). For now, focus on the fourth field, which stores the text string your system uses for the login prompt. This string is usually login, but login: is not magical; the system administrator can use a different string.

The login process does most of the session setup work. It checks the file /etc/passwd, which keeps track of whether your account requires a password for login. If your account requires a password, the login process asks you for the password. Passwords may be stored in /etc/passwd, but the more secure UNIX systems store the password in /etc/shadow.

Note

If the user ID you enter does not match any account on the system, the login process still displays a password prompt.

Secret

UNIX does not store your password anywhere—unless you've stored it in a file yourself, which is not a secure idea! A common misconception is that the second field of your account's entry, /etc/passwd, contains an encrypted copy of your password. Instead, password manipulation programs actually store an encrypted string of spaces in /etc/passwd. Your password is the key for that encryption. When you enter your password during login, an encrypted string of spaces is created from your entry, and the result is compared with the string stored in the file. If they match, you receive access to the system. Moreover, the first two characters in the password field are a randomly selected "salt" for the password, which makes it unlikely that two users with the same password have the same encryption string in /etc/passwd. There are over 2,500 possible salts, which create over 2,500 different encrypted strings for each password. This makes cracking passwords very hard (but not impossible). Your account is far more likely to be violated because you carelessly guarded your password than because someone cracked /etc/passwd.

When the system is satisfied that you are who you claim to be, it sets up your login session. Each session is assigned a numeric user ID and group ID. (The numeric user ID differs from the name you use to log in, your *login name,* which is also sometimes called a user ID.) These IDs control your permissions for accessing files. The system also starts an environment in which you can run commands. Command environments, which are called *shells,* are discussed in Part II.

UNIX maintains three levels of security for its resources:

- *Owner.* Owner security controls whether the owner of a resource can read, write, and/or execute the resource. The numeric user ID identifies the owner. Usually, there is one login name per user ID.

- *Group.* Users can be assigned to *groups* in UNIX. Users who work together on a project should be assigned to the same group. Group security gives users in a group read, write, and/or execute access to common resources but can deny access to other users.

- *World.* World security controls read, write, and/or execute access for all users. For example, if world read access is given to a file, anyone can look at it. (Only root can access all local files regardless of their access restrictions.)

Understanding Files Related to User Accounts

Three important files maintain information about user accounts: /etc/passwd, /etc/group, and /etc/shadow. Of these, /etc/passwd is the most important.

The /etc/passwd file

Each entry in /etc/passwd has seven fields, which are separated by colons. Figure 1-1 shows my passwd entry on my home machine. Table 1-1 describes the fields.

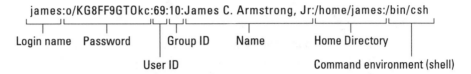

Figure 1-1: An /etc/passwd entry

Table 1-1	Fields in /etc/passwd
Field	*Description*
Login name	I use james as a login name. This field is unique within the file — nobody else can use this login name.
Password	This field stores the encrypted key to my password. Notice that the string's salt is o/. If you want to break my password, use this salt. (To make it easy for you, "Raptor" is the password. This is *not* my normal password!)
User ID	This field stores my numeric user ID. Any file I create is associated with my user ID.
Group ID	This field stores my numeric group ID. Any file I create is associated with my group ID.
Name	This field stores my name. Some sites impose different requirements on the format of this field. I've opted to include just my name here.
Home directory	This field specifies which directory is my *home directory*. When I start a session, the system places me in this directory.
Command environment (shell)	This field specifies which command environment (shell) I use. See Part II for more information about shells.

The login process isn't the only user of /etc/passwd. Because /etc/passwd is the only file that relates a user ID string to a number, processes such as ls and who need to access it to provide names for the permission numbers they get.

The /etc/group file

This file relates numeric group IDs to strings. Figure 1-2 shows the four fields of /etc/group. As in /etc/passwd, colons separate the fields. Table 1-2 describes the fields of /etc/group.

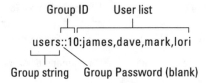

Figure 1-2: An /etc/group entry

Table 1-2	Fields in /etc/group
Field	*Description*
Group string	This field lists the group's name as it will appear in a directory listing.
Group Password	Groups can have passwords, although using passwords with groups is unusual. In Figure 1-2, this field is blank, meaning no password is assigned. When a group requires a password, you are asked for it when you use the newgrp command. Chapter 2 describes this command.
Group ID	This field lists the numeric group ID.
User list	This field lists the users in the group by login name. Names are separated by single commas.

Users can belong to more than one group and can switch between groups as needed.

The /etc/shadow file

On some secure systems, passwords are stored in /etc/shadow. On these systems, an encrypted password string follows the user ID string. The /etc/shadow file may also include other entries related to password and account expiration; you'll find these documented in more depth in Part XI. This file is accessed only by the passwd and login commands and is often protected from access.

Understanding Important UNIX Accounts

Each UNIX system reserves several special accounts, often including root, bin, uucp, and lp. The accounts reserved by your system may vary.

The root account

The root account is the most important account on any system. Although some systems may use a login name other than "root" for this account, user ID 0 is *always* the UNIX superuser. root is not bound by any access restrictions that you impose.

Normally, root is reserved for administrative purposes. Some programs may want to invoke the root account to guarantee access to resources, however.

The bin account

Users almost never use this account. The entry exists in /etc/passwd so that someone other than root can own standard UNIX utilities.

The uucp account

UNIX systems were originally networked with other systems via the uucp command. The letters *uucp* stand for "UNIX-to-UNIX copy." One UNIX system would call another and log in to the system as uucp. Then, a user could transfer files and execute commands. More advanced networking commands have superseded uucp, but uucp still exists and is used by sites that can't afford the wiring for networks. You'll find more information on uucp in Part VI.

The lp account

On some systems, the lp account prevents conflicts on remote printing devices. The printing commands communicate with a central print spooler, and that spooler prints the documents accordingly. The lp account monitors this process.

Other accounts

Some software products require certain accounts to monitor their package. Daemons use other accounts. Your machine's /etc/passwd file lists any such accounts.

Summary

This chapter gave you an overview of the login process and described the related files. Its key points were the following:

▶ You use a tty when you log in, and the getty process places the login: prompt on your screen. After you type your login name, the login process starts. This process asks you for your password.

▶ The /etc/passwd file (or /etc/shadow on some systems) maintains your password. UNIX uses an elaborate encryption scheme to hide your password. Information about all users on the system — including their login names, numeric user and group IDs, home directories, and command environments (shells) — is stored in /etc/passwd. The file /etc/group maintains lists of groups to which users belong.

▶ Your account is assigned numeric user and group IDs that control your permissions to access resources.

▶ UNIX maintains three levels of read, write, and execute security for all resources: owner, group, and world.

▶ UNIX maintains several important accounts for itself. The most important is the root account, which has no access restrictions. Others include bin, uucp, and lp. Some systems maintain other accounts to monitor software and system processes.

Chapter 2 looks in detail at all the commands used to monitor and manipulate user accounts.

Chapter 2

Manipulating Your Account

In This Chapter

▶ Managing UNIX accounts

▶ Changing your password, full name, and shell

▶ Getting (and understanding) information about an account

▶ Changing things about other accounts on the system

▶ Examining the system

Sometimes, as a user, you may need different permissions, or you may be required to change certain characteristics of your account. You should change passwords on a regular basis, for example. Knowing the right tools for these jobs is important.

Changing Your Account

As Chapter 1 explained, the password entry for a user has seven fields. You can alter some of them as a user, but others are fixed. Those fields are as follows:

Field	Changeable?
Login name	Not changeable
Password	Changeable
User ID	Not changeable
Group ID	Not changeable
Name	Changeable
Home directory	Not changeable
Command environment (shell)	Changeable

Note

Unlike user accounts, the *root* account can change the "Not changeable" fields simply by editing the /etc/passwd file.

Login name

The *user name* is a text string that uniquely identifies an account. The system administrator assigns your user name when you first obtain your account (although a good system administrator will ask you for ideas). During my career, I've had several different user names. Originally, UNIX accounts were identified by the user's initials, so my first account was *jca*. In graduate school, the students used their first names, so my account was *james*. (My current account on my home machine is still *james*.) At some places I've worked, the user account was the first initial and the last name; at others, it was the first name and last initial. Because user accounts can have a maximum of eight significant letters, I was *jarmstro* at the first location, and *jamesa* at the second.

Duplicate user names create a tricky situation. A good administrator checks for duplicates, but accidents happen. For example, duplicates may occur if the administrator tries to use more than eight characters in the name: *jarmstrong* is the same to the system as *jarmstroff*. When duplicate user names crop up, the system uses the first appearance of the user name in the /etc/passwd file and ignores the subsequent appearances.

Tip

Maintaining order in /etc/passwd is important. Although adding accounts at the end of /etc/passwd is standard procedure for many administrators, it may be wise to sort the file alphabetically to ensure that no duplicates occur. Chapter 12 shows other ways of handling this problem.

Password

Passwords are your key to security on a system. *Guard them!*

When selecting a password, try to select a string that is easy for you to remember but that is not something obvious. At various times, I've used my mother's maiden name, algorithms derived from birthdays, and various spelling tricks.

As UNIX has evolved, password checking has become more stringent. Previous versions of UNIX enabled you to select any string as a password — even a short string such as *ax*. Current versions of UNIX force you to use at least six characters in your password. Some systems also force you to use both upper- and lowercase characters, and others force you to use at least one nonalphanumeric character.

To change your password, use the passwd command:

```
$ passwd
Enter old password:
Enter new password:
Re-type new password:
```

The system may prompt you for your old password. It then asks for your new password. To make sure you typed what you thought you typed, the system asks again for the new password. If the two entries don't match, your password remains unchanged.

Tip

Of course, if you repeat the typo, you're out of luck. That's why it is useful to verify the password before logging out. You can use the `su` command, introduced later in this chapter, to test your new password. If you did mistype it and can't figure out what it is, you'll need to ask your system administrator for help.

The only users who can change your password are those who already know your password (they can use your account to log on to the system) and those who know the *root* account password. *root* can change any password on the system without knowing the current passwords.

Unfortunately, users frequently select passwords that are easy to crack. One of the more common mistakes is to repeat the account name and append a single digit, usually a 1. For example, a bad password for the account *jamesa* would be *jamesa1*. Other mistakes include using office telephone numbers, license plates, or other strings that can be easily associated with a user. For the system administrator, some tools are available on the Internet to determine whose passwords are easily broken. Crack is the best tool for that job and is available from `ftp.cert.org`. Another program available at `ftp.cert.org` is a tool that you can add to the `passwd` program to perform extra checks when you change your password. You need *root* access to install this enhancement.

Hints for Good Passwords

You may have difficulty choosing easily remembered passwords that others will find hard to figure out. Here are some tips to help you avoid passwords that are easy to crack:

■ If you have to write down your password to remember it, choose a different password.

■ Use upper- and lowercase characters. Use numbers. Use punctuation if you can. (Warning: Some UNIX versions reportedly enable you to enter passwords with punctuation but fail to accept these passwords for login.)

■ Don't base the password on personal information, such as the name of a family member, the name of a pet, or your license plate number.

■ Use at least six characters in your password. The longer the password, the harder it is to crack.

■ Do not use words from a dictionary or place names.

You can use spelling tricks to obscure your password. One of my favorite spelling tricks is to convert the letter o to 0 (zero), l to 1, and e to 3. Simple words, such as *Jersey*, become *J3rs3y*. Another trick is to use sound-alikes: *hesit8* is a possible password. You can also use logical meanings; for example, knowing that a vertical bar (|) means "or" and an exclamation point (!) means "not," you can create the password *2b|!2b*.

User and group IDs

User and group IDs are integer values that only the system administrator can change. You really don't want to change them anyway because the system uses these numbers to identify who you are. If you change them, the system no longer knows who you are, and you can't access your own files.

The user ID is supposed to be a unique identifier. I have seen systems, however, in which different logins shared user IDs to give a group of users identical access but at the same time to log that access and maintain some security by not sharing passwords. When multiple logins share the same user ID, a system attempts to resolve the user ID number into the first login name assigned to that number in the /etc/passwd file.

The group ID converts to a string in the /etc/group file. Groups are intended to be shared across some of the user community. Groups are the accounts of people who work together on a project or who are classified in a similar fashion. Consequently, any number of users may have the same group ID.

In the /etc/group file, the system uses the first entry that matches the group ID.

User IDs and group IDs are integer values between 0 and 65,535. Originally, these values were implemented as short integers, two bytes long. They were treated as *unsigned values,* meaning all 16 bits were used to determine the value. (Computers need one bit to indicate whether a value is positive or negative, so a signed short integer would have a range of –32,768 to 32,767. The unsigned data type allows the same range of values, but by keeping them positive, it makes representation and understanding easier.)

When the system administrator assigns an account, assigning a unique user ID is important. Some tools check the /etc/passwd file to determine whether an ID has already been used. If the administrator manually updates the file, she should use the editing tool to search for the number before adding it.

These numbers do more than identify you — they determine who owns files and processes. When any user creates a file, the file is automatically assigned an owner and a group owner. These are the same values as the user ID and the group ID. File ownership can be changed, of course, but only by *root*. The owner can change the file group ownership, but only to another group to which the owner belongs.

Story: Tricks with Group IDs

A clever trick I once saw was to assign a group ID as a two-digit number and assign the user ID as a four-digit number in which the first two digits were the same as the group ID. This made management of user IDs easier. For example, if I were assigned to a group named sysdev with a group ID of 33, I'd be given the next available user ID, 33*XX*. Unfortunately, if I changed projects, my group ID would change, and my user ID would be out of sync.

Secret

These ownership change restrictions are new features of UNIX that enhance security. Older versions of UNIX enabled users to change the ownership of a file to anybody, but this created a security hole. Users would change the ownership of a file to a secure ID and use it to exploit the system. Now, if you need to change the ownership of a file, the file's prospective owner needs to copy the file to his or her own space. The copy command creates a new file, owned by the copier. If you want to manipulate the copied file, you need to know the new owner's password.

Name

The fifth field in /etc/passwd is the full name field. This field is supposed to contain the name of the account's owner. UNIX does not dictate this field's format, so anything goes. Some mail and printing programs use this field to obtain a user's real name.

Originally, System V UNIX had an unusual format for this field. The field contained a four-digit number, followed by a dash, the user's name, and another four-digit number in parentheses. Here's an example from an account I used to have:

```
9990-James C. Armstrong(8933)
```

The first number was an account number on a mainframe used by Bell Labs, and the second number was the associated box number. This way, their original UNIX systems could submit batch jobs to the mainframe and get output.

Berkeley UNIX had a formula in which the name was followed by a comma and some comments. On a Berkeley UNIX machine, the full name field for my account might be

```
James C. Armstrong, author
```

You may still find this format on BSD machines.

I currently include only my name in the field. My mail and printing tools can retrieve the information easily.

Some sites let you change this field yourself. The command is chfn for "change full name":

```
$ chfn
Default values are printed inside of `[]`.
To accept the default, type <return>.
To have a blank entry, type the word `none`.

Name [James Armstrong]: James C. Armstrong, Jr.
Password:
$
```

The chfn command is not present on every UNIX system. To determine whether it is available to you, type **man -k chfn** to see whether a man page exists. If that fails, try running the command. If you get "Command not found," the command is not available to you.

The command prompts you for your password as a security feature.

If chfn is not available to you, you need to ask your system administrator to change this field. This change may be a low-priority request, so please be patient with your system administrator.

Home directory

The sixth field in /etc/passwd specifies your home directory. This field must contain a valid UNIX pathname. You should own the directory specified in this field, and you should have full access permissions to this directory.

When you start your command shell, you are placed in this directory. Furthermore, other commands may need startup files based in this directory. You don't want to change it!

If your home directory does not exist when you log in, the system warns you and then places you in the root directory.

If a change is needed, the system administrator must make the change.

Startup command shell

The last field in /etc/passwd is a command. When the login process is completed, the text in this field executes as a command. Usually, the command starts a *shell,* an environment in which you execute your commands. Part II discusses command shells.

Story: Interesting Uses of the /etc/passwd File

I have seen a few interesting commands in the /etc/passwd file. One site had the following passwd entry:

```
who::65535:65535:Who
command:/:/bin/who
```

This meant anyone could determine who was on the system by logging in as who.

I know of one company that changes the shell to /bin/exit in entries for employees who quit. Then, if someone tries to log in to the system with that account, even with the password, the system immediately terminates the session!

Another useful trick is to make the shell the passwd program on a POP-server-only account. This enables users to change their password without special software or login access.

You can change this command with the chsh program. The ability to change your shell is also discussed in the next section. If no command is specified, the /bin/sh command is used.

Changing Accounts on the System

Logging in to the system is one way to change the session permissions on the current line. You can change these session permissions in many other ways too, as described in this section.

login

When the getty program receives input, it executes the login command. As a user, you can also execute this command. The normal procedure is to type **login** followed by the user name. The login command then prompts you for the password.

Most login programs do not allow more than three failed attempts before exiting. Of course, the normal exit takes you back to getty, where you can start again. Some login programs log these failed attempts, though.

Caution

login terminates the current session, so use it only when you have finished working in your current session and someone else is ready to take over the terminal. Some people opt to use login to terminate their sessions.

su

You can also change the session with the su command. This command is often called the "superuser" command, but it really stands for "switch user ID." The epithet originated because this command gains root permissions on a system.

Normally, su takes an argument, a new user name. It then asks for a password. If the password matches the user name, su changes the session ownership and group ID to those of the new user. The environment for the previous user is inherited, including the current working directory and any environment variables.

If you are already in root, you do not need to enter a password to switch user IDs.

If you specify no argument for su, the command assumes that you are attempting to access the *root* account. It compares the password entered to that of the *root* account. If they match, the system grants you root permission.

The – flag is another useful option. When you use this flag, the system gives you the login shell and environment of the specified account. This is useful if you're temporarily borrowing someone's terminal. Using su - without an account gives you the complete root environment, assuming you know the password!

The su command has other options. The two you need to know are -c and -f.

With -c, su runs the next argument as a command with the permissions specified and then exits. For example, if I needed to remove Brian's file (and knew Brian's password), I'd type the following:

```
$su brian -c "rm hisfile"
Password:
```

I still need to provide the password to run the command.

The -f option is passed to the subsequent shell. If the destination shell is the C shell, -f says to skip the initialization file. For Bourne (and Bourne-family) shells, -f is not a useful option.

The su command can log its actions. Only *root* can access the log file. This log file is a dubious tool for tracking break-ins, though. After all, the savvy cracker knows to clean up the file.

Story: Pitfalls of the su Command

In my first job, we were selling a product that was fairly large and took a lot of time to install. Some of the work needed to be performed as *root*. The work was prone to error, so the installation manuals had "deinstall" and reinstall instructions. Those instructions included ways to change directories to the base directory for the product, change to the *root* ID, and remove the hierarchy with rm -rf *. This happened quite some time ago, so those machines were much slower than machines are today. The instructions also indicated that the removal could take as long as 15 minutes.

During the first installation, the customer support engineer ran into some problems and needed to perform this deinstall and reinstall procedure. He changed directories, went to *root*, and typed in the fateful command. He then took a coffee break and returned to the computer room 15 minutes later.

Back at the main shop, we received a phone call. "What does it mean when the computer says, Cannot remove /unix, text file busy?" As what had happened became clear, the support engineer became more panicked.

Can you guess? The engineer typed su - instead of su to become *root*. This meant that the engineer ran the command rm -rf * at the base of the entire system, effectively removing UNIX from the computer.

The story has a happy ending. We sent down an engineer with the UNIX boot tape, and she spent the weekend reloading and rebuilding the system. She stayed there while the product was installed, just to make sure it didn't happen again.

Moral: Be careful when you're *root*! UNIX assumes that you know what you're doing. If you don't know what you're doing, you can end up in a serious mess.

The `su` command has some advantages over `login`. First, if you need to do something quickly, you can avoid the startup scripts of a new session. Second, the previous session remains "under" the `su` session, and you can return to it by exiting the `su` session.

newgrp

Just as you can use other user and group IDs with `su`, you can use another group's permission with `newgrp` by typing **newgrp** and the group name.

Modern `newgrp` commands treat an absent password differently than older versions. In the past, the lack of a password in `/etc/group` meant that you could change to any group in which you were listed. This is no longer the case. If the password field of the group file is empty, you cannot use `newgrp` to become that group unless you are *root*.

When you enter `newgrp`, if the file has a password specified, the system asks for a password. When it is verified, you are given access.

exit

To terminate a session, the usual command is `exit`. You can give it a parameter; the parameter is returned to the calling process for its use. (This is useful when you write shell scripts.) In some shells, you can terminate a session by pressing Ctrl-D, which signifies the end of the file.

Examining the System

Sometimes you may need to know who is on the system or that someone was recently on the system. Some commands check the system for you.

who

The most common of these commands is `who`. POSIX mandates that `who` be part of every UNIX system.

The `who` command is simple: Just type **who**, and the system lists the users currently logged in.

```
$ who
james     tty1     Aug  2 16:51
taylor    tty4     Aug  2 18:20
chill     tty3     Aug  2 16:33
```

The output is a list of users currently logged in to the system, their terminal lines, and the date they logged in. POSIX requires `who` to have several options, which are listed in Table 2-1. These options can dramatically change the output of who.

Table 2-1	Options of who
Option	*Result*
-b	Prints the time of the last reboot
-d	Prints a list of dead processes that have not been respawned
-H	Prints column headers
-l	Lists tty lines waiting for a user
-m	Prints information about the current terminal only
-p	Lists all active processes spawned by init
-q	Lists only the user names and a count of users
-r	Lists the current run state of the system
-s	Lists the user, tty, and time of login (default)
-t	Lists the last time the system clock was changed
-T	Lists the state of each terminal line (+ indicates that the line is writable, and − indicates that the line is not writable)
-u	Lists the idle time for each terminal

On Linux, not all these features are implemented. Similarly, some of these options are not present on BSD systems. To determine which options you have, check the man page for who.

Here is the output for who -THu:

```
$ who -THu
USER     MESG LINE      LOGIN-TIME    IDLE   FROM
james    +    tty1      Aug  2 16:51  old
taylor   +    tty4      Aug  2 18:20  .
chill    -    tty3      Aug  2 16:33  old
```

Only taylor has been active. The users james and chill have not accessed their tty lines in over a day. Furthermore, chill has been denied access to the line.

The who command is useful and powerful for checking system states.

w

Another system-checking command is w. It is not present on every system, so check for its availability by entering **man -k w**.

The who command gives you login information. The w command tells you what the users are doing. The standard w output looks like this:

```
5:07pm  up 4 days, 15:04,   8 users,  load average: 1.17, 1.49, 1.27
User       tty        login@  idle   JCPU   PCPU  what
taylor     ttyp0      2:29pm   2      40      7   -csh
chill      ttyp1      1:54pm          2       2   -csh
anns       ttyp2      5:02pm         38      38   -csh
cedric     ttyp3      4:47pm          2       2   rlogin -8 mpgn.com.
wes        ttyp4      5:03pm                      -csh
abs        ttyp5      5:03pm          1       1   -csh
david      ttyp6      2:54pm         32       2   -csh
james      ttysa      5:07pm          1           grep jca
```

The first line gives you the current time, how long the machine has been up, the number of users, and the load on the machine. The next line contains the headers. The third and subsequent lines list the users and what they are doing. Each entry has seven fields, described in Table 2-2.

Table 2-2   Fields in w Output

Field	Content
User	The user name associated with the tty
tty	The tty entry
login@	The original login time
idle	The time since the user last typed anything, in minutes
JCPU	The total CPU time used by all processes on that terminal
PCPU	The total CPU time for all active processes on that terminal
what	The name and arguments for the current process

In the previous output example, most users were running the C shell. Only cedric and james were doing other things. Indeed, taylor had been away from his machine for a couple minutes. anns used her C shell session fairly intensively, but taylor's processes logged the most CPU time.

Table 2-3 describes w's three options.

Table 2-3   Options of w

Option	Result
-h	Suppresses headers
-l	Displays long form (default)
-s	Displays short form

The short form output (w -s) looks like this:

```
   5:07pm  up 4 days, 15:04,    8 users,  load average: 1.17, 1.49, 1.27
User     tty  idle  what
taylor   p0     2  csh
chill    p1        csh
anns     p2        csh
cedric   p3        rlogin
wes      p4        csh
abs      p5        csh
david    p6        csh
james    sa        grep
```

You can check a particular user by typing **w username**. For example, if I want
to see what taylor is doing, I type **w taylor**.

last

The last command determines when someone was last logged in to the
system. Without arguments, last lists, in reverse order, the last people to log
in to the system. This list can be extremely long. Here's an example:

```
$ last
james    tty1                     Wed Aug  2 16:51   still logged in
root     tty1                     Tue Aug  1 23:32-05:53  (06:20)
runlevel  ~                       Tue Aug  1 23:31
reboot    ~                       Tue Aug  1 23:31
shutdown  ~                       Wed Aug  2 05:57
runlevel  ~                       Wed Aug  2 05:57
james    tty1                     Sat Jul 15 21:49-crash (17+08:08)
james    tty1                     Wed Jul 12 09:44-09:51  (00:06)
james    tty1                     Wed Jul 12 06:53-09:08  (02:14)
james    tty1                     Tue Jul 11 17:08-21:10  (04:01)
```

The duration of each session is listed, as well as the original login dates and
times. On my home machine, I have 406 entries. Netcom, a large public-
access machine, has over 29,000 entries in its last file for only 12 days of
accounting!

You can tell last to truncate output by specifying a number as an option. For
example, last -25 lists the last 25 people to log in. By typing a name or a tty,
you can check the last time a given user logged in or who has used a
particular tty. On Netcom, if I look for my logins, I find the following:

```
$ last jca
jca      ttysa    NETCOM-sf5.netco Sat Aug 12 17:07   still logged in
jca      ttys2    NETCOM-sf8.netco Thu Aug 10 17:41-18:00  (00:19)
jca      ttyqc    NETCOM-pa8.netco Tue Aug  1 21:42-22:10  (00:27)
```

Secret

The last command is important for system administrators checking who was logged in and at what times. It relies on the /etc/utmp file, which logs logins and system reboots. When you enter **last reboot**, you see a listing of the last times the system was rebooted. On Netcom, I find the following:

```
reboot     ~                          Tue Aug  8 02:03
reboot     ~                          Fri Aug  4 12:35
```

finger

The finger command is also an interesting command to use to determine whether a user is on the system. I discuss finger in more detail in Chapter 19. By typing **finger *userID*** (as in **finger jca**), you receive a lot of information, including the last login time for that user.

uptime

The last interesting command is uptime. You've seen the output in the w command; uptime is the first line of w output, as shown in the following example:

```
5:43pm  up 10 days, 11:52,  7 users,  load average: 0.01, 0.03, 0.02
```

I include uptime in my shell startup script because it gives me a feel for how stable the system has been.

Summary

This chapter has shown you how to manage your user account and login session. Its key points were the following:

▶ The /etc/passwd file knows everything about your account: your user name, password, user ID, group ID, full name, home directory, and startup command.

▶ You can alter your account's password with the passwd command, your full name (on some systems) with the chfn command, and your startup command (on some systems) with the chsh command shell.

▶ Change the ownership of your login session with su or login.

▶ Use another group's permissions with newgrp.

▶ Use who to see who else is on the system, use last to see who has logged in recently, and use w to see what other users are doing.

In Chapter 3, you will be introduced to the theory of command shells.

Part II

Command Shells

Chapter 3

Introducing Command Shells

In This Chapter

▶ Looking at the history of command shells

▶ Understanding command environments

▶ Understanding how UNIX shells work

When you use UNIX, odds are that you are working interactively with the computer. To do this, your computer must have a program that takes your input, feeds it to the computer, and then processes your output. This program is called a *shell*. In this chapter, I discuss the available shell options and how you can use shells to maximize your computer's efficiency.

Taking a Historical Perspective

In the dim and distant past, most interaction with computers consisted of submitting a job to a computer and waiting for the output. When I was a freshman in college, a typical programming scenario involved my typing the statements of a program on punch cards and feeding them into a card reader for the IBM 370 at the Triangle Universities Computing Center (TUCC) to process. This program would be surrounded by some cryptic commands in a language called JCL. I'd then have to wait patiently for the operators to bring my printout to the pickup area.

I admit that the chad from the punch cards was useful for parades, but as a programming paradigm, this scenario was the pits. You spent so much time waiting for your output that your productivity was low, no matter how fast you typed out the punch cards or paper tape.

The logical alternative was to work directly on a computer. TUCC provided this opportunity with the TSO lab, but only upperclassmen could use this resource, so I had to wait until my junior year to use it.

UNIX was developed to enable users to interact directly with the computer, rather than depend on a computer lab operator to bring output to them. (Actually, UNIX was developed so that some hackers at Bell Labs could play a computer game more easily, but that's beside the point.) To provide the user with this ability, a special program called a *shell* would sit between the user and the central processing unit (CPU). The shell would read the user's input and run commands to process it.

The first shell developed was the Bourne shell; it's still used as the default shell on most UNIX systems. After that came the C shell from Berkeley, developed for BSD UNIX. Bell Labs developed the Korn shell, and BASH is a freely distributed UNIX shell that combines the features of both C and Korn shells. POSIX defined a default shell for its systems that closely resembles the Korn shell. Unless I tell you otherwise, the examples in this book are based on the POSIX shell.

Understanding Command Environments

Each command is associated with an environment. Environment variables are created when a user session begins, and these variables are passed to all executed commands unless you or someone else explicitly specifies otherwise. Environment variables typically include vital information that is shared between programs but that needs to be defined differently for each user.

When a user logs in, UNIX automatically sets some environment variables, including HOME, SHELL, TERM, and PATH. These four variables have specific uses, as outlined in Table 3-1.

Table 3-1	Environment Variables
Variable	*Purpose in the Shell*
HOME	Specifies the user's initial starting directory. Typically, all files belonging to that user are kept in this directory.
SHELL	Stores the full path to the standard shell for that user. This path is derived from the last field of the user's entry in /etc/passwd.
TERM	Specifies the user's terminal type. This path is used for any program that needs escape sequences for graphics.
PATH	Lists directories, separated by colons. When you type a command, the system searches the directories listed here for it.

The system ensures that environment variables are passed successfully from process to process, although a clever programmer can change that. The environment is usually stored in strings in the form {VARIABLE}={value}. For example, here's the starting environment on my home machine:

```
HOME=/home/james
SHELL=/bin/csh
TERM=xterm
PATH=/usr/local/bin:/usr/bin:.:/bin
```

The user or the system administrator can add other variables as well. I've added several variables to my environment that I can access during regular use of my machine, including DISPLAY, CGFLAGS, HOST, and TZ. Other programs have added variables, such as VENDOR and WINDOWID. Each variable is set up as a string.

Manipulating your user environment enables you to expand the functionality of some programs and improves your UNIX productivity.

Understanding How Shells Work

Shells are moderately complicated programs simply because of what they do: shells maintain your user environment, manipulate I/O streams, oversee processes running in the background, and run commands.

Because a shell is an interpreted environment, you can consider each shell's command structure its own programming language. Indeed, experienced UNIX users program shell scripts as often as they write programs.

Maintaining the environment

As I mentioned before, the environment is a series of strings maintained by the system for you, the user. In most programs, you can access this array of globally declared character strings. The shell is one of the primary programs that you can use to maintain the environment.

Each shell has built-in commands to add, change, or delete elements of this array. The Bourne shell views environment variables as a subclass of variables that are *exported* to other programs. The C shell maintains environment variables in an entirely different hierarchy. Subsequent chapters explain these differences.

Manipulating I/O streams

One of the shell's trickiest jobs is correctly maintaining input and output. Perhaps the biggest boon of UNIX was the *pipe*. A pipe enables data to be passed (port) from one command to another. Before UNIX, you had to create and delete temporary files so that one program could use the output of a previous program as input. The code for this looked like the following:

```
OS> attach output tempfile1
OS> run command
OS> attach input tempfile1
OS> attach output tempfile2
OS> run command2
OS> remove tempfile1
OS> attach input tempfile2
OS> run command3
OS> remove tempfile2
```

This process was very confusing, to say the least. In a UNIX shell, the command sequence to accomplish the same task is simpler:

```
$ command | command2 | command3
```

The vertical bar (|) tells UNIX to pipe the output from one program to another in UNIX.

Of course, maintaining I/O streams goes beyond pipes. You can run a program with a different file for input or output. Additionally, you can choose from two types of output: standard output and standard error. Redirecting those streams to the appropriate files is part of the shell's job.

Supervising jobs

With modern shells, you can run multiple commands simultaneously and switch between those commands. The shell must track each command and its environment. When a command runs in the background, the shell needs to notify you after the background command is complete.

Each shell has a different technique for manipulating jobs. You need to determine which approach works best for you.

Running commands

Finally, the most important task that a shell performs is running a command. Each shell has some built-in commands that it can execute without creating new processes. Not all commands are built-in, however. To locate these commands, the shell uses the PATH variable to check each directory for an executable file that matches the name of the command. When a file is found, it is executed. If no file is found, the shell generates an error.

Therefore, you need a good PATH variable because shells use this to look for commands. Without PATH, running commands is very difficult.

Summary

This chapter illustrated some of the ideas that went into making the first UNIX shells, and it explained various aspects of the UNIX shell environment. It covered the following topics:

▶ *Shells* are programs that enable you to interact directly with computers by feeding your input to the computer and processing the output.

▶ Four standard variables are automatically set when the user logs in for a session: HOME, SHELL, TERM, and PATH. You also can set additional environment variables.

▶ You can redirect I/O streams with UNIX pipes.

▶ The most important task of a shell is to run commands.

The next two chapters examine different aspects of the shell. Chapter 4 examines each shell mentioned here, highlighting the similarities and differences between them. Chapter 5 explains how to use the shell as a programming language and how to write shell scripts to handle repetitive tasks.

Chapter 4

Understanding Shells: An Overview

In This Chapter

▶ Exploring the common shell features

▶ Introducing the Bourne, C, Korn, and BASH shells

▶ Working with built-in commands

▶ Using the chsh command

S hells are programs that enable a user to interact with the computer. Many standard shells are available with UNIX — certainly too many to be covered in one book! I've narrowed down the list to four important shells:

■ The *Bourne shell* is the original UNIX command shell. It's basic but functional.

■ The *C shell* is Berkeley's addition to shells. It builds on the Bourne shell with a C-like command syntax. It also keeps a history of the commands you execute.

■ The *Korn shell* is similar to the C shell but keeps the control flows consistent with the Bourne shell.

■ *BASH* is the "Bourne Again shell," the UNIX shell from the Free Software Foundation.

POSIX-compliant shells are based on the Korn shell; the Free Software Foundation is working to make the BASH shell POSIX-compliant. You should be aware of how the POSIX-compliant shells work because they are the next generation of UNIX shells.

Common Shell Features

The basic principle behind a shell is to parse user input into a series of commands and arguments. Therefore, shells are *language interpreters,* and the shell programming language is an *interpreted language*. One archaic example of an interpreted language is BASIC. Another involves the old IBM-5100, which came with an APL interpreter. The shell languages are more powerful because they include the capability to execute previously existing commands.

Note

You can consider any interactive computer system a language interpreter. DOS, for example, interprets your input and then runs a command based on that input. Even graphical user interface (GUI) environments have these features; the input may not come from a keyboard, but it still has a definition and is interpreted by a program.

Many other command interpreters exist in the UNIX environment, including some shells (such as tclsh and tk). However, because those interpreters are used less often than the four described here, I have omitted them from this chapter.

Every shell in UNIX makes use of the PATH environment variable. This is a list of directories on a system, separated by colons, that the shell uses to find commands for execution. The shell searches the PATH until the command is found, and then it executes the command. If an account uses the following PATH

```
PATH=/usr/bin:/bin:.:/usr/ucb:/home/james/bin:/usr/local/bin
```

and the user enters **elm**, the shell takes the following steps to find a command called elm in the directories listed in PATH:

1. The shell searches for an executable file named /usr/bin/elm.

2. If it can't find that file, the shell looks for /bin/elm.

3. If it can't find that, the shell looks for ./elm.

4. If it doesn't find that, the shell looks for /usr/ucb/elm.

5. If the shell comes up empty-handed, it looks for /home/james/bin/elm.

6. If it can't find that, the shell looks for /usr/local/bin/elm.

7. If it still hasn't found the correct command, the shell returns an error.

The directory . refers to the current working directory. If this specification is not in your PATH, you can't execute files in your current directory.

You can avoid a PATH search by specifying a fully qualified path. This is a path that includes a directory and a file. The following code lists some examples:

```
/usr/local/bin/elm
./myprogram
bin/forecast
```

In these cases, the shell attempts to find the program and execute it. If it can't find or run the program, you receive an error. For a command not found, you'll see badcommand: command not found. For a program you can't run, the error is badcommand: Permission denied.

In all shells, you can place multiple commands on a command line just by separating them with semicolons.

Wildcard matching

The shell matches an asterisk (*) to any string that consists of zero or more characters. A question mark (?) specifies a single-character match, and square brackets ([ ]) are matched by the contents in the brackets. Each wildcard acts on the names of the files in the current directory.

The command `echo g*` provides a list of all files that begin with the letter *g*. Other useful expansions are `*.c` for all C source files and `*.o` for object files.

If you've made a mess of your PATH variable and have "lost" the `ls` command, `echo *` also gives you a list of all files in the current directory.

To obtain all files with a single-character suffix, you can use the `echo *.?` command. Similarly, if you want to see a list of all C source and object files, `*.[co]` does the trick.

Substituting commands

Each shell supports command substitution. When a command is enclosed in backquotes, the output of that command is passed to the program as arguments. For example,

```
$ echo Output of date is `date`
Output of date is Sat Aug 19 11:38:10 PDT 1995
$
```

Command substitution takes any arbitrarily valid UNIX command, including pipelines. If no output exists, nothing is substituted.

The Bourne Shell

The Bourne shell is the first shell for UNIX systems. Ken Thompson wrote the original version, but Steven Bourne expanded on Thompson's idea and made the shell his own. The Bourne shell pioneered many of the features commonly considered UNIX features. It was ubiquitous, and knowledge of this shell became mandatory for anyone who claimed to know UNIX.

It still is.

Although the POSIX shell has superseded the Bourne shell as the standard UNIX shell, both the POSIX shell and the Korn shell build on the concepts that originated in the Bourne. Furthermore, many shell scripts are still written for the Bourne shell, so to understand them, you must understand this shell.

Redirecting I/O

The Bourne shell introduced the capability of I/O redirection. This means that on any command line, you can redirect input so that it comes from an existing file and can redirect output to send it to a file. The greater-than (>) and less-than (<) signs accomplish these tasks.

Standard input and output

To have the input come from an existing file rather than from the mouse or keyboard, type < after the command name, followed by the name of a file. The program uses the contents of that file as *standard input* and proceeds accordingly.

Similarly, to send the output to a file, type > after the command, followed by the name of the file in which you want to store the output. You can tell the shell to perform either or both tasks in any order. The following listing illustrates several examples of input and output redirection:

```
$ ls > list-of-files
$ mail Dave < message
$ filter < inputfile > outputfile
$ filter > outputfile < inputfile
```

The first line of the preceding example uses the ls command to produce a listing of the files in the current directory (Chapter 7 discusses this command further) and to put that list (the output) into the list-of-files file. The next line uses mail to send a message to Dave. The last two lines illustrate that order is not important: In both cases, the filter program takes the input file and produces the output file.

Note

Although order is not important to the shell, providing the input filename first and then providing the output filename is customary. This practice makes shell commands easier to read and decipher.

Appending to files

When you redirect output to an existing file, you destroy the contents of the file and create a new file that contains only the output. Sometimes, however, you want to keep the data originally stored in the destination file and add more via the output. To do this, you must use the > redirection directive. When you use two greater-than signs, the shell appends the output to the file if possible. If the file does not exist, using this directive performs the same task specified by the >.

Redirecting error messages and using /dev/null

Suppose that you have redirected output to a file, but the program still puts error messages on your screen. Why is this happening?

Most likely, the program is trying to use the wrong type of output. UNIX programs have two types of output available by default, *standard output* and *standard error.* Redirection directives, however, apply only to the standard output type.

Without redirection, both standout output and standard error are sent to your terminal device. With redirection, standard error remains pointed at your terminal. You can fix this in the Bourne shell by using the format 2> as the directive to redirect standard error output:

```
$ filter < inputfile > outputfile 2> errorfile
```

The preceding example shows the `filter` command sending error messages to a separate file. In special cases, redirected I/O can point to a file named `/dev/null`. This file is the ultimate garbage can in UNIX: Anything sent to it disappears and cannot be recovered. Similarly, if you are running a program that needs an input stream but has no input, you can use `/dev/null` for that.

So, if you don't care to see the error messages from `filter`, type the following:

```
$ filter < inputfile > outputfile 2> /dev/null
```

Using file descriptors

The 2 that redirects standard error output in the preceding example is a *file descriptor.* The number 2 specifies the standard error output type. Standard input and standard output also have file descriptors: 0 and 1, respectively.

If you want to merge the output and error files, don't list them separately on the command line; otherwise, UNIX creates a race condition for the output. A race condition means that the system will not necessarily put the output in the file in the order you expected. Instead, merge the file descriptors with this format: #>&# (replace the number signs with the appropriate file descriptors). This statement tells the shell to merge the first file descriptor with the second. For example, if you want standard errors and standard output from the `filter` program to go to the same file, you'd revise the preceding example as follows:

```
$ filter < inputfile > outputfile 2>&1
```

Order is important! When the shell parses the command line, it follows these steps:

1. The shell runs the `filter` program.
2. The shell changes the source of the standard input to `inputfile`.
3. The shell changes the destination of the standard output to `outputfile`.
4. The shell changes the destination of the standard error output to the same location to which it sends the standard output.

If the command reads `filter < inputfile 2>&1 > outputfile` instead, the destination for standard error output becomes the same as for standard output, and standard output changes. The standard error remains the same as the original standard output.

Advanced shell users can open files and use more than these three file descriptors. Chapter 5 discusses the other file descriptors.

Pipes

An even more powerful feature of the shell than I/O redirection is its capability to create pipes. A pipe is a UNIX tool that sends the output of one command directly to the input of another. The symbol to create a pipe is a vertical bar (|).

To take the output produced by the ls command and send it through the filter program, type the following statement:

```
$ ls | filter
```

Pipes, by default, use the standard output type. To pipe standard error instead, type 2 before the | symbol, as follows:

```
$ ls 2| filter
```

Command lines can become difficult to read when multiple forms of redirection are used. For that reason, you commonly see parentheses included to group commands.

```
$ ls | (filter > outputfile 2> /dev/null) 2>&1
```

The preceding command tells the shell to pipe the output of ls to filter. The output of filter is then placed in the file outputfile and the errors are ignored. The errors of ls are also sent to the filter program.

Pipelines (a term used to refer to a string of commands linked with pipes) are not restricted to two commands — you can splice any number of commands together. The following example shows a four-stage pipeline that sends a user e-mail containing the full name of another user in all uppercase letters.

```
$ grep user1 /etc/passwd | cut -d: -f5 | tr `[a-z]´ `[A-Z]´ | mail
user2
```

The four commands are joined by pipes, eliminating the need for temporary files.

Note

The grep, cut, tr, and mail commands are described in subsequent chapters.

Managing the environment

The Bourne shell maintains a single set of variables. These variables are defined with simple statements: *name=value*. The following example shows how some of these variables are assigned:

```
$ MY_NAME=James
$ MY_FULLNAME="James C. Armstrong, Jr."
$ MY_TEAM="Rangers FC"
```

The shell can use these variables in commands when you precede them with a dollar sign:

```
$ echo $MY_TEAM
Rangers FC
$
```

To use these variables in other programs, you must make them available to the programs. In this case, you use the command export, followed by the name of the variables:

```
$ export MY_NAME MY_TEAM
$ subprogram
James likes Rangers FC
$
```

subprogram looks at the variables and produces the output. If the variables are not exported, the shell may generate an error when it runs this program.

Variables can be given default values in assignments. Chapter 5 discusses advanced uses of variables.

Performing jobs

The Bourne shell does not maintain any form of job control, but it does enable you to run commands in the background. That means that when you fire off a command, you don't have to wait for the command to finish before starting another. Just append an ampersand (&) to the command to run it in the background.

The C Shell

Although the Bourne shell was a pioneer in UNIX shells, it lacks several features that would make it easier to use. So, when developers at the University of California, Berkeley, obtained a license to build their own form of UNIX, they decided to build a more intuitive shell. The author of the C shell is Bill Joy, who became one of the founders of Sun Microsystems, the most successful company to be built around UNIX.

Joy designed the C shell to maintain a syntax similar to that of the C programming language. This feature makes the programming structures of the C shell familiar to programmers and easy for them to use. (I use the C shell in my home environment.) Joy also incorporated a history mechanism and an aliasing mechanism for frequently used commands into the C shell.

Even though the POSIX specification does not include any information on the C Shell, this shell will probably remain a fixture in UNIX for years to come. It is an extremely popular shell with users, and it is still evolving. The version I use is tcsh.

Differences from the Bourne shell

The C shell's basic function is similar to the Bourne shell's; the internal implementation, however, is different. Instead of searching a path repeatedly, the C shell maintains an internal hash table for finding commands. As a result, several built-in commands have been added to the C shell that report on this hash table. In addition, when a new file is added in this environment, you must use the rehash command to rebuild the hash table.

Redirecting I/O

Another big difference between these shells is in I/O redirection. The C shell does not support a separate redirection for standard error. Instead, you must combine the standard output and standard error into a single stream of output, as illustrated in the following example:

```
% filter < inputfile >& outputfile
% (filter < inputfile > outputfile) > errorfile
```

The second command shows the standard C shell technique for saving standard error to a different file: By enclosing the first command in parentheses, the command is executed in a subshell, and the standard error becomes the standard output of the subshell.

The C shell supports several internal variables that govern its behavior. The noclobber variable controls I/O redirection. When this variable is set to true, the C shell does not overwrite existing files unless you insert an exclamation point after the redirection sign. If the specified file exists, you'd use the following format to overwrite it: command >! file.

When you want to append output to a file, the behavior of noclobber is not intuitive. If noclobber is set to true when you want to append, the system prevents you from creating a file. In this situation, inserting an exclamation point after the redirection sign again overrides noclobber's behavior.

Different variables

The C shell supports local shell variables and environment variables. Use the set command to create local shell variables. You can also assign values to existing variables with set. Here, I've set some variables in the C shell:

```
% set MY_NAME=James
% set MY_FULLNAME="James C. Armstrong, Jr."
% set MY_TEAM="Rangers FC"
```

These variables are now local to the program. Unfortunately, there is no easy way to export them to the environment. Instead, the C shell supports a setenv command that enables you to add variables to the environment. The format you use to type in the data is setenv NAME value. For example, if I want MY_NAME and MY_TEAM to be variables in the environment, I'd use the following C shell commands:

```
% setenv MY_NAME James
% set MY_FULLNAME="James C. Armstrong, Jr."
% setenv MY_TEAM "Rangers FC"
```

You also can use a numeric variable. The @ command is an example of a numeric variable. By using the @ command, you can set arithmetic variables and perform arithmetic operations (in the Bourne shell, you need to use the expr command for this task).

The C shell supports a C-like syntax, so unary operators such as ++ increment the variable. The following example shows how you can use numeric variables and unary operators to perform some simple C shell arithmetic:

```
% @ a=1
% @ b=3
% @ c=$a + $b
% @ d=$a - $b
% @ d++
% echo $a $b $c $d
1 3 4 -1


bash-2.01$ csh
everything% @ a=1
everything% @ b=3
everything% @ c=$a+$b
@: Badly formed number
@: Expression syntax
everything% @ c=$a + $b
everything%
```

Manipulating history

Being able to manipulate the shell's history is one of the biggest advantages of using the C shell. The Bourne shell has no concept of a history, so if you make a typo in a long command, you need to retype the whole command. In contrast, the C shell's history feature enables you to modify just the previous command.

To use this feature and access the shell history, you need to set a history retention level. This level determines the number of previously entered commands stored in the shell's memory. You set the history variable by specifying the number of commands you want it to store.

The C shell then saves each command with an event number. You can view these event numbers by using the history command, which lists all the commands in your shell history with their associated event numbers. To retrieve commands by using their event numbers, type an exclamation point followed by the number. To repeat the command you just entered, type !!. The following example shows how to use the history command:

```
% history
2 15:14 ls
3 15:14 cat c4
4 15:15 who
5 15:15 mail
6 15:15 history
% !4
who
james tty1  Aug 2 16:51
% !!
who
james tty1  Aug 2 16:51
```

You can search the history list as well. By typing an exclamation point followed by some characters, you command the C shell to search for the most recent history event that begins with those characters and execute it. To search for a word anywhere in the history, use the **!?word** syntax to specify your search items.

You can edit a previous command stored in the shell history by using the ^ character. This character enables you to replace a regular expression with text in a way similar to the way you use an ed editor. (For more information on ed, see Chapter 10.) If you mistype something, it's easy to correct, as the following example shows:

```
% mial dave
mial: Command not found.
% ^ia^ai^
mail dave
```

Using the history feature to correct a typo is much easier than retyping the command, as you must do in the Bourne shell. This is especially true when you need to correct a long command.

The history feature also enables you to extract *pieces* of old commands. The syntax for this task is fairly complicated, but you can use shortcuts to simplify the process. First, you type the command's event number, and then you follow it with a colon and a number representing the field in the command when the words of the command are separated by spaces.

Suppose that you had a history like the following:

```
5 15:15 vi file1 file2 file3 file2
```

You could type **!5:2** to get file2. You could also specify ranges such as **!5:3-** to get file3 file2 or **!5:1-3** to get file1 file2 file3.

The most common shortcut is to grab the last word of the last command. The format for this is !$.

Once you become accustomed to using the history feature, you'll be glad to have it. Using the history list is one way to speed your work in a C shell.

Using aliases

Another improvement that the C shell offers over the Bourne shell is its capability to create aliases for common commands. I'm a heavy user of aliases for repeated tasks, and I often enhance existing commands with aliases (sometimes called *overloading* commands).

To create an alias in the C shell, type **alias**, followed by the command that you want to assign an alias to and the replacement string. For example, because I often mistype the cd command with the two keys next to it, I just create an alias for it: alias xs cd (check your keyboard). I also use my gerp typo as an alias for grep.

To list your existing aliases, type **alias**. (This command comes in handy for users with less-than-perfect memories.)

The usefulness of aliases extends beyond typos, however. For example, I've assigned an alias to the ls command so that when I type ls, the shell performs both the ls command functions and the -F flag functions by default. Similarly, I've changed vi so that it brings up my vi sessions in an xterm. (For more information on vi, see Chapter 11. For more information on X commands and xterms, see Part VIII.)

Here's a list of all the aliases I have on my home machine:

```
+w          (chmod !:0 !:1)
+x          (chmod !:0 !:1)
-w          (chmod !:0 !:1)
addpath     (set path = ( $path !* );source /home/james/bin/patrunc)
cd          (cd !*;pathprompt;rehash)
cls         clear;ls
cptree      (pushd !:1 ; cd .. ; tar cfp - !:1 | (cd !:2 ; tar xvfp -
            ) ; popd)
env         setenv
gerp        grep
ls          (ls -F)
lso         (source .aliases)
mail        dmail
pathprompt  (set prompt="\!: $cwd$id")
popd        (popd !*;pathprompt)
pushd       (pushd !*;pathprompt)
q           (/usr/lib/sendmail -bp)
r           restorewind
rmcore      (find . -name core -print -exec rm \{\} \;)
term        (xterm -bg black -fg blue -bd red -ms green -cr yellow -fn
            7x13 -g =80x29+0+90 &)
vf          cd
vi          xterm -cr purple -ms black -bd green -bg cyan -fg red -T
            `vi !*´ -g 80x22 -e vi !*&
xs          cd
```

You can remove an alias with the unalias command.

Accessing directory stacks

The C shell maintains a hierarchy of directories that you can access. Use the `dirs` command to list the current directory stack. You can use other commands to access the hierarchy as well. The `pushd` command works the same way as the `cd` command, except that it adds the current directory to the stack. Similarly, `popd` retrieves a directory level and removes the previous directory from the top of the stack.

Controlling jobs

The C shell has a more advanced concept of job control than the Bourne shell. In the C shell, you can suspend a running job by pressing Ctrl-Z. Then you can move the job into the background with the `bg` command or into the foreground with the `fg` command.

You also can examine your current jobs by typing **jobs**. The resulting list provides you with a job's reference number, which you can use to apply any job control command to the job.

The Korn Shell

The Korn shell is Bell Labs' successor to the Bourne shell and is becoming quite popular. David Korn is the author of the shell, which — like the C shell — builds on the original Bourne shell.

Manipulating history

The Korn shell supports a history syntax, as does the C shell. The Korn shell's history variable determines the level of history retention, and the history command prints that history. This is where the similarity with the C shell ends, however.

To access previous commands and events in the Korn shell, press Escape at the command line, and you're in history mode. You can search for older commands by typing a slash mark (/) and a pattern, or you can step through the commands incrementally by pressing - and +. When you find the command that you want, press Enter to execute it.

You also can edit the command with your favorite editor if you've set an `EDITOR` variable. Another way to specify this setting is with the `set -o` command. Then, after you've found the command, you can use your standard editor commands to move along the line and make changes. (For more details on editor commands, see Part IV.)

The Korn shell history mechanism has a distinct advantage over the C shell's: You don't need to remember event numbers or complicated syntaxes to pull words or pieces from commands. Instead, you can run a complicated command in the Korn shell, return to edit it, and save the command to a file under a new name. This is an excellent start to building commands.

Using aliases

The Korn shell supports aliasing, but its aliasing feature differs slightly from the C shell's. To create an alias in the Korn shell, specify the name followed by an equal sign and the value. You can't perform replacements in the alias.

Table 4-1 shows some of my common aliases in the Korn shell and C shell formats.

Table 4-1 Creating Aliases in the Korn and C Shells	
Korn Shell Format	*C Shell Format*
alias ls='ls -F'	alias ls ls -F
alias xs=cd	alias xs cd
alias vi='xterm -e vi'	alias vi xterm -e vi

In both shells, you can check a list of aliases by typing **alias**.

Using functions

The Korn shell enables you to create functions, which are more powerful than aliases. (This capability was also incorporated into the Bourne shell.) To create a function in the Korn shell, use a format such as the one shown in the following example:

```
my_func()
{
pwd
ls
}
```

This function enables me to type **my_func** on the command line at any time and view the current directory (pwd) and a listing of all files therein.

More details about functions are available in Chapter 5.

Controlling jobs

The Korn shell offers job control, using the same command syntax as the C shell. If you know how to use job control for one of these shells, you don't need to learn it for the other.

The BASH Shell

The BASH (or Bourne Again) shell basically combines the features of the C shell and the Korn shell. BASH was developed by the Free Software Foundation, maker of the GNU tools described in Part X. BASH is a free tool, so anyone who wants to use it can grab it via file transfer protocol (FTP) and build it on his or her system.

Built-in Commands

In Chapter 3, I told you that the most important task that a shell performs is running commands. Typically, this involves using the PATH variable to search for and locate the command and then executing it. Some commands, however, are built into the shell itself; a separate program does not execute the command. Thus, built-in commands execute much faster than programs because the shell does not have to find a program before it can run the command. More important, when you execute a built-in command, the shell does not waste time loading and starting a program. One of the more time-intensive UNIX actions is loading and starting programs. Using built-in commands definitely speeds up your shell's execution time.

Another disadvantage of executable file commands is that they cannot affect the shell's environment. Because of this, commands such as cd must be built into the shell. After all, what's the point of executing a command to change a directory if that affects only the command, not the shell?

Different shells have different commands built into them; you may find commands in the Korn shell that you won't find in the Bourne shell. Table 4-2 lists the built-in commands for three of the shells discussed in this chapter: the Bourne shell, the C shell, and the Korn shell.

Table 4-2   Built-in Shell Commands

Command	Bourne Shell	C Shell	Korn Shell
%		X	X
.	X		X
:			X
@		X	
alias		X	X
bg		X	X
cd	X	X	X
chdir	X	X	
dirs		X	

Command	Bourne Shell	C Shell	Korn Shell
echo	X	X	X
eval	X	X	X
exec	X	X	X
exit	X	X	X
export	X		X
fc			X
fg		X	X
getopts	X		X
glob		X	
goto		X	
hash		X	
hashstat		X	
history		X	X
jobs		X	X
kill		X	X
let			X
limit		X	
login	X	X	
logout		X	
newgrp	X	X	X
nice		X	
nohup		X	
notify		X	
onintr		X	
popd		X	
print			X
pushd		X	
pwd	X		X
read	X		X
readonly	X		X
rehash		X	
repeat		X	

Continued

Table 4-2   *(continued)*

Command	Bourne Shell	C Shell	Korn Shell
return	X		X
set	X	X	X
setenv		X	
shift	X	X	X
source		X	
stop		X	
suspend		X	
test	X		
time		X	
times	X		X
trap	X		X
type	X		
typeset			X
ulimit			X
umask	X	X	X
unalias		X	X
unhash		X	
unlimit		X	
unset	X	X	X
unsetenv		X	
wait	X	X	X
whence			X

For more information on specific commands, check the manual pages on your system.

The chsh Command

Use the chsh command to change your default shell in UNIX. When you execute this command, the program checks an administrative file to make sure that you entered a valid shell. If you did, it changes the last field in /etc/passwd for you. Your system asks for your password before it makes the change.

Summary

In this chapter, you learned about the four most common shells available on UNIX systems: the Bourne shell, the C shell, the Korn shell, and BASH. You also learned the command that enables you to change your default shell, and you learned why some commands have been built into the shell. In addition, these topics were covered:

▶ You use PATH variables to run commands from executable files. Built-in commands do not have to go through this process to execute.

▶ UNIX has wildcards that you can use to match a search item with a specific character or string of characters.

▶ Command substitution techniques enable you to use the output of commands as the arguments in a program.

▶ In UNIX, you can specify that input comes from and output goes to a file rather than the user. This is called standard input and output.

▶ Pipes enable the shell to use the output of one command as the input of another.

▶ You can use shells to interact directly with your computer. Several different types of shells are available.

▶ The C shell, Korn shell, and BASH are all based on the Bourne shell, which is the original standard for UNIX shells.

▶ You can use a technique called aliasing in the C shell, Korn shell, and BASH to help you execute the correct command functions when you make typos or to group various command functions under one command.

In Chapter 5, you will be introduced to shell programming.

Chapter 5

Shell Programming

As Chapter 4 explains, shells are really interpreted languages. Consequently, you can write programs in a shell language and run them as you would any other program. This chapter uses the Korn shell to discuss basic programming techniques. It concludes with some sample programs.

You can view everything you type into a shell as a program. You can use the shell's history capability to save commands to files and then use them to build programs.

Understanding Shell Variables

One of a program's primary purposes is to manipulate data. That data is stored in variables, so programs need to manipulate variables.

The Korn shell supports several variable types, including arrays and integers. The typeset command indicates the type; if you don't use typeset to specify the type of a variable, it is considered a string. Shell variables are assigned by specifying *name=value*.

Arrays

The Korn shell enables you to create arrays. You can use the `set` command to create an array with the `-A` flag. Follow the flag with the name of the variable and then a list of values, each value separated by a space. The following is an example of an array assignment:

```
$ set -A states Delaware Pennsylvania "New Jersey"
```

Consider arrays in the Korn shell associative: You can add new members with array indexes beyond the current scope. You can add the 50th state to the previous example with `states[49]=Alaska`.

Note

Array indexing in the Korn shell starts with index 0, so the 50th element has an index of 49.

Referencing variables

You can access variables in the Korn shell in several ways. In every case, you use a dollar sign ($) to indicate that the following string is the name of a shell variable and that you want to associate some value with it. Variable names must start with a letter of the alphabet or an underscore and can be followed by letters, numbers, or underscores. `My_House` is a fine variable name, but `1stree` and `Go>there` are not.

The following list describes 19 methods for accessing variable data. In each syntax example, *name* is a variable name, *pattern* is a pattern, and *value* is an alternate value.

- **$*name*** — This is the simplest means of accessing the variable. When the shell encounters `$name`, it replaces this with the value of the variable. The following example shows the simple substitution. When the variable is not set or is undefined, a `NULL` string is returned.

  ```
  $ myhouse=Colonial
  $ echo My house is $myhouse
  My house is Colonial
  ```

- **${*name*}** — Sometimes, just using the name format is inadequate. Examples include situations in which you need to prepend the variable to another string without any spaces between the two strings. The curly braces separate the variable name from the surrounding context, making substitution easier. The following example illustrates the reasons why such substitutions may be necessary.

  ```
  $ prefix=anti
  $ echo to keep a car warm, use $prefixfreeze
  to keep a car warm, use
  $ echo to keep a car warm, use ${prefix}freeze
  to keep a car warm, use antifreeze
  ```

In the first case, even though you wanted the variable $prefix, because you did not include a space, the shell went looking for a variable named prefixfreeze. It didn't find one and returned a NULL. By surrounding the variable name in curly braces, you can obtain the value and append the string.

- **${*name[n]*}** — This accesses the *n*th element of the array variable. If the element is not set, this returns NULL. In the example at the beginning of the "Arrays" section, you can list a single element of the states array with $ echo ${states[1]} and expect to see Pennsylvania.

- **${*name[*]*}** — This syntax lists all the values of the array elements, separated by spaces. In the states example, this would result in Delaware Pennsylvania New Jersey Alaska.

- **${*name[@]*}** — In the previous item's example, the third element of the array, New Jersey, has an embedded blank. This blank makes it difficult to determine whether *New* and *Jersey* are part of the same element or are different elements of the array. When a subsequent command needs to parse the values of the variable, it treats them as separate elements.

The {name[@]} construct circumvents this. When enclosed in double quotation marks, elements are passed intact, without splitting on spaces. The following example illustrates this using a for loop, which is described later in this chapter.

```
$ for state in "${states[@]}"
> do
> echo $state
> done
Delaware
Pennsylvania
New Jersey
Alaska
$
* @BL:${name:-value} -This syntax is replaced with the value of
the name variable or, if undefined or zero length, the value
specified in the curly braces. This is useful if you need to
generate something on expansion, even if the variable is not set,
as the following example illustrates.
$ state=California
$ echo I live in ${city:-unknown}, ${state:-unknown}
I live in unknown, California
```

- **${*name–value*}** — By omitting the colon from the previous syntax, you test only for the variable's existence. If you've set city as a zero-length string, the output from the previous echo statement becomes I live in , California.

- **${*name=value*}** — If name is undefined, it is assigned the value given. Then, the value of name is substituted. If a colon is present before the equal sign, name also is reset if it is of zero length. The following example shows this replacement.

```
$ echo Today is ${day}
Today is
$ echo Today is ${day=Saturday}
Today is Saturday
$ echo Today is ${day}
Today is Saturday
```

- **${*name?value*}** — This syntax halts execution if the variable name is undefined and presents *value* as an error message. If this is in a shell program, execution terminates at this point.

- **${*name+value*}** — This expression works exactly opposite to ${name-value}. If ${name} is defined, *value* is substituted. If ${name} is not defined (or with ${name:+value} zero length), a NULL string is substituted.

- **${*name#pattern*}** — This expression presents the value of ${name} with the shortest leftmost pattern deleted. Patterns may include any character sequence, variable, command substitutions, and wildcard expressions. Only the first occurrence of a matching string is deleted.

```
$ MY_NAME="James C. Armstrong"
$ echo ${MY_NAME#James}
 C. Armstrong
$
```

The Bourne shell provides some simple types of pattern matching. An asterisk (*) matches zero or more characters. A question mark (?) matches a single character. Square brackets ([ ]) match any single character enclosed in the brackets.

The Korn shell adds five more types of pattern matching. An asterisk (*) followed by a pattern or list of patterns matches zero or more occurrences of that pattern. A plus (+) matches one or more occurrences of that pattern. A question mark (?) matches one or fewer occurrences. An at sign (@) matches exactly one occurrence, and an exclamation point (!) matches exactly zero occurrences.

These characters can produce some interesting effects. Consider a directory with the files speedtrap, speedzone, speed.c, speed.o, speed.1, speed.1.c, speed.1.1, and speed. The following example shows the appropriate pattern matches:

```
$ echo speed*(zone|trap)
speed speedtrap speedzone
$ echo speed+(.1|.c)
speed.c speed.1 speed.1.c speed.1.1
$ echo speed?(.1|.c)
speed speed.c speed.1
$ echo speed@(.1|.c)
speed.c speed.1
$ echo speed!(.1|.c)
speed speed.o speedtrap speedzone
```

The advanced pattern-matching features of the Korn shell are also used in variable matchings.

■ **${*name*##*pattern*}** — This functions the same as ${name#pattern}, except that the longest leftmost match is deleted.

■ **${*name*%*pattern*}** — This is the same as ${name#pattern}, except that the shortest rightmost pattern is deleted.

■ **${*name*%%*pattern* }** — In this case, the longest rightmost pattern is deleted.

■ **$*** — The entire set of command-line or shell parameters is echoed.

■ **$@** — The entire set of command-line or shell parameters is echoed, but the individual values are not split by spaces.

■ **${#@}** — This returns an integer count of the number of words that would result from $@.

■ **${#*}** — This returns an integer count of the number of words that would result from $*.

■ **${#*name*}** — This returns the integer value of the length of the string in the variable name.

■ **${#*name*[*]}** and **${#*name*[@]}** — These expressions return the number of elements in the array variable name.

Using the typeset command

The typeset command defines types and manipulates variables in the Korn shell. Variables can be integers or strings, and data conversions can be forced upon assignment. The syntax is

```
typeset [ -LRZilrtux [n] ] [ name[=value] ] ...
```

Table 5-1 describes the typeset command's flags.

Table 5-1   Flags for the typeset Command

Argument	Meaning
-L [n]	The variable is left-justified, so any leading blanks are eliminated. If an additional number is specified, the variable is padded with spaces until it reaches the specified length.
-R [n]	The variable is right-justified and padded with leading spaces until it reaches the specified length. All trailing whitespace is eliminated.

Continued

Table 5-1   *(continued)*

Argument	Meaning
-Z [n]	The variable is right-justified and padded with leading zeros. This flag is used for numeric fields.
-i	The variable is of type integer. This is very useful for arithmetic operations. The Korn shell doesn't need variables to be defined as integers, but by doing so, you speed up calculation times.
-l	The variable is converted to lowercase letters when assigned.
-r	The variable is read-only, which means you cannot assign values to it after the initial assignment.
-u	The variable is automatically converted to uppercase on assignment.
-x	The variable is automatically exported to the environment.

Secret

The -Z flag is particularly useful if your system supports it (Solaris does not), as the following example illustrates:

```
$ typeset -i -Z2 chapter=1
$ while
> [ $chapter < 5 ]
> do
> mkdir chapter${chapter}
> let chapter=chapter+1
> done
$ ls
chapter01 chapter02 chapter03 chapter04 chapter05
```

Note

The export command is just an alias to typeset -x.

I provide examples for the use of typeset later in the chapter.

Assigning values to variables

You normally assign values to variables by listing the variable followed by an equal sign and a value. There is another common way to obtain a value, though. The read command assigns user input as the value of variables. Where read appears, a list of variables follows. The input is broken into words and spaces and assigned to each variable listed. If more words exist than variables, the remaining words are assigned to the last variable.

For example, you may see the following in a program:

```
echo "Month and Day of birth?"
read mon day rubbish
```

When the preceding code is executed, you see the following:

```
Month and Day of birth?
```

The program then reads your input to the program and assigns values to the mon, day, and rubbish variables. The rubbish variable exists for one reason: to gather any excess information from the input and ignore it.

Deleting variables

To remove a variable from the script, use the unset command. After unset, list the variables you want destroyed. After the command executes, the variables are undefined.

Using Command-Line Arguments and Shell Parameters

A shell script should include a *command type* on its first line. This is a left-justified string beginning with #!. The UNIX operating system finds this and executes the subsequent command with the arguments as parameters.

For Korn shell scripts, the command is usually #!/bin/ksh. For POSIX-compliant systems, it may be /bin/sh instead.

The arguments passed are considered positional parameters. You can access them by specifying a number, such as $2, to give to the second argument. If more than nine arguments exist, you need to enclose the number in curly braces. This is shorthand for $argv[2].

You can change positional parameters with the set and shift commands. The set command, followed by a list of strings, changes the positional parameters to those listed. set has several flags. To obtain the full list, see the Korn shell manual page. The shift command deletes the first parameter and reassigns all the remaining parameters to the previous spot. If a number is also specified, the first *n* parameters are eliminated. The following example illustrates set and shift in use:

```
$ set January February March April May June
$ echo $*
January February March April May June
$ shift
$ echo $*
February March April May June
$ shift 3
$ echo $*
May June
```

The control flow structures include shortcuts for using positional parameters, so if you assign parameters, they are manipulated with greater ease in a program.

Using Functions

Functions in programs provide tremendous savings in terms of maintenance. By including groupings of frequently used commands in a function, you don't need to type the same commands repeatedly. If a change is needed, you need to make it in only one place.

Both the Korn and Bourne shells now support functions, making the C shell pretty out-of-date for programming purposes.

You can define functions easily in the Korn shell: simply follow the keyword `function` with a name and a list of commands in curly braces. Functions can call other functions, including themselves.

Note

A function's ability to call itself is *recursion*. Recursion is a powerful concept in programming because it makes coding some complicated programs easier.

The following is an example of a function that changes a directory and lists the files:

```
$ function clist {
> cd $1
> ls
> }
```

Now, when I call `clist`, the current directory changes to the argument directory or my home directory, and I see a listing of files in that directory.

Using typeset to manipulate functions

The `typeset` command has four options to manipulate functions. Each option involves the `-f` flag. When used alone, `typeset -f` lists the currently defined functions for the shell script. The predefined alias `functions` is the same command.

With the `-ft` flag, a trace of the function is initiated on the next call. This gives a listing of each command when it is executed with the fully expanded variables. When you are debugging your functions, this is a handy tool. After the function call is completed, tracing is turned off.

With the `-fx` flag, the functions listed are exported to any child shell scripts. You cannot export functions to separate invocations of `ksh`, though.

The last flag is `-fu`, which designates the listed functions as autoloading functions. Autoloading functions are kept as tags. When these functions are called, the shell looks on the `FPATH` variable for a file with the same name as the function and loads that file to invoke the function.

Autoloading functions

Autoloading functions have some advantages over standard functions. By creating a directory with autoloading functions, you can use the same function in multiple shell scripts without needing to copy that function to every script. Furthermore, the shell does not need the function, and memory is saved by not loading the function.

Autoloading is recommended for frequently used functions, particularly those that appear in multiple scripts.

Deleting functions

You can delete functions with the unset command. You need to specify the -f flag so that the shell knows you are deleting a function, not a variable.

Using Arithmetic and Conditions

The Korn shell supports built-in arithmetic functions. The let command indicates that the arguments that follow are an expression to be evaluated. The simplest expression is a single term, usually an integer value.

You can write integers as a string of digits or in any base format. The format is radix#number, where radix is any number up to 26. The most common radixes are 2 (binary), 8 (octal), and 16 (hexadecimal).

The simple mathematical expressions are addition (+), subtraction (-), multiplication (*), integer division (/), and integer remainder (%). The let command takes the two operands and assigns them to the variable.

One nice feature of let is that it doesn't need the dollar sign to identify a variable, so you can write commands such as let sum=x+7, and let looks for the variable x and adds 7 to it. The let command also takes expansion of other let expressions by enclosing them in double parentheses. You can create fairly complicated expressions this way.

The let command is not limited to simple arithmetic. Table 5-2 shows the complete set of operations for let.

Table 5-2   Korn Shell Arithmetic Operators

Operator	Syntax	Result
!	!exp	Returns 1 if exp evaluates to 0; otherwise, returns 0
!=	exp1!=exp2	Returns 1 if exp1 evaluates to a value different from exp2; otherwise, returns 0
%	exp1%exp2	Returns the remainder of the division of exp1 by exp2

Continued

	Table 5-2 *(continued)*	
Operator	**Syntax**	**Result**
%=	Var%=exp	Assigns the remainder of the division of `var` by `exp` to `var`
&	exp1&exp2	Returns the bitwise AND of `exp1` and `exp2`
&&	exp1&&exp2	Returns 1 if both `exp1` and `exp2` are nonzero; otherwise, returns 0
&=	var &= exp	Assigns the bitwise AND of `var` and `exp` to `var`
*	exp1 * exp2	Multiplies `exp1` by `exp2`
*=	var *= exp	Multiplies `exp` by the value of `var` and assigns the result to `var`
+	exp1 + exp2	Adds `exp1` and `exp2`
+=	var += exp	Adds `exp` to the value of `var` and assigns the sum to `var`
-	-exp	Negates `exp` (called *unary minus*)
-	exp1 - exp2	Subtracts `exp2` from `exp1`
-=	var -= exp	Subtracts `exp` from the value of `var` and assigns the remainder to `var`
/	exp1 / exp2	Divides `exp1` by `exp2`
/=	var /= exp	Divides `var` by `exp` and assigns the remainder to `var`
<	exp1 < exp2	Returns 1 if `exp1` is less than `exp2`; otherwise, returns 0
<<	exp1 << exp2	Shifts `exp1` left `exp2` bits
<<=	var <<= exp	Shifts the value of `var` left by `exp` bits
<=	exp1 <= exp2	Returns 1 if `exp1` is less than or equal to `exp2`; otherwise, returns 0
=	var = exp	Assigns the value of `exp` to the variable `var`
==	exp1 == exp2	Returns 1 if `exp1` is equal to `exp2`; otherwise, returns 0
>	exp1 > exp2	Returns 1 if `exp1` is greater than `exp2`; otherwise, returns 0
>=	exp1 >= exp2	Returns 1 if `exp1` is greater than or equal to `exp2`; otherwise, returns 0
>	exp1 > exp2	Shifts `exp1` right `exp2` bits
>=	var >= exp	Shifts the value of `var` right by `exp` bits

Operator	Syntax	Result
^	exp1 ^ exp2	Returns the exclusive OR of exp1 and exp2
^=	var ^= exp	Assigns the bitwise exclusive OR of var and exp to var
|	exp1 | exp2	Returns the bitwise OR of exp1 and exp2
|=	var |= exp	Assigns the bitwise OR of var and exp to var
||	exp1 || exp2	Returns 1 if either exp1 or exp2 is nonzero; otherwise, returns 0
~	~exp	Returns the bitwise complement of exp

Note

Shell redirection characters need to be enclosed in single quotation marks to be understood.

Conditions of let

Besides using the let command for assignments, you can use let to evaluate conditions. Like C, the Korn shell can assign any value to a variable, and the expression itself has a value that can be used. Often, for ease of programming, Korn shell conditions use the (( )) syntax for control flow.

Of course, you can assign conditional results to variables, and you can use the results of arithmetic calculations for conditions. Performing an action while decrementing a value is a good example of this. The following illustrates a simple case:

```
$ let x=5
$ while
> (( x-=1 ))
> do
> something
> done
$
```

This example starts with the value of 5 and decrements it until it equals zero. For each iteration, it performs the something function.

Shortcuts

The most common shortcut is one that eliminates the word *let* from your shell programs. When you declare your variables as integers, any assignment is automatically treated as an arithmetic assignment. You use typeset -i to declare and assign the variable, and it then becomes usable as an integer. Or you can use the keyword integer (an alias for typeset -i) and declare the variables as integers. Then, expressions such as x=y+z make sense as arithmetic expressions.

Additional conditions

Beyond the arithmetic conditions are file existence conditions. The test command is a legacy of these conditions. You specify the flag and a filename within square brackets. A 1 is returned if the test is true, and a 0 is returned if it is false. Table 5-3 lists these conditions.

Table 5-3   File Tests

test Operator	Meaning
-b	The file is a block special file
-c	The file is a character special file
-d	The file is a directory
-e	The file is executable
-f	The file is a regular file
-r	The file is readable
-s	The file is of nonzero length
-t n	The number is associated with a terminal device
-w	The file is writable

These conditions may be negated with an exclamation point or combined with -a for AND and -o for OR.

Control Flow

At the heart of a programming language stands the capability to control the execution sequence of commands. This is called *control flow,* and the Korn shell comes with four standard methods of controlling the sequence in which instructions are executed. Each method has its advantages and disadvantages. The choice of flow format is up to you, the programmer.

Conditional execution

Two commands exist that execute blocks of code conditionally: the if statement and the case statement. The if statement is usually used for easy evaluation where there are two branches; case statements are more useful with multiple branches.

if statements

The if statement executes a condition and, according to the results, executes a block of code. The syntax is as follows:

```
if
statement_list
then
statement_list
{ elif
statement_list
then
statement_list }
[ else
statement_list ]
fi
```

The Korn shell allows multiple commands in any condition. The last command is evaluated and the return code is checked for truth or falsehood. Truth is a nonzero return code.

When a command is true, it executes the second statement_list. Anything can be included in that list, including other if statements. This can be optionally followed by any number of elif clauses. An elif clause is one that is tested only if all previous tests are false and a subsequent statement_list executes. Finally, a terminal else statement_list can execute if all previous conditions are false. The if statement terminates with the keyword fi.

The following is an example of a simple if statement that prints out the type of file.

```
if
    [ -f $file ]
then
    echo $file is a regular file
elif
    [ -d $file ]
then
    echo $file is a directory
elif
    [ -c $file ]
then
    echo $file is a character special file
elif
    [ -b $file ]
then
    echo $file is a block special file
else
    echo $file is unidentified
fi
```

Note

For ease of reading, I have indented statements. This is a good programming style because it helps make your shell scripts easy for others to maintain.

if statements can be arbitrarily long.

Fast if statements

An alternative to the traditional if statement is to link two statements with a conjunction. The && conjunction executes the commands following the conjunction if the first command returns true. The | | conjunction does the opposite, executing the second case only if the first returns false. For example, [-f $file] && echo The file $file exists tests for the existence of a file. If the file is found, it echoes a statement that the file exists.

case statements

If you end up with multiple elif clauses in your if statement, you should check to see whether the statement is a candidate for a case statement. The case statement is similar to switch in the C programming language, but it has more power because it includes pattern matching in the labels.

The syntax for a case statement is as follows:

```
case value in
pattern) statement_list ;;
(pattern) statement_list ;; }
esac
```

The value can be anything, but it is usually a variable. Patterns are matched against that variable with the Korn shell pattern matching. Multiple patterns can be separated by vertical bars.

A good example of a case statement resolves actions according to the day of the week, as the following code illustrates:

```
dow=`date `+%w``
case "$dow" in
1|2|3|4) echo Another working day;;
5) echo TGIF! ;;
0|6) echo I live for the weekend;;
*) echo What day is $dow
esac
```

This example uses the date command to get an integer that represents the day of the week (Sunday=0, Monday=1, and so on). Then, it uses the case statement to print a message for the day. On Monday through Thursday, it says it is just another working day. On Friday, it exclaims "TGIF!," and on the weekend, it expresses a decent life philosophy.

Note

The case statement also includes a default case. Because the asterisk matches anything, including it as the last pattern catches all expressions that were unmatched.

By using pattern matching, the case statement can handle most combinations. You can combine two variables in the case statement and any number of patterns attached for matching.

Loop statements

The other significant control structure is for looping commands. You use a *loop* when you need to execute a block of commands repeatedly in the same section of code. The for loop modifies a single variable per execution, and the while loop executes a block while a condition is valid.

for statements

The for loop uses a list of values for a variable and executes a block of code for each of those values. The syntax is as follows:

```
for var [ in list ]
do
    statement_list
done
```

The list can be anything from the values of a variable to an expansion of filenames. If no list is provided, the function's positional parameters are used.

The following example shows a for loop that goes through the command-line arguments and echoes them to the screen.

```
for arg
do
    echo $arg
done
```

for loops are extremely powerful. You may want to write a program that performs a spelling check on a file. Instead of running the program for each file, you could place the whole program in a loop, as in the previous example, and use a variable for the filename.

This is actually an ideal use for a function. Create a function named spellcheck that does everything you want, including making the call to spellcheck in the for loop.

You are not required to use the variable passed to the command block, as the following example (which echoes the string Beat Carolina three times) demonstrates:

```
for i in 1 2 3
do
    echo Beat Carolina
done
```

The i variable is never used in the loop.

while statements

The `while` loop executes a block of statements while a condition is true. That condition may also be another block of statements. The return value of the last statement is checked for truth or falsehood. The syntax is as follows:

```
while
    statement_list
do
    statement_list
done
```

`while` lists are often used when the number of iterations is nondeterministic. An example is the following script, which checks to see whether a file exists and, while it exists, sleeps:

```
while
    [ -f $file ]
do
    sleep 10
done
```

This kind of loop might be used while a user is waiting for a resource to become available.

Breaking loops

The Korn shell provides two easy ways to break out of loops. The `break` command terminates execution of a loop, and the `continue` command terminates the current iteration of the statement block.

The break command

The `break` command is useful to terminate a `while` loop when a condition is no longer valid. In the previous example, the `while` loop could have been written as an infinite loop to be broken when the file no longer exists, as follows:

```
while
    true
do
    if [ ! -f $file ]
    then
        break
    fi
    sleep 10
done
```

The continue command

You use `continue` when you no longer need to execute a statement block but when you may want to continue testing the block on other conditions. An example is to ignore the `/dev/null` file in any list of files:

```
while
    file=$filelist[$i]
    (( $i < ${#filelist[*]} ))
do
    if
        [ "$file" == "/dev/null" ]
    then
        continue
    fi
    action
done
```

The program skips over the value but continues to test other values.

Using the getopts Command

One very useful command for programming is getopts, which parses the command line for flags and is used to assign variables. The syntax is as follows:

```
getopts option-string variable [ arg ... ]
```

Note

Flags are command-line options and are usually designated with a minus sign; for example, -i is a flag for typeset. Sometimes, these flags have arguments associated with them. Programs need to interpret these flags and change their behavior accordingly. Other names for flags are arguments and options.

The *option-string* is a list of possible letters and numbers for flags. If an argument is expected to accompany the flag, a colon must follow the letter. The variable is assigned the letter for the option.

The getopts command returns true while it can discern arguments. It is customary to include getopts in a while loop and parse the data with a case statement. Here is what getopts looks like:

```
while
    getopts o:i:ltr optletter
do
    case $optletter in
    o)    oflag=1; oval=$OPTARG;;
    i)    iflag=1; ival=$OPTARG;;
    l)    lflag=1;;
    t)    tflag=1;;
    r)    rflag=1;;
    *)    echo Illegal option $optletter
    esac
done
```

The getopts command includes two special environment variables, OPTARG and OPTIND. The OPTARG variable is set to the next word in the arguments if an optional value is expected, and OPTIND is the numerical index of the argument.

The getopts command also parses array variables, so you can use it within a function to parse the function's arguments or to parse user input.

Advanced I/O

The Korn shell provides some basic commands for manipulating input and output streams. You can open and close files for reading and writing.

Note

Because of the high-level nature of shell programming, if your program needs to use file I/O extensively, I strongly recommend that you write it in a compiled programming language. For more information on programming in the UNIX environment, see Part IX.

You can open files in two ways: using the exec command or using the <> redirection symbol. When using exec, you need to specify a file number (your choice) and redirection followed by a filename. For example, you could open a file named inputfile with exec 3<inputfile, and you'd use the redirection structure 3< to read data from that file. Opening output is the same: exec 4> outputfile.

You can close files by appending an ampersand (&) followed by a minus sign (–) to the redirection. For example, after finishing with inputfile, use 3<&- to close the file.

The <> redirection command closes standard input and output and reopens them with the named file.

Traps

Sometimes, you need to interrupt the execution of a program. UNIX interrupts programs by passing signals, and this results in the asynchronous execution of signal-handling code within a program. The shell provides a similar capability with the trap command. The syntax is as follows:

```
trap "statement-list" signal-list
```

When the shell receives a signal on the signal-list, it executes the statement-list, which is usually cleanup commands and an exit command. The signals are specified by integers, usually 1 (hang up), 2 (interrupt), and 15 (terminate). Other usable signals are 16 (user1) and 17 (user2).

If you have a shell daemon, you may want the capability to turn debugging on and off without interrupting the process. The following example illustrates a clever means of doing this:

```
integer debug=0
function debugger
{
```

```
debug=1-debug
if
    $debug
then
    set -x
else
    set +x
fi
}
trap "debugger" 16
```

When the user1 signal is sent to the process, debugging is toggled on and off.

Debugging

You can debug shell scripts in two standard ways. One is to include many echo statements, which enable you to track what is going on. This method is imperfect.

Fortunately, the Korn shell provides a more advanced interface for tracking the actions of a script. When you set the -x flag, the shell echoes the command as executed, including variable expansion. The -v flag echoes commands before execution.

You can set the variables with the set command. To turn off debugging, use a plus sign instead of a minus sign.

Sample Shell Scripts

Two shell scripts provided here are samples of shell programming in the Korn shell.

Set path in all caps.

The first script is a path truncator. You need to run this as a function within your shell session for it to work. The second script imitates the behavior of the uuto command, a tool to send files via UUCP.

PATH truncator

Often, a PATH variable grows in a UNIX session as you add different directories. Entries may be duplicated or may point to nonexistent directories. Removing these entries speeds your shell's execution. The following is the source code to the path truncator script:

```
newpath=""
for elem in `echo $PATH | sed `s/:/ /g``
do
    if
```

```
            [ -d $elem ]
        then
            bad=0
            for nelem in `echo $newpath | sed `s/:/ /g``
            do
                if
                    [ $elem == $nelem ]
                then
                    bad=1
                fi
            done
            if
                [ $bad == 0 ]
            then
                newpath=${newpath}:$elem
            fi
        fi
    done
done
PATH=${newpath}
unset newpath elem nelem
```

Examine this script. First, it creates a variable `newpath` with a null string.
Then, it uses a `for` loop to look at each element of the current `PATH` variable,
one at a time. Next, it uses command substitution with a pipe to echo the
`PATH` and convert the colons to spaces. It then checks to see whether the
element is a directory. If it is, the script looks at the elements of `newpath`, and
if the current element of `PATH` is already in `newpath`, the script indicates that
the element is bad. After looping through the `newpath`, if the element isn't
bad, the script adds the element to the `newpath`. When the script finishes
looking at `PATH`, it sets `PATH` to `newpath` and removes the variables.

This program is not optimal. See whether you can find ways to make it better.
Here's a hint: Look at the `break` and `continue` commands.

uuto using Korn shell

The `uuto` command is an old UNIX command that is meant to be an easy
front end to UUCP. *UUCP* is discussed in Part VI. The idea is to take `uuto` and
build an easy command. The `uuto` command's input is a list of files, followed
by a destination. That destination is in the form *machine!user*. The
following example illustrates a simple script:

```
#!/usr/bin/ksh
# or whatever is required on your system
function usage
{
echo uuto -D machine!user files ...
}
if (( ${#@} < 2 ))
then
    echo Must have more arguments.
```

```
        usage
        exit
fi
dest=none
mflag=""
while
        getopts mD: KEY
do
        case "$KEY" in
        D) dest=$OPTARG;;
        m) mflag="-m";;
        *) echo Illegal argument; usage;;
        esac
done
destmachine=`echo $dest | cut -d! -f1`
destuser=`echo $dest | cut -d! -f2`
if
        [ "$destmachine" == "" ]
then
        echo A remote host must be specified.
        usage
        exit
fi
if
        [ "$destuser" == "" ]
then
        echo A remote user must be specified.
        usage
        exit
fi
host=`hostname`
for file
do
        uucp ${mflag} -n${destuser} $file
${destmachine}!~/receive/${destuser}/${host}
done
```

This command is a bit more complicated than the first example. If you are familiar with uuto, note that the syntax has changed slightly; I now expect the destination to appear as a flag on the command line, and you can send mail to yourself when transfer is complete (-m).

First, I wrote a function named usage. This echoes a usage line. When I need to terminate the program quickly, I call this function to inform the user how to use it. For the main program, I first confirm that arguments exist, and then I use getopts to parse the flags. I require a -D flag for the user; the -m flag is optional. If I get anything else, I echo the usage line and exit.

Next, I break the destination into a user and machine name. I use com
line substitution and parsing tools to separate on the exclamation
then confirm that I have two valid pieces. When that's done, all
the files on the command line. I step through them using a f
uucp with the appropriate command-line arguments.

Summary

Programming the Korn shell is a useful skill for any UNIX user. Later in the book, I provide examples of Korn shell programs that solve problems. Wes Morgan talks about writing Korn shell scripts for administration in Chapter 52.

This chapter covered the following topics:

- Ways to assign shell variables in the POSIX shell
- POSIX shell arrays
- How to name variables
- How to handle unassigned variables
- POSIX shell extensions to wildcard matching
- Defining variable types
- Accessing command-line arguments
- Functions
- Arithmetic
- Conditions
- Control flow
- File I/O
- Signal traps

In the next chapter, you will be introduced to file system theory.

Part III

File System Navigation

Chapter 6

Introducing the File System

Computers have two basic purposes: data manipulation and data storage. Most programs primarily manipulate data, but in the end, the data usually ends up stored somewhere. On UNIX systems, that storage location is the file system. Most books on UNIX discuss the file system from the user's perspective, teaching how to navigate and locate information. Although this book presents that information to you, I feel you should understand what happens underneath those commands so that you know why you use certain commands in various situations.

Understanding File System Structure

Most UNIX systems have more than one file system. Each file system is a separate section of a physical device, usually a hard disk. Hard disks are partitioned into segments, and those segments are then formatted into file systems.

Story: File System Alternatives

I have seen a file system built on a floppy disk. The old UNIX PCs enabled you to do this. At that time, they had 10 megabytes of hard disk, and sometimes the extra storage was useful. I've also heard that some systems have had the root file system on RAM. This would make the machine blindingly fast.

Some UNIX systems support a journaled file system. AIX, IBM's UNIX for its PCs and larger machines, supports this concept. Although journaling requires an extra layer of software, it enables you to create file systems that span disks. A good administrator can optimize system performance by mapping file systems across multiple disks, a technique called *striping*. Good use of journaling enables faster disk access. Because file systems are spread across multiple disks, however, a failure of one disk can prove catastrophic because it can affect more than one file system. This is why you should always make thorough backups.

The hard disk is a physical device, just like a monitor and a keyboard. It comprises numerous platters of nonvolatile memory, and disk read/write heads move over those platters to archive and retrieve data. The platters also rotate.

File systems built on disks have three components: an i-node table, a superblock, and data storage blocks. The *superblock* oversees the file system and is normally not directly accessible to the user except through some programming calls. The data stored on the hard disk for the superblock is usually a mirror of the superblock structure in kernel memory. The important tracked information is a list of free i-nodes, free data blocks, and superblock statistical flags. Some important flags are read-only and modified. If the file system is set as a read-only file system, you are not allowed to modify it, even as root. The modified flag is set when the file system changes, which happens, for example, when a file is created or deleted from the disk. At that time, you must write out the superblock to the disk, or else the new file may be lost and/or corrupted.

A separate superblock resides in kernel memory for every locally mounted file system. Each mounted file system resides in a devices table in the kernel and has a unique identifier associated with it.

Using I-Nodes

Each disk entry in a file system is associated with an i-node. *I-nodes* manage disk entries and contain all the administrative information for files. This data is used in the kernel's *i-list,* a listing of all the i-nodes associated with open files on the system. The i-node includes several key data elements.

Four elements of the i-node are pointers to other i-nodes. Two maintain a hash chain for finding i-nodes, and two maintain a free list of i-nodes for file creation. When an i-node entry in the kernel table is no longer needed, the i-node is added to the free list, and when a new entry is needed, the first i-node on the free list is used. The hash table is only kernel-resident because the data has no meaning on the disk itself.

The next two data entries are integer values — the device number and the i-node number — that uniquely describe the i-node. The *device number* refers to the physical device on which the i-node is stored. (For journaled file systems, this refers to the logical device.) The *i-node number* is the unique i-node within the device. This is an index into the i-node table physically stored on the device, but when the kernel accesses an i-node, it is stored in a hash table. These data points are stored only in the kernel entry, as they are deduced from the i-node table on disk.

Following the integer value entries, the i-node stores critical information about a file. The first data point is a reference to the type of file.

Secret

Every disk entry in UNIX is a file, and every peripheral device has a file. UNIX needs to differentiate between remote peripherals and regular disk entries. UNIX supports two types of peripherals, a raw device and a character special device. A *raw device* enables block transfers of I/O, and a *character special device* enables single character transfers. Your keyboard, screen, and terminal are all character special devices, whereas a hard disk is usually a raw device.

Raw devices usually have two filenames; one is used for sequential transfer of data, and the other is used for random access.

Each peripheral device is associated with a device driver, and therefore each device i-node has two numbers: an index into a device driver table and a unique identifier for the driver's specific device. These are the major and minor numbers, respectively. If you can learn how to write device drivers, you never will need to worry about unemployment!

The most common file types are standard files and directories. A *standard file* is a set of data stored on a disk. It can be a document, a program, or just data, and you can use standard tools to access it. A *directory* is a special file that references the data. It has names associated with i-nodes. When you access a filename, you receive an i-node and use the i-node table to identify the file.

Other types of files are named pipes, symbolic links, and peripheral devices. Each has special means of access.

Each file contains ownership and access permissions, which are stored in three separate entries: a user ID associated with ownership, a group ID associated with group ownership, and a permissions entry. Standard permissions assign read, write, and execution access based on your user ID, group ID, and world status. I discuss permissions more fully in Chapter 7.

The i-node tracks the size of the file. This size is stored in bytes and blocks. (Some systems may have varying block sizes for different file systems. In these cases, a size for the block is also stored.) When the file changes size, the data in the i-node also changes. This information is kept in the i-node so that when a user requests the size of the file, the system does not need to open the file and count the size.

Access times are also tracked. Each i-node has three times associated with it: the time of the last access, the time of the last modification, and the time of creation. Of these three, the time of last modification is most often used, but each time has its uses. Chapter 7, which discusses the find command, illustrates some of those uses.

The i-node also keeps a count of directory entries. You can consider each entry a *link*. Links are vital to UNIX systems; they enable multiple directory entries to share the same set of data. POSIX requires that a minimum of eight directory entries be allowed per file. By tracking the number of links, the system knows whether to respond to a delete request by deleting only a directory entry or by deleting the file from the disk. When the link count drops to zero, the file is marked for deletion.

Secret

When writing a program, if you want to create a temporary file but don't want to worry about cleanup, you can open the file in your program and immediately unlink the filename. This reduces the link count to zero, but the file still exists on the disk until you close the file descriptor.

Note

When writing programs, you can move a file more easily by creating a link between the old file and the new file and then deleting the old file. Because the i-node tracks the count of links, the deletion removes only the older directory entry.

The last interesting data stored in the i-node consist of a list of blocks containing data. Without this, you wouldn't have a file. Implementations differ among file system types, but the basic structure is a list of blocks followed by indirection blocks. An *indirection block* is simply a list of blocks: when a file uses all the standard blocks in a list, it needs to add block numbers to an indirection block to access a file. Block numbers need not be contiguous or even in numerical order. Each indirection block can maintain either 128 or 256 entries, depending on the size of a block. File systems need to support three levels of indirection, which means that the largest file can be 16 million blocks in size for a 16-gigabyte file.

By supporting multiple levels of indirection, the i-node can track large files without costing space for small files. Typically, an i-node keeps only ten direct block addresses before it needs indirection. Although systems vary widely, the average file size is usually in the neighborhood of four blocks. This means that the block addresses for most files are stored in the i-node without relying on indirection.

Indirection is one of the techniques that adds flexibility to UNIX.

Working with Links

POSIX requires the support of two kinds of links: a hard link and a symbolic link. I've discussed hard links previously. A directory entry that points to the same i-node as another directory entry is considered a *hard link*. Hard links are very efficient, but they have their limits. Hard links can be made only on the same file system; this restricts their use. When a hard link is created, the file to which it points must already exist. Directories can't be hard-linked.

Symbolic links are different. A *symbolic link* is a special file that includes the path to a different file. That path can point to anything: a directory, a file residing on another file system, or even a nonexistent file. The file containing the path is flagged as a symbolic link in the i-node, so when you access it, you get the data for the file named in the link instead.

UNIX programmers at the University of California, Berkeley, added symbolic links for BSD UNIX. With the addition of networking to UNIX, symbolic links have become even more powerful. You can point a symbolic link to a directory on a remotely mounted file system, and you can establish a link from there to another entry. Multiple links in a path can lead to a file. You can use a symbolic link to access a file without knowing the exact location of that file.

Unfortunately, a symbolic link is slower than a hard link. To resolve the path, you must open the file and resolve the name.

Some systems limit the number of symbolic links in a path. POSIX requires that the maximum allowed be at least 20, but the actual maximum depends on implementation. Of course, you can combine symbolic links and hard links in a path.

Summary

This chapter covered the basics needed to understand how file systems work. It introduced the following topics:

- ▶ The file system structure
- ▶ I-nodes
- ▶ File permissions
- ▶ Hard links
- ▶ Symbolic links

The next chapter presents the basics of using the file system.

Chapter 7

Finding and Identifying Files

In This Chapter

▶ Using the ls, find, xargs, which, and whereis commands to find files

▶ Using the ls, file, wc, head, tail, cat, more, and od commands to identify files

On my UNIX system at home, I have over 110,000 directory entries pointing to over 100,000 files. (I have Linux installed with the complete source.) With this much information spread across 2 gigabytes of storage, I am often looking for a specific file, or set of files, without knowing exactly where it is. Furthermore, I sometimes find an older file and don't know what it is.

The specific numbers are 110,533 directories and 110,339 files. I found these numbers by using the tools I describe in this chapter, and I tell you how at the end of Chapter 9. See whether you can figure out how I did this before you reach the end.

Fortunately for me, UNIX provides tools that enable me to search for files, and after I've found a file, UNIX enables me to examine the file to determine its size, its type, and other pertinent information. This chapter examines the tools most commonly used for those tasks.

Although these tools are usually generic enough for the tasks, UNIX is a hacker's operation system, and occasionally an experienced programmer writes a program to perform these tasks.

Finding Files

Because UNIX provides several tools for searching a file system, the user must use the right one. Knowing the right tool, and the reasons why it is the right tool, is a sign of a UNIX expert.

When thinking about finding a file, you should remember how a UNIX file system is structured. At the bottom is a root directory identified solely as /. Files are always identified by name and are included at the end of a path. Directories are intermediate locations in a path and are separated by slashes.

For example, a file with the full name /usr/james/mailbox is just the file mailbox, located in a directory named james, which is in a directory named usr, which is in the root directory. To continue the tree analogy, think of files as leaves and directories as branches.

Note

On some systems, I have seen a symbolic link /root that points to /. Although I don't use it myself, the mnemonic link is a useful trigger for some users.

You can mount other file systems on the tree. Their roots are standard directories. Some standard mount points are /usr, /home, and /var/spool. You should mount file systems when the disk needs under a specific directory are larger than the current disk's capacity or when you need to segregate data.

Secret

If you have two or more hard disks, keep your two busiest file systems on separate disks. These are usually the root file system and the /usr or /home file system. By keeping these on separate disks, you speed I/O. The disk heads do not need to search from one partition to another continually.

The tree hierarchy becomes somewhat confusing with the addition of symbolic links. At this stage, think of the tree as magic. When you reach a symbolic link, you are magically transported to a different part of the tree. Keep this structure in mind when considering the commands in this chapter.

Using the ls command

One of the most commonly executed commands is ls, which gives you a listing of all the files in a directory. Older ls commands provided this information in a single column; currently, ls lists names in multiple columns, the number of columns depending on the length of the longest name.

The syntax is ls, followed first by command options and then by a list of files. You can use wildcard expansion. If no files are provided, ls operates on the current working directory.

Note

ls is one of the first UNIX commands and illustrates a guiding principle for UNIX commands: Keep the command name short and easy to remember. This practice has been criticized in the past because sometimes the short names do not make sense. In this case, think of ls as an abbreviation for list.

Listing 7-1 shows a listing of the files in the bin directory under my home directory.

Listing 7-1: Output of ls

```
CShells
Shells
adbook
banner
checkem
crons
desk
```

```
gruber
gzip
mailedit
mst3k
munge
mydate
olvwm
op
parsit
patch
patrunc
procmon
satno
screensaver.sh
sendmail.cf
shar
shipit
showbowls
showquakes
sortem
src
testprocess
wchance
wishlists
xloadimage
xv
xv.old
yes
```

As you can see, this directory contains 35 visible directory entries. It also contains three entries that are hidden from normal view: ., .., and .hidden. The files are sorted in alphabetical order, one entry per line. This is the default behavior.

Secret

Any filename beginning with a dot is considered hidden from normal view. The ls command does not show these files unless you use a special flag. Experienced users often create dot files and directories for more sensitive materials. These may include personal files or administrative files.

The first two hidden files are included in every directory. The . file is a directory entry that points back to the current directory. The .. file points to the current directory's parent. Because every directory contains an entry for these files, commands that may access the file tree do not need to contain a special option for accessing these directories. Instead, any tool accessing the tree just needs to find the entry in the directory and parse it accordingly.

Note

Normally, the . and .. directories had importance only at the start of a path, but . and .. produce some interesting effects when combined with symbolic links. If I have a save directory in my current directory, the path save/.. points back to my current directory. But, if save is a pointer to /users/save, save/.. points to /users. Later, this chapter shows an interesting trick for resolving chains of symbolic links.

Story: Unscrupulous Root Access

One common trick that unscrupulous users employ to obtain root access is to copy a shell program to a directory when they've been lent root permission by a system administrator and change it to a `set-UID` program owned by root. This is usually a dot file such as `...` or `.sh`. Administrators have become aware of this trick and now search out these files for deletion. A friend of mine recently found a further way to obtain root access. She had access to a file system debugger and changed the i-node associated with the `..` entry to a directory that included her `.sh`. This directory had no locations pointing to it, so standard UNIX search tools would never find it. As a result, when my friend needed a root shell, she simply changed directories to `~/bin/..` and typed `./.sh` to become root. Her administrators never figured it out.

You may need to know more about a file than just its name. The `ls` command includes 21 command-line flags that change its behavior. Some are associated with finding files, and some determine information about files. This section discusses flags used to find files, and a following section discusses flags used to identify files. The flags discussed are all defined in the XPG4 specification for POSIX compliance. Your site may have a slightly different set of flags. To determine what is available to you, use the `man` command.

The number of flags included also illustrates a guiding principle in developing UNIX commands: Instead of creating many little commands to perform each task, one command should have multiple options, resulting in tremendous power for a single program. The `ls` command, with 21 options, has 2,097,152 possible flag combinations. Although some combinations are incompatible, this one program is still equivalent to over two million commands in an environment where flags don't exist!

Using multiple-column format

As you can see from the previous section, a single column has some limitations. If a directory's entries outnumber the lines on your screen, the listing scrolls off the top of the page. The `-C` flag creates multiple-column output, with the sorting order going down columns. Listing 7-1 shows a single-column listing; Listing 7-2 shows the same directory in multiple-column format.

Listing 7-2: Output of ls —C /home/james/bin

```
CShells    gruber     op              sendmail.cf    testprocess
Shells     gzip       parsit          shar           wchance
adbook     mailedit   patch           shipit         wishlists
banner     mst3k      patrunc         showbowls      xloadimage
checkem    munge      procmon         showquakes     xv
crons      mydate     satno           sortem         xv.old
desk       olvwm      screensaver.sh  src            yes
```

Examining directories recursively

The -R flag not only enables you to examine the contents of the specified directory, but also gives you a listing of each directory under the tree. The output can be quite large because it looks at every file under the specified directory. My machine has over 110,000 directory entries. Fortunately, Listing 7-3 illustrates a smaller section.

Listing 7-3: Output of ls -RC /home/james/bin

```
CShells    gruber      op                 sendmail.cf   testprocess
Shells     gzip        parsit             shar          wchance
adbook     mailedit    patch              shipit        wishlists
banner     mst3k       patrunc            showbowls     xloadimage
checkem    munge       procmon            showquakes    xv
crons      mydate      satno              sortem        xv.old
desk       olvwm       screensaver.sh     src           yes
/home/james/bin/CShells:
2pr            eastit      mailomit     scc        uupicker
allgodit       footit      mailzap      shv        zooboy
backup2        godit       mroot2       test2
combinelists   inttest     open         tester
data1          linkup      restorewind  trivit
dumpit         linkx11r5   rotatem.sh   urgent
/home/james/bin/Shells:
addrolo    dmail      killron     quirk        selectsc    showrecvs
allofem    dmail2     metamail    runx         sendit      showscores
alter      dmail3     mknewdb     sammi        shcdlink    showstand
backup     flibber1   patrunc     sample       showbigyear testhoops
backup1    flibber2   patrunc2    savethem     showmaxyear tpr
collect    frame      pgsize      scc          showpoll    unlock
davesscc   gerp       pollhoops   selectpoll   showrec     xoit
/home/james/bin/src:
active     foo.c      parsit.c    shar         vtwm-5.1.tar
calcit     gruber.c   procI.c     sortem.c     wchance.c
calcit.c   op.c       satno.c     thoughts
/home/james/bin/src/shar:
Makefile   shar.1     shar.shar   unshar.1     uushar.c
README     shar.c     unshar      unshar.c     who@where.c
/home/james/bin/wishlists:
addbookfile  dodd       fileproc2    narback     restorewind
bigcal       dofile     filesback    outmailer   runthelot
calc2+       doit       filestruct   quark       scanthem
clockwally   dols       gamer        quark2      tarministore
dirproc      dropkick   geese        quark3      zoot
dirproc2     f2         messfor      rabbits
dod          fileproc   mosquito     rback
```

Many files are still specified, so I included the -C option. The output first lists the files in the current directory and then essentially performs an ls -R on each directory in the sort order.

The column widths differ among directories because the lengths of the filenames differ.

Seeing hidden files

The -a flag shows all files in a directory, including those meant to be hidden. Listing 7-4 shows the output of the hidden files.

Listing 7-4: Output of /bin/ls -aC /home/james/bin

```
.           crons      olvwm            sendmail.cf    wchance
..          desk       op               shar           wishlists
.hidden     gruber     parsit           shipit         xloadimage
CShells     gzip       patch            showbowls      xv
Shells      mailedit   patrunc          showquakes     xv.old
adbook      mst3k      procmon          sortem         yes
banner      munge      satno            src
checkem     mydate     screensaver.sh   testprocess
```

The three hidden files mentioned earlier in the chapter are displayed.

Forcing directory display

The -f flag forces the arguments to be interpreted as directories and presents all the files in the order that they appear in the directory. This disables several flags for list order and automatically enables the flag to view hidden files. Listing 7-5 shows the output.

Listing 7-5: Output of /bin/ls -fC /home/james/bin

```
.           Shells        screensaver.sh   mydate         munge
..          gzip          desk             shipit         mst3k
src         xv            procmon          wishlists      showbowls
op          gruber        sortem           parsit         banner
patch       olvwm         shar             testprocess    mailedit
satno       adbook        crons            showquakes     .hidden
yes         wchance       patrunc          checkem
CShells     sendmail.cf   xloadimage       xv.old
```

This is actually a very fast form of output because the program just reads the directory and pumps out the filenames in the order found, saving the time needed to sort the data.

Generating comma-separated output

The -m flag produces a listing of comma-separated files. This may be useful for inclusion in documents. Listing 7-6 shows this output.

Listing 7-6: Output of /bin/ls -m /home/james/bin

```
CShells, Shells, adbook, banner, checkem, crons, desk,
mst3k, munge, mydate, olvwm, op, parsit, patch, patrunc , sortem, src,
testprocess, wchance, wishlists, xloadimage, xv, xv.old
```

The `ls` command still breaks each line at 80 characters. This is determined from either your terminal settings or the `COLUMNS` environment variable.

Changing unprintable characters

On occasion, you may accidentally create filenames with unprintable characters. This can cause some confusion on directory listings, so the `-q` option prints those characters as question marks.

Reversing the order

When you specify the `-r` flag, your listing appears in reverse order from the specified sort options. Listing 7-7 illustrates a reverse-order search. This is often used in conjunction with the `-t` flag to list the newest files last.

Listing 7-7: Output of /bin/ls -Cr /home/james/bin

```
yes            src            screensaver.sh  olvwm       desk
xv.old         sortem         satno           mydate      crons
xv             showquakes     procmon         munge       checkem
xloadimage     showbowls      patrunc         mst3k       banner
wishlists      shipit         patch           mailedit    adbook
wchance        shar           parsit          gzip        Shells
testprocess    sendmail.cf    op              gruber      CShells
```

Sorting in time order

The `-t` flag sorts the files in time order, with the most recently modified first. With this flag, you can determine which files are oldest. Listing 7-8 illustrates the time sort.

Listing 7-8: Output of /bin/ls -tC /home/james/bin

```
mailedit    xloadimage    mydate       screensaver.sh    satno
showbowls   CShells       mst3k        gzip              wchance
banner      wishlists     patrunc      procmon           testprocess
munge       Shells        showquakes   desk              gruber
xv          src           shar         olvwm             adbook
checkem     yes           shipit       sendmail.cf       parsit
xv.old      crons         sortem       op                patch
```

The file `mailedit` is the most recently modified file, and `patch` has remained unchanged the longest. The order of the directories is based on the time their contents changed.

Sorting by status change

The `-c` flag modifies the `-t` flag by sorting according to the most recent status change. When you change ownership or permissions, the file's status change data is updated. Listing 7-9 shows the effects of `-c`.

Listing 7-9: Output of /bin/ls -ctC /home/james/bin

```
desk            crons          checkem       op       olvwm
shipit          patrunc        xv.old        patch    wchance
sendmail.cf     xloadimage     munge         satno    CShells
screensaver.sh  mydate         mst3k         yes      wishlists
procmon         parsit         showbowls     gzip     Shells
sortem          testprocess    banner        xv       src
shar            showquakes     mailedit      gruber   adbook
```

Note

The -c option is ignored unless -t is also specified. The order of Listing 7-9 has changed significantly from that of Listing 7-8 because the status change times are different from the modification times.

Sorting by access time

Besides modification and status change times, UNIX keeps a last access time value for each file. By specifying -u with -t, you sort on access time. Listing 7-10 shows what happens when you do.

Listing 7-10: Output of /bin/ls -utC /home/james/bin

```
CShells     showbowls   xloadimage   adbook          shar
Shells      banner      olvwm        wchance         crons
src         munge       op           sendmail.cf     mydate
wishlists   xv.old      patch        screensaver.sh  parsit
xv          checkem     satno        desk            testprocess
mailedit    gzip        yes          procmon         showquakes
patrunc     shipit      gruber       sortem          mst3k
```

The most recently accessed file is CShells (previously shown to be a directory), and the least recently accessed is mst3k. Normally, directories are seen earlier in these listings; for example, when a file in a directory is accessed, that directory is usually also accessed.

Performing another multiple-column search

Besides using -C for producing columns, ls uses the -x flag to sort across each line. Listing 7-11 shows the results of that search.

Listing 7-11: Output of /bin/ls -x /home/james/bin

```
CShells         Shells        adbook      banner        checkem
crons           desk          gruber      gzip          mailedit
mst3k           munge         mydate      olvwm         op
parsit          patch         patrunc     procmon       satno
screensaver.sh  sendmail.cf   shar        shipit        showbowls
showquakes      sortem        src         testprocess   wchance
wishlists       xloadimage    xv          xv.old        yes
```

If both the -C and -x flags are specified, the last flag listed takes precedence, and the former is ignored. Because you can create an alias for ls that includes one of the flags, you can override the flag you selected in your alias.

Generating single-column output

By specifying the -1 flag, you force single-column output. This is the default on my system, but on others, multiple-column output is the default. See Listing 7-1 for a sample of single-column output.

Using the find command

A more powerful command for finding files is find. The syntax for find is somewhat arcane, however. You start with find, followed by a listing of files and a listing of expressions. Each expression is evaluated down the list in list order until one evaluates as false and evaluation halts. You normally list directories as the second argument, although files are also checked. Files are examined recursively.

When an expression requires a numeric value, you can express it in three possible fashions. If preceded by a plus sign (+), the expression is true, and the value for the file must be greater than the specified number. If preceded by a minus sign (–), it must be less than the number. If no sign is present, it must match the number.

Use find to find files, usually with patterns specified. find has other applications, too, including pruning file trees according to time.

Note

The find command is resource intensive. If you can trim your initial conditions at all, you'll help other users and speed the command's execution.

Creating output

Interestingly, find produces no output unless you explicitly ask for output. To produce output, include the -print expression. This always evaluates as true, so execution proceeds down the list of expressions.

Output is the file currently being examined, with one name per line. You may note a difference between find . -print and ls -R1. Listing 7-12 shows their output side by side.

Listing 7-12: Output of find . -print and ls -Rf1

```
./src                              . .
./src/shar                         src
./src/shar/README                  op
./src/shar/shar.c                  patch
./src/shar/unshar.1                satno
./src/shar/unshar.c                yes
./src/shar/uushar.c                CShells
./src/shar/who@where.c             Shells
./src/shar/unshar                  gzip
./src/shar/shar.shar               xv
./src/shar/shar.1                  gruber
./src/shar/Makefile                olvwm
```

```
./src/satno.c                    adbook
./src/active                     wchance
./src/wchance.c                  sendmail.cf
./src/sortem.c                   screensaver.sh
./src/vtwm-5.1.tar               desk
./src/.newsrc                    procmon
./src/calcit.c                   sortem
./src/thoughts                   shar
./src/op.c                       crons
./src/foo.c                      patrunc
./src/calcit                     xloadimage
./src/procI.c                    mydate
./src/parsit.c                   shipit
./src/gruber.c                   wishlists
./op                             parsit
./patch                          testprocess
./satno                          showquakes
./yes                            checkem
./CShells                        xv.old
./CShells/combinelists           munge
./CShells/dumpit                 mst3k
./CShells/eastit                 showbowls
./CShells/footit                 banner
./CShells/godit                  mailedit
./CShells/mailomit               .hidden
./CShells/mailzap
./CShells/open                   src:
./CShells/rotatem.sh             .
./CShells/shv                    ..
./CShells/trivit                 shar
./CShells/urgent                 satno.c
./CShells/inttest                active
./CShells/uupicker               wchance.c
./CShells/zooboy                 sortem.c
./CShells/scc                    vtwm-5.1.tar
./CShells/2pr                    .newsrc
./CShells/allgodit               calcit.c
./CShells/data1                  thoughts
./CShells/test2                  op.c
./CShells/linkup                 foo.c
./CShells/linkx11r5              calcit
./CShells/mroot2                 procI.c
./CShells/restorewind            parsit.c
./CShells/tester                 gruber.c
./CShells/backup2
./Shells                         src/shar:
./Shells/backup                  .
./Shells/backup1                 ..
./Shells/dmail                   README
./Shells/dmail3                  shar.c
./Shells/collect                 unshar.1
./Shells/mknewdb                 unshar.c
./Shells/patrunc2                uushar.c
```

```
./Shells/flibber1              who@where.c
./Shells/flibber2              unshar
./Shells/frame                 shar.shar
./Shells/gerp                  shar.1
./Shells/killron               Makefile
./Shells/pollhoops
./Shells/quirk                 CShells:
./Shells/pgsize                .
./Shells/savethem              ..
./Shells/scc                   combinelists
./Shells/runx                  dumpit
./Shells/sammi                 eastit
./Shells/selectsc              footit
./Shells/sendit                godit
./Shells/shcdlink              mailomit
./Shells/tpr                   mailzap
./Shells/showbigyear           open
./Shells/showpoll              rotatem.sh
./Shells/showrec               shv
./Shells/showrecvs             trivit
./Shells/showscores            urgent
./Shells/showstand             inttest
./Shells/testhoops             uupicker
./Shells/xoit                  zooboy
./Shells/addrolo               scc
./Shells/allofem               2pr
./Shells/unlock                allgodit
./Shells/metamail              data1
./Shells/sample                test2
./Shells/dmail2                linkup
./Shells/patrunc               linkx11r5
./Shells/selectpoll            mroot2
./Shells/showmaxyear           restorewind
./Shells/davesscc              tester
./Shells/alter                 backup2
./gzip
./xv                           Shells:
./gruber                       .
./olvwm                        ..
./adbook                       backup
./wchance                      backup1
./sendmail.cf                  dmail
./screensaver.sh               dmail3
./desk                         collect
./procmon                      mknewdb
./sortem                       patrunc2
./shar                         flibber1
./crons                        flibber2
./patrunc                      frame
./xloadimage                   gerp
./mydate                       killron
./shipit                       pollhoops
./wishlists                    quirk
```

```
./wishlists/dirproc          pgsize
./wishlists/dirproc2         savethem
./wishlists/doit             scc
./wishlists/f2               runx
./wishlists/fileproc         sammi
./wishlists/fileproc2        selectsc
./wishlists/dod              sendit
./wishlists/dodd             shcdlink
./wishlists/dofile           tpr
./wishlists/zoot             showbigyear
./wishlists/dols             showpoll
./wishlists/filesback        showrec
./wishlists/filestruct       showrecvs
./wishlists/gamer            showscores
./wishlists/geese            showstand
./wishlists/messfor          testhoops
./wishlists/mosquito         xoit
./wishlists/narback          addrolo
./wishlists/outmailer        allofem
./wishlists/quark            unlock
./wishlists/quark2           metamail
./wishlists/rabbits          sample
./wishlists/rback            dmail2
./wishlists/restorewind      patrunc
./wishlists/runthelot        selectpoll
./wishlists/scanthem         showmaxyear
./wishlists/addbookfile      davesscc
./wishlists/calc2+           alter
./wishlists/dropkick
./wishlists/quark3           wishlists:
./wishlists/tarministore     .
./wishlists/bigcal           ..
./wishlists/clockwally       dirproc
./parsit                     dirproc2
./testprocess                doit
./showquakes                 f2
./checkem                    fileproc
./xv.old                     fileproc2
./munge                      dod
./mst3k                      dodd
./showbowls                  dofile
./banner                     zoot
./mailedit                   dols
./.hidden                    filesback
                             filestruct
                             gamer
                             geese
                             messfor
                             mosquito
                             narback
                             outmailer
                             quark
                             quark2
```

```
rabbits
rback
restorewind
runthelot
scanthem
addbookfile
calc2+
dropkick
quark3
tarministore
bigcal
clockwally

.hidden:
.
..
```

Note

The find command does not look at the .. directory and looks at . only when it is specified on the command line. Another reason the ls output is longer than find's is that ls labels each directory before traversing the directory. With find, the directory tree is present in the output.

Matching a filename

The -name expression matches filenames in accordance with the pattern provided as an argument to the expression.

Note

Wildcard matching in POSIX is defined simply. An ordinary character matches itself. A question mark matches any single character. An asterisk matches multiple characters. To match the question mark or asterisk, escape these with a backslash. For example, abc matches a?c, a*, and ?b*, but not a\?c. To match a backslash, use two backslashes.

Pattern matching includes a bracket expression. When a character or multiple characters are enclosed in brackets, the pattern matches any single character enclosed in the brackets. This can be negated (that is, set to match any character not enclosed in the brackets) if the first character is a circumflex (^). For example, *abc* matches a[bc]c or a[^c][^b], but not a[bc]. To match the brackets or the circumflex, escape them with backslashes.

Because the shell attempts to interpret these characters, if you plan to use them in a command such as find, you need to enclose the pattern in double quotation marks.

Some common name matchings are find . -name core to find all core dumps and find . -name "*.o" to find all object files (intermediate files in program compilation).

Listing 7-13 shows the output of a search for files whose name includes the word *core* from my home directory.

Listing 7-13: Output of find ~ -name '*core*' -print

```
/home/james/bin/Shells/showscores
/home/james/.data/oscores
/home/james/.data/scores
/home/james/.IA/showscores
/home/james/scoreboard
/home/james/bin2/showscores
/home/james/pine/pine3.91/pine/osdep/coredump
/home/james/pine/pine3.91/pine/osdep/coredump.fpe
/home/james/Ncaa.scores
/home/james/PME.scores
/home/james/oware/scoreboard.c
/home/james/oware/old/scoreboard.c
/home/james/.Foot/scores.c
/home/james/.Foot/scores.o
/home/james/tonetcom/WACscores
/home/james/tonetcom/BWscores
/home/james/tonetcom/MACscores
/home/james/tonetcom/Indepscores
```

Because I used a wildcard matching pattern, *core*, I found every file with *core* embedded in the name. Most of these are related to the word *score* because core is embedded therein.

Note

Only the last part of the path includes *core* because find checks only the filename and ignores any intervening directories.

Remaining on the file system

If you include the -xdev expression, the find command examines only those files that have the same device number as their parent directory. It always evaluates to true. Listing 7-14 shows a short find that illustrates this pruning technique.

Listing 7-14: Output of find . -xdev -print

```
$ mkdir dir1
$ cd dir1
$ touch myfile
$ mkdir root
$ mount external:/filesys root
$ find . -xdev -print
.
./myfile
./root
```

If -xdev were not present, the entire file tree from external:/filesys would be traversed.

Checking permissions

The -perm expression is used primarily to print files with certain permissions. You can use two techniques for defining the needed permissions for the expression. The first is to build a permissions bit pattern with the relative permissions definitions, outlined for the chmod command in Chapter 8. These include u+r, g+w for a user-readable, group-writable file. If prepended with a hyphen, this expression is true if all the bits in the pattern are set in the file's permission mask. If not prepended with a hyphen, the pattern and permissions must match exactly.

The second option is to give a precise octal pattern for permissions, such as 0555. Again, a hyphen means that the bits in the expression must all be in the file's permission; otherwise, it must be an exact match.

Going from /home/james/bin, here is a find for any world-writable files (find /home/james/bin -perm -0002 -print):

/home/james/bin/checkem

Only one file was found. This pattern is useful for the occasional security check.

Note

As a user, I find the octal patterns more useful than the bit patterns, but I am accustomed to thinking of permissions in that fashion. Other users find the pattern o+w easier to use. I suggest that you use both and determine which makes you feel more comfortable.

Searching for file types

The -type expression enables you to search for special file types. The flag is followed by one of five letters, each representing a type of file, as illustrated in Table 7-1.

Table 7-1   File Types for the find Command

Letter	File Type
b	Block special file
c	Character special file
d	Directory
f	Regular file
p	Named pipe

Listing 7-15 illustrates a search for directories that are writable by others. This search is more useful than the one for world-writable files.

Listing 7-15: Output of find /home/james -type d -perm -0002 -print

/home/james/testdir

This directory is vulnerable to an unscrupulous user. Because the world can write to this directory, anyone could come in and delete my files.

Listing files with links

You may want to find where your linked files are. By specifying the `-link` expression with a numeric argument, you can list all the files with links. Listing 7-16 shows how rarely I use links!

Listing 7-16: Output of find ~ -type f -links +1 -print

```
/home/james/bin/shipit
/home/james/Docs/IDG/bin/src/binhex
/home/james/Docs/IDG/bin/src/unxbin
/home/james/footpicks/clungit.c
/home/james/footpicks/dba.c
/home/james/footpicks/dbdump.c
/home/james/footpicks/dbedit.c
/home/james/footpicks/dbscan.c
/home/james/footpicks/deletit.c
/home/james/footpicks/emailmissing.c
/home/james/footpicks/foofoo.c
/home/james/footpicks/loadthem.c
/home/james/footpicks/loadthem.passwd.c
/home/james/footpicks/newweek.c
/home/james/footpicks/process.c
/home/james/footpicks/ripem.c
/home/james/footpicks/alter.c
/home/james/footpicks/verify.c
/home/james/footpicks/emailinstruct.c
/home/james/shipit
/home/james/hooppicks/dba.c
/home/james/hooppicks/newweek.c
/home/james/hooppicks/process.c
/home/james/hooppicks/alter.c
/home/james/hooppicks/dbedit.c
/home/james/hooppicks/dbscan.c
/home/james/hooppicks/deletit.c
/home/james/hooppicks/dbdump.c
/home/james/hooppicks/clungit.c
/home/james/hooppicks/foofoo.c
/home/james/hooppicks/ripem.c
/home/james/hooppicks/loadthem.c
/home/james/hooppicks/emailmissing.c
/home/james/hooppicks/loadthem.passwd.c
/home/james/hooppicks/verify.c
/home/james/hooppicks/emailinstruct.c
```

Each listed file is linked somewhere else on my file system.

Searching by user and group

The find command has four possible expressions to search for files according to ownership and group ownership. Two special expressions apply when the user or group numeric IDs for a file do not appear in the /etc/passwd or /etc/group files. The -nouser applies to the former case, and -nogroup applies to the latter.

These negative conditions are not as rare as you might think. As administrators delete users and groups, files associated with the deleted users may still be on the file system. The find / -nouser -print command lists all such files. Listing 7-17 shows the first 20 files found with this command on my system.

Listing 7-17: Output of find / -nouser -print

```
/home/james/Unix-Stuff/organization
/home/james/Unix-Stuff/sys
/home/elm/Overview
/home/elm/README
/home/elm/config.h.SH
/home/elm/src
/home/elm/src/Makefile.SH
/home/elm/src/a_edit.c
/home/elm/src/a_quit.c
/home/elm/src/a_screen.c
/home/elm/src/a_sort.c
/home/elm/src/addr_util.c
/home/elm/src/alias.c
/home/elm/src/aliaslib.c
/home/elm/src/args.c
/home/elm/src/bouncebk.c
/home/elm/src/builtin.c
/home/elm/src/calendar.c
/home/elm/src/curses.c
/home/elm/src/date.c
```

The other two expression primaries are -user and -group. Each takes a string, which is checked against the /etc/passwd or /etc/group file and converted to an integer. This integer is checked against every file; if a match is made, the condition returns true.

If no match is made for the string and the string is also an integer value, that integer is checked. Thus, when a user ID is deleted, if you know the ID, you can check for the files that still belong to that ID.

Listing 7-18 shows the output of a find command that looks for files on the root partition that belong to me. I found 37 files.

Listing 7-18: Output of find / -user james -xdev -print

```
/lost+found/#215572
/lost+found/#215573
/dev/console
```

```
/dev/systty
/dev/tty1
/dev/tty5
/dev/ttyp0
/dev/ttyp1
/dev/ttyp2
/dev/ttyp3
/dev/ttyp4
/dev/ttyp5
/var/spool/atjobs/c00cc79c8.00
/var/spool/lpd/dfA000Aa11755
/var/spool/lpd/dfA001Aa11761
/var/spool/lpd/dfA002Aa11767
/var/spool/lpd/dfA003Aa11773
/var/spool/lpd/dfA004Aa11779
/var/spool/mail/james
/var/spool/mail/fpicks
/var/tmp/catpg01793aaa
/var/tmp/elv_73f.1
/var/tmp/script
/var/tmp/elv_1a70.1
/usr/games/Foot
/usr/games/Foot/teams
/usr/games/Foot/solo
/usr/games/Foot/solo/statdat
/usr/games/Foot/solo/plays0
/usr/games/Foot/solo/Scores
/usr/games/Foot/solo/scores
/usr/games/Foot/solo/fscores
/usr/games/Foot/solo/week1
/usr/games/Foot/solo/datadump
/usr/games/Foot/scores
/usr/games/Foot/who.has.played
/usr/games/Foot/dumpdata
```

Checking based on file size

You also have the option to search for files according to file size. The `-size` expression followed by a number looks for files that match the given size. Because block sizes vary in different file systems on different architectures, the size is expressed in 512-byte increments, rounded up. For example, a file that is 16,745 bytes would match `-size 33`, `-size -34`, or `-size +32` because 512 · 33 = 16,896 and 16,745 is less than 512 bytes smaller than the 512 ? 33 spec.

Note

The original UNIX file systems came with 512-byte blocks.

If you want a more precise size, follow the number with the letter c, in which case the size is in bytes. (c was chosen to represent characters, but with the advent of two- and three-byte characters to accommodate non-Roman character sets, that meaning is obsolete.)

A good example is a search of a file system to find files larger than a certain threshold, such as 10 megabytes. The `find / -size +20480 -print` command illustrated in Listing 7-19 does this.

Listing 7-19: Output of find . -size -20480 -print

```
/home/james/Mail/950807/oldmail.Z
/proc/kcore
```

The first file is a compressed tar archive of some old mail, obvious to me from the title. The second is an image of the kernel in the `/proc` directory. More information on process images is available in Part V. Suffice it to say, the kernel process can be quite large.

Checking based on file times

Three expressions check against each of the three timestamps stored in a file's i-node: `atime` checks against the last access time, `-ctime` checks against the file status change time, and `-mtime` checks against the file modification time. Each expression takes a single integer that represents the number of days since the last change. The integer represents a 24-hour clock time, so `-atime 1` means any file accessed within the last 24 hours.

Checking based on different times is very useful. Some standard `find` commands look for core files and the like that are more than a week old and then delete them. Table 7-2 lists some of those standard commands.

Table 7-2   Common find Commands

Command	Purpose
`find / -name core -mtime +7`	Finds core files older than one week
`find ~ -atime +31`	Finds files not accessed for more than a month, which is useful for identifying material for archives
`find dir -ctime -1`	Finds files in a named directory that have had a status change in the last day

Interestingly, using the `find` command changes the access time for directories because they need to be opened for recursive perusal.

Listing 7-20 illustrates an interesting variant to the `find` command: `find ~ -atime +31`. It has given me a list of files that have not been accessed in the last month. There are more than I expected!

Listing 7-20: Files in My bin That Have Not Been Accessed in a Month

```
/home/james/bin/op
/home/james/bin/patch
```

```
/home/james/bin/satno
/home/james/bin/yes
/home/james/bin/gzip
/home/james/bin/gruber
/home/james/bin/olvwm
/home/james/bin/adbook
/home/james/bin/wchance
/home/james/bin/sendmail.cf
/home/james/bin/screensaver.sh
/home/james/bin/desk
/home/james/bin/procmon
/home/james/bin/sortem
/home/james/bin/shar
/home/james/bin/crons
/home/james/bin/xloadimage
/home/james/bin/mydate
/home/james/bin/shipit
/home/james/bin/parsit
/home/james/bin/testprocess
/home/james/bin/showquakes
/home/james/bin/checkem
/home/james/bin/mst3k
```

Executing commands from find

Of course, sometimes you may want to execute a command for each file found. The xargs command, discussed later in this chapter, is usually the best method, but find still provides a means to execute a command.

The -exec expression precedes a series of words that execute as a command. Everything up to a semicolon (;) is taken to be a part of the command.

Note

Because the semicolon is important to shells, you customarily escape it with a backslash.

To use the name of the file in the command, represent it with two curly braces ({}). The command is invoked in the directory where the find command executed. If you need to use paths in the command, I strongly urge you to use full paths to avoid confusion.

Table 7-3 uses two examples from Table 7-2 and builds on them to include actions.

Table 7-3   Examples of Finds with -exec

Command	Purpose
find / -name core -mtime +7 -exec rm {} \;	Finds old core files and deletes them
find ~ -atime +31 -exec mv {} /archive/{} \;	Copies files that have not been accessed in a month to an archive for older files

The second expression is similar to the first, with one exception. If the command is included in an -ok expression, you are first prompted for permission to execute the command. Usually, if the commands are nonreversible and are also likely to be few, you're better off running with -ok than -exec. If the command is likely to be executed many times, though, approving every command will be tedious. The prompt looks like this:

```
$ find ~ -name core -mtime +7 -ok rm {} \;
< rm ... /home/james/project/core > ?
```

A y indicates that you want the command executed.

Comparing files relatively

Another expression primary is -newer, which takes a filename as its argument. If the filename found is newer (that is, the modification time is more recent) than the one named, this returns true. This expression is particularly useful when you are examining source directories to acquire a listing of source files that have been modified more recently than the resultant executable file.

Note

A properly written makefile also does this for you. For more information, see Chapters 38 and 42.

In my bin directory, I want a listing of all the files newer than the showbowls program. The command to produce this list is find ~/bin -newer ~/bin/showbowls -print. Listing 7-21 shows the results.

Listing 7-21: Output of find ~/bin -newer ~/bin/showbowls -print

```
/home/james/bin
/home/james/bin/Shells/dmail
/home/james/bin/mailedit
/home/james/bin/.hidden
```

There's not much here. The directory has changed, indicating that a file has been added or deleted. Three other files have modification times more recent than showbowls.

Checking directories first

By default, when find finds a directory, it performs the actions required on the directory before checking the components of the directory. Sometimes, you would prefer to examine the directory entries before the directory itself. (One such occasion occurs when you're checking modification times and an action on a file would significantly modify the directory.) The expression that enables you to do this is -depth, and it takes no arguments.

Listing 7-22 shows a side-by-side comparison of find Shells -print and find Shells -depth -print from my bin directory. Note the difference in order when examining the files.

Listing 7-22: Comparing find Output with -depth

```
CShells      CShells/combinelists
CShells/combinelists      CShells/dumpit
CShells/dumpit      CShells/eastit
CShells/eastit      CShells/footit
CShells/footit      CShells/godit
CShells/godit      CShells/mailomit
CShells/mailomit      CShells/mailzap
CShells/mailzap      CShells/open
CShells/open      CShells/rotatem.sh
CShells/rotatem.sh      CShells/shv
CShells/shv      CShells/trivit
CShells/trivit      CShells/urgent
CShells/urgent      CShells/inttest
CShells/inttest      CShells/uupicker
CShells/uupicker      CShells/zooboy
CShells/zooboy      CShells/scc
CShells/scc      CShells/2pr
CShells/2pr      CShells/allgodit
CShells/allgodit      CShells/data1
CShells/data1      CShells/test2
CShells/test2      CShells/linkup
CShells/linkup      CShells/linkx11r5
CShells/linkx11r5      CShells/mroot2
CShells/mroot2      CShells/restorewind
CShells/restorewind      CShells/tester
CShells/tester      CShells/backup2
CShells/backup2      CShells
```

The -depth expression is always true.

Ignoring directories

Similarly, you can prune your find output with the -prune expression. If the file being checked is a directory, find does not descend the directory. An example is looking for files with the string el in them. In my bin directory, the subdirectory Shells has a file selectsc that would be found without pruning; but Shells also has el, and -prune would disable the search. Listing 7-23 shows the output.

Listing 7-23: Output of find . -name "*el*" -prune -print

```
./CShells
./Shells
./wishlists/runthelot
```

The expression -prune is always true.

Building expressions

Although the outlined expression list is quite powerful, you can make it even more powerful by building more complicated expressions. To do this, use the following four techniques: parenthesis grouping, negation, AND expressions, and OR expressions.

Parenthesis grouping

You can group an expression or set of expressions in parentheses. If the expressions within are true, the parenthetical expression is true.

Note

Because parentheses have meanings to the shell, you should escape the parenthesis characters with a backslash.

Negation

You can negate any expression with the exclamation point. When the expression returns true, it becomes false, and vice versa.

Note

If you are a C shell user, remember to escape the exclamation point, as it has special meaning to the shell.

AND expressions

Listing expressions in order is the same as a logical AND operation, but occasions may arise where you want to make it more explicit. In those cases, use the `-a` operator. If the first expression is false, the second expression is not evaluated.

OR expressions

The OR operator is the opposite of the AND operator. It is `-o`; and if the first expression is true, the second is not evaluated. This is particularly significant if the second expression includes some actions, such as `-prune -o -print`. In that case, you have no output.

Examples of combined expressions

A common cleanup technique is to remove object files and core files from a source directory. This requires a parenthetical expression and an OR, as in the following example:

```
find . \( -name `*.o´ -o -name core \) -exec rm {} \;
```

Another example might be to remove old archive files except those that include the word *important* in the name.

```
find . -atime +31 ! -name `*important*´ -ok mv {} /archive/{} \;
```

As you use UNIX, you will certainly find occasions to use some rather esoteric expressions with `find`.

Using the xargs command

One weakness with using `find`'s `-exec` and `-ok` options is that they can create quite a few processes. Process creation, outlined in Part V, is expensive: Each time `-exec` is reached, a new process is created. If the command is fairly routine, such as rm, building a list of files would be better, up to a system limit, and you could execute rm only once with all those files as arguments.

The xargs program does this. It takes lines of data (they need not be filenames) on its input and builds argument lists for the commands specified as arguments to xargs. The input values always follow the command arguments listed for the xargs command. If the input must precede an argument, such as with mv, you'll need to perform input substitution.

You commonly use xargs to accept the output of find on standard input:

```
find . expressions -print | xargs command
```

The xargs program also takes some arguments that can affect its functioning. Table 7-4 shows these arguments.

Table 7-4   xargs Arguments

Arguments	Meaning
-E *string*	This command uses the specified string to signify the end of input; everything after it is ignored.
-I *string*	Whenever the specified string is found in the list of arguments to the command, this command replaces it with the line from input.
-I *string*	This command is the same as -I, except that if the string is omitted, {} is assumed.
L *number*	This command invokes the command for each specified number of lines from input. If the last character of an input line is a space, the next line is considered a continuation of the previous one.
-l *number*	This command is the same as -L, except that 1 is assumed if the number is omitted.
-n *number*	This command invokes the command with the specified number of arguments, unless that exceeds the allowable size of the command line.
-p	This command prompts for command execution.
-s *number*	This command assumes that the maximum number of characters on the command line is *number*.
-t	This command traces the execution of commands.
-xnumber	This command terminates execution of commands if the specified number does not fit in the space available.

Most users of xargs do not invoke the command with arguments.

Guru: Writing the Command as a Shell

The -I option executes the command once per input line, creating the same problems that -exec does for find. To avoid these problems, the expert user instead writes the command as a shell script and includes that shell script as the command for xargs. For example, to move files to an archive disk, the function would be

```
#!/bin/ksh
mv $i /archives
```

The shell script is executed after a command line is filled and moves everything to the target directory.

Using the which command

The which command is a built-in shell command that is useful for finding files. It applies only to executable files, but when you are searching for the exact location of a file, it is unmatched.

The which command takes a single argument and puts the command executed for that string on standard output. With the C Shell, which is adept at translating built-in commands and aliases.

You primarily use which when you execute a command and you don't see the results you expected. You may have created a command that appears earlier on your path, or you may have an intervening alias. I've frequently used which when moving accounts to new machines and architectures to debug my operating environment.

Using the whereis command

Another useful command, introduced by BSD UNIX and not a part of the POSIX specification, is whereis. This command looks in the normal places for executable files, manual pages, and source files. I use it less frequently than which because I'm usually looking for the executable file to debug a path; but if I don't find the specific file, I sometimes fall back on whereis.

The whereis command sees around aliases, so if you've overloaded an alias, whereis finds the executable file. Table 7-5 shows the arguments that whereis takes.

Table 7-5   whereis Arguments

Argument	Meaning
-B *directory*	Looks for binaries in the specified directory
-M *directory*	Looks for manual pages in the specified directory

Continued

Table 7-5 *(continued)*	
Argument	**Meaning**
-S *directory*	Looks for source files in the specified directory
-b	Looks for binaries only
-m	Looks for manual pages only
-s	Looks for source files only
-u	Looks for unusual entries such as files that are not source files, manual pages, or binaries
-f	Signifies an end of directory listings for -B, -M, and -S

Identifying Files

The commands at the beginning of this chapter are good for finding files, but they tell you very little about the file itself. As Chapter 6 explains, a file is essentially an i-node containing administrative information and blocks of data. Commands such as ls access the i-node and provide descriptive information about the file. Other commands examine the data blocks. You can use still other commands to characterize the data in those data blocks. I'll examine the commands in that order.

Using the ls command again

As previously mentioned, ls is perhaps the most versatile command in UNIX. In this chapter, I've discussed twelve flags that modify ls's capability to locate files. The nine flags discussed in this section access the i-node and provide additional data.

Note

Some of the ls flags discussed at the beginning of the chapter (such as those that sort by time) access the i-node for information but do not present the actual data.

Providing some basic file information

The -F flag adds some basic information to the filenames in a listing. If the file is a directory, a slash is appended to the name. Executable files have an asterisk appended, and named pipes have a vertical bar (the UNIX pipe symbol).

Listing 7-24 shows the additional information I receive when I look at my bin directory with this flag (compare Listing 7-2). The single character adds a lot of value.

Listing 7-24: Output of /bin/ls -CF /home/james/bin

```
CShells/    mailedit*    procmon*          src/
Shells/     mst3k*       satno*            testprocess*
adbook      munge*       screensaver.sh*   wchance*
banner*     mydate*      sendmail.cf       wishlists/
checkem*    olvwm*       shar*             xloadimage*
crons       op*          shipit*           xv*
desk*       parsit*      showbowls*        xv.old*
gruber*     patch*       showquakes*       yes*
gzip*       patrunc*     sortem*
```

As you can see from the figure, most of the files are executable files. Four files, though, are directories: CShells, Shells, src, and wishlists. Three files are not executable: adbook, crons, and sendmail.cf. There are no named pipes.

Note

Traditionally, a user creates a bin directory under his or her home directory for executable binary files.

Secret

Although I've mentioned only three symbols, your system may define more. Mine includes the at sign (@) to indicate a symbolic link. These are extensions to the POSIX specification for UNIX.

Identifying directories

The -p flag is similar to -F, except that it identifies only directories. Use -p if you feel that the other symbols associated with file types add to the clutter.

Examining a directory

By default, if a directory is specified on a command line, the contents of the directory are listed on standard output. Sometimes, such as when you are checking ownership and access permissions, this behavior is undesirable. In these cases, use the -d flag to force ls to examine the directory without checking its members.

Listing 7-25 shows the output of ls using -d. Normally, the -d flag is combined with -l for a detailed listing or with -p or -F to highlight the fact that the file is a directory. When the -d flag is used alone, you cannot tell whether the file is a regular file or a directory.

Listing 7-25: Output of /bin/ls -d /home/james/bin

```
/home/james/bin
```

Obtaining detailed information

The -l flag provides a long list of information for each file. It opens the i-node and presents size, ownership, permissions, and times associated with the file. By default, you can break the output into five pieces.

Before listing the files, you are presented with a count of the number of data blocks consumed by all the files.

The first piece of output is a measure of permissions. It is 11 characters long. The first character indicates the type of file being listed. Five possibilities exist:

- d for directory
- b for a block special device
- c for a character special device
- p for a named pipe
- - for a regular file

The next nine characters are indications for the file's access permissions, broken into three groups of three characters. The first group is access permissions for the owner, the second is for the group, and the last is for the world. Table 7-6 shows how the characters break down within each group.

Table 7-6   Access Permission Information Provided by the -l Flag

Character	Flag	Meaning
First	-	The file is not readable.
	r	The file is readable.
Second	-	The file is not writable.
	w	The file is writable.
Third (an executable tag)	x	The file is executable.
	s	The file is executable and sets the effective user or group ID to the ownership of the file.
	S	The file is not executable and sets the user ID accordingly.

The last (eleventh) character is the optional access mode, usually a blank.

This string precedes a count of the number of links associated with the given file. The next major piece of information is the ownership of the file. If the numeric user ID from the i-node has a user name associated with it in the /etc/passwd file, that name is listed. The same goes for the group ID and the /etc/group file.

The third piece of information is the size of the file, in bytes.

The fourth piece of information is a date. This is usually the last time the file was modified. If the -u flag is included, however, the last access time is printed. If -c is specified, the last status change time appears. If the date is within the last six months, it is presented as a three-character month abbreviation followed by the day of the month and the time (in a 24-hour clock format). If the date is older, the 24-hour clock is replaced by the four-digit year.

The last piece of information is the filename. If the file is a symbolic link, the filename is followed by an arrow and the name of the file to which it is linked. To acquire information on the linked file, you must also specify the -L flag. This option is present in many versions of ls, but it is not a POSIX-required option. To determine whether your system supports that flag, type **man ls**. Listing 7-26 shows the long listing for my bin directory.

Listing 7-26: Output of /bin/ls -l /home/james/bin

```
total 5572
drwxr-xr-x    2 james     admin        1024 Apr 23 16:28 CShells
drwxr-xr-x    2 james     admin        1024 Mar 24 01:11 Shells
-rw-r--r--    1 james     admin           0 Aug 31  1991 adbook
-r-xr-xr-x    1 james     admin         637 Aug 16 19:22 banner
-rwxrwxrwx    1 james     admin         157 Jul 18 15:36 checkem
-rw-r--r--    1 james     admin          75 Aug 19  1994 crons
-rwxr-x--     1 james     admin     1597440 Mar  5  1993 desk
-rwxr-xr-x    1 james     admin       24576 Sep 25  1991 gruber
-rwxr-xr-x    1 james     admin       98304 Sep  7  1993 gzip
-rwxr-xr-x    1 james     admin         118 Aug 18 10:47 mailedit
-rwxr-xr-x    1 james     admin         406 Aug 19  1994 mst3k
-rwxr-xr-x    1 james     admin         233 Aug 11 22:46 munge
-rwxr-xr-x    1 james     admin        7804 Aug 19  1994 mydate
-rwxr-xr-x    1 james     admin      360448 Feb 24  1993 olvwm
-rwxr-xr-x    1 james     admin       32768 Sep 30  1992 op
-rwxr-xr-x    1 james     admin       24576 Apr 29  1991 parsit
-rwxr-xr-x    1 james     admin       49152 Feb 22  1991 patch
-rwxr-xr-x    1 james     admin         285 Jul 30  1994 patrunc
-rwxr-xr-x    1 james     admin      491520 Mar  5  1993 procmon
-rwxr-xr-x    1 james     admin       32768 Jul 24  1992 satno
-rwxr-xr-x    1 james     admin        1483 Sep 14  1993 screensaver.sh
-rw-r--r--    1 james     admin        8335 Oct  1  1992 sendmail.cf
-rwxr-xr-x    1 james     admin       49152 Feb  6  1994 shar
-rwxr-xr-x    2 james     admin       24576 Nov 26  1993 shipit
-r-xr-xr-x    1 james     admin         233 Aug 16 19:22 showbowls
-rwxr-xr-x    1 james     admin         427 Jul  3  1994 showquakes
-rwxr-xr-x    1 james     admin       24576 Nov 11  1993 sortem
drwxr-xr-x    3 james     admin        1024 Mar 24 01:11 src
-rwxr-xr-x    1 james     admin       32768 Apr 22  1992 testprocess
-rwxr-xr-x    1 james     admin       24576 Jul 21  1992 wchance
drwxr-xr-x    2 james     admin        1024 Mar 24 01:11 wishlists
-rwxr-xr-x    1 james     admin      753485 Jul  8 08:19 xloadimage
-rwxr-xr-x    1 james     admin     1198175 Aug  4 08:09 xv
-rwxr-xr-x    1 james     admin      822045 Jul  8 08:53 xv.old
-rwxr-xr-x    1 james     admin          34 Sep 30  1994 yes
```

This listing tells me that my `bin` directory is consuming over 5,000 blocks of disk space. Some files, such as `patch`, have remained unchanged since 1991 — over eight years. Others, such as `xv`, have been modified in the last month. Almost every file is readable and executable by the world. Some are quite large: `xv` is over a megabyte in size; some are small: `adbook` has no data associated with it.

Note

Although this is not a hard and fast rule, you can often guess which executable files are programs and which are shell scripts by the size of the file. Programs tend to be larger because they need to contain all their execution instructions in the file. Shell scripts are just a listing of directives to another program. Judging from size, I could reasonably assume that `yes` is a shell script and `xv` is a program. The precise crossover point is not well defined.

If I were to combine the `-l` flag with `-d`, I'd see a listing of the statistics for the directory itself:

```
drwxr-xr-x    7 james     admin      1024 Sep  2 09:33 /home/james/bin
```

It is a directory that anyone can look at, but only I can modify it. Currently, it needs a kilobyte of space to store all the entries. I last modified it at 9:33 a.m. on September 2.

The `-l` flag is probably the most frequently used flag for `ls`. Because `ls` is one of the most commonly used commands, this suggests that `ls -l` is the most common combination.

Note

In an informal survey of my friends who use UNIX, the most commonly aliased command was `ls -l`.

Showing groups only

Some versions of UNIX do not list the group name on the long output (Solaris 1 and 2 are good examples). This is not a weakness because you can use the `-g` flag to obtain only the group name on the listing.

Whereas the long listing includes both owner and group, the owner is replaced with white space on the `-g` listing.

Showing owners only

Similar to `-g`, the `-o` flag lists only the owner of the file. The group name is replaced with white space. In both cases, the allocated area may be shortened to provide extra information.

Providing numeric UID and GID

Sometimes, providing the numeric information for the user ID (UID) and group ID (GID) is more useful than listing the strings. In these cases, use the `-n` option. When I look at my `bin` directory with `-n`, I find that my UID is 69 and my GID is 10:

```
drwxr-xr-x    7 69        10         1024 Sep  2 09:33 /home/james/bin
```

Obtaining the i-node number

Sometimes, you need to obtain the i-node number. In these cases, use the -i flag to list the i-nodes for each file.

Consider the following case. A directory has four files, all the same size, but each file is listed with two links. How can you tell which file is linked to which?

```
total 4
-rw-r--r--    2 james      admin         6 Sep  3 15:52 name1
-rw-r--r--    2 james      admin         6 Sep  3 15:53 name2
-rw-r--r--    2 james      admin         6 Sep  3 15:52 name3
-rw-r--r--    2 james      admin         6 Sep  3 15:53 name4
```

There must be an easier way to tell them apart without actually examining the data. If the data is the same, then what?

This is clearly an application for the -i flag because the files that are linked share the same i-node. When I run ls -i on the directory, the output is

```
163971 name1   163972 name2   163971 name3   163972 name4
```

Aha! By comparing the i-node numbers, I see that name1 and name3 are linked and that name2 and name4 are also linked.

Note

I could have done this by linking name1 to another file, such as name5. An ls -l of the directory would have then yielded five files, and name1, name3, and name5 would have listed three links apiece instead of two.

Determining how many blocks are used

Although the size in characters is often useful, the number of blocks consumed is sometimes more useful. The -s flag provides information on the size of the file in blocks. Listing 7-27 shows the listing for my bin with the size in blocks provided.

Listing 7-27: Output of /bin/ls -ls /home/james/bin

```
total 5572
    1 drwxr-xr-x    2 james      admin      1024 Apr 23 16:28 CShells
    1 drwxr-xr-x    2 james      admin      1024 Mar 24 01:11 Shells
    0 -rw-r--r--    1 james      admin         0 Aug 31  1991 adbook
    1 -r-xr-xr-x    1 james      admin       637 Aug 16 19:22 banner
    1 -rwxrwxrwx    1 james      admin       157 Jul 18 15:36 checkem
    1 -rw-r--r--    1 james      admin        75 Aug 19  1994 crons
 1568 -rwxr-x---    1 james      admin   1597440 Mar  5  1993 desk
   25 -rwxr-xr-x    1 james      admin     24576 Sep 25  1991 gruber
   97 -rwxr-xr-x    1 james      admin     98304 Sep  7  1993 gzip
    1 -rwxr-xr-x    1 james      admin       118 Aug 18 10:47 mailedit
    1 -rwxr-xr-x    1 james      admin       406 Aug 19  1994 mst3k
    1 -rwxr-xr-x    1 james      admin       233 Aug 11 22:46 munge
    8 -rwxr-xr-x    1 james      admin      7804 Aug 19  1994 mydate
  355 -rwxr-xr-x    1 james      admin    360448 Feb 24  1993 olvwm
```

```
  33 -rwxr-xr-x   1 james    admin       32768 Sep 30  1992 op
  25 -rwxr-xr-x   1 james    admin       24576 Apr 29  1991 parsit
  49 -rwxr-xr-x   1 james    admin       49152 Feb 22  1991 patch
   1 -rwxr-xr-x   1 james    admin         285 Jul 30  1994 patrunc
 483 -rwxr-xr-x   1 james    admin      491520 Mar  5  1993 procmon
  33 -rwxr-xr-x   1 james    admin       32768 Jul 24  1992 satno
   2 -rwxr-xr-x   1 james    admin        1483 Sep 14  1993 screensaver.sh
   9 -rw-r--r--   1 james    admin        8335 Oct  1  1992 sendmail.cf
  49 -rwxr-xr-x   1 james    admin       49152 Feb  6  1994 shar
  25 -rwxr-xr-x   2 james    admin       24576 Nov 26  1993 shipit
   1 -r-xr-xr-x   1 james    admin         233 Aug 16 19:22 showbowls
   1 -rwxr-xr-x   1 james    admin         427 Jul  3  1994 showquakes
  25 -rwxr-xr-x   1 james    admin       24576 Nov 11  1993 sortem
   1 drwxr-xr-x   3 james    admin        1024 Mar 24 01:11 src
  33 -rwxr-xr-x   1 james    admin       32768 Apr 22  1992 testprocess
  25 -rwxr-xr-x   1 james    admin       24576 Jul 21  1992 wchance
   1 drwxr-xr-x   2 james    admin        1024 Mar 24 01:11 wishlists
 737 -rwxr-xr-x   1 james    admin      753485 Jul  8 08:19 xloadimage
1176 -rwxr-xr-x   1 james    admin     1198175 Aug  4 08:09 xv
 801 -rwxr-xr-x   1 james    admin      822045 Jul  8 08:53 xv.old
   1 -rwxr-xr-x   1 james    admin          34 Sep 30  1994 yes
```

One interesting check sums up the total number of blocks used by each file and determines whether it matches the total at the top.

Obtaining the size of the file is often useful for other reasons: No sorting flag based on file size exists, so if you need to sort by that criteria, you should use ls -ls and pipe it into a sort.

Some UNIX systems enable the creation of arbitrarily large files with sparse data elements to which intermediate blocks are not allocated until needed. In these cases, though, the file may indicate that it is 1,048,576 bytes in size. If only the first and last blocks are allocated, the actual space consumed is two blocks.

Most UNIX systems do not implement sparse allocation.

Note

Using the file command

Now that you've seen how the i-node is examined, let's look at describing the actual file contents. POSIX defines a command, file, for this purpose.

The file command takes no flags, just a list of filenames, and it attempts to determine the type of file. First, it checks the i-node file type; if the file is anything other than a regular file, the command lists the specific type. Then, if the file is a regular file, file checks the length. A zero-length file is listed as an empty file. Lastly, the first data block is checked, and a reasonable guess is made as to the file's actual contents. Sometimes, a magic number is checked; at other times, a string at the start of the file may be checked.

At no time is the output of file guaranteed to be correct. Do not rely on it for absolute certainty.

Listing 7-28 shows the output of the `file` command on all the files in my `bin` directory.

Listing 7-28: Output of file /home/james/bin/*

```
/home/james/bin/CShells:      directory
/home/james/bin/Shells:       directory
/home/james/bin/adbook:       empty
/home/james/bin/banner:       English text
/home/james/bin/checkem:      C Shell script text
/home/james/bin/crons:        ascii text
/home/james/bin/desk:         sparc demand paged executable
/home/james/bin/gruber:       sparc demand paged dynamically linked
executable not stripped
/home/james/bin/gzip:         sparc demand paged dynamically linked
executable not stripped
/home/james/bin/mailedit:     C Shell script text
/home/james/bin/mst3k:        English text
/home/james/bin/munge:        ascii text
/home/james/bin/mydate:       ELF 32-bit MSB executable SPARC Version 1
/home/james/bin/olvwm:        sparc demand paged dynamically linked
executable not stripped
/home/james/bin/op:           sparc demand paged dynamically linked
executable not stripped
/home/james/bin/parsit:       sparc demand paged dynamically linked
executable not stripped
/home/james/bin/patch:        sparc demand paged dynamically linked
executable not stripped
/home/james/bin/patrunc:      ascii text
/home/james/bin/procmon:      sparc demand paged executable
/home/james/bin/satno:        sparc demand paged dynamically linked
executable not stripped
/home/james/bin/screensaver.sh: Bourne Shell script text
/home/james/bin/sendmail.cf:  English text
/home/james/bin/shar:         sparc demand paged dynamically linked
executable not stripped
/home/james/bin/shipit:       sparc demand paged dynamically linked
executable not stripped
/home/james/bin/showbowls:    ascii text
/home/james/bin/showquakes:   Bourne Shell script text
/home/james/bin/sortem:       sparc demand paged dynamically linked
executable not stripped
/home/james/bin/src:          directory
/home/james/bin/testprocess:  sparc demand paged dynamically linked
executable not stripped
/home/james/bin/wchance:      sparc demand paged dynamically linked
executable not stripped
/home/james/bin/wishlists:    directory
/home/james/bin/xloadimage:   Linux/i386 demand-paged executable
(QMAGIC) not stripped
/home/james/bin/xv:           Linux/i386 demand-paged executable
(QMAGIC) not stripped
/home/james/bin/xv.old:       Linux/i386 demand-paged executable
(QMAGIC) not stripped
/home/james/bin/yes:          ascii text
```

Because I recently migrated from a SPARC station to a Linux machine, some of my binaries are still SPARC-based and others are Linux-based.

Using the wc command

The wc command is useful for examining textual documents. The command's name comes from *word count,* and it counts the number of bytes, words, and lines in a file.

A *word* is defined as a series of alphanumeric characters separated by white-space characters, spaces, new lines, or tabs. A *line* is a series of characters separated by new lines. The command takes a filename, or a list of filenames, as arguments. If more than one filename is listed as an argument, the command provides summary information. If no files are listed, it takes the information from standard input.

Four flags are available. If -m is specified, only the number of characters is output. If -l is specified, only the number of lines is output. If -b is specified, only the number of bytes is output. Finally, if -w is specified, only the number of words is output.

Remember that with internationalization, -m and -b may not have the same output.

The output for wc on the screensaver.sh file is

```
58      232     1483 /home/james/bin/screensaver.sh
```

The shell program is 58 lines long, with 232 distinct words.

Using the head and tail commands

Sometimes, to examine a file, you need take a look at some of its contents. head and tail are two commands used for that.

The head command examines the first few lines of a file. The first ten lines of the file are printed on standard output. The command's only argument changes the number of lines: If an integer is specified with either a dash or the -n flag, that number of lines is printed.

If no files are listed, standard input is read until ten lines are found. If multiple files are listed, the first ten lines for each file are output. Listing 7-29 shows the head of a mail file.

Listing 7-29: Output of head /home/james/Mail/joan

```
From james Sun Sep  3 08:09:34 1995
Subject: Re: First Day of the Hawks
To: joan@med.unc.edu (Joan Shields)
Date: Sun, 3 Sep 1995 08:09:34 -0700 (PDT)
```

In-Reply-To: <9509031402.AA21724@dallas.med.unc.edu> from "Joan Shields" at Sep
3, 95 10:02:52 am
X-Mailer: ELM [version 2.4 PL23]
MIME-Version: 1.0
Content-Type: text/plain; charset=US-ASCII
Content-Transfer-Encoding: 7bit
Content-Length: 507

The `tail` command is the opposite partner to `head`. By default, it shows the
last ten lines of a file. It takes three possible arguments.

If you specify `-c` followed by a positive number, output begins that many
bytes from the beginning of the file; if `-c` is followed by a negative number,
output begins that many bytes from the end of the file.

Specifying `-n` has the same effect as specifying `-c`, except that the number is
the number of lines, not bytes.

If you specify `-f`, the command does not terminate when it reaches the end
of the file. Instead, the program waits for more data to be added to the file,
and it outputs that data as it is added. Listing 7-30 is a `tail` of my UUCP log
file.

Listing 7-30: Output of tail /usr/spool/uucp/Log

```
uucico netcomsv daemon (1995-09-03 16:23:49.54 8687) Receiving D.netco4633aff
uucico netcomsv daemon (1995-09-03 16:23:51.72 8687) Receiving X.netcomsC4633
uucico netcomsv - (1995-09-03 16:23:53.28 8687) Protocol `g´ packets: sent 54,
resent 0, received 140
uucico netcomsv - (1995-09-03 16:23:53.28 8687) Errors: header 0, checksum 4,
order 3, remote rejects 0
uucico netcomsv - (1995-09-03 16:23:53.54 8687) Call complete (21 seconds 8642
bytes 411 bps)
uuxqt netcomsv daemon (1995-09-03 16:23:53.66 8689) Executing X.netcomsCd580
(rmail james@sagarmatha.com)
uuxqt netcomsv daemon (1995-09-03 16:23:53.81 8689) Executing X.netcomsC6b5e
(rmail james@sagarmatha.com)
uuxqt netcomsv daemon (1995-09-03 16:23:53.99 8689) Executing X.netcomsCb605
(rmail james@sagarmatha.com)
uuxqt netcomsv daemon (1995-09-03 16:23:54.28 8689) Executing X.netcomsC4633
(rmail james@sagarmatha.com)
uux netcomsv james (1995-09-03 16:25:01.66 8722) Queuing rmail joan@med.unc.edu
(D.ODWE)
```

Using the cat and more commands

This chapter has explained everything that you can do to determine what a
file is like, short of examining all its contents. Two good commands examine
those contents.

The simpler of the two is `cat`, which reads the files on the command line in sequence and puts their contents on standard output. If no files are listed or if the file is a single dash, standard input is read.

Note

The `cat` command is a useful tool for concatenating two files into a third file. The `cat file1 file2 > file3` command does the trick!

The `more` command is much more powerful than `cat`. At its simplest, it presents a screenful of information and waits for your input before proceeding. Table 7-7 lists command-line options that can change `more`'s behavior.

Table 7-7   Options for more

Flag	Meaning
-c	Uses the screen's terminal characteristics for faster output
-e	Exits immediately after reading the last file
-i	Allows case-insensitive pattern matching
-s	Replaces consecutive empty lines with a single empty line
-u	Replaces the backspace with a printable control character
-n *n*	Treats the screen as having *n* lines
-p *command*	Runs the specified `more` command on each file when opened
-t tags	Uses the `tags` file to find the file that matches the tag

The `tags` file is a special file created and used for software development. For more information, see Part IX.

`more` commands are related to the `vi` commands listed in Chapter 11.

Note

POSIX specifies several commands for `more`. Most you won't ever use, but the most common commands are a space, a return, q, and `:n`. Pressing the spacebar displays the next screenful of data. Pressing return adds a new line. To quit, press q. Use `:n` to move to the next file. Table 7-8 lists all the `more` commands.

Table 7-8   Commands for more

Command	Action
'	Goes to the marked location. The quotation mark is followed by a letter; two quotation marks mean go back to the previous mark.

Command	Action
[n]/[regular expression]	Searches for a pattern. If preceded by an exclamation point, prints from the next line that does not match the pattern. If no pattern is specified, uses the last pattern provided.*
:e	Loads the listed file into more.
[n]:n	Loads the next file on the command line.*
[n]:p	Loads the previously examined file.*
:t	Loads the file found with the tag from the tags file.
=^G	Shows the current position in the file.
[n]?	Searches backward. Uses the same syntax as /.*
[n]G	Goes to the end of the current file.*
[n]N	Searches backward using the last pattern.*
R	Refreshes the screen and discards any buffered input.
[n]b ^B	Moves back a screen.*
[n]d ^D	Moves forward half a screen.*
[n]f ^F	Moves forward a screen.*
[n]g	Goes to the beginning of the file.*
h	Shows help.
[n]j <SP> <CR>	Moves down the file.*
[n]k	Moves back a line.*
m	Marks a position in the file.
[n]n	Searches forward for the next instance of the last pattern.*
q :q ZZ	Quits more.
^L r	Redraws the screen.
[n]s	Skips some lines.*
[n]u ^U	Moves backward half a screen.*
v	Invokes an editor with the file.

*When you specify a number with [n], it usually means to perform the command that many times. For example, 200s means to skip the next 200 lines. The exceptions are g and G. These cases go to the specified line.

Additional POSIX options may exist, but this is what my more commands do. The ? displays the following message:

```
Most commands optionally preceded by integer argument k.   Defaults in brackets.
```

An asterisk (*) makes the argument the new default. Your more may have additional options; those listed in the online help are displayed in Listing 7-31.

Listing 7-31: Online Help's Listing of more Options

```
<space>                    Display next k lines of text [current screen size]
z                          Display next k lines of text [current screen size]*
<return>                   Display next k lines of text [1]*
d or ctrl-D                Scroll k lines [current scroll size, initially 11]*
q or Q or <interrupt>      Exit from more
s                          Skip forward k lines of text [1]
f                          Skip forward k screenfuls of text [1]
b or ctrl-B                Skip backwards k screenfuls of text [1]
'                          Go to place where previous search started
=                          Display current line number
/<regular expression>      Search for kth occurrence of regular expression [1]
n                          Search for kth occurrence of last r.e [1]
!<cmd> or :!<cmd>          Execute <cmd> in a subshell
v                          Start up vi at current line
h                          Display this message
ctrl-L                     Redraw screen
:n                         Go to kth next file [1]
:p                         Go to kth previous file [1]
:f                         Display current file name and line number
.                          Repeat previous command
--More--(10%) }
```

Using the od command

Cat, more, head, and tail all work for text, but the results are unpredictable if used on a data file. The command to display data is od, for *octal dump*. The od command takes four flags (listed in Table 7-9) and a listing of character options (defined in Table 7-10).

Table 7-9   od Options

Flag	Result
-j *n*	Skips *n* bytes from the beginning of the file
-N *n*	Displays the first *n* bytes read
-t c	Displays data in the format specified in Table 7-6
-v	Does not duplicate lines

Table 7-10   od Character Options

Character	Meaning
a	Named character
c	Character
d	Signed decimal
f	Floating point
o	Octal
u	Unsigned decimal
x	Hexadecimal

Octal dumps enable you to examine the data directly in the file, regardless of whether the characters are printable. Listing 7-32 shows the octal dump of a program.

Listing 7-32: od Output

```
0000000 314  \0    d   \0   \0        016   \0   \0 260 002   \0   \b    p 004   \0
0000020   @ 260   \0   \0        020   \0   \0   \0   \0   \0   \0   \0   \0   \0   \0
0000040 350 217 034 016   \0 270    -   \0   \0   \0 273   \0   \0   \0   \0 315
0000060 200 243    \   \v   \t    ' 213    D    $   \b 243    4   \v   \t    ' 017
0000100 267 005 330 333 020   \0    P 350 200 035 016   \0 203 304 004 350
0000120 270 035 016   \0 350 333 003   \0   \0    P 350    q 363 377    _    [
0000140 270 001   \0   \0   \0 315 200 353 367 220 220 220 220 220 220 220
0000160  \0 220 220 220    1    p    r   \0    p    p    m    r    a    w   \0    #
0000200   0   0   0   0    0   0   \0    #    B    2    C    0    D    C   \0    #
0000220   C   6   D   5    E   2   \0    #    8    B    9    9    B    5   \0    T
```

In Listing 7-32, the left column is an octal count of the number of bytes displayed. If a byte is a character, it is displayed as a character; otherwise, the octal value is displayed.

Summary

In this chapter, I illustrated several tools for finding files and for examining their contents. Of these, `ls` is the most powerful because it can do both tasks. For looking at files, `more` is quite powerful, one step removed from being an editor.

This chapter covered the following commands:

- `ls`
- `find`
- `xargs`
- `which`
- `whereis`
- `file`
- `wc`
- `head`
- `tail`
- `cat`
- `more`
- `od`

The next chapter introduces tools to manage file permissions and disk space.

Chapter 8

Understanding File Permissions
and Disk Limits

A UNIX user must often manage how disk space is used. You are responsible for the contents of your home directory, and you are responsible for maintaining the integrity of any data that you keep.

Monitoring and changing permissions ensures data integrity. By protecting files and directories, you prevent unauthorized access. A directory with world-write permission is an invitation to abuse. Where permitted, you can also change file ownership.

Managing your disk space involves knowing how much is available and how much you've used. The tools for disk management include the basic UNIX commands.

Understanding File Permissions

Every UNIX file contains a set of access permissions that defines a user's interaction with that file. This set is stored in the file's i-node as an integer. When represented as a binary number, the integer masks the file's permissions.

Note

Understanding different counting schemes helps you understand computers. The four common schemes are *decimal, binary, octal,* and *hexadecimal.* Each counting scheme uses a different *base,* which mathematicians call a *radix.* Think of a number as a row of baskets. When the number of items in a basket equals the base, the basket empties and one item is placed into the next basket.

Our normal method of counting is *decimal,* also called *base ten.* This system evolved because we habitually used our fingers for counting, so counting to ten became the norm. In other areas, we use base twelve (clocks). Mayan culture used a base of 60 for some calculations.

Computers started with *base two,* or *binary,* because the easiest way to represent a number electrically is by raising and lowering the current in a wire so that the computer reads the current as being either on or off. Each wire represents a bit. By combining wires, or bits, you can build large numbers. Representing large numbers in binary is difficult, however. In binary, I'd represent my birth date as 1100/1001/11110101000! One million would be 11110100001001000000.

The next step was to represent numbers in *octal,* or *base eight,* by grouping each binary number in groups of three, starting at the least significant digit, and applying the translation in Table 8-1.

Table 8-1   The First Sixteen Integers in Four Bases

Decimal	Binary	Octal	Hexadecimal
0	0	0	0
1	1	1	1
2	10	2	2
3	11	3	3
4	100	4	4
5	101	5	5
6	110	6	6
7	111	7	7
8	1000	10	8
9	1001	11	9
10	1010	12	A
11	1011	13	B
12	1100	14	C
13	1101	15	D

Decimal	Binary	Octal	Hexadecimal
14	1110	16	E
15	1111	17	F
16	10000	20	10

In octal, my birthday is 14/11/3650, and one million is 3641100. Computer scientists quickly developed the concept of the byte as eight bits.

Finding 256 different symbols for each digit was difficult, so a *hexadecimal* system, with *base 16,* was devised for use with bytes. Each byte could then be represented as a two-digit hexadecimal number. Hexadecimal numbers use the numerals 0 through 9 for the first ten digit values and the first six characters of the alphabet (A, B, C, D, E, and F) for the last six digit values. In hexadecimal, my birthday is C/9/7A8, and one million is F4240.

Most file permissions do not exceed 12 bits in size, where each bit is a yes/no toggle for a permission. The three highest bits set different execution behaviors. The remaining nine divide into three groups of three, outlining permissions for the owner, the group, and the world. The three permissions are reading, writing, and using. Table 8-2 shows the last nine bits and their meanings.

Table 8-2   File Permission Bits

Bit	Meaning
0400	Owner read permission
0200	Owner write permission
0100	Owner use permission
0040	Group read permission
0020	Group write permission
0010	Group use permission
0004	World read permission
0002	World write permission
0001	World use permission

To set a file's permission, add up the desired entries from Table 8-2; the resultant number is the file's permission.

Story: World-Writable Vulnerability

Previously, I mentioned that you invite abuse when you have a file to which anyone in the world can write. I have to admit that in my youth, I was one of those abusers.

In graduate school, my friends and I used a world-writable file to pull a prank on someone who annoyed us. At the time, we were using a VMS computer system that shared some characteristics with UNIX, including the use of world writing permissions. The VMS system also maintained a rigorous system of disk quotas per user. My friends and I found a world-writable administrative file that our victim owned. (We believed a bug in the mail program created this file and never cleaned it up.) To get even, we filled this file with meaningless data to eat up the guy's disk quota. Our victim had to ask the administrative group to raise his disk quota. Shortly thereafter, we'd eat his quota up again. They never figured out what was going on. Meanwhile, we looked into creating our own files within this increasingly large file.

The read bit has the same meaning for all types of files: It lets you read the contents of the file.

The write bit also has the same meaning for all files: It lets you write to the file. This includes overwriting the contents. You can't delete a file unless you have permission to write to the file's parent directory. Similarly, you can't create a new file without the same permissions. You can reduce the file to zero length, however.

Traditionally, you'll see the use bit described as an *execute bit*. I don't like that term because it doesn't apply to the directory case. When you set the use bit for a file, you can run the file as a command and literally use it as a program. But when you apply the use bit to a directory, you can simply access the contents of the directory. Listing 8-1 shows the results of such an effort.

Listing 8-1: Directory Permissions

```
% mkdir testdir
% echo some data > testdir/testfile
% ls -l testdir/testfile
-rw-r--r--  1 james    admin         10 Sep 10 12:35 testdir/testfile
% cat testdir/testfile
some data
% chmod 0200 testdir/testfile
% cat testdir/testfile
cat: testdir/testfile: Permission denied
% chmod 0644 testdir/testfile
% chmod 0444 testdir
% ls testdir
testfile
% cat testdir/testfile
cat: testdir/testfile: Permission denied
```

```
% chmod 0544 testdir
% cat testdir/testfile
some data
% rm testdir/testfile
rm: testdir/testfile: Permission denied
% chmod 755 testdir
% rm testdir/testfile
% rmdir testdir
{ precise messages may differ between Unix systems}
```

Listing 8-1 illustrates the different means of protecting the file. In every case, I attempted to use cat to read the file. When the file was created, everything was fine. I then set the file to write-only: I could not read the file. I then set the directory to read-only: I could see the file, but I couldn't read the contents. I then set the use bit: I could read the contents, but I could not delete the file. Finally, I set the permissions correctly to clean up the test.

Using sticky bits and the set-UID

The first three permission bits have special meanings. The first two change the ownership of a process when it is executed, and the last one is called a *sticky bit*.

You often need to set the user ID of a process to give users access to resources that they are not normally allowed to have. One common example is su. Properly executed, su changes your effective user ID by making a system call that is restricted to root. Similarly, commands such as lpr and uucp maintain spooling areas and control access to their spools. You also want to restrict access when sending and receiving electronic mail. When you send a message, you want it written to the recipient's mail file, but you don't want anyone to go into that mail file and alter the contents. UNIX gets around this problem by creating a mail group and running the mail delivery programs with the group ID set. The mail delivery agent can write out new mail to the file, but only the owner can read the file.

Story: A Legendary Back Door

One of the more legendary back doors in UNIX comes from the original mail design. The mail reading program ran set-UID as root so that it could deliver and read messages. It also contained the option for a shell escape while reading mail. System users soon discovered that this shell escape was a back door to becoming root without requiring the password to read the message. Depending on how old a system is, you can still occasionally find this back door. The last production system to include it, to the best of my knowledge, was AT&T's UNIX PC. On a trade show floor in 1989, I remember sending mail to myself and then receiving it as root, which truly dismayed the exhibitor!

The first bit indicates that the program runs with the file owner's permission (set-UID). The second bit indicates that the file program runs with the group's permissions (set-GID).

The last bit is the sticky bit. When the sticky bit is set, the program remains in the system's memory space after it finishes executing. This saves startup time when you rerun the program. By residing in memory, the program stays available: the kernel only needs to call the appropriate memory address to run the program.

Note

Setting the sticky bit is rare because doing so effectively reduces the available system memory by the size of the program when the program is inactive. Often, a system runs out of swap space when using a program containing sticky bits.

Checking permissions

Chapter 7 described each of the 21 flags to the `ls` command. The most common and most powerful flag is `-l`, which gives a long listing of the data associated with a file. Nine characters of each file's output describe the access permissions. If none of the three high-order bits is set, the binary of the permissions maps exactly to the string of the permissions.

```
0644                               0727

110100100                          111010111
rw-r--r--                          rwx-w-rwx
```

Each of the three high-order bits modifies the use bit that is appropriately indexed in the string. The set-UID bit modifies the user-use bit, the set-GID modifies the group-use bit, and the sticky bit modifies the world-use bit. In the first two cases, the character is set to an `s`. If the character previously was a dash for no permission, the `s` is capitalized. The sticky bit is set to `t`, which is capitalized if the world-use bit was not set. Table 8-3 shows some common permission octal, binary, and string values.

Table 8-3   Permissions Values

Octal	Binary	String
04755	100111101101	rwsr-xr-x
06700	110111000000	rws--S--
00644	000110100100	rw-r--r--
01555	001101101101	r-xr-xr-t
07777	111111111111	rwsrwsrwt
07666	111110110110	rwSrwSrwT

Secret

Perhaps surprisingly, world permissions do not override group and owner, and group permissions do not override owner permissions. You can create a file with the permission mode 066, which gives the group and world bits permission to read and write the file but denies you access to the file! Another odd permission is 422, which enables you to log how other users work with a process but prevents them from seeing the log.

Creating permissions

For UNIX files, the application that creates the file sets the default permissions. Normally, files created with editors and by redirection receive 666 permission, which enables anyone to read and write the files. Files created by a compiler or other program maker receive 777 permission, which grants complete access to anyone on the system. Directories usually receive 777 permission as well. You can change permissions after creation only if you own the file.

Default security

You can also change the default permission with a umask, which is a value set in a shell and passed to child processes. A umask is a number, usually set in octal, that sets permission when subtracted from the default creation mask. The most frequently used values are 022, 002, 026, or even 077 for secretive people.

umasks provide the best way to institute some security on your system. You can optimally implement them in shell startup scripts so that each session has the same value. My umask is 022, denying anyone else write access to my files unless I explicitly allow it by changing the permissions.

Guru: How umask Works

Strictly speaking, umask works by taking the default permissions and performing a logical AND on them. Follow step by step how this works:

1. umask = 026 (octal)

2. umask = 000010110 (binary)

3. complement = 111101001

4. default = 110110110

5. logical AND = 110100000

The permissions are therefore 640, owner read/write and group read-only.

Changing permissions

To change file permissions, use the standard command chmod. In the simplest form, chmod takes a mode-pattern and applies it to a list of files. Mode-patterns can be fairly complicated, though. The chmod command takes one command-line argument, -R, which tells chmod to apply the changes recursively down any directory hierarchies listed on the command line.

The simplest mode-pattern specifies an octal integer and assigns that value to the files. Commonly, this takes the form of a command such as chmod 644. This allows only one octal integer per command and converts all files to that permission.

Alternatively, you can use a symbolic mode change, which provides comma-separated commands for chmod to understand. The format takes a who specification, an operation specification, and a permissions specification. The specifications and operations take the form of a single letter, as outlined in Table 8-4.

Table 8-4   chmod Specifications

Specification	Command	What It Does
Who	U	Grants or denies access to the user/owner
	G	Grants or denies access to the group
	O	Grants or denies access to other/world
	A	Grants or denies access to all
Operation	+	Adds permission (for example, +r grants read permission)
	-	Subtracts permission (for example, -x denies execute permission)
	=	Sets permission
Permission	R	Specifies read permission
	W	Specifies write permission
	X	Specifies execute (use) permission
	S	Specifies set-UID permission
	X	Specifies directory access bit

The chmod commands can contain complex symbolic permission strings. Table 8-5 illustrates some of the more common strings. If the string doesn't specify a who, the command applies to all bits except those listed in the umask. If no permission is listed, the command is a no-op. The set command takes a second who specification. You can apply multiple operations to a single who list.

Table 8-5   chmod Symbolic Commands

Command	What It Does
go-w	Clears write permission from group and other
a+r	Makes the file universally readable
g=o	Sets the group permissions to those held by the world
o+r-w	Adds read and removes write permission for others

Cross-
Reference

The grammar for the symbolic representation is easily defined for yacc. (See Chapter 41 for more information on yacc.)

Listing 8-2: Grammar for the Symbolic Representation of Yacc

```
symbolic_mode   : section
                | symbolic_mode `,´ section

section         : actions
                | whos actions

whos   : who
                | whos who

who             : `u´ | `g´ | `a´ | `o´

actions         : action
                | actions action

action          : operation
                | operation perms
                | operation pcopy

pcopy           : `u´ | `g´ | `o´

operation       : `+´ | `-´ | `=´

perms           : perm
                | perm perms

perm            : `r´ | `w´ | `x´ | `X´ | `s´
```

The chmod command reports permission errors. You cannot change the permissions of a file that does not belong to you.

Changing owners and groups

You can also change permissions by changing the ownership of a file. Some UNIX systems restrict ownership and group ownership changes to root, so these commands may not work on your system.

The chgrp command changes the group owner of a file. The syntax is chgrp *group-name file-list*. The *group-name* is a string located in the /etc/group file. To make the change, you must own the file or have write permission to it. More secure UNIX systems place even greater restrictions on this command's use. The file's access permissions do not change. The group permissions apply to members of the new group, and members of the old group have access governed by the world permission bits.

Changing ownership involves the chown command, which is also used to change an owner's group. The syntax is similar to chgrp, except that the *group-name* is replaced by either an *owner-name* or a colon-separated *owner-name:group-name* combination. Again, you need to own the file to make this change.

Both commands take an optional flag, -R, which tells the command to apply its changes recursively to files located in directories listed for the command.

Understanding Disk Management

Some system administrators set quotas for their users. Although quotas are not a POSIX requirement, every system has effective quotas, even if they are not explicitly set. These quotas are based on the physical sizes of disk drives. When a disk becomes full, you the user should take the initiative to clean up your files. If you don't, your system administrator will!

Using common commands

When you start working on UNIX, four of the first commands that you learn manipulate your file tree. These commands copy, link, rename, and remove files. Each command has hidden power that most basic texts do not describe.

Story: Updating a Disk Users List

When I managed some systems at Bell Labs, I included an entry in the cron tab to update a list of the top ten disk users on the system automatically and to append the list to the message of the day. By the end of this chapter, you should be able to write that script.

Copying files

The cp command copies files. The standard syntax for this command lists two files and copies the contents of the first file into the second. The cp command is used most commonly with this one-to-one kind of copying and is restricted to copying regular files.

You can copy files in bulk, however. You can list as many files as you'd like and terminate the list with a directory. All these files are copied into the specified directory. Be aware that trees are not copied. For example, if you specify a cp *dir1/file1 dir2* command, the resultant file is *dir2/file1*, not *dir2/dir1/file1*. You can copy only regular files with this option.

Note

Many users make the error of misspelling the target directory's name. Consequently, the cp command does not know that you are trying to write to a directory. If you're copying only one file, a new file is created with the spelling error, and no error message is generated. If the misspelled file has the same name as a file that already exists, data from the misspelled file replaces data from the existing file. In effect, you lose data from the file that existed before the error. This even applies to linked files, so be careful.

Copying trees (a recent and much desired addition to UNIX) provides an even more powerful capability. By specifying the -R or -r option, you can copy intact the entire hierarchy specified by the arguments before the destination directory. For example, cp -r *dir1/file1 dir2* results in the creation of *dir2/dir1/file1*.

Note

Before the addition of the -r option, making an intact copy of a tree required either a lot of patience and shell programming or the use of the tar or cpio administrative tools.

The difference between -r and -R depends on implementation. If you specify -R, cp creates special files in the same hierarchical position as in the source. With -r, the results are not guaranteed. (If you have a raw character device, cp -r may attempt to copy the contents to a regular file and not create a new raw character device.)

Three other standard flags exist for cp: -f, -i, and -p. The -f flag suppresses messages from the system. The -i flag prompts for permission to copy the file before actually making the copy. The -p flag attempts to copy the ownership, permissions, and access time information intact to the new file.

Common errors include attempting to write to a directory where you don't have permission and attempting to copy a list of files to another file. In both cases, an error message occurs, and the original files remain intact.

Linking files

The ln command creates links between files. The most common approach is to link two filenames to each other. In that case, two directory entries exist for the file, but they share the same i-node and the same data.

You cannot create a hard link between directories. You *can* create a bulk link by providing a list of files, followed by a target directory. In this case, every file listed has a link created in that directory. If you specify the -f flag, ln forces the link. If the destination file already exists, it is removed and the link is made. You cannot have hard links between different file systems.

The last option is -s. This creates a symbolic link instead of a hard link. You can create symbolic links to directories, and links are not restricted to the same file system as the original. Currently, UNIX does not provide a command to link trees, but with a symbolic link, there is no need.

Renaming files

The mv command renames files. Usually, this command takes two arguments, an existing file, and a new location. If the new location already exists, an error message is generated.

Secret

Copying a file can be time-consuming. If the two locations are on the same file system, the fastest way to implement mv is by linking the files and unlinking the first file.

UNIX also has a bulk move capability. If the last file is a directory, you can move any number of files into that directory with a single command. If the target file already exists, that file is not moved. mv suffers from the same potential problem as cp: If you are moving a single file to a directory and you mistype the directory name, the command is still valid.

The mv command takes two arguments, and each is mutually exclusive. The -f argument forces a move. If the target file already exists, the target file is deleted. The -i option prompts for confirmation if the file already exists.

Removing files

The last common command, rm, removes files. This is a very powerful and dangerous command. It removes every file listed on the command line, with the exception of currently executing binaries and files where you lack permission.

Secret

The rm command does not actually remove the file. Instead, it removes the directory entry and reduces the link count in the i-node by one. When that link count drops to zero and the last process using the data closes the file, the operating system frees the space used.

The rm command takes four arguments. The -f argument causes rm to give no output. (Errors are normally output if permission problems exist.) The -i argument prompts you to approve each filename before deleting the file. Any novice user should use this argument. Without it, you may delete important files without the opportunity for correction. The -r and -R arguments remove entire hierarchies.

Note

If you cannot remove a file under a hierarchy, the parent directories also remain intact.

Caution

The `rm -r` command is one of the most dangerous on UNIX. This command can destroy an entire hierarchy of data. Used in the wrong place, `rm -r` can destroy months or years of work.

Understanding directory creation and obliteration

The preceding commands work primarily on regular files and require special options to work on directories. UNIX provides two commands explicitly for manipulating directories: `mkdir` and `rmdir`.

Creating a directory

The `mkdir` command creates a new directory. In its simplest form, it takes a single argument and creates a directory with that name.

Power users can create multiple directories with a single `mkdir` command by listing all the desired directories on the command line. Two arguments change `mkdir`'s behavior. The `-m` argument takes a mode, either octal or symbolic, and assigns that mode to the newly created directories. The `-p` argument forces the creation of any intermediate directories and the specified directory.

If you do not have write permission in the parent directory, the new directory is not created. If the directory already exists or if a file exists instead of a directory, an error occurs.

Using the rmdir command

The `rmdir` command removes directories, and it removes a single directory more simply than `rm`. The `rmdir` command removes empty directories on the command line. If a directory has any entries beyond . and .., `rmdir` won't remove it.

The `rmdir` command takes a single argument, `-p`, to remove all directories in a tree while they are empty.

Creating special files

UNIX provides two additional commands for making special files, `mkfifo` and `mknod`. The `mknod` command is not supported by POSIX. Check your local manual page to determine whether these commands are present on your system. (Type **man mkfifo** or **man mknod**. If your system gives you usage information, you have the command. Otherwise, you probably don't.)

The mkfifo command creates a named pipe and as many files as are listed on the command line. If the -m flag is specified, mkfifo creates them with the specified permissions.

Determining free disk space

UNIX also uses the following commands for disk management: df, du, and ulimit. The df command determines how much free disk space and how many i-nodes exist on a disk partition. The df command is important when you attempt to determine how much space is available for further work. The default df command takes no arguments and lists the amount of space used. Here is some standard output:

```
/               (/dev/hdb1      ):  260876 blocks    93059 files
/home           (/dev/sda1      ):  485400 blocks    17280 files
```

The first column contains the mount point for a given file system. Following this, the physical device being mounted appears in parentheses. (Remember that everything in UNIX is a file, including a file system!) The next number is the free block count, in 512-byte blocks. The last number shows how many files are present on that file system.

The -k option gives the file sizes in 1,024-byte blocks. The output format is different because it is based on the BSD output:

```
Filesystem       1024-blocks  Used  Available Capacity Mounted on
/dev/hdb1           1163199  972661   130438     88%    /
/dev/sda1           1003894  709330   242700     75%    /home
```

The first column contains the actual device name for a file system. The second column contains a count of the file system's actual size, in kilobyte blocks. Using these numbers, you can see that I have 1,191,115,776 bytes of storage available on the root partition and 1,027,987,456 bytes on the /home disk. The third column lists the number of used blocks, and the fourth column lists the number of available blocks. The fifth column contains a percentage of used disk space, and the last column contains the file system mount point.

Remember that one kilobyte does not equal 1,000 bytes and that one megabyte does not equal 1,000 kilobytes. The original Latin meanings of the prefixes suggest as much, but because computers work in binary, they've been replaced by increments of 2^{10}, or 1,024. Therefore, one kilobyte really equals 1,024 bytes; 1,000 kilobytes is 24,576 bytes short of a megabyte; and a gigabyte is 1,073,741,824 bytes or 73 million bytes more than the original Latin suggests.

I've already illustrated the differences between BSD and SYSV df output, and both are still very common.

The -P option gives POSIX-like output, which resembles BSD on systems that support it.

The df -t command generates the last output style. The -t option gives complete output in a SYSV-like fashion. Data is arranged in 512-byte blocks, and both block and i-node data are presented:

```
/               (/dev/hdb1      ):    260876 blocks    93059 files
                total: 2326398 blocks   301056 files
/usr            (/dev/sda1      ):    485400 blocks    17280 files
                total: 2007788 blocks   260096 files
```

Most experienced users prefer the BSD output format because it makes using tools such as sed and awk easier.

One last option, not supported by POSIX but still often found, is -i, which counts i-nodes. Here's what i-node output looks like:

```
Filesystem      I-nodes    IUsed    IFree  %IUsed Mounted on
/dev/hdb1       301056     93059   207997    31%  /
/dev/sda1       260096     17280   242816     7%  /home
```

Remember that df considers *files* and *i-nodes* to be the same because a one-to-one relationship exists between i-nodes and data blocks.

The df command can also take a file or a list of files as arguments. When those arguments are present, only file systems that contain the named files are printed on the output.

Disk usage

The df command is useful, but it applies only to file systems. To determine how an individual is using disk space, use the du command.

The du command, followed by a directory name, supplies a list of all the directories in the specified file tree. The numbers provided are cumulative for all subtrees. Listing 8-3 illustrates du on my bin directory.

Listing 8-3: Output of du ~james/bin

```
392     /home/james/bin/src/shar
2066    /home/james/bin/src
76      /home/james/bin/CShells
112     /home/james/bin/Shells
156     /home/james/bin/wishlists
2       /home/james/bin/.hidden
13550   /home/james/bin
```

Notice that only subdirectories are listed. If no argument is given, the current directory is checked. If a filename that is not a directory is given, there is no output. The number listed is the number of 512-byte blocks used by the file hierarchy.

The du command has four flags. The -k flag is similar to the -k flag for df. The output is listed in kilobyte blocks as opposed to 512-byte blocks. The -a flag gives output for all listed files. The numbers should match with `ls -ls`. Listing 8-4 illustrates this output.

Listing 8-4: Output of du ~james/bin, Truncated to Show First Ten Entries

```
22      /home/james/bin/src/shar/README
82      /home/james/bin/src/shar/shar.c
4       /home/james/bin/src/shar/unshar.1
24      /home/james/bin/src/shar/unshar.c
4       /home/james/bin/src/shar/uushar.c
8       /home/james/bin/src/shar/who@where.c
50      /home/james/bin/src/shar/unshar
172     /home/james/bin/src/shar/shar.shar
16      /home/james/bin/src/shar/shar.1
8       /home/james/bin/src/shar/Makefile
```

The `-s` flag produces a summary of the disk usage for the named directory. Instead of itemizing all the subdirectories, it produces one number:

```
13550   /home/james/bin
```

The `-x` option makes `du` ignore files located on different file systems. This way, you check only the data stored on the local disk under a given directory.

Summary

This chapter introduced file system permissions and disk limits. It covered the following topics:

▶ Checking and creating file permissions

▶ Sticky bits

▶ Changing file ownership

▶ Common disk commands

▶ Creating and obliterating directories

▶ Creating special files

▶ Determining free disk space

The next chapter teaches you how to combine disk and shell commands.

Chapter 9

Combining Disk and Shell Commands

In This Chapter

▶ Integrating file system tools

▶ Integrating the file system with the shell and accounts

▶ Counting files

▶ Counting directory entries

▶ Calculating disk hogs

This chapter covers the commands that examine entries in your directory tree. You can use two powerful tools, ls and find, to search for files and several tools to examine their contents. This chapter also shows you some tools that modify your file hierarchy.

Integrating File System Tools

The real power of UNIX tools comes not only from the tools themselves, but also from how you use the tools in concert with each other. This is called *integration*. When you mix the tools together, the combination is more powerful than the sum of its parts.

Note

UNIX tools are designed to work well together. Tools such as xargs are designed exclusively for use with other UNIX commands. This approach differs from some other operating systems, where tools are designed to stand alone. You need to decide which approach you prefer.

Suppose that you wanted to retrieve the last modification date for every file on a system that includes your user name. How would you go about doing this? A novice user might change directories, looking for files. But with over 100,000 files on a system, how long would it take to look at them all? An hour? A week?

A more sophisticated user might think that this is a job for pattern matching. `*$LOGNAME*` would match the name for a file, so `/*$LOGNAME*` would match any file in root, `/*/*$LOGNAME*` would match any file in a directory under root, and so forth. But when do you know that enough is enough?

This case calls for integration. The `find` command is ideal for finding the files. You just execute the `ls` command for each file found. The command is simple:

```
find / -name "*$LOGNAME*" -exec ls -ld {} \;
```

The `-exec` argument to `find` enables you to embed a command in the `find` command so that every time a file matches the pattern, `ls` is run against that file with the `-ld` argument. On my system at home, this takes about 12 minutes to run. A faster option is available: the `-exec` request spawns a process for each file found. An obvious solution is to use `xargs` at the end of a pipeline:

```
find / -name "*$LOGNAME*" -print | xargs ls -ld
```

Instead of running a separate `ls` command for every file found, this command runs `ls` once, with a long list of arguments for evaluation. Running the command this way reduces the system overhead. This command runs in about ten minutes. Of course, running these tests depends even more on the other users of the system. The only fair measurement is to run the tests simultaneously.

You may also want to determine how recently a file in a given directory was changed. The directory modification time does not reflect the last modified time of a component file, just the last time the directory changed. Access time is the last time anyone looked at the directory. The status change time does not reflect the last time a file changed.

You can use the `ls -l` command yet again, but you want only the most recently changed file. The best approach uses standard `ls` output, sorts it so that the least recently changed file is first, and grabs only the last entry. The `tail` command is perfect for this, and your command becomes

```
ls -ltr dir | tail -1
```

If you want to use this more than once, you'll be better off creating a K shell procedure and invoking it as follows:

```
dirmod () {
ls -ltr $1 | tail -1
}
dirmod ~/bin
drwxr-xr-x   2 james    admin        1024 Sep 10 17:39 Shells/
```

Note

This procedure can work with the `head` command and regular sorting, but remember that the first line of output is a count of blocks in a directory.

Integrating the File System with the Shell and Accounts

As previously mentioned, using the tools together increases your productivity. Having learned how to use shell, account, and file system commands individually, you should now learn how to integrate them.

The shell provides tools for input, for controlling execution flow, and for conditional execution. The accounting commands provide system access information. Although you won't usually use the three together, you can combine these tools to solve some problems.

You may want to peruse a directory and delete a file according to how old it is. You could combine a find and an rm -i, but this doesn't tell you how old the file is. A better approach might be to include the files in a for loop, print the last modified time, and ask about deletion, like this:

```
rmcheck () {
for file
do
        ls -ld $file
        rm -i $file
done
```

This function steps through the arguments, prints the latest ls -l data for the file (which gives you the last modified time), and calls rm -i, the file removal command that prompts for confirmation. This works if you just want to delete files, but what if you also need to save a file, to move a file, or to perform any other action?

In these cases, you build a more complicated function for rmcheck. (You may also need to rename it.) Print the file data with ls -l, give a menu, and prompt for input. You can then use a case statement based on the user's input.

procfile, illustrated in Listing 9-1, is an even more advanced command.

Listing 9-1: The procfile Command

```
procfile() {
for file
do
        ls -ld $file
        printmenu
        read command
        case "$command" in
        d*|D*)  rm -i $file ;;
        m*|M*)  echo "Destination:  \c"
                read dest
                mv $file $dest;;
        c*|C*)  cat $file;;
        h*|H*)  head $file;;
```

```
        esac
done

printmenu( ) {
echo d- delete the file
echo m- move the file
echo c- print the file
echo h- show the top of the file
echo " "
echo "Your command:  \c"
}
```

With this more complicated command, you can delete the file, move it to a new location, or list the contents. A simple `case` statement differentiates your commands and performs various actions. Another function includes the menu of commands in case you need it for other purposes.

Secret

This procedure not only illustrates the integration of different commands, but also provides an example of shell programming. Simple shell programs are easier to write and debug than compiled languages.

This command is expandable. You can add commands to determine the file type, change its permissions, or even give it away.

Looking at Some Examples

This section presents three examples of using commands to retrieve basic information. I explain what I did to obtain the count of my files and directories (see "In This Chapter" in Chapter 7) and to determine the top ten disk users on the Bell Labs system (see "Story: Updating a Disk Users List" in Chapter 8).

Counting files

The first example obtains a count of files on a system. By now, you should know the `df` tool. By using `df` without arguments, I can count the number of free blocks and the number of files created. I just need to add the two numbers, as follows:

```
/               (/dev/hdb1      ):  260876 blocks   93059 files
/home           (/dev/sda1      ):  485400 blocks   17280 files
```

The sum gives me the 110,339 answer provided in the Note at the beginning of Chapter 7.

Counting directory entries

I also mentioned a count of directory entries at the beginning of Chapter 7. Because directory entries are different from files (multiple directory entries may point to the same file), a count of files produced by df would be inadequate. Instead, you need to run a find and count the output, as follows:

```
find / -print | wc -l
```

This gives a count of directory entries found.

Calculating disk hogs

Calculating disk hogs proved the most complicated of these three tasks. I assumed that every directory under /home was a user's home directory and that all the files under /home belonged to that user. Thus, I concluded that du -s would provide me with the total disk usage for a user. I just needed to sort the output and take the top ten offenders, as follows:

```
du -s /home/* | sort -nr | head
```

With the -nr options, sort asks for a numerical sort in reverse order. (Chapter 12 discusses the sort command.) That top ten list would be produced every night and then added to the message-of-the-day file. That way, anyone logging in would see whether he or she was the disk hog for the day.

Note

Administrators use the "message-of-the-day" file, /etc/motd, to pass important messages to the users when they log in. The user is always presented with the file when using a standard shell.

Secret

Access to /etc/motd is part of the default shell startup scripts. An administrator can remove the relevant line, usually cat /etc/motd, because the user does not need to see the message.

Summary

This wraps up the disk commands. The next chapter deals with using editors to modify text within a file and using stream editors and filters to modify streams of data.

Part IV

Editing

Chapter 10

Editing with ed

In This Chapter

▶ Using the `ed` command

▶ Working with basic command formats

▶ Getting help

▶ Loading a file

▶ Showing data

▶ Adding, deleting, and changing text

▶ Performing searches

▶ Marking text

▶ Sending text to output and exiting

▶ Using simple regular expressions, special characters, character lists, and matching words

▶ Working with patterns

Simply put, editing is a technique by which a user alters the contents of a file or data stream. Files and data streams are usually in ASCII, but some editors can handle nonprintable data in other forms.

At the heart of editing is pattern matching. Matching arbitrary text strings is trickier than matching filenames (which is described in previous chapters). Within UNIX, a syntax called *regular expressions* has been developed to create pattern-matching strings. Regular expressions help out in both file and stream editors, and their use has expanded to other situations in UNIX where pattern matching is useful.

The two most commonly used UNIX editors are `vi` and `emacs`. Many others exist beyond these two, such as `pico` (the Pine composer), `ex` (a line-based version of the `vi` screen editor), and some commercial products. The `vi` editor is defined as part of the POSIX specification for UNIX; `emacs` is not.

Before either of these editors was developed, people used UNIX's first editor, `ed`. Even today, `ed` is the only editor guaranteed to appear on any UNIX system—if it isn't present, the system is broken. Any UNIX guru must understand `ed`, even if she doesn't use it, because other tools, such as `sed`, build on it.

Story: The Value of ed

I first seriously used UNIX in 1981 when I spent a summer at Duke University writing a statistical analysis package for the Department of Cardiology. This was an independent study project with Dr. William Smith, the first UNIX zealot that I met outside Bell Labs. I owe him a debt of gratitude because he set me on the path to becoming a UNIX guru.

I wrote the project on a PDP-11, using a very old version of UNIX. It had no full-screen editors, and ed was the only editing tool available. I became fairly adept at using ed and resisted moving to vi when it became available to me in graduate school. Even today, some of my editing techniques are based on a line-editing philosophy. I now use vi fairly regularly and have dabbled with some of the other editors, but my knowledge of ed is still useful for dealing with crashed systems. I also must admit that I'm surprised at the number of new UNIX professionals who don't know any ed or regular expressions — so many tools are consequently lost to them.

Using ed

As previously mentioned, ed is the only editor to appear on every properly configured UNIX system, and a knowledge of ed is important for using other UNIX commands. Before moving on to other editors, users who intend to become UNIX experts should at least use ed long enough to become familiar with its basic concepts.

Starting ed

You start ed by typing **ed** at the command line. You can specify a filename if you want. If you don't specify a file, a temporary file is created, and the editor manipulates an empty buffer. When you write the file, you must specify the filename for output, and that file is created.

The ed command takes only two arguments. The -p argument specifies a command prompt. By default, no command prompt is provided. I find no need for a prompt, but some users might. It serves purely as a convenience.

The -s argument suppresses some output related to editing and writing files and to shell escapes. Again, this is not a frequently used option, and its effect is merely cosmetic.

Basic command formats

The ed editor's commands are single letters, sometimes with additional text, and some have address specifications. You should consider ed a *bimodal* editor: When it is in *command mode,* you can't input text, and when it is in *text-input mode,* you can't run a command.

Note

In principle, bimodal commands are considered weaker than single-modal commands. Single-modal editors can cause problems because they don't enable you to base commands on the printable character set, so you end up with commands such as `<Control-Meta-Character>`, which may confuse novice users. Because ed should function in the starkest environment possible, it can't assume that these special characters will be available for commands and must rely exclusively on the default keyboard.

Address specifications

Address specifications are either a line number, a range specification, a mark character, or a regular expression. Addresses may have mathematical offsets.

You can use several special characters for lines. The dot (.) character refers to the current line. For many commands, the . may be omitted because the command's default refers to the current line. The dollar sign ($) character refers to the last line in the file. You don't need a special character to refer to the first line because it is always line number 1.

With ed, you can mark a location in the file with the k command. You can refer back to this mark when addressing a command.

You can address lines with regular expressions. When you enclose a regular expression in slash marks (/), the next line to match the regular expression functions as the address. If the search finds no lines to the end of the file, the search wraps to the beginning of the file and continues until either the pattern is matched or all lines in the file are exhausted.

If the regular expression is enclosed in question marks (?), the search starts at the previous line and moves backwards until it matches the expression. Again, it wraps from the beginning of the file to the end. You can repeat a regular expression search with //. POSIX does not specify a reverse-repeated search with ??, but many implementations support this.

Note

Regardless of the direction in which you're searching, the regular expression does not look at the current line until it has exhausted all other possibilities.

Note

To use a slash or a question mark in a regular expression, escape it with a backslash. For example, ?\?? looks for the last instance of a question mark in your file.

You can also specify relative addresses. If a line number is included, you can modify it with a +# or a -#. That number is added to or subtracted from the address found, and then used. If no number is specified, a number is assumed. Because these addresses are cumulative, you can specify a sequence of plus signs and minus signs to move that many lines. For example, .+++ refers to three lines after the current line, and $ - 6 refers to six lines before the end of the file. An address can begin with the arithmetic sign. In this case, the current line is assumed to be the base. When modifying an existing address, you can omit the plus sign if the number is present. For example, a pattern such as /RE/4 refers to an address four lines after the next line matching the specified regular expression.

When two addresses are separated by a comma, the operation is applied to both addresses and to all those in between them. The address specification a,++ applies the command to all lines between the line marked with the letter *a* and two lines past the current line. Similarly, ?RE?,//- applies the command to all lines between the last occurrence of a specified regular expression and the line before the next occurrence of that expression.

Two special characters represent standard ranges. The comma (,) represents all lines in the file. Note that the command entered has no parentheses. For example, use 1,51 to list lines 1 through 5. The semicolon (;) represents every line from the current line to the end of the file.

The second line in an address specification must follow the first, or else the results are undefined. Commands must appear one on a line, although three commands can optionally follow a command: p, 1 (ell), and n, which send the results of a command to output.

Getting help

The ed editor has a rudimentary help subsystem. Should you see an error (usually indicated with a single question mark), the h command gives you a brief message explaining the reasons for the error.

If you specify H, the help mode toggles on and off. When help mode is on, you'll see a short explanation whenever you encounter an error.

Loading a file

Normally, a file is listed on the command line. This file is automatically loaded into the editor's input buffer, with the current line set to the first line.

You can use the e command, followed by a filename, with the editor in command mode. Because e deletes the entire contents of the current buffer, the command asks you whether you want to do this if the buffer has not been written. (You can suppress this warning by using E instead of e as the command.) If you want to purge the buffer without writing, you must follow e with an exclamation point. When e locates the file, standard output prints a count of the number of bytes read (the -s argument suppresses this).

If the file begins with an exclamation point, the subsequent string is interpreted as a UNIX command, and the standard output of that command is loaded into the buffer for editing.

Addresses have no meaning for the e command. If you don't specify a file, e clears the buffer. The specified filename is used for path substitution in later commands.

Showing the data

Five commands show data with ed, and each shows different types of data or changes the behavior of the editor.

- The l command prints the text of the addressed lines on standard output. By default, the address is the current line. If unprintable characters are in the line, they are replaced with a three-digit octal number preceded by a slash. Long lines are split, indicated by a backslash and a new line, and the end of a line is tagged with a dollar sign. The current line is set to the last line printed.

- The n command prints the addressed lines on standard output, prepended with a number and followed by a tab. Again, the last line printed is the new current line.

- The p command works the same way as n, except that no lines are prepended.

- The P command toggles the printing of a prompt in command mode. If a -p argument is specified on the command line, that string is used as a prompt, and prompt mode is on by default. Otherwise, the prompt is an asterisk and is initially disabled.

- The = command prints the number of lines in the buffer or file, or it prints the line number specified by the address.

Entering an address on the command line, followed by a carriage return, prints the specified line and sets the current line to the last specified line. If no address is specified, the next line is printed, and the current line is incremented to that line.

Adding text

Four commands add text to the buffer. The most widely used of these commands open a new line in the buffer and enable you to keep typing. The a command places the new line behind the current line, and the i command places it before the current line. If an address is specified, the text is placed relative to that line.

A user enters text directly from the keyboard without being prompted. Lines are copied intact. The ed editor provides neither automatic line wrapping nor any of the other automatic features found in more advanced editors. To stop entering text, enter a . alone on a line. This halts input mode and returns you to command mode.

A novice user may not understand how you enter a line into a file that is just a dot. Well, it can be done fairly easily. See whether you can figure it out. If not, I explain it later in the chapter.

You can also use the r command to copy a file into the buffer. If no address is specified, the file is appended to the last line in the buffer. If you specify the line number 0, the file is added at the beginning of the buffer. The operation is similar to the e command, except that the pathname is unchanged. If no pathname exists, the pathname is set to the specified file. If no file is specified, the file at the specified pathname is reread. If the filename begins with an exclamation point, the remaining filename is treated as a command, and the standard output is substituted.

You can also copy lines of text to new locations within the file. The ed editor does not have a cut and paste feature. Instead, you need to specify a line or lines and a destination. The t command, followed by an address, copies the specified lines to the position immediately after the designated address.

The address 0 is valid to copy lines to the beginning of the file. For example, ;t0 copies every line from the current line to the end of the file to the beginning of the file.

Deleting text

The d command deletes text. It takes a range of addresses, and those lines are removed from the buffer. If you do not specify a range or an address, the current line is deleted. The new current line is the first line after the deleted segment. If the deleted range extends to the end of the file, the current line number becomes the last line in the file.

The u command relates to deletion. It undoes the effects of the previous command (except for changing the file being edited). The edit buffer and the current line are reset to the values they had before the command executed.

Note

You can undo an undo command, but after you've run a subsequent command, you can't undo a previous command.

Changing text

An editor really needs to change text within a file. The ed editor provides five different commands for changing a given line of text.

■ The c command takes an address specification and deletes the lines associated with the address from the file. It then enters input mode, and you can type in new data to replace the deleted line, ending input with a period alone on a line. If you do not specify an address, the current line is assumed.

Note

The c command followed immediately by the single dot is the same as the d command.

- The f command changes the remembered pathname to the specified path and prints the new pathname. If no path is specified, the remembered path is printed.

- The j command joins the specified lines by deleting intermediate new-line characters. If only one line is specified, the command does nothing. The current line is set to the newly combined lines. If no lines are specified, the current line and the next line are joined.

- The m command moves text from the specified addresses to the position immediately after the designated address. The designated address follows the m, and the specified addresses precede it. If you do not specify addresses, the current line is assumed. The designated address must not be between the specified addresses.

- The exclamation point (!) command, when followed by a second !, takes the current or specified lines as standard input to the command following the exclamation points and replaces that text with the standard output (and error) of the command. Within the shell command, the percent (%) character is replaced by the current pathname from memory. The ! command without the second ! is a shell escape. The command runs, but it sends the output to the screen.

Text substitution

The most complicated and most useful command for ed is the substitution command, s. This command takes an address specification and is followed by a delimiter, a regular expression, a delimiter, replacement text, a delimiter, and flags. The last delimiter and flags are optional.

A *delimiter* is a character, other than space or new line, that immediately follows the s. Normally, the delimiter is the slash (/), but you can specify any other character. I use the slash unless I am modifying paths, in which case I use either a dot or a comma. What you use is entirely up to you.

Regular expressions are strings used to match text patterns, and those text patterns are removed from the file and replaced by the replacement text.

Replacement text can be anything, including a new line escaped with a backslash (\), but some characters have special meaning. An ampersand (&) in the replacement text includes the regular expression matched in the replacement text at this point. To include an ampersand in the replacement text, escape it with a backslash. If a digit follows a backslash, a marked piece of the regular expression is included at this point. If the entire replacement string is a percent sign (%), the previous replacement string is used. If any other characters appear with the %, the sign's special meaning is lost. The delimiter character can reside in the replacement string if it is escaped.

You can use three possible flags. The g flag makes the replacement globally in the file. If you do not specify g, only the first occurrence of the regular expression is replaced. An integer replaces the regular expression up to that integer number of times in the line. The flags l, n, and p, tell the editor to run the l, n, or p command on each line in which a substitution occurs. Here are examples of replacement strings:

```
,s/RE/"&"/2n
s/james/James/
/James/s/Dave/my friend, Dave/g
```

The first command searches the entire file for a regular expression, encloses the second occurrence of each regular expression in a given line within quotation marks, and prints each changed line with the line number. The second command looks for james in the current line and capitalizes it. The last command looks for the next line with James in it and replaces every occurrence of the string Dave with the string my friend, Dave.

Secret

You should be able to guess how to enter a line with a single dot on it by now. Just place a simple text pattern, such as dot, on the line and terminate input on the next line. Then, use a substitution command to replace that text with the period: s/dot/./. That's it.

Global commands

Sometimes, you want to apply a command only to some specified lines in a file instead of to a range. For this, four commands apply commands globally to a file. They fit a matrix, and each takes a regular expression and selects lines that either match or don't match the regular expression. Two interactively prompt before applying the command list, and two apply it regardless. The commands look like these examples:

	Match RE	Don't Match RE
Prompt per line	G	V
Apply without prompting	g	v

Each global command takes a range of addresses (or uses the entire file if you do not specify a range) and checks for each line that matches the supplied regular expression. Each matching line is tagged, and the specified command runs on that line. If the interactive command runs, it prompts you at each line before the specified command executes on that line. Here are examples of global commands:

```
g/RE/p
;G/RE/s/RE2/"fish"/p{
v/RE/j
v/RE/m0
```

The first example searches the file for every line that matches the specified regular expression and then prints those lines. The second looks for the first regular expression on every line from the current line to the end of the file and prompts for permission to perform a replacement of the second regular expression with the word *"fish"* in quotation marks. The third example looks for lines without a regular expression and joins the next line to that line. The last example prompts you before moving any lines that don't include the regular expression to the front of the file.

Searching

The ed editor has no specific mechanism for searching, but consider the implications of the null command when printing. When you specify an address, that line prints, and the current line is set to that line. Thus, if you use a regular expression as your address, you effectively search to that line. Similarly, a single slash (/) repeats that search, and you can continue to enter slashes until you find the line you want.

Marking text

The k command marks the specified address with a single character. This character must be lowercase. You can subsequently address this line with the single character preceded by a single quotation mark. The current line number is unchanged.

Outputting text and exiting

To save the current buffer, use the w command. The remembered pathname is written, unless you specify a new pathname. The total number of bytes written is produced on standard output.

When you're finished, use the q command to quit ed. If the buffer has been modified since the last write, you'll see a warning, and to exit, you must add an exclamation point (!) after the q. A Q circumvents this check.

Using Regular Expressions

As you've seen, the ed editor makes tremendous use of regular expressions. The vi and emacs editors also use regular expressions, as do other UNIX commands. You need to understand regular expressions to make full use of these commands. I haven't come across many cogent explanations for the full syntax of regular expressions. Usually, beginning UNIX books simplify the regular expression syntax to the point of error.

Simple regular expressions

The simplest regular expression matches characters one to one. Any single character (except those described in the following section as special characters) is matched to the exact same character in a pattern. If more than one character is present, all the characters must match in the same order for a match to occur. Table 10-1 illustrates some simple regular expressions, text strings, and matches.

Table 10-1   Simple Regular Expressions

Regular Expression	Text String	Match?
James	James Armstrong	Yes
James	james@sagarmatha.com	No
James	Louise Jameson	Yes
James A	James ate here	No
James A	James Armstrong ate here	Yes

What Table 10-1 illustrates is important: Regular expressions are case-sensitive, and even whitespace must match exactly if the pattern is to match.

Story: Simplifying to a Fault

A case in point is my friend Dave Taylor's book *Teach Yourself UNIX*. Early in his book, he introduces regular expressions with the sentence "If you understood the * and ? of filename wildcards, you've learned the key lesson of regular expressions: special characters can match zero or more letters in a pattern." Dave goes on to explain that a single dot (.) is used the same way as a question mark (?) in filename expansion, but his writing can mislead people into thinking that the asterisk can match any number of characters. This is not the case. Dave's writing is not incorrect because he doesn't explicitly say this, but it is misleading.

Special characters

Several special characters are used in regular expressions. To match any of these characters, escape them with a backslash so that they are interpreted literally.

A single dot matches any character. The correspondence of the dot must be one-to-one for a specific character. The regular expression J.m.s matches both James and Jim's, but it does not match Jamie's. A dot alone matches any string that is one character long or longer. It does not match zero-length strings.

The circumflex (^) character matches the beginning of a line. This anchors a pattern to the beginning of a line. The regular expression ^James matches James ate with me., but it does not match I ate with James.

The dollar sign ($) character matches the end of a line. Like ^, this anchors a pattern, but to the end of a line. For example, the regular expression James.$ matches I ate with James. but not James ate with me.

Secret

So far, I have treated regular expressions as if they operate on single lines only, in which case a new line is considered a line terminator. For the purposes of editors and most stream-editing tools, this is true; but the UNIX regular expression library (the programs that interpret regular expressions) is designed to work on arbitrary strings. In these cases, a new line may be a component of either the regular expression or the text string and is matched like any other character. The ^ and $ anchors then refer to the beginning and end of the string.

Note

The ^ and $ anchors have their special meaning only when they appear at the beginning or end of a string, respectively. For example, $a matches a dollar sign followed by the letter *a* wherever that pattern occurs; similarly, b^ matches the letter *b* followed by a circumflex.

You can combine the two anchors to force an entire string to match a regular expression. The limiting case is ^$, which matches a zero-length string.

Note

The circumflex has special meaning in character lists as well.

Character lists

You can specify a range of characters to match by enclosing a list of characters within square brackets. To match this expression, a single character must be the same as one of those enclosed in the brackets.

The regular expression [aeiou] matches a single lowercase vowel. To identify two vowels in succession, use [aeiou][aeiou]. When included in a simple regular expression, a bracketed character list still forces a single-character match. For example, J[abxyz]m.s matches James but fails on Jim's.

Character lists can include ranges and negation. If a character list has two characters separated by a dash, all the characters found on the character tables between those two characters are a valid match. The ranges used most often are [0-9], which indicates all digits, and [a-z], which indicates all lowercase letters. You can combine ranges. For example, [0-9a-z] matches all digits and lowercase letters. To match any character except those in the list, include the circumflex as the first character in the list. For example, [^a-z] matches any character except a lowercase letter.

Some special cases crop up in character lists. To include a circumflex in the list to match, do not make it the first entry in the list, unless you escape it.

The dash and the close bracket have the opposite problem. If they are first in the list, they are part of the pattern; otherwise, they are used to define patterns. Again, a backslash escapes their special meaning. Of course, you must escape a backslash with a backslash to make it part of the pattern.

Note

The [a-z] range may match more than you intend unless you are using a machine that understands ASCII. IBM mainframes use a character set called EBCDIC, and the letters of the alphabet are not consecutive in that set. Thus, a range of *a* to *z* on an EBCDIC machine includes more than you'd expect.

Matching words

Because many regular expressions are used to match words, a syntax has developed that enables a regular expression to match word boundaries. *Words* are defined as a string of alphanumeric characters and underscores. The less-than (<) character, escaped, forces a match at the beginning of a word, and the greater-than (>) character forces the match at the end. For example, the regular expression \<James\> matches James Armstrong but not Louise Jameson. Single-side matches are also possible: \<James does match Louise Jameson, for example. Similarly, son\> matches Louise Jameson but not sonata.

Grouping into a pattern

You can group individual elements of regular expressions into patterns. This is particularly useful if you need repetitive patterns or if you have alternative patterns.

To group a series of elements, enclose them in parentheses (( )). Because the parenthesis is also a valid character for matching, prepend a slash to recognize the grouping. If you opt to append a backslash and an integer, the matched subpattern is flagged for use in a replacement pattern for editors.

Multiple iterations of a pattern

You can ask for zero or one occurrences of a pattern by appending a question mark. For example, Jam.?s matches both James and Jams but doesn't match Jamies.

Patterns are repeatable. Use the asterisk (*) to indicate zero or more occurrences of a pattern. For example, Ja*s matches Jas, Jaaaaas, and Js. If you use a plus sign, it must match one or more occurrences. For example, Ja+s matches Jas and Jaaaaas but not Js. (Some variants of UNIX do not support this.)

You can also limit the number of matches for a pattern match to be valid. If you enclose an integer within curly braces ({ }), a string must have exactly that many iterations of the previous pattern for the match to be true. For example, `Ja\{4\}s` matches only `Jaaaas`.

To specify a range within the braces, use two numbers separated by a comma. If the first number is missing, it matches zero iterations, up to the second number. If the second is missing, it must match a minimum of the first number of iterations. When both numbers are missing, a syntax error occurs. For example, `J\(ea\)\{2,4\}s` matches `Jeaeas`, `Jeaeaeas`, and `Jeaeaeaeas` but not `Jeas` or `Jeaeaeaeaeas`.

Alternative patterns

You can match alternative patterns by placing a vertical bar between the patterns. For example, `Ja|ime|'s` matches `James`, `Jam's`, `Jimes`, and `Jim's`. By using pattern grouping and alternatives, you can create some fairly complicated patterns. For example, you can match a header in a mail message with `^\(From:\)|\(Subject:\)`. This matches either `From:` or `Subject:` and requires the match to be anchored at the beginning of a string. Some variants of UNIX do not support this.

As regular expressions have evolved, different features have been added. Depending on how up-to-date the tools are, they may or may not support groupings, specific iterations, and word boundaries.

Regular expressions attempt to match the longest string possible. For example, when matching `J.*s` in `James came over to eat at our house.`, it matches `James came over to eat at our house` as opposed to `James`. If you are using regular expressions in an editor to perform text replacement, be careful.

Some common patterns

Table 10-2 illustrates some common patterns.

Table 10-2   Regular Expressions

Expression Description	Regular Expression
Area codes (prior to 1990)	`[2-9][01][1-9]`
Area codes (after 1990)	`[2-9][0-9]\{2\}`
Telephone numbers (U.S.)	`\<[2-9][0-9]\{2\}-[0-9]\{4\}\>`
Zip codes	`\<[0-9]\{5\}\(-[0-9]\{4\}\)?\>`
Blank lines	`^$`
Entire lines	`.*`

Summary

UNIX uses regular expressions in many locations. You need a strong understanding of regular expressions to get the full power out of some commands.

This wraps up my discussion of the basic UNIX editor, ed. The next chapter deals with the two most common full-screen editors, vi and emacs.

Chapter 11

Using Screen Editors

In This Chapter

▶ Using the vi editor

▶ Moving around the screen with vi

▶ Manipulating text with vi

▶ Working with ex mode and commands

▶ Using the emacs editor

▶ Getting help with emacs

▶ Moving the cursor with emacs

▶ Loading files with emacs

▶ Manipulating text with emacs

▶ Saving and quitting emacs

U NIX users now use screen editors as the standard tools for creating and modifying files. These editors have a lot of functionality that most users do not fully employ. This chapter helps expand your use of these editors.

Note

These editors have a lot more functionality than this chapter can cover. Both editors have been the sole topic of several books. I recommend the following books for more information: *Learning GNU emacs* and *Learning the vi Editor*.

Using the vi Editor

The vi editor was originally written by Bill Joy while he was at the University of California, Berkeley, for use in BSD UNIX. At the time, the only standard editor for UNIX was ed, which is not the best for editing programs and documents because you can operate on only a single line at a time. (Chapter 10 describes ed.)

The vi editor is based on the curses graphics package, which is a set of C library functions and macros for painting a full screen. Cursor movements and text placement functions are easy to write because the library handles the underlying hardware specifics. Without the development of the curses library, tools such as vi would be much harder to implement on a portable basis.

Getting started

To start vi, type **vi** at a command line. You can provide a list of files, a single file, or no files at all. The vi editor loads the first file specified into the buffer and repaints the screen. If you do not specify a file, a buffer is created. That buffer looks something like this:

```
_
~
~
~
~
~
~
"[NO FILE]"  1 line, 1 char
```

The first line is provided with no data, and all subsequent lines are marked with a tilde (~) to indicate that they don't exist. A status line giving a filename (or in this case, notice that no file is specified) and a count of lines and characters appears at the bottom.

If you've specified a file that already exists, its contents are loaded into the buffer, and the status line reflects those contents. The vi editor takes several possible arguments:

■ The -r option attempts to recover previous editing efforts. When a system crashes, you may not have written out the contents of the file, so vi -r attempts to recover them.

Note

Crash recovery is not an easy process. You may not see your last input reflected in the contents of, but the recovered file is at least more recent than your last writing.

Secret

Don't rely on the crash recovery. It is not guaranteed to work correctly. The only way to ensure the accuracy of your file is to write it out on a regular basis.

■ The -R argument makes the vi session read-only. You can examine the file with vi commands, but you can't save any changes that you've made to the content.

■ The -c command provides a list of commands for the editor to run before giving you control of the editor.

■ The -w command specifies the size of the editing window.

■ The -t flag uses a tags file to determine where to start the editing session.

Note

The tags file is useful in software development. A *tags file* lists each function and identifies where it resides in a file. The vi editor accesses this tags file, so vi -t takes you straight to that function in editing. You don't need to track which functions reside in which files if you use tags. Part IX contains more information on tags.

Your version may support two obsolete methods of starting the editor. You can specify a starting line with +*number*, or you can start vi at a pattern with vi -/*RE*. The -c command has superseded both.

The vi editor contains so many commands that this chapter presents only a subset of them.

vi basics

This section briefly details the commands for basic vi operation.

Moving around the screen

Many commands move you around the screen. POSIX defines 52 different commands that change cursor position. For this book's purposes, though, I need to cover only 15. The current cursor position determines where most of these commands move, so cursor positioning is important.

The four arrow keys move the cursor one space in the given direction. Table 11-1 shows which commands mimic these arrow keys. In each case, you can use a number as a prefix to implement the command that many times.

Table 11-1   Direction Commands

Command	Cursor Movement
h	Back one space
j	Down one line
k	Up one line
l	Forward one space

Some *control commands* move the text around one screen at a time. These are marked with a circumflex before a capital letter. Table 11-2 shows which commands move the screen where.

Table 11-2   Control Commands

Command	Movement
^F	Down one screen, placing the cursor at the top
^B	Back a full screen
^U	Up a half screen
^D	Down a half screen

The w, b, and e commands move the cursor to word boundaries, as described in Table 11-3.

Table 11-3	Direction Commands Based on Word Boundaries
Command	**Moves Cursor To**
w	The beginning of the next word
b	The beginning of the previous word
e	The end of the current or next word

Adding text

The vi editor is a bimodal editor, so you need to enter input mode to add text to the file. Commands do not work in input mode.

You can enter input mode four ways. Two are based on the current cursor position, and two open new lines for input. Table 11-4 shows how these commands work.

Table 11-4	Direction Commands Based on Word Boundaries
Command	**Action**
a	Opens input mode immediately after the current cursor position
i	Opens input mode immediately before the cursor
A	Opens input mode at the beginning of the current line
I	Opens input mode at the end of the current line
o	Opens a line below the current line
O	Opens a line above the current line

When you enter input mode, anything you type is entered as text. This continues until you press the Esc key. Escape terminates input mode and returns you to command mode.

Secret

You can duplicate your input by specifying a number before going into input mode. That number inserts that many occurrences of the subsequent input text. For example, 4a gives you four copies of whatever you type.

Secret

Experienced users use Escape to determine their editor's state. When a user presses Escape in command mode, it is an error, and a bell sounds. When a user presses Escape in input mode, input ends, and the cursor is placed over the last input character. Pressing i at this stage returns the editor to input mode.

Changing text

Changing text involves deleting or overwriting existing text with new text. vi includes several commands for this purpose. The most common are cc, C, r, and s.

- The cc command changes the current line. It removes the line from the input buffer and places the editor in input mode. Your input replaces the current line. A number preceding the cc command replaces that many lines, starting at the current line.

- The C command deletes text from the current cursor position to the end of the line and places the editor in input mode.

- The r command replaces a single character with the next character typed.

- The s command substitutes the current character with the characters typed until you exit input mode.

Deleting text

The two simplest ways to delete text are either a line at a time or a letter at a time.

- The dd command deletes one line, but placing a number in front of the dd command deletes that number of lines.

- The D command deletes text from the current cursor position to the end of a line.

- The x command deletes the current character, and X deletes the previous character.

Searching

You can search for regular expressions in vi. The slash (/) command followed by a regular expression moves the cursor to the next occurrence of that regular expression in your text. A question mark (?) moves the cursor back to the previous occurrence of that regular expression. If you do not supply a regular expression, the last specified regular expression is used.

Using cut and paste

Whenever you use dd or D to delete text and whenever you replace text, the deleted text goes to a buffer from which you can paste it into a new location. The p command pastes the contents of buffer after the current line, and P pastes the contents before the current line.

Note

Users experienced with editors on other platforms can consider this buffer a "clipboard." You can copy text into the buffer without deleting it. The yank command copies text. yy copies one or more lines at a time.

You can then copy these lines to a new location in the file.

Using Advanced vi Features

The real power of vi comes from using the editor's advanced features. To become an expert user, you need to learn the advanced commands.

Working in ex mode

One advanced feature of vi is calling ex commands. The ex mode is a line editor, similar to ed, on which vi is based. You can drop out of vi to perform global substitutions, set variables, or write the file. Most ex commands are the same as their counterparts in ed.

Using variables

The ex mode provides several variables that affect the editor's actions. These variables also apply to vi. The set command manipulates these variables. From vi, enter a **colon**, and type **set** followed by variable names and values.

Table 11-5 shows a short list of some important ex/vi variables. Most are on/off toggles and are set with :set var and unset with :set novar.

Table 11-5	ex/vi Variables	
Variable	*Default*	*Description*
autoindent	Off	Maintains indentation levels on new lines
autoprint	On	Writes the line after it has changed
autowrite	Off	Writes the file on a next, tag, edit, suspect, or stop command
beautify	Off	Discards nonprintable characters
ignorecase	Off	Ignores case in searches
list	Off	Marks tabs and the end of the line clearly
number	Off	Displays lines with line numbers

Variable	Default	Description
prompt	On	Prompts with a colon (the syntax is `:set tabstop=#`)
tabstop	8	Specifies the software tab stops in the file
terse	Off	Provides terse error messages
wrapscan	On	Wraps searches around the ends of the buffer

Using ex commands

Most ex commands are similar to their ed counterparts. I find that I can implement global substitutions faster using the ex substitute command, a legacy of my days with ed.

To access any ex command, type a **colon**. This gives you a prompt for ex commands. The substitution syntax is similar enough that I can type **:1,$s/pattern1/pattern2/g** to change every pattern in the file.

Two other commands, map and ab, enable you to specify abbreviations for input and to map other keys. I discuss these commands later in the chapter.

Using words, sentences, and paragraphs

The standard vi commands include several commands such as dd, cc, and yy that apply to a single line. You can apply these and other navigational commands to words, "big words," sentences, and paragraphs.

A *word* is a set of alphanumeric characters separated by punctuation or whitespace. A *big word* is a set of printable characters separated by whitespace. For example, the string ls /var/spool/mail/james has two big words and nine words. (Punctuation is considered a word.) *Sentences* contain punctuation, including a period, and whitespace. Paragraphs are based on blank lines.

The vi definitions are not perfect, but they do an excellent job.

You can change the cursor's position by words, big words, paragraphs, and sentences. Table 11-6 lists these commands.

Table 11-6	vi Commands for Moving the Cursor
Command	**Movement**
w	Moves forward a word
b	Moves backward a word

Continued

Table 11-6	*(continued)*
Command	**Movement**
e	Moves to the end of a word
W	Moves forward a big word
B	Moves backward a big word
E	Moves to the end of a big word
)	Moves forward a sentence
(	Moves backward a sentence
}	Moves forward a paragraph
{	Moves backward a paragraph

Each command can take a number as an argument and execute the command that many times. What's more, you can combine these commands with deleting, changing, and yanking text. By prepending any of these commands with d, you can delete text from the current cursor position to wherever the cursor ends up. For example, d) deletes text from the current cursor position to the end of a sentence. The same applies to c and y for changing and yanking. The y{ command copies the entire text from the beginning of the current paragraph to the current cursor position into the buffer for pasting elsewhere. The cE command deletes the text from the current position to the end of the current big word and puts the editor in input mode.

By manipulating text in grammatical pieces, you can become faster at preparing documents with vi.

Using abbreviations

To create abbreviations for use in documents, use the syntax :ab *str replacement*. By entering commonly repeated text into abbreviations, you can quickly add this repetitive text. For example, if you are writing about the ABC Widgets Company, you can create an abbreviation by typing **:ab abc ABC Widgets Company**. Then, whenever you type **abc**, it is replaced by *ABC Widgets Company.*

Caution

Make sure that your abbreviation string is not something you will likely type as a separate word; otherwise, every time you type it, you may inadvertently replace text.

The command :ab without arguments gives you your current list of abbreviations.

Secret

Abbreviations are particularly useful if you are prone to typographical or spelling errors. Just make your favorite typos an abbreviation for their correct spellings, and the replacements are automatic.

Using keyboard mapping

Even more powerful than abbreviations are keyboard mapping tricks. My keyboard has a key labeled "insert," but if I press it, it just produces a sequence of square brackets. I can map this key to make it a proper insert command by using the command :map, which takes an input string and a desired action.

You'd think that all I'd need to enter is **:map** <insert> **i**, right? Wrong. When I try that, I hear some beeping, and the mapping doesn't work.

Control characters, such as those in the insert key, need to be escaped in their own fashion. I have to type **^V**, which represents Ctrl-V, before pressing insert. I end up typing **:map ^V**<insert> **i**, and now, when I press insert, the editor is placed into input mode.

Note

The Ctrl-V command also inserts control characters into the text of a file.

You can also program the function keys. I use F1 to comment out a line of code. That's **:map ^VF1 I/*^V**<ESC>**A*/^V**<ESC>. It looks cryptic, but it works.

Similarly, you can add other commands to your list of function keys by mapping them. If you so desire, you can even emulate emacs with vi keyboard mappings.

Programming tricks

The vi editor also includes some tricks for programmers. The best is the % command, which seeks out matching pairs of parentheses, curly braces, and square brackets and confirms that everything matches up properly. I've sorted out many a programming bug with this command.

Understanding vi startup files

When you start vi, it looks for the .exrc file. This file contains the commands you want to run at startup. Usually, it includes your abbreviations, keyboard mappings, and variable settings. The name .exrc is a legacy of the ex line editor, and .exrc works for both editors.

Secret

Actually, both editors are the same. Typing :vi in ex puts you in full-screen mode, and typing Q in vi's command mode puts you in ex mode. The mode in which you begin depends on the command used to execute the command.

On-screen commands differ from startup commands primarily because you don't need to type the colon. For example, the syntax for creating abbreviations is just ab `text replacement`.

Using the emacs Editor

The `emacs` editor, the other widely used editor, was developed by Richard Stallman at MIT at about the same time that Bill Joy was developing `vi`. Because of `emacs`'s popularity, many versions are floating about in cyberspace for nearly every operating system.

The `emacs` editor also uses the `curses` library on UNIX, but the similarity with `vi` ends there. The `emacs` editor was originally based on LISP, and the `emacs` startup file still reflects its LISP-like origins. More important, `emacs` is a single-mode editor. If you start typing characters, they appear in your document. On the down side, the editing commands are fairly cryptic, at least when compared with `vi`'s.

Perhaps the hottest arguments you'll find among UNIX professionals relate to their choice of editor. Both editors have their merits, and both have weaknesses. The best editor is the one that works best for you. Try both. One person may prefer `emacs`, and the other may prefer `vi`. Neither person is wrong.

Note

The `emacs` editor has the capability to split windows and edit multiple files, read mail, or run shell commands. The `emacs` editor is also designed to work in an X Windows environment.

Getting started

Normally, to start `emacs`, type **emacs** at the command line. An `emacs` editing buffer is displayed. Because I am using Linux to write this chapter, the Linux version of `emacs` comes up:

```
GNU Emacs 19.25.1 of Wed Aug 17 1994 on adam (i486-linux) Copyright (C) 1994
Free Software Foundation, Inc.
```

Note

The `emacs` editor's commands are key combinations that use the Ctrl and Meta keys. Because `emacs` documentation refers to these keys respectively as C- and M-, so will I. For example, C-c means that you should press Ctrl-C. Furthermore, some commands use multiple key combinations. When written, the elements are separated by single commas. For example, C-x, C-c tells you to press Ctrl-X and then Ctrl-C.

Table 11-7 lists some basic `emacs` commands.

Table 11-7   Basic emacs Commands

Type	To Do This
C-x, u	Undo changes
C-x, C-c	Kill the emacs job
C-h	Call up help
C-h, t	Call up an emacs tutorial
C-h, i	Enter information that you can use to read GNU

GNU Emacs comes with absolutely *no* warranty. (Type C-h, C-w for details.) You may give out copies of emacs. (Type C-h, C-c to see the conditions.) Type C-h, C-d for information on obtaining the latest version. Without a filename as an argument, emacs opens up a scratch editor.

```
--Emacs: *scratch*        (Lisp Interaction)-All--
For information about the GNU Project and its goals, type C-h, C-p.
```

The most obvious argument to emacs is a filename. When a filename is specified, emacs loads the file for editing. When the filename is accompanied by a number following a plus sign, emacs places the cursor at that line in the buffer.

The -q option prevents emacs from loading your startup file. The -u user option loads that user's startup file. If the first argument is -t, emacs runs with that specified file as the output device.

Because emacs is based on LISP, you should expect some LISP processing options. The -f function executes a specified LISP function, and the -l file loads LISP code into the editor. Because emacs will run under X, it also takes standard X toolkit options, as discussed in Part VIII.

Because emacs is not a POSIX-supported program and so many versions of emacs are available, your system may not use these arguments. To determine what you have, type **man emacs**.

emacs basics

Because emacs is a single-mode editor, editing commands cannot be simple characters as they can in vi. The simple characters, when typed, go directly into the edit buffer. Editing commands are instead control characters, Meta characters, or both. The Escape key is also used for commands. Many commands involve two or more key combinations. One of the common starters is C-x. If you already use emacs, these commands should be second nature.

Note

Elsewhere in this book, control characters are signified by the circumflex. Because emacs documentation refers to the Ctrl and Meta keys respectively as C- and M-, so will I. For example, C-c means that you should press Ctrl-C. Furthermore, some commands use two key combinations. When written, they're separated by a comma. For example, C-x, C-c tells you to press Ctrl-X and then Ctrl-C.

Note

You may not see a Meta key on your keyboard. If not, look for an Alt, a cloverleaf, or a diamond key. Try using one of them for Meta.

Getting help

One of emacs biggest wins is its extensive help facility. At any point, you can call up help by typing C-h; any character you type while in help becomes an index into help files. The two best help indexes on my system are C-h, t for an emacs tutorial and C-h, i for a listing of all the help.

On my system, the C-h, i index includes help for other Free Software Foundation tools.

Moving the cursor

Because each character loads into the file by default, you must use Ctrl or Meta key combinations to move the cursor. Table 11-8 lists the cursor movements.

Table 11-8   emacs Cursor Movements

Key Combination	Movement
C-f	Moves forward one character
C-b	Moves back one character
C-n	Moves to the next line
C-p	Moves back one line
M-F	Moves forward one word
M-B	Moves back one word
C-a	Moves to the beginning of a line
C-e	Moves to the end of a line
M-a	Moves to the beginning of a sentence
M-e	Moves to the end of a sentence
C-v	Moves to the next page
M-V	Moves back a page
M-<	Moves to the beginning of the file
M->	Moves to the end of the file

Loading files

In emacs, you can load a file by typing C-x, C-f. You are then prompted to type in a filename. This file then loads into a buffer. You can also open a new window within your emacs session and add a file there. To do this, move the cursor to the location where you want to split the window, and type C-x, 2. Typing C-o moves the cursor across the window divider, and C-x, C-f loads a new file into that window.

You can split windows numerous times. The only restriction is the size of your screen.

Some versions of emacs support splitting a window vertically (C-x, 5). You can delete a window with C-x, 0 (zero). You can also move the window divider with C-x, ^.

The emacs editor tracks each file's buffer, so you can load a new file without destroying the older file buffer. The C-x, C-b command gives you a list of all files with buffers in the current emacs session. You can change buffers quickly from here.

Adding text

Just type. Text appears under your cursor.

Deleting text

Text deletion depends on the current cursor position. You can delete the character at the current cursor position with C-d. The Delete key removes the previously typed character. M-d deletes text from the cursor to the end of the current word, and C-k deletes text from the cursor to the end of the line. To remove the line entirely, press C-k, C-d when the cursor is on the first character in the line.

Using the Meta key, you can delete words and sentences, too. M-Delete deletes the previous word, C-x, Delete deletes the previous sentence, and M-k deletes the rest of the current sentence.

With all these deletion techniques, you may sometimes make an accidental deletion. If you do, type C-x, u, the undo command. Unlike vi's undo, emacs's undo remembers more than one command, so you can step back until you've undone the problem.

Searching

The emacs editor uses two simple search commands: C-s and C-r. C-s is a forward search, and C-r is the reverse search. As you type in the search string, emacs performs the search, and the cursor moves to the end of the search location. Repeatedly pressing C-s searches for subsequent instances.

After you've found what you want, use the Esc key to clear the search buffer. If you never find what you want, use C-g to go back to the beginning.

Saving and quitting

The command to write to a different file is C-x, C-w. This dumps the contents of the buffer to a file. C-x, C-s saves the current file, and C-x, C-c quits emacs.

Using Advanced emacs Features

Like vi, emacs is most useful when you use its advanced features. The emacs editor incorporates several customization features that help speed up your tasks.

Understanding emacs abbreviations

The emacs editor supports abbreviations, although the mechanism is slightly more complex than vi's. Type **M-x abbrev-mode** to enter the abbreviations mode. Then, type the desired abbreviation, C-x, and the expanded text. Press return, and you've created an abbreviation.

Cutting and pasting

Whenever you delete something with emacs, it goes to a clipboard from which you can later paste it into a different section of the file. The C-y command restores text under the current cursor position.

You can set a mark in the buffer with C-space or C-@, and the C-w command deletes from that mark to the current cursor position. If you don't move the cursor when you delete text, the deleted text is added to the clipboard.

If you want to copy text without deleting it, use M-w after setting the mark. This copies the text to the clipboard. M-k and M-d also copy text to the clipboard.

Using advanced input

Besides pasting text from the clipboard, you can overwrite text by entering **M-x overwrite-mode**. When you type in this mode, you replace characters one by one.

The emacs editor also tracks the margins for you and wraps the text when you reach the margin. Press M-q within a paragraph for automatic justification. You can modify several paragraphs by setting a mark and pressing M-g. You can enter automatic fill mode by typing **M-x auto-fill-mode**.

You can set the filling width either to the current cursor position with C-x, f or to a specific number with C-u, *number,* C-x, f.

Understanding the emacs startup file

The emacs editor has a startup file called .emacs. This takes a LISP-like
syntax and contains commands such as "define-key," "global-unset-key," or
"setq" and a key string followed by an attribute. Unlike vi's, this startup file
is not just a list of ex commands. Instead, you can view it as a program with a
different syntax from the editor's to set up the editor.

Using emacs as more than an editor

One reason so many people like emacs is that it functions as more than an
editor. You can read mail, read news, and run shell commands from within
emacs. Some people have actually set up emacs as their default shell.

Summary

Both vi and emacs provide a lot more functionality than I can list in a single
chapter. Indeed, entire books have been written on each.

As to which editor is better, I'm afraid I can say only that the best editor is the
one that enhances your productivity. Personally, I'm more productive in vi than
I am in emacs, but some of my friends are the opposite. Fortunately, UNIX lets us
use our editor of choice. Anything edited in vi can later be edited with emacs,
and vice versa.

I encourage you to play with both editors to determine which works best
for you.

Chapter 12

Using Text Manipulation Commands

You can use other tools besides editors to manipulate a file's text. This chapter introduces the UNIX text manipulation tools.

Simple Text Manipulation

Many tools are designed to search for text and manipulate it within files. Usually, these tools work with both named files and input streams.

Note

An *input stream* is a sequence of bytes, usually ASCII, that is received on the standard input for a tool. This can be output from another command or file redirection. Normally, when you specify a file or files on a command line, the tool opens these files and uses them as standard input. Therefore, command file file file... is the same as cat file file file... | command. The advantage of the first method is that it saves some processing time because only one program executes instead of two.

Most text manipulation commands are easy to use, but the proper use of these commands marks an expert.

Grabbing lines that match patterns

You can use three tools to grab lines that match patterns out of files or streams. The most common is grep, which has two siblings, egrep and fgrep. The standard grep format is grep pattern. Any files follow this pattern. Each line that matches the pattern is printed on standard output.

The grep command

The grep tool uses regular expressions, outlined in Chapter 10. grep may not, however, support the full functionality of regular expressions. Normally, neither the OR pattern nor grouping with parentheses nor word boundary checking with less-than and greater-than signs is supported. The one-or-more option, +, may not be supported. Fortunately, egrep handles these options.

Despite this, grep still remains a useful tool. More often than not, you are looking for a simple word or pattern and don't need the full functionality of regular expressions. I probably use grep more often than any other tool except my editor. Invariably, I'm looking for a specific line in a document or a variable in a program, and grep finds both quickly and easily.

The grep command takes several arguments. Your grep may have fewer or more — check your manual page for the details of your local system. Table 12-1 lists the options required for POSIX conformance.

Table 12-1	grep Options
Option	*Description*
-c	Writes only a count of lines on output
-e	Specifies a list of new line-separated patterns for matching
-f	Specifies a file with a list of patterns, one per line, for matching
-[I]i	Performs matches regardless of case (for example, *a* matches *A*)
-l	Writes only the files that include the pattern
-n	Writes the line number with the line
-q	Produces no output (good for error checking)
-s	Suppresses error messages
-v	Selects lines that do not match the pattern
-x	Matches only lines that entirely match the pattern

Some of these options deserve more consideration. The -e and -f options are particularly interesting. You can specify a set of patterns for matching, such as

```
grep -e "house\
barn" file
```

Then, any line that includes the pattern *house* or the pattern *barn* is listed on standard output. When specified in a file, you need only grep -f *pattern-file file*. If you are likely to look for the same set of patterns repeatedly, it is useful to list them in the file. Furthermore, if you are likely to look for the same patterns in several shell sessions, you can set up an alias, alias mygrep=`grep -f mypatternfile`, so that mygrep now always accesses that file.

Another useful option for shell programming is -q. By running grep -q, you can include the command in a condition without worrying that copious quantities of output will confuse the user. Listing 12-1 illustrates this use.

Listing 12-1: Using grep -q

```
for i in *
do
        if
                grep -iq mother $i
        then
                myprogram $i
        fi
done
```

The egrep command

The egrep command tests data lines against extended regular expressions. egrep supports OR cases, groupings, and word boundaries on most systems. The syntax is the same.

The fgrep command

The fgrep command is for "fast" greps. If the pattern is a string, not a regular expression, use fgrep, which matches only text and thereby avoids the overhead of parsing and matching regular expressions.

POSIX and grep

Future releases of POSIX will declare the egrep and fgrep commands obsolete. Instead, their functionality will be wrapped into grep. When you specify the -E flag, grep functions like egrep. When you specify -F, grep is fgrep. The functions may still exist on your machine as links.

Secret

You may think that the name of a program in UNIX is not important, and thus if you copy a command to a new name, you may expect it to function the same as it did under the old name. That does not always happen. Some programs change their behavior when they execute under different names. The vi and ex editors are an example of this: they are really the same program. The family of grep commands is similarly related.

Dividing files

UNIX provides a handy tool named split for splitting files according to size. By default, it splits files into smaller files, each 1,000 lines long, with names starting at xaa and incrementing through the lowercase letters until you have 676 files named xab, xac, and so forth.

You can specify a different name by listing it after the filename. If you are using standard input, replace the filename with a single dash.

The split command takes three arguments. The -a flag, followed by a number, specifies the length of the filename's suffix. If you specify 3, for example, the filenames start at xaaa and go through xzzz. The -b flag takes a numeric argument and splits the file into files of that many bytes. This number can be followed by a k for kilobytes or an m for megabytes. The last argument, -l, changes the number of lines present in each file. The -l and -b options are mutually exclusive.

Cutting and pasting

UNIX also provides some rudimentary tools for cutting and pasting data in a file. The cut command divides lines in files into different components. It has three primary options: cutting by bytes, cutting by characters, and cutting by fields.

List specification with cut

The cut command operates on a list of fields, which is a group of comma-separated integers and ranges. The format -b 1,5-10,15- means take the first field, the fifth through tenth field, and everything from the fifteenth field onward. These elements are then concatenated and sent to standard output.

Fields do not need to be listed in the same order as in the input, and fields can be repeated.

Byte cutting

With cut -b, you specify a list of bytes to be included in the output from the input. When cut is specified with the -n option, characters that span the byte range boundaries for long character sets are not separated.

Character cutting

To cut characters, specify the -c option with the cut list. Each character is output if it is present on the input line.

I often find cut useful for parsing input from other programs.

Note

Field cutting

The -f option to cut indicates that the list is a list of fields. This is probably the most useful option because clever specification of fields enables you to use variable length elements in output.

The field delimiter is normally a tab, but you can change this with the -d option. If the delimiter is not present on the input line, the entire line is printed on standard output unless you also specify the -s option.

One way you can use the cut command is to generate a list of groups on a system. The /etc/group file is really a set of fields separated by colons, with the group name as the first entry. Listing 12-2 illustrates the output on my home machine.

Listing 12-2: Cutting the Group File

```
$ cut -d: -f1 /etc/group
system
root
daemon
bin
mem
kmem
tty
disk
floppy
tape
admin
uucp
mail
news
lp
majordom
cron
dip
other
```

When you cut with multiple fields, each field on output is separated by the same delimiter as that found on the input.

Pasting

You can also use the paste command to concatenate the individual lines of different files on standard output. paste takes two arguments.

You follow the -d option with a list of delimiter characters. Each character in the list is used once as the delimiter until all characters are used. Then, the command starts over at the beginning of the list. If a backslash is present, the next character is changed, as shown in Table 12-2.

Table 12-2   paste Special Characters

Character	Meaning
\n	New line
\t	Tab
\\	Backslash
\0	Zero-length string

The -s option suppresses new lines when the last file's item is pasted.

Each file is read for a single line, and that line is printed followed by the next delimiter character. Standard input is represented with a single dash. To use the same file more than once, list it on the command line once per each desired use.

I can combine the output from the previous cut command in a more reader-friendly manner by using paste, as shown in Listing 12-3.

Listing 12-3: Cut and Paste

```
$ cut -d: -f1 /etc/group | paste - - - -
system  root    daemon  bin
mem     kmem    tty     disk
floppy  tape    admin   uucp
mail    news    lp      majordom
cron    dip     other
```

The output is displayed in four tab-separated columns. Listing 12-4 shows the results of specifying output delimiters.

Listing 12-4: Cut and Paste

```
$ cut -d: -f1 /etc/group | paste -d :-= - - - -
system:root-daemon=bin
mem:kmem-tty=disk
floppy:tape-admin=uucp
mail:news-lp=majordom
cron:dip-other=
```

The same data is present, but it has a different appearance.

Ordering text

For anyone using UNIX, sort is an important command. It takes lines from standard input and rearranges their order on standard output according to the specified sorting algorithm. The default sorts in the local language and alphabet (usually the ASCII character set). The sort command takes the options listed in Table 12-3.

Table 12-3	sort Options
Option	**Description**
-c	Checks that the file is sorted according to the specified algorithm.
-m	Merges files. The input is assumed to be already sorted.
-o	Specifies the name of an output file. This can be the same as an input file, so it enables sorting in place.
-u	Suppresses repetitions of lines with unique keys.
-d	Specifies that blanks and alphanumeric characters are the only significant characters for sorting.
-f	Sorts in a case-insensitive fashion.
-i	Ignores unprintable characters.
-n	Sorts in a numeric fashion.
-r	Reverses the sense of comparisons.
-b	Ignores leading blanks when looking at sort keys.
-t	Specifies a field separator character for sorting.
-k	Specifies a sort key.

Note

POSIX does not support the old options for specifying fields with *+number - number,* but these options may still be valid with your sort tool. To be certain, check your manual page.

Normally, you delimit sort fields with blank characters. Sometimes, though, you might want to sort on something different, such as when sorting fields that are colon-separated. The -t option is ideal for this.

The real tricks for sort lie with key specification. You can specify any number of keys, and they are evaluated in command-line order until one key evaluates with differences. When a difference is been found, evaluation stops. If all keys evaluate equally, the default sorting order (alphabetical, based on the local character set) is used. Here is the syntax for the sort key:

startfield[type][,lastfield[type]]

The *startfield* and *lastfield* are field numbers based on the field delimiter. You may optionally follow them with a period and a character offset into a field. If no *lastfield* is specified, the sort runs to the end of the line.

The types are b, d, f, i, n, and r, which have the same meaning as they do for the command line (see Table 12-3) and override any specifications from the command line. Listing 12-5 illustrates some simple sorts.

Listing 12-5: sort Commands

```
sort -t: -k n,3 /etc/passwd
sort -k 1.10 textfile
sort -u party.guests
```

The first command sorts the /etc/passwd file in an order based on the user ID numbers. This order enables you easily to scan the file for duplicate user IDs. The second sorts a text file in an order based on the tenth character in each line. The last sorts a file and eliminates duplicate entries.

Writing these key specifications can be tricky. You have to be familiar with the data, the separators, and the relative positions inside the file to write good keys. Unfortunately, without knowing the data, you've no easy way to design a tool that "knows" simple mnemonic instructions for sorting the data.

Eliminating duplicate text

The uniq command eliminates duplicate lines from text. Normally, this command takes input and suppresses the output of consecutive duplicate lines. (The sort -u option performs a similar task when sorting data.)

The uniq command takes the set of arguments illustrated in Table 12-4.

Table 12-4	uniq Options
Option	*Meaning*
-c	Precedes each line of output with a count of the number of its appearances
-d	Suppresses writing of nonrepeated lines
-f *number*	Ignores the first *number* fields when doing comparisons
-s *number*	Ignores the first *number* characters when doing comparisons
-u	Suppresses writing of repeated lines

The uniq command works on an input file and writes an output file. You can also include it in a command pipeline.

Changing text

You can use three commands to change text on the fly. Although you can use two of the commands on files, they are also useful for command pipelines.

Text translations

The simplest text-changing command is `tr`, for text translations. This command normally takes a string of characters as an argument and an optional second string of characters. The default action matches two strings, finds every instance of a character in the first string that appears on standard input, and replaces it with the corresponding character in the second string.

The character strings are treated as an array of characters. The entries can be somewhat complicated. Single characters represent themselves. To represent an octal number, precede it with a backslash. You also need backslashes to represent some characters (for example, a tab is `\t`). To specify a range of characters based on the local alphabet, list the two characters at either end of the range and separate them with a dash.

Note

When combining specifications, do not include the comma. That is a valid ASCII character and is included in the array.

You can use three specific techniques. You can include a class of characters between colons and square brackets like this: `[:class:]`. Table 12-5 lists valid character classes.

Table 12-5   tr Character Classes

Class	Meaning
alnum	All alphanumeric characters
alpha	All alphabetical characters
blank	All blank characters
cntrl	All control characters
digit	All digits
graph	All graphical characters
lower	All lowercase letters
print	All printable characters
punct	All punctuation characters
space	All whitespace characters
upper	All uppercase letters
xdigit	All hexadecimal digits

Unless both the `-d` and `-s` flags are specified, only `lower` and `upper` character classes can be included in the second string.

The [=equiv=] construct enables the placement of equivalent characters for localization. This does not apply to US ASCII.

The [x*n] format means *n* occurrences of the character *x* are placed in the array. This applies only to the second string.

The tr command takes three arguments. The -s argument tells tr to replace repeated characters with a single character. The -d argument tells tr to delete the characters in the first string from the stream. The -c argument tells tr to use the complement of the specified string. A *complement* is every character in the character set except those specified in the string. Listing 12-6 illustrates some common tr commands.

Listing 12-6: tr Translations

```
tr `[:lower:]´ `[:upper:]´
tr -dc `[:print:]´
tr `A-Za-z´ `N-ZA-Mn-za-m´
```

The first translation converts all lowercase letters to uppercase. (Similarly, tr '[:upper:]' '[:lower:]' translates all uppercase letters to lowercase.) The second translation deletes all nonprintable characters from the file. The last translation is an interesting case: it rotates the letters 13 characters along the alphabet.

Note

Enclosing the strings in single quotation marks is best.

Secret

The last translation illustrated in Listing 12-6 is called Rot-13 by experienced denizens of the computer networks. Rot-13 is often used to transmit off-color humor or other material that may provoke offense. Rot-13 is easy to translate — the same command that creates it decodes it — but still requires an action by the reader.

The Stream Editor

A truly useful command is the stream editor, sed, which makes complex conversions on data streams or performs *batch editing* on a file. You perform a batch edit when you list the edit instructions for the file and submit them but do not interact with the editor directly. For a command with sed's power, it takes surprisingly few arguments. The -e option precedes an editing script. The -f option specifies a file with the editing instructions. You can specify any number of -e and -f options, and their execution is dependent on their order in the command line. The -n option suppresses the output of lines unless specifically requested by an editor instruction.

Editing scripts consist of multiple editing instructions. If you've used the basic text editor ed, these instructions should be familiar. The format is the same:

```
[ address[,address]]instruction[arguments]
```

An address is simpler in sed than in ed: it is either a decimal number (referring to the line of input of all files with $ for the last line of input) or a regular expression delimited with slashes. A null address implies every line of input. Commands with no addresses also select every line of input. Commands with one address select every line that matches the pattern. Commands with two addresses select every line between the occurrences of the regular expression. After finding the second expression, sed looks for the first expression to repeat the process.

The sed editor supports the full regular expression definition on POSIX-compliant UNIX systems. Older UNIX systems may not support word boundary constructions, alternatives, or expression groupings.

When sed reads a line from input, it goes through the instructions in the list supplied on the command line or in files, and if the line is in the specified range of addresses, sed attempts to execute the instruction. Some instructions prevent the execution of subsequent instructions, and they read the next line of input and start at the beginning instead.

You should understand two concepts before reading further: the *pattern space* and the *hold space*. The *pattern space* is that buffer in sed where the current line of input is stored. Some sed instructions change this pattern space by appending the next line or by making changes to the pattern space. Please remember that the pattern space may change from instruction to instruction! The *hold space* is a temporary buffer into which you may copy all or part of the current pattern space. You can also append pieces of the current pattern space to the hold space.

Both the pattern space and the hold space must hold a minimum of 8,192 bytes to comply with POSIX.

Table 12-6 lists the editing instructions with the number of addresses expected, arguments, and a brief description of the purpose. Instructions that restart the cycle are marked with an asterisk.

Table 12-6   sed Instructions

Instruction	Addresses	Argument	Description
{ ... }	2		A listing of instructions
a	1	text	Adds the specified text to the output at this point
b	2	label	Branches to the instruction with the specified label
c	2	text	Deletes the specified text in the range and adds the deleted text to the output

Continued

Table 12-6 *(continued)*

Instruction	Addresses	Argument	Description
d*	2		Deletes all the text in the specified range
D*	2		Deletes all text from the beginning of the specified pattern to the end of the line
g	2		Replaces the contents of the pattern space with that of the hold space
G	2		Appends the contents of the hold space to the pattern space, following a new line
h	2		Replaces the contents of the hold space with that of the pattern space
H	2		Appends a new line and the contents of the pattern space to the hold space
i	1	*text*	Writes the specified text to the standard output
l	2		Writes the contents of the pattern space to standard output in an unambiguous form
n	2		Writes the pattern space to standard output and reads the next line of input
N	2		Appends the next line of input to the current pattern space
p	2		Writes the pattern space to standard output
P	2		Writes the pattern space up to a new line to standard output
q	1		Quits sed
r	1	*filename*	Copies the contents of the specified file to the standard output
s	2	*/RE/text/flag*	Replaces the text of the regular expression with the replacement text
t	2	*label*	Branches to the label if the input line has been modified

Instruction	Addresses	Argument	Description
w	2	`filename`	Writes the pattern space to the named file
x	2		Exchanges the contents of the pattern and hold spaces
y	2	`/string/string/`	Replaces each occurrence of a character in the first string with the corresponding member of the second string
!	2	`instruction`	Applies the instruction to the lines not included in the pattern space
:	0	`label`	Sets a label at this point in the instruction list
=	1		Writes the current line number to standard output
#	0		Specifies a comment

Several of these sed instructions require further explanation. The N instruction is particularly useful for making changes across multiple lines. To change a certain regular expression to another piece of text on two consecutive lines, simply include the N instruction before the s. The s instruction in sed is almost identical to the s instruction in ed. Similarities include using the ampersand (&) in the replacement text to repeat the regular expression or specifying replacement segments from the regular expression. The new line character can be part of the replacement text or regular expression if properly escaped.

Note

The sed editor does not have a join instruction as part of the POSIX definition, but you can work around this with this simple script:

```
/RE/{
N
s/\
/ /p
}
```

The N instruction appends the next line of text to the pattern with a new line in between, and the s instruction replaces that new line with a space and prints the current pattern space to standard output.

The s instruction also takes some flags. One flag is a number, which means to substitute only that occurrence of the pattern in the pattern space. The g flag indicates that the substitution should be made to every nonoverlapping pattern in that pattern space. If you specify a p flag, the new pattern space is written to standard output if a replacement occurs. The w flag, followed by a filename, indicates that the pattern space should be written to the specified file if a replacement occurs.

The {...} grouping of instructions is also useful. Instead of specifying the exact same pattern to each command, you can group instructions for a given pattern with the curly braces.

Some sed patterns are interesting. Listing 12-7 illustrates a replacement you can include in your .kshrc file if your system does not have a head command.

Listing 12-7: sed's head Replacement

```
procedure sedhead {
sed ${1}q
}
```

You can also mimic the cat -s command with sed, as illustrated in Listing 12-8.

Listing 12-8: sed's cat -s

```
# Run this file with -n
/./ {
        p
        d
        }
/^$/    p
:Empty
/^$/    {
        N
        s/.//
        b Empty
        }
```

If a line is not empty, it falls into the first instruction list. There, it is printed, the pattern space is deleted, and the remaining instructions are skipped. If the pattern space is empty, the second instruction set prints it. The third is a label and is ignored. The fourth set also applies to the empty pattern space. Here, the next line of input is read, and the s/.// deletes the new line. The sed command branches to the label Empty, the third instruction. Here, it is again tested to see whether it's empty. If it is, the fourth instruction's cycle repeats itself until it finds a line that is not empty. Then, it drops down to the fifth instruction, a print. Because this is the last instruction, the current pattern space is discarded, a new line is read into the pattern space, and execution of instructions begins again at the first instruction.

Think of sed as its own programming language, with the editing instructions as the language's statements. A well-written sed script has aspects of a well-written program: The script describes the flow of a problem through various states with modifications and output. I've touched only the surface of sed in this chapter. For more information on sed, read *sed & awk* by Dale Dougherty.

awk: A Program for Text Manipulation

After you've mastered sed, the next logical step is to learn awk, which is a programming language designed around text manipulation. At its simplest, awk examines input one line at a time to see whether the input meets any patterns listed. If it does, awk executes the instructions specified with the pattern.

Sounds the same as sed, right? The difference is that the instructions accompanying awk are much more complex. Instead of using only a single hold space, you can define variables and associative arrays. You can break input lines into fields and then use those fields in pattern matching. Instructions include formatted output and string manipulations.

The awk command has spawned several other text-processing tools for UNIX. GNU has provided an expanded awk called gawk. Larry Wall developed a program called perl that can also be used in the same fashion as awk. These two programs are not guaranteed to be part of a UNIX system, but awk should be present.

Fully explaining awk would take more space than is available here. Instead, this chapter covers some of the basics for reading and understanding awk. If you want to learn more, I recommend both *sed & awk* by Dale Dougherty and *The AWK Programming Language* by awk's three creators, Aho, Kernighan, and Weinberger.

The awk command reads input lines from standard input and writes to standard output. It takes three arguments. The first, -v, enables you to assign values to variables. To specify that the awk script is in a file, use the -f option. Finally, specify a field separator with the -F option. The field separator can be any regular expression. When the input text is broken into fields, the separator is not a component of any field. You may specify any number of variable assignments.

Following the arguments is the awk script. You usually need to enclose this in single quotation marks. No script is necessary if you specify an input file. The next items are arguments to the script.

Files are specified as arguments, but with advanced argument processing, you can add complexity to the awk script.

Story: What's in a Name?

Although the name of awk suggests the sea bird *auklet,* the bird has nothing to do with the program. And though *awk* suggests the awkward syntax of some commands, that is not the inspiration for awk's name either. Instead, awk derives its name from its three creators:

Alfred Aho, Peter Weinberger, and Brian Kernighan of Bell Labs. (If you are interested in auklets, though, I've seen two species in the area around Monterey Bay: the rhinoceros auklet and Cassin's auklet.)

The awk execution structure

The awk programs are basically a series of patterns, each followed by an action. Each pattern is usually a regular expression that is checked against an input line or a field from that line. awk has two special patterns, BEGIN and END. Actions associated with BEGIN execute before any input is read, and actions associated with END execute after the last line of input is read. These patterns are good for initializing awk variables and performing end-of-input collations. The following is a typical awk statement:

```
$3 ~ /RE/ { found_count++ }
```

The pattern in this case checks the third field of the input line and, if it matches the regular expression, executes the action. In this case, the action is to increment a counter.

awk patterns

The awk command supports the extended regular expression set defined in Chapter 10. Besides the two default patterns BEGIN and END, awk has four standard means of defining patterns.

You can use an expression (that is, a standard conditional expression found in any programming language) in place of a pattern. You can use variables defined in other awk actions (remember to initialize them in your BEGIN action or on the command line), fields from the input line, or the entire input line. Table 12-7 lists the expression operators.

Table 12-7   awk Expressions

Operator	Meaning
<	Less than
<=	Less than or equal to
==	Equal to
!=	Not equal to
>=	Greater than or equal to
>	Greater than
~	Matched by
!~	Not matched by

These operations work for both numeric data and character data. The relationships between characters are based on the local sorting criteria (in the United States, this is the alphabet). If characters match at the start, the comparison moves down the string until an unmatched pair is found. Thus,

James < Jim because *a* comes before *i* in the alphabet. If one string is an initial substring of the other, it appears ahead of the other string. For example, *stand < stands.*

Note

If you are uncertain of how awk orders words and strings, check a dictionary!

The match operators are particularly interesting. For these expressions, you specify a variable and a regular expression. The variable is tested against the regular expression to determine whether a match exists. If one does, the action executes.

Secret

The awk variables are stored as strings, even the numeric values. When awk can evaluate two strings as numbers for a comparative expression, the comparison uses the numeric evaluation. By storing the numbers as strings, however, you can also perform regular expression checks and make character comparisons between numbers and strings. To force a comparison between two numbers to be evaluated as characters, enclose the variable in double quotation marks.

The fourth type of pattern specifies a regular expression. If that regular expression matches the input line, the action runs. The awk command can span fields of the input line to match the regular expression.

The fifth type of pattern is the complex pattern. You can combine simpler patterns with && for logical AND, || for logical OR, or ! for negation. Here is a potential ambiguity:

```
! $4 ~ /RE1/ || $3 == 2
```

Does the programmer want the negation to apply to the entire expression or just to the first clause? Table 12-8 illustrates the results of this expression.

Table 12-8   How awk Interprets the Ambiguous Expression

$4 ~/RE1/	*$3==2*	*Execute Action?*
True	True	Yes
True	False	No
False	True	Yes
False	False	Yes

The awk command treats the negation as having the highest precedence, so it binds the negation tightly to the first clause. If the programmer wants the action executed only when both items are false, the pattern should read as follows:

```
$4 !~ /RE1/ && $3 != 2
```

The awk command tests each clause in the order written. If the logical operator is *or,* awk keeps testing until one of the clauses is true. If the logical operator is *and,* awk tests clauses until one is false.

The last type of pattern is the range. You can view ranges as state machines: when a line matches the first pattern, the state is "on" and the action runs. Subsequent lines run until the second pattern is matched and the state turns "off." Any previously mentioned pattern can be used in the range, but you cannot use ranges within ranges.

awk actions

When a pattern tests true, awk runs an action. Actions must be enclosed in curly braces and are a series of statements. They include assignments, conditionals, output, control flow, and function calls.

Assignments occur when an awk variable is given a value in accordance with either a string manipulation or an arithmetic or logical expression. Usually, the variable assigned precedes the equal sign and the relevant expression. Special cases, such as incrementing, exist for modifying the value of an already existing variable. Listing 12-9 illustrates some assignments.

Listing 12-9: awk Assignments

```
COUNTER=1
Tally+=$3
$2 = $3 + $4
Veracity = ( $4 ~ /RE/ && $3 ==2 ) || Tally < 10
```

Concatenation is an important expression for awk. You concatenate (join together) two strings by listing them next to each other. For example, *newstring= stringone stringtwo* creates a new string from the older variables.

The awk command has two types of conditional statements. One is an inline conditional, where an assignment is based on a condition. Readers familiar with C programming should recognize the construct:

```
(condition)?expression1:expression2
```

If the condition is true, the first expression is evaluated; otherwise, the second expression is evaluated. The other construct should also be familiar:

```
if (condition) expression1 else expression 2
```

In this case, the expressions can be groupings of statements.

Note

As in C, any expression in awk can be a condition, and a condition can be an expression. When a condition is true, the value is nonnegative (usually 1). Therefore, assigning conditions is like assigning any other expression.

The awk command provides some simple commands for producing output. The print command prints the arguments to standard output in the order provided. The printf command takes a format string, copies the arguments into the format, and provides output. If no argument exists, the entire input record is printed on standard output.

Remember that `print` takes a single expression as an argument, so multiple listed variables are concatenated before printing. To place a space between the arguments, you must explicitly included it. The command might then look the opposite of what you'd expect:

```
print v1" "v2" "v3
```

In this example, the variable `v2` seems to be enclosed in quotation marks. Actually, it stands alone and the spaces are enclosed. If `v1` was *Jane,* `v2` was *ran,* and `v3` was *home,* the output would be `Jane ran home`. But if the spaces were not enclosed in quotation marks, they'd have no significance to `print`, and the output would be `Janeranhome`.

If `print` obtains arguments separated by commas, the output has the output field separator inserted between the fields. The default uses the same separator as for input.

The `awk` `printf` command takes a format string similar to that for the C function `printf`. The first argument is the *format string,* which contains text and *replacement tokens.* A replacement token starts with a percent character (`%`), ends with a format control character, and optionally has a detail specification between. Table 12-9 lists the format control characters. The detail specifications may start with a dash, which means the input is left-justified (right-justified is the default). A number specifies how much space to use to present the data, and an optional period followed by a number indicates the precision.

Table 12-9   Format Controls

Character	*Print Expression As*
c	A single character
d	A decimal integer
e	Exponential notation
f	Floating point notation
g	Either exponent or floating point, whichever is shorter
o	Unsigned octal
s	Character string
x	Unsigned hexadecimal
%	The percent character

Listing 12-10 illustrates some `printf` output.

Listing 12-10: printf Output

```
Format  $1        output of printf(fmt,$1)
:%c:    'a'       :a:
:%d:    102.345 :102:
:%e:    102.345 :1.023450e+02:
:%f:    102.345 :102.345000:
:%g:    102.345 :102.345:
:%7.2f: 102.345 : 102.34:
:%o:    102.345 :146:
:%x:    102.345 :66:
:%6.6x: 102.345 :     66:
:%-10d: 102.345 :102        :
:%10d:  102.345 :        102:
:%s:    Reliant :Reliant:
:%10s:  Reliant :   Reliant:
:%-10s: Reliant :Reliant   :
:%10.3s:        Reliant :       Rel:
:%-10.5s:       Reliant :Relia     :
```

You can redirect output from within the awk action. If print or printf
precedes a redirection flag, output is redirected to either a command or a file.
To redirect to a file, use a greater-than sign (>) followed by a filename in
quotation marks (this overwrites the contents of the file). Use two greater-
than signs (>) to append to the file, and use a vertical bar (|) to send the
output as standard input to a command.

The next type of statement handles control flow. These are the standard if-
then-else and while statements. In awk, they function the same way as in
the Korn shell. Table 12-10 lists the control flow structures.

Table 12-10   Control Flow in awk

Statements
{ statements }
if (expression) statement
if (expression) statement; else statement
while (expression) statement
for (expression; expression; expression) statement
for (variable in array) statement
do statement while (expression)
break
continue
next
exit [expression]

With the exception of next, each of these statements is the same as for the Korn shell. The next statement interrupts the flow for the evaluation of patterns, reads in the next line, and starts evaluating it against patterns from the beginning.

The last type of awk statement is a function call. awk provides some standard functions for mathematics and string manipulation, and you can define your own functions.

You can define functions anywhere between a pattern action pair. Start with the keyword function followed by the function name and a parameter list in parentheses. These parameters are variable names that you use in the body of the function. Follow this specification with a series of statements grouped within curly braces. These statements are the same as any other action's: They are just a set of commands.

You then call functions by specifying the function name and arguments in parentheses.

Note

print and printf are functions.

You can specify return values with the return command.

Arithmetic functions

The awk command comes with a set of mathematical functions for evaluating mathematical expressions. Table 12-11 lists these functions and arguments.

Table 12-11　Arithmetic Functions in awk

Function	Return Value
atan2(y,x)	Arctangent of y/x
cos(x)	Cosine of x (x is in radians)
exp(x)	Exponent function of x (for example, e $\hat{\ }$ x)
int(x)	Integer portion of x, truncated toward 0
log(x)	The natural logarithm of x
rand()	A random number between 0 and 1
sin(x)	The sine of x (x is in radians)
sqrt(x)	The square root of x
srand(x)	Reseeds the random number generator with x

The arithmetic functions can define some valuable constants for you. For example, exp(1) defines the mathematical value e, and atan2(0,-1) returns the value for pi. Some functions are missing here, but they're defined later in the chapter.

String manipulations

More interesting than arithmetic functions are the various string manipulations available with awk. These functions exist to parse strings by breaking them into separate components and to replace different segments of strings. Table 12-12 lists the available functions.

Table 12-12   String Functions in awk

Function	Result
gsub(RE1,s2)	Substitutes s2 for RE1 globally in the input string.
gsub(RE1,s2,s3)	Substitutes s2 for RE1 in string s3.
index(s1,s2)	Returns the first position of s2 in s1.
length(s)	Returns the length of the string s.
match(s,RE)	Returns the index of the first character in s that matches the regular expression. If no character matches, returns 0.
split(s,a)	Splits the string s into the array a on the default file separator.
split(s,a,fs)	Splits the string s into the array a on the file separator fs.
sprintf(fmt,s..)	Returns the string generated by the printf format and arguments.
sub(RE,s)	Substitutes s for the first occurrence of RE.
sub(RE,s1,s2)	Substitutes s1 for the first occurrence of RE in s2.
substr(s,n)	Returns the string starting at position n of string s.
substr(s,n1,n2)	Returns the string starting at position n1 of string s, terminating after n2 bytes.

You can use these functions in assignment statements or in printing statements. Furthermore, you can nest calls in other function calls to extract information.

The gsub function is an interesting one for preparing output. You can specify a regular expression, such as an abbreviation, and replace it with another string. Listing 12-11 shows an example.

Listing 12-11: Substitutions

```
$ echo The USA is part of the UN | awk `{ gsub(/USA/,"United States")
gsub(/UN/,"United Nations")
print $0

}`
```

The output from Listing 12-11 now reads as follows:

```
The United States is part of the United Nations
```

Substrings are another useful tool. You create them by cutting out items from a string. For example, the substr("California",1,3) command returns the first three letters of the string *California*, creating the substring *Cal*.

Some functions for you

Here are some handy functions for you to use.

```
function tan(x) {
return sin(x)/cos(x)
}
function pow(x,y) {
return exp(log(x)*y)
}
function log10(x) {
return log(x)/log(10)
}
function randint(x) {
return int(rand()*x)
function grabRE(str,re) {
return (match(str,re))?substr(str,RSTART,RLENGTH):""
}
```

You can use these simple functions at any spot in an awk script.

Important variables

The awk command includes several default variables, which are listed in Table 12-13. They are assigned default values at startup, but you can change the values at any time. Several of the variables affect how records are read and parsed, so be aware of the potential changes.

Table 12-13   awk Variables

Variable	Argument	Default Meaning
ARGC		Argument count
ARGV		Argument vector from command line

Continued

Table 12-13 (continued)		
Variable	**Argument**	**Default Meaning**
FILENAME		Input filename
FNR		Record number in the current file
FS	" "	Input field separator
NF		Number of fields in the record
NR		Number of records read so far
OFMT	"%.6g"	Default format string for numbers
OFS	" "	Output field separator
ORS	"\n"	Output record separator
RLENGTH		Length of the string found in match
RS	"\n"	Record separator
RSTART		Start index of the string found by match
SUBSEP	"\034"	Substring separator

The awk command also has different variables that relate to fields and the input line. The record $0 refers to the input record. When used for input, the input field separators remain, but they are changed to the output field separators on output if needed. Individual fields are marked with the dollar sign ($) followed by their index into the record. If you are looking at an entry from /etc/passwd and you specify the input field separator as a colon, $1 is the user name, $2 is the password, and so on.

Assignments to positional variables or to the whole record change the value in the record for output.

Other variables are created at assignment time. You can access them with standard methods and assign them with standard methods.

Associative arrays

One nice aspect of awk is its capability to create associative arrays. Associative arrays differ from regular arrays in some fairly standard ways.

A *regular array* is an allocation of memory with consecutive instances of values. You find a value by specifying an index into the array. In C, the first record is 0 and subsequent record numbers are integer offsets from 0.

Associative arrays use a text string instead of an integer as an index. This string can be anything; awk tracks the actual offset into memory for that record. Listing 12-15 illustrates the usefulness of the associative array.

Field and record separators

By default, awk breaks the input stream into records at new lines and then breaks the record into fields at spaces. Both of these separators are changeable, and you'll often find it beneficial to make the change.

By specifying a different regular expression, you can create records that span multiple lines of input. This way, if you need to use two lines to present some data, you can do so. If you set the record separator to a pair of quotation marks (" "), records are broken on blank lines. Similarly, you can break fields on different patterns. My choice is usually a colon or a vertical bar, but other developers use different characters.

Output field and record separators do not need to be the same as those used for input.

Alternative input

You can read input from files other than standard input. The getline function reads a line from the specified file and adds it to a variable or treats it as a new input line.

The syntax is as follows:

```
getline [x] [<"filename"]
```

With no arguments, getline retrieves the next input record. It can add that record to a variable. It can also optionally read in the contents from a file.

Command-line arguments

The awk command provides you with access to the command-line arguments within the script. A count of arguments is stored in ARGC, and ARGV is an array of those arguments.

Programs often step through the arguments to retrieve extra data. Listing 12-12 illustrates how awk parses a command line to set a variable for later use.

Listing 12-12: Argument Parsing

```
BEGIN {
for (i=1; i<ARGC; i++) {
    if (ARGV[i]=="-t") {
        Team=ARGV[i+1]
        ARGV[i]=ARGV[i+1]=""
        }
    }
}
```

The BEGIN action looks for a set of arguments "-t team" by looking for the ."-t" flag. When it finds -t, it assigns the variable Team with the next argument. Then, both arguments are set to zero-length strings.

Note

awk treats arguments as files. Therefore, if you are passing additional information to your script via the command line, you must zero out those arguments; otherwise, awk attempts to open them as files.

Sample awk scripts

The awk command has a complexity that ranges from basic to positively arcane. Several examples on the accompanying CD-ROM show different complexity levels.

Simple awk scripts

Table 12-14 shows one- or two-line scripts that produce basic output.

Table 12-14   Simple awk Scripts

Script	Result
awk `END { print NR }´	Prints the number of lines in the input
awk "NR==$NR"	Prints the line specified by the environment variable NR
awk `{print $1}´	Prints the first word of each line
awk "/$NAME/ { lines++ } END {print lines}"	Counts the number of lines containing the regular expression defined in the environment variable NAME and prints the total when finished
awk `{print NR $0}´	Prints each line prepended with the line number

Using more complex scripts to evaluate a sample database

Because one of my loves is basketball, I've compiled the complete set of scores from the NCAA basketball tournament and several major conference tournaments into an awk database. Each line is a single record, and fields are separated with colons. Listing 12-13 lists the different fields in order. I have over 9,000 post-season tournament games listed in the file.

Listing 12-13: My Scores Database

```
Year of the game
Sorting flag, 1=conference tournament, 2=NIT, 3=NCAA
Tournament Name
Round
Game status
Winning Team
Score
Losing Team
Score
Overtimes
```

I have written several awk scripts to pull data out of this file. These are illustrated in the following sections.

Evaluating a team's record in a tournament

I use the awk script in Listing 12-14 to check a team's overall record in a tournament.

Listing 12-14: The awk Script to Read the Database and Calculate the Overall Record

```
BEGIN {
        FS=":"
        WINS=0
        LOSS=0
        LAST=0
        LASTFF=""
        LASTCHAMP=""
        LASTWIN=0
        LASTVIC=0
        TALCHAMP=0
        TALFF=0
        for(i=1;i<ARGC;i++) {
                if (ARGV[i]=="-T") TRNY=ARGV[i+1]
                if (ARGV[i]=="-t") TEAM=ARGV[i+1]
                }
        if (TRNY==""||TEAM=="")
                {
                print "Usage: "ARGV[0]": -T tournament -t team"
                exit
                }
        for(i=1;i<ARGC;i++) ARGV[i]=""
        ARGV[1]="/home/james/.data/scores"
        }
(($3==TRNY)&&($6==TEAM)) {
        WINS++
        LAST=$1
        if ($4=="1"&&($5=="R"||$5=="L"))
                {
                TALCHAMP++
                if (LASTCHAMP=="" ) LASTCHAMP=$1
                else
```

```
                              {
                              if (TALCHAMP==11)
                                        {
                                        LASTCHAMP=LASTCHAMP",\n "$1
                                        TALCHAMP=0
                                        }
                              else
                                        LASTCHAMP=LASTCHAMP", "$1
                              }
                    }
        LASTVIC=$8
        if ($4=="3"&&($5=="R"||$5=="L")&&($3=="NCAA"||$3=="NIT"))
                    {
                    TALFF++
                    if (LASTFF=="" ) LASTFF=$1
                    else
                              {
                              if (TALFF==11)
                                        {
                                        LASTFF=LASTFF",\n                    "$1
                                        TALFF=0
                                        }
                              else
                                        LASTFF=LASTFF", "$1
                              }
                    }
        LASTWIN=$1
        }
(($3==TRNY)&&($8==TEAM)) {
        LOSS++
        LAST=$1
        }
END {
        printf "\n"
        if (LAST!=0) {
                printf "Record for %s is %d-%d, ", TEAM, WINS, LOSS
                printf "last appearance in %s.\n", LAST
                if (LASTWIN!=0)
                        printf "Last win in %s over %s.\n", \
                                LASTWIN, LASTVIC
                if (TRNY!="ALL")
                        {
                        if (LASTFF!="")
                              printf "Final Four(s) in %s.\n", LASTFF

                        if (LASTCHAMP!="")
                              printf "Championships in %s.\n", LASTCHAMP
                        }
                }
        else
                {
                printf "%s never appeared in the %s tournament.\n", \
                        TEAM, TRNY
                }
        }
```

This awk script is designed to read each record of the database and to tally the overall record. In the BEGIN action, I initialize a series of variables, and I parse the command line for the team and tournament to be used. After parsing, I check to confirm that both items have been provided; if they're not there, I exit.

I scan the input for two patterns. The tournament field, field 3, must match the specified tournament in both cases. For the first pattern, if the team name is in column 6, the game is a win. I increment the count of wins, and I note the last year in which a win occurred. If the round is 1, this means it is the championship, so I increment the count of championships and add the current year to a list of championships. I note the opponent for the last victory. If I am looking at the NCAA or NIT, I also check for the last time the team reached the Final Four. Again, I increment a count and build on the list. Then, I've completed the winners cycle.

If the tournament field matches but the team appears in the loser's field, I increment the loss count and indicate that the current year was the last in which the team appeared in the tournament.

Note

I've not produced any input while reading all these records.

The last pattern is the END pattern. Here, I start producing output. I print out the record and note the year of the last appearance. If I find any wins, I note the year and the last victim. If the tournament includes a Final Four, I add the record of the last Final Fours and Championships.

The command to run this awk script is

```
$ awk -f NCAArecord -T NCAA -t Duke
```

and this produces the following output:

```
Record for Duke is 65-21, last appearance in 1999.
Last win in 1999 over Michigan State.
Final Four(s) in 1963, 1964, 1966, 1978, 1986, 1988, 1989, 1990, 1991, 1992,
1994, 1999.
Championships in 1991, 1992.
$
```

Evaluating a team's overall record against common opponents

The script in Listing 12-15 uses associative arrays to track one team's performance against its opponents.

Listing 12-15: awk Script for Comparative Records

```
BEGIN {
        FS=":"
        for(i=1;i<ARGC;i++) {
                if (ARGV[i]=="-T") TRNY=ARGV[i+1]
                if (ARGV[i]=="-t") TEAM=ARGV[i+1]
```

```
                }
        if (TRNY==""||TEAM=="")
                {
                print "Usage: "ARGV[0]": -T tournament -t team"
                exit
                }
        for(i=1;i<ARGC;i++) ARGV[i]=""
        ARGV[1]="/home/james/.data/scores"
        printf "\nAll Time Tournament Record for %s:\n\n", NAM
}
(($3==TRNY)&&($6==NAM)) {
        opp=$8
        if (wins[opp]==0&&lose[opp]==0)
                {
                sort[++number]=opp
                scrs[opp]=""
                }
        else if (((wins[opp]+lose[opp])%3)==0)
                scrs[opp]=scrs[opp]"\n
            "
        else
                scrs[opp]=scrs[opp]";"
        ++wins[opp]
        perc[opp]=(wins[opp]/(wins[opp]+lose[opp]))
        scrs[opp]=scrs[opp]" "$7"-"$9
        if ($10!=0)
                if ($10!=1)
                        scrs[opp]=scrs[opp]" "$10" OTS"
                else
                        scrs[opp]=scrs[opp]" OT"
        }
(($3==TRNY)&&($8==NAM)) {
        opp=$6
        if (wins[opp]==0&&lose[opp]==0)
                {
                sort[++number]=opp
                scrs[opp]=""
                }
        else if (((wins[opp]+lose[opp])%3)==0)
                scrs[opp]=scrs[opp]"\n

            "
        else
                scrs[opp]=scrs[opp]";"
        ++lose[opp]
        perc[opp]=(wins[opp]/(wins[opp]+lose[opp]))
        scrs[opp]=scrs[opp]" "$9"-"$7
        if ($10!=0)
                if ($10!=1)
                        scrs[opp]=scrs[opp]" "$10" OTS"
                else
                        scrs[opp]=scrs[opp]" OT"
        }
```

```
END {
        for(i=number;i>=1;-i)
                {
                max=0
                mp=0-1
                mw=0
                ml=1575
                tn="ZZZ"
                for(j=1;j<=number;j++)
                        if
(perc[sort[j]]>mp||(perc[sort[j]]==mp&&wins[sort[j]]>mw)||(perc[sort[j]]==mp&&w
wins[sort[j]]==mw&&lose[sort[j]]<ml)||(perc[sort[j]]==mp&&wins[sort[j]]==mw&&lo
ose[sort[j]]==ml&&sort[j]<tn)) {
                                max=j
                                mp=perc[sort[j]]
                                mw=wins[sort[j]]
                                ml=lose[sort[j]]
                                tn=sort[j]
                                }
                printf "against %-30s %2d-%-2d %5.3f %s\n", \
                        tn, mw, ml, mp, scrs[sort[max]]
                perc[tn]= 0-1
                }

        }
```

As you can see, this awk script has fewer startup variables to track. It just
assigns the team and tournament variables and prints the first line of output.

The patterns to be matched are exactly the same as in the previous example,
but the actions on finding the patterns are radically different. Because the
script tracks records against the same opponent, it retrieves the opponent
name first. Next, it checks to see whether the team has already played this
opponent. If the team hasn't, it increments the count of opponents and
assigns the name to an array of sort variables. It also initializes the
associative array of cores. If the two teams have played a multiple of three
times, the script appends a new line to the list of scores and several spaces
to keep the fields aligned. If the two teams have played but have not played a
multiple of three times, the script appends a semicolon. Next, it increments
the count of wins against this opponent and recalculates the overall winning
percentage. It then appends the score of the current game to the list of scores
and notes any overtime periods.

If the game is a loss, the script does almost exactly the same thing except it
increments losses instead of wins.

The script performs a lot of the work in the END action. The main action
scans the set of arrays repeatedly to determine against which opponent the
current team has the best record. As it finds teams with better records than
those specified, it replaces the data with new data. Finally, after each
iteration, it prints the record and scores and sets the percentage to an
impossibly low number, effectively eliminating the opponent from
consideration.

Note

The approach shown here is horribly inefficient, but it works perfectly well.

Note that in many cases I use the `sort` array to retrieve the team name for use in the associative arrays. This is perfectly acceptable behavior.

To run the command, you type

```
$ awk -f NCAArecvs -T ACC -t Virginia
```

and here is what you'll see:

```
All Time Tournament Record for Virginia:
against Clemson              5-1 0.833 68-63; 72-60; 49-57
                         56-54; 90-73; 69-66
against Georgia Tech         4-3 0.571 76-47; 96-67; 48-55
                         55-54; 61-70; 56-68
                         77-67
against Wake Forest          6-5 0.545 58-81; 60-79; 85-84
                         74-65; 59-57; 61-72
                         51-49 OT; 51-63; 70-66
                         61-57; 68-77
against Maryland             4-4 0.500 68-67 OT; 68-71; 66-70
                         66-65; 57-62; 73-65
                         62-85; 69-63
against Duke             3-9 0.250 68-96; 77-90 OT; 54-89
                         70-89; 78-99; 86-99
                         59-55; 109-66; 70-75
                         48-60; 58-69; 66-61
against North Carolina       3-9 0.250 77-81; 63-84; 95-93
                         68-78; 67-62; 69-75
                         45-47; 82-84 2 OTS; 92-85
OT
                         71-76; 56-74; 66-73
against North Carolina State    2-9 0.182 63-66; 69-106; 77-86
                         66-67; 51-63; 66-87
                         85-91; 75-63; 78-82
                         78-81; 64-62
against South Carolina       0-1 0.000 78-101
$
```

The output shows that Virginia performs best against opponents such as Clemson when playing in the NCAA tournament but does not perform well against the Research Triangle's basketball powers: Duke, North Carolina, and North Carolina State.

Markups for Formatting

You have a third type of text command at your disposal: text markup commands. Markups are commands that you insert into text to affect the document's final appearance. The two common markups are for `troff` and Web page perusal.

Note

Unlike Word for Windows, UNIX does not have a standard text-formatting tool. Instead, UNIX distributes the `troff` tool for producing document-quality output. Several vendors also produce word-formatting products, such as Island Write and Frame, for UNIX. I personally prefer Frame slightly over Island Write, but both packages are expensive. Frame is the best tool I've found on any platform for producing large documents such as books.

troff and manual pages

Joe Ossana wrote the original `troff` tool at Bell Labs in the early 1970s, and Brian Kernighan rewrote and modernized it to be device-independent after Joe Ossana's death. Requests in `troff` usually occur one per line, starting in the first column of a line and not including text.

Another command is the inline command, which is usually triggered by a backslash and is interpreted within the line. Listing 12-16 shows an example of some `troff` commands.

Listing 12-16: Sample troff Input

```
to North Dome and down into the valley. Overnight in Lee Vining.
Mrs. Nag may hang out in Yosemite Valley*
.sp
\fB15 July\fP: Visit Mono Lake, Boadie ghost town. Cross the
Sierras via the Sonora Pass, or Ebbets Pass... Dr. Nag returned to
San Francisco.
```

In this example, `.sp` is a `troff` command to create a line of space, and `\fB15 July\fP` makes the text string *15 July* bold.

You'll rarely use `troff` to create documents because better options exist. `troff` is most heavily used to create manual pages. Instead of including `troff` directives, however, you can include macros that `man` uses for printing the manual pages. Table 12-15 illustrates some common manual page macros.

Table 12-15   Common Manual Page Macros

Macro	Description
.B	Prints the argument in bold text
.BI	Prints the argument in bold italic text
.I	Prints the argument in italic text
.PP	Begins a new paragraph
.RE	Ends a region
.RS	Starts a region
.SH	Specifies a top-level header

Continued

Table 12-15 Common Manual Page Macros (continued)	
Macro	**Description**
.SS	Specifies a subheader
.TH	Specifies a title page header
.TP	Specifies an option space

The first macro you'll use on a manual page is .TH. This macro takes four arguments: the command name, a level, a description of the package, and the author. The .TH macro puts the respective fields in different places on each page header. Manual pages have certain fixed levels, as illustrated in Table 12-16.

Table 12-16 Manual Page Levels	
Level	**Meaning**
1	User commands
2	System calls for programming
3	Programming library calls
4	Special files and hardware support
5	System file formats
6	Games
7	Miscellaneous manual pages
8	System administration pages

The next macro you'll use is .SH. This is a section header and is repeated several times through normal manual pages. The name of the section follows the macro. Some standard section headers are NAME, SYNOPSIS, DESCRIPTION, SEE ALSO, DIAGNOSTICS, and BUGS. You can use the .SS macro to specify suboptions.

Most of the rest is just text, automatically filled and formatted. The .TP macro is useful for providing space and indentation when you list options. When you are writing a table, you should reserve the space by surrounding the table with .RS and .RE. The remaining macros listed in Table 12-15 change fonts for highlighting pieces of text.

Note

To be honest, I've found it easier to borrow another manual page as a template and fill in the respective data on that template. Odds are that you will never write a manual page unless you are involved with developing a product.

Hypertext markups

Another type of markup is the family of Simple Graphical Markup Languages, known as SGML. The most well-known is the Hypertext Markup Language, HTML. Other markup languages include VRML (Virtual Reality Markup Language) and DHTML (Dynamic HTML).

SGMLs are languages in which tags are embedded in a document; those tags are interpreted by the reader to produce the text. Embedded tags may have attributes that further describe the changes to the text.

Chapter 25 discusses HTML in greater detail.

CGI

Although not strictly a text editor, CGI (Common Gateway Interface) works with a Web program to produce a document based on the input of the reader. Chapter 26 discusses CGI in detail.

Summary

This chapter introduced you to several tools for formatting text. It made the following points:

▶ The basic text-formatting commands enable you to organize your text through sorting, cutting, and pasting.

▶ The sed and awk commands provide you with a powerful method for programming input.

▶ The markup tools enable you to format the appearance of text from within the document.

The next chapter ties all the text-processing tools together with the other UNIX development tools.

Chapter 13

Editing in Perspective

In This Chapter

▶ Understanding how stream editors work in pipes

Editors — tools used to create and manipulate text files — are some of the most widely used tools in UNIX. Furthermore, they integrate with other UNIX tools. Every stream editing tool discussed in Chapter 12 works with standard input, alters text as instructed, and writes to standard output. This design enables you to join the editing tools in pipelines with other tools in practically infinite combinations.

Stream Editing in Pipes

One of the most common commands used in the pipelines is `grep`. You may want to run a command but are not interested in all the output. Instead, you may want to see only certain lines of output. One of my hobbies is basketball and football picking contests. I've written a fairly extensive set of software to run these contests. One of my programs produces a listing of everyone's picks in the current round and some summary information. Sometimes, however, I want to see only one person's picks. To do this, I run the program `dbdump` and pipe the output through `fgrep`, as follows:

```
$ dbdump | fgrep ""James C. Armstrong"
James C. Armstrong, Jr. PSU 2    UWS 6    Fla 24    TAM 7    TIE
```

In this round, I've picked Penn State by 2, Washington by 6, Florida by 24, Texas A&M by 7, and a tie in the last game. This doesn't tell me much because I don't know who is playing in which game. I know the tag on the line is `Game`, so I can expand the command and use `egrep` instead of `fgrep`, as follows:

```
$ dbdump | egrep 'Armstrong|
Game                    OSU-PSU  UND-UWS  Fla-LSU  TAM-TxT  Wyo-Tls
James C. Armstrong, Jr. PSU 2    UWS 6    Fla 24    TAM 7    TIE
```

That makes a bit more sense. I've picked Penn State over Ohio State, Washington over Notre Dame, Florida over Louisiana State, Texas A&M over Texas Tech, and Wyoming and Tulsa to tie. Because `dbdump` also produces a summary of picks, I can see how my picks stack up against the average of everyone else's picks. Knowing the nature of the output, I know that the word *Mean* appears in the summary. Thus, I add that word to the egrep list, as follows:

```
$ dbdump | egrep 'Armstrong|Game|Mean'
```

```
Game                           OSU-PSU  NDU-UWS  Fla-LSU  TAM-TxT  Wyo-Tls
James C. Armstrong, Jr. PSU 2    UWS 6   Fla 24   TAM 7    TIE
OSU  18 PSU   6                Mean: OSU  3.4 Deviation:   5.3
NDU  13 UWS  11                Mean: NDU  1.8 Deviation:   6.8
Fla  22 LSU   2                Mean: Fla 12.3 Deviation:   6.8
TAM  24 TxT   0                Mean: TAM 12.3 Deviation:   5.3
Wyo  18 Tls   5       TIE  1 Mean: Wyo  6.8 Deviation:   6.8
```

I guess I'm the only one brave enough to pick a tie in the Wyoming game. I'm also bucking the trend in both the Ohio State-Penn State game and the Notre Dame-Washington game. (Clearly, I'm not a prognosticator — the only game I picked correctly was Florida's win over LSU.)

What's interesting about these commands is how you can easily substitute them for each other. You can perform the previous routine with a sed command that also results in our not needing to know some of the tags. Listing 13-1 shows the appropriate sed script.

Listing 13-1: sed Script for egrep Commands

```
1 {
  p
  d
  }
/Armstrong/ {
          p
          d
          }
/Mean/ {
        p
        d
        }
```

Naturally, I can include this command in a function and pass an argument, as follows:

```
function dbperson ()
        dbdump | egrep "${1}|Game|Summary"
        }
```

With this, the command dbperson Armstrong produces the expected output.

Another example is to read a list of newsgroups. Normally, you have a listing of newsgroups in the .newsrc file in your home directory. The standards call for a newsgroup name to be followed with a colon if the newsgroup is read and an exclamation point if it is not read. To retrieve a list of all the newsgroups I read, I need to find each line that has a colon. Sounds simple, right? Wrong. The output is quite messy:

```
$ fgrep : ~/.newsrc
rec.sport.basketball.college: 1-143914
alt.sports.college.acc: 1-2348
alt.sports.college.big10: 1-288
alt.sports.college.big10.purdue: 1-37
alt.sports.college.big10.northwestern: 1-8
alt.sports.college.pac10: 1-50
alt.sports.college.pac10.ucla: 1-12
alt.sports.college.conference-usa: 1-89
alt.sports.college.atl10: 1-31
alt.sports.college.big-east: 1-337
alt.sports.college.sec: 1-19
ca.earthquakes: 1-16640
ba.singles: 1-45681
rec.sport.football.college: 1-182553
rec.sport.soccer: 1-200818
news.admin.net-abuse.announce: 1-1035
netcom.shell.mail: 1-297
clari.news.trouble: 1-11441
clari.sports.basketball.college: 1-5526
clari.sports.briefs: 1-8173
clari.sports.football.college: 1-3244
netcom.shell.announce: 1-6
netcom.announce: 1-256
netcom.shell.netnews: 1-452
netcom.pops.announce:
netcom.netnews: 1-9071
rec.outdoors.national-parks: 1-2816
sci.geo.earthquakes: 1-4020
alt.disasters.earthquake: 1-483
alt.support.non-smokers.moderated: 1-114
ba.consumers: 1-488
ba.food: 1-33693
ba.general: 1-38630
ba.news: 1-2356
ba.news.config: 1-526
ba.news.group: 1-1214
ba.politics: 1-35451
comp.os.linux.answers: 1-437
rec.arts.drwho: 1-110703
```

The numbers after the colon list the articles read. To generate only the list of newsgroups read, I have to eliminate those numbers. This is a job for cut:

```
$ fgrep : ~/.newsrc | cut -d: -f1
rec.sport.basketball.college
alt.sports.college.acc
alt.sports.college.big10
alt.sports.college.big10.purdue
alt.sports.college.big10.northwestern
alt.sports.college.pac10
```

```
alt.sports.college.pac10.ucla
alt.sports.college.conference-usa
alt.sports.college.atl10
alt.sports.college.big-east
alt.sports.college.sec
ca.earthquakes
ba.singles
rec.sport.football.college
rec.sport.soccer
news.admin.net-abuse.announce
netcom.shell.mail
clari.news.trouble
clari.sports.basketball.college
clari.sports.briefs
clari.sports.football.college
netcom.shell.announce
netcom.announce
netcom.shell.netnews
netcom.pops.announce
netcom.netnews
rec.outdoors.national-parks
sci.geo.earthquakes
alt.disasters.earthquake
alt.support.non-smokers.moderated
ba.consumers
ba.food
ba.general
ba.news
ba.news.config
ba.news.group
ba.politics
comp.os.linux.answers
rec.arts.drwho
```

I cut on the colon simply because that marks the end of a newsgroup name. I wanted only the information before the colon, field one. Still, these results are not useful. For a start, the netcom groups are not available off netcom, so I need to eliminate them from the list. In addition, the list is not well ordered. To eliminate the netcom groups and reorder the list, I must add two more commands to the pipe, as follows:

```
$ fgrep : .newsrc | cut -d: -f1 | fgrep -v netcom | sort
alt.disasters.earthquake
alt.sports.college.acc
alt.sports.college.atl10
alt.sports.college.big-east
alt.sports.college.big10
alt.sports.college.big10.northwestern
alt.sports.college.big10.purdue
alt.sports.college.conference-usa
alt.sports.college.pac10
alt.sports.college.pac10.ucla
alt.sports.college.sec
```

```
alt.support.non-smokers.moderated
ba.consumers
ba.food
ba.general
ba.news
ba.news.config
ba.news.group
ba.politics
ba.singles
ca.earthquakes
clari.news.trouble
clari.sports.basketball.college
clari.sports.briefs
clari.sports.football.college
comp.os.linux.answers
news.admin.net-abuse.announce
rec.arts.drwho
rec.outdoors.national-parks
rec.sport.basketball.college
rec.sport.football.college
rec.sport.soccer
sci.geo.earthquakes
```

That's better, but the list is still too long. Adding the `paste` command should cut the length of the output in half.

```
$ fgrep : .newsrc | cut -d: -f1 | fgrep -v netcom | sort | paste - -
alt.disasters.earthquake        alt.sports.college.acc
alt.sports.college.atl10        alt.sports.college.big-east
alt.sports.college.big10        alt.sports.college.big10.northwestern
alt.sports.college.big10.purdue alt.sports.college.conference-usa
alt.sports.college.pac10        alt.sports.college.pac10.ucla
alt.sports.college.sec  alt.support.non-smokers.moderated
ba.consumers    ba.food
ba.general      ba.news
ba.news.config  ba.news.group
ba.politics     ba.singles
ca.earthquakes  clari.news.trouble
clari.sports.basketball.college clari.sports.briefs
clari.sports.football.college   comp.os.linux.answers
news.admin.net-abuse.announce   rec.arts.drwho
rec.outdoors.national-parks     rec.sport.basketball.college
rec.sport.football.college      rec.sport.soccer
sci.geo.earthquakes
```

That looks even better, but the appearance of the columns is poor. `awk`'s `print` can take care of that in the following manner:

```
$ fgrep : .newsrc | cut -d: -f1 | fgrep -v netcom | sort | \
paste - - | awk '{ printf "%-32s%-32s\n", $1, $2}'
alt.disasters.earthquake        alt.sports.college.acc
alt.sports.college.atl10        alt.sports.college.big-east
alt.sports.college.big10        alt.sports.college.big10.northwestern
alt.sports.college.big10.purdue alt.sports.college.conference-usa
```

```
alt.sports.college.pac10        alt.sports.college.pac10.ucla
alt.sports.college.sec          alt.support.non-smokers.moderated
ba.consumers                    ba.food
ba.general                      ba.news
ba.news.config                  ba.news.group
ba.politics                     ba.singles
ca.earthquakes                  clari.news.trouble
clari.sports.basketball.college clari.sports.briefs
clari.sports.football.college   comp.os.linux.answers
news.admin.net-abuse.announce   rec.arts.drwho
rec.outdoors.national-parks     rec.sport.basketball.college
rec.sport.football.college      rec.sport.soccer
sci.geo.earthquakes
```

That looks much better.

Note

This approach illustrates a fairly standard approach that UNIX experts take when building these commands: They test each step of the pipeline before appending the next command.

Another way to combine these tools is to build a list of indexes for output from a find command. A find on a full file system results in a lot of output, and you may end up with a file larger than you can easily manage. This is a call for split:

```
$ find / -xdev -print | split
$ ls
xaa xag xam xas xay xbe xbk xbq xbw xcc xci xco xcu xda xdg xdm
xab xah xan xat xaz xbf xbl xbr xbx xcd xcj xcp xcv xdb xdh xdn
xac xai xao xau xba xbg xbm xbs xby xce xck xcq xcw xdc xdi xdo
xad xaj xap xav xbb xbh xbn xbt xbz xcf xcl xcr xcx xdd xdj xdp
xae xak xaq xaw xbc xbi xbo xbu xca xcg xcm xcs xcy xde xdk
xaf xal xar xax xbd xbj xbp xbv xcb xch xcn xct xcz xdf xdl
```

Now, you can use grep -l to find files that contain needed patterns, and you can edit them accordingly. Suppose you want to see what files are near files with the word *james* in their names. You can use fgrep -l james * to obtain a list of the files with that word and use command substitution to edit those files:

```
$ vi ~/james `fgrep -l james *`
```

Another editing trick uses the concept of a here document in a shell program to feed commands to an editor. Here's an example:

```
hostname=`uname -n`
ed shellprogram insert  EOF
;/ADDUNAMEHERE/$hostname/g
w
q
EOF
```

Although you could use sed, it does not do an inline replacement of a file. You would need an additional command to copy the file that sed created to overwrite the original file.

Summary

You can place editing commands in both pipelines and shell commands in many ways. This chapter provided an overall perspective of editing in the UNIX environment and taught you

▶ Pipeline techniques

▶ How to use editing commands in command substitution

▶ How to use editing commands in here documents

The main topic of Part V is process management. This is the last component of basic UNIX that you need to understand before moving on to the advanced topics of networks, X Windows, and administration.

Part V

Processes

Chapter 14

Introducing Processes and Scheduling

In This Chapter

▶ Understanding processes

▶ Managing resources

▶ Scheduling

▶ Understanding what happens when the machine boots

To understand the real secrets behind the operation of UNIX, you need to understand the nature of processes in UNIX. To understand processes, you need to understand the nature of the resources available on a computer and how an operating system manages those resources. The single most important resource on a computer is the central processing unit (CPU), and the management of process scheduling on the CPU is the operating system's biggest concern.

Understanding Processes

A *process* stands at the heart of any operating system. Simply put, a *program* is a collection of machine commands fed through a CPU to perform manipulations of data. Each *process* is a uniquely identified program. Processes need to access many different resources on the computer.

The operating system manipulates a *process image,* which is the code and data sections of a process that define the execution environment. The code section includes the actual CPU instructions, both the lines of code compiled and written by the user and the code generated for the system. This system code enables the program and the operating system to communicate.

Secret

The heart of the operating system lies in something called the *kernel.* The kernel is a special program that continuously runs while the computer is up. It maintains all the tables used to track processes and other computer resources. It is, in fact, the operating system itself. On UNIX machines, the kernel is usually a file named either /unix or /vmunix, which is loaded at boot time and immediately spawns some important processes, such as init.

The data associated with a process also makes up part of the process image. Some of this data is kept in *registers,* which are memory locations that the CPU can quickly access and are sometimes built into the CPU for faster access. Also present are *malloced data locations,* which are pieces of memory used by the program to store data not kept in registers. The third type of data is *stack data,* an area allocated by the process for variables in a program.

Registers are very important for processes. Four registers that have special functions are usually allocated:

- The PC register, or program counter, points to the line of code currently being executed.
- The PS register refers to the processor status.
- The SP register points to the top of the stack.
- The FP register points to the current frame on the stack.

The *stack* regulates how a program manages some of its memory. Stack variables are automatically allocated to a program when it runs and are usually the variables that the programmer defines. When a process makes a call to a function or subroutine, a new frame is placed on the stack. Part of each frame is a pointer to the base of the previous frame, making returns from function calls easy. It is important to know the location of the current frame and the top of the stack.

Other memory is added to the process from the heap. This is dynamically allocated, and its use differs from process to process. Allowing dynamic memory enables a programmer to increase processes as needed.

Processes usually reside in memory while executing or awaiting execution. This memory is the random access memory (RAM) that is usually displayed at boot time. A portion, sometimes significant, of the RAM is reserved for the kernel. System users can access the remaining RAM for processes. Several processes can occupy the RAM at the same time.

Note

This setup differs significantly from the architecture of early PC operating systems such as DOS, which supported only a single program in memory at any given time.

Because nothing fixes a process size, the memory needs all of the current processes to exceed the available memory allocated for user processes. In earlier architectures, this problem could not be resolved. In UNIX, it is resolved by *paging.*

Process memory breaks down into segments called *pages.* Each page is a fixed size that depends on the machine and the operating system. The operating system tracks each page, determines the last time a page was accessed, and uses some heuristics to predict when the page will likely be accessed next. If all available pages are in use and a new page is needed, the least useful page is swapped out of memory, and the new page is allocated.

Swapping out a page means that it is written onto the hard disk in a special partition, called the *swap area,* which must be defined when the operating system is loaded. If no partition is available, you can use some special techniques to define regular UNIX files as swap files.

The page remains swapped out until needed, at which time it is swapped back into the computer's memory. Paging algorithms usually look at code sequentially and retain code and data pages of a process that reside next to the current page in preference to other pages of a process. You can fool this heuristic by using any command that requires jumping to a new code or data location, such as one that accesses a different variable or calls a new subroutine.

Note

One nice side effect of paging is that a process can use more memory than is installed on a machine, if needed. As different pages of memory are needed, they are paged in while lesser-needed pages are paged out.

Some pages are immune from being swapped. These are called *nonpreemptable pages.* Usually, the kernel and swapper processes use them. Some kernels have recently been written with preemptable pages, enabling them to be swapped in and out as needed.

Processes operate in one of two modes: *user mode* and *system mode.* System mode is entered when a process is executing system calls, handling interrupts, or handling traps. User mode is entered when the process is executing user-defined code. The kernel tracks the amount of time a process spends in either mode.

System mode is significant. The process executes system code to access resources that are shared among processes for operations such as directing disk input or output, adding memory from the heap to the memory available for the program, or accessing other system information. System mode is also used for executing interrupt handlers, such as those caused by signals and traps from system calls.

When a system call occurs, the current set of register values (called a *vector*) is saved, and a new stack frame is loaded from the system data area. Next, the system code specific to the stack executes. When the system call is complete, the original register vector is restored.

Interrupts are means by which system hardware interacts with a process. The most common interrupt is the clock. A clock interrupt triggers the processor scheduling algorithms in the kernel. The next most common interrupt is input from a disk, which must be processed immediately. The least common is terminal input, or what you type at your keyboard.

Clock interrupts come roughly once every one-hundredth of a second. These time slices of the CPU are the maximum allotted to a process before a new process can replace it. (I discuss details of CPU scheduling later in the chapter.)

Each process has a related entry in the kernel's process table. This table is an array of process structures. The fields of a structure include the following:

- A process status flag
- A priority
- A resident time for scheduling
- A CPU's usage amount
- A nice flag
- The user ID of the process
- The effective user ID
- The group and effective group IDs
- The process group
- The process ID and parent process ID
- The size of the swappable image
- The size of the text and stack
- An array of pending signals

The kernel needs to track all this data and more for the system to operate properly. An even larger structure is tracked per process for usage information.

Creating a process

You create a new process in UNIX only by the `fork` system call. When a process executes a `fork`, it checks available memory to see whether the process has enough room. If sufficient memory is available, the current process image is copied into a new process image, and a new entry in the process table is created. A new user table entry is also created; all its values are initialized to zero. A unique process ID is assigned to the new process, and the parent process ID is set to the forking process.

Each process must have a unique process ID. This number tracks the resource use requests for the kernel. It also provides a unique handle by which user tools can access the process.

When initialization of the kernel tables is complete, the process is added to the list of processes available for execution and awaits scheduling like any other process.

Closely related to `fork` is the `exec()` system call. Exec is usually called after `fork` and overlays the process's text and data segments with new text and data segments, creating an entirely new process image. The register values for the process are reset to the beginning of the process.

Terminating a process

When a process finishes, it calls the `exit()` system call, which frees all the resources it currently uses, such as memory and kernel table entries, and *disowns* its children. Then, the process clears its own text segment from memory and becomes a *zombie*.

Note

Zombie processes are just what they sound like, undead processes that can fill the kernel's process table and eventually freeze the system. Parents are supposed to clean up their dead children, but if a parent does not execute any code to do this, zombies result.

Finally, the process's parent must clean up after the child process. Usually, the parent process receives `SIGCHLD`, which is a UNIX signal that notifies a process that one of its child processes has died.

Disowned children become orphaned processes owned by `init`. When they die, `init` cleans them up.

Secret

To clean up zombies, you can determine the appropriate parent of the zombies and send a `SIGCHLD` manually, as described in Chapter 16. If that fails, killing the parent forces the `init` process to clean up the zombies.

Managing Resources

An important job of a process is resource management. The normal resources available to a process are disks and remote devices. Each remote device has a *device driver:* a piece of code linked into the kernel that manages the physical hardware. A device driver for a disk drive may issue directives to the device for reading data from or writing data to the disk and may buffer that I/O until it is ready to write the data or present it to a process. Writing device drivers is not easy.

The kernel manages most resources through tables. These tables include a *mount table,* which tracks disk partitions mounted on the system; a *file table,* which tracks open files; and an *i-node table,* which tracks i-nodes currently in use.

Interprocess communication (IPC)

Kernel resources are also tracked. The most common use for these resources is interprocess communication (IPC). Several IPC tools are available in UNIX.

The most commonly used IPC tool is the socket. Programs connect to sockets by requesting a bind to a specific address. Data passed to and from that address passes from socket to socket.

Other means of IPC include signals, pipes, message queues, semaphores, and shared memory.

Signals

The original means of IPC were signals. A *signal* indicates a condition existing within a process that requires the attention of the process. Most signals force core dumps to indicate that a problem has occurred. The signals that you need to familiarize yourself with include SIGINT, SIGTERM, SIGKILL, and SIGHUP.

- SIGINT is the interrupt signal and is usually sent from the keyboard to the foreground process when you press Ctrl-C. It interrupts the execution of a process without dumping core.

- SIGTERM is the terminate signal and is another means for a program to request termination. Another process usually sends SIGTERM. Two different signals exist for this purpose so that each can be caught.

- SIGKILL is an uncatchable signal that immediately terminates the process execution, leaving no time for cleaning up the process. (The original manuals described it as "Terminate with extreme prejudice.")

- SIGHUP is the hang-up signal and is sent to processes when the terminal line drops or when another I/O stream unexpectedly closes.

Each process contains a special signal-handling code linked into the process image. A programmer can override these actions by trapping a signal and attaching a routine to that signal. The kernel notes when a signal arrives by setting a bit, and the signal handler is called when convenient. Some processes may reach priority levels where they ignore all signals, including SIGKILL.

Pipes

I introduced pipes in a preceding chapter when I discussed shells. You can also create pipes by processes for IPC. Pipes come in two classes. The first, pipe(), is created by a system call. The pipe() initializes a kernel structure to pass information between processes. The calling process returns two file descriptors, one for reading information and one for writing information. Then, the process forks, and the communication channel opens between the two processes.

Note

These pipes work only between processes that have a parent-child relationship.

The other type of pipe is named pipe. In this case, a special directory that is attached to the kernel's pipe structure is created. This enables two unrelated processes to communicate over a pipe. The processes each need to open the pipe like a regular file, one opening it for reading and one for writing. I/O then occurs normally.

Secret

In UNIX systems that support sockets, an internal pipe is implemented as two connecting sockets.

System V IPC

System V UNIX introduced a more powerful and more complicated form of IPC. The means of IPC in System V include message queues, semaphores, and shared memory. The calls allow for a more complicated means of passing data than just passing a stream.

Message queues

A *message queue* is essentially a mechanism in which one process attaches a piece of information with defining flags and another process searches for information that matches the desired flags. Different flags can enable multiple processes to examine or write to the same message queue, and messages can be read out of order.

Semaphores

Semaphores are a means of passing flags from process to process. When one process has a certain state, it may raise a semaphore to indicate that it has reached that state. Any other process on the system can look for that flag and act accordingly.

Shared memory

Shared memory enables multiple processes to access the same piece of physical memory. An example of shared memory is a small database file: Multiple database access programs can use the same file, and any time one process changes a piece of data, it is automatically updated for all other processes using the same file.

For a single process, shared memory works in the same fashion as `mallocing` memory except that the shared memory also needs an address.

Scheduling

Process scheduling is the trickiest aspect of an operating system. UNIX administers scheduling by adding new processes to a run queue and examining the run queue for the best process to run. A subroutine in the kernel, called the *switcher,* saves the registers of the current process and loads the new process registers. The selected process is removed from the run queue, and the selected process becomes the running process.

The switcher is normally invoked once each second, but it may be invoked more often if the running process needs kernel resources, such as disk input or output. While a process is waiting for those resources, it moves off the CPU; when those resources become available, the process is restored to the run queue.

Process priorities are recalculated every second. The formula increments the CPU usage each clock tick and divides that by two for every second of running. For example, a process that uses the CPU for 60 ticks in a second gets 60 added to its priority before division by two. The process with the lowest priority is the best process to run.

The initial priority computation yields a value between 60 and 100. This is further adjusted by the nice value for a process, which is added to the priority to determine the actual process priority.

The superuser may subtract nice values to reduce the priority of important processes. The lowest superuser priority is 40.

Priorities below 40 are assigned to processes as a result of system states. These lower priority values force the process to use a critical system resource before it disappears, such as reading the data being returned from the disk before the disk cache is cleared. When the critical situation is cleared, a regular process priority is recomputed.

Some critical priorities are 0 for the swapper, 20 for blocked I/O, and 30 for handling the death of children. Priorities below 25 cannot be interrupted by signals. (These numbers may be different on your system owing to improved machine capabilities, but the underlying logic remains the same.)

Process scheduling is an important part of operating system design. For more information, I recommend reading the following books: Stallings's *Operating Systems,* Tanenbaum's *Structured Computer Organization,* and Silberschatz and Galvin's *Operating System Concepts.*

Understanding What Happens When the Machine Boots

When a machine boots, it loads the kernel. The kernel first creates the `init` process, which monitors the system's run state and immediately accesses the `init` table stored in `/etc/inittab`. This can start system daemons and `tty` monitors. It also executes the `rc` scripts for the specified run level. These scripts are important for monitoring the system's state. The most commonly encountered script is the one that cleans up after crashes for editors. Other scripts clean up temporary files and enable network services.

The `init` process is the grandparent of all processes on UNIX. Because it spawns every process from the `inittab` file, every process can trace parentage back to `init`. As a result, one of `init`'s functions is to clean up after zombie processes.

Summary

This chapter explained the inner workings of the UNIX kernel for process scheduling and resource management to help you understand how the kernel creates and manages processes. The specific topics included

▶ Run queues

▶ Process tables

▶ Memory management

▶ Paging

▶ Process creation

▶ Process death

▶ Interprocess communication (IPC)

▶ Boot-time services

▶ Process scheduling

The next chapter describes the tools used to examine and manipulate processes and IPC.

Chapter 15

Examining Processes

In This Chapter

▶ Understanding ps

▶ Examining all terminal processes

▶ Formatting the output

▶ Using specific output formats

▶ Combining flags

▶ Understanding the ipcs command

This chapter introduces you to the two tools most commonly used to examine processes and kernel resources.

Often, you may want to know what you or other users on the system are doing. The ps command provides you with a window into what the kernel is doing.

Understanding ps

The ps command is perhaps the most commonly used administrative command. It gives you a glimpse into the process table and enables you to see what is running, what state your processes are in, and what is eating CPU memory.

Secret

The name of the ps command has a simple origin: *process status.*

The syntax for ps is just ps followed by options. Each argument to ps must relate to a flag.

Normal ps output, without arguments, gives you a list of all processes associated with the current tty.

Note

The ps command in System V differs a lot from that in BSD. I am using the POSIX definitions here, which are based on System V. Your machine may not support some options. For more information on your options, type **man ps**.

The default output looks like this:

```
$ ps
   PID    TTY  TIME CMD
 16767  pts/1  0:00 ps
 18029  pts/1  0:00 -ksh
```

The output has four columns. The first, PID, contains the process ID. The second, TTY, ties the process to a specific tty. The third indicates how much CPU time the process has used, and the last column identifies the command being run.

The ps command takes many options, which modify the output. Table 15-1 lists these options, and the next few sections describe them in detail.

Table 15-1   Options for ps

Flag	Purpose
-a	Provides information on all processes associated with a terminal
-A	Provides information on all processes
-d	Provides information on all processes except session leaders
-e	Provides information on all processes (same as -A)
-f	Generates a full listing
-g *list*	Provides information on all processes associated with the listed group or groups
-G *list*	Provides information on all processes associated with the listed group numbers
-l	Generates a long listing
-n *name*	Provides information on all processes associated with the listed command names
-o *format*	Provides information with entries in the specified format
-p *list*	Provides information on the listed processes
-t *list*	Provides information on processes associated with the listed terminals
-U *list*	Provides information on all processes associated with the listed user IDs
-u *list*	Provides information on all processes associated with the listed user names

Examining all terminal processes

In a UNIX system, many processes are not tied to specific terminals. These are *daemons* and other administrative processes. With the -a option, you can eliminate them from a listing and examine only the interesting processes that are tied to a terminal. The output has the same format as the default:

```
$ ps -a
   PID    TTY   TIME CMD
 16767  pts/1  0:00 ps
 18029  pts/1  0:00 -ksh
```

Because I am the only user logged into the system, only my processes appear.

Some implementations of ps may omit the session leaders from the output. Session leaders are the shells that are the parent of all processes on a tty.

Examining all processes

Use the -A flag to examine all the processes on a system. The output can be fairly long:

```
$ ps -A
   PID    TTY   TIME CMD
     0      -  11:45 swapper
     1      -  24:35 init
   514      -  61371:35 kproc
   771      -  28:09 kproc
  1028      -   0:00 kproc
  1371      -   0:00 qdaemon
  1624      -   1:16 cron
  1793      -   0:00 errdemon
  2153      -   0:00 kproc
  2626      -   1:28 routed
  3071      -  24:52 syncd
  3457      -   0:00 kproc
  3647      -   0:30 syslogd
  3893      -   0:00 srcmstr
  4447      -   0:00 uprintfd
  4682      -   0:11 inetd
  5205      -   2:17 snmpd
  5470      -   0:00 writesrv
  5943      -   0:00 in.pmd
  6245      -   0:00 infod
  7633      -   0:00 httpd
  7892      -   0:00 httpd
  8051      -   0:05 radiusd
  8658      -   0:00 httpd
  8818      ?   0:00 tsm
  9173      -   0:00 httpd
  9454      -   0:00 httpd
 10415      -   0:00 portmap
```

```
10866     -   0:02  radiusd
11073     -   0:45  named
11290     -   0:00  in.pmd
12499     -   0:01  httpd
13684     -   0:03  sendmail
14032     -   0:00  httpd
16797   pts/1 0:00  ps
17772     -   0:00  telnetd
18029   pts/1 0:00  ksh
```

Note

This is the same output as that produced by the -e flag. The -A flag has superseded -e, but many ps commands still support -e.

Examining processes associated with a group

You can identify processes that belong to a given group defined in /etc/group. The -G argument (or optionally -g) followed by a list of group IDs gives a listing of those processes. The list may be comma- or space-separated, but it must be a single argument. Therefore, if spaces are present, you should enclose them in quotation marks. Here is a sample listing:

```
$ ps -G 0
   PID   TTY  TIME CMD
     0     - 11:45 swapper
     1     - 24:35 init
   514     - 61375:25 kproc
   771     - 28:09 kproc
  1028     -  0:00 kproc
```

The 0 group is the root group. This provides a list of the processes associated with root.

Formatting the output

I have not seen one POSIX specification, the -o option, implemented. Were this option available, it would enable you to specify a list of fields for output. Table 15-2 lists the available fields.

Table 15-2	-o Fields for ps
Field	*Description*
args	Command arguments
comm	Name of the command
etime	Elapsed time of the process
group	Effective group ID of the process

Field	*Description*
nice	Nice value for the process
pcpu	Recent percentage of CPU usage
pgid	Process group ID
pid	Process ID
ppid	Parent process ID
rgroup	Real group ID of the process
ruser	Real user ID of the process
time	CPU time for the process
tty	Controlling terminal for the process
user	Effective user ID of the process
vsz	Size of the process in virtual memory

You must specify a header for each field. The format is *field=header*. To specify more than one field/header pair, use a comma-separated list or a space-separated list enclosed in double quotation marks. You can specify any number of field/header pairs in a single option, and you can list multiple options on a command line.

Examining specific processes

The -p flag for ps enables you to list specific process IDs and obtain their status. This is useful if you are tracking a potential problem, such as a runaway process that is eating CPU time as fast as a bear eats berries. The list format is the same as that for group listings:

```
$ ps -p "12499, 17772"
   PID    TTY  TIME CMD
 12499     -   0:01 httpd
 17772     -   0:00 telnetd
```

The two processes are the http daemon for serving Web pages and the telnet daemon.

Examining processes associated with a specific tty

The -t option enables you to see all the processes associated with a specific terminal. You must follow the flag with a terminal name. Use the same comma- or space-separated list as that used for group listings. The output looks something like this:

```
$ ps -t \?
   PID    TTY   TIME CMD
  8818      ?  0:00 tsm
```

The question mark indicates a process that expects to be connected to a terminal but is not.

Examining processes associated with a user

The -U option examines processes belonging to a specific user. The format is the same as the -G command, with a similar string format:

```
$ ps -U 200
 UID   PID     TTY  TIME CMD
 200  9454       -  0:00 httpd
```

The user ID (UID) appears with the output in the first column. This user fired off an http daemon.

Using specific output formats

The ps command provides two longer output formats: full output and long output. The -f flag specifies full output, which looks like this:

```
$ ps -f
   USER   PID  PPID  C   STIME    TTY   TIME CMD
  james 18029 17772  0 20:25:36  pts/1  0:00 -ksh
  james 18361 18029  4 20:59:19  pts/1  0:00 ps -f
```

Table 15-3 describes the fields.

The -l flag specifies long output, which looks like this:

```
$ ps -l
     F S UID   PID  PPID  C PRI NI ADDR   SZ   WCHAN   TTY  TIME CMD
200001 R 212 11962 18029  3  61 20  881  116   pts/1  0:00 ps
241801 S 212 18029 17772  0  60 20 622e  280   pts/1  0:00 ksh
```

The fields are a bit different.

Each header has a specific meaning. To understand the output, you need to recognize each field. Table 15-3 lists those fields.

Some of the fields are useful; some are not. The WCHAN, in particular, requires the use of a kernel debugger to interpret.

Table 15-3   ps Headers and Fields

Header	-o Field	Meaning
ADDR	(none)	Address of the process
C	(none)	Processor usage for scheduling
CMD	comm,args	Command name (arguments are included with -f)
F	(none)	Flags associated with a process
NI	nice	Nice value
PID	pid	Process ID
PPID	ppid	Parent process ID
PRI	(none)	Process priority
S	(none)	State of a process
STIME	(none)	Start time for the process
SZ	vsz	Size of the process
TIME	time	Cumulative execution time for the process
TTY	tty	Controlling terminal for the process
UID	ruser	User ID of the process owner
WCHAN	(none)	Event for which the process is waiting

Combining flags

You can combine the flags for ps. Most often, you'll combine -f or -l with other options. Some long pieces can be created by combining -Af, as the following example illustrates:

```
$ ps -Af
    USER   PID  PPID   C    STIME   TTY  TIME CMD
    root     0     0 120   Aug 16     -  11:45 swapper
    root     1     0   0   Aug 16     -  24:36 /etc/init
    root   514     0 120   Aug 16     -  61386:59 kproc
    root   771     0   0   Aug 16     -  28:10 kproc
    root  1028     0   0   Aug 16     -   0:00 kproc
    root  1371  3893   0   Aug 16     -   0:00 /etc/qdaemon
    root  1624     1   0   Aug 16     -   1:16 /etc/cron
    root  1793     1   0   Aug 16     -   0:00 /usr/lib/errdemon
    root  2153     1   0   Aug 16     -   0:00 kproc
    root  2626  3893   0   Aug 16     -   1:28 /etc/routed -q
    root  3071     1   0   Aug 16     -  24:53 /etc/syncd 60
    root  3457     1   0   Aug 16     -   0:00 kproc
```

```
    root  3647  3893  0  Aug 16    -  0:30 /etc/syslogd
    root  3893     1  0  Aug 16    -  0:00 /etc/srcmstr
    root  4447     1  0  Aug 16    -  0:00 /etc/uprintfd
    root  4682  3893  0  Aug 16    -  0:11 /etc/inetd
    root  5205  3893  0  Aug 16    -  2:17 /usr/sbin/snmpd
    root  5470  3893  0  Aug 16    -  0:00 /etc/writesrv
    root  5943  4682  0  Sep 18    -  0:00 in.pmd
    root  6245  3893  0  Aug 16    -  0:00 /usr/lpp/info/bin/infod
    root  7633 14032  0  Oct 06    -  0:00 httpd-child
    root  7892 14032  0  Oct 06    -  0:00 httpd-child
    root  8051 10866  0  Sep 25    -  0:05 radiusd
    root  8658 14032  0  Oct 06    -  0:00 httpd-child
    root  8818     1  0  Sep 19    ?  0:00 /etc/getty /dev/console
    root  9173 14032  0  Oct 06    -  0:00 httpd-child
     tom  9454     1  0  Oct 01    -  0:00 bin/httpd -d /usr/tmp/websk
    root 10415     1  0  Sep 07    -  0:00 /usr/etc/portmap
    root 10866     1  0  Sep 25    -  0:02 radiusd
    root 11073     1  0 11:28:09    -  0:45 /etc/named
    root 11290  4682  0  Sep 22    -  0:00 in.pmd
   james 11967 18029  4 21:02:06 pts/1  0:00 ps -Af
    root 12499 14032  0  Oct 06    -  0:01 httpd-child
    root 13684     1  0  Sep 23    -  0:03 sendmail -bd -q30m
    root 14032     1  0  Oct 06    -  0:00 httpd-root
   james 16064 18029  2 21:02:06 pts/1  0:00 mail -s ps -Af
james@sagarmatha.com
    root 17772  4682  0 20:25:35    -  0:00 telnetd
   james 18029 17772  0 20:25:36 pts/1  0:00 -ksh
```

You can also combine the two output formats:

```
$ ps -lf
    F S   USER  PID  PPID C PRI NI ADDR  SZ WCHAN   STIME  TTY TIME CMD
200001 R  james 11966 18029 3 61 20 881 116  21:01:28 pts/1 0:00 ps -lf
241801 S  james 18029 17772 1 60 20 622e 280 20:25:36 pts/1 0:00 -ksh
```

Summary of ps

The process status command shows a lot of data associated with processes. Some of the data may seem meaningless, such as WCHAN, but you can interpret most of the data with a bit of experience.

Understanding ipcs

The other commands useful for managing resources are the ipcs and rpcinfo commands. The ipcs command examines the IPC tables, and rpcinfo examines remote procedure call (RPC) information. (RPC and rpcinfo are discussed in Chapter 19.)

The ipcs command checks the status of various interprocess communication tools. The format is ipcs followed by arguments. The default output is as follows:

```
$ ipcs
----- Shared Memory Segments -------
shmid    owner      perms     bytes      nattch     status
----- Semaphore Arrays -------
semid    owner      perms     nsems     status
----- Message Queues -------
msqid    owner      perms     used-bytes  messages
```

As you can see, I have no IPC running on my machine.

Table 15-4 lists the options to ipcs.

Table 15-4	ipcs Options
Option	**Description**
-a	Checks all IPC
-c	Lists IPC creator
-h	Lists help
-i *id*	Lists IPC associated with the specified IPC ID
-l	Lists IPC limits
-m	Lists shared memory segments only
-p	Lists creator's process ID
-q	Lists message queues only
-s	Lists semaphores only
-t	Lists time of creation
-u	Lists summary information

Summary

This chapter introduced you to two tools for checking system resources: ps and ipcs. It explained

▶ How to use ps to check process tables. You can find out the details of your own processes with ps and produce longer listings with ps -l and ps -f.

▶ How to use the different column headers (such as PID, PPID, and C) for ps.

▶ How to examine IPC channels and how to differentiate between IPC for message queues, semaphores, and shared memory.

The next chapter illustrates how to use the POSIX shell for managing processes. It will teach you how to manipulate jobs from the command line and what each of the different signals are.

Chapter 16

Managing Processes

In This Chapter

▶ Scheduling processes

▶ Manipulating the job queue

▶ Terminating processes

This chapter introduces you to the techniques that a UNIX expert uses to manage processes. At its simplest, process management is a job for the shell. The POSIX shell includes built-in commands for managing the processes that you spawn from your terminal session. Job management involves more than these commands, though. UNIX provides you with the tools necessary to schedule jobs, alter priorities, catch signals, and alter some resources.

Scheduling Processes

Although you can run commands from your terminal session immediately, sometimes you may want the computer to run a process for you at a different time. Coming back at 3 a.m. may be difficult, but you may want a reminder of a meeting. You may want to schedule a regular cleanup of your directory space, but the time it takes makes doing it from your login scripts undesirable.

Fortunately, UNIX provides job-scheduling tools. With at, you can specify an exact time to run a command. With batch, you can request that the computer run a process when it is not as busy. With crontab, you can schedule regular times to run your own administrative processes.

Caution

Some sites may disable job scheduling. One of my biggest frustrations with my current Internet service provider (ISP) is that I cannot schedule a routine administrative program. Because I use elm and filter to process my mail on that machine, I'd like to run a summary of the filter results once per day and mail them to my home machine. That's not allowed! Instead, I have to put this command in my login script. If I am away from my mail for a significant period of time, that administrative file can get fairly large. Oh, did I mention that the ISP bills for disk space used over allowance?

Story: The Days of Pure Batch Environments

Not surprisingly, at, batch, and crontab were some of the earliest UNIX job management commands. In the 1960s when UNIX was first being developed, most computers operated in a batch mode. You would write your program, include the program with the data, and submit a job. Operators would schedule larger jobs for late night times, so if you were performing large calculations (such as simulating the flight of a spacecraft), you would submit the job, go home, and obtain the output the next day.

Although I am an experienced UNIX user, I have some idea of what those days must have been

like. As an undergraduate at Duke University, most of my coursework was performed on large mainframes in batch mode. Near finals, receiving the output of your programs would take hours.

Personally, I'm glad that computers are now more interactive. I don't think I could have remained a computer professional in the pure batch environment. That doesn't mean I don't use at, batch, and crontab, though. I'm glad that such scheduling capability is in my hands, not in the hands of an operator.

The at command

The at command schedules single jobs to run at a specified time. This command also manages your pending job queue. The syntax is as follows:

```
at options time-spec
```

The at command manages multiple job queues. The default job queue is a. The job queue b is used for batch jobs, which are described later in the chapter. Your system may have other job queues defined. Ask your system administrator or examine your manual page for at. Table 16-1 describes the six options at takes.

Table 16-1   at Arguments

Option	Description
-f file	Specifies a file that contains the job
-l	Lists the jobs on the queue
-m	Sends mail to the user when the job is run
-q queue-name	Specifies a queue name
-r atjob	Deletes the specified at job
-t time	Specifies the time to run the job, using the time format defined in the touch command

Normally, at runs without arguments and with only a time specification on the command line. Unless you specify the -f option, at reads standard input to build the job to be submitted. Listing 16-1 shows an example of running at.

Listing 16-1: Running at

```
$ at noon
ls | elm james
Control-D
Job c00cecd54.00 will be executed using /bin/sh
$
```

I've requested that the ls command run in my current directory at noon and that the output be mailed to me. When typing in commands, you can terminate input with either a single dot or Ctrl-D.

The Ctrl-D character is also called EOF (end-of-file). Take care if you opt to end the commands with this character because if you accidentally press it twice, your shell receives the next EOF, which is a signal to terminate. For this reason, I recommend using the single dot instead of EOF.

Some systems may not honor the single dot, and you'll be forced to use EOF.

After I've finished entering the commands, at returns a job number. This is a unique ID that I can use to reference the job at a later date.

What at has done is build a file in the atjobs directory in the system's spool directory. This file is a listing of commands to run in the Bourne shell. The file can look very large because the first commands rebuild your current execution environment. Listing 16-2 shows the at job created in Listing 16-1.

Listing 16-2: An at Job as Defined in the File

```
#! /bin/sh
# mail     james 0
umask 22
LOGNAME=james; export LOGNAME
MAIL=/var/spool/mail/james; export MAIL
MACHTYPE=i386; export MACHTYPE
CGFLAGS=\-g; export CGFLAGS
HOSTTYPE=i386\-linux; export HOSTTYPE
PATH=/usr/local/bin\:/usr/bin\:/home/james/bin\:/usr/lib/uucp\:/usr/bin/X11\:/h
home/james/bin/CShells\:/home/james/bin/Shells\:\.\:/bin\:/home/james/Docs/IDG/
/bin; export PATH
HOME=/home/james; export HOME
SHELL=/bin/csh; export SHELL
USER=james; export USER
VENDOR=ibm; export VENDOR
HOST=duke; export HOST
OSTYPE=linux; export OSTYPE
PWD=/home/james/Docs/IDG/chapter16; export PWD
SHLVL=4; export SHLVL
BASH=/bin/sh; export BASH
TZ=PST8PDT; export TZ
```

```
WINDOWID=20971533; export WINDOWID
TERMCAP=vs\|xterm\|vs100\|xterm\ terminal\ emulator\ \(X\ Window\ System\)\:\
\:AL\=\\E\[\%dL\:DC\=\\E\[\%dP\:DL\=\\E\[\%dM\:DO\=\\E\[\%dB\:IC\=\\E\[\%d\@\:U
UP\=\\E\[\%dA\:\  \:al\=\\E\[L\:am\:\
\:bs\:cd\=\\E\[J\:ce\=\\E\[K\:cl\=\\E\[H\\E\[2J\:cm\=\\E\[\%i\%d\;\%dH\:co\#80\
\:\    \:cs\=\\E\[\%i\%d\;\%dr\:ct\=\\E\[3k\:\ \:dc\=\\E\[P\:dl\=\\E\[M\:\
    \:im\=\\E\[4h\:ei\=\\E\[4l\:mi\:\        \:ho\=\\E\[H\:\
\:is\=\\E\[r\\E\[m\\E\[2J\\E\[H\\E\[\?7h\\E\[\?1\;3\;4\;6l\\E\[4l\:\
\:rs\=\\E\[r\\E\[m\\E\[2J\\E\[H\\E\[\?7h\\E\[\?1\;
3\;4\;6l\\E\[4l\\E\<\:\
\:k1\=\\EOP\:k2\=\\EOQ\:k3\=\\EOR\:k4\=\\EOS\:kb\=\^H\:kd\=\\EOB\:ke\=\\E\[\?1l
l\\E\>\:\ \:kl\=\\EOD\:km\:kn\#4\:kr\=\\EOC\:ks\=\\E\[\?1h\\E\=\:ku\=\\EOA\:\
    \:li\#24\:md\=\\E\[1m\:me\=\\E\[m\:mr\=\\E\[7m\:ms\:nd\=\\E\[C\:pt\:\
\:sc\=\\E7\:rc\=\\E8\:sf\=\\n\:so\=\\E\[7m\:se\=\\E\[m\:sr\=\\EM\:\
\:te\=\\E\[2J\\E\[\?47l\\E8\:ti\=\\E7\\E\[\?47h\:\
\:up\=\\E\[A\:us\=\\E\[4m\:ue\=\\E\[m\:xn\:km\:"
"; export TERMCAP
cd /home/james/Docs/IDG/chapter16 || {
        echo `Execution directory inaccessible` >&2
        exit 1
}
ls | elm james
```

As mentioned previously, the file rebuilds the environment through
numerous commands that define and export variables. After defining the
environment variables, at attempts to change directories to the invocation
directory. If it fails, it logs an error message. Only after the environment is
duplicated does my command, ls | elm james, appear.

Note

The at command includes only your environment variables, not your shell
variables. If you need some of your shell variables, you need to define them
in the input to at or export them to your environment before calling at.

Time specifications

The at command allows for a fairly free-form time specification. Listing 16-3
shows the syntax. You can specify a date, a time, or an increment. Only the
time is mandatory, although some special keywords are reserved, as defined
in Table 16-2.

Listing 16-3: Syntax for at Time Specification

```
time-spec      : time | time date | time increment | time date increment |
now-spec ;
now-spec                  : "now" | "now" increment ;
time           : clock24 | clock24 tz | clock24hr ":" minute
                 | clock24hr ":" minute tz | wall-clock ampm
                 | wall-clock ampm tz | wall-hr ":" minute ampm
                 | wall-hr ":" minute ampm tz | "noon" | "midnight" ;
date           : month day | mon day "," year | weekday | "today" |
"tomorrow " ;
increment      : "+" number period | "next" period ;
period         : "minute" | "minutes"
```

```
                         | "hour"  | "hours"
                         | "day"   | "days"
                         | "week"  | "weeks"
                         | "month" | "months"
                         | "year"  | "years" ;
clock24                  : (four digit 24 hour clock time)
clock24hr                : 0-23
minute                   : 0-59
tz                       : (time zones recognized)
wall-clock               : (four digit 12 hour clock time)
ampm                     : "AM" | "PM" ;
wall-hr                  : 1-12
month                    : recognized 3 character months
day                      : recognized days of a month
year                     : two digit year
weekday                  : recognized 3 character day
```

Table 16-2   at Keywords

Keyword	Meaning
midnight	12:00 a.m. or 0:00
noon	12:00 p.m.
now	The current day and time
today	The current date
tomorrow	The day following the current day
minutes	The units of the increment as minutes
hours	The units of the increment as hours
days	The units of the increment as days
weeks	The units of the increment as weeks
months	The units of the increment as months
years	The units of the increment as years

You can combine the three types of time specifications.

Specifying time

You must specify a running time for each job that at runs because the time is a mandatory field for the at job. The at command supports both the 24-hour clock (as used in the military) or the 12-hour a.m.–p.m. clock. Times can be specified with four digits, two two-digit numbers separated by a colon, or a two-digit hour. You can optionally follow times with a time zone, as long as your system recognizes the time zone. Listing 16-4 shows some valid time specifications.

Listing 16-4: at Time Specifications

```
at 1530
at 3:30 PM
at 1 EST
at 5 AM UTC
```

If you do not specify a date, the at job runs in the next 24 hours.

Three special times are defined for at users. Providing the word noon tells at to run the job at 12 p.m. If you specify midnight, the job runs at 12 a.m. If you specify now, the job runs immediately. You can increment times, as explained later in the chapter.

Specifying dates

If you don't want the job to run in the next 24 hours, you must specify a date for the job. The date specification must follow the time specification. The date is defined as a month followed by a day. The month can be either a three-character month abbreviation or the full name of the month, followed by a date in that month. You may optionally specify a year if it is preceded by a comma. If you do not specify a year, the current year is assumed unless the date has already passed, in which case next year is assumed.

Note

Unfortunately, date specification is not as friendly as time specification, particularly to non-United States citizens. The British day-month-year format is not supported. Also not supported is the MM/DD format for abbreviating dates. (Some sites may support these dates as an extension to the POSIX specification.)

Here are some valid dates:

```
Dec 9
Aug 3, 1997
September 29
```

You can also specify a day of the week by using the three-character abbreviation for the day. For example, you can specify an at job with at 3am Tue.

You can also follow dates with increments.

Specifying increments

You can increment the specified time and date. Increments enable you to offset jobs. Follow the time and date specification with a plus sign, a number of units, and a unit specification. Listing 16-5 shows some valid increments.

Listing 16-5: at Increment Specifications

```
at now + 2 hours
at midnight Tue + 1 month
at 3am Mon + 1 week
at 1am Dec 9 + 1 year
at noon + 1 week
```

Some versions of `at` enable you to specify an increment without a time: `now` is assumed. This is not supported by the POSIX specification but is an addition.

Output from at

When an `at` job runs, any output is mailed back to you. Consider the case where I've requested an `at` job that is an `ls -CF` of my `bin` directory. Listing 16-6 shows the resultant mail message.

Listing 16-6: Output from an at Job

```
  N   4   Oct 9  system admin         (21)    Output from your job
c00ced246.00
Return-Path: <root>
Date: Mon, 9 Oct 95 12:06 EDT
To: james
Subject: Output from your job c00ced246.00
CShells/          gzip*             procmon*          testprocess*
Shells/           mailedit*         satno*            wchance*
adbook            mst3k*            screensaver.sh*   wishlists/
banner*           munge*            sendmail.cf       xloadimage*
checkem*          mydate*           shar*             xv*
crons             olvwm*            shipit*           xv.old*
desk*             op*               showbowls*        yes*
f1*               parsit*           showquakes*
f2*               patch*            sortem*
gruber*           patrunc*          src/
```

The first line of output is how the mail message appears in the `elm` mail reader. Your mail reader may show a different notification.

The message is sent from root, the user ID that runs the `at` jobs. Any standard output is collected from the `at` job and mailed back to the user. If no output is generated, no mail is sent unless you specify the `-m` flag.

If the command has output and you don't want it mailed back to you, you can redirect it to a file.

You might think that running an `at` job as root is a security hole. Nope. The `at` job first sets the effective user ID to that of the person who requested the job.

Retrieving a listing of pending jobs

You can obtain a list of pending `at` jobs by specifying the `-l` flag. The output is system-dependent, but every form of `at` should list the date of the job, the owner, and the job ID. There is no easy way to determine the specific commands of the `at` job, short of visually examining the actual job file. Listing 16-7 shows the output of `at -l`.

Secret

All at jobs are stored in the /var/spool/atjobs directory, which is usually protected so that only root can access or read the contents.

Listing 16-7: Output of at -l

```
Date                    Owner    Queue    Job#
03:00:00 12/09/95       james    c        c00d02834.00
```

I have one job queued up for 3 a.m. on December 9.

Deleting jobs

To delete a job, run at -r job-ID. There is no output to indicate that you have deleted the job.

Note

You can delete only jobs that you have requested unless you are root.

Submitting a file

If you have already written a shell script, you can specify that as a file on the command line by using -f. You must write the file in the Bourne shell to be properly understood.

This is sometimes quite useful, particularly if your at job is complicated. Essentially, when running at without -f, you are writing your shell program at the command line without the benefit of feedback from the shell, which tells you whether your commands worked. You can write your script and test it before running it with at.

Secret

If you are denied access to the crontab command, you can circumvent this by using at -f. Write all your commands into this shell script, and append the command at -f shell-file now + 1 day. When you run your shell script, it automatically registers the next time to run. The only problem is that the time may gradually shift because the value of now changes if at cannot run the job immediately.

Different time specifications

You have the option of specifying the time in the same format as that allowed by the touch command. The format is

```
[[CC]YY]MMDDhhmm[.SS]
```

where CC is the two-digit century, YY is the last two digits of the year, MM is the two numbers identifying the month, DD identifies the day, hh is the hour (24-hour clock), mm is the minutes, and ss is the seconds. The command at -t 200112091927 schedules a job for 7:27 p.m. on December 9, 2001. (Pure optimism prompts me to think that this computer will still be running on that date and at that time.)

The batch command

The batch command is very similar to the at command: it enables you to request that the computer run a command, or series of commands, at a later time. The batch command takes no arguments; instead, you type **batch** and enter the commands. When finished, use EOF to terminate input, as follows:

```
$ batch
ls | mail -s ls james
EOF
Job E00ced263.00 will be executed using /bin/sh
$
```

The batch command then schedules the job for the next time available on the job queue. The preceding job was scheduled as follows:

```
$ at -l
Date                    Owner    Queue    Job#
03:00:00 12/09/95       james    c        c00d02834.00
09:26:00 10/16/95       james    c        c00cef9ba.00
09:35:00 10/09/95       james    E        E00ced263.00
```

On my Linux system, the queue for batch jobs is E; this differs from POSIX, which specifies queue b for batch jobs.

The batch command is the same as at -q b -m now.

Disabling and enabling at and batch

A user's ability to run at and batch jobs is directly affected by the presence of two files in the /usr/lib/cron directory. If the at.allow file is present, only those users whose IDs appear in that file can queue at jobs. Similarly, if at.deny is present, users whose IDs appear in that file are denied access to at and batch. The system administrator should be the only one able to edit these files.

The crontab command

The crontab command resembles at. The crontab command manages tables of commands run by the cron daemon and schedules regularly running jobs, such as cleanup or other administrative tasks.

The crontab command takes either one of three arguments or the name of a file. If you specify a file, that file is considered the contents of the user's crontab. Table 16-3 defines the three arguments.

Table 16-3	crontab Options
Argument	**Meaning**
-e	Edits a copy of the user's crontab entry or creates a new entry for the user. When the editor is finished, the new table is installed for the user.
-l	Lists a copy of the user's crontab entry on standard output.
-r	Removes the user's crontab entry.

The EDITOR environment variable specifies the preferred editor for the -e option. If no EDITOR variable exists, vi is assumed.

Although changing the crontab entry on the current machine with the -e option is useful, sometimes you need to transfer your entry to a new machine. To do this, you create the output with crontab -l, modify it as needed for the new environment, transfer the file to the new machine, and install it there.

Note

I keep a copy of my crontab entry in a separate file under my home directory simply as a backup. Consequently, I prefer to edit that file and load it with crontab file instead of using the -e option. You should use whatever approach you find most comfortable.

Secret

All crontab entries are stored in the /var/spool/cron/crontabs directory. Usually, they are not readable by anyone with root. If you have an entry and you edit it in that directory, the cron daemon does not register it; you need to use crontab if you want to use the file.

crontab entry formats

The crontab command is just a table with time specifications and commands that run on a regular basis. Listing 16-8 shows the news crontab on my Linux system.

Listing 16-8: The News crontab

```
# DO NOT EDIT THIS FILE - edit the master and reinstall.
# (crons installed on Wed Apr 12 14:59:09 1995)
# (Cron version—$Id: crontab.c,v 2.13 1994/01/17 03:20:37 vixie Exp $)
0,15,30,45 *  1-31 *  0-6    /usr/lib/newsbin/input/newsrun
#30 8   1-31 *  1-5    su news -c `/usr/lib/newsbin/input/newsrunning off`
#00 17  1-31 *  1-5    su news -c `/usr/lib/newsbin/input/newsrunning on`
#40 *   1-31 *  0-6    su news -c `/usr/lib/newsbin/batch/sendbatches`
59 0    1-31 *  0-6    /usr/lib/newsbin/expire/doexpire
10 8    1-31 *  0-6    /usr/lib/newsbin/maint/newsdaily
00 5,13,21  1-31 *  0-6    /usr/lib/newsbin/maint/newswatch | mail james
```

Note

The netnews system, described in Chapter 20, uses `crontab` extensively to monitor and load new news articles.

The time specifications are five space-separated fields before the command. The first time specification is the minutes field, followed by hours, day of the month, month of the year, and day of the week. Each field is numerical. Minutes are between 0 and 59, hours are between 0 and 23, and days of the week start at 0 (where 0 is Sunday).

The asterisk means do not check against this field. In Listing 16-8, the `newsrun` command runs every hour at 15-minute intervals. The `doexpire` command runs once per day at 59 minutes past midnight, and `newsdaily` runs at 8:10 a.m. daily. The `newswatch` command runs daily at 5 a.m., 1 p.m., and 9 p.m.

If a number sign (#) is present, the line is commented out, and the `cron` daemon ignores everything following the #.

Controlling access to cron

The `cron.allow` and `cron.deny` files in the `/usr/lib/cron` directory control access to the `cron` tables. If a user name is present in the `cron.allow` file, that user can use `crontab`. If the user name is in `cron.deny`, that user is denied access. If both files are missing, anyone can use `crontab`.

The nohup command

Any process running off a terminal sends a hang-up signal when that terminal session ends. The `nohup` command enables a user to run a program and make it immune from hang-up signals. The syntax is `nohup` *command*.

Normally, commands that run with `nohup` are placed in the background. They run through to completion, even if you have logged out. Any output that normally would go to standard out is sent instead to the `nohup.out` file in the current directory. If that directory or its `nohup.out` file is not writable, the output is appended to a `nohup.out` file in your home directory.

Note

I find `nohup` particularly useful when I am compiling large software projects. Because `nohup` saves the output for me, I can examine it at my leisure.

The nice command

Like `nohup`, the `nice` command precedes a command and affects the running of that command. In the case of `nice`, you specify a value by which the command's priority is incremented when a CPU's scheduling is calculated. This `nice` value is a positive number, although the flag makes it look negative:

```
$ nice -10 make
```

Commands run with nice may take longer to complete because they are automatically considered lower-priority commands.

The root user may specify a negative increment, which lowers the priority value of the process and makes it run faster.

The POSIX committee has made the -number syntax obsolete and has instead specified a flag, -n, to precede the nice value, as follows:

```
nice -n 10 make
```

This helps clear up a potentially confusing syntax for specifying negative increments. Originally, the syntax looked like this:

```
nice --10
```

Now, it looks like this:

```
nice -n -10
```

 The maximum absolute value of the increment is 20. Some systems with special scheduling algorithms may support higher values.

Job Control

The POSIX shell supports job control. To enable the job control commands, specify a set -m or set -o monitor in your startup script.

Consider each command you type at the command line a job. Some commands, such as cd, return instantly and directly affect the shell's working environment. Others may take longer and do not need you to provide input. Running those commands in an interactive session robs you of time that you could productively use to perform other tasks. Ideally, you may want to run such commands in the background or even in batch mode. Sometimes, though, you may wish to track the results of the command or may require notification for the end of the job.

Job control is a mechanism for tracking the processes that spawn from your current terminal session. Any number of jobs may be running at a given time. These jobs may be running, stopped, or in other states. You can use several commands for managing these jobs.

Running a job in the background

A new user might first face the problem of how to run a command in the background. Putting a job in the background enables you to continue to use your terminal session while the command is running. Appending an ampersand (&) to the command when you type it in the command line is the standard way to do this. The shell returns the job number and the process ID for the command:

```
$ make&
[2] 20054
$
```

Now, the `make` command is considered a background job. It will continue to run in the background until it has finished or until its job status changes.

Note

The `make` command builds software packages from source code. It can take a lot of time and is a perfect candidate for running in the background.

If the job requires no input from you, it continues running in the background until completion. If the command needs input, however, the job status changes to suspended, and you receive a notification on your screen. That notification looks something like this:

```
[1]  + Suspended (tty input)  amfoot 0
```

In this case, the program `amfoot` has suspended itself, seeking some input. You need to move it into the foreground and provide the input.

Interrupting a running job

If you've started a job without placing it in the background and want to place it there, you are not out of luck. Just type Ctrl-Z. The job suspends itself, and you can then manipulate it however you please. The suspended job is placed in the background in a suspended state, and you regain control of your terminal session.

Ctrl-Z is called the suspend key, and you can address it with the `stty` command. The `stty` command creates your terminal session settings. Most of the `stty` information is fairly arcane, and you need not pay it any attention. The `susp` character, though, is one of the important characters. Type **stty -a** to obtain a complete listing of the characters, and use the one assigned to `susp`.

The other important characters are `intr`, `quit`, `erase`, `kill`, `eof`, `start`, `stop`, `werase`, `echo`, `echoe`, and `echok`. (The last three are toggles.) These characters perform special terminal functions, as described in Table 16-4.

Table 16-4	Important Characters in stty
Character	*Description*
`intr`	Sends the interrupt signal to the running process, terminating it.
`quit`	Sends the quit signal, causing the process to abort.
`erase`	Deletes the previously typed character, enabling you to back up on input.

Continued

Table 16-4 *(continued)*

Character	Description
kill	Deletes the entire line of input.
eof	Marks the end of input.
start	Handles control flow to the physical device by enabling you to stop and restart.
stop	Restarts the display of a stream of input.
werase	Erases the input back to the last whitespace character.
echo	Tells the terminal to echo your input back to the screen. This feature is turned off for password entry and the like.
echoe	Tells the screen to echo back the results of an erase. This usually removes the character from the display.
echok	Tells the screen to echo back the results of kill, restoring the line to the original clean state.

Note

You can change each one of the terminal settings listed in Table 16-4 with stty: just specify the setting and the desired character. You'll usually find these setting changes in a shell startup script.

The jobs command

You can examine the state of your jobs with the jobs command. Typing **jobs** gives you a list of all the jobs running off your terminal session.

```
$ jobs
[1]  - Running                xterm -cr purple -ms black -bd green -bg cyan
-fg red -T vi c16 -g 80x22 -e vi  ...
[2]    Running                make
[3]  + Suspended (tty output) vi chapter
$
```

I have three jobs running off this terminal session: one xterm, one make, and one vi session. Each job has a number associated with it.

The jobs command takes two options: -l, which includes the process ID with the job number, and -p, which replaces the job number with the process ID. The following example shows the results of -l.

```
$ jobs -l
[1]  - 13672 Running                xterm -cr purple -ms black -bd green -bg
cyan -fg red -T vi c16 -g 80x22 -e vi  ...
[2]    20054 Running                make
[3]  + 20147 Suspended (tty output) vi chapter
$
```

You can use the process IDs with the `ps` command, described in Chapter 15, to obtain more information on how the process is executing.

Job numbers

Job numbers provide a means for the shell to track each process. The job number can be considered the head of a group of processes because your job spawned any commands, whether in a pipeline or as part of the job.

The `fg`, `bg`, and `wait` commands, described in the following sections, each address a job number. Addressing the job number involves prepending the number with the percent sign (%). The shell also recognizes several special job numbers, as defined in Table 16-5.

Table 16-5   Special Job Numbers

Job Number	Meaning
%number	The job with the specified number
%string	The job whose command begins with the specified string
%?string	The job whose command contains the specified string
%%	The current job
%+	The current job
%-	The previous job

The concept of the current and previous jobs is interesting. Did you notice how the `jobs` command listed one job with a plus sign (+) and one with a minus sign (-)? The plus job is the current job, meaning it is the last job to receive a change in its status. The previous job is the job that was current before that.

You can use a job number for the `jobs` command. This is a convenient way of converting the job number to a process ID. Listing 16-9 illustrates a convenient function for this task. (This function is included on the CD-ROM that accompanies the book.)

Listing 16-9: The jtopid Function

```
$ jtopid () {
> jobs -p %${1}
> }
$ jtopid 2
20054
```

In this function, you pass a single job number, and it echoes out the current process ID (PID). You can then use that PID in any usual fashion, such as `ps -lp `jtopid 2``.

The fg command

The `fg` command moves jobs to the foreground. When a job is suspended and seeking terminal input or output (as job 3 is in the listings in the preceding "The jobs command" section), you can bring it forward with `fg %3`. The job then runs in the foreground, either displaying what it needs on the terminal or receiving the input it expects. After it has done this, you can again suspend the job with Ctrl-Z and manage it later.

Any job on the listing provided by `jobs` is available for you to move into the foreground, even if it is already running in the background.

Note

If only one job is on the listing, you do not need to specify a job number with the `fg` command. Similarly, if no job number is specified, the current job is assumed.

The bg command

You can resume a suspended or stopped job in the background with the `bg` command. You specify an appropriate job number, and the job then runs in the background to termination or until it again needs terminal input.

Note

After you've pressed Ctrl-Z, this is the current job. You don't need to specify a job number to place the current job in the background.

Story: Adventures in Swapping

The ability to switch back and forth between processes has interesting applications. To move quickly between two processes, I once wrote a simple alias: `alias swap='bg;fg %-'`. This placed the last job in the background and brought the previous job to the foreground.

I wrote this because a couple of friends and I were attempting to crack the adventure game.

We'd execute a command in adventure, then suspend and swap, and then write the effect in a different file. Then, we'd suspend and swap, and try a new command. We kept at this until we figured it out.

Of course, we could have found the source and made use of that, but where's the fun in doing it that way?

Story: Taking Advantage of X Windows Features

I often take advantage of some of the X Windows features in my shell sessions. Most notably, I've written an alias for my editor that brings up vi in a separate xterm window, giving me access to both my shell and the vi session at the same time. One of the unfortunate side effects, though, is that this is just a background process to the initial shell. I often forget that I'm running the vi in the background, type wait, and wonder why a process is taking so long to complete before I realize that the vi process is also in the background.

The wait command

The last notable job management command is wait. When you enter wait, you suspend the execution of the shell until all the background jobs are completed. This includes any stopped jobs, so make sure that all the background jobs are running when you start the wait.

The wait command can also receive a job number, and it suspends execution of the shell until the specified job has completed.

Although you can suspend wait, doing so makes no sense. Instead, end the wait with the interrupt key and retype it as needed.

Terminating Processes and Resources

Sometimes you may need to terminate a process or clean up some resources. You should find two commands useful for this task: kill and trap.

The kill command

The kill command is a built-in shell command that sends a signal to a process. If no signal is specified, the SIGTERM signal is sent by default. The syntax is as follows:

```
kill [ signal ] job | PID
```

You can specify either a job number or a process ID. You can kill only processes that you have started unless you have root permission.

The kill command can take one of two arguments. The -l argument gives you a short list of standard signals. The -s argument enables you to specify a signal to send to the process. In each case, you do not need to include the initial *SIG* in the signal name. Alternatively, you can specify the signal number and send it to the process.

Signals

As described in Chapter 14, a *signal* is a flag sent from one process to another (or to itself), notifying the process of a condition that may need attention. Table 16-6 lists some common UNIX signals, their meanings, and their default actions. Understanding these signals is important to understanding why a process fails or succeeds.

Note

Specific signals can vary from system to system, so you need to check your own manual pages to determine what the numbers are on your system.

Table 16-6   Signals

SIG	Meaning	Default
HUP	The tty has hung up	Terminates processing
INT	User interrupt	Terminates processing
QUIT	Abort processing	Terminates and dumps a core
ILL	Illegal instruction	Terminates and dumps a core
TRAP	EMT trap	Terminates and dumps a core
ABRT	System aborts	Terminates and dumps a core
IOT	IOT trap	Terminates and dumps a core
FPE	Floating point exception	Terminates and dumps a core
KILL	Kill	Terminates immediately
USR1	User-defined signal	Ignores
SEGV	Segmentation violation	Terminates and dumps a core
USR2	User-defined signal	Ignores
PIPE	Pipe failure	Terminates and dumps a core
ALRM	Alarm clock	Ignores
TERM	Terminate	Terminates processing
CHLD	Death of child	Is system dependent
CONT	Continue processing	Resumes execution
STOP	Stop the process	Suspends execution
TSTP	Stop the process	Suspends execution
TTIN	Background process needs input	Notifies the user
TTOU	Background process needs output	Notifies the user
XCPU	CPU limit exceeded	Terminates processing
XFSZ	File size limit exceeded	Terminates processing

SIG	Meaning	Default
WINCH	Window size changed	Ignores
PWR	Power failure imminent	Ignores

You can trap signals by changing the default actions. Only SIGKILL and SIGSTOP cannot be caught in a program.

You are not likely to see many of these signals, but if you do, they imply that something is seriously wrong with the program you are running. Table 16-7 describes some of these signals more fully.

Table 16-7   Detailed Meanings of Some Important Signals

Signal	Meaning
SIGILL	An illegal instruction has been sent to the CPU. This can result from an illegal branch in the machine code of a program, such as attempting to execute a line of data.
SIGTRAP	A process breakpoint trap has been triggered. The ptrace system call controls this, which is useful for debugging.
SIGEMT	This is an emulator failure.
SIGFPE	You have attempted to perform an illegal arithmetic operation, such as attempting to take the logarithm of a negative number.
SIGBUS	You have an error on an I/O bus. This usually results from an attempt to read or write beyond the boundary of the program's memory.
SIGSEGV	This is a segmentation violation, the bane of software developers! It means you have attempted to access a segment of memory in an illegal fashion. Examples include assigning a value to a part of the code segment or reading from address zero. Several software tools are available in UNIX to track memory usage and fix this problem. If you see a segmentation violation in a program, it usually means that the programmer has not properly tracked all the memory!
SIGPIPE	The program has attempted to read or write to a pipe after the other end of the pipe has exited. This signal helps to terminate pipelines when a command in the pipeline has failed.
SIGALRM	A programmer can set an alarm clock in a program to allow you a certain amount of time to perform an action. I use this in my football program to simulate a delay of game penalty.
SIGCHLD	Originally, this was a death-of-child signal, but now it means that the status of a child process has changed.

Continued

Table 16-7	*(continued)*
Signal	**Meaning**
SIGTSTP	This is a request from the terminal to stop a process. When you press Ctrl-Z, you are sending this signal to the process.
SIGCONT	This tells a process to resume execution. Either the fg or bg command sends this to a process, and the shell can either call the internal system call wait for a foreground process or call nothing for a background process.

The kill -l command

The kill -l command gives you a list of supported signals on your system. For my Linux system at home, the output is this:

```
$ kill -l
 1) SIGHUP      2) SIGINT      3) SIGQUIT     4) SIGILL
 5) SIGTRAP     6) SIGIOT      7) SIGBUS      8) SIGFPE
 9) SIGKILL    10) SIGUSR1    11) SIGSEGV    12) SIGUSR2
13) SIGPIPE    14) SIGALRM    15) SIGTERM    17) SIGCHLD
18) SIGCONT    19) SIGSTOP    20) SIGTSTP    21) SIGTTIN
22) SIGTTOU    23) SIGIO      24) SIGXCPU    25) SIGXFSZ
26) SIGVTALRM  27) SIGPROF    28) SIGWINCH   30) SIGPWR
$
```

My Linux system supports all the signals listed in Table 16-5 and a few more.

The actual kill

After you have determined which process will receive a signal and what signal you intend to send, you perform the kill by typing the following:

```
$ kill -s signal process
```

Either the process ID or the job number is a valid target for the kill command. You can specify multiple processes or jobs on the command line.

Normally, you first attempt to kill with the SIGTERM signal. This signal, a request to terminate, is the default. For example, if you've selected job 2 for termination, you enter the following:

```
$ kill %2
```

If the job terminates, you receive a message back asynchronously:

```
$
[2]    Done                    make
$
```

If you don't see that message, you need to move to heavier measures, using SIGKILL. You can use two approaches (either works):

```
$ kill -s KILL %2
```

or

```
$ kill -9 %2
```

In each case, the process should terminate. If not, you have a serious system problem and should contact your system administrator.

Note

As explained in Chapter 14, the process sometimes reaches a priority level where not even a KILL signal can interrupted it. These cases usually resolve themselves quickly, and the process terminates.

Story: Resolving a Hang-Up

When I was working at Bell Labs and we were using System V Release 2, we had a situation in which a uucico process was hanging on a port that had already hung up. Because the process did not know about the hang-up, it continued to lock the port, so we could not use UUCP. This glitch terminated all our incoming and outgoing mail.

Initially, we tried kill and kill -9, but neither command freed up the port. A quick look at the process table with ps -l showed that the actual process priority was about 15, which meant that it was waiting for input or output on the port and was unable to accept any signals. Because another uucico process with which our process was communicating had exited and disconnected from the line, our uucico process would never be able to answer that I/O request and would remain at priority 15 until the system rebooted.

Under normal circumstances, a system administrator might have performed the reboot, but we were developing large applications at our site. Rebooting the system could have cost us a day or more of development time, and we were under the gun to meet a deadline.

Here's where things got bizarre. We went into the system with the /etc/crash utility, which is a little-used utility that enables an administrator to observe the kernel's tables in a cleanly organized fashion while the system is running. This enabled us to determine the actual index into the process table for the uucico process. Next, we looked at the source code and the crash data to determine the actual physical address in the kernel where the process priority value was stored.

The /etc/crash utility is an analysis tool, not a debugging tool, so we actually had to change the data in the running kernel. The adb tool was perfect for this (adb is the initial UNIX debugger). We ran adb and loaded the kernel. All we had to do was set the value of the address where we thought we saw the priority to a number greater than 25. This meant that on the next scheduling iteration, it would see the KILL signal, exit, and free the port.

It worked. The port was freed, we kept working, and we were able to receive our incoming and outgoing mail.

Trapping signals in the shell, revisited

Now that I've explained what signals are and how they are used, you should have a better understanding of why a process might want to trap a signal and perform some actions. Usually, these actions are cleanup actions, but sometimes they serve other purposes.

As its name implies, the `trap` command traps the signals. It takes a list of signals and a string to execute. (That string can be a function call.) For example, you might see

```
trap 1 2 15 'cleanup;exit'
And later
function cleanup () {
# Perform some stuff to clean up a program
}
```

By setting the trap, you've told the shell that should it receive either a hang-up signal (1), an interrupt (2), or a terminate (15), you want it to clean up anything it is doing and then exit.

You can also implement some data passing between shells with traps and functions, as follows:

```
trap USR1 'getmessage'
function getmessage () {
opid=`sed 1q $messfile`
mess=`tail +2 $messfile`
# Act on the message
echo $pid > $messfile
echo $response > $messfile
kill -s USR1 $opid
}
```

The `getmessage` function expects a message to be present in `$messfile`. The first line is the process ID of the sending function, and the rest is the message. When the shell receives a `USR1` signal, it automatically goes to the `getmessage` function and grabs the data from that file. It may need to do some processing, and it sets up the `$messfile` to send the response and sends the `USR1` signal back to the calling process to let it know the response is ready.

Trapping signals in programs

There are means of trapping signals in software programs. Again, these are normally used to trap failures and clean up, with the notable exception of `SIGALRM`. UNIX system calls provide a means whereby you can send yourself a signal at a later time and perform an action when that signal arrives.

I am currently using that feature in my regular job. I have written some code that provides data to another process, and the absence of data is also important to that process. If my program cannot be reached, the process does not know about the change of state.

Therefore, I've written a signal handler that cleans up the data and then calls the alarm clock to wait for 60 seconds. During that time, any process can poll my program and determine that the relevant data has been taken down. After 60 seconds, my program receives the SIGALRM signal that I've requested, catches it, and calls my finalexit function. This does the last cleanup and exits properly.

Summary

This chapter introduced the UNIX tools that manage processes, focusing on tools that

▶ Schedule processes at requested times

▶ Time formats for at

▶ Defer execution of processes

▶ Schedule regular processes

▶ Ignore hang-up signals

▶ Change process priorities with nice

▶ Manage jobs

▶ Change jobs from the background to the foreground, and vice versa

▶ Wait for jobs to finish

▶ Terminate jobs

▶ Understand signals

▶ Trap signals

The next chapter pulls all the new process management knowledge together and puts it into the big picture of UNIX.

Chapter 17

Putting a Process in Perspective

In This Chapter

▶ Writing shell functions for process manipulation

▶ Using tools to reformat output

This chapter explains how a process fits into the overall scheme of UNIX and how to use the various tools to examine processes and other resources.

Using Shell Tools

The last chapter introduced a Korn shell function to convert the shell's job number into a process ID (PID). This is one example of how you can integrate a shell into the analysis of processes.

Another more useful approach for sorting output comes from a ps command, but it suffers because sort order is not specified. Some ps commands give output sorted by PID and others by CPU time. Neither of these is truly optimal.

Therefore, I've written a small program called sortps. It is a Korn shell script that takes one or two arguments and gives me the ps output sorted on a field. Listing 17-1 shows the shell script.

Listing 17-1: The sortps Script

```
sortps (){
if
    [ X$1 = X-r ]
then
    revorder=1
    shift
else
    revorder=0
fi
ps -A -o ${1},pid,comm,args > /tmp/ps.$$
sed 1q /tmp/ps.$$
if
```

```
    [ "$revorder" -ne 0 ]
then
    tail +2 /tmp/ps.$$ | sort -nr
else
    tail +2 /tmp/ps.$$ | sort -n
fi
}
```

What this script does is simple. It examines the first argument, and if the script finds a -r, it assumes the output is in reverse order. That argument is then shifted out. The new first argument becomes the first option listed in the -o argument for ps. The output of ps is saved to a temporary file. Because the first line of output is the headers, I use sed to print it to standard output. The remaining output is the process data. Because the sort field is also the first field, the sort command is simple. The -n option sorts the data numerically, if possible.

Secret

The $$ construct is useful for creating a temporary file. It is the shell variable for the process ID of the current shell. Because this value is unique, the risk of conflict is small.

Caution

If you write to a file system that different systems share, a conflict may arise if two systems call the same routine with common process IDs.

Secret

Another UNIX trick is illustrated in Listing 17-1. In the first comparison, both strings are prepended with an X. Consequently, a comparison does not mistake the -r as a flag to the comparison, and if $1 is not defined, the value still exists for comparison.

The code in Listing 17-1 is far from perfect. For one, it does not clean up after itself. You can accomplish this simply by adding the line rm /tmp/ps.$$ at the end of the function.

Furthermore, this code never performs a sanity check on its arguments. If no arguments are given, it crashes with a bad format string. Similarly, if the sort option is not a valid format string option, an error occurs.

Listing 17-2 illustrates a means of improving this and expanding the functionality.

Listing 17-2: Enhanced sortps

```
function sortps (){
if
    [ X$1 = X-r ]
then
    revorder=1
    shift
else
    revorder=0
fi
if
```

```
    [ $# -eq 0 ]
then
    echo Error:  Too few arguments
    return
fi
optstring=""
while
    [ $# -ne 0 ]
do
    case "${1}" in
    ruser|user|rgroup) optstring=${optstring}${1}, ;;
    group|pid|vsz) optstring=${optstring}${1}, ;;
    pgid|pcpu|ppid) optstring=${optstring}${1}, ;;
    nice|etime|time) optstring=${optstring}${1}, ;;
    tty|comm|args) optstring=${optstring}${1}, ;;
    *) echo Bad request ${1}
    return;;
    esac
    shift
done
optstring=${optstring}pid,comm,args
ps -A -o ${optstring} > /tmp/ps.$$
sed 1q /tmp/ps.$$
if
    [ "$revorder" -ne 0 ]
then
    tail +2 /tmp/ps.$$ | sort -nr
else
    tail +2 /tmp/ps.$$ | sort -n
fi
rm /tmp/ps.$$
}
```

Here's what has happened: The new `while` loop and `case` statement enable you to specify more than one field to be added and sorted. The field name is checked, and if it is a valid name, the argument is appended to the `optstring` variable.

This program enables you to specify a command such as `sortps vsz etime` to sort according to the largest processes and the greatest elapsed time. This can be useful for determining who is hogging a system.

You can create other tools. You can use the `jtopid` function (shown in Listing 16-9 and included on the accompanying CD-ROM) to generate a `ps` listing based on the job number. Listing 17-3 shows a function that does this.

Listing 17-3: ps from a Job Number

```
jobps () {
jno=${1}
shift
ps $* -p `jtopid $jno`
}
```

This function expects the job number as the first argument. It then shifts the arguments, so you can specify any normal ps arguments after the job number, and they will be passed to ps. Finally, the call to jtopid is incorporated into the command line for the ps call.

A sample call is jobps 2 -1, which gives the long listing for job number 2.

My UNIX system, Linux, does not support the -o option for ps; other versions of UNIX don't support it yet, either. Because each output field has a fixed width, however, you can use cut and paste to mimic -o. Listing 17-4 shows one such function.

Listing 17-4: Using Cut and Paste to Mimic -o

```
function pseudooptps () {
integer j
ps -ef > /tmp/ps.$$
j=1
for i
do
    case $i in
    USER) cut -c1-8 /tmp/ps.$$ > /tmp/ps.$$.$j ;;
    PID) cut -c9-14 /tmp/ps.$$ > /tmp/ps.$$.$j ;;
    PPID) cut -c15-20 /tmp/ps.$$ > /tmp/ps.$$.$j ;;
    C) cut -c21-24 /tmp/ps.$$ > /tmp/ps.$$.$j ;;
    STIME) cut -c25-33 /tmp/ps.$$ > /tmp/ps.$$.$j ;;
    TTY) cut -c34-40 /tmp/ps.$$ > /tmp/ps.$$.$j ;;
    TIME) cut -c41-46 /tmp/ps.$$ > /tmp/ps.$$.$j ;;
CMD)    cut -c47- /tmp/ps.$$ > /tmp/ps.$$.$j ;;
*)      continue
    esac
    j++
done
case $# in
1)      cat /tmp/ps.$$.1 ;;
2)      paste /tmp/ps.$$.1 /tmp/ps.$$.2 ;;
3)      paste /tmp/ps.$$.1 /tmp/ps.$$.2 /tmp/ps.$$.3 ;;
esac
rm /tmp/ps.$$*
}
```

Although definitely a kludge, this approach to making a viable -o imitator can work. The command to obtain the output is pseudooptps PPID CMD.

Summary

This chapter taught you the basic techniques for combining job and process commands — most notably the `ps` command — with other UNIX commands. You should now be able to

▶ Write functions to incorporate job control commands such as `jtopid`

▶ Write commands to sort `ps` output

This completes my discussion of the basics of UNIX. In the next section, you'll learn the basics of networks, both local area networks such as Ethernet and wide area networks such as the Internet. Subsequent chapters introduce you to other advanced features of UNIX.

Part VI

Networking and Communications

Chapter 18

Understanding Communications

This chapter traces the history and evolution of computer systems from their use in data processing to their role as communication engine.

The Evolution of Computers

Computers — machines that perform calculations — have been around for over a thousand years. The most common example of a primitive computer is the *abacus,* a series of rocks or beads on strings that can perform addition, subtraction, multiplication, and even division.

More powerful than the abacus is the *slide rule,* which is also a type of computer. Slide rules enable you to perform more complicated calculations, including logarithms and exponentiation, than do abacuses. In my youth, I learned the slide rule well enough to perform these calculations as fast as a friend could type them into an HP scientific calculator.

Many people consider the first real computer to be Charles Babbage's Analytical Engine, developed around 1830 in England. This was a very primitive analog computer in which calculations were resolved through different gears.

The first famous use of computers came in World War II. The Germans sent important military communications by radio, and to protect the security of those communications, they developed an encoding system that they believed impregnable. Early in the war, the British, with the help of Polish refugees, were able to break this code. They used a stolen version of the German Enigma machine to decrypt messages and used computers to decrypt the keys for Enigma. Alan Turing, a professor at Cambridge who is considered to be the father of modern computer science, was a leader in this effort.

Story: A Tough Decision

The intelligence provided by Enigma was sometimes too good to be used: The British knew practically every German action as fast as Hitler did. Did they dare risk acting too swiftly to counter a German threat and having the Germans discover that the code had been broken?

Winston Churchill faced this decision during the Blitz on November 14, 1940. Enigma had provided the British with the knowledge that the Germans were going to bomb the city of Coventry. This city was away from the bulk of the British defenses, so any strong defensive effort might have suggested to the Germans that their encryption was not secure. Meanwhile, Enigma continued to provide other valuable information.

It must have been a horrible night. German bombs destroyed the center of historic, beautiful Coventry and killed over 400 people. But Enigma remained safe so that the British could win the battle of the Atlantic, survive, and (with the help of the Soviet Union and the United States) defeat Germany.

After World War II, American inventiveness continued to advance the electronic computing device. Transistors — and later integrated circuits — replaced tubes and made the machines faster and more reliable. These machines, however, remained combinations of computational engines and information storage and retrieval systems. These were important functions, but toward the 1970s, the role of computers began to change, and UNIX stood at the forefront of that change.

By the end of the 1960s, setups of large computers that many users shared were being replaced by smaller computers that sat on each user's desk. Users no longer waited idly for their time slot on the mainframe; they could instead be more productive at their desks.

This situation created its own headaches, though. The computers needed to share many resources, such as account names, passwords, and other administrative files. Furthermore, when one user worked with another, having separate computers was useless unless those computers could automatically pass information to each other. In short, computers needed to learn how to communicate.

This need led to the development of the *local area network* (LAN). Initially, users passed simple files to each other through a system called "Sneaker-Net" in which a user copied material from the first machine to a transportable medium (such as a floppy disk), walked over to the second machine, inserted the medium, and copied the data to the correct location on the second machine. As you might imagine, this process was slow.

Note

I've heard arguments that the PC created the need for the LAN and that the LAN created the need for the PC. This is a classic chicken-and-egg problem. Regardless of which came first, neither technology would have taken off without the other.

UNIX solved this problem with an application called *UUCP,* which stands for *UNIX-to-UNIX CoPy.* UUCP used modems and telephone lines to call from one UNIX system to another to send files and commands. UUCP was the first means by which UNIX computers communicated.

Since UUCP's development, other LAN technology, such as Ethernet, has superseded it. This new technology enables the sharing of files and file systems across multiple machines in a local network. Modern workstations come equipped with Ethernet technology, so all you need to do is plug the wire into the back of the computer and administer some files to the network. PCs do not provide this luxury; you need to purchase a separate Ethernet card for your machine and administer it. Because a wide range of quality exists among PC components, you should first check to see which boards your flavor of UNIX supports.

Caution

One of the hardest hardware tasks I've ever undertaken is configuring a PC to work properly on a network.

Cross-Reference

Chapter 19 discusses how to use your local area network to its fullest.

As soon as computers could talk locally, what would keep them in check? If I can share my data with my coworker in the next office, why shouldn't I be able to share it with a fellow researcher in the next state or the next continent?

This idea bore the *wide area network* (WAN). UNIX quickly grew to accommodate this, using the same tools, such as UUCP, that it used for a LAN. If a telephone can dial a machine 20 feet away, why not dial a machine 7,000 miles away? If a computer can ask another machine to run a command, why not have that computer ask a third computer to run another command?

Thus, the first real WAN in the UNIX world was based on UUCP. Since those days in the 1970s, the WAN has evolved into something more advanced and pervasive. We now call it the Internet, and it contains many tools and services. (The Internet is discussed in Part VII.) Surprisingly, the technology underlying LANs and the Internet is exactly the same. Both use the Internet Protocol to transmit data in packets. Ethernet protocols are built on top of the Internet Protocol, as are protocols such as FTP, Gopher, HTTP, and those used for transmitting electronic mail and netnews.

Story: Worldwide Communication

In my opinion, the real future of computers is not so much in data storage, retrieval, and analysis systems as in a new means of communication. The evolution of networks (particularly the WAN networks for e-mail, netnews, and the World Wide Web) supports this view. Today, I regularly exchange e-mail with my friend Brad Edelman in Perth, West Australia, and with friends in Scotland, South Africa, and Brazil. The communication is nearly as fast as a telephone call.

The Network Is the Answer

What constitutes a network of computers? A general definition would be *a group of computers that communicate with each other.* Your telephone is a simple computer on a network of switches that transfer data from one node to another according to the address specified by a user. Cable television is a similar type of network.

For the purposes of this book, which is concerned entirely with UNIX computers and the communication that goes on between them, the definition of networks is restricted to *machines that communicate either across telephone lines or via a local collection of wires called an Ethernet.*

To establish a machine on a network via telephone lines, you need to install a modem. Some machines come with modems built in; others require you to attach a modem to a serial port on the machine and then to attach the telephone line to the appropriate port on the modem.

Note

Many modems are on the market. I use a US Robotics Sportster 28,800 Data/FAX modem, which does an excellent job for me.

To work on a UUCP network, you first must give your computer a host name different from the names of other machines that you communicate with and different from the names of all the machines that they communicate with to prevent naming conflicts. Next, you need to administer UUCP on your machine. I discuss this later in the chapter.

Attaching the Ethernet to a machine is similar to attaching a modem. If the machine comes with an Ethernet port, your job is easier. If it does not, you need to install an Ethernet board. You'll usually see one of two types of connectors. If you have something that looks like a telephone line socket, you're running a 10 Base T connection and need to run the appropriate wire from the machine to a concentrator. If you have something that looks like a serial connector, you need a transceiver. After you get one, you can either attach the line to a concentrator or, if you have a round adapter, run a wire to every machine on your local network.

Each machine on your network needs a unique IP address. The `/etc/hosts` file administers this, and these addresses are usually of a rigid local format. Chapter 19 provides more details on this.

LANs versus WANs

The primary difference between a LAN and a WAN is in the administration and the services provided. Usually, every machine on a LAN is available to an administrator: You or someone at your site controls every machine on the LAN.

WANs are cooperative ventures. You attach your LAN to a WAN, and you can then provide or receive services for every site on the WAN. Traditionally, you'll want to include a firewall between your LAN and the WAN to prevent abuse. *Firewalls* are machines on your LAN that you've made available but through which no protocols can pass. The firewall acts as a collector and transmitter between your local machines and the rest of the world.

Some of the typical resources available on the LAN are login information, shared file systems, remote procedures, and local socket communications. Across a WAN, you'll find services such as File Transfer, Archie, Netnews, and the World Wide Web. Some services, such as e-mail, span both networks.

UUCP

UUCP is the original UNIX networking application. It transfers files from one UNIX machine to another and runs commands on one UNIX machine at the request of another. Mike Lesk at Bell Labs originally wrote UUCP to facilitate communication among machines at Bell Labs. It spread quickly.

The version of UUCP discussed in this book is HoneyDANBER, written by Peter Honeyman, David A. Nowitz, and Brian E. Redman. A more recent version is called Taylor UUCP and is distributed with Linux, but the documentation for Taylor UUCP is not as extensive as HoneyDANBER's.

The life cycle of a UUCP transfer

The command to request a UUCP transfer is usually uucp. You use this command to request the transfer of a file from your current machine to a destination on a remote machine. A job then queues.

At regular intervals, the system attempts to place a call to the remote machine. It opens the device, dials the appropriate numbers, and expects a connection. At the heart of these actions is something called a *chat script,* which is simply a list of expect-send patterns. When the calling process sees the expected pattern, it sends the send pattern.

After the connection is established, the data is transferred. The header of the transfer usually contains the location for the file. If a command is set to run, a command file is also transferred.

When the transfer is complete, the called system may transfer files back to the calling system. This tradeoff continues until all the transfers are complete. Then, the line is broken, and both sides run any requested commands and cleanup.

You can prevent the transfer of files from a called machine to the calling machine by modifying the Permissions file.

The commands

Several commands are associated with UUCP. The most common request the queuing of jobs. Others perform the actual transfers or are front ends to the uucp commands.

uucp

The most common UUCP command is uucp. This command queues a file transfer request. The syntax is simple:

```
uucp flags file destination
```

Table 18-1 lists the flags for uucp. The format of the file and the destination are the same. You need to specify a machine or a list of machines separated with exclamation points and followed by the path to a file. If the origin file is on the local machine, you don't need to specify machine names.

Table 18-1	uucp Options
Flag	**Meaning**
-c	Do not copy the file to the spool directory (default)
-C	Force the copy of the local file to the spool
-d	Make all the necessary directories for the transfer (default)
-f	Do not make intermediate directories for the file copy
-j	Write the job ID string to standard output
-m	Send mail to the requester when the copy is complete
-n user	Notify the named user on the remote machine when the copy is complete
-r	Do not start the transfer immediately; just queue the job

Because the exclamation point is significant to the C shell, you must escape it with a backslash (\).

You can use uucp to copy files from any machine in the local UUCP network to any other machine. If I'm on the machine redtail and want to copy the file nest to the machine peregrine, the command is

```
uucp ./nest peregrine!~/nest
```

The tilde (~) in the destination file tells uucp to place the file in the public directory. This is site-specific but is usually /var/spool/uucppublic. If I were on the machine merlin and nest was in my home directory, I'd need to run the following command:

```
uucp redtail!~james/nest peregrine!~/nest
```

If redtail has normal permissions, I'd be unable to perform this command because I wouldn't have remote access to my home directory.

Similarly, if I wanted to ship the file to the machine buteo and if buteo spoke only with peregrine, the command would be

```
uucp ./nest peregrine!buteo!~/nest
```

The machine peregrine would need to be configured to enable uucp to be executed through it.

uux

If, instead of wanting to move a file, I wanted to run a command, I'd use uux. This requests the execution of a file on a remote machine. The syntax is similar to uucp:

```
uux flags command-string
```

Table 18-2 describes the uux flags. The command-string has the same machine path format as uucp, but instead of a destination file, it has a command and arguments. For example, to retrieve the date on redtail, I'd use the command uux redtail!date. If allowed, the command would run on redtail, and I'd receive mail telling me the date.

Table 18-2   uux Options

Flag	Meaning
-	Make the standard input to uux the standard input to the command on the remote machine.
-p	Make the standard input to uux the standard input to the command on the remote machine.
-j	Write the job ID to standard output.
-n	Do not notify me if the command fails.

Secret

Most machines are configured to allow only rmail and rnews to run on them.

Secret

The uux command is usually hidden in the execution of commands such as rmail and rnews. These commands transfer information, and within themselves, they may build a uux request and run it.

uucico

At the heart of UUCP is the uucico command. This command stands for *UNIX-to-UNIX Call in Call out*. This is the program that actually communicates. A UUCP transfer requires a uucico to run on both the host and destination machine. You will probably never need to run uucico, but in case you do, Table 18-3 lists its arguments.

Table 18-3	uucico Options
Argument	*Meaning*
-rnumber	Role number (1 for master, 0 for slave)
-xnumber	Debugging level
-ddir	Spool directory
-s name	System name

The command operates in either master mode or slave mode. Master sends data down to the slave, which saves the data on the local machine. The -x option debugs UUCP, as discussed later in the chapter. Only the -s flag is mandatory.

uuxqt

The other command you should never need to run is uuxqt. It normally executes at the end of the uucico command and is executed at sporadic intervals by the UUCP daemons. It takes a single argument, -x, followed by a number for the debugging level.

uuto and uupick

Two commands that are useful for transferring files are uuto and uupick. The uuto command takes a file or list of files, a destination machine, and a user and sends the files to the destination machine.

The uuto command takes two arguments. The -m argument tells UUCP to send mail to the sender when the transfer is complete. The -p argument tells uuto to copy the source file to the spool directory.

Destinations take the form machine!user. This expands to a UUCP request so that it can transfer the files to $PUBDIR/receive/user/system on the destination machine, where user is specified on the command line and system is the system on which you ran uuto.

The uupick command grabs the files sent by uuto. The only command-line argument is -s system, which restricts the search to machines from the specified system.

The uupick command browses the public spool directory for receive/user, where user is the user name of the person running uupick. It then looks for systems and files. When it finds a file, it prompts the user for the disposition of the file. Table 18-4 lists all the available uupick commands.

Table 18-4 **uupick Commands**

Command	Action
new-line	Goes to the next entry.
d	Deletes the current entry.
m *dir*	Moves the current entry to the specified directory. If no directory is specified, this command moves the file to the current directory.
a *dir*	Moves all the files from this system to the specified directory. If no directory is specified, this command moves the files to the current directory.
p	Writes the content of the file to standard output.
q	Exits uupick.
<EOF>	Exits uupick.
!*command*	Runs the specified command.
*	Writes a usage summary for the commands.

The uuto and uupick commands complement each other and are useful tools if you work on several machines separated by UUCP.

The following example illustrates how uuto sends the file nest from redtail to peregrine:

```
uuto nest peregrine!james
```

On my peregrine account, I'd receive mail telling me nest had arrived. I'd then enter uupick and see the following:

```
$ uupick
from redtail: file nest ?
m
$
```

Then, when I did an ls, I'd find the file nest.

Story: UUCP-Separated Machines

Working on several machines separated by UUCP describes my situation at Bell Labs quite well. I was working on a project with seven other engineers, and we had among us a pair of 3B20s, a 3B5, and a 386. Our local network was UUCP-based, so we'd end up transferring files from machine to machine via uuto and uupick. In 1990, we began being placed on an Ethernet-based LAN and shared file systems across machines.

Note

You can also use `uuto` and `uupick` to transfer files on the local machine between users. For example, to send `nest` to the user `dave` on my local machine, `redtail`, I'd enter

```
uuto nest redtail!dave
```

He'd then place `nest` wherever he wanted with `uupick`.

The files

UUCP expects data in several files. Table 18-5 lists each file and the contents of the file.

Table 18-5   UUCP Files

File	Contents
Systems	A list of systems and the chat scripts for UUCP
Dialers	A list of the chat scripts for various modems
Devices	A list of the devices with modems for use by UUCP
Permissions	The system permissions file for UUCP
Dialcodes	The list of dial code expansions for area codes in UUCP
Poll	A list of machines to be polled by UUCP

Each file interacts with the others. The `Systems` file identifies a device for calling a remote system. That device must be in the `Devices` file, and it usually has a `Dialer` associated with it, so you need to check that in the `Dialers` file. In addition, an area code designator may prepend the telephone number specified by the `Systems` file, and you need to expand that in the `Dialcodes` file. The format of each is discussed later. Each file accepts comments when a line is prepended with the number sign (#).

The Systems file

The most important file is the `Systems` file. Each machine that UUCP can contact must have at least one entry in this file. If no entries are present, the system can't be contacted. Each entry has six fields, described in Table 18-6.

Machine names must be unique in the first seven characters; machines named `scotland1` and `scotland2` would be considered the same machine.

Table 18-6   Systems File Fields

Field	Purpose
Machine Name	This is the actual name of the remote machine. Any number of entries can have the same machine name.
Schedule Field	This specifies the times when the call can be made.
Device Field	This specifies the kind of device to make the call.
Speed	This specifies the preferred speed at which the connection should be made.
Remote Telephone Number	This identifies the telephone number for connecting to the remote machine.
Connection Chat Script	This is the sequence of expect-send patterns for initiating communication between the two machines.

Schedule Fields can be complex. They take a two-letter abbreviation for the day of the week and a 24-hour clock time specification. Any number of schedule specifiers can be present as long as they are comma-separated and have no embedded spaces. For example, SaSu0700-1500 means call only on Saturday and Sunday between 7 a.m. and 3 p.m. If the second number is less than the first, that means the time period wraps around midnight, but be careful: Sa2300-0700 does not mean from 11 p.m. Saturday to 7 a.m. Sunday; it means from 12 a.m. to 7 a.m. Saturday and again from 11 p.m. to midnight Saturday.

Schedule Fields can take three special day abbreviations: Wk means any weekday, Any means at any time, and Never means never.

The specified device is checked in the Devices file for any matching devices at the specified speed. If one is present, it is then checked for availability; if it is available, UUCP uses it for the call.

The telephone number is usually just that: a telephone number to be dialed. If alphabetical characters prepend it, the Dialcodes file is checked for matches, and those numbers are prepended.

The last field is the *chat script*. Chat scripts are rather complex, and they control how the communication process is started. You have a pattern that you expect to see, and when you see that pattern, you send a string. In case the pattern is not found and the system times out, you can have alternative sends enclosed between dashes. An example of a simple chat script is

in:—in: uduke *word*: *password*

This tells the system to look for the string `in:`. When `in:` is found, the script sends the string `uduke`. If `in:` is never seen, the script sends a new line — every chat script send sequence is terminated with a new line — and waits for `in:`. After sending `uduke`, the script looks for `word:`. When `word:` is found, the script sends *password*.

Note

You should recognize that this is a standard login process!

Chat scripts can become complex because you may need to navigate dial-up switches and extra security before making the connection. Table 18-7 lists the escape sequences available in chat scripts.

Table 18-7	Chat Script Escapes
Escape	*Description*
`" "`	Expects a null string; is useful at the beginning of a call
`EOT`	Ends transmission
`BREAK`	Sends a break down the line
`\b`	Sends a backspace
`\c`	Suppresses the new line at the end of the send string
`\d`	Delays for one second
`\K`	Sends a break
`\n`	Sends a new line
`\N`	Sends a NULL
`\p`	Waits for less than a second
`\r`	Returns
`\s`	Sends a space
`\t`	Sends a tab
`\\`	Sends a backslash
`\nnn`	Sends the ASCII character with the specified octal value

These escape sequences can be useful for sending data down a line.

Note

Chat scripts don't need to communicate to a `uucico` process. A chat script can look like this:

```
in:--in: james word: mypassword $
echo\sSuccess\s|\smail\sjames@redtail $ exit
```

This script performs a normal login and sends me mail telling me it worked.

The Devices file

The Devices file has five fields and specifies the physical devices for communication. Table 18-8 lists those fields.

Table 18-8	Devices File Fields
Field	**Purpose**
Device Type	This identifies the device type. It is one of the two keys from the Systems file.
Dataport	This is the entry in the /dev directory that is associated with the device.
Dialer Port	This is a vestige of the days when modems required separate dialers.
Speed	This is the speed of the device.
Dialers	These are dialer scripts for accessing the device.

Some systems accept the specification Any for the speed of a device. The dialer scripts are found in the Dialers file.

The Dialers file

The Dialers file identifies scripts for accessing devices. It associates the dialer listed for a device with the chat script to communicate with that device. (Ideally, I'd love to see a higher-level protocol developed, but because UUCP is fast becoming obsolete, there's no real profit in such a protocol.) The Dialers file has three fields, listed in Table 18-9.

Table 18-9	Dialers File Fields
Field	**Purpose**
Dialer Name	The string to associate the entry in Devices with the chat script
Translation Table	A field to translate to older devices (obsolete; maintained for backward compatibility)
Chat Script	The sequence of expect-send patterns to communicate with a device

There is one important addition to Table 18-7's list of escapes for the chat script. In the Dialers file, the escape \T inserts the telephone number from the Systems file at this point.

The Dialcodes file

The `Dialcodes` file is a simple string to the area code translation file. It has two fields, the tag and the numerical dialing prefix.

`Dialcodes` need not apply to area codes only. I could create a dial code called `glasgow` and equate it to 01144141. Then, I'd just need to include `glasgow2612461` in the `Systems` file to reach that number in Glasgow, Scotland.

The Permissions file

The `Permissions` file is an important one for configuration. It consists of a series of attributes and values that indicate the permissions associated with incoming and outgoing UUCP calls. Table 18-10 describes the attributes.

Table 18-10   Permissions File Attributes

Attribute	Description
CALLBACK	This is a yes/no option. When it is set to yes, communication occurs only when your machine initiates the call. The default is no.
COMMANDS	This is a list of valid commands associated with a MACHINE name. The list is colon-separated and is usually just rmail and rnews.
LOGNAME	This is a specific login name for UUCP. You can tie any attributes to the login name unless otherwise specified.
MACHINE	This is a specific machine name for UUCP. You can tie permissions to a machine name.
MYNAME	This is the name you specify for UUCP on an outgoing call. Setting this is useful if you have a different name for other purposes.
NOREAD	This enables you to specify a list of directories to UUCP that are not accessible for reading. These directories should be a subset of those that READ specifies.
NOWRITE	This enables you to specify a list of directories to UUCP that are not accessible for writing. These directories should be a subset of those that WRITE specifies.
PUBDIR	This specifies a public directory for reading and writing. The default is /var/spool/uucppublic.
READ	This specifies a list of directories accessible for reading by UUCP. The default is PUBDIR.
REQUEST	This is a yes/no flag that specifies whether a remote machine can request files from your machine. The default is no. By saying yes, you permit others to run commands such as uucp mymachine!file othermachine!file.

Attribute	Description
SENDFILES	This is a yes/no flag that specifies whether your machine sends files to a remote machine when the remote machine initiates the call. This attribute is tied to the LOGNAME only. A third option, call, says to send files only when you initiate the call.
VALIDATE	This is a yes/no flag tied to LOGNAME only. It validates the ID of the calling machine when set to yes.
WRITE	This is a list of directories to which a remote machine can write. The default is PUBDIR.

Normally, each line is a separate entry, but if the previous line is broken with a backslash before the new line, the two (or more) lines are treated as a single entry.

Caution

If both sites set CALLBACK to yes, they will never pass data. If you set CALLBACK to yes and the other site sets SENDFILES to call, the other site never transmits its data to you.

The Sysfiles file

The Sysfiles file specifies different support files for different services. I've never seen it used.

The Poll file

The Poll file specifies times for polling a remote system. You list the system name followed by a tab and a list of the hours during which you initiate the call. The hours are based on the 24-hour clock and are integers from 0 to 23. You need to run the polling daemon.

Administration of the line

Not only do you need to set up the UUCP support files, but you also have to administer the line. This administration has two different approaches; the one you take depends on whether you're going to be a one-way or a two-way UUCP connection.

The getty

A one-way connection means that you either always initiate the call or always wait to be called. In the former case, you need to remove the entry for the getty from the inittab. In the latter case, the default getty program in the inittab is adequate for the purpose. The standard /etc/inittab entry looks like this:

```
1n:23:respawn:/etc/getty tty 9600
```

The fields are colon-separated. The first two characters are a unique ID for the `inittab` entry. The second field indicates what run states are used. The third field indicates how the command should run; `respawn` tells the init process to restart the command when it exits. The last field contains the actual command and arguments.

A two-way connection involves a slightly different process, `uugetty`. In Chapter 1, I spoke a bit about the role of `getty`. If a `tty` is intended to be two-way, you need a technique to remove the `getty` process and restart it when the line is freed. This is not possible with the regular `getty` in `/etc/inittab`.

The `uugetty` command resolves this problem. Normally, `uugetty` resides in `/usr/lib/uucp`, and it sits on the line waiting for input, just like `getty`. If it receives a signal that an outgoing UUCP process is using the line, however, it shuts itself down until the UUCP is completed.

The `uugetty` process has arguments similar to `getty`'s plus an additional argument. If a `-r` is present, `uugetty` waits until it sees a carriage return before displaying the login prompt.

The daemons

Four daemons normally accompany UUCP. Table 18-11 lists the daemons, their recommended frequency, and their functions.

Table 18-11   UUCP Daemons

Daemon	Frequency	Function
The administration daemon	Daily	Gives a snapshot of UUCP's state, including the length of the current queues, to the UUCP administrator and checks the log file for any attempts to steal the `/etc/passwd` file.
The cleanup daemon	Daily, in off-hours	Cleans up log files and runs the `uuclean` process to bounce any messages from the queues that have not been delivered. It also removes any core files.
The polling daemon	Hourly	Examines the `Poll` file and sets up UUCP requests to poll a remote system.
The hourly daemon	Hourly	Examines the job queue and attempts to deliver outstanding requests.

Testing UUCP

OK, now that you've performed all the required administrative tasks, how do you know everything is working properly? Three commands in the UUCP package test and report on the data online.

Two of these commands, uulog and uustat, are historical records of UUCP traffic. They access the log and status files and report their data accordingly. The third command is uutry, which is a shell script to fire uucico and generate output.

The uutry command

The uutry command is a shell script supplied with HoneyDANBER UUCP to test the UUCP connection. It requires a UUCP-named machine on the command line and can take two optional arguments.

The -r argument forces the removal of the status file. This file includes data indicating how long to wait before retrying the connection. Removing it guarantees that uutry will attempt the connection. The -x # argument causes uutry to override the default debugging value of -x.

The uulog command

The uulog command prints the log files for the system. It takes one argument, -s *system*. If you do not specify a system, uulog displays the complete log.

The uustat command

The uustat command is more powerful than uutry and uulog. This command reports the status of UUCP on a system. Table 18-12 lists uustat's command-line options.

Table 18-12	uustat Options
Option	**Description**
-q	Writes the number of jobs queued for each machine.
-k *ID*	Deletes the specified job ID from the queue.
-r *ID*	Rejuvenates the specified job ID. The relevant files are touched to reflect the current time. (This prevents the deletion of any queued jobs when a machine is down.)
-s *system*	Reports the details for the specified system only.
-u *user*	Reports the jobs for the specified user only.
-a	Gives a detailed listing of all jobs. (Non-POSIX)
-m	Reports on the connection status of machines. (Non-POSIX)

Summary

This chapter introduced you to the basics of networking. It covered the following topics:

▶ The history of computers and networks

▶ The differences between LANs and WANs

▶ How to administer UUCP, how to set up the port for UUCP, and how to enter the appropriate information in the files

▶ How to test UUCP with uutry

▶ How to check UUCP's status with uustat and uulog

The next chapter takes networking to the next level, moving beyond technology that relies on modems and telephone lines to discuss the local area network and the commands available to LAN users.

Chapter 19

Understanding and Using Networks

The Network Model

Networking is frighteningly like an onion. As you find a layer and peel it away, it all still looks the same, and it can make you cry!

Seriously, any networking application is built in layers. The designers decide which layers to use for building, but each layer has its own role. The International Organization for Standardization (ISO) has specified a seven-layer model. Table 19-1 lists these layers, with examples.

Table 19-1   The ISO Seven-Layer Model for Networking

Layer	Purpose	Example
7	Application	Network File System (NIS)
6	Presentation	External data representation
5	Session	Remote procedure calls
4	Transport	Transmission Control Protocol
3	Network	Internetwork Protocol
2	Data link	Ethernet
1	Physical	Ethernet

The physical and data-link layers

Underneath all the other layers lie the physical layer and the data-link layer. Strictly speaking, these layers are out of the scope of any operating system design, but you need a basic understanding of them to comprehend fully the marvel of networking.

Ethernet exemplifies these layers. They define exactly how one machine transfers a data packet to another and even how the same machine transfers a data packet between protocols. Ethernet can run across any number of media, including twisted pair cables, thick and thin net, and microwave. Its operation is the same, although interfaces between different media require definition. Failures at the physical level include problems such as improperly terminated networks or malfunctioning boards.

Ethernet has a standard test path called the *loop-back interface,* which essentially tests whether you can communicate with your local Ethernet. For more details, see the section on testing the network.

To facilitate networking, each machine must have a unique Ethernet address. Fortunately for all of us, this is hardwired into the machine when it is manufactured. The address is a unique 48-bit address. The first 24 bits are assigned to a hardware vendor and uniquely identify the hardware. The vendor is responsible for ensuring that the last 24 bits are unique.

These Ethernet addresses (also called Media Access Control addresses) are usually represented as six one- or two-digit hexadecimal numbers, each separated by a colon, such as

```
8:0:20:9e:32:a0
```

Data is transferred in packets, which are distinctly initialized and terminated strings of bits defined in the data-link layer. A packet should include a checksum and a network-specific address. Machines on the network can then examine the packet and determine whether it is intended for them. The checksum confirms that all the data in the packet is correct. Should the checksum not match, the packet is rejected.

An alternative to Ethernet is an X.25 network. These are not uncommon, but Ethernet is the de facto standard for UNIX.

The network layer

The network layer builds on the data-link layer and tries to smooth over the differences between different data-link layers to enable higher networking layers to communicate freely without worrying about the hardware specifics of remote machines.

The de facto standard for UNIX is the Internetwork Protocol (IP), which is responsible for the actual transmission of packets from one machine to another. There are no guarantees of order or even of success. This is the purview of high-level protocols.

The IP works with datagrams, which are collections of data similar to Ethernet packets. When the data-link layer can handle a packet the size of a datagram, the packet and datagram are synonymous. If the datagram is larger than the maximum packet size, the IP is responsible for breaking the datagram into packets of the appropriate size and transmitting them accordingly.

Note

By performing this fragmentation at the network layer, higher-level protocols do not need to worry about data loss due to fragmentation.

The IP also requires addresses, called IP addresses. These need to be unique across a network but not between networks (a machine on one network can have the same IP address as a machine on another network). A single machine can have multiple IP addresses, particularly if it acts as a route between networks.

IP addresses are 32-bit numbers, usually broken into four dot-separated decimal numbers from 0 through 255. An example of a standard IP address is 192.9.201.100. If your network is not connected to the world, you can designate any address you like, keeping to the one-machine-per-address scheme. If you connect to the world, you need to acquire a unique IP address. These addresses are allocated by the Network Information Center.

The format of the IP address is four octets. Usually, the first three octets refer to the network, and the last octet refers to the host. Unless you create a specific route, you cannot communicate with a machine whose first three octets are different from your own. You can communicate only through a route specified by either a router or a software route on a gateway machine.

When you ask for an IP address for accessing the Internet, you need to know which class of address you want. Addresses come in three classes; Table 19-2 illustrates their differences.

Table 19-2   Internet Address Classes

Class	Network Octet	Host Octet	First Octet Range	Number of Hosts
A	1	3	1–126	16,387,064 (254^3)
B	2	2	128–191	64,516 (254^2)
C	3	1	192–233	254

Internet octet values 0 and 255 are reserved for the formation of broadcast addresses. Primary octet 127 is used for loop-back testing, and 224 through 254 are currently reserved.

Note

The current scheme has built-in limits to the numbers of addresses. Although these limits may seem large now, all these addresses will eventually be assigned, and a new scheme will be needed.

Class A addresses are rare. Even Class B addresses are uncommon. If you have a small company with a few hundred machines, you'll commonly request multiple Class C addresses. Over 2 million Class C addresses are available, as opposed to 16,000 Class B addresses and 126 Class A addresses.

The transport layer

The next layer up is the transport layer. The two most common transports in UNIX are Transmission Control Protocol (TCP) and User Datagram Protocol (UDP). Transport layers primarily divide user buffers into datagrams and monitor the transmissions for order and correctness.

Transport layers such as TCP ensure that data and commands arrive and are processed in the appropriate order. Should a datagram arrive that is incomplete or out of order, the transport layer sends back a message requesting retransmission. UDP is a faster, but less reliable, mechanism. UDP does not check for packet order. TCP is considered a stated protocol; UDP is stateless.

The transport layer introduces the concept of port numbers to networking. A data packet is uniquely identified by the IP address and port of origination as well as the IP address and port of the target. The port number must be unique and identifies a service on the remote machine. Table 19-3 lists some common services and their port numbers.

Table 19-3	Common Service Port Numbers
Service	*Port Number*
Electronic mail	25
File transfer	20 and 21
Netnews	119
Time	37
X400 mail	103 and 104

Ports numbered under 1,024 are reserved for superuser services. Any user can use port numbers higher than that.

Traditionally, you connect to a port by attaching a socket. Sockets are a means of initiating interprocess communications across networks.

The session layer

Most common protocols appear at the session layer, including the mail protocol SMTP and the netnews protocol NNTP. The different network services each have their own protocol definitions, service ports, and transport mechanisms.

The /etc/services file defines the different sessions allowed on a UNIX machine. It defines the port number associated with the session and the underlying transport mechanism. Here are two lines from my /etc/services file:

```
finger          79/tcp
sunrpc          111/tcp
```

This example shows two of the services available on my machine. The first field defines the service type. finger is a means of acquiring some basic information about a user from a remote site. To make finger work properly, you need to have the finger daemon running (this is configured in the inetd.conf file). The inetd daemon waits for incoming requests and runs the finger daemon when they occur. finger communicates on port 79 and uses TCP as its transport layer protocol.

The second service is Sun RPC. RPCs are *remote procedure calls,* discussed later in this chapter. Sun RPC enables one program to request that another program execute a procedure call. This is a good means for transmitting data across the network.

Note

You can use the telnet command (discussed later in this chapter) to access any of these ports. If the remote site enables your site to connect and if you know the protocol, you can make queries by hand. This is an excellent means for debugging a problem.

The presentation layer

The presentation layer is basically a data-processing layer: It converts data from a form used by an application to a machine-independent representation.

A common presentation layer is XDR, which stands for *external data representation* and is a library available with most UNIX installations. It has a series of routines, callable from the application program, that open data streams and perform data conversions. In this way, a piece of data found on an Intel-based system is not different from one found on a SPARC system. (Those two platforms have different byte ordering for integers.)

XDR is defined by DARPA's Network Information Center in RFC 1041. This is a functional definition of the interface.

Story: Daily Network Use

I've never attempted to quantify the daily amount of interaction I have with a network. At my current job, my home directory is mounted on my local machine from a remote file server. Every time I access any data in my home, I use a network service. I use NIS to transmit account information, so every time I need any accounting information, that's a network access. I also use e-mail, netnews, Web, and other Internet services in my job.

Secret

Many of the network's actual communication techniques and protocols are defined in RFCs (Requests for Comments). An RFC enables those who are interested in a specific interface to have input into the design and specification of that interface. RFCs have been created since the late 1960s and even predate UNIX.

As a regular UNIX user, you do not need to care about RFCs any more than you need to care exactly how the device driver writes data onto the disk. But should you become interested in developing an application that communicates with others on the network in a friendly fashion, you need to understand the RFC process so that you can help in the design of the protocol your application uses.

The application layer

The top layer for networking is the application layer, which is where the user actually interacts with the network.

You can interact in many ways without even thinking about it. Sending e-mail to a remote site is one. If you share data by mounting file systems on multiple machines, you are using an application that interacts with the network.

Using RPC

As I mentioned previously, RPCs (remote procedure calls) are one of the more common network services. By implementing a service as an RPC, the developer can keep a centralized location that performs the hard calculations and uses remote sites for display and interaction.

One of the hottest buzzwords in the modern computing community is *client/server applications,* and RPC is one means of implementing these. The server machine can sit and wait for RPC calls, process data accordingly, and pass it back to the clients. The clients can interact with the user, define filters and parameters for RPC calls, and display the results.

Story: Convenient Monitoring

In my current job, I am a member of a team of developers working on a system-monitoring product. We use RPC extensively for passing data between our different programs. This enables us to place monitoring agents on the system in question and display the data on other machines in the same network. The customer greatly benefits from this design: Instead of running from machine to machine to check status, an administrator can operate several machines that use our product from a desktop workstation.

How RPC works

When an application running RPC requests that a remote procedure execute, it first connects to a local RPC daemon that identifies the remote machine and RPC port for connection. That daemon then examines the port mapper to find the appropriate port to use for communication. For RPC, this is a well-defined port, 111. For RPC, the client can skip using a local daemon by building the local communications stub into the client program. Ports are defined in the /etc/services file for socket-based networking. The port mapper on the remote machine then connects the two daemons together and passes the request.

On the remote side, the request is passed to the appropriate program, according to the RPC number. That program then executes the requested procedure and returns the reply to the local daemon. That daemon sends the reply back to the client machine. Here are the steps for RPC procedures:

1. The client program requires RPC and calls the function to generate an RPC request.

2. The client contacts the port mapper on the server machine for the appropriate port to make an RPC request.

3. The client contacts the designated port on the server and attempts to connect to the appropriate service daemon.

4. The service daemon receives the request and dispatches the service procedure to an appropriate application.

5. The application on the server executes the procedure.

6. The application returns an answer to the service daemon.

7. The service daemon assembles the reply.

8. The service daemon returns the reply to the client.

RPC is a building block for many network services, including NFS and NIS.

Debugging RPC

Some tools besides those normally used for debugging applications can examine the RPC on a given machine. The command is rpcinfo. Table 19-4 lists the available rpcinfo arguments. (Part VIII discusses application debugging techniques.)

Table 19-4   rpcinfo Options

Option	Arguments	Description
-p	[host]	Displays the port mapper table for the local machine or the specified host
-u	host program [version]	Uses UDP to call the NULLPROC on a specified host
-t	host program [version]	Uses TCP to call the NULLPROC on a specified host
-n	portnum	Overrides what the port mapper says with -u and -t and calls NULLPROC at a specified port
-b	program version	Broadcasts to all reachable NULLPROCs
-d	program version	Deletes the local port mapper entry

Note

A NULLPROC is just that: a process that does nothing. It is a means of checking to see whether a daemon is alive.

The listing of available ports can be confusing. Listing 19-1 shows a sample.

Listing 19-1: rpcinfo -p

```
program vers proto    port
 100000    2   tcp     111  portmapper
 100000    2   udp     111  portmapper
 100004    2   udp     663  ypserv
 100004    2   tcp     664  ypserv
 100004    1   udp     663  ypserv
 100004    1   tcp     664  ypserv
 100007    2   tcp     666  ypbind
 100007    2   udp     668  ypbind
 100007    1   tcp     666  ypbind
 100007    1   udp     668  ypbind
 100028    1   tcp     668  ypupdated
 100028    1   udp     670  ypupdated
 100003    2   udp    2049  nfs
 100005    1   udp     714  mountd
```

```
100005   2   udp    714   mountd
100005   1   tcp    717   mountd
100005   2   tcp    717   mountd
100021   1   tcp    726   nlockmgr
100021   1   udp   1033   nlockmgr
100021   3   tcp    730   nlockmgr
100021   3   udp   1034   nlockmgr
100020   2   udp   1035   llockmgr
100020   2   tcp    735   llockmgr
100021   2   tcp    738   nlockmgr
100021   2   udp   1036   nlockmgr
100024   1   udp    728   status
100024   1   tcp    731   status
100036   1   udp   1020
100069   1   udp   1508   ypxfrd
100069   1   tcp   4002   ypxfrd
100001   2   udp   1957   rstatd
100001   3   udp   1957   rstatd
100001   4   udp   1957   rstatd
100002   1   udp   1958   rusersd
100002   2   udp   1958   rusersd
```

The output has five columns. The first is the registered program number. You can use this with the other rpcinfo options. The second is a version number used for synchronization. The third column indicates the underlying transport layer (TCP or UDP). The fourth field is the assigned port number. The last column is an optional program name.

You can use rpcinfo to test and delete connections. By examining the transport layer, you can test the connection with rpc -u myhost 100002 2. This attempts to connect to the rusersd daemon. If it connects, it runs the NULLPROC.

Note

You need to specify a host in this case, even if the host is the local machine.

You should see the following output:

```
program 100002 version 2 ready and waiting
```

If you attempt to access a program that doesn't exist, you'll receive an error message. Furthermore, if the nonexistent program's entry exists, it is removed from the port mapper table.

The -b option broadcasts for connections. It should be restricted to the superuser, and it is a distinctly network-intensive act.

Lastly, you can use the -d flag to delete entries from the port mapper table. This can have serious ramifications because no process can communicate with that service after deletion. This should also be restricted to the superuser.

Story: Deleting a Port Mapper Entry

The -d flag is useful when you are debugging RPC-based applications, as we have been doing on my job. When a program terminates abnormally, it does not always have time to clean up after itself. This can leave entries in the port mapper table. Because we originally used absolute program names, we encountered a problem on restart because the program number was already registered. Therefore, we each learned how to go in and manually delete the port mapper entry.

Most of the time, you don't use RPC directly, but you may have noticed two specific entries in Listing 19-1. The first, on line 13, is for NFS. This is the RPC program for handling remote file systems, discussed in the following section. The 3rd through 12th entries all deal with NIS, which is also discussed later in this chapter.

Note

For more information on RPC, I highly recommend John Bloomer's *Power Programming with RPC*.

The Network File System

The evolution of local networks brought up the issue of sharing data among machines on the network. Before the era of networks, each large computer had arrays of disks that were local to that machine only. Because everyone used the same machine, everyone accessed the same data. Now, however, each machine is separate, and many contain their own disks for local operation. Users' home directories and work environments may be distinct, but the time comes when workers need to share their information.

The Network File System (NFS) provides the cleanest solution (so far) for managing shared data between workstations. Basically, it enables a computer to mount a file system found on another machine across the network so that all the normal tools for accessing a file system work the same way on the remote machine's file system as they do on the local machine's. This means that users need not know the specific physical location of the disk on which they're working. Similarly, the local file system knows nothing about the file server on which the remote machine's file system is physically located. Its architecture and file system structure can be completely different from the local machine's. These differences are hidden under NFS.

NFS is an application built on top of XDR and RPC. It acts as a high-level interface between systems, translating the specific actions into a universal set of instructions and transmitting them to the remote machine. The remote machine then returns the results of the transactions as if it were local.

NFS servers need to be running the network server daemon, `nfsd`, which is the actual program to accept RPC calls from clients. The `rpc.mountd` daemon handles the mounting of file systems and the pathname translations.

The Virtual File System

Underlying the Network File System is the concept of a *Virtual File System* (VFS). This is a set of generic file system instructions that define a common interface to all potential file systems that can be mounted via NFS on a UNIX system. The VFS defines two sets of operations: those performed on the file system as a whole and those performed on files within that file system.

The operations performed on the file system itself are called *VFS operations*. These include requests for available disk space and inquiries into whether a file system is writable.

Virtual File System nodes

Underneath the VFS are *Virtual File System nodes,* called *vnodes* for short. The local file system equivalent to a vnode is an i-node, defined in Chapter 6. Most NFS operations are performed on vnodes, just as most file system operations are performed on i-nodes.

NFS protocol

Commands on a networked file system are transmitted from the local machine to the remote machine, using the NFS protocol. The NFS protocol has 16 commands, outlined in Table 19-5.

Table 19-5   NFS Protocol

Protocol Command	Operation Type	Action
create	Directory	Creates a new file on the remote file system
getattr	File	Retrieves the attributes of a file
link	Link	Creates a hard link on the server
lookup	Directory	Finds a named directory entry and returns a file handle
mkdir	Directory	Creates a directory on the remote file system
mount	File system	Mounts a file system

Continued

Table 19-5 (continued)		
Protocol Command	**Operation Type**	**Action**
read	File	Reads data from a file
readdir	Directory	Reads a directory on the remote file system
readlink	Link	Reads the symbolic link on the server
remove	Directory	Deletes the file from the remote file system
rename	Directory	Changes the name of a file on the remote file system
rmdir	Directory	Removes a directory from the remote file system
setattr	File	Sets the attributes of a file
statfs	File system	Retrieves the file system statistics
symlink	Link	Creates a symbolic link on the server
write	File	Writes data to a file

All these calls — except mount — are handled by nfsd on the server side. The mount command is handled by rpc.mountd. The nfsd operations rely on vnodes.

To assist with crash recovery, the NFS protocol is designed as a stateless protocol. This way, a protocol request does not need to know what commands have come before to reply to the request. This means that each protocol request must completely describe the operation to be performed. For example, the read call in UNIX does not need to know the location of the file pointer. Instead, it just reads the specified amount of data and resets the file pointer. This doesn't work with the NFS protocol: In NFS, the request must contain the file handle, the starting offset, and the length of the read.

Note

The stateless protocol is not difficult to conceptualize for a UNIX systems programmer. Programmatically, you just include an lseek before each read to ensure that the file pointer is at the correct offset.

The same differences exist between a write system call and an NFS protocol request.

A second implication of this design is that the NFS calls may send duplicate requests without harmful side effects. If you send a read call in UNIX followed by a couple of read system calls, your file pointer changes after each read, so each read is different. With the NFS protocol, you set a start offset for each read so that each time the request is received, the same data is returned.

Of course, you may see some side effects when receiving commands in a different order, especially if the commands change the underlying data. Commands such as `write`, `remove`, `rename`, and `rmdir` do this.

Note

Some versions of UNIX NFS implement caches to prevent the errors that may result from changing the data underneath a command. The `nfsd` checks for and ignores any duplicate requests.

Secret

Another beneficial side effect is that NFS RPC can use UDP as the transport layer. UDP is stateless, like the NFS protocol, and is consequently a faster protocol.

Some common UNIX commands require multiple NFS protocol requests. Table 19-6 lists some of those mappings.

Table 19-6   Some UNIX-to-NFS Mappings

UNIX Command	NFS Protocol Requests
`ls`	`getattr`, `lookup`, `readdir`, `readlink`
`find`	`getattr`, `lookup`, `readdir`
`rm *`	`lookup`, `readdir`, `remove`

The NFS protocol is entirely hidden from the user.

Using NFS

From the user's point of view, NFS is entirely transparent. You'll notice differences only when you examine the available disk space on a file system or when you examine the mount table. Instead of seeing the name of the physical device on the local machine, you'll see the name of a remote machine and the exported directory on that machine. Here's what that looks like (using `df/u1`) on `netcom`:

```
Filesystem            kbytes    used   avail capacity  Mounted on
nac1-n3:/u1          2097151 1545431  551720    74%    /u1
```

Here, the file system `/u1`, where my home directory is located, is actually an NFS-mounted file system located on the machine `nac1-n3`.

Mounting remote file systems

An administrator performs most of the work with NFS. These tasks depend on whether the machine is a client of NFS or a server.

Note

Machines can be both clients and servers.

Client machines need to mount file systems. You use the `mount` command with the following syntax:

```
mount remote-file-system mount-point [ -o options ]
```

Designate the remote file system with the machine name followed by a colon and the remote directory. The mount point must be a local directory. Table 19-7 lists the `mount` options.

Table 19-7	mount Options
Option	**Description**
bg	Retries a failed mount in the background
hard	Makes a hard mount
intr	Enables the interruption of an RPC mount
retrans=*n*	Specifies the number of times to retry transmission of an RPC request before timing out on a soft-mounted file system
ro	Mounts the file system for reading only
rw	Mounts the file system for reading and writing
soft	Makes a soft mount
timeo=*n*	Specifies the RPC timeout period in tenths of a second

Normal `mount` options are `rw`, `bg`, and `hard`. In the command, they should be comma-separated without spaces.

This command mounts the file system when run. To mount a file system automatically via NFS at boot time, you need to add an entry to the `/etc/fstab` file. This is the file systems table.

Caution

If you are using Solaris 2, these tables have all changed.

The `/etc/fstab` file has six fields, each tab-separated. Table 19-8 lists these fields.

Table 19-8	fstab Fields
Field	**Description**
Device Name	Specifies the device to be mounted. For NFS, use the `machine:remote-path` syntax.
Mount Point	Specifies the local directory.

Field	Description
File System Type	Should be set to `nfs` for NFS file systems.
Option	Specifies the options for mounting, usually `rw,bg,hard`. These options should not be separated by spaces.
fsck Pass	Should be set to zero for NFS file systems.
Sequence Number	Should be set to zero for NFS file systems.

When an NFS file system is listed in /etc/fstab, the system tries to mount the remote file system for you at boot time.

Exporting local file systems

When you are administering the NFS server, you must follow some rules. Any local file system can be exported. You can also export proper subsets of a file system, so if you have a disk mounted on /usr, you can export /usr/local. You cannot export a subdirectory of an already exported file system unless that subdirectory resides on a different physical device. Similarly, you can't export a parent of an already exported file system unless that parent is on a different physical device.

The /etc/exports file tracks the file systems available for export. It takes one entry per line and is a listing of exported file systems followed by options. Table 19-9 lists the export options.

Table 19-9   export Options

Option	Syntax	Description
access	access=host:host	Permits only the listed hosts to access the file system
anon	anon=uid	Maps unknown users to the specified UID
ro	ro	Prevents NFS clients from writing to the file system
root	root=host:host	Grants root access to the file system to the named hosts
rw	rw=host:host	Limits the hosts that can write to a file system
secure	secure	Forces the use of secure RPC to access the file system

To activate any changes to the exports table, run exportfs.

The buffer I/O daemon

One boon to NFS file systems is the use of biod, the buffer I/O daemon that is essentially a manager of the buffer cache for file access. Ideally, biod has the smarts to predict heuristically the next required I/O for a given process and to bring it into the buffer cache before a user process requests it. Then, the process simply waits for the transfer from the buffer cache. This is a faster process than disk access and is much faster than sending network protocol requests to remote machines.

Diagnostic tools for NFS

NFS maintains three files to help diagnose NFS problems. The /etc/xtab file is a listing of all exported file systems from a given machine. The /etc/rmtab file is a listing of all the host/directory pairs for a server's clients. The /etc/mtab file is the local mount table on the client machine.

Additionally, two commands help monitor NFS activity. The showmount -a command lists all the host/directory pairs that have mounted files served by this machine, and showmount -d prints directory names.

More interesting is the nfsstat command, which takes two arguments. If -c is present, it prints client-side statistics, and -s prints server-side statistics. If no argument is given, both sets of statistics are printed.

Listing 19-2 shows the nfsstat output, which contains a lot of data. First, you receive the statistics on the RPC connection. (Table 19-10 explains each header.) Then, you see the number of calls for each of the NFS protocol requests. The client-side statistics expand a bit on the RPC statistics.

Listing 19-2: nfsstat Output

```
$ nfsstat
Server rpc:
calls       badcalls    nullrecv    badlen    xdrcall
803543      0           0           0         0

Server nfs:
calls       badcalls
803543      54
null        getattr     setattr     root      lookup       readlink    read
0 0%        144387 17%  10620 1%    0 0%      372372 46%   4860 0%     258357 32%
wrcache     write       create      remove    rename       link        symlink
0 0%        0 0%        0 0%        0 0%      0 0%         0 0%        0 0%
mkdir       rmdir       readdir     fsstat
0 0%        0 0%        12941 1%    6 0%

Client rpc:
calls       badcalls    retrans     badxid    timeout   wait   newcred   timers
37019039    734         77011       1365      77360     0      0         299620
```

```
Client nfs:
calls       badcalls    nclget     nclsleep
37004138    0           37004137   0
null    getattr     setattr     root    lookup      readlink    read
0 0%    7325449 19% 122099 0%  0 0%    15322022 41% 767681 2%   7337785 19%
wrcache     write       create      remove      rename      link        symlink
0 0%        3537467 9%  454998 1%  160368 0%   244182 0%   35304 0%   64 0%
mkdir       rmdir       readdir     fsstat
49790 0%    1497 0%     1643530 4%  1902 0%
```

Table 19-10   RPC Headers in nfsstat

Field	Client/Server	Meaning
calls	Both	The total number of RPC or NFS calls made to the server or by the client for NFS
badcalls	Both	RPC requests that were rejected
nullrecv	Server	The number of times a zero-length packet is sent
badlen	Server	RPC requests that were too short
xdrcall	Server	RPC packets with malformed XDR headers
retrans	Client	The number of RPC calls that were retransmitted owing to a lack of response
timeout	Client	The number of RPC calls that timed out as a result of a lack of server response
badxid	Client	The number of RPC requests with bad transmission IDs
wait	Client	The number of calls that had to wait on a busy client
newcred	Client	The number of times client authentication had to be refreshed

Two new headers are added to the NFS statistics: nclget counts the number of times the client had to request a new client handle from the servers, and nslsleep counts the number of times the client was blocked because no client handle was available.

NFS summary

This explains the basics of NFS. The biggest enhancement to NFS is the inclusion of the automounter, discussed later in this chapter. The automounter is a merging of NFS and NIS.

For more information on NFS, I recommend Hal Stern's *Managing NFS and NIS.*

The Network Information Service

Sun Microsystems originally developed the Network Information Service (NIS) as a means of maintaining common data for administrative files across machines. It is licensed to many vendors and universities worldwide.

For more information on NIS, I recommend Hal Stern's *Managing NFS and NIS.*

Originally, NIS was called Yellow Pages, which is why many NIS commands have the prefix *yp*. Because Yellow Pages is a trademark of British Telecom, Sun had to change the name.

NIS best manages files that do not contain host-specific information. Files such as /etc/passwd are ideal for NIS, whereas files such as /etc/fstab (the list of file systems mounted on a given machine) are not. Table 19-11 lists the files that NIS can manage.

Table 19-11	**Files That NIS Can Manage**
File	*Description*
aliases	Systemwide aliases for electronic mail
bootparams	Boot parameters for diskless machines
ethers	Ethernet numbers
group	The groups file
hosts	The hosts file (addresses of machines on your local network)
netgroup	Netgroup definitions
netmasks	Network masks (used to define permissible local hosts)
networks	Network addresses
passwd	The user ID file
protocols	Network protocol names and numbers
rpc	Remote procedure call program numbers
services	Network port numbers and services

All files are usually located in the /etc directory. Some sites may maintain the mail aliases file in /usr/lib/aliases.

Some files are needed before NIS is available. You need the /etc/hosts file, which includes the addressing data for known machines on your network, before NIS can work. In this case, you need to enter only your own machine and IP address before connecting to NIS, and then the host's table managed by NIS supersedes your local file. Other files, such as /etc/passwd, may contain information specific to the host. In these cases, the NIS passwd file augments the local file. With this file, you can specify a root password local to the machine, and you can create a list of users who can gain access to the machine if NIS is unavailable or if the machine is off the network. I provide details of augmentation later in this chapter.

How NIS works

NIS is built on a client/server model, on top of RPC. Servers are the machines on the network that maintain the data files distributed by NIS. These data files are called *maps,* and a single file may be available through separate maps. Clients are machines that request and use the information contained in the maps.

You can further subdivide servers into a single master server, which maintains the canonical data, and slave servers. The master server can drive all the slaves with its data and is the sole location where you can make data changes. Slaves act as redistributors, getting the latest and greatest information from their master and servicing requests directly.

Secret

Why allow slaves? Often, NIS can be applied to large local networks. If you have a Class B Internet address and wish to maintain a single NIS database for your network, you could have 64,516 machines attempting to access your NIS server. This machine would then receive a network service request whenever any machine on that network needed to access a network map. Pretty soon, your network would collapse, and the server machine would be unable to process all the requests. By designing the network to include slaves, you can distribute the network and processor load across many machines and consequently have a faster network.

The means of accessing the files is simple. When a machine needs to know some information, such as when translating a user ID number to a name for an ls listing, it accesses the NIS map for the passwd file with an RPC. That call returns the string, and the ls program prints the appropriate string.

You can restrict access to the maps for appropriate machines by specifying a domain. A *domain* is a collection of maps that are available to that area only. A single client may access different maps from different domains, but this is quite unusual. A domain is a grouping of machines that need to share information.

Tip

I strongly advise you to use the same domain for NIS that you use for electronic mail addressing. This helps prevent confusion when you are administering a system.

Maps

Maps are the means by which NIS clients access data. Map names are usually two words, separated by a period. The first word is the name of the service, and the second is the means of access. For example, `passwd.byname` is a map that accesses the user account information by user name. Some maps have aliases, which are single words for access. Two NIS services have single-name access because they have only one keyword. Table 19-12 lists the NIS maps.

You should have noticed more NIS maps than administrative files. A one-to-one relationship does not exist; in several files, you may be looking up information according to different keys. For example, `hosts.byname` looks up host data according to a machine name, whereas `hosts.byaddr` looks up the same information according to the IP address.

Table 19-12   NIS Maps

Map	Alias	Access Method	Augments Which File?	Integration
bootparams		Host name	bootparams	Append
ethers.byname	ethers	Host name	ethers	Replace
ethers.byaddr		MAC address	ethers	Replace
group.byname	group	Group name	group	Append
group.bygid		Group ID	group	Append
hosts.byname	hosts	Host name	hosts	Replace
hosts.byaddr		IP address	hosts	Replace
mail.aliases	aliases	Alias name	aliases	Append
mail.byaddr		Expanded alias	aliases	Append
netgroup.byhost		Host name	netgroup	Replace
netgroup.byuser		User name	netgroup	Replace
netid.byname		User name	Files containing UID & GID information	Derived
netmasks.byaddr		IP address	netmasks	Replace
networks.byname		Network name	networks	Replace
networks.byaddr		IP address	networks	Replace
passwd.byname	passwd	User name	passwd	Append
passwd.byuid		User ID	passwd	Append

Map	Alias	Access Method	Augments Which File?	Integration
protocols.bynumber	protocols	Port number	protocols	Replace
protocols.byname		Protocol name	protocols	Replace
rpc.bynumber		RPC number	rpc	Replace
services.byname	services	Service name	services	Replace
ypservers		Host name	Files containing NIS server names	Replace

Note

You should view NIS data as a database. Each file is a different database, and each dot is the key used to access a record.

Secret

You can add more data to the NIS domain simply by adding dbm files for each desired map to the domain area.

The aliases refer to frequently accessed files and keys. Usually, when you are accessing the services file, you are trying to identify a port number for a specific service by name. Rather than looking up services in services.byname, you can just specify services and obtain the information.

Note

Only the ypmatch and ypcat commands use the aliases.

Note also that three integration techniques are listed. When the technique is Replace, the client machine uses only the data supplied by NIS for administration. No data in the local file is used. When the technique is Append, the administrator can configure some information on the local machine, and the NIS data augments the local data. Lastly, one NIS file, netid.byname, is derived from other NIS files and provides a quick reference to relate a user ID and group ID.

Administering the server

Managing the NIS master server is a fairly simple process. You need to designate a machine that serves NIS to clients, build the maps, and make them available. After this, you can optionally add slave servers.

Designating the machine

Designating the machine is more important than you might suspect. The machine that acts as the server (or the master server) must be highly available. If this machine is prone to hardware problems or is located on an isolated part of your network, you risk shutting down a segment of your user community or the entire network.

You should be able to access the machine easily from anywhere on your network. It needs to be up on a reasonably continuous basis. It needs to be able to process many RPC requests quickly. This machine will potentially be one of the busiest on your network.

Building the maps

As soon as you've found a machine that meets the needs of NIS, the fun begins. You need to determine whether you must partition the network into domains, and you need to build appropriate maps for each domain.

When considering whether to define domains, look at your work environment. Are the users who need access to the computer resources grouped and working on specific tasks? Are these tasks well segregated, or do you have a lot of cross-pollination between groups? Are the machines located on their own subnetwork? If you have a situation where you need, or want, to give access to resources at different levels of security, you may want to look into providing different domains.

In NIS, the server maintains the different data files to be served in a directory under /var/yp. This directory includes separate directories for each domain maintained at the site, and the different mappings and database files are kept separated, according to domain. In this fashion, you can access different maps from different domains on the same machine.

First, you need to initialize the domain. Use the domainname command; the only argument is the desired domain. On my system this would be

```
domainname sagarmatha.com
```

Story: Down Time

I've worked in a job where the machine chosen to act as the NIS server was flaky. Because I'm an early riser, I'd frequently arrive at work ahead of everyone else, and I'd find that the machine had crashed, effectively killing the network. Usually, I'd just reboot the machine, but once, when it had some serious disk problems, I spent six hours restoring the network to functionality. Those were six hours I spent on system administration, not on doing my job as a software developer. When you include the time lost by everyone else on that network, the total time lost was somewhere around a man-week.

This happened at a small company. Can you imagine the cost to a medium-size company with a couple hundred engineers if they each lost a half day of productivity?

You can check your domain with the `domainname` call and no argument:

```
$ domainname
sagarmatha.com
$
```

Note

Including the `domainname` in the `rc` startup script and keeping the `domainname` in a file, `/etc/defaultdomain`, is standard procedure. In the `rc` script, you then see the following lines:

```
if
    [ -f /etc/defaultdomain ]
then
    domainname `cat /etc/defaultdomain`
fi
```

At this stage, you may want to check your administrative files to be certain that only the desired information is contained in those files. When you are comfortable with the data being distributed by NIS, initialize the server as master with the following command:

```
/usr/etc/ypinit -m
```

This command builds the subdirectories for NIS in `/var/yp`. It also builds the complete set of administrative files for the current domain. It asks for a list of host names that are to become NIS slave servers. They don't need to be running NIS at present but should be running NIS before the maps are changed.

As soon as this command finishes, run `ypserv` manually. This starts the NIS server and makes the maps available. You may also need to include the command in the `/etc/rc` file to start the server at boot time:

```
if
    [ -f /var/etc/ypserv -a -d /var/yp/`domainname` ]
then
    ypserv
    echo -n ` ypserv´
fi
```

This tests to see that a server exists and that the NIS files are initialized before starting NIS. This code should appear after the initialization of the `domainname`.

Creating slaves

Before you create slave servers, NIS must be running on the master server. You again use the `ypinit` command to create the slave servers, but with a different argument. Use `-s master-name` to create a slave server. The appropriate files are created on the slave. The slave should have the same `domainname` set as the master, and the two should be reachable. The slave server should be on a machine listed in the master's list of available servers.

To add a new slave, modify the `ypservers` map on the master server. Create a copy of the `ypservers` file with `ypcat -k ypservers`. Edit the file and provide it as input to `makedbm`. The command to create the new server file is

```
makedbm - /var/yp/`domainname`/ypservers
```

You can then run `ypinit -s` on the new slave and run `ypserv` to start the server process.

Publishing the maps

When you modify the files on the master server to change the data distributed by NIS, you also need to make these changes available to all the NIS slave servers and clients. To do this, the normal procedure is to make the necessary changes, cd to /var/yp, and run a `make`. Within the `makefile` are the commands to build a new map and distribute it.

The command to make the new file available is `yppush`. This "pushes" the new map onto the network. There is also a pull command, `ypxfr`.

Administering the client

Administering client machines is a lot easier than setting up servers. First, make sure that the appropriate entries are in the local files so that the machine can contact any of the NIS servers. These include an entry in the /etc/hosts file identifying the local machine and some entries in the /etc/passwd file.

Set the `domainname`. This is the same as that for a server. The domain must be served by NIS.

Start the `ypbind` daemon. This command locates the best `ypserv` daemon and initializes the communication. When a `ypbind` is running, all administrative requests go through `ypbind` and an NIS server. Listing 19-3 lists a section of an `rc` file to start NIS on a client machine.

Listing 19-3: Starting NIS on a Client at Boot Time

```
if
     [ -f /etc/defaultdomain ]
then
     domainname `cat /etc/defaultdomain`
     if
          [ -d /var/yp ]
     then
          ypbind
          echo -n ` ypbind´
     fi
fi
```

This sequence of shell commands first checks to see whether a default domain is registered, and if one is, it sets the domain. It then checks to see whether NIS is available, and it starts the bind.

Caution

Starting the NIS client routines without a valid server causes the client machine to hang up until a server begins.

Merging NIS maps with local files

For the `/etc/passwd` and `/etc/group` files, you append NIS information to the entries on the local machine. The location where you append the NIS data to the file is under the control of the administrator. The magic token, a plus sign (+), indicates where you should include the data.

This token must be in the first field of the file, and I strongly advise you to include the remaining entries for that line with colons. For example, in the `/etc/passwd` file, include

`+:*:65535:65535:::`

Tip

I strongly advise you to include the asterisk; otherwise, you have an entry in your `passwd` file with no password! If NIS is not running, this leaves your machine open to hackers.

In the group file, you should include `+:*::`. For the `aliases` and `bootparams` files, appending a + at the end of the file is adequate for including NIS data in the file.

Accessing NIS from the command line

After you have created the NIS servers and clients, NIS is running on your network. You can access NIS from command lines to obtain data and administer the network, although most accesses take place directly from programs on sockets and RPC.

Routine administration

Most of the command-line commands fall under the heading of routine administration. You use these commands to create connections and administer connections.

The ypserv command

The `ypserv` command is the primary server command. It can take a single argument, `-d hostname`, which tells it to access that host name for more information on the host.

The ypbind command

The `ypbind` command acts as the agent on the client machine for contacting NIS servers. It can take up to three arguments. The `-s` option requests a secure connection. The -ypset and ypsetme commands are used only for debugging and are not recommended.

The ypxfr command

The ypxfr command requests the transfer of NIS information from a master server to a slave server. You usually invoke it from an entry in the root crontab. Table 19-13 lists the arguments.

Table 19-13	ypxfr Options
Option	**Description**
-b	Preserves the resolver flag in the map during transfer.
-c	Does not send the "Clear current map" request to the local server. Use this when the local machine's ypserv process is not running.
-f	Forces the transfer even if the master version is not more recent than the local version.
-d domain	Specifies a domain instead of the default.
-h host	Retrieves the map from the specified host even if it is not the master.
-s domain	Specifies the course domain for a map.
-C tid prog ipad port	Requests a yppush process from the remote machine to the local machine.

You must specify the map name to be transferred on the command line.

The ypxfrd daemon

This daemon, running on the master site, enables faster ypxfr request handling. It takes one argument, -v, which tells it not to fork when running multiple requests.

The ypinit command

The ypinit command creates NIS servers. The -m option creates a master server, and -s master_name creates a slave server.

The ypset command

This command forces the ypbind process to connect to the server specified on the command line. It takes four arguments. Specify -V1 or -V2 to tell ypset which protocol should be used. The -h host argument attempts to change the binding on the specified host, and -d domain changes the domain.

The yppush command

This command forces the propagation of NIS maps to slave servers. You must specify a map name in yppush. The -v option requests verbose output, and -d domain specifies a domain for the map.

Debugging

You can use three commands to access and debug NIS map information.

The ypwhich command

The ypwhich command informs you which machine is acting as the NIS server. If no maps are specified on the command line, the local server is listed for the most recent access. Table 19-14 lists the ypwhich options.

Table 19-14	ypwhich Options
Option	**Description**
-d domain	Uses the specified domain instead of the default
-m [map]	Finds the master server for the specified map
-t	Inhibits alias translation
-V1 or -V2	Uses the specified protocol
-x	Lists the alias table

Here is an example of ypwhich output from netcom:

```
$ ypwhich
localhost
$ ypwhich -m passwd
yp
$ ypwhich -x
Use "passwd" for map "passwd.byname"
Use "group" for map "group.byname"
Use "networks" for map "networks.byaddr"
Use "hosts" for map "hosts.byaddr"
Use "protocols" for map "protocols.bynumber"
Use "services" for map "services.byname"
Use "aliases" for map "mail.aliases"
Use "ethers" for map "ethers.byname"
```

The ypcat command

This command prints the values in an NIS map. The available arguments are -k for displaying the keys (including the null entries), -t to inhibit alias translation, -d domain to specify a domain, and -x to display the alias table. On netcom, the ypcat -k networks.byaddr output is as follows:

```
$ ypcat -k networks.byaddr
```

```
192.9.200 sun-ether    192.9.200       sunether ethernet localnet
127 loopback    127
125 sun-oldether       125              sunoldether
46 ucb-ether    46              ucbether
10 arpanet             10               arpa
```

The ypmatch command

The ypmatch command matches a key in a map. The arguments are the same as those for ypcat. The following is some output for ypmatch from netcom:

```
$ ypmatch jca passwd
jca:#@jca:14804:50:James C. Armstrong, Jr.:/u1/jca:/bin/csh
$ ypmatch Armstrong passwd
Can't match key Armstrong in map passwd.byname.  Reason: no such key in map.
$ ypmatch 25/tcp services.byname
smtp            25/tcp          mail
```

As you can see, ypmatch is a grep command for NIS.

End-user commands

NIS has only three significant end-user commands.

The yppasswd command

The yppasswd command changes a user's password for NIS. The syntax and actions are the same as those for passwd.

The ypchfn command

The ypchfn command changes the user's full name in the passwd map.

The ypchsh command

The ypchsh command changes the user's shell in the passwd map.

The automounter

One important addition to NFS is the automounter. Strictly speaking, this is an application built on top of NFS, not a part of NFS.

Building a large set of files in the /etc/fstab can be a nuisance, and sometimes a machine reboot hangs up because an RPC request is not properly timing out. Furthermore, you can end up building a large mount table when you may need only a few remotely mounted file systems. The automounter addresses these issues.

The automounter maintains a list of file systems to be mounted on a given directory when needed. The mount is performed automatically without direct intervention by an administrator or user. In this way, only those file systems that are needed are mounted, and they remain mounted only as long as they are needed. The NIS usually maintains these files.

Story: Waiting It Out

At a previous job, we'd have some race conditions on our network after a power failure because one machine needed to wait for another to mount, and that machine was waiting on a third machine, which was waiting on the first. None would complete the boot process until one received a `SIGINT` to terminate the RPC call.

Direct and indirect automounting

Automounting commands come in two types: *direct mounts* and *indirect mounts*. The simplest way to understand the difference is to remember that a direct mount takes place in the root directory and always has the same path, whereas an indirect mount takes place in a subdirectory and can be in different locations on different machines.

Each entry in an automount map is one line. It consists of the local mount point, any mount command-line options, and the remote file system. Essentially, this is the same as the mount command less the actual command name. Thus, you might see an automount table with the following entries:

```
/home/james          fs:/export/home/james
/home/taylor         fs:/export/home/taylor
/usr/local/bin         -ro commands:/local/bin
/usr/local/mail        majordomo:/maillists
```

Automounting has four file systems. The home directories for the users `james` and `taylor` both come from the machine `fs` and are located there in the `export` directory. The file system `/usr/local/bin` is available as read-only from commands and `/usr/local/mail` comes from the machine `majordomo`.

Now, when a user needs to access a file in `/usr/local/mail`, the automounter mounts the file system `/maillists` found on the machine `majordomo`.

If the map were an indirect map, the automounter would mount the file system on an unnamed mount point and set up a symbolic link.

How automounting works

To use the automounter, you need to create several NIS maps. The first map is called `auto.master`. This lists directories for indirect mounts and the appropriate maps for those mounts. You can also specify mount options.

The maps specified in the `auto.master` map must also be created and pushed by NIS. After this occurs, you need to run the automounter daemon on your local machine. It first advertises the available mounts in `/etc/mtab`. When a user attempts to access a file under that mount point, the kernel looks up the path and finds that it is on an automounted file system. Thus, the automounter is contacted to mount the file system on a hidden mount point and to establish a symbolic link. Then, the pathname is properly resolved.

The hidden mount point is usually on the directory /tmp_mnt. Therefore, fs:/export/home/james is mounted on /tmp_mnt/export/home/james, and a symbolic link is made to /home/james.

Secret

Using the Local Network

So far, everything this chapter has discussed deals purely with the administrative side of the local network. Because the bulk of the work is performed behind the scenes, the user's task is simple and requires less discussion. Still, each user should be familiar with some network commands and aware of the existence of the network itself.

Debugging the network with ping

Several commands debug the network. Of these, the most commonly used is ping.

The ping command sends a test packet to a remote address and waits for a response. Some variants of ping also give statistics on network performance.

Although ping is contained in /usr/sbin and is considered an administrative command, I've used it many times as a user to determine whether a remote machine is up.

Note

Table 19-15 describes the arguments to ping.

Table 19-15	ping Options
Option	*Description*
-s	Provides summary information
-l	Uses a "loose" source routing
-r	Bypasses normal routing and sends directly to the host
-R	Records the route for the test packets
-v	Specifies verbose output, which lists any packets received other than the response packets

Listing 19-4 shows examples of ping output.

Listing 19-4: ping Output

```
netcom5% ping cs.unc.edu
cs.unc.edu is alive
netcom5% ping -s cs.ucla.edu
PING cs.ucla.edu: 56 data bytes
64 bytes from Lanai.CS.UCLA.EDU (131.179.128.13): icmp_seq=0. time=54. ms
64 bytes from Lanai.CS.UCLA.EDU (131.179.128.13): icmp_seq=1. time=53. ms
64 bytes from Lanai.CS.UCLA.EDU (131.179.128.13): icmp_seq=2. time=36. ms
64 bytes from Lanai.CS.UCLA.EDU (131.179.128.13): icmp_seq=3. time=45. ms
64 bytes from Lanai.CS.UCLA.EDU (131.179.128.13): icmp_seq=4. time=40. ms
C
--13.128.179.131.in-addr.arpa PING Statistics--
5 packets transmitted, 5 packets received, 0% packet loss
round-trip (ms)  min/avg/max = 36/45/54
netcom5% ping -s ist.co.uk
PING ist.co.uk: 56 data bytes
64 bytes from isbalham.ist.co.uk (192.31.26.1): icmp_seq=0. time=339. ms
64 bytes from isbalham.ist.co.uk (192.31.26.1): icmp_seq=1. time=3102. ms
64 bytes from isbalham.ist.co.uk (192.31.26.1): icmp_seq=4. time=282. ms
64 bytes from isbalham.ist.co.uk (192.31.26.1): icmp_seq=5. time=298. ms
64 bytes from isbalham.ist.co.uk (192.31.26.1): icmp_seq=6. time=278. ms
64 bytes from isbalham.ist.co.uk (192.31.26.1): icmp_seq=7. time=291. ms
64 bytes from isbalham.ist.co.uk (192.31.26.1): icmp_seq=8. time=303. ms
C
--1.26.31.192.in-addr.arpa PING Statistics--
9 packets transmitted, 7 packets received, 22% packet loss
round-trip (ms)  min/avg/max = 278/699/3102
```

The first example shows a check to see whether `cs.unc.edu` is alive. This is
the computer science machine at the University of North Carolina. The next
test compares transmission rates between a `ping` of UCLA (400 miles south
of me) and Imperial Software in England (6,000 miles east). The `-s` option
provides a detailed report on packet transmission and reply. The fastest
round trip to England and back took 278 milliseconds, just over a quarter of a
second, and the longest took just over 3 seconds. UCLA, however, took no
longer than 54 milliseconds to respond—roughly 1/19 of a second!

Networking commands

Besides having `ping` for testing the network, you have several UNIX
commands for communicating across the network. The standard approach
prepends a normal UNIX command with an r. The following sections discuss
some of these commands.

Note

One of the bigger naming clashes occurs between BSD and System V. System
V uses an `rsh` command to access a *restricted shell*. This shell denies the user
several basic capabilities. Meanwhile, BSD uses `rsh` to access a *remote shell*.
Efforts were made to rename BSD's `rsh` "remsh," but instead, `rsh` remained
the remote shell.

Giving yourself permission

Most remote commands require that you have permission to perform the command on the remote machine. You can acquire this through the .rhosts file in your home directory. Just list each machine from which you expect to perform commands remotely on the local system in .rhosts. For example, if you have a machine chomolongma and a machine godwin and you need to run commands on godwin from chomolongma, include godwin in the .rhosts file on chomolongma.

The rcp command

The rcp command copies files between machines. This command is analogous to uucp, except that rcp uses the network to copy files directly as opposed to just queuing requests.

The format is rcp *filename1 filename2*, where filenames are specified as *host:path*. If the host is omitted, the local machine is assumed; for example. rcp amaker:/home/james/.cshrc .oldcshrc makes the copy on the local machine. If the pathname is not a full path, it is assumed to be relative to your home directory on the host machine. You can perform third-party copies, too, by specifying *user@host* instead of *host*.

Two arguments are available. The -p argument attempts to copy the file's modification times and modes. The -r argument attempts to copy the file tree under the path to a new location.

The rdist command

The rdist command is one of the most powerful networking commands. It remotely distributes commands and files to multiple machines. It takes quite a few arguments, which are listed in Table 19-16.

Table 19-16   rdist Options

Option	Description
-R	Removes extraneous files. If a directory is being copied, any files in the target directory that are not present in the source directory are removed.
-b	Performs a binary comparison before updating files.
-c *pathname hostname*	Updates each pathname on the named host. If the host is prepended with login@, that user ID is used for the remote site. If the host name is appended with :destpath, the specified pathname is sent to the new destination.
-d *macro=value*	Defines a macro with a value. Used to override macros in a distfile.

Option	Description
-f distfile	Uses the commands in the distfile.
-h	Follows symbolic links, and copies the file and not the link.
-i	Ignores unresolved symbolic links.
-m host	Limits the machines to be updated. More than one -m argument can exist.
-n	Prints the commands without executing them.
-q	Does not display files being updated on standard output.
-v	Verifies that the files are up-to-date on all hosts.
-w	Appends the whole filename to the destination directory.
-y	Does not update remote copies that are younger than the master, but issues a warning.

As you can see, rdist enables you to update copies of software on remote machines to keep those files in sync. Prior to NIS, rdist was used to distribute many sites' administrative files to network nodes.

If you specify a directory, all the contents of the directory are checked and updated.

rdist file format

One of the real powers of rdist is that it enables you to create a file that specifies a list of files for regular update. This is the distfile, mentioned in Table 19-16 with the -f and -d options. The format of the distfile is confusing at first glance, but it can be understood quickly.

The simplest distfile defines two macros, HOSTS and FILES. The HOSTS macro is a list of host names to be kept in sync with the local master machine. The FILES macro is a list of files for distribution. If you use rdist instead of NIS and have a network of four machines, the distfile shown in Listing 19-5 keeps each site up-to-date.

Listing 19-5: An rdist File

```
HOSTS = ( chomolongma godwin anapurna laotse )

FILES = ( /etc/passwd
    /etc/services
    /etc/group
    /etc/aliases
    /etc/bootparams
    /etc/ethers
    /etc/hosts
    /etc/netgroup
    /etc/netmasks
```

```
/etc/networks
/etc/protocols
/etc/rpc )
```

`${FILES} -> ${HOSTS} install;`

This file is used with `rdist -f distfile`. When run, it checks each remote machine to see whether the local copy of the file is more up-to-date than the copy on the remote machine. If it is, the local copy is sent to the remote machine and installed.

Note

Many commands are associated with `rdist`, and those commands can have many arguments.

Note

NIS and the automounter have diminished the usefulness of `rdist`, but the command is not totally obsolete. Some sites still maintain separate home directories on different hosts and platforms, and you can use `rdist` to maintain your own environment files on those platforms.

The rlogin command

One of the most popular commands is `rlogin`. This command gains access to remote machines via a login prompt. The normal syntax is as follows:

`rlogin host [ -l userID ]`

If your local host is in the `.rhost` file on the remote machine, you are logged into your own account without being prompted for a password. Otherwise, you see a password prompt.

The `rlogin` command has four arguments. With the `-l` option, you can specify a different user ID on the remote machine. The `-L` option enables you to run in lit-out mode. The `-8` option passes 8-bit characters, instead of 7. The `-e` option enables you to specify a different escape character.

The rsh command

The `rsh` command requests the running of a shell on the remote machine. The syntax for this command is as follows:

`rsh [ -l username ] [ -n ] hostname [ command ]`

For the command to run remotely, the local machine must appear in the `.rhosts` file on the remote machine. If the entry is not present, you are presented with a request for a password before proceeding.

The command can be any command that you can run from your home directory on the remote machine. If no command is present, you obtain an interactive shell on the remote machine: `rlogin machine` is synonymous with `rsh machine`. You can specify a different user name with `-l`. The `-n` option redirects input on the remote shell to /dev/null. This is sometimes needed to avoid unusual complications.

The rup command

This command enables you to check the status of a remote machine. It produces the same output as rsh *machine* uptime. You do not need to have an entry in .rhosts to run this command.

The rusers command

This is a quick command to provide a list of users on a remote machine. It is directly analogous to the users command. Table 19-17 lists the options available.

Table 19-17   rusers Options

Option	Description
-a	Reports on a machine even if no one is using that machine
-h	Sorts alphabetically by host name
-i	Sorts by idle time
-l	Gives a longer listing in the who format
-u	Sorts by the number of users

The rwho command

The last common command is rwho. This is similar to rusers, except that the output is in a slightly different format. It reports on all the machines in your network. With the -a option, users who have been idle for over an hour are reported.

Understanding Protocols

Protocols underlie all network communications. These are the formats in which commands are sent from one daemon on a machine to another daemon on a remote machine.

You may be surprised to know that most protocols are in ASCII. Although the transmission time for a string is slightly longer than for a binary value, the use of a string is convenient for both debugging and writing network programs. Network programmers can use defined strings in their code and build protocol requests accordingly.

Two common protocols are SMTP and NNTP. SMTP is the Simple Mail Transfer Protocol. Protocol commands exist in SMTP to identify the host sending mail, the sender, the recipient, and the data to be transferred.

The Simple Mail Transfer Protocol

One commonly used protocol is the Simple Mail Transfer Protocol (SMTP). The current version of SMTP was written in RFC821 in August 1982 and defines the protocol through which mail transfer programs communicate. It is an ASCII protocol with character strings as commands and numeric error responses. The transmission of the protocol is independent of the underlying transport layers. The normal transport layer is TCP on UNIX systems.

The sending system opens a communications socket to the remote machine to initiate the connection. This remote machine does not need to be the ultimate destination for the mail message; it can be an intermediary. The two machines need to shake hands, and the sending machine initiates the transfer by indicating it has mail from a user to be sent to another user. The sender always waits for confirmation from the receiver before proceeding to the next step. Finally, the sender transmits the message and closes the connection.

Table 19-18 lists the different protocol commands for SMTP, their arguments (if any), and what they do.

Table 19-18	SMTP Commands	
Command	*Argument*	*Action*
DATA		Specifies that the next lines, until a single dot appears on the line, are the actual e-mail message
EXPN	Address	Expands an e-mail alias (not always implemented)
HELO	Local name (optional)	Identifies the sending site to the receiver
HELP	Command (optional)	Obtains a listing of all the protocol commands
MAIL	Sender address	Tells the receiver to expect mail from the sender
NOOP		Performs no operation
QUIT		Terminates the communications
RCPT	Recipient address	Tells the receiver who will receive the mail
RSET		Resets the system

Command	Argument	Action
SAML		Initiates communication to send to both a terminal and a mailbox
SEND		Initiates a mail transaction to deliver data to one or more terminals
SOML		Initiates communication to send to either a terminal or a mailbox
TURN		Gives the receiving site the opportunity to switch roles with the sending site
VRFY	Address	Verifies the e-mail address (not always implemented)

Guru: Finding the Best Connection Machine

You can discover the best machine for a connection by using the `nslookup` command. This is an interactive command. You first specify that you want mail exchange records. Then, enter **q=MX** at the prompt. Next, enter the desired domain followed by a period.

The following code specifies that for my home domain, my mail should be sent to one of the uumail machines at `netcom.com`:

```
$ /usr/etc/nslookup
Default Server:
netcom22.netcom.com
Address:  192.100.81.136

> set q=MX
> sagarmatha.com.
Server:  netcom22.netcom.com
Address:  192.100.81.136

Non-authoritative answer:
sagarmatha.com  preference = 10,
mail exchanger =
uumail2.netcom.com
sagarmatha.com  preference = 10,
mail exchanger =
uumail3.netcom.com
sagarmatha.com  preference = 10,
mail exchanger =
uumail1.netcom.com
sagarmatha.com  preference = 50,
mail exchanger =
uumail4.netcom.com
Authoritative answers can be found
from:
uumail2.netcom.com      inet
address = 163.179.3.52
uumail3.netcom.com      inet
address = 163.179.3.53
uumail1.netcom.com      inet
address = 163.179.3.50
uumail4.netcom.com      inet
address = 163.179.3.54
UUCPNS1.netcom.com      inet
address = 163.179.3.221
UUCPNS2.netcom.com      inet
address = 163.179.3.222
>
```

Examining MX records can be quite helpful because it enables you to see how your mail is routed.

The SMTP commands SAML, SEND, SOML, and TURN are rarely used.

What follows is the annotated operation of the protocol. To create this, I've used Telnet to attach to a remote sendmail process, and I'm mimicking the role of the local sendmail. I am using this to send a message to james@sagarmatha.com.

```
$ telnet uumail2.netcom.com 25
Trying 163.179.3.52 ...
Connected to uumail2.netcom.com.
Escape character is `^]'.
220-netcomsv.netcom.com Sendmail 8.6.12/SMI-4.1 ready at Mon, 20 Nov 1995
13:18:26 -0800
220 ESMTP spoken here
```

This is what the remote sendmail sent me when I requested a connection. I need to respond with a HELO to announce who I am:

```
HELO aim.com
250 netcomsv.netcom.com Hello [192.172.247.173], pleased to meet you
```

The netcom machine recognizes the command and breaks out my IP address. Next, I need to tell it that I want to send some mail:

```
MAIL From: <taylor@intuitive.com>
250 <taylor@intuitive.com>... Sender ok
```

This tells me that I can send the mail:

```
RCPT To: <james@sagarmatha.com>
250 <james@sagarmatha.com>... Recipient ok
```

It will gladly forward my mail, too:

```
DATA
354 Enter mail, end with "." on a line by itself
```

Now I can enter the message:

```
From intuitive.com!taylor 15 Nov 1995 07:36:22 PST
Subject: Dinner plans?
From: Dave Taylor (taylor@intuitive.com)

Any plans for dinner tonight?

Dave
.
250 NAA08940 Message accepted for delivery
```

When I finish entering the message, a single dot tells the remote sendmail that I have completed the message. Now, all I need to do is quit:

```
QUIT
221 netcomsv.netcom.com closing connection
Connection closed by foreign host.
```

The connection is over.

Return messages

You may have noticed that each response to a protocol request was a three-digit number. Programs that communicate over the protocol look for that number to tell them whether their request was successful. Of the three digits, the first is the most important. Table 19-19 shows the common digits and their meanings.

Table 19-19	SMTP Return Code Meanings
First Digit	*Meaning*
1	Positive preliminary reply
2	Positive completion reply
3	Positive intermediate reply
4	Transient negative completion reply
5	Permanent negative reply
Second Digit	*Meaning*
1	Information
2	Connections
3	Unspecified
4	Unspecified
5	Local mail system

The third digit gives a finer-grained reply. Usually, a protocol is completely hidden from the user. I supplied the annotated illustration simply to indicate how a protocol is actually used.

The Network News Transfer Protocol

The Network News Transfer Protocol (NNTP) defines a mechanism to send netnews between sites quickly. It also works with news readers and defines protocol requests to send articles, headers, and listings from administrative files.

Many other protocols are available in UNIX. These protocols define communication across different ports. Protocols are defined in documents called RFCs (Requests for Comments). Several archive sites are available on the Internet.

Summary

This chapter discussed the many different tools for working in your local area network. It introduced the following topics:

- *The seven-layer network application model.* This defines the seven layers of network programming and helps explain the interfaces between layers. A high-level understanding of different network levels is useful for understanding how UNIX works.

- *Remote Procedure Calls.* RPCs define a mechanism through which an application on one machine can communicate with a program on a different machine.

- *The Network File System.* NFS is a mechanism that enables many separate systems to share hard disks. This gives a network greater flexibility.

- *The Network Information Service.* NIS enables an administrator to maintain a single set of files that contains all the administrative information for the local network in a single place and to share that information with other machines in the network.

- *The automounter.* This application enables you to specify a list of files to be mounted automatically on a remote machine, as needed.

- *Remote commands.* These are standard commands that are requested on one machine and run on a remote machine.

- *Protocols.* You should be aware that protocols define communication at a lower level between programs.

The next chapter introduces wide area network commands, electronic mail, and network news.

Chapter 20

Using Electronic Mail and Netnews

In This Chapter

▶ Easy Internet access with e-mail

▶ Make friends and learn lots with mailing lists

▶ The party that never ends: Usenet

This chapter introduces you to the Internet as a communications tool. To help us on our journey, I've asked my good friend Dave Taylor to take us on an exploration of the Internet. Dave is president of Intuitive Systems and is the author of several books, including *The Internet Business Guide* and *Creating Cool Web Pages with HTML.* So without further ado, take it away, Dave . . .

Odds are excellent that you've heard of the Net, or at least the World Wide Web, and you might have been thinking that because you don't have a Mac or PC on your desk, you were probably out in the cold. This is definitely not the case, and in fact, you can do a ton of things today to start exploring the Internet.

Without question, you can do a multitude of things on your UNIX system that can be useful and productive, but it's probably optimistic to think that you might find it fun and informative on a daily basis. That's where the Internet comes in handy: There's always someone with something to say and a new publication to read online.

What the Internet Is All About

If you have managed to step outside your door in the last 12 months, have flipped on a news program, or have even read a magazine, you've probably come face-to-face with the latest piece of our mutual interactive future: the Internet. Whether you see a report about the tens of millions of people connected through the speed of light (and slow phone lines) or misinformed innuendo about inappropriate uses of so-called cyberspace, the Internet has become quite the *topic de jour* in these times.

But what is the Internet, and who runs it? As it turns out, the Internet, historically, was a research and communications *network protocol,* or language, designed so that a set of computers could communicate even if one of the machines was shut down and even if one of the network wires was cut. The original motivation, perhaps distressingly, was militarism, but soon university research groups seized onto its development when they saw it had the potential to become a much greater universal system for connecting computers.

What really made the Internet — the name derives from its position as an Interconnected Network of Networks in the original design — so innovative was that it wasn't tied to a specific type of computer language, hardware design, or wire. Previous networks tended much more to allow people with, say, IBM mainframes to talk to other IBM mainframes, or Digital minicomputers to communicate with other Digital minicomputers. Few people could envision having disparate computers able to communicate, but that's really what made the introduction of the so-called *Transmission Control Protocol and Internet Protocol* (you see this written now as *TCP/IP*) such a watershed event in computer history: Any computer could quickly and easily communicate with any other computer, regardless of who made them and how much they cost!

By the early 1980s, people at schools throughout the United States and Europe were eagerly jumping on the bandwagon, and programs designed for less expert users and aimed at higher levels of traffic began to supplant the first primitive tools for letting people communicate, especially the *UNIX-to-UNIX-copy program (uucp)*. In particular, a system originally designed by some East Coast basketball fanatics quickly evolved into an essential part of the Internet: *Usenet.*

Story: The Birth of Usenet

Usenet originated between Duke University and the University of North Carolina. Because the two schools were only eight miles apart, the departments of Computer Science would share resources at the graduate level. This included opening guest lecturers and classes to graduate students of the other school. Notifying people of these events was easy if they shared the same computer system (an old UNIX utility, news, allowed important announcements to appear on a machine). Tom Truscott at Duke and Steve Bellovin at UNC devised a means to transmit those news articles between the machines at Duke and North Carolina, and from there sprang Usenet. (Basketball was only added afterward!)

I won't tell you too much about the Internet, but you should realize that the set of technologies we have today, namely the remarkable capabilities and multimillion-user environment, was the result of a remarkable evolution in software and communications that took over 20 years, and absolutely had UNIX, not PCs or Macs, as its heart and soul. Indeed, UNIX to this day is the heart and soul of the Internet.

Note

A lot of technology underlies the Internet, but none is more important than the different ports involved. Like television channels, Internet services each operate on their own assigned "frequency," or port, and hundreds of different ports are assigned for use within the Internet environment, mostly for little-known services. Nonetheless, your e-mail traffic doesn't collide with the Web page you're downloading or the remote time server you're synchronizing against because they're all operating on different ports on your network wire.

Easy Internet Access with E-mail

Other services might hog the limelight, but those of us who've spent any significant time on the Internet are well aware that electronic mail is the backbone of the network. The capability to communicate one-on-one with any of millions of other users is exciting and simple. Indeed, you can just as easily send a message to a new friend in Finland or Tokyo as you can zap off a memo to your colleague down the hall. Electronic mail in the UNIX environment has two parts: the *transport layer* and the *user agent.* Think of these as the postal service (the transport layer) with all its mysterious mechanisms to transport a letter from point A to point B, and the physical message itself with the envelope, type of paper, and handwriting of the sender (the user agent).

Neither can exist without the other, but both have plenty of options, too. In the real world, you can type a memo and FedEx it to someone overnight, or you can handwrite it on the back of a napkin and use the U.S. Postal Service to deliver it a few days later. In the same way, the Internet supports a variety of mail transport agents and a plethora of user agents for composing and reading electronic mail.

Having said that, I should be fair. You'll almost always find that the electronic mail on your system, particularly your UNIX system, is built around a mail transport agent that speaks the *Simple Mail Transport Protocol,* or *SMTP.* It's a low-level language that's designed to make it simple for mail programs to communicate with each other on the network, and if your system is set up correctly, you'll never have to worry about it.

On top of the SMTP layer can be one of a wide variety of different mail user agents, or front-end programs. Just like the wide variety of word processing programs available that all fundamentally offer the same functionality, at least a half dozen popular electronic mail programs interact with the SMTP transport agent to send and receive your e-mail. It's then up to you, your firm, and your work style to ascertain which of the options is most appropriate. If you have a graphical interface, you might nonetheless find a text-based mail program faster and easier to use anyway, particularly if you spend much of your time on the road, dialing up remotely (or using *telnet* to connect across the network). On the other hand, a well-designed graphical interface should always be easier to understand and simpler to use.

Tip

As a general rule of thumb, try to find a mail program that lets you focus on the message, not the mailer. Good software isn't in your face, and e-mail can appear remarkably complex if the user agent is poorly designed.

E-mail itself most emulates a simple memorandum: You type the name and address of the recipient (or recipients), specify a succinct subject of the message, and type the actual message itself. When you're done, a simple keystroke or two is sufficient to feed it to the mail transport program, which then routes it to each of the recipients, whether on the same computer, in the same building, or halfway around the world. It all works remarkably well, and don't be surprised if you send mail to someone far away and receive a response within mere minutes: Often messages make international trips in fractions of a second!

E-mail addresses

In the early days of the Internet, users had to figure out the route between their own computer and that of the intended recipient, resulting in !-separated addresses that specified the entire route. A typical address might have been ihnp4!hplabs!hprnd!taylor, where the computers *inhnp4* and *hplabs* were intermediate hosts that would store and forward the message as quickly as possible, and *hprnd* was the destination machine upon which user *taylor* had his account.

As the Internet became larger and the protocols supported full-time connections to the network, the mail system itself thankfully subsumed the need for intermediate routing, and now addresses are specified as the user name followed by the computer name and domain information.

Each computer on the entire Internet, therefore, has a unique *host+domain name,* and most of the domain names are assigned by a central authority, the Internet Network Information Center, or InterNIC. Domains in the United States are pulled from a couple of pies, as shown in Figure 20-1.

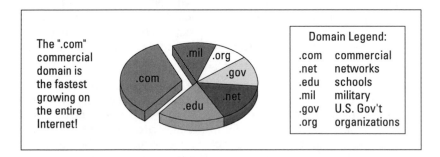

Figure 20-1: Top-level domains on the Internet

Within each top-level domain, the secondary domain typically identifies the company or organization itself. Table 20-1 shows some examples of `.com` commercial domains.

Table 20-1 Some Examples of Domain Names	
Domain Name	*Organization*
`att.com`	American Telephone & Telegraph Corp.
`best.com`	Best Communications, Inc.
`compaq.com`	Compaq Computer Corporation
`tnt-media.com`	Tracewell & Taylor Media
`visa.com`	Visa Corporation
`xerox.com`	Xerox Corporation

Many domains are worlds unto themselves, where a large corporation might have hundreds or thousands of subdomains. You can split the pie as many ways as you'd like when you set up a network (or many networks), so you'll see the gamut, ranging from division names (something like `rnd.hp.com`) to geographic areas (`burbank.nbc.com`) to weird and fun names (`killer.imagesoft.sony.com`).

When you put it all together, an e-mail address is a unique username at a unique host: *user@host.domain*. Here are a few typical e-mail addresses:

`james@sagarmatha.com`	User james at domain sagarmatha.com
`taylor@netcom17.netcom.com`	User taylor at host netcom17 in domain netcom.com
`rambaud@aol.com`	User rambaud on America Online

It's pretty straightforward for the most part. Just remember that spaces aren't allowed. (This can be a bit puzzling because America Online allows spaces for account names. So, while I'm D1 Taylor on AOL itself, my Internet e-mail address is that sans space: `D1Taylor@aol.com`.) Just about anything else goes, from dots (.) to dashes (-) to underlines (_).

Mailer programs

Mail user agents are too numerous to list here, but I can give you a brief preview of three popular ones: Berkeley Mail, Elm, and Pine. Remember that you'll use the mailer to accomplish two primary tasks: sending mail and reading mail that others have sent you.

Berkeley Mail

Berkeley Mail is a program that has been around and part of UNIX for many years, and it's a straightforward application that is line-oriented, not even taking advantage of the screen, let alone any sort of X or graphical capabilities. To read mail you may have received, simply type **mail**. Here's what I see:

```
% mail
>    1 carolyn@usenix.org Mon Aug 14 11:16   42/1383  Re: payment update
     2 zanna@usenix.org   Tue Aug 22 13:26   37/1228  Internet World
     3 webster@inlink.com Mon Sep 25 12:31   96/4666  Re: Your quotes in our si
     4 pslater@multinet.win.net Mon Sep 25 19:03   25/1039  Your book ""Creating
Cool
     5 rsage@excelsior.Eng.Sun.COM Tue Sep 26 10:02   25/994   Re: SEF Internet
SIG
     6 kcby@gpsi.com       Tue Sep 26 11:00   40/1536  Thanks, and a question
     7 LEHMAN@VM.CC.PURDUE.EDU Tue Sep 26 12:01   38/2190  Thanks!
     8 gwelz@panix.com     Fri Sep 29 06:28  261/15133 Book Intro
     9 Bob_Metcalfe@ccgate.infoworld.com Fri Sep 29 11:10   77/3395  Re[2]: Trade
Shows
    10 mall@garage.eccosys.com Tue Oct  3 22:58  177/5735
&
```

To read a specific message, enter the numeric index to the left of the message in question. If I wanted to read the mail from lehman@vm.cc.purdue.edu, for example, I'd type **7** and see the message:

```
& 7
Message  7:
From LEHMAN@VM.CC.PURDUE.EDU  Tue Sep 26 12:01:07 1995
Return-Path: <LEHMAN@VM.CC.PURDUE.EDU>
Received: from VM.CC.PURDUE.EDU (vm.cc.purdue.edu [128.210.254.40]) by
blob.best.net (8.6.12/8.6.5) with SMTP id MAA01650 for <taylor@INTUITIVE.COM>;
Tue, 26 Sep 1995 12:03:56 -0700
Message-Id: <199509261903.MAA01650@blob.best.net>
Date:       Tue, 26 Sep 95 14:00:28 EST
From: ""James D. Lehman"" <LEHMAN@VM.CC.PURDUE.EDU>
Subject:    Thanks!
To: Dave <taylor@INTUITIVE.COM>

Belated thanks for the copy of your new book. It looks great! How is it
doing so far? Our new book is scheduled to hit the shelves sometime
between December and February; I'll return the favor then.

So, how are you occupying your time? Probably just eating bon bons and
watching the ocean. The hard life of cutthroat consulting!

****************************************************************
  James D. Lehman
  Educational Computing & Instructional Development
  School of Education,  Purdue University
&
```

I have lots of options at this point, including **r**esponding to the message, **f**orwarding the message to someone else, **d**eleting the message, or **s**aving the

message to a specific folder or file. You can even **print** the message if you're
so inclined.

To send a message, either type **mail *recipient address*** at the UNIX command
line or type **mail *recipient address*** within the program. Either way, here's
what you'd see:

```
& mail james@sagarmatha.com
Subject: How about dinner tomorrow night?
My trip to Cancun has been canceled; how about dinner tomorrow night to talk
about our new Web site?  The Bangkok Pavilion at 7pm?
Dave
.
Cc:
&
```

Here you can see that the program prompted me for a subject to the
message, and when I was done entering the message itself, I simply typed a
period (.) on a line by itself to tell the program that the message was over. It
asked if I wanted to "carbon copy" (Cc) anyone, and because I didn't, it
silently and efficiently sent the message. Within seconds James is reading my
query and, no doubt, responding just as promptly!

The Elm Mail System

An alternative mail program — one that's very popular and considerably
more sophisticated than Berkeley Mail — is the Elm Mail System. Still not
needing a graphical interface like X, Elm uses the entire screen to display
incoming mail and hides much of the ugliness of the underlying mail system
on the Internet.

Here's the same mailbox, only this time I'm using Elm to read it. I started this
session by typing **elm** at the UNIX command line:

```
        Mailbox is `~/.mailbox/inbox´ with 81 messages [ELM 2.4 PL23]

      1   Aug 14 Carolyn Carr       (42)   Re: payment update
      2   Aug 22 Zanna Knight       (37)   Internet World
      3   Sep 25 Shari Peterson     (96)   Re: Your quotes in our site
M   4   Sep 25 Phillip L. Slater,   (25)   Your book ""Creating Cool Web Pages w
      5   Sep 26 Russell Sage       (25)   Re: SEF Internet SIG
      6   Sep 26 K.C. Burgess Yakem (40)   Thanks, and a question
      7   Sep 26 James D. Lehman    (38)   Thanks!
      8   Sep 29 Gary Welz          (261)  Book Intro
      9   Sep 29 Bob Metcalfe       (77)   Re[2]: Trade Shows and Boston Common
     10   Oct 4  mall@garage.eccosy (177)

        |=pipe, !=shell, ?=help, <n>=set current to n, /=search pattern
    a)lias, C)opy, c)hange folder, d)elete, e)dit, f)orward, g)roup reply, m)ail,
      n)ext, o)ptions, p)rint, q)uit, r)eply, s)ave, t)ag, u)ndelete, or e(x)it

Command:
```

To read the message from Dr. Lehman, I can either type the **7** next to the message, à la Berkeley Mail, or I can use the cursor keys to move the highlight bar down to that message and press Enter to read the specified message. Here's how it displays:

```
Message 7/81  From James D. Lehman              Sep 26, 95 02:00:28 pm EST
                                                                  Thanks!


(message addressed to Dave Taylor)


Belated thanks for the copy of your new book. It looks great! How is it
doing so far? Our new book is scheduled to hit the shelves sometime
between December and February; I'll return the favor then.

So, how are you occupying your time? Probably just eating bon bons and
watching the ocean. The hard life of cutthroat consulting!
****************************************************************
   James D. Lehman
   Educational Computing & Instructional Development
   School of Education, Purdue University
```

To send a message, the short list of menu options on the bottom of the main screen reminds me that I can type **m** to mail a message. Here's how that looks:

```
Command: Mail                            To: james@sagarmatha.com
Subject: Dinner tomorrow night?
Copies to:

Enter message.  Type Elm commands on lines by themselves.
Commands include:  ^D or `.´ to end, ~p to list, ~? for help.

My trip to Cancun has been canceled; how about dinner tomorrow night to talk
about our new Web site?  The Bangkok Pavilion at 7pm?
Dave
.
<end-of-message>

And now: s
  e)dit msg, m)ake form, h)eaders, c)opy, i)spell, !)shell, s)end, or f)orget
```

As you can see, although the underlying mail system remains the same, the design of the programs you can use to actually work with your mailbox varies considerably. Again, I encourage you to look at a mail program with a bit of a jaundiced eye. If you're like me, you'll find yourself spending a lot of time in this program each day, so make it one that is fun, that you are comfortable with, and that helps you with your daily tasks.

One of the biggest advantages of a mail reader like Elm is that you can customize it in several ways. Elm comes with several command-line arguments that can alter its function; these are described in Table 20-2.

Table 20-2 **Elm Options**

Option	Result
-?	Lists all command line options
-V	Debugs the underlying mail transport
-a	Uses -> for the screen cursor instead of inverse video
-c alias	Checks that an alias is valid
-d#	Sets the debugging level
-f file	Uses the specified file as the mailbox instead of the default mailbox
-h	Lists all command-line options
-i file	Includes the specified file in the edit buffer when sending a message
-m	Turns off the menu at the bottom of the screen, showing more messages
-s subject	Includes the specified subject on an outgoing message
-v	Prints out the Elm version
-z	Does not enter Elm if no mail is in the mailbox

The elm -z alias is one of the more common aliases for Elm, so by default, when you start Elm, it checks to see if there is any mail before proceeding.

Changing the configuration variables provides an even more powerful way to customize Elm. These variables are located in a file under your home directory, $HOME/.elm/elmrc, and you can edit this file to change the values to whatever you like. Table 20-3 lists the elmrc variables, their types, and how they affect your Elm session.

Table 20-3 **Elm Variables**

Variable	Type	Option Key Letter	Effect
aliassortby	string	l	When examining the aliases, it determines in which order those aliases are sorted. The values allowed are name, alias, or text. You can prepend each with reverse- to change the sense of the sort.
alteditor	command	j	Defines the editor used when you escape from Elm; defaults to /bin/vi.

Continued

Table 20-3 *(continued)*

Variable	Type	Option Key Letter	Effect
alternatives	ON or OFF		When set, this prevents you from receiving multiple copies of sent messages.
alwaysdelete	ON or OFF		When set, you are not prompted for confirmation to delete marked messages when you exit Elm.
alwayskeep	ON or OFF		When set to ON, always keeps unread messages in your mailbox. If set to OFF, moves unread messages to a received mailbox.
alwaysstore	ON or OFF		When set to ON, moves read mail that is not tagged for deletion to your received mailbox.
arrow	ON or OFF	a	When set to ON, changes the message cursor to an arrow, ->. This is particularly useful on machines where you can't display inverse video.
ask	ON or OFF		When set to ON, Elm asks for confirmation for or moving of messages. Setting it to OFF prevents Elm from prompting for those confirmations.
askcc	ON or OFF	w	When set to ON, Elm prompts for a CC list when you compose a message.
attribution	string		This string is included before any text to which you are replying when you send a message. This can be anything. If you include a %s, the original sender's name is included.
autocopy	ON or OFF	r	When set to ON and when you reply to mail, a copy of the message is included in your message.

Variable	Type	Option Key Letter	Effect
bounceback	integer		If you send mail along a UUCP path of more than bounceback hops, Elm automatically includes a CC to you via those remote hops. This allows you to confirm reception of the message at a remote site.
builtinlines	integer		Any message of this many lines is sent to an external pager for display.
calendar	file	c	This points to the location of your calendar file. Some configurations of Elm allow you to add notification information to a calendar file automatically.
charset	string		This specifies the character set to be used with Elm.
compat charsets	string		This lists the types of characters that can be displayed on your screen without relying on a MIME reader.
config options	string		This is a string that allows you to specify a list of Elm variables that you can manage through the Elm options string. Each variable that has an Option Key Letter specified can be managed on the screen. Just list the letters in order. To include a blank line, use a dash, and the window title is specified with a ^ .
confirmappend	ON or OFF		When set to ON, Elm asks for confirmation before appending a message to a mailbox file.
confirmcreate	ON or OFF		When set to ON, Elm asks for confirmation before creating a messages file.
confirmfiles	ON or OFF		When set to ON, Elm asks for confirmation before appending to a file outside the Mail directory.
confirmfolders	ON or OFF		When set to ON, Elm asks for confirmation before creating a file outside the Mail directory.

Continued

Table 20-3 *(continued)*

Variable	Type	Option Key Letter	Effect
copy	ON or OFF	h	When set to ON, copies of your outgoing mail are saved in your Mail directory.
displaycharset	string		This lists the character sets supported by your display.
easyeditor	command	t	This is the editor invoked with ~e from the built-in editor.
editor	command	e	This is the editor used by default or built in for composing and replying to messages.
escape	character		This is the escape character for the built-in editor.
forcename	ON or OFF		When set to ON, this forces the creation of a message file in the Mail directory using the recipient's name when saving sent mail.
forms	ON or OFF		When set to ON, Elm supports the AT&T forms protocol for mail.
fullname	string	y	This string overrides any data from /etc/passwd or .fullname when replacing the full name of the mail sender.
keepempty	ON or OFF		When set to ON, if a message file has no messages, it is retained.
keypad	ON or OFF		When set to ON, use the HP keypad for HP terminals.
localsignature	file		Specifies a file to be appended to outgoing mail messages sent on the local network.
maildir	directory	f	Specifies a directory where mail messages are retained by default.
menu	ON or OFF	m	When set to ON, a menu of command options is displayed at the bottom of the screen.
metoo	ON or OFF		When set to ON, a copy of the message sent to a mailing list is also sent to you.

Variable	Type	Option Key Letter	Effect
movepage	ON or OFF		When set to ON, the current message changes when you change pages.
names	ON or OFF	n	When set to ON, the full name is displayed instead of the e-mail address.
noheader	ON or OFF		When set to ON, none of the header is included in the editing buffer when replying to a message.
pager	command	d	Specifies which command to use builtin, as the pager. The PAGER environment or builtin+ variable overrides the selection here.
pointnew	ON or OFF		When set to ON, the current message pointer indicates the first new message; otherwise, it points to the first message.
precedences	string		Specifies precedences allowed for sending mail. These can be strings or colon-separated pairs.
prefix	string	b	When including the text of a message in a reply, this string prepends each line of the reply.
Continuedprint	command	p	This is the command used to print an e-mail message. If you include the %s string, the message file is included at that point; otherwise, it is fed into the standard input of the command.
promptafter	ON or OFF	k	When set to ON, Elm prompts to continue after the pager exits.
readmsginc	integer		When reading new messages, the screen is updated every time this many messages have been processed.
receivedmail	file		This specifies the file where received mail is retained.

Continued

Table 20-3	*(continued)*		
Variable	**Type**	**Option Key Letter**	**Effect**
remote-	file		Specifies a file to be appended to `signature` outgoing mail messages sent outside the local network.`resolve`ON or OFF When set to ON, after you have finished with a mail message, you move to the next available mail message automatically.
savename	ON or OFF		When set to ON, mail is saved in a file with the same name as the message sender (or recipient, for copies of outgoing mail). When set to OFF, mail is saved in the file specified by `receivedmail` and `sentmail`.
sentmail	file	o	Specifies a file where copies of outgoing messages are saved.
shell	command		This specifies the shell to run when requested. The SHELL environment variable overrides this variable.
sigdashes	ON or OFF	z	Specifies whether the standard dashes appear before the signature.
signature	file		Specifies a file to be appended to all outgoing messages. Overridden by `localsignature` and `remotesignature`.
sleepmsg	integer		Specifies how long a background message remains visible, in seconds.
softkeys	ON or OFF		Specifies whether the HP soft keys are to be used.
sortby	string	s	Specifies the nature of the sort of the messages in the inbox. The possible values are from, lines, mailbox, received, sent, status, and subject. Each can be prepended with `reverse-` to change the sense of the sort.

Variable	Type	Option Key Letter	Effect
textencoding	string		Specifies the text encoding for outgoing messages using MIME.
timeout	integer		Specifies how often, in seconds, Elm should check to see if there is new mail.
titles	ON or OFF		Places a title on the window with the built-in pager.
tmpdir	directory		Specifies a directory where temporary files are located.
userlevel	integer	u	Specifies the level of user sophistication. 0 is for a beginner, 1, for an intermediate user, and 2, for an advanced user. This changes how the different menus are presented.
usetite	ON or OFF		Specifies whether the termcap entries for ti and te should be used.
visualeditor	command	v	Specifies what editor to use when ~v is entered into the built-in editor.
weed	ON or OFF		Specifies whether headers should be weeded out of the message when displayed.
weedlist	string		The list of headers to be ignored.

You can modify some Elm variables through the options command, as well as by editing the .elmrc file. When in the main Elm window, enter the o command, and you are placed in a window with some options selected. Choose the option by picking the highlighted letter and then enter the appropriate value.

A third choice, Pine

Pine is a mail reader developed at the University of Washington and is aimed for more novice users to become familiar with UNIX mail. The product has been designed to be more user friendly than other mail readers, and it should enable a new user to read and send mail without needing to learn a lot of esoteric commands and options.

When you first use Pine, the program creates an electronic mail environment. This means it creates a .pinerc file and a mail directory. Starting Pine is simple: Just enter **pine** on the command line. You are presented with a standard screen:

```
PINE 3.91    MAIN MENU                    Folder: (CLOSED)  0 Messages

                      Welcome to Pine...

   a Program for Internet News and E-mail.  Pine offers the ability to:
    -Access local and remote message folders using a simple user-interface
    -Send documents, graphics, etc (via the MIME standard for attachments)

   COMMANDS IN PINE:  Available commands are always listed on the last
   two lines of the screen.  If there are more than can be displayed, the
     ""O"" command will cycle their display.  Except in function key mode,
   commands can be executed even though they are not displayed.

   PINE CONFIGURATION:  Pine has created a default configuration file for you.
    To customize pine's behavior, use the Setup/Config (""S"" then ""C""
    in Main Menu).  We also suggest seeing pine's main help (""?"" in Main
Menu).

    SPECIAL OFFER:  Would you like to receive (via e-mail) a brief document
     entitled ""Secrets of Pine"" ?


                PINE is a trademark of the University of Washington.
Request document?
Y [Yes]
N No
```

After you pass this screen, on subsequent invocations, you should end up
straight at the main menu screen, like so:

```
PINE 3.91    MAIN MENU                    Folder: INBOX  189 Messages


         ?     HELP              -  Get help using Pine

         C     COMPOSE MESSAGE   -  Compose and send a message

         I     FOLDER INDEX      -  View messages in current folder

         L     FOLDER LIST       -  Select a folder to view

         A     ADDRESS BOOK      -  Update address book

         S     SETUP             -  Configure or update Pine

         Q     QUIT              -  Exit the Pine program




      Copyright 1989-1994.  PINE is a trademark of the University of Washington.
                  [Folder "INBOX" opened with 189 messages]
? Help                  P PrevCmd                    R RelNotes
O OTHER CMDS L [ListFldrs] N NextCmd                 K KBLock
```

Pine makes extensive use of inverse video for highlighting.

The normal procedure from here to retrieve your mail is to enter **I** for the index to the default folder, your incoming mailbox. This gives you a listing of all your e-mail messages in your mailbox, in a fashion similar to Elm. What follows is my mail index. Once I've selected a message, I use **V** to view the e-mail message.

```
PINE 3.91    FOLDER INDEX                Folder: INBOX  Message 3 of 3

  +    1    Nov 19 Loren E. Miller       (969) HELP
  +    2    Nov 19 Mike Rosenberg      (3,917) Re: just a whimr
  +    3    Nov 19 Tim or Maria        (1,093) Re: ROUND THREE: PICK NOW!

















? Help       M Main Menu  P PrevMsg     - PrevPage    D Delete     R Reply
O OTHER CMDS V [ViewMsg]  N NextMsg    Spc NextPage    U Undelete   F Forward
```

Sending mail

Pine also allows for fast sending of mail. From the main menu, you can enter **C** to reach the composer. Alternatively, just include an e-mail address on the command line, and Pine starts in the composer. Here is a message being composed:

```
PINE 3.91    COMPOSE MESSAGE             Folder: INBOX  3 Messages

To      : james@sagarmatha.com
Cc      :
Fcc     : jamessave
Attchmnt:
Subject : Dinner tomorrow night?
-- Message Text --
My trip to Cancun has been cancelled; how about dinner tomorrow night to talk
about our new Web site?  The Bangkok Pavillion at 7pm?

Dave
```

```
^G Get Help    ^X Send    ^R Read File    ^Y Prev Pg    ^K Cut Text    ^O Postpone
^C Cancel      ^J Justify ^W Where is      ^V Next Pg    ^U UnCut Text  ^T To Spell
```

Getting help

Pine's biggest plus is the help system, which provides answers to any user's question. At any screen, if you enter a question mark (**?**), you go straight to Pine's help system. Information on each command or option is very detailed, and enough information is provided that even a novice can use the program. The first help screen is just a hint of what is to come:

```
PINE 3.91   HELP FOR MAIN MENU                          Line  19 of 419  4%


             GENERAL INFORMATION ON THE PINE MESSAGE SYSTEM
                   Version 3.90 (built Fri May 5 17:27:40 PDT 1995)
                          University of Washington
                               August, 1994

TABLE OF CONTENTS

          (1)  Introduction
          (2)  Pine Help
          (3)  Local Support Contacts
          (4)  Giving Commands in Pine
          (5)  Status Line
          (6)  Main Menu Commands
          (7)  Command Line Options
          (8)  Pine Configuration
          (9)  Reading News
          (10) Reporting Problems


  ----------



M Main Menu  E Exit Help     -  PrevPage      Y prYnt       B Report Bug
                            Spc NextPage      Z Print All   W WhereIs
```

In several locations, help is context-sensitive. When you are examining configuration options, requesting help further explains the meaning of the configuration variable.

Pine comes with its own built-in editor, pico, which is based on emacs but is much smaller and has a good help capability. Pine also has used the concept of multiple mail folders. This way, you can group related mail messages into different folders, and you can also use a folder to obtain remote mail using the IMAP protocol.

Customizing Pine

Just like Elm, Pine has a large list of configuration variables. You can change your configuration easily in Pine: From the main menu, request setup with **S** and **C** for configuration. You are presented with a long list of variables. Rather than consider each of them, pay attention to folder-collections, signature-file, and sort-key. You can add entries to folder-collections. Each one is implemented as a separate directory under UNIX, and mail message files can be saved in those folders. Here is an example:

```
folder-collections    = mail/[]
                         Elm Mail/[]
```

This means that I have two mail collections: a standard collection in the directory mail and a collection that I've labeled Elm in the Mail directory. The [] notation indicates that any files included in the directory should be considered mail folders.

Note

The Elm folder is, in fact, the correct location for where Elm saves mail by default.

The signature-file variable specifies a location for signatures in outgoing mail. Unlike Elm, with Pine you do not need to activate a signature file for it to be used.

The sort-key variable is an interesting implementation of the Pine variable. Instead of hiding the values and letting you guess, it lists for you all the values allowed for the sort-key:

```
sort-key               =
           Set       Sort Options
           --        ------
           ( )   Date
           (*)   Arrival
           ( )   From
           ( )   Subject
           ( )   OrderedSubj
           ( )   Reverse Date
           ( )   Reverse Arrival
           ( )   Reverse From
           ( )   Reverse Subject
           ( )   Reverse OrderedSubj
```

You move your cursor over the choices until you find the one you like, you select it, and it becomes the sorting option.

Make Friends and Learn a Lot with Mailing Lists

E-mail is a wonderful boon both for its capabilities in itself and for the added benefits it can bring you as a UNIX user. In particular, thousands (if not tens of thousands) of topical interest lists, or mailing lists, reside on the Internet. The variety of topics ranges quite as far as you can imagine, from fans of a particular video game to car salespeople, from Internet authors to deconstructionist literature students who focus on feminist interpretations of 19th century English literature — really — and a lot more.

E-mail and the computer are really ideal for mailing lists because they make sending mail to dozens of people (or hundreds of people on a list) as simple as sending it to an individual. Indeed, mailing lists are just different types of e-mail addresses, where instead of sending a message to, say, taylor@netcom.com, you'd send it to imall-chat@netcom.com and thousands of people interested in online shopping would receive your missive. The underlying mechanism is not dissimilar to a group of friends who send the club newsletter to their friends, who each then send it along to their own friends, ad infinitum. In computer terms, though, you need only send one message to the list, and the computer systems duplicate it as needed in transit. Each person on the mailing list (which is ultimately just a file on the mail server computer that lists the e-mail address of each member of the list) ends up with a personal copy in his or her mailbox, but no one had to slave over a copy machine!

Finding mailing lists

Clearly, there's lots of fun to be had on the many mailing lists available on the Internet, but how do you find them? That's a conundrum that has produced a surprising number of books in the bookstore — books that are directories of mailing lists and are almost always out of date. It is computer information, so look on the computer for these directories! What follows are a couple of spots that I recommend.

The list of publicly accessible mailing lists

Maintained by Stefanie DaSilva, this list is available through both the Web and an e-mail-based server. If you want to obtain the list through an e-mail address, send mail to `mail-server@rtfm.mit.edu` with your message containing the rather complex text:

```
send pub/usenet-by-group/news.answers/mail/mailing-lists/partXX
```

where *XX* is replaced, sequentially, by 01, 02, 03, and so on, up to 14. Needless to say, it's a huge listing when it has to be broken up into 14 parts.

A better choice, in my opinion, is to visit the World Wide Web page, which you can find at `http://www.neosoft.com/internet/paml/`. Here's how that would look if you popped over with Lynx, the slick text-only UNIX-based Web browser:

```
Publicly Accessible Mailing Lists - Index by Subject (p1 of 4)

                    PUBLICLY ACCESSIBLE MAILING LISTS

   * Intro * Sources * Contacts * Index

Index by Subject

        academics          accounting          advertising
        advertisment       agriculture         animals
        animation          anthropology        archeology
        art                astrology           astronomy
        authors            automotive          aviation
        biking             biology             birds
        boating            books               botany
        business           cats                children
        cinema             collectibles        collecting
        comics             commercial          communications
```

```
computers            crafts               cultural
dance                databases            dogs
ecology              economics            education
electromagnetics     electronics          employment
energy               engineering          entertainment
environment          family               fiction
financial            fish                 fitness
```

Unfortunately, neither the Web site nor the mailings let you do what I've always wanted: to search the descriptions of each of the thousands of mailing lists to find just those that contain a particular word or topic. Instead, you'll want to set aside some time to just browse and enjoy the remarkable diversity of interests represented by the members of the Internet community.

Your best bet, just as with the Publicly Accessible Mailing Lists information, is to use the List of Lists Web site to check things out at http://www.tile. net/tile/listserv/index.html. Here's how it looks:

```
tile.net/listserv (p1 of 2)


  Home | About | Search

                   T I L E . N E T / L I S T S E R V
                THE REFERENCE TO INTERNET DISCUSSION GROUPS.
  ──────────────────────────────────────────────────────────────

 - Alphabetical listing by description

      - Alphabetical listing by name

      - Grouped by host country

      - Grouped by sponsoring organization

      - Most popular (1000+ members)

Search by subject
n
```

Again, better organization would be a boon, but you'll find that this works pretty well.

Other ways to find mailing lists

Another way to find out about interesting mailing lists is to ask your friends and colleagues. The majority of mailing lists, in fact, are probably never publicized in central directories but can be terrific resources and a great way to make new friends. Keep your eyes open for books and magazine articles that may highlight new lists not found in the older public listings, too. New lists are born every day, it seems.

Creating your own mailing lists

After a while, you may want to form your own mailing lists. Administering a mailing list on UNIX systems calls for four approaches of increased complexity. You can keep a list in your address book, keep a list inside an aliases file, maintain the list with a link to the aliases file, or use a list manager. Each approach has its advantages and disadvantages.

Using an address book

When you're just forming a mailing list, sometimes you can just create a local entry in your address book and send mail to that entry. In BSD mail, this is simple. You add a line to the mail startup file .mailrc that says

```
alias friends dave@intuitive.com bob mark jane
```

When you send mail to friends, mailx automatically expands it to the addresses dave@intuitive.com, bob, mark, and jane. If these addresses are also aliases, they are also expanded. When you add someone new to the list, you just edit the alias in your .mailrc.

Creating aliases in Elm or Pine involves moving through their screens (or editing a file). The input is similar. Using an alias from a mail file is the fastest way to establish your mailing list. It does not require the intervention of the superuser. On the other hand, this mail alias is available only to you, and for other people to access it, you have to send them copies, and they have to keep it up to date. Adding or deleting a member can be a nightmare.

To work around that problem, the best approach is to create a single address that everyone uses. Then, you have only one location to update.

Making a sendmail alias

Each system should have a standard file, /etc/aliases, that sendmail uses to route messages. The normal procedure includes relationships between an e-mail address and an account. An example follows:

```
postmaster:    james
jca:    james
```

Mail sent to postmaster@sagarmatha.com is automatically forwarded to the user james, and mail sent to jca@sagarmatha.com is also forwarded to james. You can specify a group of addresses after the colon, too. The new address is expanded to all the addresses listed. You would have

```
friends:    dave@intuitive.com, bob, mark, jane
```

Mail sent to friends@sagarmatha.com is forwarded to all four listed addresses. Using an alias in the aliases file has several advantages. Everyone can send mail to the same address, and it is automatically forwarded to everybody on the list. The sendmail program performs the forwarding by itself, which is in theory a faster option than separate mail processes.

This approach is problematic because the /etc/aliases file is usually owned by root and only the superuser can write to it. So unless you are the system administrator, every time you need to make a change to the list, you have to track down the administrator and arrange for the change to be made. To work around that problem, create an inclusion in the /etc/aliases file that you can edit.

Including a file in /etc/aliases

Fortunately for us, the /etc/aliases file supports a syntax to include files of addresses in an alias. Instead of listing addresses, you need to use the tag :include: followed by the filename:

```
friends:      :include:/home/james/.lists/friends
```

The specified file must be world readable, but you can have it set for only the owner to write. This requires only one intervention on the part of the system administrator to place the entry in /etc/aliases. After that, you can add and delete from the file at will. This works perfectly well for a static list. If your list has a lot of turnover, though, you'll find yourself editing that file quite often. Tools are available that are designed to do this for you.

Using a list manager

Although a list manager works for any mailing list, a list manager works best automating the addition and deletion of members for publicly available lists. Another convenient function verifies that someone is a member of a mailing list before sending his or her message to the list.

Note

This latter issue has become a much greater concern in recent years. As the Internet becomes more popular, direct marketers (those same people who inevitably call you at dinner time) have taken to sending unsolicited advertising to mailing lists and newsgroups. Because most people pay for this service, this puts an inordinate amount of the cost of this advertising on the recipients and intermediate machines. Imagine if those direct marketers called collect, and you had no way to refuse the charges! This technique has been called *Spam*. Spams have been known to disable networks due to the demand on resources and are not very well received. Much of the Internet is still a cooperative effort. We strongly urge that you do not patronize any businesses that use this approach to advertising.

One of the more common list managers is *majordomo,* which is a package written by Brent Chapman in Perl and C that manages mailing lists. Subscribing and unsubscribing to a list is automated, and you can configure the lists to allow only members to post.

You can check to see if majordomo is available on your system by greping the /etc/aliases file for the word *majordomo*. If it is not there, you need to install it. This requires the efforts of the system administrator because some programs need to be run as root.

Once you have installed majordomo, creating a mailing list is relatively straightforward. It requires several entries into the /etc/aliases file per mailing list. All mail sent directly to the list name is passed to the wrapper program. This program checks permissions before forwarding the request to another program with all arguments intact. The two programs underneath are resend and request-answer.

The `resend` program is the Perl script that actually forwards the message to the mailing list. Table 20-4 illustrates the normal arguments.

Table 20-4	resend Options	
Option	*Value*	*Meaning*
-a	*passwd*	Specify the name of the file, represented by *passwd*, that contains the approval password for the list.
-A		Approve; enable list moderation by requiring an "Approved: " header to be present in the message before resending. Messages without an Approved: header will be redirected to the list owner for approval.
-C	*config-file*	Use alternate configuration file specified by *config-file* instead of the default `list-name.config`.
-d		Turn on debugging; print commands, but don't execute them.
-f	*from-addr*	Specify "sender" in the "From: " line as *from-addr* (the default is `<list-name>-request`).
-h	*host-name*	Specify host name as *host-name*.
-I	*file-list*	Bounce messages from users not listed in one of the files in *file-list*, which is a colon-separated list of pathnames to `sendmail`-style mailing lists.
-l	*list-name*	REQUIRED: Specify the name of the mailing list as *list-name*.
-M	*max-msg-length*	Specify maximum length of messages to be forwarded.
-n		Assign a sequence number to each message as it is received.
-p	*precedence*	Add "`Precedence:` *precedence*" header.
-r	*reply-to*	Add "`Reply-To:` *reply-to*" header.
-R		Delete "`received:`" lines in the header of incoming messages.
-s		Enable "administrivia" checks, to search incoming messages for common strings found in administrative messages such as "subscribe" or "unsubscribe"; such messages are then sent to the list owner rather than posted to the list.

The `request-answer` command is just an informational command that forwards the sender information on how to subscribe and unsubscribe.

Each mailing list must have several entries in the `/etc/aliases` file. For the Rangers mailing list, the entries are as follows:

```
rangers-list: ""|/usr/local/lib/listserv/wrapper resend -l rangers-list \
    -h netcom.com -f owner-rangers-list -r rangers-list \
    -I rangers-list -p list \
    -a /usr/common/majordomo/lists/rangers-list.passwd \
    rangers-list-outgoing""""
rangers-list-outgoing: :include:/usr/common/majordomo/lists/rangers-list
rangers-list-request: ""|/usr/local/lib/listserv/wrapper request-answer \
    rangers-list""
rangers-list-owner: jca
owner-rangers-list: jca
rangers-list-errors: jca
rangers-list-approval: jca
```

This means that a message sent to `rangers-list` is checked in several ways. The `-I` flag indicates that the message must be sent from an address that has already subscribed to the list, and the `-a` option points to the file containing the password that overrides that. The messages have `owner-rangers-list` on the `From` line, and all replies are sent back to the mailing list. When everything is processed, the message is sent to `rangers-list-outgoing`, which is just a standard `include` for the list of addresses.

Caution

Do not make the last address the same as the mailing list, or you enter a loop and no mail is delivered.

Now, when someone wants to subscribe, he or she sends a message to `majordomo` on this machine with the line `subscribe rangers-list`. He or she automatically subscribed at the address from which the message was sent. You unsubscribe in the same way.

You can close the list to subscriptions by creating a file `rangers-list.closed` in the `majordomo` directory. Any requests to subscribe are then forwarded to the list owner for approval. Unsubscribes process normally.

The `majordomo` list manager has some tradeoffs. It increases the security of your mailing list (although you would need to close it completely to prevent spams), but it has its costs. Instead of just being forwarded, each message requires a nontrivial amount of processing before it is forwarded to the list. Because not everyone understands majordomo commands, sometimes you will also have people who flood the list with unsubscribe requests. Overall, though, majordomo is a good approach to list management.

The Party That Never Ends: Usenet

If mailing lists are the club newsletter copied for members throughout the neighborhood, Usenet is the huge international edition sent to libraries and bookstores throughout the world. Originally, Usenet was a simple mechanism for allowing people to share messages and comment upon each other's writing and thoughts, a sort of bulletin board that spanned multiple computers. As the number of topics expanded from its initial few to dozens, then hundreds, and as the number of people joining a particular *newsgroup,* or discussion list, increased, the complexity of Usenet increased dramatically.

Note

Usenet was created in 1979 when two graduate students at Duke University, Tom Truscott and Jim Ellis, hooked their computer to another at the University of North Carolina. In 1980, there were *two* sites relaying Usenet news back and forth. At the very end of 1995, an estimated 185,000 sites were on Usenet, representing over *7.5 million* participants.

In the last few years, Usenet has exploded as a hotbed of discussion, with over 50,000 different groups ranging from specific technological topics (like programming Windows 95) to heated debates (abortion pro and con), recreational chitchat (training dogs), and social puzzles (dating angst). The most recent high-level organization of these thousands of different groups had them split into seven primary categories (not unlike the way in which top-level domains broke down the millions of computers on the Internet). Table 20-5 lists how those top domains were organized.

Table 20-5	Usenet Domains
Domain	*. . . in English*
comp.*	Computer-related topics
misc.*	A grab bag of topics
news.*	Usenet-related topics (not contemporary news)
rec.*	Recreations and hobbies
sci.*	Scientific discussion
soc.*	Social discussion groups
talk.*	Controversial and heated discussion

As you can see, the organizational scheme is pretty straightforward. But wait: A *lot* more hierarchies are out there, including the popular alt.* newsgroups that originally focused on alternative topics and are now the central spot for any random junk. This includes all the questionable and often dubious "alt.sex.*" newsgroups that represent some of the worst aspects of the Net (and some of the funniest, too). Regional newsgroups now have their own spaces, such as the following:

■ ba.* (for the San Francisco Bay area)

■ dc.* (for greater Washington, D.C.)

Organizational spaces including the following:

■ well.* for the Whole Earth 'Lectronic Link

- netcom.* for Netcom Communications Service
- ibm.* for International Business Machines
- hp.* for Hewlett-Packard

Schools have jumped into the act, too. Here are some examples:

- purdue.* for Purdue University
- ucb.* for the University of California at Berkeley
- mit.* for the Massachusetts Institute of Technology
- ufl.* for the University of Florida

You might not see all of these groups on your system, but plenty seem to trickle about. Last time I counted the number of unique top-level Usenet domains on the popular Netcom system, I found over 500!

What's also hard to grasp initially is just how much these categories can expand as you burrow your way into them, with dozens, then hundreds of sub-subtopics. For example, the comp hierarchy is for computer-related topics. Add sys (system) to the name, and you've looking at specific computer systems. Add ibm.pc, and it's IBM PCs, or comp.sys.ibm.pc.*. So how many possibilities could there be at this point? How many discussion groups can focus on PC-related topics? Here's a portion of the current list (your results may differ):

```
comp.sys.ibm.pc.demos     Demonstration programs which showcase programmer skill.
comp.sys.ibm.pc.digest    The IBM PC, PC-XT, and PC-AT. (Moderated)
comp.sys.ibm.pc.games     Games for IBM PCs and compatibles.
comp.sys.ibm.pc.games.action     Arcade-style games on PCs.
comp.sys.ibm.pc.games.adventure Adventure (non-rpg) games on PCs.
comp.sys.ibm.pc.games.announce  Announcements for all PC gamers. (Moderated)
comp.sys.ibm.pc.games.flight-sim        Flight simulators on PCs.
comp.sys.ibm.pc.games.marketplace       PC clone games wanted and for sale.
comp.sys.ibm.pc.games.misc       Games not covered by other PC groups.
comp.sys.ibm.pc.games.rpg        Role-playing games on the PC.
comp.sys.ibm.pc.games.strategic Strategy/planning games on PCs.
comp.sys.ibm.pc.hardware         XT/AT/EISA hardware, any vendor.
comp.sys.ibm.pc.hardware.cd-rom CD-ROM drives and interfaces for the PC.
comp.sys.ibm.pc.hardware.chips  Processor, cache, memory chips, etc.
comp.sys.ibm.pc.hardware.comm   Modems & communication cards for the PC.
comp.sys.ibm.pc.hardware.misc   Miscellaneous PC hardware topics.
comp.sys.ibm.pc.hardware.networking     Network hardware & equipment for the PC.
comp.sys.ibm.pc.hardware.storage        Hard drives & other PC storage devices.
comp.sys.ibm.pc.hardware.systems        Whole IBM PC computer & clone systems.
comp.sys.ibm.pc.hardware.video Video cards & monitors for the PC.
comp.sys.ibm.pc.misc     Discussion about IBM personal computers.
comp.sys.ibm.pc.programmer       Programming topics for PC users.
comp.sys.ibm.pc.rt       Topics related to IBM's RT computer.
comp.sys.ibm.pc.soundcard        Hardware and software aspects of PC sound cards.
comp.sys.ibm.pc.soundcard.advocacy       Advocacy for a particular soundcard.
comp.sys.ibm.pc.soundcard.games Questions about using soundcards with games.
comp.sys.ibm.pc.soundcard.GUS    .
comp.sys.ibm.pc.soundcard.gus    .
```

```
comp.sys.ibm.pc.soundcard.misc  Soundcards in general.
comp.sys.ibm.pc.soundcard.music Music and sound questions using soundcards.
comp.sys.ibm.pc.soundcard.tech  Technical questions about pc soundcards.
```

Probably more than you expected, eh?

Clearly, Usenet is a complex beast, and not surprisingly, the software that has evolved to help you participate in these discussions has also grown into a set of behemoths: large, complex programs with dozens of options and their own custom macro programming languages. At their most simple, though, two applications represented them: a line-based interface à la Berkeley Mail and a screen-oriented program inspired by Elm. UNIX, in fact, has over a dozen newsreaders, but the two most popular are what I'll focus on here: Rn and Tin.

Rn: A simple interface with amazing power

If you spend enough time working with UNIX, you're bound to bump into some software written by the prolific Larry Wall. In the last few years, he's focused on the development and evolution of his Perl programming language for UNIX, but prior to that, he kept busy working on the ultimate programmable Usenet application that he called Rn, a convenient abbreviation for *read news*. Like Berkeley Mail, the Rn interface design presupposes that you'll spend some time studying the system and that you want but the briefest reminder of common options at any spot. This makes it quite terse and complex, in a typically UNIX way.

Let's start by looking at the starting flags. What you see in Table 20-6 is not, by any means, the exhaustive list of options, but rather the half-dozen or so that I think are most useful for a new Rn user. Remember that just as with any other UNIX program, you can use the man page to find out more about the nuts and bolts of the program.

Table 20-6   Rn Options

Option	Meaning
-c	Checks for incoming news and indicates if any has arrived.
-e	Starts each page of an article at the top of the screen.
-hhdr	Suppresses displaying the header *hdr* in news articles shown.
-L	Leaves information on the screen as long as possible (can be weird).
-M	Forces mailbox format for all saved files. (I recommend that you always use this option.)
-m	Uses inverse video for highlighted information (if your terminal supports it).
-N	Forces normal, nonmailbox format for all saved files.
-r	Restarts within the last newsgroup you read previously.
-S	Uses subject search mode when possible.

Because you're most likely to check news every day or two, the invocation of
Rn is a great candidate for an alias of some sort so that you don't have to
remember any of these arcane options. Here's what I use:

```
alias rn="rn -L -M -m -e -S"
```

Reading Usenet news involves a couple of different phases, perhaps the most
puzzling of which is finding and subscribing to specific groups. Unlike e-mail
lists, where well-known central databases exist with choices to peruse,
Usenet newsgroups are unique and different on each site, so you need to
focus on the groups available on your own system to gain any value out of a
search. Alas, you won't find a particularly great search tool of any sort, even
though a great data file is usually a part of a Usenet installation:
/usr/lib/news/newsgroups. Fortunately, you're a UNIX pro now, so you
can easily manage to search this file by hand for any topic you'd like:

```
grep -i topic /usr/lib/news/newsgroups
```

For example, let's have a quick peek at what groups have anything to do with
UNIX by searching for the word *unix* in the file:

```
% grep -i unix /usr/lib/news/newsgroups
alt.bbs.unixbbs            UNIXBBS, from Nervous XTC.
alt.bbs.unixbbs.uniboard        Discussions about the Uniboard BBS.
alt.binaries.clip-art         Distribution of DOS, Mac and UNIX clipart.
alt.sex.bondage.sco.unix         For frustrated SCO users
alt.unix.wizards             Like comp.unix.wizards, only unmoderated.
alt.unix.wizards.free      Like comp.unix.wizards, only unmoderated.
biz.sco.binaries              Binary packages for SCO Xenix, UNIX, or ODT.
(Moderated)
ca.unix             UNIX discussion/help.
comp.bugs.2bsd           Reports of UNIX* version 2BSD related bugs.
comp.bugs.4bsd           Reports of UNIX version 4BSD related bugs.
comp.bugs.4bsd.ucb-fixes        Bug reports/fixes for BSD UNIX. (Moderated)
comp.bugs.misc           General UNIX bug reports and fixes (incl V7, uucp)
comp.os.linux            The free UNIX-clone for the 386/486, LINUX.
comp.security.unix         Discussion of UNIX security.
comp.sources.unix          Postings of complete, UNIX-oriented sources.
(Moderated)
comp.std.unix            Discussion for the P1003 committee on UNIX.
(Moderated)
comp.sys.3b1             Discussion and support of AT&T 7300/3B1/UNIXPC.
comp.unix.admin          Administering a UNIX-based system.
comp.unix.advocacy         Arguments for and against UNIX and UNIX versions.
comp.unix.aix            IBM's version of UNIX.
comp.unix.amiga          Minix, SYSV4 and other *nix on an Amiga.
comp.unix.aux            The version of UNIX for Apple Macintosh II computers.
comp.unix.bsd            Discussion of Berkeley Software Distribution UNIX.
comp.unix.bsd.386bsd.announce   Announcements pertaining to 386BSD. (Moderated)
comp.unix.bsd.386bsd.misc     386BSD operating system.
comp.unix.bsd.bsdi.announce     Announcements pertaining to BSD/OS. (Moderated)
comp.unix.bsd.bsdi.misc      BSD/OS operating system.
comp.unix.bsd.freebsd.announce  Announcements pertaining to FreeBSD. (Moderated)
comp.unix.bsd.freebsd.misc      FreeBSD operating system.
comp.unix.bsd.misc          BSD operating systems.
comp.unix.bsd.netbsd.announce   Announcements pertaining to NetBSD. (Moderated)
```

```
comp.unix.bsd.netbsd.misc        NetBSD operating system.
comp.unix.cray              Cray computers and their operating systems.
comp.unix.dos-under-unix          MS-DOS running under UNIX by whatever means.
comp.unix.internals          Discussions on hacking UNIX internals.
comp.unix.large            UNIX on mainframes and in large networks.
comp.unix.misc             Various topics that don't fit other groups.
comp.unix.osf.misc            Various aspects of Open Software Foundation
products.
comp.unix.osf.osf1            The Open Software Foundation's OSF/1.
comp.unix.pc-clone.16bit         UNIX on 286 architectures.
comp.unix.pc-clone.32bit         UNIX on 386 and 486 architectures.
comp.unix.programmer          Q&A for people programming under UNIX.
comp.unix.questions          UNIX neophytes group.
comp.unix.shell          Using and programming the UNIX shell.
comp.unix.solaris            Discussions about the Solaris operating system.
comp.unix.sys3           System III UNIX discussions.
comp.unix.sys5.misc          Versions of System V which predate Release 3.
comp.unix.sys5.r3            Discussing System V Release 3.
comp.unix.sys5.r4            Discussing System V Release 4.
comp.unix.ultrix             Discussions about DEC's Ultrix.
comp.unix.unixware           Discussion about Novell's UNIXWare products.
comp.unix.user-friendly         Discussion of UNIX user-friendliness.
comp.unix.wizards            For only true UNIX wizards. (Moderated)
comp.unix.xenix.misc          General discussions regarding XENIX (except SCO).
comp.unix.xenix.sco          XENIX versions from the Santa Cruz Operation.
comp.windows.x.i386unix         The XFree86 window system and others.
```

As you can see, you have quite a few different groups to explore!

Once you have a list of groups that you want to read, you can start up the Rn program by typing **rn** on the command line (or using the set of starting flags shown earlier):

```
% rn
(Revising soft pointers--be patient.)
Unread news in rec.arts.disney.parks            1184 articles
Unread news in ba.announce                        21 articles
Unread news in ba.seminars                        47 articles
Unread news in alt.books.technical                86 articles
Unread news in misc.books.technical               90 articles
etc.

Checking for new newsgroups...

Newsgroup alt.music.jazz.advocacy not in .newsrc--subscribe? [ynYN]
```

From this point, you can subscribe to the new group listed (alt.music.jazz.advocacy) by answering **y**, opt not to read the group with **n**, or skip the chance to join any of the many new groups with **N**. Once you're beyond the subscription invitations, you'll be shown a summary of the number of articles new in the first of the groups you read, like this:

```
******** 868 unread articles in rec.arts.disney.parks--read now? [ynq]
```

From here, you can read the articles by answering **y** for yes, but, more important, you can also pop over to a new newsgroup with the `goto` command, which is used as **g *groupname***. To join comp.sys.unix.advocacy, for example, you'd type **g comp.sys.unix.advocacy,** and assuming the group is available on your Usenet server, you'd be able to access all the articles therein.

The most common response to the prompt for the newsgroup offered by Rn, however, is to read the new messages therein by either typing **y** (for yes) or pressing the Spacebar. Generally, the most common response to any prompt in rn has the Spacebar as a convenient shortcut. To skip the specified group and move to the next newsgroup, answer **n** to the prompt, and you'll immediately be informed how many new articles are in the next group on your subscription list. Ready to unsubscribe from a group? Press **u**.

Once you're within a specific newsgroup, Rn presents you with each of the messages therein that you've not seen before (it keeps track automatically) in a manner quite analogous to Berkeley Mail. No fancy formatting, just a dump of the important — and sometimes not so important — headers and message content. One thing you'll see quite often in Usenet articles are lines prefaced by > or even >. By common convention, these denote that the lines of text are quoted and were written by someone earlier in the group. The more characters at the beginning of the line, the more times people have quoted, and requoted, the passage.

At the bottom of any individual message you have a ton of options; the most useful are outlined in Table 20-7.

Table 20-7   Rn Message Options

Keystroke	Meaning
k	Kill this discussion. Don't show me any more articles on this topic.
K	Same as k, but remember it and hide this conversational thread forever.
f	Post a follow-up article to the newsgroup.
F	Same as f, but automatically includes the text of the current message.
r	Mail a message to the author of this article.
R	Same as r, but automatically includes the text of the current message.
s	Save the message to a specified file or mail folder.
|	Feed this article to a specified program (such as lpr).
q	Quit reading this particular newsgroup.
Q	Quit Rn completely.
=	Show a summary of the unread articles in this group.

Rn is a powerful and sophisticated program, and we've only barely scratched the surface. If you want a fast application that lets you create your own custom macros and fine-tune exactly how it'll work, Rn might be your best bet.

Tin: The screen-based alternative

On the other hand, if you'd prefer a program that offers a bit more assistance in exploring the often confusing and weird world of Usenet, you'll probably join me in preferring the Tin newsreader. Tin is an unabashed clone inspired by Elm. If you're familiar with the Elm interface for reading e-mail, you'll have no problem working with Tin, even without reading any documentation. As with Rn, Tin has a plethora of different starting options, as outlined in Table 20-8.

Table 20-8   Tin Options

Option	Meaning
-h	Help shows all command-line options.
-H	A brief introduction to Tin that's also shown the first time it's started.
-q	Quick start without checking for new newsgroups.
-s dir	Save articles to specified directory. The default is $HOME/News.
-w	Quick mode to post an article and then exit Tin.
-z	Only start Tin if there's any new/unread news. If there is news to read, Tin will position the cursor at first group with unread news. Useful for putting in the .login file.

I use all the default flags when using Tin, and they work fine for me.

When you start up Tin, you're first presented with an indication that the program is checking for new newsgroups. You might figure that a few new groups are added each week because Usenet has been around and growing for years, but you'll be surprised at just how many new groups pop up each day on the Internet. Indeed, I read Usenet mostly on Netcom, and I usually have to wade through two or three dozen new group messages (where I can opt to subscribe to the group as it's announced) every other day or so.

Once you've waded through the new group messages, you'll finally be dropped right into the main program screen, as shown:

```
                    Group Selection (10)                          h=help

 1    868  rec.arts.disney.parks
 2         netcom.announce                    Announcements from Netcom Staff (
 3     21  ba.announce                        Announcements of general interest
 4     47  ba.seminars                        Announcements of Bay Area seminar
 5     87  alt.books.technical                Discussion of technical books.
 6     90  misc.books.technical               Discussion of books about technic
 7      1  com.priv
 8    207  comp.internet.net-happenings        Announcements of network happenin
 9     39  rec.arts.books.reviews             Book reviews. (Moderated)
10     31  comp.infosystems.www.users         WWW user issues (Mosaic, Lynx, et

                      *** End of Groups ***
```

If you flip back a few pages, you'll see how similar this is to Elm. This interface's consistency definitely helps you get the most out of your Internet explorations within the UNIX environment! On this display, you can see that I subscribe to ten Usenet groups and that only nine of them have new articles. (The netcom.announce group has no articles; you can tell because no second number is present on the left of the line.) The first group in my list, discussing Disney amusement parks, has a staggering 868 new articles since I last read the group. Other groups are a bit more manageable, such as ba.announce with only 21 new messages.

The first time you start up, you might see no newsgroups, or perhaps one default newsgroup. To have all the available Usenet groups shown within Tin, you'll want to **Y**ank them all in, which results in a dramatic change. The screen is now full of different groups, each with a succinct description, if available, and all prefaced by *u* to indicate that you're unsubscribed to the group. To search for specific groups, use / and type in the pattern or keyword you seek. Once you've found a group that sounds interesting, use **s** to subscribe to the group. If you later decide you don't like the group, you can **u**nsubscribe just as easily.

Tin has a three-level presentation of Usenet news, unlike Rn. The topmost level of information in Tin is the list of newsgroups to which you subscribe. Next is an overview of all articles in a specific newsgroup that you haven't seen, and the third level is an actual article from a member of the discussion group. Rn, by contrast, skips the middle level and goes straight from the overview to individual articles.

The second level shows you all the articles that are new in the group, as shown for the Usenet group rec.arts.disney.parks:

```
        rec.arts.disney.parks (275T 869A OK OH R)                h=help

 1  + 43 Urban Legends Reference Page: Disney          Kevin D. Quitt
 2  + 10 Walt on Ice WAS Re: Urban Legends Reference P  Lizz Braver
 3  + 4  FDC? FDCMuck?                                  Caleb & Michele Wa
 4  +    november trip weather?                         Randy Berbaum
 5  + 16 Fantasyland Rumor                              David Hall
 6  + 2  NOOO! Space mountain..                         Ian Grey
 7  + 7  looking for Disneyland/WDW books               Grumpstr
 8  + 3  Planet Hollywood - quality, busy times?        Francisco Lauway
 9  + 11 Bottom 10 list                                 LISA_POOH@delphi.c
10  + 8  posts that seem strangely anti-kid             LISA_POOH@delphi.c
11  +    Tampa Info Wanted                              zandrew@zandrew.se
12  + 28 Stay in or out of WDW?                         GregSacto
13  + 6  trip report oct 14-20                          Lee Whitman
14  + 3  Florida Holiday Questions                      Simon Scott
15  + 9  How long to stay at WDW?                       DVClubber
16  + 3  WDW During Christmas                           Elyn Megargee Mace

   <n>=set current to n, TAB=next unread, /=search pattern, ^K)ill/select,
 a)uthor search, c)atchup, j=line down, k=line up, K=mark read, l)ist thread,
   |=pipe, m)ail, o=print, q)uit, r=toggle all/unread, s)ave, t)ag, w=post
```

To move around at this juncture, you can use your cursor keys, j and k, to move up and down the list (just as in vi), + to move forward a page of articles, and – to move backward; finally you can also just type in the number of the article you'd like to see. The number after the plus sign tells me how many new responses are in this discussion, so you can see that numbers 4 and 11 are new and have no responses yet. In this example, I'll have a quick peek at the most recent response to article number 5 by typing in the digit **5**:

```
Fri, 27 Oct 1995 13:59:55    rec.arts.disney.parks        Thread    5 of  275
Lines 41                     Re: Fantasyland Rumor          15 Responses
dsmith@u.oregon.edu                        David Smith at The University of Oregon, Oahu

Hi,

For what?

We're talking here about the VERY FIRST two films.  If that isn't a
heritage worth keeping, then what at the Park is?

I understand that the new films need rides.  I'm all for that and have
posted several times about ways to accommodate them.  But to sacrifice
the very HEART (in a box brought by the huntsman, no less) of Fantasyland
just to stay current denys the very reason Walt came up with the whole DL
concept in the first place.  True, he wanted and expected that Lands and
attractions would change and evolve.  Heck, he actively worked on
fine-tuning most of the original ones himself.  But they were always

    <n>=set current to n, TAB=next unread, /=search pattern, ^K)ill/select,
       a)uthor search, B)ody search, c)atchup, f)ollowup, K=mark read,
       |=pipe, m)ail, o=print, q)uit, r)eply mail, s)ave, t)ag, w=post

                                    —More—(59%) [1522/2551]
```

As with Rn, Tin is a complex and powerful program, and if you opt to use it as your Usenet newsreader, I strongly recommend that you spend a week or two familiarizing yourself with the commands outlined herein and pop into the man page and documentation to learn some of the more arcane tricks and commands.

Tip

One command that I use often is | to pipe or forward an article to a colleague. Indeed, you can very easily pipe an article to a command like mail -s "check this out" james to have a copy of the article you're reading sent to your colleague.

A second visit to Pine, this time as a newsreader

Earlier in the chapter, we saw Pine as a mail reader. Pine also works as a convenient newsreader. To set up Pine as a newsreader, you just need to create a news folder in the news collections on the setup screen. Because we have news on the local hard disk, our setup is as follows:

```
news-collections        = News *[]
```

For sites where news is read via `nntp`, you need to set an nntp server and indicate that news is read via `nntp` in the news-collections. The `news-collections` should be set to `News *{nntp-server/nntp}`. This tells Pine to access netnews via `nntp`.

This configures Pine to permit access to netnews. To actually read netnews, you must use the `L` command to list the available collections of folders for pine from the mail menu. On my machine, I see the following screen:

```
PINE 3.91   FOLDER LIST                         Folder: INBOX  3 Messages


------------------------------------
Folder-collection <mail/[]>  ** Default for Saves **                  (Local)
------------------------------------


                  [ Select Here to See Expanded List ]


------------------------------------
Folder-collection <Elm>                                              (Local)
------------------------------------


                  [ Select Here to See Expanded List ]


------------------------------------
News-collection <News>                                               (Local)
------------------------------------


                  [ Select Here to See Expanded List ]



                          [Building folder list...]
? Help        M Main Menu  P PrevFldr    - PrevPage    D Delete     R Rename
O OTHER CMDS  V [Select]   N NextFldr  Spc NextPage    A Add
```

The first two listings are the mail folders defined earlier in the chapter. The last one is the news folder. To open it, I need to step down to the collection and then enter **V** to acquire the collection of folders. The list converts immediately to a listing of subscribed newsgroups. As you can see, I've subscribed to four newsgroups:

```
PINE 3.91   FOLDER LIST                         Folder: INBOX  3 Messages


------------------------------------
Folder-collection <mail/[]>  ** Default for Saves **                  (Local)
------------------------------------


                  [ Select Here to See Expanded List ]


------------------------------------
Folder-collection <Elm>                                              (Local)
------------------------------------


                  [ Select Here to See Expanded List ]


------------------------------------
News-collection <News>                                               (Local)
------------------------------------
```

```
comp.mail.pine              comp.os.unix                comp.unix.wizards
rec.sport.basketball.college
```

```
                   [Subscribed to "comp.unix.wizards"]
? Help        M Main Menu  P PrevFldr    - PrevPage    D UnSbscrbe   R Rename
O OTHER CMDS  V [ViewFldr] N NextFldr    Spc NextPage  A Subscribe
```

To read a newsgroup, I just highlight the newsgroup in question and use **V** to
expand the newsgroup into a listing of articles. On my site, there are only
four articles in rec.sport.basketball.college, so all we see is this:

```
PINE 3.91    FOLDER INDEX <News> rec.sport.basketball.college  Msg 1 of 4

    1    Oct 15 James C. Armstrong Duke Basketball FAQ
    2    Oct 15 James C. Armstrong The 1995-96 NCAA Basketball Picking Contest
    3    Nov 16 James C. Armstrong Duke Basketball FAQ
    4    Nov 18 James C. Armstrong Basketball Picking Contest: Standings after tw
```

```
          [News group "rec.sport.basketball.college" opened with 4 messages]
? Help        M Main Menu  P PrevMsg     - PrevPage    D Delete      R Reply
O OTHER CMDS  V [ViewMsg]  N NextMsg     Spc NextPage  U Undelete    F Forward
```

Reading a message is another V command.

Posting news

Posting news with Pine is as simple as reading. You can use the `reply`
command to send a message to a newsgroup. The Pine composer again
composes the message, but this time a Newsgroups line appears in the
header. When you send the message, it is posted as

Summary

In this chapter, you have been introduced to the basic tools of the Internet, electronic mail, and netnews. You should have a good understanding of the following:

▶ The origins of the Internet and how the different services developed

▶ How to use electronic mail, including understanding the Berkeley mail reader, Elm, and Pine

▶ How to access Usenet with Rn, Tin, and Pine

The next chapter begins a new part: UNIX and the Internet. I'll cover the history of the Internet and the basics of how it works.

Part VII

UNIX and the Internet

Chapter 21

Introduction to the Internet

UNIX was the backbone of networking before the Internet began and remains so today. UUCP provided a basic network in the early 1980s that exchanged e-mail and netnews; later developments with packet switching led to the Internet as we know it. Without UNIX, we would not have the World Wide Web.

History of the Internet

Probably the biggest revolution in how we live at the end of the millennium is the rise of the Internet and the expansion of computer networking to home uses. Computer networking is not a new concept. Back in 1962, JCR Licklider of MIT wrote some memos discussing a network similar to the Internet that people could use to access data remotely from any connected computer. Licklider was no crank; shortly after writing about his "Galactic Network," he became the first head of the computer research program at the Defense Advanced Research Projects Agency (DARPA).

Meanwhile, the concept of packet switching was also being developed at MIT by Leonard Kleinrock. By 1965, the first circuit-switched network was created between two computers, one in Massachusetts and one in California. The connection was made using regular telephone lines and on-demand telephone calls. Though small, it ably demonstrated that computers could communicate and share data but that a packet-switched network would be much more efficient.

Packet switches were first developed by BBN, in accordance with a specification from DARPA, and were installed in September 1969 at UCLA. The Stanford Research Institute (SRI International) provided the second node of the new ARPANET. The first application for ARPANET, electronic mail, was introduced in 1972. ARPANET was the groundwork for the Internet.

Around this time, the original UNIX was being created at Bell Labs in Murray Hill. Mike Lesk, one of the original UNIX engineers, created a package of tools called UUCP (UNIX-to-UNIX Copy) to enable UNIX machines to communicate.

UUCP was another variant of a circuit network in which one machine initiates communication, usually via a telephone line, with another machine. UUCP was widely available in UNIX source distributions and became the tool for the next major Internet application: network news.

In the mid-70s, researchers began codifying the rules for a machine to be part of ARPANET. The original protocol, NCP, was proving inadequate for the task of networking, so a new protocol was being developed. This protocol, TCP (Transmission Control Protocol), would, by the early 1980s, become the basis for communications on ARPANET.

The University of California, Berkeley, was one of the original customers for Bell Labs' UNIX. At Berkeley, researchers started work on a group of intermachine communication commands called sockets. These sockets would soon enable UNIX machines to communicate with non-UNIX machines by using protocols established with ARPANET.

Berkeley distributed its version of UNIX, BSD, to other universities, and this enabled UNIX machines to be a part of ARPANET.

UUCP networking continues to this day, but packet-switched networks are the norm. TCP enabled the creation of black boxes to act as information switches. These have become today's gateways and routers. TCP's protocol also enabled retransmission in case of failure, which makes communications more reliable.

Other networks were blooming at the same time. Several departments of the U.S. government were building networks. The National Science Foundation sponsored CSNET for the computer science community. Academic mainframes were linked with BITNET. JANET was developed in the United Kingdom for the U.K.'s academic community. These were fairly disjointed networks, with the occasional gateway to enable some internetwork communication.

To facilitate internetwork communication, a newer, low-level protocol was developed: the Internet Protocol (IP). This became part of the TCP, so you often see "TCP/IP" as the communications protocol. In 1981, an agreement was made to allow the U.S. government's various networks to share the ARPANET infrastructure without metering. At this time, the acceptable use policy (AUP) for the NSFNET was created, prohibiting use of NSF's backbone for purposes "not in support of Research and Education." This no-commercial-use philosophy is still widespread, although it is no longer the policy.

This backbone was the first step toward creating a unified, publicly available network of computers throughout the world.

By 1990, the growth of the Internet was such that other protocols for wide area networks were replaced by TCP/IP. The growth of UNIX as an inexpensive option to mainframe computers resulted in many servers being UNIX-based. The Internet was used to exchange e-mail, netnews, files, terminal sessions, and many other applications. DARPA's role in the Internet became smaller, and in the early 1990s, the NSF backbone was privatized, eliminating the restrictions in the initial AUP.

The application that draws the most people to the Internet is the World Wide Web (WWW or "the Web"). In terms of the Internet, it is a relatively new application. Tim Berners-Lee is the grandfather of the Web, designing a system in which documents can include embedded links to other, arbitrary documents. His initial idea was a notebook program written in 1980; not until 1989 did he published a proposal for information management that grew into the Web. The initial Web work was done on a NeXT machine in 1990. In 1991, a line-mode browser, www, became available to some UNIX clients, namely RS6000 and Sun4. In 1992, the browser was available by anonymous FTP. Other early browsers include viola and erwise.

The first well-known browser, Mosaic, was initially released from the NCSA by Marc Andreessen in February 1993 for UNIX machines running X. By the end of the year, versions of Mosaic for Windows and Macs were also available. Also in 1993, CERN announced that its WWW technology would be freely usable by anyone. With the standards open, anyone could develop working tools. This approach enabled the Web's fast growth.

People often confuse the Web with the Internet. The Web is a large part of the Internet, but the Internet also encompasses other applications. For me, personally, e-mail is probably the most important application because it keeps me in touch with friends on all continents.

Netscape was founded in 1994 by Jim Clark and Marc Andreessen, and produces the most popular browser on UNIX systems. As this book goes to press, a major antitrust trial is underway against Microsoft for its alleged attempt to wrest the browser market from Netscape. Microsoft's browser, Internet Explorer (IE), is available for some UNIX platforms but is not widely used in UNIX environments. (In the hit logs for my site, which gets around 20,000 hits per day, I see no hits from IE on UNIX.)

The Internet has become a buzzword for investors, too, as they see a potential gold mine in the frontiers of cyberspace. This has reached ludicrous levels: When Zapata oil company announced that it was going into the Internet business, its stock price promptly soared.

How It Works

When you use an Internet application, whether it is e-mail, the Web, or any of the other tools, you are acting as a client in a client/server model. Your program connects to a remote program, using a known address and known port, and sends commands. It then reads responses and acts accordingly. Therefore, to form a connection, two pieces of information — the remote machine's address and the connecting port — are required.

Finding the port

As mentioned in Chapter 19, services are associated with port numbers; usually, these associations are outlined in the /etc/services file. In this file, you see the port numbers of common Internet services, such as e-mail, netnews, and the Web. Table 21-1 lists some of the common Internet services and their associated ports.

Table 21-1	Internet Service Ports
Port	**Service**
20 & 21	File transfer using ftp
23	telnet (remote terminal access)
25	Electronic mail
37	time
43	whois
53	Domain Name Service
69	Trivial ftp
70	gopher
79	finger
80	World Wide Web
103 & 104	X400 mail
110	Post Office
113	User verification
119	Netnews
161	Simple Network Management

Usually, these port numbers are hard-coded into programs, as they don't change. If you want to receive mail from the Internet, for example, you need to set up your server to listen to port 25. Similarly, if you want to send e-mail, your message must go out to port 25. In some cases, such as IRC, a port number can be specified on a command line, and some Web servers listen to different ports. Those ports can be indicated in the Web site address, as discussed in Chapter 24.

On some systems, a master daemon runs, listening to several ports. This is the inetd daemon, which uses a configuration file called /etc/inetd.conf. This file lists the types of services you want on your system and specifies how the server process should run. The inetd daemon then spawns a server when a request is entered, and that server handles those requests.

Listing 21-1 shows my `inetd.conf` file. I've commented out most of the services because I don't want my home machine to act as a general server.

Listing 21-1: /etc/inetd.conf

```
#
# inetd.conf   This file describes the services that will be available
#              through the INETD TCP/IP super server.  To re-configure
#              the running INETD process, edit this file, then send the
#              INETD process a SIGHUP signal.
#
# Version:     @(#)/etc/inetd.conf      3.10      05/27/93
#
# Authors:     Original taken from BSD UNIX 4.3/TAHOE.
#              Fred N. van Kempen, <waltje@uwalt.nl.mugnet.org>
#
# Modified for Debian Linux by Ian A. Murdock <imurdock@shell.portal.com>
#
# Modified for RHS Linux by Marc Ewing <marc@redhat.com>
#
# <service_name> <sock_type> <proto> <flags> <user> <server_path> <args>
#
# Echo, discard, daytime, and chargen are used primarily for testing.
#
# To re-read this file after changes, just do a 'killall -HUP inetd'
#
#echo       stream    tcp     nowait    root       internal
#echo       dgram     udp     wait      root       internal
#discard    stream    tcp     nowait    root       internal
#discard    dgram     udp     wait      root       internal
#daytime    stream    tcp     nowait    root       internal
#daytime    dgram     udp     wait      root       internal
#chargen    stream    tcp     nowait    root       internal
#chargen    dgram     udp     wait      root       internal
#
# These are standard services.
#
ftp         stream  tcp     nowait  root    /usr/sbin/tcpd  in.ftpd -l -a
telnet      stream  tcp     nowait  root    /usr/sbin/tcpd  in.telnetd
#gopher     stream  tcp     nowait  root    /usr/sbin/tcpd  gn

# do not uncomment smtp unless you *really* know what you are doing.
# smtp is handled by the sendmail daemon now, not smtpd.  It does NOT
# run from here, it is started at boot time from /etc/rc.d/rc#.d.
#smtp       stream  tcp     nowait  root    /usr/bin/smtpd  smtpd
#nntp       stream  tcp     nowait  root    /usr/sbin/tcpd  in.nntpd
#
# Shell, login, exec and talk are BSD protocols.
#
#shell      stream  tcp     nowait  root    /usr/sbin/tcpd  in.rshd
#login      stream  tcp     nowait  root    /usr/sbin/tcpd  in.rlogind
#exec       stream  tcp     nowait  root    /usr/sbin/tcpd  in.rexecd
#talk       dgram   udp     wait    root    /usr/sbin/tcpd  in.talkd
#ntalk      dgram   udp     wait    root    /usr/sbin/tcpd  in.ntalkd
#dtalk      stream  tcp     wait    nobody  /usr/sbin/tcpd  in.dtalkd
#
```

```
# Pop and imap mail services et al
#
#pop-2    stream  tcp     nowait  root    /usr/sbin/tcpd    ipop2d
#pop-3    stream  tcp     nowait  root    /usr/sbin/tcpd    ipop3d
#imap     stream  tcp     nowait  root    /usr/sbin/tcpd    imapd
#
# The Internet UUCP service.
#
#uucp     stream  tcp     nowait  uucp    /usr/sbin/tcpd    /usr/lib/uucp/uucico
-1
#
# Tftp service is provided primarily for booting.  Most sites
# run this only on machines acting as "boot servers." Do not uncomment
# this unless you *need* it.
#
#tftp     dgram   udp     wait    root    /usr/sbin/tcpd    in.tftpd
#bootps   dgram   udp     wait    root    /usr/sbin/tcpd    bootpd
#
# Finger, systat and netstat give out user information which may be
# valuable to potential "system crackers."  Many sites choose to disable
# some or all of these services to improve security.
#
# cfinger is for GNU finger, which is currently not in use in RHS Linux
#
#finger   stream  tcp     nowait  root    /usr/sbin/tcpd    in.fingerd
#cfinger  stream  tcp     nowait  root    /usr/sbin/tcpd    in.cfingerd
#systat   stream  tcp     nowait  guest   /usr/sbin/tcpd    /bin/ps -auwwx
#netstat  stream  tcp     nowait  guest   /usr/sbin/tcpd    /bin/netstat -f inet
#
# Time service is used for clock syncronization.
#
#time     stream  tcp     nowait  nobody  /usr/sbin/tcpd    in.timed
#time     dgram   udp     wait    nobody  /usr/sbin/tcpd    in.timed
#
# Authentication
#
#auth     stream  tcp     nowait  sys     /usr/sbin/in.identd in.identd -l -e -o
-N
#
# End of inetd.conf
```

The only services I want on my home machine are FTP and Telnet. This enables me to access my e-mail remotely via Telnet and to copy files.

The `inetd.conf` file has a separate line per entry. If the line starts with a number sign (#), it is a comment and is ignored. Otherwise, the line is an entry and contains the seven fields listed in Table 21-2.

Table 21-2   /etc/inetd.conf Fields

Field Number	Description
1	Service name — identifies the type of service, such as FTP for file transfer protocol
2	Socket type — is either stream (`stream`) or datagram (`dgram`)
3	Protocol — specifies whether the service uses `tcp` or `udp` (universal datagram)
4	`wait`/`nowait` — applies to datagrams only; specifies whether `inetd` waits for connections to clear
5	User — is the user name for the daemon
6	Server program
7	Server program arguments

As you can see in Listing 21-1, the server is often the same but has different arguments. The `tcpd` command is a server manager; it spawns the argument listed, which is the actual server process.

Finding the remote address

As the previous section explains, finding the service port is easy. A limited number of services are available, so keeping a table on each server is not difficult. Moreover, to facilitate communication, those services need to be on well-known ports, so hard coding port numbers is not unreasonable.

Hosts are different. There are several million computers and domains on the Internet. Domains are added every day, so it is unrealistic to keep a table on each machine. You may want to communicate with any of those machines at any time, so it is unrealistic to hard code machine names.

The solution is the Domain Name Service (DNS). This is a protocol that runs on port 53 and resolves a unique domain name into a unique address. Each machine broadcasts its address, so finding the connection is not difficult when you have that address.

Finding DNS information

Most DNS information is determined with a program, but there are tools to debug the DNS system. The steps to resolve a name to an address are as follows:

1. The program sends a request to the local DNS server. (In UNIX, this is usually found in `/etc/resolv.conf`.)

```
domain       sagarmatha.com
search       chomolongma.sagarmatha.com sagarmatha.com
nameserver   207.126.112.31
nameserver   206.86.8.69
```

The relevant information is contained in the `nameserver` lines. This example lists two machines, identified by their IP address. In this case, the first name server is 207.126.112.31, which is found on `hostname.com`. I help administer this machine, so I know the DNS is reliable. The second name server is at Best Internet and is a backbone name server.

The other keywords, `domain` and `search`, are used to identify the local domain name and to search for host name lookup if the name is not a fully qualified domain name.

2. If the name server has the relevant IP address in its local cache, it returns that data. Otherwise, it starts to query zones.

Each domain is really a subdomain of a zone. You can look at a machine's fully qualified domain name to determine the breakdown. For `www.sagarmatha.com`, you start at the top-level domain to find the `.com` domain. Within the zone file for the `.com` domain is a pointer to the relevant name server for `sagarmatha.com`. The local name server then queries that name server for the appropriate information for the `sagarmatha.com` domain. This query finds an IP address for `www.sagarmatha.com`: 207.126.112.31.

3. The zone file lists alternative name servers, should the primary fail. If none of the name servers responds, the request is an unresolved domain.

The command `nslookup` can be used to debug name services. You start it as an interactive session. A session is shown in Listing 21-2.

Listing 21-2: nslookup

```
$ nslookup
Default Server:  hostname.com
Address:  207.126.112.31

> set debug
> www.sagarmatha.com.
Server:  hostname.com
Address:  207.126.112.31

;; res_mkquery(0, www.sagarmatha.com, 1, 1)
------
Got answer:
    HEADER:
        opcode = QUERY, id = 62068, rcode = NOERROR
        header flags:  response, auth. answer, want recursion, recursion avail.
        questions = 1,  answers = 1,  authority records = 2,  additional = 2

    QUESTIONS:
        www.sagarmatha.com, type = A, class = IN
    ANSWERS:
    -> www.sagarmatha.com
        internet address = 207.126.112.31
```

```
        ttl = 259200 (3 days)
AUTHORITY RECORDS:
-> sagarmatha.com
   nameserver = limbo.intuitive.com
   ttl = 259200 (3 days)
-> sagarmatha.com
   nameserver = ns.above.net
   ttl = 259200 (3 days)
ADDITIONAL RECORDS:
-> limbo.intuitive.com
   internet address = 207.126.112.31
   ttl = 259200 (3 days)
-> ns.above.net
   internet address = 207.126.96.162
   ttl = 169770 (1 day 23 hours 9 mins 30 secs)


------

Name:    www.sagarmatha.com
Address: 207.126.112.31
```

This listing shows a debug session for discovering the IP address for
`www.sagarmatha.com`. It shows that a request is made to `hostname.com` to
resolve the address with the `res_mkquery` function call. It found the answer
in the local cache (which makes sense because the DNS is served at that
machine).

Other information is specified in DNS. The most common identifies which
machine is designated to receive mail for a given address. It does not need to
be the same machine. To get this information, set the query to MX, as
illustrated in Listing 21-3.

Listing 21-3: MX Records for lucent.com

```
> set q=MX
> lucent.com.
Server:  hostname.com
Address: 207.126.112.31

Non-authoritative answer:
lucent.com      preference = 10, mail exchanger = ihgw1.lucent.com
lucent.com      preference = 10, mail exchanger = ihgw2.lucent.com
lucent.com      preference = 10, mail exchanger = algw1.lucent.com
lucent.com      preference = 10, mail exchanger = algw2.lucent.com
lucent.com      preference = 10, mail exchanger = cbgw1.lucent.com
lucent.com      preference = 10, mail exchanger = cbgw2.lucent.com
lucent.com      preference = 10, mail exchanger = cbgw3b.lucent.com
lucent.com      preference = 10, mail exchanger = cbgw3.lucent.com

Authoritative answers can be found from:
lucent.com      nameserver = cbgw1.lucent.com
lucent.com      nameserver = algw1.lucent.com
lucent.com      nameserver = ihgw1.lucent.com
ihgw1.lucent.com        internet address = 207.19.48.1
ihgw2.lucent.com        internet address = 207.19.48.2
algw1.lucent.com        internet address = 205.147.213.1
algw2.lucent.com        internet address = 205.147.213.2
```

```
cbgw1.lucent.com          internet address = 207.24.196.51
cbgw2.lucent.com          internet address = 207.24.196.52
cbgw3b.lucent.com         internet address = 207.24.196.53
cbgw3.lucent.com          internet address = 207.24.196.53
```

This lists eight machines at an equal level of preference for receiving e-mail. Note that it says the answer is "Non-authoritative." It says this because the answer came from the DNS of hostname.com and is based on the information stored locally in the cache. For an authoritative answer, I'd need to query the name servers listed for lucent.com. The nslookup command provides me with those machine names and addresses.

Several commands are associated with nslookup. They are listed in Table 21-3. (Table 21-4 lists the set options for nslookup.)

Table 21-3   nslookup Commands

Command	Action
Name	Determines the information for a given name.
name1 name2	Determines the information for name1, using name2 as the server.
Help	Lists the commands.
set OPTION	Sets the specified option. Options are listed in Table 21-4.
server name	Sets the default server to the specified machine.
lserver name	Sets the default server to the specified machine, using the initial server to resolve the name.
finger user	Fingers a user at the default host.
Root	Sets the current default server to the root.
ls domain [> file]	Lists addresses in the domain. The ls -d command gives all the information for a domain.
view file	Sorts an ls output file and views it with more.
exit	Exits the program.

Table 21-4   set Options in nslookup

Option	Meaning
all	Print all options.
[no]debug	Enable or disable debugging.
[no]d2	Perform extended debugging.
[no]defname	Append the domain to each query.
[no]recurse	Ask for a recursive query.

Option	Meaning
`[no]vc`	Always use a virtual circuit.
`domain=NAME`	Set the default domain.
`srchlist=N1 [/N2/...N6]`	Set the domain to *N1* and search list to *N1*, *N2*, and so forth.
`root=NAME`	Set the root server to *NAME*.
`retry=X`	Set the number of retries to *X*.
`timeout=X`	Set the timeout to *X* seconds.
`querytype=X`	Set the query type. (Command can be abbreviated q.) Query types are A, ANY, CNAME, HINFO, MX, NAPTR, NS, PTR, PX, SOA, SRV, TXT, WKS.
`port=X`	Set the port for the query.
`type=X`	Set a synonym for query type.
`class=X`	Set the class of the query.

Serving DNS information

UNIX machines can be set up to serve DNS queries. Doing so is a fairly simple process.

First, you set up your system to run `named`. This is often automatically configured for you; if not, it is usually a matter of putting the command in an `/etc/rc` file. The `named` command reads the file `/etc/named.boot`. This file contains a list of configuration commands. Each line that begins with `primary` directs DNS to set up DNS for the domain in the second argument, using the third argument as the filename. For example,

```
directory    /etc/namedb
primary      jamesarmstrong.com  jamesarmstrong.com
```

This sets up the domain `jamesarmstrong.com` by looking at the file `jamesarmstrong.com` in the directory `/etc/namedb`. Listing 21-4 is the DNS file for `jamesarmstrong.com`.

Listing 21-4: DNS File for jamesarmstrong.com

```
;; don't forget trailing dots.
$ORIGIN jamesarmstrong.com.
@      IN      SOA     limbo.intuitive.com. james.jamesarmstrong.com. (
                       980707  ; this file's version -- change every edit
                       43200   ; refresh twice a day
                       1200    ; retry refresh every 20 minutes
                       604800  ; expire after 1000 hours (over week)
                       259200  ; minimum TTL of 3 day
                       )


;  This is a list of all of the named servers for this domain.   The first
```

```
;    is the primary (us) and the rest are our various secondaries
;
;    WARNING: cannot list as a nameserver any machine that forwards to mac

@        IN      NS      limbo.intuitive.com.
@        IN      NS      ns.above.net.

; A record for IP connections
@            IN   A      207.126.112.31
localhost    IN   A      127.0.0.1

; The MX records are used only to direct mail for the customer domain to
; Best. Note that it is important to have two mx records for each domain,
; one of each form.

@            IN   MX  5  limbo.intuitive.com.

www          IN   A      207.126.112.31
             IN   MX  5  limbo.intuitive.com.
ftp          IN   CNAME www
```

The initial line sets up the authority record for `jamesarmstrong.com`. It indicates the name server location, authority for the domain, a version number, and refresh times. The refresh numbers indicate how frequently name server caches should check back for updates. If you are likely to have some turnover, set the TTL time low; otherwise, set it high. Three days is usually good.

The NS records point to the specific name server locations; Listing 21-4 shows `limbo.intuitive.com` as the primary DNS and `ns.above.net` as the secondary. The A records specify the actual IP addresses; the at sign (@) means that no name is necessary (that is, it will answer to `jamesarmstrong.com`). MX records are for receiving mail. `www` is broken out as a separate machine, and `ftp` is shown to use `www` as the canonical name CNAME.

DNS can be a black art; often the best approach is to copy other domains' information files.

Sample communication

One advantage of the `telnet` command is that you can use `telnet` to communicate on alternate ports. You can specify the machine name and port number, and `telnet` will connect to the remote port. The next two listings are examples of this communication.

Sending mail

Listing 21-5 shows a `telnet` session to send some mail. Before running this `telnet` command, I used `nslookup` to find the correct host for the MX record.

Listing 21-5: Mail by Telnet

```
$ telnet proxy3.cisco.com 25
Trying 192.31.7.90...
Connected to proxy3.cisco.com.
Escape character is '^]'.
220 proxy3.cisco.com ESMTP/smap Ready.
-EHLO sagarmatha.com
250-(sagarmatha.com) pleased to meet you.
250 8BITMIME
-MAIL From: james@sagarmatha.com
250 james@sagarmatha.com... Sender Ok
-RCPT To: sjackson@cisco.com
250 sjackson@cisco.com OK
-DATA
354 Enter mail, end with "." on a line by itself
-From: james@jamesarmstrong.com
-To: sjackson@cisco.com
-Subject:  Mail test
-
-This is a test of sending email by telnet.
-.
250 Mail accepted
-QUIT
221 Closing connection
Connection closed by foreign host.
```

Here, I've used `telnet` to connect to a mail server at Cisco Systems to send some e-mail to a friend. I identify my server as `sagarmatha.com`, and then I use the SMPT protocol commands to send my message. Cisco responds with acknowledgements to each command.

Requesting a Web page

You can also use `telnet` to request a Web page. In this case, the protocol insists that you send all your commands before the server responds with your output (see Listing 21-6).

Listing 21-6: Using Telnet to Get a Web Page

```
$ telnet www.sagarmatha.com 80
Trying 207.126.112.31...
Connected to www.sagarmatha.com.
Escape character is '^]'.
GET /index.html 1.1
Host:  www.sagarmatha.com
Agent: telnet

HTTP/1.1 200 OK
Date: Mon, 16 Nov 1998 03:24:24 GMT
Server: Apache/1.2.6
Connection: close
Content-Type: text/html

<html><head><title>Sequoia Consulting Home Page</title></head>
<body bgcolor=#ffffff>
```

```
<center><img src=Everest.jpg></center>
<pre>



</pre>
<center><h1>Welcome to Sequoia Consulting</h1></center>
<pre>



</pre>
Sequoia Consulting is an unincorporated business held by James C. Armstrong,
Jr.
Most of my work has been developing proprietary system software, such
as the event generator and log file scanner for Sun's SyMON product.
I prefer to work on a lower level, away from user interfaces, but
have been known to do a good job designing and implementing GUI's, too.
Unfortunately, since most of my work is done under contract for
different companies, you can't see the actual work.  I have done some
work for the public domain, including the software for the Duke
Basketball Report's BBS.
<p>
<ul>
<li><a href=galleries>Take a look at the Sagarmatha Studios</a>
<li><a href=Trips>Read James's Travellogues.</a>
<li><a href=dbrboard>Look at the DBR Bulletin Board</a>
<li>Picking Contests
<ul>
<li><a href=footpicks>The Football Picking Contest</a>
<li><a href=hooppicks>The Basketball Picking Contest</a>
<li><a href=ACC>The ACC Basketball Picking Contest</a>
<ul>
<li><a href=Duke>The Duke Basketball Picking Contest</a>
<li><a href=WakeForest>The Wake Forest Basketball Picking Contest</a>
<li><a href=UNC>The UNC Basketball Picking Contest</a>
</ul>
<li><a href=Kentucky>The Kentucky Basketball Picking Contest</a>
<li><a href=BigEast>The Big East Basketball Picking Contest</a>
<li><a href=Big10>The Big Ten Basketball Picking Contest</a>
<li><a href=Big12>The Big Twelve Basketball Picking Contest</a>
<li><a href=Pac10>The Pac Ten Basketball Picking Contest</a>
</ul>
<li><a href=http://www.sagarmatha.com.br>Waldemar Niclevicz's Sagarmatha Site in
Brazil</a>
</ul>
<p>
My personal webpage is at <a
href=http://www.jamesarmstrong.com/>http://www.jamesarmstrong.com/</a>.
<p>
<center>
<img src=/cgi-bin/Count.cgi?md=5|df=sagarmatha>
</body></html>
Connection closed by foreign host.
```

As you can see, this actually sends the source of the Web page. Were this request sent by a browser, it would have been up to the browser to interpret this page, format it, and display it.

Summary

This chapter explained

▶ The history of the Internet

▶ How to identify ports for services

▶ How to get IP addresses for domain names

▶ How connections work at the protocol level

The next chapter introduces some of the older Internet tools: FTP, Telnet, and Gopher.

Chapter 22

Internet Tools

In This Chapter

▶ Remote file-system access with FTP

▶ Finding files on the network with Archie

▶ The menu of a thousand dishes: Gopher

▶ The World Wide Web

▶ The future of the Internet

This chapter gives you a chance to travel beyond the confines of your own computer system by teaching you how to explore and enjoy the world's largest computer network, the Internet. Odds are excellent that you've heard of the Net, or at least the World Wide Web, and you may have been thinking that because you don't have a Mac or a PC on your desk, you're probably out in the cold. The good news is that definitely is not the case. In fact, you can do a ton of things — today — to start exploring the Internet.

Without question, you can do many useful and productive things on your UNIX system, but it's probably optimistic to think that you might find it fun and informative on a daily basis. That's where the Internet comes in handy: You'll always find someone who has something to say and a new publication to read online.

Remote File-System Access with FTP

When you're done chatting with your colleagues and peers on Usenet, you may want to add some new applications to your system, print a few standards documents, or move your own files from one account to another. You'll want to use the remote hard disk of the Internet: FTP, the File Transfer Protocol.

FTP has been around longer than just about any other Internet service, although you couldn't tell by the complete lack of evolution of the UNIX interface. It's not just rough around the edges; it still looks as though you're busy debugging the program.

Nonetheless, the capabilities offered by FTP are valuable. I continually use it to transfer graphic files, documents, and applications from system to system. FTP also is easy to use (fortunately). You simply log in to the remote system that you want to work with, and you issue a simple command or two to send files to the remote machine or to retrieve files from that system.

Let's have a look:

```
% ftp gatekeeper.dec.com
Connected to gatekeeper.dec.com.
220- *** /etc/motd.ftp ***
   Original by: Paul Vixie, 1992
   Last Revised: Richard Schedler, April 1994
   Gatekeeper.DEC.COM is an unsupported service of Digital Corporate Research.
   Use entirely at your own risk - no warranty is expressed or implied.
   Complaints and questions should be sent to <gw-archives@pa.dec.com>.
   EXPORT CONTROL NOTE: Non-U.S. ftp users are required by law to follow U.S.
   export control restrictions, which means that if you see some DES or
   otherwise controlled software here, you should not grab it. Look at the
   file OOREADME-Legal-Rules-Regs (in every directory, more or less) to learn
   more. (If the treaty between your country and the United States did not
   require you to respect U.S. export control restrictions, then you would
   not have Internet connectivity to this host. Check with your U.S. embassy
   if you want to verify this.)
   Extended commands available via:
    quote site exec COMMAND
   Where COMMAND is one of:
    index PATTERN   - to glance through our index (uses agrep). example:
           ftp> quote site exec index emacs
   This FTP server is based on the 4.3BSD-Reno version. Our modified sources
   are in /pub/DEC/gwtools.
220 gatekeeper.dec.com FTP server (Version 5.181 Fri Jun 16 12:01:35 PDT 1995)
ready.
login:
```

Now you have two options:

- If you have an account on the remote machine, you can go ahead and enter your login name and password, just as you would in a regular login.

- If you don't have an account on the remote machine but are connecting to a system that offers anonymous access, use **anonymous** or **ftp** as the login name. Then, when you are prompted for a password, use your e-mail address.

Tip

Save yourself some typing. When you specify your e-mail address as a password for anonymous FTP access, you need to type only through the at symbol (@) because the host name and domain information already are accessible to the FTP server at the other end. Instead of typing **taylor@ netcom17.netcom.com**, for example, you could type **taylor@** and save a few keystrokes.

After you log in, it's not too exciting. The system displays the prompt `ftp>`. At that point, you can type any of the commands listed in Table 22-1, which seems to list a great many commands, but you probably will use just a few of them. Typically, you connect to a remote site, use a combination of `dir` and `cd` to move to the specific directory that contains the files that you seek, and then use `get` or `mget` to pull the files onto your own system.

Table 22-1   FTP Commands

Command	Meaning	Example
`ascii`	Transfer subsequent files as text	`ascii`
`binary`	Transfer subsequent files as binary images	`binary`
`cd`	Change directories on the remote system	`cd /pub`
`dir`	Show the files in the current directory on the remote site	`dir`
`get`	Get a file from the remote server	`get test.c`
`lcd`	Change directories locally	`lcd /tmp`
`mget`	Get a set of files; specify pattern with an asterisk (*)	`mget *.gif`
`mput`	Put a set of files; specify pattern with an asterisk (*)	`mput *.c`
`prompt`	Disable or enable prompts (the command is a toggle)	`prompt`
`put`	Send a file to the remote site	`put me.gif`
`quit`	Quit FTP, closing the connection	`quit`

The following is sample output from an ftp session:

```
Ftp> dir
200 PORT command successful.
150 Opening ASCII mode data connection for /bin/ls.
total 52
dr-xr-xr-x  2 0    0      8192 Apr 14 1995 docs
-rw-r--r--  1 0    1      3086 Oct 7 16:28 gatekeeper.home.html
lrwxrwxrwx  1 0    0        20 Apr 14 1995 home.html -> gatekeeper.ho
me.html
dr-xr-xr-x  2 0    0      8192 Jul 29 19:23 includes
dr-xr-xr-x  2 0    0      8192 Jul 29 21:04 info
dr-xr-xr-x  2 0    0      8192 Apr 14 1995 orgs
dr-xr-xr-x  2 0    0      8192 Jun 16 22:44 pics
dr-xr-xr-x  2 0    0      8192 Apr 14 1995 util
226 Transfer complete.
539 bytes received in 0.34 seconds (1.5 Kbytes/s)
ftp> cd util
250 CWD command successful.
ftp> dir
200 PORT command successful.
```

```
150 Opening ASCII mode data connection for /bin/ls.
total 2
-r--r--r--  1 0    0      1538 Nov 20 1993 archieplexform.html
226 Transfer complete.
84 bytes received in 0.0016 seconds (51 Kbytes/s)
```

Now that you know what's there, you can get it with the get command, as follows:

```
ftp>get archieplexform.html
200 PORT command successful.
150 Opening ASCII mode data connection for archieplexform.html (1538 bytes).
226 Transfer complete.
local: archieplexform.html remote: archieplexform.html
1609 bytes received in 0.11 seconds (15 Kbytes/s)
ftp> quit
```

A bit of experimentation with FTP should convince you that it's a terrifically useful tool for moving large batches of files on the Internet.

To move many files at the same time, use prompt to turn off prompts; then use mput or mget. Alternatively, if you have control of the directories that contain all the files, think about building a tar archive, sending that archive to the remote system, and then using tar on the remote system (via Telnet) to unpack an entire hierarchy of files and folders.

Finding Files on the Network with Archie

When you start exploring the capabilities of FTP, you quickly realize that FTP is a great way to wander about the network and copy files to your local system. But you still face the dilemma that users of computer networks have faced from the very beginning: How do you know where to look for a file? What machine, of the thousands possible, has the file that you seek, and where is the file on that machine?

Enter Archie, a distributed FTP archive database system developed at McGill University in Canada. The Archie system works as a huge database of all the files and directories available on all the registered FTP sites in the world. The database contains more than 3.1 million files.

Nonetheless, Archie is a fairly simple-minded program. Because it simply indexes filenames and paths to those files, only a smidgen of information is available for each known file. If you have a program called Windows Emulator for X, for example, and save it in a file called windows-emulator-4-X.tar, odds are good that people who are searching for a Windows Emulator demonstration program will find it. If, however, you decide that windows-emulator-4-X.tar is too long a filename and instead name the file win-em-x.tar, it will be almost impossible for people to know what the file contains.

Archie has a few options worth discovering. Most notably, you invoke the program (and search its database) by using the command archie *search-*

string. By default, the command lists only exact matches of the pattern. The -c flag, however, matches either uppercase or lowercase entries. The -e flag forces exact matches — the default for most installations, unfortunately, but some sites have other default actions; it's up to your local system administrator. The -s flag has Archie consider the search pattern as a possible substring; -r requests a search for the specified regular expression; and -l produces a listing of the results in a format suitable for use with other programs. One final flag of interest, the -L flag, lists all archie servers known to the program.

You don't have Archie on your system? Good news: you can telnet to archie.rutgers.edu, archie.sura.net, or archie.unl.edu to work directly with the Archie database (if you can connect; these sites usually are quite busy). If you aren't directly on the Internet, you can send electronic mail to Archie at any of the three URLs listed. Use prog *search-string*, and ensure that the last line of your message is quit so that the remote site knows when to stop reading your mail for commands.

Let's look at how Archie works by looking for a UNIX utility called newmail. The first step is to find out what archie servers are registered with the application. You can do this with the -L flag, as follows:

```
% archie -L
Known archie servers:
    archie.ans.net (USA [NY])
    archie.rutgers.edu (USA [NJ])
    archie.sura.net (USA [MD])
    archie.unl.edu (USA [NE])
    archie.mcgill.ca (Canada)
    archie.funet.fi (Finland/Mainland Europe)
    archie.au (Australia)
    archie.doc.ic.ac.uk (Great Britain/Ireland)
    archie.wide.ad.jp (Japan)
    archie.ncu.edu.tw (Taiwan)
 * archie.sura.net is the default Archie server.
 * For the most up-to-date list, write to an Archie server and give it
   the command `servers'.
```

In the preceding example, you can see that the default server is at Suranet (archie.sura.net). Now try looking for that program, as follows:

```
% archie newmail
Host plaza.aarnet.edu.au
  Location: /usenet/comp.sources.unix/volume25
      FILE -r--r--r--  15049 Dec 20 1991 newmail
Host gum.isi.edu
  Location: /share/pub/vmh/bin
      FILE -rwxr-xr-x    104 Jul 9 18:26 newmail
Host venera.isi.edu
  Location: /pub/vmh/bin
      FILE -rwxr-xr-x    104 Jul 9 11:26 newmail
Host pith.uoregon.edu
  Location: /pub/Solaris2.x/bin
```

```
       FILE -rwxr-xr-x    46952 Oct 27 12:09 newmail
   Location: /pub/Sun4/bin
       FILE -rwxr-xr-x    65536 Oct 27 12:10 newmail
Host ee.utah.edu
   Location: /screen/bin
       FILE -rwxr-xr-x    57344 Oct 11 1992 newmail
```

Many FTP archives on the Internet have versions of this program, although it doesn't look as though it has changed much in the past few years. As you may recall, the suffix of the host name tells you where things are, so you can see that you have even matched an archive site in Australia (.au). Following is the same listing formatted more succinctly with the -1 flag:

```
% archie -1 newmail
19911220000000Z 15049 plaza.aarnet.edu.au
/usenet/comp.sources.unix/volume25/newmail
19930709182600Z  104 gum.isi.edu /share/pub/vmh/bin/newmail
19930709112600Z  104 venera.isi.edu /pub/vmh/bin/newmail
19931027120900Z 46952 pith.uoregon.edu /pub/Solaris2.x/bin/newmail
19931027121000Z 65536 pith.uoregon.edu /pub/Sun4/bin/newmail
19921011000000Z 57344 ee.utah.edu /screen/bin/newmail
```

Archie is a very useful system, and some nice Web-based interfaces are available if you live and die by your Web browser, but the biggest problem is that it's almost always busy — indeed, too busy to return results. That situation can be very frustrating, so be warned.

The Menu of a Thousand Dishes: Gopher

If you're like me, you're starting to get a bit overwhelmed by the options available for finding and perusing information on the Internet. And I haven't even talked about how to get to the Web from UNIX. A couple of years ago, a sharp team of programmers at the University of Minnesota asked the same question and realized what they wanted was a "gofer" — a program that would "go for" things but not make you have to think about what, where, or how. As a gopher was also the school mascot, the Gopher program was born.

Of all the systems that are accessible from the command line in UNIX, I think that Gopher is the easiest to use. Its simple menu-based interface enables you to step through information sources, seamlessly flipping between systems on the Internet. You can customize the program, too. As you travel through what's called *gopherspace*, you can mark interesting locations with a bookmark (simply select the item and press **a**) and then jump directly to your bookmarks by pressing **v**.

If you don't have the Gopher UNIX client on your system, you can still use it by logging in as gopher at consultant.micro.umn.edu, gopher.uiuc.edu, or panda.uiowa.edu. Use telnet to connect.

Let's have a quick look at how to work with Gopher within the UNIX environment. To get started, simply type **gopher** to jump to the default gopher

server for our system, which happens to be the birthplace of Gopher: the
University of Minnesota.

```
Internet Gopher Information Client 2.0 p15
          Root gopher server: gopher2.tc.umn.edu
 --> 1. Information About Gopher/
   2. Computer Information/
   3. Discussion Groups/
   4. Fun & Games/
   5. Internet file server (ftp) sites/
   6. Libraries/
   7. News/
   8. Other Gopher and Information Servers/
   9. Phone Books/
   10. Search Gopher Titles at the University of Minnesota <?>
   11. Search lots of places at the University of Minnesota <?>
   12. University of Minnesota Campus Information/
Press ? for Help, q to Quit, u to go up a menu          Page: 1/1
```

The sixth entry, Libraries/, looks interesting, and because it ends with a
slash, you can infer that it's a listing for another menu of options. Entries
that end with <?> are programs. Entries that end with ` . ´ are files.

To move to a specific location, you can type the corresponding number or use
the familiar v i j and k keys to move up and down. Pressing Return chooses the
specific item, so press **jjjjj** to move down five items (the arrow drops to point
at item 6), and then press Return, changing the screen to the following display:

```
Internet Gopher Information Client 2.0 p15
                Libraries
 --> 1. University of Minnesota Libraries/
   2. Electronic Books/
   3. Electronic Journal collection from CICnet/
   4. Government Information/
   5. Government Information/
   6. Library Catalogs via Z39.50/
   7. Library Card Catalogs via Telnet/
   8. Library Systems in the Twin Cities/
   9. Library of Congress Records/
   10. MINITEX Veronica service/
   11. Newspapers, Magazines, and Newsletters /
   12. Reference Works/
Press ? for Help, q to Quit, u to go up a menu          Page: 1/1
```

Reference Works sounds interesting, so press **12**. The arrow pointer drops to
the last item. Then press Return to see the following screen:

```
Internet Gopher Information Client 2.0 p15
                Reference Works
 --> 1. ACM SIGGRAPH Online Bibliography Project/
   2. American English Dictionary (from the UK) <?>
   3. CIA World Fact Book 1991/
   4. Current Contents/
   5. ERIC-archive.
```

```
 6. ERIC-archive Search <?>
 7. LEGI-SLATE Gopher Service /
 8. Periodic Table of the Elements/
 9. Roget's Thesaurus (Published 1911)/
10. The Hacker's Dictionary/
11. U.S. Geographic Names Database/
12. U.S. Telephone Area Codes/
13. US-State-Department-Travel-Advisories/
14. Webster's Dictionary/
Press ? for Help, q to Quit, u to go up a menu          Page: 1/1
```

If you're starting to get the impression that gopherspace offers a great deal to see and find, you're absolutely right; it's a rich, interesting, and very fast environment to explore. Finding things in gopherspace can be a puzzle, just as finding files in the FTP archives can be confusing, so a program that's the equivalent of Archie is available for Gopher users. That program is called Veronica, and although it's very useful, it often is very slow or unbelievably busy.

When you're traveling around in gopherspace, you can easily save bookmarks for any interesting spots that you find by using the set of commands listed in Table 22-2.

Table 22-2   Gopher Bookmarking Commands

Command	*Meaning*
a	Add current item to the bookmark list
A	Add current directory/search to bookmark list
v	View bookmark list
d	Delete bookmark/directory entry

To start the Gopher program with your set of bookmarks rather than with the default Gopher page of links, simply add the -b flag. It's a great alias for C and Korn shell users (alias gopher 'gopher -b'). Gopher may lack the visual pizzazz of the Web, but a remarkable amount of information is available in gopherspace (particularly from the U.S. government), and Gopher is *much* faster than the Web.

The Future of the Internet

There's no question that the Internet is growing and evolving at a fantastic rate. With the interest of the major commercial firms such as America Online, Yahoo, and the Microsoft Network; with the expanding infrastructure of companies such as Bell Atlantic, MCI, and various cable TV ventures; and with the investment of millions by venture capital firms and entrepreneurs, predicting the future of the Internet is impossible. One sure bet, however, is that the Internet will be less an environment in which you type commands in a command shell and much more a graphical environment in which you use a mouse or touch screen (or wireless remote, headset, or mind link?) to select a range of video, audio, and graphic elements.

This trend has already had a major impact on the services I've discussed in this chapter. FTP is still heavily used, as it's the protocol that Web browsers use to transfer files; but Archie and Gopher have all but been replaced by Web-based search tools such as Yahoo, Lycos, and AltaVista.

Summary

This chapter introduced older Internet tools:

- ▶ FTP
- ▶ Archie
- ▶ Gopher

The next chapter presents newer Internet tools.

About the Author: *Dave Taylor is president of Intuitive Systems, an interface design firm that specializes in usability and online information presentation. He's a prolific author and programmer who created the Elm mail system, wrote* Creating Cool Web Pages with HTML *and* Teach Yourself UNIX in a Week, *and cowrote* The Internet Business Guide. *His firm is online at* `http://www.intuitive.com/`.

Chapter 23

Getting the Most from Your Web Browser

This chapter looks at some of the browsers available for UNIX and discusses the advantages of each. It also explains how to customize Netscape.

Browsers

To surf the Web, you need a browser. The job of the browser is to make requests in HTTP, get pages, and interpret the HTML to display pages. HTML tells the browser how to highlight text, display images, and set up links between pages.

The initial browsers were primarily text oriented. Lynx, discussed later in the chapter, is a good example of a text browser. Shortly after these debuted, Motif-based browsers appeared. The most popular was Mosaic, which was developed at the University of Illinois.

Mosaic's primary engineer was Marc Andreessen. He left Illinois to join Netscape, which was formed to create Web software. Netscape's browser has gone through several generations of development. Today, the most common form you see is the Netscape 4 browser, although Netscape 3 is still frequently seen.

In early 1998, Netscape moved to an open source model. The Mozilla organization has running source code for Web browsers.

Lynx

Lynx has a long history, dating back to Earl Fogal at the University of Saskatchewan. Lynx uses `curses` graphics to display the text of a Web page and establish links. The simplest way to use Lynx is to specify a URL, as follows:

```
lynx http://www.sagarmatha.com
```

The output looks like this:

```
                      Sequoia Consulting Home Page (p1 of 2)

                  [INLINE]




               Welcome to Sequoia Consulting



     Sequoia Consulting is an unincorporated business held by James C.
     Armstrong, Jr. Most of my work has been developing proprietary system
     software, such as the event generator and log file scanner for Sun's
     SyMON product. I prefer to work on a lower level, away from user
     interfaces, but have been known to do a good job designing and
     implementing GUI's, too. Unfortunately, since most of my work is done
     under contract for different companies, you can't see the actual work.
     I have done some work for the public domain, including the software
     for the Duke Basketball Report's BBS.

-- press space for next page --
  Arrow keys: Up and Down to move. Right to follow a link; Left to go back.
 H)elp O)ptions P)rint G)o M)ain screen Q)uit /=search [delete]=history list
```

In the preceding example, `[INLINE]` appears at the top of the page; this tells you that an image is present there. If you press the spacebar, you see the rest of the page:

```
                      Sequoia Consulting Home Page (p2 of 2)
       * Take a look at the Sagarmatha Studios
       * Read James's Travellogues.
       * Look at the DBR Bulletin Board
       * Picking Contests
             + The Football Picking Contest
             + The Basketball Picking Contest
             + The ACC Basketball Picking Contest
                  o The Duke Basketball Picking Contest
                  o The Wake Forest Basketball Picking Contest
                  o The UNC Basketball Picking Contest
```

```
              + The Kentucky Basketball Picking Contest
              + The Big Ten Basketball Picking Contest
              + The Pac Ten Basketball Picking Contest
          * Waldemar Niclevicz's Sagarmatha Site in Brazil

       My personal webpage is at http://www.jamesarmstrong.com/.

                            [INLINE]



Commands: Use arrow keys to move, '?' for help, 'q' to quit, '<-' to go back.
  Arrow keys: Up and Down to move. Right to follow a link; Left to go back.
  H)elp O)ptions P)rint G)o M)ain screen Q)uit /=search [delete]=history list
```

You can use the arrow keys to step to the highlighted text. Each instance of highlighted text is a link. If you press the right arrow button, you can visit a linked page:

```
         Sagarmatha ACC Basketball Picking Contest (p1 of 2)

                            [INLINE]




       All contestants must be registered to compete in the 1998-9 ACC
       Basketball Picking Contest. Registration is simple, its purpose is to
       create a unique ID for you, so that your picks can be tracked. It will
       offer you a cookie. If you do not accept cookies, or if you use
       multiple machines, remember your ID and password.

                            Register

                         Manage Your Picks

                         Examine Results



(Form submit button) Use right-arrow or <return> to submit.
  Arrow keys: Up and Down to move. Right to follow a link; Left to go back.
  H)elp O)ptions P)rint G)o M)ain screen Q)uit /=search [delete]=history list
```

The `lynx` command has quite a few options (see Table 23-1). The most useful is the `-source` option. When you specify `-source` on a Web page, `lynx` does not format the page but simply delivers the source to standard output. You can use this to see how someone wrote her page, or you can use it as standard input into a parsing program. Listing 23-1 shows the source to my home page, as found by `lynx`.

Table 23-1   lynx Options

Option	Description
-	Reads the arguments from standard input
-anonymous	Specifies an anonymous account
-auth=*ID:PASSWD*	Specifies an authorization ID/password pair
-book	Starts the session at the bookmark page
-buried_news	Scans news articles for references and makes them links
-cache=*##*	Specifies the number of documents to be cached in memory
-case	Enables case-sensitive string searches
-cfg=*FILENAME*	Specifies a Lynx configuration file
-child	Exits when the left arrow key is pressed from within the starting file
-crawl	Moves to subsequent pages
-display=*DISPLAY*	Sets the *DISPLAY* variable for X programs
-dump	Puts the formatted output on standard out
-editor=*EDITOR*	Enables edit mode on pages
-emacskeys	Enables emacs-like cursor movements
-enable_scrollback	Toggles compatibility with scrollback keys
-error_file=*FILE*	Reports HTTP access codes to the specified file
-force_html	Forces the first document to be interpreted as HTML
-ftp	Disables FTP access
-get_data	Sends form data from standard input
-head	Sends the HEAD request
-help	Shows the lynx syntax
-historical	Uses old style comments terminator
-homepage=*URL*	Sets the home page as different from the start page
-image_links	Includes links for all images
-index=*URL*	Sets the default index page
-link=*NUMBER*	Sets the starting count for the -crawl files
-localhost	Disables remote URLs
-locexec	Enables local execution only

Option	Description
-mime_header	Prints the MIME header of the document
-minimal	Minimizes comment parsing
-newschunksize=*NUMBER*	Specifies the number of articles in a news listing
-newsmaxchunk=*NUMBER*	Specifies the maximum number of articles in a list before chunking
-nobrowse	Disables directory browsing
-noexec	Disables local program execution
-nofilereferer	Disables transmission of Referer header when the referer is a file
-nofrom	Disables transmission of From headers
-nolist	Disables link list feature in dumps
-nolog	Disables mailing of error messages to document owners
-noprint	Disables print functions
-noredir	Disables automatic redirection
-noreferer	Disables sending Referer headers for all calls
-nosocks	Disables SOCKS proxy
-number_links	Forces the numbering of links
-post_data	Sends form data, using the POST method
-print	Enables print functions
-pseudo_inlines	Toggles fake ALT strings
-raw	Toggles default setting of 8-bit character translations
-realm	Restricts access to URLs to those in the starting realm
-reload	Flushes the cache on the proxy server
-restrictions	Sets restrictions
-resubmit_posts	Forces resubmission of forms with a POST method
-rlogin	Disables rlogin commands
-selective	Requires the presence of a .www_browsable file before browsing a directory
-show_cursor	Shows the cursor on the screen
-source	Is the same as -dump, but outputs HTML source
-startfile_ok	Enables use of non-HTTP start file
-telnet	Disables Telnet commands

Continued

Table 23-1 *(continued)*	
Option	**Description**
-term=*TERM*	Specifies the terminal type
-trace	Turns on WWW trace
-traversal	Walks to the HTTP links from the start file
-underscore	Toggles underline format in dumps
-validate	Accepts on HTTP URLs
-version	Prints the version
-vikeys	Enables vi-like key movement

Listing 23-1: Lynx: Viewing the Source

```
$ lynx -source http://www.sagarmatha.com
<html><head><title>Sequoia Consulting Home Page</title></head>
<body bgcolor=#ffffff>
<center><img src=Everest.jpg></center>
<pre>




</pre>
<center><h1>Welcome to Sequoia Consulting</h1></center>
<pre>



</pre>
Sequoia Consulting is an unincorporated business held by James C. Armstrong,
Jr.
Most of my work has been developing proprietary system software, such
as the event generator and log file scanner for Sun's SyMON product.
I prefer to work on a lower level, away from user interfaces, but
have been known to do a good job designing and implementing GUI's, too.
Unfortunately, since most of my work is done under contract for
different companies, you can't see the actual work.  I have done some
work for the public domain, including the software for the Duke
Basketball Report's BBS.
<p>
<ul>
<li><a href=galleries>Take a look at the Sagarmatha Studios</a>
<li><a href=Trips>Read James's Travellogues.</a>
<li><a href=dbrboard>Look at the DBR Bulletin Board</a>
<li>Picking Contests
<ul>
<li><a href=footpicks>The Football Picking Contest</a>
```

```
<li><a href=hooppicks>The Basketball Picking Contest</a>
<li><a href=ACC>The ACC Basketball Picking Contest</a>
<ul>
<li><a href=Duke>The Duke Basketball Picking Contest</a>
<li><a href=WakeForest>The Wake Forest Basketball Picking Contest</a>
<li><a href=UNC>The UNC Basketball Picking Contest</a>
</ul>
<li><a href=Kentucky>The Kentucky Basketball Picking Contest</a>
<li><a href=Big10>The Big Ten Basketball Picking Contest</a>
<li><a href=Pac10>The Pac Ten Basketball Picking Contest</a>
</ul>
<li><a href=http://www.sagarmatha.com.br>Waldemar Niclevicz's Sagarmatha Site in
Brazil</a>
</ul>
<p>
My personal webpage is at <a
href=http://www.jamesarmstrong.com/>http://www.jamesarmstrong.com/</a>.
<p>
<center>
<img src=/cgi-bin/Count.cgi?md=5|df=sagarmatha>
</body></html>
```

Lynx is quite powerful, and although I prefer a graphical browser for surfing
the Web, I find Lynx's capabilities tremendous for script writing. Chapter 27
illustrates one use of Lynx in a shell command.

Netscape

Originally, the most popular X Windows browser for the Web was Mosaic. In
1994, several of Mosaic's developers helped form a new company, backed
with venture capital and managed by the founder of SGI. This new company,
Netscape Communications, set out to make a product-quality browser and to
make Internet browsing easier and more widespread.

Microsoft saw this as a challenge and started its own browser development
effort. To compete against Netscape, Microsoft gave its browser away for free
and later incorporated it into Microsoft's own operating system. As this book
is being written, the Justice Department is involved in a court case with
Microsoft, alleging that its browser marketing strategy is a violation of the
Sherman Antitrust Act.

Note

As a proponent of open systems, I hope the Justice Department prevails.
Open source and open standards enable faster development of ideas and
technology. Microsoft's closed source and proprietary standards strategies
are contrary to this view.

Netscape's browser has undergone several revisions. Currently, the two most
commonly found browser versions on UNIX are Netscape 3 and Netscape 4.

Netscape 3

Netscape 3, developed in 1996, is the older release. It supports JavaScript and Java applets, and it understands the majority of current HTML commands. Figure 23-1 shows Netscape 3's start screen.

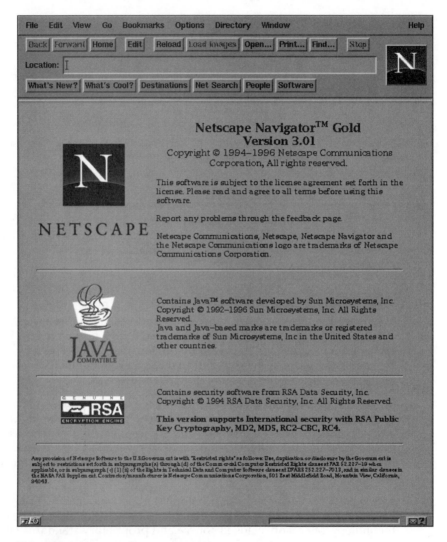

Figure 23-1: Netscape 3's start screen

Netscape 4

Netscape 4 is a more recent release. It supports a more recent version of both JavaScript and Java. The latest release, 4.5, was made public in the last quarter of 1998. Figure 23-2 shows Netscape 4's start screen.

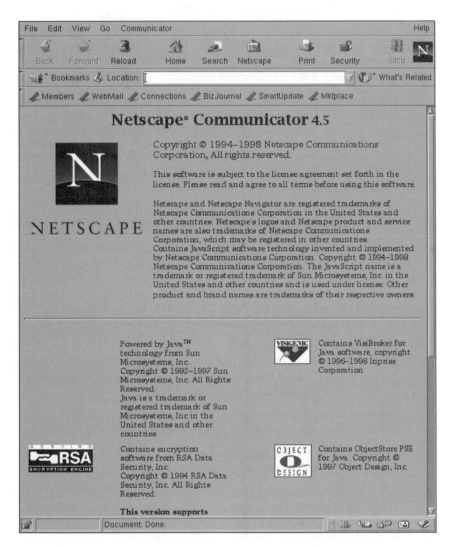

Figure 23-2: Netscape 4's start screen

Comparing the two

I regularly use Netscape 3.02. For someone who prefers to use the most modern technology available, it may seem to be an odd choice, but my reasons are well grounded.

Netscape 4.5 does not work well on Linux or other variants of UNIX. None of the Netscape 4 versions works well. Apparently, development efforts have been dedicated to optimizing the Windows version of the browser at the expense of the UNIX and Macintosh versions. Indeed, Netscape 4 seems a regression in quality from Netscape 3.

I first noticed this change when I discovered that Netscape 4 ignores the command-line geometry arguments for window placement. I set up an alias for `netscape` so that the browser window appears in the upper-left corner of my screen. When I first ran Netscape 4, however, the window popped up in random places. This surprised me, so I reset my alias and tried again. Placement was still random. I then tried to type the placement on the command line, but I still got random placement.

This is a minor irritant. Were I to continue with Netscape 4, I could simply move the browser window to my desired position every time I started a new browser.

The major irritant, and the problem that has led me to keep Netscape 3 as my default browser, is the rendition of forms. A form is a means of inputting data for an interactive Web site. I do a lot of interactive Web site development, so I noticed this problem quickly. In Netscape 3, colors are rendered correctly on all form items. Figure 23-3 shows the Duke Basketball Report introductory page properly rendered.

Netscape 4 does not render the colors correctly. In Figure 23-4, note that the button labeled "Read the Boards" has the default gray background color instead of the royal blue. This looks sloppy.

Also looking bad is the rendition of radio buttons in Netscape 4. In Figure 23-5, note that the radio buttons all have the dark blue background.

In Netscape 4, the radio buttons have the same lack of color as the "Read the Boards" button (see Figure 23-6). This also looks sloppy.

If this weren't enough to force me to retreat from Netscape 4, the mailto bug in 4.5 would definitely cause me to go back to a previous version. When you click on a link that has a mailto URL, the browser crashes because of a bus error. I've not found a single mailto URL on the Web where this does not happen.

Netscape 4.5 may be adequate for Windows, but it should never have been released for Linux. The product is unusable.

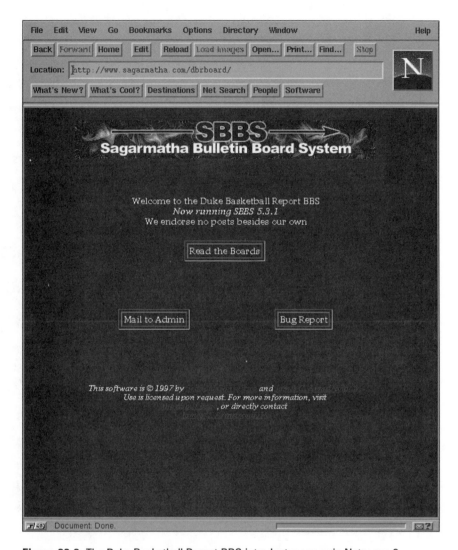

Figure 23-3: The Duke Basketball Report BBS introductory page in Netscape 3

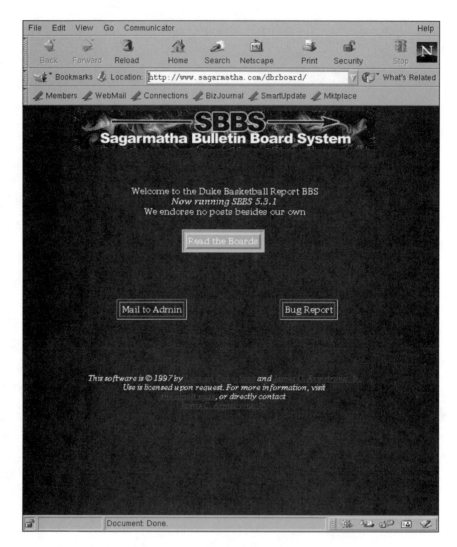

Figure 23-4: The Duke Basketball Report BBS introductory page in Netscape 4

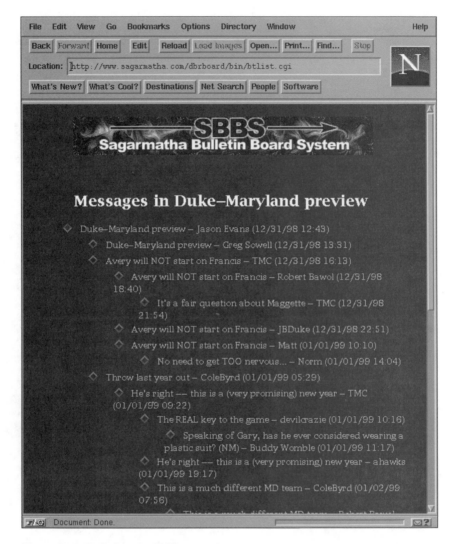

Figure 23-5: Radio buttons in Netscape 3

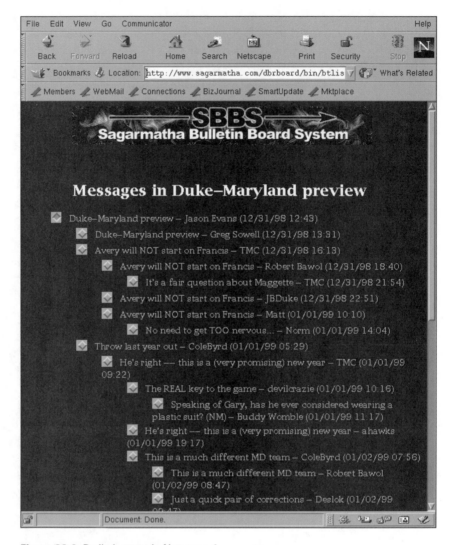

Figure 23-6: Radio buttons in Netscape 4

Mozilla

So what options exist for a UNIX user? Netscape has moved to an open source model. *Open source* means that anyone can get a copy of the source and modify it as needed. If you make an enhancement or a bug fix, you can submit it to mozilla.org, and it could become part of the Mozilla browser.

The advantage to this is that you can get a working browser. The new browser contains a faster layout engine. (Historically, browsers have been slow at placing tables. This browser has a new algorithm for laying out tables and is much faster.) In addition, bug fixes come out faster.

The disadvantages are that you must either build the browser yourself (and the necessary development environment is not easy to establish) or download binaries that have 30-day licenses. For more details, visit the Mozilla home page, `http://www.mozilla.org`.

AOL's recent acquisition of Netscape may bring about some changes in Netscape's browser. AOL recently announced that it intends to continue its business relationship with Microsoft, making Microsoft's browser the default browser for AOL users.

The Mozilla open source will continue. I suspect it will eventually become the browser of choice for UNIX users. If it does not, someone, somewhere, will start his own open source browser efforts.

Customizing Netscape

Netscape is fairly customizable. In Netscape 4, select Edit⇒ Preferences to get a listing of all the preferences. In Netscape 3, select the Options menu, and pick one of the entries. Figures 23-7 and 23-8 show the customization options.

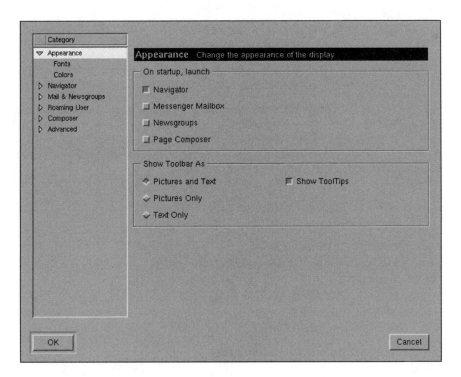

Figure 23-7: Netscape 4 Preferences window

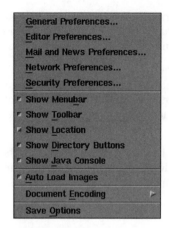

Figure 23-8: Netscape 3 Options menu

The following examples use Netscape 3. (The Netscape 4 process is similar.)

General Preferences

General Preferences include the basic preferences, such as your home page location, preferred fonts, applications, and file manipulations. The window comes with five tabs. You usually need to examine only the first two.

You can set your default home page on the Appearance tab (see Figure 23-9). You visit the home page when you first start up your browser or when you select the Home button on the button bar. To set this page, enter its URL in the Home Page Location box, select the Home Page Location radio button, and click OK.

In Figure 23-9, my home page is set to http://www.sagarmatha.com/. This is the home page for my consulting services and also the location for many of my CGI toys.

You also have some ability to customize the links so that they change color when you select them. You can have them revert after a period of time. I use 15 days.

At the top of the Appearance tab page, you can select the appearance of the toolbar. I prefer the buttons to have text only, but you can display pictures, as shown in Figure 23-10.

Select OK to make your changes.

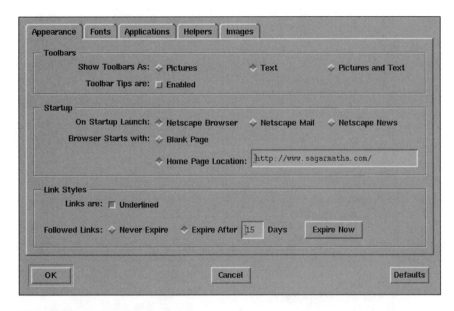

Figure 23-9: Setting the home page

Figure 23-10: Tool bar with images

Editor Preferences

Use Editor Preferences to set your preferences for Netscape Composer. Composer is an HTML generation tool that enables you to type text into a window and produce (publish) Web pages. This is useful if you have an account on an ISP where you publish Web pages but where you do not have shell access.

Select the Publish tab and enter the URL for publication, your user name, and your password. When you select the Publish button in Composer, it attempts to send your page to the ISP.

Mail and News Preferences

Mail and News Preferences are for selecting your mail server, outgoing SMTP server, and your netnews server. Netscape provides tools that enable you to interact with e-mail and netnews from your browser. Figure 23-11 shows a setup to read mail from a remote machine.

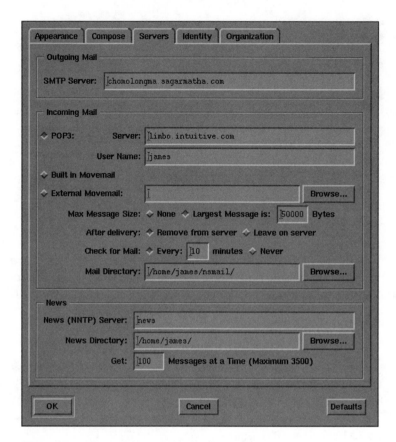

Figure 23-11: Netscape customization for e-mail

Network Preferences

The Web has the capability to transmit cookies. A *cookie* is a piece of data generated at a Web site and stored on the user's machine. It is returned to the Web site when the user revisits the site.

I use cookies in several places. My sports-picking contests give you a cookie that contains an ID code that enables you to reenter the contests without needing to remember a password. I also use the cookie in my bulletin board system to retain your posting name.

Cookies are most often used to provide advertisers with demographics. You can opt to refuse cookies from the Network Preferences screen. Select the Protocols tab to see the options shown in Figure 23-12.

By asking for an alert, you can optionally refuse to accept the cookie. Note that some sites flood you with cookies — I have seen as many as 50 on a single site when the site owners have set up their server to send a cookie with each response. Because I write CGIs that manipulate cookies, I need to watch them.

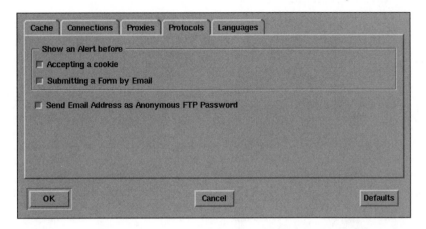

Figure 23-12: Network Preferences

You also have the option to receive a warning before submitting a form by e-mail and before sending your e-mail address. One common harvesting technique used by spammers to get e-mail addresses is to include an image on a page that is received via FTP, as follows:

```
<img src=ftp://site/image.gif>
```

The spammers can then look at their FTP logs to collect e-mail addresses for their unsolicited junk mail. If you don't want to get on spammers' lists, you may want to disable this feature.

Security Preferences

You probably won't do much changing here, but this is where you track your digital certificates for secure transmissions. Digital certificates are one of the security methods used to ensure that a site is what it claims to be. Using these, you can feel confident that when you submit your credit card number to amazon.com, it really is going to Amazon.com, Inc.

Bookmark Management

One of the more powerful features of your browser is its capability to remember sites you have visited and to enable you to return to those sites. When you find a site you'd like to return to, press Alt-A or select Bookmarksﬁ Add Bookmark from the menu bar. The site is added to the end of the list of bookmarks.

I have found over 200 sites that I use as references. A 200-entry menu is a bit excessive, so I break it down into submenus. Figure 23-13 shows my Bookmarks menu.

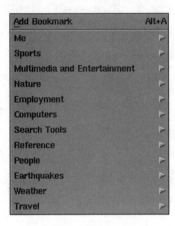

Figure 23-13: My bookmarks

When I select any entry, I find lists of bookmarks or even further menus underneath. I use Windowⓕ Bookmarks to organize my set of bookmarks. This option gives me a list of those bookmarks. Figures 23-14, 23-15, and 23-16 illustrate the manipulation of bookmarks.

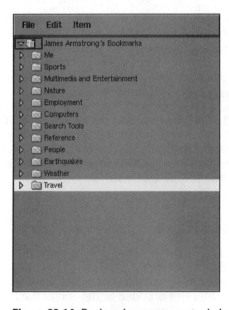

Figure 23-14: Bookmark management window

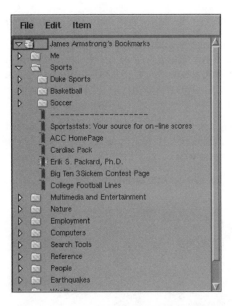

Figure 23-15: The Sports folder expanded

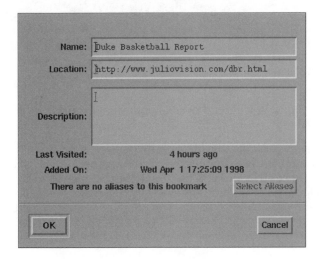

Figure 23-16: Properties of the Duke Basketball Report bookmark

After I select an item, I can change its name by selecting Itemfi Properties.

A couple of interesting options are available for a bookmark. You can ask the browser to visit each link and give you a status on the link. Some bookmarks will be marked as modified since your last visit and some will be marked as unreachable. You can use this option to clean up your list of bookmarks or to reacquaint yourself with a site.

To run a link check from the Bookmark management window, select Filefi What's New? The process can take some time; a window displays its progress. Figure 23-17 shows the link check working.

I can expand any entry for a list of the bookmarks.

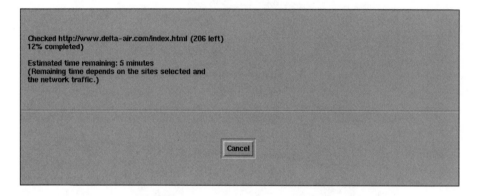

Checked http://www.delta-air.com/index.html (206 left)
12% completed)

Estimated time remaining: 5 minutes
(Remaining time depends on the sites selected and
the network traffic.)

Cancel

Figure 23-17: Link-checking status

Note

Before checking links, you should disable your cookie checker, or you are likely to get flooded.

You also can save your links to a file. I do this on a regular basis (usually monthly, but sometimes less frequently). The file generated is in HTML. With some minor editing of headers and footers, I use the page as a list of links on my Web site. Figure 23-18 shows the resulting Web page. You can visit the latest version at `http://www.jamesarmstrong.com/hotlist.html`.

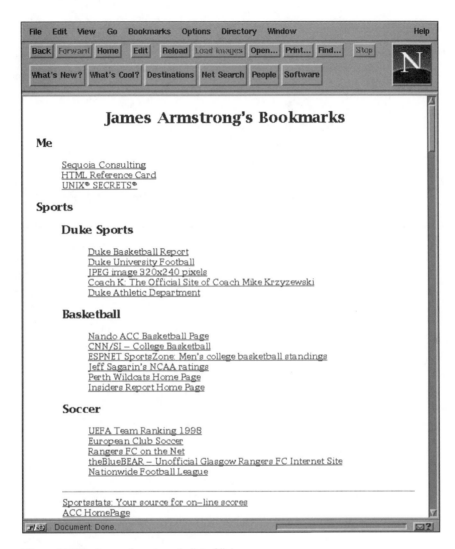

Figure 23-18: James Armstrong's list of links

Summary

This chapter introduced the UNIX Web browsers and covered the following topics:

▶ Lynx

▶ Differences between Netscape 3 and Netscape 4

▶ How to customize Netscape

▶ How to manage bookmarks

The next chapter explains how to manage an Apache Web server for UNIX.

Chapter 24

Configuring and Using a Web Server

In This Chapter

▶ Basic Apache configuration

▶ Password protection

▶ Multiple virtual domains

This chapter introduces the two primary Web servers for UNIX. It explains how to configure Apache and gives you a brief look at Netscape's Enterprise server.

Apache

The most popular Web server on the Internet is the Apache Web server. According to a January 1999 survey of Web sites, Apache is used by more Web sites than all other Web servers combined. Netcraft (http://www. netcraft.com/) performs a regular, automated survey of Web sites, and it revealed that 2,202,571 Web sites run Apache. Microsoft's Web server stood at 947,915 but was losing market share. (Internet Information Server dropped from 23.5 to 23.3 percent of the market from December 1998 to January 1999.)

You can determine what server is running on a platform simply by using telnet. To do so, open port 80, make a HEAD request, and examine the results. Listing 24-1 shows the results of an example request.

Listing 24-1: Seeing a Server Using Apache

```
$ telnet www.idgbooks.com 80
HEAD / HTTP/1.0

HTTP/1.1 200 OK
Date: Sat, 16 Jan 1999 18:38:42 GMT
Server: Apache/1.3b3
Connection: close
Content-Type: text/html
```

This shows that `www.idgbooks.com` is running Apache 1.3b3. If you are unable to use `telnet`, the Netcraft site has a database of its survey results. Just access `http://www.netcraft.com/cgi-bin/Survey/whats` and enter the host to determine what server a particular site is running.

Among the sites running Apache is the Royal Family. If Apache is good enough for Her Majesty Queen Elizabeth II, perhaps it is also good enough for your Web site?

What is Apache?

Apache is a freely available Web server developed in an open source mode. Volunteers manage the project, using the Internet, and develop the server without direct financial compensation.

Apache came about as a result of Netscape. In 1994, Netscape hired Rob McCool, who developed the NCSA Web server while working for the National Center for Supercomputing Applications. When he left NCSA, the development of the Web server stalled, so webmasters began developing their own bug fixes and enhancements. Several webmasters got together to start sharing their patches with the world. This Web server ("a patchy" Web server, get it?) was first released in April 1995. The current release is 1.3.4.

Apache has brought many different ideas to the Web server community. It is easy to configure with an HTML-like syntax, and with different modules, it is very flexible. Apache has been ported to most UNIX systems and even to Windows.

Note

Dave Taylor and I share a Web server on which we host over 40 domains. This server runs an earlier version of Apache, 1.2.6.

One downside of Apache is the lack of a formal support organization. If you have a problem with Apache, you usually need to consult a newsgroup, where only a few hundred thousand people are willing to provide assistance.

Getting Apache

Apache is available for free. You can download it from the Apache Web site or from one of Apache's mirror sites. It may even be installed with your operating system. (Red Hat Linux includes the Apache Web server by default.)

The downloaded file size is 1.3MB. You'll want to move it to an appropriate directory, where you will `gunzip` the file and then use `tar` to extract the contents.

Installing Apache

Apache installation is phenomenally simple. First, an automatic configurer builds Apache's configuration; then, you call `make` and `make install`. The

configuration program takes an argument that specifies the path prefix for
Apache. Listing 24-2 shows the results of an installation.

Listing 24-2: Apache Configuration and Installation

```
$  ./configure --prefix=/usr/local _/apache1.3.4
Configuring for Apache, Version 1.3.4
 + using installation path layout: Apache (config.layout)
Creating Makefile
Creating Configuration.apaci in src
Creating Makefile in src
 + configured for Linux platform
 + setting C compiler to gcc
 + setting C pre-processor to gcc -E
 + checking for system header files
 + adding selected modules
 + doing sanity check on compiler and options
Creating Makefile in src/support
Creating Makefile in src/main
Creating Makefile in src/ap
Creating Makefile in src/regex
Creating Makefile in src/os/unix
Creating Makefile in src/modules/standard
$ make
===> src
make[1]: Entering directory `/home/james/bin/src/apache/apache_1.3.4´
make[2]: Entering directory `/home/james/bin/src/apache/apache_1.3.4/src´
===> src/regex
sh ./mkh  -i _REGEX_H_ regex2.h regcomp.c regerror.c regexec.c regfree.c >
../include/hsregex.h
sh ./mkh  -p regcomp.c >regcomp.ih
gcc -I.  -I../os/unix -I../include  -DLINUX=2 -DUSE_HSREGEX `../apaci` -
DPOSIX_MISTAKE   -c regcomp.c -o regcomp.o
gcc -I.  -I../os/unix -I../include  -DLINUX=2 -DUSE_HSREGEX `../apaci` -
DPOSIX_MISTAKE   -c regexec.c -o regexec.o
gcc -I.  -I../os/unix -I../include  -DLINUX=2 -DUSE_HSREGEX `../apaci` -
DPOSIX_MISTAKE   -c regerror.c -o regerror.o
gcc -I.  -I../os/unix -I../include  -DLINUX=2 -DUSE_HSREGEX `../apaci` -
DPOSIX_MISTAKE   -c regfree.c -o regfree.o
rm -f libregex.a
ar cr libregex.a regcomp.o regexec.o regerror.o regfree.o
ranlib libregex.a
<=== src/regex
===> src/os/unix
gcc -c  -I../../os/unix -I../../include   -DLINUX=2 -DUSE_HSREGEX `../../apaci`
os.c
gcc -c  -I../../os/unix -I../../include   -DLINUX=2 -DUSE_HSREGEX `../../apaci`
os-inline.c
rm -f libos.a
ar cr libos.a os.o os-inline.o
ranlib libos.a
<=== src/os/unix
===> src/ap
gcc -c  -I../os/unix -I../include   -DLINUX=2 -DUSE_HSREGEX `../apaci`
ap_execve.c
```

```
gcc -c  -I../os/unix -I../include    -DLINUX=2 -DUSE_HSREGEX `../apaci`
ap_cpystrn.c
gcc -c  -I../os/unix -I../include    -DLINUX=2 -DUSE_HSREGEX `../apaci`
ap_signal.c
gcc -c  -I../os/unix -I../include    -DLINUX=2 -DUSE_HSREGEX `../apaci`
ap_slack.c
gcc -c  -I../os/unix -I../include    -DLINUX=2 -DUSE_HSREGEX `../apaci`
ap_snprintf.c
gcc -c  -I../os/unix -I../include    -DLINUX=2 -DUSE_HSREGEX `../apaci`
ap_fnmatch.c
rm -f libap.a
ar cr libap.a ap_execve.o ap_cpystrn.o ap_signal.o ap_slack.o ap_snprintf.o
ap_fnmatch.o
ranlib libap.a
<=== src/ap
===> src/main
gcc -c -I../os/unix -I../include    -DLINUX=2 -DUSE_HSREGEX `../apaci`
gen_test_char.c
gcc  -DLINUX=2 -DUSE_HSREGEX `../apaci`   -o gen_test_char gen_test_char.o  -lm
-lcrypt
./gen_test_char >test_char.h
gcc -c -I../os/unix -I../include    -DLINUX=2 -DUSE_HSREGEX `../apaci`
gen_uri_delims.c
gcc  -DLINUX=2 -DUSE_HSREGEX `../apaci`   -o gen_uri_delims gen_uri_delims.o -
lm -lcrypt
./gen_uri_delims >uri_delims.h
gcc -c -I../os/unix -I../include    -DLINUX=2 -DUSE_HSREGEX `../apaci` alloc.c
gcc -c -I../os/unix -I../include    -DLINUX=2 -DUSE_HSREGEX `../apaci` buff.c
gcc -c -I../os/unix -I../include    -DLINUX=2 -DUSE_HSREGEX `../apaci`
http_config.c
gcc -c -I../os/unix -I../include    -DLINUX=2 -DUSE_HSREGEX `../apaci`
http_core.c
gcc -c -I../os/unix -I../include    -DLINUX=2 -DUSE_HSREGEX `../apaci`
http_log.c
gcc -c -I../os/unix -I../include    -DLINUX=2 -DUSE_HSREGEX `../apaci`
http_main.c
gcc -c -I../os/unix -I../include    -DLINUX=2 -DUSE_HSREGEX `../apaci`
http_protocol.c
gcc -c -I../os/unix -I../include    -DLINUX=2 -DUSE_HSREGEX `../apaci`
http_request.c
gcc -c -I../os/unix -I../include    -DLINUX=2 -DUSE_HSREGEX `../apaci`
http_vhost.c
gcc -c -I../os/unix -I../include    -DLINUX=2 -DUSE_HSREGEX `../apaci` util.c
gcc -c -I../os/unix -I../include    -DLINUX=2 -DUSE_HSREGEX `../apaci`
util_date.c
gcc -c -I../os/unix -I../include    -DLINUX=2 -DUSE_HSREGEX `../apaci`
util_script.c
gcc -c -I../os/unix -I../include    -DLINUX=2 -DUSE_HSREGEX `../apaci`
util_uri.c
gcc -c -I../os/unix -I../include    -DLINUX=2 -DUSE_HSREGEX `../apaci`
util_md5.c
gcc -c -I../os/unix -I../include    -DLINUX=2 -DUSE_HSREGEX `../apaci` md5c.c
gcc -c -I../os/unix -I../include    -DLINUX=2 -DUSE_HSREGEX `../apaci` rfc1413.c
rm -f libmain.a
```

```
ar cr libmain.a alloc.o buff.o http_config.o http_core.o http_log.o http_main.o
http_protocol.o http_request.o http_vhost.o util.o util_date.o util_script.o
util_uri.o util_md5.o md5c.o rfc1413.o
ranlib libmain.a
<=== src/main
===> src/modules
===> src/modules/standard
gcc -c  -I../../os/unix -I../../include   -DLINUX=2 -DUSE_HSREGEX `../../apaci`
mod_env.c
gcc -c  -I../../os/unix -I../../include   -DLINUX=2 -DUSE_HSREGEX `../../apaci`
mod_log_config.c
gcc -c  -I../../os/unix -I../../include   -DLINUX=2 -DUSE_HSREGEX `../../apaci`
mod_mime.c
gcc -c  -I../../os/unix -I../../include   -DLINUX=2 -DUSE_HSREGEX `../../apaci`
mod_negotiation.c
gcc -c  -I../../os/unix -I../../include   -DLINUX=2 -DUSE_HSREGEX `../../apaci`
mod_status.c
gcc -c  -I../../os/unix -I../../include   -DLINUX=2 -DUSE_HSREGEX `../../apaci`
mod_include.c
gcc -c  -I../../os/unix -I../../include   -DLINUX=2 -DUSE_HSREGEX `../../apaci`
mod_autoindex.c
gcc -c  -I../../os/unix -I../../include   -DLINUX=2 -DUSE_HSREGEX `../../apaci`
mod_dir.c
gcc -c  -I../../os/unix -I../../include   -DLINUX=2 -DUSE_HSREGEX `../../apaci`
mod_cgi.c
gcc -c  -I../../os/unix -I../../include   -DLINUX=2 -DUSE_HSREGEX `../../apaci`
mod_asis.c
gcc -c  -I../../os/unix -I../../include   -DLINUX=2 -DUSE_HSREGEX `../../apaci`
mod_imap.c
gcc -c  -I../../os/unix -I../../include   -DLINUX=2 -DUSE_HSREGEX `../../apaci`
mod_actions.c
gcc -c  -I../../os/unix -I../../include   -DLINUX=2 -DUSE_HSREGEX `../../apaci`
mod_userdir.c
gcc -c  -I../../os/unix -I../../include   -DLINUX=2 -DUSE_HSREGEX `../../apaci`
mod_alias.c
gcc -c  -I../../os/unix -I../../include   -DLINUX=2 -DUSE_HSREGEX `../../apaci`
mod_access.c
gcc -c  -I../../os/unix -I../../include   -DLINUX=2 -DUSE_HSREGEX `../../apaci`
mod_auth.c
gcc -c  -I../../os/unix -I../../include   -DLINUX=2 -DUSE_HSREGEX `../../apaci`
mod_setenvif.c
rm -f libstandard.a
ar cr libstandard.a mod_env.o mod_log_config.o mod_mime.o mod_negotiation.o
mod_status.o mod_include.o mod_autoindex.o mod_dir.o mod_cgi.o mod_asis.o
mod_imap.o mod_actions.o mod_userdir.o mod_alias.o mod_access.o mod_auth.o
mod_setenvif.o
ranlib libstandard.a
<=== src/modules/standard
<=== src/modules
gcc -c  -I./os/unix -I./include   -DLINUX=2 -DUSE_HSREGEX `./apaci` modules.c
gcc -c  -I./os/unix -I./include   -DLINUX=2 -DUSE_HSREGEX `./apaci` buildmark.c
gcc  -DLINUX=2 -DUSE_HSREGEX `./apaci`    \
      -o httpd buildmark.o modules.o modules/standard/libstandard.a
main/libmain.a ./os/unix/libos.a ap/libap.a regex/libregex.a  -lm -lcrypt
```

```
make[2]: Leaving directory `/home/james/bin/src/apache/apache_1.3.4/src'
make[1]: Leaving directory `/home/james/bin/src/apache/apache_1.3.4'
make[1]: Entering directory `/home/james/bin/src/apache/apache_1.3.4'
===> src/support
make[2]: Entering directory
`/home/james/bin/src/apache/apache_1.3.4/src/support'
gcc -c -I../os/unix -I../include   -DLINUX=2 -DUSE_HSREGEX `../apaci`
htpasswd.c
gcc  -DLINUX=2 -DUSE_HSREGEX `../apaci` htpasswd.o -o htpasswd  -L../os/unix -
L../ap -los -lap  -lm -lcrypt
gcc -c -I../os/unix -I../include   -DLINUX=2 -DUSE_HSREGEX `../apaci`
htdigest.c
gcc  -DLINUX=2 -DUSE_HSREGEX `../apaci` htdigest.o -o htdigest  -L../os/unix -
L../ap -los -lap  -lm -lcrypt
gcc -c -I../os/unix -I../include   -DLINUX=2 -DUSE_HSREGEX `../apaci`
rotatelogs.c
gcc  -DLINUX=2 -DUSE_HSREGEX `../apaci` rotatelogs.o -o rotatelogs  -
L../os/unix -L../ap -los -lap  -lm -lcrypt
gcc -c -I../os/unix -I../include   -DLINUX=2 -DUSE_HSREGEX `../apaci`
logresolve.c
gcc  -DLINUX=2 -DUSE_HSREGEX `../apaci` logresolve.o -o logresolve  -
L../os/unix -L../ap -los -lap  -lm -lcrypt
gcc -c -I../os/unix -I../include   -DLINUX=2 -DUSE_HSREGEX `../apaci` ab.c
gcc  -DLINUX=2 -DUSE_HSREGEX `../apaci` ab.o -o ab   -L../os/unix -L../ap -los -
lap  -lm -lcrypt
sed <apxs.pl >apxs \
    -e 's%@TARGET@%httpd%g' \
    -e 's%@CC@%gcc%g' \
    -e 's%@CFLAGS@% -DLINUX=2 -DUSE_HSREGEX `../apaci`%g' \
    -e 's%@CFLAGS_SHLIB@%%g' \
    -e 's%@LD_SHLIB@%%g' \
    -e 's%@LDFLAGS_SHLIB@%%g' \
    -e 's%@LIBS_SHLIB@%%g' && chmod a+x apxs
make[2]: Leaving directory `/home/james/bin/src/apache/apache_1.3.4/src/support'
<=== src/support
make[1]: Leaving directory `/home/james/bin/src/apache/apache_1.3.4'
<=== src
$ make install
make[1]: Entering directory `/home/james/bin/src/apache/apache_1.3.4'
===> [mktree: Creating Apache installation tree]
./src/helpers/mkdir.sh /usr/local/apache1.3.4/bin
mkdir /usr/local/apache1.3.4
mkdir /usr/local/apache1.3.4/bin
./src/helpers/mkdir.sh /usr/local/apache1.3.4/bin
./src/helpers/mkdir.sh /usr/local/apache1.3.4/libexec
mkdir /usr/local/apache1.3.4/libexec
./src/helpers/mkdir.sh /usr/local/apache1.3.4/man/man1
mkdir /usr/local/apache1.3.4/man
mkdir /usr/local/apache1.3.4/man/man1
./src/helpers/mkdir.sh /usr/local/apache1.3.4/man/man8
mkdir /usr/local/apache1.3.4/man/man8
./src/helpers/mkdir.sh /usr/local/apache1.3.4/conf
mkdir /usr/local/apache1.3.4/conf
./src/helpers/mkdir.sh /usr/local/apache1.3.4/htdocs
mkdir /usr/local/apache1.3.4/htdocs
./src/helpers/mkdir.sh /usr/local/apache1.3.4/icons
```

```
mkdir /usr/local/apache1.3.4/icons
./src/helpers/mkdir.sh /usr/local/apache1.3.4/cgi-bin
mkdir /usr/local/apache1.3.4/cgi-bin
./src/helpers/mkdir.sh /usr/local/apache1.3.4/include
mkdir /usr/local/apache1.3.4/include
./src/helpers/mkdir.sh /usr/local/apache1.3.4/logs
mkdir /usr/local/apache1.3.4/logs
./src/helpers/mkdir.sh /usr/local/apache1.3.4/logs
./src/helpers/mkdir.sh /usr/local/apache1.3.4/proxy
mkdir /usr/local/apache1.3.4/proxy
<=== [mktree]
===> [programs: Installing Apache httpd program and shared objects]
./src/helpers/install.sh -c -s -m 755 ./src/httpd
/usr/local/apache1.3.4/bin/httpd
./src/helpers/install.sh -c -m 644 ./src/support/httpd.8
/usr/local/apache1.3.4/man/man8/httpd.8
<=== [programs]
===> [support: Installing Apache support programs and scripts]
./src/helpers/install.sh -c -s -m 755 ./src/support/ab
/usr/local/apache1.3.4/bin/ab
./src/helpers/install.sh -c -m 644 ./src/support/ab.1
/usr/local/apache1.3.4/man/man1/ab.1
./src/helpers/install.sh -c -m 755 ./src/support/apachectl[*]
/usr/local/apache1.3.4/bin/apachectl
./src/helpers/install.sh -c -m 644 ./src/support/apachectl.1
/usr/local/apache1.3.4/man/man1/apachectl.1
./src/helpers/install.sh -c -s -m 755 ./src/support/htpasswd
/usr/local/apache1.3.4/bin/htpasswd
./src/helpers/install.sh -c -m 644 ./src/support/htpasswd.1
/usr/local/apache1.3.4/man/man1/htpasswd.1
./src/helpers/install.sh -c -s -m 755 ./src/support/htdigest
/usr/local/apache1.3.4/bin/htdigest
./src/helpers/install.sh -c -m 644 ./src/support/htdigest.1
/usr/local/apache1.3.4/man/man1/htdigest.1
./src/helpers/install.sh -c -m 755 ./src/support/dbmmanage[*]
/usr/local/apache1.3.4/bin/dbmmanage
./src/helpers/install.sh -c -m 644 ./src/support/dbmmanage.1
/usr/local/apache1.3.4/man/man1/dbmmanage.1
./src/helpers/install.sh -c -s -m 755 ./src/support/logresolve
/usr/local/apache1.3.4/bin/logresolve
./src/helpers/install.sh -c -m 644 ./src/support/logresolve.8
/usr/local/apache1.3.4/man/man8/logresolve.8
./src/helpers/install.sh -c -s -m 755 ./src/support/rotatelogs
/usr/local/apache1.3.4/bin/rotatelogs
./src/helpers/install.sh -c -m 644 ./src/support/rotatelogs.8
/usr/local/apache1.3.4/man/man8/rotatelogs.8
./src/helpers/install.sh -c -m 755 ./src/support/apxs[*]
/usr/local/apache1.3.4/bin/apxs
./src/helpers/install.sh -c -m 644 ./src/support/apxs.8
/usr/local/apache1.3.4/man/man8/apxs.8
<=== [support]
===> [include: Installing Apache C header files]
cp ./src/include/*.h /usr/local/apache1.3.4/include/
cp ./src/os/unix/os.h /usr/local/apache1.3.4/include/
cp ./src/os/unix/os-inline.c /usr/local/apache1.3.4/include/
chmod 644 /usr/local/apache1.3.4/include/*.h
```

```
<=== [include]
===> [data: Installing initial data files]
Copying tree ./htdocs/ -> /usr/local/apache1.3.4/htdocs/
./src/helpers/install.sh -c -m 644 ./conf/printenv[*]
/usr/local/apache1.3.4/cgi-bin/printenv
./src/helpers/install.sh -c -m 644 ./conf/test-cgi[*]
/usr/local/apache1.3.4/cgi-bin/test-cgi
Copying tree ./icons/ -> /usr/local/apache1.3.4/icons/
<=== [data]
===> [config: Installing Apache configuration files]
./src/helpers/install.sh -c -m 644 ./conf/httpd.conf-dist[*]
/usr/local/apache1.3.4/conf/httpd.conf.default
./src/helpers/install.sh -c -m 644 ./conf/httpd.conf-dist[*]
/usr/local/apache1.3.4/conf/httpd.conf
./src/helpers/install.sh -c -m 644 ./conf/access.conf-dist[*]
/usr/local/apache1.3.4/conf/access.conf.default
./src/helpers/install.sh -c -m 644 ./conf/access.conf-dist[*]
/usr/local/apache1.3.4/conf/access.conf
./src/helpers/install.sh -c -m 644 ./conf/srm.conf-dist[*]
/usr/local/apache1.3.4/conf/srm.conf.default
./src/helpers/install.sh -c -m 644 ./conf/srm.conf-dist[*]
/usr/local/apache1.3.4/conf/srm.conf
./src/helpers/install.sh -c -m 644 ./conf/mime.types
/usr/local/apache1.3.4/conf/mime.types.default
./src/helpers/install.sh -c -m 644 ./conf/mime.types
/usr/local/apache1.3.4/conf/mime.types
./src/helpers/install.sh -c -m 644 ./conf/magic
/usr/local/apache1.3.4/conf/magic.default
./src/helpers/install.sh -c -m 644 ./conf/magic
/usr/local/apache1.3.4/conf/magic
<=== [config]
make[1]: Leaving directory `/home/james/bin/src/apache/apache_1.3.4'
+--------------------------------------------------------+
| You now have successfully built and installed the      |
| Apache 1.3 HTTP server. To verify that Apache actually |
| works correctly you now should first check the         |
| (initially created or preserved) configuration files   |
|                                                        |
|    /usr/local/apache1.3.4/conf/httpd.conf              |
|                                                        |
| and then you should be able to immediately fire up     |
| Apache the first time by running:                      |
|                                                        |
|    /usr/local/apache1.3.4/bin/apachectl start          |
|                                                        |
| Thanks for using Apache.      The Apache Group         |
|                               http://www.apache.org/   |
+--------------------------------------------------------+
```

You are now ready to start Apache on your system.

Basic configuration

At the heart of the Apache run-time configuration is the httpd.conf file. Within this file, you can specify the directives that tell the server how files are to be delivered from your machine.

When you install the server, a default httpd.conf file is installed at the appropriate location. You do not need to edit this file to start serving documents. As a backup, a copy of your initialized httpd.conf file is also installed as httpd.conf.default.

Caution

Do not change the httpd.conf file!

Another file that is installed is the mime.types file. This file is a listing of MIME types and their file suffixes. When the server grabs a file, it looks at the suffix to determine the file type. It passes the file type in the header of the message sent to the browser, and the browser uses the information in that header to interpret the rest of the data.

If you mix up your MIME types, browsers will not know how to interpret your data. Table 24-1 lists some common MIME types.

Table 24-1	Common MIME Types	
Suffix	**Type**	**Meaning**
.html	Text/html	An ASCII document with HTML markups. Browsers interpret these markups to lay out a page.
.txt	Text/plain	An ASCII document. The browser displays just the subsequent data.
.jpg	Image/jpeg	An image encoded with JPEG.
.js	Application /x-javascript	A JavaScript to be interpreted.
.midi	Audio/midi	An audio file in MIDI format.

Secret

You may wonder why you need a MIME types conversion. After all, the browser knows the URL it has requested, so it can interpret the URL, right? Wrong.

The server can manipulate the URL to generate and gather the data from a file other than the one specified. (In some cases, the specified URL isn't even a file.) Even so, when it is a file, the server owners might not have opted to use standard names. You may want to allow suffixes other than the standard to describe your files. If so, you need to edit the MIME types file.

Note

Older versions of Apache included two more configuration files, access.conf and srm.conf. With Apache 1.3, these files are all rolled into a single httpd.conf file.

Of course, you may not want the configuration to be exactly the default created at installation. In that case, you'll need to enter the `httpd.conf` file and change some of the variables. Two common changes are to change the basic document root (when someone requests a file, you prepend this root to the URI to find the file) and to specify different files as the defaults within a directory.

After you make any changes, you must restart the server. Find the process ID (PID) of the initial server process (Apache may spawn several processes; look for the oldest PID) and send it a hang-up signal:

```
$ kill -HUP PID
```

This tells Apache to reinitialize itself from the configuration files.

Apache 1.3 includes a control process, `Apachectl`. You can specify the argument `restart` to restart the server with the new configuration.

Setting a Web root

Setting the Web root is simple. Within the `httpd.conf` file, look for the string `DocumentRoot`.

```
$ cd /usr/local/apache1.3.4/conf
$ grep DocumentRoot httpd.conf
# DocumentRoot: The directory out of which you will serve your
DocumentRoot "/usr/local/apache1.3.4/htdocs"
# This should be changed to whatever you set DocumentRoot to.
#    DocumentRoot /www/docs/host.some_domain.com
```

In the preceding default installation, the document root is set to `/usr/local/Apache1.3.4/htdocs`. To change it to `/web/sagarmatha.com`, edit the file to change the root, as follows:

```
$ grep DocumentRoot httpd.conf
# DocumentRoot: The directory out of which you will serve your
DocumentRoot "/web/sagarmatha.com"
# This should be changed to whatever you set DocumentRoot to.
#    DocumentRoot /www/docs/host.some_domain.com
```

After a quick restart, Apache is now serving out of `/web/sagarmatha.com`.

Ordering searches

When a request comes in for a directory, normally you do not want to serve up the contents of the entire directory. Instead, you want to serve up a single file from that directory. Figure 24-1 shows what happens if you don't have a file specified.

To view a listed file, click it.

Note

There are occasions when providing a directory listing is entirely appropriate. A good example is using HTTP to access an FTP archive. Visitors can use their browsers to navigate the FTP file system until they find a specific file.

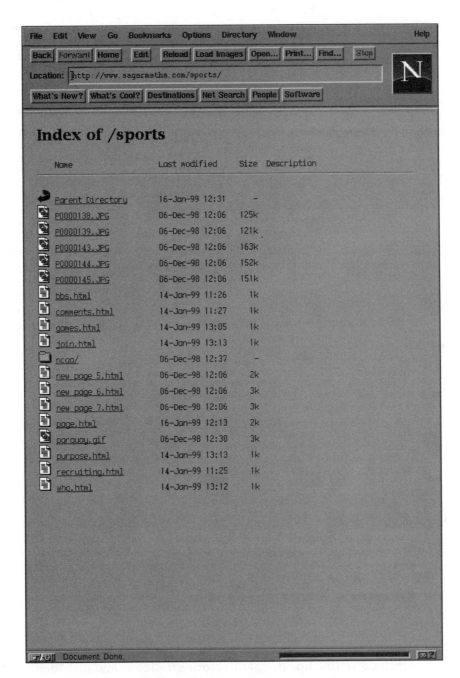

Figure 24-1: A directory listing on a server

By default, Apache looks for a file named index.html. If this file exists in a directory, its contents are displayed. Sometimes, this is not enough. If you allow people to upload files from Windows systems, their files may have three-letter suffixes, so you may want to add index.htm. Some people like to call their indexes homepage.html. FrontPage users end up forced into default.htm. Fortunately, Apache handles this easily. Look for the DirectoryIndex tag in the httpd.conf file, as follows:

```
$ grep DirectoryIndex httpd.conf
# DirectoryIndex: Name of the file or files to use as a pre-written
HTML
DirectoryIndex index.html
```

Add any files you desire, in any order.

```
$ grep DirectoryIndex httpd.conf
# DirectoryIndex: Name of the file or files to use as a pre-written HTML
DirectoryIndex index.html index.htm homepage.html default.htm index.cgi
```

Now, the system will look for additional files if index.html is not found.

Note

In the preceding example, I included index.cgi. You can include a CGI program on your Web site. If it is found and if you have enabled CGI execution for any .cgi file, the Apache server will run the program.

Advanced configuration

The Apache configuration is a powerful tool; the server understands over 200 run-time directives. Although you may never use most of them, they do enable you to customize the server to a great extent. Examples include setting up special directories for icons and providing password-protected pages.

Setting up password protection

You may have some confidential data on a page. You can protect this data with Apache by setting the directory to require the user to enter a password.

Go to the `httpd.conf` file, and create a `Location` directive. Within that directive, specify a realm for the authorization, a type of authorization, and the password file, as follows:

```
<Location /traffic>
AuthName traffic
AuthType basic
AuthUserFile /web/sagarmatha.com/traffic/.htpasswd
Require valid-user
Allow From All
</Location>
```

This example sets up the requirement that any user who wishes to see the traffic for my Web site must be authorized. I've given the name `traffic` to the authorization realm with `AuthName`. `AuthType basic` is a standard authorization. (The only alternative is `digest`.) `AuthUserFile` indicates where the password file is located.

The `require` directive indicates that anyone visiting the site must enter a user ID and password; if the password is valid, the visitor is given access. The `allow` directive specifies the host names and IP addresses that can access these pages. I've left it open to any site because I travel, and I've set up password protection.

When you set this up, you need to create a password. Use the `htpasswd` command, as follows:

```
$ htpasswd -c /web/sagarmatha.com/traffic/.htpasswd userID
Password:
Password:
```

The `-c` flags tells `htpasswd` to create the file. The next argument is the file for the passwords followed by the desired user ID. Last, you need to enter the password twice.

Caution

If the file exists and you use `-c`, the file is truncated, and your new entry becomes its only entry.

Now, when users attempt to visit `http://www.sagarmatha.com/traffic`, they are asked for a password, as illustrated in Figure 24-2. Failure is greeted with an error (see Figure 24-3). Success shows the page (see Figure 24-4).

Enter username for /home/james/sagarmatha/traffic at www.sagarmatha.com:
User ID:
Password:
OK   Clear   Cancel

Figure 24-2: Asking for the password

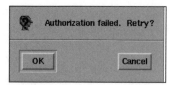

Figure 24-3: Failure

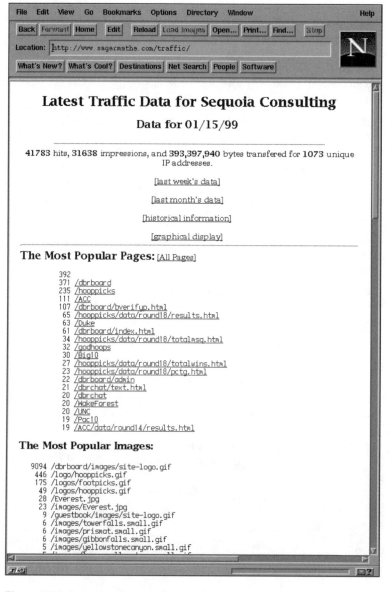

Figure 24-4: Access to the page is granted

You can set a single access name for multiple locations. Then, you can enter a password only once for access to those locations.

Setting up a CGI bin

Web servers are designed to serve static pages. Any file located under the document root can be served. These documents usually do not change.

For dynamic documents, however, you need to run programs. These programs are called CGIs (Common Gateway Interfaces). On many servers, CGIs are located in a single directory, /cgi-bin/, and are managed by the site administrator.

Two directives affect a cgi-bin. One is ScriptAlias:

```
ScriptAlias /cgi-bin/ "/usr/local/apache1.3.4/cgi-bin/"
```

This replaces the /cgi-bin/ with a fully qualified path. Note that it is outside the document root. When a request for a cgi-bin comes in, it looks for the file in this directory.

The other directive is <Directory>:

```
<Directory "/usr/local/apache1.3.4/cgi-bin">
    AllowOverride None
    Options None
    Order allow,deny
    Allow from all
</Directory>
```

This sets up access permissions. In this example, the directory is designed to be accessed by all.

Note

The ScriptAlias and <Directory> directives are set up by default.

Permitting global CGI

If you trust your users, you can allow them to create CGI programs anywhere in their Web site. To do this, simply enable the cgi-script handler, as follows:

```
AddHandler cgi-script .cgi
```

This is commented out by default. You also need to include ExecCGI in the Options for the specified directory. Usually, you enable this for /, which works for all sites.

Server-side includes

Server-side includes enable a normally static HTML page to include some output from programs. Often, they are used to add a date stamp or a counter to a page. To enable server-side includes, uncomment the AddType and Handler, as follows:

```
AddType text/html .shtml
AddHandler server-parsed .shtml
```

To include output, the files need the suffix .shtml. If you want all files to have this capability, add .html to the list, as follows:

```
AddHandler server-parsed .shtml .html
```

You also need to include server-side includes in the directory's Options line.

Setting up a virtual host

Virtual hosting is common for ISP Apache servers. A *virtual host* is a machine that can serve Web sites for multiple domains. I help run such a machine; its default name is intuitive.com, but it includes sagarmatha.com, juliovision.com, sportsstats.com, and jamesarmstrong.com, to name a few. All these domains are served from a single Web server.

I use a name-based scheme for virtual hosting. This enables each site to share the IP address space (useful, since we have only one!). I configure the DNS to point all the domain names to the same IP, and then I configure the Web server.

The first configuration task is to tell the Web server that this server will provide virtual hosts. The configuration directive NameVirtualHost is used, as follows:

```
NameVirtualHost 207.126.112.31
```

Whenever the server sees a request for this IP address, it checks for the Host: in the header of the HTTP request and then matches it against a virtual host directive. These directives look like this:

```
<VirtualHost 207.126.112.31>
ServerName www.sagarmatha.com
DocumentRoot /web/sagarmatha.com
ServerAdmin webmaster@sagarmatha.com
ErrorDocument 404 /update.html
ErrorLog /log/sagarmatha.com/error_log
</VirtualHost>
```

This example creates a separate admin ID for errors and a unique error log. I've also added a special document to be returned when a 404 (file not found) error occurs.

Because the site hosts over 50 domains, I've modified the default logging for the Web server to include the host information and some extra information. The details of the LogFormat directive are listed later in the chapter. The log file is

```
LogFormat "%h %l %u %t \"%r\" %s %b %{Host}i \"%{Referer}i\" \"%{User-Agent}i\""TransferLog /log/httpd/combined_log
```

The %{Host}i includes the host information in the log; the preceding information is the default log information. Referer and User-Agent are also additional fields.

I have written a program that nightly breaks this log file into separate access_log files for each host. The program appears in Chapter 27.

All the options

Apache understands 193 directives. Table 24-2 lists them all.

Table 24-2   Server Directives

Directive	Module	Purpose
AccessConfig	core	Specifies the location of the `access.conf` file.
AccessFileName	core	Specifies the name of the access control file. This file is used if overrides are allowed on a directory path.
Action	mod_actions	Specifies a CGI script to be called for an action type (either a MIME type or a handler).
AddAlt	mod_autoindex	Specifies a string to be displayed for fancy indexing for a file extension, in image loading is disabled.
AddAltByEncoding	mod_autoindex	Specifies an ALT string by MIME encoding.
AddAltByType	mod_autoindex	Specifies an ALT string by MIME type.
AddDescription	mod_autoindex	Adds a description string for a file for fancy indexing.
AddEncoding	mod_mime	Specifies an encoding type for a file extension.
AddHandler	mod_mime	Specifies a handler for a given file extension.
AddIcon	mod_autoindex	Specifies an icon file to be displayed for a file.
AddIconByEncoding	mod_autoindex	Specifies an icon to be displayed for a file with a specific MIME encoding.
AddIconByType	mod_autoindex	Specifies an icon to be displayed for a MIME type.
AddLanguage	mod_mime	Adds a language for a file extension.
AddModule	core	Enables the use of a compiled module.
AddModuleInfo	mod_info	Sets a string to be used when information on a module is requested.
AddType	mod_mime	Adds a MIME type for a given file extension.
AgentLog	mod_log_agent	Creates a log file of agents that make requests of the server.

Continued

Table 24-2   *(continued)*

Directive	*Module*	*Purpose*
Alias	mod_alias	Sets up a relationship between a URL and a directory outside the document root.
AliasMatch		Has the same function as Alias, but allows regular expressions in the URL.
allow	mod_access	Sets the host names that can access a directory.
AllowCONNECT	mod_proxy	Specifies the port numbers for the proxy to use the CONNECT method.
AllowOverride	core	Sets the override options in an access file. Options include None, All, AuthConfig, FileInfo, Indexes, Limit, Options.
Anonymous	mod_anon	Sets a list of user IDs allowed access without a password.
Anonymous_Authoritative	mod_anon	When set to on, denies access if a user is not matched by the Anonymous directive.
Anonymous_LogEmail	mod_anon	Logs the password provided (usually an e-mail address) in the error_log.
Anonymous_MustGiveEmail	mod_anon	Requires a nonblank password.
Anonymous_NoUserID	mod_anon	When set to on, enables users to send empty ID fields.
Anonymous_VerifyEmail	mod_anon	When enabled, checks password for an at sign (@) and a valid domain.
AuthAuthoritative	mod_auth	When set to off, enables authentication to pass to other modules if authentication fails.
AuthDBAuthoritative	mod_auth_db	Allows Berkeley DB for the authentication database. Functions the same as AuthAuthoritative.
AuthDBGroupFile	mod_auth_db	Performs same function as AuthGroupFile for Berkeley DB.
AuthDBMAuthoritative	mod_auth_dbm	Performs same function as AuthAuthoritative for DBM.
AuthDBMGroupFile	mod_auth_dbm	Performs the same function as AuthGroupFile for DBM.

Directive	Module	Purpose
AuthDBMUserFile	mod_auth_dbm	Performs the same function as AuthUserFile for DBM.
AuthDBUserFile	mod_auth_db	Performs the same function as AuthUserFile for Berkeley DB.
AuthDigestFile	mod_digest	Sets the file for digest authentication.
AuthGroupFile	mod_auth	Sets a file that lists users in a group.
AuthName	core	Specifies the name of an authorization domain.
AuthType	core	Specifies the type of authorization (basic or digest).
AuthUserFile	mod_auth	Sets the name of the file in which authorization passwords are stored.
BindAddress	core	Specifies the address for which the server listens.
BrowserMatch	mod_setenvif	Sets an environment variable to a value if the User-Agent string matches a regular expression.
BrowserMatchNoCase	mod_setenvif	Has the same function as BrowserMatch, except enables case-insensitive matching.
BS2000Account	core	Specifies the account of the nonprivileged BS2000 user.
CacheDefaultExpire	mod_proxy	Sets the time limit in hours for a fetched document to expire.
CacheDirLength	mod_proxy	Sets the number of characters in a proxy cache subdirectory.
CacheDirLevels	mod_proxy	Sets the number of subdirectory levels in the cache.
CacheForceCompletion	mod_proxy	Sets the percentage of completion required when a client cancels a request to force the proxy to complete the collection of data.
CacheGcInterval	mod_proxy	Specifies how frequently to check the cache to delete files if the proxy cache exceeds the maximum cache size. Time is in hours.
CacheLastModified Factor	mod_proxy	Sets an estimated expiration time.

Continued

Table 24-2 *(continued)*

Directive	Module	Purpose
CacheMaxExpire	mod_proxy	Sets maximum time to cache a document without requesting an update.
CacheNegotiatedDocs	mod_negotiation	If set, enables content-negotiation documents to be cached by proxy servers.
CacheRoot	mod_proxy	Sets the root directory for the cache.
CacheSize	mod_proxy	Sets the size of the cache in kilobytes.
CheckSpelling	mod_speling	If set, attempts to perform spell checking on URLs that are not found.
ClearModuleList	core	Removes all the modules from the active module list.
ContentDigest	core	Specifies whether the Content headers are to be generated.
CookieExpires	mod_usertrack	Sets the expiration time for cookie tracking. Defaults to seconds, but formats such as "2 weeks" work.
CookieLog	mod_log_config	Sets the filename for logging cookies.
CookieTracking	mod_usertrack	Enables or disables cookie tracking.
CoreDumpDirectory	core	Specifies the directory should the server dump a core.
CustomLog	mod_log_config	Sets the filename for the custom log.
DefaultIcon	mod_autoindex	Specifies a default icon to be displayed for a file.
DefaultLanguage	mod_mime	Specifies a default language.
DefaultType	core	Specifies the default MIME type for a document.
deny	mod_access	Specifies the host names that are denied access to a directory.
<Directory>	core	Creates a group of directives for a specific directory.
<DirectoryMatch>	core	Has the same function as <Directory>, but allows for regular expression matching in the directory name.

Directive	*Module*	*Purpose*
DirectoryIndex	mod_dir	Sets a list of files to be examined when a directory is specified.
DocumentRoot	core	Specifies the root for all documents served.
ErrorDocument	core	Specifies a document to be served when an error is generated.
ErrorLog	core	Specifies the location of an error log.
Example	mod_example	Demonstrates the content handler.
ExpiresActive	mod_expires	Enables the generation of an Expires header in an HTTP response.
ExpiresByType	mod_expires	Sets the expiration time by MIME type.
ExpiresDefault	mod_expires	Sets the default expiration time.
ExtendedStatus	mod_status	Indicates whether the server tracks detailed status information.
FancyIndexing	mod_autoindex	Sets a flag to turn on or off fancy indexing when examining a directory.
<Files>	core	Specifies a group of directives for access control by filename. Regular expressions can be included with <Files ~ *RE*>.
<FilesMatch>	core	Has the same function as <Files> but allows for automatic regular expressions.
ForceType	mod_mime	Forces a type for a file. Usually used inside a <Directory> or <Location>, so you don't need to include file extensions.
Group	core	Sets the group ID under which the server runs.
Header	mod_headers	Enables the expansion of HTTP response headers.
HeaderName	mod_autoindex	Specifies the name of a file to be inserted at the top of an index listing.
HostNameLookups	core	Enables DNS lookups to set Remote_Host.
IdentityCheck	core	Requests that a user's identity be checked when the server is accessed.
<IfDefine>	core	Groups directives if a condition is met.

Continued

Table 24-2 *(continued)*

Directive	*Module*	*Purpose*
`<IfModule>`	core	Groups directives if a module is loaded (or not loaded).
`ImapBase`	mod_imap	Sets the default base for use with image map files.
`ImapDefault`	mod_imap	Specifies the default response for an image map request.
`ImapMenu`	mod_imap	Specifies the action if an image map is called without valid coordinates.
`Include`	core	Specifies additional configuration files to be loaded.
`IndexIgnore`	mod_autoindex	Specifies a list of files to be ignored by the fancy index.
`IndexOptions`	mod_autoindex	Specifies the options for fancy indexing. Table 24-3 lists these options.
`IndexOrderDefault`	mod_autoindex	Specifies the default sort order for indexes.
`KeepAlive`	core	Enables Keep-Alive requests, which keep the socket open for multiple requests. (Normally, HTTP requests that the connection be closed when the request is terminated.)
`KeepAliveTimeout`	core	Specifies the number of seconds for the connection to stay open.
`LanguagePriority`	mod_negotiation	Sets the language priorities.
`<Limit>`	core	Sets authorization directives on HTTP methods.
`LimitRequestBody`	core	Sets a limit on the size of an HTTP request.
`LimitRequestFields`	core	Sets a limit on the number of header fields in a request.
`LimitRequestFieldsize`	core	Sets a size limit on each header field.
`LimitRequestLine`	core	Sets a limit on the size of a request line.
`Listen`	core	Sets a port and IP address for listening.
`ListenBacklog`	core	Sets a limit on the queue length for pending connections.
`LoadFile`	mod_so	Links in the named object files when the server is started.

Directive	Module	Purpose
LoadModule	mod_so	Links in the object file and adds the name of the module to the list of active modules.
<Location>	core	Provides access control by URL.
<LocationMatch>	core	Has the same function as <Location>, but assumes regular expressions in the URL.
LockFile	core	Sets the name of a lock file for Apache.
LogFormat	mod_log_config	Sets a format for the transfer log. With a nickname, can be used with CustomLog.
LogLevel	core	Sets the desired level for messages in an error log. Levels are similar to syslog.
MaxClients	core	Sets a limit on the number of simultaneous requests.
MaxKeepAliveRequests	core	Sets a limit on the number of requests for a connection.
MaxRequestsPerChild	core	Sets the number of requests a child process can handle.
MaxSpareServers	core	Sets the number of idle child servers allowed.
MetaDir	mod_cern_meta	Specifies the directory where meta information is stored.
MetaFiles	mod_cern_meta	Enables metafile processing.
MetaSuffix	mod_cern_meta	Sets a suffix for metafile information.
MimeMagicFile	mod_mime_magic	Specifies the location of a file for converting file magic numbers to MIME types.
MinSpareServers	core	Specifies the minimum number of spare servers that must be running at any time.
MmapFile	mod_mmap_static	Specifies the memory map configuration files (experimental).
NameVirtualHost	core	Sets an IP address for virtual hosts.
NoCache	mod_proxy	Sets a list of documents not cached by the proxy.
NoProxy	mod_proxy	Provides a list of sites that receive served documents directly.

Continued

Table 24-2 *(continued)*

Directive	Module	Purpose
Options	core	Specifies which server features are available for a particular directory. Options are All, ExecCGI (enables CGI execution), FollowSymLinks (follows symbolic links even if the destination is outside this directory), Includes (enables server-side includes), IncludesNOEXEC (disables #exec and #include in server-side includes), Indexes (returns a formatted listing of the directory), MultiViews (enables content negotiation), and SymLinksIfOwnerMatch (follows a link only if the owner matches).
order	mod_access	Sets the order in which allow and deny requests are evaluated.
PassEnv	mod_env	Specifies environment variables to be passed to CGI scripts.
PidFile	core	Specifies a file to hold the process ID.
Port	core	Specifies the port on which to listen.
ProxyBlock	mod_proxy	Provides a list of sites where connections are blocked.
ProxyDomain	mod_proxy	Sets the default domain to which the proxy server belongs.
ProxyPass	mod_proxy	Maps remote servers into the local URL space.
ProxyPassReverse	mod_proxy	Enables Apache to adjust the URL on an HTTP redirect.
ProxyReceive BufferSize	mod_proxy	Sets the buffer size for outgoing connections.
ProxyRemote	mod_proxy	Defines a list of remote proxy servers you use.
ProxyRequests	mod_proxy	Enables or disables the use of Apache as a proxy server
ProxyVia	mod_proxy	Controls the addition of the Via header to the HTTP request from the proxy.
ReadmeName	mod_autoindex	Specifies the name of a file whose contents will be appended to the end of the index listing.

Directive	Module	Purpose
Redirect	mod_alias	Tells the server to redirect requests for a URL to a new location.
RedirectMatch	mod_alias	Has the same function as Redirect, but allows regular expressions in the URL.
RedirectPermanent	mod_alias	Tells the server to refer to the redirect as permanent.
RedirectTemp	mod_alias	Tells the server to refer to the redirect as temporary.
RefererIgnore	mod_log_referer	Adds strings to be ignored by the referer log.
RefererLog	mod_log_referer	Specifies the location of the referer log.
RemoveHandler	mod_mime	Removes a handler, usually in an access file or \<Directory\>.
require	core	Specifies which authenticated users can access a directory.
ResourceConfig	core	Specifies the resource configuration file.
RewriteBase	mod_rewrite	Sets the base URL for per directory rewrites.
RewriteCond	mod_rewrite	Defines a rule condition for rewriting.
RewriteEngine	mod_rewrite	Enables or disables the rewrite engine.
RewriteLock	mod_rewrite	Sets the rewrite lock file.
RewriteLog	mod_rewrite	Specifies the location of the rewrite log.
RewriteLogLevel	mod_rewrite	Specifies the verbosity of the log (0 is nothing; 9 logs all actions).
RewriteMap	mod_rewrite	Creates a rewriting map.
RewriteOptions	mod_rewrite	Sets options for rewrites. Currently, only inherit is available.
RewriteRule	mod_rewrite	Specifies the actual rewriting.
RLimitCPU	core	Sets the maximum number of seconds for the CPU.
RLimitMEM	core	Sets the maximum memory size.
RLimitNPROC	core	Sets the maximum number of processes for a user.

Continued

Table 24-2   *(continued)*

Directive	Module	Purpose
Satisfy	core	If both the allow and require policies are used, specifies whether either or both must be satisfied to enable access.
ScoreBoardFile	core	Specifies the location of the scoreboard file.
Script	mod_actions	Creates an action when a file is requested with a specific method.
ScriptAlias	mod_alias	Sets a directory where scripts are stored for execution.
ScriptAliasMatch	mod_alias	Has the same function as ScriptAlias, but allows regular expressions in the URL.
ScriptLog	mod_cgi	Specifies the location of the script log.
ScriptLogBuffer	mod_cgi	Specifies the size of the buffer logged.
ScriptLogLength		Specifies the maximum size of the script log.
SendBufferSize	core	Sets the size of the TCP buffer.
ServerAdmin	core	Sets the e-mail address of the server's administrator.
ServerAlias	core	Sets alternative names for the server.
ServerName	core	Sets the name of the server.
ServerPath	core	Sets the legacy URL pathname for the host.
ServerRoot	core	Sets the root directory for server configuration files.
ServerSignature	core	Provides a signature to a serviced request. Used for debugging proxies.
ServerTokens	core	Sets the amount of detail sent on the Server line in the response header.
ServerType	core	Sets the type of server. Should be stand-alone, but inetd is sometimes used.
SetEnv	mod_env	Sets an environment variable to be passed to a CGI script.
SetEnvIf	mod_setenvif	Sets an environment variable if an attribute matches a regular expression. Attributes are Remote_Host, Remote_Addr, Remote_User, Request_Method, and Request_URI.

Directive	Module	Purpose
SetEnvIfNoCase	mod_setenvif	Has the same function as SetEnvIf, but enables case-insensitive matches.
SetHandler	mod_mime	Sets a handler for all files in a `<Directory>`, a `<Location>`, or an access file.
StartServers	core	Specifies the number of servers to be started when the main server starts.
ThreadsPerChild	core	Sets the number of Windows threads allowed.
TimeOut	core	Sets the timeout in seconds for Apache to wait.
TransferLog	mod_log_config	Sets a location or command for the transfer log.
TypesConfig	mod_mime	Sets the location of the `mime.types` file.
UnsetEnv	mod_env	Removes environment variables passed to CGI scripts.
UseCanonicalName	core	Tells a server to use the previously set ServerName and Port if the server needs to create a URL that refers to itself.
User	core	Sets the user ID under which this server runs.
UserDir	mod_userdir	Specifies the user directory for URLs with ~user.
`<VirtualHost>`	core	Groups directives for a virtual host.
XBitHack	mod_include	Controls the parsing of HTML documents.

Table 24-3 lists the Apache server indexing options.

Table 24-3 Indexing Options	
Option	**Purpose**
FancyIndexing	Turns on fancy indexing
IconHeight=*pixels*	Includes the HEIGHT option on the IMG tag for icons
IconsAreLinks	Makes the icons links for the file in the index
IconWidth=*pixels*	Includes the WIDTH option on the IMG tag

Continued

Table 24-3 *(continued)*

Option	Purpose
NameWidth	Enables you to specify the width of the column of filenames
ScanHTMLTitles	Extracts the `<title>` tag from HTML documents in an index
SuppressColumnSorting	Prevents the fancy index from enabling the column headings to be links for sorts
SuppressDescription	Prevents the fancy index from listing file descriptions
SuppressHTMLPreamble	Forces the index to use a specified HEADER file if specified
SuppressLastModified	Suppresses the listing of the last modified date in directory listings
SuppressSize	Suppresses the listing of size in a fancy index listing

Tables 24-2 and 24-3 list a lot of options. Not every option is always available; some modules are not automatically compiled into the server. Table 24-4 lists the module status.

Table 24-4   Module Status

Included	Not Included
core	mod_anon
mod_access	mod_auth_db
mod_action	mod_auth_dbm
mod_alias	mod_cern_meta
mod_auth	mod_digest
mod_autoindex	mod_example
mod_cgi	mod_expires
mod_dir	mod_headers
mod_env	mod_info
mod_imap	mod_log_agent
mod_include	mod_log_referer
mod_log_config	mod_mime_magic

Included	Not Included
mod_mime	mod_mmap_static
mod_negotiation	mod_proxy
mod_setenvif	mod_rewrite
mod_status	mod_so
mod_userdir	mod_speling
mod_usertrack	

To include an extra module, you must reconfigure the system. Add the --enable-*module=name* to the configure line to include these modules in your build. You may also need to include an AddModule directive.

Logging

The Server provides a standard log file in an access_log. This file includes the seven fields listed in Table 24-5.

Table 24-5	Common Log Format
Field	**Description**
host	The host that made the request
ident	The identify of the user if requested
authuser	The authorized user
date	The date and time the request was made
request	The request made
status	The return code (200 is successful)
bytes	The number of bytes transmitted

This format is called the Common Log Format. Some alternative log formats are promoted by other server vendors.

You are not restricted to this log format. The LogFormat directive changes the format of the transfer log. It takes arguments similar to printf in C. Table 24-6 lists the common arguments.

Table 24-6	Log File Literals
Literal	*Description*
a	Remote IP address
b	Bytes sent
f	Filename
{ENV}e	Contents of the environment variable ENV
h	Remote host
{header}i	Contents of the specified header line
{header}o	Contents of the outgoing header line
l	Remote log name from identd
{note}n	Contents of the note from another module
p	Canonical part of the server servicing the request
P	Process ID of the child server
r	First line of the request
s	Status of the request
t	Time of the request
{format}t	Time formatted in strftime format
T	Time taken to service the request
u	Remote user
U	URL path requested
v	Canonical server name

Each argument can have a range of return codes specified. If the return code is not matched, that item is not logged. The Common Log Format is "%h %l %u %t \"%r\" %s %b".

For my virtual user site, I've extended that format to include the Host from the headers, the User-Agent, and the Referer.

Netscape Enterprise Server

Another common server is the Netscape Enterprise server. This server is licensed from Netscape Communications and was also designed by Rob McCool. It has a completely different configuration scheme and has the capability to write dynamic objects for inclusion in the server, too. Its interface is called NSAPI.

NSAPI

NSAPI is the programming interface for adding modules to the Netscape Enterprise server. These modules are configured in the `obj.conf` file.

The best reference for NSAPI is *Programming Applications for Netscape Servers* by Kaveh Gh. Bassiri.

Summary

This chapter introduced Web servers, concentrating on the Apache Web server. It covered the following topics:

▶ How to find and build the Web server

▶ Basic configuration

▶ Advanced configuration

▶ Web server directives

▶ Log file formats

The next chapter provides a brief overview of HTML.

## Chapter 25

Introduction to HTML

In This Chapter

▶ HTML document structure

▶ URL construction

▶ Color definitions

▶ Document headers

▶ Document body tags

This chapter gives you a brief introduction to HTML. This is not an exhaustive study of HTML, but a short description of the HTML tags and their options. To gain a more thorough understanding of page design, read *Creating Cool HTML 4 Web Pages* by Dave Taylor.

Document Structure

In markup languages such as HTML, the directives are interspersed in the document with the document's text. HTML interpreters read the document, find the tags, and perform the actions. Your browser is one type of HTML interpreter.

Usually, the document itself is divided into two sections: a document header and a document body. The header includes the overall descriptive information for the document, such as the title, and occasionally some other tags. The body contains the text of the document with the markup commands.

An HTML document is usually enclosed between two tags: <HTML> and </HTML>. These tags delimit the beginning and the end of the document. An optional attribute, VERSION, may appear in an <HTML> tag.

HTML tags

The markups in an HTML document are called *tags*. Tags are enclosed within angle brackets (less-than and greater-than signs). Most tags enclose an area of text; a slash (/) preceding the tag distinguishes the closing tag, which marks the area's end, from the leading tag, which marks its beginning.

As previously mentioned, the tag for HTML is <HTML> . . . </HTML>. Tags are case- insensitive. Following convention, I use capital letters for all my tags.

A tag may be accompanied by attributes. These attributes are additional pieces of information that modify a tag's action. Some tags, such as the hyperlink tag, require attributes. In other cases, the attributes are optional. When an attribute has a value, the attribute value pair is separated by an equal sign (=). Attributes are separated by whitespace (so tags can wrap across lines) and must be enclosed entirely within the angle brackets.

With the exception of text in certain tags, linefeeds are ignored by HTML interpreters. Your entire document can be one line, but I recommend breaking it across multiple lines for readability's sake.

URLs

Any address on the Internet can be specified by a Uniform Resource Locator (URL). A URL includes several pieces of data in the following form:

```
method://server[:port]/file[#anchor]
```

The :port and #anchor are optional. The *method* can be any of those listed in Table 25-1.

Table 25-1	URL Methods
Method	**Meaning**
http	Use the hypertext transfer protocol (the most common protocol on the Internet) to access the specified Web documents.
file	Access the file on the local system or on the specified server.
finger	Use the finger protocol to access data on a remote server.
ftp	Use the FTP protocol to get files from a remote server. You can modify the server to include default login and password information: `ftp://private:password@myserver/afile`.
gopher	Use the Gopher protocol to access information.
mailto	The following information is an e-mail address.
news	Use NNTP to read the specified newsgroup.
telnet	Use Telnet to access the remote server.

The server is a machine name that can be interpreted through DNS or your local name resolution software. The port specifies the Internet port for connection; 80 is the default port for HTTP. Sometimes, you will see 8080, 8000, or other ports. An anchor is a technique used within an HTML document to access data at a location other than the start of the document.

Colors

Colors have a unique specification in HTML. As described in the Part VIII, HTML uses the hexadecimal system to define colors. These RGB values are preceded by a number sign (#) in HTML.

HTML also recognizes some colors by name, as listed in Table 25-2. These may be browser specific, so be careful when using them. (On UNIX, apparently, netscape recognizes any color named in the RGB file, which includes about 700 colors. It is dangerous, however, to rely on those names.) I strongly urge you to use RGB values, even for the most obvious colors.

Table 25-2   Some Well-Known Color Names

aqua	black	blue	fuchsia
gray	green	lime	maroon
navy	olive	purple	red
silver	teal	yellow	white

Document Header

The document header contains information that describes the document. The HTML tag is ⟨HEAD⟩ ... ⟨/HEAD⟩; no attributes are allowed. Within the document header, the most common tag is the title. The ⟨TITLE⟩ ... ⟨/TITLE⟩ tag surrounds the document title, which appears in the document's window frame. Figure 25-1 shows the document title produced by the following example:

```
<HTML><HEAD><TITLE>My Document</TITLE></HEAD>...
```

Figure 25-1: The title of a Web page

You can also enclose a new BASE within the header. The ⟨BASE⟩ tag has no closing tag and needs an HREF attribute that lists a URL to use as the base for all incompletely qualified URLs in the document (see the following example).

For example, if a subsequent anchor points to `myfile.html` and the base is `http://www.yourserver.com/yourpages/`, the anchor accesses the URL `http://www.yourserver.com/yourpages/myfile.html`.

```
<BASE HREF=http://www.yourserver.com/yourpages/>
```

The tags `<BGSOUND>` and `<EMBED>` are used to place multimedia — usually a backing soundtrack — on Web pages. The `<BGSOUND>` tag works with Explorer, and `<EMBED>` works with Netscape.

The `<LINK>` tags enable you to specify related documents. These tags have four attributes: `HREF` for the URL, `REL` for the relationship, `REV` for the reverse relationship, and `TITLE` for the link title. Table 25-3 lists the relationships.

Table 25-3   LINK Relationships

Relationship	*Description*
Copyright	A link to a copyright statement for your site
Glossary	A link to a glossary for your site
Help	A link to a help document for your site
Home	A link to your home page
Index	A link to an index for your site
Next	A link to the next sequential page
Previous	A link to the previous sequential page
Toc	A link to a table of contents for your site
Up	A link to your parent document

Note

I've not seen `<LINK>` used.

Another tag is the `<META>` tag. The `<META NAME=Keywords CONTENT=...>` tag is often used to provide keywords to describe your site. An `HTTP-EQUIV` attribute can specify a client pull dynamic document, described in a following section.

Caution

Owing to the abuse of keywords, most search engines now ignore the `<META>` tag when indexing sites.

A full header might look like this:

```
<HEAD>
<TITLE>My Document</TITLE>
<META NAME=Keywords CONTENT="Armstrong, Sagarmatha">
<BASE HREF=http://www.sagarmatha.com/james/>
<LINK HREF=/homepage.html REL=home>
<EMBED SRC=/mytheme.mid>
</HEAD>
```

Document Body

The document body is more interesting than the document header; here is where you can perform fancy layouts and include content.

First, though, you need to enclose your document in a `<BODY>` tag. The `<BODY>` ... `</BODY>` tag set should surround your data. The `<BODY>` tag accepts five color specifications and a background pattern specification. Table 25-4 lists the colors.

Table 25-4	Color Specifications
Attribute	**What Field?**
ALINK	The color of an active link
BGCOLOR	The color of the page background
LINK	The color of the unvisited links
TEXT	The color of the text
VLINK	The color of the visited links

Any combination can be specified. The `BACKGROUND` attribute takes the URL specified as an image and tries to set the browser background to that image. For example, a `<BODY>` tag can look like this:

```
<BODY BACKGROUND=/parquay.gif TEXT=#ff0000 LINK=#ffff00 VLINK=#ff0000>
```

This example sets the background to `parquay.gif`, the text and the visited links to red, and the unvisited links to yellow. (There's no accounting for taste.) Other tags are included within the body.

Hyperlinks

The way the Web works is by hyperlinks. A hyperlink is an area of text or an image that is highlighted to indicate that clicking the text or image causes a new document to be loaded. Without links, you would need to type each URL manually as you visited sites.

Hyperlinks are also called anchors in HTML and are marked with the `<A>` tag. This tag needs one of two attributes: an `HREF`, which points to a new document, or a `NAME`, which marks the location within the current document as significant. The `NAME` attribute enables the appending of *#name* to a URL to load the document at the specified location.

A link to the Duke Basketball Report looks like this:

```
<A HREF=http://www.juliovision.com/dbr.html>This goes to the Duke
Basketball Report</A>
```

By default, this appears blue and underlined on a Web page. Anchor tags can surround any amount of text. A common error is to forget the closing </A> tag; its absence makes the rest of the document the hyperlink.

Comments

Yes, HTML has comments. In some cases, such as JavaScript, you place the JavaScript within a comment. Server-side includes also are included within comments.

A comment is not a closed tag. Instead, the tag starts with <!-- and ends with -->. The comment text is included between the start and end of the comment. Originally, browsers required that comments be on a single line, but some modern browsers accept multiple-line comments. Still, because you don't know what browsers will visit your site, you should treat all comments as single-line entities. A typical comment might look like this:

```
<!-- This page is copyright me! -->
```

Headers

Headers are tags that enable you to change the emphasis for certain parts of the text, usually section headers of documents. There are six header levels, 1 through 6, where 1 is the largest header. Each header can have an ALIGN attribute, which aligns the header to the left, right, or center of the page. It can also have a CLEAR attribute, set to left, right, or all, which lowers the header until that side of the page is clear. The CLEAR attribute is useful when the header follows an image that has text flowing around it.

The header tag is <Hnumber> . . . </Hnumber>, where number is the level of the header. Figure 25-2 shows the headers created by the following HTML:

```
<H1>The Top Level</H1>
The text for the top.
<H2 ALIGN=center>The Second Level</H2>
More text for the second level.
<H3 ALIGN=right>The Third Level</H3>
Third level text.
<H4>The Fourth Level</H4>
Fourth level text.
<H5>The Fifth Level</H5>
Fifth level text.
<H6>The Sixth Level</H6>
Sixth level text.
```

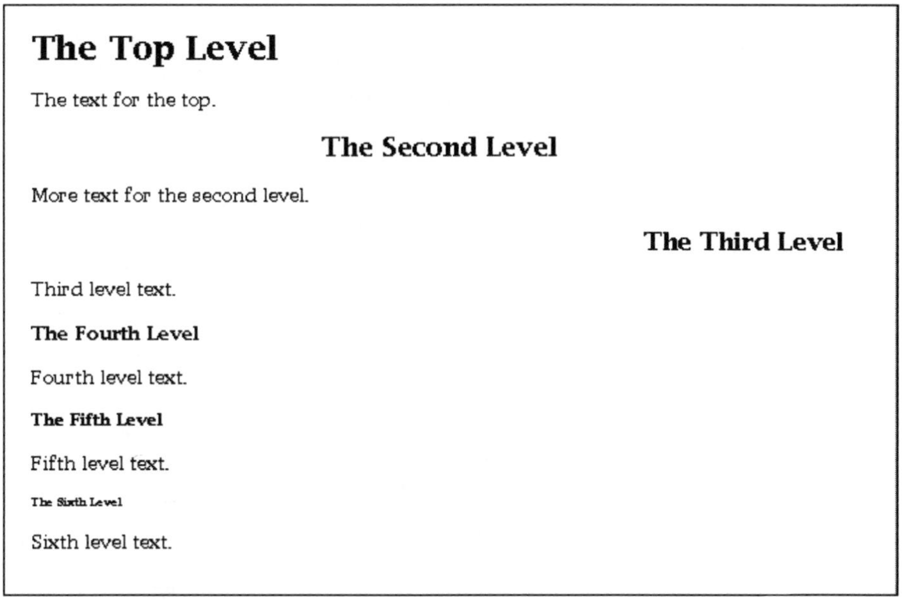

The Top Level

The text for the top.

The Second Level

More text for the second level.

The Third Level

Third level text.

The Fourth Level

Fourth level text.

The Fifth Level

Fifth level text.

The Sixth Level

Sixth level text.

Figure 25-2: Headers on a Web page

Fonts

Of course, the real fun in Web pages is the ability to change the style of the text, using different fonts. Tables 25-5 and 25-6 list HTML's font and emphasis tags. Most do not have attributes. Each tag has a closing tag.

Table 25-5	Physical Font Styles
Tag	**Meaning**
<B>	Make the enclosed text bold.
<BIG>	Make the enclosed text big.
<BLINK>	Make the enclosed text blink.
<I>	Make the enclosed text italic.
<S>	Strike through the enclosed text.
<STRIKE>	Strike through the enclosed text (same as <S>).
<SMALL>	Make the enclosed text small.
<SUB>	Make the enclosed text subscript.
<SUP>	Make the enclosed text superscript.
<TT>	Set the enclosed text in a monospace font.
<U>	Underline the enclosed text.

Table 25-6   Logical Font Styles

Tag	Meaning
`<ABBREV>`	Mark up abbreviations.
`<ACRONYM>`	Mark up acronyms.
`<AU>`	Mark the author name.
`<CITE>`	Mark up a citation.
`<DEL>`	Deleted text for legal documents.
`<DFN>`	Mark up a definition.
`<EM>`	Emphasize the text.
`<INS>`	Highlight inserted text.
`<KBD>`	Mark up keyboard input.
`<LANG>`	Alter the language context.
`<PERSON>`	Mark a person's name.
`<Q>`	Mark a short quotation.
`<SAMP>`	Set the text in sample format.
`<STRONG>`	Strongly emphasize the text.
`<VAR>`	Highlight a variable.

Physical font styles give more specific direction to the browser on how to display the enclosed text. For example, a `<B>` guarantees the text is bold. With logical font styles, the browser decides how the text should be displayed. Figure 25-3 shows how the following page is displayed:

```
<B>Bold Text</B><BR>
<BIG>Big Text</BIG><BR>
<BLINK>Blinking Text</BLINK><BR>
<I>Italic Text</I><BR>
<S>Strike Text</S><BR>
<STRIKE>Strike Text</STRIKE><BR>
<SMALL>Small Text</SMALL><BR>
Base text<SUB>Subscript Text</SUB><BR>
Base text<SUP>Superscript Text</SUP><BR>
<TT>Teletype Text</TT><BR>
<U>Underlined Text</U><BR>
<ABBREV>Abbreviation Text</ABBREV><BR>
<ACRONYM>Acronym Text</ACRONYM><BR>
<AU>Author Text</AU><BR>
<CITE>Cited Text</CITE><BR>
<DEL>Deleted Text</DEL><BR>
<DFN>Definition Text</DFN><BR>
```

```
<EM>Emphasized Text</EM><BR>
<INS>Inserted Text</INS><BR>
<KBD>Keyboard Text</KBD><BR>
<LANG>Language Text</LANG><BR>
<PERSON>Person Text</PERSON><BR>
<Q>Quoted Text</Q><BR>
<SAMP>Sample Text</SAMP><BR>
<STRONG>Strongly emphasized Text</STRONG><BR>
<VAR>Variable Text</VAR><BR>
```

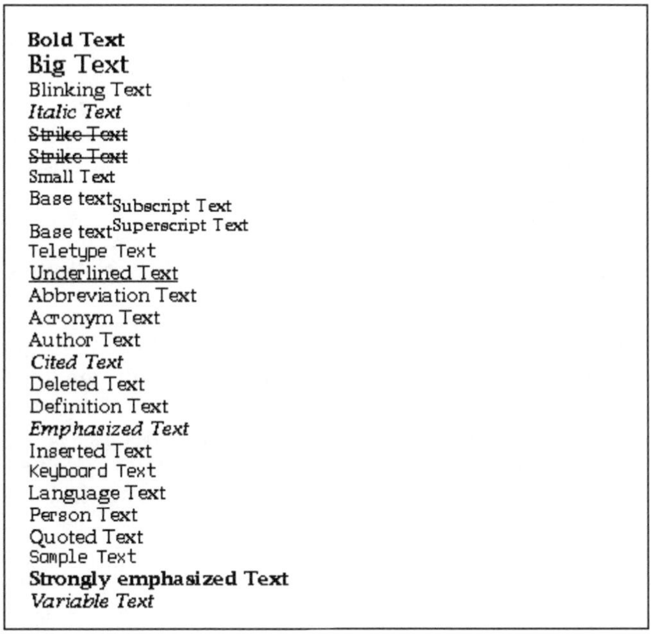

Bold Text

Big Text

Blinking Text

Italic Text

~~Strike Text~~

~~Strike Text~~

Small Text

Base text_{Subscript Text}

Base text^{Superscript Text}

Teletype Text

Underlined Text

Abbreviation Text

Acronym Text

Author Text

Cited Text

Deleted Text

Definition Text

Emphasized Text

Inserted Text

Keyboard Text

Language Text

Person Text

Quoted Text

Sample Text

Strongly emphasized Text

Variable Text

Figure 25-3: How Netscape renders fonts

These font tags can be nested. For example, if you want bold, italic text, use `<B><I>`Bold, italic text`</I></B>`. The order isn't important; `<I><B>`Bold, italic text`</B></I>` is the same as the previous example.

The two special cases are the `<BASEFONT>` and `<FONT>` tags. The `<BASEFONT>` tag sets the default font size. Fonts range from 1 through 7 in size. The `BASEFONT` tag takes as an attribute `SIZE`. If no size is specified, no change occurs.

The `<FONT>` tag is more interesting. The `<FONT>` tag takes three attributes: `COLOR`, `FACE`, and `SIZE`. The `SIZE` attribute can be absolute or a relative offset: `<FONT SIZE=+2>` increases the size of the text by two steps. The `FACE` attribute sets the style of the font, so terms such as *Roman* are used to specify a Roman font. The `COLOR` attribute sets the foreground color of the text.

Secret

You can trick people into thinking a link exists with `<FONT COLOR=#0000ff><U>Text</U></FONT>`. The underlined blue text looks like a link.

Separators

HTML specifies several means of separating text. The three with which this book is concerned are those that make paragraphs, end filling of text, and draw lines.

The `<P>` tag starts a paragraph of text. Although a `</P>` tag is defined to end a paragraph, these tags are rarely seen; a new `<P>` to start a new paragraph automatically includes a `</P>` if a preceding paragraph exists. When a new paragraph is started, a blank line separates the new paragraph from the previous one. The `<P>` tag takes an `ALIGN` attribute that works like that of a header, except that it aligns the entire contents of a paragraph.

The `<BR>` tag has no closing tag. It tells the HTML interpreter to stop filling text and to start on a new line. The `<BR>` takes a `CLEAR` attribute similar to that of a header to clear the space near images.

The `<HR>` tag creates a horizontal line. It takes up to five attributes. The `ALIGN` attribute specifies the line's alignment. By default, the line has a three-dimensional look; `NOSHADE` makes it appear flat. The `SIZE` attribute specifies the height of the line in pixels. The `WIDTH` attribute specifies the width of the line in either pixels or a percentage. The `COLOR` attribute specifies the line's color if your browser supports that. Figure 25-4 shows several examples of horizontal lines.

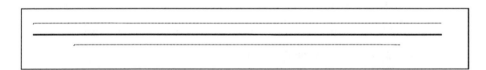

Figure 25-4: Different horizontal lines

Text offsets

In addition to changing the text's font, you can change the text's offsets. The three common offsets are `<BLOCKQUOTE>`, `<CENTER>`, and `<PRE>`.

The `<BLOCKQUOTE>` tag forces the enclosed text to be formatted with wider margins on both sides of the text. The `<BLOCKQUOTE>` tags can be nested. The `<CENTER>` tag forces the enclosed text and images to be centered. The `<PRE>` tag tells the HTML interpreter to present the data as is; do not do any text formatting or filling. The `<PRE>` tag is sometimes used to generate space, as follows:

```
<PRE>
```

```
</PRE>
```

It can be useful for presenting tables on older browsers. Only <PRE> takes an attribute, WIDTH.

Images

Of course, the real way to make a page exciting is by embedding images in the text. The <IMG> tag is used to embed images. The <IMG> tag takes several attributes, which are listed in Table 25-7.

Table 25-7   IMG Attributes

Attribute	Action
ALIGN	Specifies the image alignment
ALT	Displays this text if the image can't be loaded
BORDER	Specifies the border around the image in pixels
HEIGHT	Specifies the height of the image
HSPACE	Specifies the horizontal space to surround the image
ISMAP	Indicates that an image map exists
LOWSRC	Specifies a low-resolution image to load and display while the higher-resolution image is loading
SRC	Specifies the image's URL
USEMAP	Specifies a name of a map to be used
VSPACE	Specifies the vertical space around the image
WIDTH	Specifies the image's width in pixels

Specifying a WIDTH and HEIGHT is useful for faster page layout. If the interpreter knows the size of the image, it can lay out text around the image while the image loads. If these attributes are not specified, the interpreter must see the file's size data before filling text. Specifying an alignment causes the interpreter to lay out text around the image. VSPACE and HSPACE specify the amount of whitespace that surrounds the image. A bit of whitespace helps the image stand out.

Special characters

In HTML, characters such as the less-than sign (<) have special meaning. This makes including these characters in text without using the <PRE> tag difficult. In addition, many characters from non-English languages are not represented in the standard ASCII character set.

HTML, therefore, has a series of escape sequences for characters. These sequences, composed of an ampersand (&) followed by a short string and a semicolon (;), tell the interpreter to display the special character. There are quite a few of these characters, including different formats for upper- and lowercase. Table 25-8 lists a few of these characters.

Table 25-8 Some Escape Sequences for Characters

Escape	Character
<	<
>	>
&	&
"	"
	Nonbreaking space
®	Registered trademark symbol
©	Copyright symbol
Á	Uppercase *A* with an acute accent
á	Lowercase *a* with an acute accent
À	Uppercase *A* with a grave accent
Ä	Uppercase *A* with an umlaut
Ã	Uppercase *A* with a tilde
ß	Lowercase German sharp *s*

Lists

An easy way to organize information on a Web page is to build the information into a list. HTML has several types of lists; three of them are of interest here.

The <OL> list is an ordered list. Each list item is numbered. The <UL> lists are unnumbered, each list item being marked with a bullet, circle, or square. Both <OL> and <UL> lists need closing tags, and each list item must be marked with <LI>.

The <OL> lists can have a start number specified with START, and the TYPE is one of five choices: A for capital letters, a for lowercase letters, I for uppercase Roman numerals, i for lowercase Roman numerals, and 1 for integers. The <UL> lists have only a TYPE attribute, which can be circle, disc, or square. Figure 25-5 shows various types of lists.

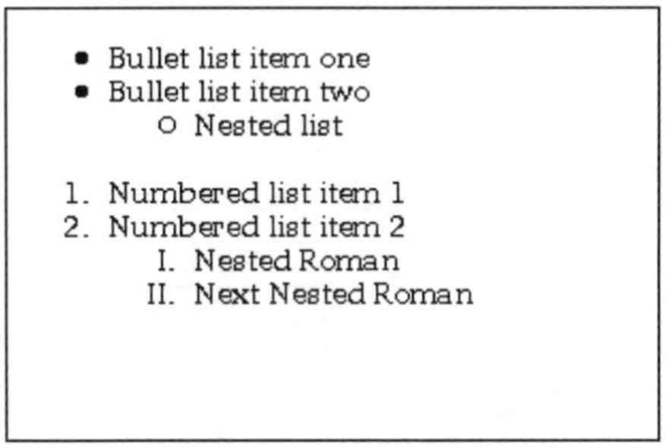

- Bullet list item one
- Bullet list item two
  - Nested list

1. Numbered list item 1
2. Numbered list item 2
    I. Nested Roman
    II. Next Nested Roman

Figure 25-5: Different types of lists

The third type of list, the definition list, is more complex. The leading tag is <DL>, and the list must terminate with </DL>. Each list item has two components, a <DT> ... </DT> and a <DD> ... </DD>. The <DT> element specifies the term to be defined, and <DD> specifies the definition. Figure 25-6 shows the definition list created by the following example:

```
<DL>
<DT>Nitrous</DT>
<DD>Containing Nitrogen</DD>
<DT>Nitty-gritty</DT>
<DD>The essential facts</DD>
</DL>
```

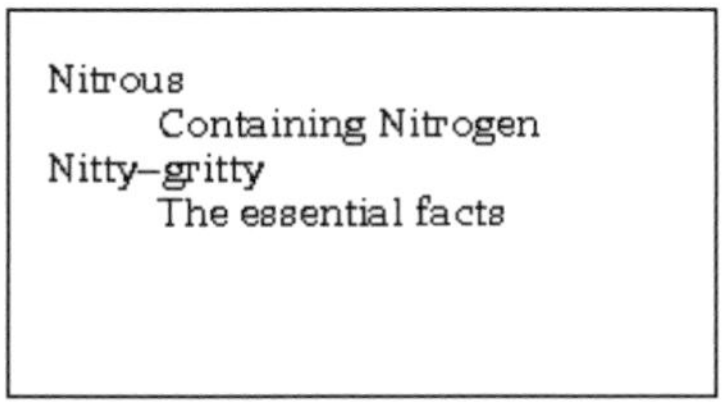

Nitrous
        Containing Nitrogen
Nitty-gritty
        The essential facts

Figure 25-6: A definition list

Secret

You don't need both <DT> and <DD>; <DL> can be used for indenting items.

Tables

Another layout mechanism is tables. A table is just a grid, where each column has the same width in each row. Rows can have different heights, depending on the contents of the row.

Tables must be grouped in <TABLE> ... </TABLE> tags. The TABLE tag can have several attributes, which are listed in Table 25-9.

Table 25-9   TABLE Attributes

Attribute	Action
ALIGN	Specifies the table alignment on the page
BGCOLOR	Specifies the table's background color
BORDER	Specifies the border width in pixels
CELLPADDING	Specifies the whitespace on the edges of each cell
CELLSPACING	Specifies the width of the lines between cells
WIDTH	Specifies the table's width in percentage or pixels

Within the table are table rows, and within the rows are table data cells. Rows are surrounded by <TR> ... </TR> tags; cells are marked by <TD> ... </TD> tags. Rows can have ALIGN and VALIGN attributes for horizontal and vertical alignment. Cells have the same alignment options. Cells also have the following attributes: COLSPAN to span the cell across more than one column, ROWSPAN to span more than one row, HEIGHT and WIDTH to specify cell size, and NOWRAP to force cells not to wrap text. The ROWSPAN and COLSPAN attributes can result in some interesting tables, as the following example and Figure 25-7 illustrate.

```
<TABLE BORDER=2 CELLSPACING=2>
<TR>
<TD COLSPAN=2>This spans two columns</TD>
<TD ROWSPAN=2>This spans two rows</TD>
</TR>
<TR>
<TD>A single column</TD>
<TD>Another single column</TD>
</TR>
</TABLE>
```

Figure 25-7: A sample table

You can do other neat tricks with tables. To create text on a background, specify a single-celled table with a background color, no CELLSPACING, and no BORDER. To create an alert, specify BGCOLOR for the <TABLE>.

Another trick is to mat photographs, as illustrated by the following example and Figure 25-8:

```
<TABLE BGCOLOR=#ffcccc BORDER=0 CELLPADDING=10>
<TR>
<TD><IMG SRC=/images/leela.gif>
</TD>
</TR>
</TABLE>
```

Figure 25-8: A matted photograph

Frames

Frames can divide your document window into separate fields. Frames require <FRAMESET> tags. Do not include a <BODY> tag. The <FRAMESET> tag takes COLS or ROWS, in pixels or percentage. The <FRAMESET> tag surrounds <FRAME> tags, which need an SRC attribute for the page to load in a frame, a NAME for the frame, NORESIZE to prevent resizing, and SCROLLING to set a scroll bar.

My DBR Chat pages use frames, as shown in the following example and Figure 25-9:

```
<HTML><HEAD><TITLE>DBR Chat</TITLE>
</HEAD>
<FRAMESET ROWS=75,*,120>
```

```
        <FRAME NAME=logo NORESIZE SRC=logo.html>
        <FRAMESET cols=75%,25%>
                <FRAME NORESIZE NAME=text SRC=text.html#end>
                <FRAME NAME=list NORESIZE SRC=list.cgi>
        </FRAMESET>
        <FRAME NAME=input NORESIZE src=input.html>
<NOFRAMES>
You need a browser that understands frames to get DBR Chat.
</NOFRAMES>
</FRAMESET>
</BODY>
</HTML>
```

Forms

Forms are a means of collecting input from browser users for CGI programs. A form includes several types of input fields. The input is passed as a query string to the program.

A form must be surrounded by <FORM> ... </FORM> tags. Two attributes are mandatory: ACTION indicates the URL of the CGI program to be executed, and METHOD is either GET or POST, indicating the HTTP method for data transmission.

Data is input via the <INPUT> tag. This is a single tag, so it does not need a closing tag. There are several possible attributes, but they have different meanings based on the context. There are ten types of input.

Checkbox input

A checkbox is a data structure in which you can select one or more boxes and submit the data. Checkboxes are a form of the <INPUT> tag; they need the TYPE attribute set to checkbox. Each one must have a NAME and a VALUE and may have an optional attribute, CHECKED, which means the form initially has the box checked when loaded. Multiple choices may share a NAME, but each should have a unique value. Each checked box is transmitted as NAME=VALUE to the CGI, so the CGI must understand that multiple variables are sharing the same name.

Radio button input

A radio button is similar to a checkbox, except that only one radio button can be selected for each variable name. These buttons behave analogously to those used on a car radio to change stations: As you press in a button, the previously pressed button pops out. Radio buttons use the same attributes as checkboxes, except that the TYPE is set to radio.

Note

Personally, I usually don't like frames.

Figure 25-9: An example of frames

Submit button

Normally, you use a submit button to submit a form. To create a submit button, set the attribute TYPE to submit; a button appears with the VALUE attribute as text. An optional NAME can be set; otherwise, the variable name is SUBMIT.

A form can consist of a single submit button, and multiple submit buttons can be included in a single form. When multiple submit buttons are present, the CGI needs to examine the value of the submission variable to determine the appropriate action.

Reset button

A reset button can be included on a form. When an <INPUT> is set to TYPE=reset, the button resets the form to the initial state.

Hidden input

The hidden input is a useful type of CGI variable. When an <INPUT> type is set to hidden, no action is visible to the browser. Nonetheless, the NAME/VALUE pair set as attributes is passed to the CGI.

Hidden variables are useful when you have multiple screens of input or when you are correcting errors in forms. By setting previously entered information in hidden variables, you don't need to worry about keeping state on your local server (nor about data timeout and the like). Instead, pass the values like this:

```
<INPUT TYPE=hidden NAME=id VALUE=12345>
```

The appearance of the data on the screen doesn't change.

Image input

An image <INPUT> is similar to the submit button, except that an additional SRC attribute is needed to identify the image. You will get x and y coordinates in the CGI script.

Text input

You can accept a single line of text input with TYPE=text. A VALUE attribute prefills the text area. The SIZE attribute sets the number of characters displayed, and MAXLENGTH sets the string's maximum length.

Password input

A TYPE=password is the same as a text input, except that when the user types in data, asterisks appear instead of the typed characters. This prevents anyone from seeing the password displayed.

Multiline text input

The `INPUT TYPE=text` accepts only a single line of input. Type a carriage return, and if you're lucky, you are moved to the next `TEXT` input. (If you are unlucky, the form submits prematurely.) If you want a larger input area, use `<TEXTAREA>` tags. The attributes are `COLS` for the number of columns, `ROWS` for the number of rows, and `NAME` for the name. Also present is `WRAP`, which can be set to `physical` (which includes carriage returns at the appropriate locations), `off` (which does not wrap text until you type a carriage return), and `virtual` (which wraps text at the appropriate locations but does not pass carriage returns to the CGI unless the user explicitly enters them).

My BBS program includes `<TEXTAREA>` tags for the message input. The form is

```
<TEXTAREA WRAP=virtual NAME=message COLS=80 ROWS=10></TEXTAREA>
```

If you include text between the tags, that text is the initial text displayed.

Selection list input

The last type of input is the selection list. This list can be either a pull-down menu or a scrolling list, depending on the configuration. The list is created by the `<SELECT>` tag. The attributes are `MULTIPLE` (which makes multiple selections possible), `NAME`, and `SIZE`. Set the `SIZE` attribute to 1, and you have a pull-down menu. Set it to more than 1, and you have a scrolling list with that many items displayed. The `<SELECT>` tag requires a closing tag.

Each item in a selection list must be marked with an `<OPTION>`. You set a `VALUE` attribute for the option, and if `SELECTED` is set, that option is the default selection. The closing `</OPTION>` tag is optional.

Style sheets

Style sheets are the coming attraction in HTML. Styles give you much greater control over how a document is displayed. Styles can be set in a style sheet, as follows:

```
<STYLE TYPE=text/css>
<!--
INDENT { font: 12pt text-indent: 0.2i }
-->
</STYLE>
```

This is an example of a valid multiline comment.

This example creates a style called `INDENT` that forces the use of a 12-point font and a text indent of one-fifth of an inch. Several tags, most notably `<P>`, enable the specification of a `CLASS` attribute, as follows:

```
<P CLASS="INDENT">
```

The paragraph is rendered in a 12-point font and indented one-fifth of an inch.

A default CLASS is BODY, so if you specify a style for BODY, that will be the default style for the document.

Each type of style must be followed by a list of style attributes in curly braces ({ }). Table 25-10 lists some style attributes. The name becomes the value for the CLASS attribute.

Table 25-10   Style Attributes

Attribute	Meaning
background	The URL for either a background pattern or a background color.
color	The text color.
font	A combination of size and family.
font-family	A searchable list of font families. The first family found is used. Examples include Roman, Courier, and Helvetica.
font-size	The size of the font. Can be points (pt), inches (in), centimeters (cm), or pixels (px).
font-style	Italic or normal.
font-weight	Either extra-light, light, demi-light, medium, demi-bold, bold, or extra-bold.
line-height	Vertical separation of lines of text.
margin-left	The left margin of the document.
margin-right	The right margin of the document.
margin-top	The top margin of the document.
text-align	Left, center, or right.
text-decoration	Text enhancement specifications.
text-indent	Desired indent for the text.

Dynamic Documents

You can create dynamic documents purely in HTML. If you use the <META> tag, set the attribute HTTP-EQUIV to Refresh and set CONTENT to a string containing the number of seconds before reloading, a semicolon separator, and the URL to be loaded, as follows:

```
<META HTTP-EQUIV=Refresh CONTENT="15;URL=/nextfile.html>
```

This example tells the browser to wait 15 seconds before loading and displaying `nextfile.html`.

I use this to forward people from an old Web site, `http://www.sagarmatha.com/james/`, to a new one, `http://www.jamesarmstrong.com/`. The Web page is

```
<HTML><HEAD><TITLE>James Armstrong's Home Page</TITLE>
<META HTTP-EQUIV=Refresh
CONTENT=15;URL=http://www.jamesarmstrong.com/>
</HEAD>
<BODY LINK=#FFFF00 VLINK=#FF0000 BGCOLOR=#000000 TEXT=#FFFFFF>
<PRE>




</PRE>
<CENTER>
<FONT SIZE=+2><I>James has moved <a
HREF=http://www.jamesarmstrong.com/>his page</A> to <A
HREF=http://www.jamesarmstrong.com/>http://www.jamesarmstrong.com/</A>
.<P>
</I>Please update your bookmarks.
</CENTER>
<PRE>



</PRE></FONT>
If your browser supports it, you will be transported to the new page
location momentarily.
</BODY></HTML>
```

Example of a Web Page

No page includes all the components described in the preceding sections, at least not if it is a page worth viewing. My philosophy on page design is to keep pages small, fast to load, and not too "busy." I like my corporate home page (shown in Figure 25-10); it includes some basic layout, a couple of images, some nested lists, and some links, as follows:

```
<html><head><title>Sequoia Consulting Home Page</title></head>
<body bgcolor=#ffffff>
<center><img src=Everest.jpg></center>
<pre>
```

```
</pre>
<center><h1>Welcome to Sequoia Consulting</h1></center>
<pre>


</pre>
Sequoia Consulting is an unincorporated business held by James C.
Armstrong,
Jr.
Most of my work has been developing proprietary system software, such
as the event generator and log file scanner for Sun's SyMON product.
I prefer to work on a lower level, away from user interfaces, but
have been known to do a good job designing and implementing GUI's,
too.
Unfortunately, since most of my work is done under contract for
different companies, you can't see the actual work.  I have done some
work for the public domain, including the software for the Duke
Basketball Report's BBS.
<p>
<ul>
<li><a href=galleries>Take a look at the Sagarmatha Studios</a>
<li><a href=Trips>Read James's Travellogues.</a>
<li><a href=dbrboard>Look at the DBR Bulletin Board</a>
<li>Picking Contests
<ul>
<li><a href=footpicks>The Football Picking Contest</a>
<li><a href=hooppicks>The Basketball Picking Contest</a>
<li><a href=ACC>The ACC Basketball Picking Contest</a>
<ul>
<li><a href=Duke>The Duke Basketball Picking Contest</a>
<li><a href=WakeForest>The Wake Forest Basketball Picking Contest</a>
<li><a href=UNC>The UNC Basketball Picking Contest</a>
</ul>
<li><a href=Kentucky>The Kentucky Basketball Picking Contest</a>
<li><a href=Big10>The Big Ten Basketball Picking Contest</a>
<li><a href=Pac10>The Pac Ten Basketball Picking Contest</a>
</ul>
<li><a href=http://www.sagarmatha.com.br>Waldemar Niclevicz's
Sagarmatha Site in Brazil</a>
</ul>
<p>
My personal webpage is at <a
href=http://www.jamesarmstrong.com/>http://www.jamesarmstrong.com/</a>
.
<p>
<center>
<img src=/cgi-bin/Count.cgi?md=5|df=sagarmatha|dd=G>
</body></html>
```

Figure 25-10: The Sequoia Consulting home page

Summary

This chapter introduced HTML and discussed the following topics:

▶ HTML document structure

▶ URL construction

▶ Color definitions

▶ Document headers

▶ Document body tags

▶ Tables

▶ Frames

▶ Forms

▶ Style sheets

▶ Dynamic pages

The next chapter introduces CGI programming, the back engine for Web pages.

Chapter 26

Writing Clean CGIs

In This Chapter

▶ Learn about CGI

▶ Understand the CGI environment

▶ Understand how documents are made

▶ Learn how to get data from the browser

This chapter introduces you to the basics of CGI programming. Web sites become much more useful when they are able to return documents created according to input from the user. These dynamic documents are often created by programs run on the server. The Common Gateway Interface (CGI) enables these programs to run.

Note

To understand several concepts in this chapter, you must understand programming. Chapter 35 describes the software development process, and Chapters 36 and 37 discuss some programming languages. The examples in this chapter are in shell programming and C, although other languages are acceptable.

Overview: CGI Programming

The Common Gateway Interface (CGI) enables the server to run programs that generate documents to display on a client's browser. Often, these programs take input from browsers, using the <FORM> tags in a parent document. Of course, input is not necessary, nor is it necessarily sent from a <FORM>.

Guru: Use Your Language of Choice

I've heard more often than I care to mention that Perl is the only acceptable language for programming CGIs. That is hardly the case. I personally prefer C because it gives me better tools to access the system, but your choice of language should be based on the problem you need to solve, not on some rhetoric.

The HTTP method that calls a CGI is either GET or POST. A POST method tells the server that the necessary input is being transmitted in the body of the HTTP request, whereas a GET method retrieves input that is part of the URL. The following two requests produce the same results:

```
$ telnet www.sagarmatha.com 80
GET /traffic/showday.cgi?date=990104 HTTP/1.0
```

and

```
$ telnet www.sagarmatha.com 80
POST /traffic/showday.cgi HTTP/1.0
Content-length: 11

date=990104
```

The GET method includes the data on the URL. The question mark separates the URL from the data, so the file requested is /traffic/showday.cgi. The data is date=990104.

In the POST method, the URL is just the file. The Content-length header reports how many bytes of data are included in the body of the request, so the server knows how many more bytes to read to finish the request. In this case, 11 bytes match date=990104.

Note

For a CGI to execute, your server must be configured to run CGIs. In Apache, you accomplish this either by adding the handler for CGIs

```
AddHandler cgi-script .cgi
```

or by placing them in a specific script alias directory. For the preceding examples, the ScriptAlias would be

```
ScriptAlias /traffic/ "/web/sagarmatha.com/traffic/"
```

If neither AddHandler nor ScriptAlias is set, the .cgi file is treated as a plain text file, and the contents of your executable are displayed by the browser.

You can transmit more than one variable in a <Form>, as illustrated in Chapter 25. To do so, separate the listed *name=value* pairs with ampersands (&), as follows:

```
date=990104&host=sagarmatha.com&file=agents
```

The preceding example contains three variables: date, host, and file. The ampersands are discarded. This leaves the ampersand and the equal sign as special characters; these characters need escapes, as explained in the next section.

Secret

One interesting trick is that with the GET method, the arguments can also be treated as command-line variables. If you include a URL such as /traffic/showmon.cgi?9812, the value 9812 is passed as argv[1] to the program.

Server-side includes

Another means of creating dynamic documents is server-side includes. A server-side include forces the server to examine a document for commands. The server looks for a special token, `<!--#exec`. If it finds this token, it parses the comment to find a command. It then executes the command and places the output in the document.

To use server-side includes, the Web browser must be configured to parse documents. The handler is server-parsed, as follows:

```
AddHandler server-parsed .shtml
```

To parse all files, use the following line:

```
AddHandler server-parsed .html .shtml
```

This increases CPU usage in the server, so you should avoid it unless you have a machine capable of handling the load. The server-side include's full syntax is as follows:

```
<!--#exec cmd="command to be run"-->
```

The spacing is vital to the parse. Everything between the quotation marks is treated as a command and is run in a shell (/bin/sh -c "*command*"). The output is then transmitted without alteration to the browser, so server-side includes may not be nested.

Server-side includes work well with counters and possibly dynamic lists. I've used server-side includes to generate the items for a list, as follows:

```
<select name=teams size=10>
<!--#exec cmd="/home/james/teamlist basketball"-->
</select>
```

The server-side include then performs a quick examination of a file and produces output, as follows:

```
#!/bin/sh

if
        [ $1 == basketball ]
then
        filename=/home/james/database/scores
fi
...
awk 'BEGIN {FS=":"} {printf "%s\n%s\n", $3, $5}' $filename | sort -u |
awk '{printf "<option value=%s>%s\n",$0, $0}'
```

This simple shell program runs some `awk` commands on a colon-separated database and lists two entries, one per line. It then sorts the entries and eliminates duplicates. Lastly, it formats the entries as `<options>` for a `<select>`. When this is included in the form, the output becomes

```
<select name=teams size=10>
<option value="Alabama">Alabama
<option value="Auburn">Auburn
<option value="Birmingham Southern">Birmingham Southern
<option value="Clemson">Clemson
<option value="Furman">Furman
<option value="Georgia">Georgia
<option value="Georgia Tech">Georgia Tech
<option value="Kentucky">Kentucky
<option value="Mercer">Mercer
<option value="Millsaps">Millsaps
<option value="Mississippi A&M">Mississippi A&M
<option value="Naval Training Station">Naval Training Station
<option value="Newberry">Newberry
<option value="Tennessee">Tennessee
<option value="Tulane">Tulane
</select>
```

Now, I no longer need to update a list as I add scores to the database file. Instead, whenever the HTML file that uses the database is accessed, the program produces an up-to-date list.

Getting data from the browser

As previously mentioned, data comes to the CGI from the browser via one of two methods. The GET method includes the data on the command line. In this case, the server converts the data to an environment variable, QUERY_STRING. This string then needs to be parsed. The POST method takes the string as standard input. It must be read into a buffer to be parsed. Some characters may be encoded. Table 26-1 lists some common encodings.

Table 26-1   Character Escapes in QUERY_STRING

Code	Character
+	space character
%09	tab
%20	space
%22	"
%23	#
%25	%
%26	&
%28	(
%29	)
%2f	/
%3a	:

Code	Character
%3b	;
%3c	<
%3d	=
%3e	>
%3f	?
%40	@
%5b	[
%5d	]
%5e	^
%60	'
%7b	{
%7c	|
%7d	}
%7e	~

Clearly, the coding of an ASCII character is just a percent sign followed by the hexadecimal number for the character. Thus, creating a reverse mapping is easy.

I've written many CGI programs and have faced the problem of building a CGI environment many times. With Dave Taylor, I wrote a series of routines to build a CGI environment structure. From the programmer's perspective, there are two routines:

```
void build_cgi_env(void);
char *get_value(char *);
```

The `build_cgi_env` routine builds an environment list either from the `QUERY_STRING` or from standard input. These name-value pairs are placed in a linked list. The `get_value` routine returns the value associated with a string.

Underlying the routines is the CGI environment structure. Listing 26-1 is the complete header file, `cgi.h`, that defines the structure.

Listing 26-1: cgi.h

```
static char cgi_h_id[]="$Id: cgi.h,v 1.2 1998/05/24 16:15:59 james Exp
$";

/*
 * $Log: cgi.h,v $
 * Revision 1.2  1998/05/24 16:15:59  james
 * Added RCS Identification Strings for tracking purposes
 *
 *
```

```
*/

struct cgienv {
        char *cgivar;
        char *cgival;
        struct cgienv *next;
        };

void *sbbs_malloc(int);
```

Basically, a single structure with three elements is defined. Two elements are the variable name (cgivar) and the value (cgival). The third is a link to the next item in the list (next). The sbbs_malloc routine is just a wrapper around malloc to catch errors.

The CGI does not need to include cgi.h unless you want to use the sbbs_malloc routine. Early in the program, a call to build_cgi_env must be made. Often, this is one of the first lines in the program.

Build_cgi_env is a fairly complicated program designed to read first the QUERY_STRING and then the input until a query string is found. It is fairly clumsy, but it works. The code follows:

```
#include <stdio.h>
#include <stdlib.h>
#include <string.h>
#include "cgi.h"

static char build_cgi_env_c_id[]="$Id: build_cgi_env.c,v 1.2
1998/05/24 16:15:58 james Exp $";

/*
 * $Log: build_cgi_env.c,v $
 * Revision 1.2  1998/05/24 16:15:58   james
 * Added RCS Identification Strings for tracking purposes
 *
 *
 */

struct cgienv *cgienvlist;
char newch;
```

newch is used as the next character in the parse. It must be declared globally so that the decoding routines can see it.

```
void build_cgi_env(void)
{
char *cp;
int found,cl,unread,bytes_read,retc;
char *start_p,*stop_p,*eqp,*p,*q;
char *tmpvarnam;
char tstring[3];
struct cgienv *cgistep;

cgienvlist=NULL;
```

The program first initializes the environment to have no variables.

```
memset(tstring,0,3);
if (!(((cp=getenv("QUERY_STRING"))!=NULL) && (sbbs_strlen(cp)>2)))
```

The program grabs the QUERY_STRING from the environment. If the QUERY_STRING doesn't exist or if its length is too short, the program assumes the CGI variables are coming from standard input.

```
    {
    if ((cp=getenv("CONTENT_LENGTH"))==NULL)
```

The CONTENT_LENGTH variable is the environment variable set by the server to report how long the query string is.

```
        {
```

If there is an error (No CONTENT_LENGTH), something is wrong. The program reports the error and exits. The html_head routine creates the header, and table_error reports the error on screen.

```
            html_head(1);
            table_error("<h2>Error:  No content length.\nNo
arguments or information to parse.</h2>");
            exit(1);
            }
      cl=atoi(cp);
      cp=(char *)sbbs_malloc(cl+1);
```

The cp variable is the program's content buffer.

```
      unread=cl;
      bytes_read=0;
```

The program uses unbuffered input. Although the program should be able to read the entire quantity in a single read() call, that isn't guaranteed. The program must do as many reads as necessary, so it tracks the number of unread bytes.

```
      while (unread)
            if ((retc=read(0,cp+bytes_read,unread))>=0)
                  {
                  bytes_read+=retc;
                  unread-=retc;
                  }
            else
```

Of course, errors can happen.

```
                  {
                  html_head(1);
                  table_error("<h2>Error: failed reading from
CGI stream</h2>");
                  exit(1);
                  }
      }
cp[cl]='\0'; /* unless your special malloc zeroes */
```

At this stage, the program has built a copy of the query string in memory.

```
start_p=cp;
tmpvarnam=NULL;
do
        {
```

The program's first break is on the ampersands (&). Each ampersand signifies the end of a name-value pair.

```
stop_p=strchr(start_p,'&');
if (stop_p==NULL)
        stop_p=strchr(start_p,'\0');
```

The stop_p marks the end of the string. The last name-value pair does not have an ampersand.

```
eqp=strchr(start_p,'=');
```

Each name-value pair must have an equal sign. If no equal sign is present, the QUERY_STRING is corrupted, and an error must be reported.

```
if (!eqp)
        {
        html_head(1);
        table_error("<h2>Corrupt query string</h2>");
        exit(1);
        }
eqp++;
if (tmpvarnam) free(tmpvarnam);
```

tmpvarname is the area to hold a copy of the variable name.

```
tmpvarnam=sbbs_malloc(eqp-start_p+1);
memset(tmpvarnam,0,eqp-start_p+1);
strncpy(tmpvarnam,start_p,eqp-start_p);
```

The program initializes the value.

```
cgistep=cgienvlist;
found=0;
while (((!found)&&(cgistep))
        if (!strcmp(cgistep->cgivar,tmpvarnam))
                found=1;
        else
                cgistep=cgistep->next;
```

The program searches the list of variables for a copy of this variable. If there are two assignments to the same variable, the program appends subsequent values to the list. This is needed for <input type=checkbox>.

```
if (found)
        {
        cgistep->cgival=realloc(cgistep-
>cgival,sbbs_strlen(cgistep->cgival)+2+stop_p-eqp);
        strcat(cgistep->cgival," ");
```

The program separates each value with spaces. This may lead to problems if values are allowed to have embedded spaces.

```
                for(p=cgistep->cgival+sbbs_strlen(cgistep-
>cgival),q=eqp;q!=stop_p;p++,q++)
                {
                switch (*q)
                    {
                case '&':html_head(1);table_error("<h2>Bad
parse</h2>");exit(1);

                case '+':newch=' ';break;
                case '%':strncpy(tstring,q+1,2);atox(tstring);
                        q+=2; break;
                default        :newch=(*q);
                    }
                if (newch=='`') newch='\'';
                (*p)=newch;
                }
        (*p)=0;
        }
```

This `for` loop may look a little odd. What it does is convert the encoding from CGI to ASCII. Let's take a closer look at the `for` loop:

```
for(p=cgistep->cgival+sbbs_strlen(cgistep->cgival),q=eqp;
```

The character pointers p and q are initialized. The q pointer is the first character after the equal sign, and p is the first new space in the `cgival` string.

```
q!=stop_p;
```

The loop terminates when q reaches `stop_p`.

```
p++,q++)
```

Each step through the loop, the program increments by one character. The body of the loop is a switch statement. If it finds a plus sign (+), it converts it to a space. If it finds an ampersand (&), a parse error occurs. If it finds a percent sign (%), it uses the `atox()` function to convert the next two characters from hex to ASCII. All other characters are copied straight to the string.

```
        else
                {
```

The loop is almost the same for new values. A new structure is added to the list, and then the name is assigned and the value computed.

```
                cgistep=(struct cgienv *) sbbs_malloc(sizeof(struct
cgienv));
                cgistep->next=cgienvlist;
                cgistep->cgivar=sbbs_malloc(sbbs_strlen(tmpvarnam)+1);
                sbbs_strcpy(cgistep->cgivar,tmpvarnam);
                cgistep->cgival=sbbs_malloc(stop_p-eqp+1);
                cgienvlist=cgistep;
```

```
                        for(p=cgistep->cgival,q=eqp;q!=stop_p;p++,q++)
                            {
                            switch (*q)
                                {
                            case '&':html_head(1);table_error("<h2>Bad
parse</h2>");exit(1);
                            case '+':newch=' ';break;
                            case '%':strncpy(tstring,q+1,2);
                                    atox(tstring);
                                    q+=2;
                                    break;
                            default           :newch=(*q);
                                }
                            if (newch=='`') newch='\'';
                            (*p)=newch;
                            }
                        (*p)=0;
                        }
                if (*stop_p) start_p=stop_p+1;
                else start_p=stop_p;
```

After the structure is parsed, the program moves the front of the parser to the end of the name-value pair.

```
                } while (*start_p);
```

The program runs the loop while there is data.

The CGI environment builder sets up the linked list of values. These values are hidden from the programmer and are found by calling get_value(). Get_value looks through the list of CGI variables and returns the value, if found, or NULL if no value is found.

```
#include <stdio.h>
#include "cgi.h"

static char get_value_c_id[]="$Id: get_value.c,v 1.2 1998/05/24
16:15:59 james Exp $";

/*
 * $Log: get_value.c,v $
 * Revision 1.2  1998/05/24 16:15:59   james
 * Added RCS Identification Strings for tracking purposes
 *
 *
 */

extern struct cgienv *cgienvlist;
```

build_cgi_env **builds the** envlist.

```
char * get_value(var)
char *var;
{
struct cgienv *cgistep;
int found;
```

```
cgistep=cgienvlist;
```

The program steps through the linked list until it matches the argument to the variable name.

```
found=0;
while ((!found)&&(cgistep))
        if (!strcmp(var,cgistep->cgivar))
                found=1;
        else
                cgistep=cgistep->next;
```

If it finds the variable name, it returns the value

```
if (found)
        return cgistep->cgival;
return NULL;
}
```

Thus, if you have a <select> such as the preceding one, you need the following code to gather the team name:

```
char *teamname;

build_cgi_env();
teamname=get_value("teams");
```

Now, you can use teamname anywhere in your code.

In addition to the QUERY_STRING and CONTENT_LENGTH variables, several other environment variables are available to the CGI. These are listed in Table 26-2.

Table 26-2 CGI Environment Variables

Variable	Use
AUTH_TYPE	The type of authentication if the script needs authentication.
CONTENT_TYPE	The MIME type of the incoming request (usually application/x-www-form-encoded).
HTTP_REQUEST_METHOD	The method used for the request (usually either GET or POST).
REMOTE_ADDR	The IP address of the requesting system.
REMOTE_HOST	The host name of the requesting system. If Reverse DNS fails, this is the IP address.
REMOTE_USER	The remote user's name if the requesting site is running identd and your server is collecting the data.
SCRIPT_FILENAME	The full path to your script.

Continued

Table 26-2   *(continued)*

Variable	Use
SCRIPT_NAME	The path and name of the CGI program (argv[0] in C and C+).
SERVER_PORT	The port for your server (usually 80).
SERVER_PROTOCOL	The HTTP protocol understood by your server.

You can use environment variables any way you would normally use them.

Story: Perils of Environment Variables

When Dave and I were working at The Internet Mall, we had some problems with our CGI environment processing. Things were working perfectly until Microsoft released Internet Explorer 3.0. Afterward, we sometimes got core dumps in our programs and other times did not.

Our CGI programs used the value of the submit variable to determine actions; this enabled us to have multiple submit buttons for a single form. The problem was that Microsoft's browser enabled you to submit a form by entering a carriage return when in a text input field. At the time, Netscape did not — a carriage return moved you to the next text input. Needless to say, this behavior was not clearly documented anywhere.

Every now and then, we'd get zero content returned to the browser, and we'd find a core dump in the server's CGI directory. We were perplexed.

I added a number of logging statements to the code, and I worked with one of our Windows users to see whether we could duplicate the error. His repeated testing never hit the problem, but we were still getting several reports per day of people hitting this bug. Because we were attempting to build an online commerce product, this bug was very frustrating.

Finally, I duplicated the problem one morning. Our Windows user always used tabs to move from field to field and always used the mouse to click a submit button. I tried using the carriage return to move from field to field and hit the failure.

When a carriage return was used to submit a form, the submit variable was never sent to the server, so build_cgi_env never set it in the CGI variable list. When we requested the value of submit, get_value returned NULL. We had assumed the submit variable was being set because we assumed you had to click a submit button to submit a form. Therefore, we never bothered to check whether the value was non-NULL. Our code usually read as follows:

```
build_cgi_env();
submit=get_value("submit");
if (!strcmp(submit,"Action"))
```

When we did the string comparison, we passed a NULL as the first argument, and this caused a segmentation violation. After discussing some options, we came up with this fix:

```
build_cgi_env();
if (!(submit=get_value("submit")))
     {
     html_head(1);
     table_error("<h2>You have
submitted a form without hitting a
submit button<br>Please go back an
select a submit button</h2>");
     exit(1);
     }
if (!strcmp(submit,"Action"))
```

We later tried to redesign as much as we could to avoid having multiple submit buttons for the same form. In many areas, though, this was difficult or required an awful kludge.

Returning data to the browser

Browsers need to be told the type of data they are receiving so that they can display it properly. Browsers use MIME to define the data types. Web pages are usually `text/html`. Images come across as `image/gif` or `image/jpeg`. Separate MIME types exist for other data types.

The server usually determines the MIME type by examining the file extension. Table 26-3 lists some of the conversions for a standard Apache server.

Table 26-3	Recognized MIME Types
Extension	**MIME Type**
.bin	application/octet-stream
.cpio	application/x-cpio
.dir	application/x-director
.doc	application/msword
.exe	application/octet-stream
.gif	image/gif
.htm	text/html
.html	text/html
.jpe	image/jpeg
.jpeg	image/jpeg
.jpg	image/jpeg
.js	application/x-javascript
.latex	application/x-latex
.man	application/x-troff-man
.mid	audio/midi
.midi	audio/midi
.mov	video/quicktime
.mpeg	video/mpeg
.mpg	video/mpeg
.pdf	application/pdf
.qt	video/quicktime
.ra	audio/x-realaudio
.rtf	application/rtf
.sh	application/x-sh

Continued

Table 26-3   *(continued)*

Extension	MIME Type
.shar	application/x-shar
.t	application/x-troff
.tar	application/x-tar
.tcl	application/x-tcl
.tif	image/tiff
.tiff	image/tiff
.txt	text/plain
.wav	audio/x-wav
.xbm	image/x-xbitmap
.xml	text/xml
.xwd	image/x-xwindowdump
.zip	application/zip

The browser looks at the MIME type and determines the action needed to display the data.

When you have a .cgi program, the server does not know what MIME type to attach to the output. It is the responsibility of the CGI programmer to add a `Content-type:` header to each set of output. This must be the first output of your program and should include a valid MIME type. Usually, this is `text/html`, but some CGIs produce images or other multimedia data. In those cases, the CGI programmer must set the appropriate `Content-type:` header.

The server parses the header and adds a few of its own headers. My Apache server adds these headers:

```
Date: Sat, 23 Jan 1999 17:16:11 GMT
Server: Apache/1.2.6
Connection: close
```

You can add any headers you want. After you complete the headers, you must include two consecutive carriage returns. These separate the document header from the data.

Story: Watch That Suffix!

If you get the file suffix wrong, you may have unexpected results. I once saved a file with .htlm as the suffix. The two figures displayed here show the results. The first shows the file saved with the .htlm extension; the second shows the file with the proper .html extension

```
<html><head><title>Africa Trip Itenerary</title></head>
<body bgcolor=#000000 text=#00ff00>
<center><h1>Africa Trip, 1999</h1><br>
<font size=-1>Pass One, January 22, 1999</font></center>
<pre>

</pre>
<center>
<table cellspacing=2 cellpassing=5 border=2>
<tr><td align=center><b>Day</b></td><td align=center><b>Date</b></td><td align=center><
<tr>
<td>
Tue
</td>
<td>
Sept. 21, 1999
</td>
<td>
CO 4420 SFO->LHR 1630->1030 +1 $922.50 (RT)
</td>
<td>
On flight
</td>
<td>
US
</td>
</tr>
<tr>
<td>
Wed
</td>
<td>
Sept. 22, 1999
</td>
```

Africa Trip, 1999

Pass One, January 22, 1999

Day	Date	Activity	Overnight	
Tue	Sept. 21, 1999	CO 4420 SFO->LHR 1630->1030 +1 $922.50 (RT)	On flight	US
Wed	Sept. 22, 1999	Arrive London, recover	London	UK
Thu	Sept. 23, 1999	Fly to Paris, BM173, 0810->1020 $125.60 LHR->CDG	Paris	UK->FR
Fri	Sept. 24, 1999	Paris->Amsterdam by train	Amsterdam	FR->NL
Sat	Sept. 25, 1999	Fly to Nairobi, KL 565, 1035->2015 $948 (RT) AMS->NBO	Nairobi	NL->KY
Sun	Sept. 26, 1999	Fly to Entebbe, UG 573, 1100->1205, $288 (RT) NBO->EBB	Sheraton Hotel Kampala	KY->UG
Mon	Sept. 27, 1999	Lake Bunyonyi	Far Out Island Camp	UG
Tue	Sept. 28, 1999	Bwindi	Buhoma Luxury Camp	UG

A notable difference created simply by a typo in the filename.

I have a simple routine that prints the header:

```
static char html_head_c_id[]="$Id: html_head.c,v 1.2 1998/05/24
16:16:00 james Exp $";

/*
 * $Log: html_head.c,v $
 * Revision 1.2  1998/05/24 16:16:00  james
 * Added RCS Identification Strings for tracking purposes
 *
 *
 */

void html_head()
{
        static called=0;

        if (called) return;
        called=1;
        printf("Content-type: text/html\n\n");
}
```

I use the static variable to determine whether I have printed the header. This way, I don't end up with an extra copy of the header in the document. The call is `html_head();`.

Cookies

A Web site uses cookies to send identification data to a browser. The browser stores that data and returns it to the server when a page is requested. This data is usually used as a unique identifier, such as a user ID, and may be used to set different levels of access.

Note

I have several cookies. Using UNIX and Netscape, you can examine your cookies by looking at the cookies file in the `.netscape` directory. I won't copy my cookies here, because in many cases, they are encrypted passwords for different levels of access.

I use cookies in several of my CGI applications. I've written the Duke Basketball Report Bulletin Board, which can be found at `http://www.sagarmatha.com/dbrboard/`. To post a message to the bulletin board, you must click one of two buttons: "Queue and Save Name" or "Queue The Post." The only difference between the two is cookies; when you opt to save your name, I send back three cookies to the browser. One holds the posting name, one holds the e-mail address, and one holds the password string. If you've saved your name, those three fields are prefilled for you the next time you post.

Setting cookies is easy. You just include the cookie in the header, as follows:

```
Content-type: text/html
Set-cookie: dbrboard_name=James;PATH=/;EXPIRES=Wednesday 29-SEP-1999
23:58:59 GMT
```

This puts the dbrboard_name cookie in my browser, and it will be delivered until September 29, 1999. You can have multiple Set-cookie lines in a header.

Cookies have three parts: a name=value pair, a path, and an expiration header. If no expiration header is present, the cookie is valid for the browser session only. The PATH determines the URLs that get the cookie sent back.

You need a CGI to understand the cookies, too. Cookies are delivered in the HTTP_COOKIE environment variable; all cookies for the domain are included there. This may require some parsing to get the cookie value.

```
cookie=getenv("HTTP_COOKIE");
if (cookie)
        {
        buffer=(char *)malloc(strlen(cookie)+1);
        strcpy(buffer,cookie);
        p=strstr(buffer,"dbrboard_name");
        if (p)
                {
                q=strchr(p,'=');
                if (q)
                        {
                        if (p=strchr(q,';')) (*p)=0;
                        q++;
                        cookie_name=(char *)malloc(strlen(q)+1);
                        strcpy(cookie_name,q);
                        }
                else
                        {
                        cookie_name=(char *)malloc(1);
                        cookie_name[0]=0;
                        }
                }
        else
                {
                cookie_name=(char *)malloc(1);
                cookie_name[0]=0;
                }
        free(buffer);
        }
}
```

This segment of code shows how I look for the dbrboard_name cookie in the posting program. First, I grab the HTTP_COOKIE from the environment. If it is there, I make a copy of the cookie variable, and I look for the cookie name in the string. If the name is present, I look for the equal sign, which separates the name from the value. Cookies are separated by semicolons (;), so I look for that separator. If this is the last cookie in the list, the separator does not need to be there. I null out the semicolon and advance one character from the equal sign. The variable q now points to the value, so I copy the value to the variable. If any step fails, I set the variable to a zero-length string.

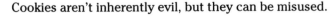 Cookies aren't inherently evil, but they can be misused.

Caution

Besides the Duke BBS system, I use cookies in my sports picking contests. These cookies are used to track user IDs so that an individual can enter picks without needing to log in each time.

Server push

Server push is one means of creating a dynamic document with CGI. (Client pull is another, purely HTML, means of creating a dynamic document.) With server push, a CGI program produces multiple documents, each separated by MIME headers.

The key to a server push is to specify the overall type for the data as `multipart/mixed`. When a multipart header is specified, a boundary must also be specified. This boundary separates the different internal documents.

```
Content-type: multipart/mixed;boundary=---X-X-X---
```

Each document must have its own Content-type header, so you see this in the browser:

```
Content-type: multipart/mixed;boundary=---X-X-X---

---X-X-X---
Content-type: text/html

document

---X-X-X---
Content-type: text/html

document
```

Any number of documents can be included in the multipart document.

Caution

You should include the `sleep` command between each document. The browser displays documents as fast as it receives them, so if no `sleep` is present, the browser user has no time to view the contents of the intermediate documents.

Redirection

The last output header usable in CGI is `Location:`. When this is present, it tells the browser to load a different URL. This is handy when you have moved a Web page. An example is

```
Content-type: text/html
Location:  http://www.jamesarmstrong.com/
```

This tells the browser to load the page `http://www.jamesarmstrong.com/` instead of the requested page.

One neat trick with the `Location:` header is to create a randomizer. If you have a list of Web sites and someone calls your `random.cgi`, it selects one at random and includes it in the header as a `Location:` redirection.

Real-World Examples of CGI

This section contains two examples of CGIs. The first is a series of applications to examine traffic data for a Web site. The second is part of a system of applications in a sports picking contest. To understand fully how these applications are developed, you should first read Chapter 35 to understand the software development process.

Traffic analysis

One of the most common requests from a Web site's owners is to understand the traffic that visits their site — particularly if they are serving ad banners or have other revenue tied to the site. Even without that impetus, owners are usually curious about their site's visitors.

The problem

The problem is fairly simple. Each site has the ability to receive log files; these log files can be in the Common Log Format (CLF). Solving the problem becomes a matter of organizing the files and processing them to get the correct data.

Solution architecture

The architecture for this solution quickly sorted itself out. The log files are just UNIX files. A mechanism was needed to organize the files by day.

We opted to create separate directories called `/log/domain` on a per-site basis. Each hosted domain received its own `access_log`, `referer_log` and `agent_log` files. To store the files on a daily basis, we created directories named after each date: for example, `990101` contained files for January 1, 1999. Because we also wanted to have weekly and monthly reports, we created week ranges. The directory `990103990109` contained the files for the week of January 3, 1999, through January 9, 1999. Last, we created monthly files whose names followed the format `9901` to keep monthly log files.

Chapter 27 outlines in detail the creation of these files.

The next question was what tools to use to parse the files. Although we initially leaned toward C programming because it is faster, a quick analysis of the problem showed that shell scripts were more appropriate. Because the CLF is a well-known format, existing shell tools were more than adequate for the job. Programs such as `awk`, `sed`, and `cut` could handle the parsing, and `sort` could handle output.

Solution design

The design quickly came out. We wanted to show the total traffic to the site (basically a count of the requests and page requests), the most popular sites, the most frequently executed programs, the referring sites, the frequent visitors, and the agents used. Fortunately, these came out of the CLF pretty easily.

Each log entry was a request, so a count of the lines revealed the number of hits on a site. We could grep the file to remove requests for images and come up with a reasonable count of page requests. This was perhaps the most fudging done in the analysis. Our steps to solve this were as follows:

- We looked for .cgi to find the programs and counted them.
- We looked at the first field to see who the visitors were and counted them.
- We looked at the referer_log and agent_log to see those fields.

The next step was to look at the data flow. Because we prefer to have known defaults, we decided the last day's traffic would be the default. We'd place an index.cgi program in a directory to count the previous day's traffic. Because the daily, weekly, and monthly counts would be similar, that would be a single program. We wanted the index page to include links to the last week's and the last month's data and a link to a data archive.

Each log dump would include a listing of requested files, images, CGIs, visitors, and a bar graph of hourly traffic. With the design basics down, we were ready to code.

Solution coding

The first file coded was the actual log dump because this would be common to each formatting. We would pass it an argument, the log directory, and produce pages accordingly. The dumplog.cgi program came out with some basic headers and then a sequence of log file grinding.

```
#!/bin/sh

#
# Traffic Analysis program written by Dave Taylor and made generic by
# James Armstrong.
#
# $Id: dumplog.cgi.sh,v 1.6 1999/01/02 22:42:14 james Exp $
#
# $Log: dumplog.cgi.sh,v $
# Revision 1.6  1999/01/02 22:42:14  james
# Changes; dumplog fixes y1999 problem.
#
# Revision 1.5  1998/11/25 17:36:05  james
# Speed the delivery of pages
#
# Revision 1.4  1998/07/15 02:27:10  james
# Major changes to traffic, including links to complete lists and
```

```
# graphical representations of traffic history.
#
# Revision 1.3  1998/04/26 14:32:12  james
# Minor changes to appearance and layout
#
# Revision 1.2  1998/04/19 21:11:47  james
# Cleaner CGI listings.
# Dynamic width bar graph
#
# Revision 1.1.1.1  1998/04/19 18:05:45  james
# Initial creation of hostname.com traffic management system
#
#
logdir=$1
Host=`pwd | cut -d/ -f4`

logfile=$1/access_log
logyr=`echo $1 |rev | cut -d/ -f1 | rev | cut -c1,2`

if
        [ -f ${logfile}.gz ]
then
        gunzip $logfile > /dev/null 2>&1
        zipped=1
else
        zipped=0
fi
```

This section of the program gets the log directory and prepares the log file. If the file is stored in `gzip` format, the program `gunzips` the file and includes a flag to remind it to zip the file back up when done.

The `logyr` variable determines the year of the log file for later use. The code uses the `rev` command to reverse the character order (for example, `/logs/sagarmatha.com/990101` becomes `101099/moc.ahtamragas/sgol/`) so that the cut gets the last piece of the directory (`101099`). This is reversed (`990101`), and then the first two characters (`99`) are cut.

Note

We wrote the program this way because the site did not have `basename` installed.

```
echo "<font size=5><B>The Most Popular Pages:</B></font>"
echo "<a href=/traffic/longpages.cgi?${logdir}>[All Pages]</a>
```

This sets up the header for the page list. A subsequent addition was `longpages.cgi`, which produces a list of all the pages.

```
echo "<BLOCKQUOTE><PRE>"
awk '{print $7}' $logfile | egrep -vi
'(\.jpg|\.jpeg|\.gif|\.cgi|\.GIF|\.mid)' | \
   sed 's/000/\//;s./$..p;s/~//g' | \
   sort | uniq -c | sort -rn | head -20 | awk '{printf "%7d <a
href=%s>%s</a>\n", $1, $2, $2}'
echo "</BLOCKQUOTE></PRE>"
```

This code is as ugly as it looks. The awk command, print $7, produces a list of the URLs requested from the server. The egrep command removes files with image or CGI suffixes. Sometimes, a browser sends a request for 000 for the home pages, so the program converts this to slashes and removes trailing slashes from directory names.

After the program cleans up the requests, it sorts them. The uniq -c command produces a listing of the number of times each entry was listed. The program then sorts them in reverse numeric order and takes the top 20 for display.

Last, awk makes each listing a link. The input format is

```
Count          URL
```

And the awk command produces

```
Count <a href=URL>URL</a>
```

This way, if a page becomes popular, it can be viewed from this list.

```
echo "<font size=4><b>The Most Popular Images:</b></font"
echo "<Blockquote><pre>"
awk '{print $7}' $logfile | egrep -i '(\.jpg|\.jpeg|\.gif)' | sort |
uniq -c | sort -rn | head -20
echo "</blockquote></pre>"
```

The images are listed similarly, except that links are not created.

```
echo "<font size=4>The Most Popular CGI Scripts:</font>"
echo "<a href=/traffic/longcgi.cgi?${logdir}>[All CGIs]</a>"

echo "<BLOCKQUOTE><PRE>"
awk '{print $7}' $logfile | grep '\.cgi' | cut -d\? -f1 | sort | uniq
-c | sort -rn | \
  sed 's/%3A/:/g;s/%2F/\//g' | head -10
echo "</BLOCKQUOTE></PRE>"
```

CGI requests are also counted, but execution without variables is nonsensical.

```
echo "<font size=4>Most Common Visitors by Machine</font>"
echo "<a href=/traffic/longvisit.cgi?${logdir}>[All Visitors]</a>"

echo "<BLOCKQUOTE><PRE>"
awk '{print $1}' $logfile | grep -v $Host | sort | uniq -c | sort -rn
| head -10
echo "</BLOCKQUOTE></PRE>"
```

For the visitors count, we wanted to see how often a remote site made requests of the server. The first entry in the logfile is the requesting domain or IP address. The program grabs it, eliminates the site's own requests, and performs a sort/uniq/sort to get the top ten.

```
echo "<font size=4>The Most Common Top-Level Domains</font>"
echo "<a href=/traffic/longtop.cgi?${logdir}>[All Top-level
Domains]</a>"

echo "<BLOCKQUOTE><PRE>"
awk '{print $1}' $logfile | grep -v 'hostname.com' | rev | \
   awk -F. '{ print $1 }' | rev | grep -v '[0-9]' | \
   sort | uniq -c | sort -rn | head -10
echo "</BLOCKQUOTE></PRE>"

echo "<font size=4>The Most Common Second-Level Domains</font>"
echo "<a href=/traffic/longsecond.cgi?${logdir}>[All Second-level
Domains]</a>"

echo "<BLOCKQUOTE><PRE>"
awk '{print $1}' $logfile | grep -v 'hostname.com' | rev | \
   awk -F. '{ print $1"."$2 }' | rev | grep -v '[0-9]' | \
   sort | uniq -c | sort -rn | head -20
echo "</BLOCKQUOTE></PRE>"
```

Top and second level domains are similar requests; the program performs a reverse on the name, removes the last or second-to-last dotted element, rereverses, eliminates IP addresses, and does the sort.

```
maxhits=100
for time in 01 02 03 04 05 06 07 08 09 10 11 12 13 14 15 16 17 18 19
20 21 22 23 00
do
  hits="`grep 19${logyr}:$time $logfile | wc -l`"
  if
        [ "$hits" -gt "$maxhits" ]
  then
        maxhits=$hits
  fi
done
```

The traffic bar graph is interesting. To set a maximum number of hits in a given hour, we used a range.

```
if
        [ "$maxhits" -gt 0 ]
then
        echo "<font size=4>Traffic by time of day:</font>"
        echo "<BLOCKQUOTE>"
        echo "<center>"
        echo "<table border=0 cellpadding=0 cellspacing=0>"
        echo
"<tr><td><b>Hour </b></td><td><b>Hits</b></td><td> </td></tr
>"
```

```
divfactor=1
mulfactor=1
if
        [ "$maxhits" -gt 500 ]
then
        divfactor=`expr $maxhits / 500`
        divfactor=`expr $divfactor + 1`
fi
if
        [ "$maxhits" -le 250 ]
then
        mulfactor=`expr 500 / $maxhits`
fi
```

If there are no hits, the graph makes no sense. If the hits exist, the program establishes scaling factors for the bar graph.

```
for time in 00 01 02 03 04 05 06 07 08 09 10 11 12 13 14 15 16 17 18
19 20 21 22 23
        do
                hits="`grep 19${logyr}:$time $logfile | wc -l`"
                #echo -n "<TR HEIGHT=20><TD width=30 height=20
align=left>"
                echo -n "<TR><td align=right>$time </td><TD
align=right>$hits </td><TD align=left>"
                hits=`expr $hits \* $mulfactor`
                hits=`expr $hits / $divfactor`
                /bin/echo -n "<img src=bar.gif width=$hits height=20
vspace=1 alt=\"---\">"
                echo "</TD></TR>"
```

The graph is a single image, extended to a width calculated from the number of hits and the scaling factors.

```
done
        echo "</table>"
```

The bar graph itself is organized into a table to establish the layout on the screen.

```
        echo "</center>"
        echo "</BLOCKQUOTE>"
fi
gzip $logfile > /dev/null 2>&1
```

The program is finished with the access log, so it zips the file up.

```
logfile=$logdir/agent_log

gunzip $logfile > /dev/null 2>&1

echo "<font size=4>Most common browsers:</font>"
echo "<a href=/traffic/longbrowsers.cgi?${logdir}>[All Browsers]</a>"
echo "<blockquote><pre>"
```

```
sort $logfile | uniq -c | sort -rn | head -10

gzip $logfile > /dev/null 2>&1
```

The program presents the agent log data in a similar fashion. The `awk` command is not needed because the log is just a list of agents.

```
logfile=$logdir/referer_log

if
        [ X$zipped = X1 ]
then
        gunzip $logfile > /dev/null 2>&1
fi

echo "</blockquote></pre>"

echo "<font size=4>Your most useful links:</font>"
echo "<a href=/traffic/longlinks.cgi?${logdir}>[All Links]</a>"
echo "<blockquote><pre>"

grep -v $Host $logfile | sort | uniq -c | sort -rn | head -10 | awk
'{printf "%7d <a href=%s>%s</a> %s %s\n", $1, $2, $2, $3, $4}'
gzip $logfile > /dev/null 2>&1
echo "</blockquote></pre>"
```

We did a little more to the `referer` file. We didn't care to see how often the site referred to itself; instead, we found the external references interesting.

```
echo "<HR SIZE=1>"
echo "<P>"
```

`Dumplog` is the heart of the code. Next, we set up the `index.cgi` to get the default when someone accesses the directory.

```
#!/bin/sh

#
#   simple traffic analysis routines...
#
# Traffic Analysis program written by Dave Taylor and made generic by
# James Armstrong.
#
# $Id: index.cgi.sh,v 1.5 1999/01/11 18:54:12 james Exp $
#
# $Log: index.cgi.sh,v $
# Revision 1.5  1999/01/11 18:54:12  james
# Change the copyright year
#
# Revision 1.4  1998/07/22 16:36:28  james
# Creating the output for day, week, and month caused the load time of
# the page to be unacceptable.  Instead, the default is now to load
# only the previous day's data, and the links at the top will get the
```

```
# previous week's and previous month's data.
#
# Revision 1.3   1998/07/15 02:27:10   james
# Major changes to traffic, including links to complete lists and
# graphical representations of traffic history.
#
# Revision 1.2   1998/06/27 22:34:13   james
# Make entries more generic.
#
# Revision 1.1.1.1  1998/04/19 18:05:45   james
# Initial creation of hostname.com traffic management system
#
#

Host=`pwd | cut -d/ -f4`
```

The program determines the host from the current working directory and uses `cut` to pull it out.

```
yesterday=`/web/bin/traffic/yesterday`
```

The program gets yesterday's date in the desired format from the `yesterday` program.

```
logdir=/log/${Host}/${yesterday}
```

It creates the log directory for later use.

```
if
        [ -f Sitename ]
then
        Site=`cat Sitename`
else
        Site="This Site"
fi
```

The program gets a text string for the site name from the file `Sitename`.

```
echo "Content-type: text/html"
echo ""
```

The standard content header is displayed.

```
echo "<HTML><HEAD><TITLE>Traffic Data for $Site"
echo "</TITLE></HEAD><BODY BGCOLOR=#FFFFFF>"
```

The file headers are displayed.

```
echo "<CENTER>"
echo "<h1>Latest Traffic Data for $Site</h1>"
echo "<h2>"
yr=`echo $yesterday | cut -c1-2`
mn=`echo $yesterday | cut -c3-4`
dt=`echo $yesterday | cut -c5-6`
echo "Data for $mn/$dt/$yr"
echo "</h2>"
```

The program uses cut on the yesterday variable to get the date.

```
echo "<HR WIDTH=80% HEIGHT=1>"

./transfer.cgi $logdir
```

The transfer.cgi program builds the header for the data.

```
curdir=`pwd`
cd $logdir
cd ..
weekcnt=`\ls -1 |grep '^............$' | wc -l`
moncnt=`\ls -1 |grep '^....$' | wc -l`

if
        [ "$weekcnt" -gt 0 ]
then
        lastweek=`ls -1 | grep '^............$' | tail -1`
        echo "<p><a href=/traffic/showweek.cgi?${lastweek}>[last
week's data]</a>"
fi
```

This creates the link to last week's data.

```
if
        [ "$moncnt" -gt 0 ]
then
        lastmon=`ls -1 | grep '^....$' | tail -1`
        echo "<p><a href=/traffic/showmon.cgi?${lastmon}>[last month's
data]</a>"
fi
```

This creates the link to last month's data.

```
cd $curdir

echo "</font>"
echo "<P>"
echo "<a href=history.cgi>[historical information]</a>"
```

The history.cgi program builds a listing of all available data.

```
echo "<P>"
echo "<a href=graph.cgi>[graphical display]</a>"
```

The graph.cgi program provides a graphical display of traffic.

```
echo "</CENTER>"
echo "<HR>"

./dumplog.cgi $logdir
```

The dumplog program appears at the beginning of this section, "Solution coding."

```
echo "<CENTER>"
echo "<h3>&copy; `date '+%Y'`, $Site</h3>"
echo "<font size=2>all rights reserved: this information is
confidential</font>"
echo "</BODY>"
echo "</HTML>"

exit 0
```

The program ends with a footer. The index is pretty basic, setting up the calls to the requisite functions.

Yesterday.c is a C program that provides yesterday's date. It is trivial and not illustrated here. The transfer.cgi program is more interesting. It provides the summary of the transferred data.

```
#!/bin/sh

#
# Traffic Analysis program written by Dave Taylor and made generic by
# James Armstrong.
#
# $Id: transfer.cgi.sh,v 1.6 1998/11/25 18:48:14 james Exp $
#
# $Log: transfer.cgi.sh,v $
# Revision 1.6  1998/11/25 18:48:14  james
# An even better count
#
# Revision 1.5  1998/11/25 17:36:24  james
# A better estimate of impressions.
#
# Revision 1.4  1998/10/31 13:00:34  james
# Kevin's web site had some unusual hostnames passed in.
#
# Revision 1.3  1998/07/22 21:27:52  james
# Cleaned up the naming of awk scripts and included them in the
# Makefile and release build.
#
# Revision 1.2  1998/06/27 22:34:13  james
# Make entries more generic.
#
# Revision 1.1.1.1  1998/04/19 18:05:45  james
# Initial creation of hostname.com traffic management system
#
#
logfile=$1/access_log

if
        [ -f ${logfile}.gz ]
then
```

```
        gunzip $logfile > /dev/null 2>&1
        zipped=1
else
        zipped=0
fi*
```

First, the program prepares the log file.

```
total="`wc -l < $logfile`"
```

The wc program provides a count of the lines in the log file, which is also a count of the hits.

```
echo "<b>$total</b> hits, <b>"
# egrep 'txt|htm|cgi' $logfile | grep -v Count.cgi | wc -l
awk '{print $7}' $logfile | egrep -vi
'(\.jpg|\.jpeg|\.gif|\.GIF|\.mid)' | wc -l
echo "</b> impressions, and <b>"
```

The awk command gets the requested URLs; egrep filters out the nonpage requests; and then wc counts them. This provides a count of presented pages.

```
awk -f /web/bin/traffic/script1.awk $logfile
```

The awk script provides a count of the number of transferred bytes. On some sites, this is much larger than MAXINT.

```
echo "</b>"
echo "bytes transfered "
echo "for <b>"
awk '{print $1}' $logfile | sort -u | wc -l
echo "</b> unique IP addresses."
```

The count of unique IP addresses gives a rough estimate of the number of individuals who have visited your site.

```
if
        [ X$zipped = X1 ]
then
        gzip $logfile > /dev/null 2>&1
fi
```

This repacks the file. Many other auxiliary programs were used to provide other views of the data.

How it looks

As soon as the traffic programs are installed, you can get the traffic data for any site you host. Figure 26-1 shows sagarmatha's traffic data for January 22, 1999.

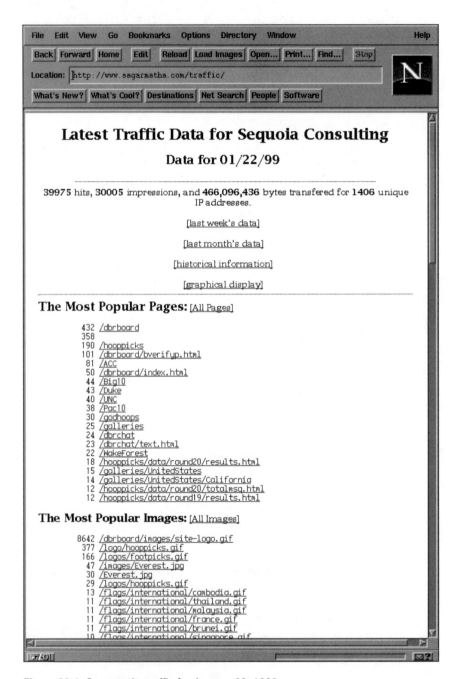

Figure 26-1: Sagarmatha traffic for January 22, 1999

The graph of traffic time shown in Figure 26-2 also looks nice.

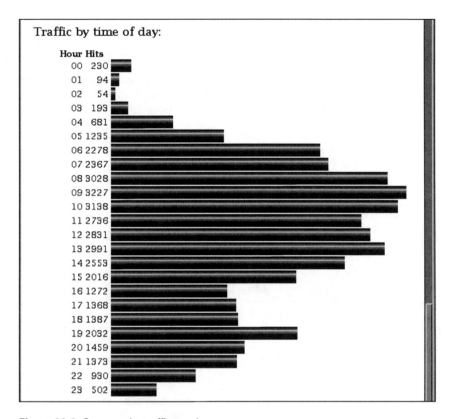

Traffic by time of day:

Hour	Hits
00	230
01	94
02	54
03	193
04	681
05	1235
06	2278
07	2367
08	3028
09	3227
10	3138
11	2736
12	2831
13	2991
14	2553
15	2016
16	1272
17	1368
18	1387
19	2032
20	1459
21	1373
22	930
23	502

Figure 26-2: Sagarmatha traffic graph

Picking contest

Chapter 36 shows the development process to generate the e-mail system for a sports picking contest. Since writing the first edition of *UNIX Secrets,* I have migrated the picking contests to a Web-based interface. Though the whole system is too complex to be described in detail here, I shall illustrate the use of cookies more clearly with the login and registration processes.

The problem

To run the picking contest properly, I wanted each picker to have a unique ID and to make his or her access to the system as seamless as possible.

Solution architecture

You might think the architecture was resolved in the design of the e-mail system, but some fundamental changes were necessary. One big change was a move away from a monolithic aggregate file. Instead, I opted to use the file system to organize my data. Under the data directory, there would be a registrants directory containing one file per registration. This would make it easy to change registrations directly, if needed.

Another big change was how results were made available. With the e-mail version, results were mailed to contestants. This would not work well with the Web version; instead, I created Web pages for the contestants to visit.

Therefore, the back end changed a bit. Registration and pick entry had to be entirely revamped. I handled result generation in a similar fashion, but instead of sending the results to a mail program, I wrote them to a file with appropriate HTML.

The registration and login system seemed ideal for cookies. I also decided to use C as the programming language.

Solution design

I had to design the technique for storing a registration. Each registrant needed the same information collected for the e-mail system, plus a few more fields. Table 26-4 lists the registrant fields.

Table 26-4   Registrant Data Fields

Field	Type	Count	Description
given	char	256	Contestant's first name
surname	char	256	Contestant's surname
email	char	256	Contestant's e-mail address
alias	char	256	Contestant's alias (the name that appears in the contest)
password	char	256	Contestant's encrypted password
wins	int	1	Total wins
losses	int	1	Total losses
winvsspread	int	1	Wins against the spread (football)
lossvsspread	int	1	Losses against the spread (football)
tievsspread	int	1	Ties against the spread (football)
sendresults	int	1	Flag to send mail to the contestant when results are entered
sendnotice	int	1	Flag to send mail to the contestant when new rounds are entered
sendlate	int	1	Flag to send mail to the contestant when entries are due
sendstory	int	1	Flag to send mail to the contestant when I produce news
square	int	1	Sum of squares of results (basketball)

Solution coding

As soon as I decided what data to include, writing four programs was a simple matter. The first program would present a registration form, the second would register a new user, the third would log in a new user via a cookie, and the fourth would register a new user with password verification.

Registration input form

The registration form program is simple; it just produces the HTML needed for a registration form. Listing 26-2 is the source code. Some files are not illustrated here. Custom.h is a custom header for the program, html_title is a function to print out a title to a Web page, and addlogo provides a standard header to each page.

Listing 26-2: Registration Input Form

```
#include <stdio.h>
#include "custom.h"

main()
{
html_head();
html_title("Registration");
addlogo();
printf("You must register before entering the picking contest.\n");
printf("Your first and last names are required, as is a password.\n");
printf("All other fields are optional.\n");
printf("<p>If you accept cookies, and use the same browser from
the\n");
printf("same machine, you should never need to log in to make
your\n");
printf("picks.\n");
printf("<p><center><form action=registerme.cgi method=post>\n");
printf("<input type=hidden name=change value=0>\n");
printf("<table border=0 cellspacing=0 cellpadding=10
bgcolor=#bbbbff>\n");
printf("<tr><td>\n");
printf("<table border=0 cellspacing=0 cellpadding=5
bgcolor=#bbbbff>\n");
printf("<tr><td align=right>First Name:</td>\n");
printf("<td align=left><input type=text name=given
size=20></td></tr>\n");
printf("<tr><td align=right>Last Name:</td>\n");
printf("<td align=left><input type=text name=surname
size=20></td></tr>\n");
printf("<tr><td align=right>Desired Alias:</td>\n");
printf("<td align=left><input type=text name=alias
size=20></td></tr>\n");
printf("<tr><td align=right>E-mail Address:</td>\n");
printf("<td align=left><input type=text name=email
size=20></td></tr>\n");
```

```
printf("<tr><td align=center><input type=checkbox name=sendr
value=yes></td>\n");
printf("<td align=left>Send notice when results are
entered?</td></tr>\n");
printf("<tr><td align=center><input type=checkbox name=sendn
value=yes></td>\n");
printf("<td align=left>Send notice when new rounds are
entered?</td></tr>\n");
printf("<tr><td align=center><input type=checkbox name=sendl
value=yes></td>\n");
printf("<td align=left>Send notice if a round is about to
close?</td></tr>\n");
printf("<tr><td align=center><input type=checkbox name=sends
value=yes></td>\n");
printf("<td align=left>Send pick descriptions and news?</td></tr>\n");
printf("<tr><td align=right>Password:</td>\n");
printf("<td align=left><input type=password name=pw1
size=20></td></tr>\n");
printf("<tr><td align=right>Repeat Password:</td>\n");
printf("<td align=left><input type=password name=pw2
size=20></td></tr>\n");
printf("<tr><td align=center colspan=2>\n");
printf("<input type=submit value=\"Register Me\">\n");
printf("</td></tr></table>\n");
printf("</td></tr></table>\n");
printf("</form>\n");
printf("<p><form method=post action=%s/bin/reloc.cgi>\n",BASEDIR);
printf("<input type=hidden name=dest
value=http://www.sagarmatha.com%s/>\n",BASEDIR);
printf("<input type=submit value=\"Home Page\">\n");
printf("</form></center>\n");
addfooter();
html_end();
exit(0);
}
```

Figure 26-3 shows the form generated by Listing 26-2.

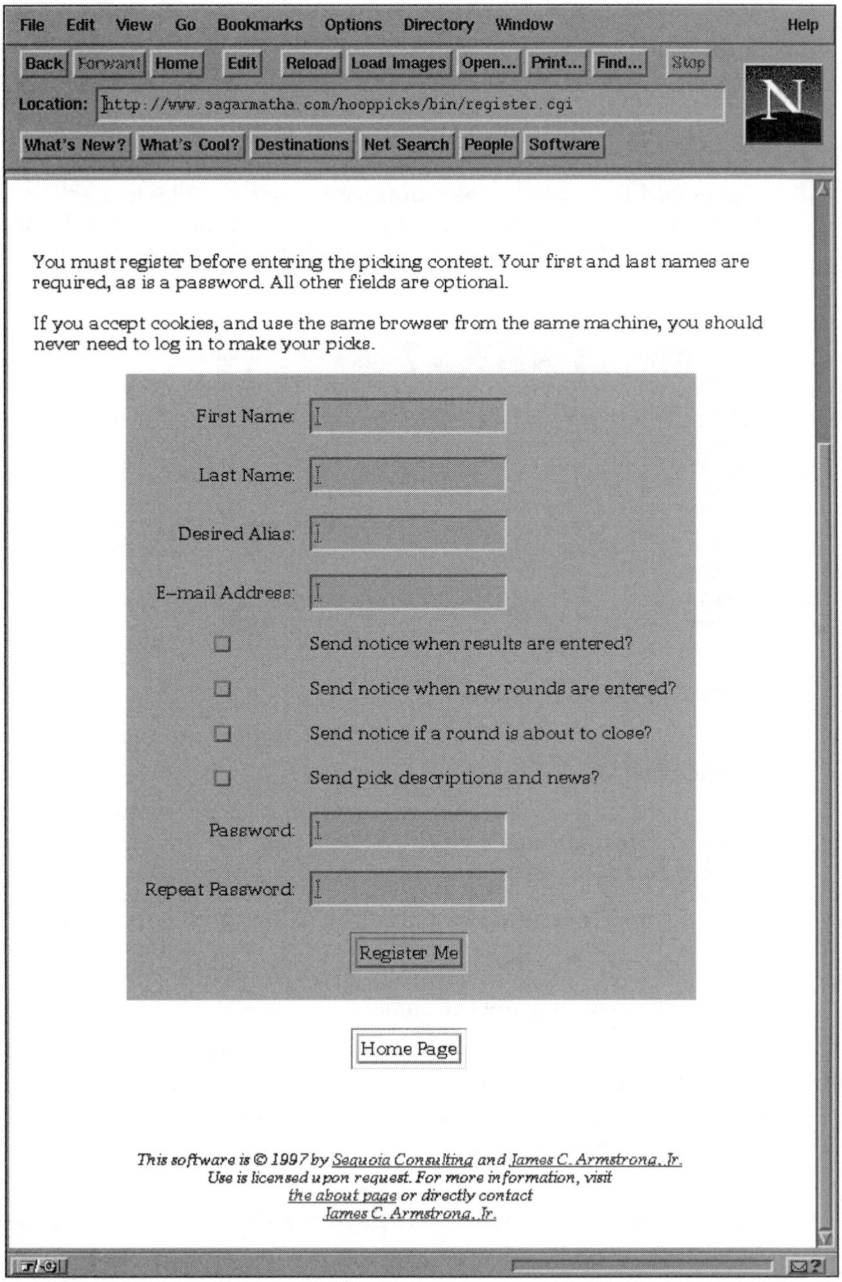

File   Edit   View   Go   Bookmarks   Options   Directory   Window   Help

Back Forward Home   Edit   Reload Load Images Open... Print... Find...   Stop

Location: http://www.sagarmatha.com/hooppicks/bin/register.cgi

What's New? What's Cool? Destinations Net Search People Software

You must register before entering the picking contest. Your first and last names are required, as is a password. All other fields are optional.

If you accept cookies, and use the same browser from the same machine, you should never need to log in to make your picks.

First Name:

Last Name:

Desired Alias:

E-mail Address:

☐   Send notice when results are entered?

☐   Send notice when new rounds are entered?

☐   Send notice if a round is about to close?

☐   Send pick descriptions and news?

Password:

Repeat Password:

Register Me

Home Page

This software is © 1997 by Sequoia Consulting and James C. Armstrong, Jr. Use is licensed upon request. For more information, visit the about page or directly contact James C. Armstrong, Jr.

Figure 26-3: The registration form

If everything checks out, the program determines whether this is a new registration or a changed registration. The chg flag is set for changes. If it is a change, the program reads the old data in from the registrant file and updates the fields with the new values. If it is a new registration, the program gets a new sequence number and builds a new registrant. When all is set, the program produces a CGI header, sets a cookie, and writes out the new record. Figure 26-4 shows the cookie notification screen. The last action is to create the Web page inviting the user to enter the picking contest. Figure 26-5 shows that page. Listing 26-3 is the source code for this program. Again, some files, such as picks.h, are not shown here.

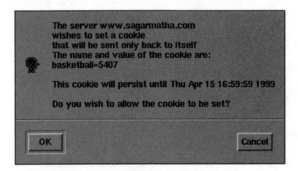

Figure 26-4: Cookie presentation

Registration

When the user completes the registration form generated by Listing 26-2, the system performs some simple verification of the data and then saves it to the file and generates a cookie.

First, the program needs to gather the data from the form with the get_value() calls. It then checks to make certain that all the fields are entered. Every field is required. The two password entry fields are compared to make certain they are the same.

The program checks the field lengths to make certain they are under 250 characters. If everything checks out, the program steps through all the existing registrations. It checks to see whether the selected alias is already in use. If it is, the program flags it.

If an error is found, the program reproduces the registration screen with the user's input. Error messages are flagged so that the user can make the needed changes.

Figure 26-5: Successful registration

Listing 26-3: Pick Entry Program

```c
#include <stdio.h>
#include <sys/types.h>
#include <fcntl.h>
#include <dirent.h>
#include <limits.h>
#include "picks.h"

main()
{
FILE *fpi;
int seqno;
char *given,*surname,*alias,*pw1,*pw2,*email;
char *sendr,*sendn;
char *sendl,*sends;
char *change,*oldid;
int err;
DIR *dp;
struct dirent *entry;
struct regist compar,newmember;
int fd;
int chg;
char filename[PATH_MAX];
char errmess[PATH_MAX];
int tmpwins,tmpwvs,tmplvs,tmptvs,tmpsq,tmplos;

#ifdef DEBUG
html_head();
#endif
build_cgi_env();
given=get_value("given");
surname=get_value("surname");
email=get_value("email");
alias=get_value("alias");
sendr=get_value("sendr");
sendn=get_value("sendn");
sendl=get_value("sendl");
sends=get_value("sends");
pw1=get_value("pw1");
pw2=get_value("pw2");
change=get_value("change");
oldid=get_value("oldid");
chg=atoi(change);
err=0;
if ((!given)||(!strlen(given)))
        {
        err=1;
        html_head();
        html_title("Incorrect registration");
        addlogo();
        table_error("A First Name must be supplied");
        }
```

```
if ((!surname)||(!strlen(surname)))
        {
        err=1;
        html_head();
        html_title("Incorrect registration");
        addlogo();
        table_error("A Last Name must be supplied");
        }
if ((!pw1)||(!strlen(pw1)))
        {
        err=1;
        html_head();
        html_title("Incorrect registration");
        addlogo();
        table_error("A Password must be supplied");
        }
if ((!pw2)||(!strlen(pw2)))
        {
        err=1;
        html_head();
        html_title("Incorrect registration");
        addlogo();
        table_error("A Password must be repeated");
        }
if ((pw2)&&(pw1)&&(strcmp(pw1,pw2)))
        {
        err=1;
        html_head();
        html_title("Incorrect registration");
        addlogo();
        table_error("Passwords must match");
        }
if ((given)&&(strlen(given)>250))
        {
        err=1;
        html_head();
        html_title("Incorrect registration");
        addlogo();
        table_error("Your given name is too long.<br>Please keep it
under 250 characters");
        }
if ((surname)&&(strlen(surname)>250))
        {
        err=1;
        html_head();
        html_title("Incorrect registration");
        addlogo();
        table_error("Your last name is too long.<br>Please keep it
under 250 characters");
        }
if (((!alias)||(!strlen(alias)))&&(given)&&(surname))
        {
```

```
            alias=(char *)malloc(strlen(given)+strlen(surname)+2);
            strcpy(alias,given);
            strcat(alias," ");
            strcat(alias,surname);
            }
if ((alias)&&(strlen(alias)>250))
        {
        err=1;
        html_head();
        html_title("Incorrect registration");
        addlogo();
        table_error("Your alias is too long.<br>Please keep it under
250 characters");
        }
if ((email)&&(strlen(email)>250))
        {
        err=1;
        html_head();
        html_title("Incorrect registration");
        addlogo();
        table_error("Your e-mail address is too long.<br>Please keep
it under 250 characters");
        }
if ((pw1)&&(strlen(pw1)>250))
        {
        err=1;
        html_head();
        html_title("Incorrect registration");
        addlogo();
        table_error("Your password is too long.<br>Please keep it
under 250 characters");
        }
if (!chg)
        {
#ifdef DEBUG
        printf("Before opendir\n");
#endif
        if ((dp=opendir(REG_DIR))==NULL)
                {
                err=1;
                html_head();
                html_title("Incorrect registration");
                addlogo();
                table_error("System Error:  Unable to open the
registrants directory.");
                }
        else
                {
#ifdef DEBUG
                printf("Before readdir loop\n");
#endif
                while (entry=readdir(dp))
```

```
                              {
                              if (!strcmp(entry->d_name,".")) continue;
                              if (!strcmp(entry->d_name,"..")) continue;
#ifdef DEBUG
                              printf("Looking at %s\n",entry->d_name);
#endif
                              sprintf(filename,"%s/%s",REG_DIR,entry-
>d_name);
                              if ((fd=open(filename,O_RDONLY,0))<0)
                                   {
                                   err=1;
                                   html_head();
                                   html_title("Incorrect registration");
                                   addlogo();
                                   table_error("System Error:  Unable to
open a registrant file.");
                                   }
                              if (read(fd,(char *)&compar,sizeof(struct
regist))!=sizeof(struct regist))
                                   {
                                   err=1;
                                   html_head();
                                   html_title("Incorrect registration");
                                   addlogo();
                                   table_error("System Error:  Unable to
read a registrant file.");
                                   }
                              close(fd);
#ifdef DEBUG
                              printf("Comparing &gt;%s&lt; to
&gt;%s&lt;<br>\n",alias,compar.alias);
#endif
                              if (!strcmp(alias,compar.alias))
                                   {
                                   err=1;
                                   html_head();
                                   html_title("Incorrect registration");
                                   addlogo();
                                   sprintf(errmess,"The alias %s is
already in use, please select another",alias);
                                   table_error(errmess);
                                   }
                              }
                    closedir(dp);
                    }
          }
if (err)
      {
      printf("<p><center><form action=registerme.cgi
method=post>\n");
      printf("<input type=hidden name=change value=%s>\n",change);
```

```
        if (chg) printf("<input type=hidden name=oldid
value=%s>\n",oldid);
        printf("<table border=0 cellspacing=0 cellpadding=10
bgcolor=#bbbbff>\n");
        printf("<tr><td>\n");
        printf("<table border=0 cellspacing=0 cellpadding=5
bgcolor=#bbbbff>\n");
        printf("<tr><td align=right>First Name:</td>\n");
        printf("<td align=left><input value=\"%s\" type=text
name=given size=20></td></tr>\n",(given)?given:"");
        printf("<tr><td align=right>Last Name:</td>\n");
        printf("<td align=left><input value=\"%s\" type=text
name=surname size=20></td></tr>\n",(surname)?surname:"");
        printf("<tr><td align=right>Desired Alias:</td>\n");
        printf("<td align=left><input value=\"%s\" type=text
name=alias size=20></td></tr>\n",(alias)?alias:"");
        printf("<tr><td align=right>E-mail Address:</td>\n");
        printf("<td align=left><input value=\"%s\" type=text
name=email size=20></td></tr>\n",(email)?email:"");
        printf("<tr><td align=center><input type=checkbox name=sendr
%s value=yes></td>\n",(sendr)?"checked":"");
        printf("<td align=left>Send notice when results are
entered?</td></tr>\n");
        printf("<tr><td align=center><input type=checkbox name=sendn
%s value=yes></td>\n",(sendn)?"checked":"");
        printf("<td align=left>Send notice when new rounds are
entered?</td></tr>\n");
        printf("<tr><td align=center><input type=checkbox name=sendl
%s value=yes></td>\n",(sendl)?"checked":"");
        printf("<td align=left>Send notice if a round is about to
close?</td></tr>\n");
        printf("<tr><td align=center><input type=checkbox name=sends
%s value=yes></td>\n",(sends)?"checked":"");
        printf("<td align=left>Send pick descriptions and
news?</td></tr>\n");
        printf("<tr><td align=right>Password:</td>\n");
        printf("<td align=left><input type=password name=pw1
size=20></td></tr>\n");
        printf("<tr><td align=right>Repeat Password:</td>\n");
        printf("<td align=left><input type=password name=pw2
size=20></td></tr>\n");
        printf("<tr><td align=center colspan=2>\n");
        printf("<input type=submit value=\"Register Me\">\n");
        printf("</td></tr></table>\n");
        printf("</td></tr></table>\n");
        }
else
        {
        if (chg)
                {
                seqno=atoi(oldid);
                sprintf(filename,"%s/%d",REG_DIR,seqno);
```

```
                    if ((fd=open(filename,O_RDONLY,0))<0)
                            {
                            html_head();
                            html_title("Registration");
                            addlogo();
                            printf("Unable to open old record\n");
                            exit(0);
                            }
                    if (read(fd,(struct regist *)&newmember,sizeof(struct
regist))!=sizeof(struct regist))
                            {
                            html_head();
                            html_title("Registration");
                            addlogo();
                            printf("Unable to read old record\n");
                            exit(0);
                            }
            close(fd);
            tmpwins=newmember.wins;
            tmplos=newmember.losses;
            tmpwvs=newmember.winvsspread;
            tmplvs=newmember.lossvsspread;
            tmptvs=newmember.tievsspread;
            tmpsq=newmember.square;
            }
        else
            {
            if ((fpi=fopen(SEQFILE,"r"))==NULL)
                    {
                    html_head();
                    html_title("Registration");
                    addlogo();
                    table_error("Unable to register
successfully");
                    table_error("No seqfile");
                    exit(0);
                    }
            else
                    {
                    fscanf(fpi,"%d",&seqno);
                    fclose(fpi);
                    seqno++;
                    if ((fpi=fopen(SEQFILE,"w"))==NULL)
                            {
                            html_head();
                            html_title("Registration");
                            addlogo();
                            table_error("Unable to register
successfully");
                            table_error("Unwritable seqfile");
                            exit(0);
                            }
                    else
```

```
                                   {
                                   fprintf(fpi,"%d\n",seqno);
                                   fclose(fpi);
                                   tmpwins=0;
                                   tmpwvs=0;
                                   tmplvs=0;
                                   tmptvs=0;
                                   tmpsq=0;
                                   tmplos=0;
                                   }
                         }
                 }
        printf("Content-type: text/html\n");
        printf("Set-cookie: %s=%d;PATH=/;EXPIRES=Wednesday, 15-Apr-
1999 23:59:59 GMT\n\n",COOKIE,seqno);
        html_title("Registration");
        addlogo();
        strcpy(newmember.given,given);
        strcpy(newmember.surname,surname);
        strcpy(newmember.alias,alias);
        strcpy(newmember.email,email);
        strcpy(newmember.password,encrypt(pw1));
        newmember.wins=tmpwins;
        newmember.winvsspread=tmpwvs;
        newmember.lossvsspread=tmplvs;
        newmember.tievsspread=tmptvs;
        newmember.sendresults=(sendr)?1:0;
        newmember.sendnotice=(sendn)?1:0;
        newmember.sendstory=(sends)?1:0;
        newmember.sendlate=(sendl)?1:0;
        newmember.square=tmpsq;
        newmember.losses=tmplos;
        sprintf(filename,"%s/%d",REG_DIR,seqno);
        if ((fd=open(filename,O_WRONLY|O_CREAT|O_TRUNC,0666))<0)
                {
                table_error("Unable to open new registration");
                }
        else
                {
                if (write(fd,(char *)&newmember,sizeof(struct
regist))!=sizeof(struct regist))
                        {
                        table_error("Unable to write new
registration");
                        }
                close(fd);
                }
#ifdef FOOT
```

```
        printf("Welcome to the Sagarmatha Football Picking
Contest.\n");
#endif
#ifdef HOOP
        printf("Welcome to the Sagarmatha Basketball Picking
Contest.\n");
#endif
        printf("You have been assigned a membership ID of
<b>%d</b>\n",seqno);
        printf("If you use a different browser, different\n");
        printf("machine, or do not accept cookies, \n");
        printf("you will need to remember this ID\n");
        printf("and the password you entered to \n");
        printf("access the membership area.\n");
        printf("<pre>\n\n\n\n</pre>\n");
        printf("<center><table cellpadding=20 border=0
bgcolor=#bbffbb>\n");
        printf("<tr><td>\n");
        printf("<form action=members.cgi method=post>\n");
        printf("<input type=submit value=\"Members Only\">\n");
        printf("</form></td></tr></table>\n");
        printf("</center>\n");
        }
addfooter();
html_end();
exit(0);
}
```

Cookie login

The cookie login is easy. The program checks to see whether the member ID is being passed to the site by a hidden CGI variable. It then checks to see whether the HTTP_COOKIE variable is set; if so, the program extracts the cookie value. It next checks to see whether the cookie value is properly registered.

If this user isn't a member, the program puts up a login screen. This screen prompts the user for her member ID and password. It also provides a means for a user to register. If everything checks out OK, the program produces the membership page shown in Figure 26-6. Listing 26-4 is the source code.

Figure 26-6: Login screen

Listing 26-4: Source code to membership page

```c
#include <stdio.h>
#include <unistd.h>
#include <stdlib.h>
#include <string.h>
#include <limits.h>
#include <errno.h>
#include "picks.h"

main()
{
char *memberno;
char *buffer,*p,*q;
char filename[PATH_MAX];

build_cgi_env();
memberno=get_value("member");
if ((!memberno)&&(getenv("HTTP_COOKIE")))
        {
        buffer=(char *)malloc(strlen(getenv("HTTP_COOKIE"))+1);
        strcpy(buffer,getenv("HTTP_COOKIE"));
        p=strstr(buffer,COOKIE);
        if (p)
                {
                q=strchr(p,'=');
                if (q)
                        {
                        if (p=strchr(q,';')) (*p)=0;
                        q++;
                        memberno=q;
                        }
                }
        }
if (memberno)
        {
        sprintf(filename,"%s/%s",REG_DIR,memberno);
        if (access(filename,F_OK))
                memberno=NULL;
        }
html_head();
if (!memberno)
        {
        html_title("Please Login");
        addlogo();
        printf("We cannot identify you (perhaps you don't accept\n");
        printf("cookies, or perhaps you are not registered.\n");
        printf("Or, perhaps your membership has expired.)\n");
        printf("You can enter by specifying your membership ID\n");
        printf("and password, or by registering.\n");
```

```
        printf("<p><center>\n");
        printf("<form method=post action=verify.cgi>\n");
        printf("<table cellspacing=0 cellpadding=5 border=0
bgcolor=#bbffbb>\n");
        printf("<tr><td align=right>Member ID:</td><td>\n");
        printf("<input type=text size=10 name=memberno></td></tr>\n");
        printf("<tr><td align=right>Password:</td><td>\n");
        printf("<input type=password name=password
size=10></td></tr>\n");
        printf("<tr><td align=center colspan=2>\n");
        printf("<input type=submit value=\"Verify Membership\">\n");
        printf("</td></tr></table></form></center>\n");
        printf("<pre>\n\n\n\n</pre><center>\n");
        printf("<form method=post action=register.cgi>\n");
        printf("<input type=submit value=Register>\n");
        printf("</form></center>\n");
        }
else
        {
        html_title("Members Area");
        addlogo();
        printf("<center><h1>Welcome</h1></center><p>\n");
        printf("This area is accessible only by registered
entrants\n");
        printf("to the Sagarmatha picking contest.\n");
        printf("You can make your picks from here, or modify\n");
        printf("your registration.  Eventually, I plan on\n");
        printf("incorporating the round summaries, and an\n");
        printf("ability for you to examine your previous picks\n");
        printf("to see trends in your picking.\n");
        printf("<p><center>\n");
        printf("<table border=0><tr>\n");
        printf("<td align=center>\n");
        printf("<form method=post
action=%s/bin/newpicks.cgi>\n",BASEDIR);
        printf("<input type=hidden name=id value=%s>\n",memberno);
        printf("<input type=submit value=\"Make Picks\">\n");
        printf("</form>\n");
        printf("</td><td align=center>\n");
        printf("<form method=post
action=%s/bin/dumplist.cgi>\n",BASEDIR);
        printf("<input type=hidden name=id value=%s>\n",memberno);
        printf("<input type=submit value=\"Show Picks\">\n");
        printf("</form>\n");
        printf("</td></tr><tr><td align=center>\n");
        printf("<form method=post
action=%s/bin/pickhist.cgi>\n",BASEDIR);
        printf("<input type=hidden name=id value=%s>\n",memberno);
        printf("<input type=submit value=\"Pick History\">\n");
        printf("</form>\n");
```

```
        printf("</td><td align=center>\n");
        printf("<form method=post
action=%s/bin/login.cgi>\n",BASEDIR);
        printf("<input type=submit value=\"Other Account\">\n");
        printf("</form>\n");
        printf("</td></tr><tr><td align=center>\n");
        printf("<form method=post
action=%s/bin/chregister.cgi>\n",BASEDIR);
        printf("<input type=hidden name=id value=%s>\n",memberno);
        printf("<input type=submit value=\"Change Registration\">\n");
        printf("</form>\n");
        printf("</td><td align=center>\n");
        printf("<form method=post
action=%s/bin/reloc.cgi>\n",BASEDIR);
        printf("<input type=hidden name=dest
value=http://www.sagarmatha.com%s/>\n",BASEDIR);
        printf("<input type=submit value=\"Home Page\">\n");
        printf("</form>\n");
        printf("</td></tr></table>\n");
        printf("</center>\n");
        }
addfooter();
html_end();
exit(0);
}
```

Keyboard login

The login page is even easier than the cookie check. The program doesn't
check the cookie, and it doesn't look for a hidden variable. Instead, it reads
the ID and password from input, encrypts them, and makes a comparison. If
the comparison is successful, the program presents the member screen
(Figure 26-7). If it is not, the program presents the login screen again. Listing
26-5 is the source code.

Listing 26-5: Keyboard Login Program

```
#include <stdio.h>
#include <limits.h>
#include <sys/types.h>
#include <fcntl.h>
#include "picks.h"

main()
{
char filename[PATH_MAX];
char errmess[PATH_MAX];
int err,fd;
struct regist member;
char *memberno;
```

```
build_cgi_env();
sprintf(filename,"%s/%s",REG_DIR,get_value("memberno"));
err=0;
html_head();
if ((fd=open(filename,O_RDONLY))<0)
        {
        err=1;
        sprintf(errmess,"ID not found.");
        }
else
        {
        if (read(fd,(char *)&member,sizeof(struct regist))!=sizeof(struct
regist))
                {
                err=1;
                sprintf(errmess,"Unable to read member file.  ");
                }
        else
                {
                if
(strcmp(encrypt(get_value("password")),member.password))
                        {
                        err=1;
                        sprintf(errmess,"Password does not match.");
                        }
                }
        }
if (err)
        {
        html_title("Please Login");
        addlogo();
        table_error(errmess);
        printf("We cannot identify you (perhaps you don't accept\n");
        printf("cookies, or perhaps you are not registered.\n");
        printf("Or, perhaps your membership has expired.)\n");
        printf("You can enter by specifying your membership ID\n");
        printf("and password, or by registering.\n");
        printf("<p><center>\n");
        printf("<form method=post action=verify.cgi>\n");
        printf("<table cellspacing=0 cellpadding=5 border=0
bgcolor=#bbffbb>\n");
        printf("<tr><td align=right>Member ID:</td><td>\n");
        printf("<input type=text size=10 value=%s
name=memberno></td></tr>\n",get_value("memberno"));
        printf("<tr><td align=right>Password:</td><td>\n");
        printf("<input type=password name=password size=10></td></tr>\n");
        printf("<tr><td align=center colspan=2>\n");
        printf("<input type=submit value=\"Verify Membership\">\n");
        printf("</td></tr></table></form></center>\n");
        printf("<pre>\n\n\n\n</pre><center>\n");
        printf("<form method=post action=register.cgi>\n");
        printf("<input type=submit value=Register>\n");
        printf("</form></center>\n");
```

```
            }
    else
            {
            html_title("Members Area");
            addlogo();
            printf("<center><h1>Welcome</h1></center><p>\n");
            printf("This area is accessible only by registered entrants\n");
            printf("to the Sagarmatha picking contest.\n");
            printf("You can make your picks from here, or modify\n");
            printf("your registration.  Eventually, I plan on\n");
            printf("incorporating the round summaries, and an\n");
            printf("ability for you to examine your previous picks\n");
            printf("to see trends in your picking.\n");
            printf("<p><center>\n");
            printf("<table border=0><tr>\n");
            printf("<td align=center>\n");
            printf("<form method=post action=%s/bin/newpicks.cgi>\n",BASEDIR);
            memberno=get_value("memberno");
            printf("<input type=hidden name=id value=%s>\n",memberno);
            printf("<input type=submit value=\"Make Picks\">\n");
            printf("</form>\n");
            printf("</td><td align=center>\n");
            printf("<form method=post action=%s/bin/dumplist.cgi>\n",BASEDIR);
            printf("<input type=hidden name=id value=%s>\n",memberno);
            printf("<input type=submit value=\"Show Picks\">\n");
            printf("</form>\n");
            printf("</td></tr><tr><td align=center>\n");
            printf("<form method=post action=%s/bin/pickhist.cgi>\n",BASEDIR);
            printf("<input type=hidden name=id value=%s>\n",memberno);
            printf("<input type=submit value=\"Pick History\">\n");
            printf("</form>\n");
            printf("</td><td align=center>\n");
            printf("<form method=post action=%s/bin/login.cgi>\n",BASEDIR);
            printf("<input type=submit value=\"Other Account\">\n");
            printf("</form>\n");
            printf("</td></tr><tr><td align=center>\n");
            printf("<form method=post
    action=%s/bin/chregister.cgi>\n",BASEDIR);
            printf("<input type=hidden name=id value=%s>\n",memberno);
            printf("<input type=submit value=\"Change Registration\">\n");
            printf("</form>\n");
            printf("</td><td align=center>\n");
            printf("<form method=post action=%s/bin/reloc.cgi>\n",BASEDIR);
            printf("<input type=hidden name=dest
    value=http://www.sagarmatha.com%s/>\n",BASEDIR);
            printf("<input type=submit value=\"Home Page\">\n");
            printf("</form>\n");
            printf("</td></tr></table>\n");
            printf("</center>\n");
            }
    addfooter();
    html_end();
    exit(0);
    }
```

Figure 26-7: Successful login

Results

The pages produced are illustrated in Figures 26-3 through 26-7.

Debugging CGI

Unfortunately, CGI debugging isn't easy. Normally, you just run your program in a debugger or examine the core file with a debugger to find out what failed. With a CGI program, this is difficult. I use two approaches to debugging CGIs.

The first is to print out debug files. Often, I print reams of data in debug files to see what is happening. This includes dumps of the CGI environment variables, the arguments to functions, and the like. Always, I remember to call `fflush` after each print; that ensures the data is printed to the file before a core dump.

The second is to use a debugger. To do this, I need to set up the environment variables. I set the `CONTENT_LENGTH`, `HTTP_COOKIE`, and `QUERY_STRING`. I use the first method to print out these values before execution.

Summary

This chapter examined some basic CGI applications and showed you

▶ What a CGI is

▶ How to get variables from the CGI environment

▶ How to return documents

▶ How to send server push documents

▶ How to use cookies

▶ How to perform redirection

The next chapter wraps up the discussion of Internet functionality.

Chapter 27

Getting the Most from the Internet

In This Chapter

▶ Integrating UNIX tools with the Internet

▶ Using finger to get data

▶ Combining Lynx and text manipulation to generate mail

▶ Managing server log files

As soon as you've learned how to use the Internet, you can integrate its use into your daily work routine. No, this chapter isn't about how to surf; it's about how to integrate the Internet applications with other UNIX tools to increase your productivity. This chapter introduces two programs that integrate Internet applications with other UNIX applications.

Combining Tools

As previously described, the magic of UNIX is its capability to combine tools to generate more powerful commands. You can easily integrate any command to access or use the Internet with other UNIX commands.

An interesting example is the finger command. finger enables you to see the state of another user on another machine. The USGS has a slightly modified finger command that gives a report on earthquakes. Access the account quake on andreas.wr.usgs.gov to get a listing of the latest earthquakes in northern California, as shown in Listing 27-1.

Listing 27-1: Earthquake Data

```
$ finger quake@andreas.wr.usgs.gov
[andreas.wr.usgs.gov]
Login name: weekly                          In real life: USGS N. Cal. Quake
Report
Directory: /we/weekly                    Shell: /bin/csh
Last login Thu Dec 31 13:13 on ttyp4 from garlock
```

New mail received Thu Jan 28 13:19:44 1999;
  unread since Wed Sep 30 15:39:48 1998
No Plan.

Login name: quake   In real life: Recent Preliminary
Earthquake Info
Directory: /seis/quake   Shell: /bin/csh
Last login Tue Feb 17, 1998 on ttyp3 from kapulu.wr.usgs.g
No unread mail
Plan:
                        RAPID EARTHQUAKE LOCATION SERVICE
                U.S. Geological Survey, Menlo Park, California.
           U.C. Berkeley Seismological Laboratory, Berkeley, California.
              (members of the Council of the National Seismic System)

Below is a list of magnitude 2 or greater earthquakes recorded by the
USGS Northern California Seismic Network and the UCB Berkeley Digital
Seismic Network during the last 3 days. All times are in UT (ie.,
Greenwich Mean Time). This is 8 hours ahead of PST or 7 hours ahead of
PDT. This catalog is valid for Central and Northern California
(approximately north of San Luis Obispo along the coast and 37 degrees
N at the Nevada border).

Magnitudes are reported as local magnitude (Ml) or coda duration
magnitude (Md) for small events. Depth is in kilometers. Q is
location quality, where the quality of the location solution is
A-D (A=good, D=bad), and `*´ indicates the solution is from an
automated system and has not been reviewed by staff.

Note: This is PRELIMINARY information. Earthquakes before 00:00 UT
today which occur > ~50 km outside the boundaries of the network will
not be listed unless reviewed by seismologists.

Similar catalog information is available via finger quake@ these machines:
geophys.washington.edu, fm.gi.alaska.edu, eas.eas.slu.edu, gldfs.cr.usgs.gov,
seismo.unr.edu, eqinfo.seis.utah.edu, scec.caltech.edu, tako.wr.usgs.gov,
seismo.berkeley.edu

WWW access: for these lists, maps, and more go to http://quake.usgs.gov

Updated at Thu Jan 28 22:22:08 GMT 1999 a.k.a. Thu Jan 28 14:22:08 PST 1999
****

```
DATE-(UTC)-TIME   LAT    LON     DEP   MAG  Q   COMMENTS
yy/mm/dd hh:mm:ss deg.   deg.    km
----------------------------------------
99/01/26 06:02:42 37.92N 122.29W 4.0  2.0MD  A*   3 mi NNW of Berkeley, CA
99/01/26 07:46:04 38.83N 122.80W 1.3  2.2MD  A*   2 mi N   of The Geysers, CA
99/01/26 09:01:50 38.82N 122.78W 1.4  2.7MD  A*   2 mi NE  of The Geysers, CA
99/01/26 16:23:50 37.52N 118.81W 4.8  2.2MD  B*   8 mi WSW of Toms Place, CA
99/01/27 02:31:30 38.81N 122.81W 1.4  2.1MD  A*   1 mi N   of The Geysers, CA
99/01/27 03:58:42 37.25N 121.64W 6.3  3.8Ml  B*   9 mi N   of Morgan Hill, CA
```

```
99/01/27 12:42:02  37.61N 118.86W   5.3 2.4MD  B*   7 mi ESE of Mammoth Lakes,
CA
99/01/28 06:33:18  38.89N 123.01W   0.0 2.4MD  B*   6 mi N   of Cloverdale, CA
99/01/28 10:50:34  40.54N 123.85W  20.7 2.5MD  A*  13 mi E   of Hydesville, CA
99/01/28 10:52:15  40.54N 123.85W  21.9 2.2MD  B*  13 mi E   of Hydesville, CA
99/01/28 16:43:59  38.89N 123.00W   0.7 2.1MD  B*   6 mi N   of Cloverdale, CA
99/01/28 21:54:30  40.43N 122.07W  15.7 2.3MD  B*  11 mi ENE of Cottonwood, CA

Login name: help                        In real life: quake info
Directory: /we/system/help              Shell: /bin/csh
Never logged in.
Unread mail since Thu Nov 30 14:57:30 1995
No Plan.
```

Northern California is seismically active; as you can see, five small earthquakes occurred on January 28 alone.

You can generate your own finger information files simply by creating a .plan file in your home directory. If your site enables finger access, that file is reported. You can also write a cron job to update the .plan file regularly.

Using the Web with Shell Programs

This section contains two examples of programs that use the Web: my program to generate weather reports for an upcoming vacation and a program to manipulate Web server log files.

Receiving weather forecasts by e-mail

Sometime in the next year, I hope to take a vacation to Africa. Should I take this trip, it would be nice to be aware of the weather so that I know what to pack. Several sites on the Web provide good weather forecasts. I suppose I could visit them each day, but sometimes I might be too busy, or the site might be down when I try. The logical solution is to write a program that surfs the site for me, gathers the data, and sends me a report via e-mail.

I spent some time looking for the right location. Initially, I used a gopher server, but that is now obsolete. I have used different Web sites, including usatoday.com and weather.com. I've found excite.com's weather site the most reliable when I send my requests.

The weather program uses Lynx to get the forecast. Because each city has its own forecast page, I need to fetch each page and parse it. Parsing the HTML source code turns out to be easier than parsing the output. Unfortunately, the Web site is not always up, so sometimes the results are erroneous. The awkittrip.awk file is a simple awk script that formats the output. Listing 27-2 shows my weather report's source code.

Listing 27-2: Weather Forecast Mailer

```
#!/bin/sh
#
# $Id: tripweather.sh,v 1.9 1998/12/14 16:27:46 james Exp $
#
# Tripweather is essentially the same as forecaster, except this collects
# data for South America.
#
cd /home/james/frio/.data
cp default/trip .
sed -e `/^#/d´ trip | cut -d: -f1 > cities
sed -e `/^#/d´ trip | cut -d: -f2 > publish
rm trip
maxcit=`cat cities| wc -l`
current=0
rm -f /home/james/frio/.tmp/awkdata2.jca
rm -f /home/james/frio/.tmp/awkdata.jca
#
# Here, I've set up the environment.  The trip file is a listing of
# URL segments and city names, for the output.
#
BASEURL=http://www.excite.com/weather/forecast/city
export BASEURL
while
        [ $current -lt $maxcit ]
do
        current=`expr "$current" + 1`
        city=`tail +$current cities | sed 1q`
        publish=`tail +$current publish | sed 1q`
        lynx -source $BASEURL/?forecast=${city} > \
                /home/james/frio/.tmp/secondbase
        #
        # Here I grab the page
        #
        high=`grep High /home/james/frio/.tmp/secondbase |\
                egrep -v `winds|level´ |\
                sed 1q |\
                cut -d\> -f3 |\
                cut -d\< -f1`
        low=`grep Low /home/james/frio/.tmp/secondbase |\
                egrep -v `level|cloud´ |\
                sed 1q |\
                cut -d\> -f3 |\
                cut -d\< -f1`
        #
        # The parse is quite crude; I've dumped the source and found
        # the locations of keywords.  I then use sed and cut to
        # remove the extraneous data.
        #
        lin=`grep -n Low /home/james/frio/.tmp/secondbase |\
                egrep -v `level|cloud´ | sed 1q | cut -d: -f1`
        lin=`expr "$lin" + 3`
```

```
                    forecast=`tail +$lin /home/james/frio/.tmp/secondbase |\
                         sed `/^</,$d´ |\
                         cut -d\< -f1`
               #
               # I echo the data to a file so I can sort the data
               #
               echo ${high}:${low}:${publish}:${high}:${low}:${forecast}:${folk} > \
                         /home/james/frio/.tmp/awkdata.jca
               #
               # I do it again for tomorrow´s forecast.
               #
               high=`grep High /home/james/frio/.tmp/secondbase |\
                         egrep -v `level|winds´ |\
                         tail +2 |\
                         sed 1q |\
                         cut -d\> -f3 |\
                         cut -d\< -f1`
               low=`grep Low /home/james/frio/.tmp/secondbase |\
                         egrep -v `level|cloud´ |\
                         tail +2 |\
                         sed 1q |\
                         cut -d\> -f3 |\
                         cut -d\< -f1`
               lin=`grep -n Low /home/james/frio/.tmp/secondbase |\
                         egrep -v `level|cloud´ |\
                         tail +2 |\
                         sed 1q |\
                         cut -d: -f1`
               lin=`expr "$lin" + 3`
               forecast=`tail +$lin /home/james/frio/.tmp/secondbase |\
                         sed `/^</,$d´ |\
                         cut -d\< -f1`
               echo ${high}:${low}:${publish}:${high}:${low}:${forecast}:${folk} > \
                         /home/james/frio/.tmp/awkdata2.jca
               rm /home/james/frio/.tmp/secondbase
          done
          rm cities publish
          #
          # I just need to sort the files by temperature to get the output
          #
          sort -t: +0 -1nr +1 -2nr /home/james/frio/.tmp/awkdata.jca >\
                  /home/james/frio/.tmp/awkdata3.jca
          sort -t: +0 -1nr +1 -2nr /home/james/frio/.tmp/awkdata2.jca >\
                  /home/james/frio/.tmp/awkdata4.jca
          #
          # I prepare a file for mailing with the forecast.
          #
          cat << EOF > /home/james/frio/.tmp/wereport.james
          From weather `date`
          Date: `date`
          From: weather@jamesarmstrong.com (Trip Weather)
          To: james@sagarmatha.com, jca@jamesarmstrong.com
          Subject: Trip Weather
```

```
EOF
echo Today\'s forecast: > /home/james/frio/.tmp/wereport.james
echo " " > /home/james/frio/.tmp/wereport.james
#
# Awktrip.awk takes the data and prints it in a nice format
#
awk -f /home/james/frio/.bin/awkittrip.awk \
        /home/james/frio/.tmp/awkdata3.jca > \
        /home/james/frio/.tmp/wereport.james
echo " " > /home/james/frio/.tmp/wereport.james
echo Tomorrow\'s forecast: > /home/james/frio/.tmp/wereport.james
echo " " > /home/james/frio/.tmp/wereport.james
awk -f /home/james/frio/.bin/awkittrip.awk \
        /home/james/frio/.tmp/awkdata4.jca > \
        /home/james/frio/.tmp/wereport.james
echo " " > /home/james/frio/.tmp/wereport.james
echo "-- " > /home/james/frio/.tmp/wereport.james
cat /home/james/.signature > /home/james/frio/.tmp/wereport.james
cp /home/james/frio/.tmp/wereport.james \
        /home/james/frio/WeatherReport.trip
/usr/sbin/sendmail james@sagarmatha.com < \
        /home/james/frio/.tmp/wereport.james
rm /home/james/frio/.tmp/awkdata* /home/james/frio/.tmp/wereport*
#
# All done!
#
```

The trip file shown in Listing 27-3 is simple:

Listing 27-3: Trip File

```
63740:Nairobi, Kenya
63714:Lake Nakuru, Kenya
63705:Entebbe, Uganda
63789:Serengeti, Tanzania
63980:Seychelles
67107:Antsirabe (Lemurs)
03772:London
07149:Paris
06240:Amsterdam
67083:Antananarivo, Madagascar
63791:Kilimanjaro, Tanzania
```

The numbers are codes for the different cities. The output shown in Listing 27-4 is simple:

Listing 27-4: Weather Forecast

```
Today's forecast:

Entebbe, Uganda              95/67   Passing clouds.
Seychelles                   88/79   Cloudy. Thunder Storms.
Kilimanjaro, Tanzania        86/67   Breezy. Many clouds.
Lake Nakuru, Kenya           84/65   Passing clouds.
Antsirabe (Lemurs)           83/73   Clouds.
```

```
Serengeti, Tanzania            82/63  Sunny.
Nairobi, Kenya                 82/60  Windy. Scattered clouds.
Antananarivo, Madagascar       78/66  Clouds. Light rain.
Paris                          51/45  Low clouds.
London                         51/44  Scattered clouds.
Amsterdam                      44/30  Blustery. Many clouds.

Tomorrow's forecast:

Entebbe, Uganda                96/66  Breezy. Sunny.
Antsirabe (Lemurs)             86/72  Windy. Clouds.
Seychelles                     86/72  Cloudy.
Kilimanjaro, Tanzania          86/69  Breezy. Mid level clouds.
Serengeti, Tanzania            86/67  Mid level clouds.
Lake Nakuru, Kenya             84/65  Sunny.
Nairobi, Kenya                 82/60  Breezy. Scattered clouds.
Antananarivo, Madagascar       77/64  Breezy. Overcast. Light rain.
Paris                          47/35  Low clouds.
London                         46/35  Breezy. Scattered clouds.
Amsterdam                      41/33  Windy. Sunny.
```

This program combines the World Wide Web, electronic mail, and UNIX text manipulation tools to produce a clean weather report for a group of cities.

Managing traffic data

As Chapter 24 describes, we have created a special log file format for my company's Apache Web server so that we can have a single log file for multiple domains. We need to parse that file into separate files for each domain before processing the log entries for that domain. Our log file processing occurs nightly so that we can have up-to-date traffic data. The log file format is fairly long. A typical entry is as follows:

```
res-152-16-201-120.dorm.duke.edu - - [28/Jan/1999:14:48:57 -0800] "GET /duke.gif
HTTP/1.0" 200 1738 www.uncbasketball.com "http://www.uncbasketball.com/"
"Mozilla/4.03 [en] (Win95; I ;Nav)"
```

This tells us the request came from the machine res-152-16-201-120. dorm.duke.edu at 2:48 p.m. on January 28. The URL is http://www. uncbasketball.com/duke.gif, requested from the uncbasketball.com Web site. The page making the request is http://www.uncbasketball.com/ and the browser is Netscape Navigator 4.03 running on Windows 95. We collect this detail for each request made to the server; the log files are on the order of 50 megabytes per day.

To parse these log files, we need to look at the host field, which is the eleventh text field on each line. That makes it easy for awk to examine. I do this with a for loop, using awk to get the host, trimming the log file as much as I can, and sorting the entries to a unique list. Within that loop, I build an awk script to match the list of hosts, and from there I build a separate access_log, referer_log, and agent_log with text manipulation tools such as cut, paste, and awk. The code for this program is shown in Listing 27-5.

Listing 27-5: Log File Parser

```
#!/bin/sh
#
# The apache web server was running out of file descriptors
# because we opted to have four logfiles per virtual domain, one
# each for the access log, agent log, error log, and referer log.
# This worked fine when we had less than 60 some virtual domains,
# but since Linux has a hard coded 256 limit to the number of file
# descriptors per process, we had a catastrophic failure when we
# added the domain that pushed us over 256.
#
# Ugly.
#
# So, after a short period of investigation, we found the LogFormat
# directive in Apache, which allowed us to create a combined log
# format that included the Host requested, Agent, and Referer.
# Since the Agent and Referer information was now combined with
# the Access log, we no longer needed to keep separate agent and
# referer logs.  And since we could now grab lines out of the log
# based on the host, we could combine all those logfiles into a
# single logfile.  Voila!  250+ file descriptors for logfiles is
# now reduced to 2.
#
# Or, to put it another way, Apache Rocks.
#
# Now, however, we have to add extra processing to the supersaver
# script to break the combined logfile into the respective pieces.
# This will allow the saver script to work as before with but a
# minor modification.  Supersaver copies the logfile, kickstarts
# apache (to start a new file), then breaks the file down first by
# host, then it carves it down into the three logfiles for saver
# and the traffic system.
#

cd /log/httpd

mv combined_log combined_log.use

kill -HUP `cat /var/run/httpd.pid`

cd /web

for i in `ls | grep \\\.`
do
        touch /log/$i/access_log
        touch /log/$i/agent_log
        touch /log/$i/error_log
        touch /log/$i/referer_log
done

for i in `awk `{print $11}´ /log/httpd/combined_log.use | \
        cut -d: -f1 |\
```

```
                cut -d/ -f1 |\
                sed -e `s/^www.//;s/^WWW.//;s/\.*$//;s/^\"//;s/"$//´ |\
                sort -u`
do
        if
                [ X$i = X- ]
        then
                echo \$11 \~ /^$i\$/ { print \$0 } > /tmp/awker
        else
                j=`echo $i | sed -e `s./.\\/.´´
                echo \$11 \~ /$j/ { print \$0 } > /tmp/awker
        fi
        awk -f /tmp/awker /log/httpd/combined_log.use > /tmp/tmp_log
        cut -d\" -f4 /tmp/tmp_log > /tmp/l1
        awk `{print $7}´ /tmp/tmp_log > /tmp/l2
        target=`echo $i | tr `[A-Z]´ `[a-z]´`
        if
                [ -d /log/$target ]
        then
                cut -d\  -f1-10 /tmp/tmp_log > \
                        /log/$target/access_log
                paste /tmp/l1 /tmp/l2 |\
                        sed -e `s/          / -> /´ |\
                        awk `$1 != "-" { print $0 }´ > \
                        /log/$target/referer_log
                cut -d\" -f6 /tmp/tmp_log > /log/$target/agent_log
        else
                cut -d\  -f1-10 /tmp/tmp_log > \
                        /log/hostname.com/access_log
                paste /tmp/l1 /tmp/l2 |\
                        sed -e `s/          / -> /´ |\
                        awk `$1 != "-" { print $0 }´ > \
                        /log/hostname.com/referer_log
                cut -d\" -f6 /tmp/tmp_log > \
                        /log/hostname.com/agent_log
        fi
        rm -f /tmp/l1 /tmp/l2 /tmp/tmp_log /tmp/awker
done

rm /log/httpd/combined_log.use

for i in `ls | grep \\\.`
do
        if
                [ -d /log/$i ]
        then
                /web/bin/traffic/saver /log/$i
        fi
done
```

When the parsing is complete, the saver program performs the daily backups. Each Sunday morning, it combines the files for the last week, and on the first of each month, it combines the files for the last month. Listing 27-6 shows the daily backup script. Several supplementary programs that generate date formats are not illustrated here.

Listing 27-6: Daily Backup

```
#!/bin/sh

dt=`date `+%d``

yesterday=`/web/bin/traffic/yesterday`

mkdir $1/$yesterday
chmod 777 $1/$yesterday

mv $1/access_log $1/$yesterday
mv $1/agent_log $1/$yesterday
mv $1/error_log $1/$yesterday
mv $1/referer_log $1/$yesterday

#
# This has backed up the files
#

cd $1/$yesterday

total=`wc -l < access_log`
total2=`egrep -i ` / |html|cgi´ access_log | wc -l`
total3=`awk -f /web/bin/traffic/script2.awk access_log |\
        sed -e `s.,..g´`
total4=`awk `{print $1}´ access_log | sort | uniq | wc -l`

cp ../graph/data /tmp/graph
echo ${yesterday}:${total}:${total2}:${total3}:$total4  |\
        sed -e `s. ..g´ > /tmp/graph

#
# This builds the graph file entry
#
awk -f /web/bin/traffic/script3.awk /tmp/graph > ../graph/data
rm /tmp/graph

#
# This removes initial zero days.
#

dow=`date `+%w``

#
# Build the week file
#

if
        [ $dow -eq 0 ]
then
        # Weekly processing
        lastweek=`/web/bin/traffic/lastweek`
```

```
        mkdir $1/$lastweek
        chmod 777 $1/$lastweek

        for i in `/web/bin/traffic/lastweekdays`
        do
                if
                        [ -d $1/$i ]
                then
                        cd $1/$i
                        gunzip * > /dev/null 2>&1
                        for j in `ls`
                        do
                                cat $j > $1/$lastweek/$j
                        done
                        gzip * > /dev/null 2>&1
                fi
        done

        cd $1/$lastweek

        gzip * > /dev/null 2>&1
fi

#
# Build the month file
#

if
        [ $dt -eq 1 ]
then
        lastmonth=`/web/bin/traffic/lastmonth`

        mkdir $1/$lastmonth
        chmod 777 $1/$lastmonth

        cd $1

        rm -f *.gz
        gunzip ${lastmonth}??/*
        rm -f ${lastmonth}/*
        for i in agent error access referer
        do
                cat ${lastmonth}??/${i}_log > ${lastmonth}/${i}_log
        done
        gzip ${lastmonth}??/*

        cd $1/$lastmonth

        gzip * > /dev/null 2>&1

fi
```

```
cd $1

#
# Remove old files and directories
#
find ?????? -mtime +45 -type f -print | xargs rm -f
rmdir * > /dev/null 2>&1
```

Summary

This chapter explained how to integrate Internet tools with UNIX tools. It covered the following topics:

▶ Using finger to get data

▶ Using Lynx and text manipulation tools to generate mail

▶ Managing server log files

The next chapter introduces the X Windows system.

Part VIII

The X Window System

Chapter 28

Understanding X Windows

In This Chapter

▶ The history of X Windows

▶ The imperatives behind X Windows

▶ The structure of an X program

▶ Window managers

This chapter introduces you to X Windows, the windowing system used by most UNIX systems. Most applications for UNIX are written for X Windows, and most UNIX users go through an X interface as opposed to a command-line interface.

The History of X Windows

As you may realize, most of these tools have been around for a while. The first public version of X was made available in 1984. Since that time, X has evolved into the de facto standard for UNIX systems.

X Windows was originally developed at Project Athena, a group within MIT that receives funding from Digital Equipment and is responsible for some of UNIX's features. Back in 1984, companies were racing to develop the first graphical user interface. Apple had its Apple II computers, which were considered user-friendly. Microsoft had DOS, a UNIX-like system that lacked multiprocessing and multiple-user capabilities, and UNIX had its standard command-line interface. Each interface had its weaknesses, the main weakness being that each was not completely user-friendly. Performing even simple tasks was considered beyond noncomputer users. In the mid-80s, Apple introduced the Macintosh computer, Microsoft followed with Windows, and UNIX had X.

Note

In hindsight, the results of the last 12 years should have been obvious to the pundits. Apple concentrated on the user-friendly market but lacked the applications. UNIX, which had an interface designed by engineers for engineers, remained the choice for serious computer professionals. Microsoft, focused on business applications, rose to dominate that market and, because that is the biggest market, rose to dominate the desktop despite having less overall functionality on its systems.

The first commercial release of X Windows was X10.4, made available in 1986, and some applications were based on it. One year later, X11 was made available. Since that time, five more releases — X11R2 through X11R6 — have been made available. Each contains enhancements of and bug fixes for previous releases.

The Imperatives behind X Windows

Any graphical user interface has some basic features. It should control the entire screen and present its data in a reasonable form, taking advantage of the resources available. The keyboard should interact with the display in a sensible fashion. A pointer device, usually a mouse, should control a graphical cursor and should be used to access resources displayed on the screen.

Each of the three competitors do this in one fashion or another.

X has many advantages over its competitors on other platforms. Both Macintosh and Windows are tied to their platforms and vendors. You can't take a Windows program and run it on a Macintosh without also loading some emulation program; even then, the program's performance is comparatively poor. In the first two cases, the windowing system is built into the operating system itself. Though performance improves this way, portability does not. In contrast, X Windows uses a client/server model. The screen is controlled by a separate program that runs in the UNIX environment. It acts as the screen server. Other applications communicate with this server, and the server displays the results of the communication. Furthermore, the server controls the keyboard and the pointer and sends the actions generated by those devices to the appropriate client program.

This has some real advantages. You do not need to execute your commands on the local machine: You can initiate communications on a remote server just as easily as you can on your local workstation. Moreover, if you run multiple X servers attached to multiple displays, your computer can actually run several different sets of windows.

Because X has received acceptance from every major UNIX vendor, multiple hardware platforms provide a fairly common interface to the system. To use Windows, you are restricted to Intel systems, and Macintosh's excellent interface is tied to the Apple hardware. Because the underlying X interface definition is standard, porting applications from one UNIX platform to another is easy.

Story: Hidden Traps

That's in theory, at least. I've ported some X-based applications to various platforms and have always found hidden traps waiting to spring on you at unexpected moments — usually when you're giving a demonstration for your boss! These glitches are often resolved quickly, however, and then you have an application that runs on multiple platforms.

As a result of this portability, you can run the output of one platform's application on another platform's display. The only difficult porting issue is writing the X server to communicate with the graphics card and monitor.

Story: X on the Internet

The X protocol even works across the Internet. When my friend Matthew Merzbacher was working on his thesis at UCLA, he needed to test an X-based application's usability across the Internet. I opened up my local server in San Francisco to accept X input from his client in Westwood. Though the performance across our 9,600-baud connection to the Net was slow, we were able to demonstrate that his application would work across the Internet.

Because X is not built into the kernel, it is easier to extend. As you add resources, you just need to reconfigure a program, not rebuild the operating system.

X is also flexible. Because almost everything you see on the screen results from the commands of client programs, you can write your own clients to perform any actions you want within the limits of your monitor's and server's capabilities. Several tools written for X are both commercial and public domain applications.

The Structure of an X Program

X programs are based on the client model. The program's first action should be to open a connection to the specified server. After that connection is established, your client should initialize its desired interface and then enter a loop waiting for input. Actions taken by your program should then be based on that input.

This is termed *call-back programming.* Your input loop is usually established as an infinite loop, and you call routines based on the input. Input can take several forms not considered in command-line programming. When a mouse moves over an object, that is an event. (All mouse motion is potential input.) When a portion of your display is covered or uncovered by another application, this is also potential input. Mouse clicks are definitely input, as are the most common callbacks. Keyboard input is also input.

Callback programming is a feature of object-oriented programming. Instead of having a sequential listing of code that runs in a standard, orderly fashion, object code is called more haphazardly. When an object is touched, the callback is called, and more actions are performed. Of course, callbacks can change other callbacks, as needed.

Secret

Strictly speaking, object-oriented code is still a sequential listing of code, but there are different types of input.

Underlying everything is a protocol. The X protocol is very big; it fills one of the volumes of O'Reilly's definitive set of books on X. Each client program sends and receives protocol requests. If you desire, you can write your client to handle the protocol directly.

Note

Some applications, such as those designed to record and play back X events, need to handle the protocol directly.

The next layer up is the X libraries. These are standard calls to library functions that interpret X protocol requests sent to you and that format and send X protocol requests back to the server. These are routines that enable you to draw images on the screen. When I performed some hacks on a public domain X program, I used X library calls to draw some symbols directly on the screen. Two volumes of the O'Reilly books are devoted to X library programming.

On top of the X libraries lie the X toolkit intrinsics. These are higher-level calls designed to draw specific objects called *widgets.* Each widget has a series of resources, such as color, shading, size, and fonts, associated with it. Normally, these are defined in a program, but you can override them by setting resources in a special file. (I discuss this in Chapter 29.)

The basic widget set is implemented at this level. Some applications still use the Athena widgets, although they have been superseded. X toolkit intrinsics fill two volumes of the O'Reilly series.

The top level is the widget level. The most common widget set is Motif, although others exist. Motif defines a style and appearance common to window interfaces and controls, such as buttons and lists. The Motif library is a series of calls to define this interface in a standard fashion, although other aspects of the interface, such as defining resources, fall back to the X toolkit intrinsics. Motif fills two more volumes of the O'Reilly books.

An alternative interface, which is declining in popularity, is XView programming.

Window Managers

One common application for each server is a *window manager.* Window managers are programs that do not normally create their own objects on the screen but instead manage the layout and placement of other applications. Three common window managers are mwm, twm, and olwm. Each places a border around the application and enables you to manipulate the application's placement on the screen. I personally prefer twm because it is the least intrusive window manager, but you may feel another manager fits your needs better.

I discuss window managers in Chapter 30.

Summary

This chapter introduced the basics of X Windows. It covered the following topics:

▶ The history of X

▶ X's strengths and weaknesses when compared with other interfaces

▶ How X Windows programs work

▶ The terms *X library, X toolkit,* and *widgets*

The next chapter covers how to start X on your display, basic configuration, and some common programs. It introduces the common argument set for most programs and some basic commands.

Chapter 29

Getting Started with X

In This Chapter

▶ The basic commands to start X

▶ The xinit command and the .xinitrc file

▶ Some basic X Windows clients

▶ Resources

▶ The .Xdefaults file

▶ The X display manager

X Windows is a complicated system, and a good grounding in the basics of X is essential before beginning. This chapter should give you enough to get started.

The Basics of X

The X Windows system is a client-server–based system in which clients send protocol requests to the server so that it can perform actions on the screen and the server preprocesses multiple forms of input for client programs.

A protocol communication between server and client underlies everything and is initiated by opening a socket on the client side to the server. If no server is present, the client notes an error and fails. A server can run without clients, but you just have a screen without programs. A single client can attach to any number of servers, if it is so configured, and a single server can have any number of clients. The former case is unusual, but the latter case is by design.

Because the underlying protocol is machine-independent, I can run an application on a Sun workstation that sends protocol requests to an SGI X server, and I have a reasonable expectation that the protocol requests should succeed. If both sides of the communication are implemented properly, it works.

A protocol session

The communication between client and server is fairly intricate. To bring up a window on an X server, the client must first initiate the connection. It sends a protocol request to the server asking for permission to connect. If the server sends a rejection or does not answer, the client is denied access and exits, usually with an error message. If accepted, the server sends back a reply indicating that it has given permission.

The client then sends a request to create a window. A `CreateWindow` protocol request includes attributes for the window, such as background pixmaps, window gravity, event masks, and the like. Each of these terms defines an underlying aspect of X applications that usually does not concern the end user.

A client's request to allocate colors for the window relates to the window creation. Even black and white windows have two colors. The server then replies to the request for colors and returns pixel values for color.

The client next requests a graphical context. Applications manage graphical contexts for drawing their output on the screen. Abbreviated *GC*, a graphical context includes pixels to represent the background and foreground colors, line width, and other characteristics of the application. Next, the application requests that the window be "managed" by the server. It then waits for the expose events that accompany management.

Note

You can create any number of objects in X, but none is displayed until management of the object is passed to the server. If you've never used X, you can think of *manage* and *unmanage* as *display* and *hide*.

When the server displays the window, an expose event is sent back down the socket to the client. Only when the application receives the initial expose event should it start to draw any objects on the screen. This is because a window manager may allow a user to determine some of the display characteristics of the window, and drawing before those characteristics are set may result in incompatibilities.

Now, the standard communication continues. As expose events are sent back to the client, more drawing occurs. Eventually, with the graphical interface completed, other interaction can begin between the client and the server, and between the server and the user.

Determining the link up

The `DISPLAY` environment variable determines which server a client's connection targets. `DISPLAY` usually breaks down into two components, separated by a colon. The first component is a machine name, found in either `/etc/hosts` or the NIS hosts map. If the machine name is absent, the local machine is assumed. Similarly, if an IP address is known but the machine hostname is not, an IP address can be placed here.

The screen number comes after the colon. Almost always, this is 0, but if the host is supporting multiple screens, the number is determined based on the lowest available integer when the server is initialized. So, on my home machine, the DISPLAY environment variable should be set to duke:0, although :0 is perfectly adequate.

When a server is established, it opens up a socket and accepts connections on that socket. The port number is usually 6000. If the machine has multiple screens, the port number is determined by adding the display number to 6000. So, duke:2 would listen to port 6002, waiting for a connection.

Closing the session

No specific protocol is required to close a session with X Windows. Instead, when you kill a program running on the screen, it just dies. The server must recognize that the client has died and clean up any windows displayed on the screen.

You don't even need to worry about closing the socket. When a program exits, the operating system automatically closes the socket for you. The client just needs to clean up after itself like any other program (by deleting any temporary files, for example).

Similarly, if an X Windows server shuts down for any reason, the client receives a socket disconnect. Usually, it should shut down gracefully when this happens.

Some clients may use a SetCloseDownMode request to preserve any abstractions created in the server, pending a new connection. This is rarely used. Accompanying it is the KillClient protocol request, which tells the server to free those abstractions.

Error recovery

Sometimes, the server does not understand a protocol request. When this happens, the server sends an error message back to the client program. The X server then refuses any further protocol requests from that client. Normally, the client program then reports the error message and exits gracefully.

The xinit Command and the .xinitrc File

The server command for X Windows is usually X, but I cannot recommend running this program from the command line. While X may start X on your system, no clients are running, so any input you give is lost, and no windows are on your screen. You can attempt to run some X clients remotely on your display, but your machine may not be configured correctly. Instead, the best thing to do, if you can, is to kill the server from a remote window.

If that proves impossible, the only option is to reboot.

Fortunately, X Windows comes with commands that you can use to prevent this from happening. The normal command to start is `xinit`, which checks to start the appropriate server and makes certain that at least one client program is running. On my system, the default client is an XTerm, an application that gives me a shell prompt. I can fire other applications from there.

The `xinit` command starts the normal X server found on your system. You can specify an alternative server by listing it on the command line. This is useful if you are designing your own X server and want to test it. The syntax is usually something like `xinit -- Xtest`. Two dashes indicate that the next argument is a server name. You can also specify a full path.

The `xinit` command starts on the default display, `:0`. You can also specify an alternative display with the `-display` argument, followed by the display name. You can start X on a remote display, if the permissions match, but this is a fairly unusual event.

You can also specify a client program or just arguments to a client program. These must immediately follow the `xinit` command, and the server and display arguments must follow. An example might be this one:

```
xinit /usr/bin/X11/twm
```

This starts the window manager `twm` automatically. Presumably, you have configured `twm` to allow input that starts other applications.

The real win for `xinit` is its capability to configure a startup file, `.xinitrc`. In this file, you normally list applications to run at startup. This usually includes a window manager, some XTerms, and other clients. Listing 29-1 shows the contents of my `.xinitrc`.

Listing 29-1: My .xinitrc

```
#!/bin/sh
xclock -bg grey20 -fg gold -hd aliceblue -hl orange -geometry =80x80-0+0 -update
1 & #run a clock
twm&
xterm -fn 7x13 -bg navy -fg gold -g =80x24+0+100&
xterm -fn 7x13 -bg black -fg yellow -g =80x24+33+66&
xterm -fn 7x13 -bg darkslategrey -fg skyblue -g =80x24+66+33&
xterm -fn 6x10 -bg brown -fg ivory -g =80x24+100+0&
xset s 300&
xhost + > /dev/null 2>&1
xload -bg forestgreen -fg white -g =250x100+0+0&
/home/xearth/*/xearth -label -fork
xterm -fn 9x15 -bg brown -fg yellow -ms green -cr black -bd red -C -n console \
 -title "`/bin/hostname` Console" -g =80x4+0+0 -iconic
#Run xterm in foreground - when this exits, server exits
```

My startup script is fairly complex. I describe each command listed in more detail later in this chapter or in subsequent chapters. I first start a clock, followed by my window manager. Next, I start four XTerms, and I run an `xset` command and an `xhost` command. These set my screen to blank out after five minutes and allow others access to my screen. I then fire an `xload` command, followed by `xearth`. My last command is an XTerm. Each of these commands has a myriad of arguments. Fortunately, all X Windows programs have a standard set of arguments.

Those of you with experience programming the shell may recognize this as just another shell script, and that is exactly what it is.

Secret

Strictly speaking, the `.xinitrc` file is also a client of the X server. When `xinit` starts, it initializes the environment, executes the server, and executes the client. The `.xinitrc` file is an executable file deemed to be the only client. So, when the last command finishes, `xinit` finishes and cleans up. For this reason, most commands are placed in the background by terminating the command with an ampersand (&). The last command is usually a foreground command; otherwise, the server terminates when it terminates. As another option, you can include a `wait` command at the end, which forces you to terminate all the commands before the server exits.

You can do some fairly weird stuff when programming your `.xinitrc`. If you call the `.xinitrc` from within the `.xinitrc`, you may never leave the X server until you reboot or actually kill the process. If you've forgotten to place all the commands in the background, you may find that your startup finishes at the last command, and when you exit that application, your "initialization" continues. Worse, if all of the commands are in the background and you start all of them, the script finishes, and the X server then dies, leaving you where you started!

The `xinit` command forks, executes the startup script, and allows it to run to completion. When the startup script finishes, `xinit` finishes, and the server terminates.

Story: The Unknown Key Sequence

IBM's AIX server is not this simple. When the `xinit` process finishes, the server remains up, and you need to either log in remotely to kill it or reboot the machine. Some key sequence did exist that involved simultaneously pressing three keys, but this was not well documented. This resulted in some consternation the first time that I tried to log out of the RS 6000. Apparently, the key combination is obvious to users of Microsoft Windows, but for those of us who had been using UNIX and X for nearly a decade, the combination was so counterintuitive that none of us would have guessed it in a million years. We spent four months going to other machines to kill the X server before someone found that document reference. You could have knocked us over with a feather.

You can specify an alternative to the standard .xinitrc file. If you have an alternate script that you want to test, you can run it on the command line, like so:

```
xinit ./test.xinitrc
```

As a more sophisticated approach, you can assign a filename to the XINITRC variable. When xinit starts, it checks that variable for a filename and only accesses .xinitrc in your home directory if that variable is not defined. Finally, if none of these approaches work, your xinit process starts an XTerm for you, and you can enter any further commands from there.

Using startx

As another, more friendly approach to starting an X server, you can use the startx command. This is a shell script distributed with X11 that performs some normal checking before starting the server through xinit. It first checks to see if a startup file is in the home directory, and if not, it checks to see if a system startup file exists. It does the same again for the server startup files. Other than that, startx takes the same arguments as xinit, and it passes those arguments to xinit.

The one advantage startx has over xinit is that startx checks for system default files if your user defaults are not present. Because I have my .xinitrc, I don't need to run startx, but it is a good habit.

Standard arguments

As mentioned previously, most X clients have a standard set of arguments. Table 29-1 lists these arguments.

Table 29-1   X Windows Client Arguments

Option	*Argument*	*Meaning*
-background	*color*	Sets the background color of the window to the specified color
-bd	*color*	Sets the border color of the window to the specified color
-bg	*color*	Same as -background
-borderwidth	*integer*	Sets the width of the window's border to the specified number of pixels
-bordercolor	*color*	Same as -bd
-bw	*integer*	Same as -borderwidth
-display	*display specification*	Runs the client on the specified display

Option	Argument	Meaning
-fg	color	Sets the window's foreground color to the specified color
-fn	font	Uses the specified font for displaying text
-font	font	Same as -fn
-foreground	color	Same as -fg
-g	geometry specification	Defines the window size and placement on the screen
-geometry	geometry specification	Same as -g
-iconic		Starts the application in an iconified form
-name	string	The name of the application
-reverse		Reverses foreground and background colors
-rv		Same as -reverse
+rv		Does not reverse foreground and background colors
-synchronize		Used for debugging
-title	string	The window title
-xrm	resource specification	Includes the resource specified in the application

In .xinitrc, you should see several of these arguments. Each XTerm, for example, has its own set of colors. I use different colors on my display to help me organize my activities. A window that is gold on navy, for example, is my primary working window. Yellow on black is one for reading and responding to mail. Other pairings have different meanings.

The XTerms sometimes also list alternate fonts. Font specifications in X are quite varied. The fixed width fonts usually come with an n by m specification, which defines the width and height of the characters in pixels. Figure 29-1 shows the largest size on my display.

In each case, the terminal also displayed a smaller than normal size. I used the geometry specification to restrict the window to 4 rows and 40 columns. The geometry specification is one of the most useful. You can determine the size of a window in an x by y format. The first number is the number of horizontal pixels; the second is the number of vertical pixels. (If the window displays text, they are columns and rows.) So, a clock with a geometry of 80·80 is an 80-pixel square. The last two numbers are offsets. The first is a horizontal offset in pixels, the latter a vertical offset. A plus indicates an offset from the left side or top of the screen, and a minus indicates an offset from the right side or bottom of the screen. Table 29-2 shows some basic offsets.

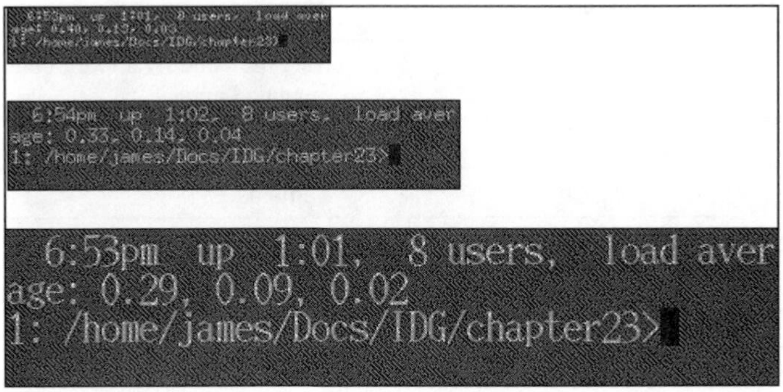

Figure 29-1: Font sizes

Table 29-2	Common Geometry Offsets
Offset	*Location*
+0+0	Top-left corner
+0-0	Bottom-left corner
-0+0	Top-right corner
-0-0	Bottom-right corner

The geometry string must be a continuous string with no spaces. Because the two formats have different indicators, you can specify a size without a location, or a location without a size. Figures 29-2 through 29-5 show the xlogo command in various sizes and positions.

A First Client XTerm

The most common client application you are likely to run with X Windows is an XTerm. At its simplest, it just attaches a terminal device to an X window. Because the concept of a terminal device is intrinsically attached to the UNIX concept of standard input and standard output, the XTerm lets you run any UNIX command in a window.

If that was all that an XTerm did, it would be a very powerful command. What makes the XTerm amazing is the X additions that accompany the application. You can add scrollbars to an XTerm and retain more data than the default provided by the screen size. You have menus that you can raise from an XTerm. You have the ability to cut and paste data between XTerms, and between an XTerm and other X Window applications.

Figure 29-2: xlogo -g =70·70+0+0

Figure 29-3: xlogo -g =120·90-0+0

Figure 29-4: xlogo -g =200·200-0-0

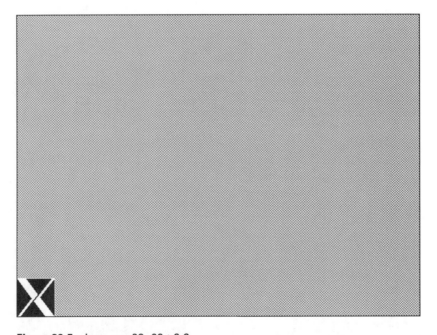

Figure 29-5: xlogo -g =60·60+0-0

XTerm menus

One big differentiating feature of an XTerm over a normal window is the presence of menus that alter the behavior of the XTerm. Three menus are available. One controls the sending of signals to a process, one controls the options available for the XTerm, and the last controls alternative fonts. The first two menus have some toggles, and below them are commands. The last menu is just a listing of commands. We'll examine each in turn.

Note

The menus you see with your XTerm may be different from mine. These menus are implementation-dependent and can be altered from one version of X to another.

The main window has ten options. The top three are toggles, the next six are commands to send signals to the process, and the last is the Quit command. Table 29-3 lists these menu options.

Table 29-3   First XTerm Menu

Option	Result
Secure Keyboard	When selected, any keyboard input is sent to this window, regardless of the pointer's location. The window's colors are inverted to remind you of this.
Allow SendEvents	Allows the sending of events to the application.
Redraw Window	Forces the window to be redrawn. This is useful if some output has scrambled the display.
Send STOP signal	Sends the STOP signal to the application.
Send CONT signal	Sends the CONT signal to the application.
Send HUP signal	Sends the HUP signal to the application.
Send INT signal	Sends the INT signal to the application.
Send TERM signal	Sends the TERM signal to the application.
Send KILL signal	Sends the KILL signal to the application.
Quit	Terminates the XTerm and kills the application in the XTerm.

The signals are very useful. If you have started a process in an XTerm and that process needs to be halted, you can use the menu to interrupt and kill the process.

The second menu is the largest. I have over 21 options on my XTerm. Table 29-4 examines these options.

Table 29-4   Second Menu Options

Option	Result
Enable Scrollbar	When selected, the window has a scrollbar and can access more information.
Enable Jump Scroll	When scrolling, the text jumps to a new location with the click of the middle mouse button.
Enable Reverse Video	Reverses the sense of foreground and background colors.
Enable Auto Wraparound	When selected, automatically wraps text when it exceeds the line length.
Enable Reverse Wraparound	When selected, backs up the cursor past the first column and places it on the last column of the previous line.
Enable Auto Linefeed	When a line exceeds the number of columns, a line feed is automatically included in the text.
Enable Application Cursor Keys	The arrow keys function with the application.
Enable Application Keypad	The keypad keys work with the application.
Scroll to Bottom on Key Press	When a key is pressed, the window automatically jumps to the bottom of the scrolled data.
Scroll to Bottom on TTY Output	When output is sent to the XTerm, it should automatically jump to the bottom of the scrolled data.
Allow 80/132 Column Switching	When emulating a terminal that allows both 80- and 132-column mode, you are permitted to make that switch.
Enable Curses Emulation	When selected, the window emulates the curses library.
Enable Visual Bell	When you make an input error that normally results in a beep, the screen flashes.
Enable Margin Bell	When you reach the end of the window on input, the bell either sounds or flashes.
Show Alternate Screen	If your application permits multiple screens on a `tty`, this allows the switching of screens.
Do Soft Reset	Resets the state of the XTerm.
Do Full Reset	Resets the screen to the state before the application started.
Reset and Clear Saved Lines	When a line is saved, it resets the lines and clears them.
Show Tek Window	Shows the Tektronix window format.

Option	Result
Switch to Tek Mode	Changes the current window to one emulating a Tektronix terminal.
Hide VT Window	When the Tek window is shown, this hides the VT format window.

When brought up on your screen, this menu can be somewhat baffling. I recommend that you experiment with the options to determine what works best for you.

Secret

Each toggle option also has an associated command-line argument and an associated X resource. Once you've found a configuration you like, you can make this permanent by either creating an alias for XTerm or by setting the resources in your local resource file.

The last window enables you to change the font size of a window. Each XTerm has several fonts built in. Table 29-5 lists those menu items and the associated fonts.

Table 29-5   Font Selection Menu

Menu Option	Resultant Font	Font Sample
Default	The starting font	Now is the time
Unreadable	nil2	▬▬
Tiny	5·7	Now is the time
Small	6·10	Now is the time
Medium	7·13	Now is the time
Large	9·15	Now is the time
Huge	10·20	Now is the time

The XTerm allows two additional entries, Escape Sequence and Selection, both of which can be set by the application.

Story: Creative Use of the Font Menu

I've seen some coworkers use the font menu creatively: One would start a large make in a window and shrink it to the unreadable font. You still see some motion and know that when the motion stops, the make is complete. I've not used the fonts this way myself. I prefer to use them to change the window size when I am demonstrating some of my work to other people. I personally prefer a smaller font size when I'm working, and most people have difficulty reading it.

XTerm cut and paste

A graphical interface's capability to cut and paste text between different applications in different windows may stand as its most basic advantage. X Windows includes this capability by implementing a buffer in the server where you can store copies of text. Any application can access that buffer for reading, writing, or both by using the proper protocol sequences (or higher level library calls).

The XTerm is no exception to this. Indeed, by including this capability in an XTerm, X Windows automatically extends the cut and paste capability to any program in UNIX that uses standard input and output.

Within an XTerm, you can write to the buffer by selecting text with your pointer device. If you wish to cut out a word, just place the pointer over the word and double-click the left mouse button. The word is highlighted in inverse video, and placed in the buffer. A triple-click highlights the entire line. To copy a passage, such as a sentence, start with the mouse at the beginning of the passage, press the mouse button, and drag the mouse until the entire passage is highlighted.

Note

Strictly speaking, the capability in an XTerm is not cut, but copy, because the highlighted text remains intact.

Tip

If you are copying a sentence or are copying on word boundaries multiple words, you can use the double-click combined with the drag. If you keep the mouse button pressed after the second click, when you drag the mouse, each new word is highlighted. The same applies to keeping the button depressed after the third click of a triple-click.

Secret

If you over-click, keep clicking until you quadruple-click. This resets the clicking sequence.

Caution

If you use line numbers in vi (like I do) and if you drag over multiple lines, those line numbers are included in the buffer. I always disable line numbers before using the mouse to copy text.

Once you have placed the text in the buffer, you can paste it wherever you want. This time, the location of the pointer is not important. Instead, you need to position the text cursor where you'd like in the window. Clicking the middle button immediately sends the entire contents of the buffer to the standard input of the application.

Caution

This can produce some unusual results for an application like vi that is not in insert mode. For example, the text that you expect to input will be treated as commands.

The text remains in the buffer after the pasting, and you can paste the same text any number of times. Only when you add new text to the buffer is the old text purged.

XTerm scrolling

When you add a scrollbar to an XTerm, you have the ability to access previous lines of data. Figure 29-6 illustrates a basic XTerm, and Figure 29-7 illustrates an XTerm with a scrollbar.

Note

The highlighted area is called a *thumb*.

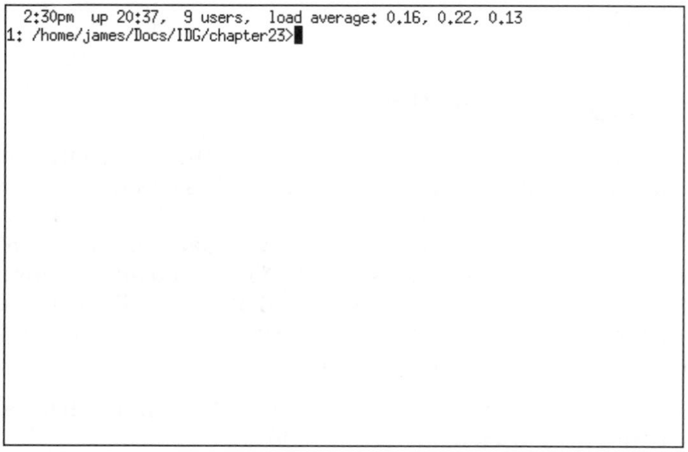

```
 2:30pm  up 20:37,  9 users,  load average: 0.16, 0.22, 0.13
1: /home/james/Docs/IDG/chapter23>█
```

Figure 29-6: A normal XTerm

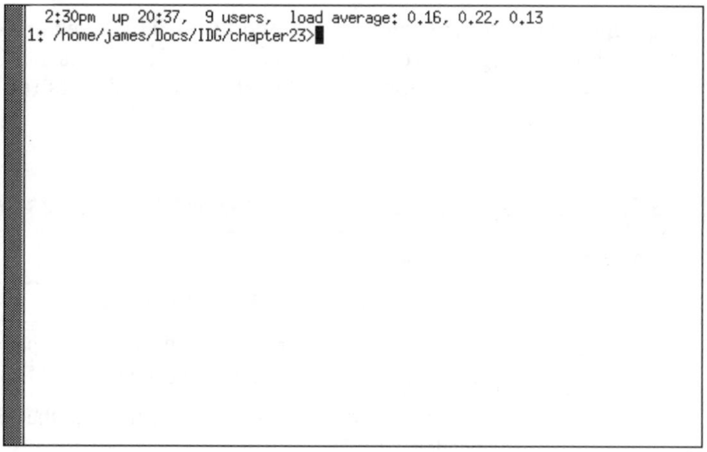

```
 2:30pm  up 20:37,  9 users,  load average: 0.16, 0.22, 0.13
1: /home/james/Docs/IDG/chapter23>█
```

Figure 29-7: An XTerm with a scrollbar

As you fill the XTerm with data, the scrollbar shrinks to show a highlighted section and an unhighlighted section. By moving that highlighted section, you can access previous data.

The direction of the thumb depends on the pointer. To move the thumb, place the pointer over the scrollbar. Clicking the left button causes the thumb to move down, scrolling to the most recent information. Clicking the right button causes the thumb to move up, toward older information. Clicking the middle button brings the thumb to the pointer. By pressing the middle button and holding it down, you can drag the thumb up and down.

Jump scroll moves the thumb immediately to the location of the pointer when you press the middle button.

XTerm startup option

Normally, when you start an XTerm, it looks for the SHELL environment variable and runs that program in the XTerm. This creates an impression that an XTerm is just a tool to create a shell. This is not the case. You can use an XTerm to execute any command. Two that I use fairly often are an alias for vi that executes the text editor in a separate XTerm and an alias for mail that executes elm in its own XTerm. (Similarly, that elm configures its editor to run an editor in yet another XTerm.) I am sure I've just scratched the surface of what people can run in separate XTerms.

You run the separate command with the -e option. (Table 29-6 lists all the options.) The two aliases in my .cshrc file are

```
alias vi "xterm -bg cyan -fg red -T `vi \!*´ -g 80x22 -e vi \!*&"
alias mail "xterm -bg red -fg white -g =80x32-0-0 -exec
/usr/local/bin/elm"
```

I use the geometry to control the size of my editing. The sizes are different at work, where I have a larger screen (home is 640x480, work is 1280x1024), my vi commands are 50 lines long, and my elm is 40. This lets me see and gather more information at a glance.

Table 29-6   XTerm Options Beyond the Standard X Windows Options

Option	Argument	Meaning
-132		Enables the window in 132-column mode.
-L		Indicates that the XTerm is called by init. It places a getty in the shell and should only be used in /etc/inittab.
-b	*integer*	Sets the border width between the text and the edge of the window.
-cr	*color*	Sets the highlight color of the cursor.
-cu		Enables a fix to curses.
-e	*command arguments*	Runs the command in the XTerm.

Option	Argument	Meaning
-fb	*font*	Specifies the font to be used for bold characters.
-i		Starts the XTerm as an icon.
-j		Enables jump scrolling by default.
-ls		Forces the XTerm to run a login shell.
-mb		Enables the margin bell. The margin bell is disabled by default.
-ms	*color*	Sets the color of the I-beam pointer.
-n	*name*	Sets the name of the XTerm.
-nb	*integer*	Sets the distance in characters for the margin bell.
-rw		Enables reverse wraparound.
-s		Allows the XTerm to scroll synchronously with the display.
-sb		Enables the scrollbar by default.
-si		Disables positioning the cursor at the bottom of the display when the XTerm receives output.
-sk		Positions the cursor at the bottom of the display when a key is pressed.
-sl	*integer*	Specifies the number of lines to be saved when the text scrolls off the top of the display.
-t		Causes the XTerm to start in Tektronix mode.
-T	*string*	Gives the window a title. This appears on the icons when the window is iconified.
vb		Enables the visible bell.

The number of options available to XTerms may seem incomprehensibly large, but this is actually a feature of X Windows. Each option has a sensible default, so the command xterm has reasonable behavior. The large set of options lets you customize your environment greatly.

You can include any number of these arguments with an xterm command.

Story: The Dark Side

I prefer a darker background on the screen and a strong contrast between the background and the foreground. This results in color combinations like red on black, yellow on blue, and so forth. I also prefer a smaller font than most people. This has resulted in my display being called the "Darth Vader" among my coworkers.

XTerm resources

Resources can manage an XTerm as well as command-line arguments. *Resources* are strings that modify the behavior of X Windows. These *X Resources* are set in the .Xdefaults file and can be viewed as a technique for eliminating the need to repeat the same command-line arguments.

You have 72 resources defined for X terminals. These range from color and font specifications to the actual definitions of the label strings on the menus. Here are some resources associated with XTerms:

XTerm.JoinSession

*SimpleMenu*menuLabel.font

*SimpleMenu*HorizontalMargins

*SimpleMenu*Cursor

*mainMenu*securekbd*Label

*mainMenu*logging*Label

*mainMenu*suspend*Label

*mainMenu*interrupt*Label

*mainMenu*terminate*Label

*mainMenu*quit*Label

*vtMenu*scrollbar*Label

*vtMenu*reversevideo*Label

*vtMenu*reversewrap*Label

*vtMenu*appcursor*Label

*vtMenu*scrollkey*Label

*vtMenu*allow132*Label

*vtMenu*visualbell*Label

*vtMenu*altscreen*Label

*vtMenu*hardreset*Label

*vtMenu*tekshow*Label

*vtMenu*vthide*Label

*fontMenu*fontdefault*Label

*VT100*font1

*SimpleMenu*BackingStore

*SimpleMenu*menuLabel. vertSpace

*SimpleMenu*Sme.height

*mainMenu.Label

*mainMenu*allowsends*Label

*mainMenu*redraw*Label

*mainMenu*continue*Label

*mainMenu*hangup*Label

*mainMenu*kill*Label

*vtMenu.Label

*vtMenu*jumpscroll*Label

*vtMenu*autowrap*Label

*vtMenu*autolinefeed*Label

*vtMenu*appkeypad*Label

*vtMenu*scrollttyoutput*Label

*vtMenu*cursesemul*Label

*vtMenu*marginbell*Label

*vtMenu*softreset*Label

*vtMenu*clearsavedlines*Label

*vtMenu*tekmode*Label

*fontMenu.Label

*fontMenu*font1*Label

*fontMenu*font2*Label

*VT100*font2	*fontMenu*font3*Label
*VT100*font3	*fontMenu*font4*Label
*VT100*font4	*fontMenu*font5*Label
*VT100*font5	*fontMenu*font6*Label
*VT100*font6	*fontMenu*fontescape*Label
*fontMenu*fontsel*Label	*tekMenu.Label
*tekMenu*tektextlarge*Label	*tekMenu*tektext2*Label
*tekMenu*tektext3*Label	*tekMenu*tektextsmall*Label
*tekMenu*tekpage*Label	*tekMenu*tekreset*Label
*tekMenu*tekcopy*Label	*tekMenu*vtshow*Label
*tekMenu*vtmode*Label	*tekMenu*tekhide*Label
*tek4014*fontLarge	*tek4014*font2
*tek4014*font3	*tek4014*fontSmall

You can customize each resource listed. For example, you could change the fonts and labels associated with the font menu to generate unusual results. Similarly, you can set default foreground and background colors for applications.

Kterm

An application closely related to the XTerm is the kterm. This is a command used to display Kanji and Kana characters (characters used in East Asian languages). It takes arguments similar to XTerm, but adds a few entries to the second menu. These entries enable different character sets and modes for translation.

Odds are that you won't see a kterm unless you exchange e-mail in any of these character sets. Some sites in Japan and Korea, however, send MIME-encoded mail that requires a kterm to display even basic Roman characters.

Resources

To an X Windows program, a *resource* is a means of defining an X Windows object's attribute. Because every application comprises these objects, they each require resources to be set. An example of a resource is a font for a label, a background color, or physical dimensions.

Most programs define a set of resources in their source code. These definitions are the reasonable defaults for a program. Beyond that, some resources are defined in an application's default file. You can customize these resources on a system-wide basis. This way, every default XTerm comes up in 9·13 font, for example. Most systems rely on the default resources, however. Lastly, each user can customize the applications by setting his or her own resource values and loading them to the local X server.

Command-line arguments always override system default and user default resources.

Resource names

Each resource must have a name. X Windows takes a hierarchical approach to naming: An application has a top-level name, followed by a hierarchy of resources. Resource levels are separated by dots, so you end up with something like XTerm.background to specify a background for XTerms. Individual objects in an application may have another layer, such as XTerm.fontMenu. background.

Usually asterisks are included in resource names. These are wildcard matches, using the same method as for shell wildcard expansion. So, some resources, as illustrated in the resources mentioned previously, include wildcards.

Resource values

Resource values depend highly on the actual resource. In some cases, they are actual strings that appear on the display. Others are font names, colors, or just flags. Anything can be a resource. It does not need to relate to an X object. An example of this is XTerm.JoinSession, which defines whether multiple ttys can attach to a single XTerm.

Finding the defaults

Usually, the system X resources reside in the applications default directory. On my system, this is located at /usr/lib/X11/app-defaults. Within that directory, every application with specified defaults has its own file. That file must be the same name as the application name, defined in the source of the program. Here is a list of all these files:

Bitmap	Bitmap-color	Chooser	Clock-color	Editres
Editres-color	Fresco	Ghostview	KTerm	XClipboard
XClock	XConsole	XIdle	XLoad	XLogo

```
XLogo-color      XMem          XTerm         XbmBrowser-color    Xfd
Xfm              Xmag          Xman          Xmh                 Xtetris
Xtetris.bw       Xtetris.c
```

The name of the application does not need to be related to the name of the program executed. If I were to rename the Xmag command to magnifying-glass, I'd still need to look at the Xmag resource file and locate resources in the server named Xmag.*.

Resource formats

One of the smallest X resource files is that for the xclock command. The actual application name is Clock, and it includes five resources in the file:

```
Clock*Background:      grey
Clock*BorderColor:      light blue
Clock*hour:            yellow
Clock*jewel:      yellow
Clock*minute:      yellow
```

This defines the five colors used by a default clock. The overall background is gray, with a light blue border. The hour and minute hands are yellow, and the second marker is yellow. Figure 29-8 illustrates what a default clock looks like.

Figure 29-8: A clock using the default values

Changing these defaults can cause a system-wide change to the image. If we were to specify a white background, for example, we would need to run xclock -xrm "Clock*Background: white" and Figure 29-9 shows the result.

```
Sat Nov 25 10:29:48 1995
```

Figure 29-9: A clock with a white background

You can make these changes permanent by changing your own system defaults file.

The .Xdefaults File

The location for your customizations is the `.Xdefaults` file, which is located in your home directory and is automatically loaded when the X server comes up. You can add any customizations you desire to this file, and whenever those applications are invoked, your customizations are present.

Let's take the case of the XTerm. You have used it for a bit and played with the menus to customize the screen. You've decided you like having the scrollbar present, with jump scrolling and a memory retention of 96 lines. You could create an alias guaranteeing that this always happens:

```
alias xterm='xterm -j -sb -sl 96'
```

Whenever you call for an XTerm, you see one with a scrollbar, jump scrolling, and 96 lines of memory. When you run another application, it pops up an XTerm for input, and this time, it lacks the scrollbar! Now, you have to go to the menus and recustomize the window how you like it.

To solve this problem, place some entries in your `.Xdefaults` file so that when any application creates an XTerm, you get the defaults you want. In this case, you need to add the lines:

```
XTerm*scrollBar: True
XTerm*jumpScroll: True
XTerm*saveLines: 96
```

Now, when this loads onto the X server with `xrdb` (which I cover later in this chapter) and whenever any application brings up an XTerm, you'll see the scrollbar, jump scroll, and 96 lines of memory.

Guru: Using Command-Line Arguments Carefully

Using your `.Xdefaults` file to specify arguments doesn't always work. When you use a command-line argument, it overrides the X defaults file. If you are writing a tool that others expect to use, please make certain that if you invoke another X application, you don't use command-line arguments that override a user's defaults unless they are absolutely necessary.

Secret

If you find a default is not to your liking for certain applications, most X applications support the plus (+) before an argument to turn off certain characteristics. So, with the resources specified previously, if I needed a terminal without a scrollbar for a special application, I'd run xterm +sb.

Finding the resource names

Unfortunately, you have no easy way to determine a resource name. If the application has been installed properly, you can look at the resource file in /usr/lib/X11/app-defaults, but that only lists the resources that the programmer could customize.

In the case illustrated previously, none of those three resources were in the resource file for XTerms on my system.

The next step is to check the manual page. In the case of an XTerm, the manual page listed resources, and from there I found the three resources I needed to set.

If the manual page is not adequate, the task is a lot harder. In this case, you need to check the source code for resource specifications. This requires some expertise in X Windows programming, but you can make some reasonable guesses.

You can grep the source code for the string *resource*. An X application may have a structure XtResource, which is a listing of supported resources. Parsing this structure should give you a listing of all the supported resources.

If you already know one resource, you can use grep to find all the references to that resource in the source code. Look around there; usually resources are defined together.

If all else fails, use the strings command on the executable file. This gives you a listing of all the strings compiled into the code, and because resource names are strings, they should all be present. Usually, the best way to process this output is to look for all the lines starting with an asterisk (*). Looking at an XTerm gives the following resources:

*reverseVideo	*iconName	*title	*tekGeometry
*waitForMap	*visualBell	*useInsertMode	*utmpInhibit
*termName	*ttyModes	*tekStartup	*saveLines
*scrollKey	*scrollTtyOutput	*sunFunctionKeys	*scrollBar
*multiScroll	*autoWrap	*reverseWrap	*nMarginBell
*pointerColor	*multiClickTime	*marginBell	*loginShell
*logFile	*logging	*jumpScroll	*boldFont
*curses	*cursorColor	*cutNewline	*charClass
*cutToBeginningOfLine	*internalBorder	*alwaysHighlight	*c132
*vt100.geometry			

The resources I set are all in this listing.

If all of these methods fail, you have one last alternative. If you can find the name of the person who wrote the application, you can e-mail that author and wait for a response. A politely worded request has a much better chance of a response, but you have no guarantees that the author still uses the same e-mail address. Failing this, you are out of luck.

Some applications are much more generous than others. Some applications automatically add their default configuration to your .Xdefaults file so that you can always check to see if the data are already present. Programs that have configuration screens should be like that already.

Comments

The .Xdefaults file supports comments. When a line begins with an exclamation point, the X server considers it a comment and ignores it.

xrdb

Once you have changed all the resources to the form you like, you try to invoke the program, and the changes are not present. Why?

Odds are you have not told the X server about the new defaults. While the server reads the .Xdefaults at boot time, no mechanism automatically re-references the .Xdefaults file when it changes. Fear not, for X Windows provides a tool to reload the defaults, xrdb.

Strictly speaking, the resources are kept in a database maintained by the X server. Hence, the xrdb command means *X resources database.*

The xrdb command loads resource files. The syntax is as follows:

```
xrdb [ options ] [ filename ]
```

The xrdb command runs the filename through the C preprocessor to change the fields listed in Table 29-7 to reasonable defaults. These are usually site-specific.

Table 29-7   Preprocessor Variables for the xrdb File

Field	Meaning
HOST	Sets to the hostname where xrdb executes.
WIDTH	Sets to the width of the screen in pixels.
HEIGHT	Sets to the height of the screen in pixels.
X_RESOLUTION	The horizontal resolution in pixels per meter.
Y_RESOLUTION	The vertical resolution in pixels per meter.

Field	Meaning
PLANES	The number of bit planes for the screen.
CLASS	The type of screen. One of StaticGray, GrayScale, StaticColor, PseudoColor, TrueColor, or DirectColor.
COLOR	Only defined if the CLASS is one of the color displays.

You may see other variables depending on your implementation. (On my system, I have 40.)

Like other X applications, xrdb takes many options, which are listed in Table 29-8.

Table 29-8   xrdb Command-Line Arguments

Option	Argument	Meaning
-help		Gives a brief listing of options and arguments.
-display	display string	Specifies the host and screen for the connection.
-cpp	filename	Uses the specified file for preprocessing the input instead of the C preprocessor.
-nocpp		Does not preprocess the file.
-symbols		Lists the symbols defined for the preprocessor.
-query		Lists the current resource values kept in the server.
-load		Replaces the resource values in the server with the ones in the command.
-merge		Merges the resources in the command with those in the server. If a duplicate exists, the new value replaces the server value.
-remove		Removes the resources from the server.
-edit	filename	The resources are copied into the specified file in an editable format. If the file already exists as a resource file, the new values are merged in correctly, retaining order, comments, and preprocessor lines.
-backup	string	When used with -edit, the previous copy of the file is copied to a new name with the specified string as a suffix.

Continued

Table 29-8 *(continued)*

Option	Argument	Meaning
-Dname [=value]		This option is passed to the C preprocessor.
-Uname		This option is passed to the C preprocessor.
-Idirectory		This option is passed to the C preprocessor.

The name of the file to be processed follows the arguments. If no file is given or if a - is given, xrdb takes the standard input and loads that as the new resources.

When you have edited a new resource file, the best procedure is to merge it into the existing database with xrdb -merge file. If you like those options and want to make them permanent, the command is xrdb -edit ~/. Xdefaults.

More Basic Clients

So far, we've only looked at two of the possible clients for X: the XTerm and xrdb. While an XTerm is a powerful command, many other applications are available for specific tasks. Much of the rest of this section deals with the many applications available on X systems.

The applications covered in the rest of this chapter are fairly basic but include several examples of each to show exactly how variable the X applications can be.

XClock

Usually, on every screen you'll find a clock. Next to XTerms, XClock seems to be the most common application in an initialization file. The normal command to see a clock in X is xclock.

The default clock is analog, updated every minute. Figure 29-10 shows the default clock.

Sat Nov 25 10:32:40 1995

Figure 29-10: xclock

The clock is a standard clock face, with an hour hand and a minute hand. Pointer clicks have no effect on the display, and no menus are raised from the screen.

An XClock has many options. It has the standard X toolkit options that allow for color, display, and size. Beyond that, Table 29-9 lists the other options for a clock.

Table 29-9   XClock Options

Option	Argument	Result
-analog		Shows the standard clock face (default).
-digital		Shows a digital clock that displays the date and time.
-d		Same as -digital.
-chime		Sounds the clock once on the half hour and twice on the hour.
-help		Displays a list of the XClock's syntax and options.
-hd	color	Specifies the color of the clock's hands.
-hl	color	Specifies the color of the outline for the clock's hands.
-padding	integer	Specifies the distance from the window border to any portion of the XClock display.
-update	integer	Specifies the number of seconds between updates. If less than 60, a jewel appears as the second hand.

The differences between an analog clock and a digital clock are purely in the representation of the data. On screen, the two look radically different, as Figure 29-11 shows, but the underlying mechanisms are the same.

Figure 29-11: xclock -digital

Digital clocks are affected by font changes. You can specify any number of fonts for the clock, and it resizes automatically. Figure 29-12 shows an XClock with a different font.

Sat Nov 25 10:32:40 1995

Figure 29-12: xclock -d -fn lucidasans-bold-24

You can also specify varying geometries for a clock. You can make a very small clock by specifying -g 30·30 (Figure 29-13), or an uneven geometry, such as 250·100 (Figure 29-14).

Figure 29-13: xclock -g =30·30

Figure 29-14: xclock -g =250·100

What's interesting about the second example is how the clock centers itself in the display area. The full width is not used, but instead, the circle of the face is placed in the middle of the screen and the rest is used for padding. For a digital clock, if not enough space is allocated, the string is just truncated.

XClock resources

The application name for a clock is XClock, and there is a very short applications default file. The only resource is one to allow input, and it is set to false: XClock.input: false.

Fortunately, the manual page lists a few more resources that are available. Table 29-10 lists those resources.

Table 29-10   XClock Resources

Resource	*Result*
*width	Specifies the width of the clock
*height	Specifies the height of the clock
*update	Specifies the number of seconds between updates
*foreground	Specifies the foreground color of the clock
*background	Specifies the background color of the clock
*hand	Specifies the hand color for the clock

Resource	Result
*highlight	Specifies the highlight color for the hands of the clock
*analog	A Boolean resource to specify either an analog or digital clock
*chime	A Boolean resource to specify if the clock chimes
*padding	An integer to specify the padding between the clock and the window
*font	Specifies the font for a digital clock
*reverseVideo	Specifies if the clock is to use inverse video

You can modify any of these resources, and include them in your
.Xdefaults file.

Other clocks

You'll find some other clocks on X Windows systems. On my system, they are
rclock and oclock.

The rclock clock is a smaller version of an xclock. It displays an analog
clock and accepts only -display, -g, -bg, and -fg as command-line arguments. The icon is the digital mode for the clock, and it does not have a
separate digital mode. Figure 29-15 shows an rclock.

Figure 29-15: rclock

An oclock uses some advanced X features to create a transparent window
for the clock. The clock is analog, but the disk of the clock provides all
there is to the window. It takes similar arguments to xclock, as listed in
Table 29-11. Figure 29-16 shows an oclock.

Table 29-11	oclock Options	
Option	**Argument**	**Result**
-minute	color	Specifies the color for the minute hand
-hour	color	Specifies the color for the hour hand
-jewel	color	Specifies the color for the second jewel
-backing	backing-store	Selects the level of backing store

Continued

Option	Argument	Result
Table 29-11	*(continued)*	
-shape		Uses the shaping extensions to X to create an oval window
-noshape		Causes the clock not to reshape itself
-transparent		Causes the clock to consist of only the jewel, hands, and border

Figure 29-16: oclock

If you are using multiple systems, I recommend using the xclock, as this is almost always present. If you use the same system on a regular basis, check out the other clocks and determine which you like best.

Another clock I've heard about is moonclock. This clock puts the hands on the face of the moon.

Xhost

You can control access to your server with the xhost command. When a server is brought up to control a display, by default anyone on that machine has access to the server, and consequently to the display.

Story: Two Common Mistakes

One of the most common mistakes when logged into a remote machine is to bring up your X applications on that machine's primary display because that is the default. This can sometimes result in some embarrassment, depending on the nature of the application you've just displayed on the other person's screen.

The next most common mistake is setting the DISPLAY environment variable correctly but not enabling display on your own server. You can easily fix this with Xhost.

Xhost is a simple program designed to permit and deny access to the server running on a display. The arguments are simple (see Table 29-12).

Table 29-12   Xhost Options

Argument	Meaning
+*hostname*	Permits access to the server for the specified host
-*hostname*	Denies access to the server for the specified host
+	Allows access for all to the server
-	Denies access for all to the server

The command has no resources or other options.

Xlogo

Another simple command is Xlogo, which displays the standard X logo where specified by the geometry. Figures 29-2 through 29-5 illustrate the different appearances of Xlogo. The only arguments it accepts are the standard toolkit arguments. Table 29-13 lists the allowed resources for Xlogo. The application name is Xlogo.

Table 29-13   Xlogo Options

Resource	Meaning
*width	The width of the window with the logo
*height	The height of the window with the logo
*foreground	The foreground color of the logo
*background	The background color of the logo
*reverseVideo	Boolean, specifies if the sense of the foreground and background colors should be reversed

The xlogo command is useful for testing different aspects of the server, notably the color map and the geometry specifications.

Xrefresh

Sometimes, the screen and the X server are confused about what should and shouldn't be present. For this reason, the xrefresh command was written. It tells the X server to repaint the whole screen or the area specified by the geometry argument. Table 29-14 lists the arguments for Xrefresh, and Table 29-15 lists the resources used.

Table 29-14   Xrefresh Options

Option	Argument	Meaning
-white		Paints the entire screen white before refreshing
-black		Paints the entire screen black before refreshing
-solid	color	Paints the entire screen in the specified color before refreshing
-root		Repaints the root window before refreshing
-none		Refreshes the windows without repainting the background
-geometry	geometry string	Repaints only the specified area of the screen
-display	display string	Repaints the specified display

Table 29-15   Xrefresh Resources

Resource	Type
*black	Boolean
*white	Boolean
*solid	color
*none	Boolean
*root	Boolean
*geometry	geometry string

One bug is that Xrefresh allows multiple background refreshes.

Xwininfo

The last command to consider is xwininfo. This is not strictly a command to create an X window, but instead, it provides data about windows on the display.

Normally, you execute Xwininfo from a command prompt. It then prompts you to select a window with the mouse, and it reports the results of the search. Listing 29-2 shows the results of clicking on the root window.

Listing 29-2: Xwininfo Output

```
$ xwininfo
xwininfo: Please select the window about which you
          would like information by clicking the
          mouse in that window.
ZZZ
xwininfo: Window id: 0x2b (the root window) (has no name)
ZZZ
  Absolute upper-left X:  0
  Absolute upper-left Y:  0
  Relative upper-left X:  0
  Relative upper-left Y:  0
  Width: 640
  Height: 480
  Depth: 8
  Visual Class: PseudoColor
  Border width: 0
  Class: InputOutput
  Colormap: 0x27 (installed)
  Bit Gravity State: ForgetGravity
  Window Gravity State: NorthWestGravity
  Backing Store State: NotUseful
  Save Under State: no
  Map State: IsViewable
  Override Redirect State: no
  Corners:  +0+0  -0+0  -0-0  +0-0
  -geometry 640x480+0+0
```

The command has several options that modify the information retrieved. Table 29-16 lists those options.

Table 29-16   Xwininfo Options

Option	Argument	Result
-display	display string	Examines windows on the specified display.
-help		Prints a help string.
-id	id	Prints the information about the window specified by the ID.
-name	name	Prints the information about the window specified by the name.
-root		Prints information about the root window.
-int		All window IDs should be printed as decimal values.
-tree		Shows the current parent and children of the current window.

Continued

Table 29-16	*(continued)*	
Option	*Argument*	*Result*
-stats		Shows statistics for the specified window.
-bits		Shows information about the raw bits of the window.
-events		Shows the event mask for the window.
-size		Shows the sizing information for the window.
-wm		Shows the window manager's information about the window.
-all		Shows as much information as possible.

You'll use Xwininfo most often for debugging X applications. Using this, you can examine what the server thinks is the appropriate information about the window.

The X Display Manager xdm

Normally, you start X with the xinit or the startx command, but you can start X with other options. The most common option is to use the X display manager, xdm, which assumes that you have already started an X server on a display and are waiting for login information. It prompts for a login ID and a password, and when correct, it executes the .Xsessions file in the user's home directory. When the user exits the session, xdm cleans up the server and displays the login window again.

To run xdm, you need to disable the gettys and place an entry in the /etc/rc startup file for xdm. It has its own configuration files and uses them to know where to start servers and where to place the login prompts.

Note

The xdm command is a bit of a nightmare, in my opinion. The idea is decent, but the implementation is weak. I know of no site that normally runs xdm on workstations (it is necessary for X terminals), and I know no engineers who like it!

xdm Configuration

The bulk of the work with xdm comes in setting up the system to use the display manager. These files are usually kept in /usr/lib/X11/xdm, but the -config command-line option on xdm can change this.

The xdm-config file

The `xdm-config` file contains all the resources used by xdm, including the names of other files, if they are not in their default locations. xdm loads this file into the appropriate server when it starts up.

Some of these resources determine the locations of other files. As we examine these files in detail, the resource name is mentioned. Other resources handle the display features, particularly for the login window. In every case, the name of the application is `DisplayManager`.

You can set some resources specifically for a display (for example, the title header for the login screen). In these cases, the display name immediately follows the `DisplayManager` name:

```
DisplayManager._0.title: Login to local machine
```

The Xservers file

The `Xservers` file is a configuration file that specifies on which devices to run X servers and the xdm login window. The syntax for the file is the display number, followed by a keyword to indicate if it is local, and the command to execute the server, with arguments. For the local machine, the line would be

```
:0 local /usr/bin/X11/X
```

With X11R4, the `Xservers` file became obsolete for all but the local display. If the local entry is not in the `Xservers` file, the xdm process can still support remote displays on X Terminals and other workstations.

The resource to identify the `Xservers` file is `DisplayManager.servers`.

The Xsession file

The `Xsession` file starts the clients on the local server after a successful login attempt. It is usually a shell script that performs some default tasks, such as looking for a local `.xsession` file. If no `.xsession` is present in the user's home directory, a default XTerm is usually executed.

The resource to identify the `Xsession` file is `DisplayManager*session`.

An administrator can reconfigure the `Xsession` file to create a standard login session for users. Depending on the timing of the call to the user's `.xsession`, this configuration can execute before the user sets up anything else local.

The Xresources file

The `Xresources` file is a collection of X resources to be loaded into the X server when a user successfully logs in. This allows the administrator to create a consistent user environment. The resource to identify the `Xresource` file is `DisplayManager*resources`.

The xdm-error file

The xdm-error file is a transcription of errors found in xdm, such as server hang-ups or missing files. The resource for this file is DisplayManager. errorLogFile.

The Xaccess file

The Xaccess file helps control access to xdm by remote clients. This is just a listing of hosts that can request a login prompt from an xdm. It accepts standard UNIX wildcards. If you precede it with an exclamation point, it excludes the following hosts. The resource for Xaccess is DisplayManager.accessFile.

User files for use with xdm

The user needs to configure some files to alter the defaults provided by the administrator and xdm. The startup scripts should check each file for xdm, although a particularly zealous system administrator can write the scripts to ignore the users' desires.

Each of the following files is in the user's home directory.

The .xsession file

The .xsession file is an executable program that sets up the user's desired session. It is analogous to the .xinitrc script for xinit, except this program can be anything executable.

Note

It is not unusual to link .xinitrc and .xsession to acquire a common interface regardless of the startup methodology.

Unlike the .xinitrc file, the .xsession file must have the execute bit set. To make certain of that, use the chmod +x .xsession command.

The .Xresources file

This file specifies the resources to be loaded into the server at startup time. Again, this is analogous to .Xdefaults and may be linked to .Xdefaults. The files are named differently because .Xdefaults is used when the server boots, and .Xresources is used when you attach to a server.

The .xsession-errors file

This file is created each time you access an X server through xdm. The .xession-errors file is just a log of the session and can be used to diagnose problems in .xsession or .Xresources.

Starting xdm

Once you have properly configured xdm, you can execute it from the command line as root. Table 29-17 lists the command-line options.

Option	Argument	Meaning
-config	*filename*	Uses the specified file for configuration information
-nodaemon		Tells xdm to suppress normal daemon behavior
-debug	*integer*	Specifies a debug level for xdm
-error	*filename*	Specifies and error file for xdm
-resources	*filename*	Specifies a replacement resource file for xdm
-server	*filename*	Specifies a replacement for DisplayManager.servers
-session	*filename*	Replaces the DisplayManager*sessions resource

Table 29-17   xdm Options

When you invoke xdm, the screen goes blank and is replaced by the xdm login prompt. xdm continues to run between sessions, until it is manually killed.

If you wish to make xdm a permanent feature of your site, you need to place it in a startup file. Near the end of the last startup file /etc/rc.local, include the following:

```
if [ -f /usr/bin/X11/xdm ] ; then
    /usr/bin/X11/xdm; echo -n xdm
fi
```

Now, when you boot, xdm comes up automatically on your display.

XDMCP

Underneath xdm is the XDMCP for *X display manager control protocol.* This protocol waits for connections, checks them against the Xaccess file, and if allowed, starts a server on the requesting client, followed by the xlogin prompt.

You need XDMCP in the case of arbitrary shutdown of clients. Older versions of xdm required a SIGHUP to terminate a connection if a user's machine suddenly crashed. That SIGHUP may not happen, and xdm may think a session is still going on. Reconnection efforts would lead to undefined results.

With XDMCP, the system knows when to clean up after crashes. In this way, if a machine abruptly shuts down, xdm can reconnect cleanly and easily.

My Session

At the start of this chapter, I illustrated my .xinitrc file. Now that you understand the basics behind starting X, you are ready to see what the commands do. Listing 29-3 shows my login session.

Listing 29-3: My Login Session

```
#!/bin/sh
xclock -geometry =60x60-0+0 -update 1 &       #run a clock
twm&
xterm -fn 7x13 -g =80x24+0+100&
xterm -fn 7x13 -g =80x24+33+66&
xterm -fn 7x13 -g =80x24+66+33&
xterm -fn 6x10 -g =80x24+100+0&
xset s 300&
xhost + > /dev/null 2>&1
/home/xearth/bin/xearth -label -fork
xterm -fn 9x15 -C -n console -title "`/bin/hostname` Console" \
    -g =80x4+0+0 -iconic
#Run xterm in foreground - when this exits, server exits
```

This should start five XTerms, a clock, and xearth. Four of the XTerms are staggered diagonally across the display, and the fifth is iconic. On the screen, it looks like Figure 29-17.

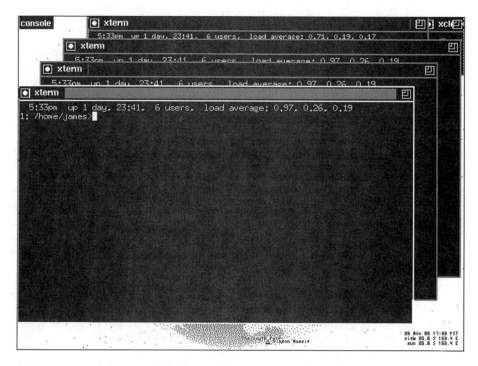

Figure 29-17: My screen at startup

Although dark, you can see the four Xterminals that have started as well as the clock and the background.

Summary

In this chapter, you have learned about the basics of getting started with X. You should be aware of the following:

▶ The basic ideas behind X, including how the protocol works, how the system determines which X server to use, what happens when a session is terminated, and how X handles errors

▶ How to use `xinit` and `startx`, including how to write an `.xinitrc` file

▶ What the standard application arguments are and how to use them

▶ How to make the full use of the XTerm, including understanding the various menus, how to use cut and paste, the different command-line options and resources, and the capability to scroll

▶ What resources are, how to set them, how to find them, and how to load them into a running X server

▶ Some other basic clients like xclock, Xhost, Xlogo, Xrefresh, and Xwininfo

▶ How to start and use the X Display Manager

The next chapter introduces you to window managers.

Chapter 30

Using Window Managers

Window managers are vital to the look and feel of X. The window manager controls communication between applications, how you start applications from X, and the appearance of applications on the screen.

Why Use a Window Manager?

You do not need to run X with a window manager. You could very easily design your .xinitrc script to bring up an xterm, a clock, and any other applications you may want to use. You can use the geometry option to place the windows where you want. Just moving your pointer over the application enables you to use the keyboard and buttons for input. When you move the pointer over the background and use the keyboard, nothing happens. This seems like what you'd want, right?

Suppose, though, you misconfigured your .xinitrc and ended up stacking the windows. Or you've run out of screen real estate and can't place a new application without covering another application. Worse, you've called up an application in the wrong size. A window manager helps you overcome these potential problems.

Note

Remember that the X server is a manager for the physical display only. It receives output requests to display on-screen and manages input requests by directing input to the appropriate device and application.

Several window managers are available. Some are commercial products, such as Sun's olwm and Motif's mwm. Others, such as twm, are in the public domain. Sometimes, arguments between proponents of different window managers can become quite heated; when you find a program that works, it is human nature to encourage others to use your system. Remember that the best window manager is the one that enables you to be productive. Because we all have different work habits and styles, different people feel more productive with different window managers. Newer window managers — called virtual window managers — can manage more space than is available on-screen. In virtual window managers, you can move from screen to screen to see different setups.

Note

I admit a bias toward `twm`. I prefer the look of the window borders, the customizing technique, and the icon management. Of course, it was also the first window manager I used, and it is publicly available.

Window managers manage the windows that X displays. They usually do this by creating a border around a window. This border can take input and is used for commands such as `iconify` or `move`. The window manager also takes the input sent to the root window and performs actions accordingly.

A normal window manager performs the following tasks:

- Repositions windows on your screen
- Manages default positioning of windows
- Manages the resizing of windows
- Manipulates the stacking order of windows
- Manages the conversion of windows to icons, and vice versa
- Refreshes the display
- Creates an easy method to start some programs, such as Xterm

Secret

Everything is a window to X, including the background. The background is called the *root window*. Several programs manipulate this root window, and I discuss them in the next two chapters. None takes input; only the window manager receives input from the root.

Taking a Look at the Big Three

Many window managers are available; I've examined at least ten in the last couple of years. Most are available in the public domain, and many are incremental advances on existing window managers. Of all these window managers, three stand out in terms of the commonality of usage. They are the Motif Window Manager, Open Look Window Manager, and Tab Window Manager.

The Motif Window Manager

The Motif Window Manager is distributed by OSF and is available for a licensing fee on many UNIX platforms. It is the largest of the three window managers in terms of execution size and is very powerful.

A Motif Window Manager session has several notable characteristics. The border surrounding a window is large and is broken at the edge into eight resize pieces. By moving your pointer over one of those edge pieces and pressing the first mouse button, you can drag the edge to enlarge the window. The side pieces increase their particular side, and the corner pieces enable an increase in two dimensions. A larger border box, which lies at the top of the window, includes several areas for clicking your pointer. These create menus with different potential actions. You can resize, move, iconify, raise, or lower windows from these menus. You can even destroy the window, effectively killing the application running in the window. Other buttons iconify the window and maximize the window.

Users familiar with Microsoft's Windows products may be most comfortable with Motif.

Another notable characteristic of Motif is the icon appearance. The Motif Window Manager gathers the icons along one side of your screen. The icon for each window looks the same: a square with four smaller square buttons inside. The application name is also identified. You can make a window reappear from an icon by moving your pointer over the icon and clicking a button. The management menu appears, and you select Maximize to repaint the window. A double-click performs this task automatically.

Caution

Please remember that you can customize each window manager, so your manager's behavior may not match that described here.

Because the Motif Window Manager is part of the Motif package, you may not often find it on home UNIX systems. Vendors of higher-end workstations, such as Hewlett Packard and Digital, have licensed Motif from OSF, so the window manager does appear on these systems. You start Motif with the command mwm.

The Open Look Window Manager

The Open Look Window Manager is available on most Sun workstations. It is tied to several Sun proprietary libraries, so it is not as widely available on other platforms as Motif. It is distributed with Open Windows on every Solaris platform (see Figure 30-1).

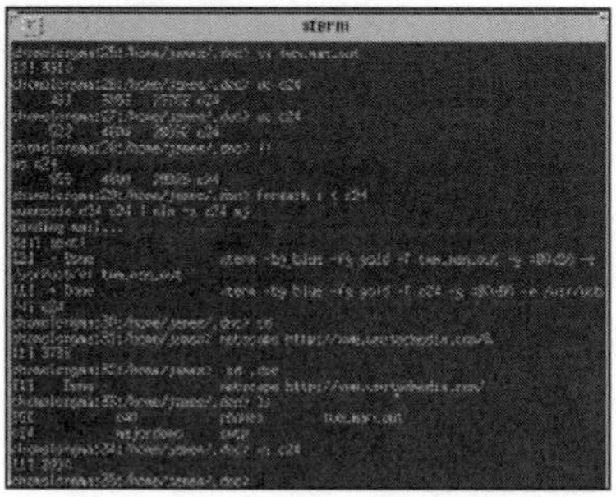

Figure 30-1: A window managed by Open Windows

You should immediately notice that a window managed by Open Look has a different appearance from one managed by Motif. The border is not as strong or prominent on the Open Look window. Instead of having a large tab that you click to resize the window, the Open Look window has little corner tags like those used to hold photographs in some photo albums. It also has a small triangular button to display the pop-up menu containing the window controls. Double-clicking the triangular button iconifies the window.

Secret

The Open Look environment does not normally include buttons to terminate programs. Instead, you need to pull down the menu from the window manager border and select the Quit option to end a program. The window manager sends a SIGTERM to the application, telling it to quit. This is particularly frustrating if you use a window manager that does not have the Quit option on the menu. The only way to kill the program is to go to a different shell, determine the process ID, and use the kill command.

When Motif is compared with Open Look, Motif stands out because it creates the illusion of three dimensions. The border of the Motif window has a three-dimensional feel, whereas Open Look has a flat appearance.

Secret

You can create a three-dimensional appearance in Open Look by specifying the -3 option on the command line when invoking the window manager.

Open Look has its own distinctive icons as well. Like Motif, the Open Look Window Manager groups the icons on one side of the window, each in a square. Figure 30-2 shows a typical icon. Clicking the icon restores it to full size.

Figure 30-2: An Open Look icon

The Open Look Window Manager is often invoked from within a startup script with the olwm command. Table 30-1 lists the command-line arguments.

Table 30-1   Open Look Window Manager Command-Line Arguments

Option	Argument	Description
-2d		Uses the two-dimensional look
-3d		Uses the three-dimensional look
-bd	*color*	Specifies the border color
-bg	*color*	Specifies the background color
-c		Uses the click-to-focus mode

Option	Argument	Description
-click		Uses the click-to-focus mode
-depth	depth	Specifies the depth of the monitor
-display	display	Runs olwm on the specified display
-dsdm		Uses the drop site database management service
-f		Uses the focus-follows-pointer mode
-follow		Uses the focus-follows-pointer mode
-fn	font	Uses the specified font for window titles
-fg	color	Specifies the foreground color
-multi		Manages all windows on the screen
-name	name	Uses the name to look up resources
-nodsdm		Does not use the drop site database management service
-single		Manages windows on a single screen
-syncpid	pid	Sends a signal to the specified process ID when it finishes initializing.
-syncsignal	signal	Sends the specified signal instead of SIGALRM (must be a number)
-visual	class	Specifies the class of the screen
-xrm	resource-string	Specifies a resource on the command line

The Tab Window Manager

The Tab Window Manager is my first choice for window managers. It is a smaller executable file and has a smaller screen presence than either Motif or Open Look. It is a publicly available window manager and is found on nearly every platform (see Figure 30-3).

Note

The original author of the Tab Window Manager is Tom LaStrange, and the original name was "Tom's Window Manager." Because of an influx of e-mail requests, the name was changed to Tab.

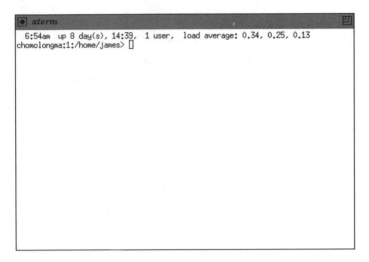

Figure 30-3: The Tab Window Manager

The first thing you'll notice about this window manager is the size of the
borders: They are almost nonexistent. The only real mark of the window
manager is the bar at the top of the window that includes the window name
and the two control spots. On the left is an iconify button: click it, and the
window is iconified. On the left is the resize button: click it, and a mouse drag
enables you to resize. The twm also gives you menus off the root window. See
Table 30-2 to learn how to perform the basic tasks in twm.

Table 30-2   Basic Tasks in twm

To Do This	*Do This*
Reposition windows on your screen	Move the pointer to the name bar on the window. Click the first button, and drag the window to the new position.
Manage default positioning of windows	Move your pointer to the position where you want the window, and click a button there. (By default, when you request a new window, twm gives you a skeleton of the window.)
Resize windows	Move the pointer over the resize icon on the frame, click the first mouse button, and drag the pointer until you've sized the window properly.
Manipulate the stacking order of windows	Move the pointer over the name bar on the window. Click the middle button to raise the window to the top of the stack; click a second time to lower it to the bottom.
Convert windows to icons	Click the iconify icon on the window frame.

To Do This	Do This
Convert icons to windows	Click the icon.
Refresh the display	Using the first button, click while over the root window. The default window includes a refresh command. Pull the pointer over that command, and release the button.

You can create an easier way to start some programs, such as Xterm, via some menus on the root window. You can customize these starts by writing a startup script.

The icons for the Tab Window Manager are a lot smaller, too. By default, they appear where you iconify the window, but you can move them by clicking the middle button over the icon and dragging it to a new location. The icons are also just large enough to include the name of the iconified application, so they take less screen space than Motif or Open Look.

The `twm` command starts the Tab Window Manager. `twm` has only five options, as outlined in Table 30-3.

Table 30-3   twm Command-Line Options

Option	Argument	Description
-display	display	Runs the window manager on the designated display
-s		Manages only the default display
-f	filename	Uses the specified file as the `twm` startup file
-v		Prints error messages when an unexpected X event occurs
-q		Doesn't print errors

An additional feature of the Tab Window Manager is the icon manager. All applications are listed in the icon manager and can be iconified and reopened from that manager. Figure 30-4 shows the icon manager. Display the icon manager by pressing the middle mouse button while over the root window and selecting icon manager.

When using the icon manager with other variables, you can eliminate the need to keep icons on the screen.

Figure 30-4: The twm icon manager

Customizing a Window Manager

Window managers are already powerful applications, but you can extend their power even further with some basic customizations. Many window managers use the following format for defining customizations, although these are specifically for `twm`.

Customizations fall into three basic types. First, you can set some basic variables, such as fonts for menus and the like. Second, you can set some basic key bindings that describe the functions performed when the window manager receives certain inputs. Finally, you can define your own menus and include them where desired.

`twm` comes with its own default startup file. This file defines the basic colors and fonts that the window manager can use and also describes the default menu. Your own customizations should be included in a file named `.twmrc` and kept in your home directory. Alternatively, you can include it as a command-line argument in your `.xinitrc` script.

Setting variables

With `twm`, you set variables in one of three ways, depending on the variable. For toggles, you list the variable on the line; negating a toggle involves prepending that toggle with *No*. Normal variables require the value to follow them on the line. Other variables can take a list of values that are grouped in curly braces ({ }).

Note Other window managers may have different assignment formats: Some require a colon, and others require an equal sign. The best bet is to examine the manual page for the window manager of choice.

Many variables control the operation of the window manager; Table 30-4 outlines twm's variables. Other window managers have similar variables. To retrieve the appropriate listing, examine the manual page. The Colors variable has subvariables listed in Tables 30-5 and 30-6.

Table 30-4   twm Variables for Customization

Variable	Type	Action
AutoRaise	list	Automatically raises the window to the top when you place the pointer over the window. The application's name should appear in quotation marks within the list.
AutoRelative Resize	toggle	Makes the window's rubber band automatically contract from the nearest edge to start the resizing. (Normally, when you resize a window, the pointer must cross an edge of the window before the rubber band appears.)
BorderWidth	pixels	Specifies the width of the border in pixels. The default is 2.
ButtonIndents	pixels	Specifies the indent for the two title buttons, iconify and resize.
ClientBorder Width	toggle	Tells the window manager to use the client-specified border width instead of the one specified by BorderWidth.
Colors	list	Sets the colors for specific traits. Table 30-5 provides a list of each possible color trait and includes expanded traits such as BorderColor.
Constrained MoveTime	integer	Defines the number of milliseconds between clicks before a constrained move operation can occur. (Constrained moves enable movement only in the horizontal or vertical direction.) The default is 400.
Cursors	list	Defines the cursors for each location. Each location should have a cursor associated with it. The locations are Frame, Title, Icon, IconMgr, Move, Resize, Menu, Button, Wait, Select, and Destroy.
Decorate Transients	toggle	Indicates that transient windows should have title bars.
Default Function	function	Specifies a function to execute when an event is received and no binding is found. Must be set after all fonts are assigned.

Continued

Table 30-4   *(continued)*

Variable	Type	Action
DontIconify ByUnmapping	list	Specifies a list of windows that should not be iconified by unmapping the window.
DontMoveOff	toggle	Indicates that windows should not be moved off the screen.
DontSqueeze Title	list	Provides a list of windows that should have full-length title bars.
ForceIcons	toggle	Specifies that icon pixmaps in the Icon variable should override client-supplied pixmaps.
FramePadding	integer	Specifies the padding between the title bar decorations and the window frame.
Grayscale	list	Specifies the colors for use on a gray-scale display. See Colors.
IconBorder Width	integer	Specifies the border width for icons.
IconDirectory	string	Specifies a directory to be searched if a bitmap file cannot be found.
IconFont	string	Specifies the font for the application name displayed in the icon.
IconifyBy Unmapping	list	Indicates which applications should be iconified by unmapping. Applications can be remapped through the icon manager. If no list is provided, all applications are iconified by unmapping.
IconManager DontShow	list	Specifies a list of applications that should not be listed in the icon manager.
IconManager Font	string	Specifies the font to use in the icon manager.
IconManager Geometry	string	Specifies the geometry for the icon manager. The default number of columns is 1.
IconManagers	list	Creates a list of icon managers. Each item in the list has four terms: the window name, the icon name (optional), the geometry, and the number of columns. This variable can create multiple icon managers.
IconManager Show	list	Specifies a list of applications to appear in the icon manager. Overrides the IconManagerDontShow variable.

Variable	Type	Action
IconRegion	string	Specifies the region of the screen for icons. Five strings must be included: a geometry string, a vertical gravity string, a horizontal gravity string, a grid width, and a grid height. I use IconRegion 840x150+400+0 North West 20 10, which allocates the top-right part of my screen for icons. The icons start at the top-left, with the icon grid being 20 · 10 pixels.
Icons	list	Specifies bitmaps to use as applications icons.
Interpolate MenuColors	toggle	Specifies that menu colors can be described in the menu definitions.
MakeTitle	list	Specifies a list of windows on which title bars should be placed. Used to override NoTitle.
MaxWindowSize	string	Specifies the largest allowable window on a system.
MenuFont	string	Specifies the font for use on menus.
Monochrome	list	Specifies a list of colors for a monochrome monitor. See Colors.
MoveDelta	integer	Specifies the number of pixels the pointer must move before the window moves.
NoBackingStore	toggle	Indicates that menus should not include backing store. This is used with fast servers.
NoCaseSensitive	toggle	Indicates that icons in the icon manager should be sorted in a case-insensitive fashion.
NoDefaults	toggle	Indicates that the default buttons on the title bar should not be supplied.
NoGrabServer	toggle	Tells twm not to grab the server when you use menus and move windows. Normally, the display is frozen until the operation is complete. This enables other applications to continue to display output.
NoHighlight	list	Specifies applications whose borders should not be highlighted to track pointer movement.
NoIconManagers	toggle	Indicates that no icon manager should be created.
NoMenuShadows	toggle	Indicates that menus should not create shadows.
NoRaiseOn Deiconify	toggle	Specifies that windows should not be raised to the top of the stack when deiconified.
NoRaiseOnMove	toggle	Specifies that a window should not be raised when moved.

Continued

Table 30-4   *(continued)*

Variable	Type	Action
NoRaiseOn Resize	toggle	Specifies that a window should not be raised when resized.
NoRaiseOnWarp	toggle	Specifies that the window should not be raised when the pointer is "warped" into the window.
NoSaveUnders	toggle	Tells the window manager not to request that menus be saved to the server.
NoStackMode	list	Specifies a list of applications whose requests to pop to the top of the stack should be ignored.
NoTitle	list	Specifies a list of applications that should not receive title bars.
NoTitleFocus	toggle	Tells twm that the keyboard focus should not be changed when the pointer enters a window.
NoTitle Highlight	list	Indicates that the highlighting in the title bar that indicates which window has focus should not be used for the specified list of applications.
OpaqueMove	toggle	Tells the window manager to move the entire window when a move is being made instead of a frame and reset.
Pixmaps	list	Specifies the pixmaps to be used with each field. The only one currently specified is the TitleHighlight.
Priority	integer	Indicates the priority of twm.
Random Placement	toggle	Indicates that new windows without a specified geometry should be placed in the screen in a pseudorandom fashion. If this variable is not set, the user must drag the outline.
ResizeFont	string	Specifies the font used in the window to indicate the resizing of another window.
Restart PreviousState	toggle	Tells the window manager to attempt a restart in the same state the previous window manager exited. Used to keep iconified applications iconified.
SaveColor	list	Specifies the colors to be kept as pixel values in the root window.

Variable	Type	Action
ShowIcon Manager	toggle	Tells the window manager to display the icon manager when the window manager begins.
SortIcon Manager	toggle	Indicates that the applications in the icon manager should be sorted alphabetically.
SqueezeTitle	list	Specifies a list of applications that have minimalist title bars. By default, the title bar stretches across the top of the window. Each entry can have a justification: left, right, or center. You can also specify a ratio to indicate placement.
StartIconified	list	Specifies a list of applications that are to start as icons.
TitleButton BorderWidth	integer	Specifies the width of the border surrounding title buttons in pixels.
TitleFont	string	Specifies the font to be used for the name in the title bar.
TitlePadding	integer	Specifies the padding between buttons, text, and highlighted areas in the title bar.
UnknownIcon	string	Specifies the icon used when no other icon is specified.
UsePPosition	string	Indicates whether program-requested locations should be honored (either on, off, or nonzero).
WarpCursor	list	Specifies a list of applications for which the pointer should be warped into the window when deiconified.
WarpUnmapped	toggle	Specifies that any iconified windows in the warp ring should be deiconified when accessed.
WindowFunction	function	Specifies the function to execute when a window is selected from the menu. Must be set after you've set all the fonts.
WindowRing	list	Specifies a list of windows for warping pointers.
XorValue	integer	Specifies the value to be used when windows are moved and resized.
Zoom	integer	Indicates the number of outlines to be drawn when a window is iconified or deiconified.

Table 30-5   Color Variables

Color Trait	Action
`DefaultBackground`	Sets the default background color of the root window
`DefaultForeground`	Sets the default foreground color for the root window
`MenuBackground`	Sets the background color for menus
`MenuForeground`	Sets the foreground color for menus
`MenuShadowColor`	Sets the color for the menu shadow
`MenuTitleBackground`	Sets the background color for the menu title
`MenuTitleForeground`	Sets the foreground color for the menu title
`PointerBackground`	Sets the background color for the pointer
`PointerForeground`	Sets the foreground color for the pointer

Table 30-6   Color List Variables

Variable	Type	Action
`BorderColor`	string/list	Specifies a border color for use by windows not running as icons. When the optional list is specified, different applications can have different border colors.
`BorderTile Background`	string/list	Specifies the default background color in the gray pattern of unhighlighted borders. The optional list is the same as `BorderColor`'s.
`BorderTile Foreground`	string/list	Specifies the foreground color for the border tile.
`IconBackground`	string/list	Specifies background colors for icons. The default applies to all icons but can be overridden by entries in the list.
`IconBorderColor`	string/list	Specifies the border color for icons. The default applies to all icons but can be overridden by entries in the list.
`IconForeground`	string/list	Specifies the foreground color for icons. The default applies to all icons but can be overridden by entries in the list.
`IconManager Background`	string/list	Specifies the background color for each application in the icon manager. The list overrides the default.

Variable	*Type*	*Action*
IconManager Foreground	string/list	Specifies the foreground color for each application in the icon manager. The list overrides the default.
IconManager Highlight	string/list	Specifies the color for the highlight in the icon manager. This can be application-specific.
TitleBackground	string/list	Specifies the background color for the title bar. The list overrides the default.
TitleForeground	string/list	Specifies the foreground color for the title bar. The list overrides the default.

The management of color is of particular interest. Although most variables take a single argument or a list, Colors variables can have variables nested inside. Consider this case:

```
Color
{
    TitleForeground      "blue"
    TitleBackground "hotpink"
    BorderTileForeground "#d0cf11"
    BorderTileBackground "#007777"
    IconBackground "limegreen" { "XTerm" "yellow" }
    IconForeground "orange" { "XTerm" "brown" }
    IconBorderColor "black" { "XTerm" "blue" }
    BorderColor     "red" { "XClock" "yellow" }
    MenuForeground       "seashell"
    MenuBackground       "forestgreen"
    IconManagerBackground     "pink" { "XTerm" "blue" }
    IconManagerForeground     "brown"    { "XTerm" "gold" }
    MenuTitleForeground      "gold"
    MenuTitleBackground      "red"
    MenuShadowColor      "yellow"
}
```

This example tells twm that the titles should be blue on hotpink in all cases. The border tiling for an unhighlighted window should be the two RGB specifications. Icons should be orange on limegreen unless they are xterms, in which case they should be brown on yellow. The icon border should be black, unless it is an xterm, in which case it should be blue. Menus are seashell on forestgreen. The icon manager is brown on pink except for xterms, which are gold on blue. Window borders are red when the pointer is over them except for the clock, which is yellow. Menu titles are gold on red, and the menu shadow is yellow.

Binding keys

You can also customize the Tab Window Manager by attaching actions to keystrokes and button presses. These key bindings are fairly simple, although at first glance they may not be intuitive. Key bindings should follow variable definitions in the startup file, but the order is not mandatory.

The syntax for a key binding is simple. You need the key name followed by a context and a function. The fields are separated by a colon. You must use the appropriate quoted keysym abbreviation (see the section on xmodmap) to specify the key name. Buttons are Button1 through Button5. You can modify the key symbol by following it with an equal sign and one of the following words: shift, control, lock, meta, mod1, mod2, mod3, mod4, or mod5. All these except the mods can be abbreviated to the first letter. The mods are abbreviated m1 through m5.

Contexts are where the pointer is located. You can list more than one context so long as you connect them with the word *or*. Valid contexts are window (w), title (t), icon (i), root (r), frame (f), or iconmgr (m).

Functions are predefined and listed in Table 30-7.

Table 30-7 twm Functions

Function	Argument	Action
!	*string*	Executes the string as a command. The string must be in quotation marks.
f.autoraise		Toggles whether the selected window is automatically raised when entered by the pointer.
f.backiconmgr		Warps the pointer to the previous column of the current icon manager.
f.beep		Sounds the keyboard bell.
f.bottomzoom		Resizes the window to fill only the bottom half of the screen.
f.circledown		Lowers the topmost window that occludes another window.
f.circleup		Raises the bottommost window.
f.colormap	*string*	Rotates the color map to one of the next, prev, or default values.
f.deiconify		Deiconifies the selected window.
f.delete		Attempts to delete the selected window.
f.deltastop		Enables a user-defined function to quit if the pointer has moved more than MoveDelta pixels.

Function	Argument	Action
f.destroy		Disconnects the X server from the application in the selected window.
f.downiconmgr		Warps the pointer to the next row in the icon manager.
f.exec	*string*	Passes the argument string to /bin/sh for execution.
f.focus		Moves keyboard focus to the selected window. If the selected window is already in focus, this removes the focus.
f.forcemove		Enables moves off the screen despite the DontMoveOff variable.
f.forwiconmgr		Warps the pointer to the next column of the icon manager.
f.fullzoom		Resizes the selected window to the full size of the display, or restores the original size if already fully zoomed.
f.function	*string*	Executes the user-specified function.
f.hbzoom		Is synonymous with f.bottomzoom.
f.hideiconmgr		Unmaps the current icon manager.
f.horizoom		Resizes the current application to the full width of the display.
f.htzoom		Is synonymous with f.topzoom.
f.hzoom		Is synonymous with f.horizoom.
f.iconify		Iconifies the selected window or deiconifies the selected icon.
f.identify		Displays a summary of the name and geometry of the selected window.
f.lefticonmgr		Is same as f.backiconmgr, except that it does not change rows.
f.leftzoom		Resizes to fill only the left half of the display.
f.lower		Lowers the selected window.
f.menu	*string*	Raises the named menu. You can nest cascading menus.
f.move		Repositions the selected window.
f.nexticonmgr		Warps the pointer to the next icon manager.
f.nop		Performs no operation.
f.previconmgr		Warps the pointer to the previous icon manager.

Continued

Table 30-7 *(continued)*

Function	Argument	Action
f.priority	*string*	Sets the priority of the client owning the selected window to the value of the string.
f.quit		Stops execution of twm.
f.raise		Raises the selected window.
f.raiselower		Raises the selected window to the top of the stack; if it is already at the top, lowers it.
f.refresh		Repaints the display.
f.resize		Resizes the selected window.
f.restart		Kills twm and restarts it on the screen.
f.righticonmgr		Is same as f.nexticonmgr, except that it doesn't change rows.
f.rightzoom		Resizes the selected window to fill the right half of the screen.
f.saveyourself		Sends the SAVEYOURSELF message to the selected window.
f.showiconmgr		Maps the icon manager.
f.sorticonmgr		Sorts the entries in the icon manager alphabetically.
f.title		Sets the title of a menu.
f.topzoom		Resizes the window to fill the top half of the screen.
f.unfocus		Resets focus to pointer-driven.
f.upiconmgr		Warps the cursor to the previous row of the icon manager.
f.vlzoom		Is synonymous with f.leftzoom.
f.vrzoom		Is synonymous with f.rightzoom.
f.warpring	*string*	Warps the pointer to the next or previous window in the WindowRing variable, according to the string (either next or prev).
f.warpto	*string*	Warps the pointer to the window with the specified name.
f.warptoiconmgr	*string*	Warps the pointer to the specified icon manager.
f.warptoscreen	*string*	Warps the pointer to the specified screen.
f.winrefresh		Repaints the selected window.
f.zoom		Resizes the selected window to be the full height of the screen.

A sample binding looks like this:

```
Button1 : title : f.move
```

This calls the `move` function when button one is pressed in the title bar.

```
"F1" = c : root : f.warpto "xbiff"
```

This causes the pointer to warp to the `xbiff` window when the Ctrl key and the F1 key are simultaneously pressed and the pointer is over the root window.

Caution

The window manager obtains access to these keys before any application program, so if you need any of the keys, make sure you don't map them to the window manager.

Customizing functions

You can define your own functions as combinations of other `twm` functions. You need to specify the keyword `Function` followed by a name and a list of commands in parentheses, as follows:

```
Function "move-and-lower" { f.move f.lower }
```

You can now specify this with `f.function "move-and-lower"`.

Adding buttons to the title bar

You can add additional functions to your title bar by adding buttons. Buttons are added from the left or the right with `LeftTitleButton` or `RightTitle Button` followed by a recognized bitmap, an equal sign, and a function, as follows:

```
LeftTitleButton    "boat" = f.identity
```

Valid button icons are `:dot`, `:iconify`, `:resize`, `:xlogo`, `:delete`, `:menu`, and `:question`.

Creating menus

Lastly, you can customize menus with the Tab Window Manager. You must identify each menu with the keyword `Menu` followed by a case-sensitive name. You can optionally specify two colors as the foreground and background colors. Then, specify a listing of menu entries between curly braces ({ }).

Menu entries are strings and functions. To create cascading menus, use functions that are other menus. Optionally, you can specify foreground and background colors between the string and function. For example,

```
Menu "Clients"
{
    "Clients"    f.title
    "Utility"    f.menu "Utility"
    "Xterm"    f.menu "XTERM"
}
```

This raises a menu with two selectable entries and the title "Clients". Each entry then can bring up another menu, in a cascade.

The "Utility" menu looks like this:

```
Menu "Utility"
{
        "Utility"        f.title
        "Mail"           !"/home/james/bin/vmail&"
        "News"           !"/home/james/xreader/procI&"
        "Redraw"         f.refresh
        "Restart"        f.restart
        "ScreenSave Off"         !"xset s 0 &"
        "ScreenSave On" !"xset s 2 &"
        "XGames"         f.menu "XGames"
        "Xbiff"          !"xbiff -bg purple -bd white -fg yellow -
geometry =80x80-85+0 &"
        "Xclock"         !"xclock -bg grey20 -fg gold -hd aliceblue -hl
orange -update 1 -geometry =80x80-0+0 &"
        "Xeyes"          !"xeyes -fg blue -center red -outline
forestgreen -g 75x50+538+0 &"
}
```

This window contains ten entries and a title. Some entries kick off programs; others kick off twm functions.

A standard twm menu, TwmWindows, gives you a listing of every window. When a window is selected, it is deiconified and raised unless WindowFunction is set to a different value.

Using Other Window Managers

Besides the three main window managers listed previously, several other window managers may be of interest. Rather than describing each in detail, I've listed them in Table 30-8.

Table 30-8   Other Window Managers

Window Manager	Origin
xwm	The original X window manager
gwm	The GNU window manager
uwm	The universal window manager
swm	The Solbourne window manager
fvwm	A virtual window manager (can look like Windows)
olvwm	The Open Look virtual window manager
tvtm	Tab virtual window manager

You can find source code for these and other window managers on the accompanying CD-ROM.

Using Virtual Window Managers

Three of the window managers listed in Table 30-8 — fvwm, olvwm, and tvtm — are virtual window managers. Other window managers are restricted by the physical size of your screen, but not the virtual window managers! These are given a fixed amount of screen space to manage, usually larger than the physical screen. This enables you to spread out your applications into various areas and then move from virtual screen to virtual screen. With this kind of window manager, you could have one location where you are working on a project, another area where you are composing documentation, and a third area where you have a continuously running e-mail session.

Despite my preference for the Tab Window Manager, I found that the Open Look Virtual Window Manager was the best for my productivity when I was using a virtual window manager. Again, your mileage may vary.

Comparing Looks and Feels

Beyond being just a window manager, each system gives X Windows a particular "look and feel." Definitions of how certain X window widgets should look to comply with a certain system actually exist. The two common looks and feels are Motif and Open Look.

Note

Motif has effectively won the war between looks and feels. Sun, the primary backer of Open Look, has conceded that Motif is needed and has developed the Common Desktop Environment so that it can have a similar desktop to other UNIX platforms.

Motif

OSF developed Motif, which is the most common look and feel for any X application. Motif buttons have a three-dimensional appearance, including shading and the illusion of depression when selected. The scroll bar has two arrow buttons at either end, and the thumb is a darker band.

You can find the complete Motif definition in *OSF/Motif Programmer's Guide* and *OSF/Motif Style Guide*.

Sun and AT&T developed Open Look as a definition of a look and feel for an X interface. The differences between Motif and Open Look are numerous. The most obvious is that Open Look buttons are rounded and have no shadows. The interface has no three-dimensional feel.

You can find the Open Look interface definition in *Open Windows Programmers' Guide*.

One major advantage of Open Windows is the inclusion of a decent desktop, illustrated in Figure 30-5. There are easy shortcuts to each application, and the olwm menus are designed to work in this environment.

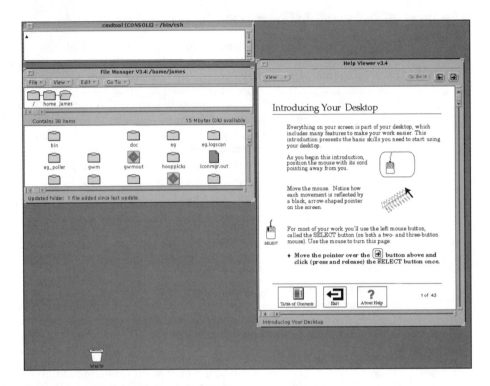

Figure 30-5: The Open Windows desktop

The Common Desktop Environment

The next generation desktop is the Common Desktop Environment (CDE). It was originally developed at Hewlett Packard and works as a virtual environment. Sun has adopted it as CDE for Solaris.

CDE is based on Motif instead of Open Windows. You can execute various programs from a control panel located on one side of the screen (by default, the bottom). You can also move among three different virtual screens, called *rooms*. Figure 30-6 illustrates the starting CDE environment.

Figure 30-6: The Common Desktop Environment

Summary

This chapter introduced window managers and different styles for X Windows. It described

▶ The reasons why window managers are needed

▶ The basics of what a window manager should do

▶ The appearance of the three main window managers

▶ How to customize the Tab Window Manager

▶ The common styles for X Windows

▶ The UNIX desktop options

The next chapter continues the tour of X applications.

Chapter 31

Common X Applications

This chapter begins a survey of X applications available to the X user by covering the common desktop-type applications.

I've broken this chapter into two categories: applications normally run on desktops and applications used to customize desktops.

Desktop Applications

Besides Xterm and Xclock (discussed in Chapter 29), you may want to run several other applications on your desktop. Some of these applications should start up when you begin your X session, and others should be readily available.

A manual page browser

One of the most useful utilities in UNIX is the manual pages. As you might expect, one of the first X utilities is a manual page viewer.

The xman utility displays manual pages in a separate window. It takes advantage of X's capability of using multiple fonts to reformat the page in an attractive fashion. The execution is not exactly intuitive: When you invoke xman, you don't immediately specify a manual page. Instead, xman pops up an initial window, illustrated in Figure 31-1. The window has three buttons. Help provides the same view of an xman help screen as clicking Manual Page. When you are on the manual page, you can browse directories and select pages to be displayed.

Figure 31-1: The initial screen for xman

When the manual page first comes up, you see the help page for xman. It includes instructions for use. Two menus are accessible: Options and Sections. You can open the menus by moving the pointer over the menu button and clicking the leftmost pointer button or by pressing Ctrl and the left or right pointer button anywhere in the display.

To access a manual page, open a directory from the Options menu and scroll to search for the appropriate page. When you see what you want, select the option, and the manual page is formatted and displayed. Figure 31-2 illustrates this.

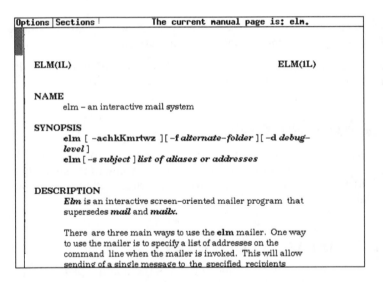

Figure 31-2: The Elm manual page in xman

Use the scroll bar to look down the page. You can search for new manual pages by selecting the search option or by pressing Ctrl-S.

One of the more interesting options is to split the screen. This enables you to use the top half as your directory screen to search for commands and to use the bottom half to display the manual page. A split screen enables faster movement between related commands.

The xman command takes the standard toolkit options and a couple of others: -bothshown starts the viewer in split-screen mode, and -notopbox starts the viewer with the help window. The resources are extensive: Each menu and button has its appearance defined as a resource.

You can best define `xman` as an option off a window manager menu or as an iconic application from the startup file.

xfm: An X file manager

The X Windows File Manager, `xfm`, displays the directories and files available for use, starting in your home directory. It also brings up an application window that lists some common applications, such as a mail reader, an editor, and a manual page browser. Figure 31-3 shows the standard appearance of the screen.

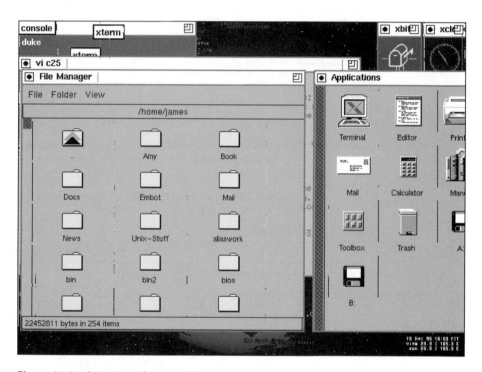

Figure 31-3: xfm's view of my world

Secret

Because `xfm` relies on a lot of support files, you need to run `xfm.install` before running `xfm`. A good system administrator ought to include this step when creating the account.

The File Manager is well designed and implemented. On the left is the listing of files in my home directory. (Directories are illustrated with folders and names; files are illustrated with a piece of paper.) Double-clicking a directory opens it for you. Double-clicking a file brings it up in an editor.

Even better, dragging a file over to one of the icons on the Applications window and dropping it in the application invokes the application with the file.

Each application in the Applications window is tied to another X-based application. Double-clicking an application brings it up on your display, so starting without a drop object is possible.

You can step through each window with your scroll bar. Each window contains a menu bar from which you can perform various tasks. In the primary window, you'll see three menus: File, Folder, and View. The File menu contains nine entries, listed in Table 31-1.

Table 31-1   The File Manager Menu

Entry	Action
New	Creates a new file in the current directory, using a pop-up window to request a name. This becomes a zero-length file but can be dragged and dropped to an editor.
Move	Provides a pop-up window prompting for a new name and then renames the file.
Copy	Provides a pop-up window prompting for a new name and then makes a copy of the file.
Link	Provides a pop-up window prompting for a new name and then makes a link to the file. The link is a symbolic link.
Delete	Deletes the selected file.
Select	Enables the selection of multiple files based on regular expressions.
Select all	Selects all files in the current directory.
Deselect all	Clears any selection.
Quit	Exits the File Manager.

The Folder menu contains six entries, listed in Table 31-2.

Table 31-2   The Folder Menu

Entry	Action
New	Enables you to create a new directory
Go to	Changes the directory displayed to the one you specify
Home	Returns to the home directory
Up	Takes you to the parent directory
Empty	Removes all the files
Close	Closes the current window

The last menu is View, which contains nine items broken into three groups. The first three items define how the file entries are viewed and are mutually exclusive. Tree displays the file tree with directories only. Click the arrows to expand a directory or to move back. Figure 31-4 shows a directory tree view.

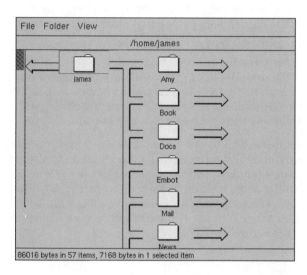

Figure 31-4: The File Manager tree

The default view is by icon, and the last option, Text, creates a view that looks like an ls list. Figure 31-5 shows the Text listing.

File Folder View				
/home/james				
[..]	1024	root	rwxr-xr-x	Fri Dec 15 10
[Amy]	1024	james	rwxr-xr-x	Fri Mar 24 03
[Book]	1024	james	rwxr-xr-x	Fri Mar 24 01
[Docs]	1024	james	rwxr-xr-x	Wed Dec 6 1
[Embot]	1024	james	rwxr-xr-x	Fri Mar 24 03
[Mail]	10240	james	rwxr-xr-x	Fri Dec 15 16
[News]	1024	james	rwxr-xr-x	Tue Jul 18 11:
[Unix-Stuff]	1024	james	rwxr-xr-x	Mon Apr 10 1
[aliaswork]	1024	james	rwxr-xr-x	Fri Mar 24 01
[bin]	1024	james	rwxr-xr-x	Sun Nov 5 0
[bin2]	1024	james	rwxr-xr-x	Fri Mar 24 01
[bios]	1024	james	rwxr-xr-x	Fri Mar 24 03
[book2]	1024	james	rwxr-xr-x	Fri Mar 24 01
[cleanup]	1024	james	rwxr-xr-x	Wed Nov 29 (
[csh]	1024	james	rwxr-xr-x	Fri Mar 24 01
22452811 bytes in 255 items				

Figure 31-5: The File Manager Text listing

The next three items are also mutually exclusive and specify the sorting order. By default, items are sorted alphabetically, but you can sort them by size or by age.

The last three items are each toggles. You can request that folders be hidden, that folders and files be intermixed (by default, all folders are displayed before files), and that hidden files (those that start with a dot) be displayed.

Within the display, you have several options. The first pointer button selects a file or folder. By pressing the button and holding it down when the pointer is over a file, you can drag the file to the Applications window and start an application, or you can move the file to a new directory by dropping it in a folder. Drags work across multiple windows. Dragging a file to the Trash in the Applications window is the same as deleting the file.

Press the third pointer buttonto open a window containing command options. The Open option attempts to bring the file up in the appropriate viewer or opens a new window if the selected object is a folder. Move, Copy, and Delete work in the same fashion as they do from the pull-down menu. Information displays a pop-up window containing all the file information, and Permissions enables you to change the permissions on a file by clicking the appropriate box (see Figure 31-6).

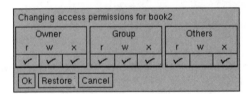

Figure 31-6: Sample permissions modification box

The Applications window provides a default list of applications (see Figure 31-7). These include a basic editor, calculator, terminal, manual page display, and mail tool. You can start each with a double-click. Clicking the third pointer button brings up a menu to modify the icons in this window.

Figure 31-7: The Applications window

Clicking the third pointer button against the background brings up the system menu, which enables you to add to the Applications window. You can modify the actions, add new applications, and start a new File Manager window.

Including the X File Manager in startup scripts is helpful, particularly for novice users unaccustomed to the UNIX command-line interface.

Customizing xfm

On-screen customization is restricted to the Applications window. Each application has several different attributes: Name, Directory, Filename, Icon, Push-Action, and Drop-Action. The Name is displayed on the application screen below the specified icon. The two other important routines are the Push-Action and the Drop-Action. These are the programs executed when the user presses the icon or drops a file on the icon.

If you want to run a program, the first word of the action must be *exec.* Other words are keywords. These are EDIT, which brings up the default editor; OPEN, which assumes the file is a directory to be opened; and LOAD, which loads a new Applications window.

This information is kept in a file, ~/.xfm/xfm-apps. Each entry in this file contains six colon-separated fields, detailed in Table 31-3.

Table 31-3	Customization Fields
Field	**Meaning**
Name	The name that appears on the screen
Directory	The specified directory for an OPEN command
Filename	The specified file for an EDIT or LOAD command
Icon	The icon to be used on screen
Push-Action	The push action (the program executed when the user presses the icon)
Drop-Action	The drop action (the program executed when the user drops a file on the icon)

More important are the techniques for customizing the File Manager display. These are kept in ~/.xfm/xfmrc. Each entry in this file contains four colon-separated fields. The first is a pattern to be matched. This isn't a regular expression or a wildcard match; it's a crippled wildcard match. An asterisk (*) may be leading or trailing, but not embedded.

The second field is the icon used to display the file on the File Manager screen. The third field is a push action, and the last field is a drop action.

Note

To specify any number of files dropped onto an icon, use $*.

When a file is encountered for display, the list of patterns in xfmrc is searched until a match is found. Then, the specified icon is displayed. Here is a sample customization:

```
*.c:xfm_c.xpm:EDIT:
```

This tells the File Manager to use the xfm_c icon to display the .c file and, when the icon is selected, to bring the file up in an editor.

Just as the xfm-apps file is an application file, you can create any number of subsequent application files by using the LOAD command:

```
newstool::xfm-news:xfm_news.xpm:LOAD:
```

This creates an icon for use on the application file that, when clicked, brings up a new application package, presumably of news tools. Here are all the available icons and pixmaps for xfm:

calc.xpm	calendar.xpm	cdrom.xpm
clipboard.xpm	compress.xpm	disk.xpm
edit.xpm	editor.xpm	find.xpm
ghostview.xpm	grep.xpm	lock.xpm
mail.xpm	make.xpm	pixmap.xpm
printer.xpm	tar.xpm	taz.xpm

tex.xpm	trash.xpm	trash2.xpm
xchess.xpm	xdbx.xpm	xdbx48.xpm
xfm_a.xpm	xfm_appmgr.xpm	xfm_apps.xpm
xfm_au.xpm	xfm_blackhole.xpm	xfm_c.xpmxfm_cc.xpm
xfm_core.xpm	xfm_data.xpm	xfm_dir.xpm
xfm_dirlnk.xpm	xfm_exec.xpm	xfm_execlnk.xpm
xfm_file.xpm	xfm_file_small.xpm	xfm_files.xpm
xfm_gif.xpm	xfm_h.xpm	xfm_icon.xpm
xfm_info.xpm	xfm_make.xpm	xfm_o.xpm
xfm_ps.xpm	xfm_symlnk.xpm	xfm_tar.xpm
xfm_taz.xpm	xfm_tex.xpm	xfm_tiff.xpm
xfm_updir.xpm	xfm_xbm.xpm	xfm_xpm.xpm
xfm_z.xpm	xfm_zip.xpm	xmag.xpm
xman.xpm	xpaint.xpm	xterm.xpm
zip.xpm	binedit.xbm	bitmap.xbm
calendar.xbm	clipboard.xbm	debug.xbm
emacs.xbm	hexdump.xbm	letters.xbm
lock.xbm	printer.xbm	sc.xbm
trash.xbm	xchess.xbm	xdbx.xbm
xfm_a.xbm	xfm_appmgr.xbm	xfm_blackhole.xbm
xfm_c.xbm	xfm_cc.xbm	xfm_cline.xbm
xfm_dir.xbm	xfm_dirlnk.xbm	xfm_dirmsk.xbm
xfm_excl.xbm	xfm_exec.xbm	xfm_execlnk.xbm
xfm_execmsk.xbm	xfm_file.xbm	xfm_filemsk.xbm
xfm_files.xbm	xfm_filesmsk.xbm	xfm_fline.xbm
xfm_h.xbm	xfm_icon.xbm	xfm_larrow.xbm
xfm_lines.xbm	xfm_lline.xbm	xfm_noentry.xbm
xfm_noentrymsk.xbm	xfm_notick.xbm	xfm_o.xbm
xfm_rarrow.xbm	xfm_symlnk.xbm	xfm_tick.xbm
xfm_tline.xbm	xfm_watch.xbm	xfm_watchmsk.xbm
xfm_wavy.xbm	xfm_wavy1.xbm	xfm_wavy_arrow.xbm
xman.xbm		

Command-line options

xfm has only two command-line options: -appmgr, which displays only the
application manager, and -filemgr, which displays only the File Manager.

xfm resources

The xfm command has several notable resources that are outlined in
Table 31-4.

Table 31-4   xfm Resources

Resource	Value	Description
bitmapPath	directory list	Specifies a list of directories to examine to find bitmaps for icon displays.
pixmapPath	directory list	Specifies a list of directories to examine to find pixmaps for icon displays.
application DataFile	file	Specifies the location of the application definition file.
configFile	file	Specifies the location of the xfmrc file.
devFile	file	Specifies the location of the mount file.
autoSave	true/false	Specifies whether xfm automatically saves changes to the application file.
doubleClickTime	integer	Sets the time interval for subtle-clicks in milliseconds.
updateInterval	integer	Sets the time interval between window updates in milliseconds.
confirm(action)	true/false	Indicates whether an action requires confirmation. Currently, the actions that do are Delete, DeleteFolder, Copy, Move, Overwrite, and Quit.
geometry	geometry string	Specifies default geometry for Applications window.
initGeometry	geometry string	Specifies default geometry for initial File Manager window.
file window. Geometry	geometry string	Specifies default geometry for subsequent File Manager windows.
*Transient Shell	geometry string	Specifies default geometry for pop-up geometry windows.
..buttonbox .?.	integer	Specifies the width in pixels for menu borderWidth buttons.
*background	color	Specifies window background colors.
*iconbox *Toggle	color	Specifies foreground color for icon (true/false).

Resource	Value	Description
*boldFont	font string	Specifies the font for bold entries.
*iconFont	font string	Specifies the font for icons.
*buttonFont	font string	Specifies the font for buttons.
*menuFont	font string	Specifies the font for menus.
*labelFont	font string	Specifies the font for labels.
*statusFont	font string	Specifies the font for status windows.
*appIconWidth	integer	Specifies the width of application icons
*appIconHeight	integer	Specifies the height of application icons.
*fileIconWidth	integer	Specifies the width of file icons.
*fileIconHeight	integer	Specifies the height of file icons.
*treeIconWidth	integer	Specifies the width of tree icons.
*treeIconHeight	integer	Specifies the height of tree icons.
*echoActions	true/false	Echoes actions to standard error (for debugging).
*show(field)	true/false	In text view, displays the following fields: Owner, Date, Permissions, and Length.
*initial DisplayType	Icons/Tree/ Text	Defines xfm's preferred initial display.
*default DisplayType	Icons/Tree/ Text	Defines xfm's preferred default display.
*defaultSortType	SortByName/ SortBySize/ SortByDate	Defines the preferred sort order.
*defaultEditor	string	Specifies the preferred editor.

For most resources, the default values are adequate, but as with any other X application, you can change the values to fit your preferences.

Mail notification

Berkeley added a little tool called biff when it wrote the BSD 4.0 distribution. This command asynchronously notified a user when mail arrived by printing a notice to the screen, sometimes with part of the mail message. With a single screen, occasions arose when such asynchronous notification was required. For example, if you were in a long-running application such as an editor, you could not otherwise receive a notice of new mail until after you exited the command.

The biff command had some problems. The notification messed up any graphical display, requiring you to redraw the screen. If you left your terminal or were showing something on your terminal to someone else and forgot to disable biff, a potentially embarrassing message might appear on your screen.

With X Windows, Berkeley's biff command is obsolete. A new command, xbiff, handles asynchronous notification of e-mail arrival. When your mailbox is empty or completely read, xbiff displays a mailbox with the flag down (see Figure 31-8a). When unread mail arrives, the flag raises and the colors reverse (see Figure 31-8b).

You can lower the flag by reading the mail or by clicking the xbiff icon.

a   b

Figure 31-8: (a) xbiff with no new mail and (b) xbiff with new mail

Caution

Ironically, the use of the flag is opposite to that of a real-world mailbox. There, a raised flag indicates that the box contains outgoing mail awaiting pickup, and the flag is lowered when the mail is delivered.

Naturally, xbiff is a customizable application. Besides the standard X toolkit arguments, xbiff also takes the arguments listed in Table 31-5.

Table 31-5   xbiff Command-Line Options

Option	Argument	Description
-help		Lists a brief summary of options.
-update	integer	Sets the frequency for update checks in seconds. The default is 30 seconds.
-file	file	Checks the specified file instead of the default mail file.
-volume	integer	Sets the volume of the bell that notifies the user of new mail.
-shape		Indicates that the shape options for X should be used if a mask bitmap is provided.

You can change the action of button presses by invoking three functions: check(), set(), and unset(). You can specify the button bindings in your Xdefault file with the following command:

```
xbiff*button1: check()
```

The check() function calls the checking routine, set() raises the flag until you unset it, and unset() lowers the flag.

The xbiff command is an ideal command for inclusion in your X startup file. Table 31-6 lists the X resources beyond the core resources.

Table 31-6   xbiff Resources

Resource	Value	Description
background	color	Specifies the background color.
checkCommand	shell command	Executes the specified shell command instead of checking the file. The string may use I/O redirection. The exit status must be 0 to indicate new mail, 1 for no new mail, and 2 to indicate that mail has been cleared.
emptyPixmap	file	Specifies the bitmap to be used when no new mail is present.
emptyPixmap Mask	file	Specifies the mask file for emptyPixmap.
file	filename	Specifies the file to monitor.
flip	true/false	Specifies whether the image should be inverted when new mail arrives.
foreground	color	Specifies the foreground color.
fullPixmap	file	Specifies the bitmap to be used when new mail arrives.
fullPixmap Mask	file	Specifies the mask file for fullPixmap.
height	integer	Specifies the mailbox height in pixels.
onceOnly	true/false	Rings the bell only once while mail is waiting.
reverseVideo	true/false	Specifies that reverse video should be used.
shapeWindow	true/false	Specifies whether shape extensions should be used.
update	integer	Specifies the update time in seconds.
volume	integer	Specifies the volume. The default is 33 percent.
width	integer	Specifies the mailbox width in pixels.

An X-based clipboard

X provides additional functionality by enabling you to cut and paste strings between applications. Normally, you do this within the X server, but the server can contain only one string in its cut buffer at any given time. When you select one string, it automatically deletes the previously selected string.

The XClipboard application solves this problem. The clipboard is a tool in which you can place more than one cut string and save those strings for recall. You can start the clipboard with `xclipboard`. A window pops up with six buttons and an indication of which page is on the board. Figure 31-9 illustrates the default starting state. As you cut strings from an application, you can paste them into the clipboard window. Similarly, you can cut from the clipboard and paste into any application that accepts pastes.

Figure 31-9: The beginning screen for XClipboard

You can have multiple clipboards within the application. This enables you to save different strings on different pages so that you can easily group related strings.

Tip

You may want to include a title within the area, but a string in the text area is not required to be from a cut and paste.

The first button, Quit, exits the application. The Delete button deletes the current page from the clipboard. If only a single page is on the clipboard, Delete clears the page. The New button creates a new page on the clipboard. Save saves the current page from the clipboard to a file. Next moves you to the next page on the clipboard, and Prev takes you to the previous page.

XClipboard is less customizable than most X applications. Besides the standard toolkit, it takes two mutually exclusive options. The `-w` option wraps entries longer than the length of the line; `-nw` does not wrap them.

The X resources for the clipboard are primarily the strings for the buttons. XClipboard works best as an iconified application from startup or as an entry off a window manager menu.

An X-based editor

One of the complaints I have heard about X is the lack of a good X-based editor. X does have an editor, called `xedit`, but seemingly few people are aware of it. Before you pass judgment on the lack of an editor in X, I urge you at least to try this application.

xedit brings up a window divided into several panes. A control pane with three buttons and a text entry area lies at the top. The three buttons do what you'd expect: Quit exits the application (with a prompt to save the file if it hasn't been saved), Save writes the file to disk, and Load places the file in the edit buffer. A text area in which you enter filenames for Save and Load follows the Load button.

The middle pane is the messages area. Any error or transactional messages are written there. The edit buffer appears at the bottom of the screen. Figure 31-10 shows the application before loading a file.

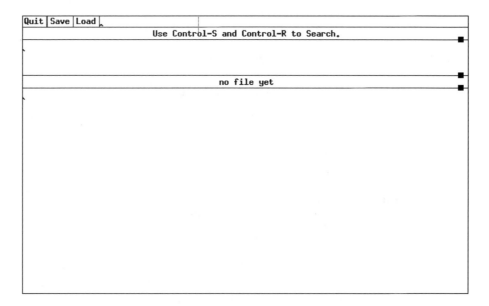

Figure 31-10: xedit before loading a file

To load a file, position the pointer over the text area beside the Load button and type a filename. When finished, click the Load button. The file is placed in the edit buffer, as illustrated in Figure 31-11.

In Figure 31-11, I've loaded the Duke Basketball FAQ into the editor. I can scroll to any location and make changes. To change the expiration date to February 29, 2000, I'd move the pointer to the end of Jan 31, backspace to remove the text, and type the new date, as shown in Figure 31-12.

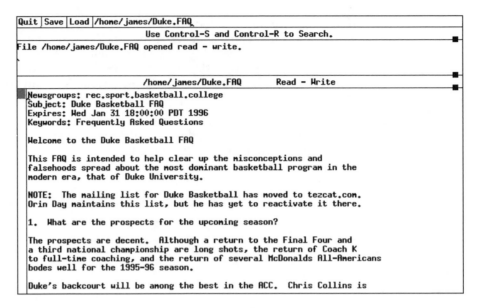

Figure 31-11: xedit with a file loaded into the buffer

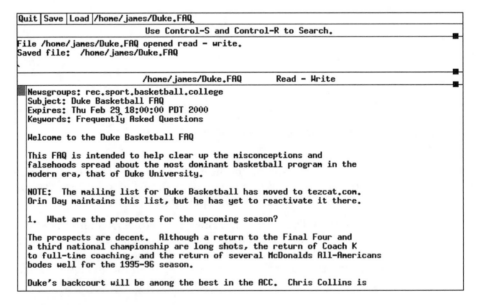

Figure 31-12: xedit updated with a write

xedit has many commands, usually related to Ctrl or Meta characters. The command set is not as complex as emacs, but it is thorough. Table 31-7 lists the xedit commands.

Table 31-7   xedit Commands

Command	Result
Ctrl-A	Moves the cursor to the beginning of a line
Ctrl-B	Moves the cursor back one character
Ctrl-D	Deletes the character immediately after the cursor
Ctrl-E	Moves the cursor to the end of a line
Ctrl-F	Moves the cursor forward one character
Ctrl-G	Resets the multiplier
Ctrl-H	Deletes the character before the cursor
Ctrl-J	Inserts a new line
Ctrl-K	Deletes characters from the cursor position to the end of the line
Ctrl-L	Redraws the display
Ctrl-M	Inserts a new line
Ctrl-N	Moves the cursor to the next line
Ctrl-O	Inserts a new line and backs up
Ctrl-P	Moves the cursor to the previous line
Ctrl-R	Searches for text backward from the current cursor position
Ctrl-S	Searches for text forward from the current cursor position
Ctrl-T	Transposes the characters on either side of the cursor
Ctrl-U	Multiplies the effect of any command by four
Ctrl-V	Moves to the next page
Ctrl-W	Deletes the selected text
Ctrl-Y	Restores the last deletion
Ctrl-Z	Scrolls up one line
Meta-B	Moves backward one word
Meta-F	Moves forward one word
Meta-I	Inserts a file at the cursor position
Meta-K	Deletes characters from the cursor position to the end of the paragraph.
Meta-Q	Forms a paragraph, eliminating embedded new lines and formatting the text accordingly
Meta-V	Moves to the previous page
Meta-Y	Inserts the selected text
Meta-Z	Scrolls down one line

Continued

Table 31-7 *(continued)*

Command	Result
Meta-D	Deletes characters from the cursor position to the end of the word
Meta-H	Deletes to the beginning of the word
Meta-<	Moves to the beginning of the file
Meta->	Moves to the end of the file
Meta-]	Moves forward a paragraph
Meta-[	Moves backward a paragraph
Meta-Delete	Deletes the previous word
Meta-Shift-Delete	Kills the previous word

The buttons also have functions. You can select text with the first pointer button, extend that selection with the third button, and insert the selected text with the second button.

xedit takes only the standard toolkit options, although you can specify the file to open on the command line, as in any other editor. xedit has three notable resources. The enableBackups resource is a toggle that creates backup files when you edit. The backupNamePrefix resource is a string that is prepended to the backed-up file, and backupNameSuffix is appended to the filename.

You do not place xedit in a startup script, but it finds its place in window manager menus and as a target in xfm.

A powerful calculator

A calculator is always a valuable tool. X provides in xcalc a calculator that emulates both Hewlett-Packard and Texas Instruments calculators. Use xcalc to start the calculator in TI mode and xcalc -rpn to start it in HP mode. Figure 31-13 shows the TI calculator. Figure 31-14 shows the HP calculator.

The TI calculator is modeled on the TI-30, and the HP calculator is modeled on the HP-10C.

Note

The HP calculator has a couple of blank keys. On the HP-10C, these keys were programmable. The xcalc option does not support programming these keys.

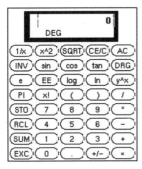

Figure 31-13: xcalc, the calculator in TI mode

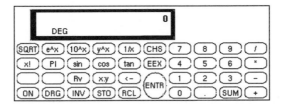

Figure 31-14: xcalc -rpn, the calculator in HP mode

The calculator works as you might expect. Move the pointer over the key, click the first button, and the key operates. The TI calculator functions with operator precedence like a program (multiplication and division are resolved before addition and subtraction). The HP calculator works around that by using reverse Polish notation (RPN).

Guru: Reverse Polish Notation

Reverse Polish notation (RPN) is different from standard notation. RPN uses an Enter key and the concept of a stack. You enter a number by typing it in and pressing Enter. The number is placed on a stack. When you perform an operation, two numbers are popped off the stack, and they are used for the operation. For example, with an RPN calculator, 2 + 3 becomes 2 <Enter> 3 <Enter> +.

You'll find it common practice in introductory computer science courses to write programs that solve mathematical problems entered in RPN and also to convert standard notation to RPN. Table 31-8 lists some conversions.

Table 31-8   Standard versus Reverse Polish Notation for Expressions

Standard Notation	Reverse Polish Notation
A+B	AB+
A-B*C	ABC*-
(A+B)*C	AB+C*
A+B+C	AB+C+ or ABC++
A/(B-(C*D)+E)+(F-G*H)	ABCD*-E+/FGH*-+

RPN has one large advantage: It eliminates the need for parentheses to group expressions.

The calculators also have keyboard accelerators. By using them, you avoid the need to move the pointer and press buttons repeatedly. Table 31-9 lists the keyboard accelerators. Table 31-10 explains each function.

Table 31-9   Calculator Functions and Keyboard Accelerators

TI Key	HP Key	Accelerator	TI Function	HP Function
SQRT	SQRT	r	squareRoot()	squareRoot()
AC	ON	Space	clear()	clear()
AC	<-	Delete	clear()	back()
AC	<-	Backspace	clear()	back()
AC	<-	Ctrl-H	clear()	back()
AC	Clear		clear()	clear()
AC	ON	q	quit()	quit()
AC	ON	Ctrl-C	quit()	quit()
INV	INV	i	inverse()	inverse()
sin	sin	s	sine()	sine()
cos	cos	c	cosine()	cosine()
tan	tan	t	tangent()	tangent()
DRG	DRG	d	degree()	degree()

TI Key	HP Key	Accelerator	TI Function	HP Function
e		e	e()	
ln	ln	l	naturalLog()	naturalLog()
y^x	y^x	^	power()	power()
PI	PI	p	pi()	pi()
x!	x!	!	factorial()	factorial()
(		(	leftParen()	
)		)	rightParen()	
/	/	/	divide()	divide()
*	*	*	multiply()	multiply()
−	−	−	subtract()	subtract()
+	+	+	add()	add()
=		=	equal()	
0–9	0–9	0–9	digit()	digit()
.	.	.	decimal()	decimal()
+/−	CHS	n	negate()	negate()
	x:y	x		XexchangeY()
	ENTR	Enter		enter()
	ENTR	Linefeed		enter()
1/x	1/x		reciprocal()	reciprocal()
x^2	x^2		square()	square()
CE/C			clear()	
EE	EEX		scientific()	scientific()
log			logarithm()	
ln			naturalLog()	
STO	STO		store()	store()
RCL	RCL		recall()	recall()
SUM	SUM		sum()	sum()
EXC			exchange()	
	10^x			tenpower()
	e^x			epower()
	Rv			roll()

Table 31-10   xcalc Functions

Function	Result
add()	Adds two numbers.
back()	Erases the last digit entered (HP mode only).
bell()	Sounds the keyboard bell.
clear()	Clears the entered number.
cosine()	Calculates the cosine of a number. If the mode is inverse, calculates the arc cosine.
decimal()	Enters a decimal point on the display.
degree()	Changes angle measurement from degree to radian to gradian.
divide()	Performs division.
e()	Produces the value for e, 2.71828.
epower()	Raises e to the specified power. In inverse mode on HP, calculates the natural logarithm.
equal()	Performs the specified calculation (TI mode only).
exchange()	Stores the currently displayed number and replaces it with any number previously in storage.
factorial()	Calculates the factorial of the specified number.
inverse()	Activates the inverse function.
leftParen()	Enters a left parenthesis (TI mode only).
logarithm()	Calculates the logarithm of a number.
multiply()	Performs multiplication.
naturalLog()	Calculates the natural logarithm of a number.
negate()	Converts from positive to negative numbers and back.
off()	Clears the state of the machine.
pi()	Produces the approximate value of pi, 3.14159265.
power()	Raises the first number to the power of the second number.
quit()	Exits the calculator program.
recall()	Places the number from storage on the display.
reciprocal()	Divides 1 by the specified number.
rightParen()	Enters a right parenthesis.
roll()	Circulates the stack (HP mode only).
scientific()	Enters the number in scientific notation.
selection()	Selects the data on the display for an X cut-and-paste buffer.

Function	Result
sine()	Calculates the sine of the specified number. In inverse mode, calculates the arc sine.
square()	Multiplies the specified number by itself.
squareRoot()	Calculates the square root of the specified number.
store()	Stores the specified number in memory.
subtract()	Subtracts the second number from the first.
sum()	Adds the current number to the number in memory.
tangent()	Calculates the tangent of the specified number. In inverse mode, calculates the arc tangent.
tenpower()	Raises ten to the specified power. In inverse mode on HP, calculates the logarithm.
XexchangeY()	Swaps the top two entries on the stack (HP mode only).

The resources for the xcalc program are extensive. Each button's string and function are defined as a resource. This gives tremendous customizing potential to the expert, but it can lead to confusion.

Note

Reprogramming the calculator can be an amusing prank.

The coding for each button is

```
*hp.button##.Label
*ti.button##.Translations
```

Use either hp or ti to indicate which mode the modification applies to and the number of the button. For the translation, indicate which button with Btn#Down and Btn#Up, where # is 1, 2, or 3, followed by the functions. For example, you could try

```
*hp.button22.Label:      x^3
*hp.button22.Translations:
<Btn1Down>,<Btn1Up>:enter()digit(3)power()unset()
```

The preceding translations create a new button to calculate the cubes of numbers.

Note

The unused buttons on the HP calculator are button21 and button22. Of course, because most of the calculator functions are tied solely to the first pointer button, you can overload each button with two more functions.

Besides the -rpn option and the standard toolkit options, xcalc supports one other option, -stipple. This adds a stipple pattern to the background of the calculator, as shown in Figure 31-15.

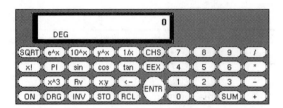

Figure 31-15: xcalc -rpn -stipple with the new "cubed" button

Table 31-11 lists the only notable xcalc resources besides button translation and core resources.

Table 31-11   xcalc Resources

Resource	Value	Description
XCalc.ti.Command.background	color	Indicates version background color (also for XCalc.hp)
XCalc.ti.Command.foreground	color	Indicates version foreground color (also for XCalc.hp)
XCalc*rpn	true/false	Indicates that HP should be the normal start (default is false)
XCalc*stipple	on/off	Indicates that background should be stippled
XCalc*cursor	string	Indicates the default pointer for the calculator

xcalc is best kept in a window manager menu, where you can easily call it up as needed.

A magnifying glass

Xmag is a handy tool for taking close-ups of different images in X. When invoked, Xmag produces a skeleton, which you can move with the pointer to any location on the screen. Click the first pointer button to magnify the area in the skeleton in a new window.

By clicking the second pointer button, you can drag the skeleton to an arbitrary size. Figure 31-16 shows an example of the magnification.

Each pixel in the selected area is enlarged to a 5 · 5 square. When the magnifier is raised, you can move the pointer to any spot in the display and press the first pointer button. You then see the location and colors of the pixel represented at the bottom of the window. You can use this to see the RGB values for a given pixel.

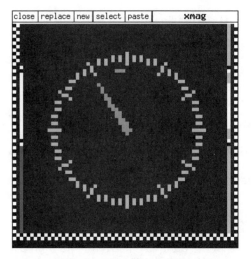

Figure 31-16: Xmag showing the clock

Five buttons stretch across the top of the display. Close causes the Xmag program to exit. Replace redraws the skeleton, enabling you to select a new area for magnification. New draws a new skeleton, and when an area is selected, it produces a new window. Select places the currently displayed image into a cut buffer. Paste restores that selected image.

The xmag label also has actions. When you click the label with the second or third pointer button, a new skeleton is drawn and a replacement is made.

To quit Xmag, either click the Close button or select q or Ctrl-C on the image.

One nice feature of Xmag is the capability to cut and paste between other bitmap-managing applications such as bitmap.

Besides the standard X toolkit options, Xmag takes two command-line options. To specify the amount of magnification, use -mag followed by an integer. The -source option followed by a geometry specification defines the size and location of the magnified region of the screen. Adding XMag as an option on a window manager menu is useful.

Customization Applications

You can use other X applications to help customize your display. These applications help you access and examine system resources, such as available colors and fonts.

Listing available colors

One of the most popular user customizations is the capability to set your own colors for your applications. I use color liberally on my desktop. At a glance, I know that the gold-on-navy window is my main working window, red-on-cyan is an editing session, and red-on-black is a mailer.

The X server, however, does not understand terms such as *red, blue,* or *yellow.* Instead, it is driven by numerical data called RGB values.

Note

Most monitors create color by using three electron guns, one each for red, green, and blue. By varying the intensity of the three primary colors, you can create any number of different colors. For the X server, though, each color is just a number indicating the intensity of the gun.

Interpretation of color is based on an RGB database. This is where X applications translate color strings into RGB values for the server. You can examine the colors available in the database with the showrgb command. It takes no arguments to show the default database.

My machine has 752 colors; Listing 31-1 shows the first 15.

Listing 31-1: Incomplete showrgb Output

```
$ showrgb
255 250 250          snow
248 248 255          ghost white
248 248 255          GhostWhite
245 245 245          white smoke
245 245 245          WhiteSmoke
220 220 220          gainsboro
255 250 240          floral white
255 250 240          FloralWhite
253 245 230          old lace
253 245 230          OldLace
250 240 230          linen
250 235 215          antique white
250 235 215          AntiqueWhite
255 239 213          papaya whip
255 239 213          PapayaWhip
```

The format for the output lists the red value, then the green, and finally the blue. After that is the string that you can use to translate the colors. The integers must be from 0 through 315.

Note

You can specify colors by their RGB values. In this case, you prepend a six-digit string with a number sign (#) and then list the three hexadecimal RGB values without spaces. For example, old lace is #fdf5e6.

You're best off running the showrgb command to examine the choice of named colors on the system. This is a tool to determine colors for experimentation.

Display characteristics

The xdpyinfo command obtains the basic information about the current display. The only argument is to specify another display by name. Listing 31-2 shows the output for my machine.

Listing 31-2: Output for xdpyinfo

```
$ xdpyinfo
name of display:      :0.0
version number:    11.0
vendor string:     X Consortium
vendor release number:    6000
maximum request size:   4194300 bytes
motion buffer size:   0
bitmap unit, bit order, padding:    32, LSBFirst, 32
image byte order:    LSBFirst
number of supported pixmap formats:    2
supported pixmap formats:
    depth 1, bits_per_pixel 1, scanline_pad 32
    depth 8, bits_per_pixel 8, scanline_pad 32
keycode range:    minimum 8, maximum 134
focus:  window 0x300000d, revert to PointerRoot
number of extensions:    12
    BIG-REQUESTS
    MIT-SHM
    MIT-SUNDRY-NONSTANDARD
    Multi-Buffering
    SHAPE
    SYNC
    X3D-PEX
    XC-MISC
    XIE
    XKEYBOARD
    XTEST
    XTestExtension1
default screen number:    0
number of screens:    1
screen #0:
  dimensions:    640x480 pixels (217x163 millimeters)
  resolution:    75x75 dots per inch
  depths (2):    1, 8
  root window id:    0x2b
  depth of root window:    8 planes
  number of colormaps:    minimum 1, maximum 1
  default colormap:    0x27
  default number of colormap cells:    256
  preallocated pixels:    black 1, white 0
  options:    backing-store YES, save-unders YES
  largest cursor:    640x480
  current input event mask:    0xd0001d
    KeyPressMask          ButtonPressMask          ButtonReleaseMask
    EnterWindowMask       SubstructureRedirectMask PropertyChangeMask
```

```
      ColormapChangeMask
number of visuals:    6
default visual id:  0x20
visual:
  visual id:    0x20
  class:    PseudoColor
  depth:    8 planes
  available colormap entries:   256
  red, green, blue masks:   0x0, 0x0, 0x0
  significant bits in color specification:   6 bits
visual:
  visual id:    0x21
  class:    DirectColor
  depth:    8 planes
  available colormap entries:   8 per subfield
  red, green, blue masks:   0x7, 0x38, 0xc0
  significant bits in color specification:   6 bits
visual:
  visual id:    0x22
  class:    GrayScale
  depth:    8 planes
  available colormap entries:   256
  red, green, blue masks:   0x0, 0x0, 0x0
  significant bits in color specification:   6 bits
visual:
  visual id:    0x23
  class:    StaticGray
  depth:    8 planes
  available colormap entries:   256
  red, green, blue masks:   0x0, 0x0, 0x0
  significant bits in color specification:   6 bits
visual:
  visual id:    0x24
  class:    StaticColor
  depth:    8 planes
  available colormap entries:   256
  red, green, blue masks:   0x7, 0x38, 0xc0
  significant bits in color specification:   6 bits
visual:
  visual id:    0x25
  class:    TrueColor
  depth:    8 planes
  available colormap entries:   8 per subfield
  red, green, blue masks:   0x7, 0x38, 0xc0
  significant bits in color specification:   6 bits
number of mono multibuffer types:    6
  visual id, max buffers, depth:   0x20, 0, 8
  visual id, max buffers, depth:   0x21, 0, 8
  visual id, max buffers, depth:   0x22, 0, 8
  visual id, max buffers, depth:   0x23, 0, 8
  visual id, max buffers, depth:   0x24, 0, 8
  visual id, max buffers, depth:   0x25, 0, 8
number of stereo multibuffer types:    0
```

The xdpyinfo command presents a lot of data. Some of the key information is the size of the display (640 · 480), the color specification (8-bit), and the screen resolution (75 dpi). Most of the information is meaningless unless you plan to develop X software.

Font selections

A very useful tool is Xfontsel, an X-based application that enables you to examine the different fonts available on the system. You start it with xfontsel, and the window appears, as illustrated in Figure 31-17.

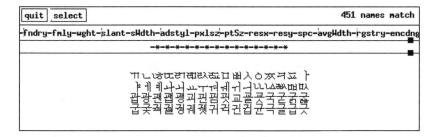

Figure 31-17: The Xfontsel application

The best way to preview a font is to pull down the menu from the listing of font characteristics and select one entry. For example, I chose the Adobe foundry for fonts in Figure 31-18.

Figure 31-18: Xfontsel looking at Adobe fonts

I've narrowed my list from over 400 fonts to just 164. Next, I look at the list of font families and choose Helvetica. This reduces my list of available fonts from 164 to just 32, as shown in Figure 31-19.

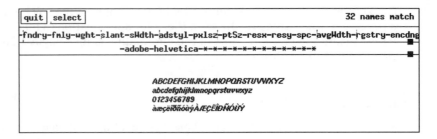

Figure 31-19: Xfontsel adobe-helvetica

I can now opt for a bold and italic version of Helvetica by selecting bold from the wght menu and o from the slant.

The list is down to eight fonts. By checking the menus, I find the next important menu is pxlsz, which defines the size of the font. I choose 18 and have only two fonts available. This is adequate. I can now click the select button, and the font becomes the clipboard string. I can paste it into any application.

To exit Xfontsel, select the quit button. Table 31-12 lists the command-line options, and Table 31-13 lists some of the X resources.

Table 31-12   xfontsel Options

Option	Argument	Result
-pattern	fontname	Includes only those fonts that match the pattern in the first window
-print		Prints the font name on standard output when quit is selected
-sample	text	Uses the text for the sample output
-sample16	text	Uses the 16-bit text for the sample output
-noscaled		Does not display the scalable fonts

Table 31-13   xfontsel Resources

Resource	Value	Description
cursor	string	Specifies the cursor to use over the application window
pattern	string	Specifies the default pattern for matches
pixelSizeList	list	Specifies a list of pixel sizes for displaying scalable fonts

Resource	Value	Description
pointSizeList	list	Specifies a list of point sizes for displaying scalable fonts
printOnQuit	true/false	Specifies whether the font should be printed when the application finishes
sampleText	string	Specifies sample text to be displayed
sampleText16	string	Specifies sample 16-bit text to be displayed
scaledFonts	true/false	If true, enables selection of arbitrary pixel and point sizes
show	true/false	If true, lists unselectable options Unselectable for each menu

The xfontsel command is most useful for previewing fonts for windows, and you should keep it in a window manager menu.

Defining fonts

All fonts in X are defined in the multiple dash style, where the dash is a separator. Most fields are not meaningful to the novice user, but four are important. The second field is the name of the font, such as Courier, New Century Schoolbook, or Times. The third field is the weight (bold or normal). The fourth field is the slant (italic or straight). The seventh field shows the size of the font in pixels. Many common fonts have aliases such as 7x13 or r24.

Listing of all fonts

One problem with Xfontsel is that it does not show aliased fonts such as 7x13. But Xlsfonts works around this problem. The normal output of Xlsfonts is a listing of fonts, as shown in Listing 31-3.

Listing 31-3: Fifteen Lines of Xlsfonts Output

```
$ xlsfonts
-adobe-courier-bold-o-normal--0-0-75-75-m-0-iso8859-1
-adobe-courier-bold-o-normal--10-100-75-75-m-60-iso8859-1
-adobe-courier-bold-o-normal--12-120-75-75-m-70-iso8859-1
-adobe-courier-bold-o-normal--14-140-75-75-m-90-iso8859-1
-adobe-courier-bold-o-normal--18-180-75-75-m-110-iso8859-1
-adobe-courier-bold-o-normal--24-240-75-75-m-150-iso8859-1
-adobe-courier-bold-o-normal--8-80-75-75-m-50-iso8859-1
-adobe-courier-bold-r-normal--0-0-75-75-m-0-iso8859-1
-adobe-courier-bold-r-normal--10-100-75-75-m-60-iso8859-1
-adobe-courier-bold-r-normal--12-120-75-75-m-70-iso8859-1
-adobe-courier-bold-r-normal--14-140-75-75-m-90-iso8859-1
-adobe-courier-bold-r-normal--18-180-75-75-m-110-iso8859-1
-adobe-courier-bold-r-normal--24-240-75-75-m-150-iso8859-1
-adobe-courier-bold-r-normal--8-80-75-75-m-50-iso8859-1
-adobe-courier-medium-o-normal--0-0-75-75-m-0-iso8859-1
```

You can obtain more information on fonts from the different command-line options listed in Table 31-14.

Table 31-14	xlsfonts Options	
Option	**Argument**	**Result**
-display	*display string*	Accesses the fonts on the specified display
-l		Lists some font attributes with the font
-ll		Lists some font properties as well as attributes
-lll		Lists character metrics
-m		Prints the minimum and maximum bounds of the font
-C		Produces output in multiple columns
-1		Produces output in a single column
-w	*integer*	Sets the width of the screen in characters
-m	*integer*	Sets the number of columns to print
-u		Does not sort output
-o		Opens fonts
-fn	*pattern*	Lists only fonts that match the pattern

Caution

When I attempted to use some of these options (most notably the -l options) on my server, the server crashed.

X display settings

The xset command sets characteristics of your X session, including definitions of bells, key clicks, and other X server attributes. You can query the attributes with xset q, as illustrated in Listing 31-4. Table 31-15 lists the xset options.

Listing 31-4: xset Output

```
$ xset q
Keyboard Control:
  auto repeat:  on     key click percent:  0     LED mask:  02000000
  auto repeating keys:  00ffffffdffffbbf
                        faffffffffdffdff
                        7f00000000000000
                        0000000000000000
  bell percent:  50     bell pitch:  400     bell duration:  100
Pointer Control:
  acceleration:  2/1     threshold:  4
```

```
Screen Saver:
  prefer blanking:  yes    allow exposures:  yes
  timeout:  300    cycle:  600
Colors:
  default colormap:  0x27    BlackPixel:  1    WhitePixel:  0
Font Path:
  /usr/lib/X11/fonts/misc/,/usr/lib/X11/fonts/75dpi/
Bug Mode: compatibility mode is disabled
```

Table 31-15   xset Options

Option	Arguments	Result
-display	*display string*	Changes the characteristics of the specified display.
b	*volume pitch duration*	Changes the characteristics of the bell. You can change the volume, the pitch, or the duration. xset b 100 1000 100 sounds like a high-pitched ping, whereas xset b 100 200 1000 sounds more like a foghorn.
bc		Sets the bug compatibility mode.
c	on/off	Enables or disables key clicks.
fp=	*font path*	Sets the font path for the server.
fp	default	Resets the font path to the default for the server.
fp	rehash	Rehashes the font path. This is useful when a new font is added.
+fp	*path*	Prepends the specified directory to the font path.
fp+	*path*	Appends the specified directory to the font path.
fp	path	Removes elements from the font path.
-fp	path	Removes elements from the fontpath.
led	on/off	Enables or disables keyboard LEDs.
m	acceleration threshold	Sets the characteristics of the pointer movement. The acceleration is the ratio of pointer pixel movement in fast mode, and threshold is the number of pixels the pointer must travel to reach the fast rate. The xset 4 2 option is a normal pointer speed, xset 10 1 is fast, and xset 2 10 is slow. the acceleratioin can be a fraction, such as xset m 10/3 3.
p	integer color	Specifies the white and black pixels.
s	*integers*	Manipulates the screen saver.
q		Prints the current information.

The manipulation of the screen saver is the most interesting option. If a single integer is given, the screen saver interval is set to that number of seconds. If no input is received during that number of seconds, the screen saver kicks in. This option has other parameters, too. The blank/noblank parameter determines whether the screen shuts off or a default background is used, expose/noexpose enables window exposures during the saver, on/off enables or disables the screen saver, activate flags automatically turn it on, and reset turns it off. Lastly, the second number is an interval in seconds to circulate any pattern to prevent burn-in.

You can place Xset commands in the startup file for initial configurations and in window manager menus for instant changes.

Managing the root window

The xsetroot command manipulates the root window and background cursor. Usually, you can set a background cursor or use a bitmap to set up a pattern. Other tools, such as xloadimage or xv, can put pictures on the background, but these are slower commands. Table 31-16 shows the xsetroot options.

Table 31-16   xsetroot Options

Option	Argument	Result
-help		Prints a usage message
-def		Restores background to the default state, a gray mesh and an X cursor
-cursor	cursorfile maskfile	Changes the background cursor to use the specified bitmaps
-cursor_ name	name	Changes the background cursor to the specified name
-bitmap	file	Sets the root window pattern to the specified bitmap
-mod	x y	Sets the grid pattern on the background to x by y, where x and y are between 1 and 16
-gray		Makes the background gray
-grey		Makes the background gray
-fg	color	Sets the foreground color
-bg	color	Sets the background color
-rv		Reverses the sense of foreground and background
-solid	color	Sets the root window to be the solid color
-name	string	Sets the name of the root window
-display	display string	Sets the root window on the specified display

xsetroot commonly appears in xinit files, although xsetroot -def is a good window manager menu entry.

Customization Hints

The commands described in the previous section enable you to customize your display. The three normal customization files are the startup file, .xinitrc; the window manager startup file, .twmrc; and the File Manager applications file, .xfm/xfm-apps. Three sample startup files are illustrated in the following sections. Each file is enhanced in the next section for a more advanced interface.

A good .xinitrc

The .xinitrc file sets up your X windows session. Therefore, it should contain the commands that you always expect to be displayed. Listing 31-5 lists an .xinitrc file.

Listing 31-5: A Sample .xinitrc File

```
twm&
xsetroot -solid navy
xsetroot -cursor_name trek
xman -iconic&
xclipboard -iconic&
xclock -update 1 -g =80x80-0+0&
xbiff -g =80x80-85+0&
xfm&
xset m 4 2
xset b 50 400 200
xhost +
xterm -g =80x24+0+200&
xterm -g =80x24+200+0&
xterm -C -g =80x4+0+0 -iconic
```

This .xinitrc file starts the twm window manager and several clients. It uses an xbiff and a clock next to each other to track mail and the time, it starts a clipboard and manual page browser iconically, it sets some default pointer speeds and bell sounds, and it starts both a couple of xterms and the File Manager. (Normally, you would start only a File Manager or the xterms.) Figure 31-20 shows the screen.

The session continues until you deiconify the console xterm and exit. I personally prefer this approach to one where you need to exit every application or where you use the window manager to terminate the X session.

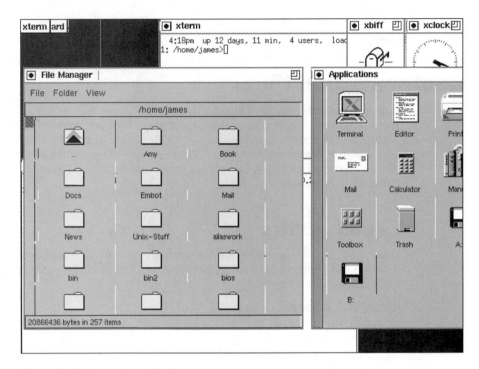

Figure 31-20: A good start for X

A good .twmrc

Many customizations are available for the window manager. Rather than showing all the colors, fonts, and key bindings that I prefer, Listing 31-6 includes only the key bindings to raise windows off the background and their menus.

Listing 31-6: A twm Startup File

```
Button1 =     : root  : f.menu "Applications"
Button2 =     : root  : f.menu "TwmWindows"
Button3 =     : root  : f.menu "Customizations"
Menu "Applications"
{
    "Applications"     f.title
    "Manual Pages"     !"xman&"
    "Clipboard"        !"xclipboard&"
    "Editor"      !"xedit&"
    "Calculator"       !"xcalc&"
    "HP Calculator"    !"xcalc -rpn&"
    "Magnifier"        !"xmag&"
    "Font Selector"    !"xfontsel&"
    "X Terminals"      f.menu "XTerms"
}
```

```
Menu "Customizations"
{
    "Customizations"       f.title
    "Backgrounds"             f.menu "Background"
    "Settings"            f.menu "Settings"
    "Controls"            f.menu "Controls"
}
Menu "XTerms"
{
    "Terminals"        f.title
    "BIG"              !"xterm -fn 7x13 -g =80x59-0-0 &"
    "HUGE"             !"xterm -fn 12x24 -g =80x33+0+0 &"
    "lower"             !"xterm -fn 7x13 -g =80x28-0-0 &"
    "small"            !"xterm -fn 5x8 -g =80x28-0-0 &"
    "upper"            !"xterm -fn 7x13 -g =80x29+0+93 &"
}
Menu "Background"
{
    "Backgrounds"       f.title
    "Defaults"         !"xsetroot -def"
    "Red"              !"xsetroot -solid red"
    "Green"             !"xsetroot -solid green"
    "Blue"             !"xsetroot -solid blue"
}
Menu "Settings"
{
    "Settings"       f.title
    "Fast Mouse"      !"xset m 10 1"
    "Slow Mouse"      !"xset m 2 4"
    "Fast blanking"     !"xset s 2"
    "Normal saver"      !"xset s 900"
}
Menu "Controls"
{
    "Controls"           f.title
    "Redraw"            f.refresh
    "Restart"             f.restart
    "Window Ops"          f.title
    "(De)Iconify"           f.iconify
    "Lower"              f.lower
    "Move"              f.move
    "Raise"              f.raise
    "Refresh Window"      f.winrefresh
    "Resize"           f.resize
    "Quit twm"           f.quit
}
```

This sets up a series of cascading menus to control your screen. The first button controls applications, and a series of xterms in different sizes can be invoked from a submenu. The second is the standard twm Windows menu. The last is a series of settings, which has three separately cascading menus. The first controls the background, the second controls the X server settings, and the last controls the window manager.

Note

You may want to customize the Background and Settings menus first.

A good .xfm/xfm-apps

Rather than listing the complete applications file, I'll list the two lines you can add to include the font selector and the magnifier:

```
Magnifier:::xmag.xpm:xmag:
Font Selector:::xfm_wavy.xbm:xfontsel:
```

This adds two icons for the magnifier and font selector, as shown in Figure 31-21.

Figure 31-21: A customized File Manager

You can accomplish this directly from the File Manager, too.

Summary

This chapter introduced several important X applications and explained

▶ How to use the xbiff command to give notice of pending mail

▶ How to use and customize the calculator

▶ How to obtain a listing of all available fonts

▶ How to select fonts graphically

▶ How to edit a file with an X-based editor

▶ How to obtain a listing of every available color

▶ How to change the settings in the X server

▶ How to set a background pattern

▶ How to use and customize the File Manager

▶ How to save multiple strings on a clipboard

▶ How to display manual pages

The next chapter completes the survey of basic X commands.

Chapter 32

Advanced X Programs

In This Chapter

▶ More tools for X Windows

▶ Multimedia commands for X Windows

▶ Games available under X

▶ Debugging tools under X

This chapter completes the look at X tools. Although this book discusses a lot of applications, many more are available from FTP sites. Watch the `comp.sources.x` newsgroup for new applications and for upgrades to existing applications, and check FTP archive sites.

Advanced Tools for X Windows

Several more categories of tools are available for X. These tools have many uses. Some display system characteristics; others change them. Still others bridge the gaps between incompletely implemented applications.

Displaying the system load

The `xload` command provides an ongoing graphical display of the system load. Figure 32-1 shows the current load on my machine.

Figure 32-1: Xload output

This program is not interactive; it just displays the ongoing system load. The load displayed is the same as the current load identified by uptime. (For more information on the uptime command, see Chapter 2.)

Table 32-1 lists the few xload options that enhance the default X toolkit options.

Table 32-1	xload Options	
Option	*Argument*	*Result*
-hl	color	Specifies scale and text color
-label	string	Uses the specified string instead of the machine name
-nolabel		Removes the label from the chart
-scale	integer	Includes at least the specified number of scale lines
-update	integer	Updates the display once every specified number of seconds

Only a couple of xload resources are worth describing. XLoad*Label *Justify specifies how to justify the label at the top of the display. Use left, center, or right as values (the default is left). XLoad*showGrip hides or displays the handle used to change the relative sizes of the window's label and graph ; it defaults to false. XLoad*internalBorderWidth specifies the width between the two areas; it defaults to zero. I use Xload in my .xinitrc script.

Monitoring free memory

Xmem is related to Xload, but it shows the available memory on the system instead of the system load. Figure 32-2 shows an Xmem graph.

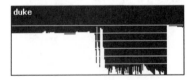

Figure 32-2: An Xmem graph

As you can see, at one point I kicked off a program that used nearly all the memory available on my machine. The huge canyon in the middle of the chart with a couple of spires denotes when the memory was used.

Xmem takes the same arguments as Xload and uses similar resources.

Watching the idle time

The Xidle application completes the trio of system monitors. This application reports idle time on the system, as illustrated in Figure 32-3.

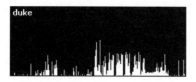

Figure 32-3: Xidle output

Figures 32-1, 32-2, and 32-3 were all shot over the same time period on the same machine. Notice how they seem to show related behavior.

Xidle takes the same arguments as Xload and Xmem and also uses similar resources.

Actually, the three use much of the same code and just display different information gleaned from the UNIX kernel.

Secret

Displaying fonts

Another handy tool is the X font displayer, Xfd. Given a font name, Xfd displays the font in a window on the screen, as shown in Figure 32-4.

```
            -Misc-Fixed-Bold-R-Normal--15-140-75-75-C-90-ISO8859-1

Quit  Prev Page  Next Page

                        Select a character

range:  0x0000 (0,0) thru 0x00ff (0,255)
upper left:  0x0000 (0,0)
```

	◆	▓	⊣	⊢	⊤	⊥	°	±	⊓	⊔	⌐	⌐	⌐	└	┼
─	─	─	─	─	┤	┤	⊥	⊤	│	≤	≥	π	≠	£	·
	!	"	#	$	%	&	'	(	)	*	+	,	─	.	/
0	1	2	3	4	5	6	7	8	9	:	;	<	=	>	?
@	A	B	C	D	E	F	G	H	I	J	K	L	M	N	O
P	Q	R	S	T	U	V	W	X	Y	Z	[	\	]	^	_
`	a	b	c	d	e	f	g	h	i	j	k	l	m	n	o
p	q	r	s	t	u	v	w	x	y	z	{			}	~	
	¡	¢	£	¤	¥	¦	§	¨	©	ª	«	¬		®	¯
°	±	²	³	´	µ	¶	·	¸	¹	º	»	¼	½	¾	¿
À	Á	Â	Ã	Ä	Å	Æ	Ç	È	É	Ê	Ë	Ì	Í	Î	Ï
Ð	Ñ	Ò	Ó	Ô	Õ	Ö	×	Ø	Ù	Ú	Û	Ü	Ý	Þ	ß
à	á	â	ã	ä	å	æ	ç	è	é	ê	ë	ì	í	î	ï
ð	ñ	ò	ó	ô	õ	ö	÷	ø	ù	ú	û	ü	ý	þ	ÿ

Figure 32-4: Output of xfd -fn 9x15bold

Notice that the displayer translated the alias `9x15bold` into a full X font name. The displayer also translates all shortcuts. In this case, the font used is `-mixed-fixed-bold-r-normal—15-140-75-75-c-90-iso8859-1`. The displayer shows all 256 characters in the font if they are printable. These characters include the extensions used beyond ASCII, where the highest bit is set. This enables the font to display characters associated with non-American English.

When you select a single character, the displayer shows you some of the character's basic specifications. To illustrate this, I'll use a variable width font, `-adobe-helvetica-medium-r-normal—12-120-75-75-p-67-iso8859-1`. First, I select the lowercase *i*, and its characteristics appear in the header (see Figure 32-5).

```
    -Adobe-Helvetica-Medium-R-Normal--12-120-75-75-P-67-ISO8859-1

 Quit  Prev Page   Next Page
                     character 0x0069 (0,105) (0,0151)
           width 3; left 1, right 2; ascent 9, descent 0 (font 11, 3)
 range:  0x0020 (0,32) thru 0x00ff (0,255)
 upper left:  0x0000 (0,0)
```

	!	"	#	$	%	&	'	(	)	*	+	,	-	.	/
0	1	2	3	4	5	6	7	8	9	:	;	<	=	>	?
@	A	B	C	D	E	F	G	H	I	J	K	L	M	N	O
P	Q	R	S	T	U	V	W	X	Y	Z	[	\	]	^	_
`	a	b	c	d	e	f	g	h	i	j	k	l	m	n	o
p	q	r	s	t	u	v	w	x	y	z	{	|	}	~	
	¡	¢	£	¤	¥	¦	§	¨	©	ª	«	¬	-	®	¯
°	±	²	³	´	µ	¶	·	¸	¹	º	»	¼	½	¾	¿
À	Á	Â	Ã	Ä	Å	Æ	Ç	È	É	Ê	Ë	Ì	Í	Î	Ï
Ð	Ñ	Ò	Ó	Ô	Õ	Ö	×	Ø	Ù	Ú	Û	Ü	Ý	Þ	ß
à	á	â	ã	ä	å	æ	ç	è	é	ê	ë	ì	í	î	ï
ð	ñ	ò	ó	ô	õ	ö	÷	ø	ù	ú	û	ü	ý	þ	ÿ

Figure 32-5: Specifications for Helvetica *i*

Now, contrast the width of the *i* with the uppercase *M,* whose specifications are displayed in Figure 32-6. The *M* requires 11 pixels in width, whereas the *i* consumes only 3. The other information presented shows the character's location within the font.

Note

If you are displaying only text, variable-width fonts give your writing a more professional appearance. For interactive uses, however, fixed-width fonts look cleaner on-screen.

Xfd uses the standard X options with a couple of minor differences. The `-fn` option identifies the font to be displayed rather than the informational font. It is also a mandatory option. Table 32-2 lists the other five `xfd` command-line options.

```
-Adobe-Helvetica-Medium-R-Normal--12-120-75-75-P-67-ISO8859-1
Quit  [Prev Page] [Next Page]
              character 0x004d (0,77) (0,0115)
      width 11; left 1, right 10; ascent 9, descent 0 (font 11, 3)
range:  0x0020 (0,32) thru 0x00ff (0,255)
upper left:  0x0000 (0,0)
```

	!	"	#	$	%	&	'	(	)	*	+	,	-	.	/
0	1	2	3	4	5	6	7	8	9	:	;	<	=	>	?
@	A	B	C	D	E	F	G	H	I	J	K	L	M	N	O
P	Q	R	S	T	U	V	W	X	Y	Z	[	\	]	^	_
`	a	b	c	d	e	f	g	h	i	j	k	l	m	n	o
p	q	r	s	t	u	v	w	x	y	z	{	|	}	~	
	¡	¢	£	¤	¥	¦	§	¨	©	ª	«	¬	-	®	¯
°	±	²	³	´	µ	¶	·	¸	¹	º	»	¼	½	¾	¿
À	Á	Â	Ã	Ä	Å	Æ	Ç	È	É	Ê	Ë	Ì	Í	Î	Ï
Ð	Ñ	Ò	Ó	Ô	Õ	Ö	×	Ø	Ù	Ú	Û	Ü	Ý	Þ	ß
à	á	â	ã	ä	å	æ	ç	è	é	ê	ë	ì	í	î	ï
ð	ñ	ò	ó	ô	õ	ö	÷	ø	ù	ú	û	ü	ý	þ	ÿ

Figure 32-6: Specifications for Helvetica *M*

Table 32-2   xfd Options

Option	Argument	Result
-box		Shows a box around each character
-center		Centers each character within the grid
-columns	*integer*	Specifies the number of columns in the grid
-rows	*integer*	Specifies the number of rows in the grid
-start	*integer*	Starts the font display from the character associated with the specified integer

Secret

Specifying a specific number of rows and columns is a back door to resizing the screen. Figure 32-7 shows the standard 9 × 15 font with a grid size of only five rows and four columns. Notice that the Prev Page and Next Page buttons are available. The smaller display does not restrict the numbers of characters that you can see.

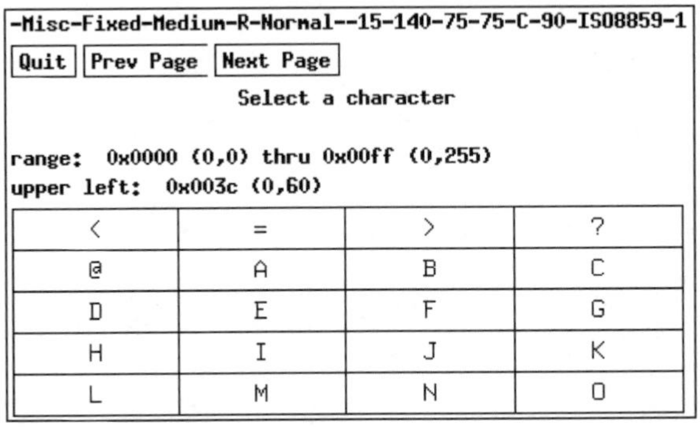

```
-Misc-Fixed-Medium-R-Normal--15-140-75-75-C-90-IS08859-1
Quit  Prev Page  Next Page
           Select a character

range:  0x0000 (0,0) thru 0x00ff (0,255)
upper left:  0x003c (0,60)
```

<	=	>	?
@	A	B	C
D	E	F	G
H	I	J	K
L	M	N	O

Figure 32-7: A smaller display

You can use the X resources listed in Table 32-3 to customize many aspects of Xfd.

Table 32-3   Xfd Resources

Resource	*Customization*
*grid.borderWidth	The size of the grid border
*quit.Label	The label for the Quit button
*prev.Label	The label for the Prev Page button
*next.Label	The label for the Next Page button
*select.Label	The label for the select widget
*metrics.Label	The label for the metrics widget
*select.Justify	The justification for the select label
*metrics.Justify	The justification for the metrics label
*range.Justify	The justification for the range
*start.Justify	The justification for the start indicator
*quit.Translations	The actions to be performed when the Quit button is selected
*next.Translations	The actions to be performed when the Next Page button is selected
*prev.Translations	The actions to be performed when the Prev Page button is selected
*Translations	Standard translations for keystrokes

The full range of customizations lets you actually change the function of the buttons. The three standard functions are Quit(), Next(), and Prev(). To change the order of the buttons on the display, just change the labels and functions.

Caution

Customizing Xfd can produce some unexpected side effects. If you deactivate the buttons and if the action is not normally allowed when you start at the beginning of the font, the only legal actions are Quit and Next Page. If Next Page and Prev Page are switched, only Quit and Prev Page will be available. You can use the keyboard translations to circumvent this problem.

The capability to change labels is very useful for translating X resources into other languages. For instance, you can quickly translate this application into French, as shown in Figure 32-8, simply by providing French translations to the English labels.

```
-Misc-Fixed-Bold-R-Normal--15-140-75-75-C-90-ISO8859-1
┌──────────┐ ┌─────────┐ ┌─────────┐
│Abandonnez│ │Ante Page│ │Vois Page│
└──────────┘ └─────────┘ └─────────┘
           Choisir un Lettre
               Metrique
range:  0x0000 (0,0) thru 0x00ff (0,255)
upper left:  0x0032 (0,50)
```

2	3	4	5	6
7	8	9	:	;
<	=	>	?	@
A	B	C	D	E
F	G	H	I	J

Figure 32-8: Xfd in French

Xfd is not a tool that should normally reside in either the X startup file or the window manager menus. Instead, you should activate it from the command line as needed.

Cutting and pasting when not supported

The Xcutsel application is a simple application that provides a cut and paste capability between applications that do not normally support cut and paste. The command is xcutsel. Figure 32-9 shows the application window.

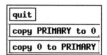

Figure 32-9: The Xcutsel application

To copy a selection, highlight it with your pointer, and press the copy 0 to PRIMARY button. To paste the selection in another location, use the pointer to select the location, and press copy PRIMARY to 0.

Note

If you have Xclipboard, you do not need Xcutsel.

Besides the standard X toolkit options, Xcutsel has two command-line options of note. The -selection name option lets you change the name of the selection. The -cutbuffer number lets you specify a different cut buffer.

Labels are resources. The Xcutsel label names are Xcutsel*sel-cut.Label (the copy PRIMARY to 0 button), Xcutsel*cut-sel.Label (the copy 0 to PRIMARY button), and Xcutsel*quit.Label (the quit button). Xcutsel is a useful application for the startup file.

Changing your pointer and keyboard

Your keyboard and pointer are remote devices to the UNIX operating system. They communicate with applications by sending a signal to a device driver that translates the signal into input for a program. When you are running X, yet another level of translation is present. The server grabs all the input and translates it into callbacks for X applications. These applications, such as an Xterm, can then send the input to other applications, and so on.

The X server contains a keyboard map and uses it to translate keystrokes into input. To change the keyboard mappings, use the xmodmap command.

Xmodmap does not display any windows on the X server, although each expression may result in callbacks to running applications. Instead, Xmodmap communicates directly with the X server, telling it how to change the standard keyboard mappings. Table 32-4 lists the xmodmap command-line options.

Table 32-4   xmodmap Options

Option	Argument	Result
-display	display string	Shows the display on which to change the mappings.
-e	expression	Executes the specified expression
-grammar		Produces a help message to describe the grammar of the Xmodmap expressions
-help		Gives a brief description of the options
-n		Does not change mappings but prints out what would change
-pk		Prints the current key map

Option	Argument	Result
-pke		Prints the current key map in the form of expressions that can be edited and fed back into Xmodmap
-pm		Prints the current modifier map
-pp		Prints the current pointer map
-quiet		Does not print out a log (default)
-verbose		Prints out each action taken by Xmodmap
-		Uses standard input instead of a file

Xmodmap works with expressions in a fixed syntax to change the mappings within the X server. The expression syntax is *command symbol=value*. Xmodmap acts on a file listed at the end of the arguments that includes all the symbolic expressions.

The most common values are KEYSYMs, taken from the KEYSYM database. You can find KEYSYMs in the header file /usr/include/X11/keysymdef.h. Some standard KEYSYMs are XK_BackSpace, XK_Escape, and XK_Num_Lock. You can modify the behavior of each key symbol. This is why separate keys for lowercase *a*, uppercase *A*, and Ctrl-A are unneeded. You can change keyboard modifiers, pointer buttons, and key codes with Xmodmap.

Working with the modifiers

Changing modifiers is relatively easy. A look at the modifier table reveals the following:

```
$ xmodmap -pm
xmodmap:  up to 2 keys per modifier, (key-codes in parentheses):

shift       Shift_L (0x32),  Shift_R (0x3e)
lock        Caps_Lock (0x42)
control     Control_L (0x25),  Control_R (0x6d)
mod1        Alt_L (0x40),  Alt_R (0x71)
mod2
mod3
mod4
mod5
```

The standard modifications are in place. The keyboard supports left and right Shift keys, a Caps Lock key, left and right Control keys, and left and right Alt keys.

Normally, you won't need to modify these values, but occasions arise when doing so is advisable. I had to modify my keyboard at work because the locations of the left Control key and the Caps Lock key are opposite of what I am accustomed to using at home. To do this, I removed the modifier functionality, remapped the keys, and added the modifier. The script is as follows:

```
remove Lock = Caps_Lock
remove Control = Control_L
keysym Control_L = Caps_Lock
keysym Caps_Lock = Control_L
add Lock = Caps_Lock
add Control = Control_L
```

You must remove the special function from the keys, or the modifiers won't change.

Working with the pointer

You probably won't need to change the pointer either, but if you do, use the following technique. First, examine the pointer with xmodmap -pp:

```
$ xmodmap -pp
There are 3 pointer buttons defined.

    Physical      Button
    Button        Code
      1             1
      2             2
      3             3
```

The pointer buttons are numbered from the left. Some pointers have only one or two buttons; others have as many as five. X works best when the pointer has three buttons.

These buttons are aligned so that your right hand's strongest finger, the index finger, is on the first button. If you use your left hand, though, your ring finger rests on the first button.

Here's where Xmodmap comes in. You can remap the buttons. The standard mapping for someone who is left-handed is

```
xmodmap -e `pointer = 3 2 1´
```

This swaps the order of the pointer buttons. Now, your left hand's index finger is on the first button.

Note

If a right-hander uses your terminal, he or she will find this very confusing!

Working with the keyboard

The biggest location for mapping is the keyboard. Each key is mapped to a specific value, and when you strike that key (or a modification of that key), the X server looks up the keystroke in the keyboard map and sends the appropriate pattern to the appropriate application. To see a complete keyboard map, use xmodmap -pk:

```
$ xmodmap -pk
There are 4 KeySyms per KeyCode; KeyCodes range from 8 to 134.

    KeyCode       Keysym (Keysym)      ...
```

Value	Value	(Name)	...
8			
9	0xff1b (Escape)		
10	0x0031 (1)	0x0021 (exclam)	
11	0x0032 (2)	0x0040 (at)	
12	0x0033 (3)	0x0023 (numbersign)	
13	0x0034 (4)	0x0024 (dollar)	
14	0x0035 (5)	0x0025 (percent)	
15	0x0036 (6)	0x005e (asciicircum)	
16	0x0037 (7)	0x0026 (ampersand)	
17	0x0038 (8)	0x002a (asterisk)	
18	0x0039 (9)	0x0028 (parenleft)	
19	0x0030 (0)	0x0029 (parenright)	
20	0x002d (minus)	0x005f (underscore)	
21	0x003d (equal)	0x002b (plus)	
22	0xffff (Delete)		
23	0xff09 (Tab)		
24	0x0071 (q)	0x0051 (Q)	
25	0x0077 (w)	0x0057 (W)	
26	0x0065 (e)	0x0045 (E)	
27	0x0072 (r)	0x0052 (R)	
28	0x0074 (t)	0x0054 (T)	
29	0x0079 (y)	0x0059 (Y)	
30	0x0075 (u)	0x0055 (U)	
31	0x0069 (i)	0x0049 (I)	
32	0x006f (o)	0x004f (O)	
33	0x0070 (p)	0x0050 (P)	
34	0x005b (bracketleft)	0x007b (braceleft)	
35	0x005d (bracketright)	0x007d (braceright)	
36	0xff0d (Return)		
37	0xffe3 (Control_L)		
38	0x0061 (a)	0x0041 (A)	
39	0x0073 (s)	0x0053 (S)	
40	0x0064 (d)	0x0044 (D)	
41	0x0066 (f)	0x0046 (F)	
42	0x0067 (g)	0x0047 (G)	
43	0x0068 (h)	0x0048 (H)	
44	0x006a (j)	0x004a (J)	
45	0x006b (k)	0x004b (K)	
46	0x006c (l)	0x004c (L)	
47	0x003b (semicolon)	0x003a (colon)	
48	0x0027 (apostrophe)	0x0022 (quotedbl)	
49	0x0060 (grave)	0x007e (asciitilde)	
50	0xffe1 (Shift_L)		
51	0x005c (backslash)	0x007c (bar)	
52	0x007a (z)	0x005a (Z)	
53	0x0078 (x)	0x0058 (X)	
54	0x0063 (c)	0x0043 (C)	
55	0x0076 (v)	0x0056 (V)	
56	0x0062 (b)	0x0042 (B)	
57	0x006e (n)	0x004e (N)	
58	0x006d (m)	0x004d (M)	

59	0x002c (comma)	0x003c (less)
60	0x002e (period)	0x003e (greater)
61	0x002f (slash)	0x003f (question)
62	0xffe2 (Shift_R)	
63	0xffaa (KP_Multiply)	
64	0xffe9 (Alt_L)	0xffe7 (Meta_L)
65	0x0020 (space)	
66	0xffe5 (Caps_Lock)	
67	0xffbe (F1)	0xffc8 (F11)
68	0xffbf (F2)	0xffc9 (F12)
69	0xffc0 (F3)	0xffca (F13)
70	0xffc1 (F4)	0xffcb (F14)
71	0xffc2 (F5)	0xffcc (F15)
72	0xffc3 (F6)	0xffcd (F16)
73	0xffc4 (F7)	0xffce (F17)
74	0xffc5 (F8)	0xffcf (F18)
75	0xffc6 (F9)	0xffd0 (F19)
76	0xffc7 (F10)	0xffd1 (F20)
77	0xff7f (Num_Lock)	
78	0xff20 (Multi_key)	
79	0xffb7 (KP_7)	
80	0xffb8 (KP_8)	
81	0xffb9 (KP_9)	
82	0xffad (KP_Subtract)	
83	0xffb4 (KP_4)	
84	0xffb5 (KP_5)	
85	0xffb6 (KP_6)	
86	0xffab (KP_Add)	
87	0xffb1 (KP_1)	
88	0xffb2 (KP_2)	
89	0xffb3 (KP_3)	
90	0xffb0 (KP_0)	
91	0xffae (KP_Decimal)	
92		
93		
94	0x003c (less)	0x003e (greater)
95	0xffc8 (F11)	
96	0xffc9 (F12)	
97	0xff50 (Home)	
98	0xff52 (Up)	
99	0xff55 (Prior)	
100	0xff51 (Left)	
101		
102	0xff53 (Right)	
103	0xff57 (End)	
104	0xff54 (Down)	
105	0xff56 (Next)	
106	0xff63 (Insert)	
107	0xffff (Delete)	
108	0xff8d (KP_Enter)	
109	0xffe4 (Control_R)	
110	0xff13 (Pause)	
111		

```
112          0xffaf (KP_Divide)
113          0xffea (Alt_R)       0xffe8 (Meta_R)
114          0xff6b (Break)
115
116
117
118
119
120
121
122
123
124
125
126
127
128
129
130
131
132
133
134
```

This is exactly how my keyboard is mapped. A second version, xmodmap
-pke, produces output that you can use to reedit the mapping:

```
$ xmodmap -pke
keycode   8 =
keycode   9 = Escape
keycode  10 = 1 exclam
keycode  11 = 2 at
keycode  12 = 3 numbersign
keycode  13 = 4 dollar
keycode  14 = 5 percent
keycode  15 = 6 asciicircum
keycode  16 = 7 ampersand
keycode  17 = 8 asterisk
keycode  18 = 9 parenleft
keycode  19 = 0 parenright
keycode  20 = minus underscore
```

I've shortened the listing a bit.

You can save this output to a file and make any changes needed. The
expression output is keycode *number* = *KEYSYM*. You can also determine the
number by examining the output of xev, the X event monitor, described later
in this chapter.

You normally won't need to change any keys. If you do, just add a keysym
command to the file.

Story: Pulling a Prank

Keyboard remapping is the basis of one of the best pranks you can pull with X. Use the -display command to pull down the key symbols for a given machine, take a -pke, save the original, and specify some remappings. Use Xmodmap to load those remappings on the remote machine and watch the fireworks. I once did this as a prank, and the victim never figured it out. He thought there were problems with the connection between his keyboard and his machine! Worse, he concluded that the problem could be fixed only by rebooting.

Sorry, Scott — it was just Xmodmap!

Xmodmap is usually placed in the X startup file so that your session has the appropriate keyboard mappings.

Displaying console messages

In UNIX, important messages are often sent to the console. When you start X on your console, those messages are still written to the display; consequently, you may need to redraw your display. To redirect these messages, you can designate one of your Xterm windows to be the console with the -C option.

You can use a third approach: the xconsole command. This creates a window where console messages are sent. Table 32-5 list xconsole's options.

Table 32-5   xconsole Command-Line Options

Option	Argument	Result
-daemon		Forces the console to place itself in the background.
-exitOnFail		Forces the application to exit if it cannot open the console.
-file	*filename*	Monitors the specified filename. This does not work on regular files.
-nonotify		Does not append an asterisk to the icon name when new data arrives in the console.
-notify		Appends an asterisk to the icon name when new data appears in the console.
-verbose		Forces the console to display an informative message on the first line of the text buffer.

Xconsole is also modified by X resources, as described in Table 32-6.

Table 32-6   Xconsole Resources

Resource	Argument	Description
XConsole*allow ShellResize	true/false	Enables the window to be resized
XConsole. translations	translation list	Enables you to use translations to clear the screen with the Clear() function.
XConsole.base Translations	translation list	Enables you to use translations to clear the screen with the Clear() function
XConsole*text. translations	translation list	Enables you to use translations to clear the screen with the Clear() function
XConsole*text.base Translations	translation list	Enables you to use translations to clear the screen with the Clear() function
XConsole*text. scrollHorizontal	flag	Indicates whether a scrollbar should be placed
XConsole*text. scrollVertical	flag	Indicates whether a scrollbar should be placed
XConsole*text.height	integer	Specifies the height of the screen in pixels
XConsole*text.width	integer	Specifies the width of the screen in pixels

XConsole is best placed in the initialization script.

Terminating applications

Occasionally, you may have a runaway application on your display. Worse, an application may have hung or be in some other state in which it cannot accept input, and you want to get rid of it. Sometimes, you can kill the application by finding a shell, locating the process ID, and sending a kill signal. Other times, you can use a window manager menu to kill the application. If these approaches fail, though, another command, xkill, can eliminate applications for you.

Secret

Strictly speaking, Xkill does not directly kill applications on your display. Instead, it tells the server to terminate the connection with the application associated with the window. For a well-written application, this event should result in the application's termination.

To specify the application connection to terminate, add a resource identifier after xkill's -id option. If you don't specify an -id option, Xkill displays a special icon and lets you select the window whose connection is to be terminated. Table 32-7 lists the other xkill command-line options.

Table 32-7   xkill Options

Option	Argument	Result
-all		Indicates that all clients with windows should be killed.
-button	*integer*	Uses the specified button to kill an application. If any is specified, any button can be used.
-display	*display string*	Runs Xkill on the specified display.
-frame		Kills all the direct children of the root window.

The only available resource is XKill*Button, which specifies the default button to use when Xkill is not given a specific application to kill.

If you use the Tab Window Manager, the function f.kill produces results similar to Xkill. Therefore, this is not a good window manager menu command. Similarly, using this in a startup script is unusual. Instead, Xkill is best invoked from a command line in dire emergencies only.

Running applications on remote machines

A last general utility is the xon command. This is similar to the rsh command, except that it is designed to be used with X. The first argument must be a remote host name. The command follows the host name. Optional arguments can follow the command. If no command is specified, Xon attempts to run the command xterm -ls on the remote machine.

As Xon runs, the environment variables DISPLAY, XAUTHORITY, and XUSERFILESEARCHPATH are passed to the remote machine. This way, any output from the command is directed to the display you specify with your desired authorizations. Table 32-8 lists the xon command-line options.

Table 32-8	xon Options	
Option	**Argument**	**Result**
-access		Runs Xhost locally to ensure that the application can be displayed on your local screen
-debug		Keeps the remote process attached to the local input, output, and error files
-name	*window*	Specifies a different application name and title for the default command
-nols		Suspects the -ls action on the Xterm
-screen	*integer*	Changes the screen number for the DISPLAY variable
-user	*user name*	Uses the specified user name on the remote machine

Xon works only if you have permission to run commands on remote machines without a password. This means that your local machine should appear in the .rhosts file on the remote machine in your home directory. For more details on local networking, see Chapter 19.

Xon is best used to bring up X terminals on multiple machines and to display them on your screen. You can use Xon in an X startup script if you normally use multiple machines; otherwise, Xon is an excellent addition to a window manager menu.

Multimedia Commands for X

Multimedia is one of the hottest topics in computing today, but what does it mean in the UNIX environment? Multimedia is the combination of images, including moving images, and sound. X, being a graphical interface, is ideal for showing images and moving pictures. The production of sound, however, is a weakness in UNIX, because none of the sound tools has reached the level of sophistication found in the image tools.

Image technology has evolved over time; current pictures and the tools that produce them are quite sophisticated. The tools are also quite numerous, so this chapter can provide a survey of only some of the available tools.

Note

This chapter looks at only those tools found with the Web. All the tools it examines are either public-domain software or shareware and should build rather easily on your machine if you have X installed. More sophisticated tools, such as Adobe PhotoShop, are available on some UNIX platforms, but these are commercial tools, and commercial UNIX software is usually very expensive.

The simplest image technology is the *bitmap,* a two-color image used for icons and other basic pictures in X. Closely related is the *pixmap,* which is just a bitmap that supports multiple colors.

The original file format for images is TIFF (Tagged Image File Format). TIFF files have the disadvantage of being incredibly large. They store information for each separate pixel without much packing or compression. Although TIFF can store 16 million colors in a single image, most displays cannot show this many colors at the same time.

The next generation of image files is GIF (Graphics Interchange Format), patented by CompuServe as an image format that is viewable on many platforms. These images have only 256 colors, which is the same number stored in most X servers. The data is stored in a compressed format to save space.

CompuServe recently attempted to enforce its patent and asked for royalties from some computer manufacturers who distributed software that decoded GIF format files. Many people misconstrued this as an effort to gather money from GIF users, but this was not the case. CompuServe is pleased with the popularity of GIF as an image format.

The generation after GIF is JPEG (Joint Photographic Experts Group). This format is even more compressed than GIF in that it can produce smaller files; it also uses more colors. According to some people, JPEG's one weakness is that it is a "lossy" format. When you convert an image to JPEG, you make a tradeoff between original image detail and compression. JPEG smoothes and changes colors to compress data to an even greater extent than GIF. You can reduce the loss, but the resulting image file may not be smaller than one created with GIF.

These are not the only image file formats. Windows has brought us the BMP format, which some UNIX tools understand. PostScript also supports color graphics. Sun Microsystems has its own raster file format for images, as does Silicon Graphics. Some tools even understand formats such as that used by MacPaint. As I discuss the tools, I'll specify what formats each supports.

The format for moving pictures is MPEG (Moving Pictures Experts Group). MPEG files are fairly standard, although other platforms have alternatives.

Creating and changing bitmaps

The Bitmap application creates and changes bitmaps that you can use for backgrounds, icons, and other pictures.

Caution

Remember that bitmaps are two colors. Those two colors can be any colors you chose, but you can display only a foreground and a background color.

To start Bitmap, type **bitmap**. The application brings up the window shown in Figure 32-10.

Bitmap comes up with a default 16×16 grid. To blacken a square, move your pointer into the grid and click the square with the first button. The second button toggles between black and white, and the third button sets the square to white.

You can hold the button down and drag the pointer to new squares, effectively clicking each square over which the pointer passes.

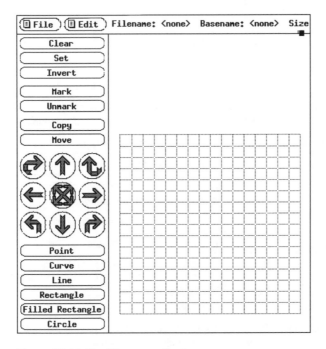

Figure 32-10: The Bitmap application

Two menus appear at the top of the window: The File menu handles overall changes to the bitmap file, and the Edit menu changes the bitmap image's appearance. Table 32-9 lists the menu options for these two pull-down menus.

Story: Images of Nature

I am particularly keen on images. One of my primary hobbies is photographing nature and wildlife. If you visit my Web site, you will see photographs of landscapes in the western United States and of animals, including a black bear, a Mojave rattlesnake, and hawks. I've used GIF for these files because I can display only 256 colors.

Table 32-9   Bitmap Menus

Menu	Option	Result
File	New	Clears the screen and loads a new file. To clear the display, select OK without specifying a file.
	Load	Loads a new file.
	Insert	Inserts a specified bitmap into the current buffer.
	Save	Saves the buffer to the specified file.
	Save As	Saves the buffer to a new file.
	Resize	Resizes the buffer. Existing cells are kept at the same location.
	Rescale	Changes the scale of the image to the newly specified scale. Recalculates and changes the position of existing cells.
File	Filename	Changes the name of the file for storage.
	Basename	Changes the base name of the bitmap for storage.
	Quit	Quits the bitmap tool. If you have made changes, you are prompted to save or discard the changes.
Edit	Image	Displays the image at the actual size (a toggle).
	Grid	Displays a grid for the image (a toggle).
	Dashed	Displays dashed or solid lines on the grid (a toggle).
	Axes	Displays the diagonals (a toggle).
	Stippled	Stipples the diagonals (a toggle).
	Proportional	Keeps the display proportional (a toggle). If this option is unset, the work area expands to fill the space.
	Zoom	Zooms the display to the marked area.
	Cut	Cuts the marked area from the display.
	Copy	Copies the buffer from the marked area.
	Paste	Pastes a copy of the marked area.

On the left side of the display is a series of buttons that help manipulate the image. These buttons perform the following tasks: clear the image, set the specified area, invert the image, mark an area, copy or move part of the image, change the orientation, and specify different figures for drawing.

Hot spots

Two buttons in the lower-left corner of the Bitmap application window add a hot spot to and remove it from the bitmap. A hot spot is important for cursors because it is the pixel in a cursor that represents the cursor's on-screen position. You can use Bitmap to create images and masks to use as cursors.

Command-line options

Bitmap supports the standard X toolkit options as well as those listed in Table 32-10.

Table 32-10	**Bitmap Command-Line Options**	
Option	*Argument*	*Result*
-axes		Turns on the major axes.
+axes		Turns off the major axes.
-dashed		Turns on the dashed lines for the frame and grid.
+dashed		Turns off the dashed lines for the frame and grid.
-dashes	*filename*	Specifies the bitmap to use for the dashes.
-fr	*color*	Specifies the color for frame and grid lines.
	filename	Specifies the bitmap to be initially loaded.
	basename	Specifies the name of the bitmap.
-grid		Turns the grid on.
+grid		Turns the grid off.
-gt	*integer*	Specifies the tolerance of the grid. If the square dimensions fall below this size, the grid is turned off.
-hl	*color*	Specifies the color for highlighting.
-proportional		Turns on the proportional mode.
+proportional		Turns off the proportional mode.
-size	*width* x *height*	Specifies the size of the grid for editing.
-sh	*integer*	Specifies the height of the squares in the editing area.
-stipple	*filename*	Specifies the bitmap to use for stippling.
-stippled		Turns on the stippling of highlighted squares.
+stippled		Turns off the stippling of highlighted squares.
-sw	*integer*	Specifies in pixels the width of the squares in the editing area.

Bitmap files

When you save a bitmap file, it is saved as a variable for a C program. This enables X11 programs to use the file as a header and to include the image in the program easily. Here is the bitmap file for the image of an X in an 8×8 bitmap:

```
#define bitmapfile_width 8
#define bitmapfile_height 8
static unsigned char bitmapfile_bits[] = {
    0xc3, 0xe7, 0x7e, 0x3c, 0x3c, 0x7e, 0xe7, 0xc3};
```

The defines tell us the actual size of the bitmap file, and the data is the highlighted bits, described in bytes. Because the width is 8 bits, each character is one line. The first, 0xc3, translates to binary 11000011. As each line is translated into binary, the following pattern emerges:

```
11000011
11100111
01111110
00111100
00111100
01111110
11100111
11000011
```

The ones form the shape of an X.

If the bitmap is wider than 8 bits, the characters fill the row. If the row is not divisible by eight, the low-order bits of the last character on the row are ignored.

Capturing screen shots

Using the script command to copy the input and output of commands in a terminal session is fairly easy. But what of the X Windows commands, which produce both images and text? Is there an easy and simple way to copy them, too?

There is. The xwd command produces screen captures for later display. To capture a screen, just invoke Xwd from a command line and grab it. Table 32-11 lists the command-line options for xwd.

Secret

Each screen capture shown in this book was originally captured with Xwd.

Table 32-11   xwd Options

Option	Argument	Result
-add	*value*	Adds the specified value to each pixel
-display	*display string*	Runs Xwd on the specified display

Option	Argument	Result
-frame		Includes the window manager frame when selecting the window
-help		Prints a summary of the command syntax
-icmap		Uses the installed color map to determine the colors for the capture
-id	*id*	Grabs the specified window ID for the capture
-name	*window name*	Grabs the specified window for the capture
-nobdrs		Does not include the window borders as part of the capture
-out	*filename*	Saves the dump to the specified file
-root		Grabs the entire display for the screen capture
-screen		Uses GetImage on the root window to process the request
-xy		Uses the XY format for saving color images

Normally, you type **xwd** at the command line with the -out specified. The cursor changes into a cross, and you select a window for the capture. If no -out file is specified, the dump goes to standard output. This is useful for copying dumps from one display to another.

Displaying screen shots

A captured screen shot is useless unless you can display it again. To do this, use the xwud command, which takes the output of the xwd command as standard input and produces a window with a copy of the screen shot. Table 32-12 lists xwud's command-line options.

Table 32-12	**xwud Options**	
Option	Argument	Result
-bg	*color*	Changes the background to the specified color if the input is a bitmap or a single-plane image.
-display	*display string*	Displays the image on the specified screen.
-fg	*color*	Sets the foreground of a bitmap or a single-plane image to the specified color.
-geometry	*geometry string*	Enables you to specify the size and position of the window.

Continued

Table 32-12 *(continued)*

Option	Argument	Result
-help		Prints a short description of the options.
-in	*file*	Uses the specified file for the input.
-new		Forces the creation of a new color map to display the image.
-noclick		Disables the pointer for terminating the image.
-plane	*integer*	Selects a single bit plane for display.
-raw		Forces the image to be displayed with the screen's current color values.
-rv		Reverses the foreground and background colors for bitmaps and single-plane images.
-std	*map type*	Uses the specified color map to display the image. Normal map types are default, best, and gray.
-vis	*visual class*	Specifies a visual class, such as StaticGray, GrayScale, or TrueColor.

Tricks you can perform with Xwd and Xwud include copying windows to a new machine. You perform this with xwd | xwud -display. Xwud is best used to display a newly saved capture to make certain that the screen capture you took is the one you want.

Printing screen shots

You can also print the screen shots that you take. The xpr command takes the screen shot as standard input and produces an image on certain printers. You can either print from standard input or include the filename on the command line and print the file. Table 32-13 lists xpr's command-line options.

Table 32-13 xpr Options

Option	Argument	Result
-append	*filename*	Appends the output to the specified file.
-compact		Compresses white pixels on PostScript printers.
-device	*device*	Specifies the output device. Normally, you'd use ps for PostScript output.

Option	Argument	Result
-header	*string*	Specifies the string to be printed as an image header.
-height	*number*	Specifies the height of the output in inches.
-landscape		Prints the image in landscape mode.
-left	*number*	Specifies the size of the left margin in inches.
-noff		When combined with -append, places the image on the same page as the previous image.
-output	*filename*	Sends the output to the specified file.
-portrait		Prints the image in portrait mode.
-report		Prints debugging information about the image.
-rv		Reverses the foreground and background colors.
-scale	*integer*	Specifies the scale for printing the image.
-split	*integer*	Splits the window onto several pages.
-trailer	*string*	Specifies the string to be printed as an image footer.
-top	*number*	Specifies the size of the top margin in inches.
-width	*number*	Specifies the width of the output in inches.

Xpr is now rarely used because other tools can perform conversion to different formats, such as PostScript, for printing.

Displaying images, Part 1

The four previous commands all handle simple images, such as bitmaps or screen shots. The real world of multimedia, however, includes the advanced graphics formats described previously in the chapter. Displaying those pictures is the job of the xloadimage command.

To display an image on the screen, type **xloadimage** followed by the image name on the command line. Figure 32-11 shows one of my photographs.

I took this photograph of a black bear just outside Banff in Alberta, Canada. When you use Xloadimage, the full-size picture is displayed, so if it is bigger than the display, you must scroll around the image to see the full picture. When you finish looking at the picture, press a pointer button or a key on the keyboard, and the image goes away.

Figure 32-11: Xloadimage's display of a bear

When I brought up the image, Xloadimage gave me the following debugging information in the invocation window:

```
brown.gif is a 567x418 GIF image with 256 colors
  Compressing colormap...250 unique colors
  Using private colormap
  Building XImage...done
```

This tells me that the image is a GIF file with the dimensions specified in pixels.

Xloadimage supports many types of images, including Sun Rasterfiles, GIF, JPEG, TIFF, X Windows dumps, PC Paintbrush, MacPaint, bitmaps, and pixmaps. Table 32-14 lists `xloadimage`'s command-line options.

Table 32-14   xloadimage Options

Option	Argument	Result
-border	color	Sets the background not covered by the image to the specified color.
-configuration		Displays the image path, suffixes, and supported filters when images are read.

Option	Argument	Result
-default		Uses the default root weave as the image.
-debug		Talks to the X server synchronously.
-delay	*integer*	Automatically advances to the next image after the specified number of seconds.
-display	*display string*	Shows the image on the specified display.
-dump	*type file*	Dumps the image in the specified format. Used for image conversion.
-fit		Forces the image to use the current color map.
-fork		Disassociates Xloadimage from the shell.
-fullscreen		Uses the full screen to show the image.
-geometry	*geometry string*	Sets the size and location of the window in which the image is displayed.
-goto	*name*	Makes the specified image the next image displayed.
-help		Gives information about an option.
-identify		Identifies the supplied image.
-install		Installs the image's color map when the window is focused.
-list		Lists the images on the image path.
-onroot		Displays the image on the root window.
-path		Displays information about the program configuration.
-pixmap		Forces the use of a pixmap as a backing store.
-private		Forces the use of a private color map.
-quiet		Provides no output.
-supported		Lists the supported image types.
-type	*typename*	Forces loading of the image as a specific type.

Continued

Table 32-14 *(continued)*

Option	Argument	Result
-verbose		Provides detailed information about images (default).
-view		Views the image in a window (default).
-visual	*visualname*	Forces the use of visual type, such as GrayScale, to display the image.
-windowid	*ID*	Sets the background pixmap of the specified window.
-at	*x,y*	Sets the coordinates to load the base image.
-background	*color*	Specifies the background color.
-brighten	*integer*	Specifies a multiplier to brighten the image. The default is 100.
-center		Centers the image when loaded.
-clip	*x,y,w,h*	Clips the image before loading it. Starts at *x,y*, and saves the specified width and height. A 0 for width or height indicates the rest of the image.
-colors	*integer*	Specifies the maximum number of colors used to display an image.
-dither		Dithers the image to monochrome.
-foreground	*color*	Specifies the foreground color.
-gamma	*gamma value*	Uses the specified gamma correction for the display. Normal corrections are 2.0 to 2.5.
-global		Applies the options to all images.
-gray		Converts the image to grayscale.
-halftone		Converts the image to halftone.
-idelay	*integer*	Sets the delay for the image to the specified number of seconds.
-invert		Inverts the colors of the monochrome image.
-merge		Merges this image onto the base after processing.
-name	*name*	Forces the next argument to be the image name.

Option	Argument	Result
-newoptions		Resets the global options.
-normalize		Normalizes the color image.
-rotate	*integer*	Rotates the image *integer* degrees clockwise. The integer must be a multiple of 90.
-shrink		Shrinks the image to fit the display.
-smooth		Smoothes the colors of an image. Useful after zooming.
-tile		Tiles the image on the background to create a full-screen image.
-title	*string*	Changes the title of the image.
-xzoom	*integer*	Zooms the x-axis to the specified percentage.
-yzoom	*integer*	Zooms the y-axis to the specified percentage.
-zoom	*integer*	Zooms the image to the specified percentage.

Xloadimage's many, varied options provide the UNIX explorer hours of study.

Using the initialization file

You can initialize Xloadimage with a startup file, .xloadimagerc, located in the user's home directory. This file has three variables: path, extension, and filter. The path is a list of directories searched for a specific image. It has the following form:

```
path = ~/images .
```

Directories are separated by whitespace. When you specify an image, this path is checked to find the image.

The extension is a listing of the image file's possible suffixes. The format is as follows:

```
extension = .gif .GIF .jpeg .jpg
```

Again, options are separated by whitespace. When an image is requested, these extensions are applied to the name as the path is searched.

Filters are commands that you can use before displaying an image. They have the syntax command suffix and are listed in pairs, as follows:

```
filter = uncompress .Z
```

If the command needs options, you must enclose the command in double quotation marks.

The pound sign (#) indicates comments.

Converting images with Xloadimage

To convert images to new formats, use the `-dump` option on the command line. You must specify a format (`gif`, `jpeg`, and `tiff` are normal formats) and, occasionally, an option. JPEG in particular has a lot of possible options for dumping the file. After the format, you must specify the output filename.

For example, the command to convert my bear image to JPEG is this:

```
xloadimage -dump jpeg,quality=80 bear.jpg brown.gif
```

You can write shell scripts to perform bulk conversions.

Displaying multiple images with Xloadimage

Xloadimage displays images in sequence based on their place on the command line. The `-delay` and `-idelay` options indicate how long an image should remain on-screen before the next image is displayed. The options listed after `-at` in Table 32-14 apply to individual images and can be placed between image names.

Displaying images, Part 2

Another tool for displaying images is Xv, the X image viewer. Xv provides a graphical interface for displaying images.

Note

Xv is a shareware program. This means that you can try it out for free. If you like it, you should send a check to the program's writer for the requested amount.

Xv is used in a fashion similar to Xloadimage: You specify a file or list of files after the `xv`, and the specified files are displayed in a window. Figure 32-12 shows a waterfall displayed with Xv.

Christine Falls is located in Mount Rainier National Park in Washington. Xv automatically scales the image to fit the display.

Although Xv has many command-line options, its real benefit is in the windows. By clicking the third pointer button, you can bring up a listing of all the images to be displayed with this command. From this window, you can alter the displayed image, change colors, convert the image format, crop the image, and perform many other commands. You can even examine a series of images and select one to be displayed on your root window. Figure 32-13 shows the Xv command window.

Figure 32-12: Christine Falls with Xv

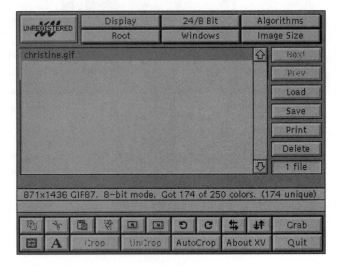

Figure 32-13: The Xv command window

Managing multiple images

When multiple images are listed on a command line, you can step through them on the command window simply by clicking the Next or Prev buttons. You can also scroll through the list and double-click any image to display it.

You can also move an image to the root window. Across the top of the Xv window is a series of pull-down menus. The Root menu enables you to move the image onto the root window in several different formats.

Using the visual schnauzer

One of the more interesting tools for Xv is the visual schnauzer. This tool is basically a preview tool for multiple images. You can reach the schnauzer from the Windows pull-down menu or by selecting Ctrl-V on the image. Figure 32-14 shows the schnauzer on my images directory.

Figure 32-14: A preview of some of my images

From this collection of previews, I can select any image and display it. For example, if I select `nyssa.gif`, the main image is changed to Nyssa's face, as shown in Figure 32-15. She's a pretty cat, isn't she?

When you add images to or delete images from the directory, click the Update button to create new thumbnail images.

Figure 32-15: One of my cats

Underlying the schnauzer is the .xvpics directory, where a smaller version of each full-size image is stored. A copy sized to fit in the area on the schnauzer is made of every image.

Changing formats

Changing formats in Xv is a snap. Just select Save from the command window. Figure 32-16 shows the Save window.

The GIF pull-down menu enables you to select from a wide variety of formats, including GIF, TIFF, JPEG, BMP, and PostScript. When additional information is needed, a dialog box appears, and you just answer the questions.

Changing colors

One of the more interesting features of Xv is the capability to edit the color map. To do this, select Color Editor from the Windows pull-down menu, or press *e* within the image display. Figure 32-17 shows Xv's color editor.

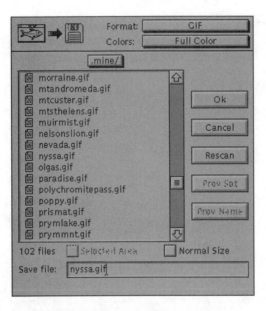

Figure 32-16: The Xv Save window

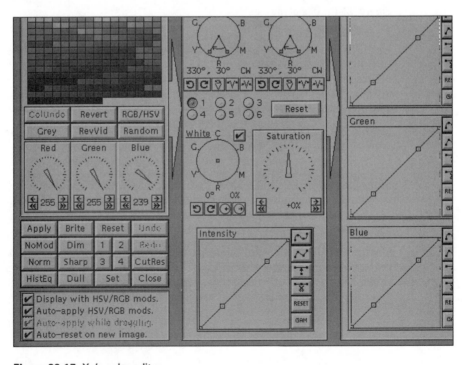

Figure 32-17: Xv's color editor

You can use the color editor to adjust the individual cells or to change the overall settings within Xv. To experiment, I inverted the intensity of the color green on my cat, producing a rather psychedelic image of Nyssa (see Figure 32-18).

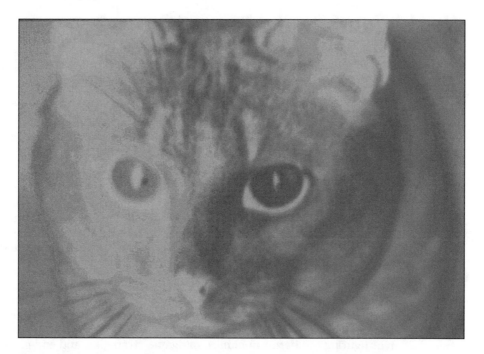

Figure 32-18: A psychedelic cat (though black and white doesn't do it justice)

Xv is similar to Xloadimage in that exploring all the different options and tricks can provide hours of entertainment for the UNIX hacker.

Going to the movies on your UNIX machine

As previously mentioned, the standard format for movies is MPEG, but commands such as xloadimage and xv do not display MPEG files. The appropriate command for doing so is mpeg_play.

The mpeg_play command places the image in a small window that is repeatedly updated. Essentially, MPEG is a format in which a series of still pictures are linked to produce the appearance of motion.

Secret

Don't feel cheated by MPEG's "appearance of motion." The real movies work the same way.

Several arguments are related to the technical details of displaying MPEG files, but the only one of interest is `-quiet`, which suppresses the debugging information provided by default.

Would You Like to Play a Game?

Currently, one of the more common uses for computers is to play games. Although this mainly falls into the realm of PCs, several games and amusing programs are available for X Windows users.

Some of the following programs are proper games, and others are amusing programs that exploit the features of X. You may want to include some of these in your window manager menu files.

An amusing puzzle

The essence of a good game is simplicity with many variations. The rules should be easy to learn, yet the strategy should require some thought. This is why most adults do not find tick-tack-toe an interesting game: They have learned all the possible variations, so they can never lose. Between two evenly matched players, the result is always a draw.

In contrast to tick-tack-toe is a game such as chess. The rules to move pieces are simple and can be described in a single page, but the various strategies involved in chess fill volumes of books. No single set of moves from the beginning can lead to a guaranteed victory. Chess players have spent their lives figuring out better openings, midgame strategies, and end-game positions.

A third type of game keeps players off balance by introducing an element of luck. Card games, dice, and other random drawing contests are nondeterministic games. Both poker and Monopoly are good examples of nondeterministic games using simple rules but requiring thoughtful strategy.

Story: Checkmate!

I'm no longer a game player. In the past, though, I beat rogue, one of the older UNIX-based games, and I once beat DUCHESS — the Duke University Computer Chess Program — shortly after it was World Champion. (I opened with a double fianchetto, which was not in its opening book at the time, and managed to mate it with Bh8 followed by Qg7++ after it castled.

I'll occasionally play a game or two with the computer now, but I find interacting with other human beings — either in person or over the networks — more entertaining.

A fourth type of game is the deterministic puzzle. Its rules are simple, but it has enough combinations to provide a challenge. The X Windows game Puzzle is an example of this type.

Puzzle is a 4 × 4 square with 15 sliding tiles. The game starts with the tiles in a random placement, and you slide them to place them in order. Figure 32-19 shows a starting position.

Figure 32-19: Starting position for Puzzle

Clicking a tile moves it into the open space. You can move up to three tiles at a time by clicking a tile, which pushes the tiles in front of it into the open space. For example, after the 3 tile is clicked, the puzzle looks like Figure 32-20.

Figure 32-20: Making a move in Puzzle

You move the tiles until you have them in numerical order, as shown in Figure 32-21. This is the winning position.

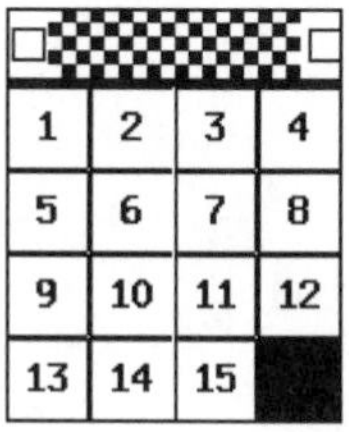

Figure 32-21: Winning position in Puzzle

To restart the puzzle, click the boxes at the top. Clicking the middle button on the checkerboard ends the Puzzle program.

As you can see, the rules for Puzzle are fairly simple, and after you get the hang of it, solving the puzzle is a matter of time. My strategy is to try to fill the top two rows correctly before maneuvering the bottom tiles into position. I work with pairs of tiles, trying first to mate them and then to slide them as a group into position.

You can customize Puzzle. You can specify the number of tiles with the -size WxH option, change the size of the window with the -geometry option, specify the screen with -display, and increase the speed of tile movement with -speed.

Tetris for X Windows

If you've spent time in a video arcade, you know that one of the longest lasting games is Tetris. This is a game in which different shapes fall and you have to try to place them in a space-optimal fashion. In arcades, you have a joystick-type device to move the pieces, and you can use the buttons to change the orientation and speed the placement.

X Windows has its own version of Tetris. Figure 32-22 shows the starting state.

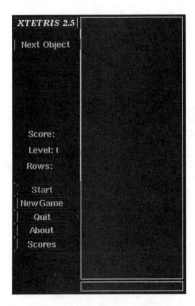

Figure 32-22: Xtetris starting state

Click Start to start a game. As the blocks fall, you can move them left or right by clicking the left or right mouse buttons. Pressing Shift while clicking causes the block to rotate. Clicking the middle mouse button causes the block to drop immediately.

Caution

If you have remapped your pointer buttons, the results may not be intuitive!

As a row is filled, it drops off the bottom of the display. As more blocks fall, the blocks start appearing faster. When the screen is filled and there is no longer any room for falling blocks, the game ends. Your score is calculated according to the nature of the blocks that have fallen and their orientation. Figure 32-23 shows a game of Xtetris in progress.

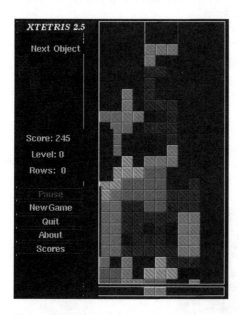

Figure 32-23: Xtetris in progress

As you can see, I'm not very good at this game!

Xtetris takes several options, which are described in Table 32-15. The game also has many X-resource customizations available. To see them, examine the /usr/lib/X11/app-defaults/Xtetris file.

Table 32-15 Xtetris Options		
Option	**Argument**	**Result**
-boxsize	*integer*	Specifies the width of the falling objects.
-bw		Uses the monochrome X defaults.

Continued

Table 32-15 *(continued)*		
Option	**Argument**	**Result**
-color		Uses the color X defaults.
-noscore		Runs Xtetris without displaying your score. The score file appears when the game is finished.
-score		Displays the score file.
-speed	*integer*	Sets the game's speed. The default is 10; higher numbers are faster (assuming your processor can support the faster speeds).

Xtetris is not distributed with every UNIX system. If you want a copy, you'll find one on the CD-ROM accompanying this book, or you can use Archie and FTP to find the latest source code.

Mazes

The Maze program is an X11 demonstration program that repeatedly creates and solves mazes. Figure 32-24 shows one such maze.

Figure 32-24: A maze to be solved

Do you think you can solve this maze? Figure 32-25 shows the solution.

Figure 32-25: A solved maze

The command-line options are simple. If -S is specified, the window fills the screen. The -r option reverses the video.

The three pointer buttons have different meanings. The left button clears the window and restarts the maze. The middle button is an on/off toggle. The right button tells the program to exit.

The generated mazes are actually easy to solve. They use the algorithm of keeping your hand on the right (or left) wall and following that wall to the exit.

Secret

Eyes to watch the cursor

A clever little application is the Xeyes program, which creates a pair of eyes that you can place anywhere on the screen. The eyes follow the cursor wherever it goes on the display. Figure 32-26 shows the eyes.

Figure 32-26: Xeyes

One nice feature of Xeyes is the capability to use the -shape extension to create a transparent window, which makes the eyes appear to float on the display.

Different colors may be set. Xeyes is a clever program to include in a startup script, particularly if you are prone to losing your pointer.

An example of gas dispersion

One little demonstration program is Xgas, which produces a window with two chambers. You can set the temperature of the two chambers to any value from 0 through 500, using the sliders. When you start, you can use the first pointer button to create a gas molecule. The molecule starts moving randomly until it hits a wall and bounces. The second pointer button places all available molecules at the given spot, and they disperse from there.

The hotter the wall, the faster the molecule moves after bouncing. With walls set to zero, everything eventually slows down. Walls at 500 cause the molecules to move faster.

Figure 32-27 shows the start, and Figure 32-28 shows the chambers after they have been running for a while. I've set the left chamber to 500 and the right to 0.

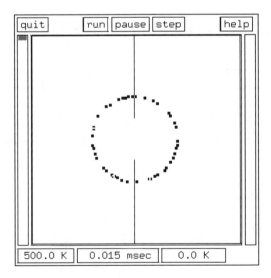

Figure 32-27: Xgas after five steps

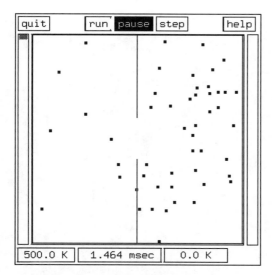

Figure 32-28: Xgas after running for a while

After Xgas has run for a while, the gas molecules begin to congregate on the colder side of the chamber. They do this because they become denser as they move slower.

One item you may want to change on the command line is the maximum number of molecules. The default is 50, but with the -mm option, you can set this to any number. Be warned, though: The larger the number, the slower the program.

A view of the Earth

One interesting program is Xearth, which provides a display of Earth from space. By default, this appears on the root window, as shown in Figure 32-29. I've iconified all the windows to produce the full effect.

The viewpoint is directly in line between the Earth and the sun. Xearth graduates the shading of the planet according to its angle to the sun. Thus, the edge of the planet is darker than the center.

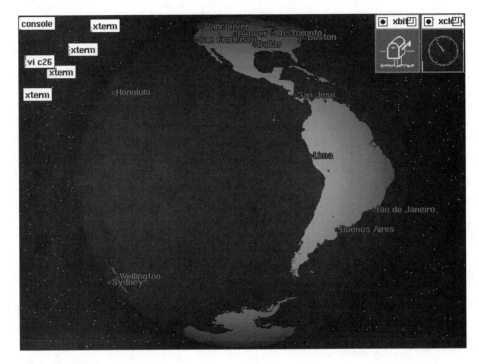

Figure 32-29: A view of Earth from space

The xearth command takes many options; Table 32-16 lists some of the most notable.

Table 32-16   xearth Options

Option	Argument	Result
-fork		Runs Xearth in the background.
-gif		Writes out the image as a GIF file.
-label		Provides a label giving the time and position in the window's bottom-right corner.
-mag	*integer*	Specifies how much to magnify the Earth's image. xearth -pos `orbit 1.5 35´ -mag 4 gives a good simulation of an orbiting capsule.
-mono		Displays the Earth in monochrome.

Option	Argument	Result
-pos	*position specification*	Enables you to change your position on the Earth. There are three different formats: The sunrel argument keeps your position relative to the sun. The fixed argument, followed by a latitude and longitude, lets you look down from a position above the specified location. The orbit argument, with an orbital period in hours and an inclination in degrees, gives you a continuously changing perspective, as if you were on a space station.
-sunpos	*specification*	Indicates where the sun should be positioned.
-time	*integer*	Specifies the starting time, expressed in seconds since the UNIX epoch.
-timewarp	*integer*	Specifies the amount by which time is accelerated.
-wait	*integer*	Specifies the frequency of updates.

I place an Xearth in my X initialization file.

The phases of the moon

You can display not only the Earth, but also the moon. The xphoon command gives an image of what the moon looks like at the present time and places it on the root window, as shown in Figure 32-30.

Again, a few command-line options can customize the display. The -b option turns off the Earth-light feature, making the dark half black. With -t followed by an integer, you can have Xphoon update the view once every specified number of minutes. With -i, the process forks itself into the background and gives you the process ID.

Xphoon simply modifies and loads the bitmap of the moon onto the screen. It works well in a startup file.

Note

I'd love to see a program like this for Mars or Jupiter. (I'd hope the Jupiter program keeps up with Jupiter's moons.) If you know of any such programs, please let me know.

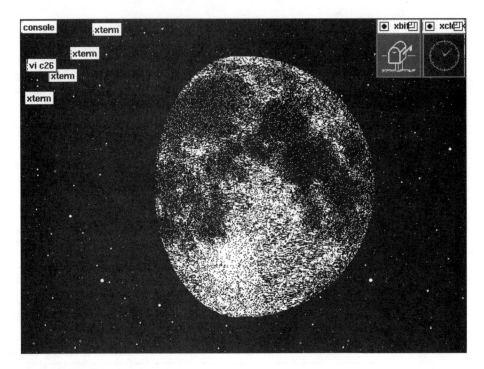

Figure 32-30: The moon

A cockroach infestation?

During part of my youth, I lived in Mendham, New Jersey, which is about 45 miles west of New York City, and I loved to visit Manhattan. One feature of New York City that you won't find in any guides to the city is the cockroaches. They're everywhere. Wherever a drop of moisture exists, *periplaneta americana* is not far behind.

It might surprise you to know that roaches can infest your screen, too. The program Xroach creates virtual cockroaches that hide under your windows. When you iconify a window, they scurry about, finding new places to hide. Figure 32-31 shows them scurrying. The xroach command has some amusing options, which Table 32-17 lists.

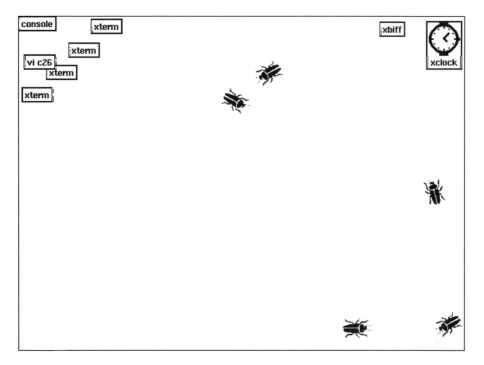

Figure 32-31: Cockroaches!

Table 32-17   xroach Options

Option	Argument	Result
-display	*display screen*	Puts the roaches on the specified display.
-rc	*color*	Makes the roaches the specified color.
-rgc	*color*	Specifies the color of a dead roach. I recommend yellowgreen.
-roaches	*integer*	Places the specified number of roaches on the screen. The default is 10.
-speed	*decimal*	Gives the roaches a speed. The default is 20 (for winter, use 5; for summer, use 30).
-squish		Enables you to kill roaches by clicking them with the pointer button.

Perhaps most disgusting, the roaches appear to eat their dead comrades.

Secret

Xroach has variations, the most notable being Xbaby, in which infant humans crawl around the display.

Other games

Many other games are available for UNIX. Use Archie and FTP to find them. Some of my favorites include Xsol, the Canfield solitaire card game, and Spider, a two-deck variation of Canfield. Other games include Xtank, a battle game for multiple users on a network.

Debugging X

A few commands help you understand what the X server is doing at any given time. I've grouped them under the term *debugging,* although strictly speaking they're not really debugging tools. They examine X events and properties, and you can use them to measure the display's speed.

Monitoring X events

The xev command monitors X events. Xev creates a window, and whenever an X event occurs in that window, Xev displays a report on your invocation screen. Figure 32-32 shows the Xev window, and Listing 32-1 shows the output generated when I move the pointer into the window, click the first button, and type my name.

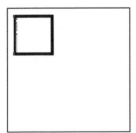

Figure 32-32: The Xev window

Listing 32-1: Xev Output

```
Outer window is 0x3400001, inner window is 0x3400002

PropertyNotify event, serial 6, synthetic NO, window 0x3400001,
    atom 0x27 (WM_NAME), time 191011030, state PropertyNewValue

PropertyNotify event, serial 7, synthetic NO, window 0x3400001,
    atom 0x22 (WM_COMMAND), time 191011030, state PropertyNewValue
```

```
PropertyNotify event, serial 8, synthetic NO, window 0x3400001,
    atom 0x28 (WM_NORMAL_HINTS), time 191011030, state PropertyNewValue

CreateNotify event, serial 9, synthetic NO, window 0x3400001,
    parent 0x3400001, window 0x3400002, (10,10), width 50, height 50
border_width 4, override NO

MapNotify event, serial 10, synthetic NO, window 0x3400001,
    event 0x3400001, window 0x3400002, override NO

ConfigureNotify event, serial 11, synthetic NO, window 0x3400001,
    event 0x3400001, window 0x3400001, (0,0), width 178, height 178,
    border_width 0, above 0x1803c56, override NO

ReparentNotify event, serial 12, synthetic NO, window 0x3400001,
    event 0x3400001, window 0x3400001, parent 0x1803fd7,
    (0,21), override NO

ConfigureNotify event, serial 12, synthetic YES, window 0x3400001,
    event 0x3400001, window 0x3400001, (390,32), width 178, height 178,
    border_width 2, above 0x1803fd7, override NO

MapNotify event, serial 12, synthetic NO, window 0x3400001,
    event 0x3400001, window 0x3400001, override NO

VisibilityNotify event, serial 12, synthetic NO, window 0x3400001,
    state VisibilityUnobscured

Expose event, serial 12, synthetic NO, window 0x3400001,
    (0,0), width 178, height 10, count 3

Expose event, serial 12, synthetic NO, window 0x3400001,
    (0,10), width 10, height 58, count 2

Expose event, serial 12, synthetic NO, window 0x3400001,
    (68,10), width 110, height 58, count 1

Expose event, serial 12, synthetic NO, window 0x3400001,
    (0,68), width 178, height 110, count 0

PropertyNotify event, serial 12, synthetic NO, window 0x3400001,
    atom 0x93 (WM_STATE), time 191015168, state PropertyNewValue

EnterNotify event, serial 15, synthetic NO, window 0x3400001,
    root 0x2b, subw 0x0, time 191031192, (105,149), root:(497,183),
    mode NotifyUngrab, detail NotifyAncestor, same_screen YES,
    focus NO, state 0

KeymapNotify event, serial 15, synthetic NO, window 0x0,
    keys:  43  0   0   0   0   0   0   0   0   0   0   0   0   0   0   0
            0  0   0   0   0   0   0   0   0   0   0   0   0   0   0   0
```

```
MotionNotify event, serial 15, synthetic NO, window 0x3400001,
    root 0x2b, subw 0x0, time 191031499, (103,171), root:(495,205),
    state 0x0, is_hint 0, same_screen YES

LeaveNotify event, serial 15, synthetic NO, window 0x3400001,
    root 0x2b, subw 0x0, time 191031549, (77,205), root:(469,239),
    mode NotifyNormal, detail NotifyNonlinear, same_screen YES,
    focus NO, state 0

EnterNotify event, serial 15, synthetic NO, window 0x3400001,
    root 0x2b, subw 0x0, time 191035169, (10,171), root:(402,205),
    mode NotifyNormal, detail NotifyAncestor, same_screen YES,
    focus YES, state 0

KeymapNotify event, serial 15, synthetic NO, window 0x0,
    keys:  43  0  0  0  0  0  0  0  0  0  0  0  0  0  0  0
            0  0  0  0  0  0  0  0  0  0  0  0  0  0  0  0

MotionNotify event, serial 15, synthetic NO, window 0x3400001,
    root 0x2b, subw 0x0, time 191035209, (12,163), root:(404,197),
    state 0x0, is_hint 0, same_screen YES

MotionNotify event, serial 15, synthetic NO, window 0x3400001,
    root 0x2b, subw 0x0, time 191035269, (13,161), root:(405,195),
    state 0x0, is_hint 0, same_screen YES

MotionNotify event, serial 15, synthetic NO, window 0x3400001,
    root 0x2b, subw 0x0, time 191035509, (13,160), root:(405,194),
    state 0x0, is_hint 0, same_screen YES

MotionNotify event, serial 15, synthetic NO, window 0x3400001,
    root 0x2b, subw 0x0, time 191035589, (13,159), root:(405,193),
    state 0x0, is_hint 0, same_screen YES

ButtonPress event, serial 15, synthetic NO, window 0x3400001,
    root 0x2b, subw 0x0, time 191037129, (13,159), root:(405,193),
    state 0x0, button 1, same_screen YES

ButtonRelease event, serial 15, synthetic NO, window 0x3400001,
    root 0x2b, subw 0x0, time 191037339, (13,159), root:(405,193),
    state 0x100, button 1, same_screen YES

KeyPress event, serial 15, synthetic NO, window 0x3400001,
    root 0x2b, subw 0x0, time 191038229, (13,159), root:(405,193),
    state 0x0, keycode 50 (keysym 0xffe1, Shift_L), same_screen YES,
    XLookupString gives 0 characters:  ""

KeyPress event, serial 17, synthetic NO, window 0x3400001,
    root 0x2b, subw 0x0, time 191038499, (13,159), root:(405,193),
    state 0x1, keycode 44 (keysym 0x4a, J), same_screen YES,
    XLookupString gives 1 characters:  "J"
```

```
KeyRelease event, serial 17, synthetic NO, window 0x3400001,
    root 0x2b, subw 0x0, time 191038579, (13,159), root:(405,193),
    state 0x1, keycode 44 (keysym 0x4a, J), same_screen YES,
    XLookupString gives 1 characters:  "J"

KeyRelease event, serial 17, synthetic NO, window 0x3400001,
    root 0x2b, subw 0x0, time 191038659, (13,159), root:(405,193),
    state 0x1, keycode 50 (keysym 0xffe1, Shift_L), same_screen YES,
    XLookupString gives 0 characters:  ""

KeyPress event, serial 17, synthetic NO, window 0x3400001,
    root 0x2b, subw 0x0, time 191038799, (13,159), root:(405,193),
    state 0x0, keycode 38 (keysym 0x61, a), same_screen YES,
    XLookupString gives 1 characters:  "a"

KeyRelease event, serial 17, synthetic NO, window 0x3400001,
    root 0x2b, subw 0x0, time 191038879, (13,159), root:(405,193),
    state 0x0, keycode 38 (keysym 0x61, a), same_screen YES,
    XLookupString gives 1 characters:  "a"

KeyPress event, serial 17, synthetic NO, window 0x3400001,
    root 0x2b, subw 0x0, time 191038929, (13,159), root:(405,193),
    state 0x0, keycode 58 (keysym 0x6d, m), same_screen YES,
    XLookupString gives 1 characters:  "m"

KeyRelease event, serial 17, synthetic NO, window 0x3400001,
    root 0x2b, subw 0x0, time 191038999, (13,159), root:(405,193),
    state 0x0, keycode 58 (keysym 0x6d, m), same_screen YES,
    XLookupString gives 1 characters:  "m"

KeyPress event, serial 17, synthetic NO, window 0x3400001,
    root 0x2b, subw 0x0, time 191039050, (13,159), root:(405,193),
    state 0x0, keycode 26 (keysym 0x65, e), same_screen YES,
    XLookupString gives 1 characters:  "e"

KeyRelease event, serial 17, synthetic NO, window 0x3400001,
    root 0x2b, subw 0x0, time 191039119, (13,159), root:(405,193),
    state 0x0, keycode 26 (keysym 0x65, e), same_screen YES,
    XLookupString gives 1 characters:  "e"

KeyPress event, serial 17, synthetic NO, window 0x3400001,
    root 0x2b, subw 0x0, time 191039219, (13,159), root:(405,193),
    state 0x0, keycode 39 (keysym 0x73, s), same_screen YES,
    XLookupString gives 1 characters:  "s"

KeyRelease event, serial 17, synthetic NO, window 0x3400001,
    root 0x2b, subw 0x0, time 191039289, (13,159), root:(405,193),
    state 0x0, keycode 39 (keysym 0x73, s), same_screen YES,
    XLookupString gives 1 characters:  "s"

MotionNotify event, serial 17, synthetic NO, window 0x3400001,
    root 0x2b, subw 0x0, time 191041049,Terminated
```

Even a little work generates a lot of output. Table 32-18 lists the options that modify xev.

Table 32-18   xev Options

Option	Argument	Result
-bs	type	Specifies the type of backing store: NotUseful, WhenMapped, or Always
-bw	integer	Specifies the window's border width in pixels
-display	display string	Monitors events on the specified display
-geometry	geometry string	Specifies the Xev window's geometry
-id	windowID	Monitors the events on the specified window
-name	string	Specifies the window's name
-rv		Indicates that the window should be in inverse video
-s		Specifies that save-unders should be enabled

Xev is particularly useful when combined with Xmodmap because it enables you to identify the key's actual number when you type on the keyboard.

Determining window properties

The xprop command enables you to examine the properties of windows under X11. By default, xprop prints the properties of a selected window on standard output (see Listing 32-2).

Listing 32-2: The Properties of the Clock Window

```
WM_STATE(WM_STATE):
        window state: Normal
        icon window: 0x1803f92
WM_PROTOCOLS(ATOM): protocols  WM_DELETE_WINDOW
WM_CLIENT_LEADER(WINDOW): window id # 0xc0000a
WM_CLASS(STRING) = "xclock", "XClock"
WM_HINTS(WM_HINTS):
        Client accepts input or input focus: False
        Initial state is Normal State.
        bitmap id # to use for icon: 0xc00001
        bitmap id # of mask for icon: 0xc00003
WM_NORMAL_HINTS(WM_SIZE_HINTS):
        user specified location: 578, 0
        user specified size: 60 by 60
        window gravity: NorthEast
WM_CLIENT_MACHINE(STRING) = "duke"
```

```
WM_COMMAND(STRING) = { "xclock", "-bg", "grey20", "-fg", "gold", "-hd",
"aliceblue", "-hl", "orange", "-geometry", "=60x60-0+0", "-update", "1" }
WM_ICON_NAME(STRING) = "xclock"
WM_NAME(STRING) = "xclock"
```

As you can see, xprop displays a lot of information related to the window. Table 32-19 lists some of the command-line options that modify xprop's behavior.

Table 32-19   xprop Command-Line Options

Option	Argument	Result
-display	display string	Specifies the server to check
-f	name format dformat	Specifies the format and data format for the given property
-font	font	Prints the properties of the specified font
-frame		Looks at the window manager frame for the specified window
-fs	filename	Uses the specified file for property formats
-grammar		Prints detailed grammars for command-line options
-help		Prints a summary of command-line options
-id	windowID	Prints the properties for the specified window
-len	integer	Specifies the maximum number of bytes to use to display a given property
-name	window name	Prints the specified window's properties
-notype		Does not display each property's type
-remove	property	Removes the specified property from the window
-root		Prints the root window's properties
-spy		Examines properties in perpetuity, noting changes in the properties

Xprop usually checks the status of windows when you develop X applications.

Testing server performance

The last X command described in this chapter is x11perf. This command measures the speed at which the server paints unique X events. When invoking x11perf, follow the command's name with the name of a test. You can run several hundred tests. Figure 32-33 shows the standard 100-pixel ellipse test, x11perf -ellipse100. Listing 32-3 shows the test's output.

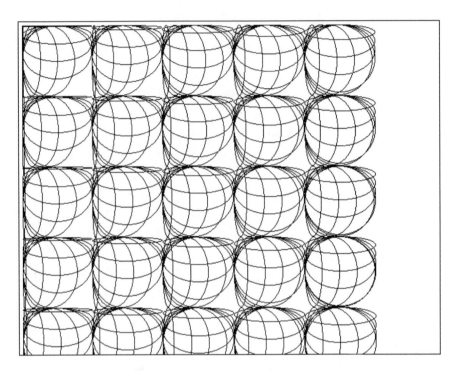

Figure 32-33: x11perf testing ellipses

Listing 32-3: Output from x11perf -ellipse100

```
x11perf - X11 performance program, version 1.5
X Consortium server version 6000 on :0.0
from duke
Mon Jan  1 13:15:23 1996

Sync time adjustment is 2.4016 msecs.

    9000 reps @    0.8306 msec (    1200.0/sec): 100-pixel ellipse
    9000 reps @    0.8381 msec (    1190.0/sec): 100-pixel ellipse
    9000 reps @    0.8827 msec (    1130.0/sec): 100-pixel ellipse
    9000 reps @    0.8387 msec (    1190.0/sec): 100-pixel ellipse
    9000 reps @    0.8471 msec (    1180.0/sec): 100-pixel ellipse
   45000 trep @    0.8474 msec (    1180.0/sec): 100-pixel ellipse
```

Several people have written programs to analyze the data of x11perf, and these interpretations have become the standard measurements for display speeds in the X environment.

Summary

This chapter finished the survey of X applications in the UNIX environment. It covered the following topics:

▶ Displaying system characteristics in graphs, such as system load, idle time, and free memory

▶ Displaying fonts and examining characteristics of letters in those fonts

▶ Performing cut and paste operations not supported by an application

▶ Changing keyboard mappings

▶ Changing the order of the pointer buttons

▶ Saving console messages to a different window

▶ Terminating applications from a remote command line

▶ Running applications on a remote machine

▶ Creating and modifying bitmaps

▶ Capturing screen images

▶ Displaying screen images

▶ Printing screen images

▶ Displaying a wide variety of images in different formats

▶ Manipulating images by changing formats, size, and aspects

▶ Manipulating the colors of images with Xv

▶ Displaying moving pictures on-screen

▶ Playing games

▶ Watching the cursor

▶ Viewing the Earth and moon

▶ Watching and squishing virtual cockroaches

▶ Monitoring X events

▶ Testing the screen's performance

The next chapter explains how to integrate X into the UNIX environment.

Chapter 33

Integrating X into the UNIX Environment

In This Chapter

▶ Using advanced startup scripts

▶ Shell programming with X

▶ Adding colors and fonts

To get the most out of your X environment, you must combine X with other UNIX commands. The normal place to do this is in scripts and startup files. You should be familiar with shell programming (see Chapter 5) to understand this chapter fully.

Exploring Sample Scripts

You should be familiar with three basic types of scripts if you want to optimize your X desktop. One type of script is invoked when the X session begins; these are the server initialization and window manager initialization scripts. A second type of script is invoked when you start an application. The application loads these resources from the server. A third type of script is executed directly as a command. Using some scripts requires a knowledge of shell programming; using others requires a knowledge of the application and its format.

Note

Strictly speaking, the resources are loaded into the server in the server initialization script, but because they are not used until an application starts, I am considering them application startup values.

Startup scripts

In Chapter 31, I showed you an X startup script based on information covered up to that point in the book. Here, I build on that basic script to show how you can exploit the full power of X even before you see your startup screen.

The two standard startups are the `.xinitrc` file and the window manager initialization file.

The first startup is a shell script. It basically tells the server what applications you want running at startup. With some programming experience, though, you can customize this to recognize different configurations and even different machines and have different setups out of the basic script.

The second startup is the window manager initialization script. This is not a shell script, but it does define key bindings, menus, and colors for your window manager.

The .xinitrc file

The `.xinitrc` that I illustrate here is quite a bit more complex than previous illustrations and may be more complex than you need.

I've designed it to be highly portable: It recognizes whether the display is color, it recognizes the size of the screen, and it performs adjustments accordingly. Listing 33-1 shows the full script.

Listing 33-1: The Complete .xinitrc Script

```
# .xinitrc written by James C. Armstrong, Jr. (c) 1996.  Feel free
# to copy and redistribute, with the copyright notice intact.
#
xdpyinfo > /tmp/xdpy.$$
#
# Save the display information to a file.  Use .$$ to keep unique
# file names.
#
width=`awk `/dimensions/{print $2}´ /tmp/xdpy.$$ | cut -dx -f1`
height=`awk `/dimensions/{print $2}´ /tmp/xdpy.$$ | cut -dx -f2`
#
# Find the width and height of the screen by grepping the data
# out of the output file.  A C program, or a yacc program, might be
# even better.
#
vid=`awk -F: `/default visual id/{ print $2}´ /tmp/xdpy.$$`
#
# There are several visual classes available, I need to get the one
# being run on the display as the default.  This is a hexadecimal
# number, but I plan to use it as a string.
#
# Next, I need to build a table to look up the string and find the
# name of the color class.
#
egrep `visual id|class´ /tmp/xdpy.$$ | egrep -v `buffer|default´ | cut
-d: -f2 | paste - - > /tmp/xdpy.2.$$
colorclass=`fgrep $vid /tmp/xdpy.2.$$ | awk `{print $2}´`
#
# I have finished with the table and Xdpyinfo output, so I can
# delete the files.
```

```
#
rm /tmp/xdpy.$$ /tmp/xdpy.2.$$
#
# Remove other customization files that may change based on
configuration.
#
rm .XDefaults .twmrc
#
# Knowing the color class, I can make any changes needed to the
# other startup files.
#
case $colorclass in PseudoColor|DirectColor|StaticColor|TrueColor)

    xearth -label -fork
    #
    # Run the earth in the background
    #
    if
        [ -f .XDefaults.color ]
    then
        cp .XDefaults.color .XDefaults
    fi
    #
    # Set up the color defaults file
    #
    if
        [ -f .twmrc.colors ]
    then
        cp .twmrc.colors .twmrc
    fi
    #
    # Set up the color specifications for TWM
    #
    # This may be different if you opt to use a different window
    # manager.
    #
    conscolor="-bg brown -fg yellow"
    xt1color="-bg black -fg red"
    xt2color="-bg darkslategrey -fg skyblue"
    xt3color="-bg navy -fg gold"
    #
    # Three xterms have different colors, this is not really
    # something suitable for X Defaults
    #
    ;;
GrayScale|StaticGray)
    xphoon -t 5&
    #
    # Show the moon in the background
    #
    if
        [ -f .XDefaults.gray ]
    then
```

```
        cp .XDefaults.gray .XDefaults
    fi
    #
    # Set up the colors for Gray Scale accordingly.
    #
    if
        [ -f .twmrc.gray ]
    then
        cp .twmrc.gray .twmrc
    fi
    #
    # Set up the gray scale specifications for TWM
    #
    # This may be different if you opt to use a different window
    # manager.
    #
    conscolor=""
    xt1color=""
    xt2color=""
    xt3color=""
    #
    # Gray Scale denies the use of colors to differentiate X Terminals
    #
    ;;
esac
if
    [ -f .XDefaults ]
then
    xrdb -merge .XDefaults
fi
#
# Load your resource customizations
#
if
    [ $width -eq 640 ]
then
    #
    # This is the small configuration
    #
    if
        [ -f .twmrc.small ]
    then
        cat .twmrc.small > .twmrc
    fi
    #
    # If there is a small configuration file to .twmrc, use it!
    #
    xclock -update 1 -g =60x60-0+0&
    xbiff -g =60x60-85+0&
    xload -g =100x50+0+0&
    xterms=.xterm.small
    #
    # Start these applications with fixed sizes due to the smaller
```

```
        # screen real estate.
        #
else
    if
        [ -f .twmrc.large ]
    then
        cat .twmrc.large > .twmrc
    fi
    #
    # If there is a large configuration file to .twmrc, use it!
    #
    xclock -update 1 -g =80x80-0+0&
    xbiff -g =80x80-85+0&
    xload -g =250x100+0+0&
    xterms=.xterms.large
    #
    # More screen space is available, so I can have a larger clock,
    # biff, and load monitor.
    #
fi
cat .twmrc.menus > .twmrc
#
# Now that I've created the appropriate initialization file, let's
# start the window manager.
#
twm&
#
# I can set the root cursor to a starship
#
xsetroot -cursor_name trek
#
# I can start a couple applications as icons.
#
xman -iconic&
xclipboard -iconic&
#
# I start the file manager.
#
xfm&
#
# The next three commands set the bell, mouse speed, and access to our
# server.
#
xset m 4 2
xset b 50 400 200
xhost +
#
# I check to see if there is a machine specific file to include,
# if so, I run it in the current environment.
#
if
    [ -f .xinitrc.`hostname` ]
then
```

```
    . .xinitrc.`hostname`
fi
#
# Last, I bring up a pair of X Terminals, and an X Terminal for the
# console.
#
. $xterms
xterm $conscolor -C -g =80x4+0+0 -iconic
```

As you can see, this startup script is fairly long and complicated. Because this script is designed to run on any number of machines and configurations, it needs to check the different sizes of the display and color options.

The program takes good advantage of several shell constructs to parse the output of the xdpyinfo command. As mentioned in Chapter 31, xdpyinfo is a tool used to acquire information about the current display. The information is output as ASCII text, is used as input into a program, and must be parsed.

Note

Of course, you could write a C program to access the server and acquire the same information, produce an executable file to create the same variables, and run it in the startup script.

The two auxiliary files govern the placement of the X terminals according to the size of the screen. The placements I like on a large screen are not possible on a small screen, so I have an alternate for the small screen. Listings 33-2 and 33-3 describe the placements.

Listing 33-2: X Terminal Placement on a Small Screen

```
# .xterms.small - A script to place two X Terminals on a small
display.
#
xterm $xt1cols -g =80x24+200+0&
xterm $xt2cols -g =80x24+0+200&
```

Listing 33-3: X Terminal Placement on a Large Screen

```
# .xterms.large - A script to place three X Terminals on a large
display.
#
xterm $xt1cols -g =80x59-0-0&
xterm $xt2cols -g =80x24+0-0&
xterm $xt3cols -g =80x28+0+150&
```

The script for the large screen places three terminals: one each in the lower two corners and one in the top-left, below the top of the screen. For smaller screens, the script places two windows overlapping each other on the top and on the side of the display.

I also provide the option to add X terminals on a per-machine basis. The test for .xinitrc.`hostname` looks for host-specific initialization files, and if they are present, it loads them into the server.

A good window manager initialization script

The window manager initialization script builds on the one shown in Chapter 31. To work with the changes made in the X initialization scripts, you must break the file into five distinct files: one for color, one for noncolor, and three based on the size of the display.

This file initializes the color variable for TWM. No other changes are required to customize colors.

Listing 33-4: Color Setup for TWM

```
#
# A .twmrc set of color specifications
#
Color
{
    TitleForeground         "blue"
    TitleBackground         "hotpink"
    BorderTileForeground    "#d0cf11"
    BorderTileBackground    "#007777"
    IconBackground          "limegreen"    { "XTerm"  "yellow" }
    IconForeground          "orange"     { "XTerm"  "brown" }
    IconBorderColor         "black"        { "XTerm"  "blue" }
    BorderColor        "red"        { "XClock" "yellow" }
    MenuForeground          "seashell"
    MenuBackground          "forestgreen"
    IconManagerBackground   "pink"         { "XTerm"  "blue" }
    IconManagerForeground   "brown"        { "XTerm"  "gold" }
    MenuTitleForeground     "gold"
    MenuTitleBackground     "red"
    MenuShadowColor         "yellow"
}
```

The .twmrc.gray file is not present because for a monochrome or gray-scale display, I want only the default colors for the window manager. You can customize a gray-scale file however you like.

Listings 33-5 and 33-6 show the different startup files for the large and small displays. The only changes specific to screen size are for the size and location of the icon area on the screen. A smaller screen gets a smaller area and different offsets.

Listing 33-5: Icon Box for a Small Screen

```
#
# IconRegion for a small screen
#
IconRegion "440x100+200+0" North West 20 10
```

Listing 33-6: Icon Box for a Large Screen

```
#
# IconRegion for a large screen
#
IconRegion "700x100+400+0" North West 20 10
```

The remaining sections of the TWM startup file are not size-dependent. These include the other startup variables and the menus and button bindings. They constitute, by far, the largest part of a good startup file, as illustrated in Listing 33-7.

Listing 33-7: Sections of the TWM File Not Dependent on Size or Color

```
#
# The TWM RC startup file, (c) 1996 James C. Armstrong, Jr, permission
# granted to redistribute and re-use.
#
RestartPreviousState
Zoom 300
#
# Set up the fonts for the various displays
#
IconFont "-*-utopia-bold-r-*-*-17-*-*-*-*-*-*"
IconManagerFont "-*-charter-bold-i-*-*-10-100-*-*-*-*-*-*"
MenuFont "-*-lucida-bold-i-*-*-14-100-*-*-*-*-*-*"
ResizeFont "-*-charter-bold-i-*-*-17-*-*-*-*-*-*"
TitleFont "-adobe-new century schoolbook-bold-i-normal—12-120-75-75-
p-76-iso8859-1"
#
# Don't ask me to place the windows, just do it!
#
RandomPlacement
#
# Keep the window borders small but manageable
#
BorderWidth 2
#
# I don't want title bars on these applications.
#
NoTitle
{
    "XClock"
    "XLoad"
    "XMem"
    "XIdle"
    "XEyes"
    "XBiff"
}
#
# My prefered key bindings for the title bars
#
Button1 =     : title : f.move
Button2 =     : title : f.raise
Button3 =     : title : f.lower
#
# My prefered key bindings for the window frame
#
Button1 =     : frame : f.resize
Button2 =     : frame : f.raise
```

```
Button3 =     : frame : f.lower
#
# My prefered key bindings for icons
#
Button1 =     : icon  : f.iconify
Button2 =     : icon  : f.move
Button3 =     : icon  : f.lower
#
# Please pull up my menus when requested.
# Remember that the TwmWindows Menu is a menu provided by the system.
#
Button1 =     : root  : f.menu "Applications"
Button2 =     : root  : f.menu "TwmWindows"
Button3 =     : root  : f.menu "Customizations"
#
# The primary Application Window is the base for most invocations.
# I have designed it to just be a pull-down menu for five sub-menus,
# one for each class of application.
#
Menu "Applications"
{
#
    "Applications"        f.title
    "User Tools"        f.menu "Tools"
    "System Monitors"   f.menu "Monitors"
    "X Terminals"       f.menu "XTerms"
    "MultiMedia"        f.menu "MultiMedia"
    "Games"             f.menu "Games"
}
#
# The tools menu brings up some fairly standard UNIX tools.  Manual
# Pages, Editors, Clipboards, and Calculators are the purview of this
# menu.
#
Menu "Tools"
{
    "User Tools"    f.title
    "Manual Pages"    !"xman&"
    "Clipboard"    !"xclipboard&"
    "Editor"    !"xedit&"
    "Calculator"    !"xcalc&"
    "HP Calculator"    !"xcalc -rpn&"
    "Magnifier"    !"xmag&"
    "Font Selector"    !"xfontsel&"
}
#
# The Monitors menu allows me to bring up one of the three graphical
# system monitors.
#
Menu "Monitors"
{
    "System Monitors"    f.title
    "System Load"        !"xload -g =200x100+0+0 &"
```

```
                "System Idle Time"      !"xidle -g =200x100+0+0 &"
                "System Free Memory"    !"xmem -g =200x100+0+0 &"
        }
        #
        # The XTerms menu allows me to add additional X Terminals at the touch
        # of a button, in various sizes.
        #
        Menu "XTerms"
        {
            "Terminals"     f.title
            "BIG"           !"xterm -fn 7x13 -g =80x59-0-0 &"
            "HUGE"          !"xterm -fn 12x24 -g =80x33+0+0 &"
            "lower"         !"xterm -fn 7x13 -g =80x28+0-0 &"
            "small"         !"xterm -fn 5x8 -g =80x28-0-0 &"
            "upper"         !"xterm -fn 7x13 -g =80x29+0+93 &"
        }
        #
        # The Multimedia menu is surprisingly sparse; few commands are really
        # useful when not acting on files.
        #
        Menu "MultiMedia"
        {
            "Multi Media"   f.title
            "Bitmaps"    !"bitmap &"
            "Images"     !"xv&"
            "Root Dump"    !"xwd -root -out $HOME/root.out"
        }
        #
        # The Games menu is a place where you can call up any games that you
        # may want to play.
        #
        Menu "Games"
        {
            "Games"          f.title
            "Eyes"          !"xeyes&"
            "Tetris"     !"xtetris&"
            "Maze"          !"maze&"
            "Puzzle"     !"puzzle&"
            "Gas"           !"xgas&"
        }
        #
        # This menu allows you to customize your Display.
        #
        Menu "Customizations"
        {
            "Customizations"    f.title
            "Backgrounds"          f.menu "Background"
            "Settings"          f.menu "Settings"
            "Controls"          f.menu "Controls"
        }
        #
        # You can select from any number of backgrounds; this includes
        # the earth and moon, and even some roaches.
```

```
#
Menu "Background"
{
    "Backgrounds"    f.title
    "The Earth"    !"xearth -label -fork"
    "The Moon"    !"xphoon -t 5 &"
    "Roaches"    !"xroach &"
    "Defaults"    !"xsetroot -def"
    "Red"    !"xsetroot -solid red"
    "Green"    !"xsetroot -solid green"
    "Blue"    !"xsetroot -solid blue"
}
#
# This menu allows you to change the default settings on your display,
# such as mouse speed or screen savings.
#
Menu "Settings"
{
    "Settings"    f.title
    "Fast Mouse"    !"xset m 10 1"
    "Slow Mouse"    !"xset m 2 4"
    "Fast blanking"    !"xset s 2"
    "Normal saver"    !"xset s 900"
}
#
# This menu provides you with a set of tools to manage other windows
# on the display through the window manager.
#
Menu "Controls"
{
    "Controls"    f.title
    "Redraw"    f.refresh
    "Restart"    f.restart
    "Window Ops"    f.title
    "(De)Iconify"    f.iconify
    "Lower"    f.lower
    "Move"    f.move
    "Raise"    f.raise
    "Kill"    f.destroy
    "Refresh Window"    f.winrefresh
    "Resize"    f.resize
    "Quit twm"    f.quit
}
#
# And, lastly, let's set up some cursors.
#
Cursors
{
    Icon    "sailboat"
    IconMgr    "box_spiral"
    Move    "shuttle"
    Resize    "gobbler"
    Menu    "spider"
```

```
Wait      "star"
Select    "trek"
Destroy   "gumby"
}
```

A lot goes into customizing the window manager, and the result is a truly powerful environment.

Customizing applications

Strictly speaking, application customization is not normally part of integrating X with UNIX. Some resources, however, can specify commands for execution under different circumstances.

My customizations do not include this. I've found that most frequently used commands are perfectly adequate for my needs, so the only two special customizations I use are to specify colors for applications in the resources file and to modify the commands for the File Manager.

Using resources

The .Xdefaults file is the normal location for resource customizations in X. Because some applications append to this file, I keep my floating customizations in a slightly different file, .XDefaults. As you can see in Listing 33-1, I build this file in my X startup script and automatically load it when I start X. Listing 33-8 shows my .Xdefaults file.

Note

Lines starting with an exclamation point are comments.

Listing 33-8: Default Colors

```
#define COLOR
!
! Allows application defaults to access color defaults
!
XLoad*background: seagreen
XLoad*foreground: white
!
! Set the colors of xload to be white on sea green.
!
XBiff*background: forest green
XBiff*foreground: yellow
!
! The mailbox is yellow on forest green.
!
XClock*foreground: gold
XClock*background: grey20
XClock*hands: aliceblue
XClock*highlight: orange
!
! Set the colors for the clock
!
```

I also added the changes to the calculator for `rpn` to the standard
`.xdefaults` file, as illustrated in Listing 33-9.

Listing 33-9: Additional Defaults

```
XCalc*hp.button22.Label: x^3
XCalc*hp.button22.Translations:
<Btn1Down>,<Btn1Up>:enter()digit(3)power()unset()
!
! Add a cubed button to the HP calculator
!
```

Most defaults are really a matter of personal taste. I recommend that you
experiment with your choices.

Changing the File Manager

One application that can undergo extensive customizations is the X File
Manager. This application should have a revamped set of drop targets and
commands in the application menu. Because you have many commands to
add, you might be better off leaving a set of basic commands at the top and
adding "special commands" at the bottom. The basic commands should
probably be an X terminal, an editor, the mailer, and other menus. You
should break the remaining commands into three other windows: `Tools`,
`MultiMedia`, and `Games`. Each menu should have easy paths back to the
others.

At the bottom of the default menu, you can include some standard backgrounds, such as `xearth`, `xphoon`, and `xroach`. These customizations result
in four defaults files, shown in Listings 33-10 through 33-13.

Listing 33-10: xfm-apps

```
#
# Standard Application defaults file for xfm.
#
Terminal:::xterm.xpm:exec xterm:
Editor:::editor.xpm:exec xedit:exec xedit $*
Mail:::mail.xpm:exec mymailer:
Tools::.xfm/xfm-tools:xfm_appmgr.xpm:LOAD:
MultiMedia::.xfm/xfm-media:xfm_gif.xpm:LOAD:
Games::.xfm/xfm-games:xchess.xpm:LOAD:
Earth:::pixmap.xpm:exec xearth:
Moon:::xfm_apps.xpm:exec xphoon:
Roaches:::debug.xbm:exec xroach:
```

You may want to create your own icons for different tools.

Note

The execution for the mailer is a program called `mymailer`. This is a shell
script introduced later in the chapter. It is used to display an `elm` mail
session in an X terminal.

Listing 33-11: Tools for xfm

```
#
# Standard Tools file for xfm.
#
Terminal:::xterm.xpm:exec xterm:
Editor:::editor.xpm:exec xedit:exec xedit $*
Mail:::mail.xpm:exec mymailer:
Defaults::.xfm/xfm-apps:xfm_appmgr.xpm:LOAD:
MultiMedia::.xfm/xfm-media:xfm_gif.xpm:LOAD:
Games::.xfm/xfm-games:xchess.xpm:LOAD:
Magnifier:::xmag.xpm:xmag:
Font Selector:::xfm_wavy.xbm:xfontsel:
Calculator:::calc.xpm:exec xcalc:
Manual:::xman.xpm:exec xman:
Compress:::compress.xpm::compress $*
Clipboard:::clipboard.xbm:exec xclipboard:
Bitmap:::bitmap.xbm:exec bitmap:exec bitmap $*
Load:::xfm_data.xpm:exec xload:
Memory:::xfm_data.xpm:exec xmem:
Idle Time:::xfm_data.xpm:exec xidle:
```

Listing 33-12: Multimedia File for xfm

```
#
# MultiMedia Tools file for xfm.
#
Terminal:::xterm.xpm:exec xterm:
Editor:::editor.xpm:exec xedit:exec xedit $*
Mail:::mail.xpm:exec mymailer:
Defaults::.xfm/xfm-apps:xfm_appmgr.xpm:LOAD:
Tools::.xfm/xfm-tools:xfm_appmgr.xpm:LOAD:
Games::.xfm/xfm-games:xchess.xpm:LOAD:
Window Dump:::hexdump.xbm:exec xwd -root -out dump.out:
Window Display:::ghostview.xpm::xwud -in $*
Display Image:::xfm_gif.xpm::exec xloadimage $*
Manage Image:::xfm_gif.xpm::exec xv $*
Show Movie:::xfm_gif.xpm::exec mpeg_play $*
```

Listing 33-13: Games File for xfm

```
#
# Games file for xfm.
#
Terminal:::xterm.xpm:exec xterm:
Editor:::editor.xpm:exec xedit:exec xedit $*
Mail:::mail.xpm:exec mymailer:
Defaults::.xfm/xfm-apps:xfm_appmgr.xpm:LOAD:
Tools::.xfm/xfm-tools:xfm_appmgr.xpm:LOAD:
Multimedia::.xfm/xfm-multi:xfm_gif.xpm:LOAD:
Puzzle:::xchess.xpm:exec puzzle:
Tetris:::xchess.xpm:exec xtetris:
Maze:::xchess.xpm:exec maze:
Gas:::xchess.xpm:exec xgas:
```

These four files enable you to create several menus that you can access with pointer clicks in the X File Manager.

Using shell scripts

Another way to integrate X with UNIX is to include X commands in shell scripts. The xterm command is ideal for making routine UNIX commands into X commands with the simple use of the -e option.

I have done this with the mymailer command, illustrated in Listing 33-14. It checks to see whether I have a DISPLAY environment variable. If I do, it starts elm in an X terminal window; otherwise, it just runs it in place.

Listing 33-14: The mymailer Command

```
if
    [ "$DISPLAY" != "" ]
then
    xterm -e elm
else
    elm
fi
```

You can similarly place this kind of wrapper around other commands.

Changes to your shell startup

Sometimes, you may start a shell remotely, such as through the rlogin command. By default, the DISPLAY variable is not set unless the parent of the shell has the variable set. Thus, you may want either to set a DISPLAY variable by default or to prompt for a display. I do this in the .profile:

```
if
    [ "$DISPLAY" == "" ]
then
    echo "Please enter a display: \c"
    read DISPLAY
    export DISPLAY
fi
```

If I just press Return, no display is set.

You can also set aliases according to the presence or absence of the DISPLAY variable, as follows:

```
if
    [ "$?DISPLAY " ]
then
    alias xv `xv -geometry =+0+0´
else
    alias xv `echo no display set for xv´
fi
```

Doing this for an X command gives it a reasonable default warning.

Automatic functions

You can also create some functions as automatic functions. The `mymailer`
command is an example of a potential automatic function (although its
inclusion in the File Manager menu precludes its being one). Another good
candidate is `vi`. In the startup script `.kshrc`, include the following:

```
typedef -fu vi
```

And in a file in the `FPATH`, have this:

```
procedure vi (){
if
    [ "$DISPLAY" == "" ]
then
    /bin/vi $*
else
    xterm -e /bin/vi $*
fi
}
```

This means that when you enter the `vi` command, you load the function that
checks the `DISPLAY` variable and either loads `vi` in an X terminal or runs `vi`
on the current screen.

Administering X

The system administrator handles most administrations of X, and currently,
few are necessary. X is loaded on almost every UNIX workstation sold, with
reasonable defaults, so that administration is not needed. The hardest
administrative task is to manage `xdm`, as discussed in Chapter 29.

Adding a color to the database

Normally, X comes with many predefined colors, which you can access with
`showrgb`. Still, you may not find the color you want, such as `myblue`. You can
experiment with color specifications to determine RGB values, but remembering them is tricky. The best approach is to add `myblue` to the RGB database.

The procedure is straightforward. You need to convert the RGB values to
decimal values. Let's say `myblue` is `1a1aee`; this converts to 26 26 238. Add
this line to `rgb.txt` in the appropriate directory. Then, remove the `rgb.dir`
and `rgb.pag` files (effectively deleting the database), and recreate the files
with the `dbm` command. Move the files to the `/usr/lib/X11` directory, and
you have added a new color.

On newer systems, a makefile handles this for you. After you've added your
color, just type **make**. When that command is complete, type **make install**,
and the job is done!

Adding a font to the database

Adding a new font is also relatively simple. You need to convert the font to the SNF format (or the appropriate format for your display). After you have created these files, you simply hook them up for display. Copy the resulting files to `/usr/lib/X11/fonts/misc`, and in that directory, run the `mkfontdir /usr/lib/X11/fonts/misc` command to rebuild the font indexes.

You may need to rehash your font path with `xset fp rehash` to pick up the new fonts.

Summary

This chapter explained how to integrate X with UNIX. It showed you the following:

▶ A complete X startup file that examines the server to determine which elements to include

▶ A window manager startup file to create menus for the TWM window manager

▶ Examples of resources

▶ Menu files for the X File Manager

▶ Examples of building shell scripts to use X

▶ How to add colors and fonts

The next chapter looks at the UNIX operating system from the perspective of a software developer.

Part IX

Software Development

Chapter 34

UNIX Is the Developer's Platform of Choice

UNIX has lasted in the market as long as it has probably because it is the favorite platform for scientists and engineers, including software developers.

Platform Advantages

For many software developers, UNIX has become the platform of choice for their work. Many factors contribute to this popularity:

- Probably the most important factor is the C programming language. C was designed concurrently with UNIX, and C takes advantage of several interfaces to the UNIX kernel to give the developer greater access to system resources. Moreover, much of UNIX is written in C. Consequently, the programming language and the operating system dovetail well. In the last two decades, C has become a popular programming language for various platforms because of its power and flexibility. C++ evolved from C, so it shares many of the advantages of C on UNIX.

- UNIX execution environments are designed to move quickly between a user environment and a system environment. System environments provide access to kernel and machine resources. When programs are able to switch quickly between the two modes, an end user's program can retain some of a system program's capabilities without requiring a privileged user account.

- Similarly, a program can have a set-UID bit that enables an entire program to run in privileged mode. By designing certain programs to run with system privileges, you can create applications that do not require the user to use a privileged account.

- The UNIX environment, particularly for C programming, usually comes with a very thorough and complete set of tools. The C compiler is ubiquitous: this tool should be available in almost every UNIX system. The compiler provides many options, including those that generate assembly language output, linkable objects, and executable programs. Some options also facilitate program debugging and performance assessment.

In recent years, some UNIX vendors have been shipping the operating system without development environments and selling the environments as add-ons. As a veteran UNIX hacker, I deplore this trend.

- UNIX has many debugging tools. When programs fail catastrophically, they leave behind files, usually named core. This core file is a dump of the program's status at the time it failed. By using a debugger, the software developer usually can find the program bug that caused the failure.

I was surprised to learn that POSIX does not include a debugger in its definition of a UNIX development environment.

- Certain UNIX tools monitor system calls and check for program portability issues. One program even reformats code for readability.

- Other UNIX tools manage source code and build libraries that applications can share. The make utility enables the developer to write rules that describe how to build complex applications.

- If you need to parse input or write lexical analyzers, tools called yacc and lex make the writing of parsers a much easier task.

- With the cflow and cxref applications, the developer can look at program flow and examine where variables are used. Some sites include a program called ctrace, which is a curses graphical interface for examining multiple files.

I discuss each UNIX development tool in the following chapters. Before I begin this survey, I discuss the development process itself in Chapter 35, outlining step by step the different states through which a software product moves and describing what is involved in each state. Then, Matthew Merzbacher provides an overview of the three most common languages for product development on UNIX: C, C++, and Perl.

Platform Disadvantages

Working with UNIX to develop software poses several disadvantages. One of the most common complaints about UNIX is that each vendor's UNIX is slightly different from everybody else's. To move your application from one platform to another, you must make changes in your code to accommodate the eccentricities of the new platform. To see how bad these can be, read the following story.

Story: AIX's Implementation of malloc

One of the more unusual flavors of UNIX was IBM's original release of AIX. Although this release had many interesting enhancements, it also had several basic UNIX interfaces that were broken. Probably the worst was its implementation of malloc, the library function that allocates memory to a process. UNIX defines malloc as a memory allocator. You pass it a single argument, which is the number of bytes needed by the application, and malloc is supposed to return a pointer to a region of memory that size or larger. If the memory is not available when the malloc call is made, malloc is supposed to return an error, and the code needs to handle that error gracefully.

AIX did not do this. Instead, its developers adopted an as-needed mechanism for memory allocation. The malloc interface returned a pointer, but no memory was actually allocated. Instead, when you needed the memory, you received it a page at a time if it was available. If no memory was available, the AIX kernel sent SIGDANGER signals to every running process on the system to enable them to clean up their memory. If no memory was freed, AIX started to kill processes, beginning with the most recently invoked process, until the need for memory was satisfied.

AIX didn't stop at just a single user's processes; it killed every process on the system, including root processes if need be! Testing revealed that any user could trigger this memory need, and consequently any user could accidentally kill some privileged processes simply with some poorly written code. This was definitely not a POSIX-compliant implementation.

Dave Taylor documented this in the February 1993 issue of *SunWorld.* When the time came for *Advanced Systems* (*SunWorld*'s successor magazine) to examine a new machine from IBM, I asked again about the memory issue. IBM had added an environment variable to the system that enabled you to force allocation of memory when malloc was called, as POSIX required. This environment variable also protected your system from being killed in a memory crisis.

POSIX and other standards are an attempt to eradicate these incompatibilities across systems. They are a good start, but incompatibilities still exist. Some companies are very inventive in how they attempt to become POSIX-compliant.

Story: Mimicking the UNIX Kernel

At another of my recent jobs, I wrote code to test Tandem's Non-Stop Kernel, which is an emulation of the UNIX kernel on top of Tandem's redundant systems. Instead of being a true kernel, Tandem's kernel essentially connected applications to another application that mimicked the UNIX kernel and performed the requisite system calls through Tandem's native operating system.

Another frequent complaint about UNIX concerns the lack of information in error messages. Compilers and other tools are required to produce information that explains why an attempt to build an executable program failed. These messages can be extremely cryptic. It has taken me awhile to grasp all the potential error messages, and on rare occasions, I see one that's new to me.

Error messages are a problem and are also platform-dependent. Unfortunately, no standards define what an error message should contain.

Summary

This chapter briefly introduced the UNIX environment for developers to help you

▶ Understand why software developers like to use UNIX

▶ Recognize strengths in development environments

▶ Recognize weaknesses in development environments

The next chapter describes the life cycle of a software product and explains how UNIX ties into this.

Chapter 35

The Development Process

In This Chapter

▶ The six stages for the development of software

Regardless of the platform of choice, the software life cycle goes through six distinct stages. Each stage requires a separate set of skills and, often, different personal temperaments; each is important, however.

The six stages are as follows:

- Genesis of the idea
- Architecting the product
- Designing components
- Writing code
- Testing the product
- Maintaining the product in the field

Because this book is about UNIX, each section highlights the features of UNIX that make the jobs easier. If you use a different platform, you need to adjust some of the comments in this chapter to fit your needs. I've had experience at each stage of the product life cycle, and although I have my own preferences, you may lean toward different preferences.

Idea

In the beginning is the problem. Sometimes, the problem comes from the sales or marketing division of your company ("Our customers see a need for a product that does. . ."). On other occasions, the problem may come from your immediate manager, or you may see the need for a specific tool yourself.

Problems are really opportunities. They provide an opportunity for you to start at the beginning of a problem and address it as you see fit. You need to know the tools that are available, and you need to do research to recognize the size and scope of the problem. A good software engineer needs to be a good problem-solver. Sometimes, the solution does not require programming; it may be a matter of hardware corrections, improved documentation, or education about how different tools can be used in concert to produce a solution. Good problem-solvers recognize these situations and seek to provide the best combination of programming, hardware, and other resources.

Consequently, it is vital for an engineer who plays this role to be a good researcher. When a problem arrives, it may involve hidden issues; the engineer needs to probe those issues. The first solution that comes to mind may not be the best; it may cause other problems in other areas.

This chapter examines a problem that I've faced. I am a member of several mailing lists related to sports. One favorite activity of the mailing lists' members is predicting the results of college football and college basketball games. When the lists started around 1991, the picking contests were fairly haphazard; results were not tracked from round to round, and no standard method was used to tally results except for manual examination of contestants' mailings. As the lists grew, this procedure was no longer viable.

The problem that you face in this chapter is how to compile people's picks, tally the results, and maintain a yearly record. Clearly, this is a software problem. Because people's picks are coming in by e-mail, some means of parsing incoming e-mail for picks is required. Because team names are varied, the solution can't be something simple, such as an awk script. Last, to ensure some permanence of the picks, some method of saving results is required.

At this stage, you have an idea where you want to go. Now you must work on a high-level solution. To differentiate this step from the application-design level, I call this procedure *architecting* the solution.

Architecting a Product

Your solution depends on software, and the platform is a UNIX platform. Now, you need to make some decisions about how you want your product to work. To proceed to the next level, you need to answer several questions.

Because UNIX is a multiprocessing, multiuser system, you need to examine the problem to see how best to take advantage of UNIX's features. You may consider networking (to see whether distributing the work across multiple machines is the answer) or threads (to use multiple CPUs of a single machine simultaneously).

You also need to break the problem — and the solution — into manageable pieces. A good architectural solution is one in which the pieces merge into a coherent, manageable solution.

Clearly, the real strengths of an architect are understanding the system and knowing how each part of the system works. For a UNIX architect, that understanding requires knowledge of networking, file systems, and interprocess communications. The best job done architecting is to design and specify the interfaces between the components; this way, different parts of the solution can all communicate easily.

Another feature of the architect is to identify commonality between tasks assigned to components and begin to suggest areas where code can be shared.

For the problem of compiling the results of a sports contest, I opted for a software solution. I may have gotten a bit ahead of myself when I started to talk about e-mail parsing, but often, that is a feature of problem solutions.

Architecting this solution involves breaking the problem into components. What is involved in a picking contest? You need to send out a list of games to be picked to the mailing list; this does not need a software solution, because UNIX comes with tools for the creation and delivery of mail. Because this is just another message, you can use them. Next, you need to compile the picks. This requires an e-mail parser, a new program. Several good tools for generic parsing and distribution of e-mail are available, such as `filter` (supplied with `elm`), and `procmail`, but this is a specific parse. You need to write a program. You also need to write a program to enter the actual game results and tally scores. Lastly, you need to track the results across rounds.

Two interfaces need definition. You need a method of storing picks when they arrive and when the results are known, and you need a method of storing people's scores across rounds.

You may opt to store the data in two files, named `picklist` and `aggregate`. Both files have fixed formats and are used by a program to tally scores. Another option is to have daemons running, using interprocess communications to transfer results from parsers to the daemon, and to read the results to tally scores. You may want to use standard files for a couple of reasons. A daemon is a slightly higher-risk program; if the daemon dies, it needs to reinitialize itself, which suggests that the daemon would need to write out data files anyway. Also, because people may make wrong picks, storing the information in a file makes changing people's picks easier.

The interfaces are files, each of which is in a specific format. Table 35-1 describes the single-round picks need fields, and Table 35-2 describes the permanent results need fields.

Table 35-1	Data Stored for Each Round
Field	**Use**
Name	The picker's name.
Key	A key string to keep each picker's picks separate. You can use this field for sorting as well, so you can place the picker's surname and initials in the field.
Picks	A list of the picks for each game.

Table 35-2   Data Passed between Rounds

Field	Use
Name	The picker's name
Key	The picker's key (refer to Table 35-1)
Wins	The number of correct picks
Losses	The number of incorrect picks
Exact	The number of exactly correct picks

These data are later converted to header files for C programs. You could have used a commercial database program, but for your purposes here, that would be overkill.

Note

As the contest grows and changes, these interfaces also need to change. Having broken the problem into smaller components and defined interfaces between those components, you are ready for the next step.

Note

At some companies, you get your first review at this stage. You prepare an architecture document and distribute it. Then, the architecture is reviewed by a committee that can give you feedback to improve your product. Don't fret; that's life in the big company. While working at Bell Labs, I was involved in creating our lab's Architecture Review Board.

Designing the Components

By this time, you can view the product as being a series of components, each of which is fairly independent of the others. If the interface design and architecture are correct, each component can proceed without concern for the others, although cross-communication usually is beneficial.

The designer requires the architect to give him or her a well-defined task. Then the designer is expected to break this task into smaller, related tasks. The designer can determine whether certain tasks are repeated in different sections of code and suggest that those tasks be functions or subroutines. By breaking the task into smaller tasks, the designer can design and implement each task separately and then build the tasks into a larger program.

When the functions and subroutines are identified, the designers should communicate to see whether those functions can be shared. If so, they have designed a library.

The designer also needs to identify the inputs to the component and the expected outputs. These inputs and outputs are often designed at the architectural stages, but subsequent needs for input and output may arise.

The strengths required of a good designer are knowledge of what UNIX can do, knowledge of the strengths and weaknesses of the language or languages chosen, and (most important) a knack for designing algorithms.

In some cases, when a design is finished, it is submitted for a design review. This review allows other people to see the design and permits the team to make improvements.

For the picking contest, look at the design for the results generator. You know that it expects to get input from the two files: one containing the picks and the other containing the results to date. You need to get the results for the games of the current round. You also need to output to the results-to-date file and to produce a report of the results.

In the picking contest, the picks are ranked in three categories: number of correct picks, percentage of correct picks, and number of exactly correct picks. Each ranking needs a separate compilation.

Clearly, the beginnings of the algorithm are

- Read inputs
- Churn results
- Produce reports
- Save the results to date

With three types of input to be read, you next need to determine a correct order. Because a marginally greater risk of error exists in the data files on disk, you may want to read those two files first. When this data is safely loaded into the program, you can prompt for the results of each game.

Now you run across a new problem: How do you know which games are being picked? The solution is simple. When you send out the picks, you need to keep a machine-readable record of the games. This is another file on disk; it required a new program to initialize it, and it would be input for this program. You can read it in after reading in the picks and results to date.

Now you can prompt for results. Each game is prompted once, and as you read in the result, you start to tally the results per person. This requires an expanded data structure so that you can track the results for a given round. Looking at the needs of the program, you may decide at this stage that the picks record and the results to date can be combined into a single data structure. Table 35-3 describes that structure.

Table 35-3	Data Needed for Each Picker
Field	*Purpose*
Name	The name of the picker
Key	The sorting key of the picker
Exact	A count of exactly correct picks
Wins	A running tally of correct picks
Losses	A running tally of incorrect picks
Round Wins	A tally of wins in this round
Round Losses	A tally of losses in the current round
Winning Percentage	Calculated from the wins and losses
Round Percentage	Calculated from the round's wins and losses
Picks	An array of picks for the current round

After you read in all the data, you will have filled many of the holes for sorting, except for the winning percentages. So you need to make a pass over all the records in the structure and calculate the percentages.

Next, you need to sort on the different fields and produce output. As a UNIX engineer, you know about the library function qsort, so you can use that function. After generating the report, you can dump the data to a file.

At this point, you have designed the specific data structures that will be used in the program, and you know what each task is, so you are ready to write the code.

Writing the Code

A great deal has already happened in the development process, and you have done very little programming. Certainly, a good architect and designer may have hacked together some prototypes, but that's not even close to the task of writing product-quality code.

The coder should receive from the designer a well-defined specification for the program. The external interfaces should be well defined. If libraries are involved, the exact order for calling the libraries should be listed. Data structures should be defined.

At this stage, the coder should be someone who is meticulous and pays attention to detail. Good code needs to consider all the alternatives and to be prepared for bad input and any other errors that may occur. The worst possible result is for a program to catastrophically fail at the customer's site.

Further, the coder should be aware of the resources that UNIX provides to facilitate coding and to use within the code to improve its quality. The coder also should be knowledgeable about debugging software because debugging is invariably part of the job.

In writing the results generator, if you improved the efficiency of the code by combining structures and took advantage of several debuggers when problems arose, these would result in changes to the code.

One decision the coder faces is whether to use the C libraries or the system calls in UNIX for I/O. Programmers frequently face this decision. I've developed a rough set of guidelines:

- If the data being read or written includes non-ASCII data, I usually opt for the system calls.

- If the data is fixed-length records, I prefer system calls.

- If the data is primarily ASCII data, and if each read or write is of variable length, I look for C library calls. These calls eventually also call the system calls, but they provide buffering, which should optimize the use of the system calls.

When coding is complete, some sites require code reviews. You meet with your peers, who look at your code to try to find bugs before they occur. When the code is finished, it needs to be tested.

Testing the Code

While the code is being written, the tester should not be idle. The tester needs to prepare to test the code, and to do so, he or she should be aware of what the code is expected to do and should deduce the possible reasonable boundary conditions for the code. During the writing of code, the tester should write the test plan, which is often reviewed.

When the code is complete, the tester is responsible for ascertaining several things:

- Does the code do what it is intended to do?

- Does the code function cleanly within the environment?

- Does the code handle boundary conditions properly?

- Is the code ready to be shipped to customers?

To handle these conditions, the tester often needs to write programs to test the code. By writing these programs, the tester avoids the tedious task of testing and retesting software on subsequent releases. The test harness reports back to the tester any bugs that may be introduced in a new release. This means that the tester needs only to confirm the existence of bugs.

As you may expect, the tester and the coder have a close relationship. Because the role of the tester often leads to finding mistakes made by the coder, this relationship can get a bit touchy, particularly when deadlines are imminent. The tester needs a good sense of diplomacy and people skills. The coder needs to realize that no one is perfect and that bugs always exist.

In a good, functional development environment, the tester and coder are members of the same team, working together to make the product the best it can be when it reaches the customer. Dysfunctional development environments are ones in which the coders and testers have an antagonistic relationship. Usually, the real losers in this conflict are the customers. I have worked in both environments, and sadly, I must report the latter type tends to be more common.

When the code is finished and passed by the testers, it is ready to be deployed to the customer. You have a product, but the task isn't over yet.

Maintaining the Product

After you send the product to customers, you need to maintain the product for those customers. This usually requires a tiered approach.

The first tier is telephone support. Telephone-support people need good people skills because they are customers' first point of contact. Support people need to filter out problems that are related to incorrect use of the product, basic product inquiries, and (occasionally) basic UNIX questions.

If the support people can't solve the problem, the problem usually goes to the second tier. The second tier handles the more complicated use issues for the product. They need to be more familiar with the actual product and are charged with finding ways to make the product work for the customer.

The third tier handles problems in the product. They usually need to duplicate what the customer has done and begin to debug the product. If the problem is too complex for the third-tier people, it usually goes back to the coder.

Product support is one of the most thankless jobs in the product life cycle. You spend your days with customers, who often are upset about problems that they are having. You need patience to help these people. If a problem is a real problem, you need to forward it to the appropriate level.

Supporting the product at the coder's end is not much fun. Usually, you spend your time looking at code written by someone else. You are given a narrow scope in changing this code, and if the change doesn't work, you become the lightning rod for criticism.

The one area of maintenance that offers the best prospects is when new releases are due. At this time, the customer usually is allowed to make suggestions for improving the product, and the development cycle begins all over again.

Summary

This chapter introduced the life cycle of a software product, explaining each phase of that life cycle. Although you can see each step as being as a discrete phase in the cycle, in the real world, a product frequently moves from one phase to another in a disorderly fashion, and jobs can be duplicated or shared. At this point, you have been introduced to the following phases of the design process:

▶ Originating the idea

▶ Working as a software architect

▶ Deciding interfaces between components

▶ Designing a software product

▶ Writing code

▶ Testing the software

▶ Managing the loop between testing and coding

▶ Achieving teamwork

▶ Maintaining the product

In the next chapter, Dr. Matthew Merzbacher introduces two common programming languages for UNIX: C and C++.

## Chapter 36

Programming Languages on UNIX: C and C++

In This Chapter
▶ C
▶ C++

This chapter introduces two common programming languages for UNIX systems: C and C++. This is not a tutorial on the languages, just a high-level overview of the concepts included therein. Dr. Matthew Merzbacher, Assistant Professor of Computer Science at Mills College, wrote this chapter.

Basic Programming in C

As UNIX was being developed, C was being developed, and for many years, C was the only language of choice for development on UNIX systems.

Introduction

Dennis Ritchie of AT&T Bell Labs created the C programming language in the early 1970s to combine the expressiveness of a high-level language with the efficiency of assembler programming. At the time, languages such as IBM's PL/I, which included capabilities to do almost anything, were in vogue. The AT&T team took a different view, believing that languages should be simple, elegant, and efficient, whereas extensions should be limited to library routines. This same philosophy inspired the original design of UNIX by the same group. C was efficient enough to be used in place of assembler language for the development of UNIX, leading to UNIX's portability and wide success.

Over the years, C became the preeminent programming language for most tasks for several reasons. ANSI, the American National Standards Institute, standardized C so that a C program that runs on one machine will most likely run on other machines without modification. Further, because C is a small language, C compilers have been written for every popular architecture (and many unpopular ones). Many operating systems come bundled with a C compiler and no other programming languages. C is also flexible, making it well-suited for software development. C programs can invoke libraries written in other languages, such as Pascal and Fortran, enabling programmers to use the vast array of previously written library software.

In recent years, C++ has displaced C as the most common programming language for new software development. C++, discussed later in this chapter, is derived from C. Consequently, almost any legal C program compiles under C++ without modification. Thus, many programmers start by learning C before moving on to C++.

C is also popular among programmers because it is powerful yet terse. Much of the design was intended to make programming faster and, as a result, C is very lenient in allowing certain syntactic structures. This leniency is both attractive and dangerous. The world is full of C programmers who have lost many hours of sleep because they wrote

```
if (i = 1) {
```

instead of

```
if (i == 1) {
```

The latter checks to see whether the variable i is equal to 1, whereas the former first assigns the value of 1 to i and then checks to see whether the result of the assignment is nonzero (which it is). Thus, you have both an assignment and a check in one—not the programmer's intention.

Still, the principal advantage that C has over other languages is its speed. Whereas PL/I has a code/assembler ratio of 25 (meaning that one line of PL/I yields 25 lines of assembler), C's ratio is closer to two! Therefore, C programs tend to yield short assembler code. Of course, these numbers vary for different architectures (for example, a RISC machine might have a 1:4 ratio). This relative simplicity of C has enabled compiler makers to focus on optimization, so the code that is generated tends to be highly efficient. Lastly, because C is a relatively simple language, the process of compiling is very fast.

Note

Throughout this chapter, I use ANSI C.

A first C program

I'll start with the first program that most C programmers write:

```
#include <stdio.h>
main(){                    /* this is a comment */
    printf("Hello World!\n");    /* print a pithy message */
}
```

This program, when compiled and executed, yields the following output:

```
Hello World!
```

Before examining the program in detail, I'll explain how to turn a C program into an executable. Under UNIX (and in many other operating systems), the C compiler is called `cc`. Before compiling, save your program to a file whose name ends in `.c` (dot-c), such as `hello.c`. Then, compile the program by typing the following code at the prompt:

```
% cc hello.c
%
```

If you don't encounter any errors, the program is compiled, creating an executable file called `a.out`. You'll see another prompt, and you can do an `ls` to see whether this worked. By default, all C compilers create `a.out`. You can then execute the program by typing this:

```
% a.out
Hello World!
%
```

Of course, if you want to call your executable file something other than `a.out`, you can rename the file at this point, but you can also make the C compiler do this for you, as follows:

```
% cc -o hello hello.c
```

The `-o hello` option tells the C compiler to create an executable file called `hello` instead of `a.out`.

Now, let's look more closely at the program itself. Note that comments start with a `/*` and end with a `*/`. This is always true, and comments can extend beyond a single line. Anything inside the comments is ignored, no matter what. Although C programs are typically indented and spread over multiple lines for readability, they need not be. Thus, the following program is the same as the one written at the beginning of this section:

```
#include <stdio.h>
main() { printf("Hello World!\n"); }     /* the same program */
```

In fact, most spacing isn't needed, but this code would be entirely unreadable without the spaces.

Note

Many C programmers take advantage of this feature to put multiple "conceptually grouped" statements on a single line, but it makes for code that is difficult to read. I advise against this.

At the beginning of the program is the line `#include <stdio.h>`, which tells C to include the standard input and output library headers. Although it isn't strictly required for this program, it's always a good idea to include `stdio` (pronounced *standard I-O*) whenever any input or output is needed.

The real program starts with the word main( ), which says that this is the main part of the program. OK, so it's the only part of the program, but just wait a bit! You place the body of the main program inside braces ({ and }), which are the block delimiters in C. Whenever a new block of code begins, it starts with an opening brace, and a closing brace ends the block. These are the same as begin and end in Pascal. In this case, only one statement is inside the block, and it is a printf statement, which is used for output in C. This particular output is the string Hello World! followed by a return (that's what the \n is for). Without the \n, the program would run like this:

```
% a.out
Hello World!%
```

And your next prompt would be on the same line as the output of the program. Every statement in C is terminated with a semicolon (;).

Getting started with variables in C

C has several standard types for variables. All variables must be declared before they are used, as in most programming languages. Here's an example of some variables and their declarations:

```
main() {
    int myScore;      /* myScore is a variable containing a single integer */
    int yourScore;    /* so is yourScore */
    char myInitial;   /* myInitial is  a single character */

    /* you can declare lots of variables of the same type at once */
    char yourInitial, anotherCharacterVariable;

    yourScore = 6;    /* sets yourScore */
    myScore = yourScore * 2;    /* I have twice what you have */
    myInitial = `J´;
    yourInitial = `M´;

    /* print the score */
    printf("The final score is:\n");
    printf("%c: %d, %c: %d\n", myInitial, myScore, yourInitial, yourScore);
    if (myScore > yourScore) { printf("I win!\n); }
  }
```

If run, this program would print the following:

```
The final score is:
J:      12, M:      6
I win!
```

This program illustrates several new concepts. Variable names are subject to length limitations (typically 16 or 32 characters), and they must start with a character and contain only characters, digits, and underscores. This program contains two integer variables (myScore and yourScore) and three variables that can contain a single character each. The program assigns a value (6) to `yourScore` and then calculates `myScore` from that value. It then sets `myInitial` and `yourInitial` to J and M, respectively. In C, single characters are delimited with single quotation marks, whereas strings are delimited by double quotation marks. The program then prints the final score using a fancier version of the `printf` statement that is described later. Then, a conditional block of code executes only if the condition holds. In this case, the condition that `myScore` is greater than `yourScore` does hold, and the block with the `printf("I win!\n")` also executes.

C has several other common types in addition to `int` and `char`, including `float` for floating-point numbers and `double` for double-precision floating-point numbers. You can also use `long` and `short` integers in C by writing either `long int x` as the declaration or just `long x`. Depending on your machine, these use more or fewer bits for representing integers and therefore have greater range or require less space.

Caution

Steer clear of `long` and `short` unless you absolutely need them. They make your code less portable.

Note

Unless portability is a concern, it is usually easier to use `double` for all floating-point variables.

Fancier types: arrays and structures

One of the distinguishing features of C is that arrays begin with element zero. This means that the first element of an array is number 0, and the *n*th element of an array is numbered *n*-1:

```
#include <stdio.h>
main() {
    int grades[3];           /* an array of three elements, numbered 0, 1, 2 */
    char initials[2];
    grades[0] = 10;     /* legal */
    grades[-1] = 9;     /* illegal -- negative index */
    grades[3] = 12;     /* illegal -- array goes from 0 to 2 */
    /* two statements on one line - not very readable */
    initials[0] = `J`; initials[1] = `A`;
    printf("Student #0 has grade %d\n", grades[0]);
}
```

Elements of the array are just like individual variables, as the example shows. Anywhere that you might use an integer, you can now use a single element of the array.

Grouping several variables together under one name is frequently convenient. For example, suppose a student has a first initial, last initial, midterm grade, and ten lab grades. You can define a new structure that relates all these parts, called fields:

```
struct student {
    char firstInitial, lastInitial;
    int midterm, labs[10];
};          /* you must have the final semicolon */
```

This defines a new type with four fields, one of which is an array. Such declarations of new types should go between the #include <stdio.h> and the beginning of the main program. To declare and use a variable of this type, write the following:

```
main() {
    struct student goodOne;    /* declares a variable "goodOne" of
                                  type "struct student" */
    goodOne.firstInitial = `T´;    /* sets a field */
    goodOne.labs[5] = -33;    /* sets another field (the sixth lab
                                 score) */
    /* lines can be split in the middle */
    printf("Your sixth lab score is: %d\n",
    goodOne.labs[5]);
    }
```

Structures enable a single variable to have several fields, which is convenient.

Casting and assignment

One of C's features is that it enables variables of one type to be directly assigned to another, doing the "right thing" most of the time. For example:

```
int i;          /* an integer */
double f;       /* a double-precision floating-point number */
i = 3;
f = i;          /* f = 3.0 */
f = f + 1.7;    /* f = 4.7 */
i = f;          /* i = 4 (the remainder is dropped) */
```

Sometimes you must explicitly convert data from one type to another. You can achieve this by *casting*. You most commonly cast when division on integers occurs.

```
f = 3/4;          /* this is integer division and f = 0, due to integer
                     rounding */
f = 3.0/4.0;      /* this is floating-point division, f = .75 */
f = i/4;          /* integer division again */
f = ((float) i)/4.0;  /* convert i to a float and do floating-point
                         division */
```

Tip

When in doubt, cast explicitly to the correct type. Don't count on C to do it for you unless you are certain that C will do it correctly.

One of the most common operations in programming is to increment or decrement an integer variable by one. C has four special operations for this:

```
i++;      /* increment i by one */
++i;      /* also increment i by one */
i--;      /* decrement i by one */
--i;      /* also decrement i by one */
```

The difference between the two versions of each operation is that the first does the increment *after* returning the variable, whereas the second does it *before* returning the variable. If the operations are the only thing done, as shown here, there is no difference. Consider this:

```
i = 1; j = i++;    /* after this, i == 2, j == 1 */
i = 1; j = ++i;    /* after this, i == 2, j == 2 */
```

Flow control

C has the flow control constructs found in most block-structured languages. Those are for loops, while loops, case statements (called switch in C), and if-then-else statements. The if-then-else enables conditional execution:

```
if (x > 10) {
     ...  /* this code executed if x is greater than 10 */
     }
else {
     ...  /* this code is executed if x is less than or equal to 10 */
     }
```

The else part of the if-then-else is optional. If only a single statement is in the then block or the else block, you can omit the braces:

```
if (x > 10) printf("x is greater than 10\n");
```

Consistently placing the braces around a single statement ensures that you won't forget to add the braces if you decide to add a second statement to the then block. Note that the word *then* does not appear in any conditional statements in C.

The conditional expression must always be in parentheses. It can be a compound expression involving logical AND (&&), logical OR (||), and logical negation (!). Suppose you have three Boolean expressions, called A, B, and C. Each of these expressions is either true or false. Consider the compound expression:

```
if  (A && B || !C)
```

In C, operator precedence gives the logical OR lowest precedence, followed by logical AND, and then logical negation, which has the highest precedence. With full parenthesization, the preceding example has the same meaning as

```
if  ((A && B) || (!C))
```

which you can read as "If both A and B hold or if C doesn't hold or both." It does not have the same meaning as

```
if  (A && (B || (!C)))
```

which is interpreted as "A and either B or not C (or both)."

What does it mean for an expression to hold or not hold? Well, obviously,

```
(x > 3)
```

holds, if the variable x is, for example, 5. C is more general, however. Any nonzero expression is considered to be true in C, and any expression equal to zero is false. This means that you could write

```
if (x) {
```

which means "if x is not zero." Moreover, assignment statements return their assigned values, which explains why the example of a disaster in the introduction is a problem.

C has conditional looping structures, the most general being the for loop. Here's an example to print the first ten squares:

```
for (i = 1; i <= 10; i++) {      /* repeat ten times */
    printf("%d squared is %d\n.", i, i*i);
    }
```

The code inside the block executes repeatedly (in this case, ten times). Before starting, i is set equal to 1. Each time through, before the block executes, i is checked to see whether it is still less than or equal to 10. If the condition holds, the block executes. After this, i is incremented by one, and the loop starts over, checking whether i is less than or equal to 10 again.

The general format of the for statement is three semicolon-separated expressions. The first is an assignment, to be done once before the loop starts. The second field is a condition, to be checked each time before the block executes. The loop executes as long as the condition holds. The third field is a modification statement, to be done each time after the block executes. Each of these fields is optional, so you could legally write

```
for (;;) ...
```

which would not set anything beforehand, would check no condition each time through, and would not modify anything afterward. This would cause an infinite loop because it has no termination condition.

C also has while loops:

```
while (x > 2) {
/* do this as long as x is greater than 2 */
    }
```

which is equivalent to:

```
for (; x > 2; ) {
/* do this as long as x is greater than 2 */
    }
```

I have shown how C enables you to use `for` in place of `while`, another example of C's flexibility. Flexibility does not necessarily imply clarity. Be careful!

Pointers and dynamic variables

Pointer variables contain addresses of locations where data is stored, as opposed to the data itself. Any data type can have a pointer to it, as follows:

```
int *p;             /* p is a pointer to an integer */
char *s;            /* s is a pointer to a character */
struct student *t;  /* t is a pointer to a student */
```

This allocates space for three pointers, but not for the locations to which they point. To do that, the storage must be allocated using a memory allocation function. The most popular function is `malloc()`, which takes a number of bytes to allocate and returns a pointer to those bytes:

```
s = (char *) (malloc(1));            /* assumes 1 byte per char */
p = (int *) (malloc(sizeof(int)));   /* independent of int size */
t = (struct student *) (malloc(sizeof(struct student)));
```

You cast the result of the `malloc` statement to the appropriate pointer type. In the preceding example, the first line allocates one byte of memory and makes s point to it. The second line allocates however many bytes an `int` needs and makes p point to that location. The third line allocates enough bytes for a record and makes t point to that record.

To use pointers, you must *dereference* or *chase* them:

```
*s = `X´;         /* assigns the byte to which s points */
*p = -14;
*p = (*p)++;    /* p now points to a location holding -13 */
p = 33;         /* don't do this - you're overwriting the pointer */
/* the following statements do the same thing */
(*t).labs[3] = 100;
t->labs[3] = 100;
```

The `free()` library routine makes possible the deallocation of space:

```
free(s);
free(p);
free(t);
free(t);        /* a very bad idea to free the same space twice */
```

Novices need pointers for three tasks. The first is to handle input, described in the next section. The second is to pass parameters to functions, described in the section after that. The third is to refer to strings. In C, strings are arrays of characters, and arrays are pointers to chunks of contiguous storage. Thus, the following statements are equivalent:

```
char str[10];    /* a "string" of 10 characters */
char *str;     /* an unallocated string */
str = (char *) malloc(10);     /* space reserved for 10 characters */
```

The second statement has the advantage that the size of the string can be adjusted at execution time instead of during compilation. By convention, strings are *null-terminated* in C. This means that the last character of the string should be a special character equal to zero, called null, that can be written as `\0`.

```
str[0] = `H`;     /* we can use the array notation, even if */
str[1] = `i`;     /* we declared the string using char *str */
str[2] = `\0`;    /* NULL terminator */
```

To print out a string, use `printf()` with the %s format, as follows:

```
printf("The string is: %s.\n", str);
```

Notice that you don't indicate that you're passing a `char` pointer to `printf` because that is what is expected for a string. This prints

```
The string is: Hi.
```

In C, double quotation marks define static strings. To copy a static string into a variable more easily than one character at a time, use `strcpy()`:

```
char str[10];               /* enough space for 9 characters */
strcpy(str, "A String");       /* copies "A String" into str */
strcpy(str, "A Long String");    /* disaster - not enough space */
```

The `strcpy()` command does not allocate any space for the string, and you must either have already used `malloc` to allocate or have declared the string as an array. Other string functions provide more sophisticated operations, but they are beyond the scope of this chapter.

Tip

Try to be flexible with your strings. When in doubt, allocate more storage than you could possibly need, and remember that the null terminator takes up one character, so leave room.

Story: Don't Forget the Terminating Null Character

Recently, when I was debugging a program, an unusual intermittent error kept popping up. After spending a few hours looking at the program, I found the problem. When allocating memory to copy a string, I was allocating only the length of the string itself and not including the space for the terminating null character. This wrote beyond the end of my array and trashed another variable. To correct this, I revised the line as follows:

```
str=malloc(strlen(inbuf)+1)
```

Input and output

The previous section shows how to use printf() for output. The printf() command takes a format string and variables and prints nicely formatted output. The format string indicates the look of the output and any literal data. Variable spots are indicated with %c for character, %d for integer, %f for floating point, and %s for string data.

```
printf("My name is %s, and I am %d feet tall\n", name, height);
```

In the preceding example, name must be a string, and it replaces the %s in the output string. height must be an integer, replacing the %d. printf() has many more sophisticated options to control other output characteristics, such as the width of the output fields.

For input, scanf() is like printf(). It takes a format string and variables and waits for the user to type in values. The values are read into the variables. Typically, the format string is simpler for scanf because you are just giving a list of variables for input:

```
int first, second, third;
printf("Please enter three integers: "); /* no carriage return */
scanf("%d %d %d", &first, &second, &third);
printf("The sum of the numbers is %d\n", first + second + third);
```

This prompts the user to type in three numbers that are read into the variables as soon as the user presses Enter. Notice the ampersand (&) in front of the variable names. If you read in scalar variables, such as floats, ints, and chars, you must prepend the variable with &. This passes a pointer to the variable instead of the variable itself for reasons described in the next section. Strings, on the other hand, must *not* have the ampersand:

```
int score;
char name[80];
printf("Enter a score and a name\n");
scanf("%d %s", &score, name);
```

Be careful to allocate enough space for any strings you may read. If you don't, your program will crash.

Tip

If your program crashes with a "Bus Error," you most likely forgot to put an & in front of a scalar variable in a scanf statement.

Functions

I have already used several common C functions, but you can design your own. A function has a return value and some number of parameters and should be declared before invoked:

```
int max(int a, int b) {              /* returns the larger of two numbers
*/
    if (a > b) return a;
```

```
    else return b;
    }
```

This is a function that takes two integer parameters and returns the larger when invoked. For example,

```
x = max(y, 3);
```

If a function doesn't return anything meaningful, it is a procedure and should be declared to return a special null-type called `void`:

```
void annoy(int n) {        /* repeatedly prints an annoying message */
    int i;              /* a local variable */
    for (i = 0; i < n; i++) {
        printf("Ain't I annoyin'?\n");
    }
}
```

Variables declared inside the function are local to that function and available only within it. Variables declared outside functions are global. A global variable is available to all functions declared after the variable; in addition, you can pass it as a parameter to any function, as demonstrated in the previous examples.

You can modify parameters, but those modifications are restored on exit. C functions are therefore said to be "call-by-value." If you need to modify a parameter inside a function, you must fool C by passing a pointer to the parameter instead of directly passing the parameter itself:

```
void paramExam(int x, int *y) {  /* y is a pointer, x is not */
    x++;      /* will not be reflected in the outside program */
    (*y)++; /* will be reflected outside */
    }
main() {
    int i, j;
    i = 0; j = 3;
    paramExam(i, &j);       /* put the & to pass a pointer to j */
    printf("%d %d\n", i, j); /* will print "0 4" */
}
```

Now you should understand why `scanf` expects the ampersand in front of its scalar arguments: because it modifies the variables, of course. You should also know why pointer arguments, such as strings, do not need the ampersand.

Software engineering in C and UNIX

One of the strengths of C is that you can break code into multiple files. You can place each function into its own file and compile it separately, saving time in the long run. If you take this approach, you must declare the function headers in the files where they are used. Breaking up the previous example, you would have a file called, perhaps, `param.c`:

```
void paramExam(int x, int *y) {  /* y is a pointer, x is not */
    x++;     /* will not be reflected in the outside program */
    (*y)++; /* will be reflected outside */
    }
```

You would also have a file called `main.c`:

```
void paramExam(int x, int *y); /* declare function */
main() {
    int i, j;
    i = 0; j = 3;
    paramExam(i, &j);     /* put the & to pass a pointer to j */
}
```

Because you use `paramExam` in `main()`, you must declare it in that file. To compile your program, you must compile each file with the `-c` flag:

```
cc -c param.c
cc -c main.c
```

This creates two object files, `param.o` and `main.o`. To combine the object files, you must link them:

```
cc -o myProgram param.o main.o
```

Although this uses three compilation steps instead of one, each step is faster. Further, suppose you now modify `main.c`, but not `param.c`. You only need to recompile `main.c` and relink without recompiling `param.c`.

```
cc -c main.c
cc -o myProgram param.o main.o
```

Secret

The make program, described in Chapter 38, helps automate this task. Break your programs into pieces to save yourself trouble.

GNU C

Some UNIX systems come with a C compiler included, but most do not. Although you can buy a commercial C compiler, using the free gcc program provided by the Free Software Foundation (FSF) is just as easy (and cheaper). This compiler is part of a combined free gcc/g++ (free C++) package and is included on the CD-ROM accompanying this book.

To learn more about C

This section has provided a brief introduction to C, but the best way to learn is to practice. As a reference guide, nothing is better than the original source: *The C Programming Language, 2nd Edition,* by Brian Kernighan and Dennis Ritchie.

C++: An Object-Oriented Extension to C

In recent years, C++ has surpassed C in popularity for new programming projects on UNIX systems.

Introduction

The C++ programming language originated as an extension to C. Designed by Bjarne Stroustroup of AT&T Bell Labs in the early 1980s, C++ has gained wide acceptance in the programming community for four key reasons:

- The C++ language offers several extensions over "Standard C." The most important of these extensions is object-orientation, which enables better organization of both programs and data.

- Compilers for C++ are widely available, and the language is now standardized by ANSI, the American National Standards Institute.

- You can compile most C programs directly in C++ with few or no modifications. Many C programmers take advantage of the flexibility of C++ to learn a bit at a time instead of jumping into object-oriented programming and a new language from the start.

- C++ programs typically retain the efficiency of C. Because the developers of C++ made their design decisions with efficiency in mind, C++ is suitable for environments where code speed is a concern.

This fourth advantage, however, is also a concern. Purists argue that C++ compromises too many of the fundamental advantages of object-oriented programming. Like C, C++ is flexible, and this flexibility invites abuse. Further, design decisions made in the name of efficiency and compatibility with C interfere with the object-orientation. Thus, thinking of C++ as an object-directed version of C is better than thinking of it as a fully object-oriented language. This is a distinction that becomes more apparent with C++ programming experience.

I can draw one last parallel between programming in C and C++. I have trumpeted the flexibility of C++. You can use that flexibility, as you can that of C, to great advantage or to great confusion. For best results, C++ should be used with discipline. This discipline adds extra structure to what C offers and makes designing, coding, and debugging easier.

In 1998, ANSI officially standardized C++, codifying several new features and assuring programmers that their standard C++ programs would be portable between machines.

A first C++ program

As usual, the first C++ program I will explore is the "Hello World" program:

```
#include <iostream>
using namespace std;
main() {
  cout << "Hello World";    // print a friendly greeting
  cout << endl;         // followed by a carriage return
}
```

The first line includes the C++ I/O Stream library, which is used for input and output. This library takes the place of the old stdio library, although you can still use stdio. The second line enables you to use the library without additional syntax. The program sends the string Hello World to cout, the console output, followed by a return. The output operator (<<) sends data to an output stream. Unlike standard C's printf, this program contains no clumsy output format string. A following section ("I/O in C++") describes the iostream library in more detail.

A word on libraries

The new standard specifies that C++ libraries do not have the .h at the end of their names. Under this approach, however, you must include the line

```
using namespace std;
```

after the #include statements. Before standardization, this was all done with a single file. Thus, the example program used to read as follows:

```
#include <iostream.h>
main() {
  cout << "Hello World";    // print a friendly greeting
  cout << endl;         // followed by a carriage return
}
```

Some compilers are not yet compliant with the standard in this regard, so many programmers still use the "old" style. This book uses up-to-date standard C++.

Comments in C++

The first C++ feature to consider is a new way of commenting code. In addition to the C-style commenting, which is delimited by /* and */, C++ accepts single-line comments that start with // and extend to the end of the line. For example:

```
int myAge;    // This is a comment that extends to the end of the line
int yourAge;    /* This is a comment, too, but it needs to be
          terminated */
```

Most programmers use /* and */ for multiple-line comments and // for single-line comments.

I/O in C++

C++ features a library with new operators for input and output. To use these operators instead of the conventional C `printf()` and `scanf()`, add the following line to the start of the program:

```
#include <iostream>
```

The input operator is <<, and the output operator is >. Although these operators still retain their original C meaning of right-shift and left-shift, they also take on the responsibility of I/O operators. This technique of using a single operator to mean different things in different contexts is called *operator overloading* or *polymorphism* and is an important feature of object-oriented programming and C++. As an example of input and output, consider the following short program:

```
#include <iostream>
using namespace std;
main() {
    int number;
    cout << "Please enter an integer: ";     // prompt for an integer
    cin > number;                // read the integer into "number"
    cout << number << " squared is "     // several pieces of output
<< number*number << endl;     // can be strung together
    }
```

This program reads in a single integer and prints out the integer and its square. The program is nearly self-explanatory. `cin` and `cout` are like `stdin` and `stdout` in C: They are predefined streams linked to the console for input and output, respectively. Notice how stringing together several << operators enables both strings and variables to generate output simultaneously. Similarly, you can input several variables at one time with several > operators:

```
cin > variable1 > variable2 > variable3;
```

Lastly, the symbol `endl` specifies the end-of-line. This puts a return onto the output (compare it with the first line, which does not have a return). You can also use the conventional C alternative of \n.

The `iostream` library enables much more sophisticated formatting control, which is beyond the scope of this book.

You can use both the `iostream` library and the C `stdio` library in C++ programs, although you must take care to avoid buffering problems if a program uses both libraries together. In general, sticking to one I/O library per program is best.

Note

Many C programmers are already adept with the C standard I/O library and stick to `printf()`, `scanf()`, and related procedures, never using the C++ I/O mechanism.

Strings in C++

With its new standard, C++ now has a very useful string library. In addition to being efficient, the library enables you to do the following tasks easily:

- Create, assign, copy, and delete strings
- Convert between `chars`, C-style strings (in double quotation marks), and string variables
- Compare two strings
- Concatenate two strings
- Find the length of a string
- Locate and replace a substring within a string

To use strings, you must include the string header file. Then, creating a new string is as easy as creating a variable of any other basic type.

```
#include <string>
using namespace std;

main() {
  string hi("hello");     // creates and initializes a new string
  string lo="greetings";    // an alternative initialization
  string g(lo);          // a third alternative
  string es="";          // the empty string
  string es2=0;          // also the empty string
  string s;         // initialized to empty string
}
```

String variables may be assigned like any other type.

```
  string name("Fred");
  name = "Flintstone";    // changes name
```

C++ manages all the storage allocation, preventing accidents. Similarly, the I/O operators (<< and >) have been overloaded for strings. Thus, string I/O is easy.

```
#include <iostream>
#include <string>
using namespace std;

main() {
  string s;
  // read a word at a time from cin
  // print each word on its own line
  while (cin > s)
    cout << s << endl;
}
```

The + operator is overloaded for strings to enable their concatenation. Comparison operators (==, >, and so forth) are also overloaded for strings.

```
string hi("hello");
string lo="greetings";
string r = hi + ` ´ + "world";      // concatenate three strings
r += `!´;                           // this works too! (r = "hello world!")
r = string(3,`!´);                  // r = "!!!";
if (hi == "hello") ...
if (lo > "great") ...
if (lo < hi) ...
```

The library has several other functions, demonstrated in the following example:

```
cout << hi.find("ll");      // returns 2 (position of leftmost "ll")
cout << hi.find(`l´);       // works, thanks to autoconversion
cout << hi.rfind(`l´);      // rfind searches from the end (returns 3)
cout << lo.find("g");       // returns 0 (position of leftmost `g´)
cout << lo.find("g", 5);    // returns 7 (leftmost `g´ beyond 5).
cout << hi.find("x")        // returns string::npos

string s("Testing!");
cout << s.substr(2, 5);     // "sting"
cout << s[3];               // `t´
s.replace(2,2,"eth");       // s == "Teething!"
s.erase(1,4);               // s == "Ting!"
s[1] = `a´;                 // s == "Tang!"
s.insert(1,"w");            // s == "Twang!"
```

Memory allocation in C++

C++ has two functions to handle dynamic memory allocation: new and delete. Although the traditional C allocation routines, malloc() and free(), are still available, new and delete are safer and easier to use. Consider the following:

```
int *p;

// allocate a new uninitialized integer and make p point to it
p = new int;
delete p;    // release the memory
// allocate another integer, initialize it to 6 and make p point to it
p = new int(6);
delete p;    // release the memory
```

The new function automatically returns a pointer to the specified type, enabling C++ to check for potential type incompatibility. It also allocates sufficient storage for the particular object, obviating the use of sizeof(). Moreover, new enables inline initialization of the allocated object, as shown in the example. More sophisticated objects can have initialization functions (called *constructors*), which are automatically invoked upon creation, in addition to cleanup functions (called *destructors*), which are invoked upon deletion of an object. I describe these later in the chapter.

You can also use `new` and `delete` to allocate arrays of objects:

```
int *a;         // pointers and arrays are related in C and C++
a = new int [5];    // allocate an array of five integers
cin > a[0];    // read in the first entry of the array
a[4] = a[0] + 1;    // set the last entry (arrays are indexed as in C)
delete [] a;    // release the memory for an array
```

Object-orientation and classes in C++

Before changing the name to C++, Stroustroup first called his new language "C with Classes," which emphasizes what he felt was the most important feature. A *class* is like a `struct` in C or a `record` in Pascal because it defines a new type composed of several fields. In addition to the data fields, a class can have functions, called *methods,* built into it. This is the heart of object-oriented programming because it enables the programmer to associate functions solely with the data that those functions access. Here is an example of a simple class definition:

```
class Person {
private:
    int age;     // every person has an age
    char *name;     // and a name
public:          // the methods below are publicly accessible
    void setAge(int a);     // declare a method to set the age
    void printAge();     // declare a method to print the age
    // etc.
};          // don't forget the semicolon!
```

Reading this declaration, C++ creates a new type, called `Person`. Variables of that type have two fields, `age` and `name`, and several methods that deal with that field. Because the fields are above the `public` indicator, you cannot access them from outside the class. The only way to change the age is through the `setAge()` method, which is also part of the class. This feature of object-oriented languages, called *encapsulation,* enables the programmer to protect the data in a class from improper access. The implementation of `setAge()` might, for example, check for improper data, such as a negative age.

So far, I have declared the class, but I have not defined the bodies of the methods. Although you can define methods inside the class, it is clearer to declare them outside, like this:

```
// the body of setAge()
void Person::setAge(int newAge) {
    if (newAge < 0)     // check for valid data
        cerr < "Improper age: " << newage << endl;
    else
        age = a;     // age refers to the age field of the Person
}
```

Note a few things: Because methods are part of the class, you don't declare the class fields inside the methods. Each method body is declared with a name formed from its class (Person) and method, separated by two colons. For example, if class A has a method B, that method is referred to as A::B(). Here is an example of the other method that I have defined for Person:

```
// the body of printAge()
void Person::printAge() {
    cout << name << "'s age is " << age;
}
```

Now that I have declared the new class, I can declare and use variables of that class type:

```
main() {
    int x(33);          // a new integer, initialized to 33
    Person p;           // a new person
    Person *q;          // q is a pointer to a person
    p.setAge(x);        // set p's age to 33
    q.setAge(x+5);      // SYNTAX ERROR!  q is a pointer
    q = new Person;     // allocate q
    p.printAge();       // print p's age
    q->setAge(10);      // set q's age.  As in C, use -> to follow pointers
    delete q;           // release allocated memory
}
```

Two special methods associated with each class are called the *constructor* and the *destructor*. The constructor is a method that is automatically invoked when a new variable of the class is created. The destructor is automatically invoked when the object is destroyed, either by a delete call for pointers to variables or by C++ directly when static objects go out of scope (for example, for variables declared inside a function when that function exits).

Note

Destructors are rare unless pointers are being used, but constructors are common and mostly used to initialize fields.

The name of a constructor method is the same as the name of the class, whereas the destructor method has the name of the class prepended with a tilde (~). Because these two methods have an unusual status, they don't have return values. Listing 36-1 illustrates this.

Listing 36-1: C++ Code

```
class Person {
private:
    int age;    // a field
    char *name;    // another field
public:         // the methods below are publicly accessible
    Person();    // a constructor declaration
    ~Person();    // a destructor declaration
    void setAge(int a);
    void printAge();
    ...         // etc.
};
```

```
Person::Person() {    // the body of the constructor
    name = new char;    // allocate space for the empty string
    name[0] = `\0´;    // initialize name to the empty string
    age = 10;        // give a default value to age and print a message
    cout << "You just created a new person with no name!\n";
}

Person::~Person(){    // the body of the destructor
    cout << "In the Destructor";
    delete name;        // clean up the allocated storage
}

main() {
    Person p;    // the constructor is called automatically here
    Person *q;    // no constructor is called, because no object is allocated
    new q;    // now the constructor is called
    delete q;    // calls the destructor for q
}            // the destructor for p is called automatically here
```

Default arguments in C++

The setAge() method has a single integer argument, but suppose you want to allow the user to omit the argument. That is, if the programmer writes

```
p.setAge();
```

you want to call setAge with a default argument. C++ makes this possible by altering the header to the method. The new header reads

```
Person::setAge(int a = 10)
```

This says that setAge() takes a single integer parameter, which, if not specified, defaults to 10. If functions have multiple arguments, the arguments with default values must come after the nondefault arguments.

Secret

Default arguments enable you to update functions easily and safely. If, at some stage of development, a function needs more arguments, you can add them to the end of the argument list with default values. Old invocations of the function will still work, using the default values.

Overloading and polymorphism in C++

Sometimes it's useful to have a function that can take arguments of several different types and do the "right thing" based on the types. For example, consider absolute value in C, where abs() takes an integer and returns an integer and dabs() takes a double and returns a double. Absolute value has different names depending on the argument and return value. C++ enables you to give both versions the same name. It decides which version to invoke according to how you use it. This is called *polymorphism* or *function overloading.* Here is what the three versions look like:

```
int absolute(int a) { return abs(a); }        // the integer version
double absolute(double d) { return dabs(d); }    // the double version
double d = -3.5;
cout << absolute(d);     // invokes the double version
cout << absolute(-3);    // invokes the integer version
```

C++ enables function polymorphism, as shown in the preceding example, but it also enables polymorphism on all the traditional operators, such as +, *, %, <<, and so on. This technique, called *operator overloading,* enables you to define a version of + for the class Person that enables an integer to be added to a Person, and vice versa. Presumably, the result would be something meaningful to the programmer, such as the sum of the integer and the person's age.

```
cout << p + 5;     // print p's age in 5 years
p.setAge(p+1);     // add 1 to p's age!
```

Tip

Though operator overloading looks snappy, it yields code that is terribly difficult to read. It is an example of something that is more clever than useful.

Parameter passing in C++

In C, you often use pointers to pass function parameters. This is necessary if the value of the parameter is changed inside the function, but it is awkward because you must refer differently to pointer variables and nonpointers. C++ has a feature called a *reference,* which provides the benefits of a pointer without the bulk.

```
void incrementByOne(int &i)  // The & identifies i as a reference
{ i++; }
main() {
int j(1);                    // j = 1;
incrementByOne(j);           // note: not &j, but just j
}
```

Without the & for the reference, incrementByOne() would update the parameter, but the change would be overwritten when the function exited, and j would remain unchanged. I have been using references since the beginning of the chapter in the input operator >. The second argument to > is a reference that avoids the unsightly—and, to new programmers, confusing—pointers used by scanf().

Secret

Use references for efficiently passing large structures that must be changed inside functions. This enables C++ to avoid copying the entire structure on or off the stack upon function entry or exit.

Constant parameters and variables

One common objection to C is that it is too permissive. It gives the programmer so much latitude that checking for unintentional errors, such as overwriting of variables that are supposed to remain constant, is impossible. C++ has a mechanism for declaring variables and parameters as constant that compels the compiler to guarantee that those variables will not be modified. You can use this mechanism to implement read-only parameters as follows:

```
void silly(const int i) {
cout << i;     // this is fine
i = i * 2;     // this will be flagged as illegal by the compiler
}
```

Note

Using constants is a good way to control data access between members of a programming team. Team members need only agree on interface and then can independently concentrate on implementation.

Constants are important with the addition of references. References enable write access to data from functions without pointers. Declaring a parameter as a constant reference means that the storage savings of references can be realized along with the compiler's guarantee that the function will not change the parameter:

```
void someFunction(const Person &p);    // saves time and space,
guarantees read-only
```

Caution

Converting an existing program to include constants is nearly impossible. You must use them from the start of implementation.

Inheritance

Consider a larger application, perhaps a personnel system for a company. Such a system would naturally include several different classes, such as `Employee`, `Manager`, and so on. I have already gone to the trouble of declaring (and presumably refining and debugging) a `Person` class. It would be nice to leverage my previous work and take advantage of the class relationships, noting that an `Employee` is a `Person`. This capability, called *inheritance,* is a fundamental aspect of object-oriented programming and is available in C++.

To create a new class `Employee` that is derived from `Person`, write this:

```
class Employee: public Person {
public:
    int salary;                    // Employee-specific field
    void setSalary(int  s) {    // Employee-specific methods go here
        salary = s;    // method bodies can go in the class definition
    }
};
```

One distinction is that I have made `salary` a public field of `Employee`, making it available for access outside the object, if desired. This declaration says that everything public in `Person` (that is, the methods) should also be public in `Employee`. There is no way to take private information from `Person` (that is, the fields) and make it public in `Employee`. That would violate the object-oriented encapsulation of `Person`. To access the private fields, I must use the methods provided by `Person`, such as `setAge()`. For example,

```
main() {
    Employee e;
    e.setAge(34);  // legal, since e is an Employee, which is a Person
    e.setSalary(55667);
};
```

I could then use the same approach to create and use a `Manager`, who is an `Employee`. If I add the restriction that manager salaries should always be over 70,000, I will need a new version of `setSalary` for managers that overrides the default from `Employee`:

```
class Manager: public Employee {
// manager-specific data here
public:
    void setSalary(int s);    // Manager-specific override of an
inherited method
};

void Manager::setSalary(int s) {
if (s < 70000)
    cerr << "insufficient managerial salary\n";
else
    salary = s;
}
```

Inheritance is a powerful mechanism, but it can lead to confusion. It is often better to sidestep the inheritance mechanism and use inclusion, illustrated in the following code:

```
class Manager {
public:
    Employee e;    // a manager has all the aspects of an employee
void setSalary(int s);
};
```

Note

Many C++ programmers never use inheritance at all.

The disadvantage of this approach is that access to the methods of `Employee` occurs through an extra level of indirection:

```
main() {
    Manager m;
    m.e.setAge(15);    // An extra `e.´ because we don't use
inheritance
}
```

Friend functions

Some methods relate two (or more) classes. Therefore, including such a function in only one of the classes is inappropriate. When a function needs access to the private members of more than one class, you should declare that function as a *friend function* to each of those classes. Friend functions are declared inside all the classes to which they need access, although the body of the function lies outside any of the classes.

For example, suppose I add a boss field to the Person class and an array of employees to the Manager field. I would like to be able to write a function managers(Manager m, Employee e) to establish the boss-worker relationship between a manager and an employee. This function needs access to private members of both the Employee and the Manager classes.

The C++ Standard Template Library

In addition to the string type, C++ has several other useful extensions. These extensions have been packaged together in a standardized library called the Standard Template Library (STL). The STL includes additional types (vectors, sets, matrices, and so forth) and algorithms (sorting, searching, matrix operations, and so forth). As its name suggests, the STL is a generic library package; its types and functions can be applied to any base type. For example, you can create a vector of ints, a vector of chars, a vector of doubles, a vector of a user-defined type, or a vector of any other type.

To show off the STL, I present a short demonstration of vectors. Vectors are like arrays in that they are an ordered list of items that enable efficient access to individual elements. Vectors have a big advantage, however, over arrays in that they automatically grow as need arises when new elements are added. To use vectors, include the <vector> header file and use the std namespace:

```
#include <vector>
using namespace std;
```

To create a vector of integers, declare the vector as you would any other type:

```
vector<int> i_vec;
```

This declares a variable i_vec, which is an initially empty vector of integers. The <int> indicates that it is a vector of integers. To add new elements to the end of i_vec, use the push_back() method:

```
  i_vec.push_back(3);    // put 3 at end
  i_vec.push_back(1);    // then put a 1
  i_vec.push_back(2);    // lastly, a 2
// i_vec now contains three elements
  // step through vector & print
  for (int ix = 0; ix < i_vec.size(); ix++)
    cout << i_vec[ix] << " ";
  // prints: 3 1 2
```

Like other types, vectors can be assigned with = and compared with ==, as follows:

```
vector<int> vecA, vecB;

vecA.push_back(3);  vecA.push_back(2);
vecB = vecA;           // vecB = (3, 2)
vecB[1] = 0;           // vecB = (3, 0)
if (vecA == vecB) cout << "same!" << endl;
```

The comparison operator, ==, does an element-by-element comparison of the two vectors. In this case, they are not equal.

The STL also contains useful algorithms. One such algorithm is sort(), which sorts a vector in place:

```
#include <vector>
#include <algorithm>     // for sort()
using namespace std;

vector<int> vec;
vec.push_back(3);
vec.push_back(-17);
vec.push_back(0);

sort(vec.begin(), vec.end());     // vec now contains (-17, 0, 3)
```

As you can see, vectors are a very flexible structure that saves a lot of recoding time. For most programming tasks, the STL may already have a version of what you need. Check it out!

GNU C++

The Free Software Foundation (FSF) offers a free GNU version of C++, called g++, which runs on a myriad of machines. See Part X for further details about the FSF and GNU products.

C++ and the Internet

Several Usenet newsgroups are wholly or partially dedicated to C++. In addition to consulting the primary newsgroups comp.lang.c++ and gnu.g++.help, you can address architecture-specific questions to architecture-specific newsgroups, such as comp.os.ms-windows. programmer.misc. Before posting to any group, read the frequently asked questions (FAQ) document. The FAQ for comp.lang.c++ is particularly thorough and is a good secondary learning tool for C++.

For more information on C++

This section has provided an introduction to C++, but considerable detail has been omitted or glossed over. You can find several good books on C++ in your local bookstore. The ultimate reference for C++ is the *Annotated Reference Manual (ARM),* cowritten by Ellis and Stroustroup. This is not suitable for beginners but is a good arbiter of disputes.

Summary

This chapter introduced the two most popular programming languages for UNIX systems. It explained the basics of the following topics:

▶ Writing and compiling a C program, including how to write conditional statements, looping, and the command for compilation

▶ Reading and understanding C++ programs, including the changes in C++ that make it radically different from C, how classes work, and the nature of inheritance

The next chapter introduces two other widely used languages, Java and Perl.

Chapter 37

More Programming Languages: Java and Perl

This chapter introduces two more programming languages for UNIX systems: Java and Perl. Like the last chapter, this chapter is not a tutorial on the languages, but a high-level overview of the concepts included therein. Java and Perl are the two languages most commonly used for writing programmed pages on the World Wide Web. Again, Dr. Matthew Merzbacher, Assistant Professor of Computer Science at Mills College, wrote this chapter.

Introduction to Java

Java is an object-oriented programming language that, on the surface, resembles a concise version of C++. Java is much more than that, however. Designed at Sun Microsystems in the 1990s, Java has become the de facto standard for sophisticated Web page design because it has all the advantages of a conventional programming language (including syntax that is very much like C/C++) coupled with other desirable features, including

- An intermediate compiled form that is interpreted later

- Secure and safe execution

- A set of reusable modules for common tasks, called the Application Program Interface (API)

These features make Java particularly well-suited for use in programmed World Wide Web pages. Java is not just for Web page animation, though. It is just as powerful as conventional languages such as C and C++, but it is easier to program.

Java is portable on many levels. Most commonly, Java's intermediate form, called *bytecode,* is transmitted to remote machines, where it is executed. This is what happens in the Web, where the remote machine is a Java-ready browser. Java source code is also portable. Further, because so much of Java is defined in the API, running Java on a new machine is only a matter of providing the support for the API. Thus, Java is designed to be fully platform-independent. In practice, multiple versions of Java have arisen, and a heated debate is underway over the future capabilities of Java.

Java is more object-oriented than C++. Whereas any C program can run legally under C++, all Java programs consist exclusively of classes and methods that operate on those classes. Unlike C++, Java cannot have functions that stand alone outside a class. Thus, some of the most important advantages of Java are the following:

- Java serves as a better C++ because it
  - Has cleaner syntax.
  - Has a better memory management model.
  - Is more restrictive to protect programmers.
- It's secure.
- It's useful for Web programming.
- It's interpreted through a virtual machine (again, enhancing security).
- It's platform-independent.

I will comment on each of these points in this chapter.

A first Java program

As always, I will use the "Hello World!" program to help explain several key concepts.

```
class HelloWorld {
  public static void main(String args[]) {     // a simple program
    System.out.println("Hello World!");
  }
}
```

To run this program, first save it in a file called HelloWorld.java. The name of the class and the name of the source file must match. Then, compile the source into bytecode:

```
javac HelloWorld.java
```

To run the program, type

```
java HelloWorld
```

Several things about this program catch the eye. Output in Java is very different from that in C or C++. In Java, you produce output by calling methods on the predefined output stream System.out. The println() method takes a string and prints it, followed by a newline character. (If you don't want a new line, use the print() method instead.) Another difference is that the main() program, as promised, is a method in the HelloWorld class, not a separate function. Moreover, main() takes an array of string as its parameter. This is for any command-line arguments.

Comments

Like C++, Java supports both inline comments, which start with a // (slash-slash), and block comments, which appear between /* (slash-star) and */ (star-slash). Further, comments starting with /** (slash-star-star) and ending with */ are called *documenting comments* and are used for automatic generation of HTML documentation in support of Java code. Thus, you can simultaneously document Java programs internally and externally.

Applets and applications

Java programs can take two forms: applet or application. An *application* is like a C++ program. It has a main() method and is launched from the command line like an executable program. An *applet* is a special Java class used by Web browsers. Essentially, it is a main() program that is launched by a browser instead of from the command line. Applets are inherently graphical, whereas applications are not.

When an applet runs (in response to a Web page access), the bytecode for the applet is copied from the server to the client Web browser. The browser interprets the applet, protecting the system where the browser is running from any damage. Java's security features protect the client from any hostile actions in the program.

To create an applet, you must replace main() with a method called paint() and specify that the program is an applet by indicating that the class is a type of applet. Lastly, you must change the output to use graphical output primitives instead of System.out. Here is the HelloWorld.java program rewritten in applet form:

```
import java.applet.Applet;       // like a #include -- allows Applet
import java.awt.Graphics;        // allows Graphics calls

public class HelloWorld extends Applet {    // note - an Applet now
  public void paint( Graphics g ) {         // a simple program
    g.drawString("Hello World!", 25, 25);
// the numbers control the text position in the window
  }
}
```

To run this applet, compile it as before, using `javac`, and create an HTML file that invokes it:

```
<html>
<applet code="HelloWorld.class" width=300 height=50>
</applet>
</html>
```

Save this as a file (for example, `hello.html`). Now use a browser to open this file and the applet runs. Alternatively, you can use a program to view the applet directly instead of running it through a browser:

```
appletviewer hello.html
```

The rest of this chapter shows applications only, but the concepts presented apply equally well to applets.

Data types in Java

Java has four types of objects: primitives, arrays, classes, and interfaces. *Primitives* include the basic types, such as `int`, `boolean`, `char`, and `double`. These are identical to the same-named types found in C and C++. Variables having these types can be changed and used with the same kind of operations as those in C and C++.

The remaining three Java types are called reference data types because variables having these types only refer to underlying data. That is, all reference type variables are really pointers. This is a primary distinction between Java and most other languages.

At the center of Java is the creation of classes, just as in C++. A class contains public and private information (typically, data members are private, whereas functions may be either public or private). After a class is defined, you can use the class in other programs, creating new variables of that class type with the `new()` command, just as you can in C++. For example, consider the class `Person`, defined (of course) in `Person.java`:

```
public class Person {
  private int age;
  private String name;

  public  Person(String n) {
    name = new String(n);          // use new() to make a copy
    age = 0;
  }

  public  Person(String n, int a) {
    name = new String(n);
    age = a;
  }

  public void print() {
```

```
    System.out.println("My name is " + name + " and my age is " +
age);
  }
}
```

This class has three methods: two constructors and a `print()` method. The first constructor builds a `Person` given only a name; the second expects both a name and an age. Notice the use of the + to print several things in the `print()` method. In Java, the + operation concatenates two strings together. Java is very flexible about converting things into strings when necessary, so you can create a long output string literally by using the sum of the parts. To use this class in another program, you could write something like this:

```
public class Populate {
  public static void main(String args[]) {
    Person p1 = new Person("Fred");        // Fred is 0
    Person p2 = new Person("Albert", 91);
    p1.print();                    // all about Fred
    p2.print();                    // and Albert
  }
}
```

Arrays are managed in a similar fashion in Java. Unlike C and C++, Java requires that you provide the size of the array when you allocate it, not when you declare it:

```
char x[];                 // no size
x = new char[10];         // now we know the size
float y[] = new float[3];          // declare and allocate an array
int z[] = {1, 2, 3};      // Java allocates automatically for you,
when you initialize
```

As in C and C++, array indexes start with zero, so z[0] through z[2] are available for use in the preceding example. Unlike C and C++, Java provides run-time checking of array boundaries, so the interpreter would detect (and object to) constructions such as z[10].

Object-oriented programming

Objects are "things" manipulated by a program. In Java, almost everything is an object; except for primitive types, all Java variables are objects. As I have explained, objects have data and methods to access the data. This organization facilitates the design process, as you can construct your program one piece at a time, testing each piece's methods and then combining the pieces together.

Even better, you may discover that someone else has already created and debugged the type of object that you need. If so, you can reuse that code instead of writing your own from scratch — it's like stealing, but it's encouraged. This is a key benefit of object-oriented programming (other benefits are beyond the scope of this chapter). Objects are set to the special value "null" unless otherwise indicated.

Wrapper classes

Because Java is almost entirely object-based, all primitive types have corresponding classes called *wrapper classes*. Wrapper classes provide object functionality around the existing primitive type. For example, Integer is a wrapper for int:

```
Integer i = new Integer(3);
```

Wrapper classes seem pointless, and they are troublesome. To change a variable (such as i, in the preceding example), you must reallocate it as follows:

```
Integer i = new Integer(i.getValue()+1);
```

Wrapper classes, however, enable any Java variable to be an object. This enables programmers to assume that Java variables have certain common properties (such as the ability to be stored in a vector or to be converted to a string). I discuss this further in a following section.

Garbage collection

I have shown you how to allocate memory with new( ) but not how to deallocate memory. Java has no explicit memory deallocation operator. Instead, the Java Virtual Machine (JVM) is responsible for reclaiming memory when it is no longer needed. How does it know when to do this? While your program is running, the JVM determines which memory cells are still accessible through any variable. If a memory location is no longer accessible, JVM deallocates it. This is called *garbage collection*.

Garbage collection releases the programmer from having to worry about memory management. When you want storage, you allocate it. When you're done with it, Java figures it out. This entails some performance penalty, but it's worth it. Here's a simple example:

```
Integer a = new Integer(7);    // allocates memory
a = new Integer(8);            // the first memory (7) can now be
deallocated
Integer b = a;                 // b refers where a refers (8)
a = new Integer(9);            // the second memory cannot be collected
```

In the last line, although a now points somewhere else, the old value (8) cannot be released because it is still accessible through b. If b changes, the memory can be recovered. Garbage collection occurs only when necessary, so the performance penalty is not consistent.

The Application Program Interface

The Java Application Program Interface (API) includes many useful classes. Using these classes saves you a lot of time and effort. One example is the `Vector` class, which enables you to create an extensible array of objects. The following example is similar to the C++ STL example in Chapter 36:

```
java.util.Vector v = new java.util.Vector();        // empty
v.addElement(new Integer(7));        // adds a 7 to the vector, now [7]
Integer i = new Integer(3);
v.addElement(i);                     // adds a 3 to end, now [7, 3]
v.addElement(i);                     // and another, now [7, 3, 3]
v.insertElementAt(new Integer(10), 2);        // puts a 10 before
element #2, now [7, 3, 10, 3]
if (v.contains(i))...                 // true
if (v.contains(new Integer(3)))              // also true
Integer j = (Integer) v.elementAt(1);        // j = i (3)
v.addElement(new String("foo"));             // bad idea, but legal.  v
is now [7, 3, 10, 3, "foo"]
```

Vectors start empty and grow as needed. Although you can control the size to which a vector grows, you should accept release from such mundane responsibilities.

A vector can contain anything that is a Java object. Including different types in your vector, however, is generally a bad plan because recovering the components is very hard. The problem is that a vector is really only a vector of objects; Java gives no indication of what the objects are underneath. That's why I had to cast the result of `elementAt()` to an integer before assigning it to `j`.

Another clumsy aspect of the preceding example is that it uses `java.util.Vector`, which is pretty long-winded. You can use shorthand for any classes by explicitly importing them into your program. For example, add

```
import java.util.Vector;
```

to the top of the program. This enables you to write the following:

```
Vector v = new Vector();
```

If your program takes advantage of several different classes in `java.util`, you can include them all, as follows:

```
import java.util.*;
```

I recommend against this, however, because it brings all sorts of names into your program and may make your program confusing.

The Java API corresponds to C++'s Standard Template Library and more. In addition to useful classes such as `vector`, the API contains dictionaries, hash tables, math functions, SQL database interfaces, network management classes, and much more.

Inheritance

Java, like C++, enables inheritance of class definitions. That is, you can derive new classes from existing classes (either classes created by you or classes in the API). For example,

```
public class Employee extends Person {
```

This line states that an Employee is a Person. Everything that you can do to a Person, you can also do to an Employee. Presumably, new methods will be defined for Employee beyond those found in Person.

Every class in Java must extend exactly one other class. If a class doesn't extend anything, it defaults to extending a top-level class called Object. Thus, all classes are derived (either directly or indirectly) from Object and inherit Object's methods (which aren't very exciting, but I'll discuss that in a following section).

Multiple inheritance is done in Java with interfaces, but it is beyond the scope of this book.

Strings

One particularly important class is the String class. Strings represent a series of characters that should not be modified after creation. After you allocate a string, you are stuck with it. (The more flexible StringBuffer class is modifiable but less efficient.)

The String class has two special characteristics that distinguish it from other classes. First, it has the + concatenation operator. Unlike C++, Java generally prohibits operator overloading. As an exception, the + operator is automatically overloaded for the String class. Second, any characters enclosed in double quotation marks cause automatic allocation of a string. Thus, the following lines are functionally equivalent (except for the use of upper- and lowercase):

```
String s = "Hello World";              // allocate and assign
String t = new String("Hello World");   // likewise
String u = "hello" + " world";          // concatenate, too
```

Use the equals() method to compare strings:

```
if (s.equals(t))...               // true
if (s.equals(u))...               // false
if (s.equalsIgnoreCase(u))...      // true
```

Other string operations calculate the length of a string, search for substrings, and remove whitespace.

As previously mentioned, all classes are ultimately derived from the general superclass Object. In the definition of Object, Java specifies a method:

```
public String toString();
```

This method returns a string based on the object. By default, this is just the address of the object. When you create a new class, though, you should override this method with something that calculates a reasonable string, given the data in the object. For example, for `Person`, you could use the following:

```
public String toString() {
  return new String(name + "(" + age + ")" );
}
```

Thus, `toString()` for a `Person` would return the name followed by the age in parentheses. Java automatically invokes the `toString()` method whenever it needs a string version of your object. For example,

```
Person p = new Person("Pops", 102);
System.out.println(p);
```

This program would print

```
Pops(102)
```

because Java knows that `println()` needs a string, so it calls the `toString()` method for the `Person p`.

The Abstract Windowing Toolkit

One of Java's main uses is as a language for designing fancy Web pages. I have provided an example of how to write a simple applet, but Java's real strength lies in the classes and methods provided by the API for all sorts of typical window operations. Thus, Java programmers never need to worry about user interface design. Instead, they can take advantage of the Abstract Windowing Toolkit (AWT), which is an API for all graphical user interface (GUI) needs. It includes the capability to manage the following items:

- Graphic components, such as buttons, labels, lists, menus, and so on
- Container objects that hold components
- Layout managers that specify arrangements of components in containers
- Contexts for managing color, images, fonts, and so on
- Event handlers for detecting and responding to input such as mouse clicks

As the AWT's name suggests, the programmer deals abstractly with these issues. For example, instead of providing specific graphical details for a menu, you indicate only the items that you want on the menu and the methods that should be called when each item is selected. The client's Java viewer decides how to present the information. Thus, the actual display is platform-dependent, whereas your code is platform-independent. The contents of the menu don't change, but the menu's appearance changes from one client to another. The same code looks different on different machines. Moreover, the look of all Java programs is roughly the same on a particular client. Thus, if a client runs new software, the user need not learn a new interface.

Naturally, the AWT must include only characteristics that are common to all windowing systems. If you want to write a program that takes advantage of some fancy feature of a particular system, you're out of luck. There are ways to control particular aspects of presentation, but they are very likely to make your program less portable because certain clients may look ugly if you force them to present some of your data in a particular way.

Exceptions

Occasionally, something really bad happens in a program, such as division by zero in a calculation or accidental access to a null object. When this happens, Java throws an exception, which immediately halts the code and returns control outward until either the program catches the exception or Java exits. Exceptions can be used to control program behavior at the right level. The next section contains an example of intentionally throwing (and catching) an exception.

Parsing

I have provided examples of output in Java, but not of input. Input appears quite messy in Java at first glance. Actually, applets can easily handle input with the AWT. Applications, however, have a harder time. Like System.out, System.in is predefined, but it processes input at the byte level. The API contains a series of classes, however, that help manage terminal input. When used by experienced programmers, these classes are more powerful than the input mechanisms found in most languages. Here is an example program that reads a series of integers until end-of-file:

```
/* The first four lines set up a reader that will read numbers */
InputStreamReader isr = new InputStreamReader(System.in);
BufferedReader br = new BufferedReader(isr);
StreamTokenizer reader = new StreamTokenizer(br);
reader.parseNumbers();

try {                  // start a block of code, looking for exceptions
  while(true) {
    tok = reader.nextToken();
    if (reader.ttype == StreamTokenizer.TT_EOF)    // if EOF
      throw new Exception("End of File");          // throw exception
    // at this point, reader.nval contains the integer read
  }
}
catch (Exception e) {        // catches exception
```

```
    // do something clever
}
```

Notice several things here. First, the `nextToken()` method scans the input for another number. If it finds one, it puts the number in `reader.nval`, a public member of the `reader` object. In addition, the program checks for end-of-file, throwing an exception if the program finds it. Because the exception occurs inside a `try` block, the corresponding `catch` is first checked. In this case, the `catch` handles all exceptions. A `catch` can be limited to certain exceptions at your control. If the program didn't have a `catch` for this particular exception, the exception would continue to be thrown outward to the method's caller. If that caller didn't have a `catch` for the exception, the exception would continue to be thrown outward to its caller, and so on. Eventually, either the exception would be caught or Java would exit with an error.

Where to learn more

Java has many other interesting features, including

- Threads to facilitate simple concurrent execution

- File input and output

- Networking and Web access

- Graphics primitives for drawing lines, shapes, and so forth

To learn more about Java, you can either jump in and start writing simple programs (especially applets, which are very satisfying), working toward fancier stuff, or read one of several books that are available on the subject. The API is also available online through Sun (`http://www.java.sun.com`). Sun's official Java environment is called the Java Developer Kit (JDK). Several other Java versions are out there, but JDK is very popular and readily available.

Introduction to Perl

Perl, the freely available Practical Extraction and Report Language, is an all-purpose interpreted scripting language (like `awk` and `sed`) designed for text file manipulation and system management tasks. Perl has more flexibility than most languages. Thus, it is well-suited for writing system prototypes, manipulating strings, doing arbitrary precision arithmetic, and performing a host of other unrelated tasks. In the past few years, Perl has become very popular for writing programs to support pages on the World Wide Web. These Perl programs use the Common Gateway Interface (CGI) to communicate through the Web and enable programmers to make "smart" Web pages.

Perl was designed for practicality rather than for simplicity or beauty, which leads critics to claim that a typical Perl script looks more like gibberish than like a readable program.

Perl is very different from traditional programming languages such as C and C++. Perl is an interpreted language, which means that you can run anything you write immediately with the `perl` command. C and C++ are languages that need an intermediate step, compilation, before you can run the resulting program.

Perl runs on almost all platforms that run some form of UNIX and has been ported to a wide variety of other systems, such as MS-DOS, Windows, Macintosh, and VMS. Written (and rewritten and rewritten) by superdeveloper Larry Wall, Perl is useful for writing programs to extract information and generate reports. Perl is both powerful and flexible. Many programmers and system administrators use Perl exclusively instead of mixing `awk`, `sed`, shell programming, and other tools. Perl is also well-suited as a rapid prototyping language for larger projects because it is reasonably fast and has low startup programming costs. (Like `awk` and `sed` programs, Perl programs can be as brief as one line, and many one-line Perl programs are available.) Further, Perl is interpreted and comes with a full debugging environment. Perl has flourished in part because of its extensibility. For example, developers have added extensions to enable Perl to interface easily with most commercial database management systems, including Oracle, Informix, Ingres, and Sybase.

After its initial release, Perl evolved quickly as new features were added and bugs were removed. Eventually, Perl stabilized at Version 4.036 (Version 4, Patch Level 36) and that version was used for several years. Now, a new version, Perl 5, has been released. Perl 5 is a complete rewrite of Perl, with several extensions and some deletions. Almost all scripts written under earlier versions still run under Perl 5. The most notable extension to Perl 5 is the addition of object-oriented capabilities. All the examples in this chapter run under both Version 4 and Version 5.

Note

If you are new to Perl, use Perl 5. In addition to having performance enhancements, object-oriented extensions, and other new features, it is smaller and tighter than Perl 4 and — most important for new programmers — has a `-w` flag that generates warnings about questionable usage.

A first Perl program

Here is a one-line version of the "Hello World!" program, written and executed in Perl:

```
perl -e `print "Hello World!\n";´
```

The real program is inside the single quotation marks; it prints the Hello World! string followed by a return. Invoking Perl with the -e option signifies that the program is given on the command line.

Like awk and shell programs, Perl programs normally are longer than one line and are stored in files called *scripts*. For one-line tasks, however, the command-line format suffices.

Starting with scripts

Perl scripts are much like UNIX shell scripts. You start comments with a number sign (#) and continue to the end of the line. Further, Perl scripts can start with a special comment that indicates where the Perl interpreter is located:

```
#! /usr/bin/perl
```

This comment must be the first line of the file and must begin with a number sign and an exclamation point (#!). The preceding example indicates that it is a Perl script and is to be run using the Perl program found in /usr/bin. This is the most common location for Perl, but if Perl is elsewhere on your system (for example, /usr/local/bin), you'll have to change this line to reflect the correct location. If you have properly specified this line, you can make the file executable (chmod a+rx *filename*) and run the script directly, just like shell scripts. Alternatively, you can invoke Perl from the command line, but that is more cumbersome than using an executable file.

Throughout this chapter, I omit the #! line from my scripts for brevity's sake.

Note

No matter where you install Perl, you are wise to put links to Perl in /usr/bin, /usr/local/bin, and /bin. Doing so requires minimal extra space and increases the portability of scripts written on other systems.

Secret

Getting started with variables

Unlike variables in conventional programming languages such as C and Java, variables in Perl are not explicitly declared. Instead, Perl determines the variable's type by its usage, and variable types can change throughout the program (although permitting this is usually not a good idea). *Scalar variables* hold a single value, such as an integer, float, character, and string, and are always prepended with a dollar sign ($). For example,

```
$x = 1;        # create a new variable called `x` and set it to 1
$y = `A string`;   # Strings can be surrounded by single quotes
$z = "Another";    # or by double quotes
$x = $x + 2.5;    # x is now 3.5
$x = $x + $other;    # since $other is undefined, it is set to 0
   # Therefore, $x remains unchanged
```

Secret

The most common Perl mistake is to forget to put the $ in front of variables. It must always be there!

Strings work the same way in Perl as they do in shell programming. Single quotation marks prevent evaluation of their contents, whereas double quotation marks enable variable expansion:

```
$x = 1;
# perl has many methods for I/O, including print and printf
print `$x + $x = 2´,"\n";    # "\n" adds a newline & carriage return
print `$x + $x = 2\n´;    # This is a mistake
print "$x + $x = 2\n";    # print is the easiest way to do I/O,
though.
```

This code yields the following output:

```
$x + $x = 2
$x + $x = 2\n1 + 1 = 2
```

The output of the second `print` statement has a literal \n instead of a return because the \n is inside single quotation marks.

Tip

To avoid unintentional evaluation, use single quotation marks unless you want explicitly to allow variable substitution in the string.

In addition to scalars, Perl has two other data structures: *arrays* and *associative arrays* (also called *hashes*). Array variables start with an at sign (@) instead of a $, whereas hashes start with a percent sign (%). Elements of an array can be any scalar type. Perl automatically extends arrays as necessary. By default, arrays start at element 0:

```
@cheeses = (`swiss´, `roquefort´, `camembert´, `cheddar´);
print @cheeses;        # print the four cheeses in order, with no
spaces

# prints the second cheese (`camembert´, because arrays start counting
at 0).
print $cheeses[2];    # Note the $, as this is a single element
print $#cheeses;        # prints a 3, the index of the last elements
$cheeses[5] = `jack´;    # adds TWO new elements (#4 is empty, #5 is
`jack´)
```

The output of this sequence is

```
swissroquefortcamembertcheddarcamembert3
```

The output is squeezed together because I didn't print any spaces or newline characters.

Perl includes a list facility, and lists are similar to arrays (see the first line of the previous example).

Associative arrays, or hashes, enable the index of the array elements to be strings instead of integers. This enables the direct association of information with names:

```
$color{strawberry} = "red";    # color is a hash between fruit and colors
$color{plum} = purple;    # individual elements are referenced with $ and {}
$midterm{James} = 100;    # we can associate numbers with names, too.
print %color;             # the entire associative array
```

The output of the last line might be

```
plumpurplestrawberryred
```

I say *might be* because associative arrays have no guaranteed order. Defining the value for strawberry first does not guarantee that it will be saved before the entry for plum. Printing the entire array this way is not terribly useful. More often, you want to step through the array one element at a time, using a while loop:

```
while (($fruit, $shade) = each %color) {
  print "$fruit is colored:  $shade\n";
  }
```

The only guarantee about the ordering of associative arrays is that they will always be in the same order so long as they remain unmodified. As soon as an associative array is changed, though, the entire order may be upset.

Caution

Scalars, arrays, and associative arrays all have separate name spaces. Although the following example is legal, it is a terrible idea because it is unclear:

```
$cheeses[4] = `gouda´;          # assigns to the array
$cheeses = 10;                  # assigns to the scalar
$cheeses{`muenster´} = `German';    # assigns to the hash
```

Input

I have already shown you the print statement for printing output in Perl. Input is achieved through the manipulation of special variables called *file handles*. Like input in most programming languages but unlike input in sed, awk, and most other UNIX utilities, input in Perl must be explicitly controlled. Here is an example:

```
$lineOne = <STDIN>;    # read an entire line of input
print $lineOne;        # and print it out
$lineTwo = <STDIN>;    # read another line of input
print $lineTwo;        # and print it out
```

This program reads two lines of input and prints them out. No \n is needed in the print statements because it is included in the variable from the input. That is, $lineOne and $lineTwo are the entire input line, including the carriage return. Input is read from the standard input (the keyboard, unless there was command-line redirection). The expression <STDIN> is a file handle, and it refers to the place from which input is obtained.

Reading from the standard input is common, unless files are specified on the command line. For example, if I write a script called silly.pl, I would like to invoke it with no arguments and read from the keyboard. If I invoke it with arguments (for example, silly.pl mydata), I want to treat any command-line arguments as files to be read. The special file handle with no name enables me to do this:

```
$inputLine = <>;     # read from  command-line args, if any, else STDIN
{this must be part of preceding line as it is part of comment}
```

Perl is very flexible, providing defaults for almost all unspecified variables. The built-in default variable, $_ (dollar sign–underscore), is used for all operations that need a variable unless the programmer supplies one. Thus, the line

```
<>;
```

reads a line of input into $_. Similarly, the statement

```
print;
```

with no arguments, prints the contents of $_ to the standard output.

As in C, all operations in Perl have well-defined return values. Input returns false upon reaching end-of-file, which plays an important role in the next section.

File I/O

Accessing files for input and output is easy in Perl:

```
# open a file for reading
# if the open fails, print a message and exit
if (open(SCOREFILE,"Scores") != 1) {
  print "can't open Scores file\n";
  exit;
}
$total = 0;
while (<SCOREFILE>) {     # for each line of the file, reads into $_
  s/[aeiou]//g;          #   delete all the vowels in $_
  print;                 #   and print the vowel-less line (no "\n" needed)
}
close(SCOREFILE);    # close after we're done
```

The open() function opens its second argument and assigns the open file to a special variable (the first argument) called a file handle. The preceding example opens a file named Scores for reading and assigns it to the file handle SCOREFILE. Conventionally, file handle names are all uppercase, but that is not required.

To read a line from the file, put the file handle in angle brackets instead of STDIN. After the file use is completed, closing the file handle is good housekeeping, though Perl does this for you if you forget.

To open a file for writing, place a greater-than sign (>) in front of the filename:

```
open(OUTPUT, ">Outputfile");       # opens a file, overwriting it
print OUTPUT "To the file\n";      # prints to the file
print "To the screen\n";           # prints to STDOUT, still the terminal
```

The print command takes an optional file handle at the beginning. If specified, the file handle indicates where the output should be directed. To append to a file, open it with >> instead of >.

Flow control

Like shell languages and C, Perl has a full set of flow control structures, including for, while, and if-then-else. I used the while statement to step through an associative array in a preceding section. Now, let's explore other uses for while:

```
$count = 0;
while(<>) {      # reads from input  into $_ AND executes the loop if
any input was found.
  if (/Mills/) {      # if $_ contains the string "Mills" anywhere in it
    print;       # print the input line -- shorthand for "print $_;"
    $count = $count + 1;     # increment a counter
    }
  }
print "Mills appeared on $count lines.\n";     # need a "\n" on this
line
```

This simple program both prints out all lines containing the string Mills in any form (including, for example, "I went to the Millshop.") and prints a count of how many lines were printed. The while statement both reads in a new line of input and continues executing the loop until it reaches the end-of-file. This is an extremely common programming construct in Perl. The if statement checks the condition (a string match—more on that later) and executes the code in the braces if the condition holds on the current line of input.

Unlike C and Pascal control constructs, Perl control constructs require braces around their statement blocks, even when the block contains only one statement. To do a single task when a condition holds, you must use the unusual format *statement* if *condition*;:

```
print "I love you!\n" if (/chocolate/);  # a one-line if statement
```

Note

Indenting code inside blocks to indicate the extent of the blocks is helpful. Perl doesn't care whether you do this, but you will if you have to reread your code after a month or two.

Perl also has a `for` mechanism that is structured exactly like the mechanism in C:

```
for ($i = 1; $i < 10; $i++) {
  print "$i  squared is ", $i*$i, "\n";
    # put the multiplication outside the quotes


}
```

Although terminating loops prematurely is normally considered unstructured, it is necessary in a language such as Perl, where so much time is dedicated to input handling. In Perl, you do this with `next` and `last`, as illustrated in this example:

```
while (<>) {          # keep reading the input
  next if (/ignore/);
    # skip the rest of the loop if the input contains "ignore"
  last if (/done/);
    # end processing altogether if the input contains "done"
  print;              # prints the input
  ...
}
print;          # prints the line with "done" on it.
```

This prints all the input lines except for those containing `ignore`. As soon as the program finds a line containing `done`, however, the loop exits for good, and execution continues after the loop.

Operators

Perl contains operators that are common in most programming, including +, -, /, *, >, <, and so on. To handle strings, be careful to use `eq`, `ne`, `le`, and so on instead of ==, !=, <=, and the like, which are reserved for arithmetic operations. Here's a clarifying example:

```
if (3 == 3.0)...     # true
if (3 == "3.0")...
    # also true, as the "3.0" is converted to a number
if (3 eq "3.0")...
    # not true, since the string "3" is different from "3.0"
```

Regular expressions, matching, search and replace

Perl is used extensively for pattern recognition, substitution, and deletion. I have already demonstrated string matching in conditionals, but that is just the tip of the iceberg. Perl includes case-insensitive matching and a tremendous regular-expression facility that goes well beyond normal UNIX regular expressions. (For more information on regular expressions, see Chapter 10.)

```
while (<>) {          # read a line of input at a time
  last if (/UCLA/i);     # skip lines with UCLA, ucla, Ucla, uCLa, etc. anywhere
  last if (/^Cluck/);    # skip if line begins with "Cluck"
  last if (/\^Cluck/);    # skip if line contains the string "^Cluck" anywhere
  # skip if the line starts with an `A´ or `a´ and ends with a `z´
  last if (/^[Aa].*z$/);
  last if (/\d+/);       # skip if line has one or more digits on it
  last if (/[0-9]+/);    # skip if line has one or more digits (same as above)
  ...
}
```

Perl's big addition to UNIX regular expressions is the use of \w, \d, and \s to
mean alphanumeric, numeric, and whitespace, respectively. Perl also defines
\W, \D, and \S to mean nonalphanumeric, nonnumeric, and nonwhitespace,
respectively. For pattern matching, these are much more convenient than
their conventional counterparts.

In addition to matching, Perl provides a search and replace operation: s//.
Here's an example:

```
while (<>) {
  s/red/black/;    # change the first occurrence on the line of "red" to "black"
  s/green/blue/g;  # change all occurrences on the line of "green" to "blue"
  s,dbl,double,;   # we can use characters other than the / as separators
print;
}
```

Applying this example to the following input

```
Fred saw the light go red green red green red green...
He spells it "dred"!
```

produces this output:

```
Fblack saw the light go red blue red blue red blue...
He spells it "doubleack"!
```

The effect on the first line is fairly straightforward: the first *red* in *Fred* is
replaced, as are all the *greens*. The second line is odd because the *red* in *dred*
is replaced, but that leaves *dblack,* which is then itself replaced.

By default, the input for the substitution operation comes from the dollar
sign–underscore ($_) variable. To apply both matching and substitution to
other variables, use the equal sign–tilde (=~):

```
$inputLine = <>;             # read in a line of input to the variable
$inputLine =~ s/meek/park/;  # change the first occurrence in the variable
```

You can also use =~ to match variables:

```
if ($inputLine =~ /eric/) {
  ...
}
```

Special variables

One of Perl's strongest selling points — and, to its detractors, one of its greatest dangers — is its incredible flexibility and terse complexity. Much of this flexibility is achieved by setting and checking special built-in variables, such as the default input variable, $_. Perl has several others, including $. (dollar sign–period) as the current line number, $* (dollar sign–asterisk) as the default output format for numbers, and $, (dollar sign–comma) as the default output field separator for print (used in print statements with multiple arguments to print). Perl even enables you to change the default line separator for input with $/ (dollar sign–slash). By using $/, you can make Perl read in multiple lines of input with one operation.

A longer example

Before concluding, I'll show you a longer example that reads in a file of scores from sporting events and calculates the total number of points scored by each team. The program then prints the high-scoring team in lowercase letters with vowels removed. Given the following input file

```
Yahoo State: 10 : Coconut City: 3
Allensville:  7  : Fredburg: 30
Yahoo State: 36  : Fredburg: 15
```

the program produces this output:

```
The high scoring team is yhstt with 46 points
```

I've commented the program to add clarity. The program uses concepts covered throughout this chapter along with a few new themes:

```perl
# open the file for reading
if (open(SCOREFILE,"Scores") != 1) {
  print "Can't open score file";
  exit;
}

while (<SCOREFILE>) {
  s/\t| //g;                # remove tabs and spaces
  s/[aeiou]//g;               # remove vowels
  ($team1, $score1, $team2, $score2) = split(/:/);    # split the
input line using the colons
  # keep a running total for each team in an associative array
  $score{$team1} += $score1;
  $score{$team2} += $score2;
  }

$topscore = 0;              # the best score

# step through the associative array one entry at a time
while (($team, $points) = each %score) {
if ($points > $topscore) {
```

```
# if this team has more than the best-so-far
# make this team be the best-so-far
$topscore = $points;  $topteam = $team;
}
}
print "The high scoring team is $topteam with $topscore points\n";
```

The `split` command breaks the input line into pieces according to a pattern (in this case, a colon). The pieces can be assigned to an array variable or, as in this case, to separate variables.

Perl and CGI programming

Perl is widely used as a back end to pages on the World Wide Web. This means that you can create a Web page with, for example, a form on it. When a user visits the page and submits the form, he automatically invokes your Perl script, which takes action based on the input found in the form. The Common Gateway Interface (CGI) specifies how this communication occurs, but what really matters is that it can occur and that you can use it. The Perl program then prints valid HTML, which is sent back to the user's browser for presentation.

Perl is particularly well-suited for CGI because it is so flexible in handling different kinds of input, searching for and modifying strings, and performing error handling.

Obtaining Perl and useful modules

Perl is freely available — the best place to look for the most recent version is `http://www.perl.org`. This site has many Perl-related links, including directions for the Comprehensive Perl Archive Network (CPAN), which is a huge collection of useful Perl modules, including modules to help with Web access, CGI programming, and a host of other things. Perl is also included on the CD-ROM accompanying this book.

The rest and other resources

Obviously, there is more to Perl than I can present in this forum. The Perl reference card alone is 20 pages long. I have, however, given you a taste of Perl, which certainly is a language that you can learn a bit at a time. (Some would argue that that is the best way to learn anything.)

Perl's features include a full subroutine mechanism to enable code separation and reuse plus a host of library functions that include

- Mathematical functions, such as `sin()` and `sqrt()`
- String functions, such as `length()`, `substr()`, and `index()`

- Array functions, such as `push()`, `pop()`, `shift()`, and `sort()`
- File I/O operations, such as `read()`, `write()`, `open()`, and `close()`
- UNIX file system operations, such as `stat()` and `unlink()`
- UNIX system functions, such as `sleep()` and `exec()`
- UNIX networking functions, such as `bind()` and `connect()`

The primary text resources for Perl are *Programming Perl* by Larry Wall, Tom Christiansen, and Randal Schwartz and *Learning Perl* by Randal Schwartz. The former is a complete reference and has a camel on the cover (it's often called "the camel book"); the other has a llama on the cover (it's called "the llama book"). Experienced Perl programmers swear by the camel book because of its wonderful examples showing how to do almost anything that anyone would ever think of doing in Perl.

Other online resources include a manual page (over 100 pages divided into 49 sections for Version 5), Usenet newsgroups (`comp.lang.perl.misc` and `comp.lang.perl.announce`, among others), and a FAQ (available in `comp.lang.perl.misc` and by FTP from `rtfm.mit.edu`).

Summary

This chapter introduced two more popular programming languages for UNIX systems: Java and Perl. It covered the basics of the following topics:

▶ Reading and understanding Java programs (applets and applications), including the differences between Java and C++ and the features that make Java particularly useful

▶ Reading and understanding Perl programs, including the many tricks and shortcuts Perl uses to make be a fast, interpreted language

The next chapter introduces the software development environment and software integration tools.

Chapter 38

Development Tools

So far, this book has introduced the basics of software design and development and the programming languages C, C++, Java, and Perl. This chapter covers C — probably the most widely used language for software development — in greater detail. This chapter also describes the basic tools used for software development: compilers, program builders, and library archivers.

Compilers

The most important components of the software development environment are *compilers* — complicated programs that take your program (henceforth called *source code*), ascertain that you used the language correctly, and then write, in machine code, a file that you can execute.

For C, the compiler is usually cc. If you have a simple program, such as the "Hello, World" program shown in Listing 38-1, compilation is simple.

Listing 38-1: "Hello, World" Program

```
#include <stdio.h>
main()
{
printf("Hello, World\n");
}
```

If the program is saved in a file called hello.c, the command to compile the program is cc hello.c. It produces an executable file named a.out. To run the program, type **./a.out** at the command line; the program should print the string Hello, World.

The POSIX compiler c89

Even though cc is universally recognized on UNIX machines as the C compiler, it is not defined in the POSIX specification for UNIX. The name for the POSIX compiler is c89, in keeping with the format for other compiler names, such as f77 for Fortran. The digits 89 represent 1989, the year that the ISO C standard was written.

If the C standard changes over time, a new compiler, such as c99, might be created, and two compilers might be used for different stages of the standard. Fortran has had several modifications of standards since the language was introduced.

Secret

The POSIX specification requires only that c89 exist. For backward compatibility with other UNIX makefiles and the like, it makes good sense to link c89 to cc.

How the compiler works

A compiler is a very complicated program. To generate working code, it must understand the input language, and the input language must be perfectly specified. It must also know how to generate machine code for the target machine; the generated machine code must also be perfect. There is no margin for error in compilers. Table 38-1 describes the steps in a compiler's execution flow.

Table 38-1   Compiler Steps

Step	Purpose
Lexical analysis	Breaks the input into appropriate tokens for analysis. These may include variables, keywords, and constants.
Syntactic analysis	Takes the lexical tokens and attempts to discern whether the source code used the programming language correctly. The logical structures of the source code are used to examine program flow.
Intermediate code generation	Generates an intermediate form of code. This is usually executable generation code with external references unresolved.
Optimization	Optimizes the intermediate code.
Code generation	Resolves external references or generates errors. This final, unresolved executable code is the program.

Note

The definitive book on compiler design is *Principles of Compiler Design* by Alfred Aho and Jeffrey Ullman. Among compiler experts, it is called "the dragon book" because a dragon appears on the cover.

One of the goals of compiler writers is to write a better, faster compiler. This is offset by the goal of improving the efficiency of the resulting code.

Tradeoffs are unavoidable. A fast compiler usually generates suboptimal (and therefore slower) code. A highly optimizing compiler may produce fast code but takes forever to compile the program.

The most common approach to writing faster compilations involves minimizing the number of passes over the source or intermediate code. Each step listed in Table 38-1 requires some means of transmitting information to the next step; these intermediate steps generate forms of code, and each intermediate form must be reread. Each rereading is considered to be a *pass* over the code. If you can combine the steps listed in Table 38-1 into a single pass, you have a faster compiler. You usually do this by reading in the source code until you have enough characters to identify a lexical token, reading enough tokens until you have a syntactic expression, and reading enough expressions to generate the intermediate code. When this happens, the code generator essentially drives the syntactic analyzer, which in turn drives the lexical analyzer, which controls input.

C is well suited for this optimization. As each statement is parsed, intermediate code can be generated. This makes the C compiler a one-pass compiler at heart. A second optimizing pass can be added.

Note

Lexical and syntactic analysis are also called *parsing*.

The declaration block at the head of a control block in C makes one-pass parsing the right way to parse. All the variables are defined at the top of a subroutine. This enables the C compiler quickly to generate a symbol table for the block of source code; therefore, internal references can be quickly resolved. Other languages, such as PL/I, enable you to declare variables after you use them. To generate code properly from such languages, the compiler must make two passes at the source: the first to build an accurate symbol table and the second to build the intermediate code.

Note

For some languages, the work stops at the intermediate-code stage. These languages are semi-interpreted: the compiler builds an optimized set of instructions that another program then interprets and runs. S-Algol, developed at the University of St. Andrews, is one such language. This approach has advantages and disadvantages. Interpreted languages are more portable than compiled languages. Instead of needing to rebuild the compiler and recompile all the programs on a new platform, you need to rebuild only the interpreter. Similarly, because compilation is cut short at the intermediate form, building new programs is faster, so the development cycle can be speeded up. Against these advantages is a serious tradeoff in terms of execution speed for the final product. Interpreted languages are always slower than compiled languages.

Lexical analysis

Lexical analysis is the first stage in translating your source code. A lexical analyzer reads in characters and forms tokens for use by syntax analyzers. Each token is a single, logical entity. Tokens can be constants, variables, functions, keywords, operators, and punctuation. Consider the following C statement:

```
for (i=0; i<10; i++ ) printf ("%d\n",i );
```

This simple statement prints all the integers from 0 through 9. The statement has several tokens, which are described in Table 38-2.

Table 38-2   Lexical Tokens for a Simple Statement

Token	Type	Meaning
for	Keyword	Identifies a `for` loop.
(	Punctuation	Signals the beginning of the grouping.
i	Variable	Identifies a location in memory; must be defined before being used (in this case, i is an integer variable).
=	Operator	Assigns the right-hand expression to the left-hand memory location.
0	Constant	Is the constant expression 0.
;	Punctuation	Signals the end of the first expression in the `for` loop.
i	Variable	Identifies the same location in memory specified by the previous i token.
<	Operator	Is a comparison operator (less than).
10	Constant	Is the constant expression 10.
;	Punctuation	Signals the end of the second expression.
i	Variable	Again, identifies the same memory location specified by the first two i tokens.
++	Operator	Is the increment operator.
)	Punctuation	Ends the grouping specifying the `for` loop.
printf	Function	Identifies a call to the `printf` function. It must be defined before it is used. (It is defined in the `stdio.h` header file.)
(	Punctuation	Signals the beginning of the argument group.
"%d\n"	Constant	Is the constant string with a formatting character (\n).
,	Punctuation	Separates an argument.
i	Variable	Identifies the memory location.
)	Punctuation	Signals the end of the argument list.
;	Punctuation	Signals the end of the statement.

This simple statement generates 20 separate lexical tokens. When you next write a program, consider how many tokens you write; the compiler needs to understand all of them.

Usually, the lexical analyzer has a fairly easy job, even if it is worked hard. It usually obtains a list of keywords that it can identify and pass back to any parser. Included in that set of keywords are the operators and punctuation. Beyond that, the lexical analyzer needs only to pass back unrecognized strings; they can become numbers, variables, or constants.

Note

Chapter 41 examines the lex program, which generates lexical analyzers.

Syntactic analysis

The syntactic analyzer requests tokens from the lexical analyzer and attempts to build them into statements. At this stage, a grammar for the language needs to be known, and this drives syntactic analysis.

Grammars

The usual means of defining a grammar in computer science is the Backus-Naur form (BNF). BNF grammars provide an easy-to-read, concise definition of how a programming language (or any language) should be laid out. From a correct BNF grammar, you can easily write a syntactic analyzer. Thus, the real task of writing a parser is writing a BNF grammar for a language.

Each line in a BNF grammar has one object on its left side and a listing of subobjects or tokens to the right of that object. Eventually, the tokens form a master, and that master is the starting point for analysis.

Note

In the following descriptions, brackets indicate optional components, and braces indicate components that can occur zero or more times.

Listing 38-2 shows a segment of the BNF description of the C grammar.

Listing 38-2: The First Five Specifications in the C Grammar

```
translation-unit: external-declaration | translation-unit
external-declaration
external-declaration: function-definition | declaration
function-definition: [ declaration-specifiers ] declarator
    [ declaration-list ] compound-statement
declaration: declaration-specifiers [ init-declarator-list ] ;
declaration-list: declaration | declaration-list declaration
```

Note

The complete BNF for C appears in *The C Programming Language* by Brian Kernighan and Dennis Ritchie. This book is the bible for C programmers.

There are 72 rules for parsing C code. Continuing with the example in the preceding section, I now parse the following statement:

```
for (i=0; i<10; i++ ) printf ("%d\n",i );
```

In this case, I am looking for a statement. The rule is as follows:

```
statement: labeled-statement | expression-statement | compound-statement |
    selection-statement | iteration-statement | jump-statement
```

This rule is an iteration-statement: The statement can be broken into for (
followed by an optional expression, a semicolon, an optional expression, a
semicolon, an optional expression, a closing parenthesis, and a statement.
The first expression becomes an assignment-expression, which is a unary-
expression followed by an assignment-operator and another assignment-
expression.

Note

This rule shows why a construct such as a=b=1 is valid in C. The unary-
expression becomes a postfix-expression, then a primary-expression, and
then an identifier. The assignment-operator is an equal sign. The second
assignment-expression breaks down to another postfix-expression, and then
another primary-expression breaks down to a constant. The remainder of
parsing this apparently simple statement is a bit more complicated in the C
grammar. If you want to follow the construct in more detail, I suggest that you
pick up *The C Programming Language* and learn the grammar there.

Parsing techniques

Simply put, there are two parsing techniques. One is *shift-reduce parsing,*
better described as *bottom-up parsing*. In this case, the parser reads the input,
breaks it into tokens, and attempts to build the tree from the leaves. Applying
this technique to the statement in the preceding section, the parser finds the
for and starts to build an iteration-statement. Similarly, it builds the
expressions included from the ground up.

Shift-reduce parsing is implemented with a stack. Tokens are pushed onto the
stack, and when the top of the stack matches only a single rule, it is reduced
to that intermediate phase. Most C compilers use the shift-reduce technique.

The other technique is *top-down parsing*. In this case, you know that you are
building a program, so you look at the top rule. That rule tells you what you
need to make a program, so you start to look for the next rule.

This approach to parsing involves the risk of recursion and may not work on
all grammars. You can use certain tricks to modify the grammar so that it
does not infinitely apply the same rule.

Beyond simple shift-reduction are the concepts of LR parsing and LALR
parsing. In LR parsing, the compiler reads left to right on the grammar. Any
context-free grammar can be understood with an LR parser, and it finds
syntax errors faster than any other parsing technique. An LALR parser
includes some look-ahead, which helps the parser reduce components of the
grammar by giving it a sense of what is next.

Intermediate code generation

As the source code is parsed, an intermediate form of the executable file can be generated. When enough code is understood to make a statement or even a part of a statement, the compiler can write out some intermediate code.

Examining the preceding `for` statement, you see that the three internal expressions are a start condition, a continuation condition, and a per-iteration increment condition. Thus, as you parse the `for` statement, you know that the compiler can first produce the code for the start condition. Listing 38-3 shows this intermediate code, which is commented to indicate what it's doing.

Note

The example shown in Listing 38-3 assumes that the intermediate code is a pseudoassembly code. Usually, it is machine code, but the assembly code described in this section has the same function and is easier to read.

Listing 38-3: Assembly Code at the Start of the for Loop

```
define memloci,4        #Defines a 4-byte memory location for i
    Load   reg1,0        #Places the constant 0 in register 1
    Save   reg1,memloci  #Saves the value in register 1 to i
L1:                      #Label for branches
    Load   reg1,memloci  #Places the value of i in register 1
    Load   reg2,10       #Places the constant 10 in register 2
    Cmp    reg1,reg2     #Compares the registers
    BLT    L2            #If reg1 is less than reg2, branches to L2
    B      L3            #Branches to L3
L2:
```

Secret

The code in Listing 38-3 is not as efficient as it could be, but that is corrected at the compiler optimization stage.

Caution

Listing 38-3 is not assembly code for any specific processor.

As the statement is parsed, the increment section is saved to be appended after the statement is parsed. When the statement is parsed, it is recognized as a subroutine call. This means that variables must be pushed on the stack, and a call must be made to an external location, as shown in Listing 38-4.

Listing 38-4: More Assembly Code

```
L2:
    push   memloc2      #Assumes that "%d\n" is in memloc2
    push   memloci      #The second argument
    resext "printf"     #Resolves an external address
    call   extadd       #Calls printf
```

Here, it becomes a bit trickier. You don't know exactly where `printf` is located, because it is an external reference, so it is tagged with `resext` and `extadd`. When the compiler puts the entire program together in the last stage, these external addresses are resolved, or else an error is generated.

Notice that the example does not list an explicit location for the constant string. Compiler implementations may differ, but in most cases, these internal constants are grouped in a symbol table, and memory allocation is kept there.

After the compiler parses the entire statement, it adds the increment statement. Listing 38-5 shows the all the intermediate code generated for the for statement.

Listing 38-5: Final Assembly Code for the for Loop

```
define memloci,4        #Defines a 4-byte memory location for i
    Load   reg1,0        #Places the constant 0 in register 1
    Save   reg1,memloci  #Saves the value in register 1 to i
L1:                      #Label for branches
    Load   reg1,memloci  #Places the value of i in register 1
    Load   reg2,10       #Places the constant 10 in register 2
    Cmp    reg1,reg2     #Compares the registers
    BLT    L2            #If reg1 is less than reg2, branches to L2
    B      L3            #Branches to L3
L2:
    push   memloc2       #Assumes that "%d\n" is in memloc2
    push   memloci       #The second argument
    resext "printf"      #Resolves an external address
    call   extadd        #Calls printf
    Load   reg1,memloci  #Loads the value of i into the register
    Add    reg1,1        #Adds one to the value in register 1
    Save   reg1,memloci  #Saves the value to i
    B      L1            #Resumes the loop
L3:                      #Loop exits location
```

The last five lines increment i by 1 and return to the top of the loop.

Optimization

You can take a couple of reasonable approaches to code optimization. One approach is to optimize the source code as you parse it. This involves several techniques, such as eliminating unexecuted code and unraveling loops. Another approach is to optimize the resulting machine code.

Source-code optimization

You can use several techniques to optimize the source code. Often, you don't want to write the source code with these optimizations because they make the code more difficult to read and maintain. Therefore, the ideal situation is for the compiler to perform these optimizations for you. The source code is maintainable and cleanly structured, but the compiled source code is rearranged for efficiency.

The first technique is to replace function calls with function code. This technique is called *inlining functions*. One of the most expensive machine-code calls is to call a function. If the page of the program with the code is not in memory, you need to page it into memory before continuing execution.

Copying the commands of the function into the source code at the calling spot is faster and easier. Consider the following case:

```
struct *d;
void swap(void *a, void *b, unsigned int c);
{
memcpy(d,a,c);
memcpy(a,b,c);
memcpy(b,d,c);
}
...
for(...) {
    ...
    swap(var1,var2,sizeof(struct));
    }
```

You are calling the swap function each time you step through the loop — tens of times or tens of thousands of times. Each time, you push three variables on the stack, jump to a new code location, and return. Building the actual swap code straight into the for loop makes more sense.

```
for(...) {
    ...
    memcpy(d,var1,sizeof(struct));
    memcpy(var1,var2,sizeof(struct));
    memcpy(var2,d,sizeof(struct));
    }
```

For maintenance, this is not as obvious; but for execution, this is faster.

Another technique is to eliminate code that is never reached. Consider this case:

```
switch(c)
    {
case 1: ...
case 2: ...
default: ... break;
case 3:
    }
```

The code for the last case never executes. A smart compiler recognizes this fact and does not generate code for the last case.

Other cases of unreachable code are more complicated. You may have an if statement that has an else clause, both with long statement blocks that invariably reach a return or exit. In such cases, all the code from the end of the if statement to the end of the statement block or function is never reached. Recognizing every case takes some intelligence on the part of the compiler writer.

Another technique for optimizing source is to unroll loops. You can unroll both deterministic and indeterministic loops. The former can be entirely replaced, and the latter can form larger loops with fewer conditional executions. Consider the case of this `while` loop:

```
i=0;
while(i<10)
    a[i]=i++;
```

Although this is clean and easy to maintain, the looping code is inefficient. If a compiler were to rewrite this as follows, the code would be more efficient:

```
a[0]=0;
a[1]=1;
a[2]=2;
a[3]=3;
a[4]=4;
a[5]=5;
a[6]=6;
a[7]=7;
a[8]=8;
a[9]=9;
```

Note

One of the best commercial source code optimizers is the KAP preprocessor for C, sold by Kuck & Associates.

Generated-code optimization

In this type of optimization, knowledge of the machine code is essential. In many cases, the machine code is generated on a statement-by-statement basis and can result in many extraneous statements. In Listing 38-5, the generated code contains 19 lines, many of which are unnecessary. Consider these lines:

```
    Save  reg1,memloci  #Saves the value in register 1 to i
L1:                     #Label for branches
    Load  reg1,memloci  #Places the value of i in register 1
```

In this example, the compiler saved the value in register 1 to memory and then pulled out the same value. The second load can be eliminated. In addition, because the push of `memloci` is in a register, it can be replaced by a push of the register value.

Farther down Listing 38-5, you find another load of `memloci` before the `add`. That, too, can be eliminated.

Furthermore, by watching the flow of code, you see that you don't need to load 10 into register 2 on every loop iteration, so you can move that instruction before the label.

Finally, in Listing 38-6, you see that saving to `memloci` is not necessary until after the loop is finished, so you can move one save and eliminate the other.

Listing 38-6: Optimized Assembly Code

```
    define memloci,4   #Defines a 4-byte memory location for i
    Load  reg1,0       #Places the constant 0 in register 1
```

```
      Load   reg2,10       #Places the constant 10 in register 2
L1:                        #Label for branches
      Cmp    reg1,reg2     #Compares the registers
      BLT    L2            #If reg1 is less than reg2, branches to L2
      Save   reg1,memloci  #Saves the value in register 1 to i
      B      L3            #Branches to L3
L2:
      push   memloc2       #Assumes that "%d\n" is in memloc2
      push   reg1          #The second argument
      resext "printf"      #Resolves an external address
      call   extadd        #Calls printf
      Add    reg1,1        #Adds one to the value in register 1
      B      L1            #Resumes the loop
L3:                        #Loop exits location
```

As you can see, this example eliminates three lines of code from the assembly and tightens the loop for execution. Table 38-3 shows how often each assembly command would otherwise have been executed.

Table 38-3   Savings from Optimization

Command	Operations before Optimization	Operations after Optimization
define	1	1
load	33	2
save	11	1
cmp	11	11
blt	10	10
push	20	20
call	10	10
add	10	10
b	11	11

Optimizing greatly reduced the number of calls between memory and registers.

Secret

If this generated-code optimization were combined with source-code optimization to unravel the loop, the resulting executable would have only twenty push commands, ten call commands, one define command, and one save command.

Code generation

The last step in compiling a program is to generate the final code. This step is primarily a pass over the machine code to resolve any external references.

External references are pointers to variables defined outside the current block of code. These can be variables but more often are functions declared in libraries or other modules. For this reason, when an intermediate code file is generated, it includes its symbol table so that any public references it contains can be resolved.

Note

To facilitate debugging, you can retain these symbol tables in the executable as well.

When this pass is made, the compiler should have all the symbols listed in a master symbol table. If that table is not available, it must be built. It scans the machine code for tags indicating unresolved symbols and replaces those tags with symbol addresses.

In the preceding for loop, the resext and call commands are replaced by a single call command, as follows:

```
call   0x0034ab
```

0x0034ab is the address in memory for the printf function. (Your printf address may differ.)

If the symbol cannot be resolved, an error message is produced.

More compiler science

Compiler science is still undergoing research. New tricks for optimizing source and final code, as well as for speeding parsing, are always being discovered.

One debatable issue in compiler science is error recovery. When the parser finds an error in the source code, what should it do? Obviously, it needs to report an error message, but after that, what?

This discussion has two camps. Some people think that as soon as an error message is generated, the compiler should just quit. The source code needs to be corrected and needs to be clean before compilation can proceed. Other people believe that a heuristic should be applied, enabling the compiler to report the error, assume some correctional approach, and continue the compilation.

Most C compilers take the latter approach. Sometimes, I find this approach useful; but often, I just fix the first error and recompile. The problem with applying heuristics is that they can easily generate spurious error messages later.

For example, this often occurs when the compiler finds an undeclared variable. Usually, the compiler assumes the variable is declared to be an integer. If this assumption is wrong, you get more errors farther down the code, and these errors are meaningless. In this case, fixing one variable declaration results in the elimination of numerous syntax errors.

When programs were compiled on large time-shared machines in batch mode, attempting to correct code made sense. Currently, applying the right heuristics is not a bad idea, but wrong heuristics can create confusion.

Structure of an a.out file

The canonical executable file is called an *a.out file*. This file is the default output of the compiler and is in a format that is suitable for execution.

The a.out file format varies from platform to platform, but some commonality exists. All a.out files require a header to define the file, the program text, the data for the program, the relocation information, a symbol table, and a string table. The header is usually the first item so that it can be quickly accessed.

The header basically describes the file. You usually can find the specific structure in /usr/include/a.out.h. The header fields specify the sizes of the a.out file components. The header also includes the address of the entry point into the file. This entry point is the first line of executable code in the file. Another feature of the header is a magic number, which must be set correctly for the operating system to recognize the file as an executable.

The text section is the actual executable machine code, and the data segment is the data used by the program. The relocation sections are listings of locations where externally defined symbols are accessed. The relocation table is used to attach shared libraries to running programs and to resolve the references the table contains. The symbol table relates addresses in the data segment to strings in the string table. It also tracks all the variable names and functions used in the executable file. The string table is a listing of all the strings used in the program.

Several commands enable you to look at a.out files. The two most common are file and size. The size command returns the size of the different segments in the executable. If I request the size of /usr/bin/vi on my Linux machine at home, my output is

```
text  data  bss   dec     hex
98304 8192  39032 145528  23878
```

This output tells me that vi has 98,304 bytes of instructions, 8,192 bytes of data, and 39,032 bytes of symbols and strings (dec is a decimal sum, and hex is a hexadecimal sum).

Modular programming

One of the most efficient approaches to programming is modular. Almost every UNIX product is modular to one extent or another. Even modern kernels are dynamically extensible.

When you write a modular program, you are distributing the tasks of the program among several files. To compile such a program, the compiler must build several objects and then link all the objects into a single executable file. Essentially, the compilation of an object stops at the optimization phase, leaving the external symbols unresolved. After all the objects are made, the compiler can then link them and resolve external symbols.

When I modularize a program, I try to separate each function or subroutine into a single file, one per file. This makes many small source files, so I am forced to use the make utility to put these objects together.

One of the big advantages of modular programming is that if you make a small change, all you need to do to rebuild the program is build that source file into an object and then relink. Compiling large source files is time-consuming. Although the link stage also takes time, it is faster than a full recompile.

Note

Pure Software sells an incremental linker that greatly increases the speed of the relink.

Another advantage of the modular approach is that it makes building libraries easier. *Libraries* are shared pieces of code that are used in different executable files. If you take a modular approach, when someone else needs a piece of code to perform a task that you've already answered, you can share that object. If you share enough objects, you should build your own library.

Story: Spaghetti with Modules

Modular programming can also increase the efficiency of other programs. When I was working at Bell Labs, one of my first assignments was to make a certain program work. The original programmer had spent six months working on the program, and it was one large spaghetti-coded module. Rather than using normal C control structures, the programmer had liberally laced the code with goto statements with very little modularity.

I went back to my boss and told him that the task was impossible because the code was unacceptably poor and that we were better off rewriting the code from scratch. My project leader told me that we had only three weeks to turn in the product, and he didn't see how the program could be written from scratch in three weeks. I finally managed to persuade him to give me the opportunity, but I was aware that if I couldn't complete the rewrite, I would be the one who'd be in trouble.

I took the original specs and broke the job into pieces. One week later, I had a working modular prototype; two weeks later, the program was complete. (I'd like to say that I took a week off, but alas, there was other work to do.)

Perhaps more impressively, that program (composed of 11 source files) became the prototype for all the other screen programs that interfaced with that product's database. Simply by redesigning the screen and the schema, we could crank out a new program in two days.

Secret

The real secret to fast programming is theft. (Well, OK, perhaps *theft* is too strong a word, but it makes the point.) Whenever you can reuse a piece of code, do so. Reuse reduces development time because you are not reinventing the wheel, and it should reduce test time because the code should already be tested.

c89 arguments

As previously mentioned, the standard compiler for POSIX systems is c89. Table 38-4 lists several options that c89 requires to comply with the specification.

Table 38-4   c89 Options

Option	Argument	Purpose
-c		Suppresses link editing and retains the resulting object files.
-g		Produces symbolic information in the object and executable files for debugging.
-o	*filename*	Produces output to the specified file.
-s		Strips the object or executable file of the symbol table.
-D	*name* [= *value*]	Defines the symbol name for the preprocessor and assigns a value if one is specified.
-E		Expands the source to standard output, replacing all preprocessor directives, such as macros and header files.
-I	*directory*	Examines the specified directory for header files.
-L	*directory*	Examines the specified directory for libraries.
-O		Optimizes the compilation.
-U	*name*	Removes the specified name from its initial definition.
-l	*library name*	Compiles with the specified library. The library name is built by prepending lib to the name and appending either .a or .so.

In the command line, you also can specify files that have the .c prefix (for C source code), the .o prefix (for object files), and the .a prefix (for libraries). You can specify multiple source and object files.

The order of the -L and -l options is important; otherwise, option order is not a concern.

Old cc arguments

Before c89 was specified, C compilers were used, and they usually included many more options than those specified in the preceding section. Table 38-5 lists the options for the SunOS C compiler that are not listed in Table 38-4.

Note

Subsequent options for cpp, inline, as, and ld are based on the SunOS compiler. For information on options for your platform, check your manual pages.

Table 38-5   Compiler Options in SunOS

Option	Argument	Purpose
-a		Inserts code to count how frequently blocks are executed. The tcov utility produces output.
-align	_block	Forces the specified data block to be page-aligned.
-B	binding	Specifies whether library bindings are static or dynamic.
-C		Tells the C preprocessor to retain comments.
-dalign		Generates double load/store instructions.
-dryrun		Lists the commands to be run by the compilation driver.
-fsingle		Uses single-precision arithmetic in floating-point calculations.
-go		Produces additional symbol-table information for adb.
-help		Displays a help message for cc.
-J		Generates 32-bit offsets in switch-statement labels.
-M		Runs only the macro preprocessor.
-misalign		Generates code to enable loading of misaligned data.
-O1		Does postpass assembly optimization only.
-O2		Does global optimization before code generation.
-O3		Optimizes uses of external variables.
-O4		Traces effects of pointer assignments.
-p		Prepares code to collect data for profiling.

Option	Argument	Purpose
-P		Runs source code through cpp and saves it to a file with the .i suffix.
-pg		Prepares code for profiling with gprof.
-pic		Produces position-independent code.
-pipe		Uses pipes, as opposed to intermediate files, between cpp and ccom.
-Qoption	*program option*	Passes the specified option to the specified program. The program must be cpp, as, inline, or ld.
-Qpath	*directory*	Inserts the specified directory into the compilation search path; this option enables the use of alternative cpp commands.
-Qproduce	*sourcetype*	Produces the specified source type: .c, .i, .o, or .s (assembly).
-R		Merges the data and text segments for as.
-S		Produces an assembly source file.
-sb		Produces an extra symbol table for the Sun Source Code Browser.
-target	*architecture*	Compiles objects for the specified processor.
-temp	*=directory*	Uses the specified directory for temporary files.
-time		Reports execution times for the various passes.
-w		Suppresses warning messages.

Other compilers, such as GNU's C compiler, have their own options. Your best bet is to examine the manual page on your system for a complete list of options.

Story: An Ace in the Hole

The -S option once won me a bet. I bet a coworker that I could write a complicated program in assembly code in a day. I wrote the program in C and then used the -S flag to produce assembly-language output. The program ran properly the first time and truly baffled my colleague. After I collected the lunch, I told him about the -S option.

Most C compilers actually are several programs; the cc command just drives those programs. The four common programs are cpp (the C preprocessor), inline (...), as (the assembler), and ld (the link editor).

C preprocessor

The C preprocessor takes processor directives and modifies the source code for the C compiler. Table 38-6 lists the standard preprocessor directives.

Table 38-6   Preprocessor Directives

Directive	Argument	Purpose
#define name	token-string	Replaces name with the specified token-string when seen in the source code.
#define name	token-(arg,arg...) string	Replaces instances of the name with arguments with the token-(arg, arg...) string after replacing the arguments in the token string.
#undef	name	Removes all instances of the specified name's definition.
#include	"filename"	Reads the contents of the specified file and includes them at this location. Looks in the current directory.
#include	<filename>	Reads the contents of the specified file and includes them at this location. Looks only in the standard places.
#line	integer "filename"	Generates line-control information for the next stage of the compilation.
#if	expression	Includes the subsequent code up to a matching #else, #elif, or #endif only if the specified expression is true.
#ifdef	name	Includes the subsequent code as per #if only if the specified name is defined.
#ifndef	name	Includes the subsequent code as per #if only if the specified name is not defined.
#elif	expression	Includes the subsequent code if the specified expression is true and the preceding expressions are false.
#else		Includes the subsequent code if the preceding expression is false.
#endif		Ends the sense of the current #if, #ifdef, or #ifndef.

One of the most powerful directives is #define with arguments. This directive enables you to create your own inline functions. Listing 38-7 shows how this directive can be used.

Listing 38-7: A Macro for SWAP

```
#define SWAP(X,Y,Z)    {char *tmp \
    tmp=malloc(Z) \
    memcpy(tmp,X,Z); \
    memcpy(X,Y,Z); \
    memcpy(Y,tmp,Z); \
    free(tmp); }
```

Admittedly, this macro does not check for errors from the malloc. In code, however, you can include SWAP(var1,var2,sizeof(var1)) whenever you want to swap the specified values.

The C preprocessor builds a new version of the C source code that can be properly compiled. The different directives are used to include different files or to include code conditionally. The conditions are best used for portability by specifying one architecture as #ifdef.

The C preprocessor program is cpp; Table 38-7 lists the options.

Table 38-7   C Preprocessor Options

Option	Argument	Purpose
-B		Supports the C++ comment operator //. This option works even with C code.
-C		Passes all comments through the preprocessor.
-H		Prints the path names of included files, one per line, on standard errors.
-M		Generates a list of makefile dependencies on standard output.
-p		Uses only the first eight characters to differentiate among symbols. This option is included for backward compatibility. Produces a warning.
-P		Does not produce line-control information.
-R		Enables use of recursive macros.
-T		Uses only the first eight characters to differentiate among symbols. This option is included for backward compatibility. Does not produce a warning.
-undef		Removes all defined names.
-D	name	Defines the specified name.
-D	name-value	Sets the specified name to a value.

Continued

Table 38-7 *(continued)*

Option	Argument	Purpose
-I	*directory*	Searches the specified directory for include files.
-U	*name*	Removes the definition for the specified name.
-Y	*directory*	Uses the specified directory instead of the standard places for the include file.

Note

You can use the -E flag with c89 or -cc to interrupt the compilation at this stage. You can also use -P on some compilers to save the output of the preprocessor to a file.

Secret

You can also use the C preprocessor to create template letters, replacing the names as needed, as follows:

```
Dear SIR,
I am inquiring about business opportunities at YOURFIRM.
```

To produce your letter, run cpp -DSIR='Mr. Smith' -DYOURFIRM='UNIX Writers' on this file.

Compiler

Some older systems included a separate compiler called ccom. Because this program is built into the c89 or cc executable files, it is not as common.

The illustrated part of the ccom program performs the actual lexical analysis, parsing, and generation of code.

Secret

As you can see, when many executable files perform different tasks in compilation, passing certain bookkeeping information between executables is necessary. This is the origin of passing symbol-table information.

Secret

In some older versions of UNIX that supported a ccom process, the cc compiler was just a shell script that managed the executable files.

Building the assembly code

On some systems, a program called inline takes the components of assembly code and puts them together in a single assembly-language program. The program also takes some .inline directives and replaces them with code from a specified file. Table 38-8 lists the options.

Table 38-8   inline Options

Option	Argument	Purpose
-w		Displays warning for duplicate definitions
-v		Displays the names of the processed routines (verbose)

Option	Argument	Purpose
-o	*filename*	Writes to the specified file
-i	*filename*	Reads the inline code templates from the specified file

On some compilers, you can stop at this stage by specifying the -S option to cc.

Assembler

The assembler, as, takes assembly-language code and builds it into an object file for use by the link editor. The compiler and inline processor produce assembly code. The assembler takes this assembly code and produces machine code. Table 38-9 lists the options for the assembler.

Table 38-9   as Options

Option	Argument	Purpose
-L		Saves the defined labels that begin with *L*. These are usually produced by the compiler and are discarded to save space in the symbol table.
-R		Makes the initial data segment read-only.
-o	*filename*	Produces the specified object file. The default filename is a.out.

You can interrupt the compilation at this stage to produce object files with the -c option on cc or c89.

Link editor

The last compilation program is the link editor, which takes the objects generated by the assembler and combines them into programs. The link editor is often invoked separately. When you are building large programs, you usually build several objects and then use the link editor to combine them into an executable file.

You can also use the link editor to create shared libraries, which are discussed at length later in this chapter.

Table 38-10 describes the options for ld, the link editor program.

Table 38-10	Id Options	
Option	*Argument*	*Purpose*
-align	*datum*	Forces the specified datum to be page-aligned.
-assert	*keyword*	Verifies that the specified assertion is true; aborts if not true.
-A	*filename*	Performs the link in a manner that enables the object to be read by an executing program. The specified file contains a symbol table for these additional symbols.
-B	*binding*	Specifies the times for the binding of objects. Static is immediate, dynamic is at execution time, and nosymbolic tells the loader to perform no symbolic relocation.
-d		Forces the allocation of storage for uninitialized variables.
-dc		Copies initialized data from shared objects.
-dp		Forces alias definition for undefined procedure entry points.
-D	*hex*	Pads the data segment to make it the specified length (in bytes).
-e	*entry*	Defines the entry point.
-l	*library name*	Includes the specified library.
-L	*directory*	Searches the specified directory for any libraries.
-M		Produces a load map with the names of the files to be loaded.
-n		Makes the text portion of the executable read-only.
-N		Does not make the text portion read-only.
-o	*filename*	Writes the output to the specified file.
-p		Arranges for the data segment to begin on a page boundary.
-r		Generates relocation bits so that the output can be run through ld a second time.
-s		Removes the symbol table from the output.
-S		Removes all symbols except local and global symbols.
-t		Traces the execution of ld.
-Tdata	*hex*	Starts the data segment at the specified location.
-Ttext	*hex*	Starts the text segment at the specified location.
-u	*name*	Enters the name as an undefined symbol.

Option	Argument	Purpose
-x		Preserves only global symbols in the symbol table.
-X		Records local symbols.
-y	symbol	Displays each file in which the symbol appears.
-x		Makes the process a demand-pageable process.

Make and Makefiles

When you have broken source code into many separate files, the next task is to build those files into a single program. The make utility is the best one for building programs.

Make options

Make normally requires a makefile, but if no makefile is present, make attempts to build an executable file from standard rules. For example, if you have a file called hello.c and you type **make hello**, make executes cc -o hello hello.c. If a makefile is present, make looks in the makefile for a rule to build hello.

If no rule is present, make fails at this stage.

Caution

Makefiles have two standard names: makefile and Makefile. Either name is acceptable.

Note

Table 38-11 lists the make options. The table lists the POSIX arguments for make; your make may have more.

Table 38-11   make Options

Option	Argument	Purpose
-f	filename	Uses the specified file as the makefile
-e		Causes environment variables to override macro definitions in the makefile
-i		Ignores error codes in the invoked commands
-k		Updates targets that do not depend on the current target even if the current target gets an error
-n		Writes the commands that would be executed to standard output, but does not execute them

Continued

Table 38-11 *(continued)*

Option	Argument	Purpose
-p		Writes the complete set of macro definitions and target descriptions
-q		Returns zero if the target is up-to-date, without updating the target
-r		Clears the suffix list and does not use built-in rules
-S		Terminates make if any commands updating the target generate an error
-s		Does not write command lines before executing
-t		Updates the modification times for each target

If no target is specified, the first listed target in the makefile is built. Conventionally, this target is the all target, which builds all the specified executable files.

Make rules

Makefiles are a series of rules and macros that define how targets are built. The basic rule syntax is

```
target { target }: [ dependencies ] [ ; command ]
{<tab>command }
```

The target needs to start in the first column. Each subsequent command must be indented with a tab.

The most common reason makefiles fail is that they lack a tab.

Tip

I've never seen the semicolon construct in a rule.

Note

A typical rule might be as follows:

```
program: program.o
    cc -o program program.o -lmylib
```

This rule tells make that before it builds program, program.o must exist. If a rule to build program.o exists, make builds program.o accordingly; otherwise, it looks for the default rules to build a program.o. When program.o exists, make can execute the cc line to build program.

Commands can have three prefixes. A command with a minus sign (-) prefix and any errors generated by this command are ignored. A command with a plus sign (+) prefix is always executed even when the -n, -q, or -t option is specified. The at sign (@) prefix tells make not to echo the command to standard output when it is executed.

The other construct is a macro. Macros are replacements, and they have the following syntax:

```
string1 = string2
```

When $(string1) or ${string1} appears, it is replaced by the contents of string2. This works very much like shell variables.

Default macros

Table 38-12 lists several typical predefined macros.

Table 38-12	Default Macros
Macro Name	**Replacement String**
AR	ar
ARFLAGS	-rv
CC	c89
CFLAGS	-O
FC	fort77
FFLAGS	-O 1
LEX	lex
LFLAGS	
MAKE	make
YACC	yacc
YFLAGS	

You can override these macros by redefining them in your makefile, by setting environment variables of the same name, or by running make -e.

There are also five internal macros, listed in Table 38-13, whose value depends on the specific rule in question.

Table 38-13   Internal Macros

Macro	Meaning
$*	The target name, with the suffix deleted
$@	The target of the given rule; evaluated in both target and inference rules
$<	The filename that enabled the inference rule to be chosen for the target
$%	The object file member of a library
$?	The list of prerequisites that are newer than the target

The inference rules enable easier writing of rules. For example,

```
target: obj1.o obj2.o ...
    ar -rv $@ $?
```

This rule adds only the objects newer than the target to the archive.

Using these macros can help make the makefile easier to port to a system that has a different configuration.

Default make rules

Make comes with a set of default rules. Before learning the default rules, you should understand the .SUFFIXES special target. This target is a listing of suffixes that are used with these default rules. The order of the suffixes indicates the order in which the default rules are checked. New suffixes are appended to the variable. If no suffixes are specified, the .SUFFIXES list is cleared, so the only way to reorder suffixes is to clear the list and then append to the null list.

The default rules are called *inferences* because their execution is inferred by make instead of being explicitly specified in a makefile. Inferences take the form of single-suffix rules or double-suffix rules. *Single-suffix rules* are used to build a suffixless target from a file that has the specified suffix. *Double-suffix rules* build a file with the second suffix from a file of the same name that has the first suffix. Table 38-14 lists the three single-suffix rules.

Looking at the inference for .c, you should be able to see why no makefile is necessary to build program from program.c; the inference tells make to execute $(CC) $(CFLAGS) $(LDFLAGS) -o program program.c. The .f rule applies to Fortran, and .sh enables you to archive the source to shell scripts.

Table 38-14   Single-Suffix Rules

Target	Commands
.c	$(CC) $(CFLAGS) $(LDFLAGS) -o $@ $<
.f	$(FC) $(FFLAGS) $(LDFLAGS) -o $@ $<
.sh	cp $< $@ ; chmod a+x $@

The double-suffix rules are more numerous, performing quite a few default actions without your needing to include them in a makefile. (See Table 38-15.)

Table 38-15   Double-Suffix Rules

Target	Commands
.c.a	$(CC) $(CFLAGS) -c $< ; $(AR) $(ARFLAGS) $@ $*.o ; rm -f $*.o
.c.o	$(CC) $(CFLAGS) -c $<
.f.a	$(FC) $(FFLAGS) -c $< ; $(AR) $(ARFLAGS) $@ $*.o ; rm -f $*.o
.f.o	$(FC) $(FFLAGS) -c $<
.l.c	$(LEX) $(LFLAGS) $< ; mv lex.yy.c $@
.l.o	$(LEX) $(LFLAGS) $< ; $(CC) $(CFLAGS) -c lex.yy.c ; rm -f lex.yy.c ; mv lex.yy.o $@
.y.c	$(YACC) $(YFLAGS) $< ; mv y.tab.c $@
.y.o	$(YACC) $(YFLAGS) $< ; $(CC) $(CFLAGS) -c y.tab.c ; rm -f y.tab.c ; mv y.tab.c $@

You can replace any of these inferences with your own rules, and you can expand your inferences. Here is an expanded inference:

```
.SUFFIXES: .man
.man:
    nroff -man $< | col -b > $@
```

This inference shows how a clear-text version of a manual page can be generated with a makefile.

Special targets

Table 38-16 lists several special targets other than .SUFFIXES.

Table 38-16	Special Targets
Target	*Purpose*
.DEFAULT	This target cannot have prerequisites — only commands. If no other targets are built in the command line, these commands are executed.
.IGNORE	This target specifies a list of targets for which errors are ignored. If no prerequisites are given, the entire makefile is treated as though -i were the command-line option.
.POSIX	If used in the first line, this target forces make to conform with POSIX definitions.
.PRECIOUS	Prerequisites of this target are not removed if make receives a signal.
.SILENT	Prerequisites of this target have their commands silenced (they are not written to standard output).

Makefiles

Makefile writers use some fairly standard tricks to increase the power of their makefiles. I always include three special targets: clean, clobber, and tags. Here are the definitions of these targets:

```
clean:
    rm -f *.o
clobber: clean
    rm -f $(TARGETS)
tags:
    ctags $(SOURCES)
```

I use the clean and clobber targets to remove intermediate files and the target file. Usually, make rules can govern when these are re-created, but at times, dates on files can get out of sync. The last target, tags, creates a tags file for use with the vi editor. If I specify a procedure name in the command line, vi comes up with the cursor at the start of that procedure.

I also define three macros by default. The TARGETS macro is a list of all the objects I want to make in the makefile. Usually, my first rule is

```
all: $(TARGETS)
```

The SOURCES macro is a listing of all the source files. The OBJECTS macro is a listing of all the objects. If I build more than one target in a makefile, I can build these two macros from smaller macros.

Secret

Remember that make can do much more than just compile programs. Make is capable of taking rules to perform any number of tasks. As you become experienced with make, you may come up with your own conventions for what you expect to see in a makefile.

Libraries

Libraries are means by which multiple object files can be combined in a single file for retrieval in programs. Similarly, these archives can be shared among programs, as needed.

Two basic types of libraries exist: static and dynamic. *Static libraries* have their object files linked in with the executable file, and all relocation values are resolved at link time. *Dynamic libraries* are not linked in by the link editor. Instead, the external symbols are noted in the relocation table, and when the program is run, the symbols are resolved dynamically. You usually need an LD_LIBRARIES_PATH variable set so that the dynamic libraries can be found.

Static libraries

Static libraries are easy to make and maintain. When you have a series of object files that you want to share among applications, you can build an archive with the ar command. Table 38-17 lists the options for ar.

Table 38-17   ar Options

Option	Purpose
-C	Prevents extracted files from overwriting like-named files.
-T	Enables filenames to be truncated on file systems that do not allow long names.
-a	Positions new files in the archive after the specified file.
-b	Positions new files in the archive before the specified file.
-c	Suppresses the diagnostic message written when an archive is created.
-d	Deletes one or more of the specified files from the archive.
-i	Positions new files in the archive before the specified file.
-l	Places temporary files in the current working directory.
-m	Moves the named files within the archive.
-p	Writes the contents of the specified files from the archive to standard output. If no files are specified, this option writes the contents of all the files.

Continued

Option	Purpose
-q	Quickly appends files to the archive.
-r	Replaces or adds the specified files to the archive.
-s	Forces the regeneration of the symbol table.
-t	Writes a table of contents for the archive.
-u	Replaces files only if the new file is more recent than the archived file.
-v	Produces verbose output.
-x	Extracts the named files from the archive.

Table 38-17 *(continued)*

These arguments are followed by the archive name and then the filenames.

For -a, -b, and -i, the first argument is the file internal to the archive for relative positioning.

When the link editor encounters an archive, it attempts to find the objects in the archive that can resolve external references. These objects are then extracted from the archive and loaded into the final executable file. This produces larger executable files but does not risk failure caused by not finding the appropriate shared library.

Shared libraries

Shared libraries have the advantage of enabling program executable files to be smaller. A shared library has its text segments loaded into memory when needed, but only one copy is loaded for all executable files. When the text is required, the program accesses that page.

Shared libraries are usually created from the ld command. The techniques for building shared libraries vary from platform to platform. On Solaris 2, you just specify the -G flag, and a shared object is created with all the objects in the command line. It is customary to include the suffix .so (to signal that it is a shared object) or .sa (to signal that it is a shared archive).

Executables that use shared libraries tend to be smaller and faster than those that don't, but if the shared library cannot be resolved at runtime, the executable crashes. You must make certain that the LD_LIBRARY_PATH variable includes the directory where the shared library is located.

Summary

This chapter introduced the basics of converting C source code to running programs on UNIX platforms. It covered the following topics:

▶ What a compiler is

▶ The phases through which source code passes to make an executable file

▶ How to use four programs invoked from the compiler to perform specific tasks

▶ How to use different preprocessor directives

▶ The basic structure of an a.out file

▶ Why modular programming is a good idea

▶ How to use make

▶ How to build libraries

The next chapter examines how to debug and clean code.

Chapter 39

You Expect Me to Understand That?

In This Chapter

▶ Code debuggers

▶ Tools for proofreading code

▶ Tools for maintaining code

This chapter introduces techniques for debugging code and techniques for maintaining code.

Debugging Code

All software developers spend most of their time debugging their own code. As a developer, you may write code to a certain specification, and the code may work on your test data, but untested conditions usually exist, and those conditions can result in program failure. Those program failures are called *bugs*.

In an ideal situation, you are presented with a set of input data and can reproduce the problem. The ability to reproduce the error is vital to debugging. A bug that you cannot reproduce is difficult, if not impossible, to remove. (The situation also begs a question: If a bug cannot be reproduced, is it really a bug?)

One of the most common techniques for debugging is inserting statements to produce output and checking to see whether the values of the variables are accurate. Even though this approach is very low-tech, the brute-force method can still provide valuable information.

Secret

Many UNIX applications still use this approach. Look at the -x option for UUCP or the -v option for sendmail.

Note

The brute-force method of debugging is frequently used in development as well. As you write code, you can easily include the debugging statements for output.

After the brute-force method come the more subtle techniques of using debuggers. Debuggers are other programs that create a run-time environment for your program and that interact with the running program to provide you more information about the program's execution.

Debuggers work best with core files, which usually are large files that are left when a program fails catastrophically. Essentially, core files are just a dump of the system's image of the executing program at the moment of failure. Most debuggers allow you to read in a new core file at startup. The programs have commands that enable you to examine this file.

Tip

You can create a core file by sending the QUIT signal to a running process. Use kill -QUIT <pid>. (Be aware that some programs trap this signal and don't dump a core.)

Debuggers also allow you to start running a program in the debugger environment.

The basics of debuggers

The role of the debugger is simple: to provide an environment in which someone can observe the run-time data associated with a program and (ideally) provide some interaction with the program as it runs. Because the nature of machine-execution environments is different, POSIX does not require the inclusion of a debugger — even in the DEVELOPMENT utilities — to conform with standards.

Note

I hope that the lack of a debugger changes.

Note

Because the standards are not present, the two debuggers discussed in this section are found on SunOS. Although Sun has superseded this release with Solaris 2, most developers are familiar with adb and dbx. A third common debugger, gdb, is provided by GNU and is discussed in Chapter 44.

When you first bring up your debugger on a core file, you need to determine where the failure occurred. You learn this through a *stack trace,* which should provide the name of the routine in which the bug exists and a listing of procedures that called that routine. The stack trace isolates the failure location. Ideally, the debugger should pinpoint the line of code where the failure occurred, but that is not always possible.

Secret

This is a strong argument for modular programming. If your debugger provides only the name of the routine that is in error, and if you have many smaller, simple routines, isolating the cause of failure is much easier than it would be if you had a few monolithic routines.

The next feature that a debugger must have is the capability to examine memory locations. The program's variables are kept in memory and must be available to assess the cause of failure.

If the debugger is designed to be interactive, it must provide features that run the program, interrupt execution, and interactively execute single instructions. If the debugger has the capability to modify data in memory, so much the better.

The first debugger: adb

The first — and usually most ubiquitous — debugger for UNIX systems is adb. The adb debugger (the name comes from *a deb*ugger) is a powerful, though esoteric, tool. Most software developers prefer to use symbolic debuggers, such as dbx (described later in this chapter), gdb (described in Chapter 44), and sdb.

The adb tool is very difficult to use, and for many reasons, most debugging is done in other debuggers. If you are going to be supporting a product, however, or you don't have a symbol table present, you're going to need to know at least some adb.

Note

The adb tool also is useful for kernel debugging. You can make an image file writable, and the image can be /dev/kmem. In this way, you can change kernel parameters on the fly. But be careful, because you are more likely to cause a system crash.

You start adb by listing the executable and a core file (if it exists). The adb debugger does not require a symbol table, so it works fine on optimized executables. You do not get a prompt with adb, so the common procedure is to just get a stack trace. The command is $C. Here is a program that generates a segmentation fault:

```
#include <stdio.h>
#include <fcntl.h>
#include <errno.h>
int openbuffer(filename)
char *filename;
{
int fd;
if ((fd=open(filename,O_RDONLY))<0)
    {
    fprintf(stderr,"Cannot open %s, errno=<%d>\n",filename,errno);
    exit(-1);
    }
return(fd);
}
int readbuffer(fd,buffer,size)
int fd;
char *buffer;
int size;
{
int retc;
```

```
if ((retc=read(fd,buffer,size))!=size)
    if (retc<0)
        {
        fprintf(stderr,"Cannot read, errno=%d\n",errno);
        exit(-2);
        }
    else if (retc)
        fprintf(stderr,"Partial read\n");
return(retc);
}
int countchar(buffer)
char *buffer;
{
int cnt;
char *p;
p=buffer;
while(*p)
    {
    if ((*p)==`\n´) cnt++;
    p++;
    }
return(cnt);
}
main()
{
int fd;
int cnt=0;
char inbuf[1024];
fd=openbuffer("/usr/lib/libc.a");
while (readbuffer(fd,inbuf,1024)) cnt+=countchar(inbuf);
printf("Bizarre character count=%d\n",cnt);
}
```

This program is, admittedly, nonsense. The program opens the C library and
reads it in one block at a time. Then the program wants to count the new
lines that appear in each block before a null character. With adb, you get the
following:

```
core file = core-program ``badprog´´
SIGSEGV 11: segmentation violation
$C
_countchar(0xeffffa90,0xeffffa90,0x400,0x344,0x3,0x0) + 2c
_main(0x1,0xeffffefc,0xeffffff04,0x4000,0x0,0x0) + 48
```

Because the program has no symbol table, adb provides six parameters for
each function on the stack. You can see that the dump occurred in
countchar, at an address 2c into the file. By examining the countchar
routine, you see that you are making a bad comparison.

This is still difficult to track with adb, because without some understanding
of the machine hardware, you can't easily translate registers and addresses
to program variables.

The adb commands take the following form:

```
[ address ] [ , count ] command [ ; ]
```

Each command is a verb, followed by a modifier. The initial address is zero; the period character can be used to represent the current location. The default count is one. Tables 39-1, 39-2, and 39-3 list the verbs and some modifiers.

Table 39-1   adb Verbs

Verb	Result
?	Prints locations from the address in the executable file
/	Prints locations in the core file from the specified address
=	Prints the address itself
@	Interprets the address as a source address
:	Manages a subprocess
$	Prints process data
>	Assigns a value to a variable or register
Return	Repeats the preceding command
!	Shell escape

The adb tool also allows you to run a program interactively, using the : verb. Although you can glean results by using adb this way, I strongly urge you to use a symbolic debugger, if possible, to get information this way.

A symbolic debugger: dbx

Probably the most common symbolic debugger on UNIX systems is dbx, which was written at Berkeley for BSD UNIX.

To get the most out of a symbolic debugger, you need to compile a program with the -g flag; this way, information is retained in the executable file to associate program symbols with addresses. Table 39-4 lists the command-line options for dbx.

Table 39-2   Modifiers for Printing Verbs ?, /, @, and =

Modifier	Result
o	Prints 2 bytes octal
O	Prints 4 bytes octal

Continued

Table 39-2 *(continued)*

Modifier	Result
q	Prints 2 bytes signed octal
Q	Prints 4 bytes signed octal
d	Prints 2 bytes decimal
D	Prints 4 bytes decimal
x	Prints 2 bytes hexadecimal
X	Prints 4 bytes hexadecimal
u	Prints 2 bytes as unsigned decimal
U	Prints 4 bytes as unsigned decimal
f	Prints a single-precision floating-point number
F	Prints a double-precision floating-point number
b	Prints the address byte in octal
c	Prints the addressed character
s	Prints the addressed string
i	Prints the machine instruction

Table 39-3 Modifiers for the $ Verb

Modifier	Action
\<filename\>	Reads commands from the file
?	Prints the process ID
r	Prints the CPU registers
x	Prints the first 15 floating-point registers
X	Prints the next 16 floating-point registers
c	Prints a stack backtrace
e	Prints the names and values of external variables
o	Treats all integers input as octal
q	Quits adb
v	Prints all nonzero variables as octal
m	Prints the address map

Table 39-4   dbx Startup Options

Option	Argument	Meaning
-f	*integer*	Alters the initial estimate of the number of functions to be debugged. The default is 500.
-i		Forces dbx to consider standard input to be a terminal.
-I	*directory*	Adds the directory to the list of directories to search for source files.
-k		For kernel debugging.
-kdb		Special keyboard debugging.
-P	*integer*	Creates a pipeline to the dbxtool process.
-r		Runs the command immediately upon setting up dbx.
-s	*filename*	Executes the commands from the startup file.
-sr	*filename*	Executes the commands from the startup file and then removes the file.

Note

To determine whether you have dbx on your system, type **whereis dbx**. If that procedure fails, you may not have dbx; check with your system administrator.

Tip

The debugger sdb, used in System V, is similar to dbx. Check the manual page for the specific command names.

Looking at the example for adb, after compiling with -g and running, you again see a core dump. This time, you start dbx and first look at a trace of the stack with the where command, as follows:

```
$ dbx badprog
Reading symbolic information...
Read 151 symbols
program terminated by signal SEGV (no mapping at the fault address) (dbx) where
countchar(buffer = 0xeffffa90 "!<arch>\n__.SYMDEF      779501081   0  1
 100644 23764  `\n"), line 45 in "badprog.c"
main(), line 58 in "badprog.c"
```

This tells you that the error is in line 45 of the program. Load the file, and examine the lines around line 45.

```
(dbx) file badprog.c
(dbx) list 40,50
 40  char *p;
 41
 42  p=buffer;
```

```
43  while(p)
44      {
45      if ((*p)=='\n') cnt++;
46      p++;
47      }
48  return(cnt);
49  }
50
```

Line 45 accesses two variables. Check their values, as follows:

```
(dbx) print cnt
`badprog`countchar`cnt = 1034
(dbx) print p
p = 0xf0000000 "warning: core file read error: data space address too
high
<bad address>"
```

Clearly, something has gone wrong with the variable p. Because it starts as buffer, look at that:

```
(dbx) print buffer
`badprog`countchar`buffer = 0xeffffa90 "!<arch>\n__.SYMDEF    779501081
0
1    100644 23764   `\n"
```

Variable p has advanced far beyond what you desired, so you need to change the terminating condition. Because you wanted newlines until a null is reached, that means checking against null, and while(p) does not check the value of the pointer. So make the change and rerun the program.

```
$ cc -g -o badprog badprog.c
$ badprog
Partial read
Bizarre character count=662832
```

The program is debugged.

The preceding code contains an additional bug that was not triggered. Can you find it?

Interactive dbx

An advantage of using an interactive debugger is being able to use it on a running program. Often, the core dump is inadequate for illustrating problems in the code. You need to run the program and interact with the program, and dbx provides a decent environment for that purpose.

When working interactively, you need to know the commands that set breakpoints, continue execution, and step through lines of code. (A *breakpoint* is a location in the code where execution can be frozen.) This gives you the opportunity to interact with the program. You can examine the data at a given time and determine whether it is accurate. You can examine the stack to see whether the calling sequence is what you would expect.

You can also single-step through commands. By stepping through commands one at a time, you can confirm that the program variables change as you expect them to.

Also, you can set breakpoints on areas in memory. This way, execution is frozen when a variable's value changes. Using this trick is handy when you are examining memory overwrites.

dbx commands

The dbx tool has many commands. Table 39-5 lists those commands and their arguments.

Table 39-5   dbx Commands

Command	Argument	Use
^C		Interrupts execution; does not terminate the program.
run	args I/O redirection	Runs the command with the listed arguments and I/O redirection. If no arguments are specified, runs with the arguments used in the last run.
rerun	args I/O redirection	Same as run, except does not use argument history.
cont	at sourceline	Continues execution, optionally at the provided line of source. This allows you to skip or repeat instructions, if desired.
cont	signal	Continues execution as though the specified signal were received.
trace	See Table 39-6	Displays tracing information as specified in Table 39-6.
stop	at sourceline	Freezes execution before the line of source is executed.
stop	in function	Freezes execution when the function is called.
stop	variable	Freezes execution when the variable changes.
stop	if condition	Freezes execution, should the condition become true. (You can append conditions to any stop statement.)
when	condition { dbx commands }	When the condition is true, executes the dbx commands. The condition is the same as a stop-line number, function, or condition.

Continued

Table 39-5 *(continued)*

Command	Argument	Use
status		Displays all open breakpoints, traces, and when commands.
delete	*command* or *all*	Deletes the breakpoint, trace, or when command, or all stopping points.
clear	*sourceline*	Clears all stopping points associated with the specified source line or current stopping point.
catch	*signal*	Displays all signals that are currently being caught, or catches the specified signal.
ignore	*signal*	Displays a list of signals that are being ignored, or adds the specified signal to the list.
step	*integer*	Executes the next source lines, including lines inside functions. The default is one.
next	*integer*	Executes the next source lines, but does not step into functions. The default is one.
print	*expression*	Prints the value of the specified expression. This can be a variable or an evaluation of an expression.
display	*expression*	Prints a list of expressions that are currently being displayed, or adds an expression to the list of expressions to be displayed when execution stops.
undisplay	*expression*	Removes the specified expression from the list.
whatis	*identifier*	Prints the declaration for the identifier.
which	*identifier*	Prints the fully qualified name for the identifier.
whereis	*identifier*	Prints the fully qualified name for all symbols that match the identifier.
assign	*variable= expression*	Assigns the expression value to the variable.
set	*variable= expression*	Assigns the expression value to the variable.
call	*function (parameters)*	Calls the specified function.
where	*integer*	Lists the stack trace, up to the specified number of functions. The default is all.

Command	Argument	Use
dump		Displays the names and values of all the variables and parameters in the current scope.
up	*count*	Moves the stack trace up the specified number of levels.
down	*count*	Moves the stack trace down the specified number of levels.
edit	*file* or *function*	Edits the specified file or function.
file	*file*	Prints the name of the current source file, or changes the current source file to the specified file.
func	*function* or *program*	Changes the current function or object.
list	*start, end*	Lists the specified lines of the current file or 10 lines from the current line.
list	*function*	Lists the function header, as well as the five lines that surround it.
use	*directory list*	Prints or sets the list of directories to be used in the source search path.
cd	*directory*	Changes the current working directory.
pwd		Prints the current working directory.
/RE		Searches the file for the regular expression.
sh	*command*	Executes the specified command in the shell.
alias	*new-name command*	Creates an alias for a command.
]		Displays a list of signals that are being ignored, or adds the spec.
help		Accesses the dbx help system.
make		Invokes make with the name of the program.
setenv	*name string*	Sets an environment variable.
source	*file*	Runs the commands from the file.
quit		Exits dbx.
debug	*program* or *pid*	Attaches the debugger to the process.
kill		Terminates the execution of the process.
detach		Allows the process to continue without the debugger.

Table 39-6 Trace Options	
Option	*Result*
None	Displays each source line before execution
in function	Displays source only when in the named function
if condition	Displays source only if the condition is true
sourceline	Displays the line of source before execution
function	Displays the routine and source line from which the function is called, the parameters passed, and the return value
expression at sourceline	Displays the value of the expression whenever the specified source line is reached
variable	Displays the name and value of the variable whenever the variable changes

As you can see, dbx has many commands; mastering it is not an overnight task.

The dbx initialization file

You can list some commands in an initialization file, .dbxinit. These commands are executed every time you start dbx. Usually, these commands are alias commands. Here is my .dbxinit file:

```
alias a alias
a r run
a c cont
a s step
a st status
a b stop in
```

As you can see, I used the init file to shorten commands to single letters.

The art of debugging

Debugging is more of an art than a science, in my experience. Although some algorithms can make debugging simpler, I've found that debugging is more a matter of seeing the code for what it is, imagining what the code is trying to do, and determining what it actually does. Often, the hardest problems to debug actually involve rather small changes, which are easy to overlook.

Debugging also may be a matter of being a decent coder. You may look at an algorithm and see a flaw in the algorithm; this flaw might have been discovered later as a bug.

The two tricks that work the best for me, beyond using a debugger, are using a second set of eyes and the `print` statement. Sometimes, someone else can look at a program and see something that you missed, such as a double or single equal sign. As when editing a book, after a while you are reading what you thought you wrote, not what is on the paper. Also, `print` statements can be more valuable than a debugger's trace command, simply because you can easily save that output to a file.

When I use a debugger, the first thing that I do is go straight to the location where core was dumped. I determine whether a variable was misused or the data was not what I expected. I then try to find where the data may change and determine whether I made mistakes elsewhere. I may try to pare the job down to a routine or segment of code. Eventually, what I'm looking for is a line or lines of code where I made a mistake in assigning a value, or failing to assign a value, to a variable. Inevitably, that error is what a bug is.

Source coverage

Another interesting command is `tcov`, a source-code coverage routine. When a program is compiled with `-a`, as it executes, a data file is created that monitors how often lines of source are executed. This can help you determine how thoroughly you tested your code.

Caution

Because `tcov` is not a POSIX routine, it may not be available on your system; check with your system administrator.

There are two options. The `-a` option lists every line of code. (By default, `tcov` lists only the first lines of code in each continuous block.) The `-n` option lists the lines of code in order of execution.

What follows is the output of `tcov` after a successful run of the test program:

```
#####  -> #include <stdio.h>
#####  -> #include <fcntl.h>
#####  -> #include <errno.h>
#####  ->
#####  -> int openbuffer(filename)
#####  -> char *filename;
    1 -> {
    1 -> int fd;
    1 ->
    1 -> if ((fd=open(filename,O_RDONLY))<0)
    1 ->    {
#####  ->    fprintf(stderr,"Cannot open %s,
errno=<%d>\n",filename,errno);
#####  ->    exit(-1);
#####  ->    }
    1 -> return(fd);
    1 -> }
    1 ->
    1 -> int readbuffer(fd,buffer,size)
```

```
   1 -> int fd;
   1 -> char *buffer;
   1 -> int size;
 649 -> {
 649 -> int retc;
 649 ->
 649 -> if ((retc=read(fd,buffer,size))!=size)
   2 ->    if (retc<0)
   2 ->        {
##### ->        fprintf(stderr,"Cannot read, errno=%d\n",errno);
##### ->        exit(-2);
##### ->        }
   2 ->    else if (retc)
   1 ->        fprintf(stderr,"Partial read\n");
 649 -> return(retc);
 649 -> }
 649 ->
 649 -> int countchar(buffer)
 649 -> char *buffer;
 648 -> {
 648 -> int cnt;
 648 -> char *p;
 648 ->
 648 -> p=buffer;
 648 -> while(*p)
 648 ->    {
5950 ->    if ((*p)=='\n') cnt++;
5950 ->    p++;
5950 ->    }
 648 -> return(cnt);
 648 -> }
 648 ->
 648 -> main()
   1 -> {
   1 -> int fd;
   1 -> int cnt=0;
   1 -> char inbuf[1024];
   1 ->
   1 -> fd=openbuffer("/usr/lib/libc.a");
   1 -> while (readbuffer(fd,inbuf,1024)) cnt+=countchar(inbuf);
   1 -> printf("Bizarre character count=%d\n",cnt);
   1 -> }
          Top 10 Blocks
          Line    Count
           45     5950
           46     5950
           22      649
           33      649
           38      648
           48      648
           26        2
           31        2
            7        1
```

```
     15      1
  15  Basic blocks in this file
  13  Basic blocks executed
86.67  Percent of the file executed
14503  Total basic block executions
966.87  Average executions per basic block
```

Cleaning Code

When you are maintaining code, sometimes cleaning the code is more important than understanding it. People's coding styles are different, and those styles may obfuscate the actions of the code.

The cb beautifier

The cb command beautifies code; cb examines code and attempts to group the sections of code logically, to produce easy-to-read output. Table 39-7 lists the command's options.

Table 39-7   cb Options

Option	Argument	Result
-j		Joins commands that span a line
-s		Uses standard style
-l	integer	Splits lines that are longer than the specified length

I usually don't use cb, because my style is different. Here is the output of cb on the test program:

```
#include <stdio.h>
#include <fcntl.h>
#include <errno.h>
int openbuffer(filename)
char *filename;
{
    int fd;
    if ((fd=open(filename,O_RDONLY))<0)
    {
        fprintf(stderr,"Cannot open %s,
errno=<%d>\n",filename,errno);
        exit(-1);
    }
    return(fd);
}
```

```
int readbuffer(fd,buffer,size)
int fd;
char *buffer;
int size;
{
    int retc;
    if ((retc=read(fd,buffer,size))!=size)
        if (retc<0)
        {
            fprintf(stderr,"Cannot read, errno=%d\n",errno);
            exit(-2);
        }
        else if (retc)
            fprintf(stderr,"Partial read\n");
    return(retc);
}
int countchar(buffer)
char *buffer;
{
    int cnt;
    char *p;
    p=buffer;
    while(*p)
    {
        if ((*p)=='\n') cnt++;
        p++;
    }
    return(cnt);
}
main()
{
    int fd;
    int cnt=0;
    char inbuf[1024];
    fd=openbuffer("/usr/lib/libc.a");
    while (readbuffer(fd,inbuf,1024)) cnt+=countchar(inbuf);
    printf("Bizarre character count=%d\n",cnt);
}
```

Notice that the indentation and the placement of brackets are slightly different.

Portability checks with lint

The lint command is used to check for portability problems. Table 39-8 outlines lint's arguments (beyond the normal C preprocessor arguments).

Table 39-8   lint Arguments

Option	Effect
-a	Reports assignment of long values to nonlong variables
-b	Reports break statements that are not reached
-c	Notices nonportable casts
-h	Applies bug heuristics
-i	Produces .ln files for each source file
-n	Does not check compatibility against the standard library
-u	Does not complain about undefined external functions and variables
-v	Suppresses complaints about unused function arguments
-x	Reports external variables that are unused
-z	Does not complain about undefined structures

As compilers have become better at producing portability warnings, the usefulness of lint has decreased. Here is the lint output on the bad program:

```
badprog.c(45): warning: cnt may be used before set
badprog.c(60): warning: main() returns random value to invocation
environment
exit value declared inconsistently    llib-lc(236) :: badprog.c(29)
fprintf returns value which is always ignored
printf returns value which is always ignored
errno used( badprog.c(28) ), but not defined
```

In this output, the only item that is important is the first. You need to initialize cnt; otherwise, the count may be inaccurate.

Maintaining Code

One of the hardest — and most thankless — jobs in the software-development cycle is program maintenance. Invariably, a program is passed from the original developers to a maintenance team, whose task is to understand the code and be able to fix any problems that may occur in the field. Because the members of the maintenance team usually are not the people who wrote the program, the task is doubly difficult because to debug a program, they must understand some of the logic that was used to create the program.

Some tools are available to help the program maintainer. The ctags program creates a vi tags file that allows the maintainer to use vi to access routines directly. The cxref program examines the source files and provides a cross-reference for every variable accessed. Last, the nm program examines symbol tables and reports their contents on standard output.

A tags file for finding routines

The simplest of the commands is ctags. You just run ctags against a list of source files, and it produces a reference used by the -t option to ex and vi. Then when you enter the editor, you can specify a function name, and the editor opens to that function. The ctags command has several options, which are listed in Table 39-9.

Table 39-9	ctags Options
Option	**Result**
-a	Appends the tags to the existing tags file
-B	Uses backward search patterns
-F	Uses forward search patterns
-t	Creates tags for typedefs
-u	Updates the references in the tags file
-v	Produces, in standard output, an index that lists function name, filename, and page number
-w	Suppresses warnings
-x	Produces a readable index in standard output

The ctags program creates a sorted list of functions, followed by a filename and a search pattern that enables you to find the first line of the function. The following lines show a tags file:

```
Mbadprog     badprog.c    /^main()$/
countchar    badprog.c    /^int countchar(buffer)$/
openbuffer   badprog.c    /^int openbuffer(filename)$/
readbuffer   badprog.c    /^int readbuffer(fd,buffer,size)$/
```

Notice that the main function is replaced by M<filename>.

Variable cross-references

After you determine that a variable's value has gone awry, the cxref command is useful for finding all the references to that variable in your source code. The command has five options. The -c option prints a combined cross-reference for all input files; -o with a filename sends the output to the specified file; -w # specifies the width of the output; -s tells cxref to operate silently; and -t specifies the use of 80 columns.

The `cxref` command produces a great deal of output because all the symbols are cross-referenced, including those in header files that remain unused in your source. Here is a section of the `xref` file to the previous program:

```
badprog.c:
SYMBOL     FILE           FUNCTION  LINE
cnt        badprog.c          countchar  *39 45 48
           badprog.c      main     *54 58 59
countchar()
           badprog.c          --       *36
           badprog.c      main      58
errno      /usr/ucbinclude/errno.h --      *11
           badprog.c      openbuffer  12
           badprog.c      readbuffer  28
exit       badprog.c          openbuffer  13
           badprog.c      readbuffer  29
fd         badprog.c          --       18
           badprog.c      main     *53 57 58
           badprog.c      openbuffer *8 10 15
           badprog.c      readbuffer *19 25
```

The actual full output file is 456 lines long. Lines marked with an asterisk are those in which the symbol is declared.

Examining external symbol tables

The `nm` command is useful for examining external symbol tables. The `nm` command is particularly useful for determining where library functions are located, and for examining object files and determining what external references need to be resolved. The command takes several options, which are listed in Table 39-10.

Table 39-10	nm Options
Option	**Result**
-a	Prints all symbols
-g	Prints only global symbols
-n	Sorts numerically
-o	Prepends file or archive element to symbol name
-p	Prints in symbol-table order
-r	Sorts in reverse order
-u	Prints only undefined symbols

Here is an example:

```
    U _ _IO_stderr_
00000000 t _ _ _gnu_compiled_c
    U _ _ _main
00000140 T _countchar
    U _errno
    U _exit
    U _fprintf
000001b0 T _main
    U _open
00000020 T _openbuffer
    U _printf
    U _read
000000b0 T _readbuffer
00000000 t gcc2_compiled.
```

The addresses of the resolved symbols appear in the first column. The second column is symbol type, as explained in Table 39-11. The last column is the symbol label.

Table 39-11   Symbol Types

Flag	Meaning
A	Absolute address
B	Bss segment symbol
C	Common symbol
D	Data segment symbol
f	Filename
t	Static function symbol
T	Text segment symbol
U	Undefined symbol
-	Debugging symbol

Based on the nm output, to build an executable from this object, you need to resolve several external symbols.

The nm command is more interesting for extracting data from libraries. You can find the printf symbol in libc, and by grepping the output of nm -o /lib/libc.a, you get the following:

```
/usr/lib/libc.a(printf.o):00000000 I _printf
```

The printf routine is tucked into the object file printf.o in libc.a. If you so desire, you can use ar to extract a copy of the object and even disassemble it.

Commercial Products

For something as important as debugging code, you can consider several commercial products, the best of which probably is Pure Software's Purify. This product checks for memory misuse — one of the hardest problems to debug. Unfortunately, Purify is not available for every platform. To see whether your platform is supported, send e-mail to `info@pure.com`.

Two other good products are Insight and Sentinel. These products also check for memory misuse and are more widely available than Purify is.

Summary

This chapter introduced debugging tools. You should understand the following:

- How to use `adb`
- How to use `dbx`
- How to beautify code
- How to remove lint from code
- How to produce a tags file to locate functions
- How to build a variable cross-reference
- How to debug a symbol-less file
- How to examine symbol tables

In the next chapter, you learn performance-optimization techniques.

Chapter 40

You've Made It, Now Make It Fast

In This Chapter

▶ Understanding basic performance improvement techniques

▶ Understanding how to use performance measurement commands

After you've removed as many bugs as you can find from a program, management will usually complain next that the program takes too long to run. Never mind that it seems blindingly fast on your workstation, when the boss tries running it on a vintage 1986 386 workstation with 20 users, your boss will think it is slow. Your boss may even be right.

This chapter is your answer to this problem. In it, I discuss some basic performance optimization techniques and show you some tools to measure program performance.

Performance Improvement Techniques

As you saw in Chapter 38, you can take some basic approaches toward optimization. Some of these include smart usage of variables and memory that the user can take, and others are compiler optimizations. You'll find many smart compilers on the market that can optimize your code better than you could imagine.

Compiler optimizations

At its simplest, a compiler simply takes your code, parses it, and translates statements into commands that the machine understands. Most compilers, though, can go beyond that in terms of optimizing code.

Compilers can modify the executing code to unravel loops, change data references, and make general changes in code to improve performance.

Caution

Be careful with optimizing compilers because the greater the optimization, the greater the risk that the code may "break." The smart thing to do is write and test your code with no optimization to confirm that it works. Then write some test cases with known correct output. After compiling with optimization, run those test cases to confirm that the code is still correct. Almost always, your code still works when optimized, but the chance always exists that the code changes for optimization may introduce subtle bugs.

Array expansion

Consider the case where you have an array of test values and an array of input data. You want to loop through the input data to check and see if it matches a certain test value. Here is a code segment that might be used:

```
#define EXCURSION      0
#define COACH          1
#define BUSINESS       2
#define FIRST          3
#define SEATS          442
int costs[NCLASS];
struct passenger {
        int ticketprice;
        int seatnumber;
        } passengers[SEATS];
main()
...
load_prices();
load_passengers();
for(i=0;i<SEATS;i++)
        if (passengers[i].ticketprice==costs[BUSINESS]) ...
```

This code has two arrays in question. The first is an array of ticket prices for a flight, and the second is a listing of passengers. In the loop in question, you have two array references, and the second is one that you can easily eliminate.

Tip

Dereferencing an array member is always more costly than dereferencing a scalar variable. You must calculate the addresses for members of an array, usually by retrieving the address of the first member and adding an offset.

When an optimizing compiler looks at this code, odds are good that the `costs` array is changed into a series of scalar values to speed access to the memory.

Dead code elimination

You can also enhance performance by eliminating code that is never reached, for example:

```
if (a<10) {}
else if (a >30 ) {}
```

```
else if (a>5) {}
else if ( a<0 ) {}
else {}
```

Here, the last two blocks of code never execute, yet a nonoptimizing compiler creates code for the tests and for the blocks of code. This wastes disk space and potentially slows execution.

Tip

To a UNIX system, the execution is just another piece of memory for a program to manage, so shrinking the size of the executable code can result in performance improvements due to less paging of the text section of the executable file.

An optimizing compiler looks at the resultant code, and if it is smart enough, it can see where code segments are never reached. It doesn't write out code for those areas.

if restructuring

Another method for improving code is by compartmentalizing condition evaluation on if statements. Here is an if statement that we can easily restructure:

```
if (((a<b)&&(c==d)||(!strcmp(e,f)) {}
```

A nonoptimizing compiler might evaluate each clause of the if statement and then check the total condition before knowing whether to execute the statement block.

An optimizing compiler can rewrite the if statement so that minimal evaluation needs to be performed before determining if the condition should execute. Here's how you might do this:

```
if (!strcmp(e,f)) goto block;
if (b<=a) goto escape;
if (c==d) { block: }
escape:
```

The three comparisons are broken into separate statements, and the goto statements indicate when the condition is met. Notice that if strcmp returns zero, the block executes. If not, you need to test the other condition. If b is less than or equal to a, you know that you never execute the block, so you escape. Make the last comparison, then, and you've performed the same function as the ungainly if, but in potentially fewer statements.

Loop manipulation

One of the biggest areas for compiler optimization is in redesigning and rewriting looping instructions. You have two primary types of optimization: unrolling loops and merging loops.

Unrolling

An unrolled loop is simple: Instead of having a short block of code that has repeated unnecessary instructions, you have a long list of statements that are executed once. Here is a typical unrollable loop:

```
for(i=0;i<10;i++)
        square[i]=i*i;
```

In this case, you know the start and end points, and it performs a simple computation for each iteration. However, each computation also requires a second computation, the increment, and a comparison. Here's the resultant code:

```
square[0]=0;
square[1]=1;
square[2]=4;
square[3]=9;
square[4]=16;
square[5]=25;
square[6]=36;
square[7]=49;
square[8]=64;
square[9]=81;
```

This code performs exactly the same task as the two lines of code it replaces. The latter code may look longer, but it executes much faster.

Fusion

Sometimes, combining multiple loops into a single loop helps. In particular, this can occur when initializing variables. What follows is a pair of loops that could be combined:

```
for(i=0;i<10;i++)
        value[i]=myfunc(i);
for(i=0;i<12;i++)
        count[i]=0;
```

These loops cover almost the same ground, but they have a lot of overhead, and that overhead is repeated. Here is a much faster execution path:

```
for(i=0;i<10;i++)
        {
        value[i]=myfunc(i);
        count[i]=0;
        }
for(;i<12;i++)
        count[i]=0;
```

This executes faster because I've reduced the overhead of incrementing, reinitializing, and reincrementing to a single set of increments. Smart compilers can pick up on this redundant execution and optimize to eliminate the need.

Note

Both loops are actually excellent targets for unrolling.

Advanced loop management

Very smart compilers can perform an additional trick: They can attempt to manage looping code on a single page. When the looping code spans pages, you have a greater risk of system paging, particularly on heavily loaded systems. By keeping the code on a single page of memory, the system can execute the code faster.

Other advanced loop management includes partial unrolling. In this case, you might rewrite a long loop instead to have a larger body with fewer iterations. This tradeoff of larger code blocks in exchange for fewer increments and comparisons can speed up your code.

Memory management

Another feature of compiler optimizations is potentially better memory management. Memory management is a tricky issue and will likely be the cause of bugs that result from optimization.

Some examples of memory management include reusing variables, altering structure sizes, or even changing structures.

Variable reuse

Often, you have several variables in a block of code that are only needed in a section of that code. They may be temporary variables, or they may be important, but transitory, variables. Here are a pair of transitory variables:

```
int sum, count;
for (i=0;i<MAX;i++)
        if (member[i].data) count++;
printf("%d members have data\n",count);
...
sum=0;
for(i=0;i<MAX;i++)
        sum+=member[i].children;
printf("There are %d children of members.\n");
```

Programmatically, having two different variables with understandable names helps, but in this block of code you don't need two separate memory locations for these variables. Optimally, you could declare the same memory used with two different labels, but C does not allow for this structure.

An optimizing compiler, however, can recognize that the first variable, once used, is no longer needed and that the second variable is not needed until after the first is used. It can then treat the two variables as the same, and therefore reduce the size of the stack needed.

For two four-byte variables, this is not much of a savings, but the savings could be enormous over the course of a program with many redundant variables or with a highly recursive routine.

Structure manipulation

You can also improve memory management by manipulating the structures as declared. Many structures may have redundant members or have dead space. An optimizing compiler can clean that up or even reorganize and change structures.

In the previous code listing, you'll see an implied structure with members data and children. These data members are accessed separately, however, and although related, they may not be used in tandem. In this case, having two arrays (one of data and one of children) may actually be better because each one is treated as a separate entity. By doing this, the related data are more tightly packed in memory, so you have less paging when accessing the values. Similarly, the program will have less need for address resolution.

Here's another case of an unorganized structure:

```
struct person {
        char name[125];
        unsigned living_father:1,living_mother:1;
        struct person *father,*mother;
        unsigned has_sibling:1;
        char sibling_count;
        struct person *siblings;
        char address[256];
        unsigned has_job:1;
        } ;
```

An optimizing compiler may reorganize this structure to make better use of the memory required. On some systems, you can achieve faster access by placing structure elements on word boundaries. Also, you can enhance this structure by combining the bit fields into a single word. Here is what an optimizing compiler may do to improve the structure:

```
struct person {
        char name[125];
        char fill[3];
        char address[256];
        struct person *father,*mother,*siblings;
        unsigned living_father:1,living_mother:1,has_siblings:1,has_job:1;
        char sibling_count;
        char fill2[3];
        };
```

This increases the size of the structure by three bytes, but it also aligns the word structure. This takes a real risk, though, because the code may later make calculated offsets into the structure, and with the members reorganized, you have no guarantee that you'll reach the same members. Similarly, if you use this structure in I/O, the reorganization may result in bad data being read.

Variable reorganization

Another trick for memory management is to reorganize related variables onto the same page of the stack or into registers. By keeping related variables together, you reduce the risk of paging, which slows execution.

Function inlining

Another compiler trick is *function inlining*. An inlined function is one where, instead of making a function call, the code is directly inserted into the execution path. Listing 40-1 shows a good example for inlining:

Listing 40-1: A Function for Inlining

```
swapvar(int *a,int *b)
{
int c;
c=(*a);
(*a)=(*b);
(*b)=c;
}
swapvar(&val1,&val2);
```

In this example, the `swapvar` function is short and is used to swap the values of two integers. It is a perfect example for inlining.

When you inline a function, you effectively treat it as a segment of code in the local scope. Some minor changes are needed, but the net result creates a faster piece of program.

Note

This example is also perfect for use as a macro:

```
#define swapvar(A,B) {int c;c=A;A=B;B=c;}
```

Tip

Of course, a multiple pass optimizer may notice a frequently used local variable on a second pass and optimize it into a single variable.

Threading

The last optimization discussed is available on multiple-processor machines. It is the automatic implementation of threading. *Threads* are segments of code in an application that can execute concurrently with other segments. Smart compilers may recognize these partially independent pieces of code and implement them as threads.

You can also write threaded programs; you need to watch for memory that is used by more than one thread, and signals are a nightmare. But a well-threaded program will be much more efficient than a nonthreaded program.

Code optimizations

Of course, you can improve the speed of your code even before you compile it. You can use several tricks to optimize your code performance.

Reduce unnecessary computation

One trick to faster programs is to reduce the number of computations required to reach your solution. This may sound simplistic, but it's true. Consider the first example:

```
for(i=0;i<SEATS;i++)
        if (passengers[i].ticketprice==costs[BUSINESS]) ...
```

Here, the addition of a temporary variable can speed the code:

```
business_cost=costs[BUSINESS];
for(i=0;i<SEATS;i++)
        if (passengers[i].ticketprice==business_cost) ...
```

Instead of requiring the program to find the value each time, this sets a single memory location to the value. A better example would be one where you perform a constant calculation:

```
for(i=0;i<MAX;i++)
        value[i]*=pow(1+(interest/period),periods);
```

Because the variables interest, period, and periods remain constant over the iteration of this loop, the repeated calculations and repeated calls to the pow function are unnecessary. Instead, perform the calculation once and use that as the multiplier:

```
coefficient=pow(1+(interest/period),periods);
for(i=0;i<MAX;i++)
        value[i]*=coefficient;
```

Although this may have more code, it will likely execute faster.

Note

Some compilers optimize this for you, but preempting that optimization doesn't hurt!

Order conditions

When you are testing conditions, explicitly ordering those conditions may help. Consider the case where you want to search some hospital records for all the male patients over 85 who have kidney stones. You know that roughly 50 percent of the patients are male, that 5 percent are over 85, and that 10 percent have kidney stones. A first cut of the condition might be

```
if
((patient.gender==MALE)&&(patient.age>84)&&(patient.kidneystone==1))
```

If you write the condition this way, however, you depend on the compiler to perform the tests in what it figures is the optimal path. This may not be the best solution. What if you wrote the following instead?

```
if (age>84)
        if (patient.kidneystone==1)
                if (patient.gender==MALE)
```

This may not look as pretty, but by explicitly testing the hardest condition first, you reduce the number of instructions that need to execute.

To write this kind of code requires proper knowledge of the data against which you write your conditions — something that is not always the case. You *can* make some intelligent guesses.

Reduce function calls

To improve performance, you may want to reduce the number of function calls that your process makes. You can achieve this by creating macros or by inlining functions.

Caution

One of the risks of writing your own performance optimizations is that the resultant code is not always the easiest code to maintain. Many structured programming constructions can result in less efficient code. Function calls, for example, are expensive calls. You need to create a new stack frame, allocate stack memory, save the return point, and change the program counter. For a two-line function, this is a lot of work the computer must perform.

Macros

Macros are a powerful addition to the C preprocessor and can speed up your code. Listing 40-1 shows how you can write a macro for swapping variables. You can also redefine other simple functions as macros, such as reading in a buffer or making a comparison.

Inlining functions

Not only can optimizing compilers inline functions, but you can, too. For a repeated one- or two-line task, if you need fast code, you may as well just include the code in place instead of making a function call. Of course, the maintenance costs are higher this way.

Is recursion necessary?

You can also speed up your code by examining where you are using recursion to determine if it is necessary. Recursion is an extremely powerful tool and is the right answer for many problems, but repeated function calls can be expensive. I'll show you two examples where recursion is elegant but not needed.

Consider the case where you want to calculate integer exponentiation of a number. The standard recursive technique is this:

```
int pow(int base,int power)
{
```

Guru: Returning Values from Multiple Commands

Macros suffer a potential difficulty from their inability to return values from multiple commands. This can pose a problem, but a solution is at hand. You need to declare an extra variable (I use either `return_code` or `retc`) and pass it to the macro. Then assign the desired return code to that variable and test that return code in the main body:

```
#define MYMAC(A,B,C) { ...
C=function }
...
MYMAC(variable1,variable2,retc)
if (retc) {}
```

This is not as pretty as a normal function call, but it is faster and can be optimized.

```
if (power<0) { /* Error */ }
if (!power) return(1);
return (base*pow(base,power-1));
}
```

This solution shows how you can use recursion to calculate the value. Without recursion, however, you have this:

```
int pow(int base,int power)
{
int temp=1;
int i;
if (power<0) { /* error */ }
for(i=0;i<power;i++) temp*=base;
return (temp);
}
```

The code is slightly longer, and the stack frame is a bit bigger, but the result is the same and can result in fewer function calls.

Another solution is the freeing of a linked list:

```
struct list {
        struct data { ... };
        struct list *next;
        } *head;
freelist(struct list *head)
{
if (head)
        {
        if (head->next) freelist(head->next);
        free(head);
        }
}
```

This checks for any other nodes down the list before freeing the current one. By using recursion, you free a list of any length at the cost of one function call per member. You can eliminate recursion with a pointer to step down the list and free each member:

```
freelist(struct list *head)
{
struct list *next;
while (head)
        {
        next=head->next;
        free(item);
        head=next;
        }
}
```

Although again not as elegant as the recursive approach, this routine does free the entire list at the cost of an additional variable on the stack frame.

Please do not presume that I am against recursion on principle. Recursion is necessary and useful on many occasions, but when examining recursion, always check to ascertain that it is needed and cost-effective.

Use pointers and registers

You can also speed up your programs by using pointers to reference arrays and using registers to speed access to variables. Because an array is just an address of a segment of memory and the array index is just an increment to the address, you can just as easily use a pointer to step through an array, and you reduce the cost of always needing to recalculate the address by adding the increment.

For example, if you wanted to step through an array of structures to print mailing labels, you might have the following:

```
struct address {
        char name[128];
        char address[256];
        char city[64];
        char state[2];
        char zipcode[9];
        } addresses[MAX];
for(i=0;i<MAX;i++)
        {
        printf("%s\n",addresses[i].name);
        printf("%s\n",addresses[i].address);
        printf("%s, %s   %s\n",addresses[i].city,addresses[i].state,
                addresses[i].zipcode);
        }
```

This looks sensible, but for each access to the address record, you need to calculate the address of the individual record using the array address and offset. Instead, you could write

```
struct address *member;
for(i=0,member=addresses;i<MAX;i++,member++)
        {
        printf("%s\n",member->name);
        printf("%s\n",member->address);
        printf("%s, %s   %s\n",member->city,member->state,
                member->zipcode);
        }
```

In C, when you increment a pointer, it knows the size of the object to which you are pointing and adds that much to the address. By using a pointer in this fashion, you end up with quicker access to the data as you step through the array of addresses.

Another trick is to use the register declaration. Using a register forces the C compiler to store a particular value in a register throughout the scope of the variable. Registers are faster to access than stack memory. I usually assign for-loop indices and frequently accessed pointers to registers.

Note

If you request more registers than available, that's OK. The program still works, but you don't have the benefit of all variables being in registers.

Performance Improvement Commands

Two commands are useful for measuring the performance of your application. The first, prof, requires special compilation options but also provides a lot of detailed information. The next, time, requires no special compilation options but only provides the basic information about the execution profile of a process.

Detailed execution profile

You can obtain a detailed profile of your process's execution by using the prof command. This command examines a dump file that contains profiling information about the last command run and presents the data.

To profile execution, you need to compile the executable file with the -p option. Table 40-1 shows the command-line options.

Table 40-1	prof Arguments	
Option	**Argument**	**Result**
-a		Reports on all symbols, not just the external symbols.
-l		Sorts the output by symbol value.
-n		Sorts the output by number of calls.
-s		Produces a summary file.

Option	Argument	Result
-v	[-low [-high]]	Suppresses the printed table and produces the output for the plot command. The low and high numbers are the percentages to be printed.
-z		Displays routines with zero usage.

The prof command also requires the name of the executable file following the options with an optional profiling file. By default, prof examines the a.out file as the executable file, and mon.out for the profiling information.

The code lines that follow show the output of the prof command. In this output, you see that almost all the time is spent in the write system call. This is the call that produces output. If I wanted to improve the performance of this program, I'd first look at how I am handling my output:

```
%time   cumsecs  #call   ms/call   name
 36.4     0.04     172      0.23    _write
  9.1     0.05                      .div
  9.1     0.06    1452      0.01    _localeconv
  9.1     0.07    1241      0.01    _memchr
  9.1     0.08       4      2.50    _open
  9.1     0.09     154      0.06    _read
  9.1     0.10    4664      0.00    _strlen
  9.1     0.11                      mcount
  0.0     0.11    1031      0.00    .mul
  0.0     0.11    8466      0.00    .udiv
  0.0     0.11      73      0.00    .umul
  0.0     0.11    8484      0.00    .urem
  0.0     0.11      22      0.00    __big_binary_to_big_decimal
  0.0     0.11      12      0.00    __big_float_times_power
  0.0     0.11      19      0.00    __carry_out_b10000
  0.0     0.11      24      0.00    __class_double
  0.0     0.11    1452      0.00    __doprnt
  0.0     0.11       2      0.00    __filbuf
  0.0     0.11       3      0.00    __findbuf
  0.0     0.11       3      0.00    __findiop
  0.0     0.11      44      0.00    __fourdigitsquick
  0.0     0.11      12      0.00    __fp_leftshift
  0.0     0.11      11      0.00    __fp_normalize
  0.0     0.11       2      0.00    __lshift_b10000
  0.0     0.11      19      0.00    __mul_65536short
  0.0     0.11       1      0.00    __multiply_base_ten_by_two
  0.0     0.11      22      0.00    __multiply_base_two
  0.0     0.11      19      0.00    __prod_65536_b10000
  0.0     0.11      17      0.00    __right_shift_base_two
  0.0     0.11      61      0.00    __umac
  0.0     0.11      12      0.00    __unpack_double
  0.0     0.11      22      0.00    __unpacked_to_big_float
  0.0     0.11      12      0.00    __unpacked_to_decimal
```

```
0.0    0.11      2    0.00   __wrtchk
0.0    0.11    160    0.00   __xflsbuf
0.0    0.11      1    0.00   _atoi
0.0    0.11     12    0.00   _binary_to_decimal_fraction
0.0    0.11     11    0.00   _binary_to_decimal_integer
0.0    0.11      4    0.00   _close
0.0    0.11     12    0.00   _decimal_round
0.0    0.11     24    0.00   _double_to_decimal
0.0    0.11      1    0.00   _exit
0.0    0.11      3    0.00   _fclose
0.0    0.11     24    0.00   _fconvert
0.0    0.11      3    0.00   _fflush
0.0    0.11      7    0.00   _fgets
0.0    0.11      3    0.00   _fopen
0.0    0.11    209    0.00   _fprintf
0.0    0.11      3    0.00   _free
0.0    0.11      3    0.00   _freopen
0.0    0.11      2    0.00   _fstat
0.0    0.11      3    0.00   _ioctl
0.0    0.11      3    0.00   _isatty
0.0    0.11      1    0.00   _main
0.0    0.11      4    0.00   _malloc
0.0    0.11      6    0.00   _memccpy
0.0    0.11      1    0.00   _on_exit
0.0    0.11   1241    0.00   _printf
0.0    0.11      1    0.00   _profil
0.0    0.11      1    0.00   _sbrk
0.0    0.11      2    0.00   _sprintf
0.0    0.11     18    0.00   _strchr
0.0    0.11      1    0.00   _strcmp
0.0    0.11     18    0.00   _strcpy
```

The column headers should be obvious. The first (%time) is the percentage of time the system spent with a given command. The second (cumsecs) is a cumulative total of seconds spent executing commands. The third (#call) is a count of the number of calls made to a routine, the fourth column (ms/call) is the average time per call, and the last column (name) is the name of the routine.

Secret

You can break down the amount of time in a long function by using the MARK macro. You place

MARK(name);

in the code of a long routine. Include the prof.h file in the source, compile with -DMARK, and you'll receive more information.

Caution

You should run several profiles before reaching conclusions. System conditions may vary the results of the profiles' output across iterations. Only by examining the output of several runs can you start to reach any legitimate conclusions.

Simple process profile

The time command can provide some basic profile information. By prefixing a command with time, you'll see a summary of elapsed real time, user CPU time, and system CPU time on the output. The time command takes only one argument, -p, which specifies that the output goes to standard error as opposed to standard output. Here is the output of time for the dbdump command:

```
4.0 real        0.1 user        0.1 sys
```

This indicates that executing the command took 4 seconds, only 0.1 seconds were spent in user CPU time, and system CPU time took just 0.1 seconds.

Secret

Measuring the profile of a pipeline is normally unpredictable, but you can use an easy technique to check. Use the sh -c construct:

```
time sh -c `command | command`
```

The output applies to the shell and all its children.

Performance Checking Commands

You can use a couple of commands to check and improve the overall performance of an executable file. The strip command reduces the size of the executable file to the smallest possible to run, and the size command examines the size.

Shrinking the file

The strip command takes a single argument, the name of the executable file to be stripped. Stripping the file usually removes the symbol table from the file (making debugging difficult), along with any other information not vital to the execution of the program.

When we strip the dbdump executable file, its size is reduced from 49,152 to 32,768 bytes.

Using strip is the same as compiling with the -s option specified.

Examining the data sizes

The size command, when run against an executable file, reports on the size of the different areas of the executable file. Table 40-2 lists the command-line objects.

Option	Argument	Result
-A		Produces System V–compatible output
-B		Produces BSD-compatible output
-format	=sysv **or** =berkeley	Same as -A or -B
-help		Shows a summary of arguments
-d		Produces decimal output
-o		Produces octal output
-x		Produces hexadecimal output
-radix	size	For sizes 8, 10, and 16; same as -d, -o, **or** -x

Table 40-2 Options to size

When examining the dbdump executable file, I see the sizes such as:

```
text    data    bss     dec     hex
24576   8192    297160  329928  508c8
```

This means 24,576 bytes are executable text, 8,192 are allocated for data, and 297,160 bytes are the global variable data.

Commercial Products

For someone who wants to improve the overall performance of his or her products, several compilers on the market perform good optimizations. The most notable is the Kuck and Associates C Preprocessor. This acts directly on the C source code and enhances it to be highly optimized, even before the compiler makes a pass at the code. For more information on this product, send e-mail to sales@kai.com.

Summary

This chapter examined several techniques for improving the performance of software. At this time, you should understand

▶ How compilers optimize code

▶ How you can write better code

▶ What the `prof` command produces

▶ How to use `time` to check execution profiles

▶ How to shrink the size of your executable file

▶ How to examine the different areas of an executable file

In the next chapter, I discuss the tools used to manipulate a programming language and the tools used to build lexical analyzers and parsers.

Chapter 41

Designing Languages

In This Chapter

▶ Lex for lexical analysis

▶ Yacc for input parsing

Parsing input has been one of the toughest tasks for any programmer. UNIX makes this task a bit easier by adding two tools, Lex and Yacc, for input parsing.

Lexical Analysis

Lexical analysis is the simple process of extracting and analyzing words from a text. In this sense, a *word* is a string that matches a regular expression. UNIX provides a tool that can create lexical analyzers and that can be used in many fashions.

Note

You might think that it would be easier to write your own lexical analyzer, and for an experienced programmer it is not a difficult task, but you may find that writing a Lex specification is easier, and the resultant code is fast enough.

A quick example of Lex

We can use Lex to extract words from a file and write them out, one word per line. This can be useful as input to sort, to determine the most frequently used words in a text. What follows shows a basic Lex file:

```
word [A-Za-z][-A-Za-z´]*
eol \n
%%
{word}    {printf("%s\n",yytext);}
{eol}     {}
.         {}
%%
```

The basic structure of a Lex specification is first to have a set of definitions. Here, I've defined a "word" to be any string with letters, where a dash or an apostrophe can appear after the first letter. That includes contractions and hyphenated words as single words, instead of breaking them up into separate components. As you can see, the regular expression for a word is fairly simple.

I also include a definition for the end of a line. This way, I can discard the end-of-line character. Otherwise, because Lex just passes any characters it does not recognize to standard output, I would see a lot of extraneous newlines in my output. Similarly, I ask for any other unrecognized characters to be ignored. In this way, I can toss out punctuation.

After building this file, I run it on the draft of my previous chapter, and the first 10 lines of output are shown here:

```
You´ve
made
it
now
make
it
fast
After
removing
as
```

Clearly, to count the words, I just need to sort this and then pass it through `uniq -c`:

```
wordextract | sort | uniq -c
```

This produces interesting output, but the sorting is case-sensitive, so I use `tr` to convert it all to lowercase before sorting. I also need to sort the output numerically, in reverse order, to determine the most commonly used words. Here are the ten most commonly used words in the previous chapter:

```
291 the
129 of
120 a
113 to
104 is
 81 and
 77 i
 69 you
 64 code
 62 for
```

No surprises here. I performed this calculation using a pipeline. A more advanced use of Lex would be to include all this in a single C program.

Using Lex

Once you have built your Lex specification, you use the `lex` command to generate a C module. The command is this:

```
lex word.l
```

Using the `.l` suffix for Lex source files is customary. The resultant file is `lex.yy.c`, in this case a 317-line C source file. Examining it reveals that the lexical analyzer is table driven. Inside is the function `yylex()`, which is your hook into the analyzer.

You can make the program easily by compiling this C file and including the Lex library:

```
cc lex.yy.c -ll
```

This produces an executable file, `a.out`. (You can specify a named file with the `-o` filename option.) The Lex library includes a default main procedure that calls `yylex()`. The resultant executable file is your program.

The Lex command-line options

Lex only accepts four command-line options, as shown in Table 41-1.

Table 41-1	Lex Options
Option	**Result**
-c	C language output. This is implied.
-n	Suppresses summary statistics. This is the default.
-t	Writes the program to standard output. This is a way to rename the file.
-v	Writes a summary of the Lex statistics to standard output.

The Lex specification file

A Lex specification is broken into three sections, each separated by a single line with two percent signs (%%) on it. The first section is definitions. The second section is the Lex rules section, and the final section is the user subroutines section. The Lex rules section must be present, so if no definitions exist, the first characters in the specification must be the %% delimiters.

Lex definitions

A *definition* is a name followed by a substitution pattern. Any names must start in the first column because any lines with a blank in the first column are treated as C source lines and are passed intact to the output file. This passing of source allows you to establish C declarations and the like.

Optionally, you may group all your C source in %{ ... %} delimiters, and all the code between those delimiters is passed intact.

These definitions are not necessary for Lex to work, but they are helpful. If the same pattern is used in different rules, you do not need to repeat the pattern. Similarly, if you need to change the definition, there is only one place to change, not several. For example, you might define DIGIT as

```
DIGIT [0-9]
```

You can then match both ordinal and decimal numbers:

```
{DIGIT}+          /* ordinal */
{DIGIT}+.{DIGIT}*      /* decimal */
```

You can also specify Lex declarations in the definitions section. These include specifications on table sizes, states, and the definition for the text pointer.

Lex rules

The Lex rules are at the heart of Lex. Rules are enhanced regular expressions and actions. Each regular expression has an associated action, and this action is C code. The action can be arbitrarily complex, so long as it is enclosed in braces. You can break the regular expression over several lines if you use the vertical bar.

When an action is matched, several things happen. First, the yytext variable is set to the string that matched the regular expression and is null-terminated. Next, the yyleng variable is set to the length of the string. Finally, any specified actions execute. Four special actions are defined in Lex, as illustrated in Table 41-2.

Table 41-2 Lex Functions

Action	Argument	Result
|		Uses the action for the next rule for this regular expression. This must be alone in the action field.
ECHO;		Echoes the value of yytext on standard output.
REJECT;		Continues to the next expression that matched the current input.
BEGIN	state	Toggles the specified state variable.

Lex attempts to match the longest string that matches a specified regular expression. If two regular expressions of the same length match, the first expression specified is used. REJECT can force matching of the second, or subsequent, regular expressions.

Lex subroutines

With the Lex rules that follow, you can specify any routines you desire, including a main routine. This is passed intact to the lex.yy.c file and is compiled normally. In this way, you can create the entire program internal to the Lex specification file.

Lex functions and variables

Lex creates several functions that are available to the programmer. Besides the yytext and yyleng variables, there is the variable yyin. This is a file descriptor and is used for input.

The primary function is yylex. It takes no arguments and returns an integer. The return values are either 0, when end of file or a token value (for use with Yacc) is reached. You must call this to invoke the lexical analyzer.

The yymore function also takes no arguments and returns an integer. When called, it tells Lex to append the next regular expression to yytext.

The yyless function takes an integer as an argument and returns an integer. It tells Lex that the initial number of characters specified will be retained and null-terminated. They are treated as if they have not been read.

The input function takes no arguments and returns an integer. This routine returns the next character off the input for lookahead. The character is removed from the input stream.

The unput function takes an integer argument and returns that value to the front of the input stream.

All C programs require the main function. The yywrap function takes no arguments and is used for end-of-file processing. Normally, it just returns 1 to tell Lex that input is finished. To move to a new file, you need to associate yyin with a new file and return 0.

Lex table declarations

Because Lex is table driven, the size of the grammar has some limits. To determine if you are close to those limits, you can run Lex with the -v option, and it dumps the table sizes. You can change these table sizes in the definitions section of the Lex specification, as listed in Table 41-3.

Table 41-3   Lex Table Declarations

Declaration	Minimum	Description
%a	2000	Number of Lex transitions
%e	1000	Number of parse tree nodes
%k	1000	Number of packed character classes
%n	500	Number of allowed states
%o	3000	Size of the output array
%p	2500	Number of allowed positions in Lex

You can use these declarations, followed by a number, to alter the table sizes. You can also declare how the yytext value will be stored. If %array is in the definitions, yytext is a character array. If %pointer is present, yytext is a character pointer. In both cases, yytext is always null-terminated.

Lex states

Sometimes, you may need to track the state of the input and perform different pattern matches or different actions based on a state. A good example of this is the comment in C: When in a comment, you just want to ignore the input. Because comments can span lines, this requires a state change.

States are defined by the %s definition. Rules that are state-dependent need to have the state specified in angle brackets before the regular expression. When a state is declared, it is considered inactive. For example:

```
%s COMMENT
%%
<COMMENT>.       {}
<COMMENT>"/*"    {}
<COMMENT>"*/"    { BEGIN INITIAL; }
"/*"     { BEGIN COMMENT; }
```

I want to pass everything through, except for the comments and the comment delimiters, so as soon as I see the beginning of a comment, I enter the COMMENT state. Any character in the comment state is ignored until I reach the end of the comment. Then I restore the initial state. If I wanted to start in COMMENT mode, I could have placed the lines:

```
%{
        BEGIN COMMENT;
%}
```

in the definitions section of the lexical specification.

An amusing use for Lex: Valspeak

Many years ago, a couple of programs converted written prose from our normal English to that allegedly spoken as jive or as Valley Girl talk. These were just Lex translations. You can use Lex to transform text from a fixed input format to a different output format. Listing 41-1 lists the lexical transformation file for Valley Girl.

Listing 41-1: The Complete Lex Source Code for Valspeak

```
T       [" .!?,"]*

%%

" bad"              printf(" mean");
" big"              printf(" bitchin´est");
" body"             printf(" bod");
" bore"             printf(" drag");
" car "             printf(" rod ");
" dirty"            printf(" grodie");
" filthy"           printf(" grodie to thuh max");
" food"             printf(" munchies");
" girl"             printf(" chick");
" good"             printf(" bitchin´");
" great"            printf(" awesum");
" gross"            printf(" grodie");
" guy"              printf(" dude");
" her "             printf(" that chick ");
" her."             printf(" that chick.");
" him "             printf(" that dude ");
" him."             printf(" that dude.");
" can be "          |
" can´t be "        |
" should have been "    |
" shouldn´t have been " |
" should be "       |
" shouldn´t be "    |
" was "             |
" wasn´t "          |
" will be "         |
" won´t be "        |
" is "          {
                    ECHO;
                    switch(rand() % 6)
                    {
                    case 0:
                            printf("like, ya know, "); break;
                    case 1:
                            printf(""); break;
                    case 2:
                            printf("like wow! "); break;
                    case 3:
                            printf("ya know, like, "); break;
```

```
                                        case 4:
                                                printf(""); break;
                                        case 5:
                                                printf(""); break;
                                        }
                        }
" house"                printf(" pad");
" interesting"          printf(" cool");
" large"                printf(" awesum");
" leave"                printf(" blow");
" man "                 printf(" nerd ");
" maybe "       {
                        switch(rand() % 6)
                        {
                        case 0:
                                printf(" if you´re a Pisces "); break;
                        case 1:
                                printf(" if the moon is full "); break;
                        case 2:
                                printf(" if the vibes are right ");
break;
                        case 3:
                                printf(" when you get the feeling ");
break;
                        case 4:
                                printf(" maybe "); break;
                        case 5:
                                printf(" maybe "); break;
                        }
                        }
" meeting"              printf(" party");
" movie"                printf(" flick");
" music "               printf(" tunes ");
" neat"                 printf(" keen");
" nice"                 printf(" class");
" no way"               printf(" just no way");
" people"               printf(" guys");
" really"               printf(" totally");
" strange"              printf(" freaky");
" the "                 printf(" thuh ");
" very"                 printf(" super");
" want"                 printf(" want");
" weird"                printf(" far out");
" yes"                  printf(" fer shure");
"But "                  printf("Man, ");
"He "                   printf("That dude ");
"I like"                printf("I can dig");
"No,"                   printf("Like, no way,");
Sir                     printf("Man");
"She "                  printf("That fox ");
This                    printf("Like, ya know, this");
There                   printf("Like, there");
"We "                   printf("Us guys ");
```

```
"Yes,"                          printf("Like,");
", "                    {
                                switch(rand() % 6)
                                {
                                case 0:
                                        printf(", like, "); break;
                                case 1:
                                        printf(", fer shure, "); break;
                                case 2:
                                        printf(", like, wow, "); break;
                                case 3:
                                        printf(", oh, baby, "); break;
                                case 4:
                                        printf(", man, "); break;
                                case 5:
                                        printf(", mostly, "); break;
                                }
                        }
!                       {
                                switch(rand() % 3)
                                {
                                case 0:
                                        printf("!  Gag me with a SPOOOOON!");
break;
                                case 1:
                                        printf("!  Gag me with a pitchfork!");
break;
                                case 2:
                                        printf("!  Oh, wow!");
                                }
                        }
ing                     printf("in´");
.                       ECHO;
%%

main()
{
        srand(getpid());
        yylex();
}
```

The source is easy to understand: when certain words or punctuation are seen, a simple translation occurs. Thus, when you see the word *house,* it is replaced with *pad.* If I feed it as input:

```
This is my house boat, sir!
```

I receive this output:

```
Like, ya know, this is my pad boat, like, sir! Gag me with a SPOOOOON!
```

This Lex script uses a random number generator, so any consecutive runs are likely to be different. Even a second entry of the same line comes out different:

```
Like, ya know, this is like wow! my pad boat, fer shure, sir! Gag me
with a pitchfork!
```

Just for amusement, I fed the preamble of the Constitution into Valspeak to see what we'd have as the law of the land if James Madison had been from Encino:

```
We, like, the guys of thuh United States, fer shure, in order to form
a more perfect Union, like, wow, establish justice, fer shure, insure
domestic tranquility, like, wow, provide for the common defense, fer
shure, promote thuh general welfare, man, and secure the blessin's of
liberty to ourselves and our posterity do ordain and establish this
Constitution for thuh United States of America.
```

I suspect that this would certainly have changed jurisprudence over the ages.

Parsing

Lexical analysis is a small part of putting together a program to understand input. The next, more important, task is to build a parser.

As discussed in Chapter 38, parsing uses two techniques: a shift/reduce parsing approach and a top-down approach. Writing a parser that works properly for a grammar is much more difficult than writing a simple lexical analyzer. UNIX provides a tool that writes the parser for you. *Yacc,* or *Yet Another Compiler Compiler,* can take a grammar specified in a recognized fashion and produce a parser that understands the grammar.

A quick example of Yacc

A quick example of Yacc may be an oxymoron, but here is a short Yacc script:

```
%token WORD
%%
DOCUMENT : WORD
        | DOCUMENT WORD; { printf("Have a document\n");}
```

This needs a lexical analyzer that returns words:

```
%{
#include "y.tab.h"
%}
%%
.        { return WORD; }
```

This prints out the line Have a document for every character in a document.

Using Yacc

You can compile the Yacc specification into a file with the command:

```
yacc example.y
```

Note

Customarily, you'll use the .y suffix for Yacc source files.

This produces the file y.tab.c, for the previous example a C source file of 508 lines. You can also produce a header file, y.tab.h, with the -d option.

Inside that file is the yyparse() function, the actual parser. This takes no arguments and returns 0 on success and 1 on a syntax error.

You can compile this with:

```
cc y.tab.c -ly
```

This produces an a.out executable file. The Yacc library includes a default main() routine and auxiliary routines necessary to run. It does not include a yylex() routine to return tokens to the parser. You can either use one generated by Lex or write your own.

The Yacc command line

Yacc has several legal options, as listed in Table 41-4.

Table 41-4	Yacc Options	
Option	**Argument**	**Result**
-b	*string*	Uses the string as a file prefix instead of y
-d		Produces the y.tab.h header file for use by a lexical analyzer
-l		Produces code that does not use the #line constructs
-p	*string*	Uses the string as a prefix for variables, instead of yy
-t		Modifies code to include conditional debugging statements by default
-v		Writes a file containing parsing statistics

The Yacc specification file

Yacc has a specifications file similar in design to Lex but with many more options. It includes a declarations section, a rules section, and a programs section. These are analogous to the definitions, rules, and subroutines sections of Lex. Each section is separated by the double percentage signs, as in Lex. Also as in Lex, the rules section must be present, and if there are no declarations, the file must start with %%.

Yacc declarations

The Yacc declarations is the section where token names are declared, as well as operator precedences and parsing start symbols. Seven tags are used to declare values.

The `%token` construct defines tokens used in the parser. You can optionally specify a field of a union in angle brackets; this union passes information from the lexical analyzer to the parser and is explained in more detail later on. After the optional field member, you can list token names, each optionally followed by a number. These tokens are converted to #define values and used in the C code to recognize constructs. An example is

```
%token   WORD 0 SENTENCE MONTH
```

This defines three tokens that you can pass back from `yylex()`, where the token WORD assumes the integer value 0.

The `%left` and `%right` constructs also declare tokens of either left-ordered precedence or right-ordered precedence. The syntax is the same as for `%token`. The order of the precedence directives in the Yacc source defines the precedence of the operators.

The `%nonassoc` construct defines tokens that are not to be used in any form of sociativity. The `%type` construct defines the type for tokens that are nonterminals. Because they are not terminal tokens, you can't assign numerical values for the tokens.

The remaining constructs in the declarations are slightly different. The `%start` construct specifies a nonterminal symbol to be used as the start symbol. This should be the largest, most general structure defined by the grammar. If no `%start` symbol is specified, Yacc assumes it is the left-hand symbol for the first rule.

You must follow the `%union` construct with a C union declaration. For example, you might have a union:

```
%union {
        long val1;
        short sval;
        char *string;
        }
```

This changes the definition for the `yylval` structure that passes data between the parser and lexical analyzer. When a union is declared, you can specify tags on `%token` lines. So if you are passing data back, you might declare tokens such as:

```
%token <val1> TIME
%token <string> WORD
%token <sval> MONTH DATE
```

Yacc automatically keeps these union members straight for type checking in the resultant grammar.

Yacc grammar rules

At the heart of Yacc is the grammar definition. Each grammar consists of a set of rules that build to form a single, coherent whole. The format is

```
Target : Body
```

The target is the object to be built, and the body is the building definition. Bodies can be a series of tokens, both terminal tokens from a lexical analyzer and nonterminal tokens. (Nonterminal tokens are the left-hand side of the rules.) You just specify a space-separated list of tokens. You can specify alternate lists of tokens on separate lines, where each is preceded by a vertical bar. Last of all, you can specify an action, separated inside braces, that executes when the token is identified. Each rule must be terminated by a semicolon.

You can specify character literals by enclosing them in single quotes. For example, this token is the top-level token for a Yacc grammar:

```
grammar : declarations MARK rules tail
        ;
```

The MARK is the %% symbol. Because the programs section is optional, the MARK is included in the definition of the tail.

A more complicated rule might specify an action when found. Rules can be arbitrarily complex, and you can make mistakes. The most common mistake when parsing is to shift/reduce conflicts. This means that the parser is not certain whether to reduce the current stack of information to a higher construct or to continue to shift more data onto the stack. This is usually the result of an ambiguous grammar. Yacc may still generate a parser for this, but the results may not always be what you would expect.

Yacc programs

After you have specified the rules, you may optionally append C code to y.tab.c. You must precede this code with the %% separator and copy it verbatim to the file. Normally, you might declare a yylex() function here to parse input. You can also specify a main() function and a yyerror() function to complete the process. If you specify all three functions, you do not need the Yacc library or a Lex parser to compile the program.

Yacc functions and variables

Yacc creates a yyparse function for you. This function takes no arguments and returns either a 0 or a 1 for success or failure. The variables used (yytext, yylval, and so on) are all defined in the lexical analyzer.

Integrating Lex with Yacc

Lex is often tightly tied with Yacc as the lexical analyzer. The two programs are often designed to work together to produce a larger output.

Normally, when you define tokens in Yacc, you expect the yylex parser to return these tokens. This is fairly easy to set up. In Yacc, you might have a line like

```
%token INTEGER
```

This token is then used later in the grammar. In Lex, you need to define a means of returning this integer:

```
%{
#include "y.tab.h"
%}
%%
[1-9][0-9]*      { yylval=atoi(yytext); return INTEGER; }
```

You need to include the header in the Lex output so that the values for the tokens are passed properly between the lexical analyzer and the parser. You also need to build your grammar using the -d flag for Yacc to produce the appropriate header file.

A Parser for dates

For the last example, I've written a simple set of Yacc and Lex scripts that parse dates. The output is the UNIX representation of the time. I decided to take dates of the form:

```
Jan 1, 1960
1 January, 1960
1/1/60
Jan 1, 60 3:04
Jan 1, 60 3:04:05
```

The first thing I wrote was the Yacc specification. I did this so that I could define the tokens I expect to receive from yylex(). Listing 41-2 shows the specification.

Listing 41-2: The Yacc Specification for Checking a Date

```
%{
#include <time.h>

struct tm timer;
int yylval;
%}
%token COMMA SLASH INTEGER MONTERM DAYSPEC COLON
%%
DATE : DATE_SPEC { return 0; }
     | DATE_SPEC TIME_SPEC { return 0; }
```

```
         ;
DATE_SPEC : DAYOFYEAR COMMA YEAR
           | DAYOFYEAR
         ;
DAYOFYEAR : DATES
           | DAYOFWEEK DATES
         ;
DATES : MONTH DAY
       | MONTH SLASH DAY
       | DAY MONTH
       | DAY SLASH MONTH
     ;
YEAR : SLASH YR
     | YR
     ;
YR : INTEGER { timer.tm_year=yylval%100; }
   ;
MONTH : MONTERM { timer.tm_mon=yylval; }
      | INTEGER { timer.tm_mon=yylval-1; }
      ;
DAY : INTEGER { timer.tm_mday=yylval; }
   ;
DAYOFWEEK : DAYSPEC { timer.tm_wday=yylval; }
          ;
TIME_SPEC : HOUR COLON MINUTE
           | HOUR COLON MINUTE COLON SECOND
         ;
HOUR : INTEGER { timer.tm_hour=yylval; }
    ;
MINUTE : INTEGER { timer.tm_min=yylval; }
      ;
SECOND : INTEGER { timer.tm_sec=yylval; }
      ;
%%
main ()
{
timer.tm_year=95;
timer.tm_mon=11;
timer.tm_mday=9;
timer.tm_hour=19;
timer.tm_min=27;
timer.tm_sec=0;
yyparse();
printf("Integer time is %d\n",(int)mktime(&timer));
}
```

The first piece of the specification is a listing of C source code that needs to be prepended to the file. This includes a header for the time information and the external variables, including yylval. This is passed through to the output unhindered.

Next is a list of tokens I expect to receive from yylex(). Surprisingly, it is only six tokens, and three of them are standard punctuation symbols.

Note

I could have used string literals in the Yacc grammar for the colon, comma, and slash, but I opted to show how the data can be passed instead.

The other three symbols are for either the month, the day of the week, or integer values. After completing the declarations, I wrote the rules. The first rule, for DATE, builds the date and returns to the calling process when complete. This way, I don't need to spin on extraneous data. The DATE requests either a date or a date followed by a time.

The other rules are similar. You should be able to look down the list and see how they build dates. When I reach a terminal symbol, I assign the appropriate value to the time structure declared previously as a global variable.

After completing the rules, I include a basic main program for the application. This program sets up some defaults for the time structure and calls yyparse() to read the input. When complete, it reports on the UNIX time.

This example is not complete without examining the requisite Lex specification. Listing 41-3 shows the date.l file.

Listing 41-3: The Lexical Specification for Dates

```
%{
#include "y.tab.h"
extern int yylval;
%}
%%
"","        { return COMMA; }
""/"        { return SLASH; }
"":"        { return COLON; }
[1-9][0-9]*     { yylval=atoi(yytext); return INTEGER; }
Sun     { yylval=0; return DAYSPEC; }
Sunday  { yylval=0; return DAYSPEC; }
Mon     { yylval=1; return DAYSPEC; }
Monday  { yylval=1; return DAYSPEC; }
Tue     { yylval=2; return DAYSPEC; }
Tuesday { yylval=2; return DAYSPEC; }
Wed     { yylval=3; return DAYSPEC; }
Wednesday       { yylval=3; return DAYSPEC; }
Thu     { yylval=4; return DAYSPEC; }
Thursday        { yylval=4; return DAYSPEC; }
Fri     { yylval=5; return DAYSPEC; }
Friday  { yylval=5; return DAYSPEC; }
Sat     { yylval=6; return DAYSPEC; }
Saturday        { yylval=6; return DAYSPEC; }
Jan     { yylval=0; return MONTERM; }
January { yylval=0; return MONTERM; }
Feb     { yylval=1; return MONTERM; }
February        { yylval=1; return MONTERM; }
```

```
Mar       { yylval=2; return MONTERM; }
March     { yylval=2; return MONTERM; }
Apr       { yylval=3; return MONTERM; }
April     { yylval=3; return MONTERM; }
May       { yylval=4; return MONTERM; }
May       { yylval=4; return MONTERM; }
Jun       { yylval=5; return MONTERM; }
June      { yylval=5; return MONTERM; }
Jul       { yylval=6; return MONTERM; }
July      { yylval=6; return MONTERM; }
Aug       { yylval=7; return MONTERM; }
August    { yylval=7; return MONTERM; }
Sep       { yylval=8; return MONTERM; }
September         { yylval=8; return MONTERM; }
Oct       { yylval=9; return MONTERM; }
October   { yylval=9; return MONTERM; }
Nov       { yylval=10; return MONTERM; }
November          { yylval=10; return MONTERM; }
Dec       { yylval=11; return MONTERM; }
December          { yylval=12; return MONTERM; }
.         {}
"\n"      {}
```

At the top of the file lies the requisite header information, including an external definition for the yylval variable. The header is also included so that yylex() can pass symbols back to the parser.

Instead of declaring any definitions, I opted to include just the regular expressions in the lexical rules. The only complicated expression is to identify integers. These are just digits and are translated into an integer value for yylval. The rest of the regular expressions match the strings. The last two rules discard extraneous input.

Secret

Due to the flexible nature of these rules, you can recognize a date like Januaribfige is my 1st house, located at 445 Bush Street. This is actually parsed as Jan 1, 45.

To build this application, I ran the following commands:

```
yacc -d date.y
lex date.l
cc -o dater lex.yy.c y.tab.c -ly -ll
```

The yacc command reported two shift/reduce conflicts but built the parser anyway. When I ran it, I saw this output:

```
% ./dater
May 16, 1960
Integer time is -303769980
% ./dater
December 9, 1960 19:27
Integer time is -283206780
% ./dater
10/27/90 20:30
```

```
Integer time is 814850820
% ./dater
29 February 1996
syntax error
Integer time is 798812820
% ./dater
29 February, 1996
Integer time is 823231620
```

This handled the dates before the epoch cleanly. The program had trouble with the string 29 February 1996. This does not produce the error you might expect (failure to handle a leap year) but instead balks at a missing comma after February. The next run of the command shows the proper results.

Note

This program could be improved extensively.

Summary

In this chapter, you have been introduced to two powerful programming tools, Lex and Yacc. You should

▶ Be able to write a simple Lex grammar

▶ Understand how Lex works

▶ Be able to write a simple grammar for Yacc

▶ Be able to integrate Lex and Yacc

The next chapter wraps up software development by defining a software development environment and by examining the imake command for portability.

Chapter 42

Combining Tools

In the previous seven chapters, we have examined how UNIX is best used for software development. The time has come to put all this information together and show how you can use the tools together.

The Software Development Environment

For many software developers who use UNIX, the best software development environment remains their shell and the commands they have written. If this describes you, just skip ahead to the next section.

A software development environment is ideally a tool that lets you increase your productivity over the standard shell. Most of these tools are commercial products. One tool of note that is not commonly available but is not a commercial product is Cscope.

The Cscope tool

My first experiences with Cscope were at Bell Labs in the late '80s. I was poking around the machine when I found this tool that built a database from your source code and provided a curses-graphics front-end to access that database.

Note

You might expect this tool to have become more advanced, incorporating X, for example. This is not the case. The Cscope I use on my Sun workstation has the same rudimentary interface.

Cscope is not a traditional development environment. Instead, it is a handy code organizer and debugging tool. You invoke Cscope by specifying as arguments the code you want incorporated into the database. This database is retained across invocations so that when you rerun Cscope, it comes up faster. Listing 42-1 illustrates the first screen.

Listing 42-1: Cscope at the Start

```
cscope                                          Press the ? key
for
help
```

```
Find this C symbol:
Find this global definition:
Find functions called by this function:
Find functions calling this function:
Find this text string:
Change this text string:
Find this egrep pattern:
Find this file:
Find files #including this file:
```

A recent debugging exercise questioned whether all the file descriptors in a
piece of code were being properly closed. The first thing I did was use
Cscope to check for all the calls to open, fopen, popen, pipe, dup, fcntl, or
opendir. Listing 42-2 shows the results for open.

Listing 42-2: All the Calls to Open

```
Functions calling this function: open


  File                  Function        Line
1 eg_ack_event.c        ack_event        73 if


((fd=open(nodename,O_TRUNC|O_WRONLY,O
                  600))<0)
2 eg_add_event.c        add_AIL         102 if


((fd=open(fullpath,O_CREAT|O_WRONLY|O
                  _TRUNC,0600))<0)
3 eg_cull_event.c       cull_event       67 if


((fd=open(fullpath,O_RDONLY,0600))<0)
```

```
* 5 more lines - press the space bar to display more *


Find this C symbol:
Find this global definition:
Find functions called by this function:
Find functions calling this function:
Find this text string:
Change this text string:
Find this egrep pattern:
Find this file:
Find files #including this file:
```

This is a short list of calls. (As it turned out, all the other functions had even fewer entries.) So I examined each call in turn to confirm that the opened file descriptor was closed. All I need to do from Cscope is select a number, and Cscope immediately calls vi at the line specified. I just need to step through the code to confirm that a matching close exists. Listing 42-3 illustrates this.

Listing 42-3: Editing from Cscope

```
57            tcl->result="unable to open directory for purge";
58            EGevent(tcl->result);
59            free(commstr);
60            return TCL_ERROR;
61        }
62  while ((entry=readdir(dpt))!=NULL)
63        {
64            if (!strcmp(entry->d_name,".")) continue;
65            if (!strcmp(entry->d_name,"..")) continue;
66            sprintf(fullpath,"%s/%s",dbfile,entry->d_name);
67            if ((fd=open(fullpath,O_RDONLY,0600))<0)
68                    continue;
69            if (fstat(fd,&stbuf))
70                {
71                    close(fd);
72                    continue;
73                }
74            if (stbuf.st_size==0)
75                {
76                    close(fd);
77                    continue;
78                }
79            p=malloc(stbuf.st_size+1);
"eg_cull_event.c" 139 lines, 3227 characters
```

Secret

The choice of editor is set using the EDITOR environment variable.

Secret

You can edit the file from the editor selected by `Cscope`. Any changes you make are automatically updated in the database and any further accesses show correct information.

Unfortunately, `Cscope` lacks the capability to invoke the make utility from the tool and similarly lacks the capabilities of a debugger or execution environment. Despite this, I've found `Cscope` a handy tool for software development.

Note

`Cscope` is particularly handy when you've assumed maintenance of code that you did not write. By "scoping" the code, you can quickly find areas where bugs may have occurred. On an X Window system, I like to keep a debugger running in one window and `Cscope` in another.

Commercial products

As mentioned earlier, the most common software development environments are commercial products. At the end of my tenure at *Advanced Systems* magazine, I was afforded the opportunity to review the three biggest development environments for Sun workstations. I found three tools that were similar in capability, and the main deciding factor was the usability of the interface.

Note

I have to admit that I'm one of those developers who prefers to eschew these development environments. While they do make life easier for some developers, I'm one of those old-fashioned engineers who prefers to do my development with the standard tools.

Caution

Each tool has a steep learning curve before you can master it.

SoftBench

SoftBench is Hewlett-Packard's offering in the world of development environments. SoftBench comes with an extensive amount of documentation that provides a thorough coverage of the tool. SoftBench also includes the complete set of tools, including editors, compilers, and debuggers. A handy extra is an interface to electronic mail that lets a user remain in the environment when performing non-development-related tasks.

The interface itself was not the best because it took some effort to find each of the tools. Once I found the tools, though, the interface to the functions was intuitive. Of the three tools I examined, this one had the quickest learning curve.

SPARCworks

SPARCworks is Sun's contribution to the development environment game. This tool comes with a good set of documents and is the most malleable of the three tools. Unfortunately, SPARCworks did not provide an interface for creating makefiles.

At the time of the review, SPARCworks provided only an OpenLook interface and did not function well under Motif. Because the OpenLook specification requires applications to be closed through signals and not user widgets, you are forced either to use Open Windows as a window manager, to modify the window manager initialization scripts, or to kill the application from a separate window. This is definitely clumsy.

CenterLine

CenterLine, from Cambridge, Massachusetts, has two notable development environment products. The first is CodeCenter, which is primarily for the C programming language. ObjectCenter is used with C++. I looked at CodeCenter for the review.

CodeCenter takes your software and incorporates it in a database. From the tool, you can edit the source code, edit the makefile, compile, execute, and debug. CodeCenter did not include a tool for performance measurement, but it allowed you to add any tools you desired.

To come up to speed with CodeCenter required using the tutorial, as the interface was not as intuitive as one might like. The documentation is decent.

Enhancing Makefiles

For an advanced UNIX user, makefiles are surprisingly powerful. The normal developer looks at make only as a tool to compile. A makefile, however, has the power to run normal shell scripts, based on the arguments provided. For example, you can build your manual pages solely by performing `nroff` commands on each file and saving the results. Here is a simple makefile:

```
manpage:
        nroff -man manpage.1 > manpage
```

Writing your own rules

A makefile comes with many rules predefined, including those to build object files from C source. You can, however, add many rules. Consider, if you have a Pascal compiler, `pc`, and you want to build intermediate objects. You can define a rule:

```
.p.o:
        pc -c $(PFLAGS) $<
```

This runs the `pc` compiler on the dependency file. You have to assume that this Pascal compiler has C compiler–like syntax and that `-c` produces an object file.

Another rule might be to build those catman files out of the manual pages:

```
.1.cat:
        nroff -man $< > $@
```

Then you can build a list of targets:

```
all:    cp.cat mv.cat man.cat
```

If this is all that is in your makefile, when you type **make**, the output looks like this:

```
nroff -man cp.1 > cp.cat
nroff -man mv.1 > mv.cat
nroff -man man.1 > man.cat
```

This assumes, of course, that the man page sources are in the current directory.

Doing other than development

As seen previously, the makefile is capable of performing tasks other than development. Two of the most common that I've seen are software installation and directory cleanup.

Normally with software installation, you need to copy files, potentially many files, to specific locations and set permissions. You can do this via a shell script, but a makefile may do the same tasks.

Listing 42-4 shows an installation script in a makefile.

Listing 42-4: An Installation Script in a Makefile

```
BINPROG = exec1 exec2
SUPPLPROG = exec3 exec4
EXECPERM=755
DATAPERM=644
DATAFILE = data1 data2

all: $(BINPROG) $(SUPPLPROG) install

install:
        @mkdir $(PROJ)/bin
        cp $(BINPROG) $(PROJ)/bin
        @mkdir $(PROJ)/supp
        cp $(SUPPLPROG) $(PROJ)/supp
        chmod $(EXECPERM) $(PROJ)/bin/* $(PROJ)/supp/*
        @mkdir $(PROJ)/data
        cp $(DATAFILE) $(PROJ)/data
        chmod $(DATAPERM) $(PROJ)/data/*
```

When the makefile has finished building the two programs, it installs them by copying the files to specific directories and changing their permissions.

Automated dependencies

C files often rely on other files to be properly compiled, and on large applications, a change to one of these header files can demand the recompiling of several dependent files. For the makefile to work properly, you need to have the dependencies set.

A new tool, Makedepend, builds these dependencies for you. You give it the same arguments as you would a C compiler, and it parses the source files and builds the dependency lists required by make. Listing 42-5 shows a sample of the output.

Listing 42-5: Output Created by Makedepend

```
verify_rules.o: /usr/include/errno.h /usr/include/sys/errno.h
verify_rules.o: /usr/include/sys/stat.h /usr/include/sys/time.h
verify_rules.o: /usr/include/sys/utsname.h /usr/include/fcntl.h
verify_rules.o: /usr/include/sys/fcntl.h /usr/include/unistd.h
verify_rules.o: /usr/include/ctype.h /usr/include/limits.h
verify_rules.o: /usr/include/syslog.h /usr/include/sys/syslog.h
verify_rules.o: /usr/include/pwd.h /home/symon/sol2/include/tcl.h
verify_rules.o: /home/symon/sol2/cur/ail/ailP.h /usr/include/values.h
verify_rules.o: /usr/include/libintl.h
/home/symon/sol2/cur/ail/listlib.h
verify_rules.o: events.h dynlink.h ../ev/allevent.h
```

Imake Files

One of the toughest issues for UNIX programming is portability. While you might write the most portable code, some people may not be able to build your software for any number of reasons. The Imake utility attempts to address this problem.

Related to Imake is the Xmkmf utility, created for X by Jim Fulton. This tool creates the makefile from Imake.

Portability

UNIX portability is more than a matter of making code work; it involves using similar tools in similar locations. I may write a makefile to use with my application that uses the cc compiler and points to include files at /usr/include/X11. You might opt to keep different releases of X and have the headers in /usr/include/X/X11R6, or you might opt to compile with the Apogee C compiler (apcc), or to do any number of things differently. To do this properly, I need to have written the makefile cleanly, and you need to make all the appropriate changes.

Note

Larry Wall's Configure script, which accompanies the rn newsreader source code, makes a good first start at this portability issue, but it still requires you to have a good knowledge of your system, and the script must be able to run.

Imake was first written by Todd Brunhoff and was adopted for the initial releases of X Windows. Simply, Imake is a makefile builder. Given a set of program descriptions, Imake accesses a system definition file and creates a makefile to build the specified program.

Imake files have some natural advantages over makefiles. The command introduces looping and conditional constructs to program builders. It also handles the inherent nonportability of C dependencies, and it allows for easy updates of global changes. What makes Imake and its related commands truly amazing is the capability to be portable.

Imake command-line options

Imake takes several command-line options, as detailed in Table 42-1.

Table 42-1	**Imake Options**	
Option	*Argument*	*Result*
-D	*define*	Defines the specified value for the C preprocessor.
-I	*directory*	Uses the named directory as part of the search path for header files.
-T	*filename*	Uses this file as the master template file for Imake.
-f	*filename*	Uses this file as the Imake file.
-C	*filename*	Names a .c file constructed in the current directory.
-s	*filename*	Names the makefile to be generated. A dash signifies standard output.
-e		Indicates that Imake should invoke the makefile.
-v		Indicates that Imake should print the cpp command line.

The xmkmf command also takes an optional -a, which tells xmkmf to invoke the make Makefiles command on the resultant makefile. This allows you to specify a series of makefiles in a hierarchy that can be made.

How it works

Surprisingly, the C preprocessor performed much of Imake's work. Imake is rules-dependent, where you take a rule and use it to build a command. For example, you might have the rule

```
NormalProgramTarget(test,test.o,NullParameter,NullParameter,NullParame
ter
)
```

This is actually a C preprocessor directive and is expanded to further C preprocessor directives, such as

```
ProgramTargetName(test): test.o NullParameter
        RemoveTargetProgram($@)
        LinkRule($@,$(LDOPTIONS),test.o,NullParameter $(LDLIBS)
NullParameter)
```

`ProgramTargetName`, `RemoveTargetProgram`, `LinkRule`, and `NullParameter` have further expansions. Eventually, you'd end up with

```
test: test.o
        $(RM) $@
        $(CC) -o $@ hello.o $(LDOPTIONS) $(LDLIBS) $(EXTRA_LOAD_FLAGS)
```

This is a standard makefile command and can be invoked with **make test**.

Simple Imake rules

Some basic rules govern the writing of Imake. Each rule must include every argument. If no argument is desired, substitute `NullParameter`. Arguments must be comma-separated and should have no whitespace around them. You can specify variables in your arguments. Each rule must be on a single line, and rules cannot be split across lines. The following sections cover some of the default rules.

SimpleProgramTarget

`SimpleProgramTarget` takes a single argument, the name of a program, and generates a makefile for a single program. For example, Listing 42-6 shows the output for `SimpleProgramTarget(myprog)`.

Listing 42-6: An Imake File for a Simple Target

```
#      ----------------------------------------------------------------
# start of Imakefile

 OBJS = myprog.o
 SRCS = myprog.c

 PROGRAM = myprog
```

```
all:: myprog

myprog: $(OBJS)
        $(RM) $@
        $(CCLINK) -o $@ $(LDOPTIONS) $(OBJS) $(LOCAL_LIBRARIES)
$(LDLIBS)

$(EXTRA_LOAD_FLAGS)

clean::
        $(RM) myprog
```

This file has been edited down from 503 lines! Several of the variables are defined in a header to the makefile.

ComplexProgramTarget

ComplexProgramTarget takes only a single argument, the name of the resultant executable file. You need to define the SRCS variable and an OBJS variable, and the resultant output resembles SimpleProgramTarget.

NormalProgramTarget

NormalProgramTarget is a bit more powerful. It takes five arguments, but any number of these can be null arguments. The first argument is the executable name. This is followed by the object file or a list of object files, the dependent libraries, the local libraries, and the system libraries. Imake builds the line to make the program and to clean up after the program.

NormalLibraryTarget

This command takes two arguments: the name of a library and a list of object files associated with that library. The name should not have the leading lib or the trailing .a. Listing 42-7 shows an example of a normal library output.

Listing 42-7: Output of NormalLibraryTarget(mylib,mylib.o)

```
# --------------------------------------------------------------
# start of Imakefile

all:: libmylib.a

libmylib.a: mylib.o
     $(RM) $@
       $(AR) $@ mylib.o
       $(RANLIB) $@
       $(_NULLCMD_)
```

Again, I've edited this down.

A sample Imake file

Listing 42-8 shows the Imake file for the Tiff distribution with Xv.

Listing 42-8: An Imake File for Tiff

```
DEFINES=-I. -Dunix

SRCS=   tif_fax3.c tif_fax4.c tif_aux.c tif_ccittrle.c tif_close.c
        \
        tif_compress.c tif_dir.c tif_dirinfo.c tif_dirread.c   \
        tif_dirwrite.c tif_dumpmode.c tif_error.c tif_getimage.c
tif_jpeg.c \
        tif_flush.c tif_lzw.c tif_next.c tif_open.c tif_packbits.c
        \
        tif_print.c tif_read.c tif_swab.c tif_strip.c tif_thunder.c
        \
        tif_tile.c tif_unix.c tif_version.c tif_warning.c tif_write.c

OBJS=   tif_fax3.o tif_fax4.o tif_aux.o tif_ccittrle.o tif_close.o
        \
        tif_compress.o tif_dir.o tif_dirinfo.o tif_dirread.o   \
        tif_dirwrite.o tif_dumpmode.o tif_error.o tif_getimage.o
tif_jpeg.o \
        tif_flush.o tif_lzw.o tif_next.o tif_open.o tif_packbits.o
        \
        tif_print.o tif_read.o tif_strip.o tif_swab.o tif_thunder.o
        \
        tif_tile.o tif_unix.o tif_version.o tif_warning.o tif_write.o

NormalLibraryTarget(tiff,$(OBJS))

tif_compress.o: Imakefile

#if HasGcc
g3states.h: mkg3states.c t4.h
        -${RM} g3states.h
        ${CC} -traditional -o mkg3states ${CFLAGS} mkg3states.c
        ./mkg3states > g3states.h || rm g3states.h
#else
g3states.h: mkg3states.c t4.h
        -${RM} g3states.h
        ${CC} -o mkg3states ${CFLAGS} mkg3states.c
        ./mkg3states > g3states.h || rm g3states.h
#endif

depend:: g3states.h

clean::
        -${RM} mkg3states g3states.h
DependTarget()
```

The Imake commands `DependTarget()` and `NormalLibraryTarget()` and `gcc` have dependencies. When run with `xmkmf` or Imake, this generates a makefile that produces the Tiff library.

Summary

This chapter wrapped up software development by looking at some tools that you can use to speed maintenance and porting. By now, you should

▶ Recognize and know `Cscope`

▶ Be familiar with some commercial development environment products

▶ Realize the real power of make

▶ Understand Imake

▶ Know the ideas behind Imake rules

In the next chapter, I begin a survey of tools written by the Free Software Foundation that are generally available for all UNIX users.

Part X

GNU Tools

Chapter 43

I'm Not Paying for That!

In This Chapter

▶ What are GNU Tools?

▶ History of the Free Software Foundation

▶ The future

You will see in this chapter that sometimes you can get more than you pay for.

What Are GNU Tools?

GNU Tools (pronounced *new*) started to appear in the mid-1980s, beginning with a text editor named emacs, written by Richard Stallman. The emacs text editor was almost an instant success. It started as a full screen editor, with more functionality than found in vi.

With the initial success of emacs, Richard Stallman went on to found the Free Software Foundation and began working with other programmers to produce high-quality, very useful UNIX tools, most of which are replacements for the standard tools distributed with the vendor's version of the operating system.

Even though emacs was the first of the GNU Tools, it is perhaps still the most popular. The emacs editor has been ported to various platforms, including many of the UNIX variants, Microsoft Windows, and even to DOS!

Whereas vi uses a command mode and an input mode, emacs can accept text and commands at the same time. Where vi treats all text equally, modes in emacs can interpret what you are typing. For example, if you are using the C language mode, emacs automatically indents and formats your source code.

No set of UNIX tools would be complete without a shell. The GNU Tool shell, BASH (*Bourne Again Sh*ell), is compatible with the venerable sh (Bourne Shell), as well as including many of the popular features found in csh (C Shell) and ksh (Korn Shell). For example, BASH offers job control, command-line editing (with either vi or emacs commands, of course), and csh-style command history.

GNU Tools also include tools for software development. One of the critical tools is GCC, the GNU C Compiler. GCC supports the various C specifications, including ANSI C. GCC also compiles the C, C++, or Objective C languages.

For us humans, GCC can produce object code that supports various debuggers, including SDB and GNU's own GDB.

One of my favorite GNU Tools is named `less`, which is a paging program similar to `more` and `pg`, except that it adds many features, such as the capability to scroll backward through the document. It also adds the capability to jump to the top or the bottom of the document from any point within it. The `less` tool also includes all the regular expression support so that searching for strings within the document is at least as simple and powerful as we are used to in `more` and `vi`.

The GNU Tools have proved so popular that most of them have been ported to microcomputers (predominately DOS platforms).

One of the unique aspects of the GNU Tools is that they are all distributed as source code, complete with makefiles and notes for special modifications needed for some UNIX variants. In fact, the instructions for the software encourage modification of the program.

Another truly unique aspect of the GNU Tools is that they are all free. Free? Yup. Every GNU Tool is available via anonymous FTP. The Tools are also all free.

While the Tools are available free of charge, they are also free in the sense that you can share them. The license agreement lets you give a copy of the Tools to a friend, neighbor, brother-in-law, whomever without violating the agreement. The license agreement also attempts to prevent companies from taking GNU Tools, making proprietary changes to the software, and then selling them under a traditional software copyright.

The Free Software Foundation is serious about living up to its name.

The History of the Free Software Foundation

As I mentioned earlier, Richard Stallman founded the Free Software Foundation in the mid-1980s. Stallman had been working for MIT's Artificial Intelligence Laboratory when the Lab's primary operating system was licensed to a computer company, which turned around and sold the operating system as a proprietary package.

Stallman, who envisioned a world where people could share good software with each other, left the Lab and started working on the first of the GNU Tools, GNU `emacs`. He also started Project GNU, whose goal was (and still is) to create a nonproprietary operating system that lets its users use and customize it.

Two years later, GNU `emacs` was ready, and Stallman incorporated the Free Software Foundation, the world's first charitable, nonprofit group whose goal is to develop free software.

When Richard Stallman started Project GNU, he did it because he believed that software programmers should not be forced into reinventing an algorithm because some other company developed it first and copyrighted and/or patented the idea. He felt that a programmer's time is better spent developing new software instead of developing ways to achieve the same result as somebody else without doing it the same way. With this cornerstone, Stallman laid the foundation that eventually became the GNU General Public License, as well as the "copyleft" that the GNU Tools use today.

One of the founding principles of the Free Software Foundation is that the traditional software copyright isn't *right* at all.

The traditional software copyright grants the ability to use the software to the purchaser, but that's about it. If you find the software useful and would like your fellow administrators to try it out, tell them to pick up the pizza on their way over to your place because you can't give them a copy of the software legally.

For many years, the copyright did not stop many people from making copies of software and handing them over to their friends, earning these folks the name *software pirates*. Recently, however, many software producers are taking their copyrights more seriously and are beginning to prosecute pirates. With some fines being reported as high as $10,000 per infraction, many sites are taking software copyrights more seriously as well.

Fortunately, the Free Software Foundation is serious about preserving the end user's right to use the software, modify it, *and* redistribute it.

This is why the GNU Tools use a copy*left*. Whereas a copyright denies the freedoms of use and modification (and especially distribution) of software, the copyleft preserves these freedoms. The copyleft ensures that these rights continue by requiring those who redistribute the software (no matter how much of the software they have changed) to include the copyleft, which grants the very same freedoms to the next user, who also must include the copyleft in any modifications that he or she distributes, and so on.

The copyleft that Project GNU (and also the Free Software Foundation) uses was created by combining a typical copyright agreement and the GNU General Public License. The GNU General Public License is included in a separate file with each GNU Tool distribution.

The GNU General Public License is a document written in pretty straightforward legalese. Very basically, it states that the license protects certain rights of the user and also certain rights of the Free Software Foundation. The General Public License is fairly limited in that it only addresses the copying, the distribution, and/or the modification of the software. It does not apply to supporting the product, nor does it imply any warranty for the product.

For the user, the GNU General Public License protects the right to copy, modify, and distribute the software—even sell it—as long as you give the same rights to the next user as were given to you. The License also lists how to meet all of these criteria. The License does contain some major restrictions, one of which forbids any changes made to the License itself or to any of the copyright notices.

How was it that the Free Software Foundation could take a normal software copyright agreement and use it to the group's advantage? Each copyright statement includes several modifiers that specifically give up certain portions of the copyright and then allow the user to redistribute the software, as long as the very same agreement text is included.

The GNU Tools are distributed primarily as source code, accompanied by the appropriate libraries, header files, and makefiles to compile the tool. Because even the most well-written source code won't compile cleanly on every system, the Free Software Foundation collects all the changes that people make to the source in order to make it compile on that system. The FSF then includes this information in the tool's distribution, so that the next user on that system can install the tool more easily.

Armed with these principles, the Free Software Foundation has continued to pursue Project GNU's original goal of a nonproprietary operating system. The Free Software Foundation decided to model the operating system after UNIX and gave it a rather cyclical name: *GNU's Not UNIX* (GNU). In this effort, the Free Software Foundation has produced many programs, ranging from BASH (shell), to `emacs` (text editor), to NetHack (games), to the GNU C Compiler (GCC) and even `perl`.

The Future

The Free Software Foundation is still hard at work, pursuing the goal of a nonproprietary operating system. This version of GNU (GNU's Not UNIX) is pronounced with the G (*guh-new*), so as to avoid confusion with the GNU Tools.

Richard Stallman, when he was getting ready to begin with Project GNU, wrote the GNU Manifesto, a description of the goals and guiding principles of the project as well as an effort to garner support for the project. Although the Manifesto was first published in 1985 (in the March edition of *Dr. Dobb's Journal*), it remains the keystone of the Free Software Foundation today with very few changes.

The Manifesto begins by describing GNU and a very brief status of the effort. After the first couple of years, however, updating the Manifesto to keep track of the many aspects of the project became overwhelming, and now users can keep up to date with its status in the Free Software Foundation publication *GNU's Bulletin*.

In the Manifesto, Stallman explains his personal goal of freely available software and his disappointment with the rest of the software industry for forcing users to abandon a lesson that we all learned early in life: sharing.

The GNU Manifesto also describes some of the logic behind Richard Stallman's decisions about GNU. For example, the Manifesto explains that he chose UNIX as a model for GNU because the basics of the operating system were sound, and what Stallman felt was missing could easily be implemented.

When `emacs` was first developed, it was written in LISP. This proved to be a very good design decision, as the flexibility, power, and capability to add features to `emacs` have helped it become as popular as it is today.

LISP is also being used as the primary language in GNU, but it is not the only system language. C/C++ is also used for a large number of GNU applications.

The building of GNU has presented some interesting development issues for the Free Software Foundation. How can a charity attract and retain the number of quality programmers needed to build a complete operating system? As you might have guessed, this problem has affected the delivery expectations more than once. Through the effort of many people with similar beliefs as Stallman volunteering their time, however, programming expertise and materials have kept the project going.

Where this support is wonderful and impressive, it sometimes presents problems, especially in coordination of a project the size of GNU. Fortunately, UNIX (and UNIX-compatible systems) comprises a collection of individual components, and programmers who are not down the hall can more easily develop it. The kernel, of course, is a different matter. Stallman and a small group of programmers working closely together (figuratively and literally) are developing that.

The work on GNU has progressed far enough that a complete software development environment is now available. Several software companies are using this development environment to produce their own software. For example, Wind River Systems, a company that produces real-time software with GNU Tools, operates over 12,000 traffic lights in New York City with their system.

What's a UNIX-compatible system without a kernel? Not GNU, certainly. Currently, the Free Software Foundation is working on the kernel to drive its operating system.

The kernel is based on the Mach microkernel, which was developed at Carnegie Mellon University. Of course, copyrights have reared their ugly heads, so the Free Software Foundation and university lawyers have been working together for some time now to incorporate the kernel into GNU.

When GNU is finished, it will provide a complete, multithreaded, multitasking operating system available free of charge. This puts a sophisticated operating system within easy reach of schools, colleges, nonprofit groups, and so on, allowing these organizations to spend more time and money on the real work of these groups.

Because GNU will most likely be distributed as source code, like GNU Tools, users will be able to make the modifications that they need, when they need them. This means that if, by some small chance, a problem arises with the software's graphical user interface, it can be fixed immediately. This is very different from some proprietary systems where fixes are withheld until some arbitrary point in time so that the proprietary system won't appear to have bugs.

As with the GNU Tools, the port of GNU to microprocessor-based platforms won't be too far behind. When this happens, more and more small software houses will be able to produce software with high-quality tools and without a high overhead cost.

GNU Tools and information about GNU are available all over the Internet, but their primary home is in Boston. GNU Tools are available via anonymous FTP from `prep.ai.mit.edu`. If you would like more information about GNU, or if you would like to volunteer, you can contact the Free Software Foundation through electronic mail at `gnu@prep.ai.mit.edu`.

Chapter 44

Using GNU Software Development Tools

As we saw in the previous chapter, the GNU Project covers a wide variety of areas for which the GNU people created free software.

The GNU Compilers

GNU has compilers for many programming languages, including C, FORTRAN, and LISP. Also, GNU offers you some tools for easy conversion tasks.

You'll find a FORTRAN to C converter, a Pascal to C converter, a multiplatform configuration tool, and lots more.

First, the C compiler is a high-quality compiler that also supports C++ and Objective C. GNU makes a FORTRAN 77 compiler. A nice complement to this is the FORTRAN to C converter utility, also made by GNU. The GNU Project also includes a variety of LISP compilers and a few scripting languages.

The GNU group also provides other programming goodies that complement the compilers, including a C library (which supports ANSI, POSIX, 44BSD, and some of SYSV), a C++ library, and a Pascal to C converter. You'll also find packages like the GNU Regex, which gives you the functionality of the UNIX `regexp` (which compiles regular expressions).

As you can see, GNU offers everything that's needed to build a very powerful and flexible development environment.

The C, C++, and Objective C compiler

The first compiler I will talk about is the C compiler. The GNU C compiler does not just compile C programs. It has an embedded C++ compiler as well, and it also supports Objective C. Even though GCC is free, it is a very high-quality C, C++, and Objective C compiler.

C++ and Objective C are both object-oriented flavors of the C language. NeXT computers developed Objective C support to use GCC as a starting point. Later, NeXT gave that work to GNU so that it became part of the GNU C compiler project.

The C compiler itself supports traditional Kernighan & Ritchie C, ANSI C, and GNU C extensions. This compiler can generate a variety of output formats including a.out, COFF, ELF, and OSF-Rose. It can produce debugging information for COFF, ECOFF, ELF, and OSF-Rose output files.

The platforms that GCC currently supports include GNU/Linux, AIX, FreeBSD, Irix, Minix, NeXTStep, OS/2, OSF, SCO, Solaris 2, System/370, SunOs, VMS, and Windows NT.

The processors that are supported for these platforms include a29k, Alpha, Clipper, PDP-11, and i386/i486/Pentium. You can see from this that the GNU C compiler offers the advantage of great versatility.

The wide variety of platforms and processors that are supported will assure you that you can use the same C compiler to compile all your C/C++/Objective C programs on these platforms/processors. Therefore, if you develop a piece of software, you don't have to worry about the flavor of C you are using, and you don't have to be afraid of not being able to find an equivalent compiler on the platform to which you want to port your software. You also don't have to worry that a certain function will not be supported on a certain platform; that is, you can feel confident that you won't have to reinvent the wheel every time you port your software to a new platform.

You just need to get the GCC source tree on that platform and compile it. Of course, this will only work if a C compiler is already present there. This would not be the case, for example, with Solaris 2 if you didn't buy the unbundled development package.

This would be a very unfortunate situation if the GNU Project didn't make GCC binaries available for all platforms so that you only need to install it to compile the latest version of the GNU C compiler.

The binaries that are made available to people are usually old versions of the C compiler. They can still compile a newer GCC even though they are less featured and probably more afflicted with early GCC bugs than the latest version. That is why GCC will build itself in at least two stages. The first stage will have GCC compiled using the old binary, and the second stage will compile GCC using the newly compiled GCC. (GCC will compile itself using itself.)

The wide variety of platforms and processors that are supported by GCC allows you to use another very important feature of GCC. This feature is called *cross-compiling*. It means that you can use GCC to produce executable programs for another CPU type. For example, imagine that you run NeXTstep for NeXT hardware and you would like to support the same program on NeXTstep for HP-PA, Intel, and Sparc. All you have to do is cross-compile the program so that GCC generates the right code for the right CPU. This way, you can easily support multiple CPUs with one single source tree.

The GNU C compiler also offers a variety of optimization features not often encountered in other compilers. These features go from unrolling of loops to optimized multiplication by constants. As opposed to most native C compilers on UNIX machines, GCC can use all these optimization features at the same time it puts debugging information in the executable program that it produces. This is a worthwhile feature as it allows you to debug your program in the same optimization state as it will be when the final program comes out.

GCC also allows you to put inline (assembler) functions in your code. This is desirable when you want the very critical parts of your program to profit from the gain in speed of execution that assembler code gives you (assuming you optimized it).

The FORTRAN 77 compiler

The GNU people offer a FORTRAN 77 compiler, which was built using part of the source code in GCC. The f2c program, distributed with the FORTRAN compiler, converts FORTRAN to C code that GCC can then compile.

The CLISP compiler

Through GNU, you can obtain an implementation of common LISP, which is derived from the original KCL. AKCL was later developed and is now renamed and distributed by GNU as GCL. The GCL package contains everything needed to build a common LISP development environment. This includes an interpreter and a compiler that produces C code, which can then be compiled using GCC.

Future developments for this compiler include complying with the emerging ANSI standard. Version 2.0 and later include hooks to tcl/tk and an X Windows interface scripting and development tool.

The ADA95 compiler

An ADA95 compiler is distributed under the GNU public license. ADA is a language that has not had much success in the past, and the ADA community has concluded that one of the major reasons why it failed to be adopted as a development language is that no cheap high-quality compiler was available. The GNU ADA compiler changes this situation.

The ADA95 compiler includes features such as object-oriented programming support and distributed systems support.

Using GCC

GCC compiles C and C++ programs in four stages: preprocessing, compilation, assembly, and linking. Some other implementations of C++ compilers will just produce an intermediate C program that the regular C compiler compiles.

GCC—you can refer to it as G++ when talking about compiling C++ programs—really is an integrated C and C++ compiler with no intermediate C program. GCC understands several types of input files, and each type makes GCC act in a different way. Table 44-1 lists what each file is and what GCC does with it.

Table 44-1   How GCC Interacts with Different Files

Extension	Kind of File	What GCC Does to It
.c	C source files	Preprocess, compile, and assemble
.C	C++ source files	Preprocess, compile, and assemble
.cc	C++ source files	Preprocess, compile, and assemble
.cxx	C++ source files	Preprocess, compile, and assemble
.m	Objective C source files	Preprocess, compile, and assemble
.i	Preprocessed C files	Compile and assemble
.ii	Preprocessed C++ files	Compile and assemble
.s	Preprocessed Assembler source files	Assemble
.S	Assembler source files	Preprocess and assemble
.o	Object files	Link
.h	Preprocessor files	Not usually named on command line

Files ending with other suffixes will be passed to the linker (ld). Any .o files, which are object files, and .a files, which are archive files, are commonly passed to the linker.

GCC accepts several command-line options that will control the behavior of the compiler during each stage of the compilation. Here is a brief description of the options that are most used.

Note

The command-line options must be separated. For example, -d -r is very different from -dr.

First, we'll look at the general command-line options. These will affect the general behavior of GCC.

This -x <language> option explicitly specifies the language for the input files that follow. The default behavior of GCC when this option is not used is to determine the language to compile using the filename suffix. Values for <language> include c, objective-c, c-header, c++, cpp-output, assembler, and assembler-with-cpp. A -x option remains in effect until GCC encounters the next -x option or all the input files are processed.

The -x none option turns off the -x <language> option. It makes GCC go back to the default behavior of guessing languages from filename suffixes.

These two options are useful when you want only GCC to do a subset of all the four stages (preprocess, compile, assemble, and link). This way, you can tell GCC, for example, to stop after the compile stage so that you can have a look at the assembly code produced by GCC.

By using one of three options (-c, -E, or -S), you can tell GCC where to stop. The -c option makes GCC compile or assemble the input files but does not link them. The output will be an object file for each input file. The -E option makes GCC run the preprocessor on each input file but does not compile, assemble, or link the files. The output is a preprocessed source file (for each input file) that is sent to standard output. The -S option makes GCC compile the input files but doesn't assemble them. The output is an assembler source file for each input file.

Note

Some combinations of these options, such as -x cpp-output -E or -x assembler -S, will tell GCC to do nothing.

The -o <file> option overrides the default output filename for an output file. The default output filename scheme consists of replacing the suffix of the input file (but keeping its name) with the suffix corresponding to the type of the output file.

For example, if I preprocess, compile, and assemble a C file named proggie.c, GCC will name the output file proggie.o. I could have specified a -o proggie.object to override the default naming scheme.

Note

You can only specify the -o option once on the command line. This means that you should also specify a single input file when you also use -o unless you are building an executable file. It would not make sense to specify multiple input files when you can only specify the -o option once.

This is a special case to the default naming scheme. When an executable file is built, the output file containing the executable program will be named a.out by default. You can also use the -o option to override it.

The -v option makes GCC print (on standard error output) the various commands used to initiate the different stages of the compilation. It also prints the version numbers of the compiler and preprocessor.

The -pipe option makes GCC use pipes instead of temporary files between each stage of the compilation. Some assemblers will have problems with this, but the GNU assembler works fine.

This option, when used, speeds up the passing of intermediary files to the next stage, and it doesn't create temporary files, behavior that can be useful if your available disk space doesn't allow it.

The preprocessor options

First, let's define what a preprocessor can do for you:

- It includes header files in your C program. Header files are files with filenames ending in .h where you declare variables and functions.

- It defines macros that your C program uses. Macros are arbitrary definitions of C code. The preprocessor will replace all references to the macro with the corresponding C code in your C program.

- It performs conditional compilation, which compiles a piece of code in your program under certain conditions. You can do this using special directives.

- It does line control. If you use a program that rearranges multiple source files into one big file that will be compiled, line control can tell the compiler where each line originated.

These options control the C preprocessor, which runs on each C source file before actual compilation.

If you use the -E option, GCC does nothing except preprocessing. Some of these options make sense only together with -E because they cause the preprocessor output to be unsuitable for actual compilation. Table 44-2 lists the main preprocessor options and their functions.

Table 44-2   Preprocessor Options

Option	Result
-include<file>	Processes <file> as input before processing any other input file.
-imacros<file>	Processes <file> before any other input file and then discards the output. It may seem useless at first sight but really it is not. Processing a macros file means that macros and defines may be made available for use by the regular input files before they are processed.

Option	*Result*
`-idirafter<dir>`	Adds the directory `<dir>` to the second include path. The directories on the second include path are searched when a header file is not found in any of the directories in the main include path (the one that `-I` adds to).
`-iprefix<prefix>`	Specifies `<prefix>` as the prefix for subsequent `-iwithprefix` options.
`-iwithprefix<dir>`	Adds a directory to the second include path. The name of the directory that is added is created by concatenating `<prefix>` and `<dir>`, where `<prefix>` was specified previously with `-iprefix`.
`-nostdinc`	Tells GCC not to search the standard system directories for header files. Only the directories you have specified with `-I` options (and the current directory, if appropriate) are searched. This is useful when you don't want the system header files to conflict with your own header files.
`-nostdinc++`	Same as `-nostdinc` but applies to C++ standard directories.
`-undef`	Does not predefine any nonstandard macros (including architecture flags). This can be useful when you are cross-compiling a program.
`-C`	Tells the preprocessor not to discard comments. Used with the `-E` option.
`-P`	Tells the preprocessor not to generate `#line` commands. Used with the `-E` option.
`-M`	Tells the preprocessor to output a rule that the make utility can use, describing the dependencies for each object file. Each source file processed this way generates a rule that the make utility can later use to process the file again. The generated rule can be one or multiple lines using \ as a continuation character if it is multiple lines. (Using `-M` implies the `-E` option.)
`-MG`	Tells the preprocessor not to treat missing header files as an error and still output the dependency information for these missing files.
`-MM`	Like `-M` but the output mentions only the user header files included with `#include "file"`. System header files included with `#include <file>` are omitted.

Continued

Table 44-2   *(continued)*

Option	Result
-MD	Like -M but the dependency information is written to files with names made by replacing .o' with .d' at the end of the output filenames. This option does not imply the -E option, and this means that, along with producing dependency information, the compilation will continue after preprocessing if this is the desired behavior. You can use the Mach utility md' to merge the .d' files into a single dependency file suitable for using with the make' command.
-MMD	Like -MD except mentions only user header files, not system header files.
-H	Prints the name of each header file used.
-D<macro>	Defines <macro> with the string 1' as its definition. For example, -D_POSIX_SOURCE will define the macro _POSIX_SOURCE and give it a value of 1.
-D<macro>=<defn>	Defines <macro> as <defn>. All the -D' options on the command line are processed before any U' options. For example, to define the macro LOCALDIR as /usr/local', the option specifies would be DLOCALDIR-"/usr/local".
-U<macro>	Undefines <macro>. -U' options are evaluated after all -D' options. All the -U' options are processed before any -include' and -imacros' options.
-dM	Tells the preprocessor to only output a list of all the macros that are defined at the end of the preprocessing stage. This is used with —E option.
-dD	Tells the preprocessor to pass all the macros definitions to the next stage after preprocessing.
-dN	Like -dD except that the macros defined on the command line are omitted. Only the #define instructions are passed.

Note

When the -imacros option is specified, it will trigger preprocessing of <file> *after* any -D or -U option specified on the command line.

Secret

If you have different header files for different people for whom you are developing the program (or different header files for each hardware architecture you support), using the -iprefix option to change the location of the second include path is a fast way to switch to a different set of header files with minimum hassle.

The language options

These options are those related to the language in which your program is written. They control the behavior of the compiler for language issues (flavor of C, special features, and so forth). Table 44-3 lists the most used language options and their functions.

Table 44-3	Language Options
Option	**Result**
-ansi	Tells the compiler to support ANSI C during compilation. It disables some GNU C extensions (inline programs, the typedef keyword, and the like) and enables some features like the ANSI trigraphs. Of course, this does not make GCC reject all non-ANSI programs. If this is the desired effect, you must use the -pedantic option as well.
-fno-asm	Tells the compiler not to recognize asm, inline, or typeof as a keyword. This option is implied by the -ansi option.
-fno-builtin	Tells the compiler not to recognize built-in functions that do not begin with two leading underscores. The functions affected in the latest version of GCC include _exit, abort, abs, alloca, cos, exit, fabs, labs, memcmp, memcpy, sin, sqrt, strcmp, strcpy, and strlen.
-fno-strict-prototype	When a function is declared without arguments (for example, int foo ()), normal C++ compilation would have that function accept no arguments. This option tells GCC that these functions with no arguments will in fact take a number of them and to leave them as is, without trying to guess anything about their arguments.
-trigraphs	Supports ANSI C trigraphs. The -ansi option implies -trigraphs. *Trigraphs* are sequences of characters beginning with ??. For example, ??/ would represent the / character.

Continued

Table 44-3 *(continued)*

Option	Result
-traditional	Tells the compiler to support and not reject some features of traditional C. These include switches with arguments of type long, references to macros inside string constants, and so forth.
-traditional-cpp	Same as -traditional except that it will only affect features related to the preprocessor, such as references to macros inside string constants.
-fdollars-in-identifiers	Tells the compiler to allow for the use of $ in identifiers. You can use the option -fno-dollars-in-identifiers to deny the use of $ in identifiers.
-fenum-int-equiv	Tells GCC to allow conversion of int variables to enumeration types and vice-versa. The normal behavior is to allow enum to int only.
-fcond-mismatch	Permits the use of conditional statements in which the second and third argument have types that do not match. The value of such an expression is of type void.
-funsigned-char	Tells the compiler to make the char type unsigned. It is equivalent to declaring a variable of type unsigned char.
-fsigned-char	Tells the compiler to make the default behavior of char-type variables to be signed.
-fsigned-bitfields -funsigned-bitfields -fno-signed-bitfields -fno-unsigned-bitfields	These four options control whether the default behavior of bitfields will be signed or unsigned. The default behavior when none of these options is specifed is signed unless the -traditional option is specified, in which case they will be unsigned.
-fwritable-strings	Tells the compiler to store the string constant in the writable data segment of the program. Normally, they are stored in the nonwritable segment and you would receive a segmentation violation error (and a core file) if you tried to write into this string constant. This option exists for backward compatibility with old programs that assumed it was legitimate to write into string constants. (-traditional has the same effect.)

Secret

A program will be more portable if the char variables are always declared so that unsigned or signed is specified (signed char, unsigned char). This is because the char type has a default behavior (signed or unsigned) depending on the type of machine it is compiled on.

Secret

If you are trying to run a program that expects its char variables to have a certain default behavior and this default behavior is different on the machine you're trying to run it on, you can use -funsigned-char or -fsigned-char to change the default behavior of the char variables for your machine and make the program work.

Tip

Writing into constants is not a very good idea. Constants have been called constants for a reason.

The linker options

These options come into play when we arrive at the stage where the various object files, archive files, and libraries are linked together to produce an executable file. Table 44-4 lists the most used linker options and their functions.

Table 44-4 Liker Options	
Option	**Result**
<object-file-name>	This is a special option. In fact, it is not really an option. If a file is specified on the command line as an input file and this file doesn't have a recognizable suffix (.c, .h, .o, and the like), GCC will consider it to be an object file or a library and will pass the filename to the linker, which will use such files as input files and link them with the other input files.
-l<library>	This tells the linker to use the library named <library> when linking. During the link stage, the linker will search a list of directories for this library. The library specified must be in the default list of directories (a common default list is /lib, /usr/lib, /usr/local/lib). If it is not, you can still link it with the -L option, which will add directories to the default list. An example of such a library specification would be to specify -lposix if we wanted to link our program with the POSIX library. The linker would build a filename by adding lib' as a prefix to the library name and .a ' as a suffix (which would give libposix.a) and search several directories to find that library.

Continued

Table 44-4 *(continued)*	
Option	*Result*
-lobjc	You need this special case of the -l option to link an Objective C program.
-nostdlib	Don't use the standard system libraries when linking. Only the files you specify will be passed to the linker.
-static	On systems that support dynamic linking, this prevents linking with the shared libraries. On other systems, this option has no effect.

Secret

If you intend to distribute your program to other people who are possibly running an older version of your operating system, use the -static option to link your program statically as opposed to linking it dynamically. Dynamic linking will use the shared libraries on the machine that other people would use to run the program. If these are older libraries or if they have been altered (patched or enhanced), your program will not work as well for others as it did for you.

The directory options

The directory options instruct GCC what directories to search for header files, libraries, and other parts of the compiler. Table 44-5 lists the main directory options and their functions.

Table 44-5 **Directory Options**	
Option	*Result*
-I<dir>	Adds <dir> to the list of directories to search for include (header) files
-L<dir>	Adds <dir> to the list of directories to search for libraries (libraries to be linked, added with the -l option)
-B<prefix>	Tells GCC that the executable files, libraries, and data files that are part of the compiler itself can be found in <prefix>

These other parts of the compilers include such programs as cccp (the preprocessor) and ld (the linker). If the executable file is not in <prefix>, GCC tries with two standard prefixes: /usr/lib/gcc and

/usr/local/lib/gcc-lib. If the executable file is still not found in there, GCC will then try with your own PATH environment variable.

Secret

If your installation of GCC is not in a standard place, you can tell GCC where it will find the executable files and libraries it needs by setting a GCC_EXEC_PREFIX environment variable and putting the directory where GCC is installed as a value for this variable.

The warning options

The warning options change the level of verbosity for GCC when it is compiling a program. You can use them to report certain things that would make your program less portable, for example. Table 44-6 lists the most convenient warning options and their functions.

Table 44-6   Warning Options

Option	Result
-fsyntax-only	Makes GCC check the code for syntax errors and produce no output.
-W	Turns all warning messages off.
-pedantic	Makes GCC reject all programs that do not conform to strict ANSI standards. Strict ANSI programs will compile fine without this option, but certain GNU and traditional C constructs will still be accepted when it is not specified. This option also makes GCC issue all the proper warnings about nonconformance to strict ANSI.
-pedantic-errors	This option is similar to -pedantic except that it makes GCC produce errors instead of warnings about nonconformance to strict ANSI.
-Wimplicit	Warns when a function or parameter is implicitly declared.
-Wreturn-type	Warns when a function's return type defaults to int. Also warns when a function does not return a value and is not of type void.
-Wunused	Warns when a local variable is not used, when a function is declared static but is never defined, and when a result is computed and it is never used.

Continued

Table 44-6   *(continued)*

Option	Result
-Wswitch	Warns when a switch statement has an index of type enum and not all values of the enumeration are covered (the default label prevents the warning for being issued). Case labels outside of the enumeration also trigger this warning.
-Wcomment	Warns when a comment-start sequence /* appears in a comment.
-Wtrigraphs	Warns if any trigraphs are encountered (when they are enabled).
-Wformat	Warns when the arguments given to printf, scanf, and so on don't have their types match with those of the format string.
-Wchar-subscripts	Warns if an array subscript is of type char. This is because char is signed on some systems.
-Wuninitialized	Warns when an automatic variable is used without having been initialized first.
-Wparentheses	Warns if parentheses are omitted in certain contexts.
-Wall	This option is a shortcut to enabling -Wimplicit -Wreturn-type -Wunused -Wswitch -Wcomment -Wtrigraphs -Wformat -Wchar-subscripts -Wuninitialized -Wparentheses -Wtemplate-debugging.
-Wtraditional	Warns about the use of traditional C constructs.
-Wshadow	Warns when a local variable shadows another local variable.
-Wwrite-strings	Makes GCC issue a warning if the address of a const char variable is copied into a non-const type. This helps you avoid writing code that could potentially write into a constant.
-Waggregate-return	Warns when a function that returns a struct or a union is defined or called.
-Wstrict-prototypes	Warns if a function is declared or defined without having its argument types specified. Such a function is allowed if it follows a declaration in which argument types are specified.
-Wmissing-prototypes	Warns if a global function is defined without a previous prototype declaration.

Option	Result
-Wmissing-declarations	Same as -Wmissing-prototypes except that it also warns even when the definition provides a proper prototype.
-Wredundant-decls	Warns if anything is declared more than once in the same scope.
-Wnested-externs	Warns if an extern declaration is encountered within a function.
-Wenum-clash	Warns about conversion between different enumeration types (C++ only).
-Werror	Treats warnings as errors. This aborts compilation after any warning.

Secret

The -Wall option warns about C constructs. Even if they are not inherently wrong, you should avoid them and can do so easily with good C programming habits.

The debugging options

GCC allows for the use of a wide variety of options for debugging purposes. These options will help you debug your program or debug GCC itself. Table 44-7 lists the most practical debugging options and their functions.

Table 44-7   Debugging Options

Option	Result
-g	Makes GCC produce debugging information in the native format of the operating system on which you're compiling your program. You can later use this information with GDB for debugging your program.
-ggdb	Makes GCC produce debugging information in the native format, including GDB extensions. If you don't plan to use GDB to debug your programs, using the -ggdb option will likely cause problems with the native debugger.

Continued

Table 44-7 *(continued)*

Option	Result
`-g<level> -ggdb<level>`	These are variants of the `-g` and `-ggdb` options. They make GCC produce debugging information according to `<level>`. When `-g` and `-ggdb` are specified without a level, the default level is 2. Level 1 just includes minimal information without line numbers and information on local variables. This is just the bare minimum for being able to do backtraces. Level 3 includes supplementary information such as the macro definitions present in your program.
`-p`	Makes GCC generate profiling information that the `prof` utility can use.
`-pg`	Makes GCC generate code that will generate profile information when the program executes. The `gprof` utility can then use this information.

GCC allows you to use `-g` and `-0` together. Most other compilers won't let you do that.

The optimization options

These options will make your code smaller and faster. Of course, receiving that kind of service from a compiler exacts a price to pay: The compilation will take longer and consume more resources.

Don't use the optimization options in the development process. Your code will compile faster. When you're at the testing phase, adding optimization options will bring you closer to the behavior that your finished product will have (assuming you're going to optimize your final product).

Table 44-8 lists the optimization options and their functions.

If you use more than one `-0` option, with or without a level, only the last one specified on the command line is effective.

Table 44-8	Optimization Options
Option	**Result**
-0 -01	Makes GCC optimize your code by turning on two options: -fthreadjumps and -fdefer-pop. It also turns on a few more options depending on the machine you are using to compile.
-02	Makes GCC optimize even more by using about all supported optimizations that do not involve a trade-off for speed over space. For example, defining funroll-loops would speed up the execution of the loop, but the code itself would be bigger. Accordingly, -02 does not turn on -funroll-loops or finline-functions.
-03	Makes GCC optimize even more but at level, GCC does not care about space, it just maximizes code speed. Everything in 02 is turned on, and -finline-functions is also turned on.
-00	Does not make GCC do any kind of optimization. It is equivalent to not specifying a -0, -01, -02, or -03 option.

The optimization options of the form -f<option> are machine-independent. Most of these options have negative counterparts. For example, -funroll -loops has the -fno-unroll-loops negative counterpart with the obvious effect of not unrolling loops. In the same vein, most -fno-<option> options have a positive counterpart that would be -f<option>. In Table 44-9, you will find both types of options (negative or positive).

Table 44-9	Optimization Options of the Form f<option>
Option	**Result**
-ffloat-store	Makes GCC not store floating-point variables in registers. On some machines, the floating-point registers keep more precision than needed. Although excess precision is usually no problem for most programs, it may be desirable for some other programs to specify this. Such programs can, for example, rely on the definition of IEEE's floating point.
-fno-default-inline	If a C++ member function is defined within a class's scope, this option will not make the function inline only because of that.
-fno-defer-pop	Always removes the arguments to a function call from the stack as soon as the function returns.

Continued

Table 44-9 *(continued)*	
Option	**Result**
-finline-functions	All simple functions are integrated in their caller function if GCC decides the function is simple enough.
-fkeep-inline-functions	If all calls to a function are integrated (-finline-functions), GCC will still output the original function in the assembler code. This means the function is still there to be called at run time.
-ffast-math	Speeds up some calculus by violating some ANSI or IEEE rules. For example, it assumes that arguments to sqrt are nonnegative numbers.

You can obtain the counterpart of the option by adding or removing the no-prefix. In that list, the given type is the one that is not the default. This means you use them if you want to alter GCC's default optimization behavior.

Note

If all calls to a function become integrated, GCC will not output the function in the assembler code. This means that the function cannot be called separately at run time anymore.

The target options

These options all start with -m and allow a choice between hardware models or configuration. For example, if you ran some version of UNIX on Sparc hardware, you could choose to compile for old CPUs such as the Cypress CPU or choose to compile for more modern CPUs such as the SuperSparc.

Each CPU has different capabilities, and the target options let you get the best out of them. Because so many of these options exist, Table 44-10 lists only those that refer to the Motorola 68000 family of CPUs, as an example.

Table 44-10 Target Options for the Motorola 68000 Family	
Option	**Result**
-m68000 -mc68000	Generates output for a 68000. The default when GCC is configured for 68000-based systems.
-m68020 -mc68020	Generates output for a 68020 instead of the default that generates output for a 68000.

Option	Result
-m68881	Generates output that contains 68881 instructions. The 68881 processor is a floating-point unit. This option is the default unless GCC was configured not to use it.
-m68030	Generates output for a 68030. It is the default when GCC is configured for 68030s.
-m68040	Generates output for a 68040. It is the default when GCC is configured for 68040s.
-m68020-40	Makes GCC generate code for a 68040 without using any of the newer instructions that are unknown to the 68020. This allows programs to run both on 68020 and 68040.
-mfpa	Generates output that contains Sun FPA instructions for floating point.
-msoft-float	Generates output that contains calls to a floating-point library. The library is not part of GNU C. Usually, you can use the floating-point facilities of the machine you're compiling your program on, but this method won't work for cross-compilation.
-mshort	Makes the type int 16 bits wide. This is equivalent to having the type int be short int.
-mnobitfield	Does not generate code with the bit-fields instructions. It is implied by -m68000.
-mbitfield	Generates code with the bit-fields instructions. This is implied by -m68020.

These options give you a good idea of what GCC can do and are also a good way to show you how powerful and flexible GCC is.

The GNU Debugger

GNU offers a debugger that can debug C programs and C++ programs. This debugger is called GDB and works with executable files produced by other compilers than GCC as well. GDB includes partial support for other languages such as Modula-2, FORTRAN, and Pascal.

You can use GDB in many ways. Its native user interface is a command-line interface, but because Emacs has a GDB operation mode, you can use Emacs as an interface to GDB.

GDB provides you with four main services to help you find and fix a bug in your program:

- It lets you start your program and specify anything that could affect its behavior.

- It stops your programs on conditions that you have established.

- It examines what the current status of your program is when it has stopped.

- It lets you change things in your program so that you can test how different things will affect a bug and the rest of the program.

Invoking GDB

You can invoke GDB in three basic ways:

```
- gdb <program>

- gdb <program> <core file>

- gdb <program> <pid>
```

In the first way, you invoke GDB with <program> as an argument, where <program> is the name of an executable file.

In the second way, you invoke GDB with <program> and <core file>, where <core file> is the name of a core file (usually named core' but the name can also be anything else). The core file contains a snapshot of the exact status your program was in when it crashed. Invoking GDB and specifying a core file will put the program in the exact same state inside GDB.

Creating core files for some programs can be impossible. Sometimes, you need to catch an insidious type of bug that is intermittent and doesn't crash your program. The third way to invoke GDB comes in handy in these cases. In this third way, you invoke GDB with <program> and <pid>, where <pid> is a process identification number of a running process. When invoked this way, GDB will attach itself to the running process and begin examining the process, which you can then debug.

We are going to examine a sample debugging session with GDB, using the same program you saw in Chapter 39. To avoid having to flip back to Chapter 39 to see the source of the program, refer to Listing 44-1. The output follows the listing.

Listing 44-1: A Program That Generates a Segmentation Fault

```
#include <stdio.h>
#include <fcntl.h>
#include <errno.h>
int openbuffer(filename)
char *filename;
```

```
{
int fd;
if ((fd=open(filename,O_RDONLY))<0)
        {
        fprintf(stderr,"Cannot open %s, errno=<%d>\n",filename,errno);
        exit(-1);
        }
return(fd);
}
int readbuffer(fd,buffer,size)
int fd;
char *buffer;
int size;
{
int retc;
if ((retc=read(fd,buffer,size))!=size)
        if (retc<0)
                {
                fprintf(stderr,"Cannot read, errno=%d\n",errno);
                exit(-2);
                }
        else if (retc)
                fprintf(stderr,"Partial read\n");
return(retc);
}
int countchar(buffer)
char *buffer;
{
int cnt;
char *p;
p=buffer;
while(*p)
        {
        if ((*p)==`\n´) cnt++;
        p++;
        }
return(cnt);
}
main()
{
int fd;
int cnt=0;
char inbuf[1024];
fd=openbuffer("/usr/lib/libc.a");
while (readbuffer(fd,inbuf,1024)) cnt+=countchar(inbuf);
printf("Bizarre character count=%d\n",cnt);
}
```

Following is the line I input, followed by the output:

```
$ gdb badprog core
GDB is free software and you are welcome to distribute copies of it under
certain conditions; type "show copying" to see the conditions.
There is absolutely no warranty for GDB; type "show warranty" for details.
```

```
GDB 4.7 (NeXT 3.1), Copyright 1992 Free Software Foundation, Inc...
Reading symbols from /home/badprog...done.
Reading symbols from /usr/shlib/libsys_s.B.shlib...done.
Reading in symbols for badprog.c...done.
0x3dda in countchar (buffer=0x3fff89c "!<arch>\n__.SYMDEF SORTED747000476   0
45             if ((*p)==`\n´) cnt++;
```

When I enter GDB with my program and core file, GDB tells me right away where the program crashed:

```
(gdb) where
#0  0x3dda in countchar (buffer=0x3fff89c "!<arch>\n__.SYMDEF SORTED747000476
#1  0x3e40 in main () at badprog.c:58
```

The `where` command shows me the stack, so I know what called my `countchar` function. It's been called by `main`. The #<digit>s at the beginning of the lines in the stack output are frames. Issuing the command `frame 0` will switch context and give the context of the `countchar` function. Likewise, issuing `frame 1` would give me the context of the `main` function:

```
(gdb) frame 0
#0  0x3dda in countchar (buffer=0x3fff89c "!<arch>\n__.SYMDEF SORTED747000476
45             if ((*p)==`\n´) cnt++;
(gdb) list 40,50
40   char *p;
41
42   p=buffer;
43   while(p)
44          {
45          if ((*p)==`\n´) cnt++;
46          p++;
47          }
48   return(cnt);
49   }
50
(gdb) print buffer
$1 = 0x3fff89c "!<arch>\n__.SYMDEF SORTED747000476   0    1    100644  58652
```

Here, we can see that I have reproduced the same bug the program had in Chapter 39. The terminating condition is on the pointer instead of being on the character the pointer points to

```
(gdb) print p
$1 = 0x4000000<Address 0x4000000 out of bounds>
(gdb) print *p
$2 = Cannot access memory: address 0x4000000 out of bounds.
```

Trying to access memory beyond what I could access caused the problem:

```
(gdb) frame 1
#1  0x3e40 in main () at badprog.c:58
58          while (readbuffer(fd,inbuf,1024)) cnt+=countchar(inbuf);
```

Let's have a look at what the buffer was while in `main`:

```
(gdb) print inbuf
$3 =   {"!<arch>\n__.SYMDEF SORTED747000476   0    1    100644  58652
\n\
(gdb) q
```

We can see that I can indeed move from one function to another, and in this way I can examine every intermediate calling function from the main function to the function that crashed.

GDB has many more powerful features. What follows are the most important ones.

Command-line options

GDB can take command-line options, as shown in Table 44-11.

Table 44-11   Command-Line Options

Option	Result
-s	
-symbols <file>	Makes GDB read the symbols table from another file.
-c	
-core <file>	Makes GDB use <file> as a core file.
-x	
-command <file>	Makes GDB read and execute GDB commands from file <file>.
-d	
-directory <dir>	Adds <dir> to the list of directories to search for source files.
-nx	Makes GDB not execute any commands from the .gdbinit file, which contains GDB commands that execute every time GDB is started.
-batch	Makes GDB run in batch mode. This mode is usually used with the -command option. GDB will exit successfully after executing all the commands in the command file specified with -command.
-quiet	Won't print the licensing information when GDB is started.

GDB commands

GDB understands a pretty varied vocabulary. Table 44-12 lists some of these keywords that you can use while debugging a program.

Table 44-12   Some GDB Commands

Option	Result
shell \<command\>	Starts a shell and executes it.
quit	Exits GDB.
make \<args\>	Starts the make utility and passes \<args\> to make.
help	Makes GDB display help about command categories.
help \<category\>	Makes GDB display help about a category of commands.
help \<command\>	Makes GDB display full help about a command.
complete \<str\>	Makes GDB list commands that begin with \<str\>.
run \<args\>	Starts your program and passes \<args\> to it; \<args\> may contain IO redirection.
attach \<pid\>	Attaches GDB to a running process with PID \<pid\>.
detach	Detaches GDB from the running process. Note that if you exit GDB or you use the run command while you are attached to a running process, you will kill the process. So always detach when you really want to keep the process alive.

GDB enables you to debug multithreaded programs! Table 44-13 lists a set of commands used for this purpose.

Table 44-13   Debugging Commands for Multithreaded Programs

Option	Result
thread \<number\>	Makes thread number \<number\> the current thread.
info threads	Lists all the threads that are currently present.
thread apply \<list\> \<args\>	Applies a command to a list of threads; \<list\> can be a list of thread numbers or the keyword ALL, which applies the command to all threads, and \<args\> is the command to apply.

GDB allows, of course, for stopping a program under certain conditions. Before listing commands, we have to define two notions, breakpoint and watchpoint. A *breakpoint* is a pointer to a place in the code that you can set. When the code pointed to by the breakpoint executes, the programs stops. A *watchpoint* monitors an expression, and when it reaches a certain value that you decide, your program stops. You set breakpoints and watchpoints using different commands, but once they are set, the same commands used to enable them will disable and delete them. Table 44-14 lists commands for stopping a program under certain conditions.

Table 44-14   Conditional Stop Commands

Option	Result
break <function>	Sets a breakpoint at the beginning of <function>.
break <line>	Sets a breakpoint at line number <line>.
break <offset>	Sets a breakpoint at +/–<offset> lines from the point where your program stopped.
break <file>:<f>	Sets a breakpoint at the beginning of function <f> in source file <file>.
break <file>:<l>	Sets a breakpoint at line number <l> in source file <file>.
break	Sets a breakpoint at the next instruction to execute.
break <args> if <cond>	Sets a breakpoint depending on <args>, which is the same set of arguments that break can take if <conf> evaluates as TRUE.
tbreak <args>	Sets a breakpoint that will be deleted as soon as the program stops.
info break	Prints a list of all breakpoints and watchpoints that are set.
watch <expr>	Sets a watchpoint for expression <expr>. When the expression changes value, the program stops.
clear	Deletes breakpoints set at the next instruction to execute.
clear <f>	Deletes breakpoints set at the beginning of function <f>.
clear <file>:<f>	Deletes breakpoints set at the beginning of function <f> in source file <file>.
clear <l>	Deletes breakpoints set at line number <l>.
clear <file>:<l>	Deletes breakpoints set at line number <l> in source file <file>.
delete	Deletes all breakpoints.
delete <args>	Deletes breakpoints according to <args>, where <args> is a list of breakpoint numbers as given by the info break' command.
disable	Disables all breakpoints.
disable <args>	Disables breakpoints specified with <args>.
enable	Enables all breakpoints.
enable <args>	Enables breakpoints specified with <args>.

Continued

Table 44-14 *(continued)*

Option	Result
enable once <args>	Enables breakpoints specified with <args> so that they will be disabled again as soon as the program stops.
enable delete <args>	Enables breakpoints specified with <args> so that they will be deleted as soon as the program stops.

Commands are also available to step through the program, as listed in Table 44-15.

Table 44-15 Step Commands

Option	Result
continue	Resumes execution of your program until the next breakpoint is encountered. If your program stopped at that location because of a breakpoint, the breakpoint is bypassed.
continue <count>	Same as continue. The optional <count> is a number of times that the breakpoint at this location will be ignored.
step	Continues the execution of your program until a different source line has been reached.
step <count>	Same as step. The optional <count> argument makes GDB go forward in step mode <count> number of times.
next	Continues the execution of your program until a different source line is encountered in the same frame. This means that function calls will not be followed.
next <count>	
finish	Continues the execution of the program until the current function returns.
until	Continues the execution of the program until a new source line past the current line is reached. This option is used to avoid going through a loop more than once. The until' option will stop the program after the loop completes.
until <loc>	Continues the execution of the program until the location <loc> is reached. The argument <loc> can be any of the arguments that the break' command takes.

GDB allows you to handle signals sent to your programs (see Table 44-16). This is very useful as you can block a signal so that your program doesn't see it or you can stop your program on a given signal.

Table 44-16 Signal Handling Options

Option	Result
info signals	Shows the signals currently handled by GDB and how they are handled
handle <signal> <arg>	Tells GDB to handle signal <signal> as specified by <arg>, which can be one or more of these:
Pass	Lets your program see the signal
Nopass	Does not let your program see the signal
Stop	Stops your program when this signal is received
Nostop	Lets your program run when the signal is received
Print	Prints a message when this signal is received
Noprint	Doesn't print a message when the signal is received
signal <signal>	Continues execution of your program and sends the signal <signal> right away

You now have an idea of how rich the command set of GDB is. You can use many other commands. GDB also allows you to do remote debugging via serial lines or TCP/IP connections. This means that you can run GDB on one machine and debug a program running on another machine. You can do this using an extension to GDB called gdbserver.

You can operate GDB from Emacs, a popular text editor that many people also use as a development environment. Emacs has a GDB mode that makes it interface pretty intimately with GDB.

Two graphical interfaces to GDB are also available. They are not supported or distributed by GNU, but because they have been developed specifically to work with GDB, they are worth a mention. The first one is called gdbtk (ftp://ftp.cygnus.com/pub/gdb/), and the second one is called xxgdb (ftp://ftp.x.org/contrib/utilities).

The gdbtk interface is a big package that includes the interface itself, tk, and tcl. These usually go together and are a new way to make X Windows-based programs. They implement high-level primitives for building GUI elements.

The xxgdb interface is a simple package that compiles in no time. It works with GDB 4.*x,* but it should also work with older versions. This one supports two modes of operation, single and multiple windows.

The GNU Libraries

The GNU Project has made several libraries available that implement functionality that you would otherwise have to pay for if you were to receive it.

The C library

The C library offers you a full implementation of the ANSI standard and also gives you the POSIX extensions to this standard. Many of the functions in this library are improvements over their traditional implementations. For example, the C library includes a `malloc` that is faster and wastes less memory than the regular `malloc`.

The C++ library

The C++ library is a collection of classes that have been developed to work with GCC (G++). Most of them will still work with regular compilers, but they will work best with the GNU C++ compiler (although programs using these classes and compiled with regular compilers will work with no noticeable differences compared to their G++-compiled counterparts).

The NeXT object library

NeXT objects always have this reputation of being easy to use. GNU offers you the exact same functionality with this library. Although these objects will not be run-time compatible with NeXT objects, they give you the same ease of use and, more important, the same functionality (which includes distributed objects).

Development Tools

GNU not only allows you to program in C, C++, or Objective C for free but also offers you language converters. For instance, `f2c` will convert FORTRAN 77 programs to C source code. You can then compile this C code using GCC. The `p2c` converter will convert Pascal programs to C source code that can also be compiled using GCC.

GDB partially supports debugging of FORTRAN and Pascal programs using the FORTRAN and Pascal source files, but printing variables in GDB and operations similar to that will still use the C syntax.

A special development tool from GNU is called GUILE. This is an extension language that can make regular C programs extensible.

GNU offers another utility called autoconf, which is not exactly a development tool. It lets you automatically configure your make file (assuming you want to use make, which you probably do), depending on the various features of the platform you are preparing to compile your program on. The autoconf utility generates a program called configure. The autoconf utility is told about things to check for using a template file. Once the configure program is generated, running it produces output telling you what configure is looking for, and then a make file is generated. Here is output from the configure program that came with tk4.1:

```
loading cache ./config.cache
checking for a BSD compatible install... (cached) /usr/bin/install -c
checking for ranlib... (cached) ranlib
checking for prefix by ... checking for wish... no
checking how to run the C preprocessor... (cached) cc -E -traditional-cpp
checking for unistd.h... (cached) yes
checking for limits.h... (cached) yes
checking stdlib.h... yes
checking whether cross-compiling... (cached) no
checking for ANSI C header files... (cached) yes
checking for mode_t... (cached) no
checking for pid_t... (cached) no
checking for size_t... (cached) yes
checking for uid_t in sys/types.h... (cached) yes
checking for X... (cached) libraries , headers
checking for X11 header files... checking for -lXbsd... (cached) no
checking for connect... (cached) yes
checking for gethostbyname... (cached) yes
checking for sin... (cached) yes
checking for -lieee... (cached) no
checking for memmove... (cached) yes
checking whether char is unsigned... (cached) no
checking for BSDgettimeofday... (cached) no
checking for gettimeofday declaration... present
checking for strtod... (cached) yes
checking for Solaris 2.4 strtod bug... ok
checking versions in library names... ok
creating ./config.status
creating Makefile
creating tkConfig.sh
```

Story: Compiling Packages for Other Systems

The autoconf utility can save you a lot of time in maintaining configurations for various systems. Using it, I have been able to compile packages on my machine that were not even ported to it. Configure did the bulk of the job by checking what my system could do and adapted the make file in consequence.

Forthcoming GNU Development Products

As you can see, GNU is truly a great project. Without it, we would have to pay for all these high-quality tools. These tools give commercial products a run for their money. If a free software package can do something that a commercial product cannot, something is obviously wrong. If GNU did not exist at all, I could bet that the quality of the same tools in the commercial versions would be lower than what we can see today.

The GNU Project is still evolving. People are developing new software continuously. Because the people involved with the GNU Project are all volunteers, the development process does not always go as fast as it could. Solutions exist though. GNU accepts monetary gifts and free labor. If you like the GNU tools and you feel you can help them help other people like you, don't hesitate to give them a hand. Future products that we might see one day from GNU include the following:

- New releases of their current products.

- GnuStep, the GNU implementation of an object-oriented API that is currently being proposed to be standard. Right now, only an Objective C library has been completed, and a lot remains to be done so that the GnuStep project actually meets the requirements of the proposed standard.

- A C interpreter. GNU hopes (and hopefully plans) to add interpreter capabilities into GCC and GDB. GCC already generates the kind of code an interpreter could process. Much work remains before this project is finished.

Summary

In this chapter you have been presented with the following:

▶ Why GNU software is better than commercial counterparts

▶ The best features of the GNU compiler and debugger

▶ Other GNU development tools

▶ Some advantages in using the GNU development tools

The next chapter covers even more GNU tools.

Chapter 45

More GNU Tools

This chapter introduces you to more GNU tools.

GNU Language Tools

You've already seen how powerful the GNU development environment can be. As impressive as it is, the Free Software Foundation provides many more equally impressive tools and utilities.

Conversion tools

Recognizing that not all developers use C or C++ as their language of choice, GNU Tools include a handful of utilities that will take source code of some other languages and convert it into a language that is compatible with the various compilers and tools used in the GNU development environment.

These tools also provide a simplified approach for maintaining legacy applications. For example, the accounting department of a company contracted a developer to develop its software years ago. Now accounting wants changes, and the original developer is long gone and living in a country that does not honor extradition.

Fortunately, GNU Tools can process several languages and return C source code. This alleviates the need to find a replacement contractor or take someone in-house and forcing that person to learn an older language for a single department's application. What follows are two GNU Tools, F2C and P2C, that translate from one language to another.

F2C

F2C is a conversion utility that takes FORTRAN-77 source code and converts it into a C or C++ that is compatible with the GCC or G++ compilers.

P2C

Another conversion utility, P2C, converts Pascal source to C. In contrast to F2C, P2C produces only C code and offers no choice between C or C++. P2C is versatile enough to accept several of the varieties of Pascal, including Turbo Pascal, ISO, HP, and VAX variants of Pascal.

DejaGnu

All complete development environments include tools to ease the testing burden, and GNU is no exception. DejaGnu provides the framework for testing programs with a single front end for all tests. The framework is designed to be open so that it can provide flexibility. Combine this with the consistency of the universal front end, and you have an environment where you can easily write and execute tests.

DejaGnu, like many testing tools available today, uses the record-playback model of operation. You develop a script of keystrokes, mouse movements, and data to be fed to a program either by recording a session with the program under test or by programming it and then replaying the script while feeding data to the program being tested. This model has proved to be a very effective system for testing software.

This model's basic premise demands that the script be capable of interpreting the output that the program is generating under test, processing it to some extent, and sending an appropriate response. For example, any scripting software would be able to send 2 + 2 and a newline to bc (the basic calculator) so that bc would do the math. The script can then read bc's answer and compare it to the value that the tester wants to see (hopefully that value would be *4* in both cases).

By maintaining testing scripts over several different versions, you are developing a library of tests that makes regression testing relatively simple (and not nearly as painful as it can be). When developing a new version, just rerun the script that tests a module that shouldn't have changed to verify that the module really didn't change.

Using this expectation throughout the development cycle has other benefits as well. Once a module has passed its individual test and has progressed into testing with other modules, supplying the same data is possible. With luck, the module behaves the same way in both scenarios.

While this is all well and good, anyone with a bit of knowledge and training can write a shell script to do the same things. What more can you expect of DejaGnu?

In addition to the basic flow control common to the scripting programs (if/then/else and the like) along with the capability to send data to a program and expect certain responses (similar to UUCP and other communication packages), you can expect to be able to pass control between the script and the user at any time, in either direction.

Being able to switch back and forth between script control and user control presents many possibilities not available before. For example, on a network, you can write a script to rlogin from one machine to another (and supply your password). This, however, requires that your password be in the script and in clear text; it is therefore a security risk.

Expect, a Perl-based tool for chat scripts, can begin the login process, ask you for your password, and pass it directly to the remote machine without storing it in a file or anywhere on disk.

For example, consider fsck, the file system integrity checking program. It comes with two basic arguments: -y (to answer yes to all of its questions) and -n (to answer no to all of its questions). Using expect, you can write a script so that fsck will answer yes to the file systems that you want it to repair, will answer no to the one that you don't want repaired, and will ask about the ones it doesn't know about (or have been set up to receive human input).

Another major difference between expect and other record-playback tools is that expect is capable of running any UNIX program (via a spawn command), where traditional script-playback tools are only capable of playing back its script.

DLD

DLD is a set of libraries that you can link in with almost any program. When you link in the DLD library, your program gains the capability to load object files into the running executable file dynamically.

As you are aware, you can build executable files once with all the modules necessary for the program to run linked when you compile the executable file. This is called static linking, and most operating systems use it.

Static linking means that all object modules and libraries that the program will use must be available to the compiler and linker at the time they run. When you are working on a totally new system, this is not always possible. Static linking also means that if any one of the object modules or libraries is changed, the entire program must be relinked.

A step up from static linking is *dynamic linking*. Some of the UNIX operating systems, such as SunOS, use this approach. For example, SunOS version 4 uses a style of dynamic linking that could be more accurately called *load-time linking*. When the program is linked, references to external objects — not the objects themselves — are included in the executable file. Then the actual objects are loaded into memory when the executable file runs.

True dynamic linking takes a slightly different approach. Dynamic linking allows the program to add, remove, or even relocate object modules within its address space while it is running—not just as it is being loaded into memory.

DLD provides the capability to use true dynamic linking in UNIX executable files. It does this by supplying tools in the form of a collection of library routines. No new executable files or changes to the existing compiler and/or linker are necessary.

When the executable file begins linking in a new module, the DLD routines locate it, process it (to resolve all the modules references), and bring it into memory. Because UNIX does not let a process change its text segment, DLD uses the dynamic data areas (the heap) for the new modules.

Unlinking is the opposite of linking. You must pay special consideration to the memory that the linked-in module used. DLD does everything it can to clean up and recycle the memory and goes as far as undefining any global variables that the module defined.

But some things, DLD won't undo. Any global variables that the module and input/output functions modified, for example, are not reversed.

DLD is currently only available on a limited variety of UNIX systems, primarily the BSD-based ones running on midrange machines.

Flex

Flex is a replacement for the UNIX Lex program. Flex creates programs that recognize patterns in text (commonly called *scanners*). You then compile and link the scanners into a program that uses the scanner to evaluate the input for occurrences of the patterns (known as regular expressions) and to execute the corresponding section of the program.

Scanners are used in a variety of places, from compilers to the regular expression syntax available in vi. When a program runs the scanner, it analyzes the input it receives, looking for strings that match any of its defined patterns. If the scanner finds more than one matching string, it uses the one that matches the pattern best. If the strings match equally, the string matching the pattern that is defined first in the scanner is used. The matching string is then passed on to the program using the scanner to do with it as it will.

If no string matches any of the patterns, the default rule executes: The input string is simply passed on as output without processing anything.

Flex is based on the Lex program originally released by AT&T. Flex, however, has additional extensions and a few incompatibilities. The major extension has been in the area of speed: Flex has been shown to perform much faster than Lex. Flex has also been developed to be compatible with the POSIX specifications (as has the bulk of GNU Tools and GNU). You can use Flex, as you can Lex, with the yacc parser-generator.

GNATS

GNATS is a system for tracking software bugs and their resolutions. Although liberal application of the GNU design tools and testing with DejaGnu should have all but eliminated software problems, they can still appear out of the blue.

The software problem descriptions are stored in a database that is simply a directory structure based on the different categories of problems that can be tracked. For example, any bug reports submitted in the FLEX category will be kept in a GNATS directory (for example, /local/GNATS/flex) as uniquely identified text files.

The GNATS database requires an administrator, who manages the categories that are valid and the lists of who is responsible for each of the categories, their e-mail addresses, and who is authorized to submit bug reports. By keeping track of who is responsible for which category, GNATS can e-mail the bug reports to those best equipped to fix the alleged bug. Bug reports in GNATS have four possible states: open, analyzed, feedback, and closed.

- *Open* is the initial state of every bug report that is submitted. It means that the bug report has been filed in the database and that e-mail has been sent to those responsible for that category.

- *Analyzed* means that the responsible party has examined the bug, agrees that it is a bug, and is now working toward resolving the bug.

- In the *feedback* state, the responsible party has discovered and approved a resolution and has forwarded it to the original submitter of the bug report.

- A *closed* bug indicates that the submitter has received, tested, and approved the resolution.

As the GNATS system is built primarily with C programs, shell scripts, and Emacs Lisp, you can access much of the principal GNATS functionality from within Emacs (described later in this chapter).

Indent

GNU's Indent is an update to the indent included with BSD UNIX. Indent formats C source. Whereas most other indents format to the Kernighan and Ritchie style by default, GNU's Indent formats to GNU coding standards. Regardless of the style used, Indent can help any source (shown in Listing 45-1) become more readable. Of course, Kernighan and Ritchie's style, shown in Listing 45-2, is available as an option, along with many others.

Listing 45-1: Source Code When I'm Done with It

```
#include    <sys/time.h>
main() {
struct timeval    tp;
```

```
struct timezone tzp;
int    flag[40], array[6], value, count, i, switchflag, save;
for (i = 0; i < 40; ++i) {
flag[i] = 0; }
count = 0;
gettimeofday(&tp, &tzp);
srandom(tp.tv_sec);
while (count < 6) {
value = (random() / 10000) % 40;
if (flag[value] == 0) {
array[count] = value + 1;
flag[value] = 1;
++count; } }
do {
switchflag = 0;
for (i = 0; i < 5; ++i) {
if (array[i] > array[i+1]) {
save = array[i];
array[i] = array[i+1];
array[i+1] = save;
switchflag = 1; } }
} while (switchflag == 1);
for (i = 0; i < 5; ++i)
printf("%d-", array[i]);
printf("%d\n", array[5]); }
```

Listing 45-2: Source Code When Indent Is Done with It (Using the Kernighan and Ritchie Style)

```
#include     <sys/time.h>
main()
{
    struct timeval  tp;
    struct timezone tzp;
    int    flag[40], array[6], value, count, i, switchflag, save;
    for (i = 0; i < 40; ++i) {
        flag[i] = 0;
    }
    count = 0;
    gettimeofday(&tp, &tzp);
    srandom(tp.tv_sec);
    while (count < 6) {
        value = (random() / 10000) % 40;
        if (flag[value] == 0) {
            array[count] = value + 1;
            flag[value] = 1;
            ++count;
        }
    }
    do {
        switchflag = 0;
        for (i = 0; i < 5; ++i) {
            if (array[i] > array[i + 1]) {
                save = array[i];
```

```
                array[i] = array[i + 1];
                array[i + 1] = save;
                switchflag = 1;
            }
        }
    } while (switchflag == 1);
    for (i = 0; i < 5; ++i)
        printf("%d-", array[i]);
    printf("%d\n", array[5]);
}
```

Three major styles set a variety of options for formatting:

- **GNU.** This is the default style, which, as stated earlier, formats to the specification of the style used throughout the GNU project. For example, the GNU style specifies that variable definitions begin in the first column, whereas the Kernighan and Ritchie style uses the second column and the Original style uses the seventeenth column.

- **Kernighan and Ritchie.** This style was used extensively throughout the book *The C Programming Language.* For example, this style, along with the Original style, sets indentation to be four spaces, whereas the GNU style sets indentation to be two spaces.

- **Original.** This style is the original C style used by the University of California at Berkeley. For example, the Original style places its comment delimiters on blank lines, whereas the GNU and Kernighan and Ritchie styles keep their comment delimiters with the comments.

Ncurses

An important part of most software is the capability to display something: an input screen, output, or whatever. A major tool for displaying data consistently across a variety of terminals is the venerable curses.

Ncurses has been designed to emulate the functionality of the standard curses library as well as the XPG4 curses library. As such, it supports control of the overall screen, window, and pad manipulation and display, reading terminal input (including mouse movements), color, and terminfo capabilities. Ncurses is the library that will replace the 4.4 BSD curses, which is being discontinued.

To Ncurses, windows and pads are slightly special types of terminals: Neither one necessarily means an entire screen. Although a window does mean a section of the screen, Ncurses will not handle windows that overlap. A *pad* is a special window that is not constrained by the size of the physical screen, nor does it require that the entire contents of the screen be displayed.

To help troubleshoot, Ncurses can produce trace logs that track the actions that Ncurses took during the running of the program.

Smalltalk

GNU Smalltalk is an interpreted language that uses the object-oriented model. Smalltalk has been written in C in a highly portable manner and has since found itself ported to many systems, even DOS.

Smalltalk is a full-fledged language in that it contains flow control (if/then, looping, and what-not) and even supports basic thread control. It also performs the basics such as math, input/output, and string manipulation.

Smalltalk treats all of its parameters as objects, as is true with most object-oriented systems. For example, consider adding and displaying the following math statement:

```
(2 + 2) printNl !
```

The first object (2) receives a message (+) with the argument object of 2. Smalltalk then creates a new object (containing the answer 4) and prints it to the standard output. The exclamation point signifies the end of the statement, much as you use a semicolon in C.

Smalltalk imposes a class hierarchy on its objects with the goal that related objects can inherit the code of their forefathers. In this type of hierarchy, once the objects have been properly defined, you should find that you need to implement an algorithm only one time and it is inherited by the children below.

One class worthy of mention is the stream class. A Smalltalk stream is similar to the streams used in C. A stream provides a sequential view to a resource: As elements are read and written, the stream position advances until the end is finally reached. As with most other streams resources, you can set the current position, allowing random access to the information in the stream.

Additionally, a Smalltalk stream gives you the ability to write into the stream without disrupting the flow, which many systems do not allow.

This is almost a complete implementation of the Smalltalk language. The only class that is not implemented by GNU is the graphical user interface (GUI) class.

Other GNU Tools

Here we will discuss some of the other tools provided by GNU. These are usually commands for UNIX.

Bash

Bash (Bourne Again Shell) is a UNIX shell. It is, of course, the shell used in and preferred by the GNU Project. Bash is an implementation of the POSIX shell standard and contains elements of the Bourne shell, the C shell, and the Korn shell.

The POSIX Story

POSIX is the name of a family of open system standards that are based on the UNIX operating systems. A wide range of functionality is being considered for standardization, from system services to applications and even system management. Each area under consideration is assigned to an IEEE working group in the 1003 series of standards.

Working group 1003.2 deals with the Shell and Utilities standard. The focus of the group has been the interface of the shell and utilities commonly run from the shell's command prompt.

Bash, for the most part, implements the 1003.2 standard. The default setting of Bash has some differences, mostly due to the inclusion of functionality. The true POSIX standard is available through a command-line option.

Perhaps the easiest way to enjoy the flavor of the functionality of Bash is to describe some differences between it and the more familiar shells. All of the Bourne shell functionality is available in Bash, plus some extras:

- `!´ is a reserved word that inverts pipeline return values.
- Bash contains a host of environment variables, especially those involved with command history.
- Bash reads ~/.bashrc for interactive shells (and uses the $ENV variable for noninteractive shells).
- Bash has csh-like history expansion.
- Command history is a shell built-in (not a separate executable file).
- Bash contains other built-ins, such as logout, pushd, and popd.
- Bash has the capability to export functions.

Some of the C shell's functionality is present in Bash, such as job control, history expansion, and environment variables that can control the behavior of the interactive shell (such as IGNOREEOF to prevent Ctrl-D from logging you out). Although differences exist in the capabilities and options of Bash's built-ins and the C shell's, the shells have very few major differences.

Bash uses a variety of features also found in the Korn shell. In fact, the Korn shell has proved so popular that many of its features have been adopted into the POSIX standard. When this is the case, Bash follows the POSIX standard, rather than the Korn shell precedence.

The Korn shell has some features that Bash does not use. For example, the Korn shell's command history is stored in a file, whereas Bash maintains its history in memory. Another difference is in the environment variables, such as EDITOR and VISUAL, which define the default text editors. Bash does not use these variables.

The startup files that Bash uses pose another difference between it and the other shells. When you log into a Bourne Again Shell, it first looks for /etc/profile and uses it if it is there. Bash then looks to ~/.bash_profile. If that doesn't exist, Bash will use ~/bash_login. If Bash cannot find either of the bash_ files in the user's home directory, it will use ~/.profile.

GNU Chess

As with any decent operating system, several diversions are available. The first one we'll look at is GNU Chess, a curses-based game of chess, shown in Figure 45-1. The distribution also includes the resources to allow GNU Chess to be compiled with X libraries to generate an X Windows-based executable file, and even enough resources to compile it for use under DOS.

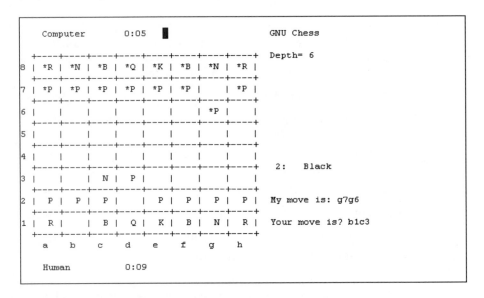

Figure 45-1: Anybody for a game of chess?

GNU Chess can control the amount of time used per turn, providing the capability to set up tournament-style play. For example, gnuchess 50 5 will set the clocks for five minutes (300 seconds) for the first 50 moves. The time controls are also useful in that they will limit how much time the computer will think about its move. The computer will think for a long time if you don't tell it when to stop.

You can move pieces in one of two ways. The first, and perhaps more familiar notation, uses a2a4, where the first letter-number pair specifies the beginning location of the piece, and the second indicates the destination. The alternate form uses the notation pf1, where the first letter indicates the piece type (p=pawn, n=knight, b=bishop, and so on). GNU Chess also permits castling and promoting of pawns.

GNU Chess has a variety of options, including the capability to switch colors (causing the computer to play the black pieces) and to force the computer to play both sides of the game.

Cpio

GNU's Cpio copies files into, or out of, an archive. An *archive* is a file that contains other files, usually compressed to some degree, along with some information about the files, such as their names, owners, and permissions. The archive file can be stored on hard disk, tape, or as part of a pipe.

The most common use for Cpio is as a replacement for the tar command. As such, Cpio is used for backing up files, normally to tape. The compression that results from using Cpio (or tar, for that matter) is not nearly as great as the compression that results from running Gzip (described later in this chapter).

Cpio works in three different modes: copy-in, copy-out, and copy-pass. In copy-in mode, Cpio copies files from an archive and into normal use. In copy-out mode, Cpio copies files out of normal use and into an archive. In copy-pass mode, Cpio copies files from one place to another, combining copy-in and copy-out modes and totally bypassing the archive file.

GNU's Cpio can understand archives of several formats, including binary files, ASCII files, tar archives, GNU tar archives, and Cpio archives. By default, Cpio writes out its archives in a binary format for compatibility with older Cpio programs.

GNU Emacs

GNU's Emacs could be considered the granddaddy of the GNU Tools. As described in Chapter 43, Richard Stallman used Emacs as the cornerstone of the GNU Project. Accordingly, don't be surprised to discover that the Emacs editor is a very versatile and full-featured text editor.

At the risk of reaching a conclusion before really getting started, Emacs does everything. Would you like to edit a large file? No problem, Emacs can handle that. Do you want to write a C program and have it indented automatically as you type? Emacs can do that. Do you want to read News without exiting the editor? Sure. How about using an editor that has been ported to most major UNIX versions, Microsoft Windows, and even DOS so that you only need to know one command set? Emacs is there for you. Will Emacs ask the boss for a raise and a better parking spot? Well, if you write the message, Emacs will send it and receive the e-mailed response from your boss (most likely, no).

Programmers designed Emacs back before the days of efficient windowing systems (such as X Windows). Even way back then, programmers needed to have several files open at once: the source code being worked on, header files, the listing of compiler errors, and the e-mail message explaining why polyester will never go out of style.

As time marched on and as natural fibers regained their rightful place atop the fashion chain, other applications began to provide some of the same services. Fortunately, Emacs is a good text editor as well.

As mentioned before, Emacs is written in Lisp — so much so that most of the functions are actually small Lisp programs. As they are programs, and not functions buried in a library, customizing any or all of Emacs's functionality is a fairly simple matter.

Through this flexibility, different modes have been added. For example, the C language mode will automatically indent and format source code as you work on it.

Despite having modes, Emacs is considered to be a *modeless editor.* This means that Emacs can accept commands as well as text at the same time. For example, to move back up one line to correct a spelling error, enter Ctrl-P, press Ctrl-F to move forward to the mistake, fix it, and then press Ctrl-N to go back down to the line you were working on.

In contrast, a vi user would need to press Escape to stop entering text, enter the letter k to move up a line, press the letter l over to the mistake, fix it, press Escape, listen for the beep, press the letter j to go back down, and press the letter a to begin adding text again.

Of course, Emacs handles many of text editing's more mundane needs as well: moving entire lines around, moving paragraphs (or larger blocks of text), undoing changes, searching and replacing (including regular expressions), word wrapping, and file merging, just to name a few of the features available.

This all comes at a price, however. Emacs is large. The compressed tar file that contains Emacs's source code and documentation is over 7.5MB in size. Running Emacs requires several megabytes of system swap space. When many copies of Emacs are running on a centralized server at the same time, the system can slow down to a crawl.

At least you won't have to exit Emacs to send mail to the system administrator to complain about the system's response time.

Finger

Finger is a program that queries a daemon running on a UNIX host for information about a user. The kinds of information typically returned include the login name, home directory, and some personalized information (such as what other humans call this user).

GNU's Finger is planned as a total replacement to BSD's Finger program. BSD's Finger was designed back when a network consisted of a small number of centralized servers on a site.

Now, as personal systems have exploded in power and popularity, sites no longer have just one or two networked computers. Now, a myriad of desktop systems are all interconnected, but most users are still logged into only one primary machine (generally the one on their desk). For example, if Mary wanted to know if Joe was logged in and what his extension is, she could go to the company phone book, look it up, and then call Joe. She could also use Finger to obtain the same information, but because Joe could be logged into any one of the dozen or so servers, Mary might be at this a while.

GNU's Finger offers an easy way around this. A singer server is installed with GNU's Finger daemon. As the daemon, it collects information about who is logged into the different hosts on the site. Now with a single Finger command, Mary can find out what's up with Joe.

As with BSD's Finger program, GNU's Finger not only displays the user's demographic information, it also displays the contents of two files located in the user's home directory. The `.plan` and `.project` files are displayed and provide a way for a user to give additional information about what the user is working on and when that user is expected to be absent. It might even include snippets of the latest Dave Barry column.

Gawk

Gawk, as you might guess, is GNU's implementation of Awk, a programming language developed by Alfred Aho, Brian Kernighan, and Peter Weinberger for UNIX.

Awk is an interpreted language, which means that the program commands are evaluated line by line, as the program runs, instead of being compiled into an executable file. Gawk uses C-like syntax and a good portion of C's functionality. For example, Awk (and Gawk) supports ARGC (the count of arguments included on Gawk's command line) and ARGV (the actual arguments that were on the command line), so the Gawk program can keep track of the arguments passed to it. Gawk also has user-defined variables, predefined string and math functions, variable conversion (such as converting a string to a numeric variable), flow control, and regular expressions.

Gawk primarily works on text files. Gawk first opens the indicated file and reads in its contents line by line (where a line is the text that is separated by a newline). Gawk then takes that line and splits it into words and processes the words according to the program. By default, words are separated by spaces and/or tabs, but you can define any separator that you want to use.

Gawk uses the words to compare against the regular expression or pattern defined in the program. Once a pattern matches, the appropriate action is taken. For example, given the input file in Listing 45-3, the program in Listing 45-4 will produce the output in Figure 45-2.

Listing 45-3: A Sample Text File

```
Hello -

This is a test data file to show the world how GAWK
is able to process a simple text file and produce
some really meaningful output.
```

Listing 45-4: A Simple Gawk Program

```
BEGIN {numwords = 0;}

{
 if ($1 ~ "Hello")
    printf("\n%s %s", $1, "World");
 else
    printf("!");

 numwords = numwords + NF;
}

END {printf("\n\nNumber of lines in data file: %d\n", NR);
      printf("Number of words in data file: %d\n", numwords);}
```

Very simply, the Gawk program in Listing 45-4 initializes its variable (in the `BEGIN` statement) and searches through the input file, looking for a line where the first word is *Hello*. (The $1 signifies the first word on the line that Gawk is processing. $2 would be the second word, and so on.) When Gawk finds what it is looking for, it prints it out along with some additional formatting. The word number counter (`numwords`) increments with the number of words found on that line (`NF`). Then Gawk produces a nice summary of the number of lines in the input file—from the number of records variable (`NR`) that Gawk keeps—and the number of words contained in the input file.

```
%gawk -f demo.gawk data.in

Hello World!!!!!

Number of lines in data file: 6
Number of words in data file: 28
%
```

Figure 45-2: A simple sample of Gawk output

You will notice that the summary from the Gawk program executes only once, instead of once per line of data like the other section of the program. Gawk allows for a section that is processed before the input file is read, and one that is processed afterward. The BEGIN section executes before the main body of the program and provides a good spot to initialize variables, set default values, and perform other preliminary activities. The END section executes after the entire data file has been processed and makes a great spot for displaying summary information, as used in the previous example.

Ghostscript and Ghostview

Have you ever downloaded a large PostScript/us file from the Internet and wanted to know what you were getting into before sending all those megabytes to the laser printer? Within five minutes of asking this question, you'll no doubt find that most of the word processing packages available today do a much better job of writing PostScript than they do of reading it.

Enter Ghostscript. Ghostscript is a package that acts as an interpreter for the Ghostscript language. Ghostscript is an *output* language that is very similar to Adobe's PostScript printing language — so much so that it can correctly interpret most PostScript files.

Ghostscript includes a basic interpreter that you can compile to run on most UNIX, VMS, and DOS machines. The interpreter will process any files that are identified on the command line as well as any input from the keyboard.

The Ghostscript package can work on such a wide variety of operating systems because it includes a library of C language procedures that provide the language's basic graphical display capabilities. You can then compile these procedures on whatever system Ghostscript is supposed to run on.

By default, Ghostscript's output goes to the screen, but you can modify the destination with command-line arguments, with commands typed in while the interpreter is running, or with an environment variable. The other possible destinations can include alternate displays (second monitors) or even printers. You can also change the interpreter's display mode (from one display resolution to another, for example) in this manner.

X Windows systems have a display option that other systems don't: Ghostview. Ghostview is an X Windows interface that provides Ghostscript a window on an X-capable terminal to draw in.

As a graphical interface, Ghostview can display colors, pop-up windows, different views of the file (landscape, portrait, and the like), different sizes of the paper (to emulate standard letter, legal, A4, and so on), zoom-in, and zoom-out.

Ghostview previews the Ghostscript or PostScript file a page at a time. This means that the window only works on the displayed page; scrolling up and down will not move you through the document. You need to use the Page menu to do that.

While on a page, you can print only that page (or the entire document), zoom in on a section of it, change the display orientation, and even adjust the size of the paper.

The Ghostview window consists mainly of the display area for the file being previewed. Also, the window contains the table of contents for the file and the Locator. The Locator displays the coordinates of the mouse pointer while in the Ghostview window. This can be very useful for correctly sizing borders around objects in the file.

Being displayed in a proper X Window allows for some additional features, such as the marking and copying of the display, as well as the use of the X Toolkit options.

Grep

GNU's Grep is similar to the standard UNIX Grep, the utility that searches through text files looking for the pattern (or string) specified on the command line. The Free Software Foundation also supplies its own version of Egrep and Fgrep. They are all one program with symbolic links from `fgrep` and `egrep` to `grep` — just like `gzcat`, `gunzip`, and `gzip`.

Grep is a powerful tool used for searching for strings within text files. While Grep will work on file types other than text, the output is generally less than useful (this is especially true of executable and other binary files). You can set up the string searching so that Grep looks for an exact match to the specified string or uses the string as a regular expression. When Grep finds a match for the string, it displays the entire line containing the match.

For example, if you wanted to scan the subject line in an archive of old e-mail quickly, you could use the following Grep command:

```
%grep Subject: 1995.Sentmail
```

Figure 45-3 shows the results of this search.

One of the major differences between GNU's Grep and the standard version is an option to include lines other than those matching the search string. With GNU's Grep, you can display an arbitrary number of lines before and/or after the line containing the match. The standard Grep will only display the matching line. In the previous example, including a few lines after the subject line might be helpful to differentiate messages with similar subjects.

Groff

Groff is GNU's entry in the list of 'roff document formatting systems. Along with the UNIX standards Nroff and Troff, Groff reads text files and formats them according to the embedded command sequences.

```
Subject: Visitor
Subject: Re: Wide Area Network Testing
Subject: Hello!
Subject: Happy Holidays!
Subject: Re: standings...
Subject: Re: Stuff Orders & Reminder
Subject: Re: Your Plans
Subject: Re: yeah, I'm going
Subject: Re: I'm baaack!
Subject: This afternoon...
Subject: How not to switch computer systems...
Subject: Oh, yeah...
Subject: Since you mentioned mailing lists...
Subject: And the details
Subject: Re: Dissolution of the Team
Subject: Month End
Subject: Just in case you don't have enough stress...
Subject: Thanks!
Subject: Re: next meeting
Subject: FYI
Subject: a question
Subject: Congratulations!
Subject: Howdy!
%
```

Figure 45-3: All the subjects talked about last year

Groff works as a front-end program, normally for GNU's version of Troff, Gtroff. Groff will take command-line options and send the file through the appropriate preprocessor, such as Geqn. Geqn reads the file and searches for specific formatting commands and processes them into the appropriate mathematical symbols.

Groff then takes the output from the preprocessors and passes it to the main processor, Gtroff. Gtroff then looks through the file for regular text formatting command sequences and for words in bold, italics, and the like and processes them. Groff then takes that output and passes it to a postprocessor (normally a program that generates PostScript) to produce the final output and send it to a printer.

Troff is better suited for producing output for PostScript printers, and Nroff works best for output to dumb terminals (Nroff is used by the man command, for example), but the Groff system is adept at many forms of output. For example, while the default output is PostScript, Groff can produce output for TeX (the Free Software Foundation's text processor, discussed later in this chapter), plain-old ASCII, and even output for X Window previewers, such as Ghostview.

Gzip, Gunzip, and Zcat

The size of the software, especially when the source code is included, poses a major hurdle to the distribution of software on the Internet, on bulletin boards, and — even the old-fashioned way — via tapes and floppy disks. A major jump is file compression utilities.

The Free Software Foundation not only uses compression, it has developed its own. Gzip is the compression software of choice for the GNU Project. Gzip uses the Lempel-Ziv algorithm (which is popular in several other compression utilities, such as the PC's PK-Zip, from PKWare). Gzip can compress a text file (such as source code) and produce a result of up to 70 percent of its original size.

The UNIX operating system also supplies a compression utility, conveniently named compress. Although compress can do a respectable job of compression, the algorithm is copyrighted and cannot be freely redistributed as Gzip and the rest of the GNU Tools can.

Compression is a very useful tool, but decompression certainly has its place in the grand scheme of things. Gzip's counterpart, Gunzip, handles this task well. In addition to understanding Gzip's format, Gunzip can also decompress files that were compressed with the standard compress.

The third member of the Gzip family is Zcat, which is a useful application that lets you view the contents of a compressed file (with either Gzip or compress), while leaving the file itself compressed.

Files compressed with Gzip have their original names preserved (along with their timestamp) and have the extension .gz appended. If this results in a filename that is too long for the file system (as with some variants of System V), Gzip will abbreviate some parts of the filename to make room for the .gz. Gzip also includes file integrity information in the form of a 32-bit checksum. When Gunzip decompresses the file, it verifies the new file's checksum against the original value.

Files compressed with compress have a .Z suffix added. The compress utility does not allow for integrity checking, making it possible for Gunzip to complain about the contents of a .Z file, when the standard UNIX decompression utility (named uncompress) will not complain. Remember that even though uncompress doesn't complain about the file it's decompressing, you have no guarantee that the file is still correct. The only way to ensure your files are intact is to use a system that uses some form of integrity checking (such as Gzip).

Ispell

GNU's spell checker, Ispell, is supplied as a separate executable file, as opposed to building the functionality into a text editor.

Ispell reads in the specified file and reports on any words that it does not find in the main dictionary or the user's customized dictionary. Ispell actually highlights the words and lets the user correct them.

While this is already a step up from some of the more basic spell checkers that only identify words they don't know, Ispell goes a step further. If any words appear in the dictionaries that are only different from the unrecognized word by a letter (such as having the *e* and *i* transposed in the word *received*), have an extra letter, are missing a letter, or even have a missing space or hyphen, these words are displayed with suggested corrections. Ispell will also make guesses based on the root of the unrecognized word.

This functionality is also used when checking the spelling of a single word on the command line. Not only is this faster than picking up a dictionary, but an "expert" makes suggestions!

Another nice feature of Ispell is that it understands the formatting commands of some of the more common formatting systems. For example, calling Ispell with the -n command-line option will force Ispell to ignore the formatting commands of the Nroff/Troff/Groff systems. Using the -t option will force Ispell to ignore the formatting commands of the TeX system.

The Ispell package includes a few other executable files, mostly maintenance-type utilities. These utilities maintain the main dictionary and manage the users' personal dictionaries.

The Ispell package also comes with a variety of dictionaries. The default dictionary is the U.S. English dictionary, but, for example, a dictionary is included for British English. The British English dictionary would allow *colour*, whereas the U.S. English dictionary would not.

Less

A maxim says that less can be more. In GNU, less is very often more than more. Less is a utility that pages through files, similar to the standard More. Less has expanded on the basic functionality of More.

The major expansion of Less is the capability to scroll backward through the file being viewed. It scrolls backward as smoothly as it scrolls forward.

Less's command set is based on the combined commands of More and vi. See Table 45-1 for a list of common key commands.

Table 45-1 Key Commands in Less

Keystroke	*Action*
Spacebar	Advances the view into the file a screen at a time
j	Moves down (toward the end of the file) one line at a time
k	Moves back (toward the beginning of the file) one line at a time
g	Goes directly to the top of the file
G	Goes straight to the last line of the file being viewed

One of my favorite features — as incidental as it is — is the capability to totally customize Less's prompt. More will always say *more,* but Less can say almost anything you want it to.

For example, I set my Less prompt with the environment variable LESS and customized the prompt with the following string:

```
-P?f%f:Standard Input. ?e(END):?pb%pb\%
```

When we translate that into English, the -P is the command-line option that indicates the following string as the Prompt string. Because it is possible to include spaces in the prompt string, this needs to be the last option passed to Less. The ?f%f:Standard Input. section first checks to see if Less is reading from a file, and if it is, it uses the filename in the prompt. If it isn't reading a file (such as a pipe), it uses the string Standard Input. as the filename in the prompt.

While the ?e(END):?pb%pb\% section looks complicated, it simply checks to see if Less is at the end of the input (either file or pipe). If it is, it displays (END) in the prompt. If it isn't at the end, Less checks to see if it knows the percentage of the file read so far, calculated at the bottom line of the display (the b part of ?pb). If it does know it, it displays it, followed by a percent sign.

As with many other UNIX programs, you can override environment variables with command-line options. This is useful if you use Less in other places besides the shell's command prompt. For example, Less is defined as the program to be used when my e-mail messages are more than 20 lines long. Inside the mailer, many of the options for the command line are impractical or unavailable, so Less's prompt is redefined as

```
-P?f%f:Email.
```

This prompt very simply identifies the input as Email in the prompt. By taking advantage of the flexibility, you can have the prompt you want, when you want it.

Nethack

Although a game of chess may be relaxing from time to time, sometimes a bit of hacking and slashing can't be beat. Nethack is GNU's foray into the fantasy gaming arena.

Unlike some games of the genre, Nethack actually has a goal (besides the extermination of the underground inhabitants trying to exterminate you). Your quest is to find the Amulet of Yendor and return it to the surface.

Nethack is a game similar to Dungeons & Dragons in design. Each character has six primary characteristics: strength, intelligence, wisdom, dexterity, constitution, and charisma. The relative strength of each characteristic helps define which skills the character possesses. Also based on these characteristics, you can choose what class of character will be played in the game. The choices include: archeologists, barbarians, cavemen (and cavewomen), elves, healers, knights, priests (and priestesses), rogues, samurai, tourists, valkyries, and wizards. For example, a high-strength characteristic with a low intelligence would make a decent barbarian, whereas high intelligence and low strength is a good start for a wizard.

As you can see, the classes extend out of the Dungeon & Dragons world, reaching into mythology, J.R.R. Tolkien's Middle Earth, and somebody's late night imagination (*tourists?*).

The playing of Nethack is similar to the playing of Rogue, the standard game found in most UNIX distributions. Both games are full-screen games, using the vi cursor movement keys as the four basic character movements (left, right, up, and down). Nethack goes a little further than Rogue in that you can set up the game to use the keys on the number pad for movement. You can even set up the game to use some more advanced graphics and controls as in an X Windows-based game.

The basic version of Nethack is curses-based and uses standard display characters to symbolize the corridors, rooms, and bad guys, as shown in Figure 45-4.

In order to find the Amulet of Yendor, your character must descend through at least 20 levels into the bowels of the Earth. While most levels will be similar to Figure 45-4, some will contain special tasks (based on your character's class) that must be completed before continuing on the quest for the Amulet. Just in case you start feeling claustrophobic, you can return to the surface to buy more supplies and gather information that may help you on your quest.

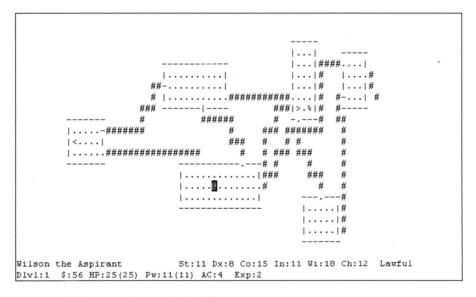

Figure 45-4: The beginning of a typical Nethack game

Perl

Perl is an interpreted language, similar in many ways to Gawk and to sed. Perl also contains a good chunk of C language–type functionality as well. If you aren't careful, you may even recognize some elements of shell programming.

Perl was designed to fill the gap that exists between writing full-fledged C programs and writing a complex shell script. Like Gawk, Perl is best suited for working with flat ASCII (text) files. Unlike Gawk, Perl has a much wider selection of predefined functions, including:

- File manipulation, like open, close, and unlink (which is a nice word that C programs use when they talk about removing a file)

- The capability to run a programs from within the Perl program (similar to shell scripts)

- Arbitrary pattern matching and replacement (like the sed program)

Like Gawk, Perl has excellent regular pattern matching and file processing. Because Perl is a program that recognizes its history — or perhaps, in a shameless-but-useful self-marketing attempt — the package contains two executable files for the conversion of programs into the Perl language. These programs, a2p and s2p, convert Awk (and Gawk) and sed programs into Perl, respectively.

For example, recall the Gawk program example in Listing 45-4. After running the a2p conversion utility, the program in Listing 45-5 is produced.

Listing 45-5: Our Gawk Program, in a Different Light

```
#!/usr/bin/perl
eval "exec /usr/local/bin/perl -S $0 $*"
    if $running_under_some_shell;
            # this emulates #! processing on NIH machines.
            # (remove #! line above if indigestible)
eval "$´.$1.´$2;´ while $ARGV[0] =~ /^([A-Za-z_]+=)(.*)/ && shift;

$[ = 1;            # set array base to 1

$numwords = 0;

while (<>) {
    chop;    # strip record separator
    \@Fld = split(` `, $_, 9999);
    if ($Fld[1] =~ "Hello") {
    printf "\n%s %s", $Fld[1], "World";
    }
    else {
    printf (("!"));
    }
    $numwords = $numwords + $#Fld;
```

```
}

printf "\n\nNumber of lines in data file: %d\n", $.;
```

As you can see, many differences exist between the two programs, but because they are now written in two different languages, we can consider this a good thing. The biggest difference between the Gawk and Perl versions is at the top of the program. The first three lines turn the Perl script into a self-executing program. As you might recall, when a file begins with #!, the shell will read the following string and attempt to execute it (after somebody changes the files permissions to make it executable, of course). In this case, we want to run Perl, so that's what is specified. Of course, we could add a similar line to the top of the Gawk script to achieve the same effect.

Since a2p doesn't know what kind of system it is running on, it also includes the next two lines just in case the first one doesn't work. The a2p program also includes comments (following the #) to describe what it is doing.

The next set of lines do a bit of housekeeping that Gawk assumes as defaults. Here, the program looks through the argument list, searching for any variable assignments that might be on the command line. Gawk also accepts these assignments but without any help from the program itself. Then Perl makes a quick initialization of the array base so that counting begins at one instead of zero.

The next set of lines brings us back to familiar ground. After initializing the word counting variable (numword), we get on with the business at hand.

Because Perl does not loop through the file the same way that Gawk does, the program needs to include the looping explicitly. The while statement uses a shorthand test that basically tells the program to keep repeating this loop until the data is exhausted.

The next line is unique to Perl. As Perl leaves the input line intact, it needs to use the chop command to remove the newline character from the line of data. Then, the script divides the line (identified by the $_) into words, up to 9,999 of them.

The rest of the script looks familiar, with the possible exception of a couple of Perl symbols: $#Fld indicates the number of elements in the Fld array, and $. keeps track of the number of lines of data read by the program.

When running the program in Figure 45-5, you will notice only one difference in the output. Perl thinks that there are 30 words, whereas Gawk counted only 28 (refer back to Figure 45-2). The difference is in the Fld array. Even when nothing is in the line of data to be counted, the element count starts at 1, not 0, so it increments the word count. Simply changing $[= 1; to $[= 0; (as well as changing every $Fld[1] reference to $Fld[0] to keep everyone looking at the same variable) will bring Perl and Gawk into agreement.

```
%demo.perl data

Hello World!!!!!

Number of lines in data file: 6
Number of words in data file: 30
%
```

Figure 45-5: Output from our Perl program

Perl also contains functionality that is very similar to sed, another utility that is included with most UNIX versions. The basic sed functionality is typified by the following string:

```
s/search pattern/replacement pattern/
```

This pattern, very simply, searches through text for the search pattern, and if it finds it, it replaces it with the replacement pattern. As you can see, when combined with the power of regular expressions and the capability to apply the search and replace command globally through a file, sed makes a powerful tool and a logical addition to the file scanning and text manipulation tools used by Perl.

Another major portion of Perl's functionality most closely resembles a shell. At first glance, the shell doesn't really seem to do much except let you run cool tools such as Perl. Well, there is a bit more to a shell than that. Shells, among other things, keep track of where you are, where to look for the cool tools, and even who you are.

Perl does, too. From within a Perl script, you can manipulate any of the shell's environment variables in the same way you would in the shell. You can even keep track of your effective user ID through use of some function calls similar to those available to C programs. This makes Perl ideal for performing security-sensitive tasks, such as password file maintenance. In fact, Perl is very often the tool of choice for many system administrators. Contrary to popular beliefs, system administrators use Perl because of the functionality, not because they enjoy learning every programming language that appears. Well, maybe they do, but this one is useful.

Many system administrators use Perl for many of the mundane, repetitive tasks that require root privileges. Perl's capability to control the running environment (as by only defining a search path to known and trusted directories) makes it very difficult to tamper with the script before it runs (such as substituting an executable file that forwards restricted information to the bad guy). Perl can also trap signals (such as KILL, HANGUP, and the like) so that the script can't be interrupted and the root permissions usurped. Keeping root privileges out of the hands of bad guys (and just about everybody else) ranks just above learning new programming languages for most system administrators.

TeX

TeX is a document formatter that reads a text file containing the text and information on how to format it. TeX also produces a device-independent output file (commonly called a DVI file), which is a binary file that can then run through a processor that produces the desired output, such as PostScript, PCL, or whatever.

Like Groff, TeX expects an input file to contain all of the necessary formatting commands by the time it is called. Unlike Groff, TeX has a rudimentary interface for processing as you work with the file, but before creating the input. This gives TeX a large measure of flexibility.

The vast majority of TeX's formatting commands reside in precompiled macros. Several formatting systems have exploited this particular feature, the most widely known being LaTeX. The LaTeX package is an add-on to TeX that includes several macros for formatting documents, making this system one of the most well known. This feature is also similar to Emacs's reliance on Lisp programs for the definition of functionality. This flexibility is the source of great study, spawning several different books on how to describe, use, and squeeze the most out of TeX.

The TeX package also includes a program for compiling your own macros, which gives a user (or a group, or a site) the ability to define standard macros for use in documentation, memos, and virtually any document.

When first starting TeX, it requests the file to be processed (if it wasn't specified on the command line). Once TeX has a file to work with, you can specify how the document will be formatted and even make changes to the document itself! (Any changes are only included in the output file; the source file remains unchanged.) Most of TeX's commands follow a control character — such as the Ctrl key, the Escape key, or the backslash (\) — so that you are always in input mode, similar to Emacs. Whenever you type anything in TeX without a control character, you are editing the output file. You can, however, call your favorite editor from within TeX so that you actually work on and save the changes you are making to the input file.

Once you finish any editing you needed to do, TeX goes off and produces the DVI file. TeX also produces a log file, which records every transaction that took place while TeX was running with that file.

As with almost every GNU Tool, you can customize TeX, in addition to defining your own macros. The environment that TeX works in depends heavily on supporting files (such as the macro files, the font definition files, and so on). TeX accepts several environment variables that can override the defaults. For example, you can define the text editor that TeX uses when you activate the edition option to work on the input file.

Other GNU Tools can also use a document formatted for the TeX system. The Info program is able to read the commands and implements a text-screen display system. Info can use any hierarchy in the document (such as a table of contents) to create a menu-driven interface so that you can read through the document, skipping forward or backward with little more than a keystroke. The Info program is a wonderful way to present online documentation.

Summary

This chapter covered several additional tools from GNU. These include language interpreters, text editors, scripting languages, diversions, and formatters.

Part XI

System Administration

Chapter 46

A Day in the Life of a System Administrator

In This Chapter

▶ Following a System Administrator through a typical day

Note

I'm not a system administrator, and I know I would not make a good one. One of my good friends, Cedric Higgins, is an excellent system administrator, so I asked him to describe one of his days. Ced's currently working at Intergraph in Mountain View, California. He received his degree in Computer Science from Southern University in Baton Rouge, Louisiana.

Strictly speaking, this chapter is not like the others you have read so far, but I hope you enjoy it.

Becoming a System Administrator

When you began your career in the technical field, you probably never thought of becoming a System Administrator. No college programs, certificate courses, or even a degree in Computer System Administration exist. So how does one become involved in System Administration?

More than likely, someone probably saw you make a backup tape, replace your hard disk, or even write a one-line shell script (`mail postmaster@ingr.com < test1`). You soon were lured into being a technical handyman around your peers, and you couldn't say "no" to lending a helping hand.

So as people often ask, what's it like being a System Administrator? Fellow workers often see you racing by their office to solve some critical problem, disks in one hand and cables draped around your neck. The rest of the chapter will give you some insight into a System Administrator's day at the office. Some of you will relate and appreciate that your day is similar. If you are not a System Administrator, after finishing the chapter, take the time to thank your Sys Admin for a job well done.

The Awakening

Like most people, your day starts at around six in the morning. You are wakened by a vibrating pager that you conveniently placed on the nightstand just some six or seven hours before. Wondering what it would be like to hear the sweet sound of a buzzing alarm clock or a traffic report on the radio, you reach for the pager and hope that it is a warning of a low battery cell. You take a peek and find that someone or something at the office is calling. Debating whether to make the call back (God forbid you attempt to dial in and learn that the Net is down), you scamper to the bathroom and throw a dash of water on your face. As you stand over the bowl, your mind begins to wonder about the page. Could it be the same user that pages you every morning at the same time? Could it be that I lost the disks in the server? Could it be that someone can't bring up their Web browser? Whatever it is, don't let it be e-mail.

While you make your morning coffee, you call the page back. A user can't print his Excel spreadsheet for a 10 A.M. meeting—a problem you can troubleshoot remotely. After you ask the user a few questions, the solution becomes clear: The printer is out of paper. While coaching the user on how to add paper to the laser printer and placing yourself on standby until the first page prints, you wonder whether you'll be granted a thank you. As the last of the brewing coffee drips into the carafe, the user gives no thanks, but instead asks, "Can you please do something about this printer not having paper?"

The Sun Rises in the East

As you watch the sunrise on your way to the office, you plan your day. As you organize your critical and noncritical tasks for the day, your pager begins to buzz. Knowing that this is the normal routine and that you have already solved one problem, you elect not to use the cellular but enjoy the morning's daylight (because you may not see it later).

When you arrive at work, you must decide whether to enter the building from the rear or the front. Your choice is determined by the number of pages that you have received during your drive. Today, you have received enough pages that you choose the rear. Using military maneuvers, you reach your desk unseen. You make sure that your key-click on your keyboard is off, and you sift through the morning's bureaucracy of yellow sticky notes (filing them as Chapter 13), voice mails, and finally e-mails. Your day begins as planned.

Making sure that your backups are completed from the night before, you often find that one or two clients failed. Not panicking, you have to determine why they failed. Was the tape bad? Was the tape drive bad? Did the software contain another bug? You never risk leaving the client without a backup and decide to make a one-off and hope tonight's backup has your fix.

Moving on to your next task requires you to be seen. Someone needs you to upgrade her machine. Wanting to finish this task early, you collect your belongings (an operating system disk and your Tech book) and head off to your destination. You are spotted as if you were Waldo by users who detain you with a slew of questions. As you acknowledge them and their urgency, your to-do list becomes longer. Finally, you make it to the user's machine for the upgrade and find her deep in work preparing to get a sales quote or a last-minute presentation. Having discussed the upgrade with her the day before (to schedule an appropriate time), you now become the Sys Admin from hell. You explain to her that you have scheduled time for this work, debate that your work is as equally important as hers, and are left alone to upgrade the machine (in fact, this is best for both of you).

As you're on your way back to your office to collect the necessary ingredients for the next few tasks, you establish a deeper rapport with some of your users. You keep your promise to give them a few minutes to answer questions that came up while you were performing your previous task. Having learned that users treasure minutes of time, you hope that they reciprocate when problems arise. Questions include such things as Internet browsing, TCP/IP, client setups, and sometimes home machines. Knowing that you can't answer every question, you write down some of the questions and promise to e-mail them later with the answers that you need to look up. As expected, your to-do list grows even longer.

High Noon

Completing a third of your planned activities and handling some extraordinary ones, you begin to become sluggish and brain dead. Realizing that it is nearly 2 P.M. (you don't go to lunch at noon because users are gone and you can do productive work without interruptions), you decide that you need a brain fix and head out for some oxygen. Promising yourself that you need to purchase a hi-tech book, you spend your lunch hour at Barnes and Noble hovering around the aisles of networks and communications. Your over-budget purchases rejuvenate you, and you succumb to your tracking device and find yourself back at the office.

Accomplishing your many tasks early only leaves way for the rest of the afternoon to develop system administration tools and monitor the tools that are in place. Deciding that you need a Perl script to accomplish some tasks, you put on your programmer's cap. As you write the first line of code (#!/usr/bin/perl), you are interrupted by someone in senior management who is frantic because his color slides are coming out with a yellow background instead of green and he needs them for a presentation right away. You add a new full blue toner cartridge to his printer. You and the manager wait for the first slide to print without conversation. Once again, truth holds true. No one converses with System Administrators about social affairs except when their best interest is at hand. Finally, the manager breaks the silence with a question about performing a procedure in a particular software package.

As you chalk up another solved problem, you face the worst situation of the day. Four users are waiting at your door, and seven messages are in your voice mailbox, all with the same complaint: The network is very slow, and some machines have descended into a black hole. As you head to the server room, the eyes of frustrated users bear down upon you. You take control of the ship and begin to steer into restoration of faith and confidence that online services will appear shortly. Performing all the basic system administration tasks, you find that one user's machine is causing the problem. Breaking open the org chart of machines, you make your way to that user's cubicle. To your amazement, you find that machine and user have moved to another cubicle. Crawling under the desk (and inhaling a good amount of dust), you find the problem: When the equipment was moved, the terminator was removed from the end of the BNC connector.

As the Dust Settles

The end of day approaches, and your Perl script remains at one line. Like most System Administrators, preparing for the evening is no easy task. This requires reading several manuals to perform an upgrade or to install new hardware or software. As you prepare, you often face those users who decide to stay late, keep you company — and require your assistance. Once again, you are plagued by interruptions such as explanations of how workstations suddenly crashed or panicked requests to help retrieve a lost file. You offer quick solutions and then return to your evening duties. Experiencing some difficulties along the way, you realize that you are leaving at the same time as you did the day before.

After patronizing the fast-food stand and greeting the cashiers by name, you make home your final destination.

The Sun Sets in the West

Settling into the comfort of home, you begin to process all of today's data. You determine that you could have solved some problems easier, and that a little planning would have prevented some of today's problems. You can't resist the temptation to dial in to finish up some tasks from home, where you aren't as likely to be interrupted.

Only a few years ago, the duties of System Administrators began to gain respect. The job has been recognized as an important part of an organization's future in the world of technology. Keeping users happy and networks running is no easy task. So next time your Sys Admin solves something for you after normal business hours, whether restoring a needed file or answering a buzzing page, give a simple smile and a word of thanks.

Summary

The next chapter delves into the actual tasks involved in system administration. You'll be introduced to the jobs of account manager, printer manager, postmaster, and hardware administrator.

Chapter 47

When Users Come Calling

Your machine room is spotless, its blinking lights strongly reminiscent of a Disney World parade. Your disks are pristine, and your printers are simply aglow with readiness. Take just a moment and savor this image, for it is about to come crashing down around you; the users have arrived.

As soon as your phone number is published in the staff directory, you will be inundated with calls for every conceivable problem, need, and situation. We'll talk about overall preparedness a bit later in this book, but let's address four fundamental, high-user impact areas of UNIX system management: account management, account deletion, printer administration, and postmaster duties. These four areas are almost guaranteed to consume the majority of your day-to-day "user time."

Account Management

Most UNIX administrators loathe account management. Someone always needs access for a week, or there is the one who collects accounts on every available system, or the one who can simply never remember his or her password. A stable, consistent method of account administration can alleviate (but never remove) some of these headaches. Account management is, all too often, an afterthought in systems administration. Many sites are happy to rely on the standard system tools and simply create and delete accounts on an ad hoc basis. We're going to take a different approach: Forethought is an absolute necessity in managing one's user base. This is especially true for those computing environments in which different levels of security are afforded to systems, software, and data. A consistent account management procedure can also ease your administration of sensitive software and data. For purposes of this chapter, I'm going to assume that we will not be using the vendor-specific user creation/deletion utilities.

Note

For purposes of clarity, I will refer to the password and group management files by their traditional names, /etc/passwd and /etc/group. Recent versions of UNIX (and add-on products, such as NIS) may keep these files in a different location, and system security features may strip passwords into a separate file. Be aware of your system's configuration while reading this chapter.

Who's out there?

The first task is to divide users (and potential users) into distinct groups, wherever possible. This is not as daunting a task as it may seem. Computationally, relatively few users have need of the proverbial entire ball of wax.

At first glance, most users would seem to be easily classified; however, things are not always as they seem. Many firms are creating cross-functional employees and teams, in which a small group of people may cover a broad spectrum of responsibilities. The best place to begin our design is, believe it or not, the organizational chart for your operation. This is an important starting point for several reasons:

■ It ensures that your account management procedures "cover all the bases."

■ Following the organizational hierarchy will help you make reasonable assumptions about computational needs.

■ Seeing the "big picture" will help you plan for future expansion. Food Services may not want a niche in your system today, but tomorrow comes all too soon.

Here's a small organizational chart, with which we'll plan our account management structure:

Executive Office			
Marketing	Technical Support	Manufacturing	Finance
Sales	Service	Suppliers	
Public Relations	R&D	Inventory	

Figure 47-1: A typical organizational chart

Our chart has already created the first major division of access categories. We'll obviously need to create user groups that reflect the work structure. Therefore, moving over to /etc/group, we create the following:

```
market:*:1000:
techspt:*:2000:
```

```
manufac:*:3000:
finance:*:4000:
exec:*:5000:
```

Those of you experienced with /etc/group have undoubtedly noticed that my example does not include group passwords. Most administrators seem to find that group passwords are quickly shared, rendering them useless. The facility is there, however, so those of you with strong password control procedures may find group passwords effective. I would recommend, however, that the lifetime of group passwords be kept rather short. A legendary maxim says, "If X persons are supposed to know a given password, the number of persons who actually know it approaches X squared." Keep that in mind as you develop your security policies.

You may have also noticed that I allocated group identifications (GIDs) in blocks of 1,000. That, too, reflects an ulterior motive: we need to reserve room to grow. Moving on to /etc/passwd, we'll simply use the GID as the base for each user's user identification (UID). This technique gives us a maximum of 1,000 users in any particular group. For most systems, this should prove more than adequate. The savvy administrator will also use these groups for access control. This, in turn, will reduce the need for group passwords and make life much easier for your users. (Using UNIX System V Release 2.*x* and 3.*x*, I grew rather tired of the newgrp command and its related headaches.)

What do I call them?

User login names (a.k.a. user names or user IDs) often cause heated discussion between you and your user base. Some people want straightforward user IDs, perhaps based on their last name. Others may want to use their nicknames, and still others may want to keep the user name from their college days (or previous employer). Again, I cannot overemphasize the importance of a consistent system. In any case, you should determine and apply a naming scheme consistently throughout your system's lifetime.

One of the more popular schemes is simply to use the first and middle initials and the last name. Under this system, Joe B. User would be issued jbuser as his user name. This is perfectly acceptable, except in those rare cases where an unsavory word may actually be created. Another crowd favorite is to add a sequence number to the user name created so that Joe B. User receives jbuser01 and Jane B. Userfile becomes jbuser02. While some potential for confusion exists in this scenario, it remains a workable option.

You may want to consider including the user's department or office designation in the user ID so that Joe B. Graf of the Marketing department becomes mkt_graf, or something similar. As long as your UNIX variant will support the use of characters such as - or _ in user names, feel free to find whatever meets your needs.

The one clear rule of user naming schemes is simple: You must select a scheme that allows you (and other users) to identify system users easily. If user `fizzbu` has a runaway database job that is consuming all available memory, you don't want to waste time trying to remember who `fizzbu` may be.

Most UNIX variants support the use of the fifth field of `/etc/passwd` as a comment. Regardless of the naming scheme you select, I strongly urge you to keep valid real names of your users in the gecos field (described in the following note). You can then use tools such as `finger` to identify users quickly.

Note

Incidentally, practice of fifth fields began in the early days of UNIX, when the fifth field was used to carry batch user identifiers to a General Electric system. The fifth field became known as the *gecos field* (*gecos* was the acronym for General Electric Comprehensive Operating System).

As with many areas of system administration, our only conclusion is to develop a scheme and stick to it!

Where can I put them?

Now that the underlying group structure is ready, we can move on to the next part of the equation: the location of the user directories. Again, a needs evaluation will pay critical dividends. Most administrators would presume that the Research and Development folks need large amounts of disk space, but what about Sales or Technical Support? The standard user creation utilities can blindly place user directories in a standard location, and the results are often painful. Careful planning at this stage can greatly alleviate problems later in the system's lifetime. We don't want to shuffle users' directories every year to battle disk space limitations. By the same token, however, we don't want to degrade performance of our power users by putting all of them on the same disk partition(s).

Our approach will be to sprinkle users about, based on their anticipated disk space needs. If the R&D folks are going to be creating 20-megabyte files by the bushel, we don't want too many of them sharing the same disk partition. Some sites use a simple rotation policy (first heavy user on `/usr1`, the next on `/usr2`, and so on), whereas others look at actual disk space consumption at the time the account is created. Your choice should be based on careful observation of user habits and trends.

Secret

System accounting records can be of great help when the time comes to chart user consumption. Our technique of matching UIDs to GIDs (with a 1,000-user range per GID) provides a built-in means by which to extract and/or sort accounting records for each operational department.

What shell will they use?

Most UNIX variants let you specify almost any program as the user's login shell. As we've discussed in earlier chapters, quite a few shells are available to the typical UNIX user. You may be in a position to allow each user his or her own choice of shell. However, almost inevitably special-purpose user IDs, using some other program as a login shell, will become necessary. We'll discuss those instances as well.

Secret

Some software packages may, for all intents and purposes, dictate a choice of shell. I have seen packages that simply would not work unless the user ran the Bourne shell. Again, be aware of your software requirements when choosing shells.

Whatever your choices of shell, your primary concern will be the configuration files. Bourne shell users will be familiar with .profile, whereas C Shell users will want to tweak their .login and .cshrc files. In any case, you need to ensure that the proper systemwide environments are created. I suggest that you build standard versions of .profile, .login, and any other configuration files needed by the shells you support, maintaining them in a standard location. (I use /usr/local/lib for such things, but some variants of UNIX provide a skeleton directory, like /etc/skel, for this purpose.) If you decide to allow users their choice of shells (whether at account creation time or interactively, via the chsh command), I strongly recommend that you install all configuration files when you create the account. This will help avoid the "I changed to csh, and now I can't run anything!" problems that plague the "login shell of the week" type of operation.

Note

Your users may want to use a shell other than those supplied by your vendor. Shells such as tcsh, bash, zsh, and ksh are available as freeware. The decision to allow or disallow additional shells is yours; however, you should inform the users if the choice of an alternative shell leaves them on their own for support. Again, make a policy and stick to it!

All right already, just do it!

Once we've decided upon a disk space rotation/placement policy, we can actually begin creating user entries for /etc/passwd.

John Q. Weeble, of the Marketing department, has just requested an account on our system. Looking at our naming scheme, we'll assign a user name of jqweeble, the GID for Marketing, and the first available UID within that group. Because jqweeble does not yet have a password, we can complete the first five fields of the /etc/passwd entry:

```
jqweeble::1001:1000:John Q Weeble,Marketing:
```

(Remember, /etc/passwd fields are separated by colons.)

Editing Configuration Files — Watch Your Step!

Never edit the /etc/passwd or /etc/group files directly! A typographical error or communications problem during such an editing session can create devastating problems. Many UNIX variants offer a command like vipw, which allows you to edit a temporary copy of the /etc/passwd file. Use it! If your system doesn't offer such a utility, use cp to make a copy of /etc/passwd, edit the copy, and replace the original.

After checking disk space availability, we decide to place jqweeble on /usr2, in the market subdirectory:

```
jqweeble::1001:1000:John Q Weeble,Marketing:/usr2/market/jqweeble:
```

Finally, jqweeble wants to use the C shell as his login shell, so:

```
jqweeble::1001:1000:John Q
Weeble,Marketing:/usr2/market/jqweeble:/bin/csh
```

Saving our work in /etc/passwd, we'll go create John's home directory.

Moving to /usr2/market (or creating it, if it does not already exist), we create a home directory for jqweeble with the mkdir command. Be sure to use chown, chgrp, and chmod to set the ownership and permission appropriately. A typical sequence of commands might look like this:

```
# cd /usr2/market
# mkdir jqweeble
# chown jqweeble jqweeble
# chgrp market jqweeble
# chmod 755 jqweeble
```

Don't forget to give him the standard startup files. Because he's using /bin/csh as his login shell, that might mean:

```
# cd /usr2/market/jqweeble
# cp /usr/local/lib/Cshrc .cshrc
# cp /usr/local/lib/Login .login
# chown jqweeble .cshrc .login
# chgrp market .cshrc .login
# chmod 700 .cshrc .login
```

If your system supports disk space quotas, this is the time to set jqweeble's quotas appropriately.

Secret

Some quota systems allow you to create a prototype user, which serves as a template for setting quotas. If your system can do this, it is a big time savings.

For some systems, you might have to jump-start electronic mail service by creating an empty mailbox for jqweeble. You could do that with:

```
# >/usr/spool/mail/jqweeble
# chown jqweeble /usr/spool/mail/jqweeble
# chgrp market /usr/spool/mail/jqweeble
# chmod 700 /usr/spool/mail/jqweeble
```

Set John's password with passwd, and he's ready to go!

Special cases

Occasionally, you'll run into some extraordinary situation. For example, a new piece of software may require its own login. As another possibility, a user may need access to files in another group. You can often handle requests of these sorts by manipulating the /etc/passwd and /etc/group files.

In our first example, a piece of software needs to be executed as a login shell. (This is not an uncommon occurrence.) You can handle this easily by creating an /etc/passwd entry just for the program in question, like so:

```
bigprog::2002:2000:BigProg
software,TechSpt:/usr/bigprog:/usr/bigprog/bp
```

In cases such as this, be sure that you set permissions on both the directory and the program itself appropriately. Set a password, and the deed is done.

Our second example comes to us by way of good old John Q. Weeble, who has discovered that he needs to access some files over in the Technical Support areas. Assuming that Technical Support does not want their files open to all users, we can address this need by adding John to the techspt group in /etc/group, like so:

```
techspt:*:2000:jqweeble
```

Some UNIX variants let users belong to multiple groups. If your system supports this functionality, your task is complete. If not, you'll need to teach John how to use the newgrp command to change his group membership back and forth.

Caution

Most UNIX variants have a length limit for lines in /etc/group. If you reach this limit, the system may silently ignore your additions! You can, however, have more than one line with the same GID. The system will take the first one that matches the user name in question. For instance:

```
biggroup1:*:7000:jbuser,mdcomp,abjack,...
biggroup2:*:7000:dilipid,buroark,adnance,...
```

If you find yourself adding a second line to /etc/group in this fashion, you may want to investigate other techniques, such as common file areas or even group user IDs.

We cannot hope to cover every possible situation in this text, but the tools and techniques described here can meet the vast majority of the needs brought to your attention.

Keeping it clean

As you may have noticed, typographical errors, truncations, and the like can wreak havoc on your /etc/passwd and /etc/group files. Your system can easily grind to a halt as a result of such errors. As mentioned previously, you can prevent some problems by working on copies of /etc/passwd and /etc/group; however, this won't protect you from subtle errors, such as an extra colon or missing character. Thankfully, most UNIX variants include utilities such as /etc/pwck and /etc/grpck, whose sole purpose is to provide a sanity check for your /etc/passwd and /etc/group files. I strongly suggest that you use these utilities regularly. You'll save yourself much heartache by nipping problems in the bud.

Automating the process

If you've actually worked through the previous sample session, you are undoubtedly muttering, "There *has* to be a better way!" Rest assured, there is, but automating this process is most definitely a matter specific to each system (and each administrator). Rather than present you with some sort of sample user addition script, I'm going to give you a set of code fragments that you can use to build your own custom script. (I'm a Bourne shell aficionado, so my fragments will assume /bin/sh.)

Generating a user name

If you've decided to use the first and middle initials and the last name to generate a user name, you can use something like this to do the trick:

```
username=`echo $firstname $midinit $lastname | tr [A-Z] [a-z] |
        awk ` NF == 3 { printf("%s%s%s",    \
              substr($1,1,1),    \
              substr($2,1,1),    \
              substr($3,1,6));
                }
           NF == 2 { printf("%s%s",    \
              substr($1,1,1),    \
              substr($2,1,7));
                }´`
```

Note the use of backslashes to continue lines. Note as well that we're assuming a maximum length of eight characters and lowercase letters.

Finding a UID

As you might expect, we're going to have holes in our UID sequences as users come and go. Needless to say, we want to reuse UIDs as they become available. Assuming that we are working within a group of 1,000 UIDs and that our UIDs match our GIDs, the following code fragment will find the first available UID in a given group:

```
lastuid=`grep :$gid: /etc/passwd |
    awk -F: `BEGIN {curuid = `"$gid"`;}
    $4 ~ /`"$gid"`/ { diff = $3 - curuid;
            if((diff > 1) && (curuid > `"$gid"`)) exit;
            curuid = $3; }
        END { print curuid; }`´
newuid=`expr $lastuid + 1`
```

This assumes that /etc/passwd is sorted by UID!

The next available UID in the group specified by $gid is stored in the newuid variable. (Be sure to add bounds checking to ensure that you don't run into the UIDs belonging to another GID.)

Setting up the home directory

Some UNIX variants, notably System V Release 4 and its derivatives, allow the administrator to maintain a skeleton user directory, which is used as a template for directories created later. Any files placed in the skeleton directory are automatically copied to any newly created user directories. If your system supports this, use it! If not, you can create the same functionality through the following steps:

1. Create a skeleton directory in a public place:

    # mkdir /usr/local/skeleton

2. Copy all of your standard startup files (.profile, .cshrc, and anything else you need) into this directory:

    # cp /usr/lib/Cshrc /usr/local/skeleton/.cshrc
    # cp /usr/lib/Login /usr/local/skeleton/.login
    # cp /usr/bigprog/.bpstart /usr/local/skeleton/.bpstart
    et cetera, et cetera...

3. If your users have any standard subdirectories (for instance, you might want all of them to have a public_html directory for their World Wide Web pages), create it in this directory:

    # mkdir /usr/local/skeleton/public_html

4. In your automated creation script, use cpio, or a similar tool, to build the user's home directory:

    # cpio -pdvm /usr/local/skeleton /usr2/market/jqweeble

Presto! You've just taken a bite from the most time-consuming part of account creation.

Tip

Be sure to maintain the standard startup files in your skeleton directory. Once you've created this and are satisfied, I recommend that you use this directory as your base for modifying the standard user startup files.

A wonderful side benefit of this is that the inevitable cries of "I accidentally deleted my `.profile`" or "My `.cshrc` file is all wrong!" can be met with, "You can retrieve a fresh copy from `/usr/local/skeleton`." Again, we're saving you time.

Account Deletion

Someone once remarked that UNIX users never really die, their files are just redistributed. Any administrator who has been faced with file retrieval requests dating back four years can vouch for the validity of this statement. Therefore, a clean, consistent deletion policy/procedure can be of significant value to the busy administrator.

Most of the account deletion utilities distributed with UNIX systems are of the take-no-prisoners variety: They will strip the `/etc/passwd` entry, delete the home directory, and be done with it. Obviously, this is not the solution for every system. Once more, we're going to examine some ideas that will allow you to tailor deletions to your needs.

Concerns

Several concerns arise from account deletion, ranging from erroneous deletion to the disposition of sensitive data. Of course, security concerns are always a significant matter as well. Our deletion scheme will need to address each of these.

Some people may simply want to change the user's password and/or login shell. This may work well for a temporary suspension, but any number of security problems can arise from with this approach. The user may have remote access privileges (through `.rhosts`, FTP, or NFS mounting), and simply changing the password may not prevent access to the data in question. By the same token, changing the login shell may actually open more security holes, depending on the trustworthiness of the locked-out shell.

We could address these issues by simply making an immediate archive of the user's file (to tape, perhaps), but that won't help us when the former user's department head wants to move some of the files to new locations. Therefore, we're going to use a short-term move, coupled with a long-term archival, to make our job easier.

Getting it done

Let's begin by setting aside a section of disk for deleted accounts. If you can spare a complete partition, only mounting it when actually deleting an account or retrieving files, so much the better. We'll work from the assumption that you can spare a complete partition for this purpose. Mount the partition as /deletion, or something similar, and create a few directories in preparation for account deletions:

```
# mount /dev/dsk/c1t0d3s4 /deletion
# mkdir crontabs atjobs mail
```

Moving to the user's home directory, use cpio or a similar tool to move their directory tree to the /deletion partition:

```
# cd /usr2/market/jqweeble
# find . -depth -print | cpio -pdmv /deletion/jqweeble
```

Don't forget that jqweeble may have cron or at jobs, too:

```
# cp /usr/spool/cron/crontabs/jqweeble /deletion/crontabs
# cp /usr/spool/cron/atjobs/jqweeble  /deletion/atjobs
```

And, finally, move his mailbox:

```
# cp /usr/spool/mail/jqweeble /deletion/mail/jqweeble
```

If you have other special needs (subdirectories in common areas, perhaps), be sure to move them to /deletion as well.

Having copied the relevant files and directories to /deletion, you may now purge them from their original locations. To finish the process, we need to remove the jqweeble entry from /etc/passwd:

```
# sed "/^jqweeble:/d" /etc/passwd > /etc/newpasswd
# cp /etc/passwd /etc/oldpasswd
# mv /etc/newpasswd /etc/passwd
```

You'll still need to check some things manually (such as /etc/group), but the bulk of your work is done. Don't forget to unmount /deletion when you're finished:

```
# umount /deletion
```

This approach gives both short-term and long-term rewards. If, for some reason, we need to retrieve any files (or restore the account) in the near future, we can simply mount /deletion and retrieve as needed. We have also placed all deleted accounts in one place. It's a simple matter to create a tape archive of just these deleted accounts each year. When you receive the inevitable request — "I need some of jqweeble's files. He left sometime in 1995." — you can simply pull your "Deletions 95" tape from the shelf and restore in a flash. The alternative — searching through monthly or weekly backup tapes until you find the last one that included jqweeble — is not worth the time or trouble. Be careful to double-check user identities; if you've reused a user name since the "original user" was deleted, you could restore files to the wrong directory, give default access to the wrong person, or create other problems.

Automating the process

To automate this process is relatively straightforward: a shell script, in this case, is a simple matter. I would, however, urge you to include some sort of log facility, saving the /etc/passwd and /etc/group entries for each deleted account. This information will be invaluable should you be required to restore files and/or accounts at a later date.

Printer Administration

Because I have discussed printer installation and configuration elsewhere in this book, this chapter's offerings will concern only the actual day-to-day questions of printer management and administration.

Default printers

Wherever possible, you should set aside a default printer for your users. If nothing else, this can serve as a fallback output device for those occasions when someone forgets to specify a printer on the command line. I suggest that a line printer, with its low cost per page, fits this need rather well. The same printer can also be used for lengthy file listings, working copies, and the like.

In the System V universe, you define a default printer with lpadmin. If we decide to make the printer named backoffice the system's default printer, we simply issue the command:

```
lpadmin -dbackoffice
```

All print requests will then default to the backoffice printer.

BSD-derived systems use the /etc/printcap entry to determine the default printer. In most cases, the printer named lp will be considered the system default printer. (You can assign multiple names in /etc/printcap. This allows you to give the default printer a more meaningful name, in addition to its designation as lp.)

If you are in the BSD universe (and, in a few cases, special System V environments), you can use an environment variable to set a default printer. In most cases, the variable in question is PRINTER. The administrator can simply insert this environment variable into the appropriate system startup files. Users can also specify their own default printer, simply by changing the value of PRINTER in their .login or .profile files. If I wanted to override the default backoffice printer with a printer named myoffice, I'd simply place the following line in my .profile:

```
PRINTER=myoffice ; export PRINTER  /* assuming /bin/sh */
```

If users perform most of their printing on a particular printer, setting this environment variable will save them quite a bit of typing!

Note

You can lessen your administrative burden significantly if you assign meaningful names to your printer queues. I suggest some combination of location and make/model. For instance, the HP LaserJet 4MP in Marketing could be named mktlj4mp, and the Apple LaserWriter in Technical Support could be known as techalw. These names will also help users to direct their special outputs to appropriate printers without your assistance.

Regardless of the number of printers you have deployed, one command should become part of your daily first-cup-of-coffee routine: lpstat -t. (BSD-derived systems may support *lpq* instead.) This command will report on the availability of every printer configured on your system. If a printer has been disabled, lpstat -t can give you valuable status information, including the system's best guess as to the reason behind the disabled status. The best tool in the administrator's arsenal is awareness, and utilities such as lpstat or lpq can put you well ahead of problems such as these.

Due to the potentially large amount of output from lpstat, some people prefer to extract only the lines detailing the enabled/disabled status of each printer. You can accomplish this with a simple pipe of lpstat -t | grep abled. You may find it worth your while to bind this to a shell command in your .profile or to an alias in your .cshrc.

Where's my printout?

Many printing problems can be traced back to the user's default printer. That's the first thing we want to check when they can't locate their output. (If the user has csh or ksh as his or her login shell, you can ask him or her to use the history shell command and read the actual lp/lpr command back to you.) Misspelled printer names or improperly capitalized options are oft-found bugaboos at this stage of the game. You also need to ensure that the user-specified options are appropriate to the printer in question. For instance, it isn't often that a line printer can actually perform in Landscape mode.

Note

If you specify per-user default printers, that information should be part of the initial information given to a new user, right beside his or her new login name and password. Some sites even create *printer maps,* floor plans of each department with the printer locations marked and labeled. This technique can be quite helpful when printers are scattered about your operation.

Assuming that the user did, indeed, direct the job to the proper printer, our detective work must begin. Before diving into the depths of the printer subsystem(s), however, be sure to check the obvious: Make sure that the printer is properly loaded with paper, has ribbon or toner, and is powered up and ready to go.

Note

If you use network-ready printers or printer servers, become familiar with the controlling software shipped with the printer. You can query many such printers remotely, so you can ascertain their status from your desk! Nothing is more annoying than making a trip to another floor (or building), only to find that the printer in question is merely out of paper or low on toner.

If the printer is ready to go and the job was sent to the proper queue, it's time to start checking the less obvious possibilities. A quick check of the queue itself often reveals the problem: Someone may have tossed a huge PostScript file to a printer with limited RAM or requested a paper size unsupported by the printer in question. System V users can check the printer queue with lpstat, like so:

```
$ lpstat -p mktglj4
no entries
$
```

BSD users would use lpq with the -P option specifying a printer:

```
% lpq -Pmktglj4
Rank    Owner      Job     Files       Total Size
1st     biguser    342     massive.ps  2938391 bytes
2nd     jqweeble   344     letter.ps   81293 bytes
%
```

As you can see in our latter example, jqweeble is waiting behind a rather large PostScript file. There really isn't much we can do for him in this particular instance. Some UNIX variants do offer queue manipulation tools, such as the SunOS lpc command, which lets the superuser move jobs up and down the printer queue(s). This, however, is not something you want to be doing on a daily basis. In the next section, we'll discuss a few preemptive measures that you can use to avoid such conflicts.

If none of these queries yields a resolution and everything seems in order, you may want to ask the user to submit the job to a different, but comparable, printer. If both jobs disappear, the problem may lie in the file itself. Believe it or not, you can create a PostScript file that never actually generates a page! Also, the file or document in question may be too large for the printer. Such jobs would pass into the void with nothing more than a quick memory-exceeded status message from the printer.

If all else fails, a careful reading of the log files can often shed some light on the intermittent problem child events. You may wish to modify your printer interface script (or /etc/printcap entry) for the problematic queue. You can direct the error messages for that particular queue to a separate log file for later evaluation.

It's just spewing garbage!

This problem — printers tossing out page after page of incomprehensible babble — is often rampant in those operations with a wide selection of printers. Someone will inevitably submit a PostScript job to a non-PostScript printer or submit an HP-GL graphic to a PostScript-only printer. In either case, your only real choice is to remove the offending job. System V users should use the `cancel` command, whereas BSD users can avail themselves of `lprm`. To avoid this sort of problem, you may wish to create a cheat sheet for your users, outlining the printer capabilities available to them. In the next section, we'll discuss methods by which the printer subsystem itself can handle this issue before it becomes a problem.

Organizing usage and avoiding problems

Printers are often the best example of resource contention, in its most classic sense. The printer can only serve one person at a time, regardless of the number of jobs queued. The organization of your printing services can relieve much of this burden, with a minimal impact on your users. As with most things UNIX, a delicate balance must be struck between ease of use and system performance. We'll talk about a few things that can help turn the tide in your favor.

First and foremost, today's graphics-capable printers are RAM-hungry beasts. It is not uncommon to see laser printers with 16, or even 32, megabytes of memory. You can use this power to your advantage by channeling print jobs to those printers best equipped to handle them. Both the System V and BSD universes provide some capability to accept or reject printouts based on file size. Those of you with BSD systems can use the `mx` parameter of `/etc/printcap` to specify a maximum size for the print jobs on each printer, whereas System V users can simply modify the printer interface scripts, which are usually found in `/usr/spool/lp`.

Controlling the actual files sent to each printer queue is tricky, but it can be done. The UNIX `file` command is your secret weapon in this particular endeavor. You may know that the `file` command refers to the `/etc/magic` file when determining the type of each file. (This, incidentally, is why plain text files are sometimes named as "English text" or "C program text" when reviewed with `file`. The initial text of the document just happens to match a different entry in `/etc/magic`.) What you may not know is that you can modify `/etc/magic`, adding or modifying entries to fit your particular needs. For instance, the PostScript standard dictates that every PostScript file will begin with the characters %!. We can use that fact to create this line for `/etc/magic`:

```
0   string    %!   PostScript document
```

The first field of /etc/magic is the offset from the beginning of the file, the second field is the type of comparison, the third field is the comparative data, and the fourth is the result of a match.

After this line is added to /etc/magic, file can tell us:

```
$ file massive.ps
massive.ps: PostScript document
$
```

The application of this approach should be obvious to System V users. A quick check of input with the file command would allow us to accept or reject print jobs based on their status as PostScript or plain text files.

Another line I've added to my /etc/magic is

```
0   short   015445      PCL document
```

This allows my printer interface scripts, with the proper coding, to accept or reject PCL graphics files as they are submitted. You can also use the file command to ward off the inevitable submission of a binary file (a compiled executable file, perhaps) to your printers. Consider the following fragment of a /bin/sh printer interface script:

```
for prtfile in $*
do
    if file $prtfile | grep "PostScript" > /dev/null
    then
      filetype="PostScript"
    elif file $prtfile | grep "data" > /dev/null
    then
      filetype="binary"
    elif file $prtfile | grep "exec" > /dev/null
    then
      filetype="binary"
    else        filetype="text"
    fi
...
... Printing decisions/referrals/denials go here
...
done
```

This single command gives us quite a bit of power to accept, route, or deny print jobs based solely on their content. That's a handy tool!

BSD administrators are not accustomed to writing printer interface scripts, but it can be done. The /etc/printcap facility includes the variables if and of, which you can use to specify, respectively, an input filter and an output filter. You could, for instance, write a small script to check the file's content (as described previously), name it /usr/local/bin/ftypeck, and specify its use in /etc/printcap with the if option, like so:

```
lp|mylaser:\
    :br#1200:fs#06320:tr=\f:if=/usr/local/bin/ftypeck:\
    :lf=/usr/adm/lpd-errs:
```

You could implement any of the techniques we've discussed in this fashion. Feel free to experiment with this facility. Close consultation with your users can pay huge dividends at this point. You may even be able to accommodate huge print jobs by deferring them with the batch command or routing them to another printer on the fly.

Note

You can use input and output filter/interface scripts to track items such as page counts, job logging (by size, type, or user), or almost anything else you might be called upon to evaluate. This is especially useful for high-cost printers, such as color laser printers or large-paper-size (drafting) printers.

Easing the logjams

Printing is something of a black hole in system administration: There never seems to be a sufficient number of printers, and they never seem to be fast enough. You *can* do a few things to clear common bottlenecks. As with any other facet of systems administration, the best approach is to monitor printer usage before implementing changes. As mentioned previously, interface scripts can amass a staggering amount of information about your printing usage. You might, for instance, write an interface script to simply log user names, file types, and file sizes. Over time, this data could provide ample proof of the need for additional printers or printer upgrades.

A careful review of your usage data should point you in the right direction for relief of your problems. Once you've generated a few weeks' worth of data, you can simply match the physical printers to the "best fit" queues. If you notice, for instance, that Marketing is printing 1,500 pages each day, it only makes sense to place a high-capacity printer in their location. As an alternative, you may simply need to upgrade their existing printer with a larger paper tray. If Technical Support is submitting heavy-duty PostScript jobs to their printer, additional RAM may ease their delays. As always, be flexible.

What else can you do? Well, some UNIX variants support the notion of printer classes, that is, groups of printers that are treated as one by the lp/lpr subsystem. If, for instance, the Executive offices are using two identical laser printers (not an uncommon situation), you may be able to group them in a single class. The lp subsystem will then route printouts to the least congested printer in the class. Those of you whose systems do not support printer classes could (surprise!) implement them with custom interface scripts. The basic layout of such an interface might look something like this:

```
determine type of data (PostScript/text/PCL/whatever)
if printer specified cannot process data type
    mark for reroute to different printer
determine size of job  if size exceeds maximum for the printer
specified
    mark for reroute to "big job" printer
if marked for reroute
    send to newly specified printer
```

```
write log entry
notify user of reroute
```

You may even wish to create a dummy printer, which does nothing but call your custom interface script for processing and rerouting. This approach has significant merit in its simplicity: Instead of maintaining multiple interface scripts, you can simply modify the single master distributor script.

Whether supported by your vendor or customized, printer classes can be a godsend to the busy office. The only caution in this area is that you should not micromanage your printing operation. Set some general guidelines and define a clear set of options for the inevitable exceptions.

Postmaster Duties

Another part of our daily walk is our role as e-mail shepherds. With the ever-increasing level of Internet participation, you are sure to be confronted with MIME data, peculiar addresses, even more peculiar mail routes, and an array of potential failure points for electronic mail. As you might expect, this can place a significant demand on your time. We'll discuss a few techniques that can ease that burden.

Privacy issues

First and foremost, you must realize the sensitive nature of postmaster duties. Very few administrators spend time inspecting the content of user files. In fact, most administrators are constrained from such inspections by both law and organizational policy. E-mail, however, is a different matter. By default, most e-mail systems include the full text of the e-mail message in their problem reports. Therefore, we find ourselves facing a large amount of sensitive and private information on a daily basis. In the interest of both user privacy and legal necessity, we should endeavor to avoid any perusal of the actual content of such e-mail. Thankfully, the UNIX utilities make this a relatively simple matter.

As you may already know, the standard for e-mail message formats (RFC 822) specifies that the headers of a message must be separated from the message's content by at least one blank line. We can use that fact to create a small shell script:

```
cat - | awk `length($0) == 0 { exit }
                  { print }´
```

This shell script will print each line until it finds a zero-length line. When it encounters a blank line, it will exit. Of course, you will need to modify this script to match your particular mailer's format for error messages. Suppose, for instance, that my mailer includes several error messages after the headers, and that it includes the message "Original message follows" before appending the original message. I could include the error messages, while avoiding the actual content, by modifying the shell script, like so:

```
cat - | awk `$0 ~ /Original message/ { print; exit }
                    { print}´
```

This script will print every line, regardless of content, until it encounters a line that includes the phrase "Original message"; at that point, it will exit.

If you encounter long error messages, you may want to modify the script to send its output to a pager, such as less or pg:

```
cat - |
awk `$0 ~ /Original message/ { print; exit }
                    { print }´ |
/usr/local/bin/less
```

Were this a cookbook, I'd finish this recipe with "season to taste." You have an enormous amount of flexibility available to you in matters such as this. Once we've customized the script to match the error message format generated by our mailer, we'll be ready to integrate it into our mail agent. Most UNIX mail agents provide a pipe facility, which allows us to divert mail messages into other programs. Supposing that our "no content" shell script is named /usr/local/bin/nocontent (and that /usr/local/bin is in our PATH), we could do the following:

```
$ mailx
1 Mailer-Daemon  12 Nov 95   25/1975  Error: non-delivery
? pipe 1 nocontent
```

and message 1 would be sent to our script for processing.

If you use a mail preprocessor, such as the public domain procmail software, you may wish to divert mailer error messages to a separate mailbox. You could even remove the user content of each message at that point, before it is placed in the "errors" mailbox, by sending it through our "nocontent" filter during preprocessing.

Before you go digging

Unless the e-mail in question is of a critical nature, it's usually worth the time to simply resend the message as is. Given the fluid nature of internetworking, it is not at all uncommon to encounter a transitory problem: A router problem may render a machine temporarily invisible to the outside world, or the receiving system may be down for repair. In any case, attempting to resend the message rarely creates problems. I suggest that you wait 30 minutes or so before dispatching a second attempt.

Following the bouncing address

Considering the vast size of the Internet, the overall performance of the electronic mail system is remarkable. In my experience, the vast majority of nondelivery errors have been traced to user error rather than system problems. A careful reading of the original destination address will, in most cases, reveal the problem. Transpositions (`.eud` instead of `.edu`) or spelling errors (`mybx.com` instead of `mybox.com`) will account for the vast majority of error messages you receive. These are usually indicated by error messages such as "No such user" or "No such host." You may wish to notify the user of the correct address, but a savvy user will recognize their error and correct it with a follow-up mailing. (If you have the luxury of presenting introductory lectures or materials to your users, it would be a very good idea to include a brief description of these error messages.) As a rule of thumb, I usually allow the first error of this sort to pass without comment. Should I see repeated errors of this type, I will contact the user with the proper address.

When dealing with errors other than mere transpositions or misspellings, you should understand the address formats expected by your mailer. Given the various address formats in use, mailer configuration is something of an ongoing project: There always seems to be something new! Unfortunately, very few rules govern the interpretation of such addresses. One is often reduced to mere experimentation when searching for the proper address. I can, however, offer a few tips that may help:

- Interpret the address backward. For instance, the address:

  `woof%backdoor::snarf@bigcorp.com`

  implies that `bigcorp.com` is the first stop on the trail. Begin your inquiries there.

- Use your Domain Name Service to verify the domain portion of the address.

- Use your Domain Name Service to verify that a system in the domain is prepared to exchange e-mail. You should look for MX (*Mail Exchanger*) DNS records.

- If the address includes % characters, you may wish to reverse the order of the elements they separate, like so:

  `backdoor%woof::snarf@bigcorp.com`

- If special characters, such as %, !, or :: are included in the address, you may need to enclose that portion of the address in quotes, like so:

  `"woof%backdoor::snarf"@bigcorp.com`

I would classify this as a last resort approach; it is rather uncommon.

Tip

A very good rule of thumb for all aspects of system administration is "Be liberal in what you accept, but conservative in what you send." Be prepared to accept rather peculiar address formats on incoming e-mail, but make every effort to simplify the addresses you place on outgoing e-mail. The postmaster on the other end of the network will thank you.

Other common errors

When someone dispatches an e-mail message to another user, that person has no way of knowing the readiness of the recipient (or the recipient's system) to process the message. As a result, you will see quite a few errors whose origin is on the remote system. In most cases, the best thing you can do is notify your counterpart on the remote system of the problem. The most common error of this sort is "Mailbox full," also reported as "Cannot append." This indicates that either the recipient's mailbox or the receiving system's mail directory is out of space. Other hints of remote problems are mentions of gateways, forwarding, or routing in the error message. Again, you should refer these to the remote postmaster.

Occasionally, the problem will lie in the network itself, rather than the sending and receiving systems. Problems of this sort are often indicated by error messages such as "Connection timed out" or "Session deferred." Most network problems are transitory in nature. Subsequent e-mail delivery sessions are usually successful. In cases such as this, you may want to consult your local network managers to ensure that the problems do not lie within your local network.

The obscure and bizarre

You can sometimes trace nondelivery of e-mail back to shortcomings or misconfigurations in other areas of the system. While these are certainly uncommon, forewarned is forearmed; therefore, I'd like to close this section with a few "war stories" from my own experience. You may never encounter situations such as these, but they illustrate the far-reaching implications of seemingly trivial configuration and installation issues. I fervently hope that you never face situations such as these.

The untouchable

I once received an error message that read "Network is unreachable." My first impulse was to check for a misspelling in the address, but the address was correct. Moreover, I was able to see the recipient system in the Domain Name System. Puzzling over this, I realized that seeing a remote network does not necessarily imply that one can actually reach the network in question. Using the freeware `traceroute` utility, I attempted to determine the route between our systems. This met with no response. Eventually, it occurred to me that every TCP/IP packet has a lifetime (Time to Live, or TTL), which is measured in hops. As a rule, every router along the path counts as one hop. It finally came to light that the remote system was buried behind 10 internal routers. My packets, with their (then-standard) lifetime of 15 hops, were exhausted before they could reach their destination. The solution was to rebuild my kernel, increasing the TTL from 15 hops to 32. Once I made this change, I never received an error of this sort again.

You can quote me on that

On another occasion, I received a "No such UUCP host" error message from a remote mailer. The address in question was of the form:

```
frump%bangate%user@company.com
```

The error was generated, however, by an intermediate system, not the system at `company.com`. After much puzzlement and several failed attempts to deliver the message, I began speaking with my counterpart at the intermediate site. As it happened, the mixed address (the percent signs) had been generated by `company.com` when the message crossed its internal PC LAN gateway. Herein lay the problem. When interpreting mixed addresses, most sites replace % with @ and attempt to parse the resulting address; however, this intermediate site went one step further. If its substitution of % with @ did not yield a valid address, it attempted to substitute ! in place of %. Naturally, this was the source of the "No such UUCP host" error. The problem then became one of getting the mixed address past the intermediate site while denying it the capability to attempt a rewriting. The solution was to enclose the mixed portion of the address in quotes, like so:

```
"frump%bangate%user"@company.com
```

This case was a perfect illustration of the maxim given a few pages ago: "Be liberal in what you accept, but conservative in what you send." Enclosing the leading portion of the address in quotes, for all intents and purposes, told intermediate sites "Hands off this part!" What could be more conservative?

Too many cooks

One of my company's senior personnel came to me with comments of "inferior systems" and "shoddy configuration." By way of demonstration, he showed me copies of his outgoing e-mail messages, as they had been received by his colleagues. Beside them, he lay printouts made when he dispatched the messages in question. Unquestionably, something peculiar was afoot. Not only was each paragraph truncated, but some individual lines of each paragraph were missing as well. A quick check of my log files revealed no inconsistencies. As far as I could tell, his messages were being processed in the same fashion as those of everyone else. I decided to send a few test messages to the respondents who had complained. These were delivered, in their entirety, without a hitch. Two days had not yet passed before the mysterious problem once more raised its head. This time, I decided to watch the user as he composed his messages.

Watching him type, I could tell that something was peculiar, but I couldn't quite put my finger on the inconsistency. Finally, I realized that he was pressing the Enter key rather infrequently. When I asked him about it, he pointed out that his terminal emulation software (running on a Macintosh) performed line wrapping. After saving his work in a separate file on the UNIX system, I examined it with the `od` command. As it happened, his terminal emulation was, indeed, wrapping the lines, but it was not transmitting a newline character to the UNIX system. This solved part of the problem. As he typed without pressing the Enter key, the UNIX system would only accept the first 255 characters of each line. Any further typing was silently discarded.

One question remained: At what point was the second truncation being performed? I went back to the list of addresses to which his mail had been truncated, and we quickly narrowed the continuation of the problem to a handful of sites. Examining the addresses, I realized that all of them were BITNET sites, and that they traversed the local BITNET gateway before being delivered. A bell rang in my mind: BITNET's protocols of that time were predicated on the notion of a card image, an 80-column Hollerith card image. My mailer was passing a nice, long line to the BITNET gateway machine, which was silently dropping everything past "column 80." Once more, we visited the terminal emulation software being used. We found that its line length was set to "the width of the window." He had been doing exactly as instructed: pressing the Enter key at the end of each line. The window was simply too wide. Coupled with the silent UNIX truncation at 255 characters and the BITNET standard of 80 characters, the picture was complete. The solution, after four days of investigation, was to merely reconfigure the terminal emulation software for a fixed 80-column window.

This incident brought home the importance of consistency in our approach to user services. I had neglected to create standard configurations for the various terminal emulation programs in use within our operation, and I had paid the price for that oversight.

The Übermailer

If you've used a UNIX system for any length of time, it's quite likely that you've found yourself in a religious discussion of various utilities. Some users like the `vi` editor, whereas others disdain `vi` in favor of Emacs or `pico`. Programmers hold heated discussions concerning the merits of the various languages or even argue the differences among compilers of the same language! Well, UNIX system administrators have their religious issues as well. One of the most volatile issues at any congregation of administrators is their choice of mail transfer agent (MTA). In the UNIX world, you'll find quite a few MTAs from which to choose: `smail`, `mailsurr`, and `mmdf` are just a few examples. Many of these packages are freely available, whereas some will be shipped with your system. Most UNIX systems, however, ship with some version of the Mother of All MTAs: `sendmail`.

Created by Eric Allman and tweaked by legions, `sendmail` has long been something of a rite of passage for the administrator. The young admin who successfully configures and manages a `sendmail` installation gains a new level of knowledge and expertise not often found outside the realm of custom kernel modification. However, any fan of adolescent movies can tell you that rites of passage are not a stroll in the park, and this is certainly true of sendmail. I will readily admit that its configuration is not necessarily simple and that its behavior is not always intuitive. But I can honestly say that I have never had a mail service need that `sendmail` could not meet. Therefore, we're going to explore the basic layout of `sendmail` and embark on a few simple configurations.

Caution

As with so many UNIX utilities, sendmail is available in several incarnations. While I will make every attempt to restrict my comments to those properties shared among all (or most) versions, your version may or may not support every technique, macro, or option discussed here. Get the documentation for your particular version and refer to it while reading this section.

Girding for battle

Because sendmail is (or will be) one of your major paths to the rest of the network, you must understand what you are doing. I suggest that a good understanding of proper address and message formats is absolutely essential *before* you embark upon sendmail configuration. If you need to sharpen your knowledge of these formats, consult the following RFCs:

- **RFC 822.** Internet Message Address Formats

- **RFC 823.** Internet Text Message Format

These formats are available (at this writing) via anonymous FTP from ftp.internic.net, in the /pub/rfc directory. In addition, you should be familiar with the delivery agents you will be using, for example SMTP, uucp, and DECNET. If RFCs exist for your agents (SMTP is defined by RFC 821, for example), secure copies of them as well; otherwise, consult your vendor's documentation.

You also need to identify the files relevant to your particular sendmail installation. The most common installations of sendmail include these files, usually installed in either /usr/lib or /etc/mail:

```
sendmail        the executable itself
sendmail.cf     the configuration file
sendmail.st     the status file
sendmail.hf     the SMTP help file
```

Some versions of sendmail also include other files. Be sure that you know what they are, where they are, and what they do. Some versions support a frozen configuration file, usually named sendmail.fc. If this file exists, changes to the configuration file will be ignored. Needless to say, you'll find frustration at hand if you ignore this particular file.

Other files are specified within sendmail.cf. For instance, the alias file is defined with an option, as is the location of the mail queue directory.

Before beginning modification of your sendmail configuration files, be sure to secure a clean set of copies elsewhere on your system. As an alternative, you can leave the default copies in place and work on separate copies during the configuration process. If you are modifying a currently operational installation, the latter option is your obvious choice. Working on separate copies allows your current configuration to continue operation while you are testing.

Set our terms

The most important concepts in `sendmail` are three: mailer, host, and user. This tuple is the goal of every `sendmail` configuration. Every valid address should resolve into these three parts: a mailer to deliver the message, a host to which it should be delivered, and the user to whom that host should deliver the message. Note that, while the mailer and host must be singular entities, the user portion of the tuple may be an address in and of itself. Consider a host sending a message via `uucp`: The mailer is (of course) the `uucp` mailer and the host is the next link in the `uucp` chain, but the user (as far as our host is concerned) can be either a user at the next host or an address relevant to the next host. Were we to say this in plain English, we might say either:

"Use the `uucp` mailer to send this to host `thatsite` for user `morgan`" or "Use the `uucp` mailer to send this to host `thatsite` for user `nextsite!morgan`."

An important part of `sendmail` configuration is knowing when a user entry is suitable for passage to its destination.

The only exceptions to the tuple rule are the error mailer, which (as a rule) only expects to receive the text of an error message, and the local mailer, which does not expect to receive a destination host (because the local mailer is on the machine conducting the processing).

Now that we understand the tuple, what are the nuts and bolts of putting it together? Well, most `sendmail` installations use nine varieties of configurable information: rules, rulesets, macros, classes, headers, mailers, options, trusted users, and precedences. Let's briefly discuss each of these before plunging into actual configuration.

Rules

In `sendmail`, each possible modification of an address is configured as a rule. Rules consist of three parts: a left-hand side (LHS) or pattern, a right-hand side (RHS) or action, and an optional comment. Whitespace is allowed, but many admins find the result confusing. I suggest that you restrict whitespace to comments. In your configuration file, rules begin with the capital letter R.

Rulesets

In and of themselves, rules are not particularly effective. The intuitive reader may also realize that processing every address through every rule could easily become rather time-consuming. The `sendmail` agent answers this concern through the notion of rulesets.

In your configuration file, rulesets begin with the notation S*n* (*n* is the ruleset number). Every ruleset must have a number. Rulesets end when another S*n* statement is encountered.

Caution

Should you accidentally delete an Sn statement, the rules in the second ruleset will become part of the preceding ruleset. Confusion will then abound.

Once sendmail enters a ruleset during processing, it will not leave until one of two things happen:

- The address is rewritten to mailer-host-user tuple.

- All rules in the ruleset have been applied.

Rulesets may be common to all processed addresses, they may only be called in certain circumstances, or they may be attached to a particular mailer definition.

Macros

Most versions of sendmail use macros for three tasks. You can use them to place unstructured information in the stream. For example, the sender name for error messages (bounce messages) is defined by a macro. You can also use macros as vectors, to dispatch information to mailers. In some installations, macros pass the host and user portions of the tuple. Finally, some macros are used only within sendmail. We'll examine the more common members of this group later. Macros are identified by the capital letter D in your configuration file.

Classes

Classes allow a single variable to reference multiple words. Classes are used almost exclusively in rewriting rules. Your configuration file identifies classes with the capital letter C.

Headers

I consider header definitions a special form of macro. Headers may be universal, in which case they are added to every message. They may also be made dependent upon the definition of the destination mailer. Any macros present in a header definition will be expanded (when possible) before the header line is added to the stream. The capital letter H designates header definitions in your configuration file.

Mailers

Mailer definitions begin with the capital letter M. The mailer definition includes the name used for this mailer in sendmail's tuple, the actual program to execute, a set of flags governing the interaction between sendmail and the mailer, rulesets to use when sending to or receiving from the mailer, and the actual command used to execute the mailer program.

Options

Identified with a capital letter O, options are internal to sendmail. Use them to define various aspects of sendmail's performance, such as the location of various files, protection modes for temporary files, or other housekeeping information.

Trusted Users

Most versions of sendmail include a command-line option for arbitrarily replacing the sender's address. As you might imagine, this is not suitable for all users. Therefore, sendmail only allows "trusted users" to invoke this option. By default, most versions of sendmail only award trusted status to user IDs root, daemon, and uucp. I do not recommend adding any user IDs to the default list. In fact, I suggest that you remove any unnecessary user IDs from the default list. A capital letter T indicates a trusted user line in your configuration file.

Precedences

Some mailers understand the notion of precedence; sendmail supports precedence by assigning numerical values to precedence levels. The major benefit of these precedences is that those precedences with values less than zero will not generate returned error messages. Precedences are specified with a capital letter P in the configuration file.

Into the fray!

Now that we've briefly defined each item used in sendmail configuration, it's time to immerse ourselves in the depths of their configuration. You may find yourself reading some of these sections several times; that's quite normal. Few of us understand sendmail upon the first reading. Remember to check the documentation for your version of sendmail at each stage of this discussion, keeping on the lookout for differences. You may also wish to consult a printout of your configuration file as we move along.

A dab of glue, a bit of duct tape

As you might imagine, sendmail cannot do its work with some latitude in its definitions and some conditional action. sendmail provides metacharacters, much like those found in the UNIX shell, to allow you this latitude. The most common metacharacters are

$*	Matches zero or more tokens
$+	Matches one or more tokens
$-	Matches exactly one token
$=x	Matches any token in class x
$^x	Matches any token not in class x

The `if/then` conditional sense is provided by the `$?` metacharacter, whereas `else` is provided by `$|`. Most uses of the conditional sense deal with macros and classes. I'll explain further when discussing those topics.

I'll mention a few other metacharacters as we discuss other topics. As a general rule, use of the dollar sign indicates a metacharacter of some sort.

Macroeconomics

The typical `sendmail` installation utilizes several dozen macros. Most are straightforward, but a few always defy explanation at a glance. Let's look at a few examples of varying complexity.

Caution

Macro names are one of the greatest divergence points among the variants of `sendmail`. For instance, I have used versions that define the `$M` macro as the default relay mailer, the masquerade name for a front-end site, and nothing at all. Read your documentation!

A simple macro does nothing more than assign a character string to a single-letter variable name. The `$n` macro (macros are referred to with metacharacter syntax) defines the name used when sending error messages, such as "Undeliverable mail" or "Can't find address." Here it is:

```
DnMAILER-DAEMON
```

We could easily rewrite this to read `DnRootmeister` or `DnThe Big Guy` if we wished to do so.

Macros may include other macros. For instance, one version familiar to me defines the host name with the `$w` macro and the domain name with the `$m` macro. It then builds the fully qualified domain name into the `$j` macro, like so:

```
Dj$w.$m
```

Macros may also be built conditionally, using the `$?` and `$|` notation mentioned earlier. For instance, consider that each of the following addresses is legal under RFC 822:

```
Wes Morgan <morgan@engr.uky.edu>
morgan@engr.uky.edu
```

Therefore, my definition of a "total name" must be able to account for the option plain text outside the address. Most `sendmail` installations define "total name" with the `$q` macro, like so:

```
Dq$?x$x <$g>$|$g$.
```

Let's take a look at that macro as if it were a high-level language program, using indentation to indicate program flow and conditionals:

```
Dq          define macro $q as:
  $?x            if $x macro is defined, then
```

```
$x <$g>          define $q as $x <$g>
$|          else
$g$.            define $q as $g$.
```

The most complex example of this sort to be found in most `sendmail`
configurations is the definition of the `Received:` header line. Take a look at
yours for some real fun with macros!

Go to the head of the class

The `sendmail` agent usually uses classes to provide the capability of
synonyms. This is especially important when a single machine may be
accepting mail for a variety of hosts. This is most often the case when
configuring a particular machine to serve as the mail gateway for an entire
domain.

Classes are defined by the capital letter C. The most common usage is the $w
class, which defines all names for a given host. For instance, suppose that the
machine `flamtap` receives mail via both `uucp` and `SMTP`. Furthermore,
suppose that it is also the domain mail server for `mydomain.com`. The
appropriate $w class definition might be

```
Cwflamtap flamtap.mydomain.com mydomain.com
```

Be careful here. If you want to accept mail for any addresses other than your
own, it may be far simpler to include them in the $w class than to attempt to
create address rewriting rules to handle the different names. Let's suppose
that the site named previously also handles mail for `bingo.com`. We may
need to redefine $w, like so:

```
Cwflamtap flamtap.mydomain.com mydomain.com bingo.com
```

Some earlier versions of `sendmail` also allow one to specify a names file with
a capital F:

```
F/usr/lib/mynames
```

You will see extensive uses of the class mechanism when building or
examining rewriting rules; they can be a great timesaver. If your version of
`sendmail` allows you to define your own classes, be sure to do so before
entering the rewriting rules. Place them before the first ruleset in the
configuration file.

Running the old option play

There's very little to say about options in a generic text such as this. Each
version of `sendmail` has its own raft of options. The only advice I can give is
to familiarize yourself with the options presented by your version of
`sendmail` and to be on the lookout for opportunities to optimize
performance. A typical `sendmail` option is the location of the spool
directory. Many versions use the Q option, like so:

```
OQ/usr/spool/mqueue
```

For the typical installation, you should have little reason to change any option settings.

Give me headers, lots of headers!

Header definitions are closely matched to mailer definitions, and `sendmail` makes every attempt to pass only relevant headers to its mail delivery agents. The syntax is similar to that used for conditional expansion in macros:

```
H?P?Return-Path: $g
```

In this example, the `Return-Path:` header will only be included if the mailer definition includes the P flag; in this case, the return path is held in the $g macro.

You may find unconditional headers, but these will not include the flag check:

```
HSubject:
```

If you wish, you can create your own headers. You may even create conditional headers based upon the mailer flags. For instance:

```
H?D?Actual-Resending-Host: $j
```

or

```
HX-Mailing-List: mylist@myhost.com
```

Be careful and considerate when creating your own headers. Remember that they will be applied to each and every piece of mail. Some users might not want funny or commercial headers. Remember, too, that other sites will have to carry these headers through to the recipients. They may not appreciate a large chunk of unnecessary header lines in every message. Finally, there is something of an Internet tradition that customized headers begin with X-, as did the X-Mailing-List header we just defined.

Rules, rules, rules

Composing a rule in `sendmail` seems a simple matter at first glance: Construct a left-hand side (LHS) that matches what we're looking for, build a right-hand side (RHS) that performs the action we want, put a comment in for the next admin, and you're done, right? I wish (for all our sakes) that it were that easy. The `sendmail` agent's myriad macros and possibilities for customization make it all too trivial to create virtual black holes, from which no address can escape. My advice to you is twofold: Tread lightly and test heavily.

sendmail lays the groundwork

The sendmail agent conducts a significant amount of preprocessing before calling your rulesets. At one time, almost every version of sendmail followed the same pattern of processing rulesets: Ruleset 3 pulled the address into the *user@host* format, then ruleset 0 resolved it to a tuple, rulesets 1 and 2 handled sender and recipient addresses (respectively), mailer-specific rulesets were applied, and ruleset 4 finally processed any remaining addresses (such as those found in Cc: headers). However, the disease known as "versionitis" has become firmly established in sendmail, and you can no longer assume that this traditional pattern is followed in their particular version. (Most versions, however, continue to use ruleset 0 for the ultimate resolution of an address and generation of a tuple.) A careful reading of your documentation and, of course, the configuration file itself, will give you a basic idea of your sendmail's program flow.

Watching the machinations

You can also learn much about sendmail's operation by using address test mode. When run with the -bt option from the command line, most versions of sendmail enter address test mode: The user merely specifies a ruleset and an address, and sendmail displays the input and output of each ruleset called. For instance, let's feed an address to ruleset 0:

```
$ /usr/lib/sendmail -bt
ADDRESS TEST MODE
Enter <ruleset> <address>
>0 morgan@mynet.com
rewrite: ruleset 3   input: "morgan" "@" "mynet" "." "com"
rewrite: ruleset 8   input: "morgan" "@" "mynet" "." "com"
rewrite: ruleset 8 returns: "morgan" "@" "mynet" "." "com"
rewrite: ruleset 6   input: "morgan" "<" "@" "mynet" "." "com" ">"
rewrite: ruleset 6 returns: "morgan" "<" "@" "mynet" "." "com" ">"
rewrite: ruleset 3 returns: "morgan" "<" "@" "mynet" "." "com" ">"
rewrite: ruleset 0   input: "morgan" "<" "@" "mynet" "." "com" ">"
rewrite: ruleset 3   input: "morgan" "@" "mynet" "." "com"
rewrite: ruleset 8   input: "morgan" "@" "mynet" "." "com"
rewrite: ruleset 8 returns: "morgan" "@" "mynet" "." "com"
rewrite: ruleset 6   input: "morgan" "<" "@" "mynet" "." "com" ">"
rewrite: ruleset 6 returns: "morgan" "<" "@" "mynet" "." "com" ">"
rewrite: ruleset 3 returns: "morgan" "<" "@" "mynet" "." "com" ">"
rewrite: ruleset 0 returns: "^V" "tcp" "^W" "mynet" "." "com"
                "^X" "morgan" "@" "mynet" "." "com"
>^D
$
```

Entering a Ctrl-D terminates test mode for most versions of sendmail.

This exercise has shown us a great deal about the operation of this sendmail installation. For instance, we see that the first step in rewriting was to tokenize the address. The second step inserted angle brackets around the remote portion of the address (@mynet.com). Finally, sendmail determined that mynet.com mail was to be delivered via the tcp mailer. It will attempt delivery to a machine accepting mail for mynet.com.

We also notice that rulesets can call other rulesets. Entrance to, and return from, each ruleset is clearly indicated in the test report. We also see that rules may be called more than once. In this example, ruleset 3 was called twice. This is not unusual. It's quite possible for rulesets to be called several times, as a thorny address is rewritten several times.

This test mode will be your best friend as you modify your sendmail configuration. I strongly suggest that you test each and every modification to exhaustion. Furthermore, I suggest that you conduct your configuration experiments on a working copy of the sendmail configuration file. Most versions of sendmail allow you to specify a different configuration file with the -C option. To test a new configuration file, you might use the command line:

```
$ /usr/lib/sendmail -bt -C$HOME/newconfig.cf
```

I should note that most versions of sendmail execute as the initiating user, *not* as root or mail, when the -C flag is used. This means that you should not actually be in a production sendmail daemon while logged in as a normal user.

Rolling our own

You can write rules to match literal text, a metacharacter, or any combination of the two. For instance, suppose that I wanted a rule that would match addresses with the hostname notmine.com. One possible LHS would be:

```
R$*<@notmine.com>$*
```

Remember that sendmail inserts the angle brackets around the remote portion of the address, as observed in the last section.

We now have a left-hand side. We need to do something with the addresses that match this pattern. Suppose that we want to replace notmine.com with bingo.com. How would we rebuild the new address on the right-hand side? Well, sendmail uses positional metachacters to store the values matched on the left-hand side. The first token matched is $1, the second is $2, and so on. We can accomplish our goal, then, with:

```
R$*<@notmine.com>$*    $1<@bingo.com>$2    map notmine to bingo
```

Notice that the @ sign in the original address was not captured by our tokens. We had to specifically include it when building the new address.

Are we finished? Not necessarily. What would happen if we were presented with the address jschmo@corp.notmine.com? Our rule is looking for the literal pattern @notmine.com in the address. It would not work if notmine.com has subdomains. How do we resolve this? Well, we need to modify the LHS to match either the domain *or* any host within that domain. It would seem that further tokenization is called for:

```
R$*<@$*notmine.com>$*    $1<@$2bingo.com>$3    map hosts to bingo
```

You'll notice that I used the $* metacharacter to match zero or more items in each instance. You may have been tempted to use $+ (matching one or more items) or $- (matching only one item) instead. A moment's thought should reveal the flaws in those approaches. Using `<@$+notmine.com>` would not match `notmine.com`, whereas `<@$-notmine.com>` would not match `machine.subdomain.notmine.com`. You don't know what addresses will be tossed into `sendmail`; therefore, you want your rules to be as flexible as possible.

Caution

Many people assume that every address will be in the nice, clean form of *username@host.domain.name*. Nothing could be further from the truth. Write your rules with maximum flexibility, and you'll be covering the bases well.

Set em up!

Individually, rules are rarely sufficient. After all, relatively few addresses can be properly rewritten in a single rule. Therefore, `sendmail` operates on the idea of rulesets. Rulesets are designated in the configuration file with a capital letter S and a number or (in more recent version) a character string:

```
S72
```

or

```
Scheck_mail
```

A ruleset does not require a closure. All rules following the ruleset designation are included in that ruleset until either the end of the configuration file is reached or another ruleset designation is found.

Let's return to our newly created rule:

```
R$*<@$*notmine.com>$*   $1<@$2bingo.com>$3   map hosts to bingo
```

If we have other local postmaster responsibilities that cannot be fulfilled by `sendmail`'s defaults, we might write additional rules, like so:

```
R$*<@*nothere.edu>$*   $1<@$2bingo.com>$3    map this domain to bingo
R$*<@$*another.net>$*   $1<@$2newname.net>$3  map another domain
R$*<@platypus.ec.com>$* $1<@platypus.new.com>$2 map a single hostname
```

Assuming that we want to process these rules for all addresses, we can either insert them into an existing ruleset or label them as a ruleset all their own. The decision point is relatively simple: If you only wish to apply these rules at a single point in processing, you can integrate them into an existing ruleset. If, however, you expect to reference these rules from several different processing steps (from several different mailer definitions, perhaps, or from both sender and recipient address rewriting), you should establish them as a separate ruleset and call that ruleset from the appropriate rules. If you take the latter approach, be sure to select a ruleset number not already in use. Our addition to the configuration file would look something like this:

```
####
# Ruleset to handle local address hackery
####
S75
R$*<@*nothere.edu>$*  $1<@$2bingo.com>$3    map this domain to bingo
R$*<@$*another.net>$*  $1<@$2newname.net>$3  map another domain
R$*<@platypus.ec.com>$* $1<@platypus.new.com>$* map a single hostname
```

Some versions of sendmail have preassigned local rulesets, which have already been integrated into the major rewriting rules. If your installation offers such rulesets, use them. It will make your locally specific rules much simpler to manage.

Talking to mailers

As mentioned previously, a successful resolution of an address yields a tuple of mailer, host, and user. You can customize the interface between sendmail and the various mailers by adjusting the mailer configuration. Let's take a look at a sample mailer configuration:

```
Mthisone, P=/bin/mailit, F=DFMPlms, S=10, R=20, A=mailit $u
  S10
  S20
```

The first entry is the sendmail name for this mailer. This name is used with the $# metacharacter to direct mail to this mailer. For instance, we might see a rule like this:

```
R$*<@$m>$* $#thisone$@$m$:$1   mail to our domain goes to /bin/mailit
```

The sendmail agent's processing always resolves to a RHS of this type, even if it is going to the error mailer. I should note that the $# metacharacter really indicates that the ruleset is to terminate immediately, the $@ metacharacter indicates that the remainder of the RHS will be returned as the value from this ruleset, and the $: metacharacter means that this rule is terminated. These meanings may seem irrelevant at this time, but their importance will become clear later.

The P entry in the mailer definition refers to the mailer program. In our example, sendmail will run /bin/mailit whenever this mailer definition is designated as the destination. If you implement a custom mailer, be sure that the program is accessible and executable by sendmail. If it is not, you've just created a virtual black hole. The F entry is the meat of the interactions between sendmail and the mailer. The flags in this entry define what the external mailer program expects to receive from sendmail. Each version of sendmail seems to have its own ideas about flag definitions, but Table 47-1 provides a common example.

Table 47-1   Sample Flag Definitions in sendmail

Flag	Definition
n	Do not insert a UNIX-style From line at the message front.
l	This mail is local; that is, final delivery will be performed.
s	Strip any quotes from address before calling mailer.
m	This mailer can send to multiple users per transaction.
F	This mailer wants a From: header line.
D	This mailer wants a Date: header line.
M	This mailer wants a Message-Id: header line.
x	This mailer wants a Full-Name: header line.
P	This mailer wants a Return-Path: header line.
E	Escape lines beginning with From in the message body with the character >.

You'll notice that several of these flags are checked in the header definitions discussed earlier. If, for instance, we wanted to include a header only in locally delivered messages, we would test for the l flag in the header definition, like so:

```
H?l?X-Msg-Delivered-By: Your friendly admin
```

Determining the proper flag and option settings for a custom mailer can be very time-consuming. Fine-tuning and repeated testing are often necessary.

The S= and R= entries refer to specific rulesets. The ruleset specified in the S= clause will be applied when sending to this mailer, and the R= ruleset will be applied when receiving mail from this mailer. You'll notice that, in this example, the specified rulesets are empty; this is perfectly acceptable. These rulesets can be very useful when your sendmail is acting as a mail gateway for other machines or networks. We'll take a look at these special rulesets a bit later.

Finally, the A= entry specifies the actual command line used to invoke this mailer. This is simply a constructed command line, with macro expansion. In our example, this version of sendmail uses the $u macro to hold the user portion of the tuple. We use it to pass the destination address to the /bin/mailit mailer. Let's tie all this together. Suppose that we have a rule like this:

```
R$*<@myhome.com>$*     $#thisone$@myhome.com$:$1
```

When matched against the address `jschmo@myhome.com`, this RHS will become

`$#thisone$@myhome.com$:jschmo`

Tip

Most versions of `sendmail` perform substitutions in the RHS in this order: parameters from the LHS ($1, $2, and so on), host names are rendered canonical, and $#, $@, and $: are processed. Keep these precedences in mind when writing new rules.

The `sendmail` agent will consult the mailer definition for `thisone`, include the appropriate headers and options, and invoke the mailer with the command line:

`/bin/mailit jschmo`

Now, will this always function properly? Well, that depends on the capability of the destination mailer, `/bin/mailit`. Suppose, for example, that the next address coming down the pipe is `woof%jschmo@myhome.com`. In this case, our rule will yield an RHS of:

`$#thisone$@myhome.com@:woof%jschmo`

which, in turn, will lead to this invocation of `/bin/mailit`:

`/bin/mailit woof%jschmo`

If `/bin/mailit` knows what to do with this address format, all is well. If, however, it does not, we've just generated a problem. What if `/bin/mailit` is expecting `jschmo@woof` instead of `woof%jschmo`? A moment's thought should be enough to realize that `sendmail` has provided for this opportunity with its custom per-mailer S= and R= ruleset applications. In this case, we need a rule that will turn `woof%jschmo` into `jschmo@woof`. Furthermore, we only need to worry about this when sending to this mailer. We need to change our mailer definition by adding a rule, like so:

```
Mthisone, P=/bin/mailit, F=DFMPlms, S=10, R=20, A=mailit $u
S10
R$+%$+        $2@$1    convert x%y to y@x
S20
```

This will rewrite the address properly when you are sending to this particular mailer. Some external mailers may need extensive rewriting upon sending or receipt of e-mail. You will probably need to consult the documentation for the external mailer in some detail to ensure working rulesets in the mailer definition.

Special mailers

The `sendmail` agent provides several special mailers, which can add great functionality to your mail processing or create major league headaches.

The first, and most common, of these is the program mailer. Most versions of `sendmail` interpret an address beginning with the | symbol as a call to the program mailer. The default program mailer is `/bin/sh`, and the user portion of the tuple is passed as its arguments. Therefore, mail to `|lp@mycom.com` would simply dump the body of the message into whatever `lp` command exists on the `mycom.com` mail handler. The security-conscious administrator will immediately see the potential problems inherent to this facility, especially if `sendmail` executes as root. It should be noted that the infamous "Morris Internet Worm" was transmitted in this very fashion. Many sites choose to disable the program mailer, whereas others substitute a secured shell in place of `/bin/sh`. The choice is yours, but be extremely careful.

Other mailers provided by `sendmail` may include a relay mailer, which may not require complete address rewriting and various local mailers.

Passing the buck . . . and getting it back

Anyone familiar with programming techniques knows the value of writing generic code and reusing it. The same technique applies to `sendmail`. Its rulesets are operational groups. It stands to reason that, while processing in one ruleset, we may wish to process the address through another ruleset. We can accomplish this with the `$>` metacharacter. Let's suppose that, for whatever reason, we want to divert addresses from the `target.net` domain into `ruleset 5` and bring its changes back to the current ruleset. We would do this with:

```
R$*<@$*target.net>$*   $>5$1@$2target.net  pass addr to ruleset 5
```

There's only one problem with this: `sendmail` will return to this rule when it completes processing in `ruleset 5`. If the address continues to match the LHS, we will have an infinite loop. We can avoid this with another metacharacter. When used as a prefix, the `$:` metacharacter directs `sendmail` to terminate this single rule but to continue processing the ruleset that contains it. This will prevent the infinite loop. The correct ruleset would be

```
R$*<@$*target.net>$*  $:$>5$1@$2target.net$3  pass addr to ruleset 5
```

Remember that the parameters from the LHS (`$1`, `$2`, and so forth) are substituted before the result is passed to another rule (or ruleset). Therefore, we do not necessarily have to pass the matching address to `ruleset 5` verbatim. We could conduct some preliminary rewriting before the pass is made. If, for instance, we wanted to rewrite any address within target.net (perhaps `corp.target.net` or `deep.subnet.target.net`) to `user@target.net` before passing it to `ruleset 5`, we could do this with:

```
R$*<@$*target.net>$*  $:$>5$1@target.net$3  pass addr to ruleset 5
```

Notice that I used `target.net` in my literal test, instead of `.target.net`. There's a simple reason for this: Had I included the period in my literal test, an address like `jschmo@target.net` would not match. I also used the `$*` metacharacter to match zero or more tokens, for the same reason. Be very careful in your use of `$*`, `$-`, and `$+`; be sure that you are using the one suited to your need.

Assuming that `ruleset 5` is properly constructed, this rule will send matching addresses to be processed by `ruleset 5`, accept that ruleset's return value, and pass that value to the next rule in its ruleset.

Gateways to the world

As you know, the Internet is not a single entity; rather, it is a collection of networks that have agreed to exchange traffic. When it comes to electronic mail, this is an important distinction to make. Many networks have single points of entry to the Internet at large, and your `sendmail` configuration may need to know how to reach these gateways. Some networks may have multiple points of entry. In these cases, you should attempt to use the gateway closest (in the network sense) to your hosts. You may even have a local gateway facility that obviates the need for any external gateways. In each of these cases, `sendmail` gives you the capability to define these gateways as part of your mail configuration.

Caution

Even if you find a gateway advertised (in Usenet, the commercial press, or by word of mouth), you should *always* secure permission to use it before sending mail through it. Some sites have been forced to remove their gateway services as a result of this word-of-mouth sort of abuse.

This task is often accomplished by the creation of local *pseudodomains*. These domain names are not officially registered but can be used within your installation. We're going to use BITNET as an example of this technique.

Caution

Be *very* careful not to allow a local pseudodomain address to leave your domain. Ensure that you do not broadcast it to other mailers, and that you do not advertise it in your DNS.

Caution

When you select a name for a local pseudodomain, be sure that it does not already belong to someone else. The `sendmail` agent will operate on the first match found by its rewriting rules. It's quite possible to pick a pseudodomain name that results in mail being dispatched to Singapore or Upper Volta!

A site I once managed needed connectivity to BITNET, but only for the exchange of electronic mail. The BITNET mavens informed me of several BITNET SMTP-capable hosts, but all of their gateways were well away from my site on the network. A bit of investigation revealed that one of the BITNET hosts at our site supported SMTP mail transfer as well. This simplified my task greatly. All I had to do was craft a `sendmail` rule that would divert BITNET mail to the SMTP mailer of the local BITNET site.

The first step was to decide on a pseudodomain. This would be used by our users to direct mail to BITNET. Well, the simplest option is often the best. I decided to use `hostname.bitnet` as the pseudodomain form. The first part of my `sendmail` rule, the LHS, then became

```
R$*<@$-.BITNET>
```

In this instance, I could use the `$-` metacharacter without fear. BITNET does not support multilevel names, so only one token would be acceptable. At this point, I had to incorporate the intermediate destination: our local BITNET site's SMTP mailer. My rule grew to:

```
R$*<@$-.BITNET>$*       $#smtp$@bitnet.mysite.com
```

I had constructed two-thirds of the necessary tuple. All that remained was to determine what address should be passed to the gateway mailer. The BITNET site's admins informed me that their mailer expected to see addresses in pure BITNET form: `user@host`. Therefore, I needed to pass neither the `.bitnet` pseudodomain nor any optional tokens (such as the user's real name). My rule took its final form:

```
R$*<@$-.BITNET>$*   $#smtp$@bitnet.mysite.com$:$1@$2   BITNET gateway
```

The final step in the process was to propagate this change to all sites running `sendmail` in my domain. Be sure to propagate your changes properly. Your users will become rather frustrated if certain mail addresses only work from certain machines.

Carefully chosen gateways can greatly improve the turnaround time for mail delivery to external networks. You can use locally implemented gateways for support of remote operations, local bulletin boards, or almost any other local need.

By any other name aliases

Almost every version of `sendmail` supports aliases. An alias may be a simple name substitution, such as rewriting `Postmaster` to your user name, or more complex, such as mailing list expansion. In either case, the general implementation of aliases is the same.

The `sendmail` agent looks for all of its aliases in one file, which is most often specified by the A option. Look for a line beginning with OA in your configuration file to learn (or change) where `sendmail` finds its aliases on your system.

The format of an alias file is a simple one:

```
alias: expansion
```

In its simplest form, one name is substituted for another, like so:

```
Postmaster: root
```

It is important to note, however, that most versions of `sendmail` are case-sensitive; therefore, we would need a few more aliases:

```
Postmaster: root
postmaster: root
POSTMASTER: root
```

Aliases may also represent several user names. Additional user names are separated by commas. Remember, however, that the maximum length of a single line is usually 255 characters. If we wanted postmaster mail to be delivered to several people, we might do something like:

```
Postmaster: root,jimbo,weenie
postmaster: root,jimbo,weenie
POSTMASTER: root,jimbo,weenie
```

If the list of names becomes unmanageable (and, believe me, it will), you will need to use the final form of aliasing: the included file. This is nothing more than a pointer to a file containing a list of addresses or user names. Suppose, for instance, that I wanted the alias `mynetstaff` to represent 25 people. That's obviously too many names to maintain in a single line of the alias file. Instead, let's create a file named `/usr/local/lists/mynetstaff` that looks like this:

```
Joe Schmo <jschmo@mynet.net>
Jane Doe <jdoe@mynet.net>
Cousin Bob In Germany <cbob@mynet.de>
Dear Old Dad <dad@myhome.org>
et cetera, et cetera...
```

Now that we've created this file, we need to point `sendmail` in its direction. We do this with the `:include:` syntax for aliasing, namely:

```
mynetstaff: :include:/usr/local/lists/mynetstaff
```

The `sendmail` agent will now dispatch mail addressed to `mynetstaff@mynet.net` to each address contained in the `/usr/local/lists/mynetstaff` file.

Note

Net tradition dictates that, if the mailing list alias `mynetstaff` exists, the alias `mynetstaff-request` will point to the person responsible for maintenance of the `mynetstaff` alias. I urge you to follow this practice. All that is required is another entry in the alias file. If user `jschmo` is responsible for the `mynetstaff` alias, point the `-request` alias to that user ID:

```
mynetstaff-request: jschmo
```

If your mailing list aliases are advertised to the outside world, providing a `-request` alias will save you considerable grief in the eyes of the net public.

If you need several mailing lists or if regular users want to manage the membership of their mailing lists, the included file approach can work rather well. Simply create a file in `/usr/local/lists` for the new mailing list alias, give ownership to the responsible user, and let users manage it to their heart's content. The `sendmail` agent will pick up changes each time the alias is called, and they won't have to ask you to make each and every change to their alias.

Note

The `sendmail` agent's mailing list alias facility is not intended for large, production-level mailing lists; furthermore, `sendmail` allows no real screening of messages destined for these aliases. (That's right. By default, anyone can send mail to these aliases.) If you have large mailing lists or require more secure access to them, consider the wide variety of mailing list managers available from Internet file archives. Some of the more popular include `majordomo`, `deliver`, `procmail`, and `listserver`.

Doing it all: a case study

This has been the briefest of introductions to the intricacies of `sendmail`. Thanks to the wide range of versions available, a comprehensive analysis is beyond the scope of this text. I'd like to conclude our discussion of `sendmail` by going through the ground-up addition of a secondary network to an existing `sendmail` configuration.

I was once asked to provide e-mail connectivity to an internal network of machines running a non-UNIX operating system. The administrators of that system had no MTA, but they had written a package capable of exchanging files over a serial link. Furthermore, they had configured the mail system on their mail hub machine to work with this file exchanger. All I had to do was find some means of integration *and* a means of advertising this network to the outside world. Finally, the addresses had to be in the form `host:user` upon receipt by their mail hub.

We faced several design issues. First, should we give this internal cluster its own domain name? You could simply look for the address of the form `host:user@mydomain.com`, but this would require considerable modification of the existing `sendmail` rulesets. I could create a pseudodomain, but that would cause problems when used from other systems, which might not be configured to recognize the pseudodomain. I decided to take the third approach: I would create a legitimate (fully qualified) subdomain and advertise it through my Domain Name Service. This required the creation and broadcast of a Mail Exchanger (MX) record for the new subdomain, which pointed to my mail system. To the outside world, a name server query would return:

```
localnet.mydomain.com  MX   mydomain.com
```

This would allow addresses such as `host:user@localnet.mydomain.com` to be directed to my mail system. Now I had to reconfigure `sendmail` to both expect and properly resolve these addresses.

Remember the `$w` class? As we discussed earlier, this class must include all names by which our host is known. By extension, this implies that `sendmail` will not accept mail addressed to hosts not listed in that class. My original `Cw` line in `sendmail.cf` read

```
Cwmydomain mydomain.com
```

I had to augment this line to support the new subdomain, like so:

```
Cwmydomain mydomain.com localnet.mydomain.com
```

Now `sendmail` would accept mail with those addresses. How would it process them? After tracing to the appropriate ruleset (ruleset zero, in this case), I needed to craft a rule (or, perhaps, several rules) that would resolve the address and send it to our custom interface. The eft-hand side of this rule was simple enough:

```
R$*<@localnet.mydomain.com>$*
```

However, how should I write the right-hand side? Should I try to rewrite the entire address in one rule or should I split it across several rules? Keeping in mind that major `sendmail` rulesets may be called several times in the course of address parsing, I decided to conduct my major rewriting in the mailer-specific rulesets. All I wanted to do in ruleset zero was direct the address to the proper mailer. Remembering the tuple rule, this became

```
R$*<@localnet.mydomain.com>$*  $#localnet$@dummy$:$1
```

Although this custom interface mailer did not require a host portion of the tuple, I decided to include a dummy host for the sake of clarity.

Finally, I needed to write a mailer definition for the custom interface `/usr/local/bin/localnet`. After consultation with the remote administrators, we decided to pass a bare minimum of headers. In addition, I needed to perform a final rewrite to pass the proper address to the remote mail system:

```
Mlocalnet, P=/usr/local/bin/localnet, F=nsFDLE, S=30, R=31,
A=localnet$u
S30
S31
```

After some exhaustive testing, we placed this into production. The users of the remote cluster were quite happy to be linked to the outside world.

Avoiding the battles

As these war stories have (hopefully) illustrated, postmaster duties can lead you into some strange, uncharted waters. The best advice I can give you is that daily attention can — and will — nip most of your electronic mail problems in the proverbial bud. Simple daily checks, using commands such as `mailq` and review of your mailer logs, can alert you to problems long before your users suffer the consequences.

Summary

This chapter has prepared you for several core system administration tasks. We've discussed

▶ User management (creating and configuring user IDs)

▶ Matching your user organization to that of your operation through UIDs, GIDs, and directory placement

▶ Customizing your printing environment with default printers and printer interface scripting

▶ Respecting your user's privacy in postmaster duties

▶ The first steps in mail troubleshooting

▶ The fundamental operation of the most popular UNIX mailer, `sendmail`

▶ Using the basic functions of `sendmail` — creating and testing your own rules

▶ Rewriting mail address (supporting subdomains, other domains, and gateways)

▶ Creating mail aliases

▶ Interfacing with mail programs or other utilities

These tools and techniques will prove their value many times over, when users come calling.

Chapter 48

Storage Tools

In this chapter, Mike O'Neill discusses UNIX storage tools.

What Are Archivers?

Archivers are programs that package a group of files in one file. They also manage the addition and removal of files from existing archives. Archivers can also be designed to produce files that are independent of specific hardware. Archivers are used to provide convenient lumps for posting to FTP or Web sites for exchange with different machines and systems or for saving backups to tapes, disks, or other media.

UNIX Archivers

UNIX has two archive formats (`ar` produced `.a` files are program libraries, not archives, no matter what the *ar* is supposed to stand for): `cpio` and `tar` files. The latter format, *tar*, stands for *tape archive*, and *cpio* stands for *copy file archives in* and *out*. These names refer to both the file formats and the commands that read and write the respective kinds of files.

Both archive formats originated with AT&T UNIX systems, but `tar` became more popular with Berkeley systems. When people who cared which format was better were debating which to use for the POSIX standard, the so-called "Tar Wars" ensued. The upshot of the Tar Wars was that extended versions of *both* formats were included in the standard. As of 4.4BSD, Berkeley UNIX has only the `tar` command, whereas System V, Release 4 has both.

As a relief from the double standard, a new command — `pax` (*portable archive exchange*), which would manipulate both formats — was made part of the POSIX standard. As of the same UNIX versions mentioned in the preceding paragraph, only Berkeley has a `pax` command (a superset of the standard).

Another command (BSD only) is called `shar`, which is short for *shell archive*. The `shar` command makes a shell script of a set of files. When run, this script recreates the files and their original directory structure.

A final command that is not nominally an archiver, but can be used as one, is `uuencode` (*UNIX-to-UNIX encode*). The command takes a binary file and produces an ASCII-only file that can be decoded with `uudecode` (*UNIX-to-UNIX decode*).

tar

Here we examine the `tar` command, which is used as a tape archiver.

The tar file format

Because one of the main purposes of an archiver is to facilitate exchange of files from one machine to another, it is an advantage to have an archive format that is simple and regular. The `tar` format fits the bill. A `tar` file consists of 512-byte blocks, which normally are written in 20-block groups. (The group size appears to be a bit of frozen history, having to do with the characteristics of a particular tape drive.) The end of the file is indicated by two blocks of zeros. (The group that contains this end-of-file marker is padded to 20 blocks long.)

Each block is either a header block or a data block. A *data block* is simply 512 bytes of the file to be archived. A *header block* is more structured, containing the information that is required to reconstruct the directory structure of the archive, access permissions, perform integrity checks, and so on. Listing 48-1 summarizes the format of the POSIX standard's extended `tar` header.

Listing 48-1: The Extended tar Header Format

```
Length (bytes)    Name
          100     name
            8     mode
            8     uid
            8     gid
           12     size
           12     mtime
            8     chksum
            1     typeflag
          100     linkname
            6     magic
            2     version
           32     uname
           32     gname
            8     devmajor
```

```
     8        devminor
   155        prefix
```

The historic `tar` header contains the first nine fields of the extended header. I can't give a detailed explanation of all these fields and their formats, so I'll just hit the high points.

Note

The following paragraphs discuss ASCII representations. Actually, the standard specifies ISO 646 codes, which are very close to ASCII but not identical. In practice, ASCII seems to be used, so the text discusses ASCII codes. If you need to know the internals of `tar` files and what the standard really says, you need more information than this chapter has space to provide.

- *All* fields are ASCII character strings. Some of the strings are always null-terminated; others are null-terminated except when they fill the entire field. Fields such as `name`, `linkname`, `magic`, and `prefix` are character strings. The numeric fields — such as `uid`, `size`, and `chksum` (check sum) — are ASCII string representations of the octal representations of the numbers in the fields. These numeric fields are supposed to be padded with (ASCII) zeros to fill each field. All of the five or six `tar` files that I examined in the course of writing this chapter, however, had blanks padding the numeric fields in their headers (both old and extended). It seems that this is one part of the standard that is honored more in the breach than the observance.

- The name field gives the filename and path of the following file. If this is an extended header, the prefix field is concatenated to the front of name (with an implicit slash between them) to give the filename and path.

- The `mode`, `uid`, `gid`, `uname`, and `gname` fields identify the context in which the original file existed and its access permissions.

- The `size` field gives the size of the file, in bytes.

- The `mtime` field gives the modification time of the file at the time when the archive was created.

- The `chksum` field is the sum of all 512 bytes in the header, each byte being treated as an unsigned number. For this addition, the 8 bytes of the `chksum` field itself are taken to be blanks.

- The `typeflag` field stores the file type — regular file, directory, link, and various more esoteric types.

- The `linkname` field contains the name of a file to which the archived file is linked.

- The `magic` field contains the null-terminated string "ustar."

- The `version` field contains the nonnull-terminated string "00."

- The `devmajor` and `devminor` fields contain system-dependent information about certain special file types.

The tar command

The options for `tar` are many and varied — and are not all the same for the System V, BSD, and various other versions (including freely distributed ones). Because `tar` is favored by Berkeley UNIX, this discussion of `tar` is based on that version and its documentation. The text mentions features that are available in other versions if they seem to be notable. Tables 48-1 and 48-2 describe some functions of `tar`.

Table 48-1   tar Options

Option	Result
-c	Creates a new tape from the given files
-r	Writes files to the end of the tape (appends to end of archive)
-t	Lists the files on the tape
-u	Adds files to the archive (to end of archive) if they are new or have been modified
-x	Extracts files from the archive

Table 48-2   More tar Options

Option	Result
-b	Next argument is the number of blocks per group.
-B	Forces input and output blocking to 20 blocks per group.
-C	`chdir` to the next argument (if it is a directory).
-f	Next argument is the name of the archive.
-h	`tar` follows symbolic links.
-H	`tar` follows symbolic links only as though they were normal files or directories.
-l	Prints error message if `tar` can't resolve the links to the specified files.
-m	Does not restore modification time; uses time of extraction instead.
-o	Does not write directory mode and owner information to archive.
-p	Restores files to their original modes.
-s	Strips leading slashes from path names.
-v	Verbose.
-w	Waits for user confirmation before acting.
-0,...9	Selects an alternative drive where the tape is mounted.

The `tar` command is invoked as follows:

```
tar [-options] [file...]
```

The files named in the command line are written to or read from the archive. If any of the names are directories, all the files within also are archived. If further directories are found, the process continues recursively. The function performed by `tar` is determined by the presence of one of the options described in Table 48-3.

Table 48-3   tar Command-Line Functions

Option	Meaning
-c	Causes a new archive to be created from the named files.
-r	Adds files to the end of an archive, which means that more than one copy of a file can exist in the same archive. When extracting occurs, the last version of a file in the archive replaces all others.
-t	Produces a listing of the names of the specified files each time they occur in the archive. If no files are given, `tar -t` lists all files in the archive.
-u	Adds files to the tape if they are not already there or if a more recent version exists.
-x	Causes the specified files to be extracted from the archive. If no file is specified, the entire archive is extracted. If a directory is specified whose contents are in the archive, the directory is recursively extracted. If possible, owner time and access permissions are restored.

Table 48-4 lists the options that modify the behavior of `tar`.

Table 48-4   Options that Modify tar Behavior

Option	Meaning
-C	Causes a `chdir` to the directory name following -C. This option is useful if you want to archive multiple directories that don't have closely related pathnames.
-v	Causes `tar` to tell you what it is going to do and to which file. With the -t option, -v provides more information about the files in the archive.
-w	Makes `tar` query the user about each action that it is about to take. Entering a word that begins with *y* causes `tar` to perform the action; any other entry causes `tar` not to perform the action.
-f	Changes the archive name from the default (/dev/rmt?). The name that follows -f becomes the name of the archive. If a hyphen (-) follows -f, the archive is written to or read from standard output. This allows `tar` to be used as the beginning or end of a line of filters.

The System V and GNU versions of `tar` have some additional options that may interest you, should those options be available to you. The following paragraphs describe only some of the extra options that may be of general interest. Table 48-5 shows some additional options in System V `tar`.

Table 48-5	Additional System V tar Options
Option	**Meaning**
-k	Followed by a number that is the size, in kilobytes, of each volume of a multiple-volume archive. This option is useful for large nontape archives on disks or other media that have limited space.
-F	Followed by the name of a list of files. This list gives the files that are to be included in the archive.
-K	Followed by the name of a list of files. This list gives the files that are to be excluded from the archive.
-A	Causes pathnames to be interpreted as being relative to the current directory, rather than absolute.

Table 48-6 shows some additional options in GNU `tar`.

Table 48-6	Additional GNU tar Options
Option	**Meaning**
-d	Causes `tar` to `diff` the files in the archive with those in the currently existing file system.
-k	Causes `tar` to keep existing files rather than replace them with files from the archive.
-z	Causes the archive to be compressed/decompressed as it is written/extracted. The compress program is used.
-Z	Same as -z.

cpio

The `cpio` command is a different archiver. It is based on the `cp` command.

The cpio file format

The `cpio` file format is not quite as simple as the `tar` format. The format has a 76-bytes-long header, a variable-length filename, and a variable-length lump of data. The end of a `cpio` archive is indicated by a header for the file. All the entries in the header are ISO 646 strings of the digits 0–7 (octal numbers), padded with the character 0, and are not null-terminated. Listing 48-2 summarizes the header format.

Listing 48-2: Extended cpio Header Format

```
Length (bytes)   Field Name

    6            c_magic
    6            c_dev
    6            c_ino
    6            c_mode
    6            c_uid
    6            c_gid
    6            c_nlink
    6            c_rdev
   11            c_mtime
    6            c_namesize
   11            c_filesize
```

- `c_magic` contains the string "070707."

- `c_dev` and `c_ino` contain fields that uniquely identify the file in the archive.

- `c_mode`, `c_uid`, and `c_gid` give the owner and access permissions at the time when the file was archived.

- `c_nlink` gives the number of links to the file at the time when the file was archived.

- `c_rdev` contains implementation-specific information that is relevant to certain special file types.

- `c_mtime` gives the modification time of the file at the time when it was archived.

- `c_namesize` and `c_filesize` give the lengths of the filename and the data, respectively, which follow the header.

The cpio command

This section follows the command as supported by System V, Revision 4. (BSD does not have it, and the GNU version is not particularly different.) Tables 48-7 and 48-8 show `cpio` options.

Table 48-7   cpio Function Options

Option	Meaning
-i	Extracts files from the standard input
-o	Creates an archive
-p	Moves (passes) files from one directory to another

Table 48-8   Other cpio Function Options

Option	Meaning
-a	Resets access times of input files after they have been copied
-A	Appends files to an archive
-b	Reverses the order of bytes in each word; used only with the -i option
-B	Blocks I/O at 5,120 bytes to a record
-c	Reads or writes header in ASCII-character form
-C	Following argument gives the size of a record, in bytes
-d	Creates directories as needed
-e	Following argument specifies how to handle a vxfs file that has extent attribute information
-E	Specifies a file that lists files to be extracted
-f	Archives the files that do *not* match the specified patterns
-G	Following argument gives a file that specifies the interface through which cpio talks to a user
-H	Following argument specifies what format the header is to be written in
-I	Specifies an input archive
-k	Tries to skip corrupted headers and I/O errors
-K	Following argument is the medium size, in kilobytes; relevant only to the -o option
-l	Used with the -p option, links files, if possible, rather than copies them
-L	Follows symbolic links
-m	Keeps preceding file-modification time
-M	Following argument is a message to be displayed when media are switched
-O	Sends the output a file; relevant only with the -o option
-r	Used with the -i option, renames extracted files interactively
-R	Following argument is the ID of a user to whom the files are assigned
-s	Swaps bytes within each halfword
-S	Swaps halfwords within each word
-t	Used with the -i option, prints a table of contents for the input archive
-T	Truncates long filenames to 14 characters
-u	Replaces a file from the archive, whether or not it is older
-v	Verbose
-V	Semiverbose; prints a dot for each file processed
-6	Processes a UNIX System Sixth Edition archive format file

The cpio command performs three basic functions, which are described in the following sections.

cpio -i [*options*] [*pattern...*]

This function extracts files from the standard input, assuming that it is a cpio archive file. The patterns are regular expressions in the notation for filename generation used by sh(1). Only the files that match one of the patterns are extracted. If no pattern is given, all files are extracted. Important options for -i are as follows:

- -d creates needed directories.

- -E introduces an argument that names a file containing a list of files to be extracted from the archive.

- -f archives all files that do *not* match the specified pattern.

- -I introduces an argument that gives the file to be used as an input archive.

- -t prints a table of contents for an archive.

cpio -o [*options*]

This function creates an archive. The list of pathnames and files is read from standard input. The archive is written to standard output. Important options for -o are the following:

- -A appends files to an existing archive (which must be specified with the -O option).

- -L follows symbolic links.

- -O introduces an argument that gives the file to which the output is to be sent.

cpio -p [*options*] *directory*

This function takes a list of files from standard input and copies them to the directory specified in the command line. Important options for -p are the following:

- -d creates needed directories.

- -l links files, if possible, rather than copying them.

- -L follows symbolic links.

The pax command

This section follows 4.4BSD. Tables 48-9 and 48-10 summarize the options of the pax command.

Table 48-9	pax Options
Option	**Meaning**
`<none>`	Lists a table of contents for an archive
`-r`	Extracts files from an archive
`-w`	Writes an archive
`-rw`	Copies files from one directory to another

Table 48-10	Other pax Options
Option	**Meaning**
`-a`	Appends files to an archive
`-b`	Following argument gives the block size, in bytes
`-B`	Following argument gives the number of bytes to which a single archive volume is to be limited
`-c`	Matches all those files that are *not* specified
`-d`	Controls matching of directories
`-D`	Similar to `-u`
`-E`	Following argument gives the number of read faults to be allowed while an archive is being read
`-f`	Specifies the name of the archive
`-G`	Following argument gives a group name on which to choose a file
`-H`	Follows only command-line symbolic links
`-i`	Renames files interactively
`-k`	Does not overwrite existing files
`-l`	Links files, if possible
`-L`	Follows all symbolic link
`-n`	Selects the first archive member that matches
`-o`	Options specific to various archive formats
`-p`	Controls preservation of access controls, owners, and access times
`-P`	Does not follow symbolic links; option is the default
`-s`	Modifies filenames with a pattern
`-t`	Resets access times

Option	Meaning
-T	Following argument gives information to control file selection, based on modification or inode-change time
-u	Ignores older files
-U	Selects a file on the basis of the following argument (a user name)
-v	Verbose
-x	Specifies the format of the output archive
-X	Does not descend into directories that have a different device ID
-Y	Similar to the -D and -u options
-Z	Similar to the -D, -u, and -Y options

The pax command performs four basic functions, which are described in the following sections.

pax [*options*] [*pattern...*]

If neither the -r or -w option is specified (list mode), pax reads an archive file from standard input and sends a table of contents for the archive to standard output.

pax -r [*options*] [*pattern...*]

The -r option causes pax to read an archive from standard input and to extract all files that match one or more of the specified patterns. If a directory is extracted, all files therein are also extracted. If no patterns are specified, all files are extracted. The pax command determines the type of the archive automatically.

pax -w [*options*] [*file...*]

The -w option causes an archive to be written to standard output. If files are named in the command line, the archive contains them; otherwise, the archive is created from a list of files read from standard input. If an input file is a directory, all its files are archived.

pax -r -w [*options*] [*file...*] *directory*

The -r and -w options, used together, cause pax to copy files to the directory named in the command line. If no files are named in the command line, a list of files is read from standard input. If one of the files is a directory, all its files are copied.

Options for pax

Some important options for pax are these:

- -a appends files to an existing archive (-w only).

- -c operates on only those files that do *not* match the specified pattern (List mode and -r only).

- -f introduces an argument that gives the file name of the archive to be used (all modes).

- -l creates links to files, if possible, rather than copying them (Copy mode only).

- -s introduces an argument that is a substitution expression of the form used by ed(1). Expression is used to modify file or archive member names (all modes).

- -x introduces an argument that specifies the output format of the archive; the default is ustar. Possible formats include:

    cpio: extended cpio

    bcpio: old binary cpio

    sv4cpio: System V, Release 4 cpio

    sv4crc: System V, Release 4 cpio, with file crc checksums

    tar: old BSD tar format

    ustar: extended tar format

Special-Purpose Archivers

This section discusses a couple of commands that aren't really archivers, but I include them because I have found their results as archives at FTP sites. These commands are intended to convert files to a format that can be transmitted over a nonbinary channel (such as e-mail). If you aren't facing this limitation, use one of the programs discussed previously.

shar

The shar command writes an archive that is a shell script. The command format is:

```
shar [file...]
```

The shar command takes the specified files and writes a shell script to standard output. When this script is run, it recreates the files and directory structure on which it was run originally.

You should be very careful with any shar files that you pick up. These files are very easily meddled with, and they can do anything that the shell can do (such as wipe out files). Before you run an unknown shar file, look at it.

uuencode and uudecode

The uuencode and uudecode commands are intended for putting binary files in ASCII-only format and later restoring the files. The following sections describe these commands.

uuencode [*file*] *name*

The uuencode command takes the given file (or standard input, if the file is omitted), converts it to ASCII-only format, and sends the result to standard output. *name* is put into a header and is the name of the file that will be recreated.

uudecode [*file...*]

This command recreates an uuencoded file with the filename that was included in the header.

Summary

This chapter introduced the archiving tools that are available on UNIX systems. You should understand the following:

▶ What tar, cpio, and pax do

▶ How to use tar

▶ How to use cpio

▶ How to use pax

▶ How to create a shell archive

▶ How to code binaries in ASCII

In the next chapter, Mike discusses compression tools.

Chapter 49

Data-Compression Tools

In This Chapter

▶ What is data compression?

▶ How does data compression work?

▶ UNIX data-compression utilities

▶ Other data-compression utilities available for UNIX

I n this chapter, you learn about data compression and about two data-compression tools. I asked Internet veteran Michael O'Neill to provide information on the theory behind data compression.

What Is Data Compression?

Data compression is the art of encoding a data file so that it occupies less space than the unencoded version. If the original file can be recovered exactly, the compression method is called *lossless;* otherwise, it is called *lossy.* Under normal circumstances, lossless compression is the only acceptable form for storage of executable, text, or program files, so general-purpose compression programs are lossless. This chapter does not deal with lossy compression.

General-purpose compression schemes work fairly well for files that contain graphics, but for serious graphic compression, special methods (including lossy ones) are used. Because such methods normally are not part of UNIX distributions, this chapter does not deal with them. The same comments apply to compression of audio.

If you want more information about compression methods, look for the Frequently Asked Questions list for the comp.compression or comp.compression.research newsgroup. This FAQ goes into much more detail than this chapter has space for and covers many topics that the chapter doesn't touch on. The FAQ also includes a short bibliography. You also can find the FAQ at the following URLs:

```
ftp://rtfm.mit.edu/pub/usenet/news.answers/compression-faq/
http://www.cis.ohio-state.edu/hypertext/faq/usenet/compression-faq/top.html
```

The compression FAQ contains information about many existing compression programs, including the compression methods that they use and where to obtain their source and/or executables.

How Does Data Compression Work?

A completely random file cannot be compressed. Compression works by exploiting regularities in the file that is to be compressed. Text files such as tables, for example, often have long strings of repeated characters (usually blanks, underscore characters, asterisks, and the like). Such strings can be replaced by an escape code, followed by the character and the length of the string. This is known as *run-length encoding* and can be very effective when it is appropriate.

A more subtle regularity that you can exploit is the fact that the letter frequencies of text vary widely. If you replace *e* and other common letters with short codes, you gain space. You need to use longer codes to represent *z* and other uncommon letters, but their rarity compensates for the longer codes, giving you a net savings in space.

This type of compression replaces a constant-length sequence (one character) with a variable-length code. Theoretically, you could make such a code have a different code for, say, each two-character sequence. In practice, such codes are rare.

Another way to compress a file is to find common subsequences of characters and replace them with shorter codes. In English, such strings as *the, wh,* and *able* are abnormally common, so you could profitably replace them with shorter codes. In practice, you would construct a dictionary of variable-length sequences of characters that occur in the file that you are compressing and assign a fixed-length code to each entry in the dictionary. The general problem of deriving an optimum coding dictionary for a given file is intractable, so in practice, various fast heuristics produce an adequate dictionary, rather than an optimum one.

Story: The Days of Slow Output

Back in the days when the Internet was still known as Arpanet, I was working where the people I worked for weren't. That was the good news. The bad news was that I had to send my results to my bosses via the Arpanet, which in those days was fairly slow (about a minute per page, as I recall). My outputs were mostly tables and printer plots that had many repeat characters, and when someone put some sort of run-length encoding online, transmission times went down by a factor of 3 to 5.

Other types of regularities occur in other types of files. Executable files have regularities that are caused by standard call and return sequences for subroutines. Program source files have high probabilities of keywords, or variable and macro names, that are specific to a given program.

Compression can be *static* (the codes are determined once for each file and do not change while that file is compressed) or *dynamic* (the codes change to follow the changing statistical patterns of the file). In between these is *block coding*. In block coding, the input file is divided into blocks, each of which is compressed separately with a static compressor.

Variable-length codes

The most common variable-length codes are Huffman and Shannon-Fano codes, the construction of which this section discusses only briefly.

Huffman codes are created in bottom-up fashion from a table of character frequencies. Initially, the codes assigned to each character are blank. The two lowest frequency characters are assigned, as codes, the binary digits 0 and 1 (one to each). Then the characters and their frequencies are merged, and the process is repeated (with the 0 or 1 being appended to the left of any bit string that is already assigned) until a string of 0s and 1s is assigned to all characters. These bit strings are the Huffman code (see Table 49-1 for a simple example).

Note

The example in Table 49-1 has been contrived so that merging always joins adjacent groups. This situation, however, is not usually the case. You can make an adaptive Huffman code by storing the code table as a tree and updating the shape of the tree as the frequencies of the characters change.

Table 49-1 Huffman Codes

	Character	*Frequency*	*Code*
Step 1	A	.1	0
	B	.1	1
	C	.2	
	D	.3	
	E	.3	
Step 2	A |	.2	0 0
	B |		0 1
	C	.2	1

Continued

Table 49-1   *(continued)*

	Character	Frequency	Code
	D	.3	
	E	.3	
Step 3	A |		0 0
	B |	.4	0 1
	C |		1
	D	.3	0
	E	.3	1
Step 4	A |		0 0 0
	B |	.4	0 0 1
	C |		0 1
	D |	.6	1 0
	E |		1 1

Shannon-Fano codes are created in top-down fashion. Initially, the codes are blank. The set of characters is divided into two subsets in such a manner that the total frequency of each subset is as close to that of the other as possible. Each member of one set is assigned the code bit 1; each member of the other is assigned 0. The process is repeated on the two subsets recursively, appending bit strings as for the Huffman construction (but to the right), stopping when a subset has only one member. See Table 49-2 for a simple example based on the same frequencies as the preceding one.

For clarity, the example shown in Table 49-2 has the order of the characters C and D changed so that the members of each subset are adjacent — which will not be the case in general.

Table 49-2   Shannon-Fano Codes

	Character	Frequency	Code
Step 1	A	.1 |	0
	B	.1 | .5	0
	D	.3 |	0
	C	.2 | .5	1
	E	.3 |	1

	Character	Frequency	Code
Steps 2, 3	A	.1 | .2	0 0
	B	.1 |	0 0
	D	.3	0 1
	C	.2	1 0
	E	.3	1 1
Step 4	A	.1	0 0 0
	B	.1	0 0 1
	D	.3	0 1
	C	.2	1 0
	E	.3	1 1

Fixed-length codes

The most common type of fixed-length codes are the assorted variations on Lempel-Ziv (L-Z) coding.

L-Z encoding, which is a bit of magic, was conceived as a theoretical result: If you let the coder run forever, it would achieve optimal compression. Eventually, a few people tried L-Z encoding and found out that it worked quite well in practice — so well that it now appears to be the method of choice for general-purpose data compression.

The trick that makes L-Z compression work is a fast, effective brute-force scheme for building the dictionary on the fly. As you scan the input file, you find the longest initial string (of the unencoded part of the file) that is already in the dictionary. Then you output the code of that string and add to the dictionary the found string and the next character from the input (which character you also output). The decoder builds its own copy of the dictionary, which it can do because the compressed file includes the characters that were added to the dictionary. Fine points such as what you do when the dictionary fills up are too involved to go into in this chapter, but the basic Lempel-Ziv coder is that simple.

Listing 49-1 shows a simple example of how L-Z coding works. The listing shows how the dictionary comes into being, but a short example can't really show how L-Z compresses so well.

Listing 49-1: A Simple Lempel-Ziv Encoding

```
Input string: abracadabra

Input string as parsed: a|b|r|ac|ad|ab|ra
```

```
Constructed dictionary:

1    a
2    b
3    r
4    ac
5    ad
6    ab
7    ra
```

```
Output string (numbers refer to dictionary entries):
abr1c1d1b3a
```

The Lempel-Ziv coding algorithm is intrinsically adaptive; no static version exists. So many variations on Lempel-Ziv coding exist that every compressor seems to use a different version. L-Z also is deeply embroiled in the highly contentious world of software and algorithm patents. The compression FAQ includes a summary of the assorted L-Z variations, as well as a list of patents for L-Z and other compression methods.

Combined methods

If you compress an already-compressed file with the same method, you won't get further compression; in fact, you are likely to get a slightly longer file. After you squeeze out whatever type of redundancy or bias a compressor removes, nothing else is left to be squeezed out. If you use two different methods, however, you can improve performance over either separately. The preferred combination is an adaptive fixed-length code followed by a static or block variable-length one. You may not have to do this yourself. As you see below, some of the currently existing programs are composite methods.

UNIX Data-Compression Utilities

Three "official" UNIX compressors exist: pack, compact, and compress. Berkeley UNIX (as of 4.4BSD) has compact and compress. System V Release 4 has pack and compress, so if you are concerned about easy compatibility, you should use compress. Your UNIX system may have compressors other than the official ones for its distribution because someone may have installed one of the public-domain or freely available versions of various UNIX commands at your site.

POSIX appears to have nothing to say about compressors or compressed file formats, so no really official UNIX compressor exists. Perhaps this situation is for the better, given the propensity of POSIX to include at least one of everything.

Note

Unlike the various archiver/compressor programs for IBM-compatibles, UNIX compressor/decompressors *replace* their inputs, so if you want a copy of the original, you have to make one explicitly. You can use the commands pcat, ccat, and zcat to view or copy a compressed file without changing it. Also, UNIX compressors are *not* archivers as are the MS-DOS programs PKZIP, ARC, ARJ, ZOO, and so on. These programs do not compress several files into one file; if you want to do so, you have to archive the files first (refer to Chapter 48).

The general form of compression commands

Each flavor of UNIX compressor generally has three forms:

- A *compressor,* which replaces uncompressed files with compressed ones and adds an extension to the filename.

- A *decompressor,* which reverses the compression process.

- A *viewer,* which decompresses a file without replacement and sends the result to standard output. The viewer allows you to view or copy the uncompressed file or pipe it to another program.

Generally, if the compressor is called X, the decompressor is called unX. The viewer is called Ycat (Y is derived irregularly from either the name of the compressor or the extension that the compressor adds to the filename).

A general comment on filenames

All the compressors that this chapter deals with replace the decompressed file with a compressed file whose name has an extension that indicates the file's compression status and the compression method used. In systems that limit the length of filenames, this may cause the filenames to be truncated or modified in various ways. If you don't work with such a system and don't import/export files to/from such a system, you don't need to worry. If you *do* need to worry, check the man pages for the compressors that you use for the exact details of filename mutation.

pack

The pack command is an old compressor that uses static Huffman coding, so its compression usually is nothing to write home about. You call pack as follows:

```
pack [options] file [file...]
```

Each file listed in the command line is replaced by a compressed version of the original, with .z appended to the filename.

The pack command has two options:

- − sends information about the encoding to standard output. You can use this option multiple times to toggle reporting on and off between files.

- -f forces compression of a file even if no space will be saved. Normally, the file would be left unchanged (but still renamed file.z).

The packed files are uncompressed with unpack, which is called as follows:

```
unpack file [file...]
```

The filenames must have the form file.z and can be specified in the command line as either file or file.z. The files are replaced by their unpacked forms, and the .z is stripped off the filename.

You can view or copy packed files in decompressed form with pcat, which has the following format:

```
pcat file [file...]
```

This decompresses the files and sends them, one by one, to standard output without altering the compressed forms of the files.

compact

The compact command uses adaptive Huffman coding and usually produces better compression than pack. The format of compact is

```
compact [-v] [file...]
```

The files are replaced by their compressed versions and renamed with a .C extension. If -v is specified, the compression percentage for each file is reported.

```
uncompact [-v] [file...]
```

This command decompacts the specified compacted files and replaces them with their decompressed versions, stripping the .C extension from the filenames. The -v flag causes uncompact to print the name of each file as it is decompressed.

If no filename is supplied with compact/uncompact, the standard input is compressed/decompressed to the standard output.

You can view or copy compacted files in decompressed form with ccat, which has the following format:

```
ccat [-v] [file...]
```

This decompresses the files and sends them, one by one, to standard output without altering the compressed forms of the files. If -v is specified, ccat prints the name of each file as it is decompressed.

compress

The `compress` command uses adaptive Lempel-Ziv compression. The format of the `compress` command is

```
compress [-cfv] [-b maxbits] [file...]
```

The files listed in the command line are replaced by compressed files that have the same names but with the `.Z` extension. If no filenames are given in the command line, input is read from standard input.

The options are

- `-b` — maxbits, which controls the size of the dictionary that `compress` uses, must be between 9 and 16. The larger maxbits is, the larger the dictionary compress can build, the greater the compression that can be attained, and the longer it takes. The default value is 16.

- `-c` writes output to the standard output without modifying any files.

- `-f` compresses files whether or not they are actually reduced in size.

- `-v` provides output information about the degree of compression for each file.

decompress

The format of the `decompress` command is

```
decompress [-cfv] [files...]
```

The files listed in the command line are replaced by decompressed files that have the same names, without the `.Z` extension. The options `-c`, `-f`, and `-v` have the same meaning as they do for `compress`.

You can view or copy compressed files in decompressed form with `zcat`, which has the following format:

```
zcat [file...]
```

This decompresses the files and sends them, one by one, to standard output without altering the compressed forms of the files. This is an alias for `uncompress -c`.

Note

If you use `compress` (or another adaptive compressor) to compress several files, the algorithm restarts with each separate file — that is, the dictionary is thrown away at the end of each file. If you want the most bang for your adaptive buck, collect the files in an archive (see Chapter 48) before you compress. That way, the adaptation spans the entire archive — theoretically. A couple of rough tests that I ran, however (using `gzip` and `tar` on a few files), indicate that the gain is small, so this method may be useful only if you are really strapped for space and need every byte.

Caution

Compressing an archive involves a safety drawback. If the compressed file is damaged, all files past the error are likely to be unrecoverable.

Other Data-Compression Utilities for UNIX

The main "unofficial" UNIX data-compression programs are gzip and its associates, gunzip and zcat. This section also briefly describes the UNIX ports or equivalents of various compression/archiver programs that are mostly used on non-UNIX systems.

gzip

The gzip program is a compression program that uses Lempel-Ziv (and, apparently, block static Huffman) compression. A rough test that I performed indicates that gzip substantially outperforms compress. The gzip program is intended to replace other UNIX decompressors, so it also decompresses files made by zip (see below), compress, compress -H (a SCO UNIX command that doesn't use the same method as the standard compress), and pack. The gzip program automatically detects the type of the compressed file and applies whatever error checking is supported by the relevant compressed format. The gzip program can decompress a zip-compressed file only if it contains a single compressed file. The gzip is a victim of creeping feature-itis. Table 49-3 describes the most important options.

Table 49-3   gzip Options

Option	Meaning
-a (ascii)	Not relevant to UNIX systems.
-c (stdout-to-stdout)	Writes output on standard output.
-d (decompress, uncompress)	Decompresses.
-f (force)	Forces compression or decompression.
-h (help)	Displays a help screen.
-l (list)	Lists various compression statistics for each file.
-L (license)	Displays the gzip license.
-n (no name)	Does not save or restore the original filename and time stamp. This option is the default for decompressing.
-N (name)	Always saves or restores the original filename and time stamp.
-q (quiet)	Suppresses all warnings.

Option	Meaning
-r (recursive)	Travels the directory structure recursively.
-S .suf (suffix .suf)	Uses the suffix .suf instead of .gz.
-t (test)	Checks the compressed file's integrity.
-v (verbose)	Verbose mode.
-V (version)	Displays the version number and compilation options.
-# (fast, best)	Controls the speed-versus-compression tradeoff.

The gzip program is accompanied by a few commands that allow you to treat a compressed file as though it were decompressed for purposes of comparing, viewing, or searching files. The gzip program is copyrighted but freely distributable under the GNU public license. Check the compression FAQ for sites where you can find the source code. The gzip command is used as follows:

```
gzip [-acdfhlLnNrtvV19] [-S suffix] [file...]
```

The main options are as follows:

- -c (stdout-to-stdout) — original files are not changed; the option sends to standard output a sequence of independently compressed versions of the files listed in the command line.

- -d (decompress, uncompress) decompresses.

- -l (list) causes various compression statistics to be listed. If the verbose option is on, more information (compression method, CRC, and time stamp) is listed.

- -r (recursive) — if any of the files in the command line are directories, gzip also compresses or decompresses the files in those directories.

- -v (verbose) displays the name and percentage of reduction for each file that is compressed or decompressed.

- -# (fast, best) — where # is a digit from 1 to 9, 1 provides the fastest compression and 9 provides the most compression. The default is 6.

gunzip

The gunzip command appears to be equivalent to gzip -d. The format of gunzip is

```
gunzip [-acfhlLnNrtvV] [-S suffix] [file...]
```

The options have the same meaning as they do for gzip.

zcat

The zcat command is identical to gunzip -c. Like the other xcat commands, zcat is used to view or copy uncompressed versions of files without altering the compressed versions. The format of zcat is

zcat [-fhLV] [*file...*]

Watch out for *zcat* being the uncompress equivalent and *zcat* called *gzcat*.

The options have the same meaning as they do for gzip.

Specialized commands related to gzip

The following sections discuss some specialized commands that are related to gzip.

gzexe [-d] [*file...*]

The gzexe command produces a shell script that acts like a compressed executable file—that is, it takes up less space but acts just as the original file would. Unlike most other UNIX compressors, gzexe does *not* replace the input file; instead, it renames the input file in the format *file~* (notice the tilde) and calls the compressed executable *file*. This is so that you can test the compressed file before wiping out the original yourself. The option -d decompresses the executable files.

znew [-ftv9PK] [*file.Z...*]

The znew command converts files that are in compress (.Z) format to gzip format, changing the file extensions appropriately. The options are as follows:

■ -f forces conversion from compress to gzip format, even if a .gz file already exists.

■ -t forces a test of the new files before the old ones are deleted.

■ -v causes output of statistics on the compression.

■ -9 uses the optimal (but slowest) compression method.

■ -P uses pipes for conversion so that less disk space is needed.

■ -K keeps the original .Z file if it is smaller than the gzip converted version.

zforce [*file...*]

The zforce command forces all gzip files to have the extension .gz, so that gzip does not try to decompress them. This is mostly for filenames that have been shortened because of file transfers. If necessary, the filename is shortened to make room for the .gz extension.

zcmp [*options*] *file1* [*file2*]
zdiff [*options*] *file1* [*file2*]

The zcmp and zdiff commands invoke the cmp or diff commands on (gzip-compatible) compressed files. The options are passed unchanged to the cmp or diff routines. If only one filename is given, the comparison is made between file1 and a decompressed version of file1.gz. If two filenames are given, they are decompressed as necessary and then handed to cmp or diff.

zgrep [*options*] [-e *pattern*] [*file...*]

The zgrep command calls grep, with the given options, on decompressed versions of the input files. If no file is given, standard input is decompressed and handed to grep. The zegrep and zfgrep commands are the same, but they call egrep and fgrep, respectively.

zmore [*file...*]

The zmore command is for viewing compressed or decompressed text files one screen at a time on a terminal. The command uses the UNIX command more, but zmore takes no options and has a somewhat different set of commands that control screen size, scrolling, and searching each time the display pauses. See Listing 49-2 for a short rundown of the zmore commands.

Listing 49-2: zmore Scrolling Commands

```
[i]      is an optional integer argument

[i] <space> Show i more lines or one screen if i is missing.

[i] ^D   Show 11 more lines (a scroll) if i is not given,
 or    otherwise set the scroll size to i.
[i] d

[i] z    If i is not given, this is the same as typing a space.
      If i is given, the window size is set to i.

[i] s    Skip i lines and display a screen.

[i] f    Skip i screens and display a screen.

q or Q   Quit displaying the current file and go on to the next
      if there is one.

e or q   When the prompt "—More—(Next file: filename)" is
      displayed this makes zmore exit.

s        When the prompt "—More—(Next file: filename)" is
      displayed this makes zmore skip the next file.

=        Print the current line number.
```

```
[i]/expr  Search for the i-th occurrence of the regular
          expression expr.

[i] n     Search for the i-th occurrence of the last regular
          expression searched for.

!command  Invoke a shell with command.

:q or :Q  Same as q or Q.

.         Repeat the previous command.
```

Ports and equivalents of various non-UNIX compressor/archivers

The world of PCs has a wide variety of compressors. The compression FAQ lists about a dozen programs that are primarily intended for MS-DOS and assorted other programs for other types of PCs. Many of these programs have been ported to UNIX or have had equivalents written for UNIX. The FAQ includes an extensive list of UNIX versions of compressors for PCs, Macintoshes, Amigas, and other machines and operating systems, as well as the FTP and Web sites at which you can obtain them (source and/or executable files). If you need one, see the FAQ for up-to-date information.

This chapter does not provide details on all of these compressors because their purpose is strictly to convert files from non-UNIX to UNIX formats and vice versa. If you don't have to perform this type of conversion, these compressors are not of interest to you, and if you do have to perform the conversion, you need more details than this chapter can provide. The following section summarizes zip — an equivalent for PKZIP, which probably is the most commonly used compressor in the MS-DOS world. It has been my experience that ZIP is the most common non-UNIX compressed-file format for files at ftp sites.

zip and unzip

The zip and unzip commands are designed to be compatible with PKware's PKZIP and PKUNZIP archiver/compressor programs for MS-DOS. This is a somewhat loose notion of compatibility, however, because version 1.x of PKZIP uses a different method (L-Z, with static Shannon-Fano coding of the entire file) from versions 2.x (L-Z with block Huffman coding of the file). The former method requires zip 1.x to decode; the latter method requires zip 2.x.

Furthermore, the command-line options do not necessarily have the same meaning. To make matters even more involved, the default behavior of each program is not the same. In particular, PKUNZIP decompresses all files into the current directory by default, whereas `unzip` reconstructs the original directory structure from the current directory down.

If you really have to use `unzip` on a PKZIP file, you should look at the detailed documentation for `zip`.

Summary

This chapter examined compression algorithms and programs. You should understand the following:

▶ The different compression techniques

▶ The relative advantages and disadvantages of each technique

▶ The basic UNIX commands

▶ Other commands for UNIX

The next chapter examines network administration.

Chapter 50

Network Services (or "Cable, Schmable, I've Got the Internet!")

In This Chapter

▶ TCP/IP

▶ IP net services

▶ The flow of network services

▶ An implementation of a network service

▶ FTP and TFTP

▶ BOOTP and RARP

Taken alone, a computer network is nothing more than dead air. As with so many other commodities, one must provide a value-added service to one's users. In the UNIX world, people usually add value through the mechanism of network services. This chapter looks at the most common network services. The chapter also discusses significant configuration and security concerns for both internal and external services.

Because the Internet Protocol (IP) is the lingua franca of the Internet's architecture, the chapter concentrates its emphasis on IP. The chapter also concentrates on a few services that are common to most UNIX variants. Discussions of Sun's RPC or Hewlett-Packard's `netdist` service are better left to texts that are more attuned to those particular flavors of UNIX.

Caution

If you are running NIS, be aware that its service configurations do *not* use the same files as a non-NIS system. Consult your NIS documentation to identify the files that are appropriate to this discussion.

Before installing or reconfiguring your network services, take a step back and consider exactly what you want to offer. As both the Internet and internal networks continue to grow, traffic levels and their accompanying congestion are sure to become issues of great import. Careful planning — and discernment of services that are necessary, not merely nifty or neat — enables you to delay or minimize the impact of network services on your clients.

Your Undivided Attention, Please . . .

Many people seem to think that *TCP/IP* is a single word, but it is not. *TCP* and *IP* represent separate layers in the chain of protocols and services that underlie today's networking.

In discussing network connections, you must consider whether the transmissions must be checked or controlled in some fashion. If the need for such control exists, the Transmission Control Protocol (TCP) is the protocol of choice. TCP enables such services as Telnet and FTP to establish a (relatively) static long-term connection. Other services, such as finger and time, merely toss their data to the network in response to a query; they don't really care whether the data is actually received. Services of that variety often use the User Datagram Protocol (UDP), which provides less robust error-checking than TCP. Both of these protocols travel on top of the Internet Protocol (IP); therefore, you may see references to both TCP/IP and UDP/IP. Keep in mind that the two protocols differ significantly in their reliability.

The protocols that your UNIX system supports usually are listed in the file /etc/protocols; the number by which the protocols are identified are those used in the actual TCP or UDP packets.

Any Port in a (Broadcast) Storm

IP network services are predicated on the ideas of *ports* and *listeners*. As you know, IP addresses are allocated on a per-system basis. How, then, do you distinguish among individual users and/or facilities of that system? IP answers that need with the notion of ports (you may also see them called *sockets*). Each end of an IP connection consists of a two-part label: the IP address of the system in question and the IP port of the particular connection in question. The client's, or end user's, port is usually assigned from an available pool of ports. On most UNIX systems, port numbers below 1,024 cannot be assigned to users in this fashion. The service itself is assigned a particular port for standardization purposes. These standard ports are identified on each UNIX system through the /etc/services file. What follows is a representative extract from one such file:

```
ftp-data    20/tcp
ftp         21/tcp
telnet      23/tcp
smtp        25/tcp
whois       43/tcp
tftp        69/udp
finger      79/tcp
```

Note

The master list of Internet standard port assignments is RFC 1700, "Assigned Numbers." This document is available via anonymous FTP from ftp.internic.net.

It seems, then, that port 23 is addressed by Telnet clients, port 79 is sought out by finger clients, and the FTP service actually uses two ports: one for interaction and one for data transfer. (The alert reader will also notice that the excerpt included a UDP/IP service, TFTP. More information on that service appears later in this chapter.) You can infer that client programs automatically direct requests to the proper port on the remote machine. How does the remote machine direct incoming requests?

The Cop on the Beat

The vast majority of UNIX systems conduct their IP services through a daemon process, usually named inetd or something similar. This daemon handles all incoming service requests, directing them to the appropriate server software through a configuration file, usually named inetd.conf. Following are a few entries from a typical inetd.conf file:

```
ftp     stream tcp   nowait root    /usr/local/etc/ftpd  ftpd -l
  -i -o
telnet  stream tcp   nowait root    /usr/etc/in.telnetd in.telnetd
name    dgram  udp   wait   root    /usr/etc/in.tnamed   in.tnamed
shell   stream tcp   nowait root    /usr/etc/in.rshd     in.rshd
login   stream tcp   nowait root    /usr/etc/in.rlogind  in.rlogind
finger  stream tcp   nowait nobody /usr/etc/in.fingerd  in.fingerd
bootps  dgram  udp   wait   root    /usr/etc/bootpd      bootpd
```

The first few entries in this file provide the basic description of the service, from the network's point of view. The first entry in this configuration file names the service. This entry must match an entry in /etc/services. The second field defines the type of socket used by this service. As you might imagine, connection-oriented services (usually, TCP) require a stream of packets. Services that send out bursts of information, such as the name service, use datagram sockets. You may also see an occasional service that uses a raw socket, which is often the case with networked printing applications.

The third field defines the protocol to be used, as listed in /etc/protocols. Although this protocol is usually either TCP or UDP, other combinations occasionally show up here.

The next few entries determine the system housekeeping needs of the service in question. The wait status field determines whether the inetd process can delegate the connection to a new invocation of the program in question, or whether it will handle the requests one at a time. A status of nowait means that the connection can be passed off to a separate invocation of the server; sendmail is a good example of this – three sendmail connections to a system with "nowait" will trigger three separate copies of sendmail running simultaneously, with the original invocation still listening for additional connections. A status of wait, on the other hand, indicates that the listening program must continue listening to the incoming port itself; it cannot spawn a copy of itself to handle the connection. The fifth field specifies the user ID under which the server program is to be executed. Security concerns play a significant role in the configuration of this particular field. Many versions of `fingerd` (the finger server) are plagued with security holes. You'll notice that the `inetd.conf` quoted earlier in this section runs `fingerd` as user `nobody`, instead of `root`.

Tip

If you don't already have a user `nobody` on your system, consider adding it. Any number of activities on any UNIX system do not require execution as `root`, and running them as `nobody` can enhance your system security.

The last two entries in `inetd.conf` determine what program will answer requests for a given service and what option (if any) should be passed to that program upon execution. The sixth field contains the full pathname of the server program. The seventh field (and, perhaps, additional fields) contains the actual command line to be used.

So What's the Big Picture?

The flow of network services follows a path something like this:

- Client user invokes program (for example, a user on `fing.com` executes `telnet foo.bar.com`).

- Client's system assigns socket from available pool ("Hey, telnet foo.bar.com, you're on socket 18342!") and sends the initial packet(s) to `foo.bar.com` ("Hey, `foo.bar.com`! Here's a request for port 23! I'm waiting on socket 18342 over here!").

- Serving system's `inetd` receives packets, checks `/etc/inetd.conf`, and spawns the appropriate piece of software. ("What's port 23? Hey, that's a telnet request. . .OK, I can do TCP. . .do I have to keep listening on port 23? No, I can pass this off. . .run `in.telnetd` as root. . .hey, `in.telnetd`! Go handle this request from socket 18342 on `fing.com`!")

- Serving software picks up connection and goes on its way ("Hey, `fing.com` socket 18342! I guess you want to log in, huh?").

- Serving system's `inetd` picks up the next request and repeats the process.

A Representative Example

This section looks at the implementation of a network service, using the example of a POP3 e-mail client. For those of you who are unfamiliar with POP (Post Office Protocol), it allows remote users to review their e-mail on their home systems. Various client software packages are available, in both commercial and freeware varieties. Those of you who are interested in implementing a POP server can retrieve the source code for popper from the FTP archive at ftp.cs.berkeley.edu.

Assuming that the server program builds cleanly, you need to modify several configuration files to get things up and running. The first of these files is /etc/services. POP3 wants to use a TCP connection and listen on port 110, so your /etc/services entry will look something like this:

```
pop3        110/tcp      # Post Office Protocol - Version 3
```

Note

Most UNIX variants allow comments in configuration files, but be sure that your particular flavor provides this functionality before you add comments to your configuration files.

Now that the /etc/services entry is installed, you can move to /etc/inetd.conf, where the actual program execution and control will take place. Remember the questions for which you must provide answers in inetd.conf:

■ What service does this program provide?

■ Is it a stream (long-term) connection or datagram (burst mode) connection?

■ What protocol is used?

■ Must I continue listening on the service's port, or can we spin this off and return to our waiting?

■ Under what user ID should this program be run?

■ Where is this program?

■ What command line should be used to run this program?

In plain English, you would say, "POP3 uses a stream connection over TCP; we don't have to wait around because popper will take over the connection; run /usr/local/etc/popper with the command line popper -s." In /etc/inetd.conf, that information looks like this:

```
pop3  stream tcp   nowait root   /usr/local/etc/popper   popper -s
```

That's all there is to it — assuming that /usr/local/etc/popper has the proper file permissions assigned. Now you're ready to get things started.

Caution

The procedure in the following paragraph varies among flavors of UNIX. Read your documentation carefully, and ensure that you are following the proper steps.

Many, if not most, varieties of UNIX allow the network services process (inetd) to be restarted on the fly. In most such cases, the administrator must send a hangup signal (SIGHUP) to the process. Sending this signal is easy to do with the kill(1) command, after you obtain the process ID (PID) of the inetd process. Following is a typical example:

```
# ps aux | grep inetd
...
190  S ??  0:03 inetd
...
# kill -HUP 190
#
```

If everything has gone well, your new POP3 server should be functional. If you don't have a client yet, how might you check this functionality? You can use Telnet to connect to any TCP/IP port on a given system. Because you know that popper should be listening to port 110, you can simply connect to that port via Telnet, as follows:

```
# telnet localhost 110
+OK UCB POP server (version 1.831beta) at localhost starting.
quit
+OK POP server at localhost signing off.
Connection closed.
#
```

It seems that you have been successful. You need to find a client and actually go through a bit of e-mail, but your initial installation was successful.

Files, Files, Getcher Files Here!

The File Transfer Protocol (FTP) is undoubtedly one of the most popular services offered on the Internet. Anyone who can recall the days of using Sneakernet or shipping disks or tapes via parcel post considers FTP to be something of a salvation. Most UNIX systems are shipped with FTP server software. Most of these default installations, however, are limited to users who have actual logins on the system in question. For those who want to make data available to the online world in general, anonymous FTP service is a necessity.

Caution

You can easily — if inadvertently — advertise important information about your system or its users when you configure anonymous FTP. Be very cautious: Configure only the minimum functionality necessary.

The first step is creating an FTP user ID. You should create this user ID like any other, except in one regard: disable login access for this account. You usually accomplish this task by entering a bogus password in /etc/passwd. I usually use something like "*LK*" because no UNIX password encryption can match that pattern. You should also specify a false login shell for FTP. I use /bin/false. Be sure to specify a home directory for the FTP user ID; I usually make it something simple, such as /usr06/ftp.

Most anonymous FTP servers execute a chroot on this directory, providing some additional security. The use of chroot, however, means that you'll have to do some special things to prepare the hierarchy.

Moving to /usr06/ftp, it's time to set up the necessary directory hierarchy. In most instances, you need the following:

- A /bin directory, holding (usually) only a copy of ls; you can usually give this copy of ls protections of 111.

- An /etc directory, which needs to hold only a (chopped) copy of /etc/passwd and /etc/group (more on this in a moment); give these copies of passwd and group protections of 444.

- A /pub directory, into which you can place files for anonymous retrieval. Many sites give these files permissions of 777, but you may choose a more restrictive approach.

You can create additional directories, but these directories are more than adequate to meet the needs of most sites.

Some varieties of UNIX may require you to create a ~ftp/dev directory or to copy additional files into ~ftp/bin or ~ftp/etc. Read your documentation carefully. The instructions in this section are quite generic.

Notice that I specified that chopped copies of /etc/passwd and /etc/group be installed in the FTP /etc directory. These copies should contain only those user IDs and groups that are necessary to provide a proper listing of the publicly accessible files; no other information should be present. Many sites, having simply copied /etc/passwd in its entirety, were dismayed to find that anonymous users had copied — and decrypted — the passwords of their users. Passwords are not necessary in these copies of the passwd and group files. Be sure to replace any true encrypted password with garbage characters.

Having done all these things, your final step is to secure the directories themselves with the appropriate permissions. Although the permissions may vary with your particular flavor of UNIX, most sites seem to use the following sets of file permissions:

```
~ftp/bin    111
~ftp/etc    111
~ftp/pub    755
```

Again, your level of file permissions depends on your need for security.

You may, if you want, open the FTP archive to direct your users' access through the use of symbolic links. You might create a directory ~ftp/users, with subdirectories for each user who has requested FTP server access. You then can move into the user's home directory and provide a link to the FTP directory tree, using something like the following:

```
# cd ~wmichal
# ln -s /usr06/ftp/users/wmichal personal_ftp
```

The user wmichal now has a subdirectory, $HOME/personal_ftp, which is linked to /usr06/ftp/users/wmichal. The user can move files in and out of

Part XI: System Administration

the FTP archive through this subdirectory, without any need for your involvement.

Caution

You may want to consider this option carefully; if you have any question about the material that users are placing in the FTP archive, you may need to assert more direct control.

At this point, you should be able to move to a remote machine and connect to your system's FTP service, logging in as anonymous.

Hey, There, Little Brother . . .

FTP actually has a baby brother of sorts. Many devices, when they are booted, need to download a configuration file into memory. This situation is where the Trivial File Transfer Protocol (TFTP) comes into play.

Caution

TFTP is inherently insecure—it is not a connection-oriented protocol, and it is easily confused and/or spoofed. I strongly recommend that you use TFTP only when absolutely necessary.

Most versions of TFTP work in a fairly straightforward manner:

- A TFTP user ID must exist in /etc/passwd.
- TFTP must have a home directory (usually, /tftpboot).
- Files that are to be retrieved are kept in /tftpboot.
- Usually, some other service must point the remote device to TFTP.

Use of TFTP is extremely common with networked peripheral devices, such as terminal servers and print servers. In some cases, actual workstations or systems are booted via TFTP.

As mentioned earlier in this section, TFTP is inherently insecure. A wise admin will not dedicate any mission-critical tasks to TFTP unless absolutely necessary.

Who Am I? Where Am I?

You already know that every system (or device) on a TCP/IP network must have a unique IP address. Given a far-flung physical network, managing the database of IP address assignments can be a real headache. Luckily, several protocols have been developed to assist you in this endeavor. The two most popular of these services are Boot Protocol (BOOTP) and Reverse Address Resolution Protocol (RARP).

In recent years, BOOTP has gained some preeminence over RARP, for one simple reason: network traffic. For whatever reason, many RARP servers answer every query that is sent to them, whether they have an answer or not. By contrast, most implementations of BOOTP respond to a request only if they have an answer to deliver. Because little need exists for these "sorry, I can't help you" messages, most vendors are supporting BOOTP. For that reason, this section is dedicated to coverage of that protocol.

The BOOTP service program is usually named bootpd, and most versions of UNIX allow you to run it on demand, via /etc/inetd.conf, or to leave it running as a background daemon. The choice is yours.

Note

Many TCP/IP network services can be run as stand-alone daemons (notably, SMTP e-mail servers, such as sendmail), which is all well and good, but the task of management remains for you. I suggest that you create dummy entries in the /etc/inetd.conf file for any services provided by stand-alone daemons. Remember to comment out these lines, and your /etc/inetd.conf will provide a nice map of your network services.

As you might imagine, BOOTP needs a configuration file; in most versions of UNIX, that file is named bootptab. You must place an entry in the BOOTP file for each machine that is to be provided an IP address. Mapping out BOOTP entries is rather simple. Relatively few configuration options are available at this level of networking, and most versions of BOOTP provide shortcuts that can reduce the size of your bootptab file (and the time required to maintain it as well).

A typical bootptab entry consists of a colon-separated list of configuration tags. Some tags require a value; others are Boolean in nature. Each bootptab entry begins with the host name of the device to be served, as follows:

mypc.wooga.com:

The tags follow, separated by colons. You can spread an entry over multiple lines by using a backward slash (\) before the end-of-line newline character. Following are some of the most common BOOTP tags.

Tag	Meaning
ds=<IP-address>	Tells the client the address of its domain name server
gw=<IP-address>	Provides the IP address of the gateway of the client's subnet (if any)
ha=<hex address>	Contains the hexadecimal hardware address of the client (must be unique)
ip=<IP-address>	Contains the IP address of the client
sm=<hexadecimal mask>	Contains the subnet mask to be used by the client
hn	Contains a Boolean flag, indicating that the client should be told its host name
tc=<template host>	Identifies the host (listed in /etc/bootptab), the configuration of which should be copied to the client

The tc tag can be very helpful. Suppose that you have several devices that will share the same gateway, DNS, and subnet mask; further suppose that you want each client to be informed of its hostname. You can create a template host in /etc/bootptab, as follows:

```
global.defaults:\
:ds=122.122.42.2:\
:gw=122.122.42.1:\
:sm=255.255.255.0:\
:hn:
```

Having constructed this template host, you can call on it from the bootptab entries for each device, as follows:

```
device1:\
  :tc=global.defaults:\
  :hw=08009ABE8347:\
  :ip=122.122.42.198:
device2:\
  :tc=global.defaults:\
  :hw=08007F347522:\
  :ip=122.122.42.199:
```

As you can see, the use of a template host can save you quite a bit of typing (and save you from the inevitable typographical errors).

Most versions of BOOTP also support a tie-in to TFTP: the Trivial File Transfer Protocol described previously. This tie-in requires the use of the following special tags, namely:

Tag	Meaning
bf=<filename>	The boot file that the client should download via TFTP
hd=<directory>	The directory to which the boot file referenced in bf is attached (usually, / or /tftpboot)

If you have, say, a remote CD-ROM drive with a boot file called bootme.cd, your bootptab entry for this device might look something like the following:

```
cdrom1:\
  :tc=global.defaults:\
  :hw=0fbd63465d9a:\
  :ip=122.122.42.200:\
  :bf=bootme.cd:\
  :hd=\tftpboot:
```

Caution

Many versions of BOOTP place a size limit on entries in /etc/bootptab; the most common limit is 1,024 bytes. Be careful.

You must visit /etc/inetd.conf, of course, and ensure that the TFTP daemon is configured. Although security concerns about TFTP are valid, it remains an important tool in some areas of system administration.

Other Standard Services

Most UNIX systems are shipped with a wide range of network services. In most cases, these services are innocuous. Several services, however, can present security problems. Notable among these services are the r commands, the most popular of which are rlogin, rsh, rcp, and rwho. Given the nature of these commands, you may want to disable them. Fortunately, this procedure is simple. Remember that every service must have an entry in /etc/inetd.conf. If you want to disable a service, simply remove (or comment out) its entry in /etc/inetd.conf.

You have a tremendous amount of flexibility in this regard. I have known sites that allowed rlogin/rsh/rcp only during working hours. At 5 P.M., a cron job (remember cron?) replaced /etc/inetd.conf with a version that disabled rlogin/rsh/rcp, sent a SIGHUP to the inetd process (forcing it to reset), and exited with a log entry. A companion script, executed at 7 A.M., reversed the process, enabling r commands for the working day. You may not need this sort of security, but it's certainly nice to know that it is available.

Other Popular Services

A plethora of network services software is available on the Internet, ranging from simple SNMP monitors to World Wide Web and Gopher servers. Before you install these products, read the documentation carefully, noting what ports are being used and what sort of connections are being made. You may even want to install services such as these on a little-used machine during the development and installation cycles, just to prevent any problems on your more dedicated systems.

The installation of services of this type is beyond the scope of this text. The most popular services are well documented, and you can call on a large body of fellow administrators for help.

Keeping an Eye on It All

Now that all these network services are humming right along, a thought may occur to you—how the heck would you know whether any of the services are being used, misused, or abused?

A moment's thought reveals the answer. Because most network services are managed through inetd, some careful modifications of inetd.conf provide the management tools that you seek.

Consider a simple example: the mere accounting of program execution. Because inetd calls whatever program you specify, you could write a program (or shell script) to generate data logging for each connection. Following is a possible script:

```
#!/bin/sh
# telnet.log - log telnet access and spawn telnetd
#
echo "Telnet executed at `date`" >/tmp/telnetlog
exec /usr/etc/in.telnetd
```

This example is trivial but illustrative of the mechanism.

Several publicly available packages allow you to exert fine control of your network services. One of the best packages of this sort is tcpd, which is also known as tcp_wrapper. This daemon, called from inetd, allows the administrator to log, double-check, and even authenticate connections before the actual service is invoked. The daemon provides for acceptance or denial of connections from particular hosts (or domains), and allows fairly complete logging to be conducted. The tcpd package is available via anonymous FTP from ftp.win.tue.nl.

What Services Am I Running, Anyway?

You may wonder what services your system currently advertises, especially when you inherit a system from another administrator. What are you to do? One of the following approaches may work for you:

- Review /etc/inetd.conf.
- Collect and review listings of /bin/ps.
- Use a network monitor.

Whichever method you choose, it's important to get a handle on things quickly. Network services can be subjugated, and you may also be concerned about the burden that these services are placing on your network.

Shutting Out the World

For whatever reason, you may want to restrict access to some of your network services, especially if you use network services such as FTP to propagate proprietary or confidential information. How can you secure your network services? The simplest approach—and, often, the one that provides the greatest flexibility within your network—is to block or pass services at the router level. Most current routers allow selective pass-through of traffic. Using filters, you can restrict the traffic that passes through your network.

Suppose that you want to disallow access to your POP3 server from outside your corporate network. Because POP3 listens to port 110, you can simply program your router not to pass any traffic addressed to (or coming from) port 110. You can restrict any or all TCP/IP and UDP/IP services in the same manner.

This step requires careful thought, however. You do not want to disable the CEO's favorite utility. Neither do you want to prevent the CEO from forwarding e-mail to his or her home. As in many other aspects of system administration, careful planning is required. If you can log the use of your network services, you'll be able to base your decisions on actual use. In any case, you'll have a very clear picture of your users' needs.

It's a Big Net Out There

The Internet is a mass of services, each of which is flinging packets hither and yon. Your job as a systems administrator is to follow the old Net maxim "Be conservative in what you send, but liberal in what you accept." If you can provide particular services to users at large, do so. By the same token, do not hesitate to restrict (or disable) services that present security concerns. TCP/IP networks are almost infinitely customizable; have fun with them.

Summary

Network services are the glue that brings your systems together into a homogenous environment. I've discussed the common architecture of UNIX network services, including

▶ The nature of TCP and UDP connectivity

▶ The procedure used in responding to network service requests via `inetd`

▶ Configuring `inetd.conf` for your services

▶ Configuring the file transfer service, `ftp`

▶ Using `bootp` and `tftp` to deliver configuration information to various TCP/IP clients

▶ Tracking and controlling your network services

Chapter 51

Crash!

Hardware Crashes

No matter what kind of hardware you have and no matter what kind of software you are running on it, at some point your system will crash. On some systems, the cursor will freeze solid, and nothing you key in or click will yield any response. On a Mac, the dreaded bomb with a lit fuse may appear. At any rate, you are (at least temporarily) dead in the water.

In the old days, a hardware crash meant just that: Hard disks rode on an air cushion, and when this vanished, the disk (which weighed many times what a modern hard disk weighs) crashed down. Another kind of crash is the *head crash,* in which the heads in the hard disk scrape away the oxide from the surface of the disk. Your hardware can fail in other, equally horrible, ways. But when a real hardware problem occurs, just how long you are idle (and how long the machine is down) is a function of how rapidly you can replace the hardware that needs to be replaced. These days, hardware is so cheap that replacement is easier than repair where desktops are concerned. If we're talking about an SGI, a Pyramid, a Sequent, or a big Sun, it's worth calling the service number and getting someone in to look at it.

By and large, a crash results in lost data and lost time. The safest thing to do is back up your work fairly frequently on some sort of external medium: floppy or tape. Daily is best; weekly is imperative. Going longer tempts fate.

However, you should take certain steps when things first freeze up.

■ Try to reboot the system. (While rebooting is much more time-consuming on a UNIX-based system than on a DOS-based system, it will occasionally solve a trivial problem.)

- Check that the power cord is plugged in securely at both ends. Don't just look. Put your dainty hand on the plugs and make sure that they are well seated. Systems are at greater risk from the cleaners and that friend of yours who tripped over the cable or trod on a connector than from true villains.

- Make sure that the power switches on your monitor and on the CPU are both turned on.

- Check all the other connectors. A short or bad connection where the phone line, modem, or printer connection is involved could have consequences beyond the scope of the actual device.

- Check the lights on any pieces of equipment that have them. (Pyramids and Suns have fault lights that really identify problems in a reliable manner.)

Now, at least, you can be fairly certain that the problem doesn't lie in an obvious oversight or blunder.

Software Crashes

Software crashes are different.

Whereas UNIX systems vary from one another, they are all based on either AT&T's System V or Berkeley's 4.3BSD or 4.4BSD. The designers of these based systems have tried very hard to eliminate the kernel bugs that might cause crashes. Throughout the hundreds of thousands of lines of code are *assertion points* and frequent *data integrity checkpoints*.

If one of these (an assertion or a check) fails, a UNIX system panics. A panic induces a controlled crash. What the panic does is write memory to a disk partition and reboot. By first writing and then rebooting, a UNIX system attempts to limit loss and preserve a trace so that later on you, or someone else, can try to diagnose the cause of the panic and crash.

If you look at your manual pages, ASSERT() will read:

```
NAME
     assert - verify program assertion
SYNOPSIS
     #include <assert.h>
     void assert (int expression);
DESCRIPTION
```

This macro is useful for putting diagnostics into programs. When it executes, if expression is false (zero), assert prints:

```
Assertion failed: expression, file xyz, line nnn
```

on the standard error output and aborts. In the error message, *xyz* is the name of the source file, and *nnn* is the source line number of the assert statement.

This may not help a great deal, but it does tell you that an assertion check is executed by using a C language macro ASSERT(). System V Release 4.1 contains just under 400,000 lines of code and about 2,500 assertions and other calls that can panic the system. If you are really lucky when your system fails, you will have a responsive vendor. The sad truth is that if you didn't purchase software support, your vendor will likely be unhelpful.

Let's go back a bit. I said that in a panic, your system will reboot. Most types of UNIX have two kinds of booting: manual and automatic. When you set up your system (or it was set up for you), it was manually booted. In general, automatic booting is what is used thereafter.

In an automatic boot, the machine executes the booting process on its own, without your intervention. In many modern systems, you just have to power up and wait for the machine to signal that it is online.

An automatic boot goes through six steps:

1. Loading UNIX into memory
2. Initializing the kernel
3. Probing and configuring the hardware
4. Creating system processes
5. Executing initialization scripts
6. Spawning listening processes

While understanding what goes on here is important, it isn't necessary for understanding crash recovery. What you need to realize in crash recovery is that while the specifics of automatic rebooting depend on whether you are running a System V–based or a BSD-based UNIX, the general flow is the same.

A few occasions will arise when you will actually want to reboot your system:

■ When you make alterations to the software or the configuration that you would otherwise only look at during bootstrapping.

■ When you want to clear the printer or modem ports which have become muddled.

■ When you need to execute fsck, the file system check and repair. (In a multiuser system, fsck should be run weekly to ensure consistency and prevent excessive fragmentation.)

SVR4-derived systems use a command called uadmin(), which gives administrative control over a few functions, including both SHUTDOWN and REBOOT. In a BSD system, reboot is called with shutdown -r. Reboot restarts your operating system. It restarts the kernel, which is loaded into memory by the PROM monitor, which transfers control to it. Although reboot can be run by the privileged user at any time, on a multiuser system, shutdown is normally used first to warn all users logged in of the impending loss of service. Normally, the system will reboot itself at power-up or after crashes.

In most multiuser systems, the system administrator should have set things up so that crash dumps are written to your system disk swap partition. The `savecore` command prevents this swap space from being overwritten on rebooting. If your UNIX vendor is clever, `savecore` executes on reboot without you having to do anything.

Looking at what the manuals say about core is instructive. In System V UNIX

> . . . the system writes out a core image of a process when it is terminated due to the receipt of some signals. The core image is called core and is written in the process's working directory. A process with an effective user ID different from the real user ID will not produce a core image.
>
> The core file contains all the process information pertinent to debugging: contents of hardware registers, process status, and process data. The format of a core file is object file specific.

In Solaris

> . . . the operating system writes out a memory image of a terminated process when any of various errors occur. The most common reasons are memory violations, illegal instructions, bus errors, and user-generated quit signals. The memory image is called core and is written in the process's working directory (provided it can be; normal access controls apply). Set-user-ID and set-group-ID programs do not produce core files when they terminate as this would cause a security loophole.
>
> The core file consists of a core structure, as defined in the <sys/core.h> file, followed by the data pages and then the stack pages of the process image. The core structure includes the program's header; the size of the text, data, and stack segments; the name of the program; and the number of the signal that terminated the process.

Should your system crash and crash dumps are not being collected, however, you can boot your BSD system in single-user mode and execute `savecore`. This is not possible on SVR3 nor SVR4. On all BSD systems and on some System V systems, however, you can write the kernel to tape prior to reboot. You can do this with the `dd` command, which converts and copies a file:

> The dd utility copies the standard input to the standard output. Input data is read and written in 512-byte blocks. If input reads are short, input from multiple reads are aggregated to form the output block. When finished, dd displays the number of complete and partial input and output blocks and truncated input records to the standard error output.

Troubleshooting

Well, here you are. The system crashed. You managed to get it back up, but what caused it? Will it happen again? One of the things that will help you out is having kept a hard copy record of the normal boot messages. If you have this in hand, when you reboot your system you will be able to see what's different. Always keep in mind that a crash is not a normal behavior. Something causes a crash, and that thing is a change. Whether it's a change in voltage as a result of an idiot with a backhoe a few blocks away, a colleague kicking a plug out, or a line of code that you've added to the system, it's still a change.

Secret

UNIX systems have a command called `syslog`, which enables you to specify how some system messages are saved and where they are saved. You specify where the messages should go using the system message logging daemon, `syslogd`. This daemon collects a variety of messages that processes send and stores them as specified in its `/etc/syslog.conf` file, the `syslog` configuration file. Many different facilities are defined, but only five of them are really important: `kern`, the kernel; `mail`, the e-mail subsystem; `lpr`, the printing subsystem; `daemon`, server processes; and `auth`, the login authentication system.

The `syslog` command has ten levels of severity, which I won't enumerate here, running from `emerg` (a system panic/crash) and `alert` (requires immediate attention) to `info` (informative material) and `debug` (information that's useful in hunting down bugs). The entries in your `/etc/syslog.conf` file will be listed in two columns like this `syslog` configuration file:

```
auth.debug          /var/saf/_log
daemon.err          /dev/console
daemon.debug
        /var/syslog/daemon
user.debug          /var/syslog/user
lpr.debug           /var/syslog/lpr
```

The first line without # prints all bugs from the authentication system in `/var/saf/_log`. The next prints all daemon errors to the console. We could put in a line:

```
.err                /dev/console
```

This would print all errors to the console. In a multiuser system, it's useful to insert something like

```
.err;daemon,auth.notice;mail.crit     /var/adm/messages
```

This will store a variety of errors and notices in `/var/adm/messages`.

Secret

The `/var` directory stands for varying data. In other words, it is a directory containing spooling, `chron`, and `uucp` data. (The `/dev` directory is the device directory of your system.) In several UNIX systems, `/var` is linked to `/usr`. So what? If you periodically monitor your `syslog` files, you will effectively have an early warning system that may prevent crashes. Flaky hardware doesn't just go nuts overnight. In general, days, weeks, and sometimes months of little glitches reveal themselves in the midrange of the warning messages.

The crit ([critical] hard device errors), warn (warnings), and notice ([noncritical] error messages) are the most important of these.

You can thus pick up on potential disasters by looking at your syslog files. Repeated info and notice messages where a single program or device is concerned are sure indications that something is wrong. Picking up on several notices is always better than picking up after a crash or panic.

It is very important that UNIX systems all differ in minor ways. Some differ in major ways.

Linux systems use a klogd daemon that keeps kernel log messages in addition to a syslogd, but not every Linux distribution does this. DEC's UNIX systems have a syslog facility in which syslog messages are directed to special files named for individual facilities. These keep only a week's messages; a crontab entry deletes older messages. IRIX has an augmented format for syslog.

I won't go into all these here, but if you're really interested in what's going on, read your system's online manual pages. They are most likely obtuse and terse, but they are full of information.

It's Not a Movie, It's crash, the Program!

Both AT&T- and BSD-derived UNIX systems have a program called crash. Because this program is machine-dependent, some manufacturers have enhanced it, and some have opted not to include it. At least one version of SVR4-derived UNIX for the 486 has elided it from the online manual pages. Nonetheless, we will spend a little time with crash because it is useful.

When your system panics, it looks for a place to dump memory. On most UNIX systems, these panic dumps are placed on the swap partition. (In some systems, a special partition is reserved for these dumps.) After a crash (panic) when the system is rebooted, it checks to see whether dump memory has been written in the appropriate partition. If there has been, that data is copied into /var/adm/crash. In general, the first image is saved as core.1, the next as core.2, and so forth. The kernel is copied from /stand/unix as unix.1, unix.2, and so forth. (Solaris uses /kernel/unix.)

Secret

A crash dump is a memory image. If you have 16MB of memory, you'll need 16MB of disk space for the dump. If you have 128MB, you'll need 128MB. If there's not enough space, you'll get a partial dump.

Examining the crash dump is important, as it will give you leads to just what caused the crash. First, apply cd to the directory where the dumps are saved. Then, enter the command

```
crash core.1 unix.1
```

Secret

If you log in as `root` or `su`, you can run `crash` while the kernel is running. Your command is then

```
crash /dev/mem /stand/unix
```

As `crash` runs interactively, it is a command-line interpreter and issues a prompt as you enter commands. The crash prompt is >, and the commands are too numerous to go into here, but the most important single crash command is ? because it will call up a complete list of which commands `crash` will accept in your system. Table 51-1 lists other widespread commands.

Table 51-1	Other Common crash Commands	
Command	*Argument*	*Result*
!		Permits you to pipe the output of a crash command to a shell command. For example, `proc ! pg` will let you see the process table, a screen at a time. (In other words, ! takes the place of │.)
-e		Displays every entry in a table, not merely the ones in use.
-f		Forces the display of data structures in full, rather than just the important fields.
-p		Interprets address arguments as physical addresses, rather than virtual addresses.
-s	slot	Forces commands that are related to processes to use process table slots rather than default slots.
-w	file	Redirects (writes) output of a command to a specified file.

What do I do first?

The first thing to do when invoking `crash` is to use the `stat` command. This prints out the kernel print buffer. As the kernel print buffer holds the last bytes that were written to the console, this permits you to read exactly what you typed before the machine crashed (panicked). (If you phone the 800-number of your vendor for support, they are going to ask you for this. They may be able to identify the problem/bug immediately.)

Second, look at the process table. This will let you know which process was running at the time the system panicked — probably the process that set off the bug.

Next, trace back in the kernel to see just which kernel functions were active during the process that initiated the panic.

If you keep at it, you may, indeed, find out what went wrong.

The crash program in action

So that you realize that I wasn't kidding about the `crash` commands, here's a brief selection from the Solaris version of `crash` examine system images:

```
as Print the address space table.
base Print number in binary, octal, decimal, and hexade-
  cimal. A number in a radix other then decimal should be
  preceded by a prefix that indicates its radix as fol-
  lows: 0x, hexidecimal; 0, octal; and 0b, binary.
buffer Print the contents of a buffer in the designated for-
  mat. The following format designations are recognized:
  -b, byte; -c, character; -d, decimal; -x, hexadecimal;
  -o, octal; -r, directory; and -i, inode. If no format
  is given, the previous format is used. The default for-
  mat at the beginning of a crash session is hexadecimal.
bufhdr Print system buffer headers.
callout Print the callout table.
ctx Print the context table.
dbfree Print free streams data block headers. If a class is
  entered, only data block headers for the class speci-
  fied will be printed.
dblock Print allocated streams data block headers. If the
  class option (-c) is used, only data block headers for
  the class specified will be printed.
defproc Set the value of the process slot argument. The pro-
  cess slot argument may be set to the current slot
  number (-c) or the slot number may be specified. If no
  argument is entered, the value of the previously set
  slot number is printed. At the start of a crash ses-
  sion, the process slot is set to the current process.
ds Print the data symbol whose address is closest to, but
  not greater than, the address entered.
file Print the file table.
help Print a description of the named command, including
  syntax and aliases.
inode Print the inode table, including file system switch
  information.
page Print the page structures.
proc Print the process table. Process table information may
  be specified in two ways. First, any mixture of table
  entries and process IDs (PID) may be entered. Each PID
  must be preceded by a `#' (pound sign). Alternatively,
  process table information for runnable processes may be
  specified with the runnable option (-r).
redirect Used with a name, redirects output of a crash session
  to the named file. If no argument is given, the file
```

```
name to which output is being redirected is printed.
Alternatively, the close option (-c) closes the previ-
ously set file and redirects output to the standard
output.
size Print the size of the designated structure. The -x
option prints the size in hexadecimal. If no argument
is given, a list of the structure names for which sizes
are available is printed.
stack Dump stack. The -u option prints the user stack. The
-k option prints the kernel stack. The -i option
prints the interrupt stack starting at the start
address. If no arguments are entered, the kernel stack
for the current process is printed. The interrupt
stack and the stack for the current process are not
available on a running system.
status Print system statistics.
trace Print stack trace. The kfp value is used with the -r
option. The interrupt option prints a trace of the
interrupt stack beginning at the start address. The
interrupt stack trace and the stack trace for the
current process are not available on a running system.
user Print the ublock for the designated process.
```

By far, the best and most extensive discussion of crash and its commands is in Berny Goodheart and James Cox's *The Magic Garden Explained* (Prentice Hall, 1994), pages 563–621.

Summary

This chapter provided a brief overview of how to handle crashes. You learned about

▶ Diagnosing hardware

▶ Diagnosing software

▶ The crash program

In the next chapter, Wes Morgan shows how to use the administration tools in concert with other UNIX tools.

Chapter 52

Tying the Tools Together for Efficiency

Throughout this book, we've explored the intricacies of UNIX systems administration. We've delved into the UNIX toolkit, tinkered with almost every aspect of the operating system, and wended our way through the maze of twisty little passages that is UNIX. At this point, we're going to move to something of a higher plane. Rather than investigate the minutiae further, we're going to talk about the mindset (philosophy would, perhaps, be a more appropriate term) behind the consistent administration of a UNIX system.

New users who have UNIX experience (new employees or transfer students, for example) often exclaim, "Wow, that isn't how it was on the box I used to use!" This is more common within the UNIX world than within the realm of other operating systems. Given the unique building-block nature of UNIX, it's only natural that each administrator casts the system in his or her image. In all but the most restrictive environments, you should feel free to do the same; however, such customizations should be preceded by careful evaluation of the existing system and its performance. Whether you have inherited your system from another administrator, are unpacking a brand-new system, or are maintaining a system that has been your responsibility for years, a consistent and ongoing evaluation process will pay dividends for the lifetime of your system.

Laying the Groundwork

Any system evaluation must begin with a thorough understanding of the beginning configuration. Therefore, I strongly recommend a complete reading of the system configuration files. In most cases, you will find that a large number of configuration settings have been untouched since the initial installation of the system. This is not necessarily a bad thing. In most cases, many of the vendor's default configurations are more than adequate for the typical UNIX system; however, you may find that these configurations are contributing to the problems that you encounter.

Of particular importance at this stage of the process is the kernel configuration. As the cornerstones of the UNIX operating system, the kernel variables can have a huge impact on the performance of your system. At this point, you should label kernel configuration files "Handle with Care." You may want to generate printouts of the various kernel configuration files. The time you spend familiarizing yourself with the myriad variables can pay significant dividends in performance analysis and system adjustments.

Note

You may want to freeze the status of all configuration files before beginning the evaluation/reconfiguration process. I usually create a directory named /etc/originals (or something similar) and stock it with the original copies of whatever critical files I may be modifying. In addition, I usually create the directory /etc/lastchange, in which I keep the immediate past version of each configuration file that I modify. With a facility of this sort, you can easily revert to either the "undo last change" configuration or the original configuration.

This is also your opportunity to discover any extraordinary modifications that may have been made to your system. If you are inheriting responsibility for an existing system, there is sure to be some peculiar login shell, output filter, or device table entry that raises questions in your mind. Take this opportunity to discover the mechanisms and functions that are unique to your system and its users.

This process also provides an opportunity for you to discern the needs, frustrations, and wishes of your users. Consultations with users often alert you to potential problems and/or shortcomings that may require your close attention during the evaluation process. Again, forewarned is forearmed.

Where Do I Start?

After consultations with users and other support staff members, you will find that three items inevitably rise to the top of the wish list: processing facilities, memory, and storage. You'll want to keep these three items in mind while you conduct your evaluation.

The first task is to ascertain the daily pushes, pulls, and grunts of your system and its users. Several UNIX utilities can assist you in gathering this sort of routine data. Primary among these are ps (or its cousins, w and top) and the various system accounting utilities (acctcom, acctprt, and the like). Most UNIX systems provide a crash-dump-analysis utility, such as /etc/crash. These utilities can often be used to evaluate a running system, instead of a crash dump. You may even find yourself checking utilities such as du, netstat, and others on a less frequent basis.

For long-term evaluations, the system accounting facilities will be your major source of information. I prefer to use ps/w/top for the "quick peek" perspective on the ebb and flow of daily operations, with /etc/crash providing an ongoing indicator of resource consumption.

As you may expect, the evaluation phase of system administration yields quite a few of its insights in a transitory matter. You may notice one item in an output listing that merits further attention, or you may see a particular error message in response to a command. You need a quick way to jot down notes for later perusal. Some administrators prefer to send themselves electronic mail messages, but I find that approach to be time-consuming, for both sending and reading. I use the following shell script:

```
#!/bin/sh
# jot - append one-line comments to log file
#
LOGFILE=$HOME/observations
if [ -z "$1" ]
then
    $PAGER $LOGFILE
    exit
fi
dtgroup=´date +´%D %T´´
echo $dtgroup """$*" >$LOGFILE
exit
```

Given this shell script, you can jot down a note as follows:

```
$ jot program biggulp - user jqweeble - drains memory
$
```

To review your log file, simply execute the shell script without arguments, as follows:

```
$ jot
12/01/95 15:59:01 program ansquare always waiting for swap
12/01/95 17:32:32 program biggulp - user jqweeble - drains memory
$
```

This shell script is very rudimentary. It may not accept characters such as parentheses or braces, but it fits your needs by providing a "scratch pad" for your observations. You can print all your observations in one sitting by printing the log file in its entirety.

Tip

Don't forget to check your spool directories for programs executed via cron and at. If you're inheriting a system, there's a good chance that some heavy-hitting programs are being executed at unusual times through these facilities.

Armed with your configuration printouts, user comments, and your online note pad, you're ready to begin.

Taking snapshots with ps

Both users and administrators often misunderstand the ps command. As originally designed, ps is nothing more than a snapshot of system activity. Unfortunately, it is often misinterpreted as being an indicator of overall system performance. The output from ps should be considered to be anecdotal information, valid only within the context of the fractions of a second in which the utility was executed. Even the most mundane cat or telnet command can be the most resource-intensive operation on your system, as far as ps is concerned. Nevertheless, the snapshots generated by ps are valuable to you. Rather than interpret them as individual data, you should use them as indicators of trends. Those trends may reflect system deficiencies that are worthy of further attention.

In keeping with the snapshot metaphor, I treat ps as a camera. If I see something interesting, I take a picture. You may notice a gradual decline in system performance over the course of an hour, or you may suddenly hit the wall with a pause measured in seconds; in either case, take a picture.

If you like, you can use a shell alias to divert a copy of the output to a disk file for later review. I use the following /bin/sh alias:

```
pdq() {
/bin/ps aux | tee -a $HOME/observations
}
```

This alias diverts a copy of the ps output to the same observations file used by the jot shell script mentioned earlier in this chapter.

A quick reading of the manual page for ps reveals several options far above the average for UNIX utilities. Although ps can certainly provide a cornucopia of information, this stage of your evaluation merits only rudimentary information. Therefore, I recommend ps aux for BSD systems and ps -ealf for those in the System V universe. When you have ascertained areas of particular interest, you can modify your default settings for ps to reflect the changes in your informational needs.

Each vendor's version of ps differs slightly in its output(s); therefore, I will not attempt to cover specific output items. Instead, several general red flags should receive your consistent attention:

■ **The memory size of each process.** Some systems report this information in two parts: the size of the data segment, and the size of the data and stack segments combined. Memory-intensive programs are often worthy of further scrutiny.

- **The run state of each process.** If programs are consistently waiting for paging, this may indicate memory conflicts; if waiting for swapping, either memory or disk space shortages could be the culprit.

- **The start time of each process.** During the millisecond in which ps interrogates the process tables, a given process may not be in a wait state. Keep an eye open, however, for programs that require inordinate amounts of time for completion.

- **The priority of each process.** Some sites enable users to change the priority of their own jobs. The indiscriminate use of this capability can create resource contention for all processes.

Again, treat the information provided by ps with the proverbial grain of salt, but be on the lookout for consistent problems of the types noted in the preceding list. Look for trends; you will find them.

System accounting files

The UNIX system accounting procedures can provide a fairly comprehensive picture of long-term use. In most cases, the accounting jobs provide daily, weekly, and monthly summaries of activity data. Your system may include utilities for on-the-fly review of accounting data. In any case, this data can serve you well during your evaluation.

Rather than attempt to address every vendor-specific item in the various accounting utilities, I provide the following points for you to consider:

- **Total use of applications.** Fifteen iterations of a small program may never lead the pack with ps, but the system accounting records may reveal that — in its overall impact — the small program consumes more resources than its more monolithic brethren do.

- **Memory consumption over time.** Some systems refer to this as KCOREMINS, or kilo-core-minutes, which reflects the consumption of main memory as a per-minute average. A program that conducts memory access in bursts may not be revealed by snapshots. Again, daily accounting can give the big picture that you need.

- **Disk I/O counts and I/O consumption over time.** Again, some applications degrade your system with a slow, steady drain, as opposed to the spike that you would see with ps.

- **Hog factor.** Some systems compute a hog factor, which measures the impact of each program in terms of a fraction of all available CPU time. Although you should take this statistic with a grain of salt, it can indicate further problems.

System accounting also provides reports of each user's activity. When reviewed under the criteria mentioned earlier, this information can be used to optimize user placements on the system. If user jqweeble is burning up the database software that resides on /usr3, moving his home directory to that file system may alleviate some disk contention.

Most accounting systems are designed to run on a nightly basis. Many of these systems (especially in the System V universe) provide utilities that can interrogate the accounting data that is currently being collected (in other words, they tell you about everything since the last execution of the accounting software). If these utilities are available to you, they can be instrumental in answering "what just happened?" questions.

Crashing the party

UNIX systems, like all other computing systems, inevitably crash unexpectedly. In preparation for that event, most UNIX systems include a crash-dump-analysis utility, most commonly /etc/crash. You also can use such a utility to inspect a running system.

Caution

It is exceptionally easy to bring your system to a halt with /etc/crash. Careful familiarization with your version of this program is essential; in addition, be careful to interrogate your system without changing its operating environment on the fly.

Use of /etc/crash is most often indicated by resource exhaustion. You may see a console message such as out of free buffers or strblks exhausted, which is a clear indicator not only that an item is under contention, but also that its limits can be changed. (Very few system error messages reflect an immovable block.) You should be familiar with the current performance tuning of your system before pulling information from the kernel with /etc/crash.

Most versions of /etc/crash provide a running peak consumption report for tunable parameters. You may see a report such as the following:

```
QTY   AVAIL  MAX
NBUF  2000    320 1900
```

This report indicates that the kernel is configured with NBUF = 2000, that 320 buffers are currently available, and that the peak demand since the last reboot was 1,900. (Given that most administrators like to give their systems — and their users — a bit of breathing room, I would definitely tune the kernel to increase NBUF; 100 spare buffers do not provide a safety margin that is adequate to my taste.)

Similar statistics are maintained for many system resources. Keep an eye out for any sudden increase in consumption. You should also keep /etc/crash in mind when you face periodic failures. If a particular problem occurs every two weeks or so, it may be caused by a slow hoarding of a particular kernel resource. The /etc/crash tool and its brethren are dangerous tools, but they can alert you to problems that are not otherwise evidenced.

If you are uncomfortable with using /etc/crash on a running system, you can use your vendor-specific utilities to generate a crash dump for analysis. Check your documentation. You may even be able to do this as part of your normal shutdown or reboot procedure.

Making Sense of It All

By this time, you're probably overwhelmed by the sheer volume of data reported to you by the various subsystems/facilities of a typical UNIX system. It's also likely that you are being asked questions like, "Are we really using that big server?" or "Do we need to budget for expansion or upgrades next year?" To answer these questions — and to keep your systems operating at peak performance — you'll have to bring a comprehensive view to the table.

Be trendy!

Now that you've located all the data-collection and reporting utilities, and you've familiarized yourself with your system's current state and/or peculiarities, what do you do with this mass of data?

Few administrators have the time to pore over every report; they simply have too many other things to do. How, then, can you best assimilate this information? The answer lies in the trends of your system's behavior, not in the raw numbers. When you become familiar with the usual comings and goings of your system, you merely need to keep an eye out for peculiarities — variations from your self-ascertained norm — and unexplained phenomena.

The first steps on this path are rather laborious, but it becomes easier with time and experience. In the beginning, you may simply want to plot certain statistics over time. You may want to plot the preceding day's CPU or disk I/O use each morning, for example. In this situation, cron can be your friend. A simple shell script can extract the necessary information from the preceding day's accounting records, piping it through plot(1) and placing a nicely printed plot on your printer each morning. While you sip that first cup of coffee, take a glance at the plot, which will alert you to anything out of the ordinary. You can examine the preceding day's accounting reports to find any culprit(s).

Over time, you will build a fairly complete picture of your system's ups and downs. These fluctuations may be tied to the nature of your business (each September brings a flood of new users to a university, for example) or to the calendar itself (fiscal-year closures in the finance department). You may even discover that different kernel configurations are appropriate for different times of the year. One site that I know of has a fiscal-year-end kernel that is loaded 60 days before the end of each fiscal year, to accommodate the extremely heavy burdens created by end-of-year reporting, archiving, and analysis.

After you map the trends of your system's use, you can begin making modifications to ease the online burden. My only advice to you in this area is to avoid the one-shot megafix approach. Kernels are notoriously finicky, and the tunable parameters often depend on one another in mysterious ways. Kernel changes should be accomplished in bits and pieces. Change only what is relevant at the time and allow the change to burn in for some time before you move to the next change. Don't be discouraged. Tuning your system's kernel to optimum condition may take weeks or even months.

The déjà vu of repetitious redundancy

As you examine your accounting records, keep an eye out for unnecessary duplication of effort. You may find that large numbers of users execute the same program, in the same fashion, at regular intervals. The users in turn are unaware of the repetition by their colleagues and coworkers. Minimization of this redundancy can pay significant dividends in system performance. Following are a few examples of this sort of redundancy:

- Each department runs a database reconciliation at the end of the day instead of running one master reconciliation each night.

- Individual users run the same reports and queries independently, instead of running one job and duplicating the output(s).

- People run two or three copies of the same program, with different data sets, at the same time.

Each problem of this type can be prevented, although some interoffice coordination may be required. You should find out what functions can be combined (or duplicated, as necessary) to minimize the impact on your system. Some potential solutions are

- Using `cron` to run the large queries and reports, such as reconciliations, after hours

- Granting users the privilege of using `at(1)` to schedule their own multiple jobs overnight

- Modifying large jobs to send copies of output(s) to several printers, rather than having people run the job several times

Experimentation (with input from your users) is the key to this piece of the puzzle. Given sufficient flexibility of scheduling, you will be amazed by the amount of redundant work being conducted on your system and the ease with which it can be minimized.

Building Your Toolbox

At times, the typical system administrator seems to be building custom programs on a daily basis. Every day brings some addition, be it a permanent integration into operations or a one-shot fix to resolve a user problem.

Over time, you'll find that a substantial portion of your system's operations are built on your custom modifications and programs. The following sections examine some of the pleasures — and pitfalls — of building your toolbox.

Don't reinvent the wheel, and don't build a luxury car

As user needs change, you will naturally come into play as the implementer of those changes. The key to effective growth is reuse of your resources. UNIX provides a wonderful toolkit for data manipulation at the shell level. Don't be afraid to use those tools to your advantage.

Many users (and some administrators) fall into the trap of believing that every need must be answered by a program written in a high-level language, such as C or FORTRAN. Such is not the case, especially with the advent of full-featured scripting languages (Perl is among the best-known examples of such a language). Even the lowly, often-maligned Bourne shell or C shell can accomplish the majority of your daily quick-and-dirty problem-solving.

Another distressing trend involves writing monolithic programs to offer a "robust" set of options. In many cases, this practice quickly becomes an unmanageable mess; resist the urge. It is far better to write small programs, each of which performs a portion of the task at hand. This approach allows you to build a library of reusable (there's that word again!) building blocks for future projects and programs. This is well in keeping with the UNIX tradition, despite the man page for ls(1), and it will greatly decrease the demands on your time.

Note

Many scripting languages are available for UNIX. It's likely that your system arrived with at least two available shells, for example. Choose a scripting language, and stick with it. Your choice — be it Perl, Tcl, or /bin/sh — will be dictated by your needs, especially if your operation has multiple administrators. If only one member of your crew knows Perl, for example, you're going to depend on that person for code maintenance. Avoid such a situation.

As you write your scripts, make every attempt to make them generic. Avoid burying specific filenames in the heart of your scripts. As an alternative, use environment variables, and set them at the beginning of the script, as follows:

```
#!/bin/sh
#
# foosh.sh - extract 4th line of specified file
#
# Set INFILE to the name of the file to process
INFILE=/etc/foobar
# Set OUTFILE to the name of the output file
OUTFILE=/tmp/foosh.out
#
awk `NR == 4 { print }` $INFILE > $OUTFILE
exit 1
```

This script is easy to reuse. All you must do is change the two lines in which the input and output files are named.

When you create temporary files, you may want to use the PID in the filename. This practice will prevent problems if and when several users execute the script simultaneously. In the Bourne shell, the variable $$ is replaced by the current PID. You might specify an output file this way:

```
OUTFILE=/tmp/foosh.$$
...
...
echo All done >$OUTFILE
```

As you develop your own library of bits-and-pieces scripts, you will discover many other methods of liberating your code from the single-use style that is all too common in today's operations.

I suggest that you maintain your library in a local area, such as /usr/local/bin, and that you keep the naming scheme consistent. I usually name my shell scripts with a suffix of .sh (or .csh, if I'm using the C shell). This scheme makes it simple for other users to get up to speed on my work.

Hey, can I borrow your wheels?

If you want to avoid reinventing the wheel, it's only natural to take a look at other admins' wheels. It's fair to assume that you are not the first administrator to face some problem; someone else may have written a solution before you ever faced the prospect of doing so.

Here's where active participation in the online world can yield real dividends. Don't be afraid to ask your mailing list and/or Usenet newsgroup correspondents for assistance. Even if you don't find a solution to your specific problem, you may find information (or, perhaps, source code that you can easily modify to meet your needs). By the same token, I urge you to help your colleagues when they post requests for help. The Internet was built on the model of cooperation, and I believe that it's important to perpetuate that tradition whenever possible.

Note

Many mailing lists (and quite a few Usenet newsgroups) are archived; many more post Frequently Asked Questions (FAQ) lists on a regular basis. Whenever possible, review these archives and postings before you dispatch your question to the online world.

Don't forget to ask about other sources of information, such as FTP archives and mail servers. The online world provides an ever-increasing number of conduits for information; become familiar with sources that are relevant to your installation.

Caution

Review outside information carefully before implementing it on your system. Every UNIX system is different, thanks to kernel tuning and vendor variety. The fix that works for Joe in Schenectady may not work on your system. Be informed, but be alert.

User groups are also a rich source of information. Several user groups publish CD-ROMs or tapes of user-contributed software, newsletters, journals, and the like. If a local user group exists for your variety of UNIX, participating in it may be well worth your time and money. If your area has no user groups, consider hosting or starting one.

Help from vendors

Your system is only as good as its operating system. I'm going to avoid the religious wars of BSD versus System V, SunOS versus Solaris, and the like. I would, however, like to discuss the help that you may (or may not) receive from vendors.

The insect world (bugs, bugs, bugs!)

Every UNIX implementation contains bugs. As a site administrator, you are not likely to have the time, resources, or source code that you would need to find and fix these bugs yourself. You can stay one step ahead of them, however.

Most vendors publish a list of known problems with their version of UNIX; some vendors call it a bug list, and others refer to it as a known problems list or something similar. In any case, make every effort to obtain current bug lists from your vendors. Some vendors may require the purchase of a software support contract; others may make the list available online. In either case, the time and/or money required will be well spent.

Familiarize yourself with the layout and contents of the lists. You don't really need to memorize them, but it's good to know your way around these documents before the world is caving in around you. If particular areas of your system are heavily used, you may want to read the pertinent portions of the bug list in detail. An academic administrator who supports a computer science lab needs to be familiar with the known bugs in the C compiler. His counterpart in the business world wants to know about the bugs hiding in database or spreadsheet software.

Some vendors place their bug reports and fixes in publicly available FTP archives, and others sponsor mailing lists. Ask your support representatives (or the mailing list/Usenet crowd) about the vendor-specific resources that are available to you. In this age of the Web, visiting your vendor's Web page is often worth the time; many vendors are posting announcements in that forum.

Places Bugs Like to Hide

When you are researching potential OS bugs, keep in mind that the interlocking motif of the UNIX operating system can cause bugs to appear in peculiar places. I once encountered a C program that yielded errors from the as(1) assembler. As I found after much testing, the bug actually lay in the cpp preprocessor. The errors introduced by cpp were not becoming evident until the final assembly of the program.

The Internet grapevine

As the infamous Intel Pentium division furor proved, the Internet is a fertile place for the dissemination of both bug information and workarounds. If online forums exist for the systems that you manage, participating is well worth your time. Vendors often make announcements in the forums that are dedicated to their systems, and other users and administrators are there to answer your questions (or confirm your suspicions, as the case may be).

Those of you who have access to Usenet should investigate the comp.sys.* newsgroups, as well as the comp.unix.* newsgroups; both hierarchies are bursting with information. In addition, look for FAQ (Frequently Asked Questions) files in relevant newsgroups; these documents may answer many of your preliminary questions.

In addition, many Internet mailing lists are dedicated to particular makes and models of computer systems. In some cases, the vendors themselves provide electronic mailing lists; be sure to ask your vendor about online support.

If you cannot find a forum for your particular make and model of system, consider creating one yourself. A few queries in relevant Usenet newsgroups can yield dozens, if not hundreds, of subscribers for such a service. Other users will be grateful for the forum, and you'll reap the benefits of the community's knowledge.

When Trouble Comes Home to Roost

Inevitably, you will find your system (and yourself) in Panic Mode. Errors will be flying by, the mundane operations of the system will be grinding to a halt, and the phone will not stop ringing. Here's where administrators earn their salt — where the time that they spent observing the normal flow of their system(s) pays its dividends.

Stemming the tide

The first task at hand during Panic Mode is to isolate the problem case(s), whenever possible. In some cases, the necessary steps are obvious. A failing disk can be dismounted, or files can be transferred from a nearly full file system. Your steps in many such cases are going to be guided by the system's error messages. At this point, you need to decide on your goal. Which of the following things do you want to do?

- Keep the system running for as many users as possible

- Let the problem run its course

- Attempt to run with the problem, resolving symptoms on the fly

- Change to a different run state

- Achieve an orderly shutdown and start over with a reboot

There is no hard-and-fast guidance in this area; your choices depend on the nature of your operation. This is where your knowledge of jobs, users, and system load will be of great value.

Note

Your system may issue error messages of varying severity; if so, you can use those severity levels as your guide. One variant of UNIX, for example, classifies messages as ERROR, WARNING, PANIC, and DOUBLE PANIC. As you might assume, a DOUBLE PANIC error message was the high sign for a quick shutdown. Be familiar with your system's error levels.

Other options might be to terminate unnecessary jobs, remove access to problematic software, or purge a bloated printer queue. After you stem the tide, you're ready to move to the next step.

Swap 'n' shop

In most environments, production-system time is at a premium. Your first priority, then, is to make the system available as soon as possible. Using the information gleaned from the error messages and/or log files, you may be able to bring the system back in a piecemeal fashion, isolating the problem areas for further study. You can lay some groundwork for this eventuality. I always try to create disk partitions of equal size, and I keep a spare partition for just such an occasion. I also keep a list of superblock locations for each file system; fsck(1) can repair a partition with any of these alternate superblocks, should the master become corrupted.

In any case, it's important to have a disaster plan in place, ready to go.

If you happen to be working in a multiple-system operation, you may be able to use other systems to provide the needed services. You might install a backup copy of that critical CAD software on a little-used system. If the workhorse system dies, CAD users could be shunted to the backup system. You should have several systems that are capable of serving as the electronic mail handler for your domain; with backups of this sort, service could be temporarily restored with a simple change to the DNS records. Other techniques include

- Bringing the system back as a stand-alone (if the troubles lie in RFS or NFS)

- Disabling unnecessary network services (if a network crash is the cause of your problems)
- Keeping a minimized kernel on hand for limited operations
- Restricting logins to the absolute minimum
- Using external network management to minimize the load on your system (isolating your system from connections outside your own network)

The key is to have these capabilities available in advance, whenever possible.

Tracking it down

After you restore what services you can, it's time to track down the problem itself. In most cases, the root cause is obvious — this disk drive failed, or that file system may be full. Here's where your friend /etc/crash can come to the rescue. You can use it not only to view items such as error messages (which most UNIX systems save in NVRAM) and memory allocations at the time of the crash, but also to check your kernel variables for shortcomings.

Be prepared to check everything; you will not often find the cause clearly labeled in this arena. I once encountered a consistent SCSI error that froze my system. Upon investigation, I found that the actual cause was a shortage of stream resources in the kernel. If the system error logs do not provide a clear indicator of the failure, you should begin by checking for exhausted kernel resources. The /etc/crash tool is perfectly suited for this task.

Note

Remember that many UNIX systems can be configured to create a crash dump automatically in response to an unexpected system failure. In some cases, this behavior is guided by yet another kernel configuration file. Find out how to enable it on your system, and do so.

You may want to run your diagnostics in stepwise fashion — that is, you may want to begin in single-user mode and work your way back through the run levels until the system is back to multiple-user mode. I suggest that you begin diagnostics in single-user mode, especially with fsck(1) and other utilities of that ilk. As you remove potential causes from your list, bring the system to the next run state, diagnose the items that are peculiar to that run state, and then repeat the process. This stepwise approach also allows you to review the information messages generated at each stage of the boot process. This, in and of itself, can alert you to problems without necessarily exposing users to further anguish.

Note

You may want to write a "system exerciser" script to put your machine through its paces. This script might include such things as generating a large number of network connections, batching up some large print jobs, exercising NFS/RFS disk links, and creating and processing a large mail queue. You are the best judge of the proper exercise for your system. This approach can help you prevent the crash/boot yo-yo mode of problem diagnosis.

Back to normal?

After you diagnose the problem and (if all goes well) discover a fix or workaround, it's time to put the users back online. I suggest that you do so in limited fashion. You may want to disable cron(1) and at(1) for the first few hours to lessen the ramp-up impact on the still-possibly-fragile system.

It would also be advantageous to avoid any unnecessary system load during the first few hours of uptime. I know of sites that automatically shut down facilities such as anonymous FTP and uucp for 24 hours after a system crash; other sites reduce the number of concurrent login session by 50 percent during ramp-up time. The value of such actions is debatable, but your actions should be guided by your needs.

Assuming that you are able to bring your system to its operational level, you need to pay close attention to its behavior for the next few hours. The period after a crash can be quite revealing, for the following reasons:

- If a user program caused the problem, a high probability exists that they will try to resume their work soon after the system returns.

- If a kernel configuration problem is to blame, it may take some time for the problem to return; that delay is a clue in and of itself.

- If the problem does not return until the next overnight period, check cron(1) and at(1) jobs for potential causes.

Remember — what *doesn't* happen can be as instructive as what *does* happen.

Note

If you have enabled system accounting, reviewing the data for the date of the crash (if available) can yield valuable clues. Keep an eye out for new programs in the listings or for new user names with heavy use attached to them.

Closing it out or letting it go

How do you tell the difference between a one-time glitch and an ongoing problem that is in need of repair? Only time can make that determination. As a rule of thumb, I wait for the second occurrence of a particular problem before I pursue the matter with vendors or repair contractors. Your needs may vary, but your definition of "closed" should be based on the use patterns of your particular system. You may want to observe for a day, a week, or even a month; this is well and good.

Be careful, however, to avoid excessive vigilance. A watched pot never boils, and you can spend months waiting for a particular set of circumstances to occur a second time. Given the wide leeway afforded typical UNIX users in their use of system facilities, you are certain to see irreproducible problems and more than your share of one-time glitches. Take them in stride; they're part of the job.

Case Studies from the Trenches

In closing this chapter, I offer a couple of war stories from my own experience. These stories are by no means representative of the problems that you will face on your system — indeed, I hope that you never face problems such as these — but the solutions indicate the mindset that a UNIX system administrator needs.

Story: The Mass Mailing

One fine morning, I walked into my office and glanced at the console of my flagship system. To my horror, it was filled with error messages such as `no space on drive 0, partition 2` and `tcp: too many connections`. When I attempted to log in, I found myself in the root directory instead of my normal home. Checking `df`, I found that both `/tmp` and `/usr/mail` were filled to bursting. Remembering the TCP/IP error messages, I used `netstat(1)` to check network connections; I found every available connection in use by SMTP, the electronic-mail facility. A quick `ps(1)` revealed more than 40 copies of `sendmail` executing on the system. No wonder things were up in the air!

The first task was to relieve the pressure. I removed the execute permissions from `/usr/lib/sendmail` to ensure that no further copies would be executed. Wending my way through the `ps(1)` listings, I killed every `sendmail` job. After I ensured that the rogue `sendmail` processes had, indeed, died, it was time to find the endpoint of this particular line.

Moving over to `/usr/mail`, I began examining the last few sets of message headers from each user mailbox. It soon became apparent that someone had sent a 75K electronic-mail message to each of my 2,100 users. As you might imagine, this message was the source of my system woes. A quick adjustment to my network interface (using a freeware program known as `tcpd` and/or `tcp_wrapper`) ensured that the offending machine could no longer bombard my system with electronic mail.

As for the overflowing mailboxes, I knew the size of the offending message (in lines), and a quick sample showed that most of my users had not received any further electronic-mail messages since the beginning of this deluge. A quickly written shell script did the following things:

- Used `tail` to see whether the last message in user X's mailbox was the mass mailing
- Used `wc -l` to obtain the length of user X's mailbox, in lines
- Subtracted the length of the mass-mailed message from the total
- Used `sed` to create a copy of the user's mailbox without the mass-mailed message

This shell script purged almost 1,200 copies of the message from `/usr/mail/*`, freeing 90MB of space in the disk partition.

At this point, it was safe to restart `sendmail`. The temporary lock created with `tcpd` would prevent the offending system from resuming its torrent of electronc mail, but other systems could continue to conduct communications normally.

At that point, making several telephone calls was in order. As it turned out, someone in an upper-level staff meeting had suggested that each employee should see a copy of a particular proposal. An overly enthusiastic staff member had constructed a list of all e-mail addresses in the domain and fired off a mass mailing. This person was taught the error of his ways.

I Wanna Be a Router!

Having recently experienced an explosion of network problems, ranging from timeouts to broadcast storms, I decided to conduct a bit of network analysis. After capturing a day's worth of Ethernet traffic, I discovered that one of my systems, for whatever reason, was configured to forward TCP/IP traffic. Because this system was not intended to function as a router, it was clear that many (if not most) of my network problems could be traced to this behavior.

I initially assumed that the solution would be a simple kernel reconfiguration, but this was not the case. After finding no tunable parameters for IP forwarding, I made a telephone call to the TCP/IP vendor and was told, "The software is supposed to do that!" I found myself facing the proverbial brick wall. The UNIX variant in question did not include a kernel debugger or binary editor at that time, and I had no source code or tunable parameter files to modify.

The first step was attempting to locate the variables that needed to be changed. The nm(1) command — little known and little documented, but incredibly useful — provided a dump of every symbol in /unix. A quick application of grep(1) to the list revealed a symbol named ipforward, which held a value of 1. A reasonable assumption was that setting this symbol's value to zero could solve the problem,

but how was I going to accomplish this without the tools to edit /unix?

You may have heard the saying, "All of UNIX is a file." That saying applies to memory as well. I realized that the running kernel was the first thing loaded into the /dev/mem file (RAM). Further, the dd(1) utility can be used on any UNIX file. The solution began to dawn on me. I created a file that contained nothing but a zero value. The nm(1) command had provided me the location of the symbol, through its offset computation. I was ready to try it. After the users logged out, I issued a dd command to patch /dev/mem with my zero-value file, using the offset from nm(1). A quick glance at my network analyzer revealed that the forwarding had stopped and that all other TCP/IP traffic seemed to be proceeding apace. Whew!

How did I finalize this process? To those of you who have read this far, the answer should be obvious: I modified the boot sequence files. Editing the appropriate files in /etc/rc.* ensured that this patch would be applied immediately upon boot. I cycled the system through several reboots, and everything seemed to be fine.

Later that week, after investigation revealed no other options, another dd session made the patch to /unix directly, making the reconfiguration permanent.

Summary

This chapter reviewed various UNIX facilities useful in elevating/maintaining your system's efficiency, including

▶ Reviewing and understanding your kernel configuration

▶ Examining system activity with `ps`

▶ System accounting programs and `/etc/crash`

▶ Detecting trends in system performance

▶ Distributing your system's load with tools such as `cron` and `at`

▶ Building your own custom toolbox, with reusability in mind

▶ Dealing with immediate trouble (crashes, slowdowns) and troubleshooting

These facilities and techniques should enable you to create and maintain an exceptionally accurate picture of your system's performance, and equip you to handle the inevitable problems that will occur.

Part XII

UNIX Flavors and Directions

Chapter 53

Flavors of UNIX

You may be running AIX or BSD, HP/UX or Ultrix, SINIX or SVR4, SunOS or Solaris, Linux or something else. For all intents and purposes, they are UNIX.

In the beginning (in 1969), Ritchie and Thompson created UNIX. In the fall of 1973, they gave a paper, and that paper was published in June 1974. The result was growing demand for this new, useful system. But AT&T didn't know how to respond to the demand, so it decided to give the system to educational institutions and research organizations at minimal cost, but with no support, no guarantees, and no bug fixes. (Yes, I know that this sounds just like your current vendor.)

As a consequence, the users — nearly all of them from universities — had to band together and cooperate. The users shared new programs, bug fixes, and clever hacks, all of which were incorporated into the next edition of UNIX from Bell Labs. (The tenth, and last, edition of the Research System appeared in 1990.)

One set of users was at the University of California in Berkeley. These users installed UNIX in January 1974. In the fall of 1975, they were running Sixth Edition. In 1975–76, Ken Thompson went to Berkeley on sabbatical, and two new graduate students, Bill Joy and Chuck Haley, arrived on campus. They were fascinated by the new system. The next autumn, George Coulouris arrived from Queen Mary College, London, and introduced Joy to em (editor for *m*ortals), his screen editor. Joy turned it into ex and that into vi — the beginning of the editors that we use now.

Why All This History?

Up to the end of 1977, all UNIX was AT&T UNIX. Then, at the beginning of 1978, Berkeley offered a tape containing a UNIX Pascal system and the ex text editor. It came on a 1,200-foot reel of 800 bpi tape for $50. Joy distributed about 30 copies. Within a few months, the Berkeley group had done more (including termcap) and offered a new tape, 2BSD (Berkeley Software Distribution). Joy shipped about 75 of those.

Simultaneously, Interactive Systems (Peter Weiner and Heinz Lycklama) produced the first commercial UNIX, and Whitesmiths (P.J. Plauger) produced the first UNIX clone, Idris.

AT&T had no control of what Berkeley or Queen Mary College did and even less control of what Interactive and Whitesmiths (and others) did. The result was a proliferation of variants. Figure 53-1 shows the early part of this family tree.

Secret

In actuality, only two types of UNIX exist, and they don't differ much. The types are those that are based on 4.2, 4.3, or 4.4BSD, and those that are based on SVR3 and SVR4. (In fact, SVR4 is closer to 4.4BSD than SVR3 was to 4.3BSD.) The fastest way to detect whether your system was derived from BDS or AT&T is to look at the print command. If you use lp to print, your system is AT&T-derived; if you use lpr, it is BSD-derived. (And if you're running OSF/1, both will work.)

Figure 53-2 shows the most recent (and much more confusing) part of the family tree.

Most commands are uniform across UNIX systems (despite propaganda to the contrary from Microsoft). The at command, for example, which executes commands at a specified time, is the same in OSF/1, SCO UNIX, SCO Xenix, SVR3.2, SVR4, and X/Open. The atq command however, which displays jobs that are queued to run at specific times, is in OSF/1 and SVR4 but not in SCO UNIX, SCO Xenix, SVR3.2, or X/Open. Using at -l in these four yields the same result.

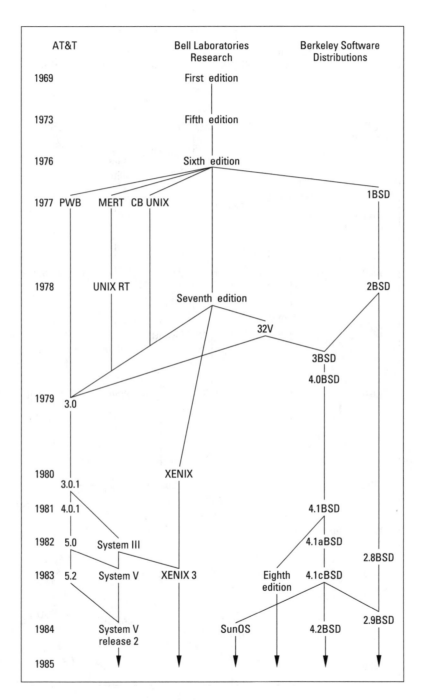

Figure 53-1: An early UNIX family tree

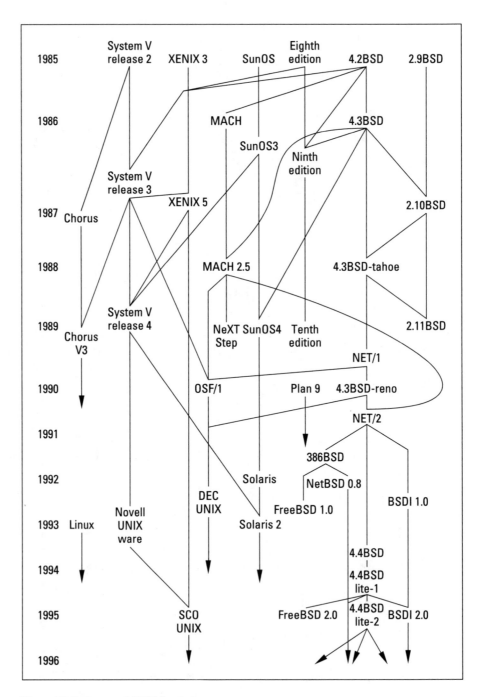

Figure 53-2: A current UNIX family tree

Why Should I Care?

There are only a few places where you might care whether your system derives from System V R3 or 4.2BSD. Chorus, for example, was derived from SVR2 in 1987. But SVR3 was strongly influenced by 4.2BSD. Thus, Chorus V3 has many BSDisms, which were derived from SVR3. Linux has elements of both SVR4 and BSD, as do OSF/1 and DEC UNIX (which was derived from it). FreeBSD, NetBSD, 4.4BSD Lite, and BSDI are purer BSDs, but because the BSDs that followed NET/2 (1991) were influenced by OSF/1, they all have some genes from SVR3.

SunOS was a fairly straightforward BSD derivative, based on 4.1cBSD (1983), but Solaris 2 (1993) has a great deal of SVR4 in it, as a result of the brief conjoining of Sun Microsystems and AT&T in UNIX International.

If you are a user, don't fret about the differences. If you are a programmer or a systems administrator, however, you must pay attention to the differences. Perhaps the best example is the command ps, report process status.

Every version of UNIX has ps. The options vary widely. The 4.4BSD system, for example, has the flags listed in Table 53-1.

Table 53-1   4.4BSD Flags

Flag	Meaning
-a	Displays information about other users' processes as well as your own.
-C	Changes the way that the CPU percentage (%cpu) is calculated, by using a raw CPU calculation that ignores resident time.
-e	Displays the environment as well.
-h	Repeats the information header as often as necessary to guarantee one header per page of information.
-j	Prints information associated with the following keywords: user, pid, ppid, pgid, sess, jobc, state, tt, time, and command.
-L	Lists the set of available keywords.
-l	Displays information associated with the following keywords: uid, pid, ppid, cpu, pri, nice, vsz, rss, wchan, state, tt, time, and command.
-M	Extracts values associated with the name list from the specified core instead of the default /dev/kmem.
-m	Sorts by memory use instead of by process ID.
-N	Extracts the name list from the specified system instead of the default /bsd'.

Continued

Table 53-1 *(continued)*

Flag	Meaning
-O	Adds the information associated with the space- or comma-separated list of keywords specified, after the process ID, in the default information display. Keywords can be appended with an equal sign (=)and a string, causing the printed header to use the specified string instead of the standard header.
-o	Displays information associated with the space- or comma-separated list of keywords specified. Keywords can be appended with an equal sign (=) and a string, causing the printed header to use the specified string instead of the standard header.
-p	Displays information associated with the specified process ID.
-r	Sorts by current CPU usage, instead of by process ID.
-S	Changes the way that the process time is calculated by summing all exited children to their parent processes.
-T	Displays information about processes attached to the device associated with the standard input.
-t	Displays information about processes attached to the specified terminal device.
-U	Displays information associated with the specified user.
-u	Displays information associated with the following keywords: user, pid, %cpu, %mem, vsz, rss, tt, state, start, time, and command. The -u option implies the -r option.
-v	Displays information associated with the following keywords: pid, state, time, sl, re, pagein, vsz, rss, lim, tsiz, %cpu, %mem, and command. The -v option implies the -m option.
-W	Extracts swap information from the specified file instead of the default /dev/swap'.
-w	Uses 132 columns to display information instead of the default (your window size). If the -w option is specified more than once, ps uses as many columns as necessary, without regard for your window size.
-x	Displays information about processes without controlling terminals.

But SVR4 has the flags listed in Table 53-2.

Table 53-2   SVR4 Flags

Flag	Meaning
-e	Prints information about every process that is running.
-d	Prints information about all processes except session leaders.

Flag	Meaning
-a	Prints information about the processes that are most frequently requested: all those except session leaders and processes that are not associated with a terminal.
-j	Prints the session ID and process group ID.
-f	Generates a full listing.
-l	Generates a long listing.
-c	Prints information in a format that reflects scheduler properties, as described in `priocntl(1)`. The -c option affects the output of the -f and -l options.
-t (termlist)	Lists only process data associated with the terminal specified in `termlist`.
-p (proclist)	Lists only process data for which process ID numbers are specified in `proclist`.
-u (uidlist)	Lists only process data for which user IDs or login names are specified in `uidlist`.
-g (grplist)	Lists only process data for which the group leader's ID number appears in `grplist`.
-s (sesslist)	Lists information on all session leaders whose IDs appear in `sesslist`.

In OSF/1, -j gives job-control information; -m displays all threads in a task; -o uses specifier to format output; and -O adds information to -o. Except for -m, these are as in BSD.

 The information from the online SVR4 manual has been left in the order in which it appears: It is unknown who decided not to place the material in alphabetical order.

Summary

In this chapter, you have seen some of the differences between BSD- and SVR4-based UNIXes. In the next chapter, I will talk a bit about Linux and the rivalry between Microsoft and UNIX.

Chapter 54

Riding the Linux Wave

The hottest news in the UNIX world in the 1990s is Linux.

What Is Linux?

For a start, Linux is not UNIX. Linux is a UNIX-like operating system, which has been developed by many developers throughout the world in an Open Source Model. Open Source means that the source code is freely shared and that you can submit your own changes. A group of engineers will examine your changes, and if they approve them, will incorporate them in the next release of Linux.

Linux began back in 1991, when Linus Torvalds at the University of Helsinki, in Finland, developed a system to exceed the standards of Minix, an older, free UNIX operating system. At the time, most UNIXes were controlled by corporations, who were fairly jealous about protecting their source code, so hacking on UNIX was discouraged.

In 1994, Linus released the first full-featured Linux kernel (The kernel is the heart of a UNIX operating system), and it has been uphill ever since. Several companies now provide a full-featured Linux prepackaged for easy installation and configuration. The most prominent are RedHat, Caldera, and SuSE. I personally use RedHat Linux on my home computer, and my Web sites are all delivered from RedHat Linux machines.

Note

Linus Torvalds uses RedHat Linux on his home computer.

Where Do You Get Linux?

The most common means of getting Linux for your computer is to purchase it from a distributor. You will get a CD-ROM and a boot floppy, and instructions for installation. Some distributors will include extra manuals. Some distributors are:

Caldera OpenLinux
(888) 465-4689
`linux@caldera.com`

RedHat Linux
(888) 733-4281
`orders@redhat.com`

S.u.S.E.
+ 911-7405331 (Germany)
`http://www.suse.com/`

Numerous other variants of Linux can be found online, or at many retailers. If you want the pleasure of loading your own Linux, there are numerous sites online where you can download Debian, RedHat, Caldera, Slackware, or other Linux distributions. The best location to start on a download would be `http://www.linux.org/`; follow the links to an appropriate FTP distribution.

Note

Some Linuxes, such as RedHat, will even install across the Internet via FTP. You just need to create an installation diskette, and follow the directions, to get the latest Linux version.

Naturally, you can look for other sources of Linux. We've included a RedHat CD in this book for your convenience.

Linux Creams Windows NT

The single biggest competitor to Linux is Microsoft, and their Windows NT product. Windows NT is quite popular, but often those decisions are based not on product quality, but on other, nonengineering reasons. (That is, "No one was ever fired for buying Microsoft.") Those of us who believe in Linux believe this will change, but we have an uphill fight. Engineering-wise, we believe the numbers are with us.

Results from *Smart Reseller*

Smart Reseller is a Ziff Davis magazine that recently published a comparison between three Linux distributions and Windows NT. The Linux distributions tested were RedHat 5.2, Caldera 1.3, and SuSE 5.3. They performed tests from the perspective of a business looking to install a server for a network. All three distributions of Linux outperformed Windows NT on less hardware.

The Linux machines were configured to run Samba, a file server that allows Windows users to mount UNIX file systems, and to share file systems served from UNIX machines. The Linux machines also ran the Apache Web server. They were not configured as Internet machines, so DNS and `sendmail` were not installed. The X Windows system was not installed, either.

Based on benchmarks, all three distributions outperformed Windows NT as a Windows file server at double-digit client numbers. At 32 clients, the worst-performing UNIX distribution outperformed Windows NT by 250 percent. Only at low loads did Windows NT 4.0 have performance comparable to Linux servers running Samba.

This was truly astonishing; one would have expected a Microsoft product to be better at communications with Windows clients, but the strength of Open Source outperformed Microsoft's engineering.

When running as a Web server, Apache running on Linux again outperformed the latest Microsoft Internet Information Server running on Windows NT 4.0, although in this case the race was closer. Once again, Windows NT would hold a slight edge against Linux/Apache combinations with low load, but as the load on the Web servers increase, the performance of Apache on Linux was between 16 percent and 50 percent better than IIS on NT, depending on which distribution was examined.

Meanwhile, Linux could be installed on less powerful hardware configurations. All three Linux distributions have minimum processor requirements of 386DX and 8 megabytes of RAM. Windows NT requires a Pentium processor and at least 64 megabytes of RAM for practical use (official minimums are a 486/33 and 16MB). Linux can be installed in as little as 120MB of hard disk, whereas NT requires 1GB (again, a practical recommendation; the official minimum is 124MB). Linux comes with software development tools for C, C++, Perl, and Tcl; others can be found on the Web. Windows NT comes with no extra software development tools.

Even more damning is a price comparison. Basic Windows NT 4.0 costs $809. This is more than ten times as expensive as any of the Linux distributions tested. For that extra money, what do you get? Less development tools, poorer performance, and the need to purchase extra hardware. Why would anyone purchase NT in preference to Linux?

Comparison by a Microsoft Certified Engineer

John Kirch is a Microsoft Certified Professional on Windows NT. In 1998, he published a Web page of his comparison between Windows NT Server 4.0 and UNIX. His Web page, relocated to `http://www.unix-vs-nt.org/`, has been translated into many languages, and it is one of the best resources when deciding between Linux and NT.

His examination is primarily from a financial perspective, as a manager might make. His conclusion is that, although some variants of UNIX may be more expensive at the outset, the maturity, reliability, and security of UNIX make it cheaper to use in the long term than NT. Since Linux's initial starting costs are lower than NT, one might reasonably conclude that, with its reliability, Linux will remain cheaper.

The first price comparison is the real price for a Windows NT server. As seen above, Microsoft charges $809 for Windows NT. This gives a five-user license. Larger numbers of users require higher payments: NT Server 4.0 Enterprise with a 50-seat license is $4,799. That's only $4,749 more than the cost of RedHat. For that difference in price, you can purchase two more Intel workstations.

Let's add to this. Suppose you want your employees to have access to e-mail. With Linux, you get `sendmail` as part of the package. Two other mail transport tools, `exim` and `qmail`, are available for free via the Internet. If you're running NT, though, the obvious choice is Microsoft Exchange Server. For your 50 clients, that's only $4,859. Just a little bit more than the cost for Linux mail tools.

The real win for Linux is in its reliability. I can say from my own experience, when I worked at The Internet Mall, our NT ad server crashed on a weekly basis. Our Linux servers did not crash during my employment. My home Linux machine has only crashed when the electric company failed. With a UPS, that "crash" was a graceful shutdown. With Windows NT, it was the "Blue Screen of Death."

In John Kirch's experience, Windows NT crashed under a variety of conditions that a UNIX system would handle without problems. There are UNIX crashes, but these are usually confined to hardware failures or experimental kernels. Because of the decision to tie a GUI into the operating system, when there is a problem with the user interface, the system can crash. Here, the genius of having the GUI system as a separate application from the operating system is obvious. A failure in an X application is not a reason for a system to crash.

Security is also a concern. While Microsoft touts the C2 security rating from the NSA, what they don't mention is that the certification for NT 3.5 came from a less stringent testing procedure — one that does not test a networked machine. Why install a server on a machine that isn't networked?

John has referred to one amusing thing in his article: Even Microsoft uses UNIX. When Microsoft bought Hotmail, Hotmail was running Sun Solaris and FreeBSD. Their Web server was Apache. Microsoft tried to migrate to NT, but found that the load of supporting 10,000,000 users was too much for NT to handle, so they had to go back to using Solaris.

Cisco systems recently moved from using Windows NT to Linux for mail servers, because Linux could do more.

Microsoft's reaction

Microsoft hasn't been sitting quietly while Linux has been gaining strength. In October 1998, two documents were leaked from Microsoft that discussed their strategy for dealing with Linux and Open Source. While Microsoft has attempted to disavow these documents as the writing of a "low-level engineer," the document had input from several key executives at Microsoft, including two that report directly to Bill Gates. The only way it could be more official would be if Bill Gates had been involved in the document.

Because the documents were leaked near Halloween, they have been named "The Halloween Documents" in the Linux community. You can see the complete documents at `http://www.opensource.org/`.

The initial and primary conclusion that can be inferred from the document is that Microsoft sees Linux, and Open Source, as a threat to their monopoly position. To quote, "Consequently, OSS (Open Source Software) poses a direct, short-term revenue and platform threat to Microsoft — particularly in server space. Additionally, the intrinsic parallelism and free idea exchange in OSS has benefits that are not replicable with our current licensing model and therefore present a long-term developer mindshare threat."

Among the observations by Microsoft is that the Open Source approach produces superior code than proprietary technologies. Microsoft has seen that commercial quality code is achievable through engineers' world-wide sharing in the development effort.

The real threat from Microsoft comes in their discussion of Linux as a threat to NT Server. The document included several bullet items, the four most significant of which I've reproduced here:

- Linux uses commodity PC hardware and, due to OS modularity, can be run on smaller systems than NT. Linux is frequently used for services such as DNS running on old 486s in back closets.

- Due to it's (sic) UNIX heritage, Linux represents a lower switching cost for some organizations than NT.

- UNIX's has perceived scalability, interoperability, availability, and manageability advantages over NT.

- Linux can win as long as services protocols are commodities.

As Eric Raymond's analysis of the Halloween Documents points out, this is the key threat to Linux. By having a service or protocol as a commodity, what Microsoft means is that the services are open and transparent. Anyone can write applications for those services. For Microsoft to win, the protocols must be closed.

Closed protocols means that to write an application, the business must have agreements with Microsoft to learn the protocol. To compete, the business must essentially gain permission from Microsoft to compete with Microsoft. Is this the best world for consumers? I think not.

Later in the Halloween Documents, Microsoft is even more explicit with the strategy of closing protocols. In the section "Beating Linux," one of the bullet items is "Fold extended functionality into commodity protocols/services and create new protocols." This is the process of closing access for businesses to compete.

We recently saw this with Microsoft's violation of their agreement with Sun for Java. Microsoft "extended" Java in a proprietary fashion. Sun sued to get an injunction against shipping the nonstandard Java and won an injunction. The court fight is still going on as this book is being written, but this is a perfect example of Microsoft's strategy to eliminate competition by extending public protocols with proprietary extensions.

What Microsoft has realized is that Open Source Software is a tremendous advantage for developing software. By sharing the tasks among potentially millions of developers, OSS has the benefits of parallel debugging, low entry costs, and extensibility.

In Halloween II, Microsoft's engineers ran Linux and saw how easy it is to use: "Contrary to popular belief, even though this was open source, I never had to touch the C code to get the core functionality working." Even the engineers recognized the performance of Linux: "I previously had IE4/NT4 on the same box and by comparison the combination of Linux/Navigator ran at least 30–40% faster when rendering simple HTML + graphics."

After reading the Halloween documents, one can sense some concern on the part of Microsoft about the growth of Linux and Apache. Open solutions are proving to be the best solutions.

Linux Myths

An engineer advocating Linux may face some common misconceptions about Linux. The two biggest concern applications and support.

While the number of applications for Linux does not yet reach the number for Windows, they are growing. Applix provides an office tool suite, and there are efforts to create a Windows emulator for Linux. Oracle has invested in Linux, and the Oracle 8.0.5 database system is available.

Support is available for Linux. Caldera and RedHat both provide free support through installation, and newsgroups exist for Linux questions. For those who are uncomfortable with support that is free, you can purchase Linux support from Caldera and RedHat beyond installation.

Summary

This chapter looked at Linux. In it, you have learned

- ▶ What Linux is
- ▶ Who Linus Torvalds is
- ▶ How to find Linux
- ▶ How Linux compares to Windows NT

The next chapter looks at the future of UNIX.

Chapter 55

The Future of UNIX

Congratulations — you've reached the end of the book. (It makes no difference whether you've read everything so far or have just flipped to the end.) This chapter discusses some of the future of UNIX.

Where Are We Going?

UNIX is more than 25 years old, yet it has a great deal of life left to live. Because UNIX is the world's first and most successful portable operating system, a great deal of money has been invested in its future, and it has many faithful adherents on engineering staffs. The two primary sources for the evolution of UNIX, however — Bell Laboratories and the University of California, Berkeley — are both out of the UNIX business. If UNIX is to thrive, the energy that went into its initial evolution must be replaced. Otherwise, UNIX will go the way of COBOL — widely used and evolutionarily dead.

Fortunately, two groups are still energetic and interested in improving UNIX: the people who are working on Linux and the Internet community.

Linux

Linux is a UNIX clone that is continually being enhanced and that is available from many FTP sites throughout the Internet. Linux was started by Linus Torvalds, a hacker in Finland. Linux is freely distributed under the same terms as the Free Software Foundation's copyleft. Also, several firms have started to distribute Linux on CD-ROM at minimal cost.

Story: My Home Linux

My home machine is a Linux machine. I have a Pentium 200 machine at home, with 64MB of RAM and 12GB of disk; it has run successfully with Linux as the operating system for more than four years without system crashes. My Linux was provided by RedHat.

Linux is intended to be used on Intel *x*86 machines, and as such, it makes an excellent alternative to Microsoft Windows. You get the full functionality of UNIX, complete with a development environment based on GNU software.

Linux can support networking, including networking between PCs that are running different operating systems. Usually, the CD-ROMs that are used to distribute Linux come with the complete set of source code.

What makes Linux important, however, is the fact that more than 100 hackers work, in their spare time, to improve the operating system. As these hackers work without the encumbrances of corporate bureaucracy, they are free to be creative in expanding and enhancing Linux. I expect several advances in UNIX technology to be started by this community.

Besides the people who are involved in further development, a large community of users is willing to provide support for Linux users. Several newsgroups exist (see Table 55-1). Also, Specialized Systems Consultants in Seattle publishes *Linux Journal* for the Linux community. You can get more information by visiting the company's Web page (http://www.ssc.com/) or by sending e-mail to sales@ssc.com.

Table 55-1   Linux Newsgroups

Newsgroup	Purpose
comp.os.linux	Discussions of general Linux questions
comp.os.linux.admin	Information on installing and administering Linux
comp.os.linux.advocacy	Discussion group on the advantages of Linux
comp.os.linux.announce	Important announcements for Linux users
comp.os.linux.answers	Help for Linux
comp.os.linux.development	Discussions of ongoing work with Linux
comp.os.linux.development.apps	Discussions of writing Linux applications and porting applications to Linux

Newsgroup	Purpose
comp.os.linux.development.system	Discussions of writing Linux system software, such as device drivers and the Linux kernel
comp.os.linux.hardware	Hardware-compatibility questions for Linux
comp.os.linux.help	Linux advice
comp.os.linux.misc	Linux topics that are not covered in other newsgroups
comp.os.linux.m68k	Discussions of Linux on Motorola chips
comp.os.linux.networking	Networks and communications in Linux
comp.os.linux.setup	Linux installation questions
comp.os.linux.x	Running X on Linux systems

Internet servers

The largest growth area in computing involves Internet access and Internet servers. UNIX is particularly well adapted for this application because much of the Internet was developed for communications among UNIX systems. (In Chapter 50, Wes Morgan discussed the techniques for bringing a system onto the Internet.)

As the Internet grows, systems are going to need to process and transmit large quantities of data. UNIX has a jump in this area because many large databases are now on UNIX systems, and all the fastest machines have UNIX ports. With portability and performance as important benchmarks, UNIX is well placed to take advantage of this market.

Multiprocessor machines

Another area in which UNIX should grow is multiprocessor machines. Single processors are capable of using only one process at a time, so multiple processors can run multiple processes. This increases system performance, but at the cost of more overhead in the kernel to manage CPU resources.

Note

Solaris 2, Sun's version of UNIX, is particularly adept at managing multiple processors with minimal overhead.

Multiple processors have the advantage of being capable of processing difficult problems in parallel. In original UNIX, for an application to process information in a parallel fashion, it would need to fork a second process, and the two processes would need to remain synchronized. The fork system call and the exec system call are both expensive, so the savings involved in parallel processing can be lost in the initialization. A single process can use no more than one CPU at any time.

Threads are a technique for improving parallelization for multiprocessor systems. A *thread* is a piece of code that can be run separately from the rest of a process and that can run in parallel. An unlimited number of threads can be associated with a process, and threads can be executed concurrently.

Many GUI programs are perfect candidates for threaded programming. Each action that comes from an X event can be a separate thread that executes to completion without preventing the GUI itself from gaining CPU time and performing other actions.

Threads are also useful in large databases. These database programs can receive requests and create a thread to handle the processing. As a result, the database can await new requests while it is still processing the old. This area has a great deal of room for growth as threads become more efficient.

Standards

Perhaps the biggest growth area, and the biggest need, involves standards and conformance with standards. The XPG4 group owns the POSIX standard for UNIX and is also responsible for compliance testing.

The most common complaint I hear about UNIX is the fact that each UNIX system is different. Sun may add one feature to UNIX, and that feature may not work with a feature created by IBM. Eventually, the features become so far out of sync that the two operating systems are no longer similar. Enforcing a rigid standard should prevent this problem from becoming more prevalent in the future.

The XPG4 spec for POSIX defines a set of commands that must be present for a system to be considered to be compliant. The spec also defines the way in which those commands must operate. Similarly, the POSIX spec includes definitions of programming interfaces that must be present for compliance. Of the two (commands and interfaces), I feel that those programming interfaces are more important to make the system compliant. If UNIX is to survive the coming competition, it must be known for compliance with standards.

Competition

The real threat to UNIX comes from external competition. The two primary competitors are Windows NT (from Microsoft) and Open VMS (from DEC).

Windows NT

Ironically, the biggest threat to UNIX is Microsoft's Windows NT product — because one of the original licensees for UNIX was Microsoft, and Xenix was Microsoft's UNIX product in the early 1980s.

Story: It's All in the Name

Experts once said that an MIS manager could not go wrong buying IBM. Even if better products were available, the name was so well known that the purchase would be safe. Microsoft has reached the same level of corporate name recognition: To be a better seller, being a better product is no longer enough.

Windows NT is targeted for the same server market for which UNIX is an ideal product. NT has a closer similarity with Windows desktop products, and the name "Microsoft" is a big selling point.

Remember that Windows NT advertises POSIX compliance.

Open VMS

Digital Equipment Corporation has a long history of antipathy to UNIX: Even while it worked with OSF on a UNIX competitor for AT&T's System V, Ken Olson, a former chairman of DEC, compared UNIX proponents with snake-oil merchants.

Not surprisingly, DEC is attempting to maintain its own operating system — VMS — for its products. The competition is not stiff.

Plan 9 (From Outer Space?)

Another interesting path away from UNIX is a new operating system called Plan 9, which is being developed by Bell Laboratories' Computing Science Research Center (headed by Dennis Ritchie) — the group that originally wrote UNIX.

The basic idea of Plan 9 is to expand beyond the UNIX kernel concept to become essentially a distributed operating system. Every object on the system is a named file, accessible through read/write operations, and these system objects can be local or remote. As a result, remote machines (including processors and other resources) are accessible to the local machine. The actual execution of applications can be distributed in a resource-smart fashion. If one user, for example, is performing several resource-intensive applications, that work is automatically distributed to other machines that are less heavily loaded.

Plan 9 is currently available for Intel platforms, MIPS, SPARC, and Motorola 68020 processors. It supports multiprocessor machines. Plan 9 is also POSIX-compliant.

If you want more information on Plan 9, check the Plan 9 Web page at `http://plan9.bell-labs.com/plan9` and read the newsgroup `comp.os.plan9`.

Summary

This chapter looked at the future of UNIX. You should

▶ Be aware of Linux

▶ Understand the basics of threads

▶ Know why standards exist

▶ Recognize competitors

▶ Be aware of Plan 9

This chapter finishes the book. I hope that you enjoyed reading this material. If you have any questions, comments, or observations, please eel free to contact me. My e-mail address is `james@jamesarmstrong.com`.

Index

continued

continued

continued

continued

continued

continued

GNU General Public License

Version 2, June 1991

Preamble

The licenses for most software are designed to take away your freedom to share and change it. By contrast, the GNU General Public License is intended to guarantee your freedom to share and change free software — to make sure the software is free for all its users. This General Public License applies to most of the Free Software Foundation's software and to any other program whose authors commit to using it. (Some other Free Software Foundation software is covered by the GNU Library General Public License instead.) You can apply it to your programs, too.

When we speak of free software, we are referring to freedom, not price. Our General Public Licenses are designed to make sure that you have the freedom to distribute copies of free software (and charge for this service if you wish), that you receive source code or can get it if you want it, that you can change the software or use pieces of it in new free programs; and that you know you can do these things.

To protect your rights, we need to make restrictions that forbid anyone to deny you these rights or to ask you to surrender the rights. These restrictions translate to certain responsibilities for you if you distribute copies of the software, or if you modify it.

For example, if you distribute copies of such a program, whether gratis or for a fee, you must give the recipients all the rights that you have. You must make sure that they, too, receive or can get the source code. And you must show them these terms so they know their rights.

We protect your rights with two steps: (1) copyright the software, and (2) offer you this license which gives you legal permission to copy, distribute and/or modify the software.

Also, for each author's protection and ours, we want to make certain that everyone understands that there is no warranty for this free software. If the software is modified by someone else and passed on, we want its recipients to know that what they have is not the original, so that any problems introduced by others will not reflect on the original authors' reputations.

Finally, any free program is threatened constantly by software patents. We wish to avoid the danger that redistributors of a free program will individually obtain patent licenses, in effect making the program proprietary. To prevent this, we have made it clear that any patent must be licensed for everyone's free use or not licensed at all.

The precise terms and conditions for copying, distribution and modification follow.

TERMS AND CONDITIONS FOR COPYING, DISTRIBUTION AND MODIFICATION

0. This License applies to any program or other work which contains a notice placed by the copyright holder saying it may be distributed under the terms of this General Public License. The "Program", below, refers to any such program or work, and a "work based on the Program" means either the Program or any derivative work under copyright law: that is to say, a work containing the Program or a portion of it, either verbatim or with modifications and/or translated into another language. (Hereinafter, translation is included without limitation in the term "modification.") Each licensee is addressed as "you."

   Activities other than copying, distribution and modification are not covered by this License; they are outside its scope. The act of running the Program is not restricted, and the output from the Program is covered only if its contents constitute a work based on the Program (independent of having been made by running the Program). Whether that is true depends on what the Program does.

1. You may copy and distribute verbatim copies of the Program's source code as you receive it, in any medium, provided that you conspicuously and appropriately publish on each copy an appropriate copyright notice and disclaimer of warranty; keep intact all the notices that refer to this License and to the absence of any warranty; and give any other recipients of the Program a copy of this License along with the Program.

   You may charge a fee for the physical act of transferring a copy, and you may at your option offer warranty protection in exchange for a fee.

2. You may modify your copy or copies of the Program or any portion of it, thus forming a work based on the Program, and copy and distribute such modifications or work under the terms of Section 1 above, provided that you also meet all of these conditions:

   a) You must cause the modified files to carry prominent notices stating that you changed the files and the date of any change.

   b) You must cause any work that you distribute or publish, that in whole or in part contains or is derived from the Program or any part thereof, to be licensed as a whole at no charge to all third parties under the terms of this License.

c) If the modified program normally reads commands interactively when run, you must cause it, when started running for such interactive use in the most ordinary way, to print or display an announcement including an appropriate copyright notice and a notice that there is no warranty (or else, saying that you provide a warranty) and that users may redistribute the program under these conditions, and telling the user how to view a copy of this License. (Exception: if the Program itself is interactive but does not normally print such an announcement, your work based on the Program is not required to print an announcement.)

These requirements apply to the modified work as a whole. If identifiable sections of that work are not derived from the Program, and can be reasonably considered independent and separate works in themselves, then this License, and its terms, do not apply to those sections when you distribute them as separate works. But when you distribute the same sections as part of a whole which is a work based on the Program, the distribution of the whole must be on the terms of this License, whose permissions for other licensees extend to the entire whole, and thus to each and every part regardless of who wrote it.

Thus, it is not the intent of this section to claim rights or contest your rights to work written entirely by you; rather, the intent is to exercise the right to control the distribution of derivative or collective works based on the Program.

In addition, mere aggregation of another work not based on the Program with the Program (or with a work based on the Program) on a volume of a storage or distribution medium does not bring the other work under the scope of this License.

3. You may copy and distribute the Program (or a work based on it, under Section 2) in object code or executable form under the terms of Sections 1 and 2 above provided that you also do one of the following:

a) Accompany it with the complete corresponding machine-readable source code, which must be distributed under the terms of Sections 1 and 2 above on a medium customarily used for software interchange; or,

b) Accompany it with a written offer, valid for at least three years, to give any third party, for a charge no more than your cost of physically performing source distribution, a complete machine-readable copy of the corresponding source code, to be distributed under the terms of Sections 1 and 2 above on a medium customarily used for software interchange; or,

c) Accompany it with the information you received as to the offer to distribute corresponding source code. (This alternative is allowed only for noncommercial distribution and only if you received the program in object code or executable form with such an offer, in accord with Subsection b above.)

The source code for a work means the preferred form of the work for making modifications to it. For an executable work, complete source code means all the source code for all modules it contains, plus any associated interface definition files, plus the scripts used to control compilation and installation of the executable. However, as a special exception, the source code distributed need not include anything that is normally distributed (in either source or binary form) with the major components (compiler, kernel, and so on) of the operating system on which the executable runs, unless that component itself accompanies the executable.

If distribution of executable or object code is made by offering access to copy from a designated place, then offering equivalent access to copy the source code from the same place counts as distribution of the source code, even though third parties are not compelled to copy the source along with the object code.

4. You may not copy, modify, sublicense, or distribute the Program except as expressly provided under this License. Any attempt otherwise to copy, modify, sublicense or distribute the Program is void, and will automatically terminate your rights under this License. However, parties who have received copies, or rights, from you under this License will not have their licenses terminated so long as such parties remain in full compliance.

5. You are not required to accept this License, since you have not signed it. However, nothing else grants you permission to modify or distribute the Program or its derivative works. These actions are prohibited by law if you do not accept this License. Therefore, by modifying or distributing the Program (or any work based on the Program), you indicate your acceptance of this License to do so, and all its terms and conditions for copying, distributing or modifying the Program or works based on it.

6. Each time you redistribute the Program (or any work based on the Program), the recipient automatically receives a license from the original licensor to copy, distribute or modify the Program subject to these terms and conditions. You may not impose any further restrictions on the recipients' exercise of the rights granted herein. You are not responsible for enforcing compliance by third parties to this License.

7. If, as a consequence of a court judgment or allegation of patent infringement or for any other reason (not limited to patent issues), conditions are imposed on you (whether by court order, agreement or otherwise) that contradict the conditions of this License, they do not excuse you from the conditions of this License. If you cannot distribute so as to satisfy simultaneously your obligations under this License and any other pertinent obligations, then as a consequence you may not

distribute the Program at all. For example, if a patent license would not permit royalty-free redistribution of the Program by all those who receive copies directly or indirectly through you, then the only way you could satisfy both it and this License would be to refrain entirely from distribution of the Program.

If any portion of this section is held invalid or unenforceable under any particular circumstance, the balance of the section is intended to apply and the section as a whole is intended to apply in other circumstances.

It is not the purpose of this section to induce you to infringe any patents or other property right claims or to contest validity of any such claims; this section has the sole purpose of protecting the integrity of the free software distribution system, which is implemented by public license practices. Many people have made generous contributions to the wide range of software distributed through that system in reliance on consistent application of that system; it is up to the author/donor to decide if he or she is willing to distribute software through any other system and a licensee cannot impose that choice.

This section is intended to make thoroughly clear what is believed to be a consequence of the rest of this License.

8. If the distribution and/or use of the Program is restricted in certain countries either by patents or by copyrighted interfaces, the original copyright holder who places the Program under this License may add an explicit geographical distribution limitation excluding those countries, so that distribution is permitted only in or among countries not thus excluded. In such case, this License incorporates the limitation as if written in the body of this License.

9. The Free Software Foundation may publish revised and/or new versions of the General Public License from time to time. Such new versions will be similar in spirit to the present version, but may differ in detail to address new problems or concerns.

Each version is given a distinguishing version number. If the Program specifies a version number of this License which applies to it and "any later version", you have the option of following the terms and conditions either of that version or of any later version published by the Free Software Foundation. If the Program does not specify a version number of this License, you may choose any version ever published by the Free Software Foundation.

10. If you wish to incorporate parts of the Program into other free programs whose distribution conditions are different, write to the author to ask for permission. For software which is copyrighted by the Free Software Foundation, write to the Free Software Foundation; we sometimes make exceptions for this. Our decision will be guided by the two goals of preserving the free status of all derivatives of our free software and of promoting the sharing and reuse of software generally.

NO WARRANTY

11. BECAUSE THE PROGRAM IS LICENSED FREE OF CHARGE, THERE IS NO WARRANTY FOR THE PROGRAM, TO THE EXTENT PERMITTED BY APPLICABLE LAW. EXCEPT WHEN OTHERWISE STATED IN WRITING THE COPYRIGHT HOLDERS AND/OR OTHER PARTIES PROVIDE THE PROGRAM "AS IS" WITHOUT WARRANTY OF ANY KIND, EITHER EXPRESSED OR IMPLIED, INCLUDING, BUT NOT LIMITED TO, THE IMPLIED WARRANTIES OF MERCHANTABILITY AND FITNESS FOR A PARTICULAR PURPOSE. THE ENTIRE RISK AS TO THE QUALITY AND PERFORMANCE OF THE PROGRAM IS WITH YOU. SHOULD THE PROGRAM PROVE DEFECTIVE, YOU ASSUME THE COST OF ALL NECESSARY SERVICING, REPAIR OR CORRECTION.

12. IN NO EVENT UNLESS REQUIRED BY APPLICABLE LAW OR AGREED TO IN WRITING WILL ANY COPYRIGHT HOLDER, OR ANY OTHER PARTY WHO MAY MODIFY AND/OR REDISTRIBUTE THE PROGRAM AS PERMITTED ABOVE, BE LIABLE TO YOU FOR DAMAGES, INCLUDING ANY GENERAL, SPECIAL, INCIDENTAL OR CONSEQUENTIAL DAMAGES ARISING OUT OF THE USE OR INABILITY TO USE THE PROGRAM (INCLUDING BUT NOT LIMITED TO LOSS OF DATA OR DATA BEING RENDERED INACCURATE OR LOSSES SUSTAINED BY YOU OR THIRD PARTIES OR A FAILURE OF THE PROGRAM TO OPERATE WITH ANY OTHER PROGRAMS), EVEN IF SUCH HOLDER OR OTHER PARTY HAS BEEN ADVISED OF THE POSSIBILITY OF SUCH DAMAGES.

*****END OF TERMS AND CONDITIONS*****

How to Apply These Terms to Your New Programs

If you develop a new program, and you want it to be of the greatest possible use to the public, the best way to achieve this is to make it free software which everyone can redistribute and change under these terms.

To do so, attach the following notices to the program. It is safest to attach them to the start of each source file to most effectively convey the exclusion of warranty; and each file should have at least the "copyright" line and a pointer to where the full notice is found.

```
one line to give the program's name and an idea of what it does.
Copyright (C) yyyy  name of author

This program is free software; you can redistribute it and/or
modify it under the terms of the GNU General Public License
as published by the Free Software Foundation; either version 2
of the License, or (at your option) any later version.

This program is distributed in the hope that it will be useful,
```